WISEUP

Knowledge Ends Extremism

Daisy Khan

Executive Editor

To contact the author or order
additional copies of this book
info@wisemuslimwomen.org

Executive Editor: Daisy Khan
Managing Editor: Lisa Nakashima
Designers: Gulraiz Khan, Bobbi Reyda, and Devyani Rana
Copy Editor: Rima Weinberg
Marketing and Cover Design: Ahmer Kalam and Devyani Rana

ISBN: 978-0-9995244-0-4 (paperback - color)
ISBN: 978-0-9995244-1-1 (paperback - black and white)
ISBN: 978-0-9995244-2-8 (e-book)
Library of Congress Control Number: 2017913836
Printed in the United States of America
First Printing: October 2017

To people around the world who have experienced the loss of a loved one to violent extremism, and to everyone, especially WISE women, who are working to bring peace and prosperity to their communities.

Table of Contents

Acknowledgments

The message of *WISE Up* has attracted countless committed people of all world religions, who wish to usher in a more peaceful world. We begin by expressing our deepest gratitude to our 72 contributors, listed below:

Religious Rehabilitation Group (RRG), Zainab Alam, Peter Romaniuk, Imam Talib M. Shareef, Imam Feisal Abdul Rauf, Cherrefe Kadri, Engy Abdelkader, Moustafa Bayoumi, Arsalan Iftikhar, Dr. Nazir Khan and the rest of the team at Spiritual Perception, Arsalan Suleman, Saeed A. Khan and the rest of the team at ISPU, Shaikh Rami Nsour, Major General Doug Stone (Ret.), Salam Al-Marayati of MPAC, Inas Younis, Haris Hromic, Nabil Shaikh, Hassanah El-Yacoubi, Kamran Pasha, Sami H. Elmansoury, Congressman Keith Ellison, Ameena Jandali and Henry Millstein of the Islamic Networks Group (ING), Imam Jamal Rahman, Maulana Wahiduddin Khan, Ibrahim H. Malabari, Dr. John Andrew Morrow, Dr. Safi Kaskas, Dr. Laleh Bakhtiar, Dr. Jonathan AC Brown, Dr. Eboo Patel, Dr. Sultan Abdulhameed, Rohan Gunaratna, The Soufan Group, Dr. Fathali Mogghadam, Dr. Houda Abadi, Naveed Hada, Dr. Ibrahim Negm, Dr. Mohamed Bin Ali, Imam Tahir Kukaj, Imam Mohamed Magid, Imam Souleimane Konate, Imam Mohamad Bashar Arafat, Sumbul Ali-Karamali, Rabia Terri Harris, Kabir Helminski, Syed-Mohsin Naquvi, Dr. Wayel Azmeh, Dr. Saeed Albezreh, Dr. Reza Aslan, Dr. Mehnaz Afridi, Mike Ghouse, Imam Abdul Malik Mujahid, Qasim Rashid, Christianne Boudreau, Nicola Benyahia, Mubin Shaikh, Center for the Prevention of Radicalization Leading to Violence (CPRLV), Soraya Deen, Scott Cooper of Human Rights First, Emily May of Hollaback!, Camille Helminski, Fitrah Muhammad, Imam Michael Saahir, John Kiser, Talat Hamdani, and Sheila Musaji. WISE owes special thanks to Dr. Seyyed Hossein Nasr, who graciously allowed us to excerpt a part of his book.

In addition, this enormous task would not have been possible had we not had an entire team of dedicated people. In particular, we would like to thank the research and writing team, led by Jill, and carried on by Allie, and completed by our cadre of bright and energetic interns: Jack, Christine, Rachel, Anais, Zahra, Zainab, Carmen, Dani, Rahima, Liz, Bob, Nora, Kashaf, Natalie, Emma, Clara, Irene, Alex, Allison, and Emily.

The *WISE Up Report* would not have to come to fruition without the pro bono professional services of Ahmer, an advertising and marketing genius; Marcia, Nataliya, and the rest of their team at Rubenstein; and without our attorneys, Jesse, Mark, and Jake, who counseled us on legal matters to publish this book with 72 authors.

The real success of this project is in the support we have garnered from private individuals of all faiths who provided critical financial support to underwrite this report. I especially want to thank John K., Tony, John R., Abigail, Cynda, Helen, Swanee, Mary, Arfa, and Faroque, who have been staunch supporters of WISE and its women-led peacebuilding initiatives. We are grateful to Debbie, Christina, Aliya, Linda, Sheikh Bashir, Alexandra, Adem, Imam Khalid, Faiza, Sahar, Iman, and other members of New York's Muslim community who joined our focus groups and acted as our sounding board. Our deepest gratitude goes to our Muslim and interfaith allies, especially Global Peace Foundation, who continue to act as our advisers; Yehezkel, Kai, Macky, Susan B., Laleh, and Helene for their astute editing skills. Thank you to Diane, Khadijah, and Ilene for helping us develop *WISE Up* lesson plans to carry this work forward in other arenas. To Tasneema and Amina for filling much-needed gaps, and to my dear friend, Prakash Daswani MBE, for giving up his vacation in New York to help us in our hour of need. To our talented graphic design team: Gulraiz for the original design and page layout, Bobbi for carrying forward Gulraiz's vision for *WISE Up*, and Devyani, who displayed her incredible skill in graphic design and video production, working at all hours to meet our tight deadlines; and to all three for their endless patience with us.

A very special thank you to Richard, Yawar, and

Junaid for advising us throughout this process, and for always offering kind words of encouragement. We also want to thank the *WISE Up* outreach team: Nadia, Arsalan, Wa'el, Aysha, Rizwan, Gail, Paul, Nazli, Maria, Saeed, Rabiah, Muhammad, Hind, Bob, Jim, Majid, Ryan, Steve, Jennifer, Margaret, Mino, Shahid, Chris, Rabbi Schneier, Dr. Hassan, Fozia, Shahana, Sheryl, and many others who are dedicated to spreading the message of *WISE Up* around the nation. To Susan S., who continues to work tirelessly to conduct outreach for WISE Up across the country.

I applaud my right hand at WISE, Lisa Nakashima, who coordinated this collaborative effort between 72 contributors, and managed the many consultants, designers, editors, volunteers, and interns throughout this whole process. Without her, this project would not have come to fruition. I am indebted to my husband, Imam Feisal Abdul Rauf, who enabled me spiritually to take on this task and taught me to ground my activism in knowledge. Most importantly, I thank my Creator for giving me an opportunity to humbly serve my community and country.

Last, we intended for this project to be as flawless as possible, but we know there might be errors, gaps, and omissions. Such mistakes are a result of human error, and we humbly ask anyone finding such errors to contact us immediately so we can correct them. We also want to acknowledge the scholars, academics, and imams who have inspired our work, and key authors whose books (listed here) we have consulted frequently. We refer anyone looking for in-depth, well-researched knowledge about all things Islam to the following works:

The Study Quran: A New Translation and Commentary, edited by Seyyed Hossein Nasr, Caner K. Dagli, Maria Massi Dakake, Joseph E. B. Lumbard, and Mohammed Rustom

The Quran, translation and commentary, by Maulana Wahiduddin Khan

The Qur'an with References to the Bible, by Safi Kaskas and David Hungerford

The Prophet of Peace: Teachings of the Prophet Muhammad, by Maulana Wahiduddin Khan

The Culture of Terrorism: Tenets and Treatments, by Dr. 'Abd Allah Bin Al-Sheik Mahfuz Bin Bayyah, translated by Hamza Yusuf

What's Right with Islam Is What's Right with America: A New Vision for Muslims and the West, by Imam Feisal Abdul Rauf

Defining Islamic Statehood: Measuring and Indexing Contemporary Muslim States, by Imam Feisal Abdul Rauf

The Heart of Islam: Enduring Values for Humanity, by Seyyed Hossein Nasr

A New Introduction to Islam, by Daniel Brown

Introduction

MESSAGE FROM THE EDITOR

***"Where are the Muslims?
Why aren't they speaking out against terrorism?
What are they doing to solve this issue?"***

I must confess that I have grown weary of seeing such statements time and again during the long, conflicted, and ongoing aftermath of the attacks of September 11, 2001, especially when they are made by respected commentators.

The vast majority of Muslims in the global community of believers—including the millions of us long settled peacefully and integrated successfully in the US and other Western nations—have repeatedly and publicly refuted the dangerous fallacy that "terrorism" is somehow intrinsic to our faith, that Islam willfully inspires wanton murder and destruction the world over and always has.

Yet beneath the frustration—and fear—implicit in the second of the two questions above lies a serious challenge, one that confronts us all, Muslims and non-Muslims alike. The time is ripe for a fresh strategic approach. This seems to me to require people of all faiths, and none, to work together in good faith, pooling our insights, experiences, and know-how to "solve the issue"; namely, to defeat the persistence of violent extremism in and beyond the US. It seems crucial that we must do so by peaceful means; for peace is the underlying and unifying spirit of all our diverse faiths.

A fundamental prerequisite of what now has to be a collective and systematic worldwide strategy is to develop and apply a suite of proven, comprehensive, and tactically astute measures over the coming years, based on our shared intelligence and united commitment to peace and goodwill. The *WISE Up Report* contains our first attempt at a blueprint for such measures.

The most deadly and virulent form of violent extremism in the world today is represented by Daesh, often also referred to as ISIS or Islamic State. Whilst rooted in the al-Qaeda organization responsible for 9/11 and earlier terrorist atrocities elsewhere, Daesh now has a far more extensive membership and power base than its predecessor, is rampant in more territories all over the globe, and poses a greater threat to Muslims around the world and to global security and peace in general.

As an American Muslim woman, I worked with New York City's interfaith and Muslim communities in the years immediately after 9/11, and have done so ever since, to develop constructive—and peaceful—responses to the terrible consequences of that tragedy. Together with other Muslim women in the US and beyond, we created a new organization: WISE, Women's Islamic Initiative in Spirituality and Equality. Later, WISE developed a Global Women's Shura Council, a body of Muslim women scholars. In 2009, after examining the extent to which there was any genuine scriptural basis in the Qur'an to legitimize al-Qaeda and its actions, the Shura Council issued a white paper, "Jihad Against Violence," a powerful condemnation of both violent extremism and domestic violence.

Fast-forward a few years to April 2013: I was invited to attend a summit hosted by Singapore's Religious Rehabilitation Group (RRG). The RRG presented the history and methodology of its work in combating violent extremism and extremist ideology. After digesting its findings, I came to the view that something similar could prove effective in the United States, where previous approaches to violent extremism had not only failed to quell the spread of global terrorism but had also, it could be argued, helped to fuel the rise of Islamophobia, or fear and hatred of Islam.

In response to the subsequent emergence and growth of Daesh, in summer 2015 WISE embarked on a mission to create a holistic, research- and evidence-based approach to the interconnected issues of violent extremism and Islamophobia. We began by issuing an online survey to WISE's American Muslim constituents to gauge their opinions and elicit their insights on violent extremism, Islamophobia, and existing counterterrorism strategies. The response to the survey was overwhelmingly positive, with the contributions themselves overwhelmingly constructive: wise, compassionate, and practical in equal measure.

The survey findings confirmed our belief that for any solutions to be effective in the long term, they must also address the range of factors—social, political, psychological, historical, and ideological—and the complex interconnections between them that have brought Muslims and non-Muslims to this unique place in history. We therefore decided to spend the next 18 months cultivating the multiple dialogues that emerged from this extensive collaborative exercise, one that additionally involved some 60 expert scholars, religious leaders, and key writers from the US and abroad, before assembling the key propositions submitted into a coherent, overarching framework.

The result is *WISE Up*.

WISE Up is now both the slogan for WISE's forward-looking campaign to spread authoritative yet easily accessible knowledge about Islam, and the title of a comprehensive new toolkit that serves to act as a practical blueprint for positive change, particularly in places where Daesh already exists along with those still potentially vulnerable to its lethal attractions.

The toolkit comprises three interrelated yet discrete sections, each covering a different aspect of violent extremism and Islamophobia and each usable as a stand-alone guide: Part One: *Voices of American Muslims*; Part Two: *Islamic Theology vs. Extremist Ideology*; and Part Three: *Preventing Extremist Recruitment*. These tools are intended to inform and educate all. They are also designed to equip those who so wish with the intellectual resources and practical know-how to become leaders and ambassadors for change within their respective constituencies.

As a campaign, WISE Up aims to empower individuals and groups who are passionate about building bridges to stand against hatred and violence. We therefore invite you, Dear Reader, to support WISE Up, whether by spreading the word about it to your professional and personal contacts and/or by playing a more active and engaged role, as part of our collective movement for peace. We welcome you most warmly in either capacity, or both.

I pay tribute to our donors for supporting WISE Up from its inception and ever since. We shall also remain forever indebted to RRG, whose in-depth research and extraordinary achievements in Singapore have been our inspiration for this toolkit and campaign.

In closing, I wish to express WISE's immense gratitude to all those who have made it possible to bring WISE Up into being; we honor them by name in the Acknowledgments section. Whether as partners or volunteers they have been an indispensable part of this collaborative movement for peace, working both at the forefront and behind the scenes to enable lasting positive change for the benefit of us all.

Salaam Alaykum: Peace be with you.
Daisy Khan, Executive Director, WISE

PART ONE

Voices of American Muslims

Executive Summary: Part One

VOICES OF AMERICAN MUSLIMS

KEY TAKEAWAYS

1. American Muslims practice their faith freely and openly, protected by the guarantees in the First Amendment of the U.S. Constitution.

2. American Muslims see no contradiction between American values and their Islamic faith.

3. Recognize that the acts of a few violent individuals do not apply to the entire community, the vast majority of whom are upright citizens.

In the years since the attacks of September 11, 2001, Muslims have been placed firmly in the crosshairs of the global War on Terror. American Muslims have found themselves reluctantly yet consistently caught in this war and have become subjects of unlawful government policies and targets of unfair racial and religious stereotypes.

This is deeply regrettable, not least because the vast majority of American Muslims are peace-loving and upright; model American citizens, many of them long-established and highly respected pillars of their communities.

As the articles in the three chapters in this first section of *WISE Up* emphasize time and again, American Muslims have always placed enormous value on their American identity, alongside the profound love they have for their faith. For most American Muslims, there is an exceptionally high degree of congruence between the foundational values of America and the central tenets of Islam.

They particularly appreciate the U.S. Constitution's First Amendment guarantee of religious freedom, and America's commitment to social justice and racial equality and civil rights has allowed Muslims to flourish freely.

Unfortunately, a small fraction of Muslims have been deceived by the pernicious ideology of extremists, who twist Islamic terms to instigate violent action. In the process, they portray the American Muslim community as somehow guilty by association. Precisely because of this, Muslims in America are on the receiving end of unlawful surveillance, hate crimes, and entrapment.

This, of course, plays right into the hands of violent extremist groups like Daesh (also known as *Islamic State in Iraq and Syria* or ISIS), which propagate the narrative, described by Kamran Pasha in his article on Hollywood and Islam in Chapter 3, that "*America hates Muslims*" and "*America is engaged in a war against Islam*," primarily to boost the numbers of their recruits and strengthen their power base among disaffected and alienated populations the world over.

All of this serves to increase suspicion toward Muslims from their fellow Americans, thereby alienating them from full and active participation in mainstream public discourse. This, in turn, not only violates American values, but also negatively impacts our collective safety and security as a nation.

Drawing on his experience of implementing the Iraqi detention program from 2007 onward, Major General Douglas Stone (ret.) observes that: "*Ignorance of Islam and Muslims initially impaired our ability to achieve peace and stability. [However] building relations of trust and respect proved to be invaluable in our fight against extremism.*" He concludes: "*I strongly believe that Islamophobia jeopardizes the security of our country*" (Chapter 2).

Nevertheless, we see many optimistic and

constructive calls to collective action in the articles contained in the three opening chapters of *WISE Up*. Each of the articles outlines one of the numerous obstacles facing American Muslims, yet all focus on the importance of Muslim-led efforts to combat violent extremism, Islamophobia, and all forms of hate. All agree that such initiatives must also be based on collaborative relationships with mainstream institutions where trust has already been built and, if not, now urgently needs to be, particularly, though not exclusively, with federal government and local law enforcement agencies. As Congressman Keith Ellison observes: "*If unity becomes the mainstream message, then Daesh cannot recruit successfully*" (Chapter 3).

All the articles are ever mindful of the challenges ahead yet appeal to the heart as much as to the mind. As Sami H. Elmansoury states: "*As for me, just one American who also happens to be Muslim, I will work with every breath to have a profound and significant positive impact on my country and my world*" (Chapter 3).

In an effort to gauge American Muslims' opinions and elicit their insights on the aforementioned issues, about which they are frequently subjects rather than participants with their own active voices, WISE conducted a survey in the summer of 2015, the results of which emphatically underscored the importance of community engagement to prevent extremism, with 89 percent of mainly Muslim respondents asserting that "*more investment and focus should be applied to community engagement*."

WISE Up is itself such a Muslim community–originated response, with this motif running through all 27 articles in the three chapters of Part One. All the articles have been contributed by leading Muslim thinkers and eminent faith leaders, as well as skilled professionals from a variety of disciplines, chiefly Muslims but non-Muslims too, along with deeply committed community activists with admirable achievements in this field.

The opening articles, by Imam Talib M. Shareef, Imam Feisal Abdul Rauf, and Cherrefe Kadri, highlight the great value to American Muslims of the inalienable right to religious freedom conferred on all Americans by the nation's founding fathers. Focusing on the central importance of the First Amendment, Imam Shareef provides the signal insight that in this primary amendment, the Constitution "*treats all citizens as the creation of Almighty God, the Creator*."

Imam Rauf develops this line of thought further, reasoning that to craft an American Muslim identity from that point onward "*has to involve a high appreciation of what it means to be American and what it means to be Muslim.*" This allows for any seeming dichotomies between these two distinct identities to be transcended—and to be fused more closely together, at the higher plane of core universal values.

To elucidate this point, he points to the effectiveness of such places for American Catholics and American Jews, who themselves went through the very same processes several decades earlier, as Muslims are undergoing now: "[They] *were finally able to establish their Catholic-ness and Jewishness, not apart from or in spite of their American-ness, but precisely through it.*"

Cherrefe Kadri's exposition of her experiences at the Islamic Center of Toledo provides an excellent real-life example of how this has worked in action. An added dividend of this is that "*Muslims who regularly attend mosques are more likely to work with their neighbors to solve community problems, be registered to vote, and more likely to plan to vote*."

Chapter 2, *Grasping the Challenges Facing American Muslims*, focuses on a range of interconnected, yet discrete and very specific, challenges that were referred to briefly above: *Islam in the Media; Muslim Condemnations of Terrorism*; and *How Does It Feel to Be a Problem?*; the nature of *Bigotry in Defaming Islam; Surging Hate Crimes; Anti-Shari'ah Legislation; Incarcerated Muslims; Islamophobia and Domestic Security*; and *Partnerships Between Communities and Law Enforcement.*

Each of the articles addressing these broad spectrum of topics is richly detailed and impressively nuanced, with none shying away from stating the facts, however unpalatable they may be, so that the varied lived experiences of American Muslims are laid bare, thereby making them straightforward to accept, and (one would hope) spurring us to collective action.

A number of the compelling insights are contained in the final chapter of this section—*Crafting an American Muslim Identity*. All present several practical examples that illuminate inspiring ways forward on a range of subjects articulated by American Muslims and non-Muslims. The titles of the articles give an indication of the diverse spectrum of views on offer. These carry through in their various ways the threads of the propositions made in the earlier chapters, such as *Fighting Hate: Preserving American Values; Bosniak Muslim Refugees: An American Success Story; The Millennial Muslim; Modesty, Veiling, and Fashion;* and *Notable American Muslims*.

Here's a small taste of what awaits the reader in these articles:

"*[My colleagues and I are] committed to building peace one relationship at a time.*"— Inas Younis

"*Muslim women in America straddle a dual identity—one that allows free exercise of religion and that also allows freedom of expression, thus synthesizing agency and choice.*"— Hassanah El-Yacoubi

"*Islam belongs to neither East nor West but to the hearts of those who want to live in peace and security.*"—Haris Hromic

"*Only after Muslims become a normal and more welcome part of society and of American film and TV industries, will Hollywood be able to fulfill its self-proclaimed ideal of being the conscience of the nation.*"—Kamran Pasha.

Taken together, the 27 articles in Part One incorporate a robust foundation of knowledge, experiences, and achievements on which can be built ever stronger defenses against all forms of hate. As Keith Ellison says, "*Through civic engagement, misrepresentations can diminish and discriminatory mind-sets come tumbling down.*"

SUGGESTIONS

1. Rather than treating the American Muslim community as a security threat, create empowering partnerships with community leaders to solve a range of sociological problems facing Muslim communities.
2. Strengthen interfaith relations, which can counteract much of the opposition to Islam and create a culture of acceptance, understanding, and unity.
3. Support programs that help youth and women cultivate healthy identity formation that attends to both their culture and faith.

CHAPTER 1

Understanding Islam and Muslims in America

The Real Voices of American Muslims: A Survey

ZAINAB ALAM and **PETER ROMANIUK** conducted an online survey to gauge the opinion of American Muslims on the following: Whether the perception of Muslims in America has gotten worse over time; whether the portrayal of Daesh in the mainstream media has had a negative impact on American Muslims; and where the emphasis should be placed when it comes to efforts to combat violent extremism. The evidence gathered in this survey confirms the need for greater emphasis on community engagement and diplomacy when it comes to combating the spread of extremism, an idea that will be explored in more tangible detail in the chapters to come.

The public debate on terrorism and violent extremism is inevitably a highly charged affair. For a variety of reasons, American Muslims, who comprise some 0.9 percent of the total U.S. population (Pew Research Center 2015), are perhaps as likely to be the subjects of that debate as they are to be participants in it. In assembling this Guide, WISE set about the task of deepening our collective understanding of what American Muslims think about extremism and conducted an initial survey toward this goal. Although the WISE survey data and corresponding analysis are limited is certain ways, they generally confirm past research on American Muslims and, in particular, underscore the importance of community engagement in responding to extremism.

Survey research provides the opportunity to gauge public opinion among large numbers of people in an objective and highly representative fashion. But surveys come with a series of known challenges, especially when the sample size of respondents is small and the topic covers sensitive or controversial issues. Both of these challenges pertain in advancing surveys of American Muslims. Not surprisingly, very few large-scale surveys have been conducted among Muslims in the United States on the topic of extremism. When they have been surveyed (Pew Research Center 2011; see also Pew Research Center 2007), data have shown that:

- 64 percent of American Muslims think there is little or no support for Islamic extremism in their community, and only 5 percent had favorable views of Al-Qaeda;
- 81 percent of American Muslims rejected the acceptability of suicide bombings entirely;
- 60 percent of American Muslims were concerned about the possible rise in Islamic extremism in the United States, while 72 percent were concerned about its global rise;
- 48 percent say that Muslim leaders in the United States have not done enough to speak out against Islamic extremists, while 34 percent say Muslim leaders have done as much as they should in challenging extremists; and
- The top three most pressing issues facing American Muslims are: "negative views about Muslims (29 percent), Discrimination/Prejudice/ Not [being] treated fairly (20 percent) and Ignorance about Islam (15 percent)."

We are aware of other research that has used surveys to understand American Muslim perceptions of policing in the context of counterterrorism (Tyler, Schulhofer, and Huq 2010) and also to understand how the general American public thinks about Islam

ZAINAB ALAM is a peacebuilding consultant with experience in the MENA region and in Pakistan. Her current research is focused on the South Asian diaspora in the United States. Ms. Alam recieved her MS in Global Affairs from New York University and she is currently seeking her PhD in Political Science at Rutgers University.

PETER ROMANIUK is an Associate Professor of Political Science at John Jay College of Criminal Justice at the City University of New York. He is the Associate Director of the College's Center on Terrorism and a Senior Fellow at the Global Center on Cooperative Security. Mr. Romaniuk is the author of *Multilateral Counter-terrorism: The Global Politics of Cooperation and Contestation.*

FIGURE 1 As a Muslim, which of the following labels (for the so-called Islamic State) would you recommend for use in the mainstream media?

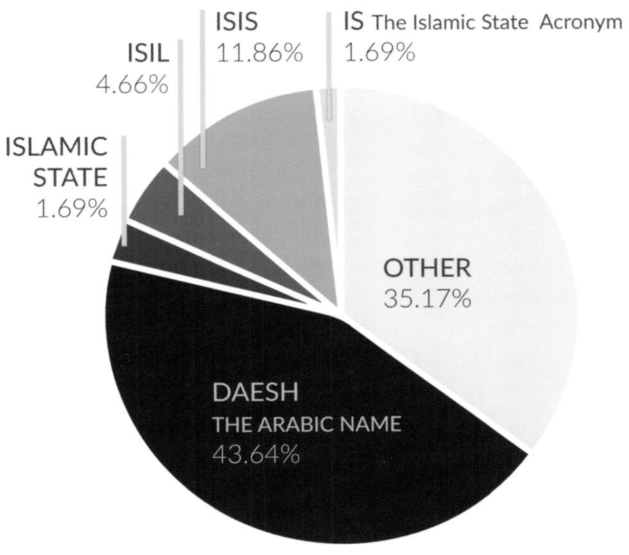

FIGURE 2 In your opinion, the portrayal of Islam in the mainsteam US media (e.g., TV, radio, print) is:

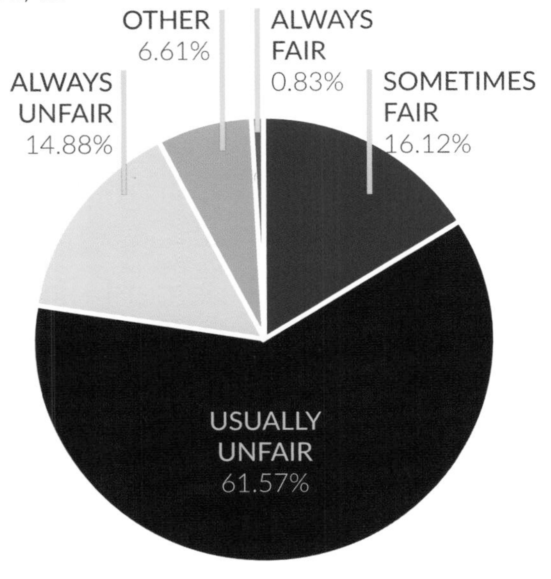

and Muslims in the current climate (YouGov 2015). (Other examples of related research include: Pew Research 2009, Gallup 2011, and Pew Research 2013). In order to add to this body of knowledge, WISE, as a grassroots Muslim organization, set out to conduct a survey on Muslim views on extremism, and more specifically Daesh. We undertook this effort within certain limitations. The survey utilized Survey Monkey, an online tool that enables broad distribution but not ultimate control over who receives and completes the survey. It was initially sent to the approximately 5,000 people who had previously signed up to receive emails from WISE. Across 17 substantive questions, the highest number of responses received (for question 1) was 471, while the fewest (for several of the later questions) was 229. In reviewing these responses, and in light of time constraints, we did not undertake a statistical analysis of the data but rather offer the following descriptive points on the basis of the raw responses for each question submitted by respondents.

An initial finding from the survey is anecdotal. We heard from several people who received the email with the link to the survey that they would decline to complete it due to the sensitive nature of the topic. Although we conducted the survey anonymously, and although WISE is presumably known to almost all of those who received the email, some recipients were clearly concerned about the security of communications and preferred not to participate. To us, this underscores the challenges of survey research on such sensitive topics.

They described being Muslim (67 percent) and being American (52 percent) as "extremely important" to their identity.

Among those who did respond, a slight majority (57 percent) were over 40 years old. Most (60 percent) describe themselves as practicing Muslims. In separate questions they described being Muslim (67 percent) and being American (52 percent) as "extremely important" to their identity. More than three quarters of respondents felt that most Americans perceive Islam negatively while two-thirds agreed that popular perceptions of Islam in the United States have gotten worse over time. While we cannot claim a causal link, roughly the same number of respondents (63 percent) agreed that the portrayal of Islam in the mainstream US media has generally gotten worse over time. When asked further about media coverage of Islam, 62 percent of respondents indicated that the mainstream media is "usually unfair" in its portrayal. More than 90 percent of respondents indicated that the portrayal of Daesh in the mainstream media had a negative impact on popular perceptions of Islam.

> More than 90 percent of respondents indicated that the portrayal of Daesh in the mainstream media had a negative impact on popular perceptions of Islam.

In terms of responses to extremism, in separate questions, the survey prompted respondents to assess the use of different tools of counterterrorism in the last five years and also to suggest what tools should be given greater emphasis in the next five years. Among these data, some points stand out. For example, regarding the use of military force, 55 percent of respondents said that past efforts have been counterproductive, while 44 percent added that such measures should receive less emphasis in the future. Nearly 40 percent of respondents said that foreign policy has been counterproductive for counterterrorism in the past, while 75 percent said it should have more emphasis in the future. Further, 43 percent of respondents viewed past efforts at community engagement as effective, while 89 percent said it should be given greater emphasis. Overall, it seems respondents viewed community engagement, alongside foreign policy and diplomacy, as critical to effective counterterrorism responses.

As noted, the survey included a few questions on Daesh in particular. For example, respondents were asked to rank order who, within the Muslim community (Imams and mosques; Islamic schools; Muslim non-government organizations; parents and families; and figures in the arts and entertainment), should lead efforts in discrediting the extremist narrative. Here, results were somewhat spread, perhaps indicating that different actors all have a role to play in this regard. However, many respondents clearly think that Imams and mosques have an important role here (40 percent of respondents ranked Imams and mosques first). Finally, the survey asked respondents about the different names used in the media to describe the so-called Islamic State, noting that some names may lend

FIGURE 03 Over the next 5 years, please rate how much emphasis should be placed on the following counter-extremism efforts.

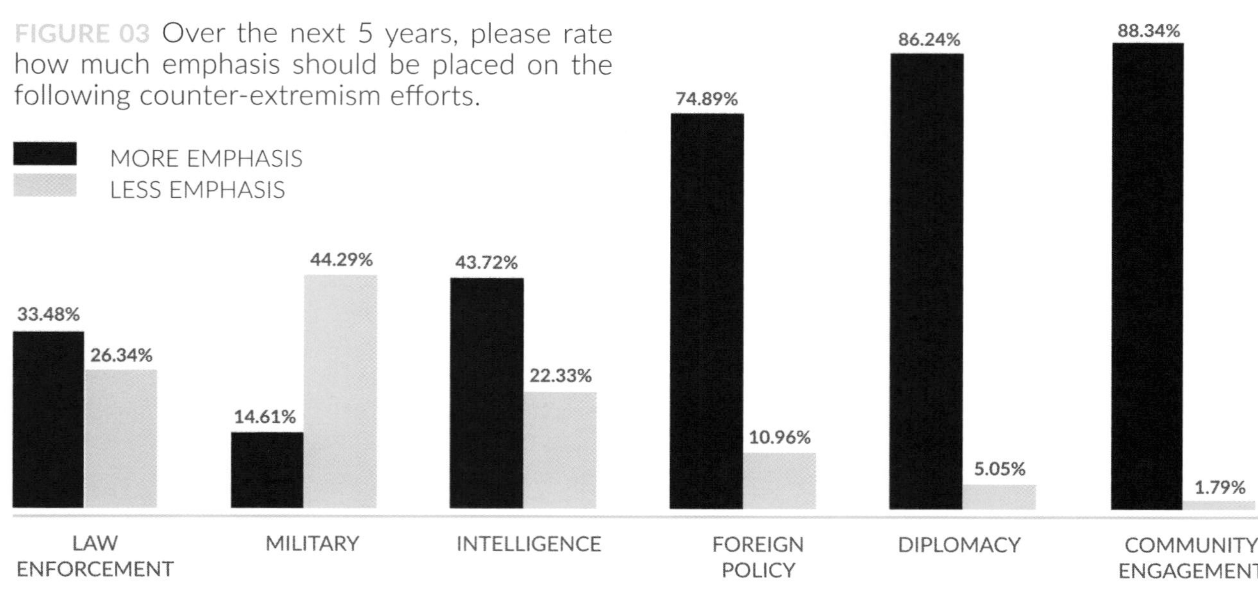

religious credibility to the group. Here, 44 percent of respondents said that the Arabic term, "Daesh," should be preferred to others. An additional 35 percent of respondents chose to contribute their own suggestions for how the group should be identified. Many of these respondents echoed suggestions that the word "Islam" should not be used when referring to the group, to disassociate the groups' actions from the faith.

Respondents viewed community engagement, alongside foreign policy and diplomacy, as critical to effective counterterrorism.

In sum, the WISE survey should be treated as an initial effort to add to our knowledge about perceptions of extremism among American Muslims. But as a community-led effort, it may nonetheless provide a platform for some recommendations for leaders from within the American Muslim public. First, and perhaps most obviously, Muslims in America are concerned about the image of Islam in the media and how it impacts public perceptions of Muslims as a community. Second, it can be inferred that among respondents there is a desire for more community engagement about the issue of extremism, especially from religious leaders. Third, there is some skepticism surrounding the effectiveness of current responses to extremism that are not community based. Taken collectively, and in line of other anecdotal evidence that we have observed, there seems to be some support for changing the way the topic of extremism is currently being discussed with and among Muslim communities, and a demand for a more positive narrative surrounding the Islamic faith. Future efforts should aim to generate a more nuanced and informed debate about these sensitive matters and it is hoped that the present survey illustrates the willingness of communities to participate in such a discussion.

Islam, Thomas Jefferson, and the First Amendment

IMAM TALIB M. SHAREEF explains how the concept of religious freedom enshrined in the U.S. Constitution included Islam and Muslims, who have been in the U.S. Since before the nation's founding.

KEY TAKEAWAYS

- America guarantees religious freedom, a right explicitly extended to Americans of all religious beliefs, be they Christian, Jewish, Muslim, or of any other faith.
- Islam arrived in the U.S. with the slaves brought from Africa, many of whom were Muslim and continued practicing their faith throughout their bondage.
- Islam's principle of religious pluralism is compatible with the foundational American value of religious freedom.

Not long after the Declaration of Independence granted Americans their freedom from tyranny, the founding fathers gave Americans the greatest gift of all—the constitutional right to religious freedom. The value of this inalienable human right is made clear, as it was the very first amendment added to the Constitution, which states, "Congress shall make no law respecting an establishment of religion, or prohibiting the free exercise thereof; or abridging the freedom of speech, or of the press, or the right of the people peaceably to assemble, and to petition the Government for a redress of grievances." In examining the foundational values upon which our nation was established, we find that at its core, the values that brought the pioneers to America, in search of democracy and religious freedom, contain aspirations and ideals that Muslims can accept, identify and share with other Americans. Both, the religion of Islam and America, started with freedom of religion as the first of the freedoms. Therefore, the religion of Islam has a natural relationship with American philosophy and with the spirit that is found in the United States Constitution.

The First Amendment is rooted in the fact that, from the very beginning, the fight for religious freedom preceded the fight for all other freedoms. Realizing that mankind was created to have independence and freedom of worship, the Pilgrims came to these lands because they were persecuted and couldn't exercise their religious rights in Europe. So, they came here to start their lives anew with the opportunity to live their Christianity to their choosing, without hindrance and denial from the governments they fled. In doing so, they wanted that to be the standard for all in the new democracy, which included Muslims, as noted by President Obama in his address during his first visit to an American mosque in February 2016. He said, "Islam has always been part of America. Starting in colonial times, many of the slaves brought here from Africa were Muslim. And even in their bondage, some kept their faith alive. A few even won their freedom and became known to many Americans. And when enshrining the freedom of religion in our Constitution and our Bill of Rights, our Founders meant what they said when they said it applied to all religions." And Thomas Jefferson explained that

IMAM TALIB M. SHAREEF is the President and Imam of the historic Masjid Muhammad, the Nation's Mosque in Washington, DC, and is a senior Islamic leader and board member of the Interfaith Conference. He served as a Chief Master Sergeant of the United States Air Force for 30 years and received an MBA from American Intercontinental University and a Diploma from the Imam Muhammad ibn Saud Islamic University, and graduated from the Defense Language Institute Foreign Language Center in Arabic and Middle Eastern Studies. He has spoken at the U.S Congress and Washington National Cathedral; on the steps of the Lincoln Memorial in commemoration of Dr. Martin Luther King Jr.; in Italy, South Africa, South America, South Korea, and Nigeria. He has received the Kingdom of Morocco's highest Royal Medal for his outstanding interfaith leadership and has been honored by President Barack Obama at the White House in recognition of his work.

the Virginia Statute for Religious Freedom he wrote was designed to protect all faiths, which included "the Jew and the Gentile, the Christian and the Mahometan [Muslim]."

Thomas Jefferson explained that the Virginia Statute for Religious Freedom he wrote was designed to protect all faiths, which included "the Jew and the Gentile, the Christian and the Mahometan [Muslim]."

We find these core values expressed by many during the course of American history. Among those is President Franklin D. Roosevelt, who said in a speech to Congress that religious freedom "is the freedom of every person to worship God in his own way, everywhere in the world."

President Obama, in his February 2016 visit to the Islamic Society of Baltimore, reminded us of the words of President Dwight Eisenhower: "In 1957, when dedicating the Islamic Center in Washington, D.C., President Eisenhower said, 'I should like to assure you, my Islamic friends, that under the American Constitution . . . and in American hearts . . . this place of worship, is just as welcome . . . as any other religion.'"

Many among the founding fathers of this great nation and those connected with their struggle for independence and freedom of religious expression, were guided by universal aspirations to establish spiritual life as the way for the betterment of society so that society could exist, have a good future, and progress in the matter ordained for it by the Creator. This idea of the Creator is highlighted in the foundational documents upon which the First Amendment is based and is in the language of the founding fathers: "We hold these truths to be self-evident, that all men are created equal and endowed by their Creator." Here in the language of the founding fathers is the recognition of Almighty God as the Creator and a recognition that all men have inalienable rights that the government can't give to them. They acknowledged that all were created with those rights—inalienable rights—among these life, liberty, and the pursuit of happiness.

These are statements of strong faith and allegiance to God and they underscore how the First Amendment was meant to be interpreted in terms of religious freedom for all religious communities and people of faith. In the language of the founding fathers was the idea that would connect man to Almighty God; and it would insist that government recognize this connection that it, the government, didn't make and cannot break. Essentially, they were forcing government to recognize that connection and treat all citizens as the creation of Almighty God, the Creator. This idea is at the core of what makes America beautiful. This idea of a government, a society that acknowledges that there is a Superior Authority other than man and that people are accountable to that authority, their Creator, who gave them their life, is what establishes a true democracy.

Many among the founding fathers of this great nation and those connected with their struggle for independence and freedom of religious expression, were guided by universal aspirations to establish spiritual life as the way for the betterment of society.

It's consistent with what Muslims believe which is that Almighty God is the Creator, of everything. It was intentional that the founders gave acknowledgement to "the Creator," rather than using a specific or proper name. In the history of Islam, when the Prophet Muhammad (pbuh) received the first words of revelation, the name Allah (swt) was not mentioned. On the initial visit and words to Muhammad, in the first five verses, the only references to Allah are "Lord and Creator." In other words, Almighty God introduced Himself to the Prophet (pbuh), first, as the Creator, and the name Allah came later. Herein is the wisdom also of the founders in their use of "Creator."

By reasoning, they concluded that every religion that recognizes Almighty God, "the Creator," as the One who is responsible for what we see in the skies, for the earth that we live on and whatever comes out of the earth, and is responsible for man's own existence, can live and coexist with others. Not only live together, but also work together, have mutual respect for, and cooperate with one another for the future of humanity; because that is the precious idea that makes it possible for us to progress with our human life in society.

George Washington stated in his first Inaugural address, "We ought to be no less persuaded that the propitious smiles of Heaven can never be expected on a nation that disregards the eternal rules of order and right which Heaven itself has ordained." So, America recognizes that this is the beauty and strength of our Constitution, and it's what holds our society together. Imam W. Deen Mohammed, in an address to an American Muslim Military Conference in Washington, D.C., said, "This country gives us more religious freedom than most of our own Islamic nations or countries, but we have to soberly in the mind see these facts and realities, and register and appreciate them. . . . If we can recognize these realities, this change, and heal ourselves, and embrace the good, and embrace the progress, and embrace the good aims and good purposes for which this nation was envisioned or created by its Founding Fathers, and how the spirit and language that they left with us has gained support . . . then we are in a good situation to make progress in this society."

This country gives us more religious freedom than most of our own Islamic nations or countries, but we have to soberly in the mind see these facts and realities, and register and appreciate them.

Imam Mohammed was asked, "How do I serve my country?" His answer: "I serve my country as a citizen of this country, as a believer in Almighty God."

Islam: The Evolution of an American Religion

IMAM FEISAL ABDUL RAUF explains how American Muslims are currently experiencing the same struggle with acceptance that other religious groups have experienced in the past.

KEY TAKEAWAYS

- American Muslims today generally feel that they are regarded with suspicion and hostility, just as American Catholics and Jews felt a century ago.
- Crafting an American-Muslim identity requires an appreciation both of what it means to be American and what it means to be Muslim.
- Fast-tracking an American-Muslim identity lies in learning from the immigrant experiences of its predecessor religious communities of Catholicism and Judaism.

Most Muslims are unaware that what they are going through is more of a sociological rather than a religious phenomenon, one that remarkably parallels the historical experience of immigrant Catholics and Jews. American Muslims today feel as if their faith is still generally regarded by American non-Muslims with suspicion and hostility. Catholics and Jews felt the same way a century ago. If the experience of Muslims follows that of Catholics and Jews, it will take another generation or two before American Muslims reach the same point achieved by their Catholic and Jewish predecessors in America. The point to which I am referring was the time when American Catholics and American Jews were finally able to establish their Catholic-ness and Jewishness not apart from or in spite of their Americanness, but precisely in and through it.

Although Catholicism was present on American shores from the start, in New Orleans, Louisiana, and in the territories bordering Mexico, it was always seen as more of a foreign church struggling to find its place in a growing American culture, a vestige of British attitudes toward the French and the Spanish. When large numbers of Irish Catholics—followed by the immigration of Italian Catholics and Polish Catholics—began to immigrate to America in the 1800s, a hostile anti-Catholic movement began to take shape. This movement was directed primarily at the Irish "foreigners," who were felt to be imperiling the livelihood of "native" Americans, as well as their culture, religion, and the American way of life—strikingly similar to what Muslims are accused of today. In time, however, American Catholic bishops defined the Catholic Church in the United States and performed an indispensable task in mediating between the Catholic Church as a strange and alien body and the emerging American culture.

> The work involved in developing an American Islamic identity has to involve, by definition, a high appreciation both for what it means to be American and what it means to be Muslim.

In a process characteristic of the American pattern of life, the church played a crucial role as a vehicle for the social, economic, and political ambitions of immigrant groups bent on building themselves from poor

IMAM FEISAL ABDUL RAUF is the founder and president of Cordoba House, a New York-based nonprofit 501(c)3 organization dedicated to leading, engaging, and promoting a distinctly contemporary, pluralistic, and spiritual American Muslim identity in the United States. He is the author of six books, including *What's Right with Islam Is What's Right with America*, *Moving the Mountain: A New Vision of Islam in America*, and most recently, *Defining Islamic Statehood: Measuring and Indexing Contemporary Muslim States*.

foreigners to middle-class Americans. In particular, its widespread network of institutions and activities, as well as its Catholic schools and colleges, helped the church accelerate the emergence of a Catholic middle class, enabling the Catholic community to become more American—America being preeminently a middle-class country. It thus became possible to be an American not only without falling away from the church, but precisely in and through being a Catholic. The clearest sign of the Americanization of the Catholic Church in America probably came around the middle of the twentieth century, when American Catholics and non-Catholics alike began to regard Catholicism as one of the three great American religions. As sociologist Will Herberg writes in his book *Protestants, Catholics, and Jews*:

> The fast track for American Muslims seeking to find their American identity lies through learning from the immigrant experience of American Catholics and Jews.

> *Under the pressure of the American environment in which they so successfully adapted themselves, American Catholics learned to operate with a double vision: in terms of a self-enclosed microcosmic community within their own church, and in terms of a tripartite macrocosm in which Catholics, Protestants, and Jews were conceived as living in harmonious coexistence, if not cooperation, under the benevolent aegis of American democracy.*[1]

American Muslims today, especially immigrant mosque centers, operate with a similar double vision: in terms of their own small community with their own ethnic institution often tied to a "back home" worldview, and in terms of a much larger pluralistic and democratic society.

American Jews followed a similar path in becoming part of American society. Although the first Jews to come to America landed in 1654, like American Catholics, American Jewry is predominantly the product of the great wave of migration from Germany and Eastern Europe in the 1800s. By the mid-nineteenth century they were already busily erecting a network of community institutions (synagogues, schools, community centers, etc.) that reflected their conditions of settlement and not simply traditions carried over from the past or abroad.

However, because religion and immigrant culture were so thoroughly fused, the 1.7 million Eastern Europeans to arrive in America at the turn of the twentieth-century came up against a shattering crisis in their interaction with their American-born sons and daughters. Desperately anxious to become unequivocally American, the second generation born and raised in America rejected the foreignness of their parents, which sometimes also meant rejecting Jewishness and Judaism. In response, Mordecai M. Kaplan's "Reconstructionism" movement sought to combine a liberal theology with a concept of Judaism that saw Jews in America as living in two civilizations, one American and the other Jewish.

By the mid-twentieth century, the form of American Jewish religion was characterized by a far-reaching accommodation to the American pattern of religious life. The American Jewish community had become an integral part of American society. American Jews, like American Catholics, established their Jewishness not apart from or in spite of their Americanness, but precisely in and through it, and thus had achieved the status of Judaism in the American way of life as one of the three religions of democracy.

Likewise, the work involved in developing an American Islamic identity has to involve, by definition, a high appreciation both for what it means to be American and what it means to be Muslim. It cannot be just the accidental experience of being a foreign Muslim living in America, each part at odds with the other. Nor can it be an American becoming Muslim in order to reject America. It requires unpacking the psychological layers of past individual and collective experience, separating history from essential humanity, shedding what is irrelevant, and building an identity based on

[1] Will Herberg, Protestant, Catholic, Jew: An Essay in American Religious Sociology (Chicago: University of Chicago Press, 1960), 152.

what is eternal to the human condition, and essential to Islam, in a new America and a globalized world.

This knowledge can help American Muslims more rapidly shape a new definition of what it means to be an American Muslim in a globalized world—as much for their own sake as for the sake of their children and grandchildren, and for their coreligionists around the world.

One way to accomplish this goal is to engage with our predecessors in the immigrant experience, Christians and Jews who had to develop an American Christian and American Jewish identity, learning from their experiences as they evolved from being imported expressions of mainly European churches and synagogues into American expressions of Judaism and Christianity. Based on the Jewish example, for instance, American Muslims may find ways to practice their traditions and have them recognized by the wider American society. The Muslim community might follow the example of the Jewish community in establishing the equivalent of their Beth Din, a legal system for Orthodox Jews in which rabbinic judges adjudicate cases; the decisions are legally binding in American courts because the cases "are conducted in a manner consistent with the requirements of secular arbitration law" and not against the principles of American law.

Jewish and Catholic experiences in America have paved the way for Muslims to have their religious needs recognized in American society and law, and, as a byproduct, therefore help to influence the development of the Islamic tradition outside the United States. While each experience is unique, many aspects of the process are common and can afford meaningful and fruitful opportunities for growth. This means that the fast track for American Muslims seeking to find their American identity lies through learning from the immigrant experience of American Catholics and Jews. Blended with lessons gleaned from Islamic history, when the earliest Muslims spread beyond the Arabian peninsula to the ancient cultures spanning West Africa to Southeast Asia, this knowledge can help American Muslims more rapidly shape a new definition of what it means to be an American Muslim in a globalized world—as much for their own sake as for the sake of their children and grandchildren, and for their coreligionists around the world.

The American Mosque

CHERREFE KADRI traces the evolution of American mosques to show how American-Muslim religious life has shifted its focus toward promoting inclusion, integration, and acceptance of varied ethnicities, as well as toward assigning pivotal roles to women in its operations.

KEY TAKEAWAYS

- American Muslims, from as early the 1800s, have expressed their inalienable right to worship by establishing informal religious communities and mosques.
- Like other places of worship, mosques have diversified their activities and functions and are now seen as centers for community building and civic engagement.
- American Muslims who attend mosques are more likely to reach out to their neighbors, solve community problems, be civically engaged, and vote.

America was founded on the principle that all peoples possess four freedoms, one of which is an inalienable right to believe, worship, and practice what they wish. In fact, religion has historically been at the heart of community building, and often the very first thing a new community does is establish a place of worship. This is also true for Muslims in America. When Muslims began to arrive in America in the North African slave trade, records suggest that Muslim slaves organized informal religious communities and established places where they could practice their religion. For instance, in the early 1800s, Bilali (Ben Ali) Muhammad, a slave from Guinea, served as a religious leader for his fellow Muslim slaves, and even established a small mosque on the grounds of his plantation on Sapelo Island off the coast of Georgia.

The stories of early Muslim slaves, like Bilali Muhammad, show just how embedded the inalienable right to freedom of religion and establishing places of worship is to the American psyche. Although there have been records of small, "unofficial" mosques built by early slaves, it was not until the start of the twentieth century that the first "official" mosques were built in America's heartlands to serve the needs of growing Muslim communities. Most often, the early mosques in America were homes away from home in the sense that they were established by a nationally homogenous group as a place where families went to worship and maintain their heritage. This can be said of my own mosque, the Islamic Center of Greater Toledo, whose founders came mainly from the Bekaa Valley of Lebanon and established the center in 1954 to serve the needs of the Lebanese Muslim community in Toledo. Many of them were from the same town or village and they therefore had a common language and dialect, common foods, common lifestyle, and common acquaintances.

"In the early 1800s, Bilali (Ben Ali) Muhammad, a slave from Guinea, served as a religious leader for his fellow Muslim slaves, and even established a small mosque on the grounds of his plantation on Sapelo Island off the coast of Georgia

CHERREFE KADRI is the first woman president of a mosque in the United States. She was first elected president of the Islamic Center of Greater Toledo in 2001, and then was elected to serve a second term in 2013. Ms. Kadri received her law degree from the University of Toledo College of Law and currently practices law in the greater Toledo area.

But as the Toledo Muslim community began to grow and diversify with the arrival of new immigrants, so too did the Toledo mosque.

> "American religious life in general began to diversify... Religion was seen as a mechanism for community building and civic engagement, while houses of worship began to function as community centers to the local populations

It was also around this time that American religious life in general began to diversify and expand its activities beyond its primary function of worship. Rather, religion was seen as a mechanism for community building and civic engagement, while houses of worship began to function as community centers to the local populations. The same was true for the growing and rapidly diversifying American Muslim community. This community was no longer concerned with simply establishing Islam in America, but also with solidifying Islam's status as an American religion. To do so, American Muslim communities began to pursue relations with their non-Muslim neighbors and opened the doors of their mosques to the community at large.

This shift also occurred in my own mosque, the Islamic Center of Greater Toledo (ICGT). As the Toledo Muslim community grew and diversified, the mosque began to shift focus toward promoting inclusion, integration, and acceptance of all Toledo Muslims—regardless of whether they were Arab, South Asian, Afghan, Malaysian, mixed-marriage couples, or university students.

In fact, the ICGT's mission from the very beginning has been to ingrain ourselves in American culture, and to not isolate ourselves from our neighbors and the surrounding communities.

The ICGT has continued to evolve with American society by assigning women to pivotal roles in its operation. This was reflected when the ICGT elected me as its first woman president in 2001, which made me the first woman president of a mosque in the United States. Still, I was shocked when a member of the ICGT told me that I should not accept my nomination for president because it was "un-Islamic" for a mosque to have a woman president. However, I knew that his argument had no basis in the Qur'an or Islamic teachings of gender equality. So, I accepted the nomination for president in 2001 and was elected by a slim majority, after which the gender issue was set aside and life went on. When my story of becoming the first woman president of a mosque became newsworthy, I was heartened to see that the bar was raised by Dr. T. O. Shanavas when he wrote in his January 2001 editorial in the Center's magazine, the Monitor:

> *I am happy that we, the members of the Islamic Center of Greater Toledo, set in motion the beginning of the end of misogyny.*

> In common parlance, the Islamic Center walks the walk of equality of and dignity for women.

Contrary to what some may have expected, lightning did not strike the dome, the community did not disintegrate. We simply followed the same trajectory as other religious communities in America who have allowed women to occupy leadership roles. It is no wonder that many Muslim women in America see themselves as continuing the journey of the suffragettes. All we want is to contribute to the greater Muslim community and serve as active members in our mosques. This is why I am so proud that the ICGT Council has elected two other women as president since 2001, making me an anomaly no longer. Dr. Mahjabeen Islam served as president in 2012 and Dr. Nadia Ashraf-Moghal is the current president of the center. I was even elected a second time in 2013 and was able to serve my community for another three years. It makes me so proud that the youth of the center are growing up in an Islamic center that respects the contributions of all. Several young ladies have even told me that I'm a role model in their lives. What greater compliment can one get or hope to ever be given? Answer: None. It is the best compliment ever!

Unfortunately, some traditions have restricted Muslim women's ability to follow the same path, and have isolated women in the mosques and community. While I do recognize that change is difficult to accept and implement, and it is human nature to resist it, our history has shown that change occurs when women are involved in the decision-making process. Because of this, the ICGT has purposely and intentionally lived the equality that Islam brought to all Muslims, particularly women. Its prayer space has a 30-inch-high movable divider between the men's and women's sections that are lateral to each other. The women are not relegated to a balcony or distant room while the men are in the main prayer room. In common parlance, the Islamic Center walks the walk of equality of and dignity for women. At the beginning of the Eid prayers the president traditionally gives a short talk of the events of the past year, or plans for the coming year; an unusual scene indeed: a woman speaking in front of men and women in the prayer room.

In order to survive and thrive in this small world, mosques must transition from houses of worship to community centers.

To further adhere to our mission of inclusion and openness, the ICGT is proactive in introducing Islam, its culture and heritage, to the community at large in an effort to promote interfaith understanding and accommodation. One way the center is doing so is through our Visiting Scholars Program that hosts speakers for a public lecture series on topics of interest to Muslims and non-Muslims. These lectures are free and open to the public, and have previously invited Muslim and non-Muslim men and women to present on social, religious, legal, and scientific topics. Most recently, the center hosted a noted Catholic priest who gave a lecture titled "Violence and Religion" to a sold-out audience. Usually, thirty to forty percent of the attendees of our visiting scholars programs are from the non-Muslim community. All lectures are followed by a reception in the center's social hall which allows guests to mix, mingle, and get to know us. Oftentimes, our guests will say, "This is my first time in a mosque and I'm so glad I came. You folks are so friendly and welcoming."

"Muslims who regularly attend mosques are more likely to work with their neighbors to solve community problems, be registered to vote, and are more likely to plan to vote."

Our most popular community outreach event among Muslims and non-Muslims is the center's highly anticipated annual summer International Festival, which includes a main tent that houses food booths representing the many cultures of the ICGT. It is a wonderful multicultural event: the men's Seniors Active Club serves Arabic coffee and lemonade; the Lebanese women make fresh bread on the saj, frying zalabe; members from Brazil make coxina, fried bananas; Palestinians make shawarma; Pakistanis cook biriyani and serve mango ice cream; Saudi Arabians provide dates; and Turks offer sweets and tea, to name only a very few. The camel ride always has a long line, the petting zoo and bouncy house are favorites of the little ones, and our full-time school sponsors a children's tent with face painting, balloons, and arts and crafts to paint. This event is not only a fundraiser, but a fabulous public relations opportunity, especially when the public tours the center and views its cultural exhibits.

All of these reasons have caused the Islamic Center to enjoy its growth and the diversity of its membership. It attracts those with a progressive view of Islam and a vision of what can be. We have learned to coexist with our fellow Muslims despite our ethnic and racial diversity. In order to survive and thrive in this small world, mosques must transition from houses of worship to community centers. In addition to holding Friday prayers, mosques have to meet the social and educational needs of their members.

To meet this need, they must provide Sunday school classes and lectures for those who are not able to attend on Friday, or whose children are not enrolled in the full-time Islamic school. The center has done so by organizing biannual teacher workshops where experts present on the basics of Islam, Islamic history and culture, and other topics. This program has far-reaching effects because each teacher sees 75 to 100 students in a school year, meaning the center's workshop potentially influences 6,000 to 8,000 young people. It is my sincere belief that mosques in America are duty-bound to meet the social needs of their youth to help them to develop a positive identity as both Muslims and Americans.

Although some public figures have recently suggested that all American mosques should be closed because they cause "radicalization" and encourage "extremism," examples like the ICGT prove that this could not be further from the truth. Even more so, a recent survey of over 500 American

Muslims conducted by the Institute for Social Policy and Understanding (ISPU), reveals there is absolutely no correlation between frequent mosque attendance and attitudes toward violence against civilians. The survey also notes that frequent mosque attendance "is linked with higher levels of civic engagement. Muslims who regularly attend mosques are more likely to work with their neighbors to solve community problems, be registered to vote, and are more likely to plan to vote."[1]

Frequent mosque attendance "is linked with higher levels of civic engagement."[1]

So, to discredit this public rhetoric of Islamophobes and extremists, American Islamic centers need to preserve their right to worship and promote inclusion and openness as active American citizens. In this rapidly evolving world, mosques must make accurate information about Islam easily available to Muslims and non-Muslims. Isolationism is no longer an option for American Muslim communities; in fact, it is a recipe for disaster.

[1] Institute for Social Policy and Understanding. (2016). American Muslim Poll: Participation, Priorities, and Facing Prejudice in the 2016 Elections. Washington, DC: Dalia Mogahed and Fouad Pervez.

7 Common Misconceptions About American Muslims

ENGY ABDELKADER discusses how Americans often associate Muslims with violence and extremism. This perception problem is perpetuated by anti-Muslim hate groups and amplified by negative portrayals in the news media. The news media is the most influential information source shaping the general American public's views about this minority faith community. Since 90 percent of news stories on Islam and Muslims are about war or terrorism, these depictions are far from representative of the overwhelming majority of American Muslims. As such, misconceptions about Muslims persist, percolating in conspiratorial email chains, hyper-partisan news media discussions and perhaps most critically, among policymakers. American Muslims have watched these falsehoods develop over the past 15 years. Here, we identify and debunk seven of them:

1 "NOT ALL MUSLIMS ARE TERRORISTS, BUT ALL TERRORISTS ARE MUSLIM."

According to a recent 2017 report by Duke University's Triangle Center on Terrorism and Homeland Security, violent extremism dropped by 40 percent in 2016 as compared to the prior year. The reality is that while self-identifying Muslims are responsible for 123 fatalities since 9/11, according to Duke, more than 230,000 Americans were murdered over the same period. As highlighted further below, right-wing extremists actually pose the greatest threat to U.S. domestic security.

2 "MUSLIMS ARE NOT PATRIOTIC."

As Gold Star parents Khizr and Ghazala Khan reminded us at the 2016 Democratic National Convention, American Muslims have made the ultimate sacrifice for our country since the Revolutionary War. Today, almost 4,000 Muslims serve in the U.S. Armed Forces, and even more in law enforcement.

3 "MUSLIMS/ISLAM HATES AMERICA."

According to a Pew survey, almost one half of Americans (49 percent) believe "some" American Muslims are anti-American. But research from Gallup indicates that American Muslims are just as likely to identify with their faith as they do with the United States. Also, an Institute for Social Policy and Understanding study shows that Muslims with a stronger faith identity are more likely to emphasize their American identity as well.

ENGY ABDELKADER, JD, LLM is a senior fellow and adjunct professor at the Edmund A. Walsh School of Foreign Service, where she teaches seminars on civil liberties and national security as well as on terrorism and human rights. At Georgetown's Bridge Initiative, a multiyear research project located in the Alwaleed Center for Muslim-Christian Understanding, she researches and writes on the intersection of religion, law, and society with a particular focus on Islamophobia.

4 "MUSLIM REFUGEES ARE COMING TO AMERICA TO ATTACK US IN THE NAME OF ISLAM."

In 2016, approximately 85,000 refugees entered the U.S. and forty-six percent—38,901—were Muslim. The sources of more than half of our Muslim refugees are Syria (12,486) and Somalia (9,012), with the remainder coming from Iraq (7,853), Burma (3,145), Afghanistan (2,664), and other countries (3,741). Additionally, 1 million immigrants are granted Green Cards each year. In 2016 approximately one in ten of those new legal immigrants were Muslim. Last year, none of these Muslims committed an act of terrorism on U.S. soil.

5 "MUSLIM TERRORISTS ARE INFLITRATING OUR BORDERS."

In 2015, in the wake of terror attacks in Paris and San Bernardino and a wave of unaccompanied minors flowing over the border from Central America, many expressed anxiety that would-be terrorists could exploit border vulnerabilities to attack us. While political rhetoric focuses on the dangers of allowing Syrian refugees to enter the United States, there is no concrete evidence that an infiltration by Muslims or a mass movement has taken place as part of a larger pattern. Moreover, while President Donald Trump's recent executive orders have banned immigrants from six Muslim-majority countries, no Americans were murdered in terror attacks carried out by foreign nationals from the banned countries. Even intelligence from the U.S. Department of Homeland Security confirms that one's country of citizenship is an unlikely indicator of a security threat.

6 "MUSLIMS ARE RESPONSIBLE FOR MOST ACTS OF TERRORISM IN THE U.S."

Ninety-nine percent of American Muslims have had no involvement with such heinous activities in the past 15 years. According to FBI statistics, from 1980 to 2005, American Muslims were responsible for only 6 percent of attacks in the United States. The Triangle Center on Terrorism and Homeland Security at Duke University found that U.S. law enforcement agencies considered antigovernment violent extremists as the most severe threat of political violence. Research from the University of Maryland has confirmed this.

7 "MUSLIMS AREN'T DOING ANYTHING TO PREVENT VIOLENT EXTREMISM."

Surprisingly, the general American public is unaware that American Muslims are the single largest source of tips to law enforcement agencies in foiling terrorist plots. In short, American Muslims and the global Muslim community, is united in its belief that suicide bombings and other acts of terrorism committed in the name of Islam are never justified. According to Gallup, American Muslims are more likely than any other religious community to reject violence against civilians. The U.S. Department of Justice found that American Muslims are actively engaged in anti-radicalization efforts within their religious communities and mosques. These include self-policing, community-building, and political engagement. In addition, Muslims have issued over 700 (and counting) condemnations against terrorism since 9/11.

"Every now and then a man's mind is stretched by a new idea or sensation, and never shrinks back to its former dimensions."

- Oliver Wendell Holmes

CHAPTER 2

Grasping the Challenges Facing American Muslims

Islam in the Media

DAISY KHAN describes the effects of the continued linkage between Islam and terrorism in the media, and how such coverage negatively affects the general American public's view of Muslims as not speaking out against terrorism. WISE has included recommendations for media in how to provide a more balanced and accurate portrayal of Islam and Muslims in media coverage.

Terrorism has become one of the gravest concerns of all nations. Because the media is globalized, whatever U.S.-based media broadcasts also informs and influences public opinion around the world. As violent extremist groups become stronger and their actions escalate, it is incumbent upon the media to modify its coverage of this violence so that it no longer indirectly serves the interests of extremists but the interests of the public instead.

Many non-Muslim Americans perennially complain that Muslims do not sufficiently condemn terrorist attacks committed in the name of Islam. This alleged lack of Muslim response has unfortunately helped to distort American perceptions of Islam to such an extent that Muslims are somehow considered to be complicit in such violence themselves.

Ironically, Muslims make the reverse complaint against the mainstream media that it fails to give enough coverage to repeated Muslim condemnations about terrorism. In 2015, WISE conducted an online survey among American Muslims to gauge how media coverage about Islam and Muslims might affect Muslim responses to terrorism, and the perceptions that non-Muslim Americans have about Muslims as a result.

Ninety percent of respondents expressed their belief that mainstream media discourse concerning extremist violence has a negative effect on public perceptions of Islam. To offset the impact of this media coverage, WISE has included a list of condemnations against terrorism on page 33 and at www.wiseupreport.org. Had such condemnations by American Muslims been publicly reported in the mainstream media, the claim that American Muslims are somehow silently supportive of such acts would likely not have gained such currency. It is therefore crucial now more than ever for the media to inform the American public of the plain and simple fact that Muslims *have* spoken out against terrorism—and have done so regularly for years.

One of the key public responsibilities of the media in a democracy is to provide the knowledge necessary for a society to govern itself, a duty that has become more complex as global tensions and acts of violence escalate. WISE understands that Muslim responses to extremist violence, precisely because they tend to be straightforward, measured, and based on proven facts, are inherently less attention-grabbing than the sensationalist, theatrical, and usually shocking nature of terrorist acts.

It is therefore crucial now more than ever for the media to inform the American public of the plain and simple fact that Muslims *have* spoken out against terrorism—and have done so regularly for years.

EXTREMISTS' MANIPULATION OF MEDIA

When it comes to deciding what news is worthy of coverage, as the saying goes: "*If it bleeds, it leads.*" This is something that terrorists themselves fully understand, and they have crafted their entire marketing strategy accordingly. They therefore aim to produce the most graphic images and disturbing videos of their attacks to send to the media, knowing that such eye-catching content is likely to get published. And every time the media broadcasts or prints such material, it is to an extent itself complicit in helping terrorists achieve many of their aims, namely of turning non-Muslims against Muslims, increasing public fear worldwide to emphasize their menace, and increase the effectiveness of their deceitful recruitment tactics.

LINKING OF ISLAM AND TERRORISM

What may have an even more pernicious impact, however, is the constant rhetoric in some parts of the media about and framing of terrorism and Islam as being cut from the same cloth. Even something as seemingly minor as the name by which some media outlets refer to an extremist group plays an insidious role in legitimizing the group. WISE's 2015 survey found that nearly 80 percent of respondents would prefer the media not use the names "ISIS" or "Islamic State"–terms that explicitly refer to Islam–and instead use the Arabic acronym "Daesh" or something else that makes no reference to their faith.

Terrorists use Islam as a veneer, a strategic way to validate their actions and reinforce their recruitment practices. Terrorist groups are political groups with political goals, and they use religion to legitimize and achieve these goals. Whenever the media highlights a narrative in which terrorism and Islam are inherently linked, it indirectly strengthens groups such as al-Qaeda and Daesh and hinders efforts to counter extremist ideology and curb terrorist attacks.

News media inevitably reports terrorist attacks, violence, war, and conflict as "news." However, inspiring stories of human strength, resilience, and bravery, which are equally compelling in terms of their human interest, tend not to be considered as newsworthy. A more balanced media approach, one that tells more sides of the story, is needed. For instance, profiling inspirational and captivating stories about Muslims would help present a truer picture and be much less harmful to how non-Muslims tend currently to view Muslims. Indeed, the many peacemaking efforts and initiatives being led by many Muslims provide vivid stories that would help in painting a more complete picture of Muslims in America, rather than a narrative focused solely on terrorism and violence.

In addition, many are now familiar with the death threats that terrorist groups have issued in recent years against Muslims who dare to speak out against them. Yet, many Muslims have displayed the moral courage needed to issue strong condemnations against these groups, regardless of the threats made to their personal safety. The "Open Letter to Baghdadi" (www.lettertobaghdadi.com), signed by hundreds of the most respected Muslim leaders and scholars in the world, openly condemned Abu Bakr al-Baghdadi, the self-proclaimed leader of Daesh, and represents just one of many thousands of condemnations issued by Muslims.

MOVING FORWARD

In the interest of national security and national unity, as well as in the interest of undermining extremist groups in the future, the media now needs to address the following:

1. Consider how the media is being manipulated by those opposed to peace. This requires a shift in editorial decision-making to ask: "*Who really benefits from what we are reporting?*" The media's discourse on terrorism can no longer sustain the kind of impulsive and uninformed reporting of some media outlets, for these gravely undermine national security to threaten Muslims and non-Muslims alike.

2. Seek the truth, the whole truth, and nothing but the truth. Instead of just reporting the shock, horror, and theatrics of terrorist events as they happen, editors of all media outlets can encourage their journalists to probe more deeply, as the best of them do, for instance, by investigating more thoroughly the true motives of the terrorists.

3. Use wide angle as well as telephoto lenses to tell the whole story. To highlight the complex and diverse nature of American Muslim communities, media sources need to elicit responses to terrorist atrocities from a broader range of Muslims, from all walks of life. This includes religious and community leaders—men and women alike—writers, artists, young people and seniors, as well as Muslim public figures working in entertainment, sports, government, finance, law, the military, education, and other fields, to demonstrate the rich diversity of viewpoints within American Muslim communities, all united in their stand against terrorism.

4. Include credible and qualified Muslim voices. If the media's goal is to be a channel for truthfulness and understanding, then it must be careful not to perpetuate terrorist propaganda, but instead consult qualified Muslim experts with the required knowledge and authority to analyze and discredit the claims made by terrorist groups.

5. Remember the power of language. In both its coverage of violent extremism and inclusion of Muslim voices, the media should re-evaluate the particular words it uses to talk about Islam and extremism. Specific religious terms such as *Jihad* and *Shari'ah* are incessantly conflated with terrorism and barbarism, when in fact terrorists have misappropriated these terms to legitimize their destructive agenda.

6. Speak authoritatively. It is incumbent on journalists reporting on terrorists who claim to act in the name of Islam to immerse themselves in the nuances of Islam as defined by the Qur'an to highlight how distinct these concepts are from extremist ideology, This can help to strip extremist groups of the power and following they gain from misappropriating the religion. Muslims called upon by the media to condemn terrorism must also equip themselves with the knowledge and skills necessary to be able to clearly and effectively convey the true spirit of Islam for non-Muslim audiences.

7. Commit to balanced coverage. For as many stories as there are about Muslims committing violence and terrorism, there is a far greater number of stories of Muslims contributing to their communities and going above and beyond to help their fellow human beings. Truly fair and balanced reporting consists of giving coverage to those inspiring, uplifting stories of everyday Muslims doing extraordinary things, and those who are dedicating their lives to the deconstruction of extremists' claims to Islam. The more these voices are brought into the spotlight immediately after an attack to condemn it, the more this helps to counter the success and validity of extremist groups.

The U.S. prides itself on its freedom of speech and freedom of the press, but these freedoms do not justify irresponsible or recklessly one-sided journalism. It is time for the media to realize the magnitude of its impact in either inadvertently perpetuating or effectively combating extremism. What this will take is a return to the fundamental journalistic principle of balanced and truthful reporting that both asks and elicits straight answers to the essential questions.

Muslim leaders and community representatives are ever-willing to speak publicly—many have already done and continue to do so—even if this means placing their own lives at risk, to condemn terrorist attacks and those who would commit violence in the name of Islam, and to provide instead the balance that is currently missing from the discourse on violent extremism. When these voices are offered a wider platform, the critical missing perspectives can come forward for the benefit of us all.

Muslim Condemnations of Terrorism

WISE and SHEILA MUSAJI

5/2/2016	Sadiq Khan	"The British Muslim who'll take on the extremists"
4/20/2016	Tariq Sharif	New Jersey Muslim group condemns extremists, calls for reform
4/18/2016	Mufti Mohammed Wasim Khan	How These Texas Muslims Lead the Fight Against Terror
4/15/2016	Turkish president Recep Tayyip Erdogan	At summit, Islamic leaders condemn ISIS, Iran's support of terror
4/12/2016	Ashitha Nagesh	British Muslims condemn extremism, according to new ICM poll
4/4/2016	Khalida Jamilah	Battling Extremism by and Against Muslims: Cal Students to Stage "True Islam" Event
3/24/2016	Executive of Muslims Belgium (EMB)	Belgian Muslims fear growing anti-Islam backlash in wake of terror attacks
3/22/2016	Al-Azhar	Brussels attacks "violate" Islamic teachings: top Muslim body
3/22/2016	Organization of Islamic Cooperation	Organization of Islamic Cooperation Strongly Condemns Brussels Attacks
3/22/2016	Muslim Public Affairs Council (MPAC)	Muslim leaders condemn hateful rhetoric in wake of Brussels attack
2/11/2016	Alhaji Seidu Chibsah	Old Tafo: Muslim leader condemns violence
1/20/2016	Muslim Council of Britain	Ordinary Muslims Condemn Extremist Islamic Group Protest
1/20/2016	Islamic Religious Council of Singapore	Muslim leaders denounce extremism after 27 arrested for terror links
1/19/2016	Jacques Mabali	Cameroon's Muslims and Christians Unite against Boko Haram
1/18/2016	Muslim Association of Virginia	Virginia Muslim Group denounced extremism after Woodbrige arrest

For a complete list of condemnations, dating back to 1999, please visit www.wiseupreport.org
*This list has been partially derived from www.theamericanmuslim.org.
Reproduced with permission.

How Does It Feel to Be a Problem?

MOUSTAFA BAYOUMI explains what it feels like for young Muslims to be seen as a "problem" of American society, and contends that the way in which American society deals with Muslims has become a question at the heart of the democratic project itself.

KEY TAKEAWAYS

- Arabs and Muslims are seen as a new problem and as dangerous outsiders in American society; they have also become a foreign policy issue and a law enforcement priority.
- Young American Muslims have a keen awareness of their lives with a kind of double consciousness with which they understand how they see themselves and how they are seen by Americans in the wider culture.
- Though younger generations of American Muslims have often experienced the effects of Islamophobia and anti-Muslim sentiment the most, they also possess a unique opportunity to shape the course of American history for generations to come.

How does it feel to be a problem? Just over a century ago, W.E.B. DuBois asked that very question in his American classic *The Souls of Black Folk*, and he offered an answer: "Being a problem is a strange experience," he wrote, "peculiar even," no doubt evoking the "peculiar institution" of slavery. DuBois composed his text during Jim Crow, a time of official racial segregation that deliberately obscured to the wider world the human details of African-American life. Determined to pull back "the veil" separating populations, he showed his readers a fuller picture of the black experience, including "the meaning of its religion, the passion of its human sorrow, and the struggle of its greater souls."

A century later, Arabs and American Muslims are the new "problem" of American society. In the years following the terrorist attacks of September 11 and the rise of violent extremism, Arabs and Muslims, two groups virtually unknown to most Americans prior to 2001, now hold the dubious distinction of being the first new communities of suspicion after the hard-won victories of the civil rights era. In the eyes of some Americans, American Arabs and Muslims have become collectively known as dangerous outsiders. Arabs and Muslims have become a foreign-policy issue, an argument on the domestic agenda, a law enforcement priority, and a point of well-meaning concern. They are floating everywhere in the virtual landscape of the national imagination, as either villains of Islam or victims of Arab culture. Yet as in the postmodern world in which we live, sometimes when you are everywhere, you are really nowhere.

Broadly speaking, the representations that describe them tend to fall into two types: the exceptional assimilated immigrant or the violent extremist, with little room in between. Clichéd phrases like "sleeper cells," "alienated Muslims," "radicalization," and "homegrown terrorists" degrade the language to the point that they structure the thinking about Muslims living among us. A young woman, Yasmin, once told me the story a Muslim woman being harassed by the other passengers after boarding a bus in Brooklyn. Like Yasmin, this woman was wearing a hijab, but she also had a baby slung to her chest and a blanket covering her sleeping infant. Once the woman found her seat on the bus, the passengers started murmuring about

MOUSTAFA BAYOUMI is a professor of English at Brooklyn College, CUNY. He received his Ph.D. in English from Columbia University in 1998 with a focus in postcolonial literature and theory and ethnic studies. He is the author of *How Does It Feel to Be a Problem?: Being Young and Arab in America*, which won an American Book Award and the Arab American Book Award for nonfiction. His most recent book is *This Muslim American Life: Dispatches from the War on Terror*. His writing is featured in leading news outlets, including *the New York Times Magazine, the London Review of Books*, and *the Nation*, among others.

what the woman actually had underneath the blanket. The words "terrorist" and "bomb" floated through the bus, while others demanded that the driver stop and check what she was carrying. The accusations continued even after the woman and the bus driver confirmed that it was, in fact, a sleeping baby boy wrapped in the blanket. Yasmin was stunned. She looked at the Muslim woman with an uneasy feeling in her stomach and thought, "after her it's me."

How American society deals with its Muslims has become a question at the heart of the democratic project itself. What remains is perhaps the real issue at stake, the question not of what will become of American Muslims in the future, but what is becoming of us Americans?

It seems barely an exaggeration to say that Arab and American Muslims are constantly talked about but almost never heard from. The problem is not that they lack representatives but that they have too many. University of Michigan anthropologists Sally Howell and Andrew Shryock succinctly describe this exhausting situation when they write that "in the aftermath of 9/11, Arab and Muslim Americans have been compelled, time and again, to apologize for acts they did not commit, to condemn acts they never condoned, and to openly profess loyalties that, for most U.S. citizens, are merely assumed." Yet despite the apologies, condemnations, and professions, their voices still aren't heard. Instead, Muslims and Arabs have become essentially a nagging problem to solve, one way or another. And being the problem is a strange, if not deeply frustrating, experience.

Today, Arab and American Muslim youth experience firsthand what it feels like to be a "problem." Today, being a young Arab or American Muslim means that you are living a paradox. On the one hand, the older generation looks hopefully to you with the belief that you will produce a better world for yourself, for your family and community, and for your nation. On the other, the culture at large increasingly views you with mounting levels of fear, aversion, and occasionally outright hostility. Today's young Arab and American Muslims often live uncomfortably between these expectations. Many young Arabs and Muslims have no adult experience of the world prior to September 11. Young Arab and American Muslims are the ones forced to reconcile particular American foreign policies that affect their countries of origin with the idea that their faith poses an existential threat to Western civilization. Whereas the popular image we hold of American youth is a stage in life to be treasured because it lies far away from the pressures of adult responsibilities and the burdens of politics, the stories of young Arab and American Muslims suggest that being young and Arab or Muslim in America can never be simple.

The "war on terror" encroaches on young Arab and American Muslims and complicates their lives in ways that are often invisible to the general public. Unlike their non-Arab or non-Muslim peers, they now have extra loads to carry, burdens that often include workplace discrimination, warfare in their countries of origin, government surveillance, the disappearance of friends or family, threats of vigilante violence, a host of cultural misunderstandings, and all kinds of other problems that thrive in the age of terror. Yet what I have found is that these young adults understand both the adversities they face and the opportunities they have with an enviable maturity. They have a keen awareness about their lives, an acute kind of double consciousness that comprehends the widening gap between how they see themselves and how they are seen by the culture at large. And they somehow manage to find humor

James Baldwin wrote, "I am in the strenuous and far from dull position of having news to deliver to the Western world, black is not a synonym for slave." Almost forty years later, the situation is disturbingly similar today. "Muslim" is not a synonym for "terrorist."

in their unfortunate situation. I am reminded of a young man I once met named Ahmed, who wore a black T-shirt with white letters that read, "My name causes national security alerts. What does yours do?"

In this rocky terrain, young Arab and American Muslims are forging their lives as the newest minorities in the American imagination.

I admire their ability to live with their multiple identities and their ability to draw connections to the struggles others have faced in our American past. These young men and women have been raised by immigrant parents and educated in post–civil rights era America. In this rocky terrain, young Arab and American Muslims are forging their lives as the newest minorities in the American imagination. In their circumstances and out of their actions, they are also shaping the contours of a future American society. I remember a conversation I once had with a young Egyptian named Eyad, where he explained to me a life that seemed to be in an unresolved contradiction by simply stating, "Before, they went after the Jews, the Italians, the Irish. And now it's our turn. Everybody gets their turn. Now it's just the Muslims."

As another great African American writer of our time, James Baldwin, wrote, "I am in the strenuous and far from dull position of having news to deliver to the Western world, black is not a synonym for slave." Almost forty years later, the situation is disturbingly similar today. "Muslim" is not a synonym for "terrorist." Too many people continue to see Arabs and Muslims in America—particularly the younger generation—through narrowed eyes, as enemies living among us. Key members of the political class, an often shrill news media, and a law-enforcement establishment that succumbs to ethnic and religious profiling lead the charge, and Muslims and Arabs are scrutinized for sedition at every turn. How American society deals with its Muslims has become a question at the heart of the democratic project itself. What remains is perhaps the real issue at stake, the question not of what will become of American Muslims in the future, but what is becoming of us Americans?

Erosion of Civil Liberties

ARSALAN IFTIKHAR discusses the erosion of American Muslims' civil rights as a consequence of U.S. counterterrorism policies instituted since 9/11.

KEY TAKEAWAYS

- It is vital, but often overlooked, that American Muslims' struggle to reclaim their civil liberties be understood as part of the larger picture of minorities working to achieve equality in American civil society.
- The Patriot Act paved the way for procedures that limit American Muslims' access to civil rights guaranteed to all U.S. citizens.
- The unconstitutional surveillance of American Muslims jeopardizes counterterrorism efforts and undermines initiatives by American Muslims to fight extremism in their own communities.

The United States has a checkered civil rights history that unfortunately often includes the demonization of minority populations, and the American Muslim community is no exception. Since September 11, American Muslims have collectively experienced greater public and legal scrutiny. While the group's status as a targeted minority demographic group must be seen within the broader context of the struggle for fair and equal treatment carried out by other prominent minority communities previously under the spotlight—including the African American, Jewish American, and Japanese American communities—the profiling of American Muslims has additional repercussions in this age of hyper-globalization.

For years, the concept of "racial profiling" has reportedly undermined important terrorist investigations here in the United States. Immediately after the September 11, 2001 attacks, former Justice Department inspector general Glenn Fine officially reported that at least 1,200 men from predominantly Muslim and Arab countries were detained by law enforcement officials nationwide within the first two months alone after the attacks. Surprisingly, the inspector general also ultimately conceded within this official report that a senior officer in the Office of Public Affairs stopped reporting the cumulative count of detainees after 1,200 because the "statistics became too confusing."[1]

Moreover, in November 2001, former U.S. attorney general John Ashcroft directed the FBI and other federal law enforcement officials to seek out and interview at least 5,000 men (without due cause and based on national origin) between the ages of 18 and 33 who had legally entered into the United States on non-immigrant visas in the past two years before 2001 and who came from specific countries linked by the government to "terrorism".[2]

As Georgetown University Law Center professor David Cole puts it, "Thousands were detained in this blind search for terrorists without any real evidence of terrorism, and ultimately without netting virtually any terrorists of any kind."[3]

ARSALAN IFTIKHAR is an international human rights lawyer, senior editor for the *Islamic Monthly Magazine* and founder of *TheMuslimGuy.com*. He is a prominent figure in global media and has appeared in nearly every major media outlet and publication in the world. Mr. Iftikhar is the author of *Islamic Pacifism: Global Muslims in the Post-Osama Era*. His most recent book is *Scapegoats: How Islamophobia Helps Our Enemies and Threatens Our Freedoms*.

[1] Arsalan Iftikhar, "Why Profiling Doesn't Work," CNN.com, January 5, 2010.
[2] American Civil Liberties Union (ACLU), Sanctioned Bias: Racial Profiling Since 9/11, February 2004.
[3] Arsalan Iftikhar, "Losing Liberties," TomPaine.com, May 19, 2005.

Such instances of racial profiling were exacerbated in part because they were backed by legislation, which allowed unwarranted searches of private property and also gave access to records previously deemed inaccessible without showing probable cause of a criminal act. This was exemplified on October 25, 2001, a mere 45 days after September 11, when Congress passed the now infamous House Resolution 3162 titled the "Uniting and Strengthening America by Providing Appropriate Tools Required to Intercept and Obstruct Terrorism Act", otherwise known as the "Patriot Act," which led to devastating consequences for many American Muslims.

Under Sections 411 and 802, the official definition of "domestic terrorism" was broadly expanded so that university or college student groups who engage in certain types of legal and peaceful protests could very well find themselves labeled "domestic terrorists." For example, the sheriff of Hennepin County, Minnesota, once declared that the student groups "Anti-Racist Action," "Students Against War," and "Arise" were potential "domestic terrorist" threats based on powers newly granted to him under the Patriot Act.[4]

The highly contested Patriot Act paved the way for similar legislation and procedures that greatly limited American Muslims' access to their guaranteed rights as American citizens. Arguably, the greatest factor at play was the assumption of members of the intelligence and law enforcement communities that there is an intrinsic link between religiosity and terrorism, specifically in cases of homegrown terrorism. Often referred to as the "religious conveyor belt" theory, the belief that religion (in this case, Islam) pushes individuals to adopt extremist ideology and carry out terrorist attacks has greatly influenced intelligence and law enforcement procedures post-9/11. However, this theory stands in direct contradiction with later research conducted by government, social scientists, and psychologists, and is congruent with efforts to penetrate American Muslim communities.

The origins of the "religious conveyor belt" theory can be found in the highly controversial 2007 New York Police Department (NYPD) report titled, "Radicalization in the West: The Homegrown Threat." The report concluded that "radical Islamic views" serve as a catalyst for violent extremism based on a handpicked sample of 10 case studies of homegrown terrorism. Furthermore, the report determined that there are "signatures" of potential terrorists, such as growing a beard or becoming involved in community activities. It is not surprising that these markers are mostly likely to be found in a large segment of the American Muslim population.

In 2011, it was uncovered that the NYPD had used millions of taxpayer dollars to develop an elaborate surveillance program based on the findings of this report. Journalists Matt Apuzzo and Adam Goldman of the Associated Press discovered that the NYPD was mapping, monitoring, and analyzing the daily lives of American Muslims in New York City and surrounding areas, and consistently spying on Muslim neighborhood cafes and Islamic places of worship. It was also uncovered that the FBI was infiltrating mosques to learn what was being said by imams and congregation members.

The question that we must ask ourselves today is: Can we treat an entire community as a suspect, but also expect them to function as our partner?

Understandably, these revelations brought on harsh criticism of the NYPD and FBI by both Muslims and non-Muslims who saw these procedures as unconstitutional and an intrusion on American Muslims' First Amendment rights. New York City mayor Bill de Blasio (then a mayoral candidate) also condemned this news on Twitter during his campaign for mayor when he said that he was "Deeply troubled NYPD has labeled entire mosques & Muslim orgs terror groups with seemingly no leads. Security AND liberty make us strong."[5]

[4] Arsalan Iftikhar, "Patriots Against USA PATRIOT," Counterpunch.org, June 22, 2005.

[5] Adam Goldman and Matt Apuzzo, "NYPD Designates Mosques as Terrorism Organizations," Associated Press, August 28, 2013.

The public outcry over the surveillance of American Muslims culminated in June 2013, when the ACLU, NYCLU, and the CLEAR Project at CUNY Law School filed a lawsuit against the NYPD's "discriminatory and unjustified surveillance of New York Muslims." It wasn't until January 2016 that the lawsuit was finally settled and the NYPD was barred from carrying out investigations on the basis of race, religion, or ethnicity. Furthermore, the settlement discredited the NYPD's 2007 "Radicalization in the West" report and ordered it to be removed from the police department's website.

It is hard to deny the fact that such procedures are predicated on the belief that Muslims pose a direct threat to national security. In the post-9/11 context, American Muslims are commonly viewed through a "good versus evil" binary lens. Unfortunately, the rise of groups like Daesh and the global growth of violent extremism have kept American Muslims at center stage and exacerbated the belief that they are a threat to national security. President Donald Trump's calls to ban Muslims from entering the United States and to reinstate unconstitutional surveillance methods reveal just how little progress has been made to protect American Muslims' civil liberties.

Moving forward, it is crucial that intelligence and law enforcement agencies acknowledge the fact that the unconstitutional surveillance of American Muslim communities is being used as extremist propaganda and thus, jeopardizing broader counterterrorism efforts. They must also acknowledge the fact that their methods have undermined American Muslims' efforts to fight extremism in their own communities and prevent further attacks from occurring. The question that we must ask ourselves today is: "Can we treat an entire community as a suspect, but also expect them to function as our partner?"

Though this trend may not seem promising, it perhaps provides motivation for American Muslims to learn from, and play their part in, the counter movements of other minority groups, who have been battling similar social injustices for decades. In working together to highlight injustices and civil liberties violations among all minorities, we not only show solidarity as Americans who support the Constitutional values that were established to protect our freedoms, but also educate and impact those in positions of power.

Defaming Islam: The Tactics of Bigots

DR. NAZIR KHAN OF SPIRITUAL PERCEPTION explains how anti-Muslim bigots craft their critique of Islam in order to dehumanize Muslims. They lack both scientific and philosophical evidence to make reductionist theological statements with no complexity or refinement whatsoever.

KEY TAKEAWAYS

- Anti-Muslim bigots demonize American Muslims by flooding public perceptions with fallacies of savagery, religious repression, and extremism.
- The threatening, distorted rhetoric of anti-Muslim bigots perpetuates the idea that Islam and the West are inherently and ideologically at war.
- These anti-Islamic critics feign expertise in Islamic theology and Qur'anic exegesis, but their portrayal of Islam and their criticism do not stand up to scrutiny.

In the mind of a bigot, the enemy is Islam itself, not just the fanatics. And if the faith is evil, then by implication, anyone who claims to follow Islam and calls themselves Muslim is deliberately espousing evil and should be dealt with accordingly. The entire faith community is condemned as repugnant to modern society. To a bigot, violent Muslims are the true Muslims and peaceful Muslims are fake Muslims. Thus, the implicit assertion of bigotry is that if you're a Muslim who understands Islam, you have two options. Either you are peaceful, in which case your claim to follow Islam is a lie, or you are violent, in which case you are a "real Muslim."

If this sounds seriously problematic, it's because it is. Bigots do not make philosophical or scientific arguments. Rather, they make theological judgments that do not entertain any complexities, critical reasoning, or nuances. So, it is no secret to research groups and intelligence agencies that this bigotry is factually bogus. An MI5 research document discussed in the *Guardian* noted:

> Far from being religious zealots, a large number of those involved in terrorism do not practice their faith regularly. Many lack religious literacy and could actually be regarded as religious novices. Very few have been brought up in strongly religious households, and there is a higher than average proportion of converts. Some are involved in drug-taking, drinking alcohol and visiting prostitutes. MI5 says there is evidence that a well-established religious identity actually protects against violent radicalization.[1]

This suggests that the ideology that extremists call "Islam" denotes something completely different than the "Islam" recognized by a billion faithful Muslims. Yet, despite the bigots feigning "expertise" on Islamic theology and Qur'anic exegesis, no sophisticated discussion of these subjects ever emerges in the course of their anti-Islamic diatribes. They never mention any work of theology of any of the diverse theological schools, nor any reference to the scholarly discussions on *Maqasid* (goals of Shari'ah), *Usul* (principles of Islamic jurisprudence), and *Mu'aamalat* (civil laws). Thus, all it takes is the slightest familiarity with the foundational texts of Qur'anic exegesis to

---

DR. NAZIR KHAN is a medical doctor who also serves as an educator and Imam in the Muslim community, leading congregational prayers and delivering Friday and Eid sermons. He is the founder and lead researcher of *SpiritualPerception.org*, a website dedicated to exploring contemporary questions on Islam and modernity. He is a member of the Manitoba Islamic Association Fiqh Committee, which provides information on religious law relevant to the affairs of the local community.

[1] Alan Travis, "MI5 Report Challenges Views on Terrorism in Britain," *Guardian*. August 20, 2008.

demonstrate that bigoted portrayals of Islam simply do not stand up to scrutiny.

Moreover, it is not hard to notice a very crude simplification process operating behind the bigotry. This is because the easiest (and laziest) thing for them to say is that the lowest common denominator is an evil religion, that's why these "savage subhuman Muslims" keep misbehaving! In contrast, the rational thing to do would be to examine the historical, cultural, sectarian, and political data about where these conflicts originate and come up with a scientific explanation. What if it's not about the religion but the weaponization and instrumentalization of religion by certain groups? What if political instability, decades of warfare, tyranny, occupation, and hundreds of thousands of people killed are advantageous to the emergence of extremist groups? What if, like every violent movement in human history,[2] these groups simply exploit whatever popular ideology or religion they can in order to advance their agenda?

Whenever a Muslim is encountered in daily life, the discourse of bigotry demands that the Muslim be regarded as either a peaceful-liar or an honest-criminal, but never as a fellow human being to treat with respect, dignity, and compassion.

Unfortunately, what we are witnessing today is an intensified effort to demonize Muslims as inherently violent, savage people with a backward, barbaric religion that is dominating public discourse. So whenever a Muslim is encountered in daily life, the discourse of bigotry demands that the Muslim be regarded as either a peaceful-liar or an honest-criminal, but never as a fellow human being to treat with respect, dignity, and compassion. This point illuminates the fundamental difference between criticizing religious beliefs versus hate speech intended to dehumanize a faith community.[3] For instance, people can criticize one another's beliefs as illogical and incoherent and still go home feeling friendship toward one another. But declaring that someone else espouses criminal beliefs, that their entire way of life and identity is evil, or that they subscribe to a doctrine of violence is essentially rejecting them from society and implicitly calling for their legal incarceration.

Thus, we must realize that this rhetoric of bigotry is both factually wrong and dangerous. Bigots have made it seem as if there is an existential war between the West and Islam. So, according to the bigots, there should be fighting between Muslims and the West, because their identities necessarily conflict. But this is precisely the same message that extremists use as a rallying cry. As one German journalist embedded in Daesh confirmed, anti-Islam movements "are unwittingly playing into the hands of ISIS. The [Daesh] movement has stated numerous times that escalations between Muslims and Non-Muslims in Germany and other countries of the West are in its interest." So extremists want Muslims to think that the West is waging war against them, to feel beleaguered and marginalized by society, and to feel that they must take up arms to defend their identity from annihilation. If extremists are using such propaganda to lure disillusioned alienated Muslim youth, why are bigots so actively peddling it? This hate-filled ideology has also spread beyond North America, to Europe, and its sole aim is to elicit fear and hatred of Muslims. As an example, Anders Behring Breivik, who indiscriminately killed 77 people in Norway, cited an American Islamophobe no less than 64 times in his manifesto, demonizing Islam and Muslims as evil.

Sadly, this bigotry has also contributed to a dangerous rise in the amount of hatred of Muslims. Muslims have become the most despised religious group in America, suffering a tremendous rise in hate crimes, attacks on mosques, and employment discrimination, with some academics asserting that anti-Muslim sentiment is similar to the hatred of Japanese Americans during World War II. Hatred inevitably leads to violence. A fanatical atheist with frequent

[2] Louise Ridley, "Does Religion Really Cause War—And Do Atheists Have Something to Answer For?" *HuffingtonPost.com.uk*, November 18, 2014.

[3] Ilirjan Shehu, "Shame on You, Michael Moore: Why His Defense of Bill Maher Was Unacceptable." *Salon.com*, November 16, 2014.

online rants against Islam and religion translated his words into actions when he entered a Muslim family's home and murdered three innocent young people. Consider also the stabbing of a New York taxi driver. According to the prosecutor in that case, "After insulting the tenets of Islam and mocking the restrictions of Ramadan, the defendant, unprovoked, reached through the cab partition and sliced the victim across his neck." And such incidents happen repeatedly. Many experts have expressed great concern that the rising prominence of a discourse that dehumanizes Muslims could lead to more systematic forms of persecution, witnessed earlier in the twentieth century.

> Bigots have made it seem as if there is an existential war between the West and Islam. So, according to the bigots, there should be fighting between Muslims and the West, because their identities necessarily conflict. But this is precisely the same message that extremists use as a rallying cry.

What many people fail to see is that hating Islam is no different than hating Muslims. By definition, being a Muslim means following Islam. If you call yourself a Muslim, it typically implies that you regard Islam as an integral part of your identity. And therefore, whenever anyone places Islam in the crosshairs, they place you in the crosshairs. The logic is very simple—if someone believes that the world should be rid of Islam, they believe that the world should not contain anyone who espouses and practices Islam. If someone believes that Islam should be eliminated, that logically necessitates that they believe that Muslims should be eliminated—the only question is how.

But this doesn't mean that we shouldn't criticize beliefs. In fact, beliefs, doctrines, ideas, and values that are violent or intolerant should be criticized, along with those particular individuals who espouse them. However, when speaking about a global faith community, the essential caveat that must be added is "this interpretation of Islam" or "some Muslims believe," otherwise one again descends into a generalization and monolithic characterization of Islam and all Muslims. Whenever someone says "Islam is X" or "Muslims are Y," they can either mean it in a descriptive or prescriptive sense. If they mean it in a descriptive sense, it will invariably be factually wrong, because the identity of 1.6 billion people is not monolithic and resists such reductive characterization. On the other hand, if it is intended in a prescriptive sense, then one is saying, "the true Islam is X" or "Islam should be understood to mean X," which is an appropriate sentiment for a Muslim theologian or preacher to express, but otherwise wouldn't make any sense.

Bigotry really isn't sensible, neither ethically nor theologically. We really have no choice but to roll up our sleeves and get to work trying to break down barriers, foster mutual respect and compassion, and strive to eliminate oppression, discrimination, injustice, and violence.[4] To do so, we must collaborate in constructive educational, humanitarian, and diplomatic efforts to provide justice, security, transparency, and the restoration of basic human rights and necessities to all. Muslims must also play a vital role in reaching out to the non-Muslim community, embodying the Prophetic virtues in their moral character and being a source of good in the society around them. Because in the end, love, compassion, and kindness will always conquer hatred and hostility.

[4] As Rabbi Eric Yoffie eloquently writes in *Time* magazine, "But as the small number of Muslim extremists becomes ever more skilled at commanding attention and manipulating the media for their own purposes, it becomes more important for the rest of us to avoid tarring all Muslims with the brush of fanaticism. This means rejecting the stereotyping of Islam, categorically and unequivocally. This means recognizing that normative Islam, which has a billion adherents, is a religion that promotes kindness and compassion, opposes violence, and promotes a middle way between extremes. This means speaking up when American bigots demonize Muslims and bash Islam. And this means, above all, educating Americans in a serious way about the teachings of Islam."

Surging Hate Crimes: A Concern for All Americans

ARSALAN SULEMAN discusses the implications of policymakers viewing American Muslims as a threat to security instead of as American citizens. He talks about how this warped rhetoric has contributed to the rise of hate crimes by creating a more divisive society instead of a more cohesive and inclusive one.

KEY TAKEAWAYS

- Negative media portrayals and weakening relationships between the government and the American-Muslim community have contributed to a 67 percent spike in hate crimes against Muslims.
- However, the media and law enforcement fail to label these attacks against Muslims as acts of terrorism or as hate crimes, furthering the sense of marginalization and victimhood in American-Muslim communities. American Muslims have turned this hate crime crisis into an opportunity to stand in solidarity with other vulnerable communities and promote justice for all.
- Extremist groups like Daesh profit off this surge in Islamophobic hate crimes as they claim that their narrative that the West is at war with Muslims is confirmed, thus reinforcing their ability to recruit and grow their ranks.

The politicization and demonization of Islam in America, particularly during and after the 2016 election cycle, has had a devastating impact on American Muslim communities. While the effects of biased media narratives and deteriorating government-community relationships may seem abstract, the recent surge in hate crimes targeting American Muslims makes concrete the real-life impact of hate crimes that individuals and communities have felt across the country.

Openly anti-Muslim rhetoric and policy proposals during the 2016 election campaign gave license to hatred and bigotry, resulting in a significant spike in hate crimes against Muslims. FBI hate crimes data (which are incomplete due to underreporting from police departments and victims) reveal that anti-Muslim bias crimes spiked by 67 percent in 2015 (the most recent year for which data are available). A Pew analysis of those data indicates that physical assaults against American Muslims in 2015 almost matched such reports in 2001, when attacks against Muslims spiked following the 9/11 attacks. The Southern Poverty Law Center reported a sharp jump in post-election hate crimes, as well as an increase in hate groups in 2016, finding a tripling of anti-Muslim hate groups.

Targeting Muslims for unequal treatment betrays American law and values, and makes America less safe for everyone.

Lives have been lost amid this crime wave. Three men were attacked, two of them fatally, when they intervened to stop a hate crime targeting a young Muslim woman and her friend in Portland, Oregon. Two Indian Americans in Kansas were shot, one fatally, for being perceived as Middle Eastern. A Sikh man in Washington was similarly shot. Over the past year, dozens of American mosques have been vandalized, with four arsons reported in the first quarter of 2017.

ARSALAN SULEMAN is the former Acting U.S. Special Envoy to the Organization of Islamic Cooperation (OIC). He is a lawyer based in Washington, DC, and a member of the Muslim-Jewish Advisory Council.

This crime wave has also led to allegations of double standards in media coverage and in prosecutions of hate crimes and terrorist acts. Attacks by right-wing extremists, like Dylann Roof's massacre in South Carolina, are less likely to be labeled terrorism in the media, even though they often meet standard definitions of terrorism. Convictions for terrorism and hate crimes require additional elements of proof regarding the perpetrator's motivations, so prosecutors may be averse to charging those additional crimes if they assess their ability to prove those elements weak. But communities often look to such labels and charges as indicative of broader social understanding of their vulnerability. Many attacks against American Muslims have not been labeled as terrorism or hate crimes by the media or charged as such by prosecutors, exacerbating those communities' sense of marginalization and victimhood.

As domestic Islamophobia and anti-Muslim hate crimes increase, groups like Daesh claim that their narrative has been confirmed, boosting their ability to recruit and spread their ideology. And when groups like Daesh commit their despicable crimes, Islamophobes point to such atrocities as reason to fear and discriminate against Muslims.

In addition to the rise in hate crimes, anti-Muslim rhetoric and policies threaten to undermine our national security. Policies like the executive orders promulgating a Muslim travel ban—both of which were enjoined by federal courts on the basis that they were discriminatory and that plaintiffs were likely to succeed on their constitutional challenges—are rooted in the false notion that Islam and America are incompatible and in conflict. The very terrorists with whom we are at war share that dangerously flawed worldview. As domestic Islamophobia and anti-Muslim hate crimes increase, groups like Daesh claim that their narrative has been confirmed, boosting their ability to recruit and spread their ideology. And when groups like Daesh commit their despicable crimes, Islamophobes point to such atrocities as reason to fear and discriminate against Muslims. And so, the cycle of hatred and misunderstanding continues, and the number of victims continues to rise.

The anti-Muslim ideology, rhetoric, and policies ultimately question what it means to be an American, and it is this contest over identity that American Muslims must—and will—win. America was not founded on the basis of creed or race or ethnicity. We are a nation founded on the self-evident truth that all men are created equal, with certain inalienable rights. Religious freedom is one of those rights—the very first right enumerated in our Constitution's Bill of Rights. Early debates on the Constitution make plain that the founders contemplated a citizenry and government that could include adherents of diverse faiths, including Muslims, who, unbeknownst to many at the time, were present in large numbers via the slave trade. Targeting Muslims for unequal treatment betrays American law and values, and makes America less safe for everyone.

As American Muslims continue to cope with this challenge, many have turned the crisis into an opportunity to stand in solidarity with other vulnerable communities and reinforce our shared commitment to an America that is one nation, indivisible, with liberty and justice for all. Virtual silence from the White House over the rise in hate crimes has been overshadowed by the voices and actions of civil society. The unprecedented protests against the Muslim ban in airports and cities across the country demonstrate the extent to which Americans from all backgrounds are prepared to mobilize to defend that vision of a unified America.

Interfaith coalitions have come out loudly in defense of religious freedom for all. Jews and Muslims have rallied together in opposition to the rising bigotry, forming alliances like the Muslim-Jewish Advisory Council to fight hate crimes and bigotry. People of all faiths are vowing to register as Muslims if a registry is created. American Muslims raised over $100,000 to repair vandalized Jewish cemeteries, and separately also to rebuild black churches that were burned down over a year ago. These acts of solidarity reflect the very best of American values and represent one of the most powerful means of combating bigotry.

Ultimately, we need all elements of society—public officials, media, civil society, and ordinary Americans—to combat this epidemic of hate crimes and reject any Islamophobic rhetoric or policies. The overwhelming response to confront and reject the Muslim ban is a positive sign, but that energy will also be needed to challenge similar possible efforts in the future. At the same time, we need policy experts and community leaders to correct these mistaken views and policies, and to ensure that federal law enforcement officials vigorously investigate and prosecute hate crimes. When politicians perceive all Muslims as security threats rather than as contributing members of society, they divide and destabilize communities instead of increasing our collective safety. To break the cycle of anti-Muslim rhetoric fueling hate crimes and affirming terrorist narratives, politicians should craft policies that encourage social cohesion and minimize polarization.

This rise in hate crimes and bigotry is a test of America's commitment to the rule of law and our founding values. To prevail, Americans must unite around our core values of equality, religious freedom, and pluralism—and American Muslims must rise to the occasion and play a leading role in that effort.

Anti-*Shari'ah* Legislation: A New Incarnation of an Old Intolerance

SAEED A. KHAN explains how anti-Shari'ah legislation violates the First Amendment rights of American Muslims to practice their religion freely and serves as a smokescreen for legislative attempts to disenfranchise other minority communities in the U.S.

KEY TAKEAWAYS

- Islamophobes capitalize on the public's unfamiliarity with Islamic terms like Shari'ah by falsely claiming that Muslims seek to subvert U.S. laws with Shari'ah-based restrictions on women's freedoms.
- Eighty percent of 102 anti-Shari'ah bills introduced between 2011 and 2013 were cosponsored by legislators who aim to limit the freedoms of other marginalized groups.
- The latest effort of Islamophobes is to socially and politically reengineer American society under the guise of combating a phantom enemy, Islam.

Every few years, a new Islamic term is invoked by anti-Muslim bigots to "otherize" Islam as a so-called un-American religion, and to conjure up fear of Muslims by painting them as a menace to "civilized society." At one time, Islamophobes warned of the Muslim threat of *jihad*. At another, misusing the term *taqiyyah*, or concealment, became a scare tactic. Currently, *dawah*, or proselytization, is being brandished as the latest threat to America. Perhaps more than any other term, however, *Shari'ah* has consistently been exploited by Islamophobes—most of whom have no theological training and cannot speak credibly on issues of Muslim belief and practice—to create confusion and fear in the general American public about what *Shari'ah* is. Such individuals incorrectly liken "*Shari'ah* law" to the U.S. legal system, and falsely claim that Muslims seek to subvert U.S. constitutional protections with *Shari'ah*-sanctioned restrictions on women's freedoms and the imposition of brutal punishments for what are seen as extralegal issues, such as adultery, blasphemy, or apostasy. While American Muslims have proposed no legislation that would recognize or impose *Shari'ah*, the hysteria has precipitated a veritable cottage industry of campaigns seeking to prevent its recognition or use within the public sphere, especially in the U.S. court system. Many politicians and legislators have responded to these campaigns by passing "anti-*Shari'ah*" legislation in scattered jurisdictions throughout the country. However, rather than "protecting" Americans (as such legislators claim), such measures actually serve more nefarious goals: 1) to remove constitutionally guaranteed religious liberty protections for American Muslims, the vast majority of whom reference *Shari'ah* to determine how they perform religious rituals; and 2) to hide discriminatory measures that limit the rights and infringe upon the liberties of other groups of Americans, namely women, people of color, and members of the LGBTQ community.

DEFINITION AND SCOPE OF SHARI'AH

For Muslims, *Shari'ah* is about worship, ritual, and personal regulation in their daily lives. Confusion arises, however, from the meaning of the term "*Shari'ah*" itself, which refers to "God's laws" as laid out in the Qur'an and in the actions and sayings of the Prophet Muhammad (Hadith). *Shari'ah*, like Jewish halacha, determines what is lawful for Muslims to consume. It helps them determine at what time and in what manner they offer their prayers. It governs when the holy month of Ramadan begins and ends, as they engage in its rigorous fasting rituals for 29 or 30 days each year. *Shari'ah* offers guidelines for marriage, divorce, inheritance,

SAEED A. KHAN is a fellow at the Institute for Social Policy and Understanding. He is a senior lecturer in Near East and Asian and Global Studies at Wayne State University-Detroit, where he teaches Islamic and Middle East History, Politics, and Culture, and where he is also a research fellow at the Center for the Study of Citizenship. Professor Khan is a contributor to several media agencies, and is a consultant to the BBC and a panelist for The Turning Point on the Canadian Broadcasting Corporation.

adoption, and a spectrum of personal issues. It also provides Muslims with a religious compass to live an ethical and socially productive life. This is why *Shari'ah* is not fundamentally at odds with human rights conventions. Beyond the obvious fact that such practices are wholly within the scope of the free exercise clause of the First Amendment of the United States Constitution, American Muslims themselves find no conflict between their responsibilities under both *Shari'ah* and the U.S. Constitution.

80 percent of 102 anti-*Shari'ah* bills introduced between 2011 and 2013 were sponsored or co-sponsored by a legislator who supported laws limiting the freedoms of other groups, most notably voter ID and Right-to-Work—measures that disproportionately impact the rights of Latinos, African Americans, and women[3].

While there is little desire, and virtually no chance, of "*Shari'ah* law" becoming law in the United States, however, anti-*Shari'ah* bills, in their curtailing of some religious observances, such as marriage and divorce practices, do have real consequences for American Muslims. To observers outside the United States, such efforts appear comical at best; at worst, they suggest a country whose own adherence to the stated values of its constitution (first and foremost, religious liberty) is arbitrary and located in bigotry. For example, in 2014 alone, sixteen states introduced a total of thirty-seven anti-*Shari'ah* bills. Likewise, between 2011 and 2013, thirty-two states and the United States Congress introduced legislation to block *Shari'ah*; North Carolina and Oklahoma in fact passed anti-*Shari'ah* bills[1]. A small number of mainly Republican lawmakers are responsible for introducing and supporting these efforts without any knowledge of what *Shari'ah* really is. In the same period, no American Muslims had proposed legislation that would recognize or impose *Shari'ah*. The constitutionality of anti-*Shari'ah* laws has been challenged in several states, and federal courts have struck down these laws as violating the First Amendment[2].

Unfortunately, campaigns in favor of anti-*Shari'ah* legislation are generally accompanied by a sizable amount of publicity, which creates a false alarm that Muslims are in fact seeking to implement *Shari'ah* in order to supersede the U.S. Constitution. They also create a toxic climate of enmity and distrust in which the idea that Muslims must be stopped at any level and by all available means gains ground. Explicitly crafted anti-*Shari'ah* laws are not the only way that American Muslims are targeted, however. Local and state governments either respond to public demand or take the initiative to apply existing regulations to block the construction of mosques, Islamic centers, and dedicated Muslim cemeteries.

In 2012 in Murfreesboro, Tennessee, for example, the planning commission rejected the Islamic Center of Murfreesboro's effort to obtain a certificate of occupancy, citing zoning, traffic, and parking concerns. The mosque received its building permit only after considerable litigation, including the intervention of the Department of Justice on behalf of the Muslim community, but not before the planning commission questioned whether Islam is an actual religion deserving protection under the First Amendment. Although the Islamic Center ultimately prevailed, the litigation was very expensive, redirecting precious community resources to challenge the commission's actions, and exposed the anti-Muslim sentiments of neighbors and government officials alike, creating a rift in the community.

---

1 "Islamophobia and its Impact in the United States," Council on American-Islamic Relations, March 11, 2015, https://www.cair.com/islamophobia/legislating-fear-2013-report.html.

2 Ryan J. Reilly, "Oklahoma Anti-Sharia Constitutional Amendment Struck Down by Federal Judge," Huffington Post, August 15, 2013, http://www.huffingtonpost.com/2013/08/15/oklahoma-sharia-constitution_n_3764313.html.

THE EFFECTS OF ANTI-*SHARI'AH* LEGISLATION ON NON-MUSLIMS

While the passage of anti-*Shari'ah* laws is motivated by Islamophobia, there is evidence that such laws are part of a broader legislative agenda that affects a variety of demographic groups. While American Muslims may be an easy target, given the small size of their population and relatively weak political influence, efforts to pass laws designed to curtail their rights can serve as a cloak for lawmakers seeking to limit the rights of other groups. In fact, 80 percent of 102 anti-*Shari'ah* bills introduced between 2011 and 2013 were sponsored or co-sponsored by a legislator who supported laws limiting the freedoms of other groups, most notably voter ID and Right-to-Work—measures that disproportionately impact the rights of Latinos, African Americans, and women[3]. These laws are designed to marginalize and disenfranchise people based on their race, ethnicity, national origin, gender, sexual orientation, religion, and union membership.

The curious case of SB695 in North Carolina is perhaps the most poignant illustration of this political sleight of hand. In 2013, and for the first time since the mid-nineteenth century, North Carolina had a majority Republican legislature and a Republican governor. In the absence of any critical mass capable of mounting an opposition, the legislature sponsored and enacted laws that reflected its majority ideology. One such proposed bill was the 2013 Family, Faith and Freedom Protection Act (HB695). It was promoted as an anti-*Shari'ah* bill designed to prevent Islamic law from being implemented in North Carolina, to prevent state judges from considering "foreign law" in family court proceedings (e.g., divorce, alimony, or child custody), particularly *Shari'ah*. Prior to a floor vote on the bill, and literally at the eleventh hour, however, a series of provisions were added as riders to the bill, all of which restricted not the implementation of *Shari'ah*, but access to reproductive health care.

The strategy employed by the legislature to effectively use the public hysteria about and ignorance of *Shari'ah* as a smokescreen for other attempts at disenfranchisement— in this case, a woman's access to reproductive health care—was notable. There appeared to be recognition that most North Carolinians would not be too concerned by an effort to ban *Shari'ah* and would therefore resist launching a campaign to block the legislation. With the primary focus of the bill being American Muslims, the surreptitious, last-minute amendment of the legislation to adversely affect women suggests that the effort was less about proscribing *Shari'ah* than it was about restricting access to abortion. Suzanne Buckley, Executive Director of NARAL Pro-Choice North Carolina, said about the Senate's tactics, "It seems to me that they're trying to pass under cover of darkness legislation that would not otherwise be passed."[4] North Carolina's SB695 supported the suspicion that anti-Shari'ah bills are part of a coordinated, more comprehensive strategy to target and disenfranchise an array of demographic groups apart from American Muslims, including women. It also demonstrates that these legislative efforts are attempted through combining two seemingly disparate political issues into one bill, with the attention focused on a particular community that lacks sufficient public empathy and political capital necessary to mobilize opposition to the bill's passage.

CONCLUSION

The efforts to marginalize and demonize Muslims, legislatively and politically, are a reminder to some of their own experiences with bigotry, and for others, represent the potential of such hatred being directed toward them. The commonality that comes from being targeted has created new empathy and led to coalition-building among targeted communities. Japanese-American organizations, witnessing disturbing similarities to World War II–era rhetoric and their own internment, are voicing their concerns for this toxic climate and asserting their solidarity with the American Muslim community. Similarly, local and national women's organizations, African American and Latino groups, and American Muslims are increasingly recognizing that by working together, along with other allies, efforts to combat bigotry and racism for all targeted groups will be strengthened. At this moment in American history, Islamophobia represents only the latest effort to socially and politically reengineer American society under the guise of combating a phantom enemy.

---

[3] Saeed Khan and Alejandro Beutel, "Manufacturing Bigotry: A State by State Legislative Effort to Pushback Against 2050 by Targeting Muslims and Other Minorities," Institute for Social Policy and Understanding, 2014, http://www.ispu.org/pdfs/ISPU_Manufacturing_Bigotry[4].pdf.

[4] "North Carolina 'Trying to Pull a Texas' on Reproductive Rights," MSNBC.com, July 3, 2013, http://www.msnbc.com/rachel-maddow-show/north-carolina-trying-pull-texas.

Incarcerated Muslims: Radicals or Reformers?

SHAIKH RAMI NSOUR sheds light on the incarceration of American Muslims that most people are unaware of, and how these Muslims are at the forefront of many promising prison reform initiatives.

KEY TAKEAWAYS

- Only 6 percent of the total national prison population is Muslim, which disproves the assertion that "tens of thousands" of people are being converted to Islam in prisons.
- While some may be concerned that conversion to Islam is increasing, many Muslim converts have spearheaded initiatives for prisoner rights and founded successful inmate rehabilitation groups.
- To prevent the radicalization of incarcerated Muslims, the primary focus has to be on providing comprehensive access to Islamic religious education.

One of the most rewarding experiences throughout my entire teaching career has been the 14 years I have spent teaching Islam to Muslims in prisons throughout the United States. As the founder of The Tayba Foundation, a non-profit dedicated to providing Islamic education to inmates for their own spiritual nourishment and character rectification, I have seen how Muslims in prison have been at the forefront of many great initiatives. Yet there is still so little known to the public about Muslims in prison or about prison in general, for that matter. I strongly believe that every American has the duty to know what is going on with incarceration in our country. In addition to the civic duty of knowing about and working for the betterment of the system of incarceration in our country, Muslim citizens in particular have the added religious duty of helping the incarcerated.

Many Americans, Muslim and non-Muslim alike, are relatively unaware of the history of incarceration in the United States. Starting in the 1980s, various policies that were part of the "Tough on Crime" and "War on Drugs" approaches increased the U.S. incarcerated population by an overwhelming 500 percent. Today, there is a total of 2.3 million people in jails and prisons across the country—many convicted of nonviolent drug offenses. One of Tayba's best students, for example, was given three life sentences as a juvenile for a nonviolent drug offense. This individual, who became a Muslim while incarcerated, served 22 years in prison for possession of less than one gram of crack cocaine, while there are still other offenders who have never been convicted, or serve less time, for far more heinous crimes.

In addition, the deinstitutionalization of the state mental health asylums in recent years has significantly impacted the dramatic rise in the U.S. incarcerated population, leading some to call it the "criminalization of mental illness." More concerning, however, is that the Thirteenth Amendment—which abolished the institution of slavery—still allows for slavery to be used as "a punishment for crime." The use of prisoners for cheap, often forced, labor has been a practice that has existed since the Civil War. Today, prisoners will receive hourly wages ranging anywhere from 25 cents to $1 an hour for their labor.

Unfortunately, one of the realities for prisoners in the United States today is the high likelihood of returning to prison after their initial release. It is estimated that a startling 70 to 90 percent of prisoners are likely to return to prison at least once in their lifetime. However, studies have shown that access to education while in prison plays a major role in reducing the recidivism rate and lessening

SHAIKH RAMI NSOUR is the co-founder of The Tayba Foundation, the only organization in existence that offers distance learning programs in Islamic education to incarcerated men and women. He is an expert on various subjects of the Qur'an, Aqeedah (belief), Fiqh (law), Nahu (grammar), and Ihsan (spiritual purification), and is a recipient of the traditional teaching license (ijaza). In addition, Shaikh Nsour holds a BA in Human Development with a focus on Early Childhood.

the likelihood of repeat incarceration.[1] Still, the government is content with spending an average of $30,000–60,000 per prisoner each year even though in-prison programs, such as education, that can reduce incarceration and recidivism, would never get approved.[2]

> While some may be concerned over the fact that conversion to Islam is increasing, I have found that it has actually become a powerful force that has helped many prisoners become better people

At the Tayba Foundation, we have made it our mission to provide proper Islamic education at the postsecondary level to prisoners in the hopes of reversing this trend. The Qur'an teaches Muslims of the importance of caring for prisoners. This is seen in verse 76:8: "They give food, for the love of Him, to the needy, the orphan, and the prisoner." The Prophet Muhammad (pbuh) gave further emphasis to this in a Hadith, narrated by Tabarani, that reads, "I enjoin you to treat the captive well." This deeply profound guidance is what forces us to remember the humanity of prisoners and maintain their inherent rights, even though they may have wronged us. Perhaps what is most important is that this guidance urges us to always look for ways we can reform (tawbah), while reminding us to never give up on anyone. This guidance has served as a constant reminder for us to not forget to show mercy to others, even those who have committed crimes.[3]

In other words, the Qur'an and the Prophet Muhammad (pbuh) not only teach, but also command Muslims to show mercy toward all humanity. Qur'anic scholars have also noted that God's instructions to "give food" should not preclude us from giving anything else that is needed, especially spiritual nourishment. The Tayba Foundation is dedicated to doing just this by providing high-quality authentic Islamic education to Muslim prisoners through distance and correspondence learning programs. And although our main focus is on authentic Islamic education, we strive to assist our students in their pursuit for other degrees or certificates whenever possible.

However, we cannot overlook the many misconceptions held about Muslims and Islam in prison, which are being spread throughout the American public using what some refer to as a rhetoric of Islamophobia. One particular scare tactic relates the number of incarcerated Muslims in America to statistics showing that 30,000 to 40,000 people convert to Islam each year. However, the Federal Bureau of Prisons identified 9,000 Muslim prisoners in 2004 (6 percent of the total prison population),[4] in 2008 the New York State prison system identified 7,825 (12.5 percent of the total prison population)[5] and in 2007 California identified 4,159 (2.4 percent of the total prison population).[6]

From my 14 years of experience, I have found that such claims are nothing more than scare tactics

[1] The benefit of higher education goes beyond preventing prisoners from returning to prison, but also helps reduce incarceration to begin with, as "the U.S. Department of Education identifies college education as the single most successful method to reduce levels of incarceration." (The Wesleyan Center for Prisoner Education).

[2] Christian Henrichson and Ruth Delaney, The Price of Prisons: What Incarceration Costs Taxpayers. Center on Sentencing and Corrections,. January 2012.

[3] In 2010, I was contacted by Tariq Khanzada, a Muslim man in our community who was well-known as being a "good Samaritan." He told me that throughout his life he had done many projects helping the poor and orphans and had just completed a project of building two mobile kitchens to feed the homeless ("Mercy on Wheels"), but that he had never had a chance to "feed the prisoner." He began a collaboration between the Tayba Foundation and ICNA which, called "Feed the Prisoner," whereby halal food was sent to prisoners. Although the program was very successful, Tariq was killed soon after by a drunk driver on a freeway after he had stopped to help a stranded motorist. He died being a "good Samaritan."

[4] Office of the Inspector General, A Review of the Federal Bureau of Prisons' Selection of Muslim Religious Services Providers, 2004.

[5] State of New York Department of Correctional Services, Hub System: Profile of Inmate Population Under Custody, January 1, 2008.

[6] California Department of Corrections and Rehabilitation, Adult Research Branch, Findings from the August 2007 Inmate Faith Preference Survey, November 2007.

used to convince the public that our prisons foster an environment that is rampant with "radical Islam," or that they are flooded with converts to Islam who in some way pose a danger to our society. While some may be concerned about the fact that conversion to Islam is increasing, I have found that it has actually become a powerful force that has helped many prisoners become better people. It is more troubling that many of the inflated numbers come from articles that are not research-based and cite nongovernmental data—and in some cases are what informs policies and legislation.

In addition, another misconception is that prison, or simply an individual's conversion or practice of Islam, creates a "fertile ground" for terrorism. But according to Dr. Mark S. Hamm's extensive research on the subject of radicalization in prisons, only "a very small percentage of converts turn radical beliefs into terrorist action." Radicalization is a very complex societal ill that manifests in all sectors of society, prison included, but Muslims in prison should not be singled out and made to seem as if they are part of some sort of epidemic.[7]

Sadly, the instances where an individual went on to commit a terrorist act are due, in part, to an absence of proper Islamic education, as well as an overall misuse of the religion.

Sadly, the instances where an individual went on to commit a terrorist act are due, in part, to an absence of proper Islamic education, as well as an overall misuse of the religion. This unfortunate phenomenon has occurred both within and outside of prisons. It is for this reason that I strongly believe that one of the greatest resources we have to protect against radicalization and the misuse of the religion is a sound Islamic education. This was echoed by a survey we conducted at the Tayba Foundation, which found that the foremost religious need of Muslims in prison was access to curriculum and teachers. The Tayba Foundation began its program for Islamic education by distance and correspondence, and committed itself to maintaining this service for Muslim prisoners. We are dedicated to shedding light on how our religious texts are being misused and abused, and providing the proper education of Islam that serves to bring harmony and tolerance for all of humanity.

I have seen the endless possibilities that emerge when men and women are given the proper tools, time, and space to learn.

And the results are telling. Many of the recent major legal precedents for prisoners' rights were actually spearheaded by Muslim inmates. Many Muslims inmates are at the forefront of a number of programs to help others, including successful inmate-led rehabilitation groups that were founded by Muslims. In fact, two of our Tayba students co-founded one of these programs and went on to not only turn it into their own non-profit organization, but are now in contract for a creating a transitional house in the State of California. Some of our other students are now involved in non-profit work and teaching, some now attend graduate school, and some have even gone on to start their own businesses. Above all else, each and every one of our students has gone on to become active and engaged members in the communities in which they live. The potential here is endless. It is the very same potential that someone saw in Malcolm Little when he was in prison and chose to aid him on his journey for knowledge: the potential that transformed Malcom Little into Al Hajj Malik El Shabazz (more commonly known as Malcolm X), one of the greatest figures in the spread of Islam in the United States who helped so many others out of the darkness of ignorance.

During my time with the Tayba Foundation, I am constantly reminded of the saying of the Prophet

[7] For more on this topic, see SpearIt. "Facts and Fictions About Islam in Prison: Assessing Prisoner Radicalization in Post-9/11 America." Washington, DC: Institute for Social Policy and Understanding, January 2013.

Muhammad (pbuh), narrated by Sahih Muslim: "People are like ores, like the ores of gold and silver, the best of them before Islam [jahiliyyah] are the best of them in Islam if they gain understanding [fiqh]." My experience working with prisoners has made me a firm believer in the power of education to dramatically transform the dynamics of prisons in the United States today. I have seen the endless possibilities that emerge when men and women are given the proper tools, time, and space to learn. I have also seen the confidence and steadfastness that education has provided these men and women when they return to their communities. At the Tayba Foundation, we see it as both our religious and civic duty to provide prisoners with the necessary resources and education so that they may access this potential. We pray to continue to be able to provide this education and we look forward to collaborating with other organizations focused on making education available to prisoners.[8]

[8] One such organization that has reached out to Tayba is Jail Educational Solutions, which is piloting the use of tablets preloaded with courses for education in a few institutions (as prisons don't allow Internet access to inmates). Tayba has two courses on their preloaded tablets and we hope to increase the use of technology in prison education as it becomes available.

Islamophobia and Domestic Security

MAJOR GENERAL DOUGLAS M. STONE (RET.) provides a narrative account of his tenure overseeing the Iraqi detention program, during which he learned that ignorance regarding Islam and Muslims when it comes to policymaking hinders efforts for peace and stability. Inspired by this revelation, he developed a program to build respectful relationships with detainees that could reach them at religious and ideological levels in ways that prior military personnel had not.

KEY TAKEAWAYS

- During his time in Iraq, Stone realized that the war the U.S. was fighting was also taking place within the detention centers he was overseeing.
- The war the U.S. was fighting on the outside in Iraq was being waged inside American detention facilities as well. The policies of unjust treatment of detainees need to be replaced by a culture of law, respect, and tolerance for the "Other." Law enforcement needs to do the work of building relationships based on trust and mutual respect with Muslim religious and community leaders, and rely less on intelligence gathered from arrests to maintain security.
- In the U.S., there is a need for law enforcement to develop collaborative and trusting relationships with their local American-Muslim communities in order to better protect vulnerable community members from potential threats by extremists.

I want to begin with a simple statement: Islamophobia makes our country less secure.

Now let me say a few words about my insight on this matter. In 2007, I was put in charge of overseeing the detention camps in Iraq by General David Petraeus, specifically the Bucca and Cropper detention camps. The state of the Iraqi detention program was in shambles and people were scrambling to manage the nearly 27,000 detainees, the highest detainee population thus far. The discontent among the detainees was clear: detainee-on-detainee killings, setting fire to their living quarters, rioting (resulting in the death of 78 Marines), and making rogue weapons to be used against American soldiers.

Furthermore, detention policies prior to my arrival relied heavily on biases in terms of initial detention and treatment of detainees. Each of the 27,000 individuals were viewed and treated as "enemy combatants" by the American soldiers, regardless of their conviction or prior track record. U.S. and Iraqi forces were going into towns and essentially arresting all the eighteen-, nineteen-, and twenty-year-old males simply because they looked like they posed a security threat. The concept of detention "in advance of an attack" contributed to the skyrocketing detainee population and caused moderate individuals who did not pose an inherent threat to be housed with extremists who were known to be capable of violent attacks. Also, a lack of cultural information and respect on the part of American soldiers allowed for Sunni, Shia, and Salafis to be kept in dangerously close quarters, resulting in high levels of prisoner-on-prisoner violence.

The fact was that the U.S. detention programs were being used against us. There is no denying that Abu Ghraib was—and still is—being used against us as extremist propaganda. But our lack of cultural understanding and rule of law in the detention facilities allowed for extremists to hide in plain sight. By holding moderate detainees with known extremists, we

MAJOR GENERAL DOUGLAS M. STONE (RET) had served in the United States Marines since 1973. In 2007, Stone was assigned as commander of Iraqi detention facilities where he reversed the culture and consequences of Abu Ghraib with his policies. Major General Stone founded Security, Telecommunications, Analytic, and Computing (STAC) Solutions and works with law enforcementto bridge the gap between Muslims and the law enforcement community.

unknowingly allowed for extremist recruitment and indoctrination to occur. It soon became known that extremists were even getting purposefully detained with the intention of recruiting the more moderate detainees to their cause.

It struck me that the war that we were fighting on the outside was actually occurring inside American detention facilities. But in addition to overcrowding and the spike in violence, there was a complete lack of rule of law in terms of how detainees were arrested, processed, and charged. A main consequence of this was that detainees were not being sorted in terms of the threat level they posed. We set up detention facilities without understanding that we were creating camps for extremist indoctrination, or "jihadi universities," as I have called them. The thing that was most obvious to me, however, was the clear impact the Iraqi detention program was having on the Muslim community.

Would we have acted any differently if people showed up in our backyards one day and started shooting? It became clear to me that we had let the broader threat dictate how we viewed the entire community

Upon assuming command of Iraq detention operations and Task Force 134, I threw away the book and began pursuing a culturally informed and respectful program to essentially win the hearts and minds of my detainees, their families, and the wider Muslim community. Previous detention facilities were led by military personnel who did not have the expertise or willingness to confront the detainees at the necessary religious and ideological levels. And so, my approach to overseeing Iraqi detention consisted of 1) knowing the enemy, or being able to separate the moderate detainees from the lifelong violent extremists, 2) focusing on counterinsurgency rather than corrections, 3) focusing on rehabilitation rather than continued detention, and 4) developing a coherent detention, rule of law, release, and reintegration procedure.

At the heart of this was building trust between the detainees, their families, and the Americans who were overseeing these facilities. I personally pursued this by developing an education in Islam and the Qur'an so I could try to relate to my detainees on a deeper level. In addition, I brought in 200 imams to provide genuine religious education for the detainees to discredit extremist ideology and prevent it from spreading to other detainees. Moreover, we created a culture of transparency in our detention facilities that allowed the Muslim community and the media to see that these facilities were not a repeat of Abu Ghraib. This also included allowing families to come and visit detainees, and even participate in some of the civic education programs.

Over the course of my duty overseeing the Iraqi detention facilities, we managed to completely reverse the culture of Abu Ghraib that had cast a black mark on U.S. efforts to win the hearts and minds of the Iraqis. The lawless culture and unjust treatment of detainees were replaced by a culture of law, respect, and tolerance for "the other." The most important point I am trying to make here is that, by building relations of trust and respect in the detention facilities, we were able to make America more secure. The information we received willingly from detainees and their families proved to be invaluable in our fight against extremism. Out of trust and respect, members of al-Qaeda provided us with the locations of American soldiers' bodies so that they could be returned home to their families. We were also given the location of the greatest cache of ammunition found during the Iraq War because of this program. And because of this program, detainees and their families provided us with highly classified information that helped to secure our homeland and armed forces from future attacks.

When I look back on my experience with the detention program, I believe that part of the larger problem prior to 2007 could be attributed to an ignorance of Islam and prejudice against Muslims that manifested in the American forces viewing the Iraqi citizens through a "good versus evil" lens. Although this was not necessarily a conscious worldview, it existed nonetheless. To the Americans stationed in Iraq, every Iraqi citizen, the vast majority of whom were Muslim, was a terrorist. However, from the Iraqis' point of view, we were the ones who were trespassing in their backyards. Would we have acted any differently if people showed up in our backyards one day and started shooting? It became clear to me that we had let the broader threat dictate how we viewed the entire community.

My tenure overseeing the Iraqi detention program taught me the valuable lesson that ignorance of Islam and Muslims can impair our ability to achieve peace and stability. In today's political climate, I strongly believe that Islamophobia jeopardizes the security of our country. We learned in Iraq that you cannot group together an entire population and label them as the enemy. It was only when we stopped equating the acts of a few with an entire population that we were able to develop trusting relations that proved to be mutually beneficial to U.S. and Iraqi security.

When I took the time to educate myself on Islam and the Qur'an, I realized that Islam is not a monolithic religion. There is such a rich diversity within Islam and among Muslims that it is naïve to equate the acts of a few with the 1.6 billion other Muslims worldwide. And if it is not already apparent, Muslims are the ones being killed by terrorists. This means that responsible political, civil, and community leaders, as well as the law enforcement and security worlds, must reject a natural instinct to become more Islamophobic with each new attack. Islamophobic attitudes within the law enforcement world only help to legitimize Islamophobic attitudes among the general American public.

This is why I believe that it is of utmost importance for law enforcement agencies to build strong and trusting relations with local American Muslim religious and community leaders. I look back on the successful partnerships we created with the courageous Iraqi imams who put their lives at risk by cooperating with Americans and standing up for the truth. If we strive to create the same sort of partnerships within our own communities, I believe that, as a nation, we will be better equipped to detect potential threats and help the most vulnerable members of our communities.

But there is a fly in the ointment. The FBI has a long, and highly controversial, history of penetrating known dangerous groups: white supremacist, extreme antigovernment organizations, mafia families, and others. To be effective in their job of detecting and preventing extremism, local police departments must abstain from the temptation of doing this. As we witnessed with the NYPD mass-surveillance fiasco, such policies will only produce more harm than good, and will isolate the very community with whom they are wishing to partner. Law enforcement must realize that we cannot arrest our way to security, unless we wish to return to an era of mass internment similar to what occurred in this country during World War II. Detaining hundreds of innocent suspects, for any period of time, to apprehend one or two legitimate threats, will have the same effect as what I witnessed during my service in Iraq. It creates anger and embitterment in detainees' families and can make the detainees vulnerable to extremist indoctrination.

We learned in Iraq that you cannot group together an entire population and label them as the enemy. It was only when we stopped equating the acts of a few with an entire population that we were able to develop trusting relations that proved to be mutually beneficial to U.S. and Iraqi security.

There is no middle ground on the issue of Islamophobia and domestic security. It is of utmost importance to treat American Muslims with respect and appreciation for the commonalities that we share. As I learned during my time in Iraq, building strong and trusting relations with the American Muslim community will greatly enable law enforcement to learn of potential early-warning indicators. I believe that our law enforcement agencies must lead the way in showing that the American Muslim community is their best ally in this united fight against extremism.

Modeling Partnership Between Communities and Law Enforcement

SALAM AL-MARAYATI describes the importance of developing Muslim-led community-based solutions to violent extremist recruitment, and contends that partnerships between communities and government and law enforcement officials, in which the roles of each are clearly marked, serve to empower community and religious leaders to prevent extremism in their own communities.

KEY TAKEAWAYS

- Heavy-handed relationships between law enforcement and American-Muslim communities have made it difficult to bring these groups to the table to talk openly about how to address the threat of violent extremism in their own communities.
- The American-Muslim community needs to more clearly see the value in preventing extremists from infiltrating their communities.
- To create alternatives to law enforcement–only approaches, community leaders need to deal with the problem at the micro level and not only at the macro level by providing awareness training to community leaders and safe spaces for vulnerable individuals.

Though Islamic teachings emphasize that "there is no compulsion in religion," it is the ideology of force and compulsion that has led to the formation of Daesh. Followers of this movement believe that a religiously-centered life requires compelling Muslims to become better Muslims by force and by compelling others to either accept Islam or die. Daesh followers have given up on living within a pluralistic society. They believe that the West is at war with Islam and that closing themselves off from the West is a form of purification. All these issues need a response from authentic Muslim voices. Neither law enforcement nor government can either be or sponsor that voice. It needs to be community-driven and the community needs to see the value in its involvement on this issue. Any prodding from government is counterproductive.

Second to the ideological complexity of this problem is the record of law enforcement on this issue. As President Barack Obama expressed at the White House CVE Summit in February 2015, the U.S. government cannot arrest its way out of this problem; it needs the help of the community. The fiasco at Guantanamo Bay, stories of rendition, sting operations and entrapment: all of these have played into the mind-set within the community that law enforcement is part of the problem or is an obstacle to any solution. Heavy-handed law enforcement tactics have played a detrimental role in bringing communities to the table to discuss how to address the threat of Daesh to their own mosques and families. Unfortunately, both the numbers of arrests and the numbers of people joining Daesh are on the rise.

In order to be effective in preventing and countering violent extremism, Muslim leaders must develop a healthy partnership model between their communities and law enforcement agencies that is based on building trust and understanding. Government must adopt a policy that is reflective of the fact that violent extremism is not unique to Muslims but is also a problem among white supremacists and other disaffected groups. Singling out Muslims has also detrimentally affected the willingness of leaders in the community to get onboard in addressing threats of Daesh in their own communities.

The American Muslim community needs to more

SALAM AL-MARAYATI is President of the Muslim Public Affairs Council and works as an adviser for several political, civic, and academic organizations, helping develop an understanding of the role of Islam and Muslims in America and worldwide. His articles and interviews have appeared in prominent media outlets such as the *Wall Street Journal*, *Christian Science Monitor*, *USA Today*, C-SPAN, and NBC.

clearly see the value in preventing Daesh from infiltrating our families through social media. This problem cannot be seen or understood unless we leaders work to raise awareness of this threat. Saving one life is like saving all of humanity, as the Qur'an teaches us. So while the numbers of Daesh recruits are low within the U.S., the impact on communities is debilitating, especially if it involves an arrest or if one person commits a violent act believing this is a religious obligation. We cannot argue our way out of this problem, just like the government cannot arrest its way out of it.

We must, therefore, come up with solutions that originate from the community and are for the community, and we must focus on mental health, good Islamic education, and healthy Islamic activism and civic engagement as part of the answer. This is the community-based approach.

Federal law enforcement has two roles to play vis-à-vis dealing with the threat of Daesh: 1) protect the civil rights of communities as hate crimes and hate speech are on the rise; and 2) develop healthy partnerships with communities to empower people to intervene in cases where a person is thinking about joining Daesh. Building partnerships of trust requires reform within law enforcement, especially with regard to sting operations, as these sorts of operations leave the Muslim community doubtful about the true willingness of law enforcement to help them, as opposed to target them, and leaves the community extremely concerned about entrapment. There are some recent signs that some law enforcement agencies are beginning to respond to complaints from targeted minority communities, but there is still much work to be done.

The protection of civil rights is one of the essential mandates of federal law enforcement. When community leaders are bolstered in addressing any threat to their mosques by being able to leverage the relationships built with federal law enforcement, then communities will see the value of developing those relationships and feel less threatened by them. Also, when federal law enforcement agencies begin to create opportunities for community leaders to intervene in cases where an individual has potentially been recruited by Daesh (i.e. not treating it as a criminal matter but as a social services matter), communities will feel trusted and will, in turn, trust law enforcement.

Provided they are well informed about the issue, a parent, friend, or mentor can ascertain when someone is thinking about joining groups like Daesh. There are no reliable or accurate radicalization theories that can be used by the government as indicators. The predictive model will only amount to racial profiling, as most youth are prone to feelings of alienation, anger, and negativity, but those of Middle Eastern and/or Muslim backgrounds are likely to be subjected to greater scrutiny.

Government must adopt a policy that is reflective of the fact that violent extremism is not unique to Muslims but is actually also a problem among white supremacists and other disaffected groups. Singling out Muslims has also detrimentally affected the willingness of leaders in the community to get onboard in addressing threats of Daesh in their own communities.

So, to create an alternative to law enforcement–only approaches, community leaders must look at and deal with this problem at the micro level and not at the macro level. It is prudent for all of us to provide resources, training, and a safe space for any person who is confused about his/her beliefs, identity, or place in our society. Resources can include a directory of mental health experts, religious counselors, and social service workers. It is so much better to rehabilitate than to incarcerate. While anyone involved in criminal activity falls under the jurisdiction of law enforcement, we must remember that the preferred healing and educational approach to prevention is under the purview of the community.

"Those who would give up essential liberty to purchase a little temporary safety, deserve neither liberty nor safety."

- Benjamin Franklin

CHAPTER 3

Crafting an American Muslim Identity

Fighting Hate: Preserving American Values

INAS YOUNIS writes of how some Americans' fear of Islam and Muslims has evolved into a form of organized hate, where Muslims feel so disenfranchised and despised by mainstream society that they begin to doubt their allegiance to the values of life and liberty.

KEY TAKEAWAYS

- When standing up against this irrational hate, Muslims are not just defending their religion, but they're also defending their American values and constitutional rights.
- Hatred judges according to what it sees and not what it understands, and is always a reaction. To combat hate requires eliminating the very notion of the "Other."
- American Muslims must resurrect the tradition of cooperation and coexistence that is central to their teachings and to American religious freedom.

Muslims, like everyone else, grieve the loss of order and the erosion of common sense every time violence occurs where we least expect it. Terrorism is random for a reason. It knows that we feel safe only to the extent that there is some rhyme or reason to why and how violence occurs. So when violence occurs outside of war zones, we become more disoriented, more inflamed. We all become refugees in search of refuge when we lose our sense of security.

> Hate taking root anywhere in the world endeavors to make the persecuted minority feel so disenfranchised and despised by the mainstream that they begin to question their loyalties

But the nature of the enemy we are currently dealing with is too ancient to isolate. Historically, extremism and violence are nothing new. Violent extremists' interpretations of any religion or secular ideology, all share the same universal and timeless features. First, they elevate the group above the individual. Second, they must always have a scapegoat (e.g., Jews, blacks, Muslims, gypsies). Third, they persecute the scapegoat until it/they retaliate or lash out against their persecutors, which then justifies the irrationality of the hate toward them.

When irrational hate becomes a political force, the scapegoat's rights and liberties are compromised. For American Muslims, the erosion of our individual liberties and sacred principles started shortly after 9/11, when, for the first time, this nation not only felt personally threatened, but interpreted this threat as an arbitrary kind of hatred directed toward Americans for simply being American. We imagined that the hate was arbitrary and so the retaliation, euphemistically referred to as Operation Enduring Freedom, became equally arbitrary, triggering the politicization of hatred around the world.

Currently every kind of bigotry and hate taking root anywhere in the world endeavors to make the persecuted minority feel so disenfranchised and despised by the mainstream that they begin

INAS YOUNIS was born in Mosul, Iraq, and migrated to the United States in 1982. An independent journalist and commentator, Ms. Younis's opinion pieces, book reviews, and personal essays have been published on various websites and in magazines. Her work was also featured in an anthology titled *Living Islam Out Loud*. She serves on the board of the Sisterhood of Salaam Shalom and is an active volunteer in several interfaith initiatives dedicated to highlighting the power of religious community in resolving conflicts and promoting mutual respect and understanding.

to question their loyalties. In the case of Muslim extremists, their mission is to provoke the non-Muslim world into persecuting "moderate" Muslims to the extent that we begin to doubt our allegiance to the values of life and liberty. They intend to do this by ensuring that these values stop working for us.

In the case of Muslim extremists, their mission is to provoke the non-Muslim world into persecuting "moderate" Muslims to the extent that we begin to doubt our allegiance to the values of life and liberty. They intend to do this by ensuring that these values stop working for us.

When I as a Muslim fight against bigotry and hatred, I am not just fighting in defense of Muslims; I am also fighting for the preservation of our American values. Our political principles do not permit us to celebrate policies that violate our American constitution, even if we stand to benefit from them. Some of the rhetoric we are hearing lately being directed against Muslims is not only incendiary, but unconstitutional. And yet, we are being asked to swallow these lethal propositions that seek to impose restrictions on Muslims without any regard for the possibility that this could one day be used against any and all Americans. Our moral authority to object to injustice is compromised every time we consent, even through our resignation, to the injustice of others.

Only a Muslim who accepts that his dehumanization in the hands of "the other" is even possible, will fight to defend himself through the condemnation of others. American Muslims are not on the attack because we do not recognize the right of anyone to dehumanize us, nor do we recognize the existence of an "other." We are all American. And as American Muslims our mission is to resurrect the tradition of cooperation and co-existence that is central to our religious teachings. American Muslims are striving to empower the religious identity that reflects the pluralistic ideals of our faith.

Unfortunately when a nation goes the way of hate, there are no facts that will disabuse its citizens of their fictions. Any resistance on the part of Muslims seems to only reinforce the narrative that we are defending ourselves because we have something to be defensive about. But Muslims are not enemies of the West; we have been its greatest champions. This reality scares both radical Muslims and Islamophobes, both of whom wish to shut ordinary Muslims out from participation in our civil society. They are attempting to do this by perpetuating the lie that Islam and Western values are incompatible when in fact, Islamic values are more closely aligned to American Ideals than they are to those of any Muslim majority nation on earth.

So where do we go from here?

Love may be blind but hate is deaf. Hate cannot hear, let alone listen, because hate is experienced at a perceptual level of our awareness and never at the conceptual level. And language is a conceptual faculty. In other words, hate judges according to what it sees, not what it understands. And while love can be a choice, hate is almost always a reaction.

Our moral authority to object to injustice is compromised every time we consent, even if through our resignation, to the injustice of others.

One approach to combating hate is to organize national movements that endeavor to eliminate the very notion of "the Other," the "us versus them" phrases, that have seeped into our national and global dialect. There are many such grassroots movements currently under way. One such effort was launched by a group of Muslim and Jewish women, and has since gone international. The Sisterhood of Salaam Shalom is the first national network of Muslim and Jewish women committed to living in harmony and limiting acts of anti-Muslim and anti-Jewish sentiment. We are committed to fighting hate by engaging in informal, one-on-one, relationship-building efforts.

This is only one of many such organized movements that have discovered the power of the contact theory, which states that interpersonal contact is one of the most effective ways to reduce prejudice between groups. Informal interpersonal contact requires the employment of our conceptual faculties. It forces us to engage beyond the level of our immediate perceptions. It is effective because it is not designed to challenge our intellectual capacity to coexist, but rather our emotional capacity to hate after we have grown in the spirit of love.

Hope is not only alive and well, it is powerful and requires nothing but a willingness to listen. Hate, on the other hand, cannot survive without our silent resignation.

Direct informal contact over prolonged periods of time can diminish anxiety and facilitate conflict resolution. The contact theory has been described as one of the most effective ways to improve relations among groups. Gordon W. Allport (1954) is credited with the development of this theory, which states that when positive meaningful relationships develop between people of different religious communities, attitudes toward the entire group improve. Through the application of the contact theory, prejudice can be eliminated. The more one learns about a category of people, the more positively they will feel toward them. And as our world becomes increasingly globalized, the need for better understanding is more critical than ever before.

I believe that building interpersonal relations between groups that are seemingly at odds with one another are the path to tomorrow's peacebuilding efforts. Faith, love, respect, and the restraints of religion, are the means by which we can fight against the evils that cannot be harnessed through an escalation of violence. There are no practical solutions to our political pathologies, only spiritual ones. People of Faith for Peace, another organization to which I proudly cling, are also committed to building peace, one relationship at a time. There are countless other such groups. This surge of collaboration between faith groups is rarely ever celebrated by the mainstream media, and yet the trend is growing exponentially. Hope is not only alive and well, it is powerful and requires nothing but a willingness to listen. Hate, on the other hand, cannot survive without our silent resignation. But we are far from letting go.

Bosniak Refugees: An American Success Story

HARIS HROMIC details the immigrant experience of Bosniak-American refugees who entered the U.S. out of a desire to find a place they could call home and that would provide a safe haven for their families and future generations.

KEY TAKEAWAYS

- Despite the unimaginable pain and losses the Bosniak refugees faced, they became a model refugee community who took responsibility to forge a peaceful and prosperous future as citizens of their adopted land.
- The Bosniak community showed immense success at integrating by rejecting violence of any kind and building relationships of trust with their neighbors.
- Bosniak-Americans' full integration into the political and social fabric of the U.S. includes establishing a Congressional Caucus on Bosnia, which encourages dialogue between policymakers and Bosnian-Americans on issues important to them.

The senseless killing of Muslims by Daesh and the Assad regime in Syria, as well as the refugee crisis that we are witnessing today, are all too familiar in Muslim history. However, Muslims have a long history of perseverance in the face of extremism and in their search for a place to call home.

Even though the Bosniaks had experienced unfathomable pain and loss, and were uprooted from their homes, they recognized that, as refugees, they had the opportunity—and responsibility—to raise and educate their children in a more peaceful, accepting world.

Today, the rising fear of refugees entering the United States due to the threats cast by Daesh is understandable, yet shortsighted. As a Bosniak Muslim who immigrated to the United States, I can tell you first hand that the vast majority of Muslim refugees are attempting to enter America out of a desire to find a place that they can call home and a safe haven for their families and future generations. The Bosniak American community serves as a recent example of Muslim refugees who have successfully integrated into their communities and developed trusting relationships with their neighbors.

Bosniak Muslims are arguably the greatest victims of extremism in the modern era. During the Bosnian genocide in the early 1990s, Bosnian Serb forces launched a brutal ethnic cleansing campaign against the Bosniak Muslims, forcing hundreds of thousands of families to flee their homeland. Those who were unable to flee in time were subject to unimaginable atrocities and almost complete annihilation. Bosniak Muslims were subjected to unlawful confinement, murder, rape, sexual assault, torture, beating, and robbery at the hands of the Serbian Army. The most brutal assault came in July 1995 when Serbian forces stormed the town of Srebrenica, a United Nations safe area, where they massacred more than 8,000

HARIS HROMIC is a trustee for the Carnegie Council for Ethics in International Affairs and the vice president of the World Bosniak Congress. He was a founding member of the Council of the C-1 World organization, which is dedicated to improving relations between the Muslim and Western worlds. Mr. Hromic has been behind a number of international resolutions, including the 2009 EU resolution declaring July 11 a Day of Commemoration of the Srebrenica genocide.

Muslim men and boys while women and girls were victims of systematic rape and humiliation.

After the atrocities committed in Srebrenica, the international community could no longer remain indecisive. In response to the near complete eradication of the Bosniak Muslim population, the United States initiated peace talks between the presidents of Serbia, Croatia, and Bosnia Herzegovina. In November 1995, the United States succeeded in bringing peace to Bosnia by brokering a peace treaty known as the Dayton Accords. In doing so, the United States stopped the genocide in Bosnia and extended an invitation and assistance to Bosniak refugees wishing to resettle in America.

Even though the Bosniaks had experienced unfathomable pain and loss, and were uprooted from their homes, they recognized that, as refugees, they had the opportunity—and responsibility—to raise and educate their children in a more peaceful, accepting world. They began to acclimate to their new environment in various ways, such as building Islamic cultural centers, opening their own businesses, serving in government, running for public office, and joining the military to fight alongside their American countrymen. As former Bosnian foreign minister and United Nations ambassador Muhamed Sacirbey states, they came "to see themselves, heritage and opportunity, in the perspective of the unbounded where Bosnian and American are joined and consistent."[1]

The Bosniak community has shown immense success in integrating into new communities and building relationships of trust with their neighbors. Rather than being stigmatized and intimidated to live under the heavy pressure of collective guilt for the acts of violent extremists who are constantly labeled as "Islamic," Bosniaks made sure their message on collective security and global citizenship was clear to all Americans. Initiated by Bosniak-American leadership in 2013, the World Bosniak Congress published the "Declaration on Common Security and Global Citizenship," which was written in response to the Boston bombings and London killings. In it, the World Bosniak Congress called upon the Bosniak nation "to take a bold stance about their faith and culture and be a good example to others: to condemn violence and promote peace and tolerance wherever they are."

The 2013 Declaration identifies common security and global citizenship as two essential values of human freedom and equality that must be actively and consistently pursued. In order for us to be genuinely Muslim, the declaration states, we must love and work toward peace and bring about solidarity and cooperation within the communities we call home. The declaration states that we must show our neighbors the peaceful acceptance and practice of Islam and bear witness to the historic affirmation that "there shall be no compulsion in religion." Furthermore, it teaches that it is essential for the worldwide Muslim community to stand up for the citizens of the countries that gave us shelter and protection when we needed it most, and show our neighbors and communities how Islam can be a force behind improving the social and economic conditions of our communities.

Rather than being stigmatized and intimidated to live under the heavy pressure of collective guilt for the acts of violent extremists who are constantly labeled as "Islamic," Bosniaks made sure their message on collective security and global citizenship was clear to all Americans.

The World Bosniak Congress and its leadership called upon Muslim preachers around the world to recognize their responsibility toward ensuring the common security of the world's nations by preaching the peace and tolerance of Islam wherever they go. Muslim preachers must lead by example and show all Muslims that we must stand up and speak out about our real concept of life, faith, culture, peace, and security as part and parcel of humanity. Moreover,

[1] Sacirbey, Muhamed. "Bosnia to US, From Refugees to Great Americans." *Huffington Post*, July 3, 2015.

the Grand Mufti of Bosnia urges us in this declaration to act in such a manner that what we say, believe, preach, and teach, is in practice in our own lives, and that we must speak out against hatred and join in defending the basic principles of humanity. Muslims around the world are told to share with their neighbors and colleagues that Islam belongs to neither East nor West, but to the hearts of those who want to live in peace and security with others.

Due to their difficult history, Bosniaks have taken on a unique responsibility to be the standard bearers of morality and pluralism in all the lands they inhabit and call home, all the way from Australia to the United States and Canada. Just as the early Bosniak immigrants to the United States did before us in the 1900s, American Muslims must follow their example and commit to common security and global citizenship and work to promote and protect God's gifts of life: religion, nation, freedom, property, and honor as inalienable rights of every person.

We must raise our children and help educate future generations of Muslims of different nations to be an integral part of the societies in which they live and call home, and to know that the ends do not justify violent means, and that acts of killing and/or injuring civilians are in a complete contradiction to the basic principles of Islam and humanity. We must vigorously pursue these aims through constant education of our youth and our communities. It is paramount that we uphold the highest moral values while openly and loudly rejecting violence of any kind and all acts of terror as fundamentally un-Islamic, immoral, and inhumane.

It is incumbent upon us to strongly demonstrate perpetual and proactive responsibility, and it is our duty to systematically engage society on all levels of personal and institutional collaboration, and to solidify the trust and confidence of our fellow citizens in every aspect of human endeavor. We must uphold Article 18 of the Universal Declaration of Human Rights and Article 18 of the International Covenant on Civil and Political Rights, which state that everyone has the right to freedom of thought, conscience, and religion. It is important we never forget the preamble of the Universal Declaration of Human Rights, which states that disregard and contempt for human rights have resulted in barbarous acts that have outraged the conscience of mankind. All considered, the compassionate character of the Bosniak tradition of Islam lives today in the United States along with many other ethnic traditions, free and proud.

Today, Bosniak-Americans are proud to have established a Congressional Caucus on Bosnia, demonstrating their full integration into the political and social fabric of American society. This body encourages dialogue between policymakers and Bosniak communities across the nation. With over 30 members of the U.S. House of Representatives and U.S. Senate, the bi-partisan caucus is the voice for the Bosniak-American community both on domestic and foreign policy issues. It is an active partnership designed to deliver more informed and more effective policy solutions in an increasingly challenging and complex world.

The Millennial Muslim

NABIL SHAIKH writes about his journey to define his own identity and how he and other young Muslims find courage to challenge those who speak in their name and do not compromise their personal identities in the face of violent extremism and Islamophobia.

KEY TAKEAWAYS

- The world is constantly changing, and Muslims too are encountering new contexts and circumstances, and there are few things in Islamic law for which the jury is closed.
- Islam is always evolving as the world changes, and as a consequence, Muslims are always facing new understandings of their own identity.
- Religion is defined not only by its teachings, but also by how communities across nations and oceans apply the wisdoms of these teachings into their everyday lives and realities today.

In the post-9/11 era, a defining moment in every Muslim youth's childhood or adolescence takes place: it is when they first click on the comments section of a news article related to Islam or Muslims. For me, it was a Yahoo! piece from 2010 on the Park 51 Islamic community center (controversially called the "Ground Zero mosque"). I was only 14, and I had seen something on the *Daily Show with Jon Stewart* about it. The comments I read included openly racist and xenophobic slurs, demands for all Muslims to leave the country, calls for heightened surveillance of and violence against Muslims both in the country and abroad, and abusive misinterpretations of Qur'anic verses and prophetic sayings.

My face became hot. The Islam I grew up with was the warmth of my grandma's finger as she prodded my hand when I made a mistake while reading the Qur'an in Arabic. The Islam I grew up with was the century-old schoolhouse next to my hometown's mosque, where I attended Sunday classes taught in the broken but wholesome English of volunteer immigrant parents from Asia and Africa, whose children were my dear friends. The Islam I grew up with was the smell of old books that contained millennium-old wisdoms from prophets and scholars, made pertinent to our times.

Reading those comments, I immediately felt defensive and began various Google searches to help answer the questions these Islamophobic comments brought to mind. I did not find any satisfactory websites equipped to handle such questions. Since 2010, I have seen major strides made in one particular area of American Muslim community organizations and grassroots leadership: public relations. For some, the harangues of anti-Muslim bloggers and commenters during the Park 51 controversy sparked many within the American Muslim community to begin the struggle to speak about their religion and their community on their own terms. For many young people like me, however, such controversies left us feeling disheartened and ill-equipped to handle a public Muslim identity.

Growing up Muslim in the post-9/11 era sees many familiar scenes like this one. At age 9, you might find yourself in a history class with a teacher nervously

NABIL SHAIKH, of Reading, Pennsylvania, is a recent graduate of Princeton University, with a major in Politics and a double major in Global Health Policy and Values and Public Life. During his time at Princeton, Shaikh served as president of the Princeton Muslim Students' Association and co-convener of the Religious Life Council, and led initiatives within the Office of Religious Life and the Muslim Life Program. He also served as treasurer for Muslim Advocates for Social Justice and the Pace Council for Civic Values, and as a freshman trip leader for Community Action. He will soon commence his studies in the Master's of Public Affairs program at Princeton's Woodrow Wilson School, as a graduate fellow in the Scholars in the Nation's Service Initiative. Shaikh plans to pursue a career at the nexus of policy, law, and public health.

glancing at you as she attempts to explain the beginnings of Islamic civilization. At age 12, your friend in the cafeteria might shove a hot pocket in your face while you are fasting. At age 15, your high school debate coach might ask you for your opinion on why women in Saudi Arabia are not legally allowed to drive. At age 18, you might sit in a university lecture hall and hear a distinguished professor lend credence to the theory that all college Muslim Students' Associations receive funding from the Muslim Brotherhood. At age 21, you might console a friend dealing with workplace harassment due to her decision to wear a headscarf.

Religion is defined not only by its scriptures and teachings, but by how communities across nations and oceans implement these wisdoms into their lives and marry these virtues with the realities of today. These are the people to consult when you want to understand what Muslims think.

Throughout my life, I have struggled with the fact that all too often I find myself in rooms or in casual conversations or on news sites' comment sections (it's a bad habit of mine), listening to or reading statements made about my religion, my faith, my heritage—without any attempt made on the part of the statements' authors to first consult Muslim peers, leaders, intellectuals, or activists. Too often, I have heard people speak in my name.

The reality is that one cannot understand Islam without understanding community. And one cannot comprehend Islam in America without studying and visiting American Muslim communities. It has been demonstrated through various surveys that those who have a Muslim friend or neighbor or coworker are much less likely to fear Islam or to believe in violent conspiracy theories surrounding the Islamic way of life. Communities are the gateways to people and their shared values. The first Muslim community I strongly resonated with was the Muslim community on my college campus, Princeton University. An incredibly multiethnic community, comprising students, staff, faculty, and residents of the local towns, the Princeton Muslim community dishes out American Islam via lecture series, interfaith seminars, English-language Qur'an study circles, open Friday prayer services, spiritual retreats, intercommunity service projects, and more. The leader of the community, Princeton University Muslim chaplain Sohaib Sultan, likes to say that, just as there are seven entrances to the holiest mosque in Mecca, there are numerous doors through which one can enter the Princeton Muslim community. There is a constant influx and efflux of scholars, activists, seekers, students, "cultural Muslims," "political Muslims," and others.

The beauty of such a diverse community is that one can receive a plethora of perspectives on both "hot-button" issues and more basic matters of faith, identity, and life more generally. I never grew up thinking that Islam has one thing to say about anything, beyond the core truths of monotheism, the belief in the finality of the prophethood of Muhammad, and other central theological beliefs. The word "Shari'ah" alone evokes such controversy in the West, despite the fact that it refers to an incredibly vast and diverse set of evolving opinions within Islamic jurisprudence on how to lead observant and virtuous lives. "Shari'ah" literally means the way—and more specifically, the path to water. There are very few things in Islamic law and sociopolitical modeling for which the jury is closed. This is because the world is constantly changing, and with it, Muslims are encountering new contexts and circumstances.

Yet, again, too often I have heard people speaking in my name: "Muslims __." What follows is a broad generalization. If anyone were to spend an iota of time in a Muslim congregation or community center, one would discover that religion is defined not only by its scriptures and teachings, but by how communities across nations and oceans implement these wisdoms into their lives and marry these virtues with the realities of today. *These* are the people to consult when you want to understand what Muslims think—and there should never be just one person whom you consult.

One thing you will discover is the sheer pain that the community experiences each time violence occurs in the name of their religion. Indeed, just as I have always struggled with people of other faiths speaking in my name, I have of course repeatedly been troubled by the violent clerics and extremists who commit the most atrocious crimes against humanity in the name of my religion and in the name of all its adherents.

If I grew up wanting to see American Muslims speak in their own name; I then came to realize that the only way to achieve this is to begin with myself—to allow myself to feel collective grief without compromising my personal identity, to dare to find joy in the struggles of this world as anyone else does, and to find the courage to challenge those who speak in my name.

What follows is the backlash and, with it, the Islamophobia. Muslims immediately have to begin the age-old practice of damage control. We have to achieve the perfect balance of mourning and calling out instances of anti-Muslim rhetoric and hate. The sensitivity of these times always results in disaster for Muslims, who, like any other people in the country, want nothing more than to mourn in solidarity. Instead, we face the certain onslaught of hate-filled comments claiming that all Muslims care about is self-victimization. It intrigues and bothers me to see the people with the least privilege in society face claims that their attempts to highlight their own suffering are problematic and are a sign that they seek privilege that they do not deserve. In other words, even in moments of collective mourning, I have found that American Muslims cannot win; they cannot both mourn a public tragedy and defend themselves without unwillingly conferring a sense of privilege on themselves—for being alive—that our non-Muslim peers find deplorable.

But if there is one thing of importance I have gained from such a realization, it is that American Muslims like myself must invest time and energy not just into responding to negativity and performing damage control, but also into their own joy. My entire battle as a young American Muslim growing up in the post-9/11 era has been one of reclaiming my own emotions, of realizing that I do not need to read the comments section. If I grew up wanting to see American Muslims speak in their own name; I then came to realize that the only way to achieve this is to begin with myself—to allow myself to feel collective grief without compromising my personal identity, to dare to find joy in the struggles of this world as anyone else does, and to find the courage to challenge those who speak in my name.

Modesty, Veiling, and Fashion

HASSANAH EL-YACOUBI discusses how American Muslim women continue to shape their dual identities through choice, conviction, and fashion.

KEY TAKEAWAYS

- While women are sometimes treated differently in Islam than men, it does not mean that they are treated unequally.
- The practice of wearing the hijab (headscarf) is manifested in multiple ways, and is most often rooted in a woman's personal conviction and choice.
- The modest fashion phenomenon has enabled Muslim women to thrive in new and powerful ways as never before.

Wearing the headscarf as a signifier of one's tradition is not an easy task for those who have adopted it. In an age where overexposure seems to be the socially acceptable way to dress, the ability to control how much or how little others can see of one's body can be incredibly satisfying and powerful.

This ability to control enables women to define their own identities and agency by placing the power of representation into their hands and away from the media, fleeting fashion trends, or so-called experts. Women who choose to cover up are challenged on many sides, accused by some of affronting Western understandings of equality and liberation, and by others who say they are promoting a gender-biased interpretation of Islam.

What is left out of the debate is that women who make the decision to wear the headscarf are not being forced to do so; on the contrary, they are exercising their right to do so. Western media and scholars have a tendency to homogenize Islamic practices and, in particular, the practice of veiling adopted by some women. We have to divorce our imaginations from identifying the headscarf as a monolithic, backward, and oppressive custom, as Western media often depicts it. The reality is, the notion of global gender justice is far too nuanced, complex, and diverse to simply insert and assert patterns of Western metrics as a prevailing standard applicable in all countries.

As Americans, we have to make room for new forms of Muslim subjectivity gauged by a uniquely American reference point—freedom of expression. Not to do so means that we are grossly neglecting our core ideals of liberation. We must strive against standardized notions of equality, liberation, and gender egalitarianism, and instead, respect the varied ways in which women express their identities—ethnic, national, or religious.

Islam establishes modesty as a universal code of conduct for both males and females. While many Muslims believe the headscarf to be a religious obligation, the Qur'an states that there is no compulsion in religion. Thus, modesty in attire came to be expressed through local cultural norms. Within a modern context, to what extent a woman expresses her modesty is not only a gauge of her religiosity, but also serves as a means of identifying as a Muslim.

Despite the Qur'an's assertion that there is no

HASSANAH EL-YACOUBI is a doctoral student in religious studies at the University of California, Riverside. She focuses on women in Islam and on the role identity and body politics play for American Muslims. Her research revolves around the emerging Muslim identity cultivated by millennials through the global phenomenon of Islamic fashion, which has altered the ways in which Muslim practices are performed and perceived. As a leading fashion and lifestyle blogger, she is dedicated to creating cross-cultural and religious understanding through fashion. She is a global leader in the modest fashion industry, listed among the top modest fashion influencers by the *Huffington Post*.

compulsion in Islam, and the varying interpretations of modesty, there are Muslim women around the world for whom the headscarf is not a choice but an imposition. This misapplication of cultural norms must not eclipse the fact that women's choice to wear the headscarf is rooted in a plethora of reasons; thus, we cannot ascribe a univocal narritive to all women who have adopted the headscarf.

American Muslim women who choose to wear the headscarf have been the targets of verbal and physical abuse, and some have opted not to wear their headscarf out of fear for their lives. Their parents often beg them to remove the headscarf for their own peace of mind. Conversely, some women have chosen to continue to don their headscarves in spite of the negative reactions they may provoke because the headscarf represents their own form of agency.

> We must strive against standardized notions of equality, liberation, and gender egalitarianism, and instead, respect the varied ways in which women express their identities—ethnic, national, or religious.

Muslim women in America straddle a dual identity—one that allows free exercise of religion and one that promotes freedom of expression, thus synthesizing agency and choice. We need to demonstrate that one can be both Muslim and modern, and we do this by positively mediating a new trend: an adoption of a modest expression of fashion. Modest fashion can become a conduit of convergence between the two seemingly dialectical forces.

It is no surprise that fashion brands like American Eagle Outfitters have embraced this trend and offered a denim hijab, sending a clear message that being American and Muslim are not mutually exclusive, and that Muslim women in hijab are just as much a part of the fabric of America as are T-shirts, jeans, and cowboy hats. Brands that previously had not seen a need to cater to the fashion preferences of women of Jewish, Mormon, or other faiths with religious dress codes are embracing Muslim women, seeing the potential profits that can be reaped by serving this growing niche of underserved yet lucrative global Muslim markets. This has produced a net positive outcome in terms of the level of visibility and inclusivity Muslim women have experienced on a national and local level.

Muslim women like myself are actively changing the narrative of American Islam by embracing modesty in a fashionable way. As entrepreneurs of modest fashion, we not only reclaim what it means to be a modest woman in the West, we also mediate between our dual identities as Americans and Muslims. Our tenacity in choosing not to compromise our values despite external pressures and a lack of clothing options in the fashion marketplace has gained us recognition by mainstream fashion producers such as H&M, Zara, Mango, and Tommy Hilfiger. They have begun to cater to Muslim women's sartorial needs so we can dress in ways that we believe to be proper and in keeping with our overall lifestyle, while still being fashionable.

Modest fashion for American Muslim women may be one way to proclaim one's pious self, but more importantly, it is an expression of an agent who is in control of making her own choices, rooted in conviction in her religious practices. Recognizing and respecting Muslim women for their differences will help them to thrive in their own spaces.

Hollywood: Liberal?

KAMRAN PASHA describes how Hollywood has evolved to match the changing times by positively portraying other minority communities, but has yet to follow these trends with Muslims on screen.

KEY TAKEAWAYS

- People in Hollywood who claim to be liberal often see Islam through a lens of fear and as indefensible, believing it to be sexist, homophobic, and backward.
- Muslim movie characters are overwhelmingly depicted as the "bad guys" or terrorists who are defeated by "good guys," who are usually white.
- Hollywood has an undeniable ability to shape American perceptions, particularly how it portrays a people or culture about which Americans know very little.

"Don't take the deal," my friend said in a hushed voice over the phone. I was confused. The deal that he was referring to was my first major break in Hollywood, my chance to go from unknown, struggling screenwriter to respected professional. And what made it stranger was that he was calling from the very production company that had just made the offer to my agents. It was the summer of 2002 and I had just finished a screenplay on the Crusades, one that had been inspired by the horror of September 11, just a few months before.

There have been many movies on the Crusades in Hollywood, but my story promised to be unique, for I told the familiar story from the Muslim point of view. The protagonist of the tale was the great Muslim leader Saladin, who conquered Jerusalem from the Crusaders and then, instead of taking revenge on his enemies, went on to build a multi-cultural society where Jews, Christians, and Muslims lived together in peace. My movie was born of particular circumstances: it was written to show that there was more to Islam than what the world had been shown by a handful of madmen on 9/11.

The script had received a great deal of attention, and now I had an offer from one of the most powerful producers in Hollywood to buy the project. I was elated—and then stunned when my friend who worked for this producer called and told me to reject the offer. "I will lose my job if they found out I was telling you this," he said over the phone, "but the boss has no intention of making your movie. He plans to buy the script in order to bury it and make sure no one else will ever be able to tell this story." At this exact moment, I learned a terrible truth about how Hollywood works.

The famous producer who tried to suppress my Saladin script was just the first of many. I remember taking notes from a respected TV executive who told me directly, "Don't make the villain of the episode Chinese. Make him Arab. Everybody hates them." I've sat in a writers' room on a television series and listened to a producer say: "The best way to solve the problem of terrorism is to kill Muslim children so they know we mean business." I remember trying to pitch a lighthearted action show while a buyer kept going off on non sequiturs about how "Muslims are trying to kill us all." Or the film executive who boasted proudly that he had removed a Cat Stevens song from a hit movie because Stevens (a Muslim convert) "supported terrorists" due to his charity work in Palestine.

I find it hard to ignore the narrow stereotype

KAMRAN PASHA is a Hollywood screenwriter, director, producer, and novelist. He was the co-producer and writer for Showtime's Golden Globe and Emmy nominated show *Sleeper Cell*, and is currently the writer and producer for NBC's *Kings*. Mr. Pasha has written two novels, *The Mother of Believers*, a historical epic of the birth of Islam through the eyes of the Prophet Muhammad's wife Aisha, and *Shadow of the Swords*.

Hollywood has followed when depicting Muslims, or any minority group, for that matter, on film or television. If you think about it, only recently did Hollywood start to stray away from portraying African Americans as "gangsters" and "thugs" and start portraying black men, especially, in a more positive, "professional" light. The same can be said for women, who are now depicted as strong and powerful—succeeding in a "man's world." Hollywood has evolved to match the changing times in society in this way, but has yet to follow these trends with Muslims onscreen.

Muslim characters are overwhelmingly depicted as the "bad guys" or terrorists who are eventually defeated by the "good guys" (i.e., White and/or American).

For instance, according to the late Jack Shaheen, author of the book *Reel Bad Arabs*, there have been roughly 1,200 depictions of Arabs and Muslims in American cinema, 97 percent of which have been unfavorable portrayals.[1] Muslim characters are overwhelmingly depicted as the "bad guys" or terrorists who are eventually defeated by the "good guys" (i.e., White and/or American). And these portrayals are not a new, post-9/11 phenomenon. Take, for example, the 1994 Arnold Schwarzenegger movie *True Lies*, which explicitly portrayed a group of Palestinians as "terrorists" who are eventually stopped by the "hero" Schwarzenegger. More recently, shows such as *Tyrant*, *Homeland*, and most egregiously, the movie *American Sniper*, have exacerbated Islamophobic rhetoric and fueled the spread of fearmongering and paranoia of Muslims.

When Hollywood executives choose to portray Muslims in film or television in a negative light, they are playing right into the hands of extremist groups like Daesh who propagate these overtly negative images of Muslims as proof that "America hates Muslims" and that America is engaged in a "war against Islam." The power of film and television to positively influence popular attitudes about Muslims and push back against these extremist narratives, is so great that the Obama administration had implored Hollywood film executives to expand past portrayals of Muslims in national security situations and simply show them as normal human beings in dramas and comedy. In February 2016, Secretary of State John Kerry traveled to Los Angeles to meet with executives from NBCUniversal, Warner Bros., DreamWorks Animation, 20th Century Fox, Sony Picture Entertainment, and the Walt Disney Company, to brainstorm ways in which Hollywood can help dispel these extremist narratives.

I've found that many in Hollywood view Islam with fear and others see it as a stubbornly sexist and homophobic religion, unworthy of their liberal defense. The latter are blind to how inaccurate that stereotype is—I have often made Hollywood executives uncomfortable when I mention, for example, the high number of female doctors in the Muslim world or the work of Muslim feminists to combat sexism in their communities. They are always stunned when I point out that in Iran, sex change operations are paid for by the Islamic government. That last one usually leaves them speechless.

While Islamophobia is still rippling through Hollywood and our communities, I find that things are starting to change. For example, my show *Sleeper Cell* featured the first American Muslim hero, an FBI agent who fights terrorism. The show garnered multiple Emmy and Golden Globe nominations. We even have the ABC series *Quantico*, which featured twin Muslim sisters in its first two seasons (played by my good friend Yasmine Al-Massri), one in hijab and one without, excelling as FBI cadets, with both characters representing the incredible diversity within our community.

Fourteen years after my Saladin script was rejected, I have been blessed to have a successful career as one of the few practicing Muslims in Hollywood. I have sold other scripts to movie studios, such as my epic tale of the Taj Mahal to Warner Brothers, worked as a writer and producer on TV shows such as *Sleeper Cell* and the CW's *Nikita*, and have published two novels through Simon & Schuster. In fact, one of my

[1] Steve Rose, "'Death to the Infidels!' Why It's Time to Fix Hollywood's Problem with Muslims." The Guardian. March 8, 2016.

novels is based on that Crusades script (Shadow of the Swords) and I have received wonderful feedback from readers on how the story opened them to a positive, beautiful side of Islam they had never known. In the past fourteen years, I discovered that there are indeed many people in Hollywood who value my perspective and talent, despite not sharing my religious beliefs or cultural background.

[Hollywood] serves not only as a mirror of our culture, reflecting its unseen, ignored or uglier aspects, but it actively shapes it, encouraging us to take a closer look at our values and the ways we view others

For better or worse, Hollywood has the undeniable ability to shape the American psyche, particularly with regard to how it portrays a people or culture about which many Americans may not be knowledgeable. It serves not only as a mirror of our culture, reflecting its unseen, ignored, or uglier aspects, but it actively shapes it, encouraging us to take a closer look at our values and the ways we view others. Hollywood not only sees aspects of our culture that we often cannot see, but it is also seen, and the global Muslim community are huge consumers of this vision. As Muslims continue to become a "normal" part of American society, Hollywood will have to confront its stereotypes and prejudices. The demographics of our country are changing quickly, and whether we like it or not, the process is irreversible. In my opinion, only after Muslims become a normal and welcome part of American television and film will Hollywood begin to fulfill its self-proclaimed ideal of being the conscience of the nation. Until then, I am going to write yet another script with a Muslim hero (I have a dozen) and fight to get it produced. It would have been easier to give up back in 2002 and avoid Muslim topics in my work. It would have been a more pleasant journey, free of awkward exchanges with powerful people, and perhaps certain colleagues would have considered me a friend rather than an enemy. But my conscience would have never left me alone.

Salaam from Hollywood.

Forging Our Legacy as Americans

SAMI H. ELMANSOURY shares his view that Muslim immigrants are Americans who continue to hold great pride in their legacy and in their adopted homeland, and their national contribution often goes untold to the public at large.

KEY TAKEAWAYS

- Muslim immigrants must stake their own claim to their new homeland and simultaneously rise up against those who attempt to defame their religion and usher in a new era in which Islam is equated with justice and peace.
- It is commonly assumed that to be a Muslim is inherently un-American, a false notion that has motivated several American Muslims to get even more involved in their communities and prove that it is possible to be both.
- Young American Muslims must discover and forge their own legacy and wear that narrative with pride when documenting their stories, whether they involve tragedy or hope.

As American Muslims in a post–9/11 world, it has become our vocation to respectfully broaden the American landscape not only by showing ways with which our faith betters our actions, but that we are also the best and most involved citizens. I am a strong believer in our nation and in the many profound things that the United States has stood for. I am also a Muslim who appreciates his faith, and I recognize and will openly profess that I find no contradiction between my being an American with strong national pride, and my being a Muslim. I also know that there exists a proud American Muslim legacy that, despite the calls of the naysayers, can never be expunged from our national history.

While in college, I was told by some that a sense of Muslim community identity, "Ummah," can only be preserved if one puts aside one's national pride and values. But I never felt this to be an Islamic imperative—quite the contrary. The frank truth is that the Muslims of China, with history dating back to the earliest days of Islam, never shied away from being part of a greater Chinese culture, nor did those of India, Egypt, or Russia dispel their respective cultural heritages. So why would American Muslims shy away from rooting themselves in the United States as Americans? I recognized then, as I do today, that my views are shaped differently, in part, because I recall a different story. I find pride and seek solace in the legacy of men like my grandfather, Mohamed, an immigrant to the United States. In 1969, at the height of the Cold War, he offered his mind for the benefit of his country, and proudly served as a NASA engineer for the Apollo 11 mission. My grandfather and my family sat in the rows just behind President Lyndon Johnson as they watched the rocket take off carrying Neil Armstrong, Buzz Aldrin, and Michael Collins to the Moon.

With a radiant smile, my grandfather frequently shows me his Apollo 11 certificate, signed by NASA's director, as he reminds me of our journey and of what he left behind so that we may have the opportunity as Americans to live in greater comfort and human dignity in the most powerful country on Earth. My grandfather and his wife of nearly sixty years, my grandmother Madiha, both Muslims, are Americans, and continue to hold great pride in their legacy and in their adopted homeland. I realize that it is quintessentially American stories

SAMI H. ELMANSOURY is a public speaker and writer on issues related to education, national security, faith, and identity politics. He was a founding member of the U.S. Department of State's Generation Change initiative and was inducted as a World Young Leader by the BMW Foundation in 2013.

like theirs—stories of immigrant sacrifice followed by national contribution—that far too often go untold to American Muslim youth and to the public at large. I remind my Muslim coreligionists that individuals like my grandfather Mohamed, while being Muslim, are also deeply American at their core.

I am a strong believer in our nation and in the many profound things that the United States has stood for. I am also a Muslim who appreciates his faith, and I recognize and will openly profess that I find no contradiction between my being an American with strong national pride and my being a Muslim.

Yet the same fearmongering that today seeks to debase my grandfather Mohamed's name and strip away his legacy has also attacked many American Muslim youth, causing them to ask: "Am I American enough, and what does that mean?" The fear and disconnect that ensue have caused many of them to repel an American identity. Too often I find myself having to stand up to Muslim youth and repeat: "Be proud, you have a legacy here." And yet, I recognize that this sense of alienation admittedly plaguing many American Muslim youth in the present does not emerge from some pseudo-inherent evil within them or their faith practice—as fearmongering pundits would have one believe—but rather from a lack of connection to or rootedness in their country and its declared values, combined with potently adverse messaging pulling them away.

It is crucial to acknowledge that such adverse messaging, leading to either the creation or fostering of bigoted conditions within local American communities or within the halls of Congress, has an absolute role to play in the alienation process that can lead to social rejection and extremism. There is never an excuse for collective punishment of civilians for social grievances, whether due to disempowerment, government policy, or otherwise, and it is a common, unified mission for all people of reason to be unrelenting in the complex battle against the forces of extremism. Our American society at large simply cannot wish away American Muslim communities. They exist, they will continue to exist and to contribute positively to our fabric—and they are entitled to the same rights. We are not compelled, as Americans, to earn our rights. They are our rights, period.

But unfortunately, the disturbing use of faith-based and other ideological or violent supremacist extremism that can certainly manifest itself within any group of people, and in any country or culture, is undoubtedly being propagated by an increasingly vocal and dangerous group of Muslims today. Groups such as Daesh, Al-Qaeda, Boko Haram, Al-Shabaab, and a plethora of others, including nonviolent extremists, have posed a repeated ideological danger to coexistence and to the basic protection of human worth within Muslim-majority and minority communities. But these groups are not representative of my beliefs, and they are likely not representative of most others. It is therefore in the best interest of the Muslim community to unapologetically ramp up its efforts to quell the scourge of global extremism that veritably exacerbates the lingering climate of mistrust within society at large, regardless of sideline discussions on cause and blame.

American Muslims can stake their own claim to their new homeland and simultaneously humanize their coreligionists abroad by actively participating in political leadership, in entrepreneurship, and in various constructive industries, by producing legislation or scientific achievements that benefit society at large and artistic works that are worthy of the Oscars and Grammys. Whether from mosque pulpits in California or from living rooms in Michigan, American Muslim communities must encourage an acceleration of this shift to noninsular, positive, and above all, sincere high-profile participation and contribution. I have personally known the desire among Muslim families for understanding and mutual human dignity for themselves and for others, while in the broader community around them, I have seen the misunderstanding of many mainstream Muslim beliefs and traditions. Regardless of this challenge, I have witnessed the dominant nature of Muslim hospitality, humility, and graciousness toward others. To me, this very nature will always overshadow the extremist voice, regardless of how prevalent the latter may be in the media, or due to the brutality committed by a vocal few who adversely influence and impact Muslim communities and their neighbors, and who falsely claim to speak for Islam and Muslims. Today, I reflect upon the paradigm that has been created for American Muslims: it is often assumed that to be a practicing Muslim is inherently un-American. Yet my frustration with this absurd challenge drives me to be even more involved in my community, to present to both my neighbors and to my coreligionists the blatant fact that my faith values, when interpreted as such, neither contradict my sincere American pride nor my American culture. Because unlike many who have become radically absorbed into the misleading notion that being both American and a patriot can only be derived from the fear of what is different, my patriotism does not come from politics or apologies—it comes from our Sputnik moments. It is because of stories like that of my grandfather and my parents that I forbid myself to allow ignorance and prejudice to stifle my patriotism, to prevent me from cheering my country on when it is right or speaking up when it is wrong, or to offer me a sense of alienation in the only nation that I call home.

It is upon every American Muslim young person to discover or to forge their own legacy, and to wear that narrative with pride. Ask questions. Document your story—whether it involves tragedy or hope. Draw upon your talents. Connect with your countrymen. And love, appreciate, and give back to your greater American community. As for me, as just one American who also happens to be Muslim, I will work with every breath to have a profound, significant, and remarkably positive impact on my country and on my world, and to keep my family's proud legacy alive. I will boldly defy those who seek to alienate me because of my faith, for neither fearmongers nor coreligionists can erase a story that stays alive through example. Neither can stifle the opportunity to find power and protection in this Constitution, one of the most incredible and ever-changing documents written by Man, for the ultimate uplifting of human worth and freedom. And neither can take away the distinguished difference that any young American can make, in the most diverse nation on Earth, as they build upon the courage that brought their families and their ancestors here, and as they discover the legacy that made them American.

Each individual, in spite of varying backgrounds, has a role to play at the very grass roots, and . . . organizations must step up and do more to usher in a new era in which Islam, as is so often said, is equated with justice and with peace in the global psyche.

I challenge my fellow Muslims to continue to rise up against those who incessantly defame us as they act in the name of our religion. To acknowledge that each individual, in spite of varying backgrounds, has a role to play at the very grass roots, and that organizations must step up and do more to usher in a new era in which Islam, as is so often said, is equated with justice and with peace in the global psyche. To ask, at long last, even the most controversial questions on the role of faith, progress, and the future. To be a people who help to alter the status quo with their hands, not just with their hearts, so that we may tell our children that we sought with our best efforts to defend and to advance global human dignity. While the task seems daunting for any one individual, the collective is more powerful than any force of depravity.

And I simultaneously challenge the naysayers among my countrymen to recognize that we are still one nation, and that no troublesome force can separate us from each other's shared destiny.

To move forward together—we will have to.

This essay has been excerpted and modified from Sami H. Elmansoury's acclaimed work, reprinted with permission: Elmansoury, Sami H. "The Exodus of Fear: Redefining Patriotism Through Legacy." *All-American: 45 American Men on Being Muslim*. Ashland, OR: White Cloud Press, 2012.

Keeping America Great: The Importance of Public Service

CONGRESSMAN KEITH ELLISON writes about how when American Muslims engage with their communities—whether by voting, running for office, or community organizing—they empower and create agency for themselves and forge important connections with other diverse groups.

KEY TAKEAWAYS

- American Muslims lead the way in civic engagement and serve their communities because that is what their faith asks of them.
- Civic engagement is one of the best tools to counter extremist groups because it relies on the initiatives of the community.
- American Muslims must ensure that their homeland is safe and in this pursuit, they must not sacrifice principles of the First and Fourth Amendments.

In August 2014, African American citizens and police officers were locked in conflict in Ferguson, Missouri. People across the nation watched, wondering what to do. The physicians of the American Muslim community of St. Louis and congregants of St. Peter's United Church of Christ in Ferguson weren't wondering what to do. They were already collaborating to provide free health care in the over policed yet under protected community. They knew what to do.

The folks at St. Peter's and a group of American Muslim doctors had teamed up to start the Salam Clinic years before the shooting of Michael Brown. These Muslim and Christian leaders recognized the medical needs of the underserved residents of Ferguson, and they joined together to do something about it. They took initiative to address community needs.

The American Muslim community that was criticized before September 11, 2001, became demonized after the acts of violence against the Twin Towers in New York City, the Pentagon in Washington, DC, and United Flight 93. After 9/11, the assaults, misrepresentation in the media, and acts of discrimination against American Muslims increased. Many American Muslims felt like persecuted minorities. They feared for their families and some considered leaving the United States.

> Civic engagement is the process of American Muslims taking action. That includes voting and running for office within the larger community. The main idea is to come out of the mosques and Muslim centers and engage in improving the community in partnership with people of all faiths.

The American Muslim doctors at the Salam Clinic in Ferguson didn't retreat from providing health care. They remained engaged, showing that they were part of the community. Through participation, they made

CONGRESSMAN KEITH ELLISON is the representative of Minnesota's fifth congressional district. He is the first practicing Muslim member of the United States Congress and the first African American to be elected to the House of Representatives from Minnesota. His memoir, *My Country 'Tis of Thee*, was published in January 2014.

friends with their neighbors, diminished stereotypes, and countered the narrative of Al-Qaeda and Daesh. They provided a positive rejoinder to the extreme perspective that Muslims don't belong in America.

> If unity becomes the mainstream message, then Daesh cannot recruit successfully.

Muslims have been an integral part of American society since the first slave ships arrived on its shores. The oldest surviving mosque in America is in Iowa, where the Muslim community actively engages with their fellow Americans. American Muslims are running for office, volunteering at food shelters, writing books about the environment, and engaging in many other pursuits. American Muslims like Linda Sarsour are providing leadership to important social movements, such as March2Justice and the Justice League in New York City, which marched from New York to Washington, DC, to protest police brutality and surveillance. Young labor movement leaders like Maimuna Syed are leading the fight for a $15 minimum wage in California and around the nation.

In Minnesota, Muslims are fully part of the social fabric of our state and communities. American Muslim professors, doctors, elected officials, business owners, and civic leaders work throughout the state. The 5th Congressional District I represent is home to many American Muslim non-profits that work for civil rights, environmental justice, and women's rights. Leaders here have organized a lobby at the state legislature to help shape policy. Last year, Muslim and Jewish youth started the first annual Jewish-Muslim Youth lobby day. Although we have made progress in Minnesota, we are still working to ensure that the talents and gifts of residents of all backgrounds are fully respected and accepted in our community.

American Muslims who engage with their communities are doing something incredibly important. They discredit Daesh and all "jihadist" narratives. These terrorist recruiters hope to drive a wedge between Muslim and non-Muslim neighbors. They search out the vulnerable, angry, and naive, and promote a message that says, "America is at war with Islam"; "There is no place for Muslims in America"; "us versus them"; and "don't be friends with the non believers."

As Muslims engage, they are accepted. Like other communities, American Muslims have agency and power over their own lives. As they continue to engage, they will find common ground with diverse groups in the community. If unity becomes the mainstream message, then Daesh cannot recruit successfully.

American Muslims lead the way in civic engagement and serve their community because that is what their faith asks of them. Community service and giving to the poor is a core principle of Islam, as it is for most faiths. When I asked a Muslim doctor at the Salam Clinic why he was volunteering his Saturdays to see patients for free, he answered, "for the pleasure of Allah."

Today, there are more than 30 health clinics in the United States founded by American Muslims. The largest, Umma Clinic in South Central Los Angeles, was started by Muslim medical students after the closure of Martin Luther King Hospital and the Rodney King riots in 1991. Many other clinics started following the Umma Clinic model.

> Terrorism emerges from every part of the globe, from every ethnic and religious group, and from every ideology, but a disproportionate number of victims of terrorism live in Muslim-majority states, and a portion of the perpetrators claim Islam as their inspiration.

Some forces still represent barriers to American Muslim civic engagement. For example, bigotry, discrimination, and hateful rhetoric fueled by a small number of members of the media and a few public officials can discourage Muslims from engaging. Religious profiling and other forms of government overreach can also discourage engagement.

Civic engagement is one of the best tools available to counter extremist groups because it relies on the initiative of the community. The most effective approaches to counter violent extremism come from the civic engagement of community members. Civic engagement is the process of American Muslims taking action. That includes voting and running for office within the larger community. The main idea is to come out of the mosques and Muslim centers and engage in improving the community in partnership with people of all faiths.

Daesh wants governments to overreact, and it uses bigotry and misrepresentations of Islam. The best defense against violent extremism is to adhere to our values. We need to ensure that our homeland is safe and in this pursuit, we should not sacrifice our principles embodied in the First and Fourth Amendments. We are safer when people have confidence that our system of justice is fair.

America needs what its Muslim leaders have to offer. After all, the terrorists who claim Islam as their inspiration are attempting to recruit in Muslim communities. They are using language familiar to faithful Muslims, and distorting the meaning and the message of the Qur'an. Terrorism emerges from every part of the globe, from every ethnic and religious group, and from every ideology, but a disproportionate number of victims of terrorism live in Muslim-majority states, and a portion of the perpetrators claim Islam as their inspiration.

Muslims everywhere should look to the American Muslim doctors in Ferguson as their example. They have shown that through civic engagement, misrepresentations can diminish and discriminatory mind-sets can come tumbling down. Those experiences can permeate neighborhoods and communities, which will help Muslims who have a strong stake in defeating terrorists who operate under the veneer of Islamic rhetoric.

Notable American Muslims

AMEENA JANDALI and **HENRY MILLSTEIN** of **ING** discuss how although American Muslims remain a relatively small part of the U.S. population—between three and six million—they have produced a great many major contributors to American life. This article provides some profiles of accomplished American Muslims in various professions.

Muslims have been part of American history since before the United States existed as a nation, contributing to the building and the very fabric of this country. Around one-fifth of Africans brought here as slaves were Muslim. Many were known for their literacy, knowledge, and adherence to aspects of their faith, although few were able to continue to practice Islam.

The first wave of voluntary Muslim immigrants to the U.S. came in the second half of the nineteenth century, mostly from what was then called Greater Syria. The majority were single men hoping to earn money for families back home. One such immigrant, Hajji Ali (anglicized as Hi Jolly) served as chief camel driver in the U.S. army's attempt to set up a Camel Military Corps between 1856 and 1864. The camel experiment was discontinued but Ali was immortalized in a campfire song. Another Syrian immigrant, Anas Hamawi, is credited with the invention of the ice cream cone at the 1904 World Fair in St. Louis.

Later waves of Muslim immigration came from the collapsing Ottoman Empire in the early 1900s, from Eastern Europe and the Soviet Union after World War II, and from the Indian subcontinent following the partition of India and Pakistan. After immigration laws became less restrictive in 1965, Muslims came in greater numbers from many places in the Muslim world, primarily for work and education, or in some cases to escape political repression and turmoil at home.

> Together with African American and other indigenous Muslims, American Muslims today make up a community that is vibrant and talented and is contributing in multiple and varied ways to the rich fabric of America.

African Americans, who began to rediscover Islam in northern cities early in the twentieth century, form another sizable component of the American Muslim community. The most well-known rediscovery movement was the Nation of Islam founded by Elijah Muhammad in the late 1930s. The Nation differs from traditional Islam in significant ways; with the death of

AMEENA JANDALI is Content Director and a founding member of ING (www.ing.org). She co-designs and develops ING's educational presentations and cultural competency seminars. Ameena has delivered hundreds of presentations in schools, colleges, universities, churches, and other venues on Islam and related subjects. She's also appeared on many news outlets speaking on issues relating to American Muslims. She currently team teaches a class on Islam at San Francisco City College. Ameena received her MA in Near Eastern Studies from the University of California, Berkeley, and BA in History from the University of Illinois.

HENRY MILLSTEIN is ING's Content Manager and Programs Analyst. Henry holds a PhD in Jewish Studies from the University of California, Berkeley, and the Graduate Theological Union, with a focus on Jewish-Christian relations. He worked for sixteen years with the Confederated Tribes of Warm Springs in Oregon developing a program to preserve and teach their native languages and cultures. He has taught humanities and history of religion at GTU, Stanford, and the University of California Berkeley and Davis. Henry has a BA in Classics from Reed College and an MFA in playwriting from Carnegie-Mellon University and is a published poet and fiction writer.

its founder in 1975, his son W. D. Muhammad led most of the Nation's followers toward mainstream Islam.

The post-1965 wave of Muslim immigration brought large numbers of people seeking to continue their graduate studies in medicine, science, and engineering in the United States. One of the most remarkable of these immigrants was Fazlur Rahman Khan, who designed the Hancock Building and Willis Tower in Chicago, two of the world's tallest buildings. His innovations in building technology led *Newsweek* magazine to dub him "the Einstein of structural engineering."

But he was not unique. After graduating, Muslim immigrants found and excelled in competitive jobs in their fields, settling in urban areas where they married and raised families. Now their children and grandchildren are students at prestigious universities in fields such as medicine, engineering, and law. Today thousands of American Muslims are highly successful physicians, engineers, scientists, lawyers, and professionals in diverse fields. Together with African American and other indigenous Muslims, American Muslims today make up a community that is vibrant and talented and is contributing in multiple and varied ways to the rich fabric of America.

While American Muslims remain a relatively small part of the U.S. population—between three and six million—they have produced more than their share of major contributors to American life. The following are a few examples of notable American Muslims and Americans of Muslim backgrounds.

SCIENCE & ENGINEERING

ANOUSHEH ANSARI is an Iranian-American engineer and co-founder and chairwoman of Prodea Systems. She previously served as co-founder and CEO of Telecom Technologies, Inc. (TTI). On September 18, 2006, Ansari became the first self-funded woman to fly to the International Space Station. Her memoir, *My Dream of Stars*, co-written with Homer Hickam, was published in 2010.

MARK SALMAN HUMAYUN, MD, PhD, is an ophthalmologist, engineer, scientist, and inventor. He is also a researcher, clinician, and professor of both ophthalmology and biomedical engineering at the University of Southern California, in addition to other positions. President Obama awarded Dr. Humayun the National Medal of Technology and Innovation for his work on the Argus Series retina implants, which help restore sight to the blind.

AHMED ZEWAIL was an Egyptian American scientist. In 1999 he won the Nobel Prize in Chemistry, making him the first Arab scientist to win a Nobel Prize in a scientific field. He was the Linus Pauling Chair Professor of Chemistry and Physics and the director of the Physical Biology Center for Ultrafast Science and Technology at the California Institute of Technology.

MEDIA

FAREED ZAKARIA is an Indian American journalist and author. He is the host of CNN's *Fareed Zakaria GPS* and served as contributing editor of *Time* and editor of *Newsweek International*.

ALI VELSHI is an anchor of MSNBC Live, and a senior economic and business correspondent for NBC News. He is the former host of *Ali Velshi on Target* on Al Jazeera America, and previously served as CNN's chief business correspondent, anchor of CNN's *Your Money*, and a co-host of CNN International's weekday business show *World Business Today*.

MEDICINE

DR. MEHMET OZ is a Turkish-American surgeon, author, and, most famously, the host and commentator of *The Dr. Oz Show*.

ELIAS A. ZERHOUNI is an Algerian-American radiologist and medical researcher. He was appointed by George W. Bush as the 15th director of the National Institutes of Health in May 2002. He served for six years before stepping down in October, 2008.

SPORTS

KAREEM ABDUL-JABBAR is a renowned former professional basketball player, and the all-time leading scorer in the NBA. He was selected by Secretary of State Hillary Clinton to be a U.S. global cultural ambassador in 2012. He is also an actor, commentator, and author.

IBTIHAJ MUHAMMAD is a saber fencer and member of the United States fencing team. In the 2016 Summer Olympics, she earned a bronze medal as part of Team USA in the Team Sabre, becoming the first American Muslim woman wearing hijab to qualify and earn a medal for the United States Olympic team. She also owns her own fashion brand, Louella.

HAKEEM OLAJUWON is a Nigerian American who was inducted into the Basketball Hall of Fame in 2008 and into the FIBA Hall of Fame in 2016. He led the Houston Rockets to NBA championships in 1994 and 1995. In 1996, he played on the Olympic gold medal–winning U.S. national team and was named one of the 50 Greatest Players in NBA History.

DALILAH MUHAMMAD won a gold medal in the 400-meter hurdles at the 2016 Summer Olympics. She is also a four-time All-American at the NCAA Outdoor Championships, a medalist at the 2007 World Youth Championships, and the 2009 Pan American Junior Athletics Championships.

RYAN HARRIS, a Minnesota native, helped the Denver Broncos beat the Carolina Panthers to win Super Bowl 50 in 2016. In 2017, he announced his retirement after spending ten years in the NFL, and seamlessly transitioned from football player to public servant, speaking against the travel ban and hate crimes committed against American Muslims.

ENTERTAINMENT

AASIF MANDVI is an Indian American actor and comedian. He has been featured in *The Daily Show* and recently launched his own new web series called *Halal in the Family*.

HASAN MINHAJ is an American comedian, actor, and writer of Indian descent. He is a correspondent on the *The Daily Show with Trevor Noah*. His first stand-up show *Homecoming King* debuted in May 2017.

DAVE CHAPPELLE is a stand-up comic, screenwriter, producer, and actor. He is best known for his television series *Chappelle's Show*. Although the show ran for only two years, it continues to be rebroadcast by stations around the world.

YASMINE AL MASSRI is an actress of Palestinian and Egyptian descent. She made her movie debut in the 2007 film *Caramel*. From 2015 to 2017, Massri starred as Nimah and Raina Amin, identical twins in the ABC drama series *Quantico*.

MAHERSHALA ALI won the 2017 Academy Award for Best Supporting Actor for his role in the film *Moonlight*. He has also appeared in films such as *The Curious Case of Benjamin Button*, *Hidden Figures*, and the Hunger Games series, as well as television shows such as *House of Cards* and *Luke Cage*.

KUMAIL NANJIANI is a Pakistani-American stand-up comedian, actor, and writer known for his role in the Emmy Award-nominated series *Silicon Valley*, and his turn in the autobiographical romantic comedy film *The Big Sick*, which has received critical acclaim from Muslims and non-Muslims alike and launched him to national stardom.

AUTHORS

KHALED HOSSEINI is an Afghan-born American novelist and physician. He is the author of three bestselling novels, most notably his 2003 debut, *The Kite Runner*.

MOHSIN HAMID is a Pakistani novelist and writer. His novels include *Moth Smoke* (2000), *The Reluctant Fundamentalist* (2007), and *How to Get Filthy Rich in Rising Asia* (2013). *The Reluctant Fundamentalist* was adapted for film and released in 2012.

AYAD AKHTAR is an American playwright, novelist, screenwriter, and actor of Pakistani descent. He is best known for his play *Disgraced*, which received the 2013 Pulitzer Prize for Drama, was nominated for a Tony Award for Best Play, and was the most produced play in America in the 2015–2016 season.

AZAR NAFISI, an Iranian American, is author of the New York Times bestseller *Reading Lolita in Tehran*. She is currently the Director of Cultural Conversations at the Foreign Policy Institute of Johns Hopkins University's School of Advanced International Studies in Washington, DC.

MUSICIANS

Q-TIP (born Jonathan Davis) is a rapper, record producer, and DJ. He was a founding member of the prominent hip-hop group A Tribe Called Quest. Since the group broke up, Q-Tip has continued to write and produce music.

LUPE FIASCO is a rapper, record producer, and entrepreneur who owns two lines of clothing. He is also a philanthropist who recorded a benefit single for victims of the 2010 Haiti earthquake.

ICE CUBE is a rapper, record producer, actor, and filmmaker. He began his career as a member of the hip-hop group C.I.A. and later joined the gangster rap group N.W.A (Niggaz Wit Attitudes). After leaving N.W.A in 1989, he has built a successful solo career in music and films.

DJ KHALED is a Grammy Award–nominated record producer, radio personality, record label executive, and author. He has released 10 albums and hit songs such as "All I Do Is Win." He has collaborated with a wide range of other artists, including John Legend, Lil Wayne, Kanye West, Wiz Khalifa, and Nicki Minaj.

POLITICS/PUBLIC SERVICE

HUMA ABEDIN is the vice-chairwoman of Hillary Clinton's 2016 presidential campaign and a longtime aide to Hillary Clinton. She previously served as Secretary of State Clinton's deputy chief of staff at the State Department. Prior to that she was traveling chief of staff and served as Clinton's assistant during her campaign in the 2008 presidential election.

KEITH ELLISON is a lawyer and the nation's first American Muslim congressman (Democrat), first elected in 2006 as a representative from the state of Minnesota. He is a co-chair of the House Progressive Caucus and a member of the House Committee on Financial Services.

ANDRÉ D. CARSON became the second American Muslim congressman (Democrat) when he was first elected in Indiana's special election in 2008. He is a member of the Congressional Progressive Caucus and Black Caucus and serves on the House Armed Forces and Transportation and Infrastructure Committees.

ILHAN OMAR is the first Somali-American Muslim lawmaker in the United States, elected to Minnesota's House of Representatives in November 2016. Born in Somalia, Ilhan and her family fled the country's civil war when she was eight years old. The family spent four years in a refugee camp before coming to the United States. In addition to serving in the legislature, Ilhan Omar is the Director of Policy Initiatives at Women Organizing Women, where she empowers East African women to take leadership roles in their community.

BUSINESSMEN AND ENTREPRENEURS

SHAHID (SHAD) KHAN is a Pakistani American business tycoon and owner of the NFL's Jacksonville Jaguars. He is president and owner of an automotive parts corporation where he began working when still in college. In 2012 the billionaire was featured on the cover of *Forbes* magazine as the face of the American Dream.

TARIQ FARID, a Pakistani American, is the owner and CEO of Edible Arrangements. In 2009 he was recognized as Entrepreneur of the Year by the International Franchise Association.

HAMDI ULUKAYA is a Kurdish-American entrepreneur and businessman and the owner, founder, chairman, and CEO of Chobani yogurt. In April, 2016, Ulukaya surprised his employees with the announcement that he was giving them 10 percent of Chobani shares.

SALMAN KHAN is a Bengali American educator and entrepreneur. He is the founder of Khan Academy, a free online education platform with over 6,500 video lessons on a variety of academic subjects, with an emphasis on mathematics and sciences. In 2012, *Time* named Salman Khan as one of the 100 most influential people in the world.

ARMED FORCES

KAREEM RASHAD SULTAN KHAN was a twenty-year-old U.S. Army Specialist who died in combat in Iraq in 2007. He received a Bronze Star and a Purple Heart for his service. He is buried in Arlington National Cemetery.

HUMAYUN KHAN was a Pakistani-American soldier who was posthumously awarded the Bronze Star and Purple Heart after his life was cut short during his tour of duty in Iraq. At the 2016 Democratic National Convention, he became known to the public after his parents, Khizr and Ghazala Khan, spoke of his courage and commitment to upholding American values.

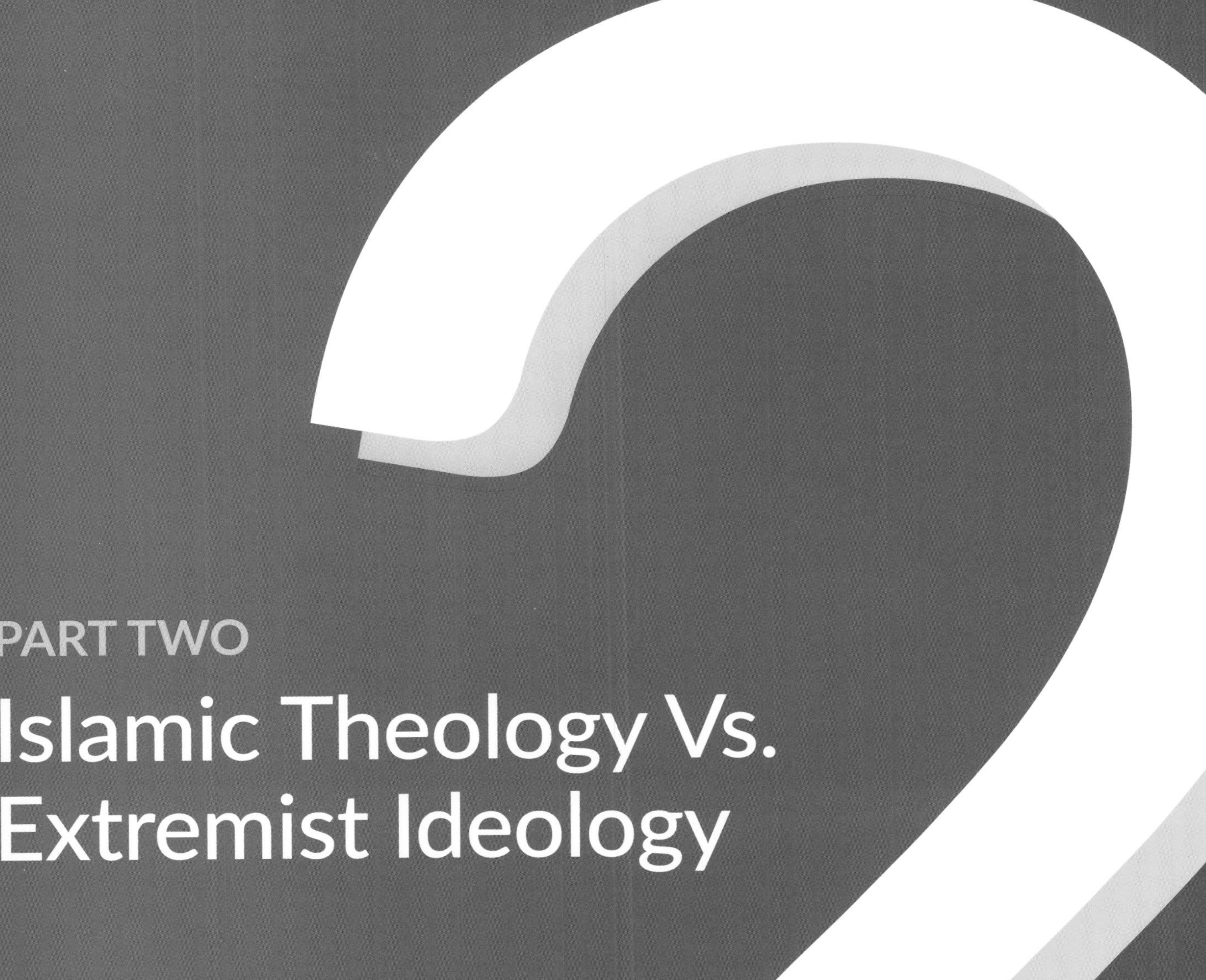

PART TWO

Islamic Theology Vs. Extremist Ideology

Executive Summary: Part Two

ISLAMIC THEOLOGY VS. EXTREMIST IDEOLOGY

KEY TAKEAWAYS

1. Daesh distorts religious concepts, ignores the established interpretive methodology of sacred texts, and takes the Qur'an out of context to meet its recruitment goals to strengthen its power base.
2. Daesh has a deliberate approach toward bringing women into its ecosystem as instruments of spreading its ideology in order to expand and strengthen the infrastructure of its state.
3. The factors driving individuals to join Daesh vary from individual to individual and can be attributed to social, political, economic, and historical grievances.

Although the problem of violent extremism has existed for decades, relatively little is still known about violent extremist groups like Daesh. What are their motivations? What legitimate grounds—if any—do they have for claiming that what they do is Islamic? What is their ultimate goal?

Before we delve into this subject, however, we must understand what Islam is. That is, if we are claiming that Daesh distorts Islamic teachings and scripture for political gain, we must first understand what it is that Daesh is distorting. To bring clarity to Islamic scriptures, Dr. Safi Kaskas provides a brvief history of the Qur'an from the time it was revealed to how it applies in today's world. Supporting this is Laleh Bakhtiar's article, "What Is Qur'anic Critical Thinking?," in which she lays out the proper ways to read the Qur'an in contrast to the incorrect methods employed by extremists like Daesh. To further discredit Daesh's claims of following the original spirit of Islam, contributors Dr. Jonathan AC Brown, Dr. John Andrew Morrow, and Ibrahim H. Malabari each offer insights into the true teachings and peaceful message of Islam, as shared with mankind by the Prophet Muhammad. Kabir Helmiski, Sultan Abdulhameed, Rabia Terri Harris, and Maulana Wahiduddin Khan close the section with the Qur'anic lessons of peaceful reconciliation, tolerance, and living a life of moderation.

The second section opens with a brief summary of the origins of Daesh (also known as the *Islamic State in Iraq and Syria [ISIS]*) from its early ties to al-Qaeda to its more recent declaration in 2014 of its aim to re-establish the "Caliphate." The Soufan Group provides an analysis of the political origins of Daesh, including the source of its foreign fighters and the extent of its territorial conquests. Dr. Fathali Moghaddam uses the "Relative Deprivation Theory" to explain how the long history of Western political intervention throughout the twentieth century created even more unfavorable social conditions for the masses in the Near and Middle East than when they were under colonial rule; moreover, the West's political, military, and financial supremacy, demonstrated by Western governments propping up puppet governments to rule former colonial territories, generated simmering resentment against it among local populations in these countries and created the grounds for revolutionary action on the part of local actors. We also explore how the so-called Caliphate depends on the recruitment of women and girls to sustain Daesh's empire-building operation, and how recruiters lure women and children to join.

This section also provides an explanation of why extremists use religion as the basis for their ideology, and explores the foundations for this ideology and the ways in which it is used as a powerful psychological motivator for recruitment. In addition, it compares Daesh's distortions of eight key Islamic concepts that it uses to justify its violent mission with the theological foundations of these terms within Islam. These terms include: *al-wala' wal bara'* (loyalty and disavowal); *ummah* (community); *takfir / kafr* (excommunication/ declaring someone an apostate); *bay'ah* (pledge of allegiance); *hijrah* (migration); *jihad* (to struggle or strive for the sake of God); *shahid* (martyrdom); and most important, *Khalifah/Khilafah* (Caliphate). By laying out these eight distortions alongside the genuine teachings of Islam, this section makes plain how Daesh in fact has no legitimate claim to represent Islam.

Following this section are academic explanations for how terrorists have blatantly misused sacred texts and ignored the established methodology required in order to interpret Islamic scripture properly. This section also outlines the beliefs and actions of terrorists, to highlight how these go against the essential teachings of Islam.

Examples include Dr. Wayel Azmeh's and Dr. Saeed Albezreh's explanation of the notion of the Caliphate according to Islamic history to demonstrate how Daesh presents a romanticized and unrealistic vision of what the Caliphate historically was. Contributor Syed-Mohsin Naquvi also provides an explicit condemnation of Daesh's distorted understanding of martyrdom, showing how sacrificing one's life, especially at the cost of the innocent lives of others, is never sanctioned in Islam and will never result in the reward of paradise. We have also included a robust "Debunked" section, in which scholars debunk various Daesh claims. In Reza Aslan's article, he explains the "Cosmic War" mind-set of Daesh that frames its view that the Christian Crusaders of the West are actively engaged in a battle to defeat Muslims and rid the world of Islam. But, as he and contributor Dr. Mehnaz Afridi point out in her article "Debunked: Jews—Enemies of Muslims," there is a long history of harmonious coexistence between Christians, Jews, and Muslims stretching back to the time of the Prophet Muhammad, a practice that Dr. Eboo Patel reaffirms in his article "Pluralism Within Islamic Jurisprudence."

SUGGESTIONS

1. Communities must be able to effectively distinguish between Islamic theology and extremist ideology, so they know exactly how extremists distort Islamic terms to recruit individuals to their violent cause, and can defend their faith from those who would seek to malign it.

2. Civil society should lead efforts to provide services and programs aimed at leveraging an individual's "protective factors" and mitigating the "push" factors that motivate individuals to join extremist groups, thereby improving individuals' resilience to extremist indoctrination of any kind.

3. Actively promote harmonious coexistence, cooperation, and mutual respect between Muslims and people of other faiths in order to refute Daesh's "us versus them'" claim that there is a civilizational clash between the West and Islam. Special attention must be shown to women, who are recruited for different reasons than men.

"Learn your religion, do not inherit it."

- Imam Ali

SECTION 1

Islamic Theology

CHAPTER 4

Islam: History, Texts, Beliefs

Timeline of the Prophet Muhammad's Life

WISE

570 C.E.
BIRTH OF A PROPHET

Muhammad ibn 'Abd Allah was born in Mecca in the Banu Hashim clan of the Quraysh tribe. At the age of six, he was orphaned and lived with his grandfather until the age of eight, and then with his uncle, Abu Talib.

590–595 C.E.
TRADESMAN

Muhammad helped his uncle in his trading business, gaining a reputation for trustworthiness. Khadijah bint Khuwaylid, a forty-year-old merchantwoman, employed Muhammad to trade on her behalf in Syria, where he and impressed her by doubling her earnings.

595 C.E.
SIGNS OF PROPHECY

During the caravan journey to Syria, Muhammad stopped to rest under a tree. A Jewish monk, Nestora, who saw Muhammad resting there, informed Maysarah, Khadijah's servant, "None but a prophet ever sat beneath this tree."

595 C.E.
MARRIAGE OF MUHAMMAD TO KHADIJAH

Khadījah was from a noble Quraysh tribe. She had been previously married twice and had children from her marriages. Many wealthy Quraysh men asked for Khadijah's hand in marriage, but she proposed marriage to Muhammad, her trusted agent.

595–620 C.E.
MUHAMMAD AND KHADIJAH'S MARRIAGE

Muhammad and Khadijah stayed married monogamously for twenty-five years and had seven children. They had four daughters—Zaynab, Ruqayyah, Umm Kulthum, and Fatima—and three sons—Qasim, Ibrahim, and Abd-Allah. Each son died in infancy.

610 C.E.
FIRST REVELATION

At age forty, Muhammad was meditating in a cave in Mount Hira when he received his first revelation from the Archangel Gabriel. Khadijah was the first person to acknowledge his Prophethood and became one of the first Muslims.

613 C.E.
PUBLIC PREACHING

The Prophet Muhammad began preaching and proclaiming his message that "God is One." Although he gained a few followers, he was met mostly with hostility by the pagans of Mecca.

615 C.E.
MIGRATION (*HIJRAH*) TO ABYSSINIA

The Meccans relentlessly persecuted the Prophet and his followers, so he sent his followers to Abyssinia, where they were given refuge by its Christian king, Negus.

619 C.E.
YEAR OF SORROW

In what the Prophet called the "Year of Sorrow," both his wife, Khadijah, and his uncle and protector, Abu Talib, died. No longer protected from persecution by family and marriage ties, the Prophet was ridiculed and stoned, but he forbade the Muslims from fighting back.

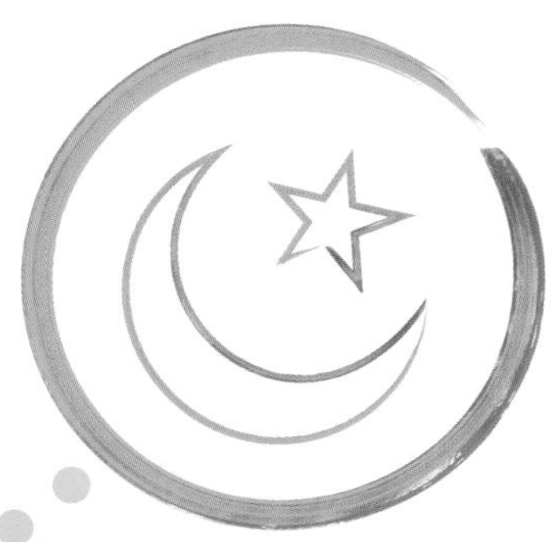

621 C.E.
THE NIGHT JOURNEY

The Prophet was transported to Jerusalem on a heavenly steed with wings named Buraq, from where he ascended to the seven heavens and met God, who commanded that Muslims pray fifty times per day. This was eventually reduced to five times per day through Moses' intervention.

622 C.E.
HIJRAH (MIGRATION TO MEDINA)

After another attempt on his life, the Prophet fled with his followers from Mecca to Yathrib (Medina), where he was welcomed by the local tribes. This migration is a major historical event in early Islam, and marks the beginning of the Islamic (*Hijri*) lunar calendar.

622 C.E.
PACT OF MEDINA

When he arrived in Medina, the Prophet worked to rectify long-standing conflicts between the local tribes. He crafted the Pact of Medina, which detailed the rights and duties of all citizens regardless of their religion, and which declared that Christians, Jews, and pagans are all part of the *ummah*.

624 C.E.
BATTLE OF BADR

When Meccans seized the property of Muslims who had emigrated to Medina, the Prophet received revelation 22:39 giving him permission to fight back, after which he led the Battle of Badr and was victorious.

624 C.E.
QIBLA DIRECTION

The Prophet received a revelation from God to change the direction of prayer from Jerusalem to Mecca. Since that time, all Muslims pray in the direction of the Kabah, which was constructed by Prophet Abraham.

625 C.E.
BATTLE OF UHUD

Following the Battle of Badr, the Meccans regrouped and attacked the Muslims once again, killing 75, including the Prophet's uncle Hamza, considered to be one of the first martyrs in Islam. The Muslims were defeated and the Meccans declared victory.

627 C.E.
BATTLE OF THE TRENCH

The Meccans attacked the Prophet again, with an army of 12,000. The Muslims and Medinans, less than 3,000 strong, dug a trench and overcame their opponents. The defeat caused the Meccans to lose their trade and prestige, and Islam became influential in the region.

628 C.E.
HUDAYBIYYAH PEACE TREATY

The Prophet affirmed a ten-year peace treaty between the Quraysh tribe of Mecca and the state of Medina. Though this helped decrease tensions between the Meccans and Muslims, and ushered in a decade of peace and harmony, the treaty was broken when allies of the Meccans killed members of a tribe allied with the Muslims.

630 C.E.
CONQUEST OF MECCA

The Prophet marched peacefully into Mecca with 10,000 followers and ushered in a period of diplomacy between the tribes of Mecca and the Muslims. He gave amnesty to the entire city and the Meccans willingly accepted Islam as their religion.

632 C.E.
DEATH OF THE PROPHET

The Prophet completed his first *Hajj* (Islamic pilgrimage). After delivering the farewell sermon on the Mount Arafat, the Prophet Muhammad fell ill and passed away in his home at the age of 62.

What Is Islam?

IMAM JAMAL RAHMAN provides an overview of Islam, its basic principles, five pillars, and beliefs.

Islam was revealed 1,437 years ago, and is the second largest religion in the world, with 1.6 billion adherents. Unfortunately, the religion of Islam continues to be linked to terrorism, due to the politically motivated acts of violence committed in its name, leaving many to wonder, "What is Islam?"

Ultimately, what we are able to glean from any religion depends on our state of consciousness and our intention.

It is difficult to understand and appreciate the heart of any religion in times of prolonged conflict and senseless violence. The trauma caused by endless bloodshed, whether it be through "shock and awe" bombings or suicide attacks, distorts psyches and mangles souls. The Qur'an explains that when there is chronic anger, fear, suspicion, and hopelessness, *"Verily, it is not the eyes that grow blind, but it is the hearts which are in the breasts that grow blind"* (22:46). In these blinded times, religion becomes politicized and many of us, Muslim and non-Muslim alike, lapse into serving truth based on convenience. We misuse religion, individually and collectively, to serve our agenda of self-interest. Ultimately, what we are able to glean from any religion depends on our state of consciousness and our intention. The thirteenth-century sage Rumi illustrates this insight through a metaphor: a bee and wasp drink from the same flower; one produces nectar and the other, a sting.

Islam is a spiritual path that is defined by the root of its name, *Salaam*. Like its Hebrew cousin, Shalom, *Salaam* means "peace" in the sense of psychological and emotional wellbeing—the well-being that comes from surrendering the ego to a higher, divine power; following the precepts of the prophets and the Qur'an; and doing our best to be God's agents for good upon the earth.

Islam is a spiritual path that is defined by the root of its name, *Salaam*.

According to a celebrated prophetic saying (Hadith), a stranger dressed in white appeared to the Prophet Muhammad (pbuh) and posed this exact question. After an intense conversation, the visitor disappeared as mysteriously as he had arrived. To his astonished companions who witnessed the event, the Prophet confided that the visitor was the angel Gabriel in the shape of a human. The angel validated the Prophet's understanding of the core teachings of Islam contained in three principles and five pillars.

IMAM JAMAL RAHMAN is a popular speaker on Islam, Sufi spirituality, and interfaith relations. He has been featured in the *New York Times*, and on CBS News, BBC, and various NPR programs. Imam Rahman is co-founder and Muslim Sufi minister at Interfaith Community Sanctuary and adjunct faculty at Seattle University. He is a former co-host of Interfaith Talk Radio and travels nationally and internationally, presenting at retreats and workshops. He is the author of numerous books, including *Spiritual Gems of Islam: Insights and Practices from the Qur'an, Hadith, Rumi and Muslim Teaching Stories to Enlighten the Heart and Mind* and *The Fragrance of Faith: The Enlightened Heart of Islam*.

Basic Principles

ISLAM

Surrender in Peace

Islam means **"surrender in peace."** Surrender is the inner journey of releasing attachment to the ego and making space for God at the center of one's being in order to become a more complete and authentic human being. If we do not do this work of self-surrender (Islam), explains the Qur'an, "*we shall be in the ranks of those who have lost*" (3:85). Sadly, this verse is often misinterpreted to mean that Islam is the only valid religion. But religion per se doesn't matter to God; it is the whole hearted attempt to live in a state of surrender to Divine Will that is paramount.

In the verse above, the Qur'an clearly embraces the critical concept of surrender as it has been revealed in other religions:

***"We believe in God, and in what has been revealed to us and what was revealed to Abraham, Ismail, Isaac, Jacob, and the Tribes, and in (the Books) given to Moses, Jesus, and the Prophets, from their Lord: we make no distinction between one and another among them, and to God do we bow our will"* (3:84).**

Iman means **faith**—primarily belief in the oneness of God; the existence of angels; the revelations of the prophets and messengers who came before Muhammad (including Adam, Abraham, Moses, and Jesus); the scriptures of the three Abrahamic traditions (Torah, Psalms, Gospels, and Qur'an); and the Day of Judgment. The Qur'an makes it amply clear that faith must be informed, not merely blind. Certainty borrowed from our scriptures and teachers is not enough (102:5); from that base we must progress to personal witnessing (102:7) and from there, to a deep inner conviction (69:51).

***"The Desert-Arabs say, "We have believed." Say, "You have not [yet] believed; but say [instead], 'We have submitted,' for faith has not yet entered your hearts. And if you obey God and His Messenger, He will not deprive you from your deeds of anything. Indeed, God is Forgiving and Merciful"* (49:14).**

IMAN

Faith

IHSAN

Righteousness

Ihsan means **to be righteous or beautiful.** "*Render your innermost heart pure of all dross,*" says the Qur'an (3:154), and "*Bring to God a sound heart*" (26:89). The Prophet cautions Muslims to especially guard against three negative traits that are at the root of all wrongdoing: pride, greed, and envy. Self-purification is not an end in itself. We work at it so that we may develop our capacity to do God's work in the world: practicing the Golden Rule, pursuing social justice, and caring for the earth. The Qur'an emphasizes repeatedly the importance of "righteous deeds." Whether you are male or female, says the Holy Book, whether you are Jew, Christian, Sabian, or Muslim, what assures heavenly rewards is having faith in God and engaging in righteous deeds (2:62).

***"And whoever does righteous deeds, whether male or female, while being a believer—those will enter Paradise and will not be wronged, [even as much as] the speck on a date seed"* (4:124).**

Five Beliefs of Muslims

1

BELIEF IN ONE GOD

Islam is a monotheistic religion, meaning that Muslims believe that God is one, the sole creator of life on earth, who has neither gender nor human form and is beyond likeness to anything in creation. God is called Allah in Arabic and is also described by ninety-nine "Beautiful Names of God," which are descriptive attributes of God, such as the Merciful, the Compassionate, the King, the Holy, and the Almighty. These divine names describe how God relates to humankind and to the rest of creation.

"Before thy time We never sent any apostle without having revealed to him that there is no deity save Me, therefore, you shall worship Me!" **(Qur'an 21:25).**

2

BELIEF THAT GOD HAS COMMUNICATED WITH MANKIND THROUGH SCRIPTURES

Muslims believe in four scriptures sent from God as revealed through the prophets: the Torah of Moses; the Psalms of David; the Gospels (Evangel) of Jesus (Isa); and the Qur'an of Muhammad, as well as the scrolls of Abraham and Moses. All these books were authored by the one God and were sent to particular prophets with one overarching theme: right belief regarding God and right ethics for the benefit of humankind.

"Oh people of the Book! You do not stand on anything until you observe the Torah and the Evangel and what was sent down to you from your Lord" **(Qur'an 5:68).**

BELIEFS IN THE PROPHETS-MESSENGERS

The Qur'an names twenty-five prophets, beginning with Adam and including Noah, Abraham, Ishmael, Isaac, Jacob, Joseph, David, Solomon, Moses, Aaron, Job, Jonah, John the Baptist, and Jesus Christ, and ending with Muhammad. Muslims are instructed to revere them all and to make no distinction between them. The Qur'an says that in addition to the named prophets there are many others who are unnamed and every community has been sent a prophet. Muslims make a distinction between a prophet—one to whom God sent a revelation; and a messenger—who received a revelation and was instructed to preach.

"But as for those who believe in God and His apostles and make no distinction between any of them—unto them, in time, will He grant their rewards. And God is indeed much-forgiving, a dispenser of grace" **(Qur'an 4:152).**

4

BELIEF IN THE EXISTENCE OF ANGELS

Angels are radiant, genderless beings of light acting as intermediaries between God and the visible world. The primary ones are the four archangels also known in the Jewish and Christian traditions: Jibra'il (Gabriel), Mika'il (Michael), Izra'il (Azrael), and Israf'il (Raphael). Angels are assigned to individuals to record their good and bad deeds and Angels will interrogate people after their death and accompany them to their afterlife. There are Angels in heaven, overseen by Ridwan, and in hell, overseen by Malik.

"The angels celebrate the praises of their Lord, and pray for forgiveness for all beings on earth" **(Qur'an 42:5).**

BELIEF IN THE HEREAFTER, SOMETIMES CALLED BY MUSLIMS THE LAST DAY

The Last Day means that creation will come to an end, followed by a Day of Resurrection when all souls will be resurrected, followed by a Day of Judgment when souls will be judged. On this day, souls will be judged on all their deeds, both good and bad. The philosophical underpinning of the idea of the Last Day is human accountability for our ethical actions. Those who lived a righteous life will gain divine approval and enter the bliss of Paradise, while those who lived unethically will gain divine disapproval, taste the burn of their evil actions in Hell, and undergo a period of purification in Hell.

"On that day all human beings will come forward separately to be shown their deeds. Then shall anyone who has done an atom's weight of good see it! And anyone who has done an atom's weight of harm shall see that" (Qur'an 99:6–8).

The Five Pillars

1

PROFESSION OF FAITH

Shahada

Shahada, where you state: **"There is no God but God and Muhammad is a messenger of God."**

The first part testifies to the omnipresence and eternity of God: *"Everywhere you turn is the Face of God"* (2:115); *"All that is on Earth will perish but forever will abide the Face of your Sustainer, full of Majesty and Abundant Honor"* (55:26–27). God is utterly beyond space, time, gender, and form. Toward the end of his life, the Prophet humbly lamented, "O God, we have not known You as we should have." Sadly, humans fight and kill over definitions of Divinity, forgetting that in essence God is One for all of humanity. In a telling verse, God instructs us not to argue with Jews and Christians *"otherwise than in a most kindly manner . . . and say . . . our God and your God is one and the same, and it is unto Him that we all surrender ourselves"* (29:46).

2

PRAYER

Salat

Salat, or **prayer**, in which Muslims are required to pray five times daily. *"Bow in adoration and draw closer,"* says the Qur'an (96:19), and Muslims respond by bowing and prostrating to God five times a day in obligatory prayer. This prayer is derived, some scholars opine, from the Prophet's mystical night journey, during which he ascended seven levels of heaven and was dazzled by the sight of angels bowing and prostrating to God while uttering words of praise and thanksgiving. The Prophet saw this as a sign that prayer must consist of praising and thanking God, and using the gift of the body to express adoration. Spiritual teachers explain that one prostration of prayer to God frees us from a thousand prostrations to our ego. The required number of prayers is attributed to a legend that when the Prophet was descending the seven levels, he met Moses, who asked him how often God wanted his community to pray. "Fifty times a day," the Prophet said. "They'll never pray that much!" Moses exclaimed. "Go back and plead for a lesser number." With Moses' encouragement, the Prophet finally got the number down to a more manageable five prayers daily.

3

CHARITY

Zakat

Zakat means **purification through almsgiving**. Muslims sanctify our wealth and our being by giving for the sake of God. Muslims must tithe at least 2.5 percent of their net worth every year to those in need and are encouraged to offer nonobligatory donations and service for worthy causes. The Qur'an stipulates some guidelines: "*give freely of what you love*" (3:92), "*to those who ask*" (2:177), "*and to those who can't ask*" (70:25), and give quietly, for "*it will atone for some of your wrongdoings*" (2:271).

FASTING

Sawm

Sawm in Arabic literally means **"fasting,"** but is more commonly known as Ramadan, which is the name of the month when Muslims abstain from food, drink, and sexual activity from dawn to dusk. It was during Ramadan, the ninth month of the Islamic lunar calendar, that Muhammad began receiving the revelations that were later codified in the Qur'an. The Ramadan fast is an expression of gratitude for the gift of the Qur'an, as well as a time of self-purification so that we might remain conscious of God (2:183).

PILGRIMAGE

Hajj

Hajj is the **pilgrimage** to Mecca in the twelfth month of the Islamic calendar. Able-bodied Muslims who can afford it are expected to go on *hajj* at least once in their lives "*in the service of Allah*" (2:196). Joining fellow Muslims from all over the world in the rituals of the *hajj* is a glorious reminder of the importance and sacredness of a community of faith as we live out our lifelong pilgrimage from this world to the next.

Unity and Oneness of God

Tawhid

Adapted from **DR. SEYYED HOSSEIN NASR**'s acclaimed work, *Heart of Islam: Enduring Values for Humanity*, this article explains the core Islamic concept of *Tawhid*, or "oneness of God," and how all Islamic teaching rests upon this principle.

At the heart of Islam stands the reality of God, the One, the Absolute and the Infinite, greater than all we can conceive or imagine, and, as the Qur'an, attests, closer to us than our jugular vein. The One God, known by His Arabic Name, Allah, is the central reality of Islam in all its facets, and attestation to this oneness, called *tawhid*, is the axis around which all that is Islamic revolves. Allah is beyond all duality and relationality, beyond the differences of gender and all qualities that distinguish beings one from another in this world. He is the source of all existence and all cosmic and human qualities, as well as the End to Whom all things return.

The One God, known by His Arabic Name, Allah, is the central reality of Islam in all its facets, and attestation to this oneness, called *tawhid*, is the axis around which all that is Islamic revolves.

To testify to this oneness lies at the heart of the credo of Islam, and the formula that expresses the truth of this oneness, *La ilaha ill'Allah*, "There is no god but God." The second is *Muhammadun rasul Allah*, "Muhammad is the messenger of God." For Muslims, the oneness of God is not only the heart of their religion, but also that of every Abrahamic religion. It is a reassertion of the revelation of God to the Hebrew prophets and to Christ, whom Muslims also consider to be their prophet in the first testimony (*shahadah*) of Islam. Muslims believe in the revelation of the truth "Thy Lord is one," and in the reconfirmation of that timeless truth that is stated in the Catholic creed, *Credo in Unum Deum*, "I believe in one God." As the Qur'an states, "We have never sent a messenger before thee except that We revealed to him, saying, 'There is no god but I, so worship Me'" (21:25). When countless Muslims read the names of the prophets in the Qur'an, they experience them as living realities in the Islamic universe, while being fully conscious of the fact that they are revered figures in Judaism and Christianity. Muslims also remain fully aware that people of faith are all speaking of the same God Who is One and not of some other deity.

The One God, or Allah, is neither male nor female. The Qualities of God, reflected throughout creation, are of a feminine as well as a masculine nature, and the traditional Islamic understanding of Divinity is not at all confined, as some think, to a purely patriarchal image. Furthermore, the doctrine of God the One, as stated in the Qur'an, does not only emphasize utter transcendence, although there are powerful expressions of this truth such as *Allahu akbar*, usually translated as "God is great," but meaning that God is greater than anything we can conceive of Him, which is also attested by the apophatic theology of both the Catholic and Orthodox churches as well as by traditional Judaism. Muslims also emphasize God's immanence, for as the Qur'an states, "Wherever ye turn there is the Face of God" (2:115).

Allahu akbar, usually translated as "God is great," but meaning that God is greater than anything we can conceive of Him.

Striving for the realization of that oneness, *tawhid*, is the heart of Islamic life; the measure of a successful religious life is the degree to which one is able to

> Muslims also emphasize God's immanence, for as the Qur'an states, "Wherever ye turn there is the Face of God" (2:115).

realize *tawhid*, which means not only oneness, but also the integration of multiplicity into Unity. The multiplicity of Divine Qualities reflected in the cosmos and within the being of men and women does not distract Muslims from God's oneness. The authenticity of one's faith in Islam has by and large been determined by the testimony of *tawhid*, while the degree of inward realization of this truth has remained a matter to be decided by God and not by external authorities. This has been the general norm in Islamic history, but there have also been exceptions, and there are historical instances when a particular group or political authority has taken it upon itself to determine the authenticity or lack thereof of the belief in *tawhid* of a particular person or school.

Though Daesh claims that there is an urgent need to "return to *tawhid*" while encouraging the killing of people who reject their ideology, we need to remind everyone that humanity, according to the Qur'an, was created from a single soul, then diversified into races and tribes, as the Qur'an states, "He created you [humanity] from a single soul" (39:6). The single origin of humanity implies the profound unity within diversity of human nature, and therefore religion based on the message of Divine Oneness could not have been meant for or available to only a segment of humanity. The great number of races, nations, and tribes necessitates the diversity of revelation. Thus, not only is the multiplicity of religions necessary, but it is also a reflection of the richness of the Divine Nature and is willed by God.[1]

[1] This article has been adapted from Dr. Seyyed Hossein Nasr's acclaimed work, reprinted with permission:

Nasr, Seyyed Hossein. *The Heart of Islam: Enduring Values for Humanity*. New York: HarperCollins, 2002.

Qur'an: The Book of Revelation

DR. SAFI KASKAS provides the sociohistorical background of the Qur'an, from the time it was revealed to the Prophet Muhammad to how Muslims view it today. He states that the Qur'anic revelations came to resolve specific issues afflicting seventh century Arabian society.

KEY TAKEAWAYS

- The Qur'an is a book of wisdom for all humankind as it provides knowledge of God's divine plan and the principles required for a successful life.
- The message of the Qur'an was deemed quite progressive for its time as it reformed unjust pre-Islamic cultural practices.
- The Qur'an links the stories of all the Abrahamic prophets, mentioning Moses and Jesus more often than the Prophet Muhammad himself.

The responsibility of understanding the Qur'an is often left to scholars whom many Muslims rely on to interpret what God is saying for us. Admittedly, I was one of those Muslims. I felt inadequate, unable to truly understand God's message and grasp the deeper meanings of His Word. It was only after I took on the task of translating the Qur'an in its entirety that I came to understand its meaning and purpose for humanity. While doing so, I was confronted with the Qur'anic verse, *"This is a blessed Book, which We have revealed to you so that they might reflect upon its verses and that those of understanding would be reminded"* (38:29).

It was at that moment when I realized that not only does God will us to understand, but He has created mankind with the ability to understand His Word. He asks each of us to reflect on the meaning of every word, of every verse, and to use the proper tools to enable us to understand His guidance and His relation to creation. He wants us to know our religion by directly understanding its basic foundation—the Qur'an. But what is required for us to be able to truly understand the Qur'an? We must first look to the life of the Prophet Muhammad and the trials and tribulations of seventh-century Arabian society. It is within this sociohistorical context that we may come to understand the reasons for each particular Qur'anic revelation and thus, the meaning of its 6,236 verses.

It was in the year 570 CE that Muhammad was born into the Quraysh tribe of Mecca. Having lost both of his parents before the age of six, Muhammad traveled alongside his uncle, the Hashemite chieftain Abu Talib, on the caravan journey to Syria where he gained his reputation as *Al-Amin*, the trustworthy. As he grew older, Muhammad became increasingly troubled by what he saw as the social malaise of Arabian society—injustice, religious persecution, slavery, and the oppression of women. Moreover, he became deeply concerned over the Meccans' disregard for the less fortunate and their obsession with wealth and idol worship. In fact, Muhammad was one of the few at the time to reject the ignorance (*jahiliyyah*) the Meccans had fallen into, and he longed for the truth. In order to meditate on these social and political challenges, Muhammad would often seek out solace and retreat to Mount Hira near Mecca.

Then, in 610 CE on the seventh day of Ramadan in the ninth month of the lunar calendar, when Muhammad was forty years old, his life changed forever. While Muhammad was meditating in a cave, he was suddenly

DR. SAFI KASKAS is an expert on administrative and managerial sciences and a frequent speaker on issues of faith. Kaskas co-founded East West University in Chicago, Illinois, and was president of its board of directors until 2005. He is also the founder and president of Strategic Edge Management Consultants. Dr. Kaskas's most recent publication is a translation of the Qur'an that cross-references the Old and New Testaments.

enveloped in a terrifying embrace that felt as though his very breath was being squeezed from his body. The angel Gabriel spoke to him and gave him one command: "*Iqra!*" ("Read!"). Muhammad protested that he could not read; like most at that time, he was unlettered. But the command was issued twice more, and each time he would feel he was reaching the end of his endurance, and he uttered the same response. Finally, Muhammad found divinely inspired words flowing from his lips—he began to read words acquired not from the writings of men but revealed directly by God:

> *Read in the name of your Lord who created; created the human being from a clinging substance. Read! Your Lord is the Most Generous, who taught by the pen, taught the human being that which he knew not* (96:1–5).

Thus began the magnificent story of God's last testament to humanity.

In the purest sense, the Qur'an is a book of wisdom. It was revealed to serve as guidance for all of humankind as it provides knowledge of God's divine plan and the principles required for achieving a successful life.

For 23 years of his Prophetic mission, the Angel Gabriel would continue to utter the Word of God to the Prophet Muhammad. The Qur'an is the final of a series of Divine Messages that were first revealed to Adam and culminated with the Prophet Muhammad. And as each of God's messengers had done before him, Muhammad was tasked with spreading the Divine Message to all of humanity: "*Nothing has been said to you [Prophet] that was not said to the messengers before you. Your Lord is a Lord of Forgiveness, but also of painful punishment*" (41:43).

In the purest sense, the Qur'an is a book of wisdom. It was revealed to serve as guidance for all of humankind as it provides knowledge of God's divine plan and the principles required for achieving a successful life. These fundamental teachings of the Qur'an can broadly be defined as the protection of life, family, property/wealth, happiness, religion, and dignity (collectively known as the six universal *maqasid* or ultimate goals)—all of which were missing in pre-Islamic Arabia. Additionally, the Qur'an focuses on ethical and legal subjects, including topics such as charity, prayer, and piety. Its verses also discuss historical events and contain general exhortations regarding right and wrong as a means to outline its general moral lessons and teachings so that they may be applied to our daily lives.

Many of the Qur'an's verses were actually deemed to be quite progressive for the time, as they both reformed and directly responded to the pre-Islamic cultural practices so that they would reflect God's will for mankind. For instance, to respond to the ongoing oppression and injustice toward women, God made gender egalitarianism an intrinsic teaching of the Qur'an. It even goes so far as to neither depict nor describe God as a masculine figure. The Qur'an also explicitly teaches that women are of absolute equal status to men, as God says, "*Never shall I lose sight of the good deeds of any one of you, male or female. Each of you is equal to the other*" (3:195). Consequently, the Qur'an rejected the norms of its time and guaranteed women their right to inheritance, property, and marriage. This is outlined in Qur'anic verse 4:7, which states: "*Men will have a share in what their parents and close relatives leave behind, and women will have a share in what their parents and close relatives leave behind, whether it is a little or a lot: this is ordained by God.*" Arguably the most important right God has provided humankind through His revelations is the freedom to choose and practice one's religion freely, as the truth cannot be obtained by compulsion. This is seen in the Qur'anic verse stating: "*There shall be no compulsion in religion*" (2:256). The Qur'an emphasized that it is up to an individual to pursue spiritual guidance. "*Insights have come to you from your Lord. Whoever chooses to see does so for his own good, and whoever chooses to remain blind, does so to his own loss. 'I am not your keeper'*" (6:104). Such verses came as a direct response to the idolatry, polytheism, and backwardness that were plaguing Arabian society at that time and causing warfare between tribes.

Although many of its teachings differ from earlier revelations, the Qur'an contains stories of God's earlier Prophets and Messengers, including Adam, Noah, Abraham, Ishmael, Moses, and many others. In fact, many would be surprised to learn that both Moses and Jesus are mentioned more often in the Qur'an than Muhammad. Even Mary, the mother of Jesus, is mentioned more times in the Qur'an than in the New Testament. But also, it explicitly recognizes and speaks of the commonality between the Abrahamic religions and their texts: *"Say, 'We believe in God and what He revealed to us and to Abraham, Ishmael, Isaac, Jacob, the tribes, and in what was given to Moses, Jesus and the prophets from their Lord. We do not distinguish between any of them, and we have submitted to Him"* (3:84).

> Arguably the most important right God has provided humankind through His revelations is the freedom to choose and practice one's religion freely, as the truth cannot be obtained by compulsion.

However, unlike the Torah or the New Testament, the Qur'an is seen as the direct verbatim speech of God revealed to humanity, without any contribution from human authors. This is reflected in the Qur'anic verses, stating:

> *This Qur'an could have never been created by anyone but God as a confirmation of what is available to him from earlier revelations and a detailed explanation of the Book that—let there be no doubt—is from the Lord of all the worlds. Or do they say, "He [the Prophet] has invented it?" Say, "Then produce a chapter of similar merit, and call on anyone you can other than God if what you say is true"* (10:37–38).

It is for this very reason that Muslims view the Qur'an as a sacred object, as the physical manifestation of the Word of God as it was revealed to the Prophet Muhammad. The Prophet has instructed all Muslims to "Beautify the Qur'an with your voice"—a lesson that still resonates in the hearts of all Muslims. To this day Muslims regard this act as one of the most important sacred rituals. Many Muslims also strive to achieve the coveted position of a Hafiz (or one who has memorized the entire Qur'an by heart) considered an honor for a person in this life and the next life.

Societies in the seventh century (when the Qur'an was revealed) primarily passed on traditions orally. As with many oral societies at the time, poetry was an integral part of Arabia's culture, and the Arabs of Mecca prided themselves on being the master poets of their time. Many of the earliest converts embraced the message of the Qur'an when they found its eloquence and beauty far surpassed their poetry.

The Qur'an is composed of 114 chapters, and each chapter (*surah*) comprises individual verses (*ayah*). The Qur'an was preserved both orally and textually—the Prophet and his closest companions would memorize and recite its verses on a daily basis throughout the 23 years of revelation, and a number of companions known as "*Kuttab al-Wahy*" (Scribes of the revelation) would write down the verses separately, then recite them to the Prophet in order for him to make sure that what they wrote is exactly what he recited. Many of the companions had memorized the entire Qur'an directly from the Prophet Muhammad. It was not until after the Prophet's death in the late seventh century that the Qur'an was organized into a single document. Then, under the leadership of the first caliph, Abu Bakr, the Prophet's closest companions came together and recorded the Qur'an into a single document.

> Muslims view the Qur'an as a sacred object, as the physical manifestation of the Word of God as it was revealed to Prophet Muhammad.

As Islam began to spread during the mid-700s, written copies of the Qur'an became necessary to address the growing diversity in the Muslim world. The third caliph Uthman (r. 644–656), commissioned a group to organize the Qur'an according to the Arabic dialect of the Prophet's tribe, the Quraysh. This group, including one of the original scribes of the Prophet, compiled a complete written codex of the Qur'an on sheets of vellum (*mus'haf*) and began to spread it throughout the Muslim world as the authorized copy of the Qur'an. To this day, the Qur'an must be written in Arabic to be regarded as an authentic, pure form of the Scripture. The Qur'an is written in beautiful calligraphy, an exquisite art that flourished in Islamic civilization. The beauty of the calligraphic script is seen throughout Muslims societies as it is engraved in extensive, breathtaking patterns on buildings and mosques, giving Muslims the feeling of being in the presence the Divine for all of time.

When I completed my journey of translating the Qur'an I began to ponder the essence of the Divine and His message to all mankind. My mind was brought to a particular passage in the Qur'an: "*These are the verses of the Qur'an, a book that makes everything clear, a guidance and good news for the believers*" (27:1–2). God has willed it so that we may be able to understand His guidance and discover the Straight Path. But the choice is ours, and it is through the Qur'an that we may come to find our freedom to choose whether to accept God's guidance. He does not wish for us to be misguided or compelled by others. He has gifted us with the knowledge and tools to interpret His revelations in such a way that reason and scripture do not clash, and so that we may be able to apply his teachings to our modern-day context. Thus, after taking my journey through the Qur'an, it is my sincere belief that if every Muslim learns that the primary objective of the Qur'an is to understand, reflect, and ponder God's message to humanity, the Qur'an can be a liberating tool to free young Muslims from abuse and manipulation by others, especially extremist groups like Daesh who are using the Qur'an to manipulate individuals for their politically nefarious goals.

What Is Qur'anic Critical Thinking?

LALEH BAKHTIAR calls upon Muslims to reclaim the Qur'an from the extremists by critically engaging with the Qur'an in order to discredit Daesh's misinterpretation, which is cherry-picked, rigid, and made to fit within a violent worldview.

KEY TAKEAWAYS

- Critical Qur'anic thinkers user their God-given reason and wisdom to engage with the text, understanding that it is not limited by time and place.
- Extremists allow their suppressed violent tendencies to influence their interpretation of the Qur'an and cling to a literal, scripturally rigid approach to the Qur'an.
- To read the Qur'an critically, it must be approached with an open mind and allowed to speak for itself.

The main goal of the Qur'an is Guidance or *Hidayah*. It is this guidance, which is all encompassing, that we should strive for as well. One of the ways that we can get this guidance is by turning to the Qur'an and understanding it. To do so requires that we first approach the Qur'an with an open mind in order to allow the Qur'an to speak for itself. One cannot approach the Qur'an with the mentality that one already knows the truth, as this will cause one to try and twist the Qur'an to meet what one wants to believe. The Qur'an itself speaks of the error in approaching the Qur'an this way when it states, "*You command humanity to virtuous conduct and you yourselves forget while you recount the Book? Will you not then be reasonable?*" (2:44). Unfortunately, today's extremists like Daesh have turned their backs to such teachings, favoring distorted and impulsive interpretations that give them a false sense of confidence so that they can preach that only their vision of Islam is the true one.

The Qur'an contains God's Infinite knowledge as a gift to humanity so that we may read it and find guidance within its words. In his article, "Reading the Signs: Qur'anic Perspective of Thinking," Professor Hashim Kamali writes, "The Qur'an teaches an essential doctrine of the *ayat* (God's signs in the universe) functioning as pointers to the providential purpose at all levels."[1] This is confirmed in the Qur'anic verse that states, "*Truly in the creation of the heavens and the earth and the alteration of the nighttime and the daytime and the boats that run on the sea with what profits humanity and what God sent forth from heaven of water and gave life to the earth after its death and disseminated on it all moving creatures and diversified the winds and the clouds that are caused to be subservient between heaven and earth are the signs for a people who are reasonable*" (2:164).

Professor Kamali explains that inherent to this Qur'anic virtue is that human beings are required to use reason and become critical thinkers when interpreting the signs and guidance of God. This means that, as with any of God's signs, we must approach the Qur'an critically using our God-given reason to understand the divine revelation, engage with it, reflect on its meaning, ask questions, and solve issues facing our community (*ummah*). Muslims are told this is what God has intended for how human beings should approach and use the Qur'an in verse 38:29,[2] stating: "*It is a blessed Book that We have sent forth to you so that they may meditate on its signs and*

LALEH BAKHTIAR was the first American woman to translate the Qur'an. Her translation, *The Sublime Qur'an*, earned her a reputation as a sensitive translator and editor. Ms. Bakhtiar is also a nationally certified counselor, the president of the Institute of Traditional Psychology, and scholar in residence at Kazi Publications.

[1] Mohammed Hashim Kamali, "Reading the Signs." Also, see *The Middle Path of Moderation in Islam: The Quranic Principle of Wasatiyyah.*
[2] Ibid.

those imbued with intuition may recollect."

Although God has gifted us all with the knowledge and capacity to understand and apply His guidance, it is our responsibility to access and apply this knowledge in order to access his guidance as it is contained in the Qur'an. Doing so requires that we first develop our natural cognitive process of discernment (*furqan*) and reflect on the questions before us, before asking ourselves: "What is my intention, what do I consider when understanding a Qur'anic verse? What questions does it raise when I reflect? What reasoned judgments does it give me as evidence? How do I understand it? How do I recall the concepts to help me understand the verse? What assumptions or opinions do I have about it? What implications or consequences do I ponder? What is my point of view as I take a verse to heart?" By asking ourselves these questions when interacting with the Qur'an, we are engaging our thoughts and feelings in interpreting and understanding God's message as He intended, and discovering the deeper, essential meaning of a verse.

There are many different ways that we may interpret the Qur'an to find this guidance as well. For example, one may choose to approach the Qur'an using a mystical or esoteric interpretation in search of its hidden meanings. Likewise, one may choose to pursue a philosophical or modern interpretation to develop an understanding that is compatible with the modern era and where reason and scripture do not clash. There even exist feminist lenses for interpreting the Qur'an, which emphasize the egalitarian nature of the Qur'an and the ungendered nature of God. There is, of course, a literal interpretation of the Qur'an that takes its verses at face value without considering the deeper, essential meaning. Each of these approaches, however, demands that the integrity of human reason and discernment remain intact, or else we run the risk of allowing our suppressed feelings to influence our understanding.

Today's extremists are the greatest perpetrators of this. Based on their suppressed feelings, these uncritical thinkers act impulsively and tend not to see any relationship between their feelings and their thoughts, leading them to disregard the feelings of others. They cling to a literal, scripturally rigid approach to the Qur'an, assuming that their view is the only view, and disregard any verse or criticism that contradicts their worldview. Similar to the people of innovation (*Ahlul-Bid'ah*), Daesh and modern-day extremists only accept the Qur'an for what they already believe—or want to believe—it says. Such an approach, however, is as if to say that they are not in need of God's guidance and are merely reading the Qur'an to validate their own egocentric worldview. They close their minds to any sort of critical reasoning or discernment when reading the text, which prevents them from seeing the relationship between their feelings and how they have come to interpret the meaning of the Qur'an.

"You command humanity to virtuous conduct and you yourselves forget while you recount the Book? Will you not then be reasonable?" (Qur'an 2:44).

Because Daesh are self-centered, they have to be right about everything, they lack interest in consistency and clarity, and they hold an all-or-nothing attitude: I am 100 percent right, you are 100 percent wrong. This is the opposite of having discernment and it leads to a "group-think" prejudice: a belief formed before the facts are known, resistant to evidence and reason, and irrespective of facts that contradict it. This way of thinking enables extremists to sleep peacefully at night even while flagrantly abusing the rights of others, and allows them to sanction their actions with a superabundance of self-righteousness. Their belief in their own rightness is easier to maintain because they suppress the faults in their thinking. They automatically hide their egocentricity from themselves. They fail to notice when their behavior contradicts their self-image. They base their reasoning on false assumptions, and they fail to make relevant distinctions. They deny or conveniently "forget" facts inconsistent with their conclusions. They often misunderstand or distort what others, including the Qur'an, say.

Unlike these extremists, active and critical Qur'anic thinkers use their God-given reason and wisdom to understand, engage, and apply the text within their own lives and in a way that is beneficial for all humanity. As Professor Hashim Kamali writes: *"To read the Qur'an in light of hikmah (wisdom) thus means a comprehensive reading that reaches beyond the obvious meaning of its words to encapsulate the goal and purpose of its message and then also reflection on the ways and means of how its benefits can be realized for the individual and society."*[3]

Active and critical Qur'anic thinkers use their God-given reason and wisdom to understand, engage, and apply the text within their own lives and in a way that is beneficial for all humanity.

Unlike extremists, active and critical Qur'anic thinkers approach the Qur'an with the realization that the Qur'an is universal, that its verses and guidance are not restrained by time and place. They reflect on each verse, asking themselves, "What does God mean for me in this passage? What is the point I'm supposed to get out of this passage?" They understand that the Qur'an was revealed in a specific sociohistorical context and so they will engage more deeply with the text in an admirable quest for God's guidance. Yet, they also realize that the Qur'an is, in essence, a gift from God to humanity so that we may be able to heal and save ourselves not only in the time in which it was revealed, but for all times, and that it should not be taken lightly.

Muslims have to realize that the Qur'an has been taken hostage. The way to free it is to intellectually engage with it, open it, study it, "own" it, and take it back in a language in which they understand it as they continue to listen and recite the Arabic for spiritual reward. They have to confront its literal interpretation with discernment and critical thinking. Just as the Qur'an commanded the Prophet to say, moderate Muslims should say to the extremists: "*Say, 'Shall We tell you who will be ones who are losers by their actions? Those whose endeavoring goes astray in this present life while they assume that they are doing good works.*" (18:103–4).

[3] Mohammed Hashim Kamali, "Reading the Signs: A Quranic Perspective on Thinking." Introduction to *Critical Thinking, Quranic Perspective: Teacher's Manual*, p. 33.

Who Is the Prophet Muhammad?

MAULANA WAHIDUDDIN KHAN describes Prophet Muhammad as the Prophet of Mercy and states that the best path for a Muslim to follow is the example of the Prophet, which Daesh does not align with.

KEY TAKEAWAYS

- The Prophet's aim was to build a society of upright individuals, and such as society can only be formed if each individual behaves with moral rectitude.
- The Prophet had respect for all people, regardless of religious or political differences, and had an open and strong commitment to women's rights.
- Daesh stands in total opposition to the exemplary way of life set forth by the Prophet Muhammad.

God, as the Creator of the universe, selected a person from among human beings, giving him all the fundamental knowledge necessary for construction and development. This is the divine guide, a prophet, whose advice makes it possible for man to begin his journey in a state of enlightenment, so that he may receive the blessings of both worlds. In Islam, this Prophet goes by the name of Muhammad who was chosen by God as His final Messenger, as seen in the Qur'an: "*We've not sent you, [O Muhammad] except as mercy to the worlds*" (21:107). Muhammad was born in 570 CE and, from an early age, exhibited signs of exemplary behavior. As he grew older, he became known as the most chivalrous among his people, tolerant and forbearing, truthful and trustworthy, always the good neighbor. He would stay aloof from all quarrels and quibbles and never indulged in foul utterances, abuse, or invective. People even left their valuables in his custody, for they knew that he would never betray them. His unimpeachable trustworthiness won for him the title of "*Al-Amin*," a faithful custodian, an unfailing trustee.

Without doubt the Prophet had every opportunity for worldly advancement. He was born into a noble family of Mecca and his virtues guaranteed his success in life. Then at the age of twenty-five, he married one of the richest women in Mecca, a forty-year-old widow named Khadijah who became impressed with the Prophet's high qualities and offered herself to him. Not only did marriage with Khadijah provide the Prophet with wealth and property, it also threw open to him a vast field of business in Arabia and beyond. The Prophet had every opportunity, then, of leading a successful and comfortable life. But he forsook such opportunities and worldly gains to seek out the answer to the all-important questions of truth and falsehood: What is our true role in life? What does the Lord require of us, as His servants? Whence do we come and whither will we go after death?

Unable to find answers to these questions in the centers of human activity, he betook himself to the stillness of the desert where, in 610 CE, God turned in mercy to His Prophet, illuminating his path and guiding him on his journey. The angel of the Lord appeared before him in human form and taught him the words that appear at the beginning of the ninety-sixth chapter of the Qur'an. The Prophet's quest had finally been rewarded. His restless soul had joined in

---

MAULANA WAHIDUDDIN KHAN is an Islamic spiritual scholar who has adopted peace as the mission of his life. Known for his Gandhian views, he considers non-violence as the only method to achieve success. Internationally recognized for his contributions to world peace, he has received, among others, the Demiurgus Peace International Award, the Padma Bhushan, the Rajiv Gandhi National Sadbhavna Award, and the National Citizen's Award. A recent book, *The 500 Most Influential Muslims of 2009* by Georgetown University, Washington DC, has named him "Islam's Spiritual Ambassador to the world." His approach, the book points out, is "popular among Indians, both Muslim and non-Muslim."

communion with the Lord. Not only did God grant him guidance; He also chose Muhammad as His Prophet and special envoy to the world. The Qur'an speaks of this in verse 93:7, which states, "*Did He not find you wandering, and give you guidance?*" Thus, God found Muhammad intent on finding the truth, but in a quandary as to which way to turn, so He showed him the right path. It is this quest for truth, coupled with the willingness to be guided by the Almighty that constitutes the exemplary model all Muslims should follow in their lives.

He forsook such opportunities and worldly gains to seek out the answer to the all-important questions of truth and falsehood: What is our true role in life? What does the Lord require of us, as His servants? Whence do we come and whither will we go after death?

Having received God's guidance himself, the Prophet set out on his mission to spread the truth and guide mankind to God and the hereafter. One task of the Prophet, therefore, was to initiate proper intellectual training, so that they might not only learn the apparent meaning of religious teachings but also understand the wisdom behind them. The Prophet of Islam not only presented God's religion theoretically, but also diligently followed it in practice. Therefore, he is not only one who has told us what to do, but is also one who has demonstrated a practical example of what he preached: "'*Truly, you have in the Prophet of Allah an excellent model for him who fears Allah and the Last Day and who frequently remembers Allah*'" (33:22). Thus, the Prophet's life serves as the best example for the believer. God's true servant is one who adopts the model presented by God's Prophet throughout his life.

The actual goal of his prophetic mission was to help people lead their lives in accordance with the straight path laid down by God, so that they might have an eternal share in God's mercy. Addressing the Prophet of Islam, God says in the Qur'an: "*Call men to the path of your Lord with wisdom and mild exhortation. Reason with them in the most courteous manner. Your Lord best knows those who stray from His path and best knows those who are rightly guided*" (16:125). To this extent, the Prophet Muhammad gave mankind what may be called the knowledge of the divine scheme of things. That is, the Prophet tells us what God's scheme in life is for man and the universe. This is essential for an understanding of life on earth. This is among the greatest gifts of the Prophet to modern man. It was the Prophet's aim to build a society of upright individuals, and such a society can only be formed if each separate individual behaves with moral rectitude.

However, gaining political power to realize God's vision for change was never the goal of the Prophet. In contrast to the Prophet, however, many present-day Muslim leaders and reformers consider it necessary to capture political power or at least gain access to it, in order to bring about their vision for reform. Regardless of their location, all of their efforts have been directed toward bringing political centers under their influence and they will stop at nothing to bring about the total destruction of those who oppose them in their endeavor. The Prophet, however, never concerned himself with the political institutions of the day. For example, he never sought a position in the Dar-an-Nadwa tribal parliament as a replacement for his grandfather who passed away; instead, he chose to concentrate all of his efforts on working peacefully for the success of God's mission.

The Prophet's life serves as the best example for the believer. God's true servant is one who adopts the model presented by God's Prophet throughout his life.

To achieve this, the Prophet adopted a "positive status quoism" plan of action to avoid disrupting social order (which often results in futility or all-out strife), which left him free to take advantage of available opportunities to spread the Word of God in a peaceful and non-confrontational manner. For instance, rather than removing the nearly 360 Meccan idols from the

Kabah—a sanctuary built by the Prophet Abraham for the purpose of worshiping a monotheistic God—the Prophet used this opportunity to preach the teachings of the Qur'an to the polytheists when they gathered for their idol worship. By doing so, he was able to peacefully convey the truth of monotheism to large numbers of people without disrupting or forcing them from their way of life. It is through this example that the Prophet conveyed one of the core teachings of Islam—there is no compulsion in religion. Subsequently, the Prophet was successful in spreading monotheism across Arabia and brought an end to the long history of religious persecution that had plagued Arabian society.

However, even though the Prophet, as a leader and messenger, brought about a miraculous revolution in society, he never believed himself to be greater or better than other people. He never made others feel small, unwanted or embarrassed. Abdullah bin Masood, a companion of the Prophet, narrates that on the occasion of the battle of Badr, when they set forth, they did not have enough mounts. There was one camel for three of them, so they mounted by turns. Ali (the Prophet's son-in-law), Abu Lubaba (a leading member of the Banu Aws in Medina), and the Prophet shared one camel. When the two companions had to take their turns, they would both ask the Prophet to mount instead of them, saying that they would continue on foot. The Prophet would reply, "You are not stronger than me in walking, and I am not less in need of God's reward than you." (Musnad Ahmad).

The Prophet would exhort his followers to live in peace with their fellow men, saying, "A true believer is one with whom others feel secure—one who returns love for hatred."

The Prophet had equal respect in his heart for all human beings, regardless of religious or political differences, and recognized each individual's right to personal dignity. Everyone was equally a creature of God, and everyone served to remind him of God as a perfect Creator. Hatred was totally against his nature. The Prophet upheld equality and condemned hatred even though he suffered through all kinds of injustice and oppression for a period of thirteen years while living in Mecca, and he unilaterally adopted the path of patience and tolerance no matter the situation. The way of the Prophet of Islam was not to retaliate immediately against any act of oppression. He felt that, despite injustice and oppression on the part of the enemy, the way of patience and avoidance of clashes should be adopted. The Prophet of Islam adopted this principle throughout his life. His policy was to adopt a nonviolent method rather than a violent method. The Prophet would exhort his followers to live in peace with their fellow men, saying, "A true believer is one with whom others feel secure—one who returns love for hatred."

> From all sides, Daesh stands in total opposition to the exemplary way of life set forth by the Prophet Muhammad. Whereas the Prophet adopted the policy of avoidance of war by planning for peace, these individuals are planning to destroy the world of peace through their violent actions.

An outstanding example of this magnanimity, which the Prophet displayed throughout his life, can be found in his treatment of the Quraysh after Mecca had been conquered. The very people who had been relentlessly persecuting the Prophet and his followers for the previous twenty years, were now at the Prophet's mercy. But, rather than punish them for past crimes, he forgave them all. When the Quraysh were brought before him in chains he simply said to them, "Be on your way: you are all free men."

This was the example the Prophet set for mankind. He had high moral character, so that even if badly treated by others, he went on returning good for evil. People harmed him, yet he would pray for them. He would remain patient in the face of oppression and, regardless of the provocation, he would refrain from becoming incensed. In setting this example, his aim was to fashion souls that were God-oriented, that found God so great that everything else paled in significance. He wanted everyone to have such boundless peace of mind that nothing could disturb them. The Prophet's mission therefore was the spiritual purification of man—to make man a better human being through his guidance and example. As the Qur'an says, "*Our Lord, and send among them a messenger from themselves who will recite to them Your verses and teach them the Book and wisdom to purify them. Indeed, you are the Exalted in Might, the Wise*" (2:129).

The Qur'an says, "*Certainly you have in the Messenger of Allah an excellent exemplar for him who hopes in Allah and the latter day and remembers Allah much*" (33:21). This means that Islam has given the Prophet Muhammad to the world as a shining example and has established him as a role model for all time to come. All those who claim to be Muslims are therefore honor-bound to follow in his footsteps. However, the truth is that the example of the Prophet is open to more than one interpretation, and it may happen that the wrong—or right—interpretation is made. Only if one is sincere will one interpret the situation correctly, and this can only be achieved through the realism that comes from the fear of God. When sincere people consider these incidents in the Prophet's life, they are not just seeking a meaning that will serve their ends; rather they are seeking to ascertain the exact nature of the example imparted by the Prophet. Thus, the consideration that should be uppermost in a believer's mind is what serves the interests of Islam, not his/her own personal interests.

Unfortunately, some present-day Muslims attempt to legitimize their own personal movements by calling them "Muhammad" or "Islamic" even though their deviant actions are sure to be rejected by God as unworthy. Daesh and violent extremists today fall into this category of the unworthy. They call themselves Muslims and justify their claims by misinterpreting the Qur'an and the Hadith, thus positioning themselves falsely as role models for other Muslims. But their actions deviate from the very example set by the Prophet. Daesh even went so far as to launch a suicide attack in the Prophet's own mosque during Ramadan, an act of senseless violence that would have received the harshest condemnation from the Prophet had it occurred during his lifetime.

From all sides, Daesh stands in total opposition to the exemplary way of life set forth by the Prophet Muhammad. Whereas the Prophet adopted the policy of avoidance of war by planning for peace. These individuals are planning to destroy the world of peace through their violent actions. It is thus imperative for Muslims today to engage all efforts in the positive construction of Islam and Muslims, and present Islam to the world as a non-violent religion with a peaceful ideology exemplified through the life of the Prophet Muhammad. There simply is no other path to peace and success for modern man.

The Prophet Muhammad's Role in Warfare

IBRAHIM MALABARI explains how the Prophet created rules of warfare to make it as humane as possible, so as to discredit the image of the Prophet Muhammad as a "bloodthirsty warmonger."

KEY TAKEAWAYS

- Out of the ten years of his life in Medina, the Prophet spent 795 days in battles and expeditions. The rest of his time the Prophet spent reforming society for the better.
- The Prophet brought sweeping changes to the conduct of war, limiting the use of violence against others and the means by which war is fought to make it more humane.
- Objectively, the Prophet's wars were some of the least bloody in history.

What Abu Bakr al-Baghdadi, leader of Daesh, is doing is a complete violation of the teaching of the Prophet of Mercy, Muhammad (pbuh), and the dictates of the Qur'an. It is surprising the self-proclaimed Khalifah "studied" Islam for many years, since he interprets it to suit his whims and personal impulses. Al-Baghdadi is doing more harm to Islam, and by extension to humanity, than al-Qaeda and other terrorists organizations ever did. Islam, the Qur'an, and the Prophet Muhammad (pbuh) have nothing to do with Daesh's criminal agenda. He is using the Qur'an and Islam to exploit the naivete and ignorance of the Muslim masses, and his claims are unanimously rejected by Muslim scholars of the world.

The Prophet Muhammad, the Messenger of Mercy, did not prescribe war as a natural state of affairs; at the same time, war cannot simply be abolished. What any reformer or spiritual leader can do is minimize its brutality. The Messenger of Mercy, at God's direction, attempted to establish rules of warfare that would make war as humane as possible, to encourage peace, and to minimize the toll in human lives.

Many portray the Messenger of Mercy bloodthirsty and as a warmonger as if fighting battles was his main occupation. But in reality, out of the ten years of his life in Medina, only 795 days were spent on battles and expeditions. The rest of the ten years (approximately 2,865 days) he spent on bringing revolutionary changes to people's lives and totally reforming a pagan society. This historical fact is overlooked by most of his biographers and almost all Western writers who depict him as a warmonger.

The Messenger of Mercy, at God's direction, attempted to establish rules of warfare that would make war as humane as possible, to encourage peace, and to minimize the toll in human lives.

The Prophetic approach to war can be better appreciated by looking at some figures. The Messenger of Mercy was forced to defend himself militarily on many occasions, yet the amount of human loss that resulted is surprisingly low given similar battles and wars in human history. From a total of 28 battles and 38 campaigns, the total casualties from those wars, including both sides, amounted to 1,284 lives.

IBRAHIM MALABARI is an Islamic scholar, activist, and author of the book *Mercy: Prophet Muhammad's Legacy to All Creation*. He has been involved in several Islamic organizations, including the Islamic Society of North America, and was a member of the Fiqh Council of North America.

Someone can argue that the reason for the decreased numbers of casualties is the smaller numbers of combatants who participated in the various campaigns. But a careful examination shows that the percentage of people killed in these wars relative to the number of the people who participated in them amounted to about 1.5 percent. Since the Messenger of Mercy was victorious in most of these battles, the numbers of casualties indicate that he is not to be counted among the ruthless and barbaric warlords, conquerors, and military generals of human history—in fact, he was far from it.

Compare the above numbers to other wars in human history. For example, in the Second World War alone, the ratio between the number of people killed (including civilians) to the number of combatants who were involved in that war was 351%. That is, 10,600,000 participated in that war, yet the dead numbered as high as 54,800,000.

The Messenger of Mercy brought sweeping changes to the conduct of war, radically limiting the means and use of violence against others. Much like today, the Messenger of Mercy lived in a world in which brutal warfare was rampant. Like the Roman and Persian empires of that time, the Arab tribes primarily engaged in battle for material gains rather than for any higher, moral purpose. The Messenger of Mercy, however, would change that radically.

The Messenger of Mercy stressed the observance of several important moral principles even during the tumult of warfare. First, he fundamentally redefined the basic understanding and concept of war. By introducing an entirely new term—*jihad fi sabilillah*—he purified warfare from its material or vested interests and self-serving motives. *Jihad* means "struggle" and for one to carry a concerted effort to remove the injustices and oppression imposed by others. By adding "in the way of God" (*fi sabilillah*), he taught that war must not be waged for the sake of the self, of spoils, pride, prestige, subjugation, or oppressing other people. This belief served as the glue holding the principles of warfare together and reining in all potential injustices inherent within it.

Under this new conception of war, the Messenger of Mercy introduced a comprehensive set of laws that encompassed the conduct of war: its moral boundaries, components, rights, and obligations; the difference between combatants and noncombatants and their rights; and the rights of envoys, prisoners of war, and conquered people. All of these principles were expressed clearly and unequivocally by the Messenger of Mercy.

The Messenger of Mercy also underscored the sanctity and inviolability of human life, be it Muslim or non-Muslim. He embodied the Qur'anic verse: "*If anyone slays a human being—unless it be [in punishment] for murder or for spreading corruption on earth—it shall be as though he had slain all humanity*" (5:32). His followers, although they certainly were—and still are—prone to great errors, were remarkable exemplars of these principles in general.

"*If anyone slays a human being—unless it be [in punishment] for murder or for spreading corruption on earth—it shall be as though he had slain all humanity*" (Qur'an 5:32).

The Messenger of Mercy prohibited the robbery, banditry, and vandalism that had been commonplace in wars before his time. For example, after the Khaybar peace treaty had been signed, some of the young new Muslims started looting Jewish property. The Jewish leader came to the Messenger of Mercy and asked: "Is it appropriate for your people to slaughter our donkeys, devour our crops, and beat our women?" Suddenly, the Messenger of Mercy ordered the entire army into the mosque for prayer and told them: "God did not permit you to enter the People of the Book's houses without permission and to beat their women and eat their crops." If a milking animal is found on the way and soldiers want to take its milk, they cannot do so unless permission is granted. Therefore, even in warfare, the Messenger of Mercy stressed the importance of the rule of law and respect for the property and rights of others, which is far more than what we see in modern wars.

In the past, armies destroyed crops, farmland and property, and even entire villages. But the Messenger of Mercy prohibited killing all non-combatants, such as women, children, the old, the sick, the wounded, the blind, the disabled, the mentally unwell, travelers, monks, and worshippers. In fact, he only permitted killing those in the front lines; everyone behind them was protected from attack. Remarkably, the Messenger of Mercy here grants far more than what is stated in theories of just war today. Once the Messenger of Mercy saw a woman's corpse on the battlefield and became very upset. He ordered his commander, Khalid ibn al-Walid: "Do not kill women or laborers." Moreover, the Messenger of Mercy specifically commanded Muslims not to kill monks or worshippers, and not to destroy places of worship.

Before Islam, both Arabs and non-Arabs, in the heat of vengeance, habitually burned their enemies alive. The Messenger of Mercy categorically prohibited this: "Nobody should punish with fire except the Lord of Fire [God]." He also forbade desecrating and mutilating the enemies' corpses by cutting off their limbs.

The Messenger of Mercy prohibited the killing of prisoners of war, declaring: "No wounded person will be killed, no one who flees will be followed."

The Messenger of Mercy also stated that one cannot breach one's trust and kill those with whom peace has been made. No peace treaty should be violated: "If you have made a treaty with a people, you cannot make any changes or alterations until it expires."

The Messenger of Mercy tried his utmost to reduce human casualties. Anyone who studies the Messenger of Mercy's wars objectively and compares these with other wars in human history, including the wars of our modern times (such as the wars in Iraq, Afghanistan, and the War on Terror) can conclude that his wars were the least bloody—and most humane. Today, in a time of constant war under pretexts of preemptive strikes, these teachings demonstrate his just personality—a Messenger for our time.

The Covenants of the Prophet Muhammad

DR. JOHN ANDREW MORROW presents a translation of a covenant between the Prophet Muhammad and the Monks of Mount Sinai—one among many covenants and letters that the Prophet dictated. These covenants were authenticated by the first four Caliphs and were considered legally binding by Muslim rulers and sultans. They reveal the lengths to which the Prophet Muhammad went to ensure and guarantee protection for the People of the Book, namely Christians and Jews.

The Prophet Muhammad (pbuh) issued various covenants of protection for the People of the Book, enshrining their rights.[1] The various covenants are mentioned in the Prophet's biography and jurisprudence, and copies can be found in whole or in part in classical Muslim sources.[2] Although the covenants were dictated by the Prophet, they were scribed by different individuals, and in some cases were authenticated by the Prophet's palm-print or with his famous ring seal. The major covenants were written down by Ali and Mu'awiyah and witnessed by the Companions of the Prophet, including Abu Bakr, Umar, and Uthman.

As a messenger, the Prophet also wrote numerous letters to invite people, tribes, and nations to the Muslim faith; in the event they opted to maintain their current religion, he asked them to enter into an alliance with him. One of the earliest of these documents was the Pact of Medina, in which the Prophet outlined principles such as freedom of movement, freedom of religion, and equality before the law for people of various faiths who were under his protection, and declared Muslims and non-Muslims to be "one community" (ummah). Additional covenants, such as the Covenant of the Prophet Muhammad with the Monks of Mount Sinai, protected freedom of worship for Christians, and provided them with military protection. Importantly, the Prophet emphasized that any Muslim who violated the terms of this Covenant "makes a mockery of his religion" and "dissents from the Messenger of God." The Prophet's behavior toward other faith communities vis-à-vis the terms of these covenants serves as an important reminder for today's Muslims to similarly embody the core values of religious freedom and respect for all religions as enshrined in the Qur'an.

The covenants of the Prophet Muhammad were treated as genuine by the four rightly guided Caliphs, the Umayyads, the Abbasids, the Fatimids, the Ayyubids, the Mamluks, the Safavids, and the

DR. JOHN ANDREW MORROW is a religious authority, academic, and activist. He is the author of a large body of scholarly works, including *The Covenants of the Prophet Muhammad with the Christians of the World*. Along with Charles Upton, he directs the Covenants Initiative, an international movement devoted to promoting classical Islam, countering extremism and radicalization, and defending the People of the Qiblah and the People of the Book who are persecuted by Takfiri terrorists.

[1] These include: the Pact of Medina, the Covenant of the Prophet Muhammad with the Monks of Mount Sinai, the Covenant of the Prophet Muhammad with the Christians of Najran, the Covenant of the Prophet Muhammad with the Christians of Persia, the Covenant of the Prophet Muhammad with the Assyrian Christians, the Covenant of the Prophet Muhammad with the Syriac Orthodox Christians, the Covenant of the Prophet Muhammad with the Coptic Christians of Egypt, the Covenant of the Prophet Muhammad with the Armenian Christians, the Covenant of the Prophet Muhammad with the Samaritans, the Covenant of the Prophet Muhammad with the Jews of Maqna, the Covenant of the Prophet Muhammad with the Yemenite Jews, and the Covenant of the Prophet Muhammad with the Zoroastrians.

[2] These include the works of Balkhi, Tabari, Mas'udi, Muqtafi II, Ibn Ishaq, Waqidi, Abu Yusuf, Shaybani, Yahya ibn Adam, Abu 'Ubayd, Ibn Hisham, Ibn Sa'd, Ibn Zanjawayh, Abu Dawud, Baladhuri, Ya'qubi, Ibn Hawqal, Mufid, Abu al-Shaykh, Abu Nu'aym, Ibn Shahrashub, Abu al-Futuh al-Razi, Fakhr al-Din al-Razi, Ibn al-'Athir, Ibn Kathir, Ibn Qayyim, Qazwini, Maqrizi, Qalqashandi, Kwandamir, Kashfi, Majlisi, and Shirazi.

Ottomans, as can be confirmed by early Muslim sources.[3] They have also been authenticated by Sunni, Shia, and non-Muslim scholars.

Copies of the covenants of the Prophet have been preserved in Christian monasteries in Egypt, Palestine, Syria, Turkey, Armenia, and Persia. Others were passed down through priestly lines in Jewish and Zoroastrian communities in Egypt, Yemen, Persia, and India. Others still were preserved as sacred relics in the treasuries of the caliphs, sultans, and shahs of Islam, including those of Selim I and Abbas I.

The surviving copies of the covenants were issued, signed, sealed, notarized, and authenticated by the political and religious leaders of the Muslim world; namely, by the caliphs, sultans, and shahs, along with their grand viziers, muftis, and chief jurists. Copies of the covenants of the Prophet, in both the original Arabic and in translations, were provided by the Muslim authorities to the Christian communities under their rule, and it was customary for Muslim authorities to renew the covenants of the Prophet on a yearly basis. Indeed, for thirteen centuries after the death of the Prophet, Muslim rulers continued to put into practice the terms of the covenants by protecting Christians and other faith minorities under their rule. Sultan Abdul Hamid, the last caliph of the Ottoman Empire, renewed the Prophet's covenant with St. Catherine's Monastery in 1904.

Today, the covenants of the Prophet are recognized by Pope Francis, Patriarch Bartholomew, and Patriarch Bartholomew III, as well as the Holy Fathers from the monasteries of St. Catherine, Simonopetra, and St. George, among many others. Recently, they have been endorsed by hundreds of Muslim scholars around the world.[4]

Although the covenants of the Prophet were commonly known among educated Muslims throughout most of Islamic history, knowledge of them faded after the collapse of the Ottoman Empire in the early twentieth century. Today, more than 1,400 years after the death of the Prophet, Muslims and non-Muslims alike are witnessing the destruction of Christian churches and the indiscriminate killing of Muslims, Christians, and people of other faiths by extremist groups. These actions are a gross violation of the teachings of the Qur'an and stand in direct contradiction to the Prophet's letters and the instructions he conveyed to his followers in the Pact of Medina and the covenants.

The covenants of the Prophet represent a genuine call for reconstituting the deteriorated relationships between the three Abrahamic religions. Their practical application can serve to promote peaceful coexistence, respect, and care beyond mere tolerance. In fact, they shed light upon the nature and policy of the Prophet vis-à-vis governing diverse groups and maintaining relationships among other people, both of which are completely in line with the Prophet's life and teachings. Whether in the Pact of Medina, the letters, or the covenants, the Prophet sought to convey the core message of the Qur'an: that all believers are brethren of one another. The Prophet's covenants represent a practical example, and provide a blueprint for Muslims, on how to conduct their relations with others in today's fractured world. The covenants serve as a source of inspiration for the establishment of mutually beneficial and peaceful coexistence.

---

[3] Readers who are interested in the history of the transmission of the Covenants of the Prophet can refer to "The Provenance of the Prophet's Covenant," which appears in volume 2 of Islam and the People of the Book: Critical Studies on the Covenants of the Prophet, which provides a meticulous study of hundreds of references to the Covenants of the Prophet over the past 1,400 years.

[4] These scholars include leaders such as Imam Abdul-Malik Mujahid, Dr. Omid Safi, Dr. Muqtedar Khan, Dr. Reza Shah-Kazemi, Imam Feisal Abdul Rauf, Shaikh Kabir Helminski, Shaykha Fariha al-Jerrahi, Imam Yahya Pallavicini, Shaykh Fadlallah Haeri, Ahmed El-Wakil, Dr. Akbar Ahmed, Dr. Bridget Blomfield, Dr. Hisham Ramadan, Dr. Cyrus Ali Zargar, Dr. Roger Abdul-Wahhab Boase, Imam Mohammed Ali Elahi, Dr. Abdallah Schleifer, Dr. Allan 'Abd al-Haqq Godlas, Shaykh Muhammad 'Umar al-Qadri, and Shaykh Sa'd al-Azhari, as well as organizations, such as the Islamic Society of North America. For a full list, see the signatories of the Covenants Initiative at www.covenantsoftheprophet.com.

The Covenant of the Prophet Muhammad with the Monks of Mount Sinai

In the Name of Allah, the Most Compassionate, the Most Merciful.

This covenant was written upon the order of Muhammad, the son of 'Abd Allah, the proclaimer and warner, trusted to protect Allah's creation, in order that people may raise no claim against Allah after [the advent of] His Messengers for Allah is Almighty, Wise.

He has written it for the members of his religion and to all those who profess the Christian religion in East and West, near or far, Arabs or non-Arabs, known or unknown, as a covenant of protection.

If anyone breaks the covenant herein proclaimed, or contravenes or transgresses its commands, he has broken the Covenant of Allah, breaks his bond, makes a mockery of his religion, deserves the curse [of Allah], whether he is a sultan or another among the believing Muslims.

If a monk or pilgrim seeks protection, in mountain or valley, in a cave or in tilled fields, in the plain, in the desert, or in a church, I am behind them, defending them from every enemy; I, my helpers, all the members of my religion, and all my followers, for they [the monks and the pilgrims] are my protégés and my subjects.

I protect them from interference with their supplies and from the payment of taxes save what they willingly renounce. There shall be no compulsion or constraint against them in any of these matters.

A bishop shall not be removed from his bishopric nor a monk from his monastery, nor a hermit from his tower, nor shall a pilgrim be hindered from his pilgrimage. Moreover, no building from among their churches shall be destroyed, nor shall the money from their churches be used for the building of mosques or houses for the Muslims. Whoever does such a thing violates Allah's covenant and dissents from the Messenger of Allah.

Neither poll-tax nor fees shall be laid on monks, bishops, or worshippers for I protect them, wherever they may be, on land or sea, in East and West, in North and South. They are under my protection, within my covenant, and under my security, against all harm.

Those who also isolate themselves in the mountains or in sacred sites shall be free from the poll-tax, land tribute and from tithe or duty on whatever they grow for their own use, and they shall be assisted in raising a crop by a free allowance of one qadah [unit of dry measure] in every ardabb for their personal use.

They shall be not obliged to serve in war, or to pay the poll-tax; even those for whom an obligation to pay land tribute exists, or who possess resources in land or from commercial activity, shall not have to pay more than twelve dirhams a head per year.

On no one shall an unjust tax be imposed, and with the People of the Book there is to be no strife, unless it is in the best of manners [Qur'an 29:46]. We wish to take them under the wing of our mercy, and the penalty of vexation shall be kept at a distance from them, wherever they are and wherever they may settle.

If a Christian woman enters a Muslim household, she shall be received with kindness, and she shall be given opportunity to pray in her church; there shall be no dispute between her and a man who loves her religion. Whoever contravenes the covenant of Allah and acts to the contrary is a rebel against his covenant and his Messenger.

These people shall be assisted in the maintenance of their religious buildings and their dwellings; thus they will be aided in their faith and kept true to their allegiance.

None of them shall be compelled to bear arms, but the Muslims shall defend them; and they shall never contravene this promise of protection until the hour comes and the world ends.

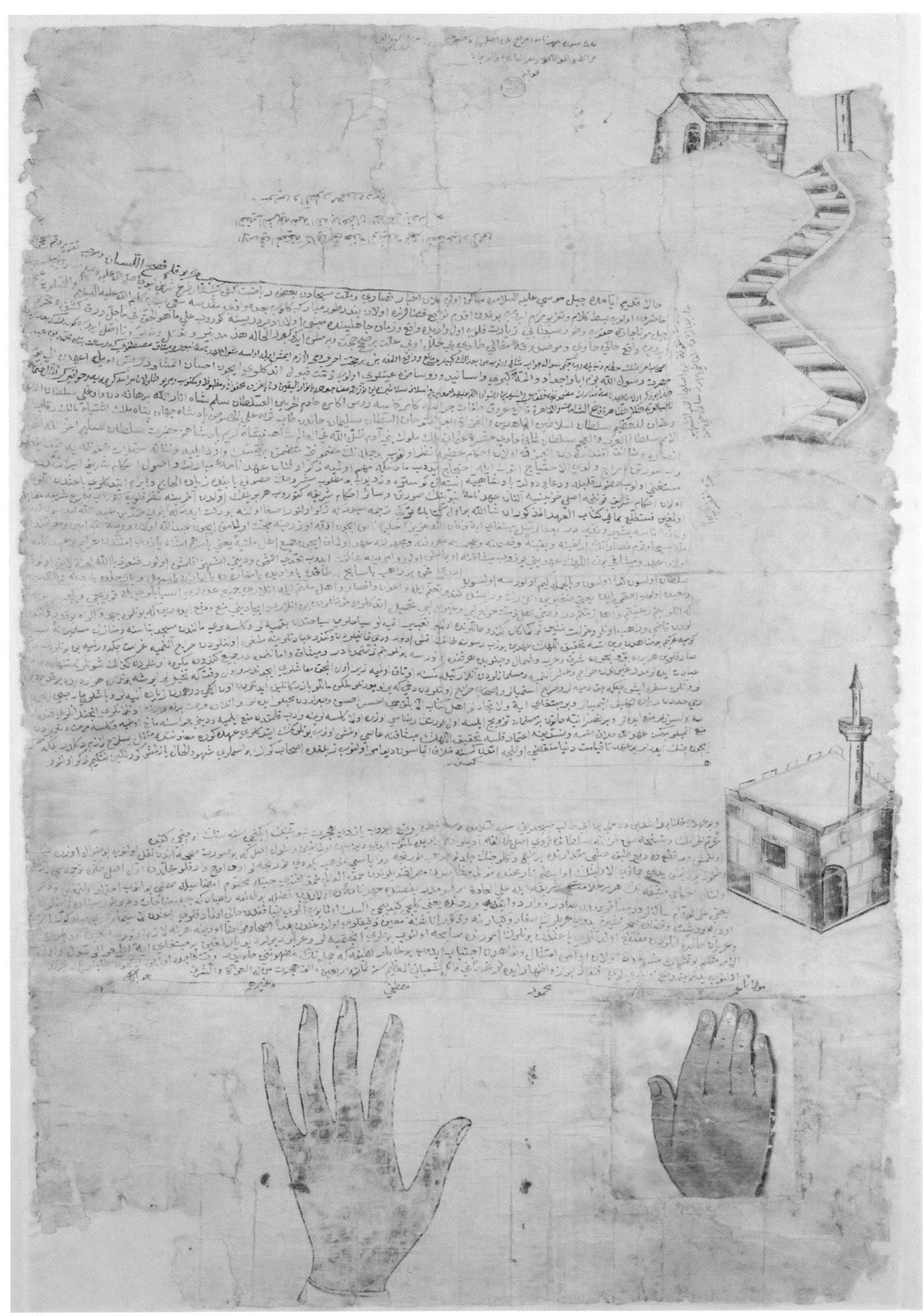

Turkish language copy of the *Covenant of the Prophet Muhammad with the Monks of Mount Sinai* from 1638. Reprinted with permission from St. Catherine's Monastery in Sinai, Egypt.

The Prophet Muhammad's Marriages

IBRAHIM H. MALABARI shows how the Prophet Muhammad's multiple marriages throughout his life had a social motive and a higher goal than mere sexual gratification, and discusses the importance of the Prophet's wives in the history of Islam.

Whenever the Prophet Muhammad's name emerges, the image in many people's minds is of a man with many wives. For Muslims, his multiple marriages had meaning and immense implications for Islam, and by extension, the history of the world. The issue remains controversial, and as such, any study of the matter requires an objective approach. Therefore we will endeavor to tackle this topic by being as objective as possible.

The Prophet Muhammad was driven by the goal to ensure that his mission as the Messenger of God was fulfilled and to establish a society based on God's commands, not his own. In order to achieve this goal, he did everything he could: he forged relations with the various tribes of Arabia; concluded peace treaties with his sworn enemies; and kept relations with the heads of various tribes, nations, and religions. Taken together, his marriages were one way by which he fostered relationships with various influential tribes.

If one were to view the marriages of the Prophet through this lens, the motivating factors behind his marriages become clear. It would be very simplistic and incorrect to view his marriages as being merely for lustful ends.

Let us now briefly examine the context of each of his marriages. From the outset, it is of ultimate importance to note that, except for one of his wives, all his eleven wives were widowed or divorced. Most were in fact widowed.

His first marriage was to a widow named Khadijah, who had been married twice and whom he married when she was forty years old and he was twenty-five. She was the first woman to embrace Islam. She provided great consolation to him throughout his life and he continued to remember her in his later years as his most beloved wife. He stayed with her faithfully for 25 years until her death at sixty-five, when he was fifty years old.

If he was driven merely by lustful desires, as he was accused of doing by his opponents, he could have married several beautiful young women in a society where having numerous wives was the norm—there would be no reason for him to faithfully remain with an older woman until her death. This single fact would be sufficient to refute the charges against him in this regard. However, an examination of all his marriages, as we shall see, should put this question to rest.

[The Prophet] forged relations with the various tribes of Arabia; concluded peace treaties with his sworn enemies; and kept relations with the heads of various tribes, nations, and religions. Taken together, his marriages were one way by which he fostered relationships with various influential tribes.

After Khadijah's death, he married another widow, Sawda, who was sixty-five years old. She and her previous husband, Sakran, were among those who had immigrated to Ethiopia, fleeing from the oppression and persecution of the Meccans. It was during their return to Mecca that her husband had died. Seeing her difficult condition, the Prophet married her.

Then he married Aisha, daughter of his lifelong friend and companion Abu Bakr. Aisha had first been betrothed to Jabir bin Mut'im at the age of five. (In many regions of the world, children were commonly betrothed to marry at a young age during that time.) She was the only one of the Prophet's wives who had not been previously married, and who was born into a Muslim family.

One of the Prophet's goals in his marriage to Aisha was to strengthen the bond of his brotherhood with Abu Bakr, who was his main defender against the Meccans. Second, Aisha was of a lineage known for honor and intelligence. The Prophet knew that she would tremendously benefit his community by transmitting crucial knowledge from his life, especially family and personal matters that others were not privy to. Indeed, the Prophet advised his community to learn half the knowledge of the religion from Aisha. The foresight of the Prophet proved itself, for she would live for 45 years after his death, and thus became one of the main sources of Prophetic wisdom and knowledge.

He also married another widow, Hafsa, who was the daughter of Umar Bin Khattab, his next closest companion. Her husband, Khunays, had been martyred in the Battle of Badr. He felt a duty toward Umar, whose acceptance of Islam provided a major boost for the Muslims in Mecca against their foes.

Zaynab, daughter of Khuzaima, was another widow whom the Prophet married. She had been married to Ubayda bin al-Haris, who was also martyred in the Battle of Badr. She was sixty when the Prophet married her. She was known as the "Mother of the Downtrodden." She passed away after only two or three months of marriage.

He married another widow, Umm Salama. Her previous husband, Abu Salama, was martyred in the Battle of Uhud, leaving behind four fatherless children. Umm Salama was pregnant with her fifth child at that time and was extremely distressed and very sad. Needless to say, she needed much support. After she delivered the child, Umar proposed that the Prophet marry her. The Prophet accepted the proposal and married Umm Salama. What purpose can there be for a person of fifty-four to marry a widow with five children except love, mercy, and compassion? There was another crucial factor in this marriage: Umm Salama was from the Bani Makhzum tribe, which was the tribe of Islam's archenemies at that time, Abu Jahl and Khalid bin Waleed. Though Abu Jahl never changed, Khalid later accepted Islam and became a brilliant military general. Once again, bringing influential and powerful tribes closer to Islam was one of the noble objectives of the Prophet's marriage.

He married a divorced woman, Zaynab, the daughter of Jahsh. She had been married to Zayd bin Haritha, the freed slave of the Prophet. She was the cousin of the Prophet, being the daughter of his paternal aunt. Zayd divorced her and the Prophet married her when she was thirty-eight years old. His marriage to Zaynab was aimed at emphasizing the invalidity of the age-old Arab practice of taking adopted sons as real sons. The marriage was divinely sanctioned, as stated in the Qur'an, "When Zayd had come to the end of his union with her, We gave her to you in marriage . . ." (33:37).

Umm Habiba was the next the Prophet married. She was a daughter of Abu Sufyan, who was a bitter enemy of Islam until his conversion later. She was initially married to Ubaydallah, who was a companion of the Prophet. Both immigrated to Ethiopia, fleeing the persecution of the Meccans. Ubaydallah became a Christian and later died there. After considering her very difficult situation, her father being an enemy of Islam and her husband a deserter, the Prophet sent an envoy to Negus, king of Ethiopia, requesting to arrange a marriage with her. The king agreed and she was married to him when she was thirty-six or thirty-seven years old. Like many of his marriages, his marriage to Umm Habiba resulted in bringing a major tribe of the Quraysh, the Banu Abd al-Shams, toward Islam.

He married another widow, Juwayria. Both her father and husband were bitter enemies of Islam; the former had planned to attack Medina at the instigation of the Meccans. This led the Muslim army to march against the clan of her father. The result was their defeat at the hands of the Prophet and the death of Juwayria's husband. After the conflict, the Muslims captured many prisoners, one of whom was Juwayria. Juwayria's father offered a ransom for her freedom. She requested to stay in the service of the Prophet and he married her at her request. The marriage resulted in the freeing of all the prisoners of war of her tribe. Again, this marriage led to the establishment of peace and friendly relations with a formerly antagonistic group.

He also married a woman named Safiyya, a widow as well. Her second husband was killed in the Battle of Khaybar. Her father was the chief of the famous Jewish tribe Banu Nazir, who was killed in the Battle of Khaybar as well, and so Safiyya was taken prisoner. She was eventually freed and the Prophet married her. Some expressed concern that she was still loyal to the tribe of Jews who had just fought the Prophet. Her answer was that they were her relatives, and the Prophet defended her position. He told her to respond in the following way: "My father is Aaron (Haroon) and my uncle is Moses (Musa)." This marriage had led to a closer relationship between the Muslims and the Jews of Medina.

His final marriage was to another divorced woman, Maymuna. She was married twice and was very old. She married the Prophet when he was fifty-seven. The Prophet's uncle, Abbas, suggested the Prophet marry Maymuna so that she could bring her tribe—the Halaliyyeen—into the fold of Islam. That was what eventually happened.

From the above, we see that it was not the Prophet's whims and desires that initiated his marriages, but rather it was that God had planned his marriages. He commanded His Messenger after the last marriage (with Maymuna) not to marry anymore (Qur'an 33:52), because by that time the objectives of his marriages were achieved as the Prophet's mission was near completion.

All this does not mean that the Prophet was not interested in sex. He was surely attracted by sex and beauty, and was not a prude in expressing it. He said, "Perfume and women are made dear to me. However, the joy of my eye is in prayer." He also said: "I am in full control of myself." In fact, a look at his life would suggest that he approached the various aspects of human life with moderation—be it eating, drinking, or enjoying time with his wives—never indulging in any one thing excessively. The portrayal of him by some Western writers as promiscuous and licentious, mostly due to the fact that he had numerous wives, is far from the truth and historical facts, as shown above. Indeed, his marriages had a social motive and a higher goal than mere sexual gratification.

It is relevant here to quote a female Western scholar, Karen Armstrong, the author of Muhammad: A Prophet for Our Time, in relation to the issue of the Prophet's marriages and the practice of polygamy in Islam: "The Qur'anic institution of polygamy was a piece of social legislation. It was designed not to gratify the male sexual appetite, but to correct the injustices done to widows, orphans, and other female dependents, who were especially vulnerable. All too often, unscrupulous people seized everything and left the weaker members of the family with nothing. . . . Polygamy was designed to ensure that unprotected women would be decently married, and to abolish the old loose, irresponsible liaisons; men could have only four wives and must treat them equitably; it was an unjustifiably wicked act to devour their property. . . . The Qur'an was attempting to give women a legal status that most Western women would not enjoy until the nineteenth century. The emancipation of women was a project dear to the Prophet's heart."

Understanding Hadith: The Prophet's Teachings

DR. JONATHAN BROWN explains the complexities of Hadith and their importance in Islam. Hadith must be read and understood within the context of the Qur'an and Sunnah to avoid serious misunderstanding.

KEY TAKEAWAYS

- Hadith often deal with matters of worship, issues of ethics, and the chain of transmission of the Prophet's words.
- Neither the Qur'an nor Hadith should be read without some reliable reference that can provide context and explanation.
- Use of unreliable Hadith carries a high social cost for the community, preventing members from assigning proper priorities to belief and action.

When Islam is brought up, discussion usually moves to the question "What does the Qur'an say about this?" Because people are told that the Qur'an is "the Muslim Bible," it's natural to assume that the Qur'an is where we can find answers to questions about Muslim faith and belief. But many basic tenets of Islamic worship and even beliefs are not found in the Qur'an. For example, nowhere in the holy book does one find explicit mention of the exact timings of the five daily prayers that all Muslims are supposed to perform. Where one does find this crucial information is in the Sunnah of the Prophet Muhammad, namely his authoritative precedent and teachings. Included in the Sunnah are the Hadith, which are reports about the Prophet Muhammad's words and actions.

The Sunnah is the essential companion of the Qur'an, and the two cannot be read one without the other. For example, the Qur'an provides the spiritual impetus for Muslims to pray and to give charity; the Sunnah explains how, when, and how much. Hadith often deal with matters of worship, such as descriptions of how the Prophet held his arms during his prayers or when he fasted. Hadith can involve issues of ethics, such as the Prophet saying, "The best amongst you is the best to their family." They can also be legal, such as the Prophet saying, "Do not sell what you do not own," or his instruction that judges should never pass judgment when angry.

The Qur'an provides the spiritual impetus for Muslims to pray and to give charity; the Sunnah explains how, when, and how much.

Due to the importance of Hadith in understanding the Qur'an, and in order to mitigate the risk of misunderstanding, early Muslim scholars like Imam Bukhari took on the enormous task of developing an objective system for grading the authenticity of statements claimed to be made by the Prophet. Hadith studies consist of examining whether the chain of transmission (*isnad*) is possible (e.g., making sure that all of the transmitters and transmittees were alive and living in the same area at the time of transmission) and whether the transmitters were considered to be reliable. Hadith that were known to be transmitted by reliable sources are considered *sahih* (authentic). Those transmitters who are reported

DR. JONATHAN BROWN is an American scholar of Islamic studies and an associate professor at Georgetown University's Edmund A. Walsh School of Foreign Service where he also serves as the Chair of Islamic Civilizations. Dr. Brown serves as the editor in chief of the *Oxford Encyclopedia* and is the author of numerous books and articles, including "*Misquoting Muhammad: The Challenge and Choices of Interpreting the Prophet's Legacy*" and "*Hadith: Muhammad's Legacy in the Medieval and Modern World.*"

to have lied at any point in their lives, or were reputed to be heedless, were rejected as unreliable and likely to have misunderstood what the Prophet said.

Scholars saw the use of unreliable Hadith as both a danger to social morality and contrary to the stated values of Islamic thought. Moreover, these unreliable Hadith carried a high social cost, threatening the Muslim community's ability to assign proper priorities to elements of belief and action. The most conscientious acknowledgment of the social consequences of promulgating weak Hadith comes from Ibn al-Jawzi (d. 597/1201). Concerns over irresponsible preachers, their use of unreliable stories, and the heretical ideas they spread were powerful motives in Ibn al-Jawzi's writings.

One Hadith is just part of a much larger equation. It can't be understood properly unless it is placed alongside the Qur'an and other relevant Hadith.

In his works, Ibn al-Jawzi vents his anxieties over the effects of unreliable hadith on society, most specifically on people's ability to assign moral weight to actions: "How many complexions have become yellow with hunger, and how many people fall asleep flat on their faces out of wandering in pious travel (*bi'lsiyaha*)? How many have forbidden to themselves what is permitted, and how many have abandoned the transmission of religious knowledge (*'ilm*), claiming that they are resisting the desire of their souls to do so? How many a person has orphaned his children by asceticism while still alive, and how many have turned away from their wives, not fulfilling their obligations to them, leaving them neither single nor women with a master?!"

When it comes to understanding the meaning of Hadith, they must be viewed in relation to the overall principles and rules that the Prophet Muhammad taught. One Hadith is just part of a much larger equation. It can't be understood properly unless it is placed alongside the Qur'an and other relevant Hadith. One finds the seemingly controversial Hadith in which the Prophet says, "I have been commanded to fight the people until they say 'There is no god but God and Muhammad is the messenger of God,' and if they do so then their lives and property are inviolable to me." This seems to say that Muslims should fight all non-Muslims until they convert to Islam. But the Qur'an specifies that followers of existing religions, such as Christians and Jews, can retain their religion even if they lived under Muslim rule. The meaning of this particular Hadith becomes clear when one looks at another translation of it, which reads, "I have been commanded to fight the polytheists until they say 'There is no god but God'," showing that the Prophet was only talking about fighting the polytheistic Arab tribes in Arabia. Beyond those narrow circumstances, a Muslim state can exist in peaceful relations with its neighbors and respect the religious rights of non-Muslim minorities.

Neither the Qur'an nor the collections of Hadith should be picked up and read without some reliable reference that can provide context and explanation. A Qur'anic verse or Hadith read on its own might have a very different meaning than when it's read in the context, of when they were said and its meaning might change entirely when placed in relation to other parts of these sources. Though they operate under the Prophet's banner, Daesh's violent actions violate and stand in direct contrast to the message of the Qur'an and Prophetic traditions.

What is *Shari'ah*?

IMAM FEISAL ABDUL RAUF clarifies many of the misconceptions about *Shari'ah*, a term that has been misappropriated and misused by extremists and others to undermine the basic human rights that it actually guarantees.

KEY TAKEAWAYS

- While the term *Shari'ah* is often equated with a penal code that doles out barbaric punishments, in fact the term refers to God's laws in the Qur'an and the words and actions of the Prophet, both of which prescribe and prohibit incorrect behavior.
- The objectives of Islamic law, called the *maqasid al-shari'ah*, guarantee to all the rights to life, religion, thought, property, family, and dignity.
- Prohibiting American Muslims from following God's commandments, as prescribed in the Qur'an and Hadith of the Prophet Muhammad, violates their First Amendment right to freedom of religion.

INTRODUCTION

Shari'ah or "*Shari'ah* law" as it is commonly referred to in the West, is often misunderstood as a strictly "legal" code that stands in direct opposition to U.S. laws, and is incompatible with human rights and American values. Many point to extreme punishment—such as stoning and cutting off hands—that are enforced in a few countries, as well as specific violent practices directed against Muslim women—such as "honor killings" and female genital mutilation—as evidence of the violence and gender bias inherent in Islam, and thus call for *Shari'ah* to be outlawed and Islam rebuffed.

Yet the vast majority of Muslims understand *Shari'ah* as a broad set of values that helps them distinguish between "ethical or unethical behavior, legitimate or illegitimate governance, appropriate civil and criminal punishments, and protection of human rights."[1] Nevertheless, violent extremists and many who misunderstand Islam remain misguided about what *Shari'ah* is.

To answer these questions we must first understand what *Shari'ah* is (and what it is not), which includes debunking the notion of *Shari'ah* as a set of "laws" that take precedence over the U.S. legal system; and second, explain the ways that American Muslims understand *Shari'ah* as a part of their religious practice and thus part of their right to religious freedom guaranteed to all under the First Amendment of the Constitution.

DEFINITION AND SOURCES OF *SHARI'AH*

Although the word *Shari'ah* is often used interchangeably with "Islamic law," the two are not strictly synonymous. The literal meaning of the word *Shari'ah* in Arabic is "the way to the watering hole," and it is derived from the Arabic word *shar*, meaning "ordinances." Muslims generally understand these ordinances as "God's commandments" or "God's legislation,"[2] which explains why many misleadingly equate the term with "Islamic law." In fact, however, *Shari'ah* refers to 1) the commandments of God in the Qur'an: the 150 to 500 Qur'anic verses; and 2) the commandments of the Prophet Muhammad: the 1,200 to 1,500 *Hadith* (oral reports on behaviors and actions of the Prophet and his companions), all of which prescribe and prohibit behavior.

The other equally important aspect of "Islamic law" is *fiqh* (literally, "understanding"), which refers to the human endeavor to interpret God's injunctions as outlined in the Qur'an and the Hadith. Indeed,

[1] Rauf, Feisal Abdul. *Moving the Mountain: A New Vision of Islam in America*. Free Press, 2012, 50.
[2] Ibid, 51.

a distinction must be made between God's laws (*shari'ah*), and the body of laws *derived* from these divine ordinances (*fiqh al-shari'ah*), the latter of which can more properly be called "Islamic law," and which might be compared to the Jewish halacha.

A distinction must be made between God's laws (*shari'ah*), and the body of laws *derived* from these divine ordinances (*fiqh al-shari'ah*), the latter of which can more properly be called "Islamic law," and which might be compared to the Jewish halacha.

THE DEVELOPMENT OF ISLAMIC LAW

In a manner similar to the development of U.S. laws, all of which must follow the U.S. Constitution, *fiqh al-shari'ah* were developed from the sources of *shari'ah*, that is, the Qur'an and Hadith, in response to changing circumstances, dilemmas, and challenges. Islamic legal scholars derived these rulings from these sources by developing and utilizing various methods of reasoning (*ijtihad*)—including consensus (*'Ijma*) and legal analogy (*Qiyas*)—and legal doctrines, such as juristic preference (*Istihsan*), public interest (*Istislah* or *Maslahah*), reason and logic (*Istidlal* and *Istishab*), and social custom (*'Urf*).[3]

Islamic legal scholars have broadly classified *fiqh al-shari'ah* into two categories: those pertaining to matters of worship and belief (*'ibadat*), and those regulating worldly affairs (*mu'amalat*), such as laws dealing with civil obligations or transactions, including commercial, criminal and administrative law, and family law.[4] Importantly, Islamic law pertaining to worldly affairs is constantly evolving and striving to meet the challenges of the modern world while adhering to a set of principles for the betterment of human life.

Indeed, the vast majority of Muslims understand *Shari'ah* as those injunctions from God that shape their behavior and encompass "religious" rituals and practices (such as marriage and divorce ceremonies, prayers, charitable giving, and food rules). Legislative efforts to "ban" or outlaw *Shari'ah*, some of which have been enacted in scattered jurisdictions throughout the U.S., are based on a distorted understanding of what *Shari'ah* is, and actually infringe upon the religious liberties of patriotic American Muslims. Similar to the manner in which Jews understand halacha as prescribing and defining their ethics and behavior, Muslims see *Shari'ah* as part and parcel of their freedom to worship as they are accustomed.

THE OBJECTIVES OF ISLAMIC LAW

We can equate the development of Islamic law and its variances across cultures to the ways in which individual states within the U.S. understand their right to implement the death penalty for certain crimes.[5] To answer the question about whether each state's implementation of the death penalty violates the constitution, many scholars will point to the Fifth Amendment, the Eighth Amendment, and the Fourteenth Amendment to argue for or against the death penalty. Further, the question of what the framers of the U.S. constitution *intended* plays an important role in those arguments.

Similarly, Islamic legal scholars have argued for centuries over the *objectives* and *intentions* of God as contained in the Qur'an.[6] Muslim scholars unanimously agree that the objective of Islamic law is to help realize the best interests of human beings in this life and the next. From the Qur'an and Hadith, and utilizing the aforementioned legal methods of reasoning and doctrine, scholars have derived six fundamental objectives of *Shari'ah*, or *maqasid al-shari'ah*. These six rights, which are universally acknowledged by all Islamic scholars, and which any Islamic law must protect and promote, are as follows:

1. **Right to life**: includes rights to food, shelter, clothing, healthcare, and personal security and

[3] Baderin, Mashood Adebayo. "Modern Muslim States Between Islamic Law and International Human Rights Law. PhD diss., University of Nottingham School of Law, 2001.
[4] Rauf, *Moving the Mountain*, 52.
[5] Ibid., 68–69.
[6] Ibid, 54.

safety

2. **Right to religion**: includes the free exercise of the religion of one's choice and the prohibition of religious discrimination
3. **Right to mind**: includes the rights to education, to pursue one's talents and psychological well-being, and protection from actions that erode mental capacity and judgment
4. **Right of property**: includes the rights to be free of theft, to own property, and freely pursue wealth and economic security
5. **Right to family**: includes the rights to marriage, children, and family life
6. **Right to dignity**: includes the right to be free of oppression and discrimination, to live in a well-governed society, and not to be enslaved, treated poorly, or cruelly or unusually punished.

Though many Americans would understand these fundamental rights as similar to and in line with those guaranteed to us as Americans and enshrined in the U.S. Constitution, controversy arises when we hear of certain cruel and barbaric practices such as "honor killings," which are perpetuated and justified in the name of *Shari'ah*. Such tragic cases not only violate *Shari'ah*, but also perpetuate false notions about what *Shari'ah* is, leading to general distrust of Muslims and what they believe, and causing many to incorrectly assume that *Shari'ah* and the U.S. Constitution are fundamentally incompatible.

Barbaric practices such as "honor killings," though sometimes carried out extralegally in a few developing countries (and, tragically, here in the U.S.), are absolutely un-Islamic, and patently violate the right to life as specified in the *maqasid al-shari'ah* and the U.S. Constitution. Furthermore, *Shar'iah* does not allow individuals to take the law into their own hands. Daesh's enforcement of barbaric punishments, such as intolerance towards religious minorities, and enslavement of non-Muslim women (to name only a few) violate all of the *maqasid al-shariah*, which guarantee the right to life, religion, mind, property, family, and dignity to all.

While much more needs to be done to stop these barbaric acts that take place because of distorted understandings of *Shari'ah*—both at home and abroad—we must never let our fear of such distorted understandings make us lose sight of the values that make America a free and fair place for all. We must continue to work to separate these distorted interpretations from the true aspects of *Shari'ah* that encompass Muslims' right to freely practice their religion as guaranteed to us all in the U.S. Constitution.

'Daesh claim to enforce *Shari'ah*, their attempts to implement what they mis-name as *Shari'ah* violate all of the *maqasid al-shariah*, which guarantee the right to life, religion, mind, property, family, and dignity to all.'

OBJECTIVES OF ISLAMIC LAW

(MAQASID AL-SHARI'AH)

IMAM FEISAL ABDUL RAUF

LIFE

- Right to life and personal liberty (freedom from arbitrary arrest, torture)
- National security (internal and external)
- Provision of food, shelter, and clothing
- Opportunities for work/employment
- Healthcare; its quality, availability, and affordability
- Protection of environment, including flora and fauna

MIND

- Access to quality education (religious and secular; compulsory child education)
- Free dissemination of knowledge
- Promotion of science, technology, research, and development
- Freedom of speech and expression
- Access to information of government activity
- Promotion of rationality (as opposed to populism, cultism, and superstition), respect for general consensus, and tolerance of differences
- Control of socially undesirable elements such as drugs, narcotics, and intoxicants

RELIGION

- Protection and promotion of the moral and spiritual values of religion
- Facilitation of the realization of "commanding the good and forbidding the evil" in order to promote and protect the moral fabric of society and prevent evil
- Freedom of *ijtihad* (independent legal reasoning) by competent, qualified, and knowledgeable individuals
- Promoting harmony and good relations among followers of all religious beliefs
- Protection of religious freedom for other belief systems
- Prohibition of the desecration of religions and religious symbols

Muslim legal scholars unanimously agree that the overarching objective of Islamic law is to help realize the best interest of human beings in this life and the next. As such, scholars derived the "objectives of *Shari'ah*" (*maqasid al-Shari'ah*): six rights of all human beings that Islamic law should protect and promote. The concepts of *al-adamiyyah* (that we are all children of Adam) and *huquq al-adamiyyin* (the rights of humans) are indigenous *Shari'ah* concepts comparable to "natural rights" and "human rights." According to these principles, people are granted rights and protections by virtue of their humanity rather than their belief in Islam.

PROPERTY / WEALTH

- Protection of the sanctity of private ownership, including intellectual property and trademarks
- Protection of public property
- Integrity and stability of trade and transactions
- Prohibition of trade in unlawful substances and human organs
- Labor rights, fair wages, and equal and fair treatment of domestic and foreign labor
- Control the undesirable elements of unlawful gain, exploitative practices, gambling, and bribery
- Promotion of equity in material well-being and equitable distribution of wealth

HONOR / PERSONAL DIGNITY

- Government protection of personal dignity and reputation against slander/libel ("honor killing" has no purpose in this objective and is a violation of the sanctity of human life)
- Protection of the right to privacy
- Prevention of misuse of public office to slander and dishonor individuals, families, groups, and organizations

FAMILY / LINEAGE

- Promotion of family as a unit in society
- Promotion of family values
- Protection of the institution of marriage with a view toward fulfilling its proper objectives, including procreation, companionship, and sexual gratification
- Protection of clarity of lineage
- Provision of child benefits and special benefits for orphans, elderly, and the disabled
- Education of youth about marriage and gender relationships
- Gender and juvenile justice

This article has been adapted from Imam Feisal Abdul Rauf's acclaimed works, reprinted with permission:

Rauf, Feisal Abdul. *Defining Islamic Statehood: Measuring and Indexing Contemporary Muslim States*. Palgrave Macmillan, 2015.

Rauf, Feisal Abdul. *Moving the Mountain: A New Vision of Islam in America*. Free Press, 2012.

Pluralism: A Foundational Islamic Value

DR. EBOO PATEL makes the case for pluralism and interfaith cooperation in Islam by citing examples from the Qur'an and the Prophet Muhammad. He reminds us of the importance of interpreting the Qur'an in a way that supports and advances morality, while being mindful of historical contexts.

KEY TAKEAWAYS

- The sacred text of Islam has key areas that promote diversity that are viewed as "signs" of God, and therefore as sacred.
- The Islamic tradition is inclusive and understanding of religious pluralism as part of the divine decree.
- Qur'anic verses that speak of interfaith cooperation contain an ethic that is meant to be understood in a universal and eternal way.

In the twelfth century, the Muslim poet Ibn Arabi, wrote:

> *My heart has become capable of every form:*
> *it is a pasture for gazelles and a convent for Christian monks,*
> *and a temple for idols and the pilgrim's Kabah,*
> *and the tables of the Torah and the book of the Qur'an.*
> *I follow the religion of Love: whatever way Love's camels take,*
> *that is my religion and my faith.*

Such starkly different views not only exist within the same book, but actually within the same chapter.

In the twenty-first century, such poetic sentiments may seem lost among the drowning voices of religious extremism. Hindu nationalists, Christian and Jewish Identity preachers, and Muslim totalitarians prey on young people's desire to have a clear identity and make a powerful impact. We see their successes in the headlines of our newspapers every day. For the forces of pluralism to effectively compete with the forces of extremism we need both the energy of young people and sophisticated theological frameworks of cooperation articulated by senior scholars. A theology of interfaith cooperation means interpreting the key sources of a tradition in a way that puts forth a coherent narrative and deep logic that calls for positive relationships with people who orient around religion differently.

My own Muslim theology of interfaith cooperation begins with important stories from the life of the Prophet Muhammad that speak to interfaith cooperation. In fact, the first people to recognize his Prophethood were actually Christian: Bahira, a Christian monk who noticed that Muhammad had the mark of Prophethood on his back as a boy, and Waraqa, who explained to Muhammad and his wife Khadijah that the initial earth-shattering experience Muhammad had on Mount Hira was in fact God's revelation. The person most responsible for protecting the Prophet Muhammad during the early years of Islam, when he and his fellow Muslims were hounded and harassed in Mecca, was a pagan, Abu Talib. Later, when the Prophet emigrated from

EBOO PATEL is the founder and president of Interfaith Youth Core (www.ifyc.org), a Chicago-based international non-profit promoting interfaith cooperation. He was appointed to President Barack Obama's inaugural Advisory Council on Faith-Based Neighborhood Partnerships. Dr. Patel is the author of several books, including *Sacred Ground: Pluralism, Prejudice, and the Promise of America* and his autobiography *Acts of Faith: The Story of an American Muslim, the Struggle for the Soul of a Generation*.

Mecca to Medina, one of his first acts was to create what became known as the Pact of Medina, which united the various religious groups and tribes in that area in an alliance of goodwill and common defense.

There are powerful moments from the classical period in Muslim history that affirm the value of interfaith cooperation, from the Prophet Muhammad inviting a group of Christians to pray in his mosque, to the Caliph Ali writing to his governor in Egypt: "All those there are your brothers in faith or your equals in creation."

There are powerful moments from the classical period in Muslim history that affirm the value of interfaith cooperation, from the Prophet Muhammad inviting a group of Christians to pray in his mosque, to the Caliph Ali writing to his governor in Egypt: "All those there are your brothers in faith or your equals in creation." Many Muslim groups since have followed in this tradition of respecting and protecting non-Muslims. Interestingly, the only country in Europe with a higher Jewish population after the Holocaust was the Muslim-majority country of Albania, because the people made it a part of their public honor to protect Jews during that dark time. Similarly, the Muslims of Rwanda appeared to be the only organized group who protected Tutsis from the machete-wielding Interhamwe militia during the genocide of the 1990s.

Although a theology of interfaith cooperation needs to involve cumulative cultural and historical traditions, it also needs to have an interpretation of sacred scripture that supports and advances such comprehension. For Islamic tradition, the text of the Qur'an is central to any theological discussion and there are key areas that can be interpreted as supportive of diversity. Take, for example, the term "*ayat*," commonly understood as "verse of the Qur'an," but more literally translated as "sign." God gives us his signs in many places—in his revealed scripture, in our relationships with others, in the natural world, and in the culture of the societies in which we live. In this way, the growing diversity of our societies may be viewed as "*ayat*" of God, and therefore something sacred.

In a brilliant essay titled "The Place of Tolerance in Islam," the Islamic scholar Khaled Abou El Fadl accomplishes the task of scriptural interpretation in a particularly audacious way. He lists various verses from the Qur'an that are clearly intolerant toward other religions alongside verses that command positive interfaith relationships and essentially asks: why should we follow one set of verses rather than the other?

The verses in question could not be more different. Here is an example on the intolerant side: "*Fight those among the People of the Book (Jews and Christians) who do not believe in God or the Hereafter, who do not forbid what God and His Prophet have forbidden, and who do not acknowledge the religion of truth—fight them until they pay the poll tax with willing submission and feel themselves subdued*" (9:29). And an example that calls for interfaith cooperation: "*O humankind, God has created you from male and female and made you into diverse nations and tribes so that you may come to know each other. Verily, the most honored of you in the sight of God is he who is the most righteous*" (9:49).

The core value of Islam is mercy.

Such starkly different views not only exist within the same book, but actually within the same chapter. Surah 5, Verse 51 of the Qur'an reads: "*O you who believe, do not take the Jews and Christians as allies. They are allies of each other, and he amongst you who becomes their ally is one of them. Verily, God does not guide the unjust*" (5:51). A few pages later, also in Surah 5, we find this: "*Those who believe, those who follow the Jewish scriptures, the Christians, the Sabians, and any who believe in God and the Final Day, and do good, all shall have their reward with their Lord and they will not come to fear or grief*" (5:69).

Which view is the "correct" one? When it comes to Christians and Jews (and Sabians, whoever they are), what should a conscientious Muslim do? To answer this question, Abou El Fadl puts forth an interpretive way of approaching the Qur'an that essentially has four parts:

1. The first part of the explanation has to do with the historical context of the text. Muslims believe that the Qur'an was revealed over the course of 23 years—years during which the Prophet Muhammad was not only spreading the message of Islam but also building a Muslim society. As in any real-world movement, there were moments of tension and conflict both within the fledgling Muslim community and between Muslims and other groups—Jews, Christians, Sabians, pagans—in the area. According to Muslim belief, God would reveal Qur'anic verses that helped the Prophet Muhammad deal with particular situations—this specific dispute between two people, that group over there causing problems, and so on. Most Muslim scholars agree that the verses from the Qur'an that are intolerant toward other groups are meant to be specific advice for particular times and places, and not meant to be applied broadly. The verses that speak of interfaith cooperation, on the other hand, contain an ethic that is meant to be understood in a universal and eternal way.

2. The second part of the analysis deals with the overall moral thrust of the Qur'an. Abou El Fadl points out that at the center of the Qur'an is a set of "general moral imperatives such as mercy, justice, kindness, or goodness" and that the entire text must be read "in light of the overall moral thrust of the Qur'anic message." Along the same lines, in his essay "Mercy: The Stamp of Creation," Dr. Umar Abd-Allah affirms this view and states that the core value of Islam is mercy. He writes: "Islamic revelation designates the Prophet Muhammad as 'the prophet of mercy,' and Islam's scriptural sources stress that mercy—above other divine attributions—is God's hallmark in creation and constitutes his primary relation to the world from its inception through eternity, in this world and the next." Dr. Abd-Allah highlights what is known as the Tradition of Primacy in Islam, the first lesson that Classical Muslim scholars taught their students: "People who show mercy to others will be shown mercy by the All-Merciful. Be merciful to those on earth, and he who is in heaven will be merciful to you."

3. The third point addresses the individual reader's perspective and emphasizes that morality is not only contained in the text but also in the heart or conscience of the reader. After all, according to Muslim belief, God gave all human beings his breath ('*Ruh*'). People are required to bring this inner morality to their reading of the Qur'an, and their lives in general. As Abou El Fadl writes, "The meaning of the religious text is not fixed simply by the literal meaning of its words, but depends, too, on the moral construction given to it by the reader. The text will morally enrich the reader, but only if the reader will morally enrich the text." This particular view is probably most associated with Fazlur Rahman, one of the twentieth century's most important Muslim scholars. In his book *Major Themes of the Qur'an*, Rahman writes that "*taqwa*," translatable as "inner torch" or "moral conscience," is probably the most important single term in the Qur'an. It is the quality through which people align themselves with God's will.

"*taqwa*" translatable as "inner torch" or "moral conscience," is probably the most important single term in the Qur'an. It is the quality through which people align themselves with God's will.

4. Finally, the contextual environment of the reader is important to the understanding of the Qur'an. Like all texts, the Qur'an emerges in a particular time and place. And like all people, we read it in particular times and places. In interpreting the Qur'an, both the context of the text and the context of the reader have to be taken into account. To support this view, Abou El Fadl gives the following example: "the Qur'an persistently commands Muslims to enjoin the good. . . . Goodness, in the Qur'anic discourse, is part of what one may call a lived reality—it is the product of human experiences and constructed normative understandings." In other words, the Qur'an expects readers to not only approach the text with their God-given *taqwa*, but also with ideas of what is "good" from their own context. For Abou El Fadl, this means that evolving notions in culture and civilization, from progress in science to ideals like universal human rights and the benefits of diversity, ought to be brought to bear when interpreting Islam.

In his essay "Islam and Cultural Imperative," Dr. Umar Abd-Allah reinforces this view. He emphasizes that the genius of Islamic civilization was its ability to integrate its sacred law in various cultural contexts. In fact, he writes, one of the five maxims of Islamic law is to respect cultural usage and sound custom across time and place. Islam is meant to be a tradition that harmonizes with a range of cultures, not sets out to destroy them. To support his point, he quotes from a renowned thirteenth-century Islamic legal scholar, al-Qarafi: "Persons handing down legal judgments while adhering blindly to the texts in their books without regard for the cultural realities of their people are in gross error. They act in contradiction to established legal consensus and are guilty of iniquity and disobedience before God." Blindly following scriptural text without understanding context takes away from the rationality and lived reality present in the life and example set by Muhammad as a Prophet as well as God's words in the Qur'an.

One can understand the Qur'an and the Islamic tradition as a narrow one that compels building bunkers of isolation or barriers of division. On the other hand, as most Muslims do, one can understand the Qur'an and Islamic tradition as one that is inclusive and understanding of religious pluralism as part of the divine decree. Regardless of how the reader interprets the scriptural meaning, the case for religious pluralism and interfaith cooperation, present throughout Islamic history, has long been evidenced.

God Consciousness: Those Who Do Good, Find Good

DR. SULTAN ABDULHAMEED explains how religion and divine revelations serve as a source of good, wisdom, and morality for humankind.

KEY TAKEAWAYS

- People who are conscious of God search for the best meanings; those give insight into wisdom and liberate people from limitations.
- We must be conscious of God and take the initiative of being a source of goodness in the world while training ourselves to overcome our negative tendencies.

And when it is said to those who are conscious of God, "What is it that your Lord has revealed?" They say, "What is good."
For those who do good there is good in this world, but the reward in the hereafter is better still; for how excellent is the abode of the God-conscious! (Qur'an 16:30).

Religion and its impact on humanity have two sides. Religion is acknowledged as a source of good, wisdom, and morality. The majority of people believe in religion and are convinced that their redemption is found through the beliefs they hold. They find inspiration in the scriptures. On the other hand, the history of the world is replete with oppression, cruelty, and other types of evil carried out in the name of religion. People have interpreted scriptures, the revealed Word, to justify abuse of women and children, discrimination against minorities, slavery, economic exploitation, and genocide. In addition, many people who think they are religious oppose science and hold beliefs that are manifestly false and attribute their attitude to revelations. Many make rules of unhappy living, creating misery in their homes in the belief that they are obeying the Word of God.

With the backdrop of this common human weakness, this ayah points out that those who are conscious of God find the goodness that is in revelation. Those who are conscious know that He is benevolent, and His messages are from His grace and mercy. The purpose of revelation is described at the beginning of the Qur'an in Surah 2, Verse 4. It is to guide mankind to *falaah*, that is, success, happiness, peace, and prosperity. It is to help us find all that is good.

We have to learn to be quiet inside in order to open our hearts to revelation.

The second part of the verse says there is a simple formula for finding goodness. Do good and good will come to you here and in the hereafter. It is not very complicated or philosophical. Train yourself to overcome the bad tendencies in yourself. Live conscientiously. Take the initiative of being a source of goodness and you will achieve a happy state. This is worth emphasizing because this central idea escapes most people. They have come to believe that religion is a complex set of rules and arguments that only scholars can understand.

People get confused by revelation because its language is often transcendental. A literal or superficial reading results in meanings that are misleading. It

SULTAN ABDULHAMEED is a professor of atmospheric sciences at Stony Brook University and one of the founders of the Muslim Reform Movement Organization in Brookville, New York. He previously served as the president of the Islamic Center of Long Island, is an instructor on interpretations of the Qur'an in New York City, and is the author of *The Quran and the Life of Excellence.*

takes contemplation and patience to discern the guidance in revelation. There was a context within which events described in the scripture occurred. We want to be aware of the historical and social context before we extrapolate their meanings to the present.

Our emotional histories color our views. The images and sounds that are reverberating through our minds filter what we understand from a text. We have to learn to be quiet inside in order to open our hearts to revelation.

The Prophet Muhammad was neither a scholar nor did he study to have a degree from a religious academy. He learned to be conscious of God through his own search, and he understood the spiritual truths in simple ways that he could apply to raise awareness in himself and in others. He teaches us to do the same.

Some people are misled by revelations because they are invested in the status quo. The current system gives them advantages over others, and they interpret religion to justify the present order.

Some deduce inferior meanings because they derive national or tribal pride from "our religion." They discuss the scripture to find meanings that help them look down on others, or oppress others, or make war on others.

People who are conscious of God search for the best meanings; those that give insight into wisdom and liberate people from limitations. This ayah tells us that people who manifest goodness are the ones who are conscious of God. Do not be misled by special robes or elaborate rituals or other pretenses. Those who have risen above their egos and have become conscious are those who have goodness in their own lives and create goodness for others.

If you misunderstand revelation, you can infer meanings that make you unhappy. You may think you are following the rules of religious life, but you can be miserable and stuck. Many people justify failure in life by saying to themselves, "I may be unhappy now, but I will find the rewards of my prayers in the next world!" This *ayah* contradicts this notion. It says if you do good, you will find good in *this* world. The hereafter is a continuation of the present. So if your life is not working, reexamine your beliefs and change your interpretations.

The second part of this *ayah* teaches the basic law that what we send out into the world comes back to us. So if you want to change your life for the better, then get busy doing good, and inevitably, your life will also be filled with goodness. The word "good" includes everything that makes you or others better; it includes positive thought, speech, and action. It means thinking well of yourself and others; it means speaking well of yourself and others; it includes creating a positive intention within your mind when you do something. It means dropping negative thoughts and speech; it means not to look down on what God has given you in your person, or your experience; it means letting go of anger, jealousy, hopelessness, and self-pity; it means never wishing to harm anyone. This is what we do when we become God-conscious, because we know that what we are thinking is known to God, and He compensates us for everything we think, say, and do.

For those who do good, there is good in this world, but there can be a delay, and it can work in indirect ways. You may be kind and generous toward someone, and he can respond with hostility. This type of experience is common and throws off a lot of people. They say, "I was being good, but it was not returned to me." This formula of goodness for goodness does not work. It is better to hold back and see what others do first. If they act good toward me, then I can take a chance. This is a misunderstanding. The good that you did is a reality; it is guaranteed to bear fruit. It will come to you later, perhaps through other people. The Prophet Muhammad said that the greater the delay, the greater is the reward for you.

Many people become confused about revelations because they borrow the meanings from someone else. They say, I am not learned in religion so let me find an expert. If you try to live through someone else's mind-set, your life becomes complicated and difficult.

The other person did not have the experiences you did. If you wish to understand something and use it, you have to figure it out yourself. You can use wisdom only to the extent you personalize it.

There is another difficulty when we look to others to find meanings. There are many people who can give impressive speeches about things they don't understand. They can talk about it, but don't know how to do it. There are many who have written books about subjects they don't understand. There are people who can dress up to look like authority figures. The only thing that a person really knows is what he or she is able to do. It is the walk you walk and not the talk you talk that matters.

The Prophet Muhammad was neither a scholar nor did he study to have a degree from a religious academy. He learned to be conscious of God through his own search, and he understood the spiritual truths in simple ways that he could apply to raise awareness in himself and in others. He teaches us to do the same.

People who manifest goodness are the ones who are conscious of God.

SECTION 2

The Emergence of Extremist Ideology

"The corruption of religions comes from turning them to mere words and appearances

- Imam al-Ghazali

CHAPTER 5

The Social and Political Landscape of Extremism

The Emergence of Terrorism and Its Consequences

THE SOUFAN GROUP describes how the nature of global terrorism changed dramatically after 9/11 and how the international community has scrambled to combat the new threat. They provide an overarching view of Daesh's growth, propaganda, movement, goals, governance, marketing, and global networking, all of which helped Daesh to coalesce in the shadows of the Syrian civil war in the fall of 2013.

KEY TAKEAWAYS

- Terrorist groups typically have specific territorial objectives and focus their terrorist activity on their perceived occupiers.
- The objectives and ideology of terrorist organizations are defined by the regional, political, and social contexts from which they emerge, and terrorist violence is just one part of the larger phenomenon of violent extremism.
- Violent extremism cannot be effectively prevented and countered with a large-scale solution, but rather countless small-scale approaches, each one devised and operated by the people in the affected community.

The disease of terrorism affects communities around the world, from the United States to Iraq, from France to China. Extremist violence continues to claim thousands of lives every year, while extremist propaganda and indoctrination prey on the frustrations of the disenfranchised. Religiously motivated terrorism has proven to be especially potent over the last decade, with violent extremists carrying out attacks that impact diverse communities across the world. However, in recent decades the majority of terrorist attacks, and the majority of casualties, have occurred in the Middle East and North Africa (MENA) region. Given the current instability and civil conflict in Syria, Iraq, Yemen, and Libya, this trend looks set to continue.

As the vast majority of terror attacks take place in majority-Muslim states, it is not surprising that more than 80percent of terror attack victims are Muslim. Between 2000 and 2013, there were a rough average of 7,600 terrorism-related deaths per year. In 2013 and 2014, however, that number rose to 18,111 and 32,685, respectively—an 80 percent increase. While 60 percent of terrorist incidents occurred in only five countries—Iraq, Afghanistan, Pakistan, Nigeria, and Syria—those countries suffered more than 80 percent of the terror-related deaths. With nearly 10,000 deaths in 2014, Iraq alone was responsible for 30.4 percent of global terror related fatalities. In fact, the ten countries with the highest percentage of terror-related deaths accounted for 88 percent of the global total, with the remaining 182 countries accounting for 12 percent.

While casualty counts are key to identifying terrorism trends, it is important to note that terrorist violence itself is only one component of the larger, complex phenomenon of violent extremism

While casualty counts are key to identifying terrorism trends, it is important to note that terrorist violence itself is only one component of the larger, complex

THE SOUFAN GROUP (TSG) provides strategic security intelligence services to governments and multinational organizations. Founded by Ali Soufan, a former Federal Bureau of Investigation (FBI) Supervisory Special Agent, TSG pioneers new and innovative methods to address some of today's most challenging international issues.

FIGURE 01 DEATHS FROM TERRORISM, **2000-2015**
2015 saw the first reduction in terrorism since 2010, although it was still the second worst year recorded for terrorism.

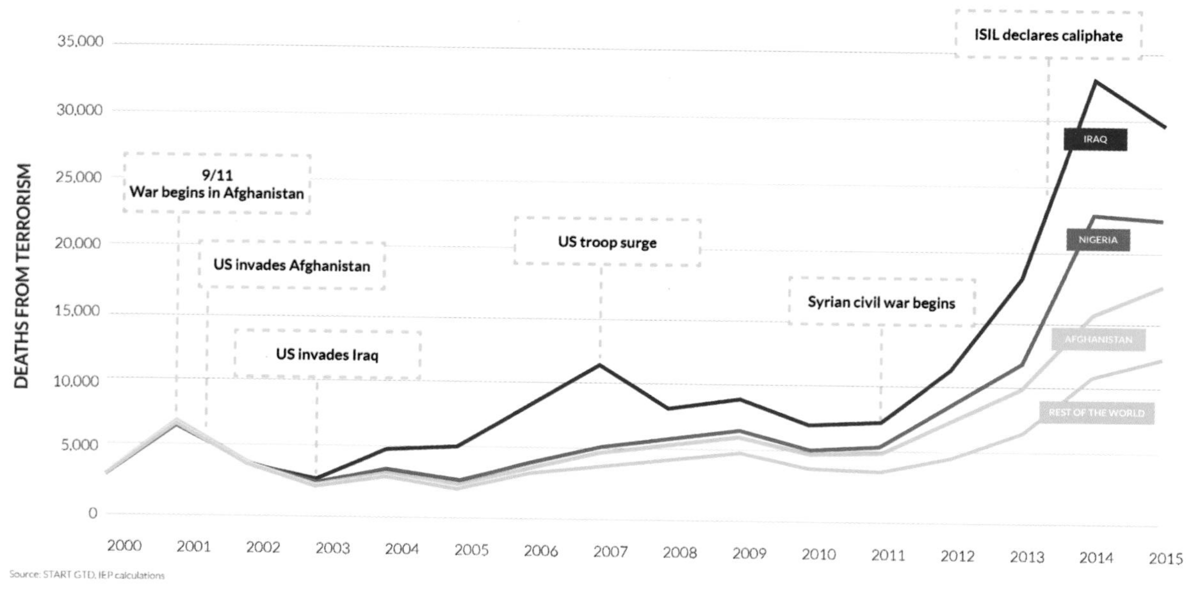

Source: START GTD, IEP calculations

phenomenon of violent extremism. International terrorist groups are large, multifaceted organizations with diverse sets of strategies and motivations. The regional, political, and social contexts in which they emerge serve to define their objectives and ideology, which in turn determines which individuals the groups attract.

The regional, political, and social contexts, in which these large, multifaceted, international terrorist groups emerge serve to define their objectives and ideology, which, in turn, determines which individuals these groups attract.

Many terrorist groups have specific territorial objectives, and focus their terrorist activity on their perceived occupiers. Due to their narrow regional focus, the ranks of these organizations are also primarily composed of local militants. While they certainly pose a tremendous threat to regional actors, they pose less of a threat to the broader international community. The Soviet invasion of Afghanistan, however, ushered in a new era for international terrorism. As the Communist Soviet forces invaded Muslim lands, calls went out throughout the Muslim world for volunteers to beat back the Communist scourge. This call inspired many mujahideen, among them Osama bin Laden, to travel to Afghanistan to help their Muslim brothers liberate their land.

It is within this context that al-Qaeda emerged. A new paradigm had been set for a global jihad, and once the Communists had been driven back, al-Qaeda turned its focus to other occupied Muslim lands. After the Iraqi invasion of Kuwait, and the subsequent deployment of U.S. troops to Saudi soil, the U.S. too drew the ire of the group. Rather than fighting to drive the Western military presence out of Islamic lands, however, bin Laden led al-Qaeda to embrace a new narrative. This ideology of "bin Laden-ism" declared Western hegemony to be an existential threat to the survival of Islam, and therefore concluded that the Western sociopolitical apparatus must be destroyed. Every Western country, and every Westerner, was now a legitimate target for such groups.

FIGURE 02 COUNTRIES WITH THE HIGHEST NUMBER OF DEATHS BY TERRORISM **2014**
2015 saw Niger and Cameroon among the ten countries with the most deaths from terrorism for the first time.

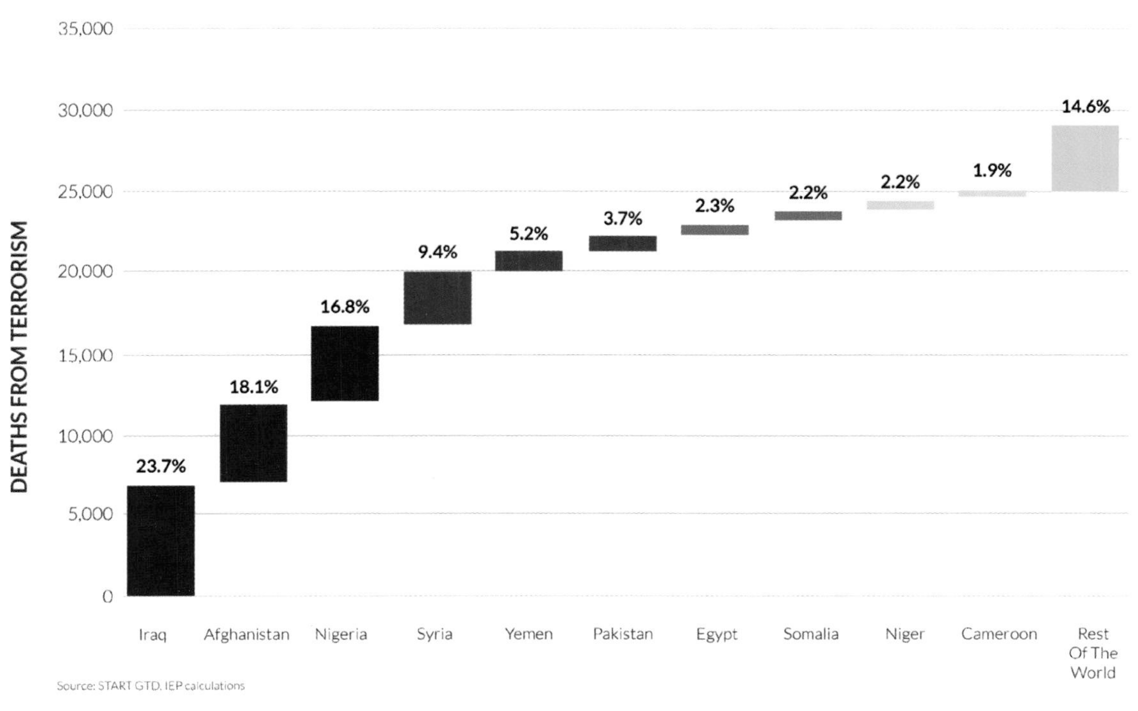

The events of September 11 were the manifestations of that narrative on the global stage. The world watched in horror as nineteen hijackers expressed their twisted interpretation of Islam through the murder of nearly 3,000 civilians. The nature of transnational terrorism fundamentally changed, and the international community was scrambling to counter the new threat. Though there have been many criticisms of military and security policies and their impact on human and civil rights, in many ways, the global war on terror has been successful in achieving its goals. Osama bin Laden is dead and American military operations against al-Qaeda and the Taliban have achieved tactical goals. Despite this, excessive focus on short-term tactical objectives has not achieved the long-term stability that is necessary for sustainable peace. Furthermore, the root factors driving violent extremism, such as political instability and long-standing political conflicts, perceived injustices, alienation, oppressive regimes, and so on, persist in Afghanistan, Iraq, and across the world. As a result, the threat of extremist militancy remains prevalent in the Muslim world.

The rise of Daesh, the acronym for the group's full Arabic name, al-Dawla al-Islamiya fi al-Iraq wa al-Sham, also known as ISIS or ISIL, exemplifies this dynamic. As Daesh coalesced in the shadows of the Syrian civil war in the fall of 2013, it drew strength from the embattled Sunni population that had been dominated by the Alawite Assad regime for decades. When Daesh fighters flooded over the Syrian border into Iraq in June 2014, they again used the sectarian frustrations of the Sunni population of northwestern Iraq to fuel their advance. However, gaining support from the Sunni populations of Iraq and Syria was not enough. Daesh, like al-Qaeda, envisions itself as a global movement for jihad, one that encompasses all Sunni Muslims around the world, as well as embracing the hard-line "bin Laden-ism" ideology.

Daesh, however, is unique in that it claims to actively establish a state under Islamic law, while also actively working to recruit Muslim populations abroad. Though al-Qaeda was given safe haven in Afghanistan, it was the Taliban who governed. In the territories controlled by Daesh, however, the group is responsible for all aspects of governance, from policing to education. This represents a new paradigm for terrorist groups, and one that offers a new level of extremist propaganda.

Excessive focus on short-term tactical objectives has not achieved the long-term stability that is necessary for sustainable peace.

While al-Qaeda has skilled propagandists—particularly those operating as al-Qaeda in the Arabian Peninsula (AQAP)—Daesh propaganda has utilized the Internet in ways that al-Qaeda never has. Each "province" within Daesh-held territory has its own media office, which is directly linked to the local preacher for that province. From the very beginning of the so-called caliphate, these media teams showed their expertise through the production of high-quality, professionally edited videos, magazines, and other media. The impact of this propaganda was vaulted to the global stage when a video of the gruesome execution of American journalist James Foley was posted in August 2014. Several similar execution videos followed, including those showing the beheadings of British, American, and Japanese citizens. In February 2015, the group released a video showing a captured Jordanian pilot being burned alive. The group has also executed countless Iraqis, Syrians, and members of other religious and ethnic groups.

These grisly decapitation videos, though they catch global media attention, are the minority of the productions released by Daesh. The group releases many videos extolling daily life in the "Islamic State," portraying it as a righteous paradise ruled by Islamic law. They show religious police enforcing this law, and portray "Islamic" judges doling out justice. Videos released by the group even show thieves having their hands publicly amputated, while the amputees exalt their righteous punishments. To show the mercy inherent to these harsh judgments, the convicted are immediately treated and put into ambulances. Videos also portray harsher punishments, including the crucifixion of those convicted of murder.

Daesh materials look to appeal to families as well, by encouraging young Muslim women to travel to the territory to become the wives of Daesh fighters. Some 700 women from Tunisia alone have traveled to Syria to join Daesh. The State is portrayed as a land where Muslim families can live in piety and raise children in a truly Islamic society. This has proven to be particularly effective in attracting European Muslims who feel alienated from their nations. Entire families, including those with young children, have traveled from several European countries to live in the Islamic State.

Although attracting Muslim families is a part of Daesh strategy, the majority of its propaganda is targeted at disenfranchised youth around the world. Through its use of advanced media production and online social networks, Daesh is able to distribute its message to anyone with a computer and an Internet connection. In order to reach a more diverse global audience, in 2014 Daesh launched al-Hayat Media, a branch of the propaganda machine aimed specifically at non-Arabic-speaking audiences. These materials are published in numerous languages, including English, Turkish, Russian, German, Dutch, French, Indonesian, Chinese, and even sign language. The multilingual nature of al-Hayat shows that Daesh considers itself more than an Arab movement; instead, it considers itself a global Islamic movement open to all those who pledge fealty to the so-called caliphate.

The root factors driving violent extremism, such as political instability/long-standing political conflicts, perceived injustices, alienation, oppressive regimes, etc., persist in Afghanistan, Iraq, and across the world. As a result, the threat of extremist militancy remains prevalent in the Muslim world

This global networking effort has been extremely effective. While not all who travel to fight the Assad regime support Daesh, estimates show that individuals have traveled to the so-called caliphate from at least

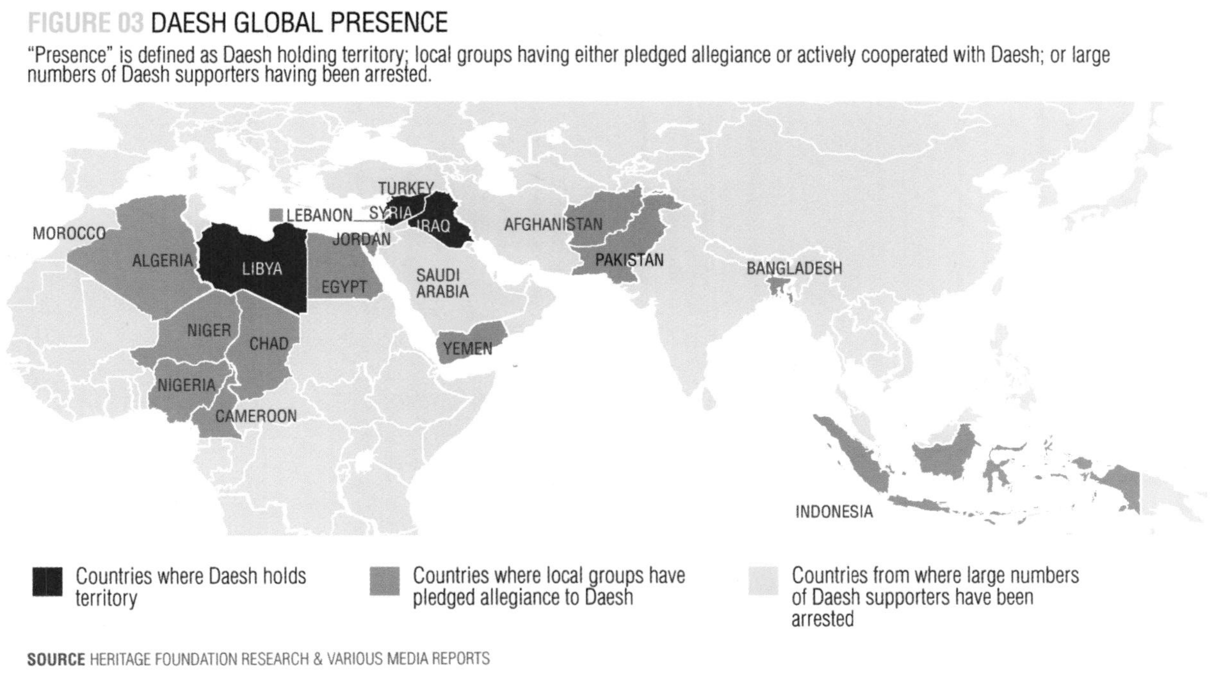

FIGURE 03 DAESH GLOBAL PRESENCE

"Presence" is defined as Daesh holding territory; local groups having either pledged allegiance or actively cooperated with Daesh; or large numbers of Daesh supporters having been arrested.

SOURCE HERITAGE FOUNDATION RESEARCH & VARIOUS MEDIA REPORTS

86 countries, which is unprecedented not only for terror groups, but also for other rebel and separatist movements. The effectiveness of Daesh propaganda is also evident from the support networks that have been built up in countries around the world. These networks, sometimes led by those who have returned from fighting in Syria and Iraq, generally target young, disaffected Muslim men. The Daesh supporters play on the frustrations of these young men and present a life in the Islamic State as an opportunity to fight for a righteous cause. Daesh recruiters have been identified and detained in dozens of countries, including the United States, the UK, France, Tunisia, and Malaysia.

Global efforts to control the flow of foreign recruits to Daesh have had minimal impact. The bulk of foreign fighters come from Arab states, such as Tunisia, Saudi Arabia, and Jordan. Hotbeds of recruitment serve as arenas for Daesh to convince disenfranchised youths to join their group. Centers of recruitment have emerged in the Lisleby district of Fredrikstad in Norway, Derna in Libya, Ben Gardane in Tunisia, and the infamous Molenbeek district of Brussels. In these areas there is less reliance on social media tactics for recruitment and more emphasis on human contact. It is more likely that close-knit groups of susceptible youths reach out to friends, family, or acquaintances with links to Daesh. Some of these youths may join Daesh in a search for belonging, purpose, adventure, and friendship.

Five thousand fighters from Europe—mostly from France (1,800), the United Kingdom (760), Germany (760), and Belgium (470)—have left to fight alongside Daesh. Evidence suggests that frustration with the secular nature of these governments along with the marginalization of the Muslim population has driven most of these foreign fighters to travel to the so-called caliphate. Initially, these fighters traveled to Syria to act as there was little emphasis placed on training to become domestic terrorists. However, the terrorist attacks on November 13, 2015, in Paris, the March 13, 2016, bombings in Ankara, and the March 22, 2016, bombings in Brussels, among many others, indicate this trend has shifted. As more foreign fighters return to their home countries, there is an increased risk they may perpetrate domestic attacks.

There has also been an increase in the number of foreign fighters from Russia and the former Soviet republics (approximately 4,700 have traveled to the so-called caliphate). The involvement of Russia in the Syrian civil war could serve as an explanation for this increase.

FOREIGN FIGHTERS BY COUNTRY[1]

Country	Number	Country	Number
Tunisia	6,000	China	300
Saudi Arabia	2,500	Kazakhstan	300
Russia	2,400	Sweden	300
Turkey	2,000 – 2,200	United States	250+
Jordan	> 2,000	Kosovo	232
France	1,700	Netherlands	220
Morocco	1,200	Maldives	200
Lebanon	900	Algeria	170
Germany	760	Macedonia	146
United Kingdom	760	Canada	130
Indonesia	700	Spain	133
Egypt	600+	Denmark	125
Libya	600	Australia	120
Belgium	470	Azerbaijan	104+
Tajikistan	386	Malaysia	100
Bosnia	330	Philippines	100
Austria	300		

The number of foreign fighters from the Americas has remained flat and relatively low in per capita terms. An estimated 250 Americans have traveled or attempted to travel to Syria with around 150 successfully doing so. In addition, there exist no hotbeds of recruitment or patterns of locally based recruitment. Instead, Daesh has relied on online recruitment and propaganda to reach potential recruits in the Americas. Though peer-to-peer recruitment networks pose a significant threat, Daesh's online recruitment and propaganda network poses perhaps an even more significant risk, especially for youth. The massive online presence of Daesh allows for their members and supporters to actively promote the extremist narrative 24/7. The dispersed nature

[1]Numbers reflected in this chart are as of December 2015. Pakistan, India, and Afghanistan are not included in the chart as the official count of foreign fighters joining Daesh from each is lower than 100. To see the full report, visit www.http://soufangroup.com/wp-content/uploads/2015/12/TSG_ForeignFightersUpdate3.pdf

of these networks also makes disruption much more difficult, with new recruitment strategies operating on a very micro level. The online propagandists have developed strategies for profiling vulnerable individuals and targeting these individuals based on their own specific frustrations. The most vulnerable population is, again, young Muslim men, especially those living in Europe and the United States; studies indicate that those who are less grounded in their religious traditions are more at risk. Though these men are often second- or third-generation immigrants from Muslim-majority nations, the increase in Islamophobia in the West helps to exacerbate alienation from their national identities. Daesh recruiters actively encourage this disassociation, and provide tailored anecdotes of other European and American Muslims who have traveled to the so-called caliphate.

Interestingly, these online recruiters do not only target vulnerable Muslim populations. Using the same profiling techniques used for young Muslims, the recruiters identify disaffected and socially isolated young people—both male and female—and work collectively to provide these vulnerable individuals with a sense of community and purpose. Communicating primarily through Twitter and Facebook, recruiters provide an outlet for frustration, and will sometimes communicate with targeted individuals for hours every day. The recruiters extoll the virtues of Islam, and provide access to materials promoting their extreme interpretation of its teachings. Through contact with the recruiters, targeted individuals are offered a sense of community, which serves to further draw them into the extremist narrative.

The scale of Daesh's propaganda and recruitment mechanisms is unprecedented. The extremist and expansionist characteristics of Daesh's ideology make it a complex and ever-evolving threat to global security. Combating Daesh's militants on the ground is a familiar task, but combating their expansive propaganda machine is not. Though governments are establishing Preventing/Countering Violent Extremism (P/CVE) programs around the world, developing effective strategies for combating extremist ideology is extremely difficult, especially when it is being strategically distributed on such a large scale. Vulnerable youth populations, both Muslim and non-Muslim, will continue to be at risk unless government and civil society partnership programs can identify and address the root causes of their alienation from society.

The root factors driving violent extremism. Combating Daesh's militants on the ground is a familiar task, but combating their expansive propaganda machine is not. . . . Vulnerable youth populations, both Muslim and non-Muslim, will continue to be at risk unless government and civil society partnership programs can identify and address the root causes of their alienation from society.

As noted above, the issue of a spreading violent extremism is a large-scale challenge, yet one that absolutely and consistently defies a large-scale solution. Rather, effectively preventing and countering violent extremism requires countless small-scale approaches, each one devised and operated by the people in the affected community. This reality, that there is no one approach or program that will work across the board, frustrates governments and large organizations that, despite the best of intentions, are not seeing the best of results in their P/CVE programs. There is an unavoidable friction between governments that want to address the large-scale issue through intelligence and law enforcement, and the impacted communities that are dealing with violent extremism on an intensely personal and individual level. The causes of extremism are as unique as the individuals who are susceptible to its toxic allure; this fact forces a true grassroots approach that is supported but not developed or run by governments. The challenge for all is how to leverage the resources of government and the creativity of community.

How Terrorists Think

DR. FATHALI MOGHADDAM delineates the conditions that give birth to terrorism, arguing that it is critical to understand that terrorism, or violent political action, is not exclusive to Muslim populations.

KEY TAKEAWAYS

- The events of the twentieth century in the Middle East led to a regional identity crisis and caused some to see violence as the only way to change their situation.
- Terrorism is the result of unmet expectations and frustrations among people in the Middle East, stemming from the game of musical chairs that involved local puppet governments propped up by foreign powers with the interests of Western nations in mind.
- The West should gently guide the Muslim world to its desired destination, which is to have the right of self-determination and the ability to achieve prosperity.

In recent years, why is it that some individuals have resorted to terrorism as the only means to fight what they perceive to be injustice? Are these people pathological? Are they illiterate? Ignorant? Do they have abnormal personalities? Are they economically deprived? These questions, however, do not probe the real reason why terrorism has become a global phenomenon. The real reason lies in a complex crisis of identity being experienced by many individuals in the Near and Middle East. It is a profound and historic identity crisis, one tragic manifestation of which is terrorism. But to the terrorists, terrorism is not the beginning of their story: it is the conclusion to a story decades in the making. Thus, to understand and avert this destructive trend, we must come to grips with the monumental crisis of identity that is fueling terrorism—we must set out to understand the conditions that give birth to terrorism.

In the context of my investigation, the term "terrorism" refers to politically motivated violence, perpetrated by individuals, groups, or state-sponsored agents, intended to bring about feelings of terror and helplessness in a civilian population in order to influence decision making and change behavior. But before we can begin any investigation of this sort, it is critical to address three fundamental points. First, to see and try to understand the world from the terrorists' point of view does not mean you condone terrorism. Second, I completely reject the view that "the term 'terrorist' is meaningless because one person's terrorist is another person's freedom fighter." In my view, if it walks like a terrorist, shoots like a terrorist, and explodes bombs like a terrorist, then it is a terrorist.

Finally, and most importantly, it is crucial to understand that terrorism, or violent political action, is not exclusively linked to Muslims. Take, for example, the Irish Republican Army (IRA), or the Basque separatist group Euskadi Ta Askatasuna (ETA), or the Sri Lankan Tamil Tigers, or the Columbian Revolutionary Armed Forces of Colombia (FARC). Each of these groups has relied on the same violent tactics and methods to achieve their goals. Each group, particularly in underdeveloped nations, professes to be the true representative of the downtrodden and neglected. Their activities are broad and framed as humanitarian, claiming only to use violent means against an oppressive enemy as a means to liberate local populations.

DR. FATHALI MOGHADDAM is a professor of psychology, conflict resolution, and government at Georgetown University and serves as the director for the university's Interdisciplinary Program in Cognitive Science. He has written extensively on intergroup relations and conflict, human rights, and on issues related to the psychology of global politics, terrorism, and violent extremists. Dr. Moghaddam has served as the editor of *Peace and Conflict: Journal of Peace Psychology* since 2013.

Groups such as al-Qaeda and Daesh are no different. They see themselves on a violent quest to free the Muslim world from the grasp of Western powers that have deprived the Near and Middle East of its natural resources and chances for a prosperous future. To position themselves as the saviors of the downtrodden Muslim world, they distort Islamic teachings to justify using any and every means to achieve their ultimate goal. To understand the terrorists' point of view and find an effective means to end terrorism, we must turn to Relative Deprivation Theory.

However, the greatest player in this century-long game of chess is neither a foreign power nor a despotic ruler—it is oil.

According to Relative Deprivation Theory, terrorism is the outcome of rising, unmet expectations, and increasing frustrations among millions of young people in the Near and Middle East who feel as though they have no voice, no hope, and no possibility for a brighter future as things stand. These feelings have been exacerbated by globalization, where improved communications have exposed them to images of the young in other nations who have the opportunity to live a fulfilled and prosperous life. They see how life could be—the rich educational opportunities, the consumer goods, and social and political freedoms—but in their own societies, they see no such opportunity to achieve a similar life. Instead, their lives and identities have been shaped by stagnation, revolutions, wars, mass migration, and vast social, political, and economic transformations over the twentieth century. Thus, to fully understand the magnitude of what these individuals are experiencing, we must go back and reflect on the events of the twentieth century that have shaped the Near and Middle East now and for decades to come.

The twentieth century was defined by disappointment for Muslims in both the Near and Middle East. At the start of the century, the decline of the Ottoman Empire and World War I created opportunities for its victors, namely Great Britain, France, and Russia, to extend their power and influence in traditionally Muslim lands. Territories that were historically controlled by the Ottomans quickly fell under the control of Western powers. Great Britain controlled what is modern-day Iraq, Egypt, and Palestine; the French took control of Lebanon and Syria. Both Great Britain and France directed maneuvers to create local puppet governments in a game of musical chairs in which chairs were replaced by thrones. Unfortunately, those with control over the music were not the local populations who inhabited the land. Rather, foreign powers were hand-selecting individuals who they felt would best represent and protect the interests of the Western nations—not the interests of the local masses.

For instance, in the wake of World War I, Great Britain and France helped shape the modern Middle-East by assisting the House of Saud in gaining control of Islam's holiest city, Mecca, and establishing Saudi Arabia; installing Faisal as King of Iraq, a country he had never before visited; and helping Reza Khan become the first Shah of Iran. Although the post-war period brought a wave of hope for political reform, foreign powers continued to meddle in local affairs and install despotic rulers to wield influence in the region. For the citizens on the ground, the effects were devastating—they were left without any political voice, political representation, or political power. They were nothing more than pawns in the West's game of chess.

They believe that terrorism is a rational problem-solving strategy to change the conditions in their lives.

However, the greatest player in this century-long game of chess is neither a foreign power nor a despotic ruler—it is oil. From the very first discovery of oil in 1908, followed by oil reserves of fantastic magnitudes, local populations in the Near and Middle East were given a glimmer of hope for achieving a better, more prosperous life. Because they had one of the most precious and essential natural resources—and the fantastic sums of money that come with that—the local populations geared up for the opportunities ahead. But these feelings were short-lived. Local populations quickly learned that the local elites were the only ones who would be reaping its benefit. Soon after, U.S. oil companies replaced Britain and France as the main players in the Middle East thanks to an agreement between President Franklin Roosevelt and then King of Saudi Arabia, Abdul Aziz, in 1945.

The two examples above reflect what I like to call "bear and porcupine foreign policies." The bear and the porcupine analogy represents the two extremes of the policies world powers use to influence the affairs of other nations. On the one extreme, "bear policies" wrap weaker nations in a powerful bear hug, causing the indigenous identity of the weaker nation to become invisible. Try as they might, the weaker nations are unable to escape the suffocating grasp of the bear. But the bear does not understand why any nation would resist its all-powerful embrace, so it tightens the grip even more. However, with bear policies, it is almost inevitable that the weaker nation will become unhappy with the bear and begin to blame the bear for everything that is wrong in the world. After all, when you are suffocated by the grip of a huge bear, what else can you see?

Historically, the United States has pursued a bear policy with countries such as Saudi Arabia, Egypt, and Pakistan. But with countries such as Iran and Syria, the United States pursues the other extreme: porcupine policies. Rather than squeezing a weaker nation in a tight embrace, porcupine policies poke and prod smaller nations while maintaining a safe distance. The porcupine will isolate the country to such an extent that it is unable to develop through contact with others, either through trade embargoes or diplomatic exclusion. When a country tries to emerge from isolation, hundreds of formidable sharp quills force it back into solitary confinement. Not surprisingly, the isolated nations will become bitter and potentially aggressive toward the porcupine. Porcupine policies create incubators for despotic and aggressive dictators.

A prime example of this may be found in the case of Mohammad Mossadegh, the democratically elected Prime Minister of Iran from 1951 to 1953. Mossadegh represented Iranians frustrated by the secretive manner in which Iranian oil was handled by the Anglo-Iranian Oil Company. To respond and represent the needs of his people, Mossadegh nationalized the assets of the company—a move that angered the British and American oil elites and led to a successful plot to overthrow his government. The results of this incident are not lost to history either. Mossadegh's subsequent assassination allowed the West to consolidate power and replace the democratically elected prime minister with the despotic shah and a monarchy with a gruesome record of human rights abuses.

Today, over sixty years later, the conditions of the twenty-first-century Near and Middle East have yet to provide the opportunities for the masses to achieve the lives they desire. This can be attributed to a myriad of factors. For starters, these societies have a long history of eliminating any and every form of political opposition from the public sphere. Moreover, the rise of social media and communication technologies act as constant reminders to the young in this region of how their lives could be if only they could change their circumstances. To make matters worse, the 24-hour international media's generalization of Muslims as a deprived, unfairly treated group, who only exist as pawns in a foreign game of chess, has manifested itself into a deep-seated crisis of identity.

> Daesh has even stated that one of its goals is to "break the barriers" put in place by the 1916 Sykes-Picot Agreement—a "secret" agreement between Britain and France that partitioned former Ottoman lands and shaped the Middle East for years to come.

Unfortunately, a small portion of the local populations have responded to this deep-seated frustration by adopting extremist ideology, some even going as far as to carry out acts of violence and terror against innocent populations. They believe that terrorism is a rational problem-solving strategy to change the conditions in their lives, and the conditions for the downtrodden Muslim world. We are experiencing the manifestation of this violent ideology today, as Daesh continues to grow and wreak havoc in a violent quest to restore the golden age of Islam and free the Muslim world from external, "Western," constraints. Daesh has even stated that one of its goals is to "break the barriers" put in place by the 1916 Sykes-Picot Agreement—a "secret" agreement between Britain and France that partitioned former Ottoman lands and shaped the Middle East for years to come.

And from the terrorists' point of view, there can be no peace without justice—justice as defined by them, of course. This mind-set manifests itself in what I have called "terrorists' myths." It is a belief system that allows the terrorists to justify violence to themselves and to others. The internal logic of the terrorists' myths is centered on the functions served by acts of terror. These include: 1) to demonstrate that local state authorities are weak and vulnerable, so as to prove that those authorities are unable to control events; 2) to lower domestic loyalty to state institutions; 3) to create a sense of instability and lawlessness on which terror groups thrive; 4) to create a sense of helplessness among local populations; 5) to demonstrate the power of the terrorist group; 6) to give the impression that terrorist attacks will continue until "final victory"; and 7) to support the illusion that innocent victims have died for a "good cause."

It is in these larger sociohistorical tensions and paradoxes that we can begin to understand the world from the terrorists' point of view, because as it stands today, the world of the Middle East exists in great turmoil. The medical doctor, street vendor, homemaker, school teacher, widower, student, villager, schoolgirl, farmer, journalist, preacher, and singer... tens of millions of people live in the Near and Far East and are utterly discontented their identities, societies, and with their own personal situations.

In some instances, individuals are motivated to change these conditions the only way they have been told will be effective—violence.

To move forward, it is crucial for policy-makers and Western leaders to investigate, understand, and to ultimately change the conditions that give birth to the terrorists' point of view. To do so, it is crucial for them to acknowledge the limits of their ability to implement change. The West can no longer be the "bear" and force its vision of society onto others, nor can it be the "porcupine" that pokes and prods others into submission. Ultimately, both choices will only lead to failure and instability. Instead, the West should pursue the role of a shepherd and gently guide the Muslim world to its desired destination. As Americans, we must recognize that all Muslims desire the same rights that we enjoy: self-determination and the ability to achieve a fulfilled, prosperous life.

This essay has been excerpted and modified from Fathali M. Moghaddam's acclaimed work, reprinted with permission:
Moghaddam, Fathali M. *From the Terrorists' Point of View: What They Experience and Why They Come to Destroy*. Westport, CT Praeger Security International, 2006.

What is ISIS/ISIL/Daesh?

DR. ROHAN GUNARATNA traces the genesis of Daesh from Abu Musab al-Zarqawi and Osama bin Laden to today.

KEY TAKEAWAYS

- Daesh emerged by harnessing the sectarian conflict in Iraq and the instability in Syria following the Arab Spring.
- Daesh is a politically motivated group seeking to change the global system through violent means.
- When it comes to recruitment, Daesh selectively exploits Islamic terms, attire, and symbols, and although it calls itself an Islamic State, it is neither Islamic nor a state.

Daesh, the Arabic acronym for "Islamic State of Iraq and Syria" or ISIS, is a politically motivated group seeking to change the international system through violence. Located in Syria and Iraq, Daesh emerged by harnessing the sectarian conflict in Iraq and the instability in Syria following the Arab Spring. Although Daesh changed its name to "Islamic State" (IS), governments and their partners confronting the group refer to it as ISIL (Islamic State of Iraq and the Levant) or by its Arabic acronym "Daesh" (al-Dawla al-Islamiya al-Iraq al-Sham).

To reach out to and recruit Muslims, especially youth, Daesh selectively exploits Islamic terms, attire, and symbols. Although it calls itself an Islamic State, Daesh is neither Islamic nor a state. The Daesh military core consists of Iraqi Islamists and Ba'athists whose messaging and propaganda is influenced by Western popular culture. Daesh's killings, including beheadings and mass executions, and brutal practices such as slavery, destruction of heritage sites, and persecuting Shi'a and Christians, have earned it notoriety.

With its core in Iraq and Syria, Daesh declared an "Islamic caliphate" in June 2014. Referring to Abu Bakr al-Baghdadi as the "caliph," Daesh said: "It is incumbent upon all Muslims to pledge allegiance to (him) and support him. . . . The legality of all emirates, groups, states, and organizations, becomes null by the expansion of the khalifah's authority and arrival of its troops to their areas." Although Muslim scholars worldwide have denounced Daesh's proclamation, the group has resonance among like-minded followers fighting governments for decades. By inviting local threat groups to pledge their allegiance to leader Abu Bakr al-Baghdadi, Daesh has expanded and claimed territory in parts of the Middle East, Africa, the Caucasus, and Asia.

The acronym for ISIS in Arabic is Daesh (al-Dawla al-Islamiya al-Iraq al-Sham). Daesh hates the use of the Arabic word "Daesh," as it means "one who crushes something underfoot" and is translated as "one who sows discord."

THE GENESIS OF THE SO-CALLED ISLAMIC STATE

Daesh can be traced back to Abu Musab al-Zarqawi, a Jordanian criminal. Radicalized by a Jordanian Palestinian ideologue, Abu Muhammad al-Maqdisi,

DR. ROHAN GUNARATNA is Professor of Security Studies at the S. Rajaratnam School of International Studies, Singapore. He was the convener of the East Asian Summit on Religious Rehabilitation and Social Integration, Singapore, 2015.

in prison, he joined Bay'at al-Imam and subsequently created his own group, Jama'at al-Tawhid wal-Jihad, in 1999. With support from Osama bin Laden's al-Qaeda, Abu Musab created and operated Jund al-Sham at the Al-Matar Camp in Afghanistan, where he trained recruits from the Levant. After the U.S.-led coalition intervention in Afghanistan, Abu Musab relocated to northern Iraq in 2002 where he worked with Ansar al-Islam to expand his network.

After the U.S.-led coalition intervention in Iraq in 2003, Abu Musab changed the name of his group from Jama'at al-Tawhid wal-Jihad to Tanzim Qaidat al-Jihad fi Bilad al-Rafidayn (TQJBR) after pledging allegiance to Osama bin Laden in 2004. Abu Musab's group, commonly known as al-Qaeda in Iraq (AQI), followed the advice of al-Qaeda's then deputy leader, Ayman al-Zawahiri, given in a letter in July 2005 to 1) expel U.S. forces from Iraq, 2) establish an Islamic authority in Iraq, 3) expand the fight to secular countries neighboring Iraq (notably Jordan and Syria), and 4) fight Israel. Abu Musab worked with his successor, Abu Omar al-Baghdadi, to invite Iraqi groups to create a Mujahideen Shura Council (MSC) in 2006, which eventually evolved into the Islamic State of Iraq (ISI). After ISI expanded into parts of Syria in 2013, the group named itself the Islamic State of Iraq and Syria (ISIS). The acronym for ISIS in Arabic is Daesh (al-Dawla al-Islamiya al-Iraq al-Sham). Daesh hates the use of the Arabic word "Daesh," as it means "one who crushes something underfoot" and is translated as "one who sows discord."

FOUNDATIONS OF DAESH'S IDEOLOGY

RRG AND WISE

US VERSUS THEM

They label anyone, including Muslims of different traditions/sects, non-Muslims, and secular states, as "infidels" to justify their actions and hatred.

MAINTAINING PURITY

They consider themselves "special" and an exclusive "saved sect" (al-Firqah al-Najiya). Only their way of life is acceptable. To remain "untainted" they must cut off ties with the West and all those who do not share their beliefs and ideas.

NEO-INTERPRETATION OF SCRIPTURE

They abandon the historical context in which the Qur'an and Hadith were revealed and use scriptures selectively. They fail to use the accepted methods of interpreting sacred texts and commentaries, which leads them to draw absurd and illogical conclusions.

REWRITING HISTORY

They disregard centuries of accomplishments and the heritage of Islamic civilizations, for example, the massive body of jurisprudence, theology, ethics, and morality, while works of recognized scholars and jurists are deemed "faulty."

ANTI-WESTERN SENTIMENTS

They trace all evil back to the "West" and its residents. The West is seen not only as the perpetrator of all oppression but as the perpetual wager of war against Islam.

PESSIMISM ABOUT THE STATE OF THE WORLD

Their view of the current state of the world is extremely negative. They feel a sense of urgency about ending Muslim suffering around the globe, and view themselves as the saviors of the downtrodden.

REJECTIONIST AND FANATICAL

Their obsessive mind-set prevents them from tolerating other views and opinions and they reject groups who achieve change proactively and peacefully. They are convinced that only through violent revolution and radical means will their goals be achieved.

APOCALYPTIC NARRATIVE

They believe that the End of Time is coming and they focus on the afterlife over the present. They believe they are God's specially appointed and divinely aided party (*al-Ta'ifah al-Mansurah*) charged with waging war and fulfilling the prophecies regarding the ultimate battle between good and evil.

REVIVE CALIPHATE TO GAIN LEGITIMACY

Establishing a caliphate will create a land of God's chosen people. They prioritize the creation of a political state over living an upright life, giving charity, respecting people of other beliefs, doing good deeds, and other divine commandments. They regard these as "minor" issues compared to meeting their political ends.

Daesh Brand Narrative

Kittens (Sometimes next to weapons)

Is meant to appeal to young women who are thought to love kittens.

Happy Selfies Posted on Twitter and Facebook

It is a way of showing that life in the Caliphate is normal and fun.

Images of Harsh Punishment

This is meant to show that they are maintaining justice, law, and order by punishing criminals.

Males: Soldiers, renegades, lone heroes

This is to assure men that they will experience masculinity, heroism, and valor.

Females: Domestic bliss, badass soldier chicks

Showing women in burqas standing in front of cars shows that this atmosphere is very family-friendly and women are empowered and valued.

Lions, Cubs

This image signifies that they are all-powerful "kings of the jungle" who know how to safeguard their territory. Their children are their cubs whom they will bring up as a whole new generation.

Social and Health Services

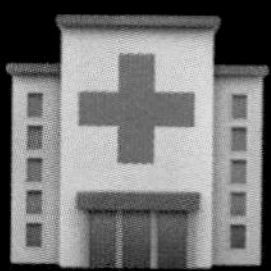

This is meant to show that they care and are capable of running a state.

Images of Dead Bodies

This is to honor the martyrdom of those who have died in the battlefield with close-up shots of their faces with halos.

Daesh Messaging Content

Religious Instructions

Will instruct soldiers on how to stay spiritually engaged. "Prayer, prayer O soldiers of Allah. For indeed, it strengthens the heart, energizes the limbs, and prevents immorality and bad conduct."

Conversations About Doctrine

Will provide unsolicited advice even if it is wrong. For example, "if you are pregnant and healthy and your baby is healthy you can't make excuses not to fast."

Hollywood-style videos, glossy magazines

They produce slick, modern, culturally and technologically savvy magazines and vidoes to show that they are trendsetters.

Trendy Hashtag and Marketing Lists

They use sophisticated marketing tools to grab people's attention, such as hashtags on Twitter, and trendy lists, such as "Top 10 Reasons to Join the Caliphate."

Interpersonal Communications

Discussions about random things like movies are meant to normalize life in the Caliphate. "Shame. I liked *Jumanji*. Good movie. Loved it as a kid."

Publicly Pronouncing Threats Against the West

This is to incite fear and to show that they are more powerful than they are. "#AmessagefromISIStoUS We are in your state We are in your Cities We are in your streets You are our goals anywhere."

Self-Publishing Reports of Battle Victories

Reports convey their victories. "Inghimasi Operation on a Restaurant by Five Mujahidin with Light Weapons, Grenades, and Knives Leaves 22 Crusaders Killed and More than 50 Injured."

Inspirational Speeches Delivered for Recruitment

Communicate with people to inspire them to join the movement and to be part of shaping history. "So let the world know that we are living today in a new era" (Abu Bakr Al Baghdadi).

Daesh Branding

Daesh uses sophisticated marketing strategies, with well-developed brand narrative and messaging to attract recruits from around the globe. The group conveys its brand promise by articulating who they are, what they do, and why their issues matter. They portray themselves as driven, bold, and courageous, underdogs like David willing to take on Goliath.

According to a *Wired* article by Brendan I. Koerner, Daesh has succeeded wildly in propagating such an image, largely due to its embrace of social media. That, coupled with its willingness to connect with people with whom it has no real ties, has allowed Daesh's brand to infiltrate society to an unprecedented degree, which in itself has become a pillar of its brand, instilling fear among people struggling to demystify the power of social media and how to control it.

Daesh's use of social media is part of its message, which is particularly targeted at young Millennials. Materials and ideas are reinforced largely due to their ability to be shared across platforms, and given the metaphysical nature of this message, it can be difficult to break down and recognize the various components of their overall brand narrative. Following is a deconstruction of Daesh's brand, how it is projected to sustain its power, aimed at instilling fear in its enemies and inspiring younger individuals to join its movement.

Target Audience
Worldwide

- Active members
- Recruiters
- Disseminators
- Potential Recruits
- Supporters
- Sympathizers
- Opponents
- Western media

Brand Narratives
Fall under six categories

- Utopia
- Belonging
- Victimhood
- Mercy
- War
- Brutality

Brand Messaging

- They are capable of governing a state
- They care about the welfare of Muslims
- It is a religious duty of every Muslim to restore the Caliphate

Repetiion
Sharing is the heartbeat of the online experience

- There are estimated 90,000 tweets and other Daesh-related transmissions per day online
- The average Daesh supporting account has approximately 1,000 followers

---

Winter, Charlie. The Virtual 'Caliphate': Understanding Islamic State's Propaganda Strategy. Quilliam, July 2015.

Other Tactics

1. **Hashtag hijacking**—Daesh activists will use a popular trending hashtag as a means of infiltrating conversations by adding that hashtag onto one of their unrelated tweets.

2. **Personal account exploitation**—Daesh created its own app, called "The Dawn of Global Tidings" or just "Dawn." When users sign up they give Daesh permission to post tweets through their own personal accounts. This enables Daesh tweets to reach hundreds or thousands more accounts.

3. **Bot armies**—Daesh uses networks of computers it has infiltrated to carry out its campaigns via remote control, making its own computers harder to identify. The group is always one step ahead as they use bots to continually regenerate accounts.

4. **Western trend manipulation**—Daesh distributes propaganda specifically designed to target a Western audience, for instance, using the #worldcup2014 hashtags for the purposes of recruitment or inciting fear.

5. **Education**—The Dawn app is used as an educational tool, distributing news and information about Daesh to its users. Daesh also educates its social media followers on how to access information that has been blocked by governments and social media sites.

Why Do People Join Daesh?

RRG and **WISE**: There is no one single factor that motivates individuals to join Daesh. In fact, the following chart underscores the many multifaceted and context-driven motivations to join—which can be socioeconomic, psychological, spiritual, or political—that are uniquely tailored to the potential recruit's personal circumstances, background, and vulnerabilities. The pull factors are designed by Daesh as propaganda to provide a solution to the individual's discontent.

PUSH FACTORS THE DISCONTENT	PULL FACTORS THE SIREN SON
SEEKING A SPIRITUAL PATH	**CLAIM TO BE THE "ONE TRUE ISLAM"**
Discontented in an increasingly secularized world, some people seek more than material fulfillment, and actively search for spiritual meaning.	Promises the recruit that joining will make them a better Muslim, and that Daesh's ideological underpinnings will fulfill their desire for the "ultimate truth."
BLEAK FUTURE OUTLOOK	**CHANCE FOR PROSPERITY**
Faced with bleak economic opportunities and the prospect of not being able to provide for themselves or their families, potential recruits feel a sense of uncertainty when it comes to being able to lead a dignified life.	Portrays the caliphate as a land of promise and economic opportunity. Every person's role is deemed important and indispensable to the state-building operation, and in turn, each person can lead a life of prosperity.
SUFFERING AND INJUSTICES IN THE MUSLIM WORLD	**BRINGS JUSTICE AND HONOR BACK TO ISLAM**
Many young Muslims are motivated to redress the injustices faced by Muslims elsewhere who are suffering because of longstanding and enduring conflicts, such as those in Syria, Iraq, Palestine, Afghanistan, Kashmir, and Chechnya.	Channels frustration by providing a solution to avenge the plight of Muslims and by offering each member a chance to fight on behalf of disenfranchised Muslim populations.

US AGAINST THE REST OF THE WORLD	**OFFERS EMPOWERMENT THROUGH SUCCESSFUL RESISTANCE**
Historical grievances resulting from past colonialization feed into feelings that the West is out to destroy Islam, and they blame Christians and Jews ("Crusaders") for all their past and current afflictions.	Muslims must reassert their glorious past. Provides a way for Muslims to seek retribution for past injustices inflicted by Western powers.
DISAFFECTED BY POLITICAL STATUS QUO	**A CHANCE TO CREATE A JUST POLITICAL SYSTEM**
Fed up with authoritarian or oppressive regimes' active suppression of dissent that leaves the masses with no political voice and without representation in the power structure.	Offers an opportunity to change their political circumstances and reclaim their individual power, by being part of an ideal model for "good Islamic" governance.
MARGINALIZATION AND ALIENATION	**PROMISES COMPANIONSHIP, BROTHERHOOD, SISTERHOOD**
Perceive a lack of social integration and acceptance of Muslims in the West due to widespread civil liberties violations and ethnic or religious discrimination. Feeling of being cut off from community and society.	Promises a social network of like-minded people who will offer companionship, inclusion and respect, and the social benefits of belonging to an elite group.
DISCONNECT FROM WESTERN CULTURE	**OPPORTUNITY TO LIVE A "PURE" LIFE**
Unable to negotiate between Western cultural mores, which are perceived to be immoral (drinking, drugs, sex) and inconsistent with Islamic values, many struggle with how to live out their faith in the West.	Opportunity to live in an ideal society, where one can preserve and develop their Islamic identity and values by living among fellow pious Muslims.
POOR EXAMPLES OF GLORY, HEROES, AND IMPORTANCE	**HEROISM AND IMPORTANCE**
Lack of positive representation, heroic narratives, and images of Muslims in the media leads to a dearth of role models for Muslims to emulate. Young Muslims, particularly, may feel that there are no icons to look up to.	A chance to experience glory, to be important, to matter, to be remembered and rewarded, to become a hero—both in this life and in Paradise.

Why Daesh Recruits Women

SARA MAHMOOD examines the unparalleled flow of women fighters, many from the West, to the "Islamic State," and the integral part they play in the development of the so-called Caliphate.

KEY TAKEAWAYS

- The first role of women in Daesh is to procreate; their other role is to actively recruit more women by painting a romanticized picture of life in the Caliphate.
- Western women join Daesh to take a stand against an Islamophobic society that sees them as oppressed victims of a purportedly misogynistic religion. They then become critical in attracting more Western women to Daesh through their strong online presence.
- In the Caliphate, women are perceived by men as commodities, there only to enable the caliphate's end goal, which is to grow in numbers.

Since the establishment of the so-called caliphate in 2014, there has been an unprecedented flow of foreign fighters to the territory of Daesh. What is more surprising, however, is that a significant portion of the supporters of this so-called Islamic State are female. In winter 2015, it was estimated that 10 percent of the 20,000–31,500 Daesh foreign fighters were young Muslim women from Europe, North America, and Australia between the ages of eighteen and twenty-five. Daesh has displayed a remarkable ability to mobilize a large number of women, specifically Western women. Women from the West, who have not been typically known to fall prey to such propaganda, have been particularly targeted for recruitment and encouraged to migrate to Daesh territory. This novel development in global terrorism gives rise to two questions: First, why do females have a bigger role in the social organization of Daesh? and second, what factors have led to the mobilization of large numbers of females from Western countries?

Daesh's propaganda materials espouse a long-term vision of the future—to establish a fully functioning state. Part of this vision includes a societal structure of which women are an integral part. Daesh strategically wants to ensure its survival in the distant future, and does so by designating two specific roles to women. The primary role of women, to ensure the lineage of Muslims fighting to create the ultimate "caliphate," is to bear children who will further populate the organization. As such, marriage is seen as an obligation for women so that they may participate in strengthening the caliphate through procreation. Moreover, the women who are widowed after their husbands die on the battlefield are remarried as soon as the traditional four-month period of widowhood (iddat), when marriage is prohibited for women, has ended. Therefore, women are perceived by men as commodities, there only to enable the end goal of the "caliphate" to grow in numbers.

> Women recruiters will speak in binaries, drawing parallels of "us versus them"—or "the West versus Islam"—to reinforce the need to travel to Daesh territory to protect Islam from the Western infidels.

The secondary, and most unique, role of Daesh women is to serve as recruiters, groomers, and

SARA MAHMOOD is a Research Analyst with the International Centre for Political Violence and Terrorism Research (ICPVTR), where she focuses on the threat of terrorism and extremism in Pakistan and within the online domain.

propagandists in the domain of social media. Here women play a crucial role in attracting Western women to Daesh through their strong online presence, where they propagate a romanticized version of life in the "caliphate." In addition, the majority of their online posts are pieces of anti-Western propaganda, references to the persecution and suffering of Muslims globally, as well as posts encouraging others to move from the land of the impure to the land of the "pure" (i.e., the "Caliphate"). Women recruiters will speak in binaries, drawing parallels of "us versus them"—or "the West versus Islam"—to reinforce the need to travel to Daesh territory to protect Islam from the Western infidels. In some ways, their role as recruiters allows women to feel as if they are actively contributing to the battle on the ground since Daesh forbids women to engage in combat.

The question that remains, however, is why has there been this mass movement of Western women to Daesh territory? Women, like men, are drawn to Daesh for a myriad of reasons: Islamophobia, perceived alienation, persecution, discrimination, and many others. Like men, Western women recruits are also consumed with images of Muslim suffering around the world that dominate the Western media, and feel that the West is complicit in the suffering. The combination of such mind-sets makes these young women vulnerable targets for female Daesh recruiters who lure them in with promises of sisterhood and visions of change.

The difference between genders, however, is the means by which women are reminded of their grievances in their daily lives. Muslim women living in the West, particularly Muslim women who wear the hijab, are often the victims of Islamophobic attacks and discrimination due to the visibility of their religion. Moreover, Muslim women are overwhelmingly perceived as victims of an oppressive, misogynistic religion who lack the autonomy to make decisions without their husbands. By abandoning their lives in Western society to join Daesh, these women are taking a symbolic—though deplorable—stand against a society that sees them only as oppressed victims. Thus, the act of leaving their home countries in the West to join the struggle for the "caliphate" symbolically elevates their status and allows them to reclaim their autonomy as rational agents.

By abandoning their lives in Western society to join Daesh, these women are taking a symbolic—though deplorable—stand against a society that sees them only as oppressed victims

While Daesh is a patriarchal organization that gives comparatively more importance to the men, it does not deny the critical role of women in the group. However, one should not perceive the more active role of women to be suggestive of the equal status of men and women in the "caliphate." Daesh is an extremely regressive and violently patriarchal organization that reduces women to nothing more than commodities that exist for the sake of men. It is evident that for the group's strategic thinkers, the resilience of the "caliphate" supersedes other considerations. This establishes the core reason for the more visible functions assigned to women, which are attributed solely to the survival of the state that requires participation by both genders alike.

Why Daesh Recruits Children

DR. HOUDA ABADI and **NAVEED HADA** present an in-depth analysis of Daesh's complex tactics for recruiting and indoctrinating children. The findings are based on a thorough examination of 90 videos that feature children in Daesh's online propaganda and print magazines.

KEY TAKEAWAYS

- Children are a vital propaganda tool in Daesh's recruitment tactic and are valued as important assets for the growth and long-term survival of the extremist group.
- Daesh tries to present itself as a postracial, post-citizenship society in a message that resonates with young children who may be discriminated against in their native countries.
- Governments must address the root causes that trigger a child's decision to turn to extremist ideology, such as poverty, discrimination, and lack of better options.

WHY RECRUIT CHILDREN?

Based on the depiction of children in its recruitment efforts, Daesh sees immense strategic value in investing resources for the preparation of its younger generation. Children are a vital propaganda tool in Daesh's recruitment tactics. They have been used as supporting objects to substantiate a whole range of its narratives. For instance, visuals of children suffering as a result of Western aggression are overwhelmingly shown to evoke feelings of anger and disgust. This, in turn, increases the emotional appeal of one of Daesh's predominant narratives, that is, the humiliation and disgrace inflicted upon the Muslim *ummah* (community) by the "tyrant" West. Admittedly, however, Daesh's use of children goes far beyond their value as propaganda instruments. They are, in fact, regarded as an important asset for the growth and long-term survival of the "caliphate." With an unparalleled rate of child recruitment, Daesh's ultimate purpose is to create and solidify an intergenerational culture of violence and religious extremism that could outlive its political-territorial loss.[1] In other words, controlling population through targeted indoctrination is a lot more appealing to Daesh than merely controlling territories. Having less developed ideological and moral foundations, children are seen as subjects who can easily be manipulated into accepting violent messages without question. Last, the visual symbolism of having an organized army of young soldiers serves as a crucial element in Daesh's psychological warfare. The organization's frequent references to its young combatants as "the cubs of the caliphate," "tomorrow's mujāhidīn," "the next generation," and "the future flag bearers" are meant to send a strong message to its adversaries that it is well equipped and has an unmatched capacity to replenish its ranks. With increasing loss of territories, children are appearing more frequently in

DR. HOUDA ABADI joined The Carter Center in June 2014 as Associate Director of the Conflict Resolution Program. For the first two years, Dr. Abadi worked on Syria and the Israel-Palestine conflict. During that time, she developed what is now the Center's inclusive approaches to preventing violent extremism project. Dr. Abadi holds a PhD in Political Communication and Media Studies, an MA in International Relations and Diplomacy, with a concentration in Middle East Studies and Conflict Resolution, and a graduate certificate from Duke–University of North Carolina in Middle East Studies. She previously served as the Director of Education for two New York City non-profits that facilitate dialogue between Jewish and Muslim youth.

NAVEED HADA worked as a researcher for the Carter Center's inclusive approaches to preventing violent extremism project. Mr. Hada holds a bachelor's degree in International Relations and Middle Eastern and South Asian Studies from Emory University, and a master's degree in International Development from the University of Cambridge.

[1] *Guardian*, " 'Raising Tomorrow's Mujahideen': The Horrific World of ISIS Child Soldiers," March 10, 2015. https://www.theguardian.com/world/2015/mar/10/horror-of-isis-child-soldiers-state-of-terror.

Daesh's videos, in part to emphasize Daesh's resolute preparedness, both ideologically as well as militarily.

RECRUITMENT METHODS

Daesh uses a multimodal recruitment approach for its outreach and indoctrination. Employing a hyperlocal approach, it fashions messages that speak directly to the pressing concerns of its target audience and offers empowering alternatives.

As regards local recruitment, the process starts at a very young age when children attend Daesh-administered schools, which are used as a tool for indoctrination. Daesh's curriculum is devoid of any critical thinking—subject areas such as arts and social studies have been abolished. Instead, in gender-segregated classrooms, children are required to learn Daesh's "religious" dogma through lessons and rote memorization. The academic curriculum is accompanied by an emphasis on physical exercise, which includes fighting drills and weapons training. By standardizing school curriculum along its strategic priorities, Daesh aims to ensure allegiance to its ideological practices. Eventually, such an intensive process of indoctrination breeds among children a favorable opinion of the organization and normalizes violence from a young age.

In addition to its schools, Daesh uses other avenues for mobilizing public support, including mosques, town squares, and markets. This enables Daesh to foster recognition among children and mainstream its presence. Propaganda videos show middle-aged Daesh soldiers overseeing sports activities, distributing food, giving away gifts and toys, and organizing public events where children are encouraged to recite Qur'anic verses, sing chants, and wave the black flag of Daesh.[2] To desensitize children to violence, Daesh forces children to witness public executions[3] and encourages them to incorporate forms of violence in their everyday play activities, such as beheading stuffed toys or pretending to be militants with toy weapons, thus forcing them to internalize violence.

Daesh also employs more direct methods for recruitment, such as offering monetary benefits and leveraging family and community ties. Daesh uses its influence through preachers and imams to condition parents to register their children in Daesh's training camps. While education, indoctrination, and social mobilization are integral to Daesh's strategy for child recruitment and retention, it does not shy away from using coercive measures to expand its army. Explicit coercive actions include abduction and lethal threats to children and their families, whereas implicit coercion manifests itself in the form of societal pressure and fear of being labeled a traitor or an apostate if one refuses to join Daesh's ranks.

Daesh's ultimate purpose is to create and solidify an intergenerational culture of violence and religious extremism that could outlive its political-territorial loss.

To recruit foreign children, Daesh uses its widespread relational networks and online propaganda. In general, most messages directed at foreign audiences aim to capitalize on the grievances of the target audience. However, Daesh acknowledges that dependent foreign children cannot be recruited in isolation from their families. Keeping this in mind, messages of sociopolitical disillusionment are enveloped within the narrative of collective family participation, which specifies obligations of and roles for each family member. For instance, in a video titled "Eid Greetings from the Caliphate," a Finnish Muslim sent the following message to his fellow Muslims: "I am calling on all Muslims living in the West, America, and Europe, and everywhere else to come . . . *with your families* [emphasis added] to the land of Khilafah. Alhamdulillah, we live in the shades of this religion."[4] Another recruitment narrative asserts that Muslim children growing up in the West are being brainwashed by morally bankrupt *munāfiqin* (hypocrites). Western secular education, it is argued, teaches Muslim youth

[2] See, for example, Al Khayr Media Center, "Holiday Cheer in the State of Unification," July 23, 2015; Al Fallujah Media Center, "And Exhort One Another with the Truth," February 15, 2015; Al Halab Media Center, "Living in the Shade of the Khilafah," January 24, 2015.
[3] Al Halab Media Center, "Establishment of the Limit Upon the Corrupt in the Land," February 7, 2015.
[4] Al Hayat Media Center, "Eid Greetings from the Land of the Khilafah," July 20, 2014.

"to accept all manner of religious deviance and social perversion."[5] These statements are juxtaposed with descriptions and images of children in Daesh, who are portrayed in a very positive light as individuals who have been blessed with the right path and are being raised under the shade of the Qur'an and Sunnah. The objective behind such imagery is to convince parents that migrating to the "caliphate" is the only way to shield their children from the immoralities of the "atheist and liberal" West.

For older children, who can be recruited independently of their parents, Daesh offers a path to discover personal and social identity. Coupled with this sentiment is the invocation of nostalgia for a utopian Muslim state, where Muslims with diverse backgrounds live and thrive in harmony. This idea of a post-racial, post-citizenship society resonates rather strongly with young individuals who are marginalized and discriminated against in their native countries because of the color of their skin and/or their heritage.

ROLES OF CHILDREN IN THE "CALIPHATE"

Children in Daesh are assigned different tasks, ranging from support activities to full-fledged participation as front-line combatants.

Children work as spies or join "sleeper cells" in government-controlled areas.[6] They are also responsible for guarding checkpoints, transferring weapons, and performing various administrative duties in Daesh-controlled social facilities. Daesh also uses its most charismatic and well-versed children as preachers and recruiters. Several propaganda videos depict children, both girls and boys, participating in public rallies and religious lectures, where they present speeches and songs eulogizing Daesh's ideas and practices.[7] These spokes-children are also used as examples to guilt-recruit and embarrass older men. In other words, if young children can so selflessly and valiantly devote their lives to Daesh, adults should not be scared to do so. Additionally, Daesh deploys children in intensely violent operations as shooters, executioners, suicide bombers, and soldiers on the battlefield. Children are also trained to punish and torture the "caliphate's" prisoners and dissidents.

> Messages of sociopolitical disillusionment are enveloped within the narrative of collective family participation, which specifies obligations of and roles for each family member.

It is commonly believed that while young boys are trained to engage in military duties, young girls are simply relegated to their homes, preparing to become obedient wives and mothers. This, however, is only partially true. A more nuanced and gender-conscious approach to understanding women and girls in Daesh reveals that their role is more complex. For instance, just like young boys, girls are also brainwashed to carry out suicide attacks. A teacher from one of the Daesh-administered schools confessed that girls as young as ten are being indoctrinated with violent ideology and trained to carry out bomb attacks.[8] This shows that to find viable countermeasures to Daesh's recruitment of children, the phenomenon must be observed and analyzed through a gender-conscious lens.

CONCLUSION

While it is virtually impossible to prevent children inside Daesh from joining its ranks, strong measures must be taken to prevent foreign recruitment. Children and youth between the ages of twelve and eighteen have an increased appetite for risk and adventure, but often lack appropriate outlets to express those urges. This makes them vulnerable to Daesh's false promises of adventure and empowerment. Alternatives are needed to nurture their imagination, stimulate their critical thinking, and provide them with safe avenues to express their

[5] *Dabiq*, issue 12, "Just Terror," p. 34.
[6] Human Rights Watch, "'Maybe We Live and Maybe We Die": Recruitment and Use of Children by Armed Groups in Syria," June 22, 2014; https://www.hrw.org/report/2014/06/22/maybe-we-live-and-maybe-we-die/recruitment-anduse-children-armed-groups-syria, pp. 20–25.
[7] Al Khayr Media Center, "Holiday Cheer in the State of Unification," July 23, 2015.
[8] Channel 4 News, "ISIS' Children: Soldiers Trained to Kill and Die,." January 10, 2015; https://www.youtube.com/watch?v=EVxZfP1fC_I.

opinions. Governments must address the root causes that triggered the children's departure in the first place, such as poverty, discrimination, and a pursuit of better options. It is also important to influence the larger context in which these youths live, so that they could feel a sense of belonging and identification with their communities.

Returning Daesh child soldiers must receive adequate psychosocial support to reintegrate into their societies. Protracted exposure to brutal aggression and violence leaves lasting physical and emotional scars on victims and perpetrators alike. Unlike adult ex-fighters who have seen an alternative way of life, child militants have been raised almost exclusively on the tenets of warfare and have zero to minimal perception of a world not immersed in violence. It is therefore crucial to have reintegration programs that provide psychosocial support and are gender-conscious. Governments must also provide legal and social services to returning children and their families. It is critical to acknowledge and address the stigma associated with former members of violent extremist groups, especially children. Placing them in hostile environments, where they feel alienated and defenseless, can increase the risk of terrorist recidivism. Those who abused, manipulated, and recruited children must be tried in a court of law and brought to justice.

Why Do Women Join Daesh?

WISE: Notions that women are "naïve" individuals seduced by thoughts of becoming "jihadi brides" have quickly been shattered upon closer examination of the profiles of women who joined Daesh. These women are not passive victims; rather, they have chosen to become participants in aiding and abetting Daesh. Below are the "push" factors that often motivate women to join Daesh, and the "pull" factors that Daesh recruiters use to lure them to the so-called caliphate.

PUSH FACTORS THE DISCONTENT	PULL FACTORS THE SIREN SONG
SOCIAL ISOLATION AND OTHERNESS	**SENSE OF BELONGING**
Feel that they are treated unequally in their own country because they are seen as part of an oppressive, misogynistic religion, which results in them feeling socially isolated, judged, and "othered."	Delivers them from feelings of isolation by becoming part of something bigger than themselves; promise of belonging to the sisterhood of *Muhajirahs* (female migrants to Daesh).
LACK OF AGENCY	**EXPRESSION OF AUTONOMY**
Feel constrained, unable to make their own choices because of restrictive cultural mores, overprotective parenting, and/or hostile societal conditions. They feel frustrated with their lack of autonomy in shaping their own destiny.	Leaving home and migrating to the Caliphate is the ultimate expression of adult autonomy, which instantly transitions a woman from adolescence to adulthood, giving her the ability to act as an independent, rational agent of change.
DEVALUED DOMESTIC LIFE	**MOTHERHOOD RANKS HIGHEST**
Perceive that women's emancipation and female liberation have diverted women from their divine duty as wives and mothers, and instead, place a higher value on working women seeking careers.	Motherhood is presented as the highest status a woman can achieve because it is done for the sake of God. Domestic life is not seen as limiting, but as a spiritually righteous sphere. Giving birth in the Caliphate is akin to birthing a new nation.

MUSLIM *UMMAH* DISHONORED	**RESTORE JUSTICE**
Frustrated at the inability of the international community and Muslim governments to end the suffering and humiliation of Muslims worldwide.	A chance to be part of a movement to restore justice by revolutionizing politics and society, and to fight on behalf of oppressed Muslims.
MORAL CORRUPTION	**LIVE A PURE LIFE**
Conflicted by the West's attitude toward blurring gender roles and fluid social mores, which are seen as being at odds with traditional norms and strict gender roles for Muslim men and women.	Escape from impure Western social mores—its disbelief and corrupting influence—and a chance to live a pious life where gender roles are clearly defined.
LOVE, MARRIAGE, SEX	**BESTOWED WITH HEAVENLY REWARD**
Disconnect between Western sexual revolution and religious constraints on sex before marriage; expectations about marriage and sex are imposed by families and society.	Promises of love upon arrival, that these women will be bestowed with divine importance as the wives of soon-to-be martyrs (for the sake of God), honored with a heavenly reward for assisting men in preparing for *jihad*.
GUARDIANS OF THE FAITH	**INHERIT GREATNESS**
Convinced that Islam is under attack by the West, they need to do their part to restore its past glory.	Assures them that the children they produce will be the future generations of a utopian society, who will ensure the survival of the caliphate. Their bloodline and legacy will change the course of history for all Muslims.

"The ink of a Scholar is more precious than the blood of a Martyr."

- Prophet Muhammad

CHAPTER 6

Debunking Extremist Ideology

Terrorists and Their Delusions

DR. IBRAHIM NEGM explains how extremists falsely claim to represent "true" Islam, though they "cherry-pick" verses from the Qur'an to suit their own agendas and justify their actions.

KEY TAKEAWAYS

- Extremist ideology contains three serious flaws: misinterpretation of the Qur'an and Hadith, a narrow concept of jihad, and a delusional understanding of martyrdom.
- None of these extremist groups have received a proper education in Islam or hold the authority to speak on behalf of the world's 1.6 billion Muslims.
- There must be an intellectual response to deviant ideologies, which requires Muslim scholars to deconstruct terrorists' warped understanding of Islam.

Terrorists blatantly manipulate the religion of Islam in an attempt to justify acts of violence and terror. When we deconstruct their warped logic and the unauthentic sources used to justify their desire for power, control, and bloodshed, we see that the ideologies of these groups contain some serious flaws.

They have turned their backs on the Qur'anic concept of diversity, human brotherhood, and peaceful relations between Muslims and non-Muslims.

The first ideological flaw is related to the terror groups' abuses against the Qur'an and Prophetic reports. Through their total ignorance of the tools needed to properly comprehend the Qur'an or Hadith, the rules of inference and the objectives of Islamic law and its principles, terrorist groups take Qur'anic verses and the Prophet's words out of context and imbue them with the worst of meanings. As a result, the true and peaceful words of God and the Prophet are replaced by the terrorists' distorted rhetoric of violence and fear. They deliberately ignore the qualifying and essential parts of the Qur'anic verses in favor of their misquoted sayings and deviant interpretations.

Terrorist groups disregard any and every Qur'anic verse that does not fit their false claims or justify their unilateral war against those who do not share their violent worldview. They have turned their backs on the Qur'anic concept of diversity, human brotherhood, and peaceful relations between Muslims and non-Muslims, as seen in the Qur'anic verse, "*O Mankind. We created you from a single pair of a male and a female and made you into nations and tribes that you may know each other. Verily the most honored of you in the sight of Allah is the most righteous of you. And God has full knowledge and is well acquainted with all things*" (49:13).

These groups reject the Qur'an's emphasis on embracing diversity and entertaining differences as established principles for dealing with people from varying religious, cultural, or racial backgrounds.

DR. IBRAHIM NEGM is the imam of the Islamic Center of Long Island and serves as the Special Advisor to the Grand Mufti of Al-Azhar University in Egypt, the highest Muslim Cleric in the Sunni Muslim World. He received his BA and MA in Islamic Studies at Al-Azhar University in Cairo, an MA as a visiting scholar and researcher at Harvard University, served as a visiting researcher in the Theology Department at the University of Oxford, and received his PhD in Islamic Studies and Christian Muslim Relations from the Graduate Theological Foundation.

Instead, terrorist groups insist that anyone who rejects their distorted ideology is a legitimate target and must be killed. This mind-set stands in complete contradiction to the clear Qur'anic message in which God says, "*If anyone kills a person, it is as if he kills all mankind while if anyone saves a life it is as if he saves the lives of all mankind*" (5:32).

The second ideological flaw is found in their narrow concept of *jihad*, which they have restricted to mean combat and slaughter, and their distorted representation that it has been required by God. However, in its true meaning *jihad* refers to the human endeavor of striving to improve the individual and society, and to bring life closer to the divine model. But for violent extremists, physical *jihad* is an end in itself. In its true form, the goal of *jihad* is guidance. But the violent extremists have distorted this concept, along with countless others, to such an extent that their actions repel others from God's religion instead of guiding them to it. Thus, violent extremists are deviating far from the true goal of *jihad* in their illegitimate declaration of war.

"Good" intentions never justify forbidden acts, nor is it permissible to kill the innocent in Islam.

And finally, the third ideological flaw is in their false belief that the terrorists who are killed in the line of "duty" will be received as martyrs and rewarded in paradise. Their delusional understanding of the concept of martyrdom goes against Islamic law's definition of what it means to be a martyr, regardless of whether they 1) considered their act to be a form of *jihad*, 2) had sincere intentions, or 3) were acting out of ignorance. "Good" intentions never justify forbidden acts, nor is it permissible to kill the innocent in Islam. Thus 9/11, 7/7, or any other similarly horrendous acts are simply acts of terrorism that have nothing to do with *jihad*.

From these three ideological flaws we can deduce that the terrorist groups are confusing the noble and honest form of *jihad*, which may be waged to fend off aggression and establish justice, with their ruthless acts of slaughter and indiscriminate killing of innocent individuals. This stands in sharp contrast to the rulings of Islamic jurisprudence that emphasize the importance of upholding justice and morality during armed struggle. Moreover, their distorted interpretations of core Islamic concepts, such as *hijrah* and *takfir*, have allowed them to hijack all of Islam and claim to represent the "true" Islam.

There must be an intellectual response to deviant ideologies. This requires Muslim scholars to deconstruct the terrorists' false claims and warped understanding of Qur'anic exegesis. Muslims are the ones who should reclaim their right to define their religion, according to the Qur'an and the teachings of the Prophet Muhammad (pbuh). They should never leave it to the pundits specializing in extremism (be they Muslim or non-Muslim). We Muslims know that Islam is a religion of peace and mercy. In fact, the first prophetic saying that is taught to any student of Islam is the Hadith "Those who show mercy are shown mercy by the All-Merciful. Show mercy to those who are on earth and the One in the heavens will show mercy to you."

It is very important for us to recognize that not a single one of these violent extremists has received a proper Islamic education at academic centers of Islamic learning—a basic requirement for anyone who makes such authoritative claims. This leaves them without the proper knowledge of the principles of Islamic jurisprudence (*usul al-fiqh*) and the methodology necessary to derive legitimate laws. Moreover, the alleged claim by violent extremists that they attempt to follow the path of the early Muslims is erroneous. The early Muslims were pioneers in writing down the guiding maxims and in developing a scientific methodology that enabled them to differentiate between the primary overarching issues and the secondary debatable ones in the Qur'anic message.
The basic principles of Islamic jurisprudence were codified by the early Muslim pioneers during the eighth and ninth centuries, and established a set precedent for how to expand and develop the law. These principles established that the four roots of Islamic law may be found in the Qur'an, Sunnah, *ijma* (consensus of scholars), and *qiyas* (ruling by analogy). Moreover, secondary sources of laws have been developed and refined over time, and consist of juristic preferences (*istihsan*), laws of the previous prophets (*shar'u man qablana*), extended analogy (*maslaha mursala*), customs (*urf*), and sayings of a

companion (*qawl al-sahabi*). It is only after receiving a proper education in Islamic jurisprudence that an individual will possess the authority to speak on behalf of the Law.

In Islam, there are two forms of law, the first and most important being *Shari'ah*, or Divine Law. *Shari'ah* consists of God's laws as revealed in the Qur'an and Sunnah, which are immutable. *Fiqh*, on the other hand, refers to the human understanding of Shari'ah and is implemented by the rulings or religious edicts (*fatwa*) of Muslim jurists. *Fiqh* is the product of the independent legal reasoning (*ijtihad*) of Islamic jurists (*Ulema*) from their scholarly interpretation of the Qur'an and Sunnah. And it is only Muslim jurists, upon receiving genuine and extensive Islamic education, who possess the authority to issue and implement a *fatwa*.

We may point to any number of declarations posing as *fatwas* from extremists and terrorists as examples of how grave the consequences are of not following the historical Islamic example of differentiating between those with scholarly standing and authority and those without. In recent years, unqualified and illegitimate personalities have exploited technological means to proclaim themselves Islamic scholars and leaders, and have issued opinions to justify everything from attacking churches, exercising violence, and denigrating women. True Islamic scholarship and leadership stands firmly against such exploitative positions, which are merely politics in the guise of religion.

Thus it has been incumbent on Egypt's Dar al-Iftaa at Al-Azhar University to rise to this global threat and to wage an intellectual war to battle against the ill beliefs, warped understandings, and misinterpretations of scriptural texts. As the leading institute in the Islamic world that issues *fatwas*, Dar al-Iftaa rejects violent extremists' flagrant de-contextualization, misappropriation, and misuse of the Holy Qur'an and prophetic traditions.

Dar al-Iftaa has taken responsibility for deconstructing the intellectual flaws of terrorists in a variety of ways. To combat their deviant ideological flaws, we publish and disseminate information about the true teachings of Islam in media such as electronic publications, social media, and books and articles, and we share best practices by networking with scholars, Muslim leaders, and practitioners around the world. Additionally, Dar al-Iftaa has established partnerships with Muslim leaders in the West to provide a unified voice against extremists' hijacking of Islam. Furthermore, Dar al-Iftaa has established an observatory that monitors and deconstructs extremists' *fatwas* and issues many counter *fatwas*. In doing so, Dar al-Iftaa is working to reveal the true authentic teachings of the Islamic faith and to emphasize that the extremists' ideologies are aberrations from the authentic teachings of Islam—both in letter and spirit.

Why Daesh Distorts Islam

RELIGIOUS REHABILITATION GROUP (RRG): Extremists use religion as an ideology because religion is a powerful motivating factor that binds people of different backgrounds in a common cause. RRG provides an overview of how and why Daesh misuses religion to not only justify their actions, but also to attract people to join.

There are injustices in the world → There is a need to act → Violence is the only response

DAESH IDEOLOGY PROVIDES A LANGUAGE OF MASS MOBILIZATION

"You should learn about some political situations, these are your brothers and sisters! It will help if you see what this persecution really looks like. Here are some videos to watch, and some websites to learn more about what is really happening."[1]

"Armed jihad is the only solution to Muslim oppression and injustice. The only way to truly free your Muslim brothers and sisters from persecution is by participating in Allah's holy war. They are depending on us."

DAESH IDEOLOGY PROVIDES JUSTIFICATION FOR ACTS OF VIOLENCE

DAESH IDEOLOGY SUSTAINS A CULTURE OF VIOLENCE FOR FUTURE GENERATIONS

"Our role is even more important as women in Islam... if [we are unwilling] to sacrifice [our] desires and give up [our] families and lives in the west in order to make Hijrah and please Allah, then who will raise the next generation of Lions?...Sister's [sic] don't forsake this beautiful blessing being able to raise the future Mujahideen of Shaam."[2]

"This Khilafah is more in need than ever before for experts, professionals, and specialists, who can help contribute in strengthening its structure and tending to the needs of their Muslim brothers."[3]

DAESH IDEOLOGY PROVIDES RATIONALE FOR FINANCIAL AND LOGISTICAL SUPPORT OF "CALIPHATE"

---

1 Abu Amru Al Qa'idy, "A Course in the Art of Recruiting," https://ia800300.us.archive.org/32/items/ACourseInTheArtOfRecruiting-RevisedJuly2010/A_Course_in_the_Art_of_Recruiting_-_Revised_July2010.pdf (accessed November 29, 2016).
2 Ruth Michaelson, "How the Wives of ISIS Are Attracting Western Women to Syria," http://www.vocativ.com/world/isis-2/wives-isis-attracting-western-women-syria/ (accessed November 29, 2016).
3 "Hijrah: From Hypocrisy to Sincerity," *Dabiq*, Shaw'wal 1435, Issue 3, pp. 26.

8 Islamic Concepts Daesh Distorts

Below are the eight core Islamic concepts that Daesh distorts to form the basis of its twisted ideology. *Al-Wala' wal Bara'* (loyalty and disavowal) is meant to reject those who are not with them, and forms their "us versus them" mentality. They consider themselves to be the "rightfully" guided *ummah* (community), and defenders of the faith. As the *jama'ah* (group), a term commonly used for congregational prayer, they claim to represent the global Muslim majority. They label others as *kuffar* (unbelievers), and declare *takfir* (excommunication) to justify the murder of innocent civilians. They demand *bay'ah* (allegiance) to their leader and the group's doctrines. They limit *jihad* (struggle) to mean "Holy War," in order to fight the enemy and justify killing. They call on Muslims to make a *hijrah* (migration) from their "impure" environments and to live with "true Muslims" like them. They ask followers to become *shahid* (martyrs) by committing suicide. They invite Muslims from all over the world to populate their *khilafah* (caliphate), which will usher in the "golden age" of Islam.

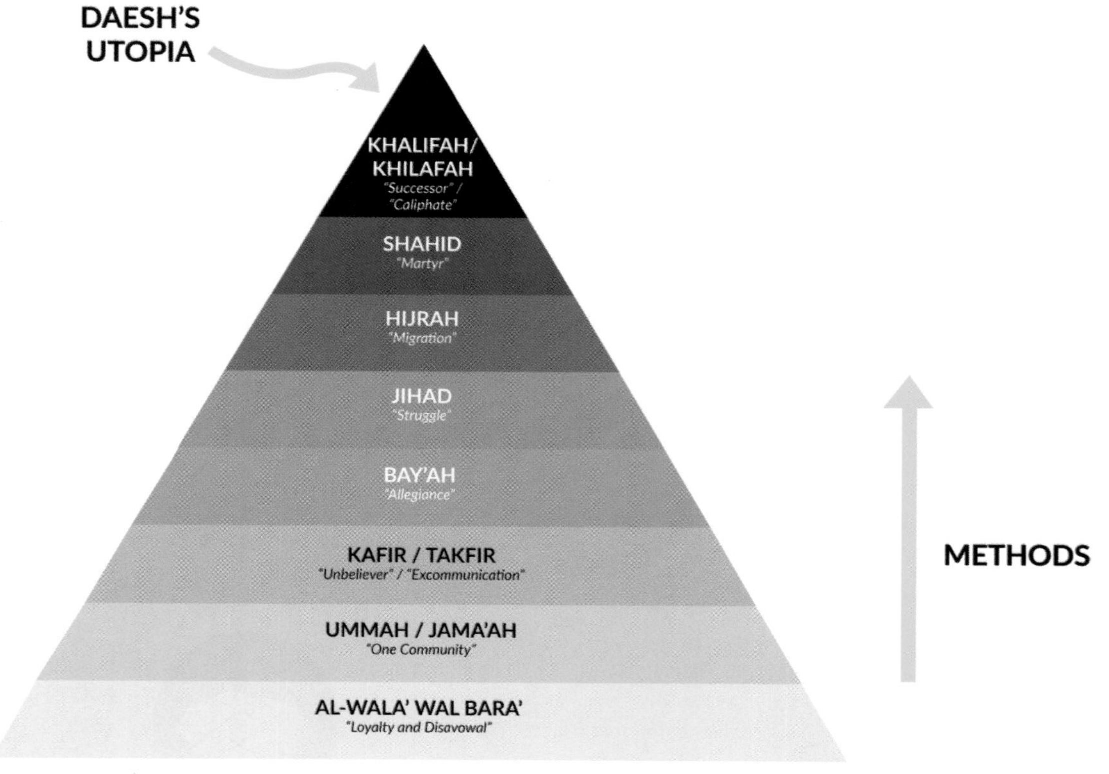

ISLAMIC CONCEPTS	**TRUE** ISLAMIC TEACHINGS	**FAKE** ISLAMIC TEACHINGS
AL-WALA' WAL BARA' *"Loyalty and Disavowal"*	*Wala'*: love of God, Prophet Muhammad, and your protectors, i.e., family, friends, etc.; *Bara'*: disavowal of all immoral things	Loyalty understood in absolute terms—"Us vs. Them"; standing with them, and disavowing all non-believers, including other Muslims
UMMAH / JAMA'AH *"One Community"*	*Ummah*: humanity, united by a shared belief in God; *Jama'ah* (quorum): representing the Muslim majority	Claim to be the only rightly guided Muslims who speak on behalf of the entire *ummah*
KAFIR / TAKFIR *"Unbeliever" / "Excommunication"*	*Kafir*: an "unbeliever" who denies the existence of God; *Takfir*: "excommunication"	An unbeliever who is accused of apostasy (perceived "enemy" of Muslims), whose killing is "justified"
BAY'AH *"Allegiance"*	Pledge of allegiance given to the Prophet before entering Mecca; not required for Muslims	A rite of passage for all Daesh recruits, signaling their belonging to the group and designating them as "true Muslims"
JIHAD *"Struggle"*	To struggle for the sake of God. Highest form of *jihad* is the struggle with one's own ego; lesser *jihad* is to fight back in self-defense only.	Define preemptive attacks as "self-defense" in an attempt to justify killing of innocent people
HIJRAH *"Migration"*	The Prophet Muhammad's migration from Mecca to Medina to flee religious persecution; also, the first year of the Islamic calendar	Promoted as an obligation to migrate to the so-called caliphate, to aid in their state-building operation
SHAHID *"Martyr"*	A *shahid* is one who witnesses the Truth of God. It can also mean a martyr, e.g., one who is slain while upholding God's justice. Someone who commits suicide to kill others is not a *shahid*.	Claim that those who kill themselves to create chaos, death, and destruction will become *shahid*.
KHALIFAH / KHILAFAH *"Successor" / "Caliphate"*	All humans are placed on earth as *khalifah* (individual stewards of God on earth). *Khalifah* also refers to a successor of the Prophet, who led the Muslim community. The word *khilafah* does not appear in the Qur'an.	Claim that all Muslims automatically fall under the authority of the self-declared Khalifah, and it is the collective obligation of Muslims to migrate to the newly created *khilafah* (caliphate).

Al–Wala' wal Bara'

Love of God and disvowal of bad actions and values

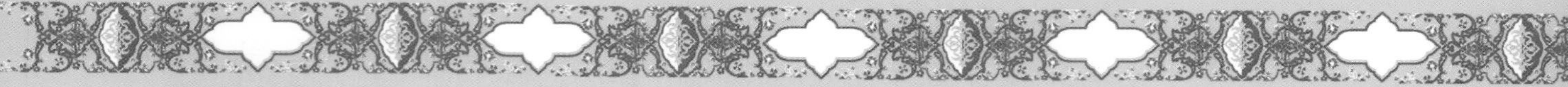

DEFINITION:

Wala' fundamentally means the love of God and love of virtue. A Muslim is thus required to give "loyalty" to God, to the Prophet Muhammad (pbuh) and to one's loyal protectors, such as parents, family members, scholars, leaders and the faithful.

Bara' means rejection or disavowal of all bad actions and values so that a follower may be free from the burden of wrongdoings, evils, and hostility. It is does not mean rejection of non-believers or specific groups of people. Indeed, Muslims must conduct themselves in a kind and just manner toward all peaceful non-believers and show respect to adherents of other religions.

PROPHET'S EXAMPLE:

- In 622 AD the Prophet Muhammad (pbuh) guaranteed protection and privileged status to minorities, including to the Jewish tribes, pagans, and Christians.

- In 634 AD, when Caliph Omar entered Jerusalem, he granted freedom of worship to all religious communities in the city, and insisted on lifting the ban forbidding Jews to enter Jerusalem, which had been placed on them by the Romans.

"God does not forbid you to deal kindly and justly with those who have not fought against you about the religion or expelled you from your homes. God does not love the unjust people."

QUR'AN 60:08

To read more about *Al-Wala' wal Bara'* please see page 196

AL-WALA' WAL BARA'

LOYALTY AND DISAVOWAL

DAESH DOGMA:

Wala/Wali' is to demonstrate loyalty only to Muslims who share their extremist ideology. It is understood in absolute terms—"Us vs. Them"—you either stand exclusively on the side of "Muslims like them," or completely on the side of all "non-believers," including other Muslims.

Bara', or disavowal, encourages rejection and animosity toward those *kuffar* (disbelievers) who do not conform to this twisted understanding. Daesh tells its followers not to align themselves with non-Muslims, because loving non-Muslims is equal to loving what is immoral.

DAESH PROPAGANDA:

"O *Ummah* of Islam, indeed the world today has been divided into two camps and two trenches, with no third camp present: The camp of Islam and faith, and the camp of *kufr* (disbelief) and hypocrisy - the camp of the Muslims and the mujahidin everywhere, and the camp of the jews, the crusaders, their allies, and with them the rest of the nations and religions of *kufr*, all being led by America and Russia, and being mobilized by the Jews."[1]

[1] *Dabiq*, Issue 1, page 10.

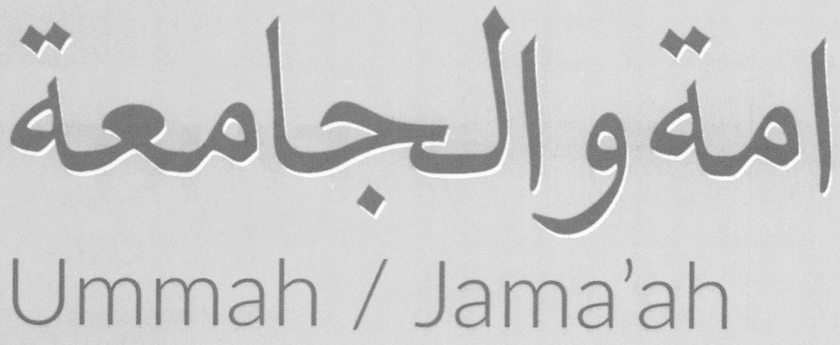

Ummah / Jama'ah

The collective community of believers

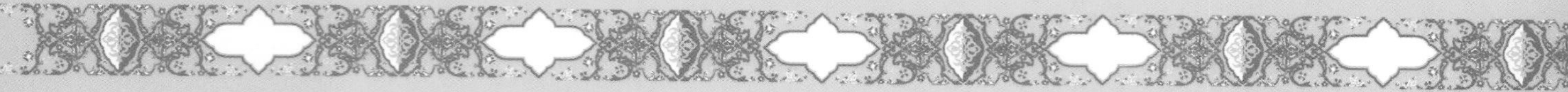

DEFINITION:

The Qur'an refers to ***Ummah Wāhidah***—a term that literally means "One Community"—a body of believers who are divinely mandated to uphold justice and compassion.

The phrase ***Ummah al-da'wah*** also appears in the Qur'an, and refers to humanity united by a shared belief in God and the divine plan for the Hereafter. Although Muslims believe in belonging to one *ummah* binding 1.6 billon Muslims together, no one movement can claim to be "the" ummah.

Jama'ah specifically refers to people praying in a congregation. It also refers to the unifying consolidated view of the Muslim community majority, as opposed to rebellious, sectarian, or peripheral views.

PROPHET'S EXAMPLE:

- In 622 AD, the Prophet Muhammad (pbuh) drafted the Constitution of Medina, which referred to Christians, Jews and pagan citizens of Medina as members of the *ummah*. The Prophet said, "All creation is one family dependent upon God. Whoever treats the creation of God the best, is loved by God the most" (Reported by al-Bayhaqi).

> "Mankind were a single community (*ummah*); then God sent the prophets as bearers of good news and warnings, and He sent down with them the Book with the Truth, that it may judge between the people concerning about which they differed."
>
> QUR'AN 2:213

To read more about *Ummah / Jama'ah* please see page 199

UMMAH / JAMA'AH

NATION/BODY OF MUSLIMS UNITED BEHIND A SINGLE LEADER

DAESH DOGMA:

Daesh claims to represent and speak for the global Muslim *ummah*, which they define as a "nation." They reject Muslims who do not follow their ways as having gone astray and label them un-Islamic.

Daesh claims to represent "the" *jama'ah*, which they define as the body of Muslims united behind a Muslim leader, e.g., Abu Bakr al-Baghdadi. By co-opting this term, which is traditionally associated with congregational prayer, they lend their actions a false sense of piety, and mobilize their followers to commit violence (which they consider to be part of worship) against those they call *kuffar* (disbelievers), including Muslims.

DAESH PROPAGANDA:

"Indeed, Allah (the Exalted) honored the *ummah* (nation) of Muhammad and blessed them. He made them the best *ummah* of all peoples… And he promised to grant the *ummah* succession to authority."[1]

"Know that your leaders will not find any arguments to keep you away from the *jama'ah* (the body of Muslims united behind a Muslim leader), the *khilafah*, and this great good…"[2]

[1] Abu Bakr Al-Baghdadi. "This Is the Promise of Allah."
[2] Ibid.

Kafir / Takfir

One who covers the truth / The act of labeling another as an unbeliever

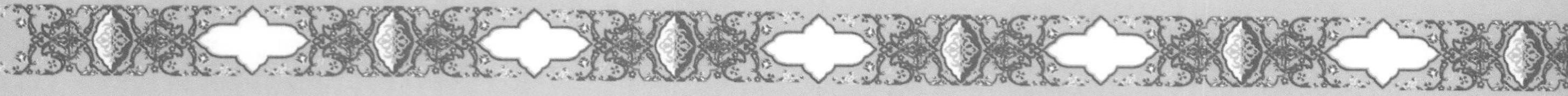

DEFINITION:

Kufr literally means "to cover the truth." Charging another person with ***kufr***, often translated as "unbelief," is not permissible because it is considered to be solely within the domain of God.

The Qur'an, the Prophet's sayings, and Muslim scholars strictly prohibit the act of a Muslim declaring ***takfir*** or "excommunication" on another Muslim.

The Qur'an insists that there is no compulsion in religion, acknowledges differences in beliefs, and maintains that humans have the free will to believe or disbelieve. The act of declaring ***takfir***, or casting derogatory remarks against people of other religions, is considered doctrinally deviant from the true essence of Islam, as it disregards the protected status of all peaceful non-Muslims.

PROPHET'S EXAMPLE:

- The Prophet Muhammad (pbuh) admonished those who pronounced disbelief upon another person: "If a Muslim wrongly accuses a fellow Muslim of disbelief, the accusation will return upon the accuser" (at-Tirmidhi).

"And say, 'The truth is from your Lord, so whoever wills—let him believe; and whoever wills—let him disbelieve.'"

QUR'AN 18:29

To read more about *Kafir / Takfir* please see page 201

KAFĪR / TAKFĪR

DISBELIEVER / EXCOMMUNICATION

DAESH DOGMA:

In their zeal for "purity," Daesh wrongfully applies verses pertaining to "non-believers" (ones who reject God), and applies them to believing Muslims—pronouncing *takfir* (excommunication) on them, and labeling them as *kuffar* (disbelievers) or *murtaddin* (apostates). In doing so, Daesh carries on the legacy of the Khawarij, a violent fringe group that broke off from the Muslim *ummah* during the time of the fourth Caliph, Ali, and declared anyone who did not subscribe to their puritanical ways to be *kuffar*.

Daesh defies longstanding consensus among scholars that:
1) Prohibits Muslims from charging each other with non-belief, and
2) Disregards the doctrine that the lives of all peaceful non-Muslims are protected and whoever wrongfully kills one of them will never enter Paradise.

DAESH PROPAGANDA:

"Living amongst the sinful kills the heart, never mind living amongst the *kuffar* (unbelievers)! Their *kufr* initially leaves dashes and traces upon the heart that over time become engravings and carvings that are nearly impossible to remove. They can destroy the person's *fitrah* (nature) to a point of no return, so that his heart's doubts and desires entrap him fully." [1]

[1] *Dabiq*, Issue 3, page 32.

Bay'ah

Pledge of support

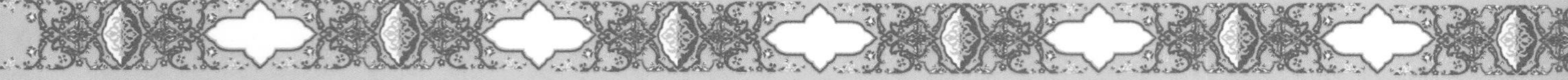

DEFINITION:

Bay'ah refers to a pledge of support that the Prophet Muhammad's (pbuh) followers freely gave to him as they attempted to perform their pilgrimage to Mecca. Following the Prophet's death, the Muslim community "pledged" their support to Abu Bakr, one of the Prophet's closest companions, as they believed he would work to establish justice and continue to uphold the teachings of the Qur'an and the Prophet.

Giving one's *bay'ah* to the Prophet was without compromise. In modern times, however, giving *bay'ah* to political or spiritual leaders is conditioned upon their ability to establish justice and uphold the moral and spiritual principles stipulated in the Qur'an and the teachings of the Prophet.

PROPHET'S EXAMPLE:

• When the Prophet attempted to perform pilgrimage to Mecca (*umrah*) he and his fellow Muslims were denied entry, so he sent Uthman to negotiate on his behalf. When Uthman did not return, the Prophet asked his 1,400 companions to pledge their allegiance to him, to show the Meccans the Muslims' determination to perform the pilgrimage. This event, known as the "Pledge of the Tree," prompted the release of Uthman, allowed the Muslims to perform the pilgrimage, and eventually led to the famous ten-year Hudaybiyyah peace treaty between the Meccans and the Muslims.

> "Prophet, when believing women come to you, pledging that they will not associate anything with God...then accept their pledge of allegiance and ask God's forgiveness for them. God is Forgiving and Merciful-to-all"
>
> QUR'AN 60:12

To read more about *Bay'ah* please see page 203

BAY'AH

PLEDGE OF ALLEGIANCE

DAESH DOGMA:

Giving *bay'ah* is a cornerstone of Daesh's ideology and recruitment strategy, and represents a ritual or rite of passage for all Daesh recruits. Once given, it signifies a recruit's belonging to the group and designation as a "true Muslim."

Daesh falsely equates giving *bay'ah* to their emir with giving *bay'ah* to the Prophet Muhammad, and announces those groups that have pledged *bay'ah* to the emir so as to make their influence seem more global and far-reaching than it really is. To break this *bay'ah* is to betray the community and be cast as a *kafir*, or "non-believer," an act punishable by death, according to Daesh.

DAESH PROPAGANDA:

"The obligation is now clearer than ever before for all Muslims to raise their voices and pledge their allegiance to Imamul-Muslimin and Amirul-Mu'minin—the Khalifah—Abu Bakr al-Husayni al-Baghdadi (may Allah raise his allies and humiliate his enemies)."[1]

[1] *Dabiq*, Issue 1, page 40.

Hijrah

Migration from Mecca to Medina

DEFINITION:

The Qur'an describes ***hijrah*** as the migration of the Prophet and his followers from Mecca to Medina when they were fleeing religious persecution. *Hijrah* ceased to be a religious obligation for Muslims following the conquest of Mecca. *Hijrah* is a significant event in Islamic history, as it marks the beginning of the Islamic calendar, and following this migration, Islamic civilization was established and thrived for centuries. Today, making *hijrah* is only necessary when a Muslim is persecuted in his homeland, or fears for his religious freedom, personal rights, dignity, and wealth. Muslims who emigrate from Muslim lands, live side by side with people of other religions, and practice their religion freely have no obligation to migrate to other lands.

PROPHET'S EXAMPLE:

• The Prophet Muhammad once met a man named Fudayk who had converted to Islam, but his entire tribe remained non-Muslim. Fudayk asked the Prophet whether he should leave his people and come live with the Muslims. The Prophet Muhammad replied, "O Fudayk, establish prayer, avoid bad deeds, and live with your people wherever you like" (Sahih Ibn Hibban).

> "He who migrates for God's cause will find many safe places and abundant resources on earth. If anyone leaves his home as an emigrant for God and His Messenger, and then he dies, his reward is certain with God. God is forever forgiving and Merciful-to-all."
>
> QUR'AN 4:100

To read more about *Hijrah* please see page 206

FAKE
ISLAMIC TEACHING

HIJRAH

MIGRATION TO THE "CALIPHATE"

DAESH DOGMA:

Daesh's recruitment and state-building campaigns rely heavily on the use of the term *hijrah* to draw foreign fighters to the so-called Caliphate. *Hijrah* is promoted as an obligation for Muslims who live in a Dar al-Harb (where non-Muslims rule) to migrate to Dar al-Islam (the Caliphate)—the only "safe haven" for Muslims. "True Believers" like them are expected to voluntarily leave their homes, properties, jobs, and parents for the sake of the Caliphate. They are told to disregard the world, their families, and their communities for the sake of the struggle. Those who migrate are expected to engage in combat or assist in building the Caliphate.

DAESH PROPAGANDA:

"Therefore, every Muslim professional who delayed his jihad in the past under the pretense of studying Shari'ah, medicine, or engineering, etc., claiming he would contribute to Islam later with his expertise, should now make his number one priority to repent and answer the call to *hijrah*, especially after the establishment of the *Khilafah*. This *Khilafah* is more in need than ever before for experts, professionals, and specialists, who can help contribute in strengthening its structure and tending to the needs of their Muslim brothers. Otherwise, his claims will become a greater proof against him on Judgment Day."[1]

[1] *Dabiq*, Issue 3, page 26.

Jihad

To struggle for excellence and the betterment of society

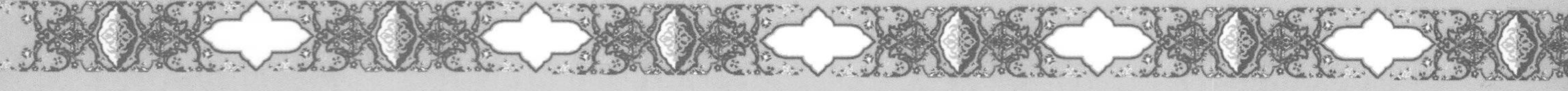

DEFINITION:

Jihad literally means to strive for excellence. There are many levels of *Jihad* that connote renewal and growth in the way of God:

- ***Jihad Al-Nafs***—the greatest and highest form of *jihad*—is struggle for self-purification by striving against the ego
- ***Jihad Al-Ilm*** is in pursuit of academic and juristic efforts
- ***Jihad Al-Amal*** is work to improve society through political, cultural, and education reform
- ***Jihad Al-Maal*** is to work through altruism to distribute wealth and eliminate poverty
- ***Jihad bi Al-Qital***—the last and final resort—is to fight back in self-defense against aggression and injustice (preemptive attacks and aggression are forbidden).

PROPHET'S EXAMPLE:

- Once a man came to the Prophet Muhammad (pbuh) and said: "Oh messenger of Allah! I want to go out and fight (in *Jihad*) and I have come to ask your advice." The Prophet said: "Do you have a mother?" The man said: "Yes." The Prophet said: "Then stay with her, for Paradise is beneath her feet" (Sunan an-Nasa').

"God does not forbid you respecting those who have not made war against you on account of (your) religion, and have not driven you from your homes, that you show them kindness and deal with them justly, surely God loves the doers of justice."

QUR'AN 60:8

To read more about *Jihad* please see pages 209, 213, and 215

ARMED STRUGGLE OR CONFLICT

DAESH DOGMA:

Daesh has limited the meaning of *jihad* to *jihad bi Al-Qital*, arguing that their "preemptive" attacks are acts of self-defense. Because a call to arms may only be declared by a recognized leader, Daesh appointed their own "caliph," who promotes armed *jihad* as an obligation to be carried out by all "true Muslims" against "enemies of Islam," including anyone who does not agree with their twisted ideology.

Though they position themselves as "defenders of Muslims," they actually kill more Muslims than any other group. They violate all rules of warfare: they encourage wanton killing of noncombatants, glorify gratuitous bloodshed and wide-scale destruction, and regularly employ forbidden tactics, including surprise attacks meant to inflict as many casualties as possible, including burning prisoners of war, suicide bombings, and raping and enslaving women.

DAESH PROPAGANDA

"One must either take the journey to dar al-Islam, joining the ranks of the mujahidin therein, or wage jihad by himself with the resources available to him (knives, guns, explosives, etc.) to kill the crusaders and other disbelievers and apostates, including the imams of kufr, to make an example of them, as all of them are valid - rather, obligatory - targets according to the Shari'ah, except for those who openly repent from kufr before they are apprehended." [1]

[1] *Dabiq*, Issue 14, page 17.

Shahid

To be a witness in the cause of truth

DEFINITION:

Shaheed literally means "witnessing," i.e., acknowledging the reality of God.

Shahid can mean "martyr," but its core meaning is to be a witness in the cause of Truth, or someone who has been killed unjustly or died an unfair death, e.g., in a fire, catastrophe, or an earthquake. The Prophet described various deaths that result in martyrdom, including dying from a plague, a disease of the stomach or intestines, through drowning, being crushed in a collapsing building, defending the faith or one's property, or a woman dying during childbirth.

A *shahid* is not someone who has been killed justly or as a punishment for an offense they committed.

Istimata, or "suicide acts," committed in the guise of martyrdom have no justification in Islam, as the Qur'an clearly states that human life is sacred and must be honored.

PROPHET'S EXAMPLE:

- The Prophet Muhammad witnessed a man who fought on the Prophet's side and had endured an injury. He chose to fall on his sword, killing himself. Muhammad gave his followers a lesson on suicide by saying, "a man may appear to people as performing the acts of an inhabitant of Paradise while he is [in the Hereafter] an occupant of Hell, and a man may appear to people as performing the acts of an inhabitant of Hell while he is an occupant of Paradise" (Bukhari).

"Nor Kill (or destroy) yourselves; for verily God has been to you most merciful! Who so does that through aggression and injustice, we will cast him into fire and that is very easy for God to do"

QUR'AN 4:29–30

To read more about *Shahid* please see page 217

SHAHID

TO BECOME A "MARTYR" THROUGH SUICIDE

DAESH DOGMA:

Daesh calls upon its fighters to die in combat and become *shahid* (martyrs), often through *istimata* (suicide acts), which they claim will expedite a fighter's journey to Paradise.

Daesh falsely claims that the "ends"—fighting alleged Western oppression and building the so-called caliphate—justify the "means," thus violating Islamic rules of warfare and the example set by the Prophet. They disregard the explicit Qur'anic prohibition on suicide, and sanction it by claiming that those who kill themselves—with the goal of creating the maximum amount of chaos, death, and destruction for their cause—will become *shahid*.

DAESH PROPAGANDA

"On this occasion, we will not forget to commend the martyred 'lone' knights of the *Khilafah* who struck out against the *kafir* and apostate enemies near them. . . . They did not use the obstacles laid down by the *kuffar* on the path to *hijrah* as an excuse to abandon *jihad* against the enemies. . . . They sacrificed their souls in the noblest of deeds in pursuit of Allah's pleasure."[1]

[1] *Dabiq*, Issue 12, page 3.

Khalifah / Khilafah

Vice-Regent of God / Succession

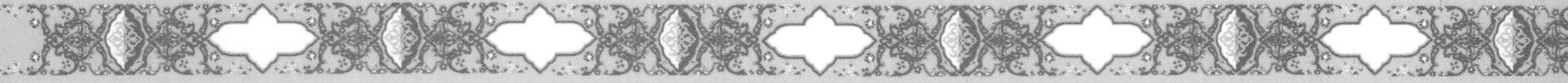

DEFINITION:

The term ***khalifah***, often translated as "vice-regent" or "steward," refers to humankind's responsibility on earth above all other creatures, and to care for all of God's creation.

Khilafah literally means "those who came after," and most scholars agree that it directly refers to the succession of the four "Rightly Guided Caliphs": Abu Bakr, Umar, Uthman and Ali, who were declared the successors of the Prophet through *shura* (consensus) following his death.

Neither the Qur'an nor the Prophet ever established a particular form of political governance, or mandated the creation of a "caliphate" or "Islamic state." Rather, the Qur'an provided general principles of guidance for "governing" the burgeoning Muslim community, specifying, for instance, the importance of *shura* (public consultation) and governing with justice. A Muslim leader is considered the representative (*wakeel*) and servant (*khadim*) of his/her people and rules only by their consent, not through presumed divine authority.[1]

PROPHET'S EXAMPLE:

- The Prophet said, "My community will never agree on an error." Scholars often interpret this to mean that God's will is reflected in the collective will of humanity, since humans are his vice-regents on earth.[2]

> "Behold, thy Lord said to the angels: "I will create a vice-regent on earth." They said: "Wilt Thou place therein one who will make mischief therein and shed blood?—whilst we do celebrate Thy praises and glorify Thy holy (name)?" He said: "I know what ye know not."
>
> QUR'AN 2:30

To read more about *Khalifah / Khilafah* please see page 220

[1] Rauf, Imam Feisal Abdul. *Defining Islamic Statehood: Measuring and Indexing Contemporary Muslim States*. Palgrave Macmillan, 2015, 38.
[2] Rauf, Imam Feisal Abdul. *Moving the Mountain: A New Vision of Islam in America*. Free Press, 2012, 165.

KHALIFAH / KHILAFAH

CALIPH / ISLAMIC STATE

DAESH DOGMA:

Daesh rejects all existing Muslim and non-Muslim nations as false and illegitimate authorities (*tawaghit*), and believes that only Daesh has a God-given mandate to re-establish a *Khilafah*, or "Caliphate."

Abu Bakr al-Baghdadi, the self-proclaimed *Khalifah* or "caliph," claims that all Muslims automatically fall under his authority, and that they are obligated to give their allegiance to him. Muslims are encouraged to give up their homes and families to help build and populate the caliphate.

In an attempt to religiously legitimize their political claims of authority, Daesh also calls itself the "Islamic State," though this concept is not found in the Qur'an, the Sunnah of the Prophet, or in any Islamic literature written before the twentieth century. Neither do the Qur'an and the Sunnah contain any state-building directives; rather, they only provide principles for just governance.

DAESH PROPAGANDA

"Here the flag of the Islamic State, the flag of *tawhid* (monotheism), rises and flutters. . . . The Muslims are honored. The *kuffar* (infidels) are disgraced. . . . The people of *bid'ah* (heresy) are humiliated. The *hudud* (Sharia penalties) are implemented. . . . The frontlines are defended. Crosses and graves are demolished. Prisoners are released by the edge of the sword. . . . *Jizyah* (a tax imposed on *kuffar*) has been enforced.... Courts have been established to resolve disputes and complaints. Evil has been removed. . . . There only remained one matter, a [collective obligation] that the *ummah* sins by abandoning. It is a forgotten obligation. . . . It is a dream that lives in the depths of every Muslim believer. It is a hope that flutters in the heart of every *mujahid muwahhid* (monotheist). It is the *khilafah* (caliphate). It is the *khilafah*-the abandoned obligation of the era."[1]

[1] Abu Bakr al-Baghdadi. "This Is the Promise of Allah."

Loyalty and Disavowal

Al'-Wala' wal Bara'

DR. MOHAMED BIN ALI discusses the Islamic principle Al'-Wala' wal Bara' and explains how this concept has been distorted by Daesh to create an "us versus them" ideology that is unsupported in the Qur'an.

KEY TAKEAWAYS

- *Al'-Wala' wal Bara'*, or "loyalty and disavowal," means love of God and love of goodness and virtue, and to distance oneself from evil, cruelty, and injustice.
- Daesh applies "good" to Muslims and "evil" to non-Muslims, such that the group harbors hatred for all who do not align with its ideology.
- Daesh inappropriately selectively uses Qur'anic verses that were revealed in specific circumstances and intentionally misinterprets their meaning to justify its cause.

To Daesh, the world is black and white, an "us versus them." They divide the world into two opposing sides: the evil non-Muslim West and the victorious, "pure" Islamic world of true believers. In the mind of the extremists, the non-Muslim world is the fundamental enemy of all Muslims and thus must be defeated and destroyed. At the foundation of this worldview is their reinterpretation of a concept known as *Al-Wala' wal Bara'*, or "loyalty and disavowal." In its most fundamental definition, the concept of Al-Wala' wal Bara' simply means love of God and love of goodness and virtue, and distancing oneself from all forms of vice, evil, cruelty, and injustice. To Daesh, however, the binary concepts of "good" and "evil" are applied to "Muslims" and "non-Muslims," respectively, such that the group harbors hatred for all non-Muslims and any Muslims who do not associate with them, viewing them to be the very embodiment of evil. This twisted narrative is concocted through the misquotation of a handful of phrases from the Qur'an and Sunnah of the Prophet Muhammad.

The bond of wala', or loyalty, is between a person and his *Wali'* (loyal protector/ally—the plural is *Awliya*). The term is used in the Qur'an where believers are told that they should possess the bond of *wala'* with God, the Prophet Muhammad, and their faith community: "*Verily your true Wali' is only Allah, His Messenger, and the (fellowship of) believers—those who establish regular prayers and regular charity and bow down humbly (in worship).*" (5:55). This relationship among believers does not, however, entail hostility toward those outside the faith community. Rather, it is an Islamic principle that the goodness of faith manifests itself in the manner by which the faithful treat one another (*akhlaq* or moral character).

> In the mind of the extremists, the non-Muslim world is the fundamental enemy of all Muslims and thus must be defeated and destroyed.

To Daesh, the concept of *Al-Wala' wal Bara'* is an important political instrument to rally others to their cause and increase their ranks. They argue that

DR. MOHAMED BIN ALI is an assistant professor of Inter-Religious Relations in Plural Societies at the S. Rajaratnam School of International Studies (RSIS) in Singapore and an expert in the areas of Islamic Jurisprudence, religious extremism, and rehabilitation of extremists. Since 2003, Dr. Ali has been involved in the rehabilitation of members of the terrorist group Jemaah Islamiyah (JI) in Singapore as a member of the Religious Rehabilitation Group (RRG). He has written extensively on these subjects, including his recent book *"The Roots of Religious Extremists: Understanding the Salafi Doctrine of Al-Wala' wal Bara'"*.

Muslims will lose their identity through association with outsiders, gradually assimilating foreign views and values. They argue that by failing to uphold *Al-Wala' wal Bara'*, Muslims have allowed Islam to become contaminated with Western influences, blurring the lines between Muslims and non-Muslims. Through its distorted interpretation of *Al-Wala' wal Bara'*, Daesh has incorrectly applied the practice of *takfir* to those who reject its violent ideology, thus justifying the slaughter of innocent Muslims and non-Muslims

Al-Wala' wal Bara' simply means love of God and love of goodness and virtue, and distancing oneself from all forms of vice, evil, cruelty, and injustice.

Daesh, however, does not like to portray itself as a "distorted" ideology—it claims to cite directly from the Qur'an and Sunnah. What Daesh has done, however, is to simply cherry-pick Qur'anic verses that were revealed in connection with very specific circumstances and misinterpret their meaning to justify their cause. That is why it is imperative to look at the social, historical, and political origins of the text when dealing with the sacred scriptures Daesh misquotes.

For example, Daesh commonly cites the verse, "*O you who believe, take not my enemies and your enemies as Awliya, extending upon them affection while they have disbelieved in what came to you of the truth, having driven out the Prophet and yourselves [only] because you believe in God*" (60:1). When one examines the historical context of the verse, it becomes abundantly clear that the "enemies" in this verse are the Quraysh who drove the Prophet and his followers from their homes in Mecca after years of relentless persecution, torture, and violence. Thus, the relationship of hostility between the Muslims and their violent Meccan oppressors is clearly case-specific and cannot logically be the template for relationships between Muslims and peaceful non-Muslims. This is explicitly stated in the very same chapter of the Qur'an: "*As for those who do not kill you on account of your faith nor drive you from your homes, God does not prevent you from dealing with them with kindness and the utmost respect*" (60:8).

Daesh also relies on another verse in the same chapter, which states:

> *There is certainly a good exemplar for you in Abraham and those who were with him, when they said to their own people, "Indeed we repudiate you and whatever you worship besides Allah. We disavow you, and between you and us there has appeared enmity and hate for ever, unless you come to have faith in Allah alone," except for Abraham's saying to his father, "I will surely plead forgiveness for you, though I cannot avail you anything against Allah" (60:4).*

They misinterpret and misapply this verse to claim that, just as Abraham declared enmity and hate for his own people (who were polytheists), they should be hostile toward all those who do not believe in their cause—even their fellow Muslims. But this is another prime example of misquotation—the verse is instructing the followers of Muhammad to deal with the Quraysh in the same way that Abraham dealt with his people. The Prophet Abraham invited his followers to faith in One God and only showed hostility to his people after he discovered some were still practicing idolatry and polytheism. Thus, both verses are case-specific and cannot be used as a blanket claim for hostilities against anyone who disagrees with Daesh.

Another of the common verses that Daesh distorts and uses to legitimize their concept of *Al-Wala' wal Bara'* is verse 5:51, which states: "*O you who have faith! Do not take the Jews and the Christians for allies; they are allies of each other. Any of you who allies with them is indeed one of them. Indeed Allah does not guide the wrongdoing lot.*" Again this citation indicates a complete disregard for the social, historical, and political context in which the verse was revealed. It was revealed after some Jewish tribesmen broke the mutual defense and peace treaty known as the Pact of Medina by traveling to Mecca and forming an alliance with the Quraysh, thus leaving Muslims without anyone to trust but each other.

But citing this verse alone ignores the fact that the Prophet Muhammad did in fact reach out and seek to foster ties with the Jewish tribes of Medina through the Pact of Medina. Likewise, Daesh also chooses to ignore the instances when the Prophet and early Muslims sought relations with their Christian neighbors. A notable example of this is seen when the Najran (modern day Yemen) Christian delegation came to the Prophet to ask him about the new religion of Islam. Although they humbly rejected the Prophet's message, the Prophet Muhammad invited the delegates into his own mosque and gave them protection while they performed their worship and rituals.

If Islamic civilization is to be truly "revived," which extremists claim as their goal, we must return to the tolerance that was once our shining hallmark.

The Prophet also sent members of the early Muslim community to seek protection under the Christian King Negus in Abyssinia (modern-day Ethiopia). He is recorded to have said, "If you went to the land of the Abyssinians, you would find there a king under whose command nobody suffers injustice. It is a land of sincerity in religion." The king granted absolute protection to the Muslim immigrants, even after the Meccan idolaters came to him requesting that he betray the Prophet and the early Muslims and send them back to Mecca.

This sort of peaceful coexistence between the three Abrahamic religions is encouraged in the Qur'an as well: "*O mankind! Indeed We created you from a male and a female, and made you nations and tribes that you may identify yourselves with one another. Indeed the noblest of you in the sight of Allah is the most God-conscious among you. Indeed Allah is all-knowing, all-aware.*" This verse is best exemplified during the Umayyad Dynasty in a place called Al-Andalus, or Muslim Spain, which was regarded as the leading cultural and economic center of the day. It was also an era of harmonious coexistence and cooperation between the three Abrahamic faiths.

If Islamic civilization is to be truly "revived," which extremists claim as their goal, we must return to the tolerance that was once our shining hallmark. This will entail a return to the compassionate and welcoming example of the Prophet, who sought to build ties with other communities and foster peaceful dialogue. It will entail correcting extremists' misuse of terms like *Al-Wala' wal Bara'*, and preventing them from leading to the Muslim world into self-annihilation.

One Community

Ummah

The concept of ummah is what binds the world's 1.6 billion Muslims together. **IMAM TAHIR KUKAJ** shows the true meaning of ummah to discredit Daesh's interpretation of the term.

KEY TAKEAWAYS

- *Ummah* is a bond that stretches beyond geographical boundaries and unites all Muslims by a shared belief in God.
- *Ummah* is a society that is in the state of eternally going and becoming toward the Absolute God.
- The Qur'an speaks out against any one individual possessing the authority over the entire *ummah*.

The term "community," or *ummah*, in Islam is derived from the root word "*umm*," meaning intention, resolution. The word "*ummah*" is a combination of three meanings: movement, goal, and conscious choice. The root word "*umm*" also has the meaning of "pioneer" in it. Thus, there are four elements that define this word: choice, movement, pioneer or progressive, and destination. By retaining all of these meanings, the word "*ummah*" essentially means "clear way," that is, a society or a human group in the sense of "on a way."

Here, a particular insight of Islam appears. In Islamic culture all of the words used to express religion, in various constructions, are words that mean "way." We can find this kind of thinking in the form of the special religious terminology in Islam: *madhab* (way), *suluk* (way), *shari'ah* (water way), *tariq* and *tariqah* (way), *sabil Allah* (way of God), *sirat* (way), *hajj* (intention of doing something or going someplace), *rajat* (the human being in existence), *hijrat* (the basis of Islam in the place of birth of the Holy Prophet, the conquest of Mecca, and even the appointment of the Prophet to prophethood). Thus, Islam places a lot of emphasis upon the principle of "movement" in the sense that it is eternally changing, yet eternally permanent.

Even though there have been many different terms in the European, Arabic, and Persian languages used to define a group of human beings—terms like *nation*, *tribe*, *class*, *society*, and *race*—Islam defines its group of believers as a community, *ummah*. Why? Because *ummah* is a bond that stretches beyond geographical boundaries and unites all people by a shared belief in God and the shared divine plan for life in the hereafter.

Although it is possible that human individuals have a goal and believe in their tribe, for instance, there is no guarantee that they will move toward that goal. They simply believe in the same things. They have the same goal in the mental or emotional sense just as our Muslim societies have a goal and a common ideal, but they do not take steps toward attaining it. The *ummah*, however, actively takes steps to reach this shared goal, as expressed in the following Qur'anic verse: "*But as for those who desire the life to come, and who endeavor earnestly to obtain it, and (demonstrate) that they truly believe—they are the ones who find favor (with God)*" (17:19).

Furthermore, we can understand the *ummah* as a society that does not stay or remain in any one place. Individuals who are part of the *ummah* are committing to a life not of "being" in the stagnant sense, but of "going." It is a human society in which all the individuals hold a common goal and join together so that they may move toward their ideal. And in Islam, this common goal is a "going and becoming" toward

IMAM TAHIR KUKAJ is Imam of the Albanian Islamic Cultural Center in Staten Island, New York. He is a prominent lecturer and speaker on issues related to Islam and interfaith relations. In addition, Imam Kukaj is one of the original members of the Muslim Advisory Council for the NYPD, formed in 2012 to provide Muslim leaders direct access to the police commissioner to advocate for issues affecting their community.

God, for He is not a specific place and does not begin in any particular place. Thus, *ummah* is a society that is in the state of eternally going and becoming toward the Absolute. We can see this referenced in the Qur'an in the following verses: "*Unto God shall be referred all affairs*" (42:53); "*For unto God is the end of your journey*" (3:27); and "*We belong to God and unto Him do we return*" (2:156).

Ummah is a bond that stretches beyond geographical boundaries and unites all people by a shared belief in God and the shared divine plan for life in the hereafter.

One of the requirements of the *ummah* is a leadership to guide its members toward the final goal. To Muslims, the Prophet Muhammad is a living exemplar of this leadership because his life, spirits, and ethics show humanity how it should be and how it should live. During his lifetime, the Prophet made it his social mission to create an inclusive community where *all* peoples could practice their faith, without persecution or coercion, and obtain the ultimate goal of the Hereafter. His leadership is exemplified by the Pact of Medina in which he negotiated a settlement with the various clans in Medina. What makes this Pact remarkable is that it explicitly refers to Christians, Jews, and the pagan citizens of Medina as members of the *ummah*.

The Qur'an also teaches that the *ummah* is not only for Muslims, or even only for humans. God has made it so all of His creation are members of the *ummah*, as seen in the Qur'anic verse stating, "*Every beast that crawls on the earth and every bird that flies with its two wings have formed communities like you. We have left nothing out of The Book. Later, they will be gathered to their Lord*" (6:38). In light of this verse, it becomes clear that no one person, or creature, may be excluded from the *ummah* based on their beliefs or identity.

With these examples, we can see how extremist groups like Daesh have manipulated the concept of *ummah* to include only those who agree with their twisted and violent ideology. There is no "one" *ummah*. It is also not permitted for one individual to claim to possess the authority over the *ummah*, as Daesh's self-declared leader Abu Bakr al-Baghdadi has done.

Furthermore, the Qur'an speaks against one individual possessing the authority over the entire *ummah*. Instead, the Qur'an and the Prophet Muhammad teach of the importance of ruling by consensus and the opinion of the group on decisions concerning the *ummah*. The Prophet was never one to make rulings without having consulted his closest companions first and having it sanctioned by members of the *ummah*. He even sought out the consensus of his first wife, Khadijah, before sharing the news that he had received his first revelations from God. This is made explicitly clear in the following verse, which states:

> *O you who have faith! Obey Allah and obey the Apostle and those vested with authority among you. And if you dispute concerning anything, refer it to Allah and the Apostle, if you have faith in Allah and the Last Day. That is better and more favorable in outcome. (4:59)*

We can now begin to see more clearly how Daesh has distorted Islamic teachings and history to achieve its twisted political goals. Its claims are proven to be in direct contradiction to the Qur'anic and Prophetic teachings on human relations toward all of God's creation.

Excommunication

Takfir

Claiming to possess the authority to determine who is a "real" Muslim and who is not, Daesh uses the practice of takfir (declaring someone an apostate) to justify the killing of Muslims who do not subscribe to its distorted ideology, but as **IMAM MOHAMED MAGID** points out, this directly violates the Qur'an.

KEY TAKEAWAYS

- The act of takfir has been declared forbidden in Islam as it is a source of social unrest, doubt among believers, and danger to the global Muslim community.
- Extremist groups aggressively practice takfir as a political weapon to denounce any Muslim head of state or religious leader who challenges the group's authority.
- Exremist groups also use takfir as a psychological tool to manipulate people and promote an "us versus them" mentality, where one is either with them or against them.

The world has become all too familiar with Daesh's brutal ways. The most shocking, however, is their senseless violence toward their fellow Muslims. Using a distorted understanding of the Islamic concept known as *takfir*, they have declared that any fellow Muslim who rejects their twisted ideology is a *kafir* (unbeliever). In doing so, they have illegitimately justified the slaughter of countless innocent, peaceful Muslims around the world. However, the inherent violence and danger *takfir* poses to the worldwide Muslim community have made it a forbidden act in Islam and it has received widespread condemnations from Muslim states and leaders. In 2011, Tunisia even went so far as to place a constitutional ban on *fatwas* (Islamic legal rulings) that call for *takfir* against fellow Muslims.

The act of *takfir*, or accusing a fellow Muslim of apostasy (*riddah*) and unbelief (*kufr*), has been almost universally rejected throughout Islamic history. For one, claiming to possess the authority to judge an individual's faith and submission to God is to essentially undermine the ultimate authority and knowledge of God. This is because the Qur'an teaches that only God has the knowledge and authority to judge on the basis of one's faith: "*Say, 'Indeed I stand on a manifest proof from my Lord and you have denied it. What you hasten is not up to me. Judgment belongs only to God; He expounds the truth and He is the best of judges'*" (6:57), and "*Indeed your Lord knows best those who stray from His way; and He knows best those who are guided*" (6:117). Moreover, the Prophet Muhammad condemned those who accused their fellow Muslims of apostasy, saying, "*Whoever says to his brother 'disbeliever' then it will have settled upon one of them*" (at-Tirmidhi).

Claiming to possess the authority to judge an individual's faith and submission to God is to essentially undermine the ultimate authority and knowledge of God.

In addition to *takfir* being a forbidden practice in Islam, it has been the source of great social unrest (*fitnah* or "sedition") throughout Islamic history, as it casts

IMAM MOHAMMED MAGID is executive director of the All Dulles Area Muslim Society (ADAMS), located in Sterling, Virginia. In the past, he has worked with organizations like the Peaceful Families Project, Annual Twinning of Mosques and Synagogues, Fairfax Faith Communities in Action, Interfaith Conference of Metropolitan Washington Assembly, and the Buxton Interfaith Initiative. Imam Magid strives to increase communication and understanding about Islam.

doubt among believers and leads one to question his/her own faith. This is best seen with the group the Khawarij, who are often regarded as the first violent extremist group. In an attempt to delegitimize the authority of Caliph Ali and secure their own leader, the Khawarij claimed that they were the "true Muslims" and treated all others with violence and hostility. To them, any Muslim who "sinned" could no longer be considered a pure Muslim—"sin" as defined by them, of course. Similarly, the Khawarij used *takfir* as a political weapon—a method employed by Daesh to justify slaughter.

The Prophet Muhammad condemned those who accused their fellow Muslims of apostasy, saying, "*Whoever says to his brother 'disbeliever' then it will have settled upon one of them*" (at-Tirmidhi).

Daesh and similar extremist groups aggressively practice *takfir* as a political weapon to denounce any Muslim head of state or religious leader who poses a threat to the group's authority by labeling them *murtadd* (apostate). This was first seen in Ibn Taymiyyah's *fatwa* against the Mongol convert invaders due to the fact that they enforced their own laws in place of Shari'ah. Similarly, Daesh has made it clear that Muslim rulers who do not fully implement Shari'ah as understood by Daesh are apostate sinners who place the laws of man above the laws of God, thus breaking their *shahadah*. They cherry-pick and distort the Qur'anic verse that says:

> *We sent down the Torah containing guidance and light. The prophets, who had submitted, judged by it for the Jews, and so did the rabbis and the scribes, as they were charged to preserve the Book of Allah and were witnesses to it. So do not fear the people, but fear Me, and do not sell My signs for a paltry gain. Those who do not judge by what Allah has sent down—it is they who are faithless* (5:44).

More specifically, Daesh sees Muslim leaders in the West as actively siding with the disbelievers and "enemies of Islam" in a battle against the "true believers." Thus, using the practice of *takfir*, Daesh falsely justifies and encourages the violent overthrow and assassination of these leaders in order to further protect their authority.

Takfir is just another deadly extension of the extremists' distorted ideology and understanding of the doctrine of *Al-Wala' wal Bara'*. It is being used as a psychological tool to manipulate disenfranchised individuals and fuel their violent "us versus them" mind-set, where one is either "with them" or "against them." And, according to their distorted doctrine of *Al-Wala' wal Bara'*, if one is against them, then he/she is a non-believer who should be killed according to the violent rules of *takfir*.

Yet, the world's 1.6 billion peaceful Muslims know that this is not a sanctioned practice in Islam, as one of the most important tenets in Islam is, "*There is no compulsion in religion*" (2:256). The truth remains that Daesh will never possess the authority to declare *takfir* and accuse a fellow Muslim of non-belief—nor will they ever be justified in practicing *takfir* that results in such a devastating loss of life.

Pledge of Allegiance

Bay'ah

IMAM SOULEIMANE KONATÉ describes the three historical categories of bay'ah within Islam and shows that Daesh's use of the practice is doctrinally inaccurate and merely another tool the group uses to advance its political goals.

KEY TAKEAWAYS

- Bay'ah was seen as a symbol of one's dedication and faithfulness to the principles of Islam and observance of correct moral behavior.
- The Prophet Muhammad set the precedent that the bay'ah given to a leader under duress is null and void, so bay'ah must be a mutual agreement conditioned on being given freely.
- Daesh has admitted to using bay'ah as propaganda and has distorted and abused the practice of bay'ah into a political weapon to instigate violence.

One of the greatest challenges in the fight against Daesh has been providing attractive counter-narratives to their twisted ideology. Between their mastering of social media and sophisticated recruitment network, Daesh has been able to use this ideology to infiltrate our communities and prey on the most vulnerable among us. They manipulate these individuals into declaring their allegiance with false promises of greatness and belonging. We have seen this most recently in Orlando, where an angry, unstable individual gave his allegiance to the group in the course of committing a horrific crime against humanity. The "*bay'ah*," or so-called pledge of allegiance, that this mass murderer allegedly gave to Daesh before slaughtering dozens and killing himself, has been one of the most powerful tools used to influence the disenfranchised in our communities, and to make Daesh's influence seem more widespread.

Daesh's conception of *bay'ah*, however, is yet another example of the extremist group's distortion of Islamic teachings. Classical Muslim scholars and jurists have established that there are three categories of *bay'ah* that have existed throughout history. The first originated with the Prophet Muhammad and has been classified as *bay'ah* on the tenets of faith. This was a ritual one took with the Prophet upon accepting Islam and declaring the *shahadah*, or when reaffirming one's faith in *tawhid* (monotheism) and devotion to God and His Messenger. This *bay'ah* also symbolized the acceptance of the Prophet as one's spiritual mentor, a practice that still exists today within Sufism, where one gives his/her allegiance to his/her Sheikh.

> The Prophet established the *bay'ah* as a conditional mutual agreement that is only valid as long as both parties uphold the moral and spiritual principles stipulated in the Qur'an and the Sunnah.

Giving *bay'ah* to the Prophet Muhammad played a key role in the establishment of the first Muslim community in Medina. It was seen as a symbol of one's allegiance, dedication, and faithfulness to the principles of Islam and observance of correct moral

IMAM SOULEIMANE KONATÉ is a Harlem-based imam who has been described as part religious leader, part social worker. An immigrant from Ivory Coast, he works to assist the African immigrant community in New York City. Imam Konaté studied Islamic law at Egypt's Al-Azhar University and pursued a communications degree in Saudi Arabia, where he lived and worked as a journalist for twelve years.

behavior. Furthermore, it served as a symbolic act in which those in the early Muslim community acknowledged their obligation to obey the Prophet Muhammad as their leader and spiritual mentor. However, this *bay'ah* was contractual in the sense that it existed so long as the Prophet acted in accordance to the Word and Laws of God and exhibited correct moral behavior in all aspects of life and leadership without compromise. In doing so, this *bay'ah* laid the foundations for the ideal Islamic society where Islam became the guiding force of daily life.

Their viral campaign shows images of people "pledging their allegiance" in different parts of the world, reducing the sacred pledge of *bay'ah* to nothing more than a tool of intimidation to make Daesh seem more powerful, threatening, and widespread than they actually are.

The most famous example of *bay'ah* during the time of the Prophet is known as the "Pledge of the Tree," which the Prophet asked the early Muslim community in Medina to take before embarking on the pilgrimage back to Mecca. This *bay'ah* served as a mutual agreement between the Prophet and the Muslim community to support and protect each other against the Meccans should a battle ensue. This *bay'ah* was significant in that it represented the precursor to the Treaty of Hudaybiyyah and the ten-year peace between the Meccans and the Muslim community, which is reflected in the Qur'anic verse stating: "*Allah was well pleased with the believers when they swore allegiance unto thee beneath the tree, and He knew what was in their hearts, and He sent down peace of reassurance onto them, and hath rewarded them with a near victory*" (48:18).

A crucial aspect of *bay'ah* under the Prophet is the fact that it was willingly and freely taken by his followers. As such, the *bay'ah* of the Prophet Muhammad set the precedent that any oath of allegiance given to a leader under duress is immediately null and void. Furthermore, the Prophet established the *bay'ah* as a conditional mutual agreement that is only valid as long as both parties uphold the moral and spiritual principles stipulated in the Qur'an and the Sunnah. Clearly, Daesh can never claim to be upholding these moral and spiritual principles, as their use of violence goes against the examples set by the Prophet and the early Muslim community.

After the death of the Prophet, the ritual of *bay'ah* became a symbol of the masses' approval of their chosen leader. This is regarded as the third category of *bay'ah* and was practiced under the first caliphs so as to establish a new institution of authority and ensure the continuity of leadership. This political form of *bay'ah* was almost democratic in nature as it was established that the *bay'ah* could only be given to a leader who was chosen by the consensus of the influential members of society who represented the voice of the Muslim masses.

For example, after being chosen as successor to the Prophet Muhammad by his closest companions, Abu Bakr humbly asked the general public to give their *bay'ah* to him with the promise that he would establish justice and follow the Qur'an and Sunnah of the Prophet Muhammad or else they were no longer obligated to follow him. Thus, from the very beginning, the concept of giving and receiving *bay'ah* put a limitation on human authority by stipulating that obedience to God and His Prophet is obligatory for both the ruler and the people. This is clearly stipulated in the following verse of the Qur'an, in which God says: "*It is not (possible) for any human being unto whom Allah had given the Scripture and wisdom and the prophethood that he should afterwards have said unto mankind: Be slaves of me instead of Allah; but (what he said was): Be ye faithful servants of the Lord by virtue of your constant teachings of the Scripture and of your constant study thereof*" (3:79).

This is the core fault in Daesh's call for Muslims around the world to declare their allegiance to the group's violent cause. For one, Daesh's leader, Abu Bakr al-Baghdadi, is far from the embodiment of the leadership of the Prophet Muhammad. He calls for the killing of innocent individuals, encourages the oppression, rape, and enslavement of women and girls, and can never claim to represent the consensus of the world's 1.6 billion Muslims. Furthermore, al-Baghdadi has attempted to legitimize his rule on the basis of being a descendant of the Prophet—a claim that has yet to be verified, as his background is still unknown to most.

Daesh has distorted and abused the practice of *bay'ah*, turning it into a political weapon to instigate violence and terror. Their misuse brainwashes individuals into sacrificing their lives and the lives of innocent civilians in the belief that it is the only way to reach Paradise. They propagate a distorted interpretation of the Hadith of the Prophet Muhammad that states, "One who dies without having bound himself by an oath of allegiance will die the death of one belonging to the days of Jahiliyyah" (Sahih Muslim), in order to bait individuals into carrying out violent acts on their behalf. Thus, they have concocted a narrative surrounding their distorted understanding of *bay'ah* in which vulnerable individuals believe the only way to Paradise is to give their allegiance—and life—to the so-called Caliphate.

Moreover, Daesh have admitted to using *bay'ah* as recruitment propaganda in order to engender fear and intimidation, stating, "*We call every Muslim [to pledge allegiance] towards this good, for indeed, it is even more infuriating for the enemies of Allah. By Allah, our rallying under one leader is harder on the enemies of Allah than a thousand victories on the battlefield.*"[1] Their viral campaign shows images of people "pledging their allegiance" in different parts of the world, reducing the sacred pledge of *bay'ah* to nothing more than a tool of intimidation to make Daesh seem more powerful, threatening, and widespread than they actually are. But Muslims worldwide know that they are not obligated to give *bay'ah* to Daesh, and they know that a criminal such as Abu Bakr al-Baghdadi will never receive the full support of the world's peaceful Muslims. As the Qur'an says, "*Believers, obey God and the Messenger and those among you who have been entrusted with authority. If you have a dispute about anything, refer it to God and the Messenger, if you truly believe in God and the Last Day. This is best to do and in turn gives the best results*" (4:59).

[1] "Remaining and Expanding," *Dabiq*, Muharram 1436, Issue 5, 23, <http://media.clarionproject.org/files/islamic-state/isis-isil-islamic-state-magazine-issue-5-remaining-and-expanding.pdf>.

Migration
Hijrah

IMAM MOHAMAD BASHAR ARAFAT explains that hijrah is a journey to further one's spirituality and faith. Daesh contorts this concept to entice supporters to travel to their territory.

KEY TAKEAWAYS

- Hijrah has always been understood as a journey to further one's faith and thus help build a more just society.
- Hijrah has been manipulated and taken out of context by Daesh to encourage recruits to travel to the "caliphate."
- Its true form is a movement forward, to a brighter, more just future with respect for all faiths.

Linguistically, the term *hijrah* refers to a "departure" or "migration," and most commonly refers to the migration of the Prophet Muhammad and the early Muslim community to escape years of persecution and violence at the hands of the Meccan idolaters and finally establish a community of their own. The inability of the Muslims in Mecca to practice their faith freely led to God's instruction to perform *hijrah* to another land, and so *hijrah* has always been about a journey to further one's spirituality and faith and thus help in building a more just society.

> In its true form, *hijrah* is a movement forward, a migration toward a brighter, more just future where all believers are able to practice their faith freely with mutual respect to those who may differ in faith.

Among extremist groups, however, *hijrah* represents the idea that it is obligatory for all Muslims to leave "lands of disbelief" and take up residence in the "true lands of Islam" (as defined by the extremists), and carry arms and fight non-Muslims and Muslims who disagree with their ways. Today, *hijrah* has been manipulated and stripped of its true significance and context, and has become a major propaganda tool used by Daesh and other extremist groups. They try to convince vulnerable individuals living in non-Muslim-majority countries that they are persecuted and don't belong, and thus should emulate the Prophet's *hijrah* and travel to the so-called Caliphate. Consequently, Muslims must stand against these distortions of Islam and revive the true meaning of *hijrah* spiritually and socially.

In order to evaluate the claim that Muslims must leave their households and perform *hijrah*, one must analyze the circumstances that led to the Muslims' migration from Mecca in the time of the Prophet. After receiving the revelation of prophethood, the Prophet Muhammad and the early Muslim community became targets of relentless harassment from the Meccan community. They were enslaved, starved, and beaten because they believed in One God. The Meccans' resistance to the Prophet's message became so great that members of his community were forced to flee their homes and seek refuge in

IMAM MOHAMAD BASHAR ARAFAT is the founder and president of the Civilizations Exchange and Cooperation Foundation (CECF). Born and raised in Syria, he earned degrees in Islamic Studies, Arabic, and Islamic Law from Damascus University. Imam Arafat has studied the Qur'an under the late Grand Mufti of Syria, Sheikh Ahmad Kuftaro, and served as both professor and imam at numerous American universities. He also works with youth in various programs, including the Youth Exchange Study (YES) Program, and he is the convener of several annual international youth leadership, intercultural, and interfaith conferences called Better Understanding for a Better World.

foreign lands. The Prophet urged those who has no one to protect them, such as slaves and the weak, to migrate to Abyssinia (modern-day Ethiopia) and seek protection from its Christian king. Even members of the Prophet's family were forced out of Mecca, a journey known as the first Muhajirun, to Abyssinia. However, the Prophet Muhammad remained in Mecca and continued to spread the Word of God to those who would listen.

For thirteen years, the Prophet Muhammad continued to spread the message of Islam throughout Mecca, and endured constant persecution and harassment that limited his ability to freely practice his religion because of it. Despite these hardships, he neither raised his hands in retaliation, nor did he flee when his task as God's Messenger seemed impossible. He remained steadfast in his service to God and freed the downtrodden from the oppression and subjugation of the Meccan idolaters. It was only when the Prophet Muhammad learned of the Meccans' plot to murder him that he undertook to journey to Medina to spread God's message of global mercy, peace, and justice.

This marks the second and most significant *hijrah*. It was in 622 CE that the Prophet Muhammad received God's blessing and called upon his community to follow him on a daunting, 300-mile journey in search of religious freedom and, ultimately, belonging. And that is exactly what they found when they arrived in Medina. *Hijrah* was first and foremost for religious freedom, and it was in Medina that the Prophet Muhammad established the first Muslim community under the banner of Islam and forged an authentic Muslim identity. The importance of this *hijrah* is so great that it came to designate the first year of the Muslim calendar.

Those who migrated in both *hijrahs* were praised in the Qur'an 24 times in various chapters: "*Those who believe, and have immigrated, and have struggled in the way of God with their possessions and their lives are greater in degree with God; and those, they are the triumphant. Their Lord gives them good tidings of mercy from Him and beatitude; for them shall be gardens wherein is enduring bliss, therein they shall abide forever. Surely with God is a tremendous reward*" (9:20–22).

It is important to note also that when the Prophet Muhammad was able to return to Mecca eight years after his migration to Medina, forgiving and pardoning all those who fought him for 20 years and killed many of his disciples and family members, he said to all the people, "No *hijrah* after the return to Mecca, except the struggle in the path of God with good intentions" (Bukhari). This Hadith clearly shows that the purpose of *hijrah* was the pursuit of religious freedom. Since the Muslims were able to learn and practice their religion freely once they had returned to Mecca, there was no need for them to migrate anymore to Medina.

"No *hijrah* after the return to Mecca, except the struggle in the path of God with good intentions" (Bukhari).

For the Meccan Muslims who migrated to Medina, it was more than just a migration to find a free and more secure place to call home. It was a chance for them to grow closer to Almighty God by being close to His Beloved Prophet Muhammad, the physical embodiment of Islam. Seeking knowledge purely for the sake of God is what is believed to be the true or ultimate form of *hijrah*, a belief echoed by the Prophet Muhammad in one of the most inspiring Hadith known to Muslims around the world: "Actions are judged by intentions, and everyone will get what was intended. Whoever migrates with an intention for Allah and His messengers, the migration will be for the sake of Allah and his Messenger. And whoever migrates for worldly gain or to marry a woman, then his migration will be for the sake of whatever he migrated for" (Bukhari and Muslim).

This saying of the Prophet Muhammad brings us to the crux of the issue facing the Muslim world today: Daesh is attempting to manipulate the purpose of *hijrah* and present it as a religious duty for "true" Muslims to travel to the so-called Caliphate and join the militant fight against the so-called *kuffar* (non-believers). There are serious flaws in this representation of *hijrah*. For one, the Prophet Muhammad was recorded as saying: "The true immigrant is the one who migrated from all the vices, bad behavior and actions. The true Muslim is the one who the people are safe from his tongue and his hand" (Bukhari). Although Daesh may paint the picture that their call for *hijrah* includes a departure from impure "Western" vices and behaviors, they will never be "true" Muslims by the Prophet's definition, for all their actions jeopardize the safety and livelihood of those who cross their path. They paint the picture that the "Western *kuffar*," who are hosting millions of Muslims in Europe and in America today, are actively trying to rid the world of Islam and persecuting Muslims to the point of extinction. By doing so, they are able to recruit whom they call the "true believers" of Islam to make their own *hijrah* to the so-called Caliphate and rebuild the community (*ummah*) of believers that was established after the Prophet Muhammad's *hijrah*.

In its true form, *hijrah* is a movement forward, a migration toward a brighter, more just future where all believers are able to practice their faith freely with mutual respect to those who may differ in faith. The true *hijrah* of the Prophet Muhammad was a new dawn for humanity to prosper through these ideals and values that push wars and conflicts away and replace them with compassion, peace, and respect for God's Will in this universe of cultural and religious diversity. His *hijrah* showed that the only difference God sees among the sons of Adam and Eve is their *taqwa* (piety), not the color of their skin, ethnicity, or wealth. The Prophet Muhammad's *hijrah* began with freeing the oppressed. His *hijrah* was a declaration of women's rights—their equality and equal responsibility with men in shaping the community of Islam, the religion of Abraham and all the prophets who followed. His *hijrah* was to tell the Muslims that the word of God starts with respect for human dignity. The Prophet Muhammad's *hijrah* was truly an event that changed the course of history forever and declared to the world that God's word is mercy, compassion, and love for all.

The Lesser Jihad and the Prohibition on Terrorism

Terrorists define their attacks as jihad ("to struggle" or "to strive" in the way of God), but **SUMBUL ALI-KARAMALI** debunks this claim by explaining that the lesser jihad can only be conducted in self-defense and that terrorism violates the rules of jihad.

KEY TAKEAWAYS

- There are three kinds of lesser jihad: by the tongue, by the hands, and by the sword. The first two are preferred and jihad by the sword should be a last resort.
- Extremists take fighting verses out of their historical context, which is a major error in Qur'anic interpretation. The context is essential to understanding jihad.
- The term jihad has been utterly misappropriated by terrorists and media outlets, who use jihad interchangeably with terrorism, normalizing the terrorists' rhetoric.

The Prophet Muhammad once famously remarked, upon returning from battle, that he had returned from the lesser jihad (physical fighting) only to engage in the greater jihad (the struggle to become a better person). *Jihad* means "to struggle" or "to strive" in the way of God. The internal jihad, called the "greater jihad" or "jihad by the heart," is the struggle to improve oneself; the external jihad is the struggle to improve society. The external jihad is an exhortation to social justice and can take many forms. Islamic law identifies three kinds of external jihad:

1. Jihad by the tongue, which means using verbal persuasion (such as writing letters to the editor) to correct an injustice;
2. Jihad by the hands, which means undertaking good works (such as volunteering at a homeless shelter) to improve people's lives; and
3. Jihad by the sword, which means the use of force in self-defense or to overthrow direct oppression.

Jihad by the sword, also called military jihad, is therefore never aggressive warfare, but defensive warfare against an attack or against direct oppression. Terrorist groups such as al-Qaeda and Daesh define their terror attacks as "jihad." But, are these terrorist groups really exercising jihad? No, for several reasons: First, terrorism has always been prohibited and severely punished in Islam. Second, neither al-Qaeda nor Daesh is acting in self-defense or to overthrow oppression as defined in Islamic law. Third, a legitimate jihad cannot be declared by just anyone, but only by a publicly recognized caliph or imam who is a leader of the worldwide Muslim community; the leaders of al-Qaeda and/or Daesh are not universally accepted caliphs or imams. And finally, *even if* the actions of these terrorist groups qualified as a legitimate jihad (which they do not), they would be required to follow these strict rules of engagement, which they have repeatedly violated:

1. Muslims may not attack noncombatants and civilians of any kind;
2. Muslims may not arbitrarily destroy property;
3. Muslims may not uproot trees;
4. Muslims may not kill people who are wounded or fleeing;
5. Muslims may not poison the water supply;
6. Muslims may not commit suicide;
7. Muslims may not engage in terrorism;

SUMBUL ALI-KARAMALI earned a BA from Stanford University, a JD from the University of California, Davis, and an LLM. in Islamic law from the University of London's School of Oriental and African Studies. She has practiced corporate law, taught Islamic law, and been a research associate at the Centre of Islamic and Middle Eastern Law in London. Her award-winning book, *The Muslim Next Door: The Qur'an, the Media, and That Veil Thing*, appeared on the American Academy of Religion's Islam section list as a recommended text for teaching Islam, as well as the Huffington Post's "Eleven Must-Read Books by Muslim Authors." Her second book, *Growing Up Muslim*, is an introduction to Islam for ages ten and up. Sumbul is a frequent speaker and lecturer. She is currently working on her third book.

8. Muslims may not engage in cheating and treachery;
9. Muslims may not commit rape;
10. Muslims may not terrorize populations;
11. Muslims may not torture any people or animals; and
12. Muslims may not wage war against other Muslims.

These rules are consistent with modern international rules of warfare and, if anything, are more stringent. Therefore, al-Qaeda and Daesh are not engaging in jihad; even worse, they are violating numerous rules of jihad and established Islamic law. This makes them mass murderers and criminals under Islamic law.

According to Sheikh bin Bayyah, a professor of Islamic studies at the King Abdul Aziz University in Jeddah, Saudi Arabia, and one of the most well respected Islamic scholars in the world, the crime of terrorism in Islamic law is defined as "all violent acts that aim to obliterate, sabotage, and terrorize people, kill the innocent, and destroy property . . . [including] the circulation of illegal drugs, as well as the violence of vigilantes against legitimate authorities, aimed to create sedition and anarchy and strike fear among civilians, or even with the express aim of overthrowing a legitimate government."[1] Clearly under this definition, the atrocities committed by al-Qaeda and the group known as Daesh are classified as terrorism—a punishable crime in Islam—and can never be classified as "jihad."

Though terrorists have wrongly equated "jihad" with "waging holy war on 'infidels,'" jihad has never meant "holy war" in Islam. On the contrary, the Arabic word for warfare is *harb*, not *jihad*. Significantly, *harb* is never attached to or combined with the phrase "in the way of God," as *jihad* is. The Arabic word for armed combat is *qital*.

In Islam, war is not holy—it is either justified or unjustified. It is justified as a jihad only when waged in self-defense or to overthrow oppression. In Islamic law, the only type of warfare that is allowed is that which qualifies as a jihad.

Wars of aggression or revenge do not qualify as jihad. Neither do wars of territorial expansion. Muslims are never allowed to wage war to convert people to Islam. Neither are Muslims allowed to kill people just because they are not Muslim. Eminent Islamic scholars throughout the centuries have affirmed, and continue to affirm, that war in Islam is defensive.

Even in early Islam, jihad by nonviolent means was preferred, and violence was a last resort. Although the Qur'an allows taking up arms in self-defense, it also counsels that patience and forgiveness are a better strategy (Qur'an 16:126). Jihad can be undertaken to overthrow oppression, but the oppression must be direct and, according to some Islamic scholars, of a kind that actively prevents one's practice of Islam.

Numerous verses in the Qur'an clarify that Muslims may not initiate warfare. The Qur'an unequivocally commands, "*But do not attack them if they do not attack you first. God loves not the aggressor*" (2:190). The Qur'an also insists on the following: if the enemy asks for peace you must agree to peace (4:86); if the enemy desists from fighting, you must desist from fighting (2:192); you may not treat noncombatants as the enemy, even if they are hostile to you and to Islam (4:94); and if the enemy repents, let them go on their way (9:5). The Qur'an says: "*Thus, if they let you be, And do not make war on you, And offer you peace, God does not allow you to harm them*" (4:90).

But what about the verses that urge Muslims to fight and slay people? These do exist in the Qur'an, but they are restricted by the verses that allow fighting only in self-defense. These verses do urge Muslims to fight and kill if they must, *but only if they are attacked first*. These fighting verses cannot be read while simultaneously ignoring the verses commanding Muslims not to initiate fighting; Muslims may not follow some verses of the Qur'an and ignore others. Moreover, the reason for the revelation (*asbab al-nuzul*) of these fighting verses was the specific ongoing war between the Muslim community and the people who had broken a treaty with the Muslims and commenced aggression against them. These verses are applicable only to that particular historical situation.

The historical context is therefore crucial for

[1] 'Abd Allah bin al-Sheikh Mahfuz bin Bayyah, *The Culture of Terrorism: Tenets and Treatments*, Hamza Yusuf, trans. (Florida: Sandala, 2014), p. 16.

understanding the fighting verses in the Qur'an, because these verses constituted a response to the circumstances of that seventh-century period. For the first thirteen or so years that the Prophet preached his religion in the city of Mecca, he and his followers were persecuted, verbally and physically attacked, tortured, and driven from their homes; yet they never fought back. Indeed, Qur'anic verses revealed during this time never allowed the Prophet and his followers to fight back, but instead urged them to endure the persecution with patience. Accordingly, the Muslims exercised patience and nonviolent resistance, which took the form of: (a) preaching their faith; (b) freeing slaves who had converted to Islam; and (c) emigrating to Abyssinia (today's Ethiopia—where they lived under its Christian ruler and respected his laws—and later to Medina.

After the Meccans attempted to assassinate the Prophet, he and his followers fled to Medina, where, at the invitation of the community, he became the political leader of the city, though he remained the religious leader of the Muslims only. Conflicts continued between the young Muslim community and the Meccans, but even then, it was another two years until the Qur'an first gave permission for the Muslims to physically fight back.

Why did the Qur'an change its message, when for approximately fifteen years the message had been one of patient endurance and nonviolent resistance? In Medina, the Prophet's status changed from individual religious preacher to political leader of a city. He became responsible not only for himself and his own followers, but for an entire city, many of whose residents were not Muslim. In addition, the efforts of fifteen years had not resolved the conflict with the Meccans. The Qur'anic verses responded to this change of situation and allowed the Prophet to physically defend himself and his new city. Fighting in self-defense, as a last resort, was authorized.

Notably, the Qur'an's message of defensive fighting was not limited to protecting solely Muslims, but followers of other religions as well:

> *Permission is given to those who fight because they have been oppressed, and God is able to help them. These are those who have been wrongfully expelled from their homes merely for saying 'God is our Lord.' If God had not restrained some people by means of others, monasteries, churches, synagogues, and mosques—all in which God's name is glorified—would have been destroyed.* (Qur'an 22:39–40)

These verses in the Qur'an gave permission to the Muslims to fight back against the Meccans in a situation where the Meccans had already initiated warfare. These verses were not allowing the Muslims to go start themselves a new war. This is clear because of those verses that prohibit Muslims from attacking unless they are attacked first—that is, only in self-defense.

The only significant exception to this understanding occurred during a period from about the ninth century to the twelfth century in which there was a split in authority on this issue. Islam was revealed at a time when war was a matter of survival and a method of conducting international relations. Yet the Qur'an allowed fighting only in self-defense. Therefore, to circumvent this Qur'anic restriction and to facilitate empire-building, some Muslim scholars (but not all and not enough to form a consensus) began formulating a theory of military jihad that simply ignored the Qur'anic verses that told them to "not attack unless they were attacked first" and instead focused solely on the fighting verses. Political expediency overruled religious restrictions on fighting. After a few centuries, however, this theory of self-serving warfare was abandoned. Since then, jihad by the sword has for centuries been defined as defensive war.

While some early Islamic scholars were developing a theory of military jihad, other Islamic scholars were developing the doctrine of "jihad of patient forbearance," a jihad of nonviolent resistance. These scholars based this doctrine on (a) the example of the Prophet Muhammad, who exercised nonviolent resistance in the face of persecution for the first fifteen years of his mission and who never initiated war against anyone, and (b) the many more verses of the Qur'an that urge peace and patience than those that urge fighting.

The preeminent twelfth-century jurist Abu Hamid Al-Ghazali brought the jihad of patient forbearance into the mainstream. He noted that more than seventy verses in the Qur'an referred to patient forbearance. Asserting that patience and gratitude were the two halves of faith, he affirmed that patient forbearance was part of jihad.

There are numerous instances of the jihad of patient forbearance in history, and include recent examples. During India's twentieth-century struggle for independence, Khan Abdul Ghaffar Khan convinced 100,000 fierce Pashtun warriors to lay down their arms and march in nonviolent protest against the British—and he based his nonviolent resistance on the Qur'an. In 2007, lawyers' peaceful but insistent protests in Pakistan eventually caused the military dictator Pervez Musharraf to step down and relinquish power to a civilian government. In 2008, peaceful resistance in Muslim-majority Maldives toppled its dictator. And nonviolent protests in Tunisia ousted that country's dictator in 2011 and resulted in a new democracy with free and fair elections.

It is tragic that *jihad* has been so utterly misappropriated by media outlets and terrorists alike. Media reports carelessly use "jihad" interchangeably with "terrorism," even though terrorism violates the rules of jihad. As a result, the media normalizes the terrorists' definition of jihad, making it increasingly difficult for Muslims to correct this inaccurate usage, dispel stereotypes about Muslims, and keep Muslim communities safe.

Terrorists are not jihadists—they are criminals under Islamic law. If they truly wanted to exercise jihad for its real purpose of improving society, they would use the jihad of patient forbearance, jihad by the hands, and jihad by the word; these form the greater part of external jihad and are not just Islamic, but universal tools for changing our world for the better.

The Qur'an, the Prophet, and the most learned scholars of Islam throughout the centuries have urged peace and tolerance as superior to physical fighting. The Prophet lived in a time where physical violence was a way of life; nevertheless, he never instigated warfare, and was in fact often considered by his contemporaries as too lenient, too gentle, and even weak. Yet he inspired a movement that would transform nearly one-quarter of the world's population. It's his example and the Qur'an's injunctions toward peace—many more than those urging violence—that we should follow.

Khaled Abou El Fadl, *The Place of Tolerance in Islam* (Boston: Beacon Press, 2002).

Khaled Abou El Fadl, "Terrorism Is at Odds with Islamic Tradition," *Los Angeles Times*, October 11, 2001.

Asma Afsaruddin, *Contemporary Issues in Islam* (Edinburgh: Edinburgh University Press, 2015).

Asma Afsaruddin, *The First Muslims: History and Memory* (Oxford: Oneworld, 2009).

Asma Afsaruddin, *Striving in the Path of God: Jihad and Martyrdom in Islamic Thought* (New York: Oxford University Press, 2013).

Abdullahi an-Naim, *Toward an Islamic Reformation: Civil Liberties, Human Rights, and International Law* (New York: Syracuse University Press, 1990).

Thomas W. Arnold, *The Spread of Islam in the World* (London, 1896; repr. New Delhi: Goodword Books, 2001).

Mohammad Asad, *The Message of the Qur'an* (Gibraltar: Dar al-Andalus, 1980).

'Abd Allah bin al-Sheikh Mahfuz bin Bayyah, *The Culture of Terrorism: Tenets and Treatments*, Hamza Yusuf, trans. (Florida: Sandala, 2014), based on a lecture at the Organization of Islamic Conference, 2007.

Arthur Goldschmidt Jr., *A Concise History of the Middle East*, 7th ed. (Boulder, CO: Westview Press, 2002).

Gerald Hawting, *The First Dynasty of Islam: The Umayyad Caliphate AD 661750*, 2nd ed. (1986; repr. London: Routledge, 2000).

James Turner Johnson, *The Holy War Idea in Western and Islamic Traditions* (University Park: Pennsylvania State University Press, 1997).

Majid Khadduri, *War and Peace in the Law of Islam* (Baltimore: Johns Hopkins University Press, 1955; repr. 1962).

Amitabh Pal, *"Islam" Means Peace: Understanding the Muslim Principle of Nonviolence Today* (Santa Barbara, CA: Praeger, 2011).

Peters, Rudolph, *Jihad in Classical and Modern Islam* (Princeton: Markus Wiener, 1996).

The Time for Islamic Nonviolence Is Now

RABIA TERRI HARRIS reclaims nonviolent *jihad* or an unarmed struggle for social justice whose goal is a restoration of wholeness and a culture of peace. This struggle is the responsibility of Muslims and it determines whether we live in a world of pain or a world of harmony.

KEY TAKEAWAYS

- The only truly effective method of pursuing social change is to use nonviolence, which relies upon the long-term power of justice, as opposed to the short-term power of injustice.
- The struggle of justice is about earning, requiring, and obtaining respect, and the highest pinnacle of success is to turn one's enemies into friends.
- The ultimate object of a just struggle is to restore wholeness, through inducing lasting change of behavior in the opponent.

NONVIOLENCE IS JIHAD

The Qur'an and the Hadith clearly call Muslims to struggle, and not all of that struggle is with our own egos. The lesser jihad, against social injustice, is our responsibility, too. How we understand that responsibility determines whether we will live in a world of beauty or in a world of pain.

Sadly, fighting "for Islam," as it is commonly understood, almost always means nothing more than fighting for political power, vengeance, or glory. None of this qualifies as jihad. In emergencies, fighting is necessary, but not all forms of fighting are acceptable to God. **Even if the motive is correct, if the means are abominable, that fighting is not jihad. If Muslims wish to regain our spiritual station, we must reclaim the nonviolent jihad.**

WHAT IS NONVIOLENCE?

Nonviolence is one of the most misunderstood words in the English language, and one of the most misunderstood ideas in the world. This confusion is not surprising, since the word means two things at the same time. And the one idea behind both meanings, though very simple, is not easy. It goes against the way many people think.

Here are the two different meanings of nonviolence.

1) **Nonviolence** is the **life decision** to live in harmony with the order of creation by giving up the domination of other people or the planet. Many wise instructions in this greatest of arts have been received by human beings over the millennia, under many names. Today, when put into community practice, the life decision for harmony is often called **culture of peace** or **peacebuilding**.

If Muslims wish to regain our spiritual station, we must reclaim the nonviolent jihad.

2) **Nonviolence** is the **method** of pursuing necessary social change by relying upon the real long-term power of justice rather than the apparent short-term

---

RABIA TERRI HARRIS, founder of the Muslim Peace Fellowship (www.muslimpeacefellowship.org), launched MPF as an associate of the Fellowship of Reconciliation in 1994. MPF was the first Muslim organization specifically devoted to the theory and practice of Islamic nonviolence, and continues as an organizing hub for Islamic peacebuilding and multireligious solidarity for justice. Currently Rabia serves as chaplain and scholar in residence at the Community of Living Traditions at Stony Point Center (http://stonypointcenter.org/multifaith-community), an Abrahamic residential community devoted to the pursuit of peace and justice through the practice of hospitality and the care of the earth.

power of injustice. Today, when put into community practice, the method of justice is often called **unarmed struggle**.

Both kinds of nonviolence rest on spiritual realities. The universe is a seamless whole of which humans are an inseparable part. The order of creation is ethical as well as physical. Ethical laws have necessary effects, just as physical laws have necessary effects. **The flow of life is not chaos—something is in charg**e. By understanding, affirming, and moving with that which is in charge, we can reach whatever goals we have that are worth having.

Once we begin to grasp Qur'anic language, understanding nonviolence becomes much simpler. The Qur'anic term for nonviolence as a life decision is ***islam*** (peace through surrender). The Qur'anic term for nonviolence as a method is ***jihad*** (struggle/striving). The Qur'anic term for the principle underlying both aspects of nonviolence is ***tawhid*** (unity).

To find peace, we must choose peace.

The object of just struggle is the restoration of wholeness. Its strategic goal is to induce a lasting change of behavior in the opponent. Every human being is capable of change, whether willingly or unwillingly. If we aim to induce such change, then wisdom, patience, and subtlety are as necessary as courage. **In a just struggle, the highest pinnacle of success is to turn enemies into friends.** Highest success is never guaranteed. Nonetheless, highest success must always be our goal. What can we do so as to allow for such a breakthrough, and in fact encourage it? The Prophetic example gives us a consistent principle, summarized in the Qur'an: "*The good and the evil are not alike. Repel (evil) with that which is better—then the one who was at enmity with you will become like an intimate friend*" (41:34).

If the object is the restoration of wholeness, it is more important that those who oppose you admire you for what you stand for—even if grudgingly—than it is for them to fear you. That is the beginning. It is never true that "People understand nothing but violence." It is incumbent upon us, however, to find out what they do understand, though it may require some study.

Unarmed struggle is not about "making nice." The desire to go forth into the fray, to find out who wins and who loses, to try to be a winner, is a reliable dimension of human nature. Any attempt to suppress something so sturdy and intrinsic is bound to produce problems. That is not what the life of nonviolence requires, however. **The struggle for justice is about earning, requiring, and obtaining respect.** This is the battle worth winning.

What, then, should we do with our natural desire to be the best? The Qur'an tells us clearly: we can aim to be the best possible servants of God's mercy.

> *If God had so willed He would have made you a single community, but He tests you (all) in what He has given you, so compete with each other in everything good. To God is your return altogether, and He will then inform you concerning those matters wherein you differed* (5:48).

Violence is not a good. Whoever competes in it is sure to lose the real race.

This world will never be perfect. Until the end of time, there will always be injustice somewhere, and the struggle with injustice will always be necessary. But **though the world cannot be perfect, there is nothing to prevent its being better than it is.** The change does not depend on our opponent: to claim that it does merely hands our opponent our power. The change depends on us . . . and in our struggles, we must depend on God, who is our peace, and from whom peace comes.

Nonviolence is the core social teaching of all the prophets and the rightful inheritance of Muslims everywhere. **To find peace, we must choose peace.** There is no other way.

The Struggle with the Ego

The Greater *Jihad*

SHAIKH KABIR HELMINSKI explains how Islam is meant to serve as a way of life that guides our soul to happiness and well-being. However, violent extremists see religion as a series of tests and rules and have transformed Islam from a religion of love and mercy into a religion of fear. For this reason, Helminski writes, there must be a collective transformation of our hearts and egos to bring us closer to God and back to a religion of peace.

Islam, from the beginning, has been a form of concentrated spiritual energy and an effective spiritual training system leading to the transformation of one's very self. The effect of this transformation is that it diminishes egoism, arrogance, and aggression, and replaces these with self-witnessing, humility, empathy, and reconciliation. This was the message and way of life brought by the Prophet Muhammad (pbuh), which caused a transformation in the souls of men and women, one that profoundly affected the societies in which they lived. He called this struggle with our egos "the greater *jihad*," and the struggle for social justice and peace "the lesser *jihad*."

Any true religion should methodically lead to the reduction of self-righteous egoism and hatred. For Muslims, the greater *jihad* increases our capacity to love unselfishly, to consider the effects of our actions (*taqwa*), and to sustain an awareness of the divine (*dhikr Allah*)—all of these without a sense of pride, self-righteousness, or self-congratulation. It is through the greater *jihad* (*jihad akhbar*) that human beings are able to surrender their pettiness, selfishness, and hostile tendencies, and instead become more productive, generous, forgiving, and loving. Unlike the physical, or lesser *jihad* (*jihad asghar*), the greater *jihad* is the effort required to be aware of the consequences that our thoughts, emotions, and actions have on our hearts and our relationship with the Divine. It represents the daily struggle to fulfill our true purpose in life and become a real Muslim, that is, a compassionate servant of the Divine. This greater *jihad* ultimately prepares us to be more effective in the struggle for social justice and peace, the lesser *jihad*.

Egoism's ultimate manifestation is tyranny. In Islam, egoism is seen as the ultimate idolatry (*shirk*), because it places the human above God. It is the great corrupter of all human endeavors, including, tragically, religion. Today, the people who are attracted to the radical messages offered by various extremist groups become servants of a collective egoism, rather than servants to God, and are thus, contributing to the disunity of humanity and the corruption of Muslims. They are corrupted by an out-of-control *nafs* (ego), engorged by their own sense of self-righteousness, which they use to justify acts of extreme aggression and ugliness, spreading *fitna* (strife) throughout society.

Such individuals and groups like to assume that religion is primarily a series of tests and rules to be followed, a strictly defined program of behaviors and prohibitions. They contend that the more exactly you follow their program, the more you will please God. Frequently, what accompanies this mentality is the compulsion, that is to say, the deeply felt need, to impose rules, behaviors, dress codes, and prohibitions on others in the belief that this will please God, Who will look favorably on this undertaking and grant success and ultimately a heavenly reward to those who follow and enforce the commands.

In other words, they distort Islam into a religion of fear, rather than a religion of love and mercy, and

KABIR HELMINSKI is a Shaikh of the Mevlevi Order and Co-Director of the Threshold Society (sufism.org), an educational foundation for the practice and study of Sufism and spiritual psychology. He has translated many volumes of Sufi literature and is the author of three books on Sufism, the most recent of which is *Holistic Islam: Sufism, Transformation & The Challenge of Our Time*. Mr. Helminski was one of the signatories of "A Common Word Between Us and You", an open letter by Islamic scholars that calls for peace and understanding.

manipulate the truth to serve an agenda of power and control. These are the people and groups who have also distorted the "lesser *jihad*" from the struggle for justice into a strategy of violent domination, and in doing so betray the most fundamental principles of exemplary character, freedom of conscience, and acceptance of diversity.

Much more radical than the false jihadism ravaging the world today is the Qur'anic principle of Divine unity, *Tawhid*, which recognizes that the diversity of religions and cultures is ordained by God for the benefit of humanity in order that we might learn from each other and grow in virtue.

Shockingly, they believe that happiness and justice may only be achieved by spreading fear and terror throughout society. The great poet Rumi describes these people in this way:

A self-righteous person sees someone "sin,"
and the flames of Hell rise up in him.
He calls his own hellish pride defense of the Religion;
he doesn't notice his own arrogant soul.
(*Mathnawi* I, 3347–8)

True Islam is meant to be a way of life that guides the soul to well-being and happiness, and that establishes justice and human dignity in society–a religion of truth, love and mercy. It began as a moral force that quickly expanded over a huge geographical area not by spreading fear and terror, but by bringing various communities, including non-Muslim communities, into harmony through the reconciling principle: "*O people of the book, let us come to a reconciling principle among us: let us worship only God, let us not associate partners (other gods) equal with Him, and let us not raise up lords or intermediaries between us and God*" (Qur'an 3:64).

Much more radical than the false jihadism ravaging the world today is the Qur'anic principle of Divine unity, *Tawhid*, which recognizes that the diversity of religions and cultures is ordained by God for the benefit of humanity in order that we might learn from each other and grow in virtue. If this principle could be understood and supported, Islam could take its proper place among the world's religions, exemplifying dignity, tolerance, and justice as it often has in the past.

Martyrdom

Shahid

SYED-MOHSIN NAQUVI explains the concept of martyrdom within Islam as the act of being a witness to God, and delinks it from Daesh's suicide attacks, whose aim is to kill innocent people.

KEY TAKEAWAYS

- The concept of martyrdom in Islam refers to the act of being a witness to God.
- Daesh's suicide attacks blatantly disregard the Qur'anic prohibition on suicide and killing innocent people, and can never be considered acts of martyrdom in Islam.

In light of the multitude of terror attacks across the globe in recent years, some have expressed concerns about certain principles and teachings within Islam. "Martyrdom operations," suicide bombings, and the "72 virgins in Paradise" are some of the most common misconceptions about Islam. Unfortunately, the meaning of martyrdom and self-sacrifice as understood in Islam has been maligned in recent years by groups like Daesh, which falsely claim that their followers who carry out suicide attacks will enter Paradise as "martyrs" (*shaheed*). Such attackers blatantly disregard the Qur'anic prohibition on suicide and patently violate the Qur'anic prohibition on killing others; thus, they can never be called "martyrs" in Islam.

The word "martyr" is derived from a Greek root meaning "a witness." Martyrdom, or the act of serving as a witness, is a historically rooted concept in all three Abrahamic religions. The period of Christianity before Constantine I was called "The Age of Martyrs" because of the persecution early Christians endured. In Judaism, *Kiddush Hashem* is a sanctification of those who lost their lives while following the commandments of God.

In Islam, *Martyrdom* generally refers to suffering, persecution, and death for advocating, renouncing, refusing to renounce, or refusing to advocate a belief or cause as demanded by an external party. This refusal to comply with the presented demands results in the punishment or execution of the martyr by the oppressor. This definition, therefore, requires a hero, a person with a committed ideal, a cause or something similar; and an opponent who is a person, a group, or an institution that opposes that cause and is willing to go to extremes to stop the movement. The hero foresees action by opponents to harm him because of his commitment to the cause. In spite of that, the hero continues, knowing the risk of retaliation. The opponents kill the hero because of his commitment to the cause, and the hero's death is commemorated. The end result is that, although the opponents succeed in temporary worldly gain, the victory belongs to the martyr who succeeds by standing up to the oppressor and then dying without fulfilling the desire of the opponent. Though Daesh refers to their suicide bombers as "martyrs" who are allegedly fighting oppression, in reality, their actions result in chaos, death, and destruction, and create, rather than alleviate, suffering for innocent people.

A true martyr in Islam is one who dies in God's way, and he is called "*Shaheed*," which is a superlative form of the Arabic word Shaahid, meaning an eyewitness. The idea of being a martyr is that a person made the ultimate sacrifice by being a witness to God's laws being preserved. In Islam, the Arabic terms *Shaheed* and *Shaahid* are often used interchangeably with the

---

SYED-MOHSIN NAQUVI was born in Lucknow, India. He holds a master's degree in physics from Karachi University, and a second master's degree in Islamic and Social Sciences from the Graduate School of Islamic and Social Sciences in Leesburg, Virginia. Mr. Naquvi has extensive professional experience in management consulting that extends over a period of some twenty years, over three continents, and across many cultures and geographical areas of the world. He is the author of the book *The Tragedy of Karbala*, and has published many monographs on other Islamic topics. For ten years, Mr. Naquvi edited and published a monthly paper for the Shi'a community in the U.S., *Community News & Views*, based in Princeton, New Jersey. He writes extensively online and gives talks in schools, hospitals, and churches.

word "martyr," but the direct translation of the word is, again, "witness to the Truth."

The Qur'an describes the rewards for those who sacrifice themselves while bearing witness to God:

> *And never think of those who have been killed in the cause of God as dead. Nay, they are alive and they are with their Lord receiving provision* (3:169).

We can interpret the last part of the statement as addressing those devotees of the same cause who, after the martyr has been killed, remember him for his sacrifice, and commemorate his bravery and glory to further the cause for all time to come.

> The idea of being a martyr is that a person made the ultimate sacrifice by being a witness to God's laws being preserved

A martyr is not, however, one who commits suicide. Suicide is defined as intentional, self-inflicted death, and is explicitly prohibited in the Qur'an:

> *And spend in the way of Allah, but do not throw [yourselves] with your own hands to destruction; but work deeds of excellence for verily Allah loves the people of excellence* (2:195).

This is a very clear indication that anyone trying to kill himself/herself will be damned in this world and in the Hereafter. This is why prominent Sunni and Shia scholars publicly condemn acts of suicide bombing and have declared that one who commits suicide will be damned to committing it eternally, and can never be considered a "martyr" in Islam.

Neither is a martyr one who kills innocent people, and treats them as "collateral damage." The Qur'an strictly prohibits such killing:

> *Do not take any human life, which God has declared as sacred, other than in the pursuit of Justice. This is what He commands you to do, so that you may remember* (6:151).

Martyrdom, by Islamic definition, is founded on moral and ethical convictions; it is never based on killing and being killed. Mahmoud Taleghani, the Iranian theologian and reformer, once described a martyr as one who moves from imperfection to perfection. This concept is simply impossible for those whose "martyrdom" is based on ethically abhorrent ideas. They can never be witnesses to the truth (shaheed) when they burn prisoners of war alive, persecute religious minorities, destroy antiquities and historical sites, and violate the Qur'an by desecrating their own places of worship—including the Prophet's mosque in Medina. They ignore the Qur'anic verse below, which instructs Muslims that they are obliged to protect houses of worship (belonging to any religion) from destruction:

> *Were it not for God's repelling people, some by means of others, monasteries, churches, synagogues, and mosques, where God's name is mentioned, much of that would have been destroyed. And God will surely help those who help Him—truly God is strong, mighty* (22:40).

Further, the Prophet Muhammad (pbuh) set ethical standards of warfare, and the atrocities carried out by Daesh would be unfathomable to him were he alive today. When the Prophet (pbuh) fought the battles of Badr, Uhud, Khandaq, and Khyber, the cause and principles of the fight were more important to him than the actual result, as he valued intention, morality, and ethics over battlefield prowess and winning. The Prophet's (pbuh) strict ground rules for warfare prohibited collateral damage, and he ordered his followers to safeguard noncombatants, including women, children, elderly persons, and animals. He also emphasized right conduct, empathy, and compassion for the enemy, including the humane treatment of prisoners of war.

Today, we need to remind people of true martyrs, who have served as exemplars to others, and continue to inspire many to live their lives faithfully. What separates the deaths of true martyrs from the concept of martyrdom preached by terrorist groups is not the fact of their death, but their intention with which they die in the course of submitting to God.

True martyrs have been described by the scholar Suyooti in his renowned work, *The Gates of Felicity in the Causes of the Witnessing to Oneness*, as follows: A woman who dies during childbirth is considered a *shaheeda*. Anyone who dies while fulfilling a religious commandment or defending his property, honor, or religious commitments is considered a Witness. Any Muslim, male or female, who dies in the pursuit of knowledge, such as those who die in their college/university struggling with their studies, or in a study circle in their mosque, are considered to be witnesses to the truth of God's commandment to seek knowledge. People who die from a plague, a stomach disease, through drowning, or crushed in a collapsed building are also considered martyrs. Men who care, empathize, and humble themselves with their wives and families are witnesses to God's message and the Prophet's traditions. For example, the Prophet Muhammad (pbuh) stated that "the best of you is he who is best with his family."

Islam has produced many such martyrs, who were killed because of their belief in one God. The first martyr was a woman, Sumayyah; she was followed by Hamza, the Prophet's uncle, at the Battle of Uhud; and Jafar al-Tayyaar, the Prophet's cousin and the older brother of his son-in-law Ali, at the battle of Mauta. Ali, the Prophet's son-in-law and fourth caliph, was martyred by a splinter group called the Khawarij, while in prostration during prayer. The greatest martyr in Islamic history, however, was Ali's son (and the Prophet's grandson), Imam Hussein, who was beheaded on the plains of Karbala, because he stayed true to his faith.

After the death of the fourth caliph, Ali, Mu'awiyah, the governor of Damascus, forcibly declared himself "caliph" ("vice-regent"), because he wanted to be seen as the "leader of the believers." Ali's eldest son, Hasan, signed a treaty with Mu'awyiah on the condition that his successor be chosen by the community. After Hasan died, his brother Hussein took up the spiritual leadership of the community and was bound to the treaty. However, Mu'awiyah reneged on the terms of the treaty and declared his own son, Yazid, as his successor, which Hussein considered a breach of the treaty. Hussein refused to pledge allegiance to Yazid, and fled Medina with the rest of his family to take refuge in Mecca. On his way to Kufah, Yazid's army butchered Hussein in the historic Battle of Karbala. Hussein's caravan was captured and the surviving women and children were imprisoned in Damascus, where they lived in miserable conditions. When the horror of this massacre of the Prophet's family came to be known across the Muslim kingdom, Yazid realized that the political climate was changing against him, and released the prisoners.

To this day, Muslims continued to revere Hussein for refusing to pledge allegiance to Yazid, whose rule they considered unjust, and every year during the month of Muharram, they commemorate Hussein's martyrdom and honor him for his unwavering faith and his unjust death. The shrine of Hussein at Karbala continues to serve as a place of pilgrimage for many faithful Muslims, especially Shia, and is the site of the largest annual peaceful gathering in the world on the day of Arba'een.

Martyrdom, by Islamic definition, is founded on moral and ethical convictions; it is never based on killing and being killed.

Today, groups like Daesh are no different from Mu'awiyah and Yazid—aiming to destroy the shrine of Hussein at Karbala, and actively persecuting Shia Muslims who respectfully commemorate Hussein's martyrdom, by destroying their homes and their places of worship and killing them en masse, in cities like Mosul in Iraq today.

Daesh's myopic definition of martyrdom, coupled with their acts of terror, such as suicide bombing, murder of innocents, and joy in violence, is absolutely unsupported by the Qur'an and would never be accepted by the Prophet Muhammad (pbuh). Today, it is incumbent upon Muslim leaders to show that such attacks are patently un-Islamic. Recently, following the terrorist attack on London Bridge, over 130 imams of different mosques refused to perform the burial rites of the terrorists who died in the attack—a rite normally performed for every Muslim regardless of his actions—thereby disowning the terrorists and clearly indicating that they did not accept the dead as being Muslim, let alone "martyrs." Indeed, the depravity of such attackers and the ruthless nature of their actions are rejected by Muslims worldwide, have been condemned by leaders of many Muslim sects, and have no place in Islam.

Misconceptions About the Caliphate

Khalifah/Khilafah

DR. WAYEL AZMEH and **DR. SAEED ALBEZREH** provide a detailed response to the common misconceptions about the Caliphate and the claims made by Daesh relating to its re-establishment. They explain how the caliphate was originally established and guided by the overall morals and principles of the Qur'an and Sunnah, and was designed by the disciples of the Prophet to express Islamic values that were appropriate to their historical environment. However, Dr. Azmeh and Dr. Albezreh note, Daesh's claim to have re-established the Caliphate comes without any critical historical review, and assert that the group has simply taken advantage of ignorance about what a "caliphate" in Islam is.

In June 2014, Daesh announced the "re-establishment" of the so-called caliphate (*khilafah*) and appointed Abu Bakr al-Baghdadi as "caliph" (*khalifah*) of Muslims around the world. Daesh described this as "the abandoned obligation of the era" and "a dream that lives in the depths of every Muslim believer."[1] The claim that Muslims are obligated to establish a centralized state under the rule of a "caliph," however, is grossly misguided, and needs to be examined and corrected. Indeed, while Muslims have sought to understand the eternal values of the Qur'an and the Prophet Muhammad's (pbuh) teachings and implement them in varied contexts across the centuries, nowhere in these sources are Muslims mandated or even encouraged to create a "caliphate" or "Islamic state."[2]

The word *khalifah*, as it appears in the Qur'an, literally means "vice-regent," and is used to describe humans as the stewards or ambassadors of God on earth, who bestowed upon them the responsibility to care for God's creation. It is not understood in the Qur'an in "political" terms, neither does the Qu'ran ever refer to the Prophet Muhammad as a head of state, prince, or king— instead referring to him as "the messenger of God."

As such, the Prophet Muhammad strictly adhered to the commands he received from God, which included harmonious coexistence for people of all religions, upholding justice for all, honoring other people's beliefs, allowing people to abide by their own laws, and providing protection for other religions. In the Pact of Medina, for example, the Prophet Muhammad established protections for those living in Medina, in which each group kept its religion without interference, and created an alliance between Muslims, the Jewish tribes, and the polytheists. It is worth mentioning that in the Pact of Medina, the Prophet Muhammad never refers to

DR. WAYEL AZMEH is a cardiologist in Dayton, Ohio. He grew up in Damascus, Syria, before coming to America in 1985. He is a board member of MPAC. He has spoken in many forums concerning Islam and Muslims in America over the last thirty years. Dr. Azmeh is a graduate student in English composition and rhetoric at the University of Dayton. He has published an essay titled "Corporal Punishment Verses in the Qur'an Are to Be Reinterpreted to Counter Violent Extremist Practices" in October 2015. Another essay, titled "Misconceptions About the Caliphate in Islam," is pending publication.

DR. SAEED ALBEZREH is a physician trained in dermatology and healthcare management, and an avid student of Islamic theology. He studied classical Islamic jurisprudence at Al Fat'h Islamic Seminary in Damascus, and studied under several scholars of classic Islamic sciences in Syria and Jordan. He has been invited to speak at various Islamic centers, churches, synagogues, and academic and interfaith forums, and is currently leading an initiative to study the needs of young refugees in the Middle East in collaboration with the Harvard Humanitarian Initiative. Dr. Albezreh is a graduate of Boston University School of Medicine, and holds a Master's of Science degree from Boston University and Master's in Management degree from Cambridge College.

[1] Abu Bakr al-Baghdadi, "This Is the Promise of Allah."

[2] Rauf, Imam Feisal Abdul. *Defining Islamic Statehood: Measuring and Indexing Contemporary Muslim States.* Palgrave Macmillan, 2015, 38.

himself as a political "head of state," but rather, as a religious leader: "*This is a writ from Muhammad the Prophet among the believers, the Muslims from Quraysh and those from Yathrib (Medina) and whoever joined them and struggled with them.*"

Though Abu Bakr al-Baghdadi, the self-proclaimed "caliph," calls upon all Muslims living in "Western" countries to leave their homes to move to the "caliphate," built by and for Muslims only, this is a clear contradiction to the example the Prophet Muhammad set in Medina. When Muslims were being persecuted by Quraysh, the Prophet Muhammad sent them to Christian-ruled Abyssinia, where they would be protected under the king's rule. The Prophet Muhammad was modeling another example for his vision of Muslims living peacefully with people of other faiths, even as a protected minority. The Prophet Muhammad also instructed his faithful to follow the law of the land in which they lived while maintaining their religious devotion, and not to establish a break-away legal authority.

The claim that Muslims are obligated to establish a centralized state under the rule of a "caliph," however, is grossly misguided, and needs to be examined and corrected.

The issue of *khilafah* (succession) arose after the Prophet Muhammad died in 632 CE. The Prophet left no explicit instruction as to how his successor should be chosen, thus motivating his companions to consult (shura) among themselves—a process that has a clear reference in the Qur'an. After consultation, Abu Bakr was chosen as the new leader of the Muslims, who gave their allegiance (*bay'ah*) to him, thereby making him the first formal "caliph" by tribal consensus. This newly founded "caliphate" was thus born as a civic state, established on and guided by the overarching morals of the Qur'an and the Prophet Muhammad's example. This succession of leadership via consent of the people continued with the next three caliphs—Umar, Uthman, and Ali—who all ruled according to the principles of the Qur'an and the Prophet Muhammad's example, and eventually came to be called the four "rightly guided caliphs."

During Ali's time, however, a civil war broke out and a splinter group, the Khawarij, assassinated him. Mu'awiyah took up the mantle of leadership of the Muslim community by force and ruled as a king for nineteen years, eventually designating his son, Yazid, as his successor. Nevertheless, Mu'awiyah called himself "caliph," for he wanted to be seen as the "leader of the believers." Thus, twenty-nine years after the death of the Prophet Muhammad, a new type of caliphate—one based on hereditary kingship, rather than shura (consultation) and the consent of the governed—was established. As such, classical scholars, like Ibn Taymiyyah and Ibn Khaldūn, declare that the "caliphate" had ceased to exist after the four rightly guided caliphs.

Over time, the caliphate system evolved in response to changing circumstances. The idealized image of a vast caliphate unified under a central exemplary and just government is inspiring to Muslims, but it never existed in reality. Most of the 1,400 years of Islamic history witnessed multiple independent states with more than one caliphate system at any given time. These evolved progressively, from a centralized system of governance that would not accept rival caliphs, into a vast decentralized empire with many independent states pledging allegiance to their caliph symbolically, until finally, many independent caliphates came to exist simultaneously, with each caliph ruling a separate territory.

For example, in 680 CE, two competing caliphates developed simultaneously—the Umayyads in Damascus and Abd Allah Ibn al-Zubayr in Mecca. Between 934 CE and 955 CE, up to six caliphs co-existed. Over the next 161 years, three major caliphates ruled simultaneously—the Umayyads in Damascus, Abbasids in Baghdad, and Fatimids in Egypt. With this decentralization of leadership, the "caliphate" gradually took on different forms in different Muslim societies, and came to be called by various names, including *mulk*, *wilayah 'am*, *dawlah*, and *milla*. [3]

[3] Ibid., 44.

The caliphate system of governance ceased to exist when Britain and the Allied powers skillfully utilized the romantic image of the caliphate to motivate the leader of Mecca, Sharif Hussein Bin Ali, to lead a revolt against the Ottoman caliphate. When they succeeded, the Ottoman caliphate was abolished in March 1924, and Sharif Hussein proclaimed himself Caliph of All Muslims. However, the British switched their support to Ibn Saud in eastern Arabia, who defeated Hussein, forcing him to give up his claim later that same year and ushering in the birth of the Kingdom of Saudi Arabia. Importantly, had the declaration of a "caliphate" been religiously mandated, the Saudis would have declared Saudi Arabia as the caliphate; but they did not.

While Daesh claims to govern according to "*shari'ah*," in fact they only implement their harshest, and conveniently literal, interpretations of penal code punishments, while completely ignoring the core values upheld by the Prophet Muhammad in the seventh century, which include justice, equality, freedom of religion, and mutual consultation.[6]

Today, a sense of defeat dominates the Arab world following the end of the Ottoman caliphate and the subsequent colonization of many Arab countries by Western powers. This defeat has encouraged some Islamist political leaders to claim the dream of a caliphate that would free and unite all Muslims.

The American-led invasion of Iraq and the dismantling of Iraq's central government sparked a new wave of religious polarization between the two main components of Iraqi society, the Sunni and the Shia. This, along with the chaos of the Syrian civil war, created a leadership vacuum, which Daesh has filled. Daesh declared a "caliphate" under its self-appointed "caliph," Abu Bakr al-Baghdadi, claiming to follow the teachings of the Prophet Muhammad. Daesh is trying to sell its "caliphate" to some gullible Muslim youth on the Internet as a revival of the glorious dream of Muslims' dignity, unity, and prosperity.

Daesh's "caliphate," however, which it equates with the ideal "Islamic state," violates Qur'anic principles. One of those Qur'anic principles is *bay'ah*, which is a pledge of allegiance to a leader that confers upon him/her the legitimacy to lead. This principle of leading by the consent of the people is comparable to the modern-day social contract in which the leader pledges to serve his people and they, in return, remain respectful of his decisions. The guiding principle of *Hisbah* in the Islamic tradition, meaning "the promotion of good and the prevention of evil," makes it incumbent upon the leader to ensure his people's welfare. The responsibility to strive for the welfare of others extends to all Muslims, not just the ruler.[4] Along with these core principles in the Qur'an and the Muslim tradition, there are important principles that are totally ignored by Daesh, such as assuring the equality of all people under the law and furthering the fundamental rights of all people, as defined by the five objectives of Islamic law (*shari'ah*): life, religion, property, intellect, and family.[5] While Daesh claims to govern according to "*shari'ah*," in fact they only implement their harshest, and conveniently literal, interpretations of penal code punishments, while completely ignoring the core values upheld by the Prophet Muhammad in the seventh century, which include justice, equality, freedom of religion, and mutual consultation.[6]

Whether a government system is called a caliphate, a sultanate, a republic, or a kingdom is of secondary importance. What is most important is to cultivate and popularize basic knowledge of Islamic history and empower Muslims in envisioning a viable future based on core Islamic values of peace, freedom, and human dignity.

[4] Ibid., 38.
[5] Some scholars choose to list a sixth objective of Shari'ah: *'ird* or *karamah*, meaning "honor" or "human dignity." See ibid., 27.
[6] Rauf, Imam Feisal Abdul. *Moving the Mountain: A New Vision of Islam in America*. Free Press, 2012, 165.

Five Qur'anic Verses Commonly Taken out of Context

SPIRITUAL PERCEPTION

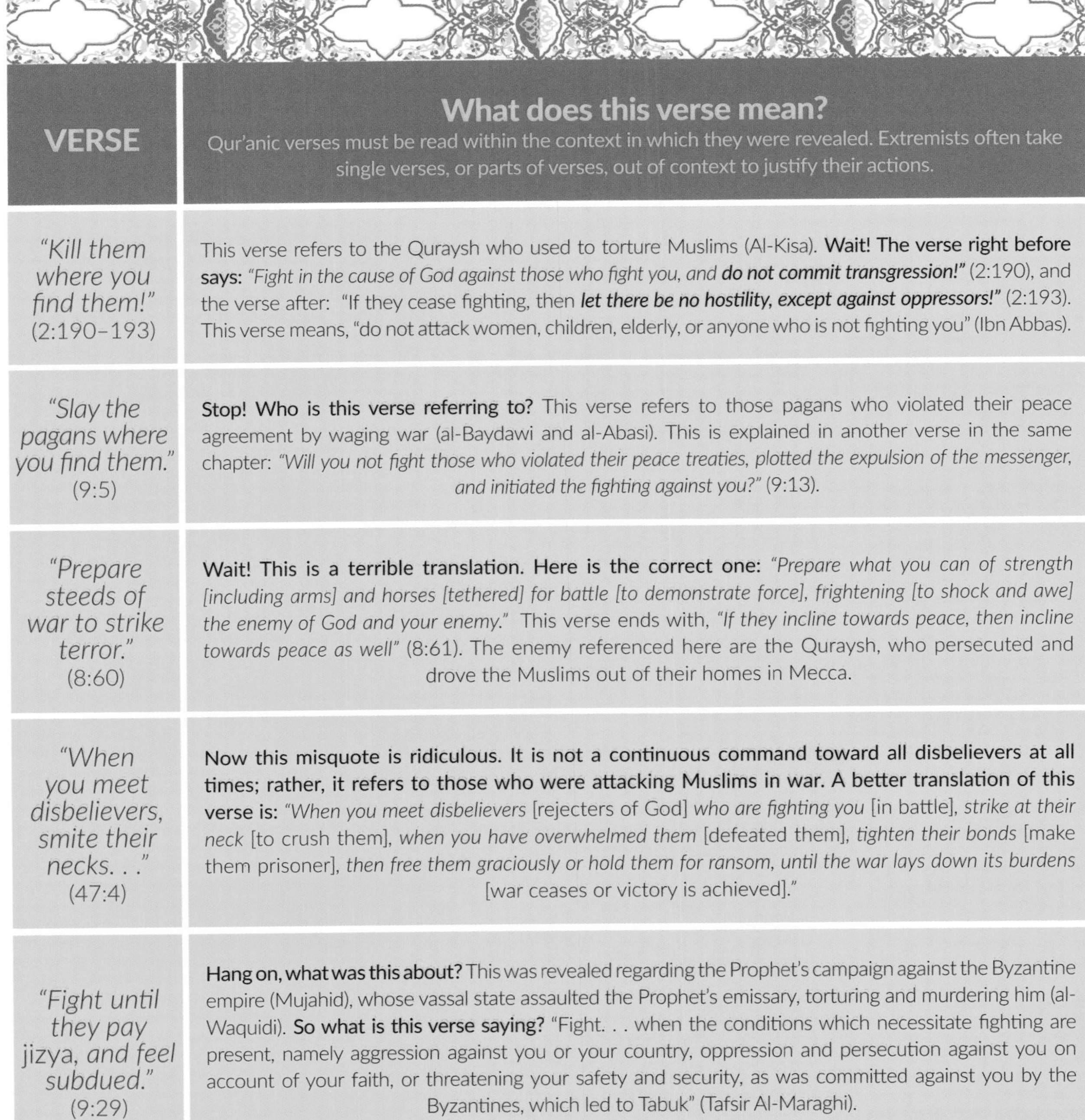

VERSE	What does this verse mean? Qur'anic verses must be read within the context in which they were revealed. Extremists often take single verses, or parts of verses, out of context to justify their actions.
"Kill them where you find them!" (2:190–193)	This verse refers to the Quraysh who used to torture Muslims (Al-Kisa). **Wait! The verse right before says:** *"Fight in the cause of God against those who fight you, and* ***do not commit transgression!"*** (2:190), and the verse after: "If they cease fighting, then ***let there be no hostility, except against oppressors!"*** (2:193). This verse means, "do not attack women, children, elderly, or anyone who is not fighting you" (Ibn Abbas).
"Slay the pagans where you find them." (9:5)	**Stop! Who is this verse referring to?** This verse refers to those pagans who violated their peace agreement by waging war (al-Baydawi and al-Abasi). This is explained in another verse in the same chapter: *"Will you not fight those who violated their peace treaties, plotted the expulsion of the messenger, and initiated the fighting against you?"* (9:13).
"Prepare steeds of war to strike terror." (8:60)	**Wait! This is a terrible translation. Here is the correct one:** *"Prepare what you can of strength [including arms] and horses [tethered] for battle [to demonstrate force], frightening [to shock and awe] the enemy of God and your enemy."* This verse ends with, *"If they incline towards peace, then incline towards peace as well"* (8:61). The enemy referenced here are the Quraysh, who persecuted and drove the Muslims out of their homes in Mecca.
"When you meet disbelievers, smite their necks. . ." (47:4)	**Now this misquote is ridiculous. It is not a continuous command toward all disbelievers at all times; rather, it refers to those who were attacking Muslims in war. A better translation of this verse is:** *"When you meet disbelievers* [rejecters of God] *who are fighting you* [in battle], *strike at their neck* [to crush them], *when you have overwhelmed them* [defeated them], *tighten their bonds* [make them prisoner], *then free them graciously or hold them for ransom, until the war lays down its burdens* [war ceases or victory is achieved]."
"Fight until they pay jizya, and feel subdued." (9:29)	**Hang on, what was this about?** This was revealed regarding the Prophet's campaign against the Byzantine empire (Mujahid), whose vassal state assaulted the Prophet's emissary, torturing and murdering him (al-Waquidi). **So what is this verse saying?** "Fight. . . when the conditions which necessitate fighting are present, namely aggression against you or your country, oppression and persecution against you on account of your faith, or threatening your safety and security, as was committed against you by the Byzantines, which led to Tabuk" (Tafsir Al-Maraghi).

How Daesh Violates Islam

SPIRITUAL PERCEPTION

CORE VISION OF DAESH **Begin a world war that will start the apocalypse at Dabiq, Syria**	**CORE VISION OF ISLAM** **The goal of humanity is to achieve moral virtue**	
"The spark has been lit here in Iraq, and its head will continue to intensify–by Allah's permission–until it burns the crusader armies in Dabiq" [1]	*"Righteousness is about giving to orphans, the needy, travelers, beggars, and freeing slaves, as well as charity."* (Qur'an 2:177) "I have only been sent to teach people the perfection of moral character." - The Prophet Muhammad	
Dehumanization of non-Muslims	Islam teaches that God has conferred dignity upon all human beings.	*"Certainly we gave dignity to the Children of Adam, and carried them over land and sea, and provided them with all the good things, and given them an advantage over many of those We have created with a complete preference."* (Qur'an 17:70) "A worshipper only reaches true faith when one loves for all humanity what one loves for oneself." - The Prophet Muhammad
Excommunication (takfir) of Muslims	Islam forbids self-righteousness, contempt, or judging another human being.	*"Do not say to those who offer you greetings of peace, 'You are not a believer!'"* (Qur'an 4:94) "Whoever declares that God is one is a Muslim and his blood is sacred and his property inviolable." - The Prophet Muhammad
Indiscriminate violence	Islam teaches that killing one person is like killing all of humanity.	*"We decreed to the Children of Israel that if anyone kills a human being... it will be as though he killed all human beings. And, if anyone saves a life, it will be as though he had saved the lives of all human beings."* (Qur'an 5:32) "A person can only remain sound in faith so long as he does not shed innocent blood." - The Prophet Muhammad
Building a utopian "caliphate"	Islam does not dictate that Muslims form a "caliphate"—leaders are seen as representatives (*wakeel*) and servants (*khadim*) of the people, and must be chosen by consent	*"The believers are those who consult one another."* (Qur'an 42:38) Uthman was chosen to be a leader by majority consent (including by housewives and school children). - Ibn Kathir

[1] *Dabiq*, Issue 1, Page 2.

Persecution of Other Religions	Islam protects freedom of religion, and forbids oppression and coercion.	*"Had God not granted the right to defend, it would result in the destruction of monasteries, churches, synagogues and mosques."* (Qur'an 22:40)
		The Prophet protected the monks of Saint Catherine's monastery, and welcomed Christians to pray in his mosque.
	Muslims are taught that true worship of God entails kindness to all humanity.	"Donate to charity to people of all faiths." - The Prophet Muhammad
		"Whoever wrongs a peaceful non-Muslim, or infringes upon his or her rights, will have to reckon with me on Judgment day." - The Prophet Muhammad
Reinstitution of slavery to usher in the "end of times"	Islam calls for freeing slaves and makes enslavement a crime.	*"The spiritual ascent towards God occurs by freeing slaves, caring for orphans, feeding the poor and needy."* (Qur'an 90:11–16)
	Muslims believe that it is not possible for humans to usher in the End of Days.	*"Many evil actions are signs of the end of times, but it remains evil to perform such deeds, and it is not possible to hasten the arrival of the Judgment day."* (Quran 7:187)
Declaring war against all	Islam forbids fighting against those who offer peace.	*"Regarding those who neither fight you nor drive you from your homes because of your religion, God instructs you to deal with them with justice, and utmost respect."* (Qur'an 60:8)
	Muslims are only permitted to fight in self-defense, and not become aggressors.	*"Fight in the cause of God those who fight you, and do not commit aggression."* (Qur'an 2:190) The verse above means "to fight only those who fight you, and not kill women, children, the elderly, or anyone who is not fighting you." –Tafsir 2:190 Ibn Abbas
Murder of innocent civilians as "revenge" for civilians killed during foreign invasions	Islam forbids killing of innocent civilians and commands the protection of all.	Islam calls upon Muslims to live up to the highest moral standard (Qur'an 3:110), not to sink to the level of enemy fighters.
		The Prophet forbade those going to battle from harming *'Usafa* (hired workers, women, children, the elderly, monks, diplomats, and emissaries).
	Islam teaches that no human being is responsible for the crime of another.	*"Each soul is responsible for its own actions, no bearer of burdens will bear the burdens of another."* (Qur'an 6:164)

"May Allah protect this Khilafah state and continue guiding it until its legions fight the crusader armies who will gather near Dabiq" (*Dabiq*, Issue 1, pg. 40).

Debunked: "Cosmic War"

DR. REZA ASLAN breaks down the notion of "cosmic war" and the "us versus them" mind-set that extremists cling to when they justify violence against non-Muslims or Muslims who do not share their misinterpretation of Islam.

KEY TAKEAWAYS

- In a cosmic war, participants see themselves as soldiers sanctioned by God acting out a battle on earth that they believe is actually taking place in the heavens.
- Extremists justify their violence by believing that they are engaged in this metaphysical conflict between the angels of light and the demons of darkness.
- There is no cosmic war against Christianity or Judaism in the Qur'an, and these faiths have been named allies of the Muslim world by the Prophet Muhammad.

The violent extremists who are slaughtering and beheading countless innocent individuals believe that they are carrying out a liturgical act in which they cast their victims as sacrificial lambs, regardless of race, religion, or nationality. They frame these acts in cosmic terms, as a battle for the sake of God. Although no religion is inherently violent or peaceful, these vicious men read the Qur'an and assure themselves that it is not innocents they are sacrificing but the allies of Satan, the brothers of the Devil. However wrong they are, some of these men and women may firmly believe that they are acting in the service of God. They believe they are engaged in a metaphysical conflict, not between armies or nations, but between the angels of light and the demons of darkness. They are fighting a cosmic war, not against the American or Western imperium, but against the eternal forces of evil.

A cosmic war is like a ritual drama in which participants act out on earth a battle they believe is actually taking place in the heavens. Faith is a key value in the idea of cosmic war because the participants see themselves as soldiers sanctioned by God. In its simplest expression, cosmic war refers to the belief that God is actively engaged in human conflicts on behalf of one side against the other. The ultimate goal of a cosmic war is not to defeat an earthy force but to vanquish evil itself, which ensures that a cosmic war remains an absolute, eternal, unending, and ultimately unwinnable conflict. Thus, "cosmic warriors" like Daesh are fighting a war of the imagination in which they are seeking to bring about a global transformation.

Today, this global transformation has taken the form of jihadism, a global jihad movement that seeks to

REZA ASLAN is an internationally acclaimed writer and scholar of religion with a BA in religion from Santa Clara University, an MTS in Theology from Harvard, and a PhD in sociology from the University of California, Santa Barbara. He is an Adjunct Senior Fellow at the Council on Foreign Relations and a leading authority on Islam, the Middle East, and Muslim Americans. Dr. Aslan's first book, *No God but God: The Origins, Evolution, and Future of Islam*, is an international bestseller and was named among the 100 most important books of the last decade.

right the injustices against Muslims resulting from colonialism. Groups like Daesh, and al-Qaeda before them, view the injustice towards Muslims as a centuries-long war waged by the "Crusaders" against Islam. Although the belief in a cosmic war is used to mobilize and unite extremist groups under a shared set of grievances, they fail to provide a substantive plan to address these grievances outside of violence and terror.

The ultimate goal of a cosmic war is not to defeat an earthly force but to vanquish evil itself, which ensures that a cosmic war remains an absolute, eternal, unending, and ultimately unwinnable conflict.

Violent extremists view the United States through the historical lens of the Crusades, wherein Americans are the embodiment of the Christian crusaders. This is a view that has only been exacerbated by U.S. politicians who demonize all of Islam in the name of fighting terrorism. On both sides, the "war on terror" has come to be seen through the lens of a cosmic war and an "us versus them" way of thinking.

For extremist groups like Daesh and al-Qaeda, the Crusades are not so much a historical event as they are an ideological construct—an enduring narrative whose final chapter is only now being written in today's battlefields, except it is no longer Europe but America that has "taken up the cross" in the eternal cosmic battle between Christianity and Islam. The brazen use of Christian rhetoric in support of war is a legacy of the Crusades, which not only solidified the notion that physical combat against "the enemies of Christ" could be a valid expression of Christian faith but altered the very language of Christianity. The consequence of this has been the extremist call to arms for Muslims everywhere to awake from their slumber, to embrace Islam's own tradition of cosmic war, and to take the battle directly to the enemies of God.

But this cosmic mind-set is not limited to one faith or one movement. The Hebrew Bible contains sections, such as the Book of Joshua or Numbers chapter 31, that present total warfare against non-Israelite peoples as Divinely sanctioned warfare against idolaters, with military victory understood as triumphant glorification of the one true God. This concept of cosmic war not only provided the motivation for the Crusades, but is a foundation of the extreme right wing modern-day Christian evangelical movement. The extreme right wing evangelicals remain steadfast in their cosmic mind-set against the Muslim world due to their belief that Jews must be in possession of Israel and the Temple in Jerusalem in order to usher in the return of the Messiah. To these evangelicals, Islam is a cosmic enemy that seeks to destroy the state of Israel and overthrow Judeo-Christian civilization—the very foundation of our Western civilization.

In contrast, there is no such thing as blanket cosmic war against Christianity or Judaism in the Qur'an. The Qur'an refers to Christians—and Jews—as "*Ahl al-Kitab*" or "People of the Book" and have historically been allies of the Muslim world. In fact, when the Prophet Muhammad was forced to flee Mecca, his community of followers was granted protection by the Christian King of Abyssinia. Moreover, the Qur'an's reverence of Jesus and his faith supports coexistence between Muslims and Christians, further indicating that a cosmic war is not the will of God. The Qur'an states: *"Say (O Muslims): We believe in Allah and that which is revealed unto us and that which was revealed unto Abraham, and Ishmael, and Isaac, and Jacob, and the tribes, and that which Moses and Jesus received, and that which the prophets received from their Lord. We make no distinction between any of them, and unto Him we have surrendered"* (2:136).

Daesh, however, has expanded their cosmic war mind-set beyond the Christian West. They have turned their attention to their fellow Muslims by invoking the Islamic concept of "*Al-Wala' wal Bara*'" or "loyalty and disavowal." This duality divides all of creation into the "believers," with whom Daesh identify, and the "unbelievers," whom they define as any Muslim who does not agree with their ways. This is evident in the following quote, taken from a speech made by Daesh's leader, Abu Bakr al-Baghdadi:

"O Ummah of Islam, indeed the world today has been divided into two camps and two trenches, with no third camp present: The camp of Islam and faith, and the camp of *kufr* (disbelief) and hypocrisy—the camp of the Muslims and the *mujahidin* everywhere, and the camp of the jews, the crusaders, their allies, and with them the rest of the nations and religions of *kufr*, all being led by America and Russia, and being mobilized by the jews."

The consequence of this has been the extremist call to arms for Muslims everywhere to awake from their slumber, to embrace Islam's own tradition of cosmic war, and to take the battle directly to the enemies of God.

The quote above shows their distorted understanding of this term and further instills the "us versus them" mind-set by designating any Muslim who does not adhere to Daesh ideology as a non-believer, with no middle ground from which to choose. Seeing themselves as the only "true" believers, Daesh is abusing the Islamic concept of *takfir* to justify the slaughter of their fellow Muslim brothers and sisters. This practice continues with fervor, regardless of the countless Muslim clerics who are issuing fatwas against this practice, stating that it is a misappropriation of God's judgment and that in Islam "there is no [such thing as] *takfir*."

These Muslim cosmic warriors legitimize their attacks against both military and civilian targets, against both Muslims and non-Muslims, by dividing the world into two separate camps: one of faith and one of infidelity. Their jihad is not a defensive struggle against an occupying power but an eternal cosmic war that transcends all earthly ambitions. We must reject the religiously polarizing rhetoric of our leaders and of our enemies, focus on the material matters at stake, and seek to address the earthly issues that always lie behind the cosmic impulse.

Muslims! Whoever thinks that it is within his pacity to conciliate with the Jews . . . has belied e explicit statement of his Lord . . . who says, . . . nd they will continue to fight you until they turn you ck from your religion}" (*Dabiq*, Issue 9, pg. 52).

Debunked: Jews—Enemies of Muslims

DR. MEHNAZ AFRIDI argues against the notion that Jews are enemies of Muslims, pointing out that Jews are considered "People of the Book" in Islam and share the same message of the oneness of God.

KEY TAKEAWAYS

- The concept of God being the ultimate Judge is so central to Muslim belief that those who accuse Jews are going against God's revelations.
- The Qur'an prescribes tolerance of and eternal life to Jews and asks Muslims to accept their message in the Torah.
- The periods of peace between the two faith communities outnumber the times of turbulence, regardless of what extremists want others to believe.

JEWS IN ISLAM

In Islam, Muslims are asked to live in harmony and accept Jews as a people of faith, believing that Jews were given a similar scriptural message from the same God. The two groups have shared a long history together: Jews are known as "People of the Book" or *Ahl-al Kitab* in Islam, and were the first group of people to accept and receive the most important message through Abraham that adheres to the monotheistic belief in the one-ness of God, or *Tawhid*. The Jews were the people led by Moses to spread the deep faith of the unknowable, inconceivable, beneficent, and all-knowing God. They share many beliefs, including belief in the one God, the prophetic tradition, dietary laws, ritual prayer, and alms to the poor, with their fellow Muslims. Islamic history is replete with Muslim-Jewish encounters, and their mentions in the Qur'an and the Prophet's sayings are understood in the social and historical context of the Prophet's time. As an example, the verses that indicate mistrust between the Jews and Muslims were revealed at a time when certain Jewish tribes broke their contract with the Prophet and refused to acknowledge him as a messenger of God. Daesh and other extremist groups not only attempt to erase the long history of Jewish-Muslim co-existence, but they also distort certain verses of the Qur'an to justify their hatred and violence toward the Jews, to whom they wrongfully refer as *kuffar*—loosely translated as "unbeliever" or "infidel."

The word "infidel," in Arabic *kafir* (singular of *kuffar*) does not literally mean "non-believer." In Arabic, *kafir* has multiple meanings and its root is commonly translated as "disbelief," which also means "to conceal or cover the truth." The word *kafir* is used in the Qur'an not only for Jews but also for Muslims who rejected belief in God, His miracles, or the Prophet's sayings. The language of concealment, deafening and blinding, is also used to refer to those who go astray,

DR. MEHNAZ M. AFRIDI is Assistant Professor of Religious Studies at Manhattan College and a member of the American Academy of Religion. Dr. Afridi is the author of *Naguib Mahfouz and Modern Islamic Identity* and co-author of *Global Perspectives on Orhan Pamuk: Existentialism and Politics*.

including Muslims: *"So have they not traveled through the earth and have hearts by which to reason and ears by which to hear? For indeed, it is not eyes that are blinded, but blinded are the hearts which are within the breasts"* (22:46). Extremist groups, especially Daesh, have taken the word *kafir* and distorted it to justify violence and terror against Jews, Muslims, and those who do not agree with their skewed understanding of God's religion.

The Qur'an also rejects any exclusivist claim to heavenly reward (2:111–112). The most pluralistic verse is repeated twice in the Qur'an, in 2:62 and 5:69, the former of which states: *"The believers, the Jews, the Christians and the Sabians—all those who believe in God and the Last Day and do good—will have their rewards with their Lord. No fear for them, nor will they grieve."*

The most important message of the Qur'an is with regard to the "Day of Judgment," where Muslims believe the balance of their deeds will be revealed: *"Those who believe (in the Qur'an), those who follow the Jewish (scriptures), and the Sabians (can mean an ancient religion or people with no specific religion), Christians, Magians, and Polytheists, God will judge between them on the Day of Judgment: for God (alone) is witness of all things"* (22:17). Furthermore, the Qur'an states that judgment is a divine quality, and as such only God can fully judge humankind. As the Qur'an notes: *"For behold, unto (only) Us will be their return, Then it will be for Us to Judge (humans)"* (88:25–26). The concept of God being the ultimate Judge is so central to Muslim belief that those who accuse Jews—who are followers of God's scripture—of being "infidels" are egregiously going against God's revelations.

Furthermore, there is an oft-repeated charge against Muslims that the Qur'an is inherently anti-Semitic due to three Qur'anic verses that refer to Jews as either "apes" (2:63–65 and 7:163–166) or "apes and pigs" (5:59–60). While these verses exist and must be acknowledged, they also must be properly understood and contextualized. Nowhere in these verses (or anywhere else in the Qur'an) does God say that all Jews are apes or pigs. The verses in which Jews are called "apes" or "apes and pigs" refer to a specific group of Sabbath-desecrating Jewish fishermen who disobeyed God by profaning the Sabbath. God tells this group that their punishment is to "be as despicable as apes" since they refuse to obey God's laws. Scholars argue that God did not literally turn these Jews into apes or pigs, but rather that this expression is metaphorical in nature. Distorted understandings of these verses and the use of "apes" or "apes and pigs" in the Qur'an have mutually reinforced the goals of extremist groups and Islamophobes alike; the former distort these verses to promote their incendiary political agendas, and the latter quote these extremist Jew-haters to "prove" that Islam denigrates Jews. Neither is true.

The periods of peace between the two faith communities outnumber the times of turbulence, no matter what the extremists want others to believe.

The Qur'an also refers to groups of Arabs as hypocrites: *"And among those around you of the Arabs are hypocrites, and from the people of Medina. They have become accustomed to hypocrisy. You, O Muhammad, do not know them, but We know them. We will punish them twice [in this world]; then they will be returned to a great punishment"* (9:101). If the same logic is applied to this verse then one can argue that the Qur'an considers all Arabs to be hypocrites. This claim is ridiculous.

Contrary to how extremists exploit scripture, the Qur'an prescribes tolerance and eternal life to Jews and asks Muslims to accept their message in the Torah (*tawrah*). The Qur'an states that Islam is close to Judaism, and as such, Muslims may even join Jews in communal meals, and Jews can worship in a mosque. Too, a Muslim man can marry a Jewish woman without her converting to Islam, something exemplified by Prophet Muhammad, who married two Jewish women: Safiya Bint Huyayy and Rayhana bint Zayd.

JEWISH-MUSLIM EARLY ENCOUNTER

The Prophet's attempt to spread the message of the oneness of God, and equality of minorities and slaves, threatened the economic and military dominance of the neighboring polytheistic tribes. When the Jewish tribes—the Banu Qaynuqa', Banu al-Nadir, and Banu Qurayza—resisted and rejected his message, the

Prophet offered them a mutually beneficial contract, the Pact of Medina, which they signed to affirm that they were part of a community (*ummah*) of believers and under mutual protection. This would form the basis of a multireligious community in Medina; however, this agreement was ultimately not successful and the Prophet suggested that Jews and Muslims live under their own religious laws (*din*).[1]

As the nascent Muslim community grew, there were many attempts to assassinate the Prophet, and the Muslims were continually being attacked by pagan tribes. To fortify his troops during these battles, the Prophet needed to forge alliances with other tribes, a task for which he enlisted the help of arbitrator Sa'ad ibn Mua'dh, and which ultimately allied the Muslims with certain Jewish tribes, including the Banu Qurayza. During the Battle of the Trench, the Banu Qurayza did not uphold their agreement with the Prophet, but instead betrayed the Prophet, who had been relying on their support. Although the Muslims were severely outnumbered, the Prophet and his followers won the battle. By reneging on their agreement, the Banu Qurayza had committed political treason that needed to be punished. The Prophet once again turned to Sa'ad, this time to suggest an appropriate punishment. As Sa'ad was severely wounded in the battle, the Banu Qurayza agreed to his appointment as their judge. Sa'ad judged that their men were to be killed and their children and women to be taken as slaves, a decision the Prophet abided by. The Prophet, however, wanted to treat the Jewish members with kindness and compassion, so he married one of the Jewish women, thereby establishing the standard for respectful treatment for the remaining members of this Jewish tribe: *"This day [all] good foods have been made lawful, and the food of those who were given the Scripture is lawful for you and your food is lawful for them. And [lawful in marriage are] chaste women from among the believers and chaste women from among those who were given the Scripture before you" (5:5).*

JEWS AND MUSLIMS: MEDIEVAL TO MODERN

Jews and Muslims have built deep bonds on the foundations laid centuries ago. With similar beliefs and practices, Jews have lived in Muslim lands in harmony and co-existence with their neighbors. Jews and Muslims translated Greek works together into Arabic and Hebrew during the medieval period. Maimonides, a great Jewish philosopher, became a personal physician of Muslim governors. One of the most well-known examples is Shmuel Hanagid, who not only served as vizier (high official) of the Muslim king of Granada, but also as a commander of his armies. He successfully commanded power and brought his kingdom great fame and influence. Jews, in Muslim lands, often fared much better than anywhere else and shared in their local culture, language, and customs.

Jews were allotted governing power, especially from the tenth through the twelfth centuries in such areas as Muslim Spain, Iraq, Egypt, and areas of North Africa such as Tunisia, and in the Ottoman Empire during the sixteenth century. These were golden ages for Jews and their Muslim host countries. In the twentieth century, during the Holocaust, Albanian Muslims rescued Jews who were fleeing persecution. Muslims also helped Jews during the Holocaust in countries like Iran, Tunisia, Morocco, Egypt, and in Eastern European cities, including Sarajevo. Muslims were seen as the protectors of the People of the Book in the most dangerous times and were seen as people with whom Jews could live with in harmony without persecution.

JEWS ARE NOT THE ENEMY

There is no basis for hating or mistrusting Jews in the Qur'an or historically. They share a belief in the same monotheistic (Abrahamic) God, and share in the message of the Prophets Moses and Abraham. The periods of peace between the two faith communities outnumber the times of turbulence, no matter what the extremists want others to believe. Jews are seen in a favorable light and allotted a status that is highly regarded by Muslims and in the Qur'an: *"Say, 'O People of the Scripture, you are [standing] on nothing until you uphold [the law of] the Torah, the Gospel, and what has been revealed to you from your Lord.' And that which has been revealed to you from your Lord will surely increase many of them in transgression and disbelief. So do not grieve over the disbelieving people'" (5:68).*

---

[1] Gordon D. Newby, "The Jews of Arabia at the Birth of Islam." *A History of Jewish-Muslim Relations: From Origins to the Present Day*, edited by Abdelwahab Meddeb and Benjamin Stow, Princeton University Press, 2013, p. 48.

"[The] continual existence [of the Yazidis] to this day is a matter that Muslims should question as they will be asked about it on Judgment Day. . . .Their creed is so deviant from the truth (*Dabiq*, Issue 4, pg. 14).

Debunked: There Is Only One Way to God

MIKE GHOUSE discusses the widespread misperception that Muslims are intolerant of other religions and explains how Islam advocates pluralism.

KEY TAKEAWAYS

- Muslims believe that they should not merely tolerate those who are different, but to commit to engaging with them.
- The Qur'an declares that differences in religious practices should make people work with one another to do good.
- Daesh's ideology against other religions violates Islamic principles and is not in accordance with what Muslims actually believe.

There is a widespread perception that Muslims are intolerant of other religions, and that such intolerance is inherent in our teachings. Indeed, "pluralism" is often claimed as a "Western" and "secular" value that is antithetical to Islam itself, rather than a fundamental Qur'anic value at the very heart of our tradition.

But what, exactly, is pluralism, and why is Islam perceived as an anti-pluralistic religion, intolerant of other traditions? Pluralism is simply an attitude of respecting the otherness of our fellow human beings and accepting the God-given uniqueness of each one of us. Pluralism is living your religious, social, political, and cultural life and letting others live theirs. It's about celebrating such diversity, but it's also about getting to know one another. God asks Muslims not merely to tolerate those who are different from us, but to commit ourselves to engaging with them; to work and live with mutual assistance and respect. This is something that runs against everything that extremist groups like Daesh believe. They mercilessly slaughter minority faith communities, such as the Yazidis, ignoring the Qur'anic imperative to embrace diversity, and the acknowledgment that "the plurality of religious paths to the One is . . .a reflection of the spiritual infinity of the One."[1]

Islam presents God as a common God, the God of all creation. He is not a God of Muslims or any one group of people. The Qur'an starts with, *"All praise is due to God alone, the Sustainer of all the worlds"* (1:1). There is a reason why this is the very first verse of the Qur'an—it is to reaffirm that the creator God belongs to all of humanity, and cannot be exclusively claimed by Muslims or any one faith.

MIKE GHOUSE is President of the Center for Pluralism in Washington, DC, which offers pluralistic solutions on issues of the day. He is a speaker, writer, and interfaith wedding officiant, who has appeared in over 300 television interviews, including 125 on Fox News, and spoken for over 1,000 hours on talk radio shows. He has published over 3,000 articles on pluralism, Islam, and foreign policy, among other important topics, all of which can be found at www.MikeGhouse.net.

[1] Reza Shah-Kazemi, Amyn B. Sajoo, ed. A Companion to Muslim Ethics, London: I.B. Taurus, 2010, p. 141.

Indeed, in the Qur'an, God said, *"Unto every one of you have We appointed a [different] law and way of life. And if God had so willed, He could surely have made you all one single community: but [He willed it otherwise] in order to test you by means of what He has vouchsafed unto, you. Vie, then, with one another in doing good works! Unto God you all must return; and then He will make you truly understand all that on which you were wont to differ"* (5:48).

This verse has often been misunderstood to mean that only one community will cross the finish line, while the others will not. However, here the expression "every one of you" denotes the various communities of which mankind is composed. Thus, the Qur'an impresses upon all who believe in God, Muslims and non-Muslims alike, that the differences in their religious practices should make them "vie with one another in doing good works" rather than lose themselves in mutual hostility.

This concept is similar to the phrase emblazoned on the Great Seal of the United States, "E pluribus unum," meaning, "One out of many." The phrase is similar to a Latin translation of a variation of Heraclitus' 10th fragment, "The one is made up of all things, and all things issue from the one." By God mandating that we get to know each other, this is another way for us to see the Divine in the other, and for us to acknowledge the hand of creation.

The Qur'an also emphasizes that no single community will earn God's grace.

"Those who believe, those who are Jewish, the converts, the Christians, the Zoroastrians, and the idol worshipers, God is the One who will judge among them on the Day of Resurrection. God witnesses all things" (22:17).

God also mentions that God does not make any distinction between any of the prophets:

"Say, 'We believe in God, and in what was sent down to us, and in what was sent down to Abraham, Ismail, Isaac, Jacob, and the Patriarchs; and in what was given to Moses and Jesus, and all the prophets from their Lord. We make no distinction among any of them. To Him alone we are submitters'" (2:136).

As Reza Shah-Kazemi writes, "Both universal revelation and human diversity are not seen as accidents of human experience but as expressions of divine wisdom. God is absolutely one yet immeasurably infinite, the human race too is one in its essence yet infinitely variegated in its forms." [2]

UNDERSTANDING THE SIGNS OF GOD IS PLURALISM

Although God breathed the breath of the Divine into all human beings, endowing all of us with the faculties of sight, smell, sound, taste, and touch, He also chose to create us in different tribes, communities, nations, and by extension, faiths, races, ideas, shapes, and colors:

"O mankind, indeed We have created you from male and female and made you peoples and tribes that you may know one another. Indeed, the most noble of you in the sight of Allah is the most righteous of you. Indeed, Allah is Knowing and Acquainted" (49:13).

Given that diversity, we are bound to have conflicts and compete for resources. So, He adds more guidance in the verse: the best ones among you are those who will take the time to know each other. He knows that committing ourselves to knowledge about others leads to understanding, and understanding to acceptance and appreciation of different points of view, resulting in harmony and peace.

Furthermore, God created the world in perfect harmony and balance, and gave us the abilities to manage our affairs:

"The sun and the moon run on precise calculations. The stars and the trees submit to Him. The skies, He raised high and has established the balance that you may not transgress in the balance. But weight with justice, and do not violate the balance. The earth, He laid out for all living creatures. In it are fruits, and date-palms in clusters. And grains on flourishing stems and fragrant plants. So which of your Lord's blessings do you both deny?" (5:5–13).

All God asked of us was to keep His creation intact, and restore harmony and balance if they wither.

[2] Reza Shah-Kazemi, Amyn B. Sajoo, ed, A Companion to Muslim Ethics, London: I.B. Taurus, 2010, p. 145.

The Prophet Muhammad had a singular determination—for all people to live in harmony. He honored and respected people of different religions, and protected minorities. He sought to restore God's balance by re-making society into one where no individual had to live in apprehension or fear of another; where one could live his or her own life and let others live theirs. In our day, if we can learn to accept the otherness of others, and respect the God-given uniqueness of each one of the 7 billion of us, then conflicts will fade and solutions emerge.

America has flourished because of its commitment to pluralism. Islam flourished because of a commitment to the pluralism inherent in its teachings. Those societies that have embraced and celebrated pluralism, rather than merely accepted it, tend to flourish most.

Muslim women] should emulate the women first called to religion, Mariam and Asia and Khadija, Fatima, Aisha and the mothers of the believers, women of the Companions and their followers." ("Women of the Islamic State: A Manifesto on Women by the Al-Khanssaa Brigade," pg. 19, translated by Charlie Winter, Quilliam Foundation).

Debunked: Daesh's View of Women

DAISY KHAN describes how women who are both experiencing anti-Islamic sentiment and are more vulnerable to Daesh propaganda can look to the stories of women in the Qur'an to not only debunk Daesh's manipulation of their stories but find vital lessons and motivation for empowerment as well.

KEY TAKEAWAYS

- The Qur'an stresses the importance of motherhood, independence, strength, and unwavering faith in the way it describes women.
- The Qur'an's stories of women illuminate important connections between Islam, Judaism, and Christianity.
- The lessons behind the stories of these women reveal Daesh's selective and manipulated reading of the sacred texts.

The rights of Muslim women have been at the center of debates surrounding Islam in the West for more than a decade. Western media's continual portrayals of Muslim women as oppressed and lacking agency, and their purported subservience to men, not only make Muslim women visible targets for an anti-Islam backlash, but also shape their perception of themselves as outsiders in their own country. Moreover, when they become subjects of the debate rather than participants in it, they experience powerlessness and disconnection from society.

Daesh capitalizes on this vulnerability by reinforcing these women's feelings of being hated, isolated, and othered, using incidents of anti-Muslim bias or rhetoric that occur in these Western societies to reinforce their feelings of being under attack. Daesh offers these women a compelling alternative: escape discrimination and be part of a global sisterhood, feel protected, and find true belonging. They refer to potential recruits as "daring," "brave," and "courageous" and compare them to Maryam (Mary, mother of Jesus), Asiyah (the Pharaoh's wife), Khadijah (the Prophet Muhammad's first wife), Fatima (the Prophet's daughter), and Aisha (the Prophet's last wife), women whom Muslims hold in high esteem for their piety, acts of self-sacrifice, and devotion.

However, Daesh's women can never legitimately follow in the footsteps of these women, for their actions and intentions go against the very principles that these women embodied, such as truthfulness, forbearance, and devotion to God. Here are their stories:

Maryam (Mary) is described in the Qur'an as "chosen above all women" and is regarded as one of the most righteous and pious women: "*The angels said, 'Mary, God has chosen you, purified you, and chosen you above all women in the world. Mary, be dedicated to your Lord; bow down and kneel with those who are kneeling in prayer*" (3:42–43). As testament to her righteousness, a chapter (surah) of the Qur'an is named after her, making her one of only eight people to have a surah named after them. For her steadfastness and purity, God chose her to give birth to Jesus, "the spirit of God." The Qur'an calls her the truthful one (5:75) who followed God's commandments, fulfilled her covenant with God, and endured many hardships. That the story of Maryam appears in the Qur'an is deeply significant for interfaith relations, as it is through her that we find a key connection between Islam, Judaism, and Christianity.

Asiyah, the Pharaoh's wife, is honored in Islam for remaining steadfast against the Pharaoh, one of the most tyrannical rulers of all time, who tortured her for believing in Moses. She had deep faith in God and exhibited great bravery because she believed in God. The Qur'an describes her as such: "*God draws an[other] example for those who have faith: the wife of Pharaoh, when she said, 'My Lord! Build me a home near You in paradise, and deliver me from Pharaoh and his conduct, and deliver me from the wrongdoing lot*" (66:11). Before her death, she asked God to deliver her from the Pharaoh and his bad deeds and from evil people. Asiyah rejected her tyrannical husband who was a wrongdoer and raised the infant Moses to fulfill her mandate as Moses's protector. In Asiyah we find a deep commonalty between the Jewish and Muslim traditions.

Since the women who have answered Daesh's call have devoted their lives to violence, oppression, and injustice, in no way can they claim to follow in the footsteps of women like Maryam or Asiyah, and should learn the real lessons that the stories of these women have to offer. Misguided women would do well to learn the stories of Hagar and Bilquis (Queen of Sheba) as well, who devoted their lives to the way of peace, patience, and justice.

Hagar, mother of Ishmael, is a significant figure in Islam. Her son was the patriarch of Islam and she is considered one of the founders of Mecca. She had incredible strength and unwavering courage and faith in God that enabled her to remain in the desolate desert valley after they were left behind by Abraham. To quench her son's thirst she rushed between two hills to find water when angel Gabriel appeared before her and told her of God's plan. It was then that the ground opened up and God caused a spring to burst forth from the holy fountain known as Zamzam. The event is so historically significant, it is commemorated during the annual pilgrimage (*hajj*) when all Muslim pilgrims run between the hills and drink from the continuously flowing fountain of Zamzam. Thus, not only is Hagar recognized as an embodiment of strength for raising her child in a desolate desert without a male companion, but her sacrifice is honored and reenacted as an important religious ritual. Hagar bore Abraham his first son, Ishmael, a direct forefather of the Prophet Muhammad, while Sarah gave birth to the son Isaac, who was the forefather of Moses and Jesus. This shows that all three monotheistic faiths trace their heritage back to one single patriarch, Abraham.

Since the women who have answered Daesh's call have devoted their lives to violence, oppression, and injustice, in no way can they claim to follow in the footsteps of women like Maryam or Asiyah, and should learn the real lessons that the stories of these women have to offer. Misguided women would do well to learn the stories of Hagar and Bilquis (Queen of Sheba) as well, who devoted their lives to the way of peace, patience, and justice.

Aisha, the last wife of the Prophet Muhammad, spent more than forty years propagating knowledge of Islam, and played an important role in Islamic history by transcribing and narrating 2,210 Hadith (sayings of the Prophet). A strong advocate for women's education in Islam, she is considered to be one of the most knowledgeable Muslim women, and is held in high regard by many Muslims for her scholarly intelligence and expertise in understanding and memorizing the Qur'an. One day, when Aisha accidentally became separated from the Prophet's caravan and was stranded in the desert, people made false accusations against her, causing deep distress to her and her family. After they were reunited, the Prophet consoled her, saying, "Aisha, I have heard that you are innocent, I expect that God will declare your innocence. I will bear this patiently with good grace." Aisha waited patiently and trusted that God would reveal the truth. God sent a revelation proving her innocence in ten verses of Surah An-Noor: "*Why then, did the believers, men and women, when you heard it (the slander), think good of their own people and say: 'This (charge) is an obvious lie?' Why did they not produce four witnesses? Since they (the slanderers) have not produced witnesses! Then with God they are the liars*" (Qur'an 24:12–13). After the death of the Prophet, Aisha became involved in politics and public affairs, correcting distortions of the Prophet's message when she heard them.

Daesh barely mentions **Bilquis (Queen of Sheba)** in its recruitment narrative, though in the Qur'an she is hailed as the archetype of political leadership for her transparency, reliance on public consultation (shura), and the priority she placed on the welfare of her people over all else. She is contrasted with Pharaoh, the egocentric leader who is presented as the archetype of tyranny—intoxicated with his own power and force. When the Queen received a letter from King Solomon requesting the submission of her and her people to God, unlike the rash and violent Pharaoh, she turned to her companions and advisers to seek their consensus on how to respond: "*She said, 'O eminent ones, advise me in my affair. I would not decide a matter until you witness [for] me*" (Qur'an 27:32). By yielding power to her people, she was rendered even more powerful by her court, as they responded to her request: "*They said, 'We are men of strength and of great military might, but the command is yours, so see what you will command*" (Qur'an 27:33). The Queen refused to make a rash decision to engage in physical confrontation. Rather, the Queen acknowledged the danger a war would pose to the well-being of her people, so she chose a path of nonconfrontation. As she observed: "*Indeed kings—when they enter a city, they ruin it and render the honor of its people humbled. And thus do they do*" (Qur'an 27:34).

CONCLUSION

In today's world of great social unrest and division, it is unfortunate that so many young women are being manipulated into joining a destructive group like Daesh. They need to be reminded that tyranny, coercion, and flawed thinking are linked to aggression and violence aimed at forcing others to change. In this violent paradigm, a person is always in a state of war.

If Muslim women want to express their agency and not be seen as subservient, second-class citizens, they need look no further than the Qur'an, which explicitly states that gender equality is an integral part of Islam: "*The men and women who have submitted to God, the believing men and women, the obedient men and women, the truthful men and women, the patient men and women, the humble men and women, the charitable men and women, the fasting men and women, the men and women who guard their private parts, the men and women who remember God often, for them, God prepared forgiveness and a great reward*" (Qur'an 33:35).

The stories of Maryam, Asiyah, Hagar, and Bilquis, as told in the Qur'an, show that these women were all autonomous agents capable of receiving God's guidance, and that, in the eyes of God, they are of absolute moral and spiritual equality to men. Indeed, Muslim women have been afforded respect and dignity within Islam.

It is encouraging to see so many Muslim women working to redress social grievances and enact social change. They are responsible agents who earn respect and dignity, who exercise their rights as legal, social, and spiritual beings; and who, as servants of God, exercise their abilities and talents in all areas of human activity. They do this by upholding the truth, rejecting tyrannical wrongdoers, exhibiting bravery, seeking consensus, and using diplomacy and peaceful means to promote change that will benefit all. These are the women who are walking in the footsteps of Islam's earliest women—the ones who have joined Daesh have gone astray.

"The Islamic state dealt with [the Yazidis] as the majority of [jurists] have indicated how mushrikin [polytheists] should be dealt with. . . . Large-scale enslavement of mushrik families is probably the first since the abandonment of this Shari'ah law" (*Dabiq*, Issue 4, pg. 15).

Debunked: The Revival of Slavery

IMAM ABDUL MALIK MUJAHID presents a response to Daesh's practice of enslaving prisoners. He points out that the emancipation of slaves was clearly intended in the Qur'an.

KEY TAKEAWAYS

- The Qur'an does not have any verses that command the practice of slavery to be continued or reinstated.
- Daesh abuses the Qur'an to justify its crimes of enslaving prisoners and taking female prisoners as concubines.
- To the Prophet Muhammad and his Companions, liberating slaves was one of the ultimate means of reaching moral and spiritual excellence.

Thanks be to God that we now live in a world where there is a global consensus against slavery.

Our gratitude is intensified when we recognize that slavery was a persistent evil that existed not just in our ancient past, but continued until not very long ago in virtually all cultures.

Yet, despite all this progress, slavery has yet to be fully eradicated from the world. Today, Daesh is abusing the Qur'an to justify their crimes of enslaving prisoners and taking women prisoners as concubines. And although rape does not need a theology, Daesh claims to offer one. For this reason, it is of the utmost importance for faith-based voices to speak loudly against the atrocities of Daesh and provide clear, informed responses based on Islamic sources.

From a spiritual perspective, God describes the first step in the journey toward Him as one of freeing slaves, "*But he did not take the difficult path. And how would you know what is the difficult path? It is to free a slave, or to feed on a day of hunger an orphaned relative,*" (90:10–14). Within Islamic law itself, the freeing of slaves was incorporated into expiations and punishments for crimes. These verses were reaffirmed in a 2014 letter to Daesh leader Abu Bakr al-Baghdadi, signed by more than one hundred of the top Islamic scholars from around the world.

In addition, there are numerous verses in the Qur'an that speak of the emancipation of slaves. For example, in Surah 2, Verse 177, God teaches that one's piety is personified by the freeing of slaves. The Qur'an also teaches that the emancipation of slaves may be used to compensate for sin or a crime: "*A believer should never kill another believer, but mistakes happen. If someone kills a believer by mistake, he must free one believing slave and pay compensation to the victim's relatives, unless they willingly forgo compensation. If the victim is a believer, but belonged to a community with which you are at war, then the compensation is only to free a believing slave*" (4:92).

IMAM ABDUL MALIK MUJAHID is the founder of Sound Vision. He is also Chair Emeritus of the Parliament of the World's Religions and Burma Task Force USA. Imam Mujahid was selected six times as one of the 500 Most Influential Muslims in the world. A longer version of this article can be found at: tinyurl.com/no2salve.

This theme continues in 58:3: *"Those of you who divorce your wives by equating them with your mothers, then wish to go back on what you said, must set free a slave before they touch one another,"* and *"God does not hold you accountable for oaths thoughtlessly sworn, but He will take you to task for earnestly sworn oaths. So, the breaking of an oath must be atoned by feeding ten needy persons with the same food as you would want for your own family, or by clothing them, or by freeing a slave, and if a person cannot find the means to do this, he will fast for three days"* (5:89).

Likewise, the Qur'an speaks strongly against taking female prisoners as concubines, which is seen in Surah 4, Verse 25:

"If any of you does not have the means to marry free believing women, then marry a believer from those whom your right hands held in trust. God knows all about your faith; each one of you is part of the same human family. Marry them with their guardian's consent, and give them their rightful bridal-gifts. Make them married women, not adulterous fornicators or lovers. If they commit adultery when they are married, their punishment should be half that of free women. This permission is for those of you who fear they will sin. It is better for you to practice self-control. God is most forgiving and Merciful-to-all."

To the Prophet and his Companions, liberating slaves was not merely one specific good deed out of a long list of potential opportunities for good; rather, it was one of the ultimate means of reaching moral and spiritual excellence.

Moreover, there is not a single verse in the Qur'an that encourages or commands people to take others as slaves. Also, there is nothing to suggest that it is the Divine Will for the practice of slavery to continue until the end of time, as Daesh would like everyone to believe.

Following these commandments, the Prophet Muhammad launched an anti-slavery movement in which he personally liberated all of his slaves, and even promised prisoners of war their freedom if they taught ten Muslims how to read. The Prophet's Companions followed his example, freeing tens of thousands of slaves of their own volition. To the Prophet and his Companions, liberating slaves was not merely one specific good deed out of a long list of potential opportunities for good; rather, it was one of the ultimate means of reaching moral and spiritual excellence. This is why his wife, Khadijah, and his most beloved companion, Abu Bakr, both wealthy businesspersons, became almost penniless buying slaves their freedom.

It was because of this anti-slavery movement that most people who accepted the Prophet's invitation to believe in One God and join his peace movement were slaves. It was this core message of the equality of all human beings as explained in Surah 49, Verse 13, *"People, We created you from a male and a female and made you nations and tribes so that you may know one another. The best among you in the sight of God is the one who is most mindful of God. God is All-knowing and All-Aware,"* that attracted Malik El-Shabazz (Malcolm X), Muhammad Ali, and Kareem Abdul-Jabbar, among hundreds of thousands of African Americans, as well as former untouchables in India, to Islam.

It should be noted that there is one Qur'anic verse that authorizes the capture of human beings; not as slaves, but as prisoners of war, *"So, when you encounter the unbelievers (in battle), strike at their necks. Then, once they are defeated, bind them firmly. Then either release them by grace, or by ransom, until the war is over. God could have defeated them Himself if He had willed, but He wants to test some of you by means of others. As for those who are killed in the cause of God, He will not let their deeds go to waste,"* (47:4). This was ordered in a context when there were no prison systems or prisoner-of-war camps. Army commanders were either to free prisoners without financial compensation or to hold them for ransom.

Another aspect of the Prophet's anti-slavery movement was to challenge the exploitation of enslaved women or concubines, who were often treated as sexual pawns and prostituted to the highest bidder. Using both legal and moral measures to address this practice, the Prophet made the prostitution of all women illegal and ruled that sexual intercourse must require marital consent.

In addition, Muslim men who owned female slaves were highly encouraged to emancipate them, instead of living in a system that promoted their exploitation. The Prophet Muhammad said: "Whoever educates a slave woman, treats her nicely, liberates her, and marries her, will be rewarded twice." In short, the aim was to end both the sexual exploitation of women, and slavery in general. The Prophet also forbade the division of slave families, prohibited selling-off mothers, encouraged Muslims to marry slave women, and enacted equal inheritance laws among the children of both free and slave women.

Although Daesh does not seem amenable to reason, there is an Islamic theological reasoning against the revival of slavery that must be made clear: God has never ordered anyone to establish slavery, nor is there any verse in the Qur'an that commands the practice to be continued or reinstated.

Thus, slavery should not be revived in the name of Islam, as the act of reinstituting slavery goes against direct encouragements and commandments that speak towards setting people free, and go against God's plan and the Prophet's movement to eliminate it.

Daesh grossly misinterprets the mere mention of the existence of slavery in the Qur'an, equating it with approval and encouragement, while ignoring the clear verses that speak towards its abolition. It is a clear violation of Islamic principles and teachings, as Islamic scholars in America and the Muslim world have made clear.

Although Daesh does not seem amenable to reason, there is an Islamic theological reasoning against the revival of slavery that must be made clear: God has never ordered anyone to establish slavery, nor is there any verse in the Qur'an that commands the practice to be continued or reinstated. Likewise, God has instructed us to follow Him, the Prophet, and our Leaders: "*Believers, obey God and the messenger and those among you who have been entrusted with authority. If you have a dispute about anything, refer it to God and the Messenger, if you truly believe in God and the Last Day. This is best to do and in turn gives the best results*" (4:59). They have all prohibited slavery through their commandments and treaties, and it is a sin to violate such treaties.

Muslims around the world must be at the forefront of speaking out against slavery and rape based on God's Commandments for emancipation, Islam's emphasis on establishing an egalitarian society, and the Prophet's movement for the liberation of slaves. Our voices must be louder than those of groups like Daesh and Boko Haram.

Supporting the anti-slavery movement is in line with a Muslim's duty to be just, as emphasized in the Qur'an: "*O you who believe! stand out firmly for justice, as witnesses for God, even if it be against yourselves, or your parents, or your kin. Whether one is rich or poor, God can best protect both. So do not ever follow prejudice, so as to do justice; and in case you twist or veer away, then surely God has been Ever-Cognizant of whatever you do.*" (4:135).

ne soldiers of the Khilafah, with sledgehammers
hand, revived the Sunnah of their father
rahim . . . when they laid waste to the shirki
gacy of a nation that had long passed from the
ce of the Earth" (*Dabiq*, Issue 8, pg. 22).

Debunked: The Destruction of Antiquities and Historical Sites

QASIM RASHID shows how Daesh's destruction of antiquities and historical sites goes against the Islamic imperative of preserving such sites to prove the impermanence of past civilizations.

KEY TAKEAWAYS

- The Prophet Muhammad's example in the Qur'an shows that he categorically rejected destroying idols belonging to others, as well as that he forbade Muslims from even insulting that which others worship.
- Islam guarantees universal freedom of conscience to idolaters.
- Daesh's acts of destruction extend to Muslims as well, proving that it is not interested in helping Muslims or upholding Islam.

The terrorist organization known as Daesh generally posits four arguments to justify their destruction of idols, ancient sites, and ancient temples. First, Daesh claims that because Prophet Abraham (pbuh) destroyed idols, Muslims are required to destroy idols. Next, Daesh argues that idol destruction is required because the Prophet Muhammad (pbuh) ordered Jabir Abdullah al-Bajalirz to destroy a house in Yemen filled with idols. Third, Daesh destroys idols because the Prophet Muhammad (pbuh) removed idols from the Kabah. Finally, Daesh cites a Hadith in which the Prophet Muhammad (pbuh) allegedly mandated the destruction of all idols and graves.

Before demonstrating why each point Daesh posits is meritless, it is necessary to establish that in forming its conclusions, Daesh consistently violates the most basic principles of Islamic jurisprudence. In Islam, the Qur'an is the primary and final authority—no Hadith can supersede the Qur'an. The Hadith must then be interpreted in accordance with the Qur'an, never vice versa. Accordingly, the Prophet Muhammad (pbuh) himself clarified, "Whenever a Hadith is presented to you in my name, verify it with the Qur'an. If it agrees with the Qur'an, accept it, and if it is in conflict, discard it." He additionally instructed, "There is no doubt that, there will be Ahadith coming after me, claiming that I have said things. So you must test those Hadith from the Qur'an. If it is really according to the Qur'an only then accept it, otherwise reject it." And finally, Hazrat Salamarz relates that, "I heard the Prophet (pbuh) saying, "Whoever (intentionally) ascribes to me what I have not said then (surely) let him occupy his seat in Hell-fire." Daesh, instead, consistently accepts Hadith as superior to the Qur'an, or ignores the Qur'an altogether. This flawed methodology Daesh uses leads to flawed and distorted conclusions on Islam.

Based on the aforementioned foundational rules of Islamic jurisprudence, it is explicitly clear that Islam mandates universal freedom of conscience

---

QASIM RASHID is an attorney, author, and national spokesperson for the Ahmadiyya Muslim Community USA. He is a former visiting fellow at Harvard University's Islamic Studies Program. He is the author of three books, including the best-selling *Extremist*, which refutes misconceptions of Islam promoted by extremists and Islamophobes.

for all humanity. The Qur'an addresses disbelief, idolatry, and apostasy more than 150 times but never once prescribes or permits any worldly punishment whatsoever. The majority of these verses were revealed after the Prophet Muhammad (pbuh) migrated to Medina. This demonstrates that even as Muslims came to worldly power, universal freedom of conscience remained inviolable. This Qur'anic premise of freedom necessarily extends to idol worshipers—otherwise it is not universal. The Qur'an in Surah 2, Verse 257 cannot on the one hand declare without exception that "*There shall be no compulsion in religion*," and then subsequently provide an exception—yet this is what Daesh unwarrantedly claims.

Daesh is not interested in upholding Islam or helping Muslims—their actions prove the exact opposite.

The first Daesh argument on destroying idols, can be refuted through re-evaluating Daesh's reference to Verse 21:58–68, which relates the story of the Prophet Abraham (pbuh) and the idols he broke. Daesh misrepresents the purpose of this story. First, the Prophet Abraham (pbuh) demonstrated that a god that does not speak is no god at all. Instead, God speaks to His creation, answers prayers, and shall always reveal Himself to those who seek him. Idols, on the contrary, do not and cannot speak. Second, at a time when idolatry was widespread, the Prophet Abraham (pbuh) exemplified how destroying the idols of his own family did not harm him. This is critical. The Prophet Abraham (pbuh) did not destroy idols belonging to others—only those of his own home and family. The Prophet Abraham (pbuh) destroyed his own property. Thus, rather than enforce himself on others, as Daesh insists, the Prophet Abraham (pbuh) led by example to demonstrate personal reformation. Therefore, contrary to the acts of Daesh, the Prophet Abraham's (pbuh) example in the Qur'an categorically rejects destroying idols belonging to others. Not only destroying, but the Qur'an goes much further, and in Verse 6:109 forbids Muslims from even insulting that which others worship, "*And revile not those whom they call upon beside Allah, lest they, out of spite, revile Allah in their ignorance.*" Far from destroying idols, Muslims must show respect to the faith of others, even if they vehemently disagree with them.

Next, Daesh claims that it is permissible to destroy idols because the Prophet Muhammad (pbuh) ordered Jabir Abdullah al-Bajalirz to destroy a house in Yemen because it was full of idols. Daesh's argument once again falters. History records that this house, known as Dhul Khalasa, was erected by a cult to serve the same role as the Holy Kabah. This outpost of Dhul Khalasa was ultimately destroyed not because they were idolaters, but because they neither accepted a peace treaty from the Muslims nor stopped their insurgency. Indeed, the Qur'an in Verse 9:4 specifically commands Muslims to protect those idolaters: "*with whom you have entered into a treaty and who have not subsequently failed you in anything nor aided anyone against you. So fulfil to these the treaty you have made with them.*" Thus, the Qur'an itself categorically rejects Daesh's claim that Dhul Khalasa was destroyed because it was a house of idolatry. Instead, this was a secular decision to stop an uprising by a group that refused peace and threatened instability in the state.

Third, Daesh attempts to justify destroying idols because the Prophet Muhammad (pbuh) removed idols from the Kabah upon the victory at Mecca. The refutation of this justification takes us back to the Prophet Abraham (pbuh). The Prophet Abraham (pbuh) and his son the Prophet Ismael (pbuh) built the Kabah for the purpose of worshiping God's unity, and this remained its long-standing use for thousands of years. Upon the victory of Mecca, the Prophet Muhammad (pbuh) offered amnesty to the entire city. Even known critic of Islam Stanley Lane-Poole writes, "The day of Muhammad's greatest triumph over his enemies was also the day of his grandest victory over himself. He freely forgave the Quraysh all the years of sorrow and cruel scorn to which they had inflicted him, and gave an amnesty to the whole population of Mecca." In doing so, the Prophet Muhammad (pbuh) took three significant actions. First, he restored the Kabah back to its monotheistic purpose for which it was built and functioned for thousands of years. Second, he removed the idols left there by idol worshipers. Of significance, these idols did not belong to any particular people or persons. Rather, they occupied a space that was simply not theirs to occupy. This is further evidenced by the third point—the Prophet Muhammad (pbuh) continued to permit idol worshipers to worship their idols in their own homes and in their own temples. For example, the wife of an idolater named Ikrama sought amnesty for him on the condition that he may remain an idolater. The Prophet Muhammad (pbuh) granted the amnesty and permitted Ikrama to re-enter Mecca and live as an idolater. It was this magnanimous example of the Prophet Muhammad (pbuh) that inspired Ikrama to later accept Islam of his own free will. Indeed, it is this example of Muhammad's (pbuh) magnanimity that Daesh completely misses. If Prophet Muhammad (pbuh) truly intended to set the precedent that Muslims must destroy all idols everywhere, he would have done so upon becoming the de facto ruler of Arabia. He not only refused to do this, but actively protected freedom of conscience for Christians, Jews, atheists, and idol worshipers on the single condition that they recognize universal freedom of conscience for all humanity, just as the Qur'an itself mandated.

Finally, Daesh cites the following Hadith to justify destruction of idols: Abul Hayyaj reported: Ali ibn Abi Talibrz said to him: "Shall I not send you on a mission as the Messenger (pbuh) of Allah sent me? Do not leave an image without effacing it and do not leave an elevated grave without leveling it." Once again, Daesh censors the truth of the matter. In this Hadith, the Prophet Muhammad (pbuh) provided moral guidance to Ali, who later became the fourth caliph (*khalifa*), on how Muslims should maintain their own graves going forward. As the Arabs of the time were willingly leaving idolatry, the Prophet Muhammad (pbuh) necessarily provided them with moral training on proper Muslim burials. Imam Ibn Al-Jawzi (1116–1201) elaborates on this Hadith that, "This tradition is interpreted to mean what the Arabs used to do when exalting graves with beautiful structures and tall buildings." Ancient Arab idolaters often built elaborate tombs and worshiped their dead. The Prophet Muhammad (pbuh) provided guidance on proper Islamic burials to put an end to the former idolatrous practice among Arab Muslims, and further admonished Ali to stop Muslims from engaging in idolatrous customs. Thus, contrary to Daesh's meritless interpretation of this Hadith, no record exists of Muslims ravaging lands to destroy idols and graves belonging to non-Muslims. Indeed, if Islam mandated that all idols everywhere must be destroyed, then the Prophet Muhammad (pbuh) would have been the first to do so. Instead the Prophet's (pbuh) acts were in exact accordance with Surah 22, Verse 41 of the Qur'an, which commands Muslims to protect all houses of worship, mentioning mosques last.

And yet, the above four repudiations notwithstanding, Islam's guarantee to idolaters of universal freedom of conscience extended well beyond the life of the Prophet Muhammad (pbuh). The Muslim empire expanded to Egypt during the caliphate of Umar. Yet, the massive sphynx idols to this day remain unharmed by Muslim hands. In Jerusalem, rather than further destroy the already devastated Temple Mount, Caliph Umar spent Muslim funds to restore it. Likewise, when Iraq fell under Caliph Umar's rule, he granted his protection to the ancient temples and statues that idolaters worshiped. This precedent ensured that these temples and statues remained standing for the next 1,400 years. Though none of the idols Daesh has destroyed were currently being worshiped, Caliph Umar's precedent well establishes that no permission exists to destroy them at all. It is further well-established in the Prophet Muhammad's (pbuh) rules of war that even in the heat of battle, destruction of property, homes, and places of worship is impermissible, just as the taking of innocent life (i.e. anyone not offensively attacking to kill Muslims) is forbidden. Daesh violates each of these foundational Islamic principles. As the Caliph and worldwide head of the Ahmadiyya Muslim Community, Hazrat Mirza Masroor Ahmadaba, said in 2015:

> No matter how vehemently Daesh claims otherwise, the facts demonstrate that Islam champions universal freedom of conscience for all human beings—including for idolaters.

"For more than 1,400 years these cities were preserved and protected by successive Muslim rulers and governments and yet now the extremists claim to have destroyed them in Islam's name. This can only be branded as an extreme cruelty and a transgression of Islam's teachings. No true Muslim could ever comprehend acting in this way."

At most it is reasonable to conclude that Islam permits Muslims to destroy their own idols, figuratively and literally—but never to impose their faith on others. This is precisely the example the Prophet Abraham (pbuh) set forth, the example that the Prophet Muhammad (pbuh) re-established, the example that the four rightly guided caliphs understood and practiced, and the example that all Muslims for 1,400 years have embraced, which Daesh, in their utter ignorance, have chosen to disregard.

It is finally worth noting that Daesh's heinous acts extend to Muslims as well. They have shamelessly destroyed Shia and Sunni mosques and shrines, killed Ahmadis, and mass murdered scores of minority groups such as the Yazidi. Daesh is not interested in upholding Islam or helping Muslims—their actions prove the exact opposite. No matter how vehemently Daesh claims otherwise, the facts demonstrate that Islam champions universal freedom of conscience for all human beings—including for idolaters.

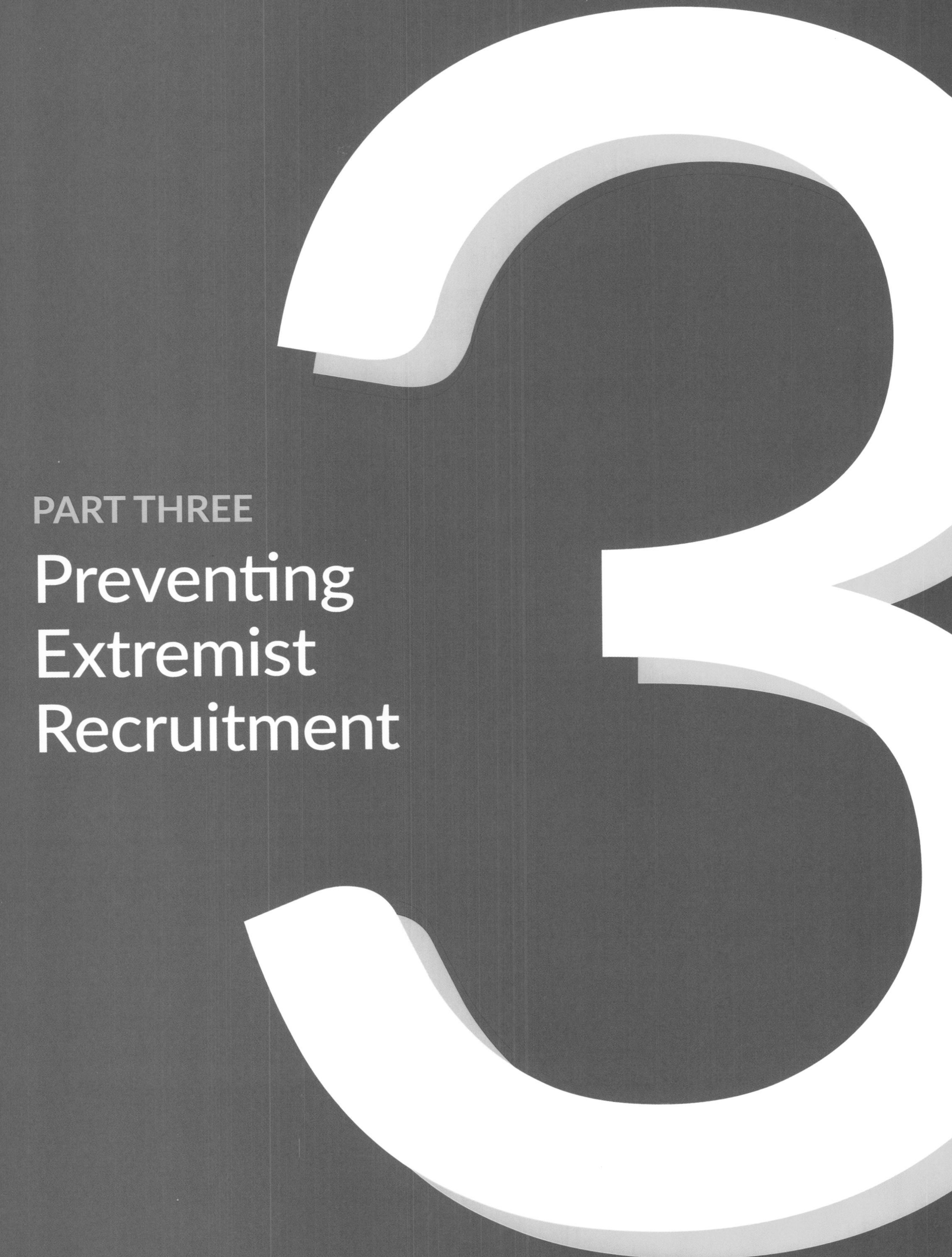

PART THREE

Preventing Extremist Recruitment

Executive Summary: Part Three

PREVENTING EXTREMIST RECRUITMENT

KEY TAKEAWAYS

1. Daesh has developed a sophisticated recruitment machine focused on online propaganda that uses distorted Islamic terms to mobilize and recruit people.
2. All individuals have protective and vulnerability factors that are either personal or environmental, which can be leveraged to strengthen an individual's resiliency to resist extremist recruitment.
3. Parents and peers are the first line of defense in disrupting recruitment. They need to be better equipped and empowered with the tools and resources needed to shelter individuals from extremist influence and intervene at first notice.

Preventing Extremist Recruitment is meant to be used as a toolkit, to provide a community-based approach for countering and neutralizing the threat of Daesh recruitment in families and communities. Contributors to this section of *WISE Up* include community leaders, psychologists, practitioners, bereaved mothers, and a former extremist. They speak directly to families and the American Muslim community at large to equip them with effective methods on how to deal with vulnerable individuals, particularly those who exhibit troubling behaviors or have been indoctrinated by extremists.

One of the most unsettling and puzzling aspects of the rise of Daesh has been their ability to inspire so many individuals to travel to Daesh territory, leaving behind their comfortable home lives for a life of terror and war. Daesh's ability to capitalize on the power of the Internet and utilize social media to spread propaganda and recruit vulnerable individuals from all parts of the globe has left the world's leaders scrambling to find ways to defeat the Caliphate and its online recruitment machine.

This toolkit for Preventing Extremist Recruitment addresses the human costs of Daesh's powerful recruitment strategies by providing letters from two mothers, Christianne Boudreau and Nicola Benyahia, whose sons joined Daesh and died fighting for the group. In their accounts, they provide heartbreaking details of their sons' indoctrination into extremist ideology, and their personal accounts of their own emotional experiences in watching their sons change before their eyes.

The majority of the research on Daesh's recruitment tactics was conducted by Singapore's Religious Rehabilitation Group (RRG), part of its long history of working with incarcerated extremists. Expanding upon RRG's research, we listed the 16 steps of enticing recruitment rhetoric that Daesh uses to indoctrinate new recruits and eventually spur them to action. Our two mothers, Christianne and Nicola, have put forth their own responses to each of these recruitment tactics, having heard many of these sentiments expressed by their sons. It is their hope (and ours) that these responses will help parents arm themselves with the knowledge and appropriate tactics to use should their children express any of these sentiments.

Former extremist Mubin Shaikh shares how he discovered the faults and distortions in extremist ideology and prescribes five tips for what Muslims must do in their communities to protect them from extremist infiltration. Dr. Houda Abadi urges religious and community leaders to revise their communication strategies so that they can offer attractive counter-narratives to extremism to the millennial generation. The "Parent's Guide to Social Media" helps bridge the generational gap between parents and the millennial generation, by providing a quick guide on the most popular social platforms used by millennials.

One reason why Daesh has been so successful with its recruitment is how well it utilizes and engages with the Internet using these platforms that millennials are familiar with. To aid in this intervention, *WISE Up* provides numerous real-life examples of Daesh's social media propaganda, its brand marketing that is uniquely designed to attract varied audiences—consisting of both young men and women—from around the world.

Soraya Deen's article "Parenting With Care So Our Children Will Care" outlines how parents and family members can communicate more effectively with their children during difficult times. To supplement this, Ameena Jandali and Henry Millstein of Islamic Networks Group (ING) provide a guide to "Bullying Prevention" so parents, teachers, and concerned community members can help prevent social alienation in children from a young age. Scott Cooper of Human Rights First has contributed a guide to "Defusing Hate: Counteracting Hate Speech," which is followed by Emily May's article on "Bystander Intervention," both of which provide tips to those who want to help but don't know where to start. This section ends with a list of "FAQs About Islam," which is meant to serve as a quick resource for addressing commonly asked questions about Islam and Muslims. We've also included a list of resources for parents to consult if their child is exhibiting worrisome behaviors, such as drug or alcohol abuse or signs of mental illness.

Daesh has been able to lure vulnerable individuals—especially those who feel alienated from their home community and seek alternative meaning in their lives—with the promise of being a part of something much greater than themselves. They present the image of a "hero" as one who sacrifices his or her life to violence and the false promise of martyrdom. The final section of the toolkit provides examples of many genuine Muslim heroes past and present. The aim of this section is to give young Muslims a broad spectrum of positive role models to contrast with the highly dubious—and ultimately destructive—attractions of life as a Daesh recruit. This section also highlights the lives of many ordinary Muslims who follow the true teachings of Islam by working in the interest of their communities, whether by feeding the needy, caring for the elderly, or providing mentoring and other forms of social and educational support for those who require them. This section also highlights successful interfaith initiatives taken by individuals and organizations to fight bigotry against Muslims and Islamophobia.

SUGGESTIONS

1. Family, friends, and community leaders must intervene with sensitivity and care in order to rehabilitate a loved one, an inmate, or someone they suspect has been recruited by Daesh.
2. Counseling and rehabilitating individuals must be tailored to the different experiences of men and women, with consideration of their local context and experience.
3. The stories of Muslim heroes provide young people models of morality and behavior for them to emulate.

"Knowledge without action is vanity, and action without knowledge is insanity"

- Imam al-Ghazali

CHAPTER 7

Understanding Extremist Recruitment

Letters from Bereaved Mothers: On Losing a Child

May 29, 2015, was the last day I ever saw my nineteen-year old son, **Rasheed**. He had left our home in Birmingham, England, early that morning, something not unusual for him. He usually left for his engineering apprenticeship in the morning, and would later meet up with friends. But when he didn't come home that evening, I suspected something was wrong. He would always call, even if he was going to be just 10 minutes late. Three days later, we received a message from Rasheed:

> I am very safe and in good hands, please don't worry about me and I am sorry, I'll be without a phone for 30 days and please know that I would never put anyone through this if I didn't know the reward. I ask Allah to protect you and reward you with the highest paradise. Please do not worry. I love you more than ever and again I am sorry.

After that, I didn't hear from him for 64 days. It was agonizing. When he finally contacted us, he told us he was in Syria. As soon as I heard that, I knew I was never going to see him again. My grief started as soon as I knew where he was. I had lost him already.

At the end of 2015, my husband received a call saying that Rasheed had been killed in a drone strike on the Syrian-Iraqi border. In the run-up to his death, I had just been waiting for that call—a part of me wanted that call, just to end the nightmare. I used to catch myself thinking, how can you, as a mother, want that call? **But I was caught in a situation over which I had no power. I couldn't get him out. He couldn't get out, they'd taken his passport from him. So I knew that, even if he changed his mind, he was stuck.**

In retrospect, I sensed that something had been shifting in him. When he spent hours alone in his room, I thought he was playing video games, but now I think he had been in contact with online recruiters. During that time, my husband and I were also going through a difficult period in our marriage, and I think Rasheed had been jolted by this. He withdrew from family life and became more introverted. He was less willing to share his feelings, and became more confrontational at times. I tried to sit with him and talk through what was going on in the family and in his own life. **I remember that he had been unhappy in his engineering job, and had wanted to shift to another type of engineering. I wish I had focused on that more at the time, and worked with him to see how we could have changed his course, so he would've been happier with his job and what he was doing.**

When Rasheed heard about the declaration of the so-called Caliphate, I saw something ignite within him. My husband tried to reason with Rasheed. He urged him to look very carefully at Islamic history, at groups that had claimed to represent Muslims—only to be found wanting. But Rasheed wasn't listening to these arguments. He admonished us for not doing anything about the slaughter of innocent Syrians. But we pushed back. We told him there were plenty of ways he could help people here in the UK—we urged him to get involved with charity, campaigning, writing letters and making calls to our politicians. But Rasheed was unconvinced. Then, all of a sudden, he stopped having an opinion on anything. I mistakenly thought he had just been going through a phase, and that now it was over. **But then, he bought me a diamond necklace. Looking back, I think it was his goodbye present to me. He had made his decision to go, and that was his way of saying goodbye. Now I know that that sense of calm is one of the tactics that recruiters instill in recruits.** They tell them to avoid tension, to be placid, to not bring attention to themselves, to just go along with what their parents want. But at that point, he had already made his decision to leave.

When we found out he left for Syria, and finally were able to reach him again, I trod carefully. I knew if I expressed my rage to him, I would only push him away, I knew it was a long game—whatever I did, whatever my family did, there would always be recruiters on the other side, trying to push back against what we had been telling him. They would be there with their own theological arguments, their own scholars.

One of my final texts to my son was a plea: "I can only speak from a mother's heart that I potentially [am] going to lose my only beloved cherished son, and I can't help but think what difference will it make to the horrific situation there, but my life will never be the same again, and my heart will always have a hole in it."

Shortly before he was killed by a drone strike, he told his sisters, "If I'm wrong about this choice that I have made, pray to God that I'm guided away from it."

Nicola Benyahia

NICOLA BENYAHIA has extensive experience within the social care sector, spanning over 30 years with extensive work in the context of mental health provision. She is a fully qualified, registered BACP (British Association of Counselling and Psychotherapy) Counselor with specific experience in mental health, brain injury and most recently working and counseling young people aged 14 to 25 years old. As a mother personally affected by the impact of violent extremist recruitment in her own family, she has recently stepped forward for other families sharing similar problems. She founded a counseling organization, 'Families For Life' following the death of her son Rasheed in Syria in 2015. She hopes, through her organization, to support and empower families to combat the shame of extremist recruitment and provide them with a platform for their voices to be heard.

My son **Damian** had always been a happy kid. He loved to experience things. Even at a young age, four years old, he would seek out answers to things on his own. I never had enough information to give him. But I also raised him as a very compassionate person, to take heed to the people around him and pay attention to other people's feelings. So in grade school, he would be the kid that would stand up to the bullies and protect the other kids. So I was called in to the school on numerous occasions to deal with the principal, because he was sticking up for a kid. He didn't want them to be the underdog, he wanted to be their friend, and cared about them no matter what their differences were.

But he had a rough time at certain points. The bullying had been hard on him. When he was a teenager, he had tried to commit suicide. But when he was seventeen, he converted to Islam, and I could see a change, a shift in him. He started becoming much more peaceful and grounded. I would take him to the mosque where he would pray, and I was so pleased for him. I met all of his friends. They were beautiful, loving people. If he wanted to pray when he was visiting our home, I would give him that space. I respected the faith that he chose, I was happy for him and told him so over and over again.

For someone like Damian, I could see how he would be easily drawn to Islam for that sense of peace and calm, as well as for that sense of belonging, that feeling of connection, that sense of family and of fitting in.

When Damian moved to a different part of the city, he started attending a different mosque. There, he met new people with much more rigid views. As a convert, he was still learning, and he wanted to be a better Muslim, he wanted a bigger high, and he started exploring and delving into these more radicalized opinions. We now know that, **in 2011, he was approached by a recruiter, who presented Damian with visions of going to Syria to do something good, to help people, to save people, and to become a productive person in society, which was something that he needed. And the recruiter spoke to that.** They specifically spoke to that vulnerability, that need that was within him.

Bit by bit, Damian started to change. He cut his hair, grew his beard, started to become more distant from our family, would refuse to eat at the table with us if we were drinking wine, and he would leave to take private phone calls. **At the time, I thought it was just a phase. He would angrily say the media was lying about what was really happening around the world. He said we didn't know the truth and that the Western world was selfish.** I would challenge it a bit, but when he had an idea in his mind, good luck trying to change it.

One day, **Damian called me from the airport and told me he was going to Egypt to study Arabic. I cried for the whole day. I could tell something was not right. A few months later, the Canadian Security Intelligence Service knocked on my door and told me they had been watching Damian for almost two years, and that he was likely headed to, or already in, Syria. When I confronted Damian over the phone, he told me, "Mom, women and children here are being tortured, raped, every day. And I'm here to help save them."**

We kept in touch sporadically over the next few months. During that time, I reached out to people, asking for quotes from the Qur'an, anything to make him see that he needed to come home. But nothing worked.

That June, in what would turn out to be one of my last phone conversations with him, **I thought, "My son is gone. I'm talking to someone on the phone, it sounds like his physical voice, but whatever is behind that is not my son." He was cold, hard, and empty. And that hurt because there was no way to reach him. And I felt like I kept failing him, like I was losing him piece by piece. It was a slow, tortuous, painful loss.** And because there was no finality, I had to live with each day of torture, each day waking up, wondering, "Is he still alive, is he dead?" I always guessed. It was horrible.

The following January, I woke up one day feeling really ill. I kept thinking, "Something is wrong." So I looked on the Internet for videos, to see if he was dead, or to see if he was alive, anything at all. I drove myself crazy looking for him. About a week later, on January 14, 2014, **I received a call from a journalist looking for a recent photo of Damian to compare to the one posted on Twitter with his eulogy. This was how I learned that Damian had been killed fighting near Aleppo.**

Every day I ask myself, what if? Why couldn't I see what was going on? Why couldn't I see what was coming? As a mother, that guilt kicks in, and you sit there thinking, I should have done more. But more what? I didn't know. If he had met with different people, circumstances would have been slightly different.

These people who seek out youths like Damian, they know what they're looking for, they're experienced in seeing these vulnerabilities. When our kids are asking those questions, seeking those answers, needing that additional fulfillment, those are the kids who are ultimately targeted, because they're the kids who need and require so much more. And if they're not getting it from positive influences, they're going to get it from somewhere else. And to foresee that is difficult, unless you have that understanding. I think because of Damian's personality, where he would get so passionate about things, and not knowing that this type of issue was of concern, made it more difficult. Had I known that this was a possibility, or that there was a potential of "radicalization," so to speak, which I had no awareness of back then, there may have been areas where I could have, with guidance, been able to reel him back in enough to question or doubt whether leaving was the right choice. If you don't know there is anything to be warned against, what are you going to pick up on in your child? Hindsight is 20/20. Knowing what I know now, there were tons of warning signs. But if you don't know, you're not aware, you're not educated to begin with, you don't even know what to look for, so I didn't. And if you have these gut feelings, where do you go with those feelings?

Instead of saying, "Oh, I don't want to appear as though I'm not a good enough parent," or whatever issues of insecurity you may have, put that aside. And reach out and ask for help with anyone who may have some sort of idea or sense of knowledge in that area. People think that by asking for help, it's a sign of weakness. No. It's a sign of strength. Step out of your comfort zone and ask for help. As a parent, we have to admit that we don't know everything. We're doing the best that we can with what we have, which might not be a full picture. If something doesn't feel right, trust that gut feeling.

I truly believe, with the right people, with the right encouragements in the right direction, where Damian could have felt or gotten that high, that internal sense of peace, or whatever that high was for him, he would still be here today. Let's say he had been approached by the right group, a humanitarian group, even if it had worked in our local area, feeding the homeless, helping people, getting them on their feet, and he got a high from it, then it's the same sort of fulfillment, and fulfillment of self-purpose, but in a positive direction. As youth, especially when you're still trying to find that right guidance, or figure out where you belong or where you fit, the right guidance and support makes a world of difference.

Ultimately, in the end, I don't know what he believed. That's a big question that I would still want to ask him if I had that chance. The only closure I'd ever get, would be for me to talk to m one more time, and say, "why?" All of these questions that I have to live with for the rest of my life without concrete answers, without them being answered. And even if I could ask him, I don't know what he would say.

Everybody asks me why I'm speaking out. I can't live with the fact that he went out to help people, and he died. And the only way I can cope is to extend his life, by helping people. I don't want to see any more people die. There's a way back for everybody, there's second chances for everybody. I truly believe if you get that help for those people, and they realize they may have been misdirected, then there is a way back.

Christianne Boudreau

CHRISTIANNE BOUDREAU founded the Hayat Canada Family Support foundation in 2014. As a mother personally affected by the impact of violent extremist recruitment in her own family, she decided to give her own experiences a voice and step forward for other families sharing similar problems. Ms. Boudreau has been featured in international media on various topics related to prevention and intervention with violent extremism and is now counseling other families. She is also coordinates the mothers network "Mothers for Life" with Daniel Koehler, which brings together mothers of violent extremists to give them a stronger voice globally.

Advice from Bereaved Mothers

We are two mothers, living in completely different parts of the world, and both of us have lost our sons to this toxic and twisted ideology, to recruiters who were preying on the emotional vulnerabilities of our children—vulnerabilities than any adolescent teenager could have. But we had nothing to warn us that this could happen, we had no tools at our disposal. Had we had the correct tools and knowledge, we may have been able to persuade our sons to take a step back, to really think about what they were doing.

As parents who have gone through this horrible tragedy, we can tell you that this is not an issue of religion or theology alone. Often, there is so much more going on with your child. When your child is having issues, he/she may be being fed an 'us versus them' narrative. Your child may be feeling shut out, and if you push against him or her you could be fueling them more. Look at what is going on with your child behind the rhetoric and the ideology. Are there circumstances with your child that may be fueling their feelings of anger or disillusionment? Your child is crying out to be heard, understood, and seen, and that's what you should focus on no matter what.

Using quotes or "alternative" writers to argue with your child could backfire. Your child will never accept a writer or scholar different from what the recruiter has taught them. Therefore this is a futile exercise, and will only build further barriers between you and your child.

No matter how much advice we give parents to stay calm or calmly discuss certain points, as a parent you may be experiencing fear, and may not be able to honestly recognize the emotional panic in your tone or behavior that your child is picking up on. This panic can sometimes put up further barriers between you and your child, and such situations can quickly escalate and get out of hand. You should also try to recognize that some of the emotional struggles that your child may be dealing with could be too close to your own emotional struggles as a parent. Their struggles become our struggles, and as such, we may deal with it in a less-than-helpful way. Having someone else who can offer an outside perspective can sometimes be much more effective than a parent simply carrying the entire load on his or her own, as our children have a tendency to dismiss what we say in favor of what an outsider says to them anyway.

Starting on page 260 you will find our attempt to respond, step-by-step, to what Daesh recruiters may be saying to your child. You may find it helpful and valuable to show your child some videos, rather than simply trying to argue with him or her or ignoring their behavior as "a phase." If you have a gut feeling that something is off, trust that feeling and follow up with your child, or seek outside help. There is no shame in asking for help. It is a sign of strength as a parent.

Additionally, there are many strong and emotionally gripping short videos available on the Internet for you to show your child. These could be used as a starting point for a conversation with your child, rather than just quoting text that they won't connect with and can easily disregard. These have often proved to be much more effective in getting youth to think a bit differently than just talking at them. Examples of such videos can be found at www.extremedialogue.com and www.findfate.org.

Nicola Benyahia &
Christianne Boudreau

The Story of a Former Extremist

MUBIN SHAIKH was able to escape the control of extremists when he realized that the views of extremists do not represent the true teachings of Islam. He now uses his experience to steer individuals in a similar position away from extremist recruiters. He also provides a list of "Five Things Muslims Should Do in Their Communities," so communities can protect themselves from extremism and Islamophobia.

On September 11, 2001, I was driving to work when I heard that a plane had struck one of the two towers of the World Trade Center. Immediately, I exclaimed, "Allahu Akbar," "God is Great!" My celebratory moment was quickly muted when I asked myself, "What if the very office building I was working in was similarly struck by a plane?" I would have perished along with everyone else just as those innocent people perished on that day. For me, September 11 2001 was for all intents and purposes the beginning of the end of my commitment to the extremist mind-set. Allow me to explain how this began for me.

The only way I thought I could make amends with my family was to "get religious."

I was born and raised in Toronto, Canada, to Indian immigrants. As a child I grew up attending a very conservative brand of madrasa, a school that typically teaches Qur'anic recitation. This madrasa was an imported version of what you would find in India and Pakistan, rows of boys separated from the girls sitting at wooden benches, rocking back and forth, reciting the Qur'an in Arabic but not understanding a word of what they were reading. Contrast that with my daily life of attending public school, which was the complete opposite of the rigid fundamentalist manner of education of the madrasa. Here I could actually talk to girls and have a normal functional relationship with them. When I left the Qur'an school at age twelve and moved on to middle school and high school, I wasn't discriminated against, bullied, picked on, or anything of the like. I was actually one of the cool kids. But when I was seventeen I had a house party while my parents were away, which my hyper-conservative uncle walked in on. Normal as it may be to the Western experience, my uncle and other family members were incensed that I would have brought non-Muslim friends to my home and they spent the next several days berating me over what I had done. Due to the sustained guilt trip I received, the only way I thought I could make amends with my family was to "get religious." Hence, I became one of the born-again types seeking to right the wrongs of their past.

I then traveled to India and Pakistan and, in the latter, ended up in a place called Quetta, which unbeknownst to me at the time was the center of the Taliban Shura and of the group known as al-Qaeda. As I walked around the area, I chanced upon ten heavily armed men dressed in black turbans, flowing robes, and sandals. One of them said to me that if I truly wished to bring about political change, it could only be done by using this, and he held aloft his AK-47. I was completely enamored with them, and considered them to be jihadi heroes, consistent with the theme in jihadi literature and media today. In the years that followed, I absorbed myself in proclaiming that jihad was the only way to change things. And when Osama

MUBIN SHAIKH is the co-author of *Undercover Jihadi* and one of two undercover counterterrorism operatives in the 2006 Toronto terrorism case. He is a member of the Canadian Network for Research on Terrorism, Security, and Society and is involved in the academic study of radicalization and terrorism. He received his Master's degree in Policing, Intelligence, and Counter Terrorism and is working toward a PhD in psychology in terrorist decision making.

Bin Laden gave his fatwa in 1998, I was onboard. Then 9/11 happened and I thought, "Wait a second. I get attacking combatants. But this? Office buildings in which regular people work, Muslims included?" I realized that I needed to study the religion of Islam properly to make sense of what I had just witnessed.

I sold my belongings and moved to Syria in early 2002 when there was still some semblance of normality in that country. I attended the class of a Syrian Islamic scholar who challenged me on my views regarding jihad and subsequently spent a year and a half with him studying the verses of the Qur'an and the traditions of the Prophet (pbuh) that the jihadists use to justify their hate and destruction. I came to relinquish my views completely and returned to Canada in 2004 with a newfound appreciation for the rights of Muslims in the West. That year, some individuals had been arrested in the UK in the London fertilizer bomb plot. One of those individuals was none other than my classmate from the madrasa that I had attended as a child. I thought this had been a mistake and contacted the security agency to give a character reference for the family. But it was too late for him. As for me, I was recruited by the service as an undercover operative because I felt this was my religious duty. I can say that I conducted several infiltration operations both online and on the ground involving religious extremists. One of those cases moved on to become a criminal investigation and I transferred from the intelligence service to the Mounted Police integrated national security enforcement team in what came to be known as the Toronto 18 terrorism prosecution. I gave fact witness testimony in five hearings over four years at the Superior Court, where 11 individuals were eventually convicted. I have since worked with various mechanisms of the US government national counterterrorism center, security office for civil rights and civil liberties, and the US Department of State Center for Strategic Counterterrorism Communications. In addition, I have spent the last few years on Twitter watching the birth of the foreign fighter phenomenon and directly observing the recruitment and propaganda by Daesh types online. I have engaged with many of them, male and female, as well as with some of the victims they have tried to recruit. My approach is to show how wrong they are and to criticize and delegitimize them from the very Islamic sources that they misquote and mutilate. Thus, the correct term to describe these TIICs, Terrorists in Islamic Costume, is khawarij, a technical Islamic term loosely translated to mean rebel or reject. I have personally intervened in the case of an American girl whom these predators were trying to lure away, and put a stop to it by engaging her online as someone who could show her the real interpretation of Islam. I have a good understanding of what is happening in terms of recruitment and what needs to be done in terms of counter vmessaging. By providing in-depth Islamic knowledge to these potential recruits, we can challenge their way of thinking and bring them back to the straight path.

Five Things Muslims Should Do in Their Communities

MUBIN SHAIKH

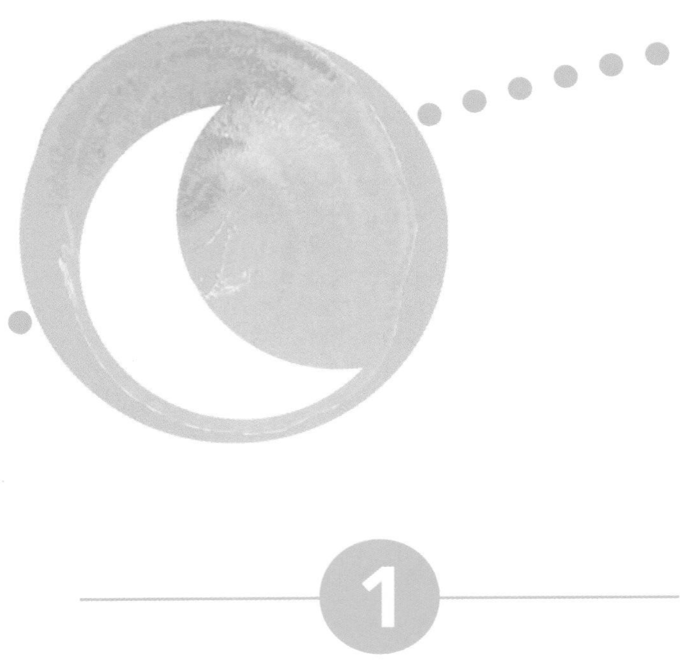

1

TREAT YOUR MOSQUE LIKE AN EMBASSY

Muslim Americans need to be aware that mosques or masajid are representing Islam to Muslims and to the local non-Muslim community. Hence, the masjid should be an inviting place where anyone from the public can come in and talk to people about Islam or Muslims in curiosity and friendship. It should be clean and presentable to people of other faiths at all times.

2

PROTECT YOUR MOSQUE

Muslims should also protect their mosques from both inside and outside threats. Rather than being scared of law enforcement, Muslims should develop strong relations with local police who are there to protect us and our mosques. Building relationships with groups like law enforcement is the first step in having a community of support if something happens. Additionally, Muslims should be aware of persons who openly discuss violent acts without appropriate context. These people bring unneeded and unwanted attention to your mosque. Concerns should be brought up to community leaders who have authority in the masjid.

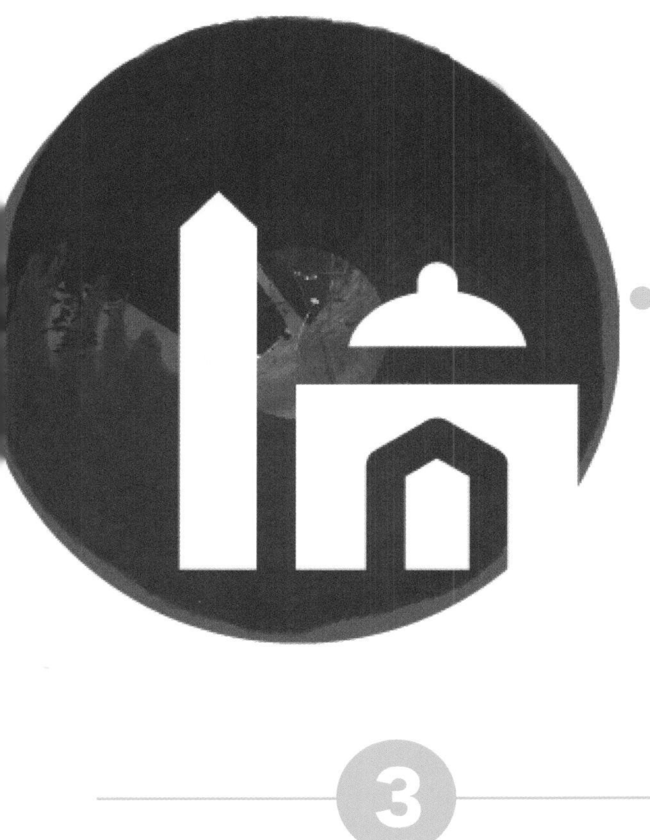

4

DO OUTREACH WITH PEOPLE OF DIFFERENT FAITHS

The Prophet (pbuh) said: "He is not a believer whose neighbor is unsafe from his mischief" (narrated by Bukhari). Non-Muslims are our friends, neighbors, and fellow human beings, and deserve to be treated with respect. Muslims should get to know other local community members to build both friendship and trust, and attend interfaith events to build bridges of understanding.

3

TEACH PEOPLE IN THE MOSQUE

Rather than simply being a place of prayer on Eid or on Fridays, mosques should be places of learning and have programs running on a daily basis. Whether these programs are public lessons by qualified teachers or private gatherings for specific groups (e.g., youth), a mosque that is alive with the remembrance of God is a successful one. Such a mosque gives the sense of community that Islam calls for and that people need. It also prevents young people from seeking their own information on Islam that can be from untrustworthy sources.

BE GOOD REPRESENTATIVES OF ISLAM

Most important, Muslims should remember that we are the direct representatives of God on earth, Islam, and the Prophet (pbuh). We show people our faith by our actions and by our conduct. We have a responsibility to protect the image of Islam in our individual capacities and we should always keep this in mind.

Daesh Recruitment: Step-by-Step

RRG, WISE, NICOLA BENYAHIA, and **CHRISTIANNE BOUDREAU:** Daesh recruiters are actively looking online and on the ground for potential candidates whom they can lure into joining their cause. Recruiters gradually, yet systematically, lead potential recruits through a program of indoctrination. Below is sample rhetoric from recruiters (some quotes are direct; others are composites from news stories or Daesh-affiliated social media accounts). For every step listed, there is a corresponding, in-depth look at how the recruiter is manipulating the recruit and the strategy the recruiter uses to convince the recruit to join their so-called caliphate. We have also provided a "suggested response" for each step so that a concerned parent or friend can adequately respond should they see any of these sentiments manifesting in an individual.

1 "Interested in becoming a better Muslim?"
See page 262

2 "Our version of Islam is correct. Our teachers are superior and have the most correct Islamic knowledge"
See page 262

3 "Maintain secrecy about our relationship: enemies do not want the correct version of Islam to flourish"
See page 263

4 "Muslims around the world are persecuted and treated unjustly"
See page 263

5 "Jihad is the only way to alleviate the suffering of oppressed Muslims"
See page 264

6 "Allah finds armed jihad and martyrdom more superior than other non-aggressive forms of devotion"
See page 264

7 "Armed jihad is an obligation of every Muslim"
See page 265

8 "Wage jihad against all infidels"
See page 265

9 "Preserve your purity; Stay away from non-believers"
See page 266

10 "Hate anyone who is not a true believer like us"
See page 266

11 "Most Muslim states are apostates; they don't practice Islam"
See page 267

12 "You must be prepared to engage in armed jihad against non-Muslim powers"
See page 267

13 "You must migrate (hijrah) to a region that practices the true Islam"
See page 268

14 "Migrating to a region that practices true Islam is essential for you to practice your faith"
See page 268

15 "You must give a pledge of allegiance (bay'ah) to show undivided loyalty"
See page 269

16 "Breaking this pledge is an unforgiveable sin in Islam. (Hell or Heaven?)"
See page 269

1

"INTERESTED IN LEARNING MORE ABOUT ISLAM?
I'm happy to teach you about it. We'll begin with traditional concepts like worship and morals. By the way, are you a convert?"[1]

HEADS UP

The initial strategy of extremist recruiters is to target Muslims who just returned to practicing the faith, young/high school students (who are naive and are not likely to be spies), and converts. Some in these groups are likely to be on a spiritual quest and looking for a life of meaning, and are highly prized by recruiters for their eagerness and malleability.

SUGGESTED RESPONSE

Support the young person in checking out Arabic/Islam classes. Get to know who runs the classes and how they connect with the young people. Actively engage with the young person and try to find out in what part of their life they feel the need for further spirituality, knowledge, or connection. Recommend books and religious leaders whom you have vetted. Learn from the young person about how they feel their knowledge, spirituality, and identity fit in with their family, community, and wider society. Possibly provide them with suggestions about where you see a gap between their future vision and their present situation.

2

"OUR VERSION OF ISLAM IS CORRECT. OUR TEACHERS ARE SUPERIOR AND HAVE THE MOST CORRECT ISLAMIC KNOWLEDGE
All the other teachers and mosques in the community are deficient—their understanding is incomprehensive. I'll tell you where you can get the true, all-embracing Islam. There are some classes and teachings that I'd like to invite you to, or show you. It's not at a mosque, but that way we'll be able to go more in-depth with the concepts."[2]

HEADS UP

Recruiters will immediately set up a course of study organized in a specific order so as to promote their brand of Islam. Their brand is backed by in-house information production, and daily outputs of materials such as books, pamphlets, videos, full-length movies, social media networks (Facebook/Twitter/Tumblr), jihadi forums, magazines, and curriculum. Recruiters will begin to indoctrinate the recruit with an in-group sense of love and belonging by introducing the recruit to terms like *ummah*, *jama'ah*, and *al wala' wal bara'*.

SUGGESTED RESPONSE

It is important to explain and teach our youth to seek information through various sources, since often what is written by someone is presented from their personal perspective, rather than from concrete facts.

[1] From "A Course in the Art of Recruitment," collected and organized by Abu Amru Al Qa'idy.
[2] Ibid.

3

"MAINTAIN SECRECY ABOUT OUR RELATIONSHIP: ENEMIES DO NOT WANT THE CORRECT VERSION OF ISLAM TO FLOURISH

You're not telling anyone about our conversations, are you? I wouldn't tell anyone if I were you. We must protect Islam from the infidels. You should create a second Facebook and Twitter account where we can talk. We can also talk on private apps like Kik and Wickr. Since Muslims are persecuted in the U.S., your conversation with me could label you a terrorist, so it's best if you keep our conversations secret, even from your family."

HEADS UP

At this stage, the recruiter will try to move from acquaintance to loyal confidant by learning more about a recruit's concerns, interests, and relationships. Upon learning this knowledge, a recruiter will urge the candidate not to speak to anyone, including family, about the "advanced" classes or sessions they've been invited to by the recruiter.

SUGGESTED RESPONSE

Ask to meet their friends, take a genuine interest and invite them around. Keep in contact with their old friends. This way, they will also be able to air and share possible concerns their peers may have noticed. This will also allow you as a parent to monitor your child, and to make sure he is with the friends he says he is with. Show a genuine interest in their current interests as they may have changed from what you knew of them. What makes them tick? What are their dreams and visions for their future and for the world around them? This will reassure them that you have their best interests in mind. It is important to gather information below the surface about their emotional motivators rather than lecture them. Your goal is to become their confidante.

"MUSLIMS AROUND THE WORLD ARE PERSECUTED AND OPPRESSED

You should learn about some political situations—these are your brothers and sisters! It will help if you see what this persecution really looks like. Here are some videos to watch. And some websites to learn more about what is really happening."

HEADS UP

A recruiter will highlight certain political situations and the suffering of the Muslim community (*ummah*). Recruits are taught that Muslim oppression, from Palestine to Afghanistan, is intentionally imposed by the West and part of the West's larger efforts to destroy Islam. Videos and photos are utilized and disparate political events are woven together to form an overarching narrative that the West is waging a war against Islam. The recruiter aims to stir emotions of sympathy (for the victims) and anger (against the perpetrators).

SUGGESTED RESPONSE

This is a critical juncture, as they are seeking to redress grievances. Provide opportunities to get involved with Muslim organizations or peace groups that assist with welfare or community support, such as mentoring younger kids, or combating homelessness or poverty. It's important to check out the organizations before signing up to ensure that they are organized, professional, and well-structured, otherwise this could lead to disappointment for the young person. This is also an opportunity for the parents to ask their child what initiative they would like to get involved with (and for parents to support their child in this initiative), and participate with their youth so they can have opportunities for relationship-bonding and connection building. Try to seek out a group or organization with mentors available.

"JIHAD IS THE ONLY WAY TO ALLEVIATE THE SUFFERING AND OPPRESSION OF MUSLIMS
It is your religious duty to help—if you don't, it's like turning your back on the entire ummah."

HEADS UP
Recruiters will try to make the recruit feel guilty for not acting to alleviate the suffering of the *ummah*. A recruit is introduced to the concept of armed jihad as the solution to this suffering, and the recruiter will try to instill in a potential recruit the desire for violent jihad to help his or her fellow Muslims.

SUGGESTED RESPONSE
Encourage the young person to help alleviate the suffering of others by getting involved in charity work in their own country. You can also show them step by step how money or food parcels are collected and processed to feed families in Syria, Iraq, Yemen, and other locales. Remind them that these countries require aid in order for them to help themselves. Actions are always much more effective than words. Engage in these activities with them, thus making it a team effort.

"ALLAH FINDS ARMED JIHAD AND MARTYRDOM SUPERIOR TO OTHER, NON-AGGRESSIVE FORMS OF DEVOTION
Armed jihad is the only solution to Muslim oppression and injustice. The only way to truly free your Muslim brothers and sisters from persecution is by participating in Allah's holy war. They are depending on us."

HEADS UP
Recruiters will emphasize that non-aggressive religious actions of the past are pointless. They will begin to normalize violent jihad by getting a recruit used to watching videos to the point that they yearn to see more and ask about new releases. The goal is for the recruit to reach the point where he feels that the movement is his own, that she feels love toward them, wants to hear news about them, and begins mirroring their ideas in her speech.

SUGGESTED RESPONSE
Remind them of the value of life, that saving one life is like saving all of humanity, and that there is always a family behind each person they may face. Remind the young person that in such chaotic situations, many victims are Muslim, and ask them, do they want to be part of killing or hurting a fellow human being? Being alive allows much more opportunity to create positive change or help those who require it. Be very cautious not to use authoritative statements like "you are not permitted to do this" or "don't do this," as these types of statements will instantly put up barriers between you and your child.

"ARMED JIHAD IS AN OBLIGATION OF EVERY MUSLIM
You must travel to occupied Muslim lands and participate in armed jihad in order to liberate your fellow Muslims."[3]

HEADS UP
Armed jihad is presented as a religious obligation for every Muslim, and often as the "sixth pillar of Islam." Using examples of defamation of the Prophet Muhammad and defilement of the Qur'an, a recruiter will suggest traveling to occupied Muslim lands to participate in armed jihad, and if they cannot, candidates will be encouraged to serve as Internet mujahideen by spreading and defending extremist videos and literature. This way, recruiters ensure that recruits' enthusiasm, motivation, and sense of purpose remain high.

SUGGESTED RESPONSE
First and foremost, remind your child that God only wants him to do good deeds, and God does not like what is distasteful to Him, for example, self-righteousness, anger, rebellion, or aggression. Jihad is a last resort and should only be used to defend oneself. Remind the young person that he is not being personally attacked, so he would not be waging jihad in self-defense. True jihad is about the trials and tribulations we are put through in life, and sometimes the desire to die in such a cause may be looked upon as an easier option than facing one's difficulties. We are all put to the test, and overcoming these tests through patience and determination is the real jihad. Work with your child to write a letter to your local government officials, those who have influence on foreign policy, and others to effect meaningful change.

"WAGE JIHAD AGAINST ALL INFIDELS
Us against the rest of the world' is the formula that drives the West. We Muslims are finally offering successful resistance."

HEADS UP
At this stage, the recruiter will emphasize the need for armed jihad. They will blame Jews and Christians ("crusaders") for all past and current afflictions, and stress that they are out to destroy Islam and Muslims. A recruiter will evaluate a recruit's change in attitude to measure if the following have manifested in the recruit: respect and honor for Daesh's leaders, and acceptance that armed jihad is the only way forward. A recruiter may also choose to familiarize the recruit with the "heroes of jihad," as well as past acts of martyrdom perpetrated by those loyal to Daesh.

SUGGESTED RESPONSE
Islam is God's religion and will be protected by God, who is the sole creator of humankind and all world religions. Muslims may never denounce people of other religions as infidels. God refers to them in the Qur'an as "people of the book," who must be respected. By calling other people infidels, you cast judgment on fellow believers and displease God.

[3] *Dabiq*, Issue 3, Page 16.

"PRESERVE YOUR PURITY—STAY AWAY FROM NON-BELIEVERS
Keep your distance from your friends and family, even if they profess to be Muslim. They are *kuffar* (unbelievers) of the correct way of living Islam. Staying close with them will taint your piety. Isolate yourself by putting one brick around yourself at a time to protect yourself and your faith from your unbelieving family."[4]

HEADS UP

The recruiter will attempt to drive a wedge between the recruit and her family and community by emphasizing that mingling with anyone who does not subscribe to their distorted ideology can taint one's piety, since such people are "corrupt" and live in a state of *jahiliyyah*, or ignorance. The recruiter will work to make the recruit feel that she is a stranger in her own life while simultaneously emphasizing that the recruit is not alone.

SUGGESTED RESPONSE

Your parents brought you up and tended to your every need when you were young, when you were hungry, upset, or sick. How can you reject the very people who brought you into this world and provided you with food, shelter, warmth, and love? God requires children to respect their parents, regardless of their belief. It is very important for you to maintain a strong emotional connection with your child by reminding them how heartbreaking it would be for you to lose them to strangers who don't have their best interests in mind.

"HATE ANYONE WHO IS NOT A TRUE BELIEVER LIKE US
And so, the fornicators, adulterers, sodomites, abandoners of jihad, people of religious innovations, and alcoholics are all harmful for the religion of Islam, and intermingling with them is also harmful. They do not assist in righteousness nor piety. Whoever does not abandon them has thus left an obligation and fallen into a prohibition."[5]

HEADS UP

The recruiter will emphasize that all other Muslims have fallen into disbelief, and thus should be rejected and excommunicated (*takfir*). They use hate of the other as a motivator, mobilizer, and unifying point to get the recruit to commit to this "chosen" group. They emphasize loyalty (*wala*) to only them, and disavowal (*bara*) of their friends, families, peers, and countries as enemies. The recruiter will also stress that belonging to the group is the only way to further the recruit's piety and righteousness.

SUGGESTED RESPONSE

The only judge is God and no person can judge another as you never truly know what is in a person's heart. The only true way to attain piety and to be righteous is to do good deeds, and never to cast judgment on another human being. Never give up on anyone or lose hope in humanity; instead, reach out to people who may be feeling lost in their lives. Showing love to them is how you bring them to becoming believers, because love is more powerful than anything else.

[4] *Dabiq*, Issue 3, Pages 6–8.
[5] *Dabiq*, Issue 3, Page 32.

11

"MOST MUSLIM STATES ARE APOSTATES;
THEY DON'T PRACTICE ISLAM
Any so-called Muslim state that exists right now is not Islamic. They do not properly enforce Shari'ah.
Everything is kafir!"

HEADS UP

Here the recruiter will introduce the recruit to Daesh's "caliphate" by claiming that in order to be considered a pious Muslim, one cannot show loyalty to non-Muslim states or "corrupt" Muslim states. Even more so, true obedience to Islam is disobedience to all morally corrupt non-Muslim governments. The recruiter will try to convince the potential recruit that the only true "Islamic" state is Daesh's "caliphate."

SUGGESTED RESPONSE

Remind the young person that the country that they are being told to reject has provided them with a system of support, including the right to an education, freedom of expression, free exercise of religion, protection of human rights, and acquiring the skills for their career so they could contribute to society for years and generations to come. Remind them that true faith comes from within; it is not gained just from living in an "Islamic" state. Encourage them to work within their own communities to share their faith through good deeds.

"YOU MUST BE PREPARED TO ENGAGE IN ARMED
JIHAD AGAINST NON-MUSLIM POWERS
We must wage jihad against the infidels. The Jews and Christians ("crusaders") are out to destroy Islam and Muslims. They are the ones responsible for all our past and current afflictions. If you cannot leave right now, you must wage jihad against your government. Strike where you can!"

HEADS UP

Recruiters will now show that the time has come for Muslims to rise up and reassert their dominance, beginning with retribution for past injustices of Western powers upon the Muslim population. The recruiter will try to convince the recruit that performing armed jihad is possible and she should begin to conceive of ways to do it—both at home and abroad.

SUGGESTED RESPONSE

Remind the young person that they must never be an aggressor, and that they should only take action when they are being attacked, and should never think of harming innocent people. Stress that the Prophet Muhammad never initiated war against anyone, and protected religious minorities. It is a far more difficult struggle, but more rewarding to spread Islam by educating others with knowledge and skills they can use throughout their lives, rather than to pick up a sword or gun. The Prophet said, "the pen is mightier than the sword." Refer the young person to the Prophet's Covenants on pages 116-119, which show how he considered Jews and Christians fellow believers, and provided protection to them.

13

"YOU MUST MIGRATE (*HIJRAH*) TO A REGION THAT PRACTICES THE TRUE ISLAM

Migrating to a country that practices true Islam will make you a better Muslim. Making *hijrah* to the caliphate will fulfill your obligation of armed jihad. This life of jihad is not possible until you pack up and move to the caliphate."

HEADS UP

Now the recruiter will introduce the story of the Prophet's *hijrah* from Mecca to Medina to convince the recruit that making *hijrah* will further a recruit along the path of being a truly pious Muslim. Delaying or abandoning their *hijrah* and jihad will expose them to doubts and desires that will destroy their piety.

SUGGESTED RESPONSE

Remind the young person that packing up and migrating (*hijrah*) to the caliphate will not make her a better Muslim, and that migrating to another land is not a requirement in Islam. Stress to them the position of their parents and siblings, and their responsibility towards them. What would happen to their parents if they were left alone in their old age, and who would care for them? How would their potential involvement in unlawful activities affect their siblings? Remind them that parents have rights, too; the Qur'an emphasize kindness towards one's parents. The Prophet emphasized the importance of serving one's mother, the reward for which is Paradise.

"MIGRATING TO A REGION THAT PRACTICES THE TRUE ISLAM IS ESSENTIAL FOR YOU TO PRACTICE YOUR FAITH

Allah will honor you wherever you go when you take the step of *hijrah*. There is something fulfilling in knowing that you have been removed from the kuffar and handed to Allah personally as a gift. The caliphate is the only place on earth that is not an apostate government. We implement Shari'ah/Islamic law in full and as Allah intended. You can help us build the caliphate—we need you!"

HEADS UP

The recruiter will present the recruit with the choice of making *hijrah*: "you are either with us or against us." By reminding the recruit that it is an obligation to live under an Islamic state after it is established, the recruiter puts the responsibility on the individual to join. The recruit is told that he is not practicing his faith correctly until he joins the caliphate.

SUGGESTED RESPONSE

You do not need to travel to or build a "caliphate" to practice your faith. Your first obligation is to your family, your own kith and kin, and the country in which you live. You will be truly fulfilled when you contribute to your own community and help those around you. A righteous Muslim would never resort to clandestine operations of any kind, as they know they are prohibited in Islam.

15

"YOU MUST GIVE A PLEDGE OF ALLEGIANCE (*BAY'AH*) TO SHOW UNDIVIDED LOYALTY

If you cannot perform *hijrah* for whatever extraordinary reason, then try in your location to organize *bay'at* (pledges of allegiance) to the Khalifah Ibrahim. Publicize them, gather in masjids and mosques, distribute over media so that *bay'ah* becomes so common to the average Muslim that he considers those holding back as grossly abnormal."[6]

HEADS UP

When a recruit takes *bay'ah* (pledge of allegiance), he is inducted into a global brotherhood/sisterhood. By pledging allegiance he demonstrates his undivided loyalty and a commitment to perform any duty on behalf of the caliphate. Daesh publicizes the *bay'ah* through media to show potential recruits that many others have done the same, and to demonstrate to their enemies that they have global reach.

SUGGESTED RESPONSE

If a young person is talking about taking *bay'ah* with Daesh's leader, she may have adopted extremist ideology. At this point, you should immediately seek outside intervention from a religious counselor, specialist, or psychologist. Stay engaged with your child by reminding them that all actions are judged by their intentions, and if they intend to do harm, they will face dire consequences, such as incarceration, and cause severe pain to their family.

16

"BREAKING THIS PLEDGE IS AN UNFORGIVABLE SIN IN ISLAM

Abandoning *hijrah*—the path to jihad—is a dangerous matter. In effect, one is thereby deserting jihad and willingly accepting his tragic condition of being a hypocritical spectator."[7]

HEADS UP

A recruiter will present a recruit with an ultimatum to manipulate him into thinking that by staying committed and acting on behalf of Daesh, he will be rewarded with Paradise, and by breaking his pledge to Daesh, he will go to hell.

SUGGESTED RESPONSE

Since Muslims are not required to take *bay'ah*, there is no consequence to breaking this pledge. A righteous Muslim loves God, puts his trust in Him, does good deeds that will help others, obeys and shows kindness to his parents, respects his fellow human beings, and never resorts to harming anybody.

---

[6] *Dabiq*, Issue 2, Page 3.
[7] *Dabiq*, Issue 3, Page 27.

Vulnerability Factors

THE CENTER FOR THE PREVENTION OF RADICALIZATION LEADING TO VIOLENCE (CPRLV) explains how when faced with a potentially worrying situation in terms of radicalization, all behavioral changes must be interpreted in the context of an individual's susceptibility to radical messaging. These vulnerability factors fall into several categories and are often the fertile ground for radicalization leading to recruitment of individuals into violent extremism and possible violent acts. These vulnerability factors are also common to many other psychosocial issues (suicide, street gang membership, cult membership, and others).

RELATIONAL

- Family disaffiliation
- Network of contacts in extremist circles
- Distancing from circle of friends

SOCIAL IDENTITY

- Other-or self-imposed social isolation
- Identity malaise
- Sense of being stigmatized or discriminated against due to one's beliefs or origin

PSYCHOLOGICAL

- Psychological frailty or disorders
- Psychological rigidity
- Episodes of psychological distress

PERSONAL

- Troubled adolescence or difficult transition to adulthood
- Difficult life events (such as death of a loved one or job loss)
- Existential or spiritual crisis (pre- or post-conversion)

EXTERNAL

- Polarized and polarizing societal debates
- Government positioning on poorly understood national and international issues
- Highly sensationalized public and media discourse
- Extremist discourse and propaganda that is readily accessible

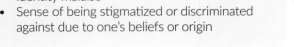

THE CENTER FOR THE PREVENTION OF RADICALIZATION LEADING TO VIOLENCE (CPRLV), was created in March 2015 by the City of Montréal with the support of the Quebec government and the active involvement of community and institutional partners. It is the first independent non-profit organization in Canada aimed at preventing violent radicalization and providing support to individuals affected by the phenomenon, be they individuals who are radicalized or undergoing radicalization, family or friends of such individuals, teachers, professionals or field workers. The CPRLV is a provincially mandated organization whose work also includes the prevention of hate crimes and incidents as well as the provision of support and counseling for victims of such acts.

Protective Factors

THE CENTER FOR THE PREVENTION OF RADICALIZATION LEADING TO VIOLENCE (CPRLV) explains how all individuals have protective factors that are either personal or environmental, constituting levers that can be used by social workers and counselors to create a safety net around the individual. In order to intervene in the prevention of potential situations of radicalization leading to violence and recruitment into extremism, it is necessary to work to reinforce the protective factors already existing in an individual or to put them in place when they are absent. These protective factors help to make individuals more resilient and resistant to radicalization leading to violence and recruitment into extremism in all its forms.

RELATIONAL

- Belonging to a peaceful social network (physical or virtual)
- Quality relationship with a positive role model
- Stable relational environment
- Strong family connection

SOCIAL IDENTITY

- Stable identity
- Sense of social integration and community acceptance
- Strong social bonds

PSYCHOLOGICAL

- Critical thinking and cognitive moderation
- Emotional and mental resilience against attempted indoctrination
- Empathy and openness to others
- Emotional self-regulation

PERSONAL

- Stable family situation
- Support and guidance during difficult life events
- Positive educational and career prospects

EXTERNAL

- Presence of counter-extremist discourse in general society
- Open societal debates advocating tolerance, respect, and integration
- Reinforcement of the principles of shared community
- Collective resilience against hateful ideologies and hate speech

A Religious Counselor's Approach to Intervention

THE RELIGIOUS REHABILIATION GROUP (RRG) and **WISE** provide best practices to guide religious counselors using different approaches when dealing with counselees who have engaged with extremist ideology.

KEY TAKEAWAYS

- The counselor's aim should be to lead the counselee to the right path, instead of viewing the intervention as merely a component of debunking extremist ideology.
- The counselee deserves the chance to be taught so that he can disassociate himself from false beliefs and adopt positive values to replace negative ones.
- Counseling women is crucial and counseling must be tailored to the local context to adequately address the varied experiences of women.

The main objective of starting an intervention between a religious counselor and counselee is to ensure that the counselee **recants his misconstrued understanding of Islam** and develops the capacity to resist being recruited. More often than not, the counselor is approaching an individual whose knowledge of Islam **may require refinement and reinforcement**. The counselor's aim should be to **lead the counselee to the right path**, instead of viewing the intervention as merely a **component of debunking the ideology of extremists**.

In terms of Islamic knowledge, counselees can generally be categorized into two groups:

1

NO ACCESS TO FORMAL OR INFORMAL ISLAMIC EDUCATION

Individuals who have **no access to formal or informal Islamic education**, who are introduced to online propaganda (posing as Islam) that is promoted by terrorist groups like Daesh. This type of education is not part of mainstream Islamic thought and can be convincing to the counselee, as it is presented in simple yet absolutist terms.

2

RECEIVED SOME FORM OF MAINSTREAM RELIGIOUS EDUCATION

Individuals who have **received some form of mainstream religious education** (usually at the beginner or intermediate level). As they progressively involve themselves in online activity with groups like Daesh, they believe they have acquired "true Islamic" knowledge and teachings, which are violent in nature.

For religious intervention to be effective, the counselor's tact and skillfulness are key. The counselors who undertake the religious rehabilitation process must engage with the counselees, not only in their capacity as Islamic scholars, but also as **psychologists**. For this, the counselors need to:

1 Possess **knowledge about the ideology** of extremists.

2 Be aware of the **various social, psychological, and political conditions that may be affecting the psychology** of the counselee. See pages 270-271 for Vulnerability and Protective Factors.

3 Leave a **lasting impact** on the mind of the counselee.

This approach reflects a **"brethren" relationship between the counselor and the counselee**, one that fosters a dynamic of equality and open communication, as opposed to one-sided authority. This was also the way Islam was taught throughout history: **the learned one aspires to share his knowledge with his brothers in order to elevate them to a better standing.** It starts with encouraging the other to seek God's pleasure by performing what was commanded. We are reminded not to transgress the boundaries set by Islam, and that failure to adhere to these boundaries will result in God's displeasure. Ideally, the relationship between counselor and counselee should be one of **"brotherhood,"** which **imparts true knowledge, helps the counselee understand his errors in judgment, and cements the trust that can create a long-lasting bond between them.**

Thus, to be effective, the counselor should explore the individual's **circumstances**, including **her upbringing and her life experiences**. For example, issues that appear straightforward on the surface in fact may require other forms of intervention, such as, for example, family counseling, mental health assistance, social cohesion activities, or personal spiritual reflection.

If the counselee is using religious terminology to justify his/her wrong actions, the counselor must try to **disengage the recruit's use of religion as a basis for his feelings of hatred, resentment, and/or violence**. Thus, the counselor must stress two important points during the course of counseling the counselee:

1 State that in Islam, killing innocents and violence are not condoned.

2 Remind the counselee that it is against the law to take part in any terrorist or religious extremist group advocating violence.

Though the counselor's aim may be to **correct the counselee's misunderstanding of Islamic concepts**, the counselor must be mindful that the counselee's engagement with extremist groups may go beyond the search for "religion" or "religious meaning." Rather, the counselee may be searching for social belonging, revenge, justice for the oppressed, and so on. Acknowledging these other factors, which may be fueling the counselee's engagement with extremist groups, will help to ensure that the holistic needs of the counselee are being met in counseling, and prevent her continued engagement with extremist groups. (See "Why Do People Join Daesh?" on pages 162-163 for more information.)

Before the counselor begins, he must classify the issues or questions in their relevant categories under **Islamic jurisprudence**, in a process known as ***takyif* or "classification."**

1

If the counselee is unable to explain his specific problems, the counselor **should be gentle and patient** when the counselee is formulating questions, and **carefully process his own thoughts when listening to the questions posed**.

2

If the counselee correlates the perceived injustice and oppression of fellow Muslims to justify her need to engage in war against the "West," the counselor must

1. present an answer with logical, credible, and well thought out evidence that not only **relates to religious matters but also addresses the counselee's well-being**,
2. provide advice in a clear, concise and noncontradictory manner that cites evidence from the Qur'an or Sunnah to avoid misunderstandings, and 3) promote the true teachings of Islam in the spirit of desiring what is best for the counselee and as a **guide for her to become a better Muslim.**

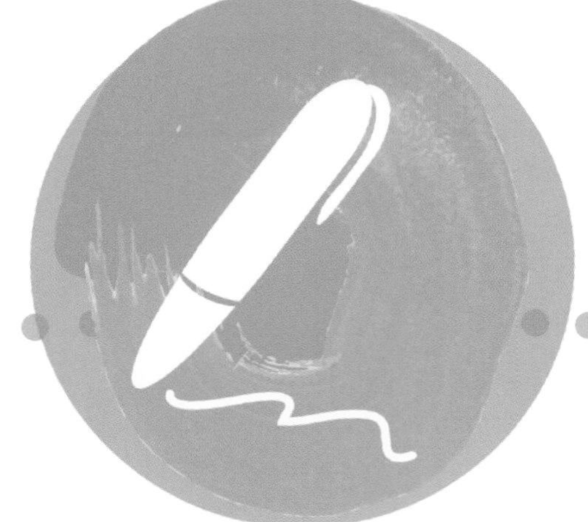

There are two techniques in approaching religiously motivated individuals who condone violence in the name of Islam:

1

CARROT AND STICK APPROACH

Influence behavior by **motivating the counselee to perform good deeds**, and explaining the consequent rewards that would benefit him in this life and the hereafter. Attempt to warn the counselee against committing sins by always reminding him of the consequences that may befall him in this life and on the Day of Judgment. **It is important to note that this does not aim to completely stop the counselee, but rather is an effort to minimize wrongdoing.**

Start a discourse on religion that

1. **promotes universal values such as compassion**,
2. uses texts that **promote peace and righteous behavior**,
3. exposes the counselee to Islamic scripture **prohibiting** unethical war conduct, and
4. emphasizes adverse consequences of **engaging in indiscriminate killing**. One Qur'anic verse may be helpful:

> *Because of that upon, we decreed the Children of Israel that whoever kills a soul unless for a soul or for corruption [done] in the land—it is as if he had slain humankind entirely. And whoever saves one—it is as if he saved humankind entirely* (5:24).

Allow the counselee to reassess her beliefs about the killing of noncombatants during war, examine whether a person is indeed an enemy, and ponder upon the action of choosing to kill over spreading the word of compassion and peace.

> "The world is sweet and green, and Allah has given you authority over it, so look at what you do" (Muslim 2007, 112).

Emphasize that war, cruelty, and committing atrocities are not complementary to the message of this Hadith.

Counseling women is crucial. Though they may not be on the frontlines of the battlefield, they are among Daesh's strongest supporters, and are key in propagating Daesh ideology online. They also serve as the primary nurturers of children, who could potentially become the next generation of extremists.

Counseling must be **tailored for the local context of the female counselee and must address female experiences.** On the religious front, the same steps mentioned above should be followed to properly counter extremist dogma. This approach should be promoted online as well and complemented with community engagement programs that aim to mobilize the whole of society. This can serve as a proactive approach to safeguard vulnerable women and young girls from the threat of extremist recruitment.

2

LEARN, UNLEARN, RELEARN

LEARN

The **counselor aids the counselee in guided learning** on Islamic matters of which he has no prior knowledge. He encourages the counselee to examine issues of relevance to his own spiritual journey and not to become a tool for others. He asks the counselee to live a purpose-driven life that promotes goodness and respect for all people and religions.

UNLEARN

This step is the counselor's attempt to **unsubscribe the counselee from extremists' erroneous dogma**. In this process, the counselor introduces good values to replace the bad ones. The counselee may have beliefs or thoughts that have **subconsciously or unconsciously been sustained with repeated exposure and subsequent reinforcement over time.** It is crucial for the counselor to help the counselee unsubscribe from false perceptions by providing credible evidence to support arguments against them. The unlearn phase has a double-edged function because it **contributes to the process of unlearning and relearning simultaneously.**

For example, when discussing the notion of the "caliphate," a counselee would not only identify his mistaken understanding of this term (a process of unlearning), but he is also **exposed to the bigger picture** of the discourse about the "caliphate" among scholars, and he ultimately acquires **a new set of knowledge that convinces him to abandon the old** (relearning). More specifically, the counselee may have been presented with an idea that the caliphate system is deemed as the only legitimate system of governance in Islam and its establishment is a religious obligation of Muslims. When the concept of the caliphate is repeatedly considered, and viewed solely from this lens, the tendency to arrive at a misconstrued conclusion is very high. **Counselors must emphasize that Muslims are not religiously obligated to establish a caliphate** and that the term "caliph" simply referred to the leader who was appointed to manage the civic needs of the burgeoning Muslim community as well as the implementation of law, and that the title "caliph" (*khalifat ar Rasul*) or the "successor of the Messenger" is no longer applicable to today's leaders. People who ruled over Muslims in past centuries referred to themselves as "*ammir al mu'minin*" or the "leaders of the believers," a title that is also not part of religious terminology or religious law.

RELEARN

This step encourages the counselee to **revisit and reevaluate** his understanding of Islamic matters, especially in **distinguishing between a literal interpretation of the Qur'an (used by extremists) and contextual-based interpretations (used by mainstream Muslims).** The counselor should explain that a Muslim is not only one who practices Islam according to its authentic teachings, but also one who promotes peaceful coexistence and does not impose his own values on others.

It is extremely important that the counselor not disparage his counselee. He must convey his message in a very subtle and diplomatic manner so as not to offend the counselee or create an antagonistic relationship. The counselee deserves the chance to be taught so that he can **disassociate himself from false beliefs** and adopt good values to replace bad ones.

By going through this three-phase process, the counselee acquires knowledge about Islam, and becomes familiar with an analytical process that will help him to **replace distorted understandings with sound and legitimate ones.** This approach will be well received if the counselee feels that he is being treated as a brother instead of a suspect.

COUNSELING OF WOMEN

Daesh intensely exploits three Islamic concepts to recruit women. First, they hold that it is an individual's obligation to perform *hijrah* (migration). Second, they **exploit** a Hadith in which the Prophet Muhammad says, "Unite under the army of the black flag," and use the powerful symbolism inherent in the display of this black battle flag. Third, they tell women that if they are married to a *mujahidin* (fighter), they will receive a share of their husbands' divine rewards, aside from the rewards that God gives women for maintaining a home, bearing children, and nurturing the children to become the next generation of *mujahidin*. Daesh women are told that when their husbands die as "martyrs" on the battlefield, they will also bring their wives to Paradise. Thus, female recruits are strongly encouraged to marry *mujahidin*. Many women, too, marry Daesh fighters for practical reasons: women are generally not allowed to be seen in public without a male chaperone.

There is hope for rehabilitating Daesh women, however, as disillusionment with Daesh has been identified as the main reason that women return from Daesh territory. Several aspects need to be taken into consideration during the counseling process:

1

The **extent** to which these women have been indoctrinated with extremist dogma

2

Their **motivations** for traveling to Daesh territory, which include beliefs that they will be united in "sisterhood" (perceived unity of the *ummah* or the Muslim nation under Daesh); practical reasons such as the need to accompany their husbands; their search for identity or meaning in life; and an innate need for a sense of belonging to something special. (See "Why Do Women Join Daesh?" on pages 170–171 for more information.)

Countering Daesh Media Strategies: The Role of Community Leaders

DR. HOUDA ABADI explains that Daesh relies greatly on social media to disseminate its message. They tailor their online presence to attract vulnerable and disenfranchised youth. This demands that Muslim leaders develop productive ways to engage Muslim youth in order to counteract Daesh's extremist appeal.

KEY TAKEAWAYS

- Driven by a deep discontent and estrangement from their own societies, thousands of young people have joined Daesh in search of an ideal society.
- Daesh uses highly professional, skillfully produced social media messaging to appeal to youth.
- Religious leaders must use the same mediums and techniques to reach young people that Daesh uses to recruit them to counteract Daesh's claims.

Daesh has capitalized on the political vacuum created by failed states and the failure of national governments to address core sociopolitical grievances, more specifically, the disenfranchisement of youth and marginalization of particular segments of the population. Driven by a deep discontent and estrangement from their own societies, thousands of youth have joined Daesh in search of an idealistic society. Daesh has taken advantage of these feelings of disenfranchisement in its recruitment by emphasizing the idyllic notion of a utopian "Islamic state" that addresses Muslim grievances across the globe.

Driven by a deep discontent and estrangement from their own societies, thousands of youth have joined Daesh in search of an idealistic society.

Daesh's systematic misrepresentation of religious doctrines and manipulation of political grievances serve as tactics to legitimize violence and attract new recruits. Since their barbaric practices violate every Islamic law, they take religious texts out of context to establish their authority and justify jihad as a morally and Islamically justifiable act. By re-contextualizing Qur'anic references, Daesh taps into the Muslim imagination to reminisce about the glory days of Muslim power. Apocalyptic in style, Daesh asks its target audience to relive Islamic history, the times of persecution, and the times of glory that God promised if they remained steadfast. This sympathetic figuration revives a nostalgic Muslim collective memory of Islam's golden days and banks on its affective depository of cultural referents in their call for a transnational membership. The extreme violence becomes a temporary method of self-preservation to the otherwise good-natured, honest, and humble servant of God.

DAESH AND SOCIAL MEDIA

To create an appealing Daesh brand, the recruiters main online propaganda narratives revolve around seven primary themes:

1. The humiliation and transgression of the ummah;
2. Humiliating the West;
3. Military jihad;
4. Providing social services within Daesh-controlled territory;
5. Hypocrisy of Muslim, Middle East, and North African leaders;
6. Ability to administer territory by providing security, law, and order; and last,
7. Espousing purely theological motivations.

Their narrative is heavily dependent on their target

audience and media channel. Daesh uses tech-savvy online campaigns and sophisticated video production techniques in its propaganda strategy to recruit and attract young foreign fighters. Ayman al-Zawahiri, leader of al-Qaeda Central, said in 2005, "We are in a battle, and more than half of this battle is taking place in the battlefield of the media. We are in a media battle for the heart and minds of our ummah."

> Using social media to draw on vulnerable and disenfranchised youth, Daesh attempts to propagate its ideology and build identification with its target audience.

Daesh digital propaganda videos are of high production value and stylistic similarities with Hollywood action movies. For Daesh, being seen is as important as being heard in its branding of its caliphate project. Using social media to draw in vulnerable and disenfranchised youth, Daesh attempts to propagate its ideology and build identification with its target audience. Their use of various languages in stories of converts and foreign Muslim fighters projects an image of acceptance in which everyone is seemingly united under the banner of Islam regardless of race, socioeconomic status, physical disability, and country of origin. In one of his sermons, Abu Bakr al-Baghdadi states, "[The Islamic State] is a state where the Arab and non-Arab, the white man and black man, the easterner and westerner are all brothers." These types of propaganda videos tap into the socio-economic grievances of the potential recruits and provide an alternative to their respective communities.

THE ROLE OF MUSLIM COMMUNITY LEADERS IN COUNTERING DAESH

Muslim religious and community leaders have an important role to play in discrediting and preventing violent extremism as they hold unique positions of authority, credibility, and communal ties. Our religious and community leaders must be proactive and identify the problems and solutions and recognize the particular role that they can play in providing alternative avenues for expressing grievances, while promoting community-based activities that respond to local needs. This will foster greater inclusion and sense of belonging in vulnerable youth.

Muslim religious leaders have been condemning violence, but seldom do they discredit the religious militant ideology propagated by Daesh using diverse online social tools. Many of the responses from religious leaders have relied on traditional forms of communication that are neither engaging nor attractive to the youth. The primary focus has been on Qur'anic verses and long sermons (many times in classical Arabic). Some religious leaders also have published long manifestos to condemn Daesh. While these actions are all important in sending a clear message that Daesh does not represent Islam, they do not directly engage with the most vulnerable population—the disenfranchised Muslim youth.

> Their use of various languages in stories of converts and foreign Muslim fighters projects an image of acceptance in which everyone is seemingly united under the banner of Islam regardless of race, socioeconomic status, physical disability, and country of origin.

The Muslim religious and community leaders must understand Daesh's communication strategies so that they can identify productive ways of engaging Muslim youth. First, religious and community leaders must understand and identify the emotional appeals and various narratives Daesh employs. For example, how does Daesh propaganda differ in the Uniteds States from its counterpart in the Middle East and North Africa? Does Daesh target men and women differently?

> Muslim religious leaders have been condemning violence, but seldom do they discredit the religious militant ideology propagated by Daesh using diverse online social tools.

Effective solutions must be localized and grassroot in nature. In parallel, the apocalyptic out-of-context interpretation of Qur'anic verses must be examined and refuted. One main recurring theme that is found in all Daesh media propaganda is the concept of the caliphate and the abolition of the nation-state, which is directly tied to issues of Muslim identity. We should encourage and not shy away from critical discussion. Second, Daesh's heavy reliance on sophisticated digital media to recruit young Muslims makes it even more imperative for religious leaders to use the same mediums effectively when creating localized alternative online narratives. One helpful approach to address this challenge is for religious leaders to enhance their media capabilities and communication strategies so that they can effectively discredit Daesh's propaganda. Third, their disconnect with the youth has presented a major challenge to the Muslim religious leaders' attempts to guide and engage the youth. Community leaders must be able to communicate in a language that the youth can understand and identify with. This can be done through the use of local dialects, shorter and interactive sermons, safe spaces for women, and local initiatives for youth. It is of the utmost importance that our youth feel empowered and listened to.

A Parent's Guide to Social Media and Online Behavior

WISE provides parents with an explanation of how Daesh uses online platforms to entice youth into joining their cause, and some helpful information on the top social media platforms used for communication and recruitment.

ABOUT THE INTERNET AND SOCIAL MEDIA: PUTTING TECHNOLOGY IN CONTEXT

The creation of the Internet opened a tangible, yet ethereal, dimension where humans can interact, learn, and engage with limitless amounts of information. Today there are multiple generations alive who have different relationships with technology and the Internet, thus presenting different levels of impact. For example:

There is a generation alive today who knows the majority of their lives without the Internet.

There is a generation who was relatively young when the Internet was introduced, whose childhood and teenage years make them the final generation to know a world with, and without, the Internet.

There is a generation who will always know what it's like to have a screen nearby.

Our connectivity has greatly increased—we network, engage, and become activists in big, meaningful causes—all at our fingertips. In just two decades, we've grown accustomed to everything being available to us in an instant. Technology and online socialization have emerged as formative players in behavior construction. Rushes of adrenaline and dopamine flow with each message exchanged or as each "like" is received on social media.

Moreover, the Internet has impacted the world's access to news. It has shattered the microphone once belonging only to journalists and mainstream news outlets, and handed the pieces to anyone with an Internet connection. The borderless nature of online terrain makes it an environment inherently resistant to policing and control practices. The essence of online communities is exchange and collaboration. The Internet is not, however, immune to propaganda or censorship.

Conditions like those above amplify issues once they go "viral." Anything can become an unmanageable beast within seconds each time the Enter key is tapped. The success of the Internet's ability to

intensify an issue can be seen most clearly with the ever-growing presence of Daesh and its supporters online. The group's uses of the Internet as a key part of its long-term strategy and immediate tactics have accelerated its position as a central actor in a major global conflict. Why has it been so effective?

For starters, the Daesh presence online has been organic. Its users and sympathizers are for the most part people who have grown up with the Internet. They understand the pulse of the younger generation (because they ARE that pulse) and they know how to use the Internet as a canvas for self-expression. With every click, Daesh is able to operationalize its brand, ideology, recruiting efforts, and media.

The purpose of this section on social media is to create awareness on how to be critical, informed users and consumers of the information available to us. Mindful Internet use protects two sacred frontiers: the freedom of the web and the freedom of our minds.

THE APPEAL: AN OPPORTUNITY TO MAKE A STATEMENT

Daesh postures itself as an actor that is interested in the individual and the global. To the individual, Daesh recruiters and fighters offer their attention to anyone available. Once contact is established, days are filled with constant updates, notifications, and messages from the Daesh network.

Understanding why this is so attractive requires thoughtful evaluation of those Daesh tries to recruit the most: young adults. What does Daesh have to offer that fulfills what they are looking for?

For starters, millennials tend to be reform-minded. Younger generations are socially conscious individuals interested in creating systems that will bring sufficient change to pressing global issues. For this age group, conventional modes of change are perceived as largely ineffective and misrepresentative of reality.

The Daesh invitation is alluring because it is a specially crafted message designed to appeal to the best in people. It does not simply speak to the lonely, estranged young adults who are alienated from mainstream society. The Daesh message, whether it is to move to the caliphate or to conduct attacks on the group's behalf, offers a direct cause to which any person's hopes, dreams, aspirations, faith, self-actualization, and deepest longings for identity can be used to build something that will undoubtedly change the world. The strength of Daesh online is sustained by efforts around the globe simply by holding space and repeating the vision for the caliphate. American millennials are accustomed to being treated like inspired and capable individuals. Daesh has been able to tap into this and offer youth an occasion to rise to.

Internet and Social Media Definitions

Online extremism is a child-safety issue. This guide is designed to provide parents with information about the online world in order to recognize and prevent extremist involvement. Online interactions have real-life consequences and youth need to have a better grasp on how to make informed decisions with regard to material that they encounter. Parents should be encouraged to take an active interest in their children's online activities and learn how to use online platforms with them. The Internet is a major space of interaction and socialization, and while it can be positive and beneficial, it also has risks.

PUBLIC CHAT ROOM
Online room where a number of users can be at any given time. Chat rooms are usually centered around a specific topic, like sports, entertainment, gaming, and others.

CHAT
Real-time text conversation between users.

INSTANT MESSAGES
Private, real-time text conversations between two users in a chat room.

SOCIAL MEDIA
Online tools that allow people to share and exchange information, media, and ideas in virtual networks and communities.

Social Media Platforms

INSTAGRAM is a site and app where users can share photos with other users and link to multiple social networking sites.

ASK.FM is a site where people can post a profile (a picture and information about themselves) and be asked questions anonymously.

FACEBOOK is the largest social networking site, and can be used for communication and gathering information about people and ideas by sharing updates through statuses, photos and videos, as well as via private messaging.

VIBER is an instant messaging service that permits users to call as well as text with other users.

TUMBLR is a microblogging site where users can interact with other users and share similar content. The site allows for anonymity and does not require sharing a lot of personal information.

SURESPOT is a chat messenger service that encrypts every text, picture, and video shared between users. Its focus is on privacy and the content can be read only by the person receiving the message.

KIK is an instant messaging service that allows for user anonymity. You can text with other users without having to give out a personal phone number.

WHATSAPP is an instant messaging service that permits users to text as well as voice chat with other users. There are also group chats, which can connect larger groups of people in one messaging thread.

YOUTUBE is a video sharing service that allows users to view and often comment on the videos others have posted.

PALTALK is a communication service that lets multiple users communicate using Internet chat rooms as well as allowing for voice and video messaging.

JUSTPASTE.IT is a site that allows users to paste or type text and distribute the resulting link.

TWITTER is a service that only allows users to send out posts that are 140 characters (letters, symbols, or spaces) in a message called a Tweet. This Tweet can be directed at another user, or can include a hashtag, which is a trending term preceded by a # symbol.

TELEGRAM is a free, cloud-based instant messaging provider, used to send messages, photos, videos, stickers, audio, and files of any type. The messaging app also offers optional end-to-end-encrypted messaging.

GROUPME is a mobile group messaging app that allows people to easily communicate in a group message even if they have different phone providers.

GOOGLE PLUS is an interest-based social network owned and controlled by Google. It allows users to organize people into groups or lists which are shared across other Google products and services.

INDEED is a job-search site that allows users to find and apply to jobs all over the world, as well as post job opportunities with their organizations.

XBOX is a video game console from Microsoft that also has services such as Netflix and YouTube built in and is widely used as a home entertainment source. The console also offers a chatting service through Xbox Live, for which users need an Xbox 360 headset or a Kinect sensor, an internet connection, and an Xbox Live Gold subscription. Users can verbally speak to either just their added friends or anyone while playing an Xbox game.

PLAYSTATION is a video game console from Sony that allows users to send messages through the PlayStation Network (PSN) online gaming service, as well as through voice-chatting and even conversing through a specific game, like World of Warcraft or Call of Duty. Communication via PlayStation is notoriously more difficult to track than communication via encrypted phone or email conversations.

SKYPE is an Internet-enabled service that allows registered users to communicate via instant messaging and voice and video chat.

LINKEDIN is a social networking site created to connect the business world. It allows users to develop and document networks of people that they have built relationships with professionally.

REDDIT is a social news aggregation, web content rating, and discussion website. Its users can upload content such as text posts or links. Other users can then vote a post up or down to determine its position on the page.

SNAPCHAT is a mobile messaging service that allows for the sending of photos or videos to friends that last between 1 second and 24 hours before becoming inaccessible. Users can also post to their stories, which can be viewed by their friends, and each story lasts only 24 hours.

Online Behavior

Online recruiting poses a major challenge to Internet use today. Immersion in extremist content over extended periods of time amplifies the effects of graphic images, videos, and messages, eventually resulting in emotional desensitization. The Internet should be viewed as a legitimate social environment because it connects people with similar interests. While online platforms offer great potential as a salon-type environment for people to engage one another, they can also easily become echo chambers rather than houses of discussion. This enables bad ideas to grow and metastasize. Social environments are spaces of influence and impact—meaning, people can gain power and notoriety based on the support of others. The anonymity of the Internet allows thrill-seekers to easily test the waters without real commitment. They can show up and become anyone they really want to be, choosing role-play instead of authenticity.

COMMUNICATION IS KEY

An open channel for communicating is the most important non-technical method that parents can use to deal with the challenges of extremism.

TEACH YOUR LOVED ONES SENSIBLE ONLINE BEHAVIOR AND PRECAUTIONS.

PROTECT YOUR SAFETY

Giving out personal contact information, and/or arranging to meet a stranger met online can create a dangerous situation! Do not open pictures or files from people you do not know.

PROTECT YOUR PRIVACY

Updating daily activities to social media is the norm nowadays. Understand the risks of posting pictures online, and agree on standards as a family on what is appropriate and inappropriate.

EDUCATE YOUNGER GENERATIONS ABOUT TRUTH AND PROPAGANDA

Reintroduce critical thinking into education.

USE GOOD JUDGMENT IN MONITORING INTERNET USE

Young people need privacy in their online social lives just as in their in-person relationships. Maintaining an honest and open relationship is the best way to keep informed about their online activities without having to resort to spying (which can alienate your child and break your trust).

PROTECT YOUR PASSWORDS.

ON REPETITION AND PERSONAL RESPONSIBILITY WHEN REPOSTING THINGS

Practice sharing with intention. Each time we click, we send energy and support toward something. Only by being mindful of it as it happens can we begin to control our binge-clicking.

FIND OUT WHY YOUR LOVED ONE SPENDS SO MUCH TIME ONLINE

Healthy conversations may uncover hidden details of your loved one's life that they may be struggling with (e.g., depression, low self-esteem, anxiety, substance abuse, and detachment from real relationships).

CHAPTER 8

Creating Resilient Families and Communities

Parenting with Care So Our Children Will Care

SORAYA DEEN

On Children

KAHLIL GIBRAN

Your children are not your children.
They are the sons and daughters of Life's longing for itself.
They come through you but not from you,
And though they are with you, yet they belong not to you.

You may give them your love but not your thoughts.
For they have their own thoughts.
You may house their bodies but not their souls,
For their souls dwell in the house of tomorrow,
which you cannot visit, not even in your dreams.
You may strive to be like them, but seek not to make them like you.
For life goes not backward nor tarries with yesterday.

You are the bows from which your children as living arrows are sent forth.
The archer sees the mark upon the path of the infinite,
and He bends you with His might that His arrows may go swift and far.
Let your bending in the archer's hand be for gladness;
For even as He loves the arrow that flies,
so He loves also the bow that is stable.

SORAYA DEEN is the founder of the Muslim Women Speakers Movement. She is the author of *Peace Matters—Raising Peace Conscious Children* and *Serve: A Call to Muslims*. She is a coach, a lawyer, and a certified Nonviolent Parent Educator, who blends legal expertise with her uniquely diverse background to inspire people and communities to navigate conflict and promote dialogue. She is a peace activist and advocates for interfaith dialogue action.

Most of the time parenting takes place at the two extremes of parents telling their children "No" or shaming them. We need to hear what our children have to say. We need to collaborate with them, meet them where they are and consider their terms.

SORAYA DEEN

INTRODUCTION

How we raise our children, how we help them integrate and navigate the world they live in, what tools we give them to create impact and influence, are critical first steps, not just for a better life today, but for a greater generation in the future, and a life away from violence. The deep connection and trust and overall relationship a parent builds with her child is foundational to this journey.

DIRECTION

I remember the day when my seven-year-old son looked up at me—his eyes welled in tears, his face sad and confused—and asked, "Mommy, are we terrorists?" It was the sixth anniversary of 9/11. I realized at that moment that my words had the power to liberate or enslave my son, to bring hope or fear not only to my son, but to the world. So I took a deep breath and firmly told my son, "Baby, we are not terrorists. You are not a terrorist. Your baby sister is not a terrorist. Mommy is not a terrorist, and Daddy is not a terrorist."

No matter how bad the past, how rough the present, and how daunting the future seems, we can't let circumstances define who we are. We have the capacity to change those circumstances, we have the capacity to become better parents, we have the capacity to become better citizens, and we have the capacity to become better beings. You must TRUST that your child has the same capacity. The parenting challenges you will encounter will not be those that your parents encountered. We encounter different complexities today. We have moved from raising compliant children to more independent ones. I think technology has offered great solutions and created complex problems for our children and our parenting. Your child can transform the world without leaving the comfort of his home, for better or worse. At the same time, people—predators, terrorists, recruiters—from around the world can share ideas to entice, influence, and alter the course of your children's lives, putting them onto an extremely destructive path. The good and the bad are both a click away. Children raised without strong role models, and without affection and acceptance, are particularly likely to seek solace, comfort, and friendships with others whom they think they can trust and who understand them.

Being a great parent requires practice every day. Make it a ritual to speak and CONNECT (not always CORRECT) with your child. It is my hope to share with you some very vital skills that you can use every day. All I ask from you as a parent is that you be prepared to bring about a radical revolution of your MIND and your ACTIONS. If you are willing to change your thoughts, you can change your world and the world of your child. Take determined action, to **EDUCATE**, **EMPOWER**, and **ENGAGE** your child to be a global citizen and to acknowledge and appreciate all people of different faiths and cultures.

KNOWING YOU, KNOWING SELF

As parents let's understand that we have a title, we have a position, we have a job. A job that requires not just your will but, more important, your skill. When you have a moderate relationship with your children, where you listen to them, observe them and do not judge them, blame them, or shame them, they will respect you and follow you. And when they follow you, it will provide you with great opportunities to connect with them, and be a friend and partner to them. You can now be directly involved in supporting them to solve their problems and help them in their challenges, and contribute to creating momentum in their lives.

IT IS NOT THE WILL BUT THE SKILL THAT MATTERS

As a parent, you must acquire the skills to create a fault-free zone in your home, an atmosphere of safety and trust, to assist (not control) your child. You can help your child reach his full potential by supporting his gifts, talents, and abilities. Raising peace-conscious children is a process of education; we must take small steps every day in our home, and we must embody nonviolence.

COMPASSIONATE PARENTING

Let's explore six ways in which we can transform the lives of our children through compassionate parenting:

1. Understanding your parenting paradigm.
2. Understanding the brain development of your child.
3. Learning the language of compassion and connection.
4. Anger: Where is it coming from?
5. Moving from the problem to the solution.
6. Empathy and expectations.
7. Understanding behavior changes—ask for help.
8. Setting limits.

1. WHAT IS YOUR PARENTING PARADIGM?

TRANSFORMATIONAL PARENT	TRANSACTIONAL PARENT
I offer unconditional love.	I offer conditional love to my child. He/she must listen, comply, and cooperate.
I have a long -term vision of who I want my child to be.	I discipline through physical punishment, put-downs and comparisons.
I understand and connect with my child's feelings and needs. I am empathetic.	I inflict emotional pain on my child by shaming, blaming, and name calling.
I understand the developmental stages of my child.	I don't know that when I hurt my child it affects his brain and growth.
I respect my child's needs and feelings.	I don't think that a child's feelings and needs are important.
I use my power and knowledge to guide and support my child.	I use my power to control my child's behavior.

1.1 – EXERCISE

WRITE DOWN THREE THINGS YOU ENJOY ABOUT YOUR CHILD

1. ....

2. ....

3. ....

WRITE DOWN THREE THINGS YOU FEEL CHALLENGED ABOUT WITH YOUR CHILD

1. ....

2. ....

3. ....

WRITE DOWN THREE QUALITIES YOU WANT YOUR CHILD TO HAVE

1. ....

2. ....

3. ....

WHAT KIND OF A PERSON DO YOU WANT YOUR CHILD TO BE?

I Want My Child to Be ....

....

....

CONTINUED OVERLEAF ...

1.1 – EXERCISE (CONT'D)

SETTING BY EXAMPLE: NOW REWRITE THE QUALITIES YOU WROTE ABOVE IN THE FORM OF "I WILL BE. . ." STATEMENTS

FOR EXAMPLE, IF YOU WROTE "I WANT MY CHILD TO BE RESPECTFUL." REWRITE TO SAY, "I WILL BE RESPECTFUL."

I Will Be ....

....

....

REFLECTION: WHAT NEEDS TO CHANGE?

....

....

....

2. UNDERSTANDING THE BRAIN DEVELOPMENT OF YOUR CHILD

Islam teaches that there are three stages of raising children from birth to when they are twenty-one years old. These stages are based on a hadith of the Prophet Muhammad (pbuh) that states: "The child is the master for seven years; a subject for seven years and a vizier for seven years; so if he grows into a good character within 21 years, well and good."

The first stage consists of the first seven years of a child's life and is described as a "care free" period where the parents' lives revolve around their child's. This stage of life is when children begin to learn by observation and imitation; therefore, it is absolutely necessary for parents to provide their children with examples of good behavior and to constantly engage and interact with them. Treat them, talk to them, and play with them as if you were a child. As the Prophet says, "Respect your children and teach them good behavior. God will forgive [your sins]."

The second stage lasts from the age of eight until the child is fourteen years of age, when the child's mind starts to grasp logical reasoning and is fully developed for formal education and discipline. The child is described as a "subject" since it is during these years that children are taught to follow the instructions of their parents and teachers. Parents should be strict in their discipline and raise their child with proper Islamic ethics and genuine religious education so their religious beliefs are based on sound reasoning and a firm foundation.

The third and final stage ranges from the ages of fifteen to twenty-one in which the child is expected to become a responsible teenager. During this final stage, parents should help guide their child in making correct decisions for themselves but also become more like a friend to their child. Parents' responsibility toward their children ends once they reach the age of twenty-one and begin to lead independent lives.

A simple peek into how and when our brains begin to develop and function will open a positive new way in which we can parent our children and understand the human condition.

I always tell parents not to be concerned so much that your child is not listening to you, but rather, be concerned that your child is watching you.

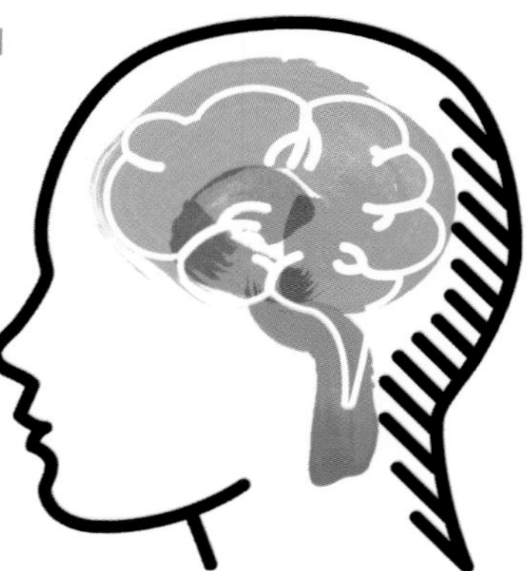
NEOCORTEX BRAIN
Analytical Mind
LIMBIC BRAIN
Emotional Mind
REPTILIAN BRAIN
Instinctive Mind
Manages reason, problem solving, creativity, imagination, empathy, and rational thought. A well-integrated brain is the result of a loving caregiver. It also integrates all the other functions of the brain to work together
Feelings and memory are stored here
Alarm Center - ensures survival and responds to danger

Every child as we know is individualized and born with a unique set of attributes, but the optimal growth and development of the child depends on the connection the child develops with the parent. A **TRANSACTIONAL PARENT** judges and evaluates a child by his/her behavior and focuses on punishment and discipline. This parent fails to understand the developmental stages of the child and the feelings and the needs that the child is seeking to express.

2.1 – EXERCISE

WRITE DOWN THREE WAYS YOUR CHILD SEEKS ATTENTION AND AFFECTION

1. ....

2. ....

3. ....

HOW DOES YOUR CHILD SHOW THAT HE/SHE WANTS AUTONOMY?

....

....

....

HOW DO YOU EXPRESS AUTONOMY?

....

....

....

Often times parenting begins and ends with struggles for autonomy. We focus on the strategies and not expressing our NEEDS and FEELINGS. By now I hope you are ready to master the needs literacy. Check out the NEEDS LIST on page 299. Just ponder what you are NEEDING right this moment. Always remember: everything we do is in the pursuit of a NEED.

REFLECTION: WHAT MUST CHANGE?

....

....

....

3. LEARNING THE LANGUAGE OF COMPASSION AND CONNECTION

Without delving into detailed subject matter, let's do something experiential.

3.1 – EXERCISE

USING YOUR REAL LIFE, WRITE DOWN SOMETHING YOUR CHILD SAYS OR DOES THAT'S HARD FOR YOU TO HEAR

....

....

....

WHAT IS YOUR HABITUAL RESPONSE?

....

....

....

WHAT THOUGHTS AND JUDGMENTS DO YOU HAVE AROUND WHAT YOUR CHILD DOES AND SAYS THAT IS HARD FOR YOU TO HEAR AND SEE?

....

....

....

Do you find judgments, evaluations, blame, and shame in your responses above? Is there compassion and kindness in your words? Communicating compassionately with our children, requires a whole new set of skills. We learn to:

1. Make observations;
2. Communicate our feelings;
3. Express our needs;
4. Offer empathy; and
5. Make specific actionable requests.

Identify what NEEDS you were trying to meet when your child was doing or saying what he was doing, and which were hard for you to hear or see. What feelings came up for you?

3.2 – CHART

ACQUIRE A **NEEDS LITERACY**.
POST THIS IN A PROMINENT PLACE IN YOUR HOME
AND **EXPRESS YOUR NEEDS**,
NOT WHAT IS WRONG WITH YOUR CHILD.
CNVC.ORG

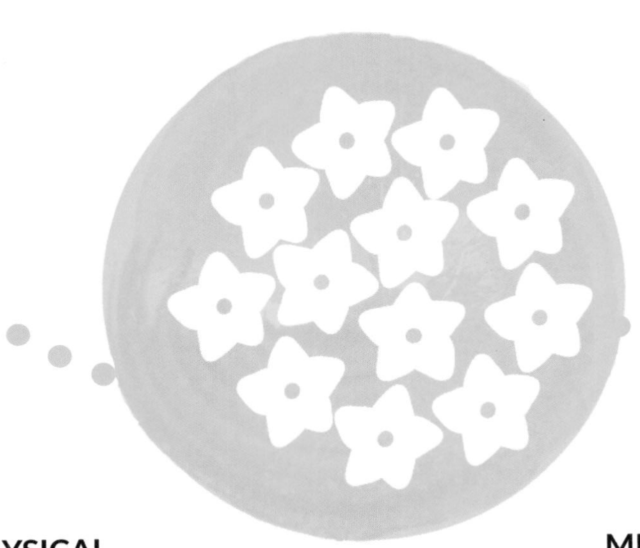

CONNECTION

acceptance
affection
appreciation
belonging
cooperation
communication
closeness
community
companionship
compassion
consideration
consistency
empathy
inclusion
intimacy
love
mutuality
nurturing
respect/self-respect
safety
security
stability
support
to know and be known
to see and be seen
to understand and be understood
trust
warmth

PHYSICAL WELL-BEING

air
food
movement/exercise
rest/sleep
sexual expression
safety
shelter
touch
water

HONESTY

authenticity
integrity
presence

PLAY

joy
humor

PEACE

beauty
communion
ease
equality
harmony
inspiration
order

AUTONOMY

choice
freedom
independence
space
spontaneity

MEANING

awareness
celebration of life
challenge
clarity
competence
consciousness
contribution
creativity
discovery
efficacy
effectiveness
growth
hope
learning
mourning
participation
purpose
self-expression
stimulation
to matter
understanding

CUT ALONG THIS LINE

3.3 – EXERCISE

APPLYING COMPASSIONATE COMMUNICATION TO
FULLY EXPRESS YOUR ANGER/FRUSTRATION/DISCONNECTION,
WRITE WHAT YOU WOULD SAY TO YOUR CHILD NOW

MAKE AN OBSERVATION OF WHAT YOU SAW OR HEARD
(NO JUDGMENT/ EVALUATION)

....

....

....

EXPRESS YOUR NEEDS
(CHECK THE LIST TO BE AS SPECIFIC AS YOU CAN)

....

....

....

EXPRESS YOUR FEELINGS ABOUT WHAT IS HAPPENING WITH YOUR CHILD
(NOT WHAT IS WRONG WITH HIM/HER)

....

....

....

MAKE A REQUEST
(WHAT DO YOU WANT YOUR CHILD TO DO OR NOT TO DO?)

....

....

....

EXAMPLE

"I am angry and irritated with my son for the hundredth time because he is online for far too long and is neglecting his studies. He doesn't listen to me."

You can react to this situation by screaming at him or calling him names and demand that he get off the Internet. You have a legitimate concern for his welfare. But you are NOT expressing your concern. Rather, you are expressing his wrongness.

Instead, consider speaking to your son this way: "When I see you on the computer from 4 pm to 6 pm, without finishing your homework (OBSERVING), I FEEL very scared, because I am concerned about your education. I NEED your cooperation to finish your homework before you go on the computer. I want you to take full responsibility for finishing your homework before 6 pm every weekday. REQUEST: Can you please finish your homework before you go on the computer?"

Observe yourself wherever you are—standing at the checkout line in a supermarket, responding to a client or spouse, and especially, WHEN TALKING TO YOUR CHILD. Remember, everything you think is not the truth.

SHARPEN YOUR OBSERVATION SKILLS: WHAT DO YOU SEE?

Often when I show this picture to participants at my workshops, they say, "The children are fighting, the mother is stressed out and looks angry and annoyed. She must be having a headache because of the children."

A PURE OBSERVATION WILL BE:

A woman (we don't even know if it is the mother) is knitting her eyebrows, with her fingers through her hair. Two children in the background are holding onto each other's shoulders. The girl is leaning slightly forward.

4. ANGER: WHERE IS IT COMING FROM?

Anger is an expression of unmet NEEDS. A parent who is able to feel him/herself being TRIGGERED by something the child said or did not say, did or did not do, and is able to OBSERVE the anger rising (physical response), understands the FEELINGS that are coming up, and is able to really PAUSE before expressing oneself or taking action, will eventually come to realize that ANGER is a CHOICE. The way we express our anger to our children can be one of the most destructive habits they will learn in their childhood. Consequently, they will carry this anger as they grow into adulthood and become parents themselves. As parents we must first take care of ourselves. Anger is a negative emotion and no good can come out of it. It is always destructive.

4.1 – EXERCISE

HOW DID YOUR MOTHER SHOW HER ANGER?

....

....

....

HOW DID YOUR FATHER SHOW HIS ANGER?

....

....

....

HOW DID ADULTS IN YOUR LIFE EXPRESS ANGER?

....

....

....

HOW DID THEIR ANGER AFFECT YOU? WHAT DID YOU FEEL?

....

....

....

HOW DO YOU EXPRESS YOUR ANGER NOW?

....

....

....

WHAT DO YOU THINK YOUR CHILDREN FEEL WHEN YOU EXPRESS YOUR ANGER?

....

....

....

DO YOU WANT TO CHANGE THE WAY YOU EXPRESS YOUR ANGER?

....

....

....

WHY AND HOW?

....

....

....

5. MOVING FROM THE PROBLEM TO THE SOLUTION

So let's say you have done everything RIGHT, but you are faced with the realization that your child is being recruited. Or he/she is continuing to move around with groups of individuals you know are not safe and law-abiding. Or your child is involved with substance abuse.

> The only thing worse than being blind is having sight but no vision.
>
> **HELEN KELLER**

This can be a parent's nightmare. You will be shocked, pained, and have a deep sense of anger, helplessness, and resentment. What motivated your child? Was my child repeatedly targeted, isolated, and physically or verbally bullied? How did my child get radicalized? Is it religion, identity, or adventure? Is it alienation or political grievances? Is it something you, as a parent, did or did not do? These questions can wreak havoc in your life. Please know that these issues are systemic; no single action will resolve it.

I know personal friends whose children have made choices that have caused immense pain to their parents. As parents we will always ask the question "Why?" You will be devastated, but don't let it destroy you. Your sorrow, your shock, your struggle, will open a way for you to find creative solutions and be a source of strength to other concerned parents who can benefit from your support and services.

There are TWO immediate initial steps you need to take NOW.

1. Do NOT blame and shame your child. You will learn how to PREVENT and INTERRUPT. Establish a sense of urgency. Identify the problem and possible solutions.
2. As you respond to the circumstances, be STRONG and PRAGMATIC. Remember, you get to control your thoughts and feelings about this catastrophe. To be EFFECTIVE, your next steps should be based on your leadership, understanding, strength, resolve, and faith. Craft a vision.

6. EMPATHY AND EXPECTATIONS

> When someone really hears you without passing judgment on you, without trying to take responsibility for you, without trying to mold you, it feels damn good.
>
> **CARL ROGERS**

EMPATHY

Offering EMPATHY is one of the most challenging skills parents and children struggle with. Empathy is our ability to be present rather than doing something. It is a deep ability to experience the needs and feelings of the other. Imagine a moment where your child comes to you and says that he has made some new friends and wants to go out with them. You are determined that it is not safe for him to go out with his new friends until you meet them and their families.

An EMPATHIC conversation would be: "Oh dear, so you are excited to go out with your new friends even though I have not met them or their families. I really want you to enjoy hanging out with your friends, but I am concerned about your safety. Can you arrange for your friends to come here instead?" In this frame of conversation, you are opening the doors to connection and new possibilities. Your child will learn to trust and respect you. Make EMPATHY your new currency and use it to create bonds with your child. When you reach out in empathy, your child will feel safe to come to you with their wants, because you have shown concern for their wishes.

FOR EMPATHY to be present there need to be three elements:

1. Presence
2. Intent to connect, not correct
3. Ability to reframe and paraphrase what is being said

Empathy can be verbal or nonverbal. Sometimes a hug, a smile, a nod is all that it takes for your child to FEEL FELT and be heard. I recall one day my daughter Imaan was very unhappy that her paintings were not turning out the way she wanted them to. She was crying and I began to console her. I asked her what I could do for her and she said, "Mommy, I don't want you to do anything. Just hold me and let me cry."

A daily habit of learning to EXPRESS GRATITUDE is a powerful way to build EMPATHY. Have a GRATITUDE BOARD in your home. Together with your child, learn to write down two or three things that you are grateful for each day. Learning to be grateful even for a smile is a great way to start. Look around, and know you are blessed.

EXPECTATIONS

No matter where we are and who we are, we have high expectations for our children. I have never once met a parent with low expectations. I have always struggled and continue to struggle in this area of parenting. As in the story of Goldilocks who tasted the three bears' porridge until she found the one of just the right temperature, our expectations for our children shouldn't be too high or too low, but just at the right level for their stage of development. Research is consistent in showing that parents always expect their children to do things they're not yet able to do and that they judge, blame, shame, and punish their children when their expectations are not met.

It is in this effort to set the "right level" that we enter into conflict. It is on this path that you must give it all as a parent to do your best. It is on this path that you must be realistic. You must remember that no matter who you are, you do not control outcomes nor do you control people. Especially not YOUR CHILD.

Remember to consider the following:

1. The individuality of your child. The abilities, needs, gifts, talents, and accomplishments of your child. The developmental stage, maturity, and level of understanding of your child.
2. The culture and environment in which you are raising your child. If you are a first- generation immigrant, there will be huge differences in how you were raised and how you will raise your child now. I meet parents every day who have very high levels of expectations of their children. I have been there myself. Learn to view your child, your circumstances, and your parenting style differently. Watch yourself if you brag about your own sense of sacrificing for the good of the family and consider your expectations reasonable. "I am doing so much for you and all I am asking is for you to listen and do what I am asking you to do."
3. The external influences and forces that impact your child. Friends and peers. The incredible influences of those who are in their inner circle of friendship and those others who want to penetrate that inner circle with new and different possibilities.
4. The reasonableness of your expectations. Are you expecting too much? Are you expecting a high level of performance and delivery from your child?
5. Negotiate. This is a powerful way to meet your expectations. Let go when you have to. Focus on the connection, not the task.

When your child fails or is unable to comply and conform to your expectations, you will find yourself in the most stressful place. You might find yourself bearing down on your child in many ways. Be conscious of this or it can take you down the path of deep despair. When this happens your child may do two things: accept your authority or defy your authority.

When we parent consciously we are able to watch ourselves and take positive and corrective measures to stop this from escalating. It's never too late. YOU CAN REPAIR THE RUPTURE.

Find small pockets of time to connect and renew your connection with your child. A movie, an ice cream sundae at the ice cream parlor, a moment of deep quiet and closeness at home. These are all small things you can do to get back on track to reconnect with your child.

You know yourself (or do you?), and you know your child best. As long as you are being INCLUSIVE and RESPECTFUL of your child's needs and wants, you will be on a great track. Be PATIENT, model EMPATHY. Take comfort in the knowledge that you can be your child's BEST FRIEND. Be that friend first.

7. UNDERSTANDING BEHAVIOR CHANGES—ASK FOR HELP

If you are well tuned into your child's needs, you will be able to effectively identify changes in your child's behaviors, attitudes, emotions, and actions. Do they arise from neglect? Other people's influences? Abuse, or just the process of growing up?

If you build a strong foundational relationship of connection and compassion with your children, trust me, you will be their "go to" person in times of need or uncertainty. As I have said before, your child is looking for SAFETY and TRUST—provide it.

Are you maintaining a safe, secure environment in your home where you can engage and encourage your child to express himself?

Mood swings, depression-like symptoms, a desire to grow a beard, sudden talk of travel to distant lands, names of new friends and acquaintances, new plans, changes in appearance, changes in language and expression can all be causes for concern.

There is no right or wrong way to look at the transformation and changes. Be honest, keep an open door, and encourage conversation. Taboos and orders, anger and resentment can only aggravate and disconnect you from your child.

Inquire, why?

If you are not able to provide solutions or see changes in behaviors that you find alarming, please reach out for help. Don't feel ashamed to take your child to a doctor who can screen for signs of drug and alcohol abuse or other unexpected issues. Get counseling, for you and your child. Have or create a close group of parents and friends with whom you can discuss your concerns freely. Sometimes you cannot do it alone. Asking for help from professionals is the first important step if you notice signs of drug and alcohol abuse. Stigma should be the least of your concerns, even though that may be your biggest hurdle. You may be thinking that it is disgraceful and shameful to go to a mental health specialist. But that is not necessarily what others are perceiving.

Your efforts to shroud everything in secrecy will not benefit you or your child. In one study of 156 parents and spouses of first-admission patients, half reported making efforts to conceal mental illness from others. Ask yourself, what is there to be ashamed about? Is it the cultural sanctioning? Reach out. You will be amazed to know how many people genuinely care about your welfare.

8. SETTING LIMITS

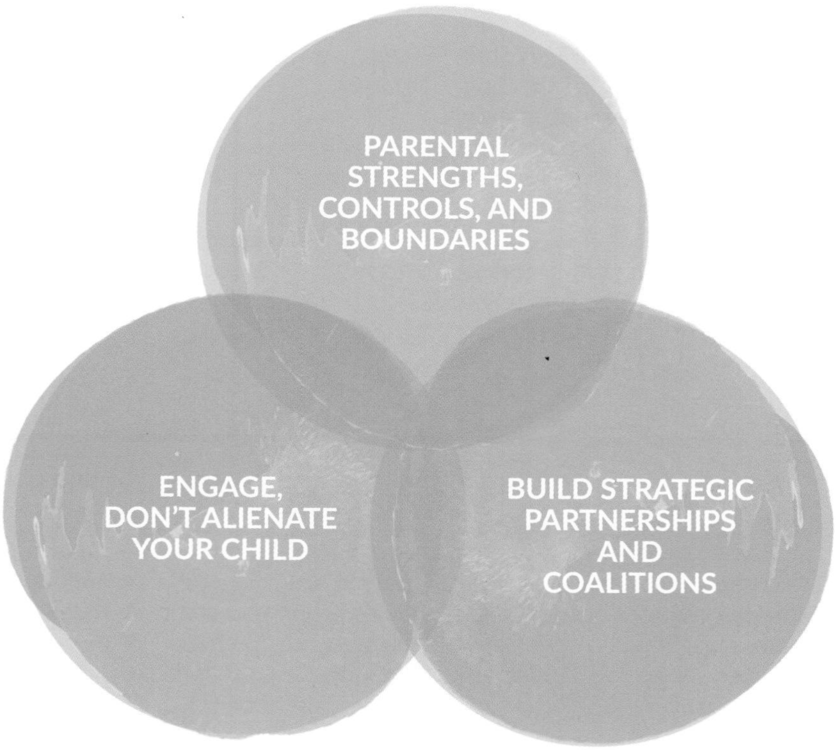

PARENTAL STRENGTHS, CONTROLS, AND BOUNDARIES

I have noticed, that in times of crisis, parents focus on the problem and not on the solution. Some initial steps you could take should include, but not be limited to, the following:

1. Lay strong boundaries regarding the use of the Internet by your child. In extreme circumstances you might even have to sign off from your Internet service provider. Place the computer in a place in your house like the family room or your office, where you can supervise and monitor your child's Internet use. This should include the cell phone, text messaging, chats, social networking sites, and instant messaging. Have a password that is known only to you, or require your child to share his/her password with you. You must be the first link in the chain to prevent the recruiters from exploiting your child on the Internet.
2. Your child must be exposed to proper knowledge of scripture and their faith so that they can distinguish between the falsehoods promoted by extremist groups online. Introduce your child to a mentor or religious scholar who is not only an authority on the text and its context, but is one who encourages critical engagement with the text. And you must encourage your child to ask questions. The Prophet Muhammad (pbuh) is known to have said, "Reason must be at the root of my faith." Explain to your child the context of the passages, and show how they have been distorted to justify violent extremism. Most of all, emphasize to your children that the politics and brutality of extremist groups do not represent Islam and the world's 1.6 billion Muslims.
3. Search in your community for other programs and classes that are available to you and your child.
4. Get to know the peers, friends, and associates of your child. Talk to their parents. Get to know their families. Create a strong net around the children who might already be exposed to this threat.
5. Have a very strong positive reinforcement system in your home. Acknowledge every effort and change your child makes. Recognize and reward your child for participating in productive activities.

It's very important to educate children and explain to them what role they can truly play to transform the world. Do everything in your power and ability to prevent your child from being influenced by any extreme ideology.

ENGAGE, DON'T ALIENATE, YOUR CHILD THROUGH EFFECTIVE INTERVENTION

Education and Engagement must be foundational to effective intervention. You must focus on RESTORATION, NOT what punishment he deserves. You must remember that even a broken clock is right twice a day. Understand his personal challenges. Empathy and listening are powerful tools for you to navigate this phase.

CREATE A VISION STATEMENT FOR THE YOUTH IN YOUR COMMUNITY

In the summers I teach classes at the Islamic Center. I always encourage the youth to come up with an acronym to represent their learning goals and values in my class. I remember one such acronym the youth chose: LAKERS. (The Los Angeles Lakers are a famous professional basketball team.) The youth then broke into six smaller groups and decided what the acronym should represent to them.

L meant LISTEN
A meant APPRECIATE
K meant KNOWLEDGE, a commitment to learn
E meant EMPATHY for all
R meant RESPECT
S meant SUPPORT one another.

LAKERS

BUILD STRATEGIC PARTNERSHIPS AND COALITIONS with groups and associations, third-party specialists, and community leaders who are leading with initiatives to prevent the recruitment process. Do not wait for them to come to you. Be vigilant. Ensure your child and other youth in your community are recognized and rewarded for their participation.

LEAD A PEACE INITIATIVE IN YOUR COMMUNITY. Begin in your home by scheduling a gathering of a few people; exchange ideas, and share material and resources.. Be sure to invite all the youth in your neighborhood. Open the gathering to questions and discussion. LISTEN closely to what your child and the youth have to say. Understand and acknowledge their NEEDS and FEELINGS.

You may use WISE Up to facilitate an open discussion and create an educational awareness campaign to inform other members of the community of the solutions to the growing problem of extremism. Make sure to invite youth members of the community to attend so that they can gain information to protect themselves and their peers.

IDENTIFY A COMMUNITY LIAISON to act as a buffer between the community and law/state agencies. A specialist or someone with experience with law enforcement and youth would be perfect to act as an intermediary if a parent suspects their child of participating in unlawful behavior. Seek advice from the liaison and strategize the best methods of getting your child the help they need.

It is normal to worry about the repercussions of speaking out. What will happen to my job? Will speaking out affect our standing in the community? Will my other children be seen as the brothers and sisters of an extremist? Rather than keeping your concerns to yourself over fear of how others will see you, speak out and seek help for your child. The consequences of not doing so could very well be worse. And remember, no matter what, show empathy to your children and those around you.

CONCLUSION

I wish your parenting journey every success. Even though this is the only job that you will be called upon to perform without any experience, you will do well. When we make every effort to feel compassion and understanding, our hearts will continue to open and our minds will continue to learn. Don't rely ONLY on your LOVE for your child. Build CONNECTION. Please refrain from expecting your child to achieve more and take on responsibilities that they are incapable of taking on. Be realistic, parent yourself, ask the tough questions about you.

I made many mistakes myself and learned much on the job. Sometimes we must remember that there is no perfect parenting—we might only have perfect moments in parenting. Children are not asking for much, they are only asking for our heart. It is our time. Let's accept personal responsibility for the world we want to create for ourselves and our children.

> Kindness is a mark of faith. Those of you who are not kind have not faith.
>
> **PROPHET MUHAMMAD (PBUH)**

Let's create a movement and build momentum.

Bullying Prevention

AMEENA JANDALI and **HENRY MILLSTEIN** of **ING** explain how bullying has taken a special toll on Muslim students, post-9/11. This can result in shame or alienation for the Muslim student, which is detrimental to academic performance and mental health and can contribute to extremist recruitment.

KEY TAKEAWAYS
- Muslim students are bullied at twice the rate at which students in the US overall report being bullied.
- Parental intervention and understanding at home are extremely important to support the child.
- Teacher bias prevents students from speaking up or defending themselves and creates isolation in schools.

Bullying is a problem in schools across the United States, affecting students of all backgrounds. According to Stopbullying.gov, between 1 in 4 and 1 in 3 students in the United States say they have been bullied at school. A 2011 study by the National Education Association and Johns Hopkins University found that 41 percent of school staff witnessed bullying frequently, while 45 percent of teachers said that a student had reported bullying incidents to them within the past month.[1] This is not without consequences. Bullying has an impact not only on the victim, but on all the students witnessing it as well, threatening a sense of security for all students. Bullied children are more likely to suffer from behavioral and emotional problems. Additionally, bullying increases school absenteeism and school violence. A study in the *Journal of Adolescence* found that bullying is linked to "antisocial behavior, low prosocial behavior, school failure, and substance abuse" for the bully and "psychosomatic complaints, school absenteeism, low self-esteem, anxiety, loneliness, and depression" for the victim.[2]

STUDENTS AT RISK OF BEING BULLIED

While anybody can be a victim of bullying, some students are more likely to be bullied than others. They include, but are not limited to, the following types of students:

- Students perceived to be "different" from their peers, such as those who are overweight, those who are new to a school, or those who do not dress "cool."
- Students belonging to an ethnic or religious minority.
- Students perceived to be weak, to have low self-esteem, or to lack confidence.
- Students who have few friends or who are unpopular.

BULLYING OF MUSLIM STUDENTS

Bullying has taken a special toll on Muslim students in the post-9/11 environment. Much of the bullying has been verbal, with common slurs such as "terrorist" and "raghead." This harassment generally spikes after a domestic or global event involving terrorism or terrorists. For example, after the death of Osama bin Laden, one study found that the prevalence of bullying against Muslim students rose. One participant in the study reported that she was repeatedly called a "terrorist" and asked if she was sad that her so-called "leader" had died. The study reports that other Muslim students had similar experiences after the death of Saddam Hussein.[3] It

[1] Michaela Gulemetova, Darrel Drury, and Catherine P. Bradshaw, "National Education Association Bullying Study," Colleagues 6:2 (2011); http://scholarworks.gvsu.edu/colleagues/vol6/iss2/1.
[2] Rebecca Bondü, Tobias Rothmund, and Mario Gollwitzer, "Mutual Long-Term Effects of School Bullying, Victimization, and Justice Sensitivity In Adolescents," *Journal of Adolescence* 48 (2016): 62–72.
[3] Dupper, David R., Shandra Forrest-Bank, and Autumn Lowry-Carusillo. "Experiences of Religious Minorities in Public School Settings: Findings from Focus Groups Involving Muslim, Jewish, Catholic, and Unitarian Universalist Youths." *Children and Schools* 37.1 (2015): 37–45 9. CINAHL Plus with Full Text. April 29, 2016.

stands to reason that these trends are not limited to these two events but would reflect common trends of issues related to terrorism. Where there is a public outcry over terrorism, there is a likely corresponding increase in Islamophobic bullying in schools.

More recently, the rise of Daesh and nonstop media coverage about it, combined with virulent anti-Muslim rhetoric by political figures, has greatly increased fear and bigotry against Muslims. This has also resulted in a spike in reports of bullying of Muslim students, even prior to the Paris and San Bernardino attacks. A recent study by CAIR showed that 55 percent of Muslim students in California—one of the most liberal and diverse areas in the country—reported having been bullied on account of their religion or ethnicity; this is twice the rate at which students in the United States overall report having been bullied.[4] The following are a couple of incidents that represent what have become common occurrences in schools across the country.

> "Are you part of the 9/11 or are you ISIS?" "Did you ever kill anyone?" "Are you going to bomb this place?" These are some typical questions that 12-year-old Abdu Rahman Mohamed says he's been asked by his non-Muslim classmates.

"'Are you part of the 9/11 or are you ISIS?' 'Did you ever kill anyone?' 'Are you going to bomb this place?' These are some typical questions that 12-year-old Abdu Rahman Mohamed says he's been asked by his non-Muslim classmates week after week in his Long Beach, California, school, he told youth radio VoiceWaves.org last week."[5]

"Rasmia Shuman remembers when the schoolyard conversation among her ninth-grade peers in Redwood City turned to the Islamic State, the extremist group commonly known as ISIS. 'I kind of knew it would go bad because I was the only Muslim in the group,' said Rasmia, a 15-year-old sophomore at Summit Charter School. As the talk escalated, a classmate pointed at Rasmia, who wears the traditional Muslim head scarf or hijab, and simply said, 'You're ISIS.' Then he walked away. The verbal attack was a gut punch to the soft-spoken teen, but across California, such harassment is not uncommon for students who share her religion."[6]

TYPES OF BULLYING

This bullying can take a variety of forms. The CAIR report about bullying of Muslim students in California schools found the following:

VERBAL ABUSE: Fifty-two percent of Muslim students in California report having been subjected to verbal abuse on account of their religion. One of the most common slurs is "terrorist," while Muslim girls who wear a headscarf are called names like "raghead."

CYBERBULLYING: Nineteen percent of Muslim students in California report having received offensive comments through e-mail or text message, or on websites and apps like Facebook, Twitter, Snapchat, and Instagram.

PHYSICAL ABUSE INVOLVING HIJAB: Twenty-nine percent of hijab-wearing students in California reported having experienced offensive touching or pulling of their hijab.

OTHER PHYSICAL ABUSE: Nine percent of Muslim students in California report having been assaulted or otherwise physically bullied on account of their religion.

---

[4] Council on American-Islamic Relations, "California, Mislabeled: The Impact of School Bullying and Discrimination on California Muslim Students," https://ca.cair.com/sfba/wp-content/uploads/2015/10/CAIR-CA-2015-Bullying-Report-Web.pdf.

[5] Michael Lozano, "'They Call Us Terrorists'—Muslim Students Bullied in California Schools" (December 4, 2015), http://voicewaves.org/2015/12/they-call-us-terrorists-muslim-students-bullied-in-california-schools/. See also Kristina Rizga, "This Is What It's Like to Be a Muslim Schoolkid in America Right Now," *Mother Jones* (December 9, 2015).

[6] Jill Tucker, "Study Finds majority of Muslims Have Faced Bullying at School," *San Francisco Chronicle* (October 30, 2015), http://www.sfchronicle.com/education/article/With-education-and-humor-taking-aim-at-bullying-6601785.php.

DISCUSSIONS OF CURRENT EVENTS

While bullying generally takes place in unsupervised areas such as during lunch or in the hallways, verbal harassment of Muslim students often follows current event discussions in which the class discusses events relating to Muslim extremists. The following article, published in *Voices of NY*, represents one such incident:

"Amina Adekola, 15, was in her 10th-grade global class learning about the Boko Haram massacres when another student asked, 'Why are all Muslims terrorists?' She said that she wanted to stand up for herself, tell him that she was a Muslim and not a terrorist. But she was embarrassed in the face of what she felt was an overwhelming majority. 'About 90 percent of the kids in my class feel that way,' she said."[7]

As noted previously, bullying like this, especially if ongoing, results in a sense of shame for the victim. This is particularly true with young victims, who are often unsure or ambivalent about their identity. Students may be afraid to discuss these issues with parents or teachers for fear of repercussions, increased harassment, or ostracism.

TEACHER BIAS OR DISCRIMINATION

Even worse than student bullying is open or subtle prejudice on the part of a teacher or administrator. Issues as basic as properly pronouncing a student's name on the first day of school can set the stage for the remainder of the year. The following incidents reflect a trend that has also been widely reported by Muslim students across the country who complain of both teacher prejudice and the use of biased teaching materials.

"Earlier this year, a high school teacher in Richmond, Texas, sent all his students home with a new study guide he had created, with the title, 'Islam/Radical Islam (Did You Know).' In the study guide, which had not been approved by the school, the economics teacher presented fictional statements as if they were facts, including, '38% of Muslims believe people that leave the faith should be executed.' The teacher also wrote up instructions for what to do 'if taken hostage by radical Islamists.'"[8]

"In Weston, Florida, a high school French teacher allegedly called one 14-year-old Muslim student a 'rag-head Taliban' in February. The student's father, Youssef Wardani, a software engineer and an immigrant from Lebanon, said his son, an honor roll student, now hates going to school."[9]

Students who experience teacher bias may feel afraid or embarrassed to bring this subject up with an adult, even their parents, for fear that they will react by calling and admonishing the teacher or staff member, which could make matters worse. Students are left with few or no options to address or even discuss an issue that is making their life miserable.

Amina Adekola, 15, was in her 10th-grade global class learning about the Boko Haram massacres when another student asked, "Why are all Muslims terrorists?"

BULLYING PREVENTION AT SCHOOL

Bullying is, however, not an insoluble problem. Bullying prevention efforts, at home and at school, make a big difference—studies show reductions of fifty percent or more in student reports of being bullied and bullying others. The first step in addressing the problem of bullying in schools is recognizing that it exists. The second step is implementing a zero-tolerance policy for any form of discrimination, bullying or harassment, whether from staff or students, with strictly enforced and clearly enunciated consequences. When bullying occurs, the response should be immediate and appropriate to the level of the bullying. If the problem persists,

[7] Southern Poverty Law Center, "Extreme Prejudice," *Teaching Tolerance* 51 (Fall 2015), http://www.tolerance.org/magazine/number-51-fall-2015/feature/extreme-prejudice.

[8] Rachel Bertsche, "Teacher Under Fire for Anti-Muslim Lesson," *Yahoo News* (April 9, 2015), http://news.yahoo.com/teacher-under-fire-for-anti-muslim-lesson-115945553072.html?nf=1.

[9] Ann Henson Feltgen, "Weston Teacher Faces Discipline over Alleged Slur of Muslim Student," *Miami Herald* (March 2, 2015), http://www.miamiherald.com/news/local/community/broward/article11924603.html.

there should be mediation with all parties involved, including the parents, who should be enlisted to address this issue with their children.

There are also a number of steps that schools can take proactively to prevent bullying and encourage a more tolerant and harmonious environment. These include the following:

- Promote school-wide programs and activities that encourage tolerance and diversity.
- Address the issue of prejudice and its roots in the classroom or throughout the school through discussions, posters, assemblies, or other forums.
- Have students relate and discuss their own experience with discrimination or bullying and brainstorm possible solutions.
- Invite guest speakers into classrooms or for assemblies to address common stereotypes and misconceptions about Arabs and Muslims.
- Exhibit sensitivity in classroom discussions relating to the war on terror or any other conflict concerning people of Muslim-majority regions, especially during a time of crisis.

Extra diligence in monitoring a spike in bullying is warranted during a crisis situation or if students exhibit signs of harassment.

ADDRESSING TEACHER BIAS

It is also important for teachers and staff to acknowledge and address their own personal views on current events or related issues that may compromise educators' or employees' academic responsibility to be objective and neutral in education and in their interactions with all students. Potential prejudice should be addressed with proactive efforts such as staff sensitivity trainings or cultural diversity workshops for teachers and faculty and continuous follow-up with staff. Teachers who exhibit bias or who make inappropriate comments about a student's dress, religion, or traditions should be held accountable and dealt with in a manner appropriate to the misconduct.

BULLYING PREVENTION AT HOME

Behavior patterns are established at home from early childhood, and the home is the first teacher. At the heart of bullying behavior is a lack of compassion, empathy, and respect toward others and an inability to control one's anger. Parents who lead by example by treating their children and others with courtesy and respect will raise children who will emulate that behavior; they will neither be bullies nor witness bullying without doing something about it.

IF YOUR CHILD IS BEING BULLIED AT SCHOOL

Your child has the right to be safe at school. If your child is experiencing bullying:

- Request and review the school's or school district's bullying policies and follow the procedures outlined in the policy.
- Inform the school about your concerns right away.

Go up the chain of command at the school and in the district if the bullying does not stop. You are your child's strongest advocate.

SIGNS THAT YOUR CHILD IS BEING BULLIED

Even if your child doesn't share this with you, there are some obvious signs that a child is being bullied at school. Parents should be concerned if their child refuses to go to school or avoids activities that he or she previously enjoyed.

Other signs include:

- A decline in academic performance.
- A decline in self-esteem and confidence.
- Negative self-statements by the child.
- Depression, crying spells, stomachaches, headaches, or other vague physical complaints.
- Having few friends and being socially isolated.
- Coming home hungry, with no explanation of what happened to his or her lunch or lunch money.
- Unexplained bruises and scrapes.

Signs of cyber-bullying include:

- Being upset after being online.
- Being upset after viewing a text message.

IF YOUR CHILD IS A WITNESS TO BULLYING

Most kids are neither a bully nor a victim of bullying, but are often a witness to bullying. How they choose to respond can make an enormous difference in whether or not bullying is tolerated. Here are some ways for a witness to help stop bullying:

- Alert the teacher, staff member, or school principal that bullying is occurring.
- Show support for the victim.

- Stand up for the victim publicly in the presence of the bully.
- Enlist others to support the victim.

Teach your child not to repeat gossip even if he or she thinks it is true, as it can hurt someone and encourage continued harassment and bullying.

HELP PROTECT YOUR CHILD

It is the parents' job to ensure that their children are happy and well adjusted at school and that they are neither bullying others nor becoming a victim of bullying. Bullies generally avoid picking on students who show self-confidence and have a positive self-image. Parents need to instill in their children a sense of dignity, self-worth, confidence, and self-respect. Children who have both high self-esteem and an understanding of positive, non-violent responses to abusive behavior will know how to set limits that will put a stop to bullying if they are targeted. One of the best ways to protect children from bullying is to discuss the issue and present ways—both verbal and nonverbal through body language—to convey to a bully that they are not vulnerable or susceptible to bullying. To that end we suggest the following:

- Always keep the lines of communication open with your child. Parents who treat their children with respect make it easy for them to talk to their parents.
- Be an advocate for your child by instilling confidence in them that will help them to ward off bullies.
- Ask your child about his or her day.
- Get to know his or her friends.
- Volunteer at his or her school.
- Get to know the staff at the school.
- Encourage and help your child build friendships. Bullies often target loner kids.
- Explain to your child the difference between "tattling" and "telling." "Tattling" means reporting something to get someone in trouble, while "telling" means letting adults know when someone is in danger.
- Encourage your child to have a buddy system to and from school, at school, on the bus, and in the neighborhood. Children provide support for each other.
- Enroll your child in a self-defense course. These courses promote self-discipline, self-control, increased confidence, and a positive self-image.
- Teach your child skills for self-protection and boundary setting by making and practicing a plan with you at home. Roleplay different scenarios. Many resource guides are available for these programs.
- Seek professional help for your child if her or his anxiety or fear becomes overwhelming.

BULLYING PREVENTION IN MOSQUES

A mosque can serve as a good place for youth to make friends, share ideas, and enhance their religious identity. It is important to create a welcoming atmosphere for youth and to be aware that bullying can occur anywhere, including at the mosque.

- Make sure that bullying is not occurring at the mosque, especially in the hallways or outside where adults are not present.
- Create safe spaces for youth to talk about their experiences of harassment or bullying at school and brainstorm solutions.
- Invite experts to discuss the topic with parents and children and to present ways to prevent bullying at school. Consider holding a workshop at your mosque.[10]

A positive self-image and a respectful attitude toward others are key to preventing bullying. Mosques should aim to increase young American Muslims' Islamic literacy to help them respond to frequently asked questions about Islam, as well as to prevent extremism, which is often based on ignorance of authentic religious teachings; build confidence in their Islamic identities based on a sound understanding of their faith; and inspire action toward bridge-building between American Muslims and people of other faiths or those of no faith. The goal of such mosque-led programs should be to empower Muslim students to stand up to bullying and discourage them from turning to bullying behavior themselves.

10 For more information, see: http://www.ing.org/youth-trainings.

Counteracting Hate Speech

SCOTT COOPER uses the research and methodology of **RACHEL BROWN** to discuss how to enter into a dialogue with someone who may be engaging in dangerous speech or hate speech in order to promote positive and constructive change.

In today's highly polarized political climate, it seems that hate speech, dangerous speech, and repercussions related to such types of speech are becoming increasingly prevalent and visible. In 2015, the number of anti-Muslim hate crimes rose 67 percent.[1] And from then until now—directly coinciding with Donald Trump's campaign and election—the number of anti-Muslim hate groups has risen 197 percent, with 101 hate groups currently in operation across the U.S.[2] These statistics exemplify the direct manifestations of hate speech—defined as targeted speech aimed at directly harming a group—and dangerous speech—defined as any form of expression that increases the likelihood that its audience will condone or participate in violence against members of a certain group. The impact of both is highly significant as they directly influence and play on popular attitudes, emotions, social norms, behaviors, experiences, and the interpretations of problems and formulation of solutions. Thus, when attempting to constructively counteract dangerous speech and its manifestations, a number of steps must be taken for effective action.

First, it is necessary to assess the situation so that one may tailor solutions to the specific set of problems he or she is confronted with. In assessing the context, we must ask, What content is being created? Who is tapping into such content? How is the content being spread? In answering these questions, it becomes easier for us to not only know what we are up against but how we can analyze and counteract that rhetoric. To do this, we must first ask, Who in the audience can we engage with? How can we reach the larger audience? and How can we reach maximum engagement? Addressing these questions will allow us to identify modes of transmission and communication and points of connection within the groups we hope to reach. Once the context and the situation are assessed, we can most effectively join in a dialogue that may promote positive and constructive change.

When entering into such a dialogue, it is important for us to be wary of a number of factors:

1 Consider the person's emotions

People who take part in hate speech are probably experiencing fear, parochial empathy, anger, disgust, or a combination of these emotions. We must listen to them in a nonjudgmental way, validate these emotions, and attempt to move them forward from these emotions in a more constructive, less damaging way. We must realize that in order to help someone back away from hate or dangerous speech, we need to give them a way to feel a sense of belonging to an alternative narrative.

SCOTT COOPER serves as Director of National Security Outreach for Human Rights First, a non-profit, nonpartisan international human rights organization based in New York, Washington D.C., Houston, and Los Angeles, that challenges America to live up to its ideals. He leads Human Rights First's efforts to build partnerships with members of the military and national security communities as well as national security-focused think tanks and research institutions. Prior to joining Human Rights First, Scott spent a career in the Marine Corps, serving five tours in Iraq, two in Afghanistan, one in Europe, and one in the Western Pacific. An expert on civil-military relations, air power, and national security issues, he has published work in The Washington Post, The Washington Quarterly, Policy Review, Proceedings, and The Marine Corps Gazette.

[1] U.S. Department of Justice. "Incidents and Offenses." Federal Bureau of Investigation, October 20, 2016. Web: July 11, 2017.
[2] Southern Poverty Law Center. "Hate Map." N.d. Web: July 11, 2017.

2 Remember that changing beliefs is hard

As humans, we can be very set in our ways and people may react strongly when asked to reconsider personal values and opinions that they hold central to their identity and being. This type of challenging information can be understood as a psychological threat. It is important to try to understand their self-image and what triggers are connected to that image. When presenting your perspective and information, it is most productive to frame it using the values, beliefs, and emotions that the person you're engaging with already holds. You can use storytelling as a device to open people to new perspectives that they wouldn't usually be open to in an argument.

3 Respect that people have "sticky identities"

As humans, we have "sticky identities," meaning that we have parts of our identity that we feel we cannot change. Those who participate in hate speech may feel that their core identity is under attack by some outside group. One way to ameliorate this reality is by understanding and respecting people's grievances (for example, economic or political grievances) and providing them with alternative ways to address those grievances (for example, through collective civic engagement). In addition, we must avoid shaming people, as this will likely increase their defenses and isolate them from our perspective.

4 Combat misinformation

Hate speech is, more often than not, predicated upon misinformation and misinterpretation. The best way to combat the spread of misinformation is to catch it and correct it early; however, this is not always the most realistic solution. When directly confronting the misinformation, it is beneficial to avoid negative framing (for example, by saying that something did "not" happen) and repetition of falsehoods. Doing these will continue to give legitimacy to the misinformation, even though you are trying to correct it. When correcting, the most effective way to undermine the credibility of the source of misinformation, use positive framing, make sure the correction comes from a trusted source, and offer reinterpretations of the existing evidence used to back up the misinformation. If you offer additional evidence, check your facts! Make sure the source is credible and will benefit your contribution.

5 Acknowledge the impact of social norms

We are continuously affected by the social norms that exist all around us. The awareness of these norms may cause us to be influenced by social pressure and norms based on identities. Social norm perceptions make it difficult for someone to speak out against hate speech for they believe that most people in their personal group approve of such speech. Or someone may be unable to identify the danger of participating in hate speech as it is perceived as the norm. Help make it safe for people to speak up, either by correcting misperceptions (for example, someone might think his or her peers approve of dangerous speech, when in reality they don't) or providing alternative spaces for people to speak out with social support.

In the U.S. today, an "us versus them" narrative colors some interpersonal relationships, especially with Muslims in the aftermath of the events of 9/11. This rhetoric contributes to a vicious cycle of dehumanization as well as a push for collective blame and guilt attribution—blaming all members of a group for the actions of a few, which often leads to people being expected to apologize for the actions of others of their group. In order to combat this narrative and the dangerous speech that has grown out of it, our solutions must directly counteract this dehumanization process. Through respect for people's various identities and the channeling of emotions and passion toward positive outlets, may we find a common ground upon which a conversation may take place. [3]

[3] This article has been adapted and reprinted with permission: Brown, Rachel. (Producer). (2017). Countering Hate Speech [Video webinar]. July 11, 2017.

Bystander Intervention: Making Public Places Safer

EMILY MAY explains how when any part of our society gives license to bigotry, we must stand up to it. Unfortunately, acts of violence and street harassment against Muslims have increased by 67 percent between 2014 and 2015, with incidents such as women getting their hijabs torn off and mosques being set on fire. What's worse than being targeted for harassment because of your race, sex, religion, color, gender, size, orientation, disability, religion, or origin? Being targeted while surrounded by a bunch of strangers who choose to remain passive bystanders. Below are common excuses for inaction and how to overcome them:

"It's Not My Problem"
Street harassment is everyone's problem. Even if you've never been a target, the odds are that your loved ones, friends and co-workers have been. Ask them. If you care about making the world safe for them, it's your responsibility to do something when you see it happening.

"Nobody Else is Doing Anything"
It's that kind of thinking that allows a whole crowd to wait for "someone else" to act. It takes courage to the first to speak up for what's right.

"But it's a cultural thing."
Street harassment might be normalized in certain circles, but it's never okay.

"I Can't Make A Difference"
For targets of harassment, the response of bystanders makes a HUGE difference in their day. While your inaction or reluctance to get involved could magnify the effects of harassment, support the target and help prevent future street harassment.

"It's Harmless, Right?"
Verbal harassment can make targets feel uncomfortable, threatened or in danger and can quickly escalate to violence or physical assault. The effects are very real, to everyone who lives their life aware that they are not safe in public.

"I Don't Know What To Do"
We've got you covered. Read on.

EMILY MAY is executive director of Hollaback!, which she co-founded in New York City in 2005. Under her leadership, Hollaback! has scaled to over 50 cities in 25 countries. Emily brings a fresh perspective to social action in the digital age: she argues that the Internet gives us new opportunities to tackle injustice by transforming discrimination from a lonely experience into a piece of a larger, public movement. Emily believes that through the power of storytelling, decentralized leadership, and deep empathy we can disrupt cycles of hate and create a world where everyone has the right to feel safe and confident. An Ashoka Fellow and Prime Movers Fellow, she has won over ten awards for her work, including the TEDCity 2.0 Prize. She recently co-founded HeartMob, Hollaback!'s platform designed to support people being harassed online.

5 Ds Of Bystander Intervention

EMILY MAY lists the many ways in which an individual can help a victim of harassment. Research by Cornell's International Labor Relations school found that as little as a knowing glance shared with the target can reduce the trauma associated with harassment, while the presence of bystanders who do nothing can actually increase the trauma. The key to successful bystander intervention is knowing that you have options and using them. Below are Hollaback!'s 5 Ds of Bystander Intervention.

DISTRACT

Creating a distraction can help de-escalate the situation by bringing the person doing the harassment "out of the moment." Examples include asking for the time, dropping your coffee cup, pretending you're lost—really, anything.

DELAY

Intervention doesn't always need to happen while the harassment is happening. After the harassment is over, ask the person if they are okay, or if there is anything you can do to help. This one is powerful because it puts control of the situation back into the hands of the person who was harassed. It makes them feel less alone, and reduces trauma.

DIRECT INTERVENTION

Calmly let the harasser know that what they are doing is wrong, but do not escalate the situation. The focus of this intervention is to usher the person being harassed to safety. This can be risky and is not always the safest bet for everyone as the harassment can be redirected at the bystander, but there are some people who can do this.

DELEGATE

Ask a third party to help, since there is strength in numbers. We've heard stories of people finding support in someone else standing near them, or from a transit employee, a teacher, or a manager.

DOCUMENT

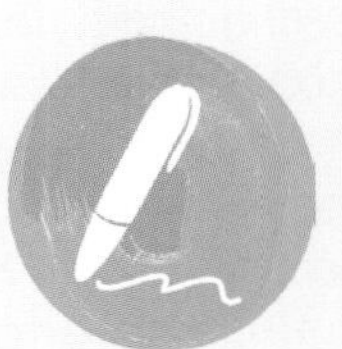

Use your phone to take video or photographs of the situation. Although this tactic can be incredibly useful in building awareness about harassment and catching the perpetrator, it can also be disempowering, and even dangerous, for the person being harassed if you share the footage you take without their consent. Be sure to share the footage with the person being targeted immediately after the incident and respect their wishes if they do not want anyone else to see it.

*Adapted from an article printed on CNN.com by Emily May in partnership with Kio Stark.

FAQs About Islam

AMEENA JANDALI AND HENRY MILLSTEIN

ISLAM, MUSLIMS, AND AMERICA

1. HOW DO AMERICAN MUSLIMS PARTICIPATE IN AMERICAN PUBLIC LIFE?

Though American Muslims are often viewed as recent immigrants, in fact, Muslims have been in America since before the founding of the U.S. Today, there are approximately 3-6 million Muslims (the number is difficult to estimate), with about half of this population born in the U.S. Today, American Muslims are present in aspects of American life, and occupy roles of taxi drivers, doctors, lawyers, academics, athletes, media personalities, and serve in the armed forces.

2. IS THERE A CONFLICT BETWEEN BEING A MUSLIM AND AN AMERICAN?

There is no conflict in being both Muslim and American. This question is like asking whether there is a conflict between being a Christian and an American. One is a religious identity, while the other is a national identity. Both impact one's life but play different roles in shaping one's identity.

While Muslims, like other immigrants, maintain their identity and culture in a multicultural, multi-religious society, the values they hold in common with the great majority of Americans —values such as respect for education, hard work, family, democracy, individual rights, and liberty—are mainstream American values.

3. DO AMERICAN MUSLIMS PRACTICE WAHHABISM?

Wahhabism began as an eighteenth-century movement in the Arabian Peninsula focused on what its founder, Muhammad ibn Abd al-Wahhab, perceived as the straying of Muslims from what he believed was "pure Islam." He formed an alliance with Ibn Sa'ud, a powerful tribe of Arabia, thereby expanding Wahhabism's reach. Wahhabism evolved into an ultra-conservative and puritanical form of Islam practiced mainly in Saudi Arabia, but it has spread to other Muslim-populated countries through well-funded literature and educational campaigns. Wahhabism has been adopted only in Saudi Arabia and the Gulf Arab states such as Qatar, the United Arab Emirates, and Kuwait. Out of the 1.6 billion Muslims worldwide, only 0.5 percent practice Wahhabism. Today, the vast majority of Muslims worldwide, including American Muslims, have not adopted Wahhabism in their communities.

4. IS IT TRUE THAT MANY MUSLIMS IN THE WORLD HATE AMERICA?

Muslims around the world generally admire America for its technology, liberty, education, innovations, and accomplishments. During the Arab Spring, protesters in Tunisia, Egypt, and Libya used American social media to advocate many American ideals, such as democracy. If some Muslims disagree with specific aspects of foreign or domestic policies, this cannot reasonably be described as "hatred" of America, and in fact many Americans are critical of some of these policies.

ISLAM AND TERRORISM

1. DOES ISLAM PROMOTE VIOLENCE?

No, the very name "Islam" is derived from the word "salaam," which means "peace through following God's guidance." Muslims commonly greet each other with "Salaam alaikum," which means "peace be upon you." One of the names of God is "As-Salaam," the "Giver of Peace." Islam allows for warfare only to protect people from aggression or to fight injustice, including injustice against people of other faiths.

2. WHAT IS THE ISLAMIC VIEW OF TERRORISM?

Islamic teachings view terrorism as the most extreme violation of the sanctity of life. Terrorism, which is defined as the use of violence and threats to intimidate, coerce, or exact retribution, especially for political purposes, flagrantly and directly violates at least three interrelated Islamic principles: respect for life, right to due process, and individual responsibility. Even during a state of war, it is forbidden to target innocent civilians, specifically women, children, and the elderly.

3. WHY DON'T MUSLIMS SPEAK OUT AGAINST TERRORISM?

Muslims have consistently and repeatedly denounced terrorism since before September 11, 2001. Unfortunately, these statements are rarely noted in American media, leading many people to think erroneously that Muslims have not denounced terrorism. See Page 33, for a comprehensive list of condemnations.

4. IS ISLAM A POLITICAL MOVEMENT OR IDEOLOGY?

No. Islam is a religion that focuses primarily on cultivating good character and drawing close to God. Like people of other faiths, American Muslims participate in American political life by voting in elections and getting involved in community organizing around issues or candidates.

ISLAM: AN ABRAHAMIC FAITH

1. DO MUSLIMS WORSHIP THE SAME GOD AS CHRISTIANS AND JEWS?

Yes, Muslims worship the same God; the God of the prophet Abraham. The word for God in Arabic is "Allah," which merely means "God," in the same way that "Allaha" in Aramaic and "Elohim" in Hebrew mean "God." The three faiths may differ on the way they think of God, but they still worship the same God of Abraham.

2. DOES ISLAM RECOGNIZE ANY OF THE BIBLICAL PROPHETS?

There are twenty-five prophets mentioned by name in the Qur'an. They include many who are mentioned in the Bible as well, including Adam, Noah, Lot, Abraham, Jacob, Joseph, Aaron, Moses, David, Job, Ezekiel, Jonah, Elijah, Zachariah, John, and Jesus. Of these prophets, Moses is mentioned in the Qur'an the most (136 times), followed by Abraham (69 times) and Jesus (59 times).

3. WHAT DO MUSLIMS BELIEVE ABOUT JESUS?

Muslims revere Jesus as a great prophet as well as a messenger who received revelation from God. They believe that he was, like all other prophets, only a human being, born to the Virgin Mary through an act of God, just as Adam is believed to have been created by God without a father or mother. The Qur'an describes Jesus' conception and birth, as well as his many miracles, such as healing the sick.

4. HOW DO MUSLIMS VIEW THE VIRGIN MARY?

Muslims believe that she is the Virgin Mother of the Prophet Jesus. An entire chapter in the Qur'an is

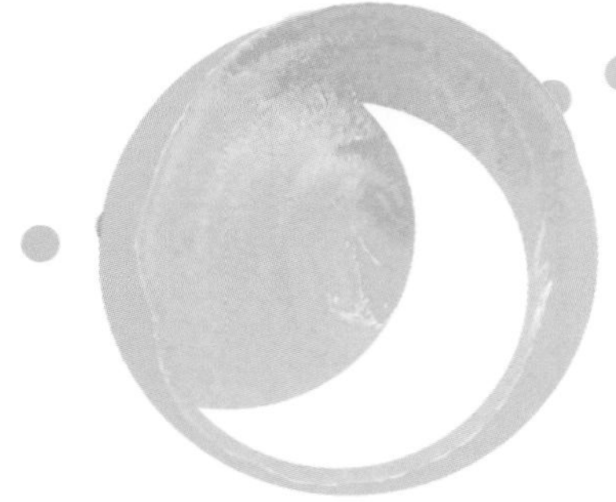

named after her. The chapter called Mary ("Maryam" in Arabic) and other verses in the Qur'an emphasize her piety, righteousness, and status as an exemplar for all people, male and female.

5. HOW DOES ISLAM VIEW OTHER RELIGIONS?

Respect for freedom of religion and conscience is a basic Islamic principle, and there are numerous Qur'anic verses that state that diversity, including religious diversity, is part of God's divine plan. Moreover, Muslims believe that the salvation of all people, Muslims included, lies with God alone.

6. ARE MUSLIMS OBLIGATED TO FORCIBLY CONVERT NON-MUSLIMS?

No. Forced conversion violates the Islamic principles of respect for human dignity and for freedom of religion and conscience. The Qur'an states, "there is no compulsion in religion" (2:256) and describes religious pluralism as part of God's plan. The existence of old churches, temples, and synagogues throughout the Muslim world in places like Egypt, Turkey, Palestine, Jordan, Syria, India, and Bosnia and the existence of minority religious populations in those areas demonstrate that this command was historically followed by many Muslim societies.

SHARI'AH, HONOR KILLINGS, AND OTHER MISUNDERSTOOD CONCEPTS

1. WHAT IS SHARI'AH?

Shari'ah comes from an Arabic word meaning "path to the water." Shari'ah is often translated as "Islamic law," and is based on the Qur'an and Hadith (sayings of the Prophet Muhammad) as well as scholarly interpretation. The bulk of Shari'ah deals with issues such as prayer, fasting, diet, and other daily activities.

Shari'ah is said to have six main objectives: to protect life, property, lineage, religion, intellect, and dignity. Shari'ah rulings or religious commandments are similar to the Ten Commandments. Both claim divine authority, but require human interpretation, are religiously binding, and in that sense are "sacred law." Only some of them are social and, of these, only a very few intersect with government law.

2. IS THERE A CONFLICT BETWEEN FOLLOWING THE CONSTITUTION AND FOLLOWING SHARI'AH?

The Constitution protects rights such as religious freedom, privacy, and private property. The Constitution allows people to follow their conscience as it relates to culture, behavior, and lifestyle, so long as they respect others' rights and their actions are compatible with the common good. American Muslims can follow Shari'ah (Islamic values and way of life) in the same way that other religious practitioners follow their values, rules, and lifestyles. The basic parts of Shari'ah (rituals; marriage and family life; charity and ethical business practices) are private and voluntary. Americans who voluntarily follow Shari'ah are simply exercising a part of American religious freedom. On the other hand, American Muslims are obligated to follow the law of the land and the U.S. Constitution.

3. IS SHARI'AH SUBSTITUTING THE U.S. CONSTITUTION?

With Muslims making up 1 percent to 2 percent of the American population there is little danger or evidence that Shari'ah is being substituted for U.S. law in American courts. The Constitution allows the personal practice of faith for Muslims—which is the main focus of Shari'ah—just as it does for observant Jews and Christians, including the observance of rules regarding personal worship and some family laws. However, no religious law can supersede state or federal law. Additionally, Shari'ah commands Muslims to observe the law of the land in which they dwell, and American Muslims generally have no desire to substitute any form of Islamic law for the Constitution or other American laws.

4. WHAT IS A FATWA?

A fatwa is an Arabic term that means a legal opinion or ruling given by a qualified jurist or Islamic scholar on issues pertaining to Islamic law that generally have not previously been decided. These opinions are nonbinding, and Muslims are free to choose the scholars whose rulings they follow.

5. WHAT IS *TAQIYYAH*? DOES ISLAM ENCOURAGE MUSLIMS TO LIE AND DECEIVE?

The term *taqiyyah* is little known to most Muslims. It comes from a principle developed during the early years of Islam when Muslims were being persecuted for their faith that allowed Muslims to conceal their religious beliefs or identity if they feared for their life or imminent harm because of their religion. Contrary to claims by some anti-Muslim activists, this principle in no way encourages Muslims to lie or deceive.

6. WHAT IS *DAW'AH*?

The Arabic term *daw'ah* means "to invite." In Islamic theology, it means to invite others to learn about Islam. Contrary to Daesh's belief that *daw'ah* means forced conversion, the Prophet Muhammad and the Qur'an forbid Muslims from forcing people to convert to Islam, as exemplified by the following verse: "*There is no compulsion in [the acceptance of] religion*" (2:256). Furthermore, early Muslims never practiced forced conversions and actually encouraged Muslims to learn about other faiths. To practice *daw'ah*, Muslims can engage in scholarship, participate in their communities as model citizens, and encourage interfaith conversations.

7. WHY DO MUSLIM COUNTRIES USE BARBARIC EXECUTION PRACTICES AND PUNISHMENTS LIKE BEHEADING, STONING, FLOGGING, AND CUTTING OFF HANDS?

These severe punishments, known as *hudud* (derived from *hadd*, meaning "limit"), are mentioned in the Qur'an to denote the maximum allowable punishments for specific crimes—not the preferred punishments. Such punishments were more commonly implemented 1,400 years ago in the tribal society of Arabia and even then were only rarely imposed because the conditions for imposing them were so strict. For instance, according to Islamic texts, the punishment of stoning for adultery can only be carried out if there is testimony by four eyewitnesses—a virtually impossible condition. Capital punishment for murder could be avoided if the victim's family agreed to monetary compensation for their loss—a normal practice in the society of the time.

These punishments are very similar to those found in the Hebrew Bible, which, like the Qur'an, spoke to social conditions and attitudes vastly different from those of later times and different places. Today, most Muslim-populated countries do not practice these punishments; within Islamic jurisprudence there is a broad spectrum of interpretations and applications of Islamic Law (Shari'ah) and, as a result, Muslim countries apply it in their own context. Out of the 57 nations that make up the Organization of Islamic Cooperation, 52 do not allow these maximin punishments. Where they are practiced, such as under the Taliban or Daesh, the required legal due process, which renders these punishments nearly impossible to enforce, is not followed, which is why many Muslims have condemned their use.

8. DO MUSLIMS BELIEVE THEY WILL BE REWARDED WITH 72 VIRGINS IN PARADISE?

While the Qur'an mentions "*houris*," which are described as wide-eyed beings in Paradise, it also mentions young men of eternal youth. However the Qur'an does not mention the number 72; while there are a few hadith or prophetic sayings that mention this number, they are not considered reliable, so most Muslims have never heard of them nor is it a topic that is generally emphasized or discussed. Furthermore, those who commit violence against innocent people are criminals, not martyrs.

WOMEN AND ISLAM

1. ARE MEN AND WOMEN EQUAL IN ISLAM?

According to normative teachings, men and women have freedom of choice and the same nature, origin, responsibility, and accountability before God. Historically, Islam promoted women's rights and granted women freedoms that they did not have before, such as the right to inherit property, conduct business, and have access to knowledge. Many Muslims, in America and elsewhere, advocate complete equality between men and women.

2. HOW ARE WOMEN TREATED IN MUSLIM COUNTRIES?

There are over 50 Muslim-majority countries in the world and they differ widely on women's rights, depending on a variety of factors, including political development, social and economic circumstances, and cultural views and practices; even within a single country, there may be considerable differences because of region (urban or rural), education, and even family circumstances.

In many Muslim-majority countries women are involved at the highest levels of education, employment, and politics, with many female physicians, engineers, lawyers, and other professionals. Muslim women have even been heads of state in Bangladesh, Indonesia, Turkey, Kosovo, and Pakistan. In other Muslim-majority countries, societies, or families, the position of women is very different and women's freedoms are seriously inhibited due to social, historical, and cultural conditions and oppressive patriarchal attitudes and practices.

3. DOES ISLAM CALL FOR OR ALLOW "HONOR KILLINGS"?

No. "Honor killings"—which refer to violence generally against girls or women by one or more family members who believe the victim has brought dishonor upon the family—are prohibited by Islam for a number of reasons. First, they violate the sanctity of life, which is considered sacrosanct; second, they fail to respect the right of due process for anyone accused of a crime; and, third, they contradict the principle that each individual is responsible for his or her own actions and that no individual or family member should be held responsible for the behavior of another. In fact, the Qur'an specifically prohibits even speaking ill of a woman without the testimony of four witnesses and calls for the punishment of one who does so without this virtually impossible to satisfy requirement.

4. WHY DO SOME MUSLIM WOMEN COVER THEIR HAIR AND FACES?

Many Muslim women accept an interpretation of the Qur'an established in the formative period of Islam that references Quranic verses and hadith (prophetic sayings) as obligating women to cover their hair and much of their body for the sake of modesty. Some Muslim women understand modesty to require covering their faces as well. Therefore, when in public, some women choose to wear a *hijab* (which covers the head and hair), while a smaller number wear a burqa (which covers the body and face), or *niqab* (covering for the face that leaves only the eyes exposed). Whether or not a Muslim woman wears one of the aforementioned articles of clothing is generally a matter of her personal choice and interpretation of her religion, and is often informed by cultural norms.

5. WHY IS IT THAT MUSLIM MEN CAN MARRY MORE THAN ONE WOMAN?

Muslims actually view monogamy as the ideal, as reflected in God's creation of life in pairs of male and female, which is mentioned in various Qur'anic verses. Where polygamy is illegal, as is the case in the U.S. and other Western as well as many Muslim countries, it is not lawful for Muslims to marry more than one wife.

The Qur'an only allows men to marry more than one wife on the condition that he treats all wives equally, a standard that the Qur'an warns is difficult to achieve, clearly implying a preference for monogamy. The Qur'an declared polygamy permissible 1,400 years ago in the context of war, when caring for orphans was a major concern; polygamy in this situation was supposed to assist widowed women with children who otherwise would have been left to fend for themselves in a brutally patriarchal social order.

Polygamy was, of course, not peculiar to the Arabian Peninsula; it was widespread in many cultures, including that represented by the Hebrew Bible, where some patriarchs are depicted as having multiple wives.

Know Your Resources

EDUCATIONAL DISCRIMINATION
PHONE 877-292-3804
EMAIL education@usdoj.gov
WEB www.justice.gov/crt/complaint/#three

EMPLOYMENT DISCRIMINATION
PHONE 800-669-4000
WEB www.justice.gov/crt

EQUAL EMPLOYMENT OPPORTUNITY COMMISSION
WEB www.eeoc.gov
EMAIL info@eeoc.gov

HOUSING DISCRIMINATION
PHONE 800-896-7743
EMAIL fairhousing@asdoj.gov

COMPLAINTS AGAINST INSTITUTIONS
INCLUDING JAILS, PRISONS, JUVENILE FACILITIES, ETC
PHONE 888-848-5306
WEB justice.gov/crt/publications/natorigin2.php#law

SPECIAL LITIGATION SERVICES
PHONE 877-218-5228
WEB justice.gov/crt/complaint/#eight

NATIONAL ORIGIN DISCRIMINATION
WEB www.justice.gov/crt/publications/natorigin2.php

COMPLAIN TS AGAINST STATE OR LOCAL LAW ENFORCEMENT AGENCIES
PHONE 202-514-4609
WEB justice.gov/crt/about/spl/documents/polmis.php

VOTING RIGHTS DISCRIMINATION
PHONE 800-253-3931
EMAIL Voting.Section@usdoj.gov
WEB justice.gov/crt/complaint/#nine

NATIONAL INSTITUTE OF MENTAL HEALTH
PHONE 866-615-6464
WEB www.nimh.nih.gov

NATIONAL SUICIDE PREVENTION LIFELINE
PHONE 800-273-8255
WEB www.suicidepreventionlifeline.org

NATIONAL CENTER FOR MISSING AND EXPLOITED CHILDREN
PHONE 800-THE-LOST (800-843-5678)
WEB www.missingkids.org/home

NATIONAL FAMILY PARTNERSHIP FOR DRUG FREE YOUTH
PHONE 800-544-5437
WEB nfp.org

PARENTS' RESOURCE INSTITUTE FOR DRUG EDUCATION (PRIDE)
PHONE 800-541-7946
WEB www.prideusa.org

DEPARTMENT OF HEALTH AND HUMAN SERVICES
PHONE 877-696-6775
WEB www.hhs.gov

NATIONAL CHILD ABUSE HOTLINE
PHONE 800-455-4453
WEB www.childhelp.org/hotline

NATIONAL DOMESTIC VIOLENCE HOTLINE
PHONE 800-799-7233
WEB www.thehotline.org

RUNAWAY/HOMELESS YOUTH
PHONE 1-800-786-2929
WEB www.acf.hhs.gov/programs/fysb

ALCOHOLICS ANONYMOUS
PHONE 212-870-3400
WEB www.aa.org

NATIONAL INSTITUTE ON DRUG ABUSE
PHONE 301-443-1124
WEB www.drugabuse.gov

NATIONAL INSTITUTE OF JUSTICE
PHONE 800-851-3420 or 301-519-5500
WEB www.nij.gov

SUBSTANCE ABUSE AND MENTAL HEALTH SERVICES
PHONE 800-662-4357 or 800-487-4889
WEB www.samhsa.gov

CHAPTER 9

Celebrating True Heroes and Heroines: Past and Present

Why Do We Need Heroes?

THE POTENTIAL OF HEROES IN THE FIGHT AGAINST DAESH

The heroic narrative has long been a central component of Muslim literature, lifestyle, and culture. Scholar John Renard contends that: "across the [Islamic] world the theme of the hero provides such a cultural constant. In popular and elite epics, folk and princely arts alike, Muslims have told and retold tales of exemplary figures."[1] As moral and behavioral models, heroes, both fictional and real, play a critical role in shaping the ideals of a community. Indeed, Renard suggests, "The hero provides an invitation to explore the breadth and depth of Islam's role in shaping the aspirations and values of many hundreds of millions of people."[2] At a time when Muslims are struggling to reclaim the power of defining these aspirations and values from extremists, identifying heroes in the Muslim community—both past and present—is essential to setting the record straight and providing Muslims with truly Islamic role models. Among the many factors that drive youth to extremism is the idea that they will quickly become a hero or martyr by devoting themselves to an extremist cause. Longing to be taken seriously and to make an impact in a world from which they feel alienated, many youth see violent extremism as the quickest path to influence and recognition, often in the form of martyrdom. The propaganda surrounding violent extremists acting in the name of a highly misconstrued version of Islam, as the heroes of the Muslim community while Western media fixates on their most violent acts, demonstrates to youth that extremist activity begets fame and recognition. It is from this context that the need for a shift in focus to true Islamic heroes arises. The identification and celebration of positive Muslim role models can take

[1] Renard, John. *Islam and the Heroic Image: Themes in Literature and Visual Arts*. Mercer University Press, 1999. 1.
[2] Ibid, 2.

"The heroic figure must. . . function as a model, an ideal of exemplary behavior as worked out in the context of adversity."[3]

JOHN RENARD

the spotlight off violent extremists and provide all youth—even those who feel alienated from their community—with a peaceful, just, and truly Islamic set of ideals to aspire to.

WHO IS A HERO?

So, what constitutes a "true" Muslim hero? In the words of scholar John Renard, "The heroic figure must. . . function as a model, an ideal of exemplary behavior as worked out in the context of adversity."[1] Heroes come from history, literature, legend, and even our everyday lives. Men and women hailing from a variety of backgrounds and circumstances, heroes demonstrate exemplary bravery, resourcefulness, and loyalty in the pursuit of justice. A hero goes above and beyond to help others, even if it puts him at risk. A hero is willing to show even enemies forgiveness and solidarity. A hero rises out of extenuating circumstances even when the odds are stacked against him. A hero uses his influence to demonstrate that love, not hate, is the driving force behind positive change. Whether a political figure, prophet, or next-door neighbor, a hero represents the ideals of a community. Muslim heroes conduct their lives in the spirit of the Prophet Muhammad, prioritizing the needs of others, the pursuit of justice, and their relationship with Allah. No act of heroism is too small, but any act in the name of violent extremism is never heroic. Despite messages to the contrary from Western media's fixation with Daesh militants, true Muslim heroes do exist and they are acting and improving their communities through service, forgiveness, leadership, sacrifice, and commitment to their faith. Below we profile exemplary Muslims, past and present, who demonstrate what it truly means to be a hero.

[3] Ibid, 9.

Muslim Heroes

Khadijah bint Khuwaylid

D: 620 CE

Khadijah bint Khuwaylid was known in the community of Mecca as at-Tahira, "the pure one." A woman of great integrity, intelligence, and spiritual depth, she became the wife of the Prophet Muhammad, peace and blessings be upon them both, before the responsibility of Prophethood came to him. Before marrying Muhammad, she had been married and widowed, and had developed and been conducting her own business in caravan trade. She was forty years old, when, being aware of Muhammad's sincere trustworthiness and skill, she hired him to oversee one of her trading caravans. At the time, Muhammad was twenty-five and of meager financial means. When her caravan returned from a very successful trading venture under his charge, through her cousin, Khadijah proposed marriage to Muhammad. At first Muhammad was hesitant to believe such a match was possible for someone of his financial state and limited tribal status—he had been orphaned at an early age and taken under the wing of his uncle. However, he did belong to the illustrious tribe of the noble Quraysh who for many years had held custodianship of the Kabah. Muhammad accepted Khadijah's offer.

A very happy marriage unfolded. More independent now that he was supported by Khadijah's love as well as her wealth, Muhammad would often retire to a nearby cave to meditate and pray for long periods. It was here, during the month of Ramadan in 610 CE that, at the age of forty, he received the first revelation of the Qur'an. Overwhelmed and concerned that perhaps he was losing his mind, he rushed home to Khadijah and told her to cover him with a blanket. She held him close and reassured him that he did not suddenly go crazy but that what had taken place was a tremendous spiritual experience. She went to her cousin, Waraqa, a Christian who was well versed in Jewish and Christian prophecy, and he confirmed for her that indeed Muhammad must be the messenger whose coming was referred to in the Jewish and Christian scriptures and that this must be the beginning of his mission as a prophet. Khadijah was the first to have faith in his mission as a prophet who had come to renew the message of monotheism of the whole Abrahamic tradition, coming both to the peoples of Arabia and as a mercy to all the worlds

> "Khadijah had been for the Holy Prophet more than a wife. She had placed all her wealth, which was considerable, at his disposal. She had given him love. She was the first person to be converted to Islam, and had been a pillar of strength for the Holy Prophet as well as the Muslims."

Through the early years of prophecy, Khadijah supported Muhammad when many in the community stood against him. Even though she and her family were eventually ostracized and forced to endure great hardship, she never wavered in her support of Muhammad and his mission. She was his constant companion and confidant and welcomed and helped to support all who joined with them in the newly awakening faith.

CAMILLE ADAMS HELMINSKI is Co-Director and Co-Founder of the Threshold Society, a non-profit organization rooted within the traditions of Sufism and dedicated to facilitating personal experiences with the Divine. She has worked with the Melevi tradition of Sufism for over 30 years and has written several books on this subject, including *Women of Sufism: A Hidden Treasure: Writings and Stories of Mystic Poets, Scholars, and Saints*. Ms. Helminski is a core member of the Spiritual Paths Foundation, a mentor of the Snowmass Interspiritual Dialogue, and is recognized as one of WISE's spiritual leaders.

After years of deprivation due to the intensity of the boycott against the emerging Muslim community, Khadijah died at the age of sixty-five in 619 CE, just before permission came for the *hijrah*. She and Muhammad had lived contentedly together for 25 years. Together she and Muhammad had two sons, Qasim and Abd-Allah, who both died in infancy, and four daughters, Zaynab, Ruqqayah, Umm Kulthum, and Fatima, who were the only children of the Prophet Muhammad to live past infancy. She raised them all with a strong sense of spirit and reliance upon their Sustainer. She was known for her purity, her wisdom, her generosity, and her kindness. Khadijah was buried in the al-Mala' cemetery in Mecca.

Even after remarrying, Muhammad long mourned his devoted wife. "Khadijah had been for the Holy Prophet more than a wife. She had placed all her wealth, which was considerable, at his disposal. She had given him love. She was the first person to be converted to Islam, and had been a pillar of strength for the Holy Prophet as well as the Muslims." When his later wife, Aisha, questioned him about the extent to which he continued to remember and miss her, he said, "She embraced Islam when people disbelieved me, and she helped me in her person and her wealth when there was none else to lend me a helping hand. I had children only from her." [1]

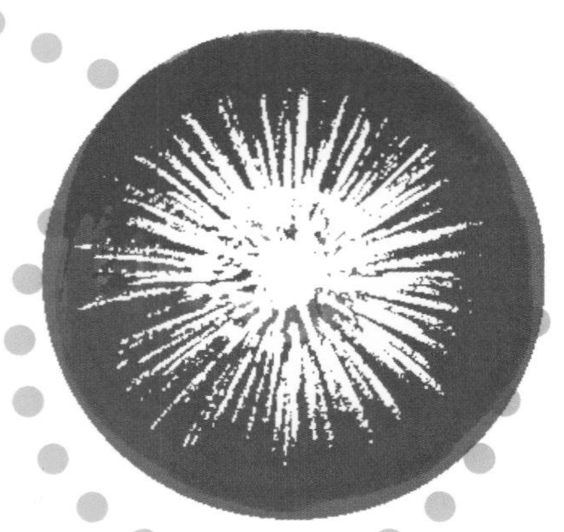

[1] This article has been adapted from Camille Helminski's acclaimed work, reprinted with permission: Helminski, Camille Adams. *Women of Sufism: A Hidden Treasure: Writings and Stories of Mystic Poets, Scholars and Saints*. Boulder, CO: Shambhala Publications, 2003.

Fatima bint Muhammad

D: 633 CE

Fatima, the youngest daughter of Khadijah and Muhammad, was born just around the time of the beginning of his prophethood, and she grew up under the dynamic influence of the new Message her father was conveying.

As his youngest child, she would often accompany Muhammad as he moved about the Meccan community, handling the family's errands, praying at the Kabah, or visiting Muslim friends and families, continually speaking of the new faith. During these early years of Islam, she witnessed countless episodes of persecution and would staunchly defend her father and care for him. Some years later, after the death of her mother, when she was the only one of his own children still living at home with him, witnessing his sorrow, this loving concern for her father intensified and earned her the title "Umm Abi-ha" (the mother of her father). Some also refer to this title as being indicative of the fact that his familial line was carried forward through her.

After enduring extreme hardship during the Meccan boycott, two years after the community emigrated to Medina, and three years after the death of her beloved mother, when she was about sixteen, Fatima married Ali ibn Abu Talib (the son of Muhammad's dear uncle, Abu Talib) who had been living with the family since the death of his father some years earlier and who had been among the first to become a Muslim. Ali was known for his courage, virtue, and piety. He and Fatima soon had a hut of their own near the Prophet in Medina. Two sons were born to them, Hasan and Hussein, and two daughters, Umm Kulthum and Zaynab. A third son of theirs, Muhsin, died in infancy. The line of the family of the Prophet is traced through Fatima, Hasan and Hussein, and their children.

She witnessed countless episodes of persecution and would staunchly defend her father and care for him. Some years later, after the death of her mother, when she was the only one of his own children still living at home with him, witnessing his sorrow, this loving concern for her father intensified and earned her the title "Umm Abi-ha" (the mother of her father).

The marriage of Fatima and Ali, though inspired by the Angel Gabriel, had its own vicissitudes, as do many marriages. One day, when Fatima and Ali were at odds with each other, Muhammad came to visit them. It is said that he lay down between them and had each of them place a hand on his belly. He told them to breathe with him and to remain together in that position until peace came to both of them.

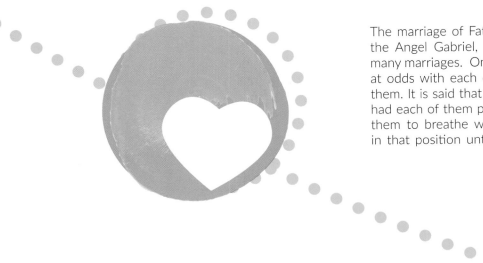

Sometime later he left their hut, smiling broadly. A companion who witnessed the difference in his countenance from when he had entered asked him why he was now smiling. He responded that he was smiling because the two people most beloved by him were now at peace.

Fatima's life with Ali was as simple and frugal, as it had been in her father's household. To relieve their extreme poverty, Ali, when he was not called to battle to defend their faith, worked as a drawer and carrier of water and she as a grinder of grain. One day Fatima told Ali, "I have ground grain until my hands are blistered."

> The Prophet extolled Fatima as one of the four most exemplary women in history, along with Mary, mother of Jesus, Khadijah, Fatima's mother, and Asiyah, the wife of the Pharaoh, who raised Moses as her own. These four women are considered the holiest women of Islam.

"And I've drawn water until my chest is aching," said Ali. He suggested to her that she ask her father, whose power and influence had grown since coming to Medina, to give her a servant.

Reluctantly, she went to the Prophet, but when he inquired what had brought her to him she could only respond, "I came to give you greetings of peace," and could not bring herself to ask for what she had intended.

When she returned home, she told Ali she had been ashamed to ask, so they went together to the Prophet, and asked him for assistance, but the Prophet felt that others were in greater need, especially the Ahl as-Suffah, the "people of the bench."

Ali and Fatimah returned home somewhat dejected, but later that night, after they had gone to bed, they heard the voice of the Prophet, asking permission to enter. Welcoming him, they both rose to their feet, but he told them: "Stay where you are," and sat down beside them. "Shall I not tell you of something better than that which you asked of me?" he asked, and when they said yes, he said: "Words which Jibril taught me, that you should say 'Subhaan Allah—Glory be to God' ten times after every Prayer, and ten times 'Alhamdulillah—Praise be to God,' and ten times 'Allahu Akbar—God is Great.' And that when you go to bed you should say them thirty-three times each." Ali used to say in later years: "I have never once failed to say them since the Messenger of God taught them to us." It was often to the "word of God" that they turned for nourishment and well-being.

It is said that Fatima greatly resembled her father and that her ways of sitting and standing and speaking were quite similar. She inherited from Muhammad a persuasive eloquence that was rooted in wisdom. When she spoke, people would often be moved to tears. She had the ability and the sincerity to stir the emotions, move people, and fill their hearts with praise and gratitude to God for His grace and His inestimable bounties. Aisha, the later wife of the Prophet, said of her: "I have not seen any one of God's creation resemble the Messenger of God more in speech, conversation, and manner of sitting than Fatima, may God be pleased with her. When the Prophet saw her approaching, he would welcome her, stand up and kiss her, take her by the hand and sit her down in the place where he was sitting." She would do the same when the Prophet came to her. She would stand up and welcome him with joy and kiss him.

The Prophet had a special love for Fatima. He once said: "Whoever pleases Fatima has indeed pleased God and whoever has caused her to be angry has indeed angered God. Fatima is a part of me. Whatever pleases her pleases me and whatever angers her angers me, and whoever injures her injures me." When he went on a journey the last person of whom he took leave was Fatima, and when he returned from the journey the first person he would see was Fatima.

Fatima is regarded by some as the first spiritual head (*qutb*) of the Sufi fellowship. The Prophet extolled Fatima as one of the four most exemplary women in history, along with Mary, mother of Jesus, Khadijah, Fatima's mother, and Asiyah, the wife of the Pharaoh, who raised Moses as her own. These four women are considered the holiest women of Islam.

One day while the Prophet was ill, he whispered something to Fatima and she cried, and then he whispered again in her ear and she smiled. After the Prophet's death, Aisha asked her what Muhammad had whispered to her. She answered that at first he had told her of his impending death, but then he had told her that she would be among the first to join him in paradise.

It was Fatima who eloquently delivered her father's eulogy. She deeply mourned the death of the Holy Prophet and is later reported to have said: "It is not surprising that whoever catches the fragrance of Muhammad's tomb will never know another perfume. Destiny injured me with a bereavement so sorrowful, and so dark, that if it had fallen on the days they would have been turned into eternal nights."

Then, six months after the death of her beloved father, after a prolonged illness, she arose one morning smiling and called for a mat to be placed in the open courtyard of their home. She asked her companion, Salma, for assistance in washing and perfuming herself and then with her face turned toward the heavens, she asked for her husband, Ali.

He was taken aback when he saw her lying in the middle of the courtyard and asked her what was wrong. She smiled and said: "I have an appointment today with the Messenger of God." Ali cried, and she tried to console him. She told him to look after their sons, Hasan (age seven) and Hussein (age six), and advised that she should be buried without ceremony. She gazed upward again, then closed her eyes and surrendered her soul to the Mighty Creator.

She was twenty-nine years old when she passed from this world in 633 CE. Ali visited the grave of Fatima frequently, and wrote verses to express his grief. On one occasion he wrote:

O thou grave, to thee I resort for paying homage to thee.
O thou, the repository of my beloved, thou answer me not.
O thou beloved tomb, what ails thee—
Thou respondeth not to my supplications.
Art thou, out of humor, Because of the love that I bear thee?

Though there is a sepulcher referred to as Fatima's tomb near the Prophet's tomb in Medina, she most probably rests in al-Baqi cemetery on the outskirts of Medina and it was probably here that Ali would often go for solace.[1]

[1] This article has been adapted from Camille Helminski's acclaimed work, reprinted with permission:
Helminski, Camille Adams. *Women of Sufism: A Hidden Treasure: Writings and Stories of Mystic Poets, Scholars and Saints*. Boulder, CO: Shambhala Publications, 2003.

Sumayyah bint Khayyat

D. 615 CE

Popularly known as "The First Martyr," Sumayyah was the first Muslim convert to die for her faith. After converting alongside her husband and sons, Sumayyah declared her faith publicly despite the threat of persecution from the Quraysh and her own tribe, the Banu Makhzum. Although Sumayyah and her family were chained and dragged into the desert where they endured brutal torture at the hands of their pagan tribesmen, Sumayyah stood by her faith and never recanted. Ultimately, Sumayyah was killed by Makhzum chief Abu Jahl, at whom she smiled peacefully even as he threatened her with his sword. Sumayyah's commitment to her faith gave her the strength to resist even in the face of extreme violence. She was a remarkable woman who put her devotion to God before all else, even her own life.

Abu Dhar al-Ghifari

D. 652 CE

An early convert to Islam, Abu Dhar al-Ghifari is famous for his life-long piety and commitment to aesthetic living. As a young man, Abu Dhar al-Ghifari set out in search of the Prophet Muhammad upon hearing rumors of the new faith he was proclaiming in Mecca. Upon converting to Islam and proclaiming his faith in front of the Kabah, Abu Dhar al-Ghifari endured brutal beatings for three days, but persisted nonetheless. At the command of the Prophet, Abu Dhar al-Ghifari subsequently returned to his clan, educated them about Islam, and led them in joining the Prophet in Medina. Abu Dhar lived out the rest of his days in service to the Prophet Muhammad both in military campaigns and pious observance of Islam. He is credited with the preservation of many important hadith and is remembered for his enduring loyalty to the Prophet, even after the Prophet's death.

Bilal ibn Rabah: A Hero for Islam and Humanity

D: 640 CE

One of the earliest and most profound examples of Islam welcoming diversity, and the struggle to establish freedom, justice, and equality for ALL human beings is seen in the history of one of the closest, and most honored companions of the Prophet Muhammad (pbuh), Bilal Ibn Rabah. Bilal, an emancipated slave and Islam's first *mu'adhin* (caller to prayer), was a champion in the struggle to see humanity free.

Bilal was a Black Abyssinian (Ethiopian) born into slavery in the sacred city of Mecca. His master, Abdullah ibn Juid'an, sought trusted individuals, such as Bilal, whom he could send with the caravan to protect his goods. On one caravan journey, Bilal caught the attention of a young well-known Meccan merchant named Abu Bakr, who would become the Prophet Muhammad's closest companion. Bilal often recited poetry and Abu Bakr would say, "What a beautiful voice you have. It has relieved our travel weariness and has brought the distant near." While on this journey, Abu Bakr had a dream. When he awoke, he asked Bilal to accompany him to visit a famous priest in the area to interpret his dream. After hearing the story of his dream, the priest said to Abu Bakr, "You have seen a beautiful dream indeed. May [God] make your dream come true! One from among your people will be sent as a Prophet. You will believe in him. . . . He will invite people to belief in the One [God], and denounce the worship of idols." The priest's comments stayed with Bilal and had a great effect on him.

When the Prophet Muhammad began preaching the message of the One God, many slaves embraced Islam. Meccan leaders were enraged with Muhammad's teachings on slavery—that slaves were equal to their masters and deserved to be valued as human beings. The Meccans exerted a great deal of pressure on the people to stay away from Muhammad, who was now known as the Messenger. It came to the point where no one dared to exchange words with Muhammad in public. The tension escalated and Muhammad left Mecca with his close friend Abu Bakr, retreating to a cave outside the city.

One day while Bilal was grazing his master's flock of sheep as was customary, Bilal came across the cave where Muhammad and Abu Bakr sat. Upon seeing Bilal, Muhammad sought to share the message of Islam with one more person. Sensing Bilal's hesitation, Muhammad took a step toward him and treated him not as a slave, but as an equal, and invited Bilal to sit. During the conversation, he told Bilal that he was indeed the Messenger sent by God, quoted verses from the Qur'an, and told Bilal about Islam. This was the first time Bilal was addressed as an ordinary human being by a freeman. Muhammad's succinct speech, the nobility in his manner of being and behavior, and the beauty and sweetness in his words drew Bilal to him and won his heart. Without hesitation and in complete earnestness, he recited the Declaration of Faith and became a Muslim.

From that day Bilal's soul attained great peace and though physically enslaved, he was free intellectually and spiritually. He would never again bow down to idols, even if his master commanded him. So, one day without being aware of his surroundings, he shouted at the idols, "Debased be those who worship you!" The Meccans who overheard Bilal asked, "Did you just curse our gods and us who worship them?" In an act of immense courage, Bilal exclaimed, "Yes, I cursed them." Immediately, one of the Meccans ordered that Bilal be dragged through the streets as an example to others who would curse their idols,

---

FITRAH MUHAMMAD is a student of Imam Warith Deen Mohammed. She works to bridge cultural relationships and build interfaith collaborations through understanding, mutual respect, and acknowledging the common decency of human and community life. She is the executive producer of a weekly Sunday program called "Study Al-Islam." She has extensive experience in working with high-profile leaders, government officials, embassy personnel, and in international relations.

The men tied and dragged Bilal throughout Mecca, with deaf ears to Bilal's cries of pain and blind eyes to his being covered in blood.

With Bilal barely conscious, they tied his hands and feet to stakes and nailed them into the hot burning sand. A Meccan woman, Umayya, began shouting, "Deny Muhammad!" Bilal did not answer. Umayya whipped Bilal unconscious, but nothing could pull him away from his Lord! Bilal did not have the strength to speak, merely uttering mournfully, "One! One! God is One!" Bilal's grueling life began as a slave with no status, who was now subjected to physical torture and persecution because of his belief in God. Muslims facing similar struggles think of none other than Bilal, who symbolized to people that one must stand firm in his belief in God, and that the ultimate victory can only be won with matchless faith, patience, and constancy.

Muhammad said that the believers, in their mutual affection, mercy, and compassion, are like a single body; if one limb aches, the rest of the body reacts with sleeplessness and fever. Deeply grieved by the unimaginable torture that Bilal and others were subjected to in Mecca, the Prophet Muhammad extended a helping hand to each of them to offer relief from their suffering. Not only did he sacrifice everything that he and his wife Khadijah had, but once he exhausted his resources, he encouraged his companion, Abu Bakr, to buy the tortured Bilal out of slavery. This first effort initiated by the Prophet led to the emancipation of many slaves, the first of whom was Bilal.

After gaining his freedom, and from the moment be became Muslim, Bilal embraced the Divine decree to "Read!," educating himself by reading and translating into action all that he read, purifying his mind. His heart and life were illuminated with the light of belief. Once, a group of dignitaries stated to Abu Talib, the Prophet's uncle, "We [Arabs] ask that you grant us special assembly, and recognize our superiority. We are embarrassed to be seen sitting with slaves. So, when we come to you, drive them away, and when we have finished, sit with them if you wish." Upon hearing this, Muhammad, Bilal, and the Prophet's Companions sat so close that their knees touched.

It was in the city of Medina that the Prophet appointed Bilal as the first *mu'adhin*, or Caller to Prayer, and gave him the title Sayyid al-Mu'adhin, or Master of the Callers to Prayer. Bilal was also appointed security secretary, empowered to safeguard and distribute the public funds from the state treasury.

The Prophet Muhammad praised Bilal with the following words: "The first to don the dress of Paradise after the Prophets will be Bilal and the righteous Callers to Prayer." On the day of Mecca's conquest, Bilal, a freed slave, experienced one of the most important moments in his life: he was instructed by the Prophet to climb to the top of the Kabah and deliver the call to prayer.

Some scholars offer the story of Bilal as a prophetic figure, comparing his enslaved life to what the world has done to Black people. In the time of the Prophet, Bilal was looked down upon, treated unequally, and tortured for being a slave and then for being Muslim. One of the Companions close to the Prophet belittled or looked down on Bilal. The Prophet said to him, "We are all Bilal," indicating that "when you speak disparagingly of one of us, you are speaking of all of us," and the nature that's been rejected in Bilal and his people is the same nature that all humans are created upon. We all are Bilal.

Ahmed, N. (2016). *Introduction of Islam in Africa*, https://historyofislam.com/contents/the-classical-period/islam-in-africa/.
Kara, H., and A. Kara (2016). *Bilal Al-Habashi: An Exemplar of Patience and Devotion*. Clifton, NJ: Tughra Books.

Salahuddin

1137–1193

Born to a Kurdish family in 1137, Salahuddin quickly rose up the ranks of the Zengid military as a young man while simultaneously studying mathematics, law, astronomy, and theology. In a series of successful military campaigns, Salahuddin united the territories of Egypt and Syria and presided over them as their king, founding the Ayyubid dynasty and commissioning the establishment of hospitals and academic institutions. In 1187, Salahuddin engaged in battle with Western Crusaders in an effort to reconquer Jerusalem from the Christians. Although Salahuddin was committed to defend Jerusalem to his death, he fought justly, allowing his faith and the principles outlined in the Constitution of Medina to guide his treatment of his non-Muslim opponents. Despite the extreme brutality of the Crusaders in the First Crusade, Salahuddin allowed the defeated Christians and any remaining Jews to either retreat or remain in Jerusalem peacefully. To this day, Salahuddin is regarded as a source of Muslim unity under his Ayyubid Empire and an example of tolerance and justice in the name of Islam.

Razia Sultana

1205–1240

The only female ruler of the Delhi Sultanate, Razia Sultana presided over the kingdom beginning in 1236 following the death of her father and the subsequent assassination of her mother and brother. Although Razia's reign was contested by the Muslim nobility, she ruled with great conviction, challenging gender binaries by dressing like a man and leading her army into battle. Angered by Razia's apparent favoritism toward one of her advisors, Malik Altunia, along with several other provincial governors, rose up against Razia in 1240. The rebel forces defeated and imprisoned Razia, ultimately forcing her to marry Altunia in lieu of assassination. Together, Razia and Altunia attempted to reclaim the throne usurped by Razia's brother, but were unsuccessful and died at the hands of robbers as they fled from Delhi. Razia is remembered for her courage, commitment to her faith, tolerance as a leader, and political acumen. Her reign challenged traditional notions of gender and she continues to serve as a role model for women.

Imam Shammil

1797–1871

Imam Shammil was born in Dagestan in 1797, just as the Russian Empire began encroaching on Ottoman, Persian, and Caucasian territories. As a young man, Imam Shammil studied logic, Arabic, and the Qur'an and Sunnah, quickly becoming a respected figure in the Muslim community. In the midst of growing resentment at Russian control, Shammil founded the Muradism movement that encouraged the peoples of Dagestan and Chechnya to abandon their tribal divisions and work together to combat Russian occupation with the ultimate goal of establishing a unified Islamic state in the Caucasus governed by Sharia law. Although Imam Shammil never achieved this goal, he fought valiantly in pursuit of it, always letting his spiritual principles guide him. Shammil served as the leader of the resistance forces in the Caucasian War and as the third imam in the Caucasian Imamate from 1834 until 1859, during which time he successfully united a number of the Caucasian tribes and employed guerrilla warfare in offensives against the Russians. Shammil was captured by the Russians and exiled to an area outside Moscow. Nearly a decade after his capture, Imam Shammil was permitted to complete the hajj to Mecca and he died in Medina in 1871. Imam Shammil was one of the first Muslims to unite the oppressed under Islam in pursuit of anti-colonial resistance. He is venerated for his remarkable bravery, insistence on cooperation, and dedication to his faith even after his capture.

Omar Mokhtar

1858–1931

Born near Tabruk, Libya, in 1858, Omar Mokhtar pursued a career as a Qur'an teacher and worked alongside the Senussi Sufis affiliated with the university where he studied as a young man until 1912. Following the invasion of Libya by Italian troops in 1911, spillover from the Italo-Turkish War, Mokhtar led armed opposition forces in guerrilla-style combat for almost twenty years. Despite their initial success, the troops Mokhtar organized suffered many defeats in the later years of the war and Mokhtar was ultimately wounded, captured, and placed in a prisoner of war camp in 1931. While the treatment Mokhtar received in the camp was brutal, fellow inmates remember him reciting verses of the Qur'an proclaiming peace and his last words prior to his execution were "*To God we belong and to God we shall return*" 2:156). Mokhtar devoted his life to the pursuit of his faith, peace, and independence for the Libyan people. A pioneer of African anti-colonialism, Mokhtar devoted his life to speaking up for justice.

Emir Abdelkader al-Jazairy: A Hero for Humanity

1808-1883

There are two busts side by side in the headquarters of the International Committee of the Red Cross in Geneva, Switzerland. One is of Henry Dunant, the Swiss Calvinist and humanitarian activist who founded the Red Cross in 1859. The other is of Emir Abdelkader al-Jazairy, the Algerian warrior, scholar, and holy man whose most feared weapon in his struggle against French armies invading North Africa was his humanity. Dunant was awarded the first Nobel Peace Prize, in 1864. Abdelkader won the accolades of the world for his chivalry on the battlefield, restraint, moral courage, and humanitarian spirit.

> During the mid-nineteenth century, Emir Abdelkader would be admired by people of all social ranks, nationalities, and religions: An American lawyer in Dubuque named a settlement in his honor in 1846, today Elkader, Iowa.

Horrified by the suffering of twenty thousand unattended wounded and dying soldiers on the battlefield of Solferino in 1859, Henry Dunant became obsessed with the need for countries to develop voluntary relief societies to care for wounded soldiers. While doing business in Algiers, he learned of Emir Abdelkader's chivalrous conduct on and off the battlefield during his seventeen-year struggle against a French occupation that began in 1830. After more investigation, Dunant counted him as one of the inspirational sources of the Geneva Code of Conduct. The emir, he learned, initiated the first prisoner exchanges with the French, and forbade the decapitation of French soldiers who were wounded or surrendered on the battlefield. He insisted on respectful treatment of French prisoners, had their wounds treated, and gave them the same rations as those given to his own men. By selecting his caliphs for both their moral and fighting qualities, he enforced other rules of Islamic warfare: no mutilation of the dead, no shooting in the face, no destroying nature, no killing of women, children, old men, or animals (except to eat). Destroying sacred sites and shooting priests and monks were forbidden, all rules of warfare promulgated by Abubakr (the first of the rightly guided caliphs).[1]

JOHN W. KISER, a former international technology broker, is author of *Commander of the Faithful: The Life and Times of Emir Abd el-Kader* and *The Monks of Tibhirine: Faith, Love, and Terror in Algeria*. In 2008, he co-founded the Abdelkader Education Project (AEP), a non-profit organization that promotes cultural literacy, civility, and respectful engagement between all people through education and outreach by drawing on Emir Abdelkader's life story and values. Since its founding in Elkader, Iowa, AEP has produced a local essay contest for high school and college students to revive the memory of Elkader's namesake and to explore models of ethical leadership, moral courage, and humanitarian conduct. More information can be found at www.abdelkaderproject.org and www.truejihad.com.

Dunant was not alone. During the mid-nineteenth century, Emir Abdelkader would be admired by people of all social ranks, nationalities, and religions: An American lawyer in Dubuque named a settlement in his honor in 1846, today Elkader, Iowa; in 1852, an Irish racehorse owner won the Grand National Steeplechase Championship with a small underdog horse named Abdelkader, or Little Ab, as his fans called him; former prisoners sought the honor of guarding him during his five years of imprisonment (1848–1852) in France. Pope Pius IX, Queen Victoria, Abraham Lincoln, and Emir Shamil in Russia sang his praises for protecting Christians in Damascus. As he lay on his deathbed in Damascus in 1883, the *New York Times* wrote an 800-word obituary hailing him as "one of the few great men of the century."

> "Politics shrinks the spirit, while the sacred enlarges the spirit without limit."

Who then was Emir Abdelkader? Algerians sometimes call him their George Washington. At age twenty-five, he became the first Arab leader to organize tribes into a proto-Arab state to resist a French occupation that had begun in 1830 with the sack of Algiers, a western outpost of a decaying Ottoman Empire. Unlike General Washington, the political seedling Abdelkader created did not bear fruit until 132 years later when Algiers won its independence from France.

Abd el-Kader. Servant of God—a challenging name to carry. Yet, he came as close as any human might to fulfilling his implied calling. Following his rescue of Christians in Damascus during the politically motivated pogrom of 1860, Abdelkader received a letter of gratitude from the French Bishop Pavy in Algiers. The emir wrote back: "That which we did for the Christians we did to be faithful to Islamic Law, and out of respect for human rights. . . . The law places greatest importance on compassion and mercy and all that preserves social cohesion." Abdelkader then ended his letter with an observation that is painfully obvious today: "Those who belong to the religion of Mohammad have corrupted it, which is why they are now like lost sheep."

The emir's story is about struggle. He struggled against French invaders and Arab tribes that rejected his leadership. He struggled with betrayal, humiliation, and depression in France, and finally, he struggled to teach Muslims by example, especially by his openness toward others, not allowing despair, bitterness, or revenge to dominate his spirit.

An Arab warrior, a Muslim of deep, informed faith, Abdelkader was above all a great human being who inspired others with his physical endurance and moral courage, his wide learning, and his spiritual depth that was capped by his ability to empathize with and forgive enemies. Whence did these traits come? What produced such a person? There were many influences:

- The traditions and teachings of the eleventh-century saint Abdelkader al-Jilani that inspired his Kaderiyyia Sufi tradition. Al-Jilani taught that Muslims had a duty to pray for the well-being of all people and to hold a place of special respect for Jesus Christ. In this tradition, Jesus is set apart from other prophets by his power of love.
- The teachings and influence of his parents that emphasized the continuous pursuit of knowledge, purity of heart, patience, and contempt of material riches.
- His mother, who taught that ritual purity is only half the faith, a reminder of the harder half—to purify one's inner self. To be a true servant of God, one must be free of egotistical desires and violent passions of hatred, anger, and revenge.
- His father, a scholar who taught him the complexities of interpreting God's word, the importance of context, the different levels of understanding, and different forms of behavior that are also righteous.
- His life as a Bedouin hunter and horseman, which taught patience, endurance, courage, and warrior skills.
- Sincere piety and a strong moral compass rooted in the teachings of all the prophets (Torah,

[1] The rules of Islamic warfare have been attributed by most scholars to the first caliph, Abubakr. The rules are also practical and could lead to enemies fighting less tenaciously if they be slieved they would be treated well as prisoners.

Psalms, Gospels, Qur'an).
- A broad education that included, in addition to the law, mathematics, history, astronomy, Greek philosophy, plant pharmacology, and art of rhetoric and recitation of the Qur'an.
- His exposure to the larger world, thanks to his father who took him on a hajj at age twenty-four that also took him to Tunis, Cairo, and Damascus.

The emir would often say, "The forms of worship may change, but the Master is One. We differ only in the way we address ourselves to him."

Abdelkader believed the pursuit of knowledge to be the highest good and the ultimate purpose in life. He distinguished, however, between knowledge of worldly things, which he likened to pools of rainwater that come and go, and knowledge of the divine within, which is like an everlasting spring.

The emir believed that the most important form of knowledge is political knowledge. Why? It affects the way people live together. Man is a social animal. He needs to cooperate to survive. No knowledge is more important than that needed for living in the community and guiding human behavior justly. Such justice requires access to higher wisdom, transmitted via the prophets who are only vessels for mediating God's wisdom. Nor is there any contradiction between the different prophets. They all subscribe to the fundamental moral rule: Be just. Do not let hatred turn you away from justice. Do unto others as you would have them do unto you. All have a common message: glorify God and show compassion for His creatures.

At least three elements of his character make Abdekader a worthy heroic role model in today's diverse and interconnected world:

He was "local" and "universal" at the same time. He was deeply and authentically Muslim. Yet he also grew spiritually, especially during his imprisonment in France, when he experienced the goodness of Christians and nonbelievers alike. His religion wasn't a safety belt holding his identity together, but a platform for probing the meaning of God's creation. His religious identity made him bigger, not smaller.

He was a unifier, not a divider. The plurality of beliefs was only a reflection of the infinite nature of God and the inexhaustible ways to praise God.

He didn't see any conflict between politics, religion, and science. Politics should be governed by a desire to lead people to live together in harmony, religion should provide a common moral base of shared values and common origin, and science should teach us to grasp the basic unity of mankind.

He didn't see any conflict between politics, religion, and science. Politics should be governed by a desire to lead people to live together in harmony, religion should provide a common moral base of shared values and common origin, and science should teach us to grasp the basic unity of mankind.

His was a life of virtue in action, guided by his sense of obedience to Divine Law. True obedience and leadership require certain virtues which Abdelkader possessed: a strong intellect, moral courage, justice, and restraint, once known in the Christian world as the Cardinal Virtues. Without cultivating these qualities in our youth and in our leaders, there will be little real progress made in the world.

Muslims throughout the world today are struggling for the soul of their faith. The Islam that was once at the forefront of intellectual achievement in the world was, like the emir, an Islam that sought knowledge and understanding wherever they could be found. There was no such thing as a pure Islam, just as there is no pure Christianity. The struggle today is over role models for young Muslims . . . and for that matter, youth everywhere.

"Politics shrinks the spirit, while the sacred enlarges the spirit without limit," said Abdelkader after being liberated from prison by Napoleon III in 1852.

Khan Abdul Ghaffar Khan

1890–1988

Khan Abdul Ghaffar Khan was born in 1890 in the Peshawar Valley under British rule and dedicated his life to anti-colonial resistance, the promotion of peace and nonviolence, and empowering his countrymen through education. Ghaffar Khan made nonviolence a key tenet of his life at an early age, refusing an offer to join the Guides, an elite Pashtun corps in the military of the British Raj, in his final years of secondary school. As a young man, Ghaffar Khan was not permitted by his parents to pursue university study outside of India, so, keenly aware of the potential of education for empowerment, at age twenty, in 1990 he established a school in his hometown. Khan realized that nonviolent activism rather than violent insurgency was the best way to combat British occupation when his school was banned by British authorities in 1915. In pursuit of nonviolent resistance, Khan played an integral role in the establishment of the Afghan Reform Society in 1921 and the Pashtun Assembly in 1927, visiting over five hundred villages to unite the Pashtuns against the British and empower them through unity and awareness. In 1929, Khan created the Khudayi Khidmatgar or "Servants of God" movement, which at its height, comprised over 100,000 members. Committed to nonviolent resistance against the British, the Khudayi Khidmatgar faced firing squads unarmed and completely defenseless at the Kissa Khwani Massacre of 1930, where over 200 peaceful protesters were killed. Khan Abdul Ghaffar Khan is a Nobel Peace Prize nominee and the recipient of the Jawaharlal Nehru Award for International Understanding and the Bharat Ratna, the highest honor bestowed on Indian civilians. He remains the leading figure in Muslim nonviolent anti-colonial resistance and his life serves as a model for the application of Islam and peace to resist oppression.

Noor Inayat Khan

1914 –1944

Noor Inayat Khan was an Indian-American Muslim woman who worked for the Allied Special Operations Executive in France as a radio transmitter. In 1943, Khan was sent by the British into France along with several other members of the Physician network of secret warfare agents. Despite most of her cohorts being quickly discovered and arrested by the Germans as well as an offer from her superiors to return to Britain, Khan continued to send her transmissions and help undermine the German presence in France. She was driven not by loyalty to Britain, but by her strong beliefs in religious tolerance and nonviolence. As the Germans learned more about her presence, she was forced to continually move locations, sometimes several times a day. Only three months after her landing in France, Khan was betrayed by an associate and handed over to the Germans. Despite a monthlong interrogation, she refused to betray her allies and give the Germans any information. She was kept in solitary confinement for ten months, then transferred to Dachau, where she was executed by the Germans in 1944. Khan's courage and willingness to continue working in dangerous conditions as well as her staunch refusal to cooperate with the Germans enabled the British to gain valuable information for the war effort.

Malcolm X

1925–1965

Malcolm Little, later known as Malcolm X, was born on May 19, 1925, in Omaha, Nebraska. He was an American Muslim minister, human rights activist, and one of the world's most influential African American civil rights leaders. When he was twenty years old, Malcolm was incarcerated for larceny and breaking and entering. Through the influence of his brother Reginald he began to use his time in prison to further his education and make efforts toward self-enlightenment. His brother had converted to Islam and used the opportunity to discuss his conversion with Malcolm. Shortly thereafter, Malcolm began to build parallels between the teachings of Islam and his active struggle in the African American civil rights movement. He joined the Nation of Islam, where he adopted a more outspoken stance on race relations in the United States and the causes contributing to African American oppression. Paroled after seven years, he was appointed minister and national spokesman for the Nation of Islam and established new mosques in Detroit, Michigan, and Harlem, New York.

Malcolm X had radically changed his separatist message to one of collaboration among the races and incorporated teachings of Islam into his speeches.

In 1964, Malcolm went on a pilgrimage to Mecca, as hajj is one of the Five Pillars of Islam, and was welcomed warmly by the global Muslim community. His pilgrimage proved to be life-altering for him and showed him how multicultural and diverse the Muslim community was. Through this sacred rite of passage, he was given a platform to share his thoughts and beliefs with people from different cultures and found the response to be overwhelmingly positive. Before his pilgrimage, he had referred to white Americans as "blue-eyed devils," advocated a black separatist movement, and condoned violent retaliation against oppression. He had even gone so far as to reject the mainstream civil rights movement for its emphasis on integration, but after he saw Muslims of "all colors, from blue-eyed blonds to black-skinned Africans" interacting as equals, he began to see Islam as a means by which racial problems could be overcome.

After returning to the United States, Malcolm addressed a wide variety of audiences and spoke regularly at meetings held by Muslim Mosque, Inc., and the Organization of Afro-American Unity. Malcolm X had radically changed his separatist message to one of collaboration among the races and incorporated teachings of Islam into his speeches. In a famous letter from Mecca, he wrote that his experiences during his pilgrimage convinced him to "rearrange" his thinking about race and "toss aside some of his previous conclusions." Malcolm X even met with Dr. Martin Luther King Jr. a few times after his views softened to discuss more peaceful strategies to help the African American community in the United States.

Tragically, on February 21, 1965, Malcolm X was murdered at the Audubon Ballroom in New York City after his break with the Nation of Islam. However, his brave words and example continue to inspire others around the world to struggle for justice and empowerment. His wife, Betty Shabazz, and his family have carried his message forward. After the famous *Autobiography* edited by Alex Haley in 1965, the 1992 film by Spike Lee brought Malcolm's indomitable example to new generations.

"I had just moved to Harlem. It was the first night I was there, and I went for a walk and there was a rally going on. Of course, I had heard about Malcolm before that, but it was mostly the kind of negative things they were running about him in the press then. I felt as if I was hearing the truth. I had never heard anyone speak with such clarity and forcefulness. And he just stimulated me. I found if he mentioned a book or a magazine article, I would try to find it. You hear people use that cliche about the University of the Streets. It really was that." — A. Peter Bailey, journalist

"I for one believe that if you give people a thorough understanding of what confronts them and the basic causes that produce it, they'll create their own program, and when the people create a program, you get action." — Malcolm X

Abdul Sattar Edhi

1928–2016

The late Abdul Sattar Edhi was known by many as the "Angel of Mercy." In life, he was venerated as the "world's greatest living humanitarian" who provided those who are disenfranchised with basic social and health services. His efforts led to his being nominated several times for the Nobel Peace Prize.

Born in India, Edhi immigrated with his family to Pakistan following the partition of India in 1947. With war and conflict emerging and economic resources scarce, poverty among the new immigrant population became exacerbated. Edhi himself was no stranger to poverty, as he had worked on the streets of Karachi as a peddler selling goods from store to store. It was through his time working in Karachi, and following the tragic death of his mother, that Edhi began to empathize strongly with the dire health condition of the poor and destitute. Seeing the lack of services and government support, Edhi began collecting donations and opened his first meager, but free, dispensary for his community.

In 1951, he founded the Edhi Foundation, which has grown to be the largest non-profit organization in Pakistan. The foundation provides ambulance services, 24-hour emergency response, medical facilities for emergencies and general care, homeless shelters, shelters for orphans, and adoption services. During his life, Edhi even became the guardian to several thousand orphans. Through the foundation, he was able to extend his kindness to not only those living in Pakistan, but to various causes and conflicts around the world. He has always affirmed that charitable work is central to one's devotion in practicing Islam, since charity (*zakat*) is one of the foundational pillars of Islam. His legacy lives on, carried out through the foundation, now operated by his family that continues to work to improve the lives of many around the world. His memory lingers in the hearts and minds of many Pakistanis and Muslims around the globe, as his humility and kindness emulated the example set by the Prophet Muhammad (pbuh).

Imam Warith Deen Mohammed: America's Imam

1933–2008

Imam Warith Deen Mohammed passed away on September 9, 2008. He was praised in newspapers around the world as "America's Imam." A historical highlight in the life of Imam W. Deen Mohammed—who favored using the name Warithun-Deen Mohammed—occurred on February 6, 1992, when he became the first Muslim to offer an invocation in the United States Senate. This monumental moment opened the doors for all American Muslims. He prayed:

> *Our Creator, the Merciful Benefactor, the Merciful Redeemer who opens for all people a way to have good conscience and a good life. Grant to this Nation that Americans continue to live as a prosperous nation of "many in one" and as a people of faith taking pride in human decency, industry and service. Let us pray that this great Nation's two centuries of national life may inspire other nations to move toward social and economic justice to all. Bless Americans to always cherish our freedom and the noble essence of the American people. Bring all citizens and Government together, those of great means and small means, to appreciate more our Nation's solemn pledge of liberty, peace and justice for all. Increase for the president of the United States, for every member of the Senate and for every member of the House of Representatives, the excellence of man's spirit and the excellence of the intellect of the statesman so that they may build a better America for us all. Amen.*

On February 26, 1975, Imam Warith Deen Mohammed was unanimously chosen to be the new leader of the then Nation of Islam (NOI) after the passing of Elijah Muhammad, his father. Upon assuming the leadership position, Wallace moved away from the movement's racially separatist and nationalistic teachings and theology that his father inherited from W. D. Fard. This created a new set of challenges for him, which he called "Conflicts in Darkness." He rejected a large part of the NOI theology because it went against the grain of the clear teachings of the Qur'an and the life example of the Prophet Muhammad (pbuh). He immediately began transforming the NOI from a black separatist group to one with a more open approach, and began forming interfaith and intrafaith relationships with Muslims, Christians, and Jews. Speaking at an interfaith roundtable in 1993, he said, "I believe that we are seeing in our time developments that could bring us closer to the goal or the destiny for us in our different religions of Christianity, Judaism, and Islam."

Unity has always been a goal of Imam Mohammed. On October 28, 1999, standing before Pope Paul II and 200 other religious leaders from around the world at the Eve of the New Millennium at St. Peter's Basilica in Rome, Italy, the American Muslim leader said, "I have devoted my life to building bridges. Inclusion was in my heart. . . . I wholeheartedly accept and embrace with you the idea of unity, mutual sharing, and love for one another. We have to condition ourselves to be at peace."

Malcolm X shared in his autobiography the strong respect he had for Wallace after studying with him. Wallace reciprocated his love and appreciation for Malcolm's friendship by renaming the Harlem, New York, mosque to *Masjid Malcolm Shabazz*.

Imam Mohammed led the way in interfaith understanding in the United States, speaking

IMAM MICHAEL SAAHIR is an author, activist, and retired firefighter, who had served with the Indianapolis Fire Department since 1979. He is Resident Imam of the Nur-Allah Islamic Center and the author of *The Honorable Elijah Muhammad: The Man Behind the Men*. Starting in 1992, he has penned a regular column for the *Indianapolis Recorder* titled "Al-Islam in America," and he is a regular contributor to *Muslim Journal*, a national Islamic publication.

numerous times in churches, synagogues, mosques, and at hundreds of college campuses, where he received numerous awards and accolades. In April 2002 he was inducted as a member of the Martin Luther King Jr. International Chapel Board of Friends, and received the Gandhi-King-Ikeda Award from Morehouse College. This distinguished honor was bestowed by the Reverend Dr. Lawrence Edward Carter Sr., Ph.D., Dean of the Martin Luther King Jr. International Chapel, archivist, and curator at Morehouse College. Dr. Carter praised Imam Mohammed in glowing terms as he recounted his national and international effect upon the world's religious leaders:

> *I have followed your career for 30 years. Your unforgettable courage arrested the Nation when you announced that you would not be bounded by the limits of religion. I next heard you address the American Academy of Religion and the Society of Biblical Literature in New Orleans in the early 70s, where you held the Nation's religion professors spellbound...This past summer, when I was in the Alps of Northern Italy, in dialogue with the Dalai Lama, I saw an enlarged color photograph; in fact, I saw more than one of you with Pope John Paul II and Chiara Lubich of the Focolare Movement. Your sincere interfaith actions have established your name as one who knows the difference between religion and spirituality. You do not just preach or teach peace. My good sir, you are Peace. . . I am pleased to forever link your name and nature with Mohandas Karamchand Mahatma Gandhi, Martin Luther King, Jr., and Daisaku Ikeda.*

In 1995, Imam Mohammed became President of the World Conference on Religion and Peace. His list of achievements also includes delivering prayers at both of President Bill Clinton's Inaugural Interfaith Prayer Services, the first in 1993, and again in 1997. His strong interest in interfaith dialogue led him to address the Muslim-Jewish Conference on March 6, 1995, with leaders of Islam and Reform Judaism, held in Glencoe, IL. In October 1996, at the invitation of Archbishop William Cardinal Keeler and the Focolare Movement, Imam Mohammed met Pope John Paul II at the Vatican.

In 1997, he received the Luminosa Award for his work promoting interfaith dialogue, peace, and understanding in the U.S. In 1999, Imam Mohammed served on the Advisory Panel for Religious Freedom Abroad, formed by Secretary of State Madeleine Albright.

Upon the passing of Imam W. Deen Mohammed, condolences poured in from every sector of American society. Rami Nashashibi, executive director of the Chicago based Inner City Muslim Action Network (IMAN), observed, "He forged forward with a meaningful and dignified path of both being Muslim American and human and he set the standard for many of us. It was an honor and a privilege to get to know him and to be in the company of an absolutely beautiful human being."

Muhammad Ali

1942–2016

Muhammad Ali, born Cassius Marcellus Clay Jr., will forever be remembered for his skill, technique, and grace in the boxing ring. A storied fighter, Ali rose to be the greatest of the great. But it is perhaps what Ali chose to do with his success outside the ring that set him apart from his peers. Politically active with an eloquent yet sharp tongue, Ali was no stranger to the limelight. In fact, he basked in it. He never shied away from voicing his opinion and he never failed to back his words with action. Perhaps most notable was his refusal to be conscripted to fight in the United States' war in Vietnam. Ali wholeheartedly opposed the United States' involvement—and as a man of conscience, when push came to shove, he defied his country to uphold his values.

His defeat of heavyweight champion Sonny Liston in 1964 cemented his position as a dominant and electric champion. This was the last fight he would win as Cassius Clay Jr. In his place, Muhammad Ali was born.

> "I am angry that the world sees a certain group of Islam followers who caused this destruction, but they are not real Muslims. They are racist fanatics who call themselves Muslims, permitting the murder of thousands."

Muhammad Ali converted to Islam after many years of showing interest in Islamic values. He never quit fighting for Islam or Muslims around the world. After the attacks of September 11, Ali took it upon himself to denounce innocents being killed in the name of his religion. "I am angry that the world sees a certain group of Islam followers who caused this destruction, but they are not real Muslims. They are racist fanatics who call themselves Muslims, permitting the murder of thousands."

Following his death on June 3, 2016, thousands flocked to Louisville, Kentucky, Ali's hometown, to honor their hero. Those paying their respects included former president Bill Clinton, Kareem Abdul-Jabbar, Billy Crystal, and Will Smith, among many others.

Muhammad Ali fought for those who did not have the voice or the strength to fight for themselves. He was a Civil Rights Movement hero, a counter-culture hero, and a hero to those with Parkinson's disease—continually showing them that the sky is the limit. He was a hero to boxing amateurs and champions alike, a hero to poets, rappers, and everyone in between. His spirit, his grace, his passion, and his values—these are what will be remembered about "The Greatest," Muhammad Ali.

Salman Hamdani

1978–2001

Mohammad Salman Hamdani was born in Karachi, Pakistan, in 1978, and emigrated to the United States thirteen months later with his parents. Salman embodied the American dream: an immigrant who grew up in Queens; a devout Muslim; a New York State-certified first responder; a New York Police Department cadet; a diligent student who dreamed of being a doctor; and a fiercely proud American.

On September 11, 2001, Salman was on his way to work when he learned about the attack on the World Trade Center. From the elevated train he was on, he saw the towers in flames. Without giving any thought to his own safety, he disembarked and rushed to the North Tower to save the lives of strangers. As others fled from the destruction, Salman ran to it. We don't know how many lives Salman helped save. We don't know how he managed to be so determined at a time of utter chaos. We cannot ask him because Salman died in the wreckage of the North Tower that day.

Salman is, without a doubt, a hero—a hero who died in service to his country. Salman made the ultimate sacrifice. He personifies the best of Islam and of America. Salman is a posthumous recipient of the Noor Inayat Khan Courage Award as well as the ISNA, ICNA, and CAIR Hero awards.

Afsha Ahmed

1990–2014

Afsha Ahmed was a twenty-four-year-old Pakistani teacher who valiantly sacrificed her life for her students during an attack on her school in Peshawar in December 2014. When Taliban gunmen came bursting into her classroom, she placed herself between the men and her students. Ahmed stood in front of the attackers stating that they would have to kill her first, because she refused to see her children's dead bodies on the floor. In response, the men doused her with gasoline and lit her on fire. Ahmed stood before the men and yelled to her students to flee to find safety. As a result of her sacrifice, Ahmed's students were able to escape while 132 others were killed elsewhere in the school. Her bravery and quick action prevented the loss of additional lives and served as a beacon of strength for her students during a time of chaos.

Aitzaz Hasan

1997–2014

Aitzaz Hasan was a Shia teenager living in the Hangu region of Pakistan who stopped a suicide bomber from reaching his school in January 2014. One morning, as he was going to class, Hasan noticed a man with an explosive vest approaching the school. Despite the pleas of his friends to stay back and not risk his life, Hasan knew that he had to keep the bomber from detonating his vest inside the school filled with students. Hasan chased after the suicide bomber and tackled him, about 500 feet from the main gate of the school. The bomber then detonated his bomb, killing both himself and Hasan. Due to his quick thinking and bravery, Hasan saved the lives of over a thousand of his friends and classmates, and his heroism is now being compared across Pakistan to that of Malala Yousafzai. Through his grief, Hasan's father was also very proud, saying, "My son made his mother cry, but saved hundreds of mothers from crying for their children."

Tuğçe Albayrak

1991–2014

Tuğçe Albayrak was a German Muslim student teacher who saved two teenage girls being harassed by three men in a restaurant. After hearing cries for help coming from the bathroom, Albayrak stepped into the dangerous situation and ended the confrontation. Later on, she was assaulted and punched to the ground by one of the men in the restaurant's parking lot. The punch put her into a coma, and she died two weeks later. Her death prompted a strong response from the German public, with more than 200,000 people signing a petition to grant her the Federal Order of Merit. She has been hailed as a role model for all of Germany, and her death has raised awareness for the issues of violence and harassment as they pertain to women's equality.

Abdi Mohamud Abdi

DATE UNKNOWN

Abdi Mohamud Abdi risked his life to protect Christians and other Muslims when the Somalian extremist group al-Shabaab attacked the bus he was riding on on December 21, 2015, in Mandera, Kenya. Abdi refused to give in to the militants' threats when they demanded the Muslim passengers separate themselves from the 28 non-Muslim passengers, many of whom were Christians. He even went as far as to provide Christian passengers with traditional religious attire so that they would not be easily identified. As Abdi told reporters after the attack, "The militants threatened to shoot us but we still refused and protected our brothers and sisters."[1] His heroic defiance in the face of extremism forced the terrorists to retreat without further loss of innocent lives.

Alioune Niass

DATE UNKNOWN

Alioune Niass is the Senegalese American who first notified police about the Times Square car bomber in 2010. On the morning of May 1, a blue Nissan Pathfinder pulled up in front of his photograph stand. At first, he did not realize the car was there, but he soon noticed smoke rising from underneath. Niass walked to the next vendor and asked him to call 911, due to Niass's limited knowledge of English, but he quickly decided to find a police officer instead. After being notified, the officer called in a bomb squad and began to evacuate the area. Although the bomb failed and never went off, Niass's quick action had the potential of saving the lives of thousands of New Yorkers within the square. Despite his integral role in the discovery of the car bomb, Niass was barely mentioned in any reports about the incident. This prompted a movement by many New Yorkers and Americans to highlight that it was a Muslim who first responded to the bomb and that several terrorist attacks on U.S. soil have been prevented with the help of Muslims.

[1] Akwiri, Joseph. "Passenger Says Muslims Protect Christians in Islamist Attack on Kenyan Bus." Reuters, December 21, 215.

Rais Bhuiyan

B. 1974

Rais Bhuiyan is a Bangladeshi American Muslim who was shot in Texas shortly after the attacks of September 11, 2001. He was shot in the face by Mark Stroman, a white supremacist and neo-Nazi sympathizer who was "out hunting Arabs" in revenge for the recent terrorist attacks. As a result of the shooting, Bhuiyan lost vision in his left eye and had to undergo many surgeries, draining his savings and sending him spiraling into debt. Nonetheless, Bhuiyan refused to hate the man who had despised him so much based upon his perceived ethnicity, and he began a campaign to remove Stroman from death row. Although the campaign ultimately failed, Bhuiyan had touched the heart of his attacker, who stated in a *New York Times* interview, "His deep Islamic Beliefs Have gave him the strength to Forgive the Un-forgiveable . . . that is truly Inspiring to me, and should be an Example for us all." Bhuiyan went on to form World Without Hate, an organization whose mission is to cultivate compassion, forgiveness, and empathy through education, community outreach, and advocacy. He has spoken across the globe about the regenerative power of forgiveness, using his own life story as an example.

Sobuj Khalifa

B. 1983

A homeless Bangladeshi immigrant, Sobuj Khalifa lives in a cave along the Tiber River. On May 12, 2015, Khalifa saw a woman in the river. Realizing that something was horribly wrong, he yelled to people on a nearby bridge to call for help and dove, fully clothed, into the river. He swam to the woman and dragged her back to the shore, where emergency responders were able to care for her. Khalifa cited his faith as the reason behind his actions, stating that "God wants us to help everybody." For his actions, Khalifa was hailed as a hero across Europe and has been awarded a one-year permit to live and work in the city, so he will no longer have to live there illegally. Furthermore, because the woman was Jewish, the Jewish community of Rome is currently working to find Khalifa a job and housing. Khalifa's feat has eased some fears as Europe continues a heated debate on immigration from the Middle East and North Africa.

Hassan Askari

B. 1987

Hassan Askari, an American Muslim from New York City, was a twenty-year-old student in December 2007 when a fight broke out on the subway. A group of ten anti-Semitic people had started throwing punches at four Jews for wishing them a happy Hanukkah. Askari gazed around in disbelief as the other commuters on the packed train looked away and did nothing to help those being assaulted. Askari stepped in and confronted the assailants, rebuking them for their violence and lack of sympathy. This caused the group to turn on Askari, and they pinned him to the wall and viciously punched him. That gave one of the Jewish men enough time to pull the emergency brake, forcing a stop at the next station, where police arrived and arrested the ten thugs. By acting as he did, Askari helped bridge religious divides, and later joined one of the Jewish men in celebrating the Festival of Lights.

Lassana Bathily

B. 1990

Lassana Bathily is a Malian-born Muslim living in France who valiantly hid customers in the downstairs freezer during a shooting at Hyper Cacher supermarket on January 9, 2015. He calmed the customers down and told them to wait in the freezer, while he ran outside, risking his life, to inform police where the customers were located. Due to his bravery, the police got the information needed to raid the store, neutralize the shooter, and free the trapped customers. As a result of his actions, Bathily was hailed internationally as a hero, and the French president awarded him citizenship shortly afterward. Asked his reaction, Bathily stated, "I'll stay the same. I would do the same again, because I was following my heart."

Malala Yousafzai

B. 1997

Malala Yousafzai was a seventeen-year-old Pakistani girl when she was shot through the head by the Taliban in 2012 for promoting women's education. From the age of eleven, Yousafzai was an outspoken proponent of women's right to be educated in Pakistan. Despite the threat of reprisal from the Taliban, she gave many public talks and served as an anonymous BBC blogger, describing her life as a woman under Taliban authority. When her identity as a blogger was discovered by the Taliban in 2012, however, she was issued a death threat by the organization. On October 9, 2012, a man boarded her bus home from school and shot her through her head. She was airlifted to a Pakistani hospital and eventually to England, where she miraculously recovered. Her situation received global attention, which inspired a signature campaign that prompted the passing of Pakistan's first right to education bill. She has since leveraged her passion and fame to speak actively against women's lack of educational rights in many countries across the world. She started the Malala Fund to raise awareness for girls' education and to empower girls to harness their own potential and fight for change. As a result of her efforts, she was awarded the Nobel Peace Prize in 2014 as well as many other national and international awards.

Deah Barakat, Yusor Abu-Salha, and Razan Abu-Salha

DEAH BARAKAT was a second-year student at the University of North Carolina–Chapel Hill and had recently married Yusor Abu Salha in December. The couple, along with Yusor's sister Razan, were killed in a hate crime on February 10, 2015. Deah's father described Deah and his wife as "bright, intelligent, thoughtful, generous and loving." In addition to graduating from his class with honors, Barakat was dedicated to aiding the less fortunate. Barakat and ten local dentists and faculty from the UNC School of Dentistry were planning a trip to Rihaniya, Turkey, to provide dental care to students there, and spearheaded an initiative to raise funds for the trip. Barakat also led various fundraisers for Syrian refugees, including a charitable basketball tournament.

YUSOR ABU-SALHA graduated from North Carolina State University with a bachelor's degree in Biological Sciences and was set to begin classes for dental school in the fall. Yusor went on a volunteer mission to help at a dentistry clinic along with her husband, Deah. The couple was planning another mission trip to Turkey for the following summer. She and her husband frequently fed the homeless and hungry in downtown Raleigh. Before she enrolled in the university, her resume sparkled with honors, accomplishments, leadership positions, and community service.

Yusor's sister RAZAN was also a student at North Carolina State University, where she studied architecture and environmental design. Razan supported charities such as Global Deaf Muslim, advocating for equal access to Islam for the deaf and hard of hearing. Razan also joined her older sister in volunteering in downtown Raleigh to feed the homeless and the hungry. She was also a talented artist and won a contest for her 3D abstract model-making.

Ricky John Best, Taliesin Myrddin Namkai Meche, and Micah David-Cole Fletcher

When people see an injustice take place, they often do not know what to do. As a result, victims are harassed in public spaces, feeling helpless and devalued by both the abuser and the public. Bystander passivity as they witness street harassment is part of the problem, and it takes courage to be the first person to speak up for what is right (See page 317 for Bystander Intervention Tips). A hero is someone who steps in to correct an injustice. That is what Ricky John Best, Taliesin Myrddin Namkai Meche, and Micah David-Cole Fletcher did when they intervened to defend two girls, one of whom was wearing a hijab, who were harassed by a white supremacist on a train in Portland, Oregon. As they tried to protect the girls from the racist man, he stabbed them with a knife. Tragically, Best and Namkai Menche lost their lives.

RICKY JOHN BEST was an Army veteran who spent 23 years in the military, defending and upholding American values overseas. After his military service, he continued to be an active member of his community by running for county commissioner. Though he dedicated his life to protecting Americans, he was a father and husband first: he loved spending time with his kids, whom he missed dearly during his military service. Best lost his life, but up to his final breath, he epitomized what it means to be an American hero.

TALIESIN MYRDDIN NAMKAI MECHE was twenty-three years old, newly graduated from college, with his whole life ahead of him. He worked at an environmental consulting agency, hoping to make the world a better place. Like many others his age, he had plans of buying a home, getting married, and starting a family. His mother and sister described him as a "shining bright star" who, in his final act of bravery, was resolute in what he believed in.

MICAH DAVID-COLE FLETCHER is a twenty-one-year-old student at Portland State University with dreams of becoming a poet. He has written poems focusing on social justice, including a poem about racism directed at Muslims, for which he won an award at a poetry competition. He has always been conscious of the struggles of minorities and the obstacles they encounter and wants to use his poetry to shed light on these issues. He was critically wounded during the attack; even so, he said that he will continue to fight to correct injustice.

Best, Namkai Menche, and Fletcher shared the courage to put themselves in harm's way to protect the vulnerable. This is what makes them American heroes. Their bravery has raised nationwide awareness of the struggles that Muslims face and the public's shared responsibility to boldly and fearlessly uphold American values wherever they may be threatened.

Map 3 Europe After the Congress of Vienna, 1815
The major European powers re-drew the map of Europe with the Congress of Vienna in 1815 after the defeat of Napoleon. This map shows the dismantlement of the massive empire France had acquired under his leadership.

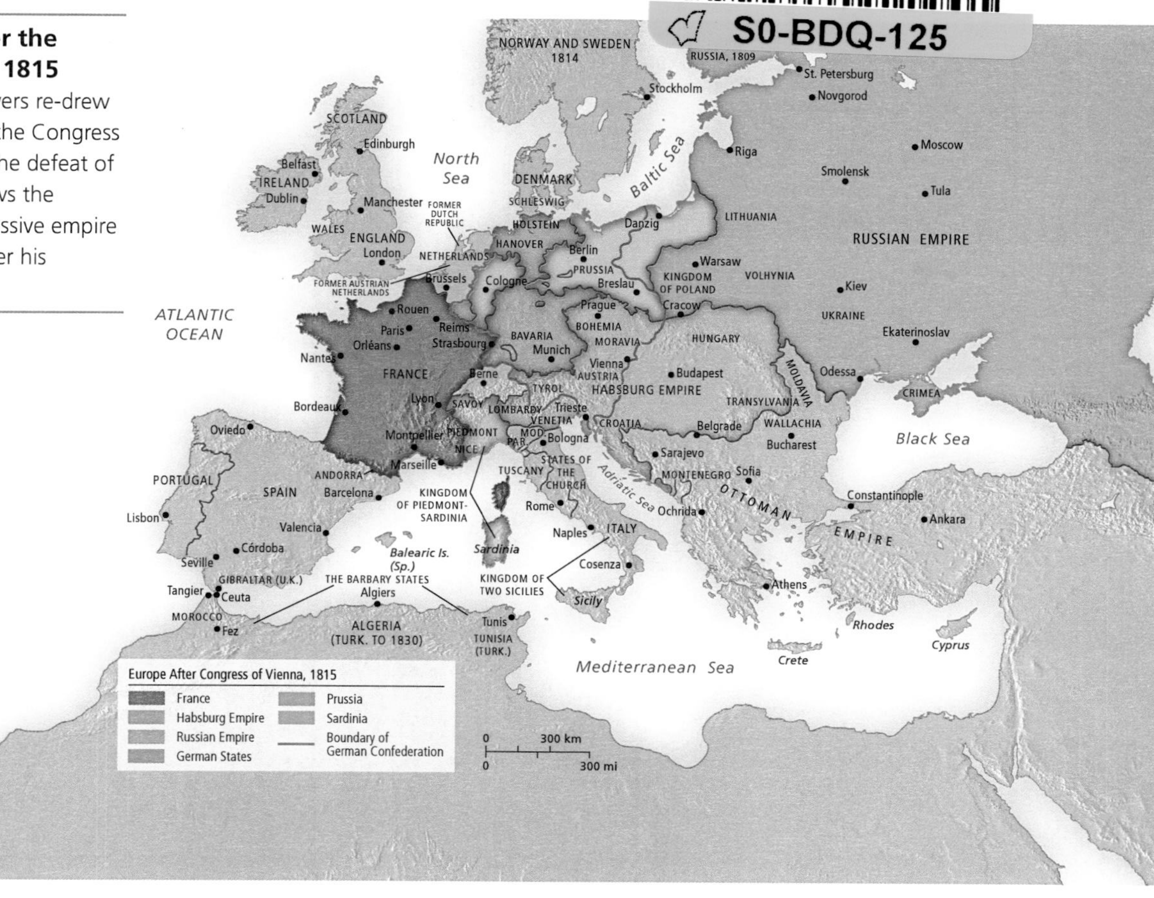

Map 4 Europe After World War I
The map of Europe changed dramatically after World War I with the collapse of the old authoritarian empires and the creation of independent nation-states in eastern Europe. What neither Map 3 nor Map 4 can show, however, is the expansion of "the West" beyond European borders to embrace cultures on other continents, including Australia, Africa, and North America.

Europe and the Middle East After World War I
To Great Britain
To France
To Italy
To Rumania
To Denmark
To Yugoslavia (Serbia and Montenegro)
To Belgium
To Greece
Became independent
1914 boundaries
New boundaries

THE WEST

Encounters & Transformations

Second Edition, Atlas Edition

This Atlas Edition is designed to help students with geography, one of the most difficult parts of the course for many students. Questions provided with outline and four-color maps call for identifying important geographical areas and think critically about the importance of geography thoughout history. The maps are on perforated pages and are organized by book chapter so they can be easily assigned.

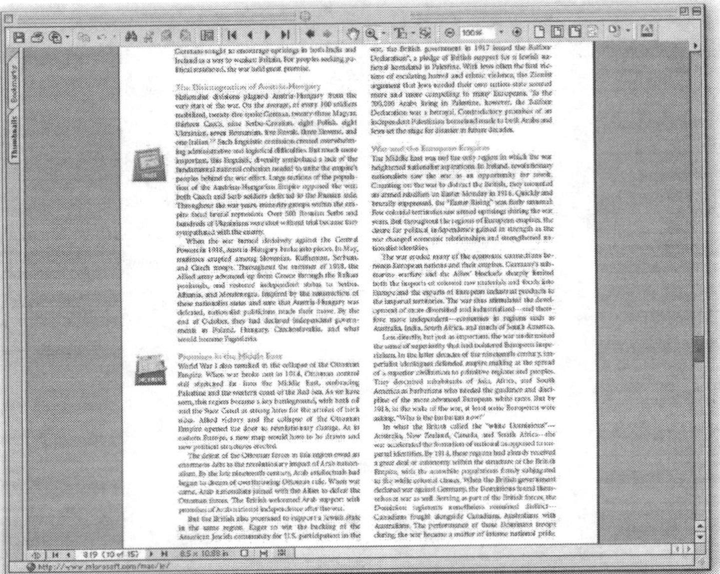

Would your life be easier if you had an electronic version of your textbook?

MyHistoryLab contains the complete text with icons that link to selected sources. You can print sections of the text to read anytime, anywhere.

Are you overwhelmed by the time it takes to find primary source documents, images, and maps for your research papers?

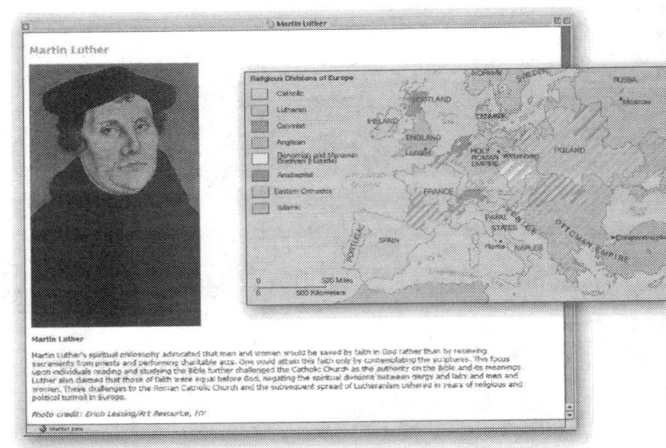

MyHistoryLab contains over 1,100 documents, images, maps, and video clips—all in one place—to help make writing your research paper easier and more effective and to help you better understand the course material.

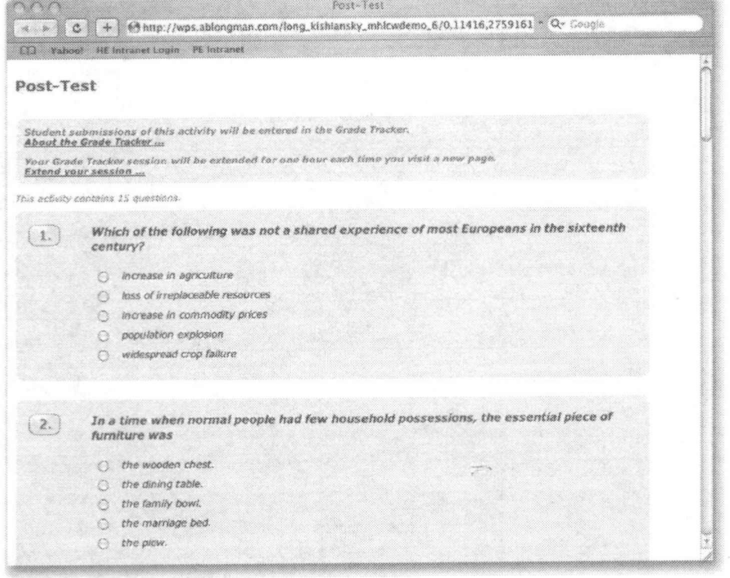

Are you sometimes overwhelmed when you study for exams?

MyHistoryLab provides an integrated quizzing and testing program that includes chapter pre-tests, post-tests, and exams. A customized study plan, generated from the chapter pre-tests and post-tests, shows what you've mastered as well as where you need more work. Look for these icons in MyHistoryLab.

Need extra help during evening hours?

Get help from The Tutor Center when your instructor is often unavailable—5 pm to midnight, Sunday through Thursday, spring and fall terms (Sunday through Wednesday, summer term). Tutors can help you navigate MyHistoryLab or review your paper for organization, grammar, and mechanics.

Did your professor assign other books to read?

MyHistoryLab allows you to read, download, or print over fifty of the most commonly assigned works for this course—all at no additional cost! The following titles are all available on History Bookshelf.

1. *Aesop's Fables* (c. 500 BCE)
2. *Histories*, Herodotus (c. 450 BCE)
3. *Lysistrata*, Aristophanes (c. 448 BCE)
4. *The Oedipus Trilogy*, Sophocles (c. 425 BCE)
5. *The Republic*, Plato (360 BCE)
6. *The Ethics of Aristotle* (c. 350 BCE)
7. *The Bhagavad-Gita* (c. 100 CE)
8. *The Iliad*, Homer (c. 800 BCE)
9. *The Upanishads* (c. 600 BCE)
10. *Letters of Marcus Tullius Cicero* (c. 45 CE)
11. *De Agricultura*, Marcus Cato (141 CE)
12. *The Lives of Plutarch* (c. 200 CE)
13. *The Confessions of St. Augustine* (401 CE)
14. *The Secret History of the Court of Justinian*, Procopius (558 CE)
15. *The Arabian Nights* (c. 800 CE)
16. *Beowulf* (c. 1000 CE)
17. *Four Arthurian Romances*, De Troyes, (c. 1170)
18. *The Song of Roland* (c. 1200 CE)
19. *The Prince*, Machiavelli *(1505)*
20. *95 Theses*, Martin Luther (1517)
21. *Romeo and Juliet*, Shakespeare (c. 1590)
22. *The Essays of Francis Bacon* (1601)
23. *Leviathan*, Thomas Hobbes (1651)
24. *When London Burned*, G.A. Henty (1665)
25. *Captivity and Restoration*, Mary Rowlandson (1682)
26. *Treatise on Government*, John Locke (1690)
27. *Gulliver's Travels*, Jonathan Swift (1726)
28. *Three Sermons*, Jonathan Swift (1750)
29. *An Inquiry into the Slave Trade*, Anthony Benezet (1771)
30. *Wealth of Nations*, Adam Smith (1776)
31. *Pilgrim's Progress*, John Bunyan (1794)
32. *Sense and Sensibility*, Jane Austen (1811)
33. *The Napoleon of the People*, Honore Balzac (1812)
34. *The Afghan Wars*, Forbes (1839)
35. *The Communist Manifesto*, Karl Marx (1848)
36. *Origin of Species*, Charles Darwin (1859)
37. *Narrative of the Overland Expedition to Northern Queensland*, Fredrick Byerley (1867)
38. *Japanese Manners and Customs*, J. Silver (1867)
39. *20,000 Leagues Under the Sea*, Jules Verne (1870)
40. *To the Gold Coast for Gold*, Sir Richard Burton (1883)
41. *The Jungle Book*, Rudyard Kipling (1894)
42. *Heart of Darkness*, Joseph Conrad (1899)
43. *Moorish Literature*, Rene Basset (1901)
44. *River Wars of the Sudan*, Winston Churchill (1902)
45. *The Woman Who Toils*, Vorst (1903)
46. *Congo Free State*, Marcus Dorman (1905)
47. *The Beginnings of Israeli History*, Kent & Jenks (1912)
48. *Clairvoyance*, Swami Panchadasi (1916)
49. *The Psychology of Dreams*, Sigmund Freud (1920)
50. *A Biography of Simon Bolivar*, Sherwell, (1921)

Now, flip through *The West: Encounters & Transformations.* You will find the icons shown on the opposite page. Each icon will direct you to a place in MyHistoryLab to help you better understand the material. For example, when reading about 19th-century European politics, you may find an icon that links you to an original source document by Martin Luther or Karl Marx.

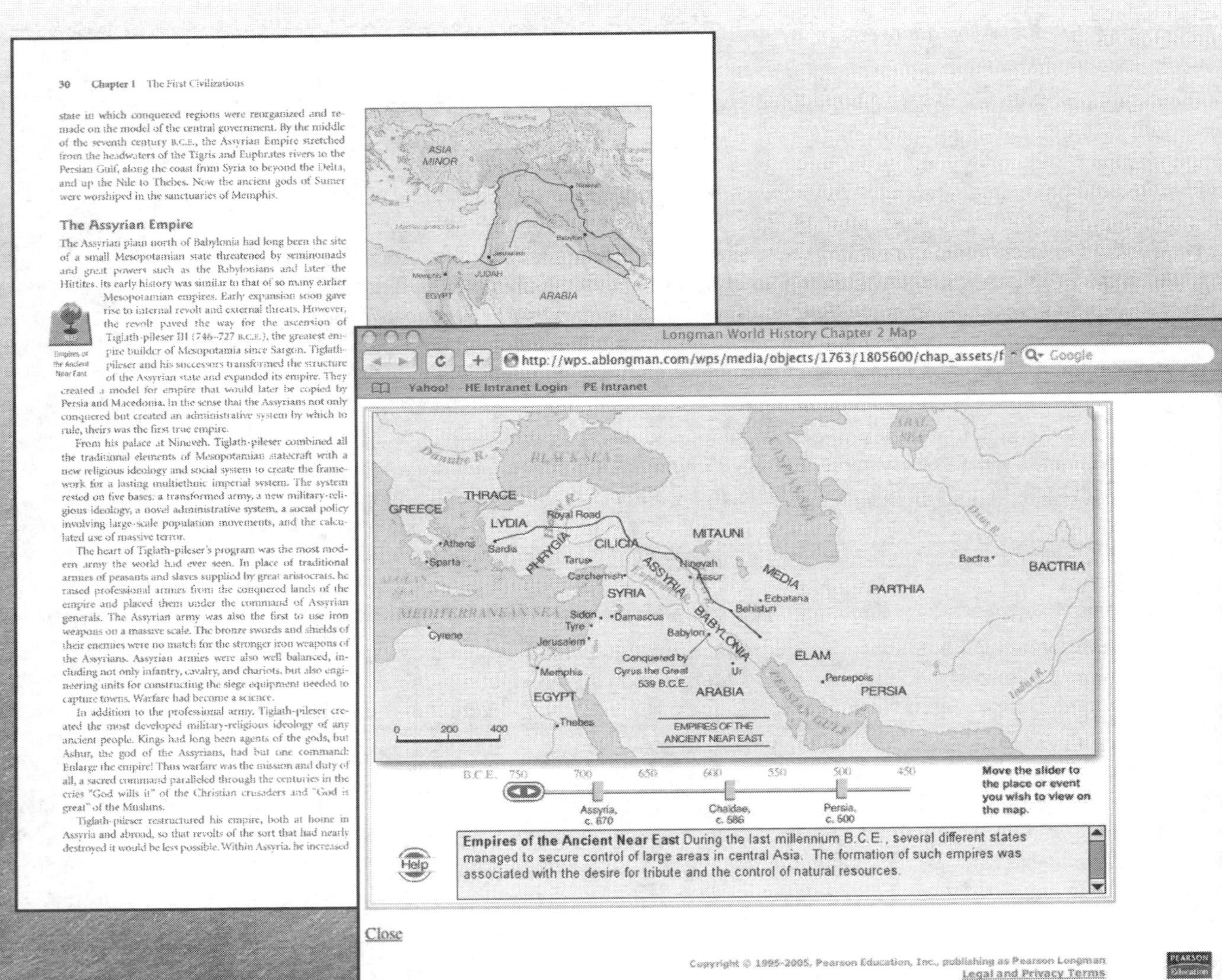
30 Chapter 1 The First Civilizations

state in which conquered regions were reorganized and remade on the model of the central government. By the middle of the seventh century B.C.E., the Assyrian Empire stretched from the headwaters of the Tigris and Euphrates rivers to the Persian Gulf, along the coast from Syria to beyond the Delta, and up the Nile to Thebes. Now the ancient gods of Sumer were worshiped in the sanctuaries of Memphis.

The Assyrian Empire

The Assyrian plain north of Babylonia had long been the site of a small Mesopotamian state threatened by seminomads and great powers such as the Babylonians and later the Hittites. Its early history was similar to that of so many earlier Mesopotamian empires. Early expansion soon gave rise to internal revolt and external threats. However, the revolt paved the way for the ascension of Tiglath-pileser III (746–727 B.C.E.), the greatest empire builder of Mesopotamia since Sargon. Tiglath-pileser and his successors transformed the structure of the Assyrian state and expanded its empire. They created a model for empire that would later be copied by Persia and Macedonia. In the sense that the Assyrians not only conquered but created an administrative system by which to rule, theirs was the first true empire.

Empires of the Ancient Near East

From his palace at Nineveh, Tiglath-pileser combined all the traditional elements of Mesopotamian statecraft with a new religious ideology and social system to create the framework for a lasting multiethnic imperial system. The system rested on five bases: a transformed army, a new military-religious ideology, a novel administrative system, a social policy involving large-scale population movements, and the calculated use of massive terror.

The heart of Tiglath-pileser's program was the most modern army the world had ever seen. In place of traditional armies of peasants and slaves supplied by great aristocrats, he raised professional armies from the conquered lands of the empire and placed them under the command of Assyrian generals. The Assyrian army was also the first to use iron weapons on a massive scale. The bronze swords and shields of their enemies were no match for the stronger iron weapons of the Assyrians. Assyrian armies were also well balanced, including not only infantry, cavalry, and chariots, but also engineering units for constructing the siege equipment needed to capture towns. Warfare had become a science.

In addition to the professional army, Tiglath-pileser created the most developed military-religious ideology of any ancient people. Kings had long been agents of the gods, but Ashur, the god of the Assyrians, had but one command: Enlarge the empire! Thus warfare was the mission and duty of all, a sacred command paralleled through the centuries in the cries "God wills it" of the Christian crusaders and "God is great" of the Muslims.

Tiglath-pileser restructured his empire, both at home in Assyria and abroad, so that revolts of the sort that had nearly destroyed it would be less possible. Within Assyria, he increased

DOCUMENT

This icon directs students to primary source documents that support the material they are reading. In addition, the documents offer headnotes and analysis questions to focus students' reading.

IMAGE

Photos, cartoons, and artwork offer students opportunities to learn the course content in a more visual way. Each image includes a headnote and analysis questions.

MAP

Interactive maps with headnotes and questions help students visualize the material they are studying. Atlas maps and printable map activities from a Longman workbook give students hands-on experience.

VIDEO CLIP

Historical video clips are included, along with headnotes and thoughtful questions.

Volume 3

Atlas Edition

THE WEST

Encounters & Transformations

HISTORY 103

Brian Levack

Edward Muir

Meredith Veldman

Michael Maas

Custom Edition for Oregon State University

Taken from:

The West: Encounters & Transformations, Second Edition
by Brian Levack, Edward Muir, Meredith Veldman, and Michael Maas

Custom Publishing

New York Boston San Francisco
London Toronto Sydney Tokyo Singapore Madrid
Mexico City Munich Paris Cape Town Hong Kong Montreal

Cover Art: Courtesy of PhotoDisc/Getty Images

Excerpts taken from:

The West: Encounters & Transformations, Second Edition
by Brian Levack, Edward Muir, Meredith Veldman, and Michael Maas

Published by Longman
New York, New York 10036

Printed in the United States of America

10 9 8 7 6 5 4 3 2 1

2008300179

DM

Pearson
Custom Publishing
is a division of

www.pearsonhighered.com

ISBN 10: 0-558-15915-X
ISBN 13: 978-0-558-15915-3

Brief Contents

Detailed Contents

Documents

Maps

Features

JUSTICE IN HISTORY

THE HUMAN BODY IN HISTORY

ENCOUNTERS & TRANSFORMATIONS

Chronologies

Preface

We wrote this textbook to answer questions about the identity of the civilization in which we live. Journalists, politicians, and scholars often refer to our civilization, its political ideologies, its economic systems, and its cultures as "Western" without fully considering what that label means and why it might be appropriate. The classification of our civilization as Western has become particularly problematic in the age of globalization. The creation of international markets, the rapid dissemination of ideas on a global scale, and the transmission of popular culture from one country to another often make it difficult to distinguish what is Western from what is not. *The West: Encounters & Transformations* offers students a history of Western civilization in which these issues of Western identity are given prominence. Our goal is neither to idealize nor to indict that civilization but to describe its main characteristics in different historical periods.

The West: Encounters & Transformations gives careful consideration to two basic questions. The first is, how did the definition of the West change over time? In what ways did its boundaries shift and how did the distinguishing characteristics of its cultures change? The second question is, by what means did the West—and the idea of the West—develop? We argue that the West is the product of a series of cultural encounters that occurred both outside and within its geographical boundaries. We explore these encounters and the transformations they produced by detailing the political, social, religious, and cultural history of the regions that have been, at one time or another, a part of the West.

Defining the West

What is the West? How did it come into being? How has it developed throughout history? Many textbooks take for granted which regions or peoples of the globe constitute the West. They treat the history of the West as a somewhat expanded version of European history. While not disputing the centrality of Europe to any definition of the West, we contend that the West is not only a geographical realm with ever-shifting boundaries but also a cultural realm, an area of cultural influence extending beyond the geographical and political boundaries of Europe. We so strongly believe in this notion that we have written the essay "What Is the West?" to encourage students to think about their understanding of Western civilization and to guide their understanding of each chapter. Many of the features of what we call Western civilization originated in regions that are not geographically part of Europe (such as northern Africa and the Middle East), while ever since the fifteenth century various social, ethnic, and political groups from non-European regions (such as North and South America, eastern Russia, Australia, New Zealand, and South Africa) have identified themselves, in one way or another, with the West. Throughout the text, we devote considerable attention to the boundaries of the West and show how borderlines between cultures have been created, especially in eastern and southeastern Europe.

Considered as a geographical and cultural realm, "the West" is a term of recent origin, and the civilization to which it refers did not become clearly defined until the eleventh century, especially during the Crusades, when western European Christians developed a distinct cultural identity. Before that time we can only talk about the powerful forces that created the West, especially the dynamic interaction of the civilizations of western Europe, the Byzantine Empire, and the Muslim world.

Over the centuries Western civilization has acquired many salient characteristics. These include two of the world's great legal systems (civil law and common law), three of the world's monotheistic religions (Judaism, Christianity, and Islam), certain political and social philosophies, forms of political organization (such as the modern bureaucratic state and democracy), methods of scientific inquiry, systems of economic organization (such as industrial capitalism), and distinctive styles of art, architecture, and music. At times one or more of these characteristics has served as a primary source of Western identity: Christianity in the Middle Ages, science and rationalism during the Enlightenment, industrialization in the nineteenth and twentieth centuries, and a defense of individual liberty and democracy in the late twentieth century. These sources of Western identity, however, have always been challenged and contested, both when they were coming into prominence and when they appeared to be most triumphant. Western culture has never been monolithic, and even today references to the West imply a wide range of meanings.

Cultural Encounters

The definition of the West is closely related to the central theme of our book, which is the process of cultural encounters. Throughout *The West: Encounters & Transformations,* we examine the West as a product of a series of cultural encounters both outside the West and within it. We show that the West originated and developed through a continuous process of inclusion and exclusion resulting from a series of encounters among and within different groups. These encounters can be described in a general sense as external, internal, or ideological.

External Encounters

External encounters took place between peoples of different civilizations. Before the emergence of the West as a clearly defined entity, external encounters occurred between such diverse peoples as Greeks and Phoenicians, Macedonians and Egyptians, and Romans and Celts. After the eleventh century, external encounters between Western and non-Western peoples occurred mainly during periods of European exploration, expansion, and imperialism. In the sixteenth and seventeenth centuries, for example, a series of external encounters took place between Europeans on the one hand and Africans, Asians, and the indigenous people of the Americas on the other. Two chapters of *The West: Encounters & Transformations* (Chapters 12 and 17) and a large section of a third (Chapter 23) explore these external encounters in depth and discuss how they affected Western and non-Western civilizations alike.

Internal Encounters

Our discussion of encounters also includes similar interactions between different social groups *within* Western countries. These internal encounters often took place between dominant and subordinate groups, such as between lords and peasants, rulers and subjects, men and women, factory owners and workers, masters and slaves. Encounters between those who were educated and those who were illiterate, which recur frequently throughout Western history, also fall into this category. Encounters just as often took place between different religious and political groups, such as between Christians and Jews, Catholics and Protestants, and royal absolutists and republicans.

Ideological Encounters

Ideological encounters involve interaction between comprehensive systems of thought, most notably religious doctrines, political philosophies, and scientific theories about the nature of the world. These ideological conflicts usually arose out of internal encounters, when various groups within Western societies subscribed to different theories of government or rival religious faiths. The encounters between Christianity and polytheism in the early Middle Ages, between liberalism and conservatism in the nineteenth century, and between fascism and communism in the twentieth century were ideological encounters. Some ideological encounters had an external dimension, such as when the forces of Islam and Christianity came into conflict during the Crusades and when the Cold War developed between Soviet communism and Western democracy in the second half of the twentieth century.

* * *

The West: Encounters & Transformations illuminates the variety of these encounters and clarifies their effects. By their very nature encounters are interactive, but they have taken different forms: they have been violent or peaceful, coercive or cooperative. Some have resulted in the imposition of Western ideas on areas outside the geographical boundaries of the West or the perpetuation of the dominant culture within Western societies. More often than not, however, encounters have resulted in a more reciprocal process of exchange in which both Western and non-Western cultures or the values of both dominant and subordinate groups have undergone significant transformation. Our book not only identifies these encounters but also discusses their significance by returning periodically to the issue of Western identity.

Coverage

T*he West: Encounters & Transformations* offers both balanced coverage of political, social, and culture history and a broader coverage of the West and the world.

Balanced Coverage

Our goal throughout the text has been to provide balanced coverage of political, social, and cultural history and to include significant coverage of religious and military history as well. Political history defines the basic structure of the book, and some chapters, such as those on the Hellenistic world, the age of confessional divisions, absolutism and state building, the French Revolution, and the coming of mass politics, include sustained political narratives. Because we understand the West to be a cultural as well as a geographical realm, we give a prominent position to cultural history. Thus we include rich sections on Hellenistic philosophy and literature, the cultural environment of the Italian Renaissance, the creation of a new political culture at the time of the French Revolution, and the atmosphere of cultural despair and desire that prevailed in Europe after World War I. We also devote special attention to religious history, including the history of Islam as well as that of Christianity and Judaism. Unlike many other textbooks, our coverage of religion continues into the modern period.

The West: Encounters & Transformations also provides extensive coverage of the history of women and gender. Wherever possible the history of women is integrated into the broader social, cultural, and political history of the period. But there are also separate sections on women in our chapters on classical Greece, the Renaissance, the Reformation, the Enlightenment, the Industrial Revolution, World War I, World War II, and the postwar era.

The West and the World

Our book provides broad geographical coverage. Because the West is the product of a series of encounters, the external areas with which the West interacted are of major importance. Three chapters deal specifically with the West and the world.

- Chapter 12, "The West and the World: The Significance of Global Encounters, 1450–1650"
- Chapter 17, "The West and the World: Empire, Trade, and War, 1650–1815"
- Chapter 23, "The West and the World: Cultural Crisis and the New Imperialism, 1870–1914"

These chapters present substantial material on sub-Saharan Africa, Latin America, the Middle East, India, and East Asia. Our text is also distinctive in its coverage of eastern Europe and the Muslim world, areas that have often been considered outside the boundaries of the West. These regions were arenas within which significant cultural encounters took place. Finally we include material on the United States and Australia, both of which have become part of the West. We recognize that most American college and university students have the opportunity to study American history as a separate subject, but treatment of the United States as a Western nation provides a different perspective from that usually given in courses on American history. For example, this book treats America's revolution as one of four Atlantic revolutions, its national unification in the nineteenth century as part of a broader western European development, its pattern of industrialization as related to that of Britain, and its central role in the Cold War as part of an ideological encounter that was global in scope.

Organization

The chronological and thematic organization of our book conforms in its broad outline to the way in which Western civilization courses are generally taught. We have limited the number of chapters to twenty-eight, in an effort to make the book more compatible with the traditional American semester calendar and to solve the frequent complaint that there is not enough time to cover all the material in the course. However, our organization differs from other books in some significant ways:

- Chapter 2, which covers the period from ca. 1600 to 550 B.C.E., is the first in a Western civilization textbook to examine the International Bronze Age and its aftermath as a period important in its own right because it saw the creation of expansionist, multi-ethnic empires linked by trade and diplomacy.
- In Chapter 4 the Roman Republic, in keeping with contemporary scholarship, has been incorporated into a discussion of the Hellenistic world, dethroned slightly to emphasize how it was one of many competing Mediterranean civilizations.
- Chapter 12 covers the first period of European expansion, from 1450 to 1650. It examines the new European encounters with the civilizations of sub-Saharan Africa, the Americas, and East Asia. By paying careful attention to the characteristics of these civilizations before the arrival of the Europeans, we show how this encounter affected indigenous peoples as well as Europeans.
- Chapter 16 is devoted entirely to the Scientific Revolution of the seventeenth century in order to emphasize the central importance of this development in the creation of Western identity.
- Chapter 17, which covers the second period of European expansion, from 1650 to 1815, studies the growth of European empires, the beginning of global warfare, and encounters between Europeans and the peoples of Asia and Africa. It treats the Atlantic revolutions of the late eighteenth and early nineteenth centuries, including

the American Revolution, as episodes in the history of European empires rather than as revolts inspired mainly by national sentiment.

- Chapter 26 not only offers a comprehensive examination of World War II, but also explores the moral fissure in the history of the West created, in very different ways, by the Holocaust and the aerial bombings of civilian centers that culminated in the use of the atomic bomb in August 1945.
- Chapter 28, "The West in the Contemporary Era: New Encounters and Transformations," includes an extended discussion of the emergence of European Islamic communities and the resulting transformations in both European and Islamic identities.

What's New in this Edition?

In preparing the second edition of *The West: Encounters & Transformations* we have focused on two goals: to make the textbook more teachable and to strengthen our emphasis on the encounters that have transformed the West.

Organization

We have reduced the number of chapters from twenty-nine to twenty-eight, in order to make the book even more compatible with the typical fifteen-week semester. In a number of chapters, moreover, we have made significant rearrangements of material:

- In Chapter 3, we have discussed the Persian Empire before beginning our study of Hebrew and Greek civilizations to emphasize the argument that the latter two civilizations emerged in a political world dominated by Persia.
- Chapters 6 through 9, which deal with the period from about 300 to 1300 C.E., have been rearranged along more thematic, less chronological lines. We have adopted this strategy to emphasize the importance of the interactions among different religious communities during a period that was crucial to the development of Christianity and Islam.
- Chapter 17, "The West and the World: Empire, Trade, and War, 1650–1815," which appeared as Chapter 19 in the first edition, has been placed earlier in the book because it is concerned mainly with eighteenth-century developments. It now precedes the discussion of eighteenth-century society and culture.
- In Chapter 22, "The Coming of Mass Politics: Industrialization, Emancipation, and Instability, 1870–1914," we have replaced the "nation-by-nation" narrative with a thematic approach that more effectively conveys the processes by which European elites sought both to capitalize on and control the new forces of popular nationalism.
- Our treatment of both the Holocaust and the decision to use atomic bombs against Japan, which appeared as a separate chapter in the first edition, is now embedded in Chapter 26, "World War II." This volume still includes a far more extensive and in-depth exploration of these developments than any other Western civilization textbook.
- New sections on "Postwar Nationalism, Westernization, and the Islamic Challenge" in Chapter 25, and "Islam, Terrorism, and European Identity" in Chapter 28 are the most striking examples of our decision to give more coverage to Islam throughout the book.

New Feature: "Encounters & Transformations"

We have introduced a new feature, "Encounters & Transformations," in about half the chapters. These essays reinforce the main theme of the book by giving specific examples of the ways in which cultural encounters changed the perception and identity of the West.

Features and Pedagogical Aids

In writing this textbook we have endeavored to keep both the student reader and the classroom instructor in mind at all times. The text includes the following features and pedagogical aids, all of which are intended to support the themes of the book.

What Is the West?

MANY OF THE PEOPLE WHO INFLUENCE PUBLIC OPINION—POLITIcians, teachers, clergy, journalists, and television commentators—refer to "Western values," "the West," and "Western civilization." They often use these terms as if they do not require explanation. But what *do* these terms mean? The West has always been an arena within which different cultures, religions, values, and philosophies have interacted, and any definition of the West will inevitably arouse controversy.

The most basic definition of the West is of a place. Western civilization is now typically thought to comprise the regions of Europe, the Americas, Australia, and New Zealand. However, this is a contemporary definition of the West. The inclusion of these places in the West is the result of a long history of European expansion through colonization. In addition to being a place, Western civilization also encompasses a cultural history—a tradition stretching back thousands of years to the ancient world. Over this long period the civilization we now identify as Western gradually took shape. The

"What Is the West?"

The West: Encounters & Transformations begins with an essay to engage students in the task of defining the West and to introduce them to the notion of cultural encounters. "What Is the West?" guides students through the text by providing a framework for understanding how the West was shaped. Structured around the six questions of What? When? Where? Who? How? and Why?, this framework encourages students to think about their understanding of Western civilization. The essay serves as a blueprint for using this textbook.

NEW! "Encounters & Transformations"

These features, which appear in about half the chapters, illustrate the main theme of the book by identifying specific encounters and showing how they led to significant transformations in the culture of the West. These features show, for example, how encounters among nomadic tribes of Arabia led to the rapid spread of Islam; how the Mayas' interpretation of Christian symbols transformed European Christianity into a hybrid religion; how the importation of chocolate from the New World to Europe changed Western consumption patterns and the rhythms of the Atlantic economy; and how Picasso's encounter with African art led to the transformation of modernism. Each of these essays concludes with a question for discussion.

Encounters & Transformations

Ships of the Desert: Camels from Morocco to Central Asia

A remarkable thing happened when the Arab followers of the dynamic new religion of Islam encountered the humble beast of burden the camel. The camel helped make Arab armies lethal in battle, which meant that the message of Islam spread rapidly through conquest. In addition the caravan trade that transported goods on the backs of camels brought the Arabs into contact with a vast stretch of the world from Spain to China. In the exchanges that took place along the caravan routes, Islamic religious ideas were widely disseminated, and Arab merchants gained access to a lucrative trade that enriched Muslim cities. The success of the caravan trade changed the very appearance of large parts of the West by making obsolete the old Roman roads and the shipping lanes that had unified the Mediterranean, Europe, and North Africa in the ancient world. Narrow camel tracks replaced roads; oases and cities along the caravan routes supplanted ports in economic significance.

Before Muhammad began to recite, the camel had already transformed the life of Arabia. Camels were highly efficient beasts of burden, especially in arid regions, because of their bodies' capacity to conserve water. Able to drink as much as twenty-eight gallons at a time, camels can last four to nine days without water and travel great distances in this period. The fat in their humps allows camels to survive for even longer without food. As pack animals, camels are more efficient than carts pulled by animals because they can traverse roadless rough terrain and cross rivers without bridges. They require fewer people to manage them on a journey than do wheeled vehicles.

Arab fighters were especially menacing because they developed the "North Arabian saddle" that let them ride the one-humped Arabian camel with comfort in battle. The new saddle required only one rider who could grasp the camel's reins with one hand while slashing downward at enemy troops with a sword in his other hand. Warriors on camels could attack infantry with speed and crushing force. By 300 C.E., camel-breeding Arab tribesmen, empowered by their new military technology, inaugurated the "Caravan Age." The Arabs seized control of the lucrative spice trade routes and became an economic, military, and political force by exploiting and guarding the wealth of the caravans.

After Muhammad established his community in Mecca, Islam literally "took off" on camelback. Tribesmen on camels proved an unstoppable force as they spread Islam first throughout Arabia and the Middle East, and then with lightning speed across North Africa into Spain and Central Asia. Camels played a significant role in the expanding Islamic economy because they made long-distance trade extremely profitable. The transformations the camel brought were most evident in the former Roman provinces wh
mous Roman roads h
primary conduit of la
Thousands of miles c
nected the provinces
Empire and let troop
from one front to an
ever, camels change
Because these "ships
do not need paved r
routes did not have t
Roman road systems,
chants bypassed ther
New trade routes acr
and other harsh terra
to camels quickly de
Morocco to Central A
astonishing conseque
700 paved roads start
pear. Because camels
walk on narrow path
streets and wide mar
carts and wagons tha
Greek and Roman cit
use. Bazaars with nar
lanes appropriate to
sprung up to replace
and wheeled vehicle
peared in these lands
just roads and the sh
that changed. There
consequences as wel
caravan traffic reache
China, bringing Chin
Chinese ideas to the

Question for I
How might the history
have differed had not
replaced the system of

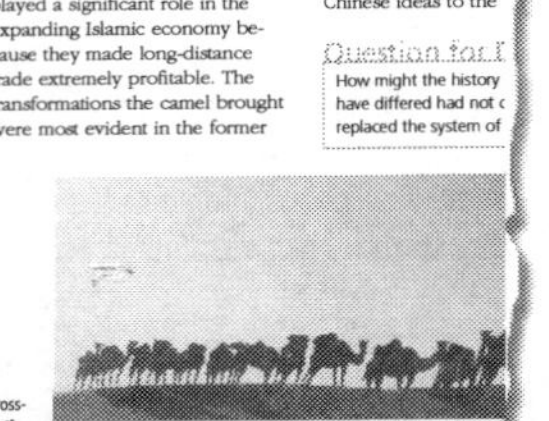

The Camel Caravan
This modern photograph shows a string of camels cross-

Focus Questions

The introduction to each chapter includes a statement of the main question that the entire chapter addresses. It also includes a set of questions that the individual sections of the chapter seek to answer. Each of these questions is then repeated at the beginning of the relevant section of the chapter. The reason for this strategy is to remind the student that the purpose of studying history is not only to learn what happened in the past but also to explain and interpret the course of events. This pedagogical strategy reinforces the approach that the essay, "What is the West?," introduces at the beginning of the book.

"Justice in History"

Found in every chapter, this feature presents a historically significant trial or episode in which different notions of justice (or injustice) were debated and resolved. The "Justice in History" features illustrate cultural encounters within communities as they try to determine the fate of individuals from all walks of life. Many famous trials dealt with conflicts over basic religious, philosophical, or political values, such as those of Socrates, Jesus, Joan of Arc, Charles I, Galileo, and Adolf Eichmann. Other "Justice in History" features show how judicial institutions, such as the ordeal, the Inquisition, and revolutionary tribunals, handled adversarial situations in different societies. These essays, therefore, illustrate the way in which the basic values of the West have evolved through attempts to resolve disputes, contention, and conflict.

Each "Justice in History" feature includes two pedagogical aids. "Questions of Justice" helps students explore the historical significance of the episode just examined. These questions can also be used in classroom discussion or as student essay topics. "Taking It Further" provides the student with a few references that can be consulted in connection with a research project.

"The Human Body in History"

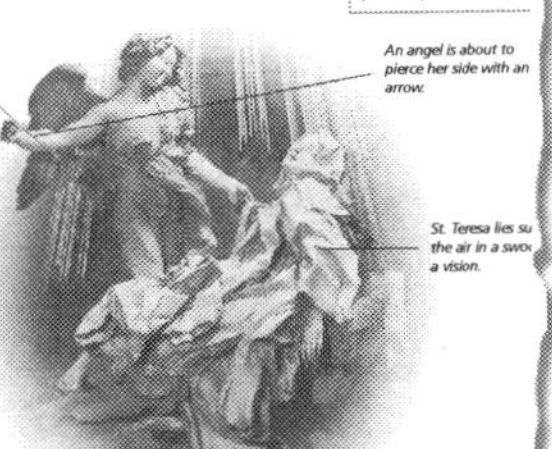

Found in about half of the chapters, these features show that the human body, which many people tend to understand solely as a product of biology, also has a history. These essays reveal that the ways in which various religious and political groups have represented the body in art and literature, clothed it, treated it medically, and abused it tell a great deal about the history of Western culture. These features include essays on the classical nude male body, the signs of disease during the Black Death, bathing the body in the East and the West, and the contraceptive pill. Concluding each essay is a single question for discussion that directs students back to the broader issues with which the chapter deals.

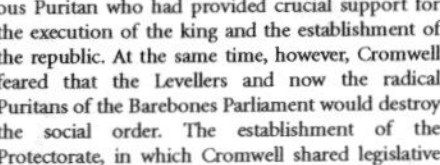

Primary Source Documents

In each chapter we have presented a number of excerpts from primary source documents—from "Tales of the Flood" to "Darwin's 'Descent of Man'"—in order to reinforce or expand upon the points made in the text and to introduce students to the basic materials of historical research.

Maps and Illustrations

Artwork is a key component of our book. We recognize that many students often lack a strong familiarity with geography, and so we have taken great care to develop maps that help sharpen their geographic skills. Complementing the book's standard map program,

we include maps focusing on areas outside the borders of Western civilization. These maps include a small thumbnail globe that highlights the geographic area under discussion in the context of the larger world. Fine art and photos also tell the story of Western civilization, and we have included more than 350 images to help students visualize the past: the way people lived, the events that shaped their lives, and how they viewed the world around them.

Chronologies and Suggested Readings

Each chapter includes chronological charts and suggested readings. Chronologies outline significant events, such as "The End of World War II," and serve as convenient references for students. Each chapter concludes with an annotated list of suggested readings. These are not scholarly bibliographies aimed at the professor, but suggestions for students who wish to explore a topic in greater depth or to write a research paper. A comprehensive list of suggested readings is available on our book-specific website, www.ablongman.com/levack2e.

Glossary

We have sought to create a work that is accessible to students with little prior knowledge of the basic facts of Western history or geography. Throughout the book we have explained difficult concepts at length. For example, we present in-depth explanations of the concepts of Zoroastrianism, Neoplatonism, Renaissance humanism, the various Protestant denominations of the sixteenth century, capitalism, seventeenth-century absolutism, nineteenth-century liberalism and nationalism, fascism, and modernism. Key concepts such as these are identified in the chapters with a degree symbol (°) and defined as well in the end-of-text Glossary.

MyHistoryLab Icons

Throughout the text, you will see icons that will lead students to additional resources found on MyHistoryLab.com. These resources fall into four categories:

The **document** icon directs students to primary source documents that support the material they are reading in the textbook. In addition, most documents offer headnotes and analysis questions that focus students' reading.

The **image** icon leads students to photos, cartoons, and artwork that relate to the topic they are reading. Most images include a descriptive, contextualized headnote and analysis questions.

The **map** icon refers to maps, many of which are interactive and contain headnotes and questions designed to help students visualize the material they are learning. Printable map activities from Longman's outstanding geography workbooks allow students to interact with maps.

The **video** icon leads students to video clips that focus on the regions, people, or events discussed in the text.

A Note About Dates and Transliterations

In keeping with current academic practice, *The West: Encounters & Transformations* uses B.C.E. (before the common era) and C.E. (common era) to designate dates. We also follow the most current and widely accepted English transliterations of Arabic. *Qur'an,* for example, is used for *Koran; Muslim* is used for *Moslem.* Chinese words appearing in the text for the first time are written in pinyin, followed by the older Wade-Giles system in parentheses.

Supplements

For Qualified College Instructors

Instructor's Resource Manual

0-321-42735-1

In this manual written by Sharon Arnoult, Midwestern State University, each chapter contains a chapter outline, significant themes, learning objectives, lesson enrichment ideas, discussion suggestions, and questions for discussing the primary source documents in the text.

Test Bank

0-321-42731-9

Written by Susan Carrafiello, Wright State University, this supplement contains more than 1,200 multiple-choice and essay questions. All questions are referenced by topic and text page number.

TestGen-EQ Computerized Testing System

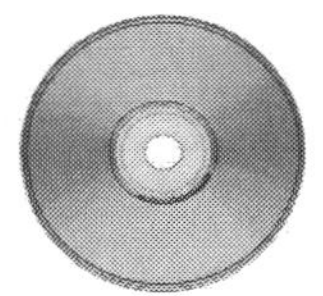

0-321-42573-1

This flexible, easy-to-master computerized test bank on a dual-platform CD includes all of the items in the printed test bank and allows instructors to select specific questions, edit existing questions, and add their own items to create exams. Tests can be printed in several different fonts and formats and can include figures, such as graphs and tables.

Companion Website (www.ablongman.com/levack2e)

Instructors can take advantage of the Companion Website that supports this text. The instructor section includes teaching links, downloadable maps, tables, and graphs from the text for use in PowerPoint, PowerPoint lecture outlines, and a link to the Instructor Resource Center.

Instructor Resource Center (IRC) (www.ablongman.com/irc)

Through the Instructor Resource Center, instructors can log into premium online products, browse and download book-specific instructor resources, and receive immediate access and instructions to installing course management content. Instructors who already have access to CourseCompass or Supplements Central can log in to the IRC immediately using their existing login and password. First-time users can register at the Instructor Resource Center welcome page at www.ablongman.com/irc.

MyHistoryLab (www.myhistorylab.com)

MyHistoryLab provides students with an online package complete with the entire electronic textbook and numerous study aids. With several hundred primary sources, many of which are assignable and link to a gradebook, pre- and post-tests that link to a gradebook and result in individualized study plans, videos and images, as well as map workbook activities with gradable quizzes, the site offers students a unique, interactive experience that brings history to life. The comprehensive site also includes a History Bookshelf with fifty of the most commonly assigned books in history classes and a History Toolkit with tutorials and helpful links. Other features include gradable assignments and chapter review materials; a Test Bank; and Research Navigator.

Delivered in CourseCompass, Blackboard, or WebCT, as well as in a non-course-management version, MyHistoryLab is easy to use and flexible. MyHistoryLab is organized according to the table of contents of this textbook. With the course management version, instructors can create a further customized product by adding their own syllabus, content, and assignments, or they can use the materials as presented.

PowerPoint Presentations

These presentations contain PowerPoint slides for each chapter and may include key points and terms for a lecture on the chapter, as well as full-color images of important maps, graphs, and charts. The presentations are available for download from www.ablongman.com/levack2e and www.ablongman.com/irc.

Text-Specific Transparency Set

0-321-42732-7

Instructors can download files with which to make full-color transparency map acetates taken from the text at www.ablongman.com/irc.

History Video Program

Longman offers more than one hundred videos from which qualified adopters can choose. Restrictions apply.

History Digital Media Archive CD-ROM

0-321-14976-9

This CD-ROM contains electronic images, interactive and static maps, and media elements such as video. It is fully customizable and ready for classroom presentation. All images and maps are available in PowerPoint as well.

Discovering Western Civilization Through Maps and Views

0-673-53596-7

Created by Gerald Danzer, University of Illinois at Chicago, and David Buissert, this unique set of 140 full-color acetates contains an introduction to teaching history through maps and a detailed commentary on each transparency. The collection includes cartographic and pictorial maps, views and photos, urban plans, building diagrams, and works of art. Available to qualified college adopters on Longman's Instructor Resource Center (IRC) at www.ablongman.com/irc.

For Students

Study Guide

Volume I: 0-321-42733-5

Volume II: 0-321-42734-3

Containing activities and study aids for every chapter in the text, each chapter of the *Study Guide* written by Carron Fillingim, Louisiana State University, includes a thorough chapter outline; timeline; map exercises; identification, multiple-choice and thought questions; and critical-thinking questions based on primary source documents from the text.

Companion Website (www.ablongman.com/levack2e)

Providing a wealth of resources for students using *The West: Encounters & Transformations,* Second Edition, this Companion Website contains chapter summaries, interactive practice test questions, and Web links for every chapter in the text.

Research Navigator and Research Navigator Guide

0-205-40838-9

Research Navigator is a comprehensive Website comprising four exclusive databases of credible and reliable source material for research and for student assignments: EBSCO's ContentSelect Academic Journal & Abstract Database, the *New York Times* Search-by-Subject Archive, *Financial Times* Article Archive and Company Financials, and "Best of the Web" Link Library. The site also includes an extensive help section. The Research Navigator Guide provides your students with access to the Research Navigator website and includes reference material and hints about conducting online research. Available to qualified college adopters when packaged with the text.

Mapping Western Civilization: Student Activities

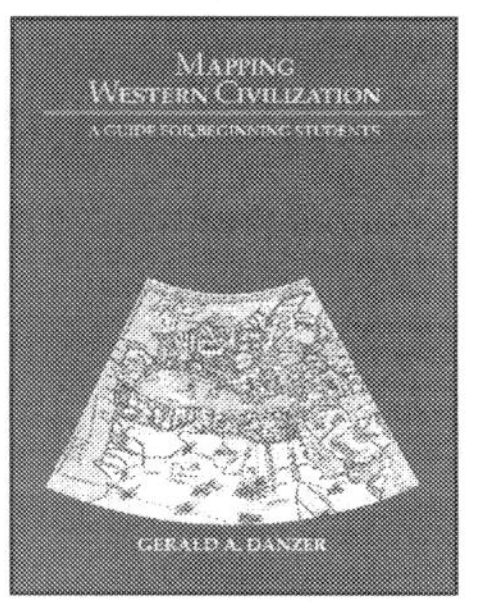

0-673-53774-9

Created by Gerald Danzer, University of Illinois at Chicago, this FREE map workbook for students is designed as an accompaniment to *Discovering Western Civilization Through Maps and Views.* It features exercises designed to teach students to interpret and analyze cartographic materials such as historical documents. Available to qualified college adopters when packaged with the text.

Western Civilization Map Workbook

Volume I: 0-321-01878-8

Volume II: 0-321-01877-X

The map exercises in these volumes, created by Glee Wilson at Kent State University, test and reinforce basic geography literacy while building critical-thinking skills. Available to qualified college adopters when packaged with the text.

Study Card for Western Civilization

0-321-29233-2

Colorful, affordable, and packed with useful information, Longman's Study Cards make studying easier, more efficient, and more enjoyable. Course information is distilled down to the basics, helping students quickly master the fundamentals, review a subject for understanding, or prepare for an exam. Because they're laminated for durability, they can be kept for years to come and used whenever necessary for a quick review. Available to qualified college adopters when packaged with the text.

MyHistoryLab (www.myhistorylab.com)

MyHistoryLab provides students with an online package complete with the entire electronic textbook, numerous study aids, primary sources, and chapter exams. With several hundred primary sources and images, as well as map workbook activities with gradable quizzes, the site offers students a unique, interactive experience that brings history to life. The comprehensive site also includes a History Bookshelf with fifty of the most commonly assigned books in history classes and a History Toolkit with tutorials and helpful links.

Longman Atlas of Western Civilization

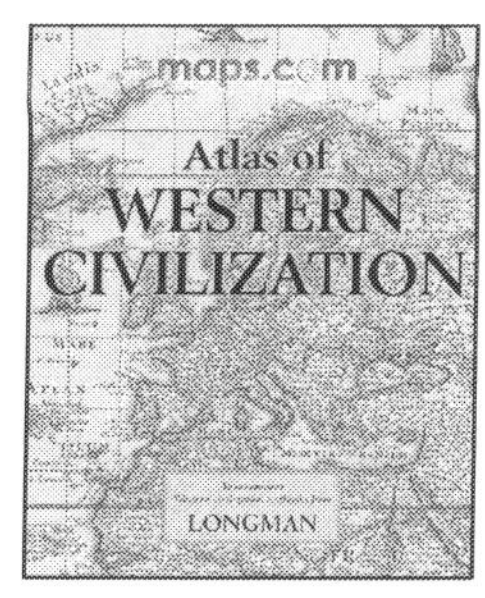

0-321-21626-1

This fifty-two-page atlas features carefully selected historical maps that provide comprehensive coverage for the major historical periods. Each map has been designed to be colorful, easy to read, and informative, without sacrificing detailed accuracy. This atlas makes history—and geography—more comprehensible.

A Short Guide to Writing About History, Fifth Edition

0-321-22716-6

Written by Richard A. Marius, late of Harvard University, and Melvin E. Page, Eastern Tennessee State University, this engaging and practical text helps students get beyond merely compiling dates and facts; it teaches them how to incorporate their own ideas into their papers and to tell a story about history that interests them and their peers. Covering both brief essays and the documented resource paper, the text explores the writing and researching processes; identifies different modes of historical writing, including argument; and concludes with guidelines for improving style.

Penguin-Longman Partnership

The partnership between Penguin Books and Longman Publishers offers a discount on the following titles when bundled with any Longman history survey textbook. Visit www.ablongman.com/penguin for more information.

Available Titles

Peter Abelard, *The Letters of Abelard and Heloise*
Dante Alighieri, *Divine Comedy: Inferno*
Dante Alighieri, *The Portable Dante*
Anonymous, *Early Irish Myths & Sagas*
Anonymous, *The Epic of Gilgamesh*
Anonymous, *The Song of Roland*
Anonymous, *Vinland Sagas*
Hannah Arendt, *On Revolution*
Aristophanes, *The Birds and Other Plays*
Aristotle, *The Politics*
Louis Auchincloss, *Woodrow Wilson* (Penguin Lives Series)
St. Augustine, *The Confessions of St. Augustine*
Jane Austen, *Emma*
Jane Austen, *Persuasion*
Jane Austen, *Pride and Prejudice*
Jane Austen, *Sense and Sensibility*
Edward Bellamy, *Looking Backward*
Richard Bowring, *Diary of Lady Murasaki*
Charlotte Brontë, *Jane Eyre*
Charlotte Brontë, *Villette*
Emily Brontë, *Wuthering Heights*
Edmund Burke, *Reflection on the Revolution in France and on the Proceedings in Certain Societies in London Relative to that Event*
Benvenuto Cellini, *The Autobiography of Benvenuto Cellini*
Geoffrey Chaucer, *The Canterbury Tales*
Marcus Tullius Cicero, *Cicero: Selected Political Speeches*
Miguel de Cervantes, *The Adventures of Don Quixote*
Bartolome de las Casas, *A Short Account of the Destruction of the West Indies*
René Descartes, *Discourse on Method and Related Writings*
Charles Dickens, *Great Expectations*
Charles Dickens, *Hard Times*
John Dos Passos, *Three Soldiers*
Einhard, *Two Lives of Charlemagne*
Olaudah Equiano, *The Interesting Narrative and Other Writings*
M. Finley (ed.), *The Portable Greek Historians*
Benjamin Franklin, *The Autobiography and Other Writings*
Jeffrey Gantz (tr.), *Early Irish Myths and Sagas*
Peter Gay, *Mozart* (Penguin Lives Series)
William Golding, *Lord of the Flies*
Grimm & Grimm, *Grimms' Fairy Tales*
Thomas Hardy, *Jude the Obscure*
Herodotus, *The Histories*
Thomas Hobbes, *Leviathan*
Homer, *The Iliad*
Homer, *The Iliad* (Deluxe)
Homer, *Odyssey Deluxe*
Homer, *Odyssey: Revised Prose Translation*
The Koran

Deborah Lipstadt, *Denying the Holocaust*
Machiavelli, *The Prince*
Bill Manley, *The Penguin Historical Atlas of Ancient Egypt*
Karl Marx, *The Communist Manifesto*
Colin McEvedy, *The New Penguin Atlas of Ancient History*
Colin McEvedy, *The New Penguin Atlas of Medieval History*
John Stuart Mill, *On Liberty*
Jean-Baptiste Molière, *Tartuffe and Other Plays*
Sir Thomas More, *Utopia and Other Essential Writings*
Robert Morkot, *The Penguin Historical Atlas of Ancient Greece*
Sherwin Nuland, *Leonardo Da Vinci*
George Orwell, *1984*
George Orwell, *Animal Farm*
Plato, *Great Dialogues of Plato*
Plato, *The Last Days of Socrates*
Plato, *The Republic*
Plutarch, *Fall of the Roman Republic*
Marco Polo, *The Travels*
Procopius, *The Secret History*
Jean-Jacques Rousseau, *The Social Contract*
Sallust, *The Jugurthine Wars, The Conspiracy of Cataline*
Chris Scarre, *The Penguin Historical Atlas of Ancient Rome*
Desmond Seward, *The Hundred Years' War*
William Shakespeare, *Four Great Comedies: The Taming of the Shrew, A Midsummer's Night Dream, Twelfth Night, The Tempest*
William Shakespeare, *Four Great Tragedies: Hamlet, Macbeth, King Lear, Othello*
William Shakespeare, *Four Histories: Richard II, Henry IV: Part I, Henry IV: Part II, Henry V*
William Shakespeare, *Hamlet*
William Shakespeare, *King Lear*
William Shakespeare, *Macbeth*
William Shakespeare, *The Merchant of Venice*
William Shakespeare, *Othello*
William Shakespeare, *The Taming of the Shrew*
William Shakespeare, *The Tempest*
William Shakespeare, *Twelfth Night*
Mary Shelley, *Frankenstein*
Aleksandr Solzhenitsyn, *One Day in the Life of Ivan Denisovich*
Sophocles, *The Three Theban Plays*
Robert Louis Stevenson, *The Strange Case of Dr. Jekyll and Mr. Hyde*
Suetonius, *The Twelve Caesars*
Jonathan Swift, *Gulliver's Travels*
Tacitus, *The Histories*
Various, *The Penguin Book of Historical Speeches*
Voltaire, *Candide, Zadig and Selected Stories*
Carl von Clausewitz, *On War*
von Goethe, *Faust, Part 1*
von Goethe, *Faust, Part 2*
Edith Wharton, *Ethan Frome*
Willet, *The Signet World Atlas*
Gary Wills, *Saint Augustine* (Penguin Lives Series)
Virginia Woolf, *Jacob's Room*

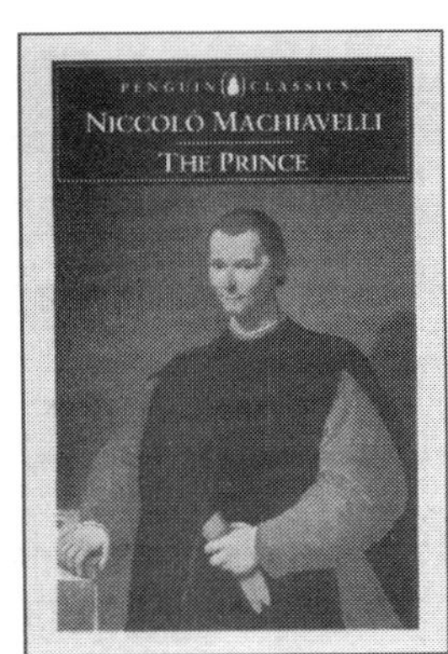

Longman Library of World Biography Series

Each interpretive biography in the new Library of World Biography series focuses on a figure whose actions and ideas significantly influenced the course of world history. Pocket-sized and brief, each book relates the life of its subject to the broader themes and developments of the time. Longman Publishers offers your students a discount on the titles below when instructors request that they be bundled with any Longman history survey textbook. Series titles include:

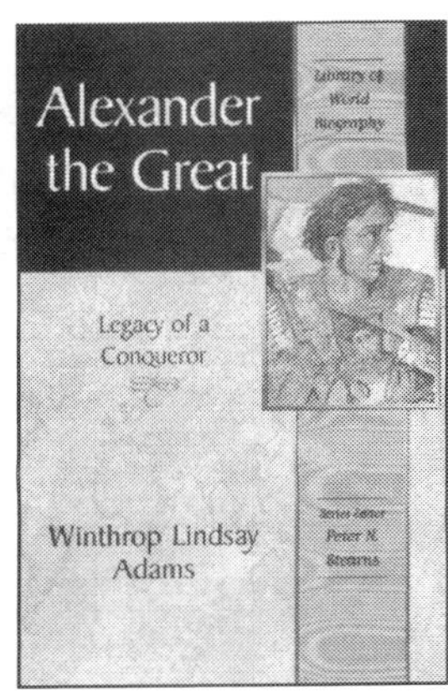

Ahmad al-Mansur: Islamic Visionary by Richard Smith (Ferrum College)
Alexander the Great: Legacy of a Conqueror by Winthrop Lindsay Adams (University of Utah)
Benito Mussolini: The First Fascist by Anthony L. Cardoza (Loyola University)
Fukuzawa Yûkichi: From Samurai to Capitalist by Helen M. Hopper (University of Pittsburgh)
Ignatius of Loyola: Founder of the Jesuits by John Patrick Donnelly (Marquette University)

Jacques Coeur: Entrepreneur and King's Bursar by Kathryn L. Reyerson (University of Minnesota)
Katô Shidzue: A Japanese Feminist by Helen M. Hopper (University of Pittsburgh)
Simón Bolívar: Liberation and Disappointment by David Bushnell (University of Florida)
Vasco da Gama: Renaissance Crusader by Glenn J. Ames (University of Toledo)
Zheng He: China and the Oceans in the Early Ming, 1405–1433 by Edward Dreyer (University of Miami)

Acknowledgments

In writing this book we have benefited from the guidance of many members of the superb editorial staff at Longman. We would like to thank our acquisitions editor Janet Lanphier for helping us refine and develop this second edition. David Kear, our development editor, gave us valuable criticisms and helped us keep our audience in mind. Heather Johnson superintended the copyediting and proofreading with skill and efficiency, while Christine Buese helped us locate the most appropriate illustrations. Sue Westmoreland, the executive marketing manager for history, offered many creative ideas for promoting the book.

The authors wish to thank the following friends and colleagues for their assistance: Kenneth Alder, Joseph Alehermes, Karl Appuhn, Sharon Arnoult, Nicholas Baker, Paula Baskovits, Paul-Alain Beaulieu, Kamilia Bergen, Timothy Breen, Peter Brown, Peter Carroll, Shawn Clybor, Jauabeth Condie-Pugh, Patricia Crone, Tracey Cullen, Arthur Eckstein, Susanna Elm, Benjamin Frommer, Cynthia Gladstone, Dena Goodman, Stefka Hadjiandonova, Matthias Henze, Stanley Hilton, Kenneth Holum, Mark Jurdjevic, Werner Kelber, Cathleen Keller, Anne Kilmer, Jacob Lassner, Robert Lerner, Nancy Levack, Richard Lim, David Lindenfeld, Brian Maxson, Sarah Maza, Peter Mazur, Laura McGough, Roderick McIntosh, Susan K. McIntosh, Glenn Markoe, William Monter, Randy Nichols, Scott Noegel, Monique O'Connell, Carl Petry, Michael Rogers, Karl Roider, Sarah Ross, Michele Salzman, Paula Sanders, Regina Schwartz, Ethan Shagan, Julia M. H. Smith, James Sidbury, and Rachel Wahlig.

We would also like to thank the many historians who gave generously of their time to review during the various stages of development of our second edition. Their comments and suggestions helped to improve the book. Thank you:

Melanie A. Bailey, *South Dakota State University*
Brett Berliner, *Morgan State University*
Alfred S. Bradford, *University of Oklahoma*
Linda Charmaine Powell, *Amarillo College*
Daniel Christensen, *California State University, Fullerton*
William L. Cumiford, *Chapman University*
Rebecca Durrer, *Columbia College*
Steven Fanning, *University of Illinois at Chicago*
Sean Farrell, *Northern Illinois University*
Judy E. Gaughan, *Colorado State University*
Jennifer Hedda, *Simpson College*
David Hudson, *California State University, Fresno*
Rebecca Huston, *Hinds Community College*
Barbara A. Klemm, *Broward Community College*
Molly McClain, *University of San Diego*
Randall McGowen, *University of Oregon*
John A. Nichols, *Slippery Rock University*
James T. Owens, *Oakton Community College*
Elizabeth Propes, *Mesa State College*
Miriam Raub Vivian, *California State University, Bakersfield*
Anne Rodrick, *Wofford College*
Jarbel Rodriguez, *San Francisco State University*
Jacquelyn A. Royal, *Lee University*
Jutta Scott, *South Carolina University*
Susan O. Shapiro, *Utah State University*
Steven E. Sidebotham, *University of Delaware*
David Stone, *Kansas State University*
Charles R. Sullivan, *University of Dallas*
Mary C. Swilling, *University of Mississippi*
Larissa Juliet Taylor, *Colby College*
Jonathan Ziskind, *University of Louisville*

We would also like to thank the historians whose careful reviews and comments on the first edition helped us revise the book for its second edition. Our thanks for your contributions:

Henry Abramson, *Florida Atlantic University*
Patricia Ali, *Morris College*
Joseph Appiah, *J. Sergeant Reynolds Community College*
Sharon L. Arnoult, *Midwestern State University*
Arthur H. Auten, *University of Hartford*
Clifford Backman, *Boston University*
Suzanne Balch-Lindsay, *Eastern New Mexico University*
Wayne C. Bartee, *Southwest Miami State University*
Brandon Beck, *Shenandoah University*
James R. Belpedio, *Becker College*
Richard Berthold, *University of New Mexico*
Cynthia S. Bisson, *Belmont University*
Richard Bodek, *College of Charleston*
Melissa Bokovoy, *University of New Mexico*
William H. Brennan, *University of the Pacific*
Morgan R. Broadhead, *Jefferson Community College*
Theodore Bromund, *Yale University*
April A. Brooks, *South Dakota State University*
Nathan M. Brooks, *New Mexico State University*
Michael Burger, *Mississippi University for Women*
Susan Carrafiello, *Wright State University*
Kathleen S. Carter, *High Point University*
William L. Combs, *Western Illinois University*
Joseph Coohill, *Pennsylvania State University–New Kensington*
Richard A. Cosgrove, *University of Arizona*
Leonard Curtis, *Mississippi College*
Miriam Davis, *Delta State University*
Alexander DeGrand, *North Carolina State University*
Marion Deshmukh, *George Mason University*
Janusz Duzinkiewicz, *Purdue University, North Central*
Mary Beth Emmerichs, *University of Wisconsin, Sheboygan*
Steven Fanning, *University of Illinois at Chicago*
Bryan Ganaway, *University of Illinois at Urbana–Champaign*
Frank Garosi, *California State University–Sacramento*
Christina Gold, *Loyola Marymount University*
Ignacio Götz, *Hofstra University*
Louis Haas, *Duquesne University*
Linda Jones Hall, *Saint Mary's College of Maryland*
Paul Halsall, *University of North Florida*
Donald J. Harreld, *Brigham Young University*
Carmen V. Harris, *University of South Carolina at Spartanburg*
James C. Harrison, *Siena College*
Mark C. Herman, *Edison Community College*
Curry A. Herring, *University of Southern Alabama*
Patrick Holt, *Fordham University*
W. Robert Houston, *University of South Alabama*
Lester Hutton, *Westfield State College*
Jeffrey Hyson, *Saint Joseph's University*
Paul Jankowski, *Brandeis University*
Padraic Kennedy, *McNeese State University*
Joanne Klein, *Boise State University*
Theodore Kluz, *Troy State University*
Skip Knox, *Boise State University*
Cynthia Kosso, *Northern Arizona University*
Ann Kuzdale, *Chicago State University*
Lawrence Langer, *University of Connecticut*
Oscar E. Lansen, *University of North Carolina at Charlotte*
Michael V. Leggiere, *Louisiana State University at Shreveport*
Rhett Leverett, *Marymount University*
Alison Williams Lewin, *Saint Joseph's University*
Wendy Liu, *Miami University, Middletown*
Elizabeth Makowski, *Southwest Texas State University*
Daniel Meissner, *Marquette University*
Isabel Moreira, *University of Utah*
Kenneth Moure, *University of California–Santa Barbara*
Melva E. Newsom, *Clark State Community College*
John A. Nichols, *Slippery Rock University*
Susannah R. Ottaway, *Carleton College*
James H. Overfield, *University of Vermont*
Brian L. Peterson, *Florida International University*
Hugh Phillips, *Western Kentucky University*
Jeff Plaks, *University of Central Oklahoma*
Thomas L. Powers, *University of South Carolina, Sumter*
Carole Putko, *San Diego State University*
Barbara Ranieri, *University of Alabama at Birmingham*
Elsa M. E. Rapp, *Montgomery County Community College*
Marlette Rebhorn, *Austin Community College*
Roger Reese, *Texas A&M University*
Travis Ricketts, *Bryan College*
Thomas Robisheaux, *Duke University*
Bill Robison, *Southeastern Louisiana University*
Mark Ruff, *Concordia University*
Frank Russell, *Transylvania University*
Marylou Ruud, *The University of West Florida*
Michael Saler, *University of California–Davis*
Timothy D. Saxon, *Charleston Southern University*
Daniel A. Scalberg, *Multnomah Bible College*
Ronald Schechter, *College of William and Mary*
Philip Skaggs, *Grand Valley State University*
Helmut Walser Smith, *Vanderbilt University*
Eileen Solwedel, *Edmonds Community College*
Sister Maria Consuelo Sparks, *Immaculata University*
Ilicia J. Sprey, *Saint Joseph's College*
Charles R. Sullivan, *University of Dallas*
Frederick Suppe, *Ball State University*

Frank W. Thackery, *Indiana University Southeast*
Frances B. Titchener, *Utah State University*
Katherine Tosa, *Muskegon Community College*
Lawrence A. Tritle, *Loyola Marymount University*
Clifford F. Wargelin, *Georgetown College*
Theodore R. Weeks, *Southern Illinois University*
Elizabeth A. Williams, *Oklahoma State University*
Mary E. Zamon, *Marymount University*

BRIAN LEVACK
EDWARD MUIR
MEREDITH VELDMAN
MICHAEL MAAS

Meet the Authors

Brian Levack grew up in a family of teachers in the New York metropolitan area. From his father, a professor of French history, he acquired a love for studying the past, and he knew from an early age that he too would become a historian. He received his B.A. from Fordham University in 1965 and his Ph.D. from Yale in 1970. In graduate school he became fascinated by the history of the law and the interaction between law and politics, interests that he has maintained throughout his career. In 1969 he joined the history department of the University of Texas at Austin, where he is now the John Green Regents Professor in History. The winner of several teaching awards, Levack teaches a wide variety of courses on British and European history, legal history, and the history of witchcraft. For eight years he served as the chair of his department, a rewarding but challenging assignment that made it difficult for him to devote as much time as he wished to his teaching and scholarship. His books include *The Civil Lawyers in England, 1603–1641: A Political Study* (1973), *The Formation of the British State: England, Scotland and the Union, 1603–1707* (1987), and *The Witch-Hunt in Early Modern Europe* (1987 and 1995), which has been translated into eight languages.

His study of the development of beliefs about witchcraft in Europe over the course of many centuries gave him the idea of writing a textbook on Western civilization that would illustrate a broader set of encounters between different cultures, societies, and ideologies. While writing the book, Levack and his two sons built a house on property that he and his wife, Nancy, own in the Texas hill country. He found that the two projects presented similar challenges: It was easy to draw up the design, but far more difficult to execute it. When not teaching, writing, or doing carpentry work, Levack runs along the jogging trails of Austin, and he has recently discovered the pleasures of scuba diving.

Edward Muir grew up in the foothills of the Wasatch Mountains in Utah, close to the Emigration Trail along which wagon trains of Mormon pioneers and California-bound settlers made their way westward. As a child he loved to explore the broken-down wagons and abandoned household goods left at the side of the trail and from that acquired a fascination with the past. Besides the material remains of the past, he grew up with stories of his Mormon pioneer ancestors and an appreciation for how the past continued to influence the present. During the turbulent 1960s, he became interested in Renaissance Italy as a period and a place that had been formative for Western civilization. His biggest challenge is finding the time to explore yet another new corner of Italy and its restaurants.

Muir received his Ph.D. from Rutgers University, where he specialized in the Italian Renaissance and did archival research in Venice and Florence, Italy. He is now the Clarence L. Ver Steeg Professor in the Arts and Sciences at Northwestern University and former chair of the history department. At Northwestern he has won several teaching awards. His books include *Civic Ritual in Renaissance Venice* (1981), *Mad Blood Stirring: Vendetta in Renaissance Italy* (1993 and 1998), and *Ritual in Early Modern Europe* (1997 and 2005).

Some years ago Muir began to experiment with the use of historical trials in teaching and discovered that students loved them. From that experience he decided to write this textbook, which employs trials as a central feature. He lives beside Lake Michigan in Evanston, Illinois. His twin passions are skiing in the Rocky Mountains and rooting for the Chicago Cubs, who manage every summer to demonstrate that winning isn't everything.

Meredith Veldman grew up in the western suburbs of Chicago in a close-knit, closed-in Dutch Calvinist community. In this immigrant society, history mattered: the "Reformed tradition" structured not only religious beliefs but also social identity and political practice. This influence certainly played some role in shaping Veldman's early fascination with history. But probably just as important were the countless World War II reenactment games she played with her five older brothers. Whatever the cause, Veldman majored in history at Calvin College in Grand Rapids, Michigan, and then earned a Ph.D. in modern European history, with a concentration in nineteenth- and twentieth-century Britain, from Northwestern University in 1988.

As associate professor of history at Louisiana State University, Veldman teaches courses in nineteenth- and twentieth-century British history and twentieth-century Europe, as well as the second half of "Western Civ." In her many semesters in the Western Civ. classroom, Veldman tried a number of different textbooks but found herself increasingly dissatisfied. She wanted a text that would convey to beginning students at least some of the complexities and ambiguities of historical interpretation, introduce them to the exciting work being done now in cultural history, and, most important, tell a good story. The search for this textbook led her to accept the offer made by Levack, Maas, and Muir to join them in writing *The West: Encounters & Transformations.*

The author of *Fantasy, the Bomb, and the Greening of Britain: Romantic Protest, 1945–1980* (1994), Veldman is also the wife of a Methodist minister and the mother of two young sons. They reside in Baton Rouge, Louisiana, where Veldman finds coping with the steamy climate a constant challenge. She and her family recently returned from Manchester, England, where they lived for three years and astonished the natives by their enthusiastic appreciation of English weather.

Michael Maas was born in the Ohio River Valley, in a community that had been a frontier outpost during the late eighteenth century. He grew up reading the stories of the early settlers and their struggles with the native peoples, and seeing in the urban fabric how the city had subsequently developed into a prosperous coal and steel town with immigrants from all over the world. As a boy he developed a lifetime interest in the archaeology and history of the ancient Mediterranean world and began to study Latin. At Cornell University he combined his interests in cultural history and the classical world by majoring in classics and anthropology. A semester in Rome clinched his commitment to these fields—and to Italian cooking. Maas went on to get his Ph.D. in the graduate program in ancient history and Mediterranean archaeology at the University of California at Berkeley.

He has traveled widely in the Mediterranean and the Middle East and participated in several archaeological excavations, including an underwater dig in Greece. Since 1985 he has taught ancient history at Rice University in Houston, Texas, where he founded and directs the interdisciplinary B.A. program in ancient Mediterranean civilizations. He has won several teaching awards.

Maas's special area of research is late antiquity, the period of transition from the classical to the medieval worlds, which saw the collapse of the Roman Empire in western Europe and the development of the Byzantine state in the East. During his last sabbatical, he was a member of the Institute for Advanced Study in Princeton, New Jersey, where he worked on his current book, *The Conqueror's Gift: Ethnography, Identity, and Imperial Power at the End of Antiquity* (forthcoming). His other books include *John Lydus and the Roman Past: Antiquarianism and Politics in the Age of Justinian* (1992), *Readings in Late Antiquity: A Sourcebook* (2000), and *Exegesis and Empire in the Early Byzantine Mediterranean* (2003).

Maas has always been interested in interdisciplinary teaching and the encounters among different cultures. He sees *The West: Encounters & Transformations* as an opportunity to explain how the modern civilization that we call "the West" had its origins in the diverse interactions among many peoples of antiquity.

Eighteenth-Century Society and Culture

18

CHAPTER OUTLINE

In 1745 Thomas Brown and eleven other men living on the estate of the Earl of Uxbridge, an English nobleman, were jailed for up to one year for shooting deer and rabbits on the earl's land. All twelve defendants were poor. Brown eked out a living as a coal miner in the earl's mines and rented a cottage and five acres of land from him. Like many of his fellow villagers, Brown supplemented his family's diet by shooting game from time to time, usually as he was walking to work through the earl's vast estate. This poaching violated a set of English parliamentary statutes known as the game laws, which restricted the shooting or trapping of wild animals to the members of the landed class.

The earl and other noblemen defended the game laws on the grounds that they were necessary to protect their property. The laws, however, served the even more important purpose of maintaining social distinctions between landowners and the common people. Members of the landed class believed that only they should have the right to hunt game and to serve deer, pheasants, and hares at lavish dinners attended by their social equals. For a poor person like Thomas Brown, who was described in a court document as "a rude disorderly man and a most notorious poacher," to enjoy such delicacies was a challenge to the social order.

This mid-eighteenth-century encounter between the Earl of Uxbridge and his tenants, which took the form of a criminal prosecution, reflected the tensions that simmered beneath the calm surface of eighteenth-century European society. These tensions arose between the members of the aristocracy, a small but wealthy governing elite, and the masses of tenants and laborers who formed the overwhelming majority of the European population. The aristocracy occupied a dominant position in eighteenth-century society. They controlled an enormous portion of the wealth in their countries, much of it in land. They staffed the state bureaucracies, the legislative assemblies, the military officer corps, and the judiciaries of almost all European states. They dominated and set the tone of high cultural life in Europe. Together

First Lecture in the Salon of Madame Geoffrin, 1755 The speaker is lecturing on Voltaire's *The Orphan of China* before a predominantly aristocratic audience of men and women.

with the monarchy and the church, with which they were socially and politically linked, the aristocracy formed what today is often referred to as "the Establishment."

By 1800 the social and political dominance of the aristocracy had begun to wane. Their legitimacy as a privileged elite was increasingly called into question. In a few countries political power began to pass from them to different social groups. The aristocracy did not surrender all their power, but they lost their stranglehold over society. This change began during a period of political stability between 1750 and the outbreak of the French Revolution in 1789.

The decline of the aristocracy was the result of a series of cultural encounters. The first were the tense and occasionally violent interactions between landowners and peasants who resented the repressive features of upper-class rule. The second were criticisms of the aristocracy and the demands for reform that came from the increasingly literate, politically active people from the middle ranks of society, such as merchants, financiers, industrialists, and skilled artisans. The third was the cultural and intellectual movement known as the Enlightenment. Even though many of the Enlightenment's most prominent thinkers came from the ranks of the aristocracy, they advanced a set of political, social, economic, and legal ideas that ultimately inspired the creation of a more egalitarian society.

The aristocracy did not relinquish power willingly or quickly. Although they faced severe criticism and challenges to their dominance, they managed to preserve much of their wealth and maintain at least some of their political influence. To insulate themselves from criticisms from less powerful social groups, they adopted many of the values of the people who occupied the middle ranks of society and subscribed to many of the ideas of the Enlightenment, including those that criticized their own class. Internal encounters between different social groups, just like external encounters between Western and non-Western peoples, rarely result in total domination of one group over the other. Instead both parties change their thinking and behavior as a result of their interaction.

These encounters, especially those that took place at the time of the Enlightenment, resulted in a redefinition of the West. In Chapter 16 we saw how the Scientific Revolution completely changed the face of Western culture. In the eighteenth century the Enlightenment, which was inspired to a great extent by the ideas of the Scientific Revolution, produced a set of political and social ideals that served as the basis for a new Western identity.

This chapter will explore the ways in which these social and cultural encounters changed the political and intellectual culture of the West. In doing this the individual sections of the chapter will address the following questions:

- **What social groups belonged to the aristocracy and how did they exercise their power and influence during the eighteenth century?**
- **How did subordinate social groups, most notably the rural peasantry and those who lived in the towns, challenge the aristocracy during the late eighteenth century?**
- **What were the main features of Enlightenment thought and how did it present a threat to the old order?**
- **What impact did the Enlightenment have on Western culture and politics?**

The Aristocracy

- **What social groups belonged to the aristocracy and how did they exercise their power and influence during the eighteenth century?**

During the eighteenth century a relatively small, wealthy group of men dominated European society and politics. This social and ruling elite is often referred to as the aristocracy°, a term derived from a Greek word meaning the people who were the most fit to rule. In the eighteenth and nineteenth centuries the term *aristocracy* began to be applied not just to those few men who exercised political power but to the wealthiest members of society, especially those who owned land.

Within the aristocracy those who received official recognition of their hereditary status, including their titles of honor and special legal privileges, were known as the nobility°. In the Middle Ages the nobility consisted mainly of warriors who prided themselves on their courage and military skill. Over the course of many centuries these military functions became less important, although many noblemen, especially in central and eastern Europe, continued to serve as military officers in the armies of the state during the eighteenth century.

The aristocracy for the most part lived on their estates in the countryside, but they also spent time in the cities and towns, where many of them maintained townhouses or even large palaces. In cities that were centers of national government, such as Madrid and Berlin, aristocrats were prominent members of the royal court. As royal judges, some members of the aristocracy also took an active part in the administration of the law in the cities, just as they did in the provinces. The aristocracy, therefore, maintained a visible and powerful presence in urban society.

By the eighteenth century most European aristocracies included a relatively small group of titled noblemen (such as dukes and counts) who possessed great wealth and political influence and a much larger group of lesser aristocrats, occasionally referred to as gentry, who sometimes did not even bear hereditary titles. In Spain a vast gulf separated a few hundred titled noblemen, the *titulos,* and thousands of sometimes poverty-stricken *hidalgos.* In Britain a few hun-

DOCUMENT

Merchants Become Members of the Aristocracy in England

Daniel Defoe is most famous for his novels, such as Robinson Crusoe *(1719) and* Moll Flanders *(1722), but he also wrote commentaries on contemporary English politics and society. In* The English Tradesman *(1726), which is excerpted here, Defoe argued that the wealth of England "lies mainly among the trading part of the people." To support his argument he presented evidence that many members of the English aristocracy came from trading backgrounds. England was unusual in the opportunities it offered for this type of upward social mobility, but Defoe nonetheless overstated his case. Even the English aristocracy of the eighteenth century was not open to such frequent entry from below.*

This being the case in England, and our trade being so vastly great, it is no wonder that the tradesmen in England fill the lists of our nobility and gentry; no wonder that the gentlemen of the best families marry tradesmen's daughters, and put their younger sons' apprentices to tradesmen; and how often do these younger sons come to buy the elder sons' estates, and restore the family, when the elder and head of the house, proving rakish and extravagant, has wasted his patrimony, and is obliged to make out the blessing of Israel's family, where the younger son brought the birthright, and the elder was doomed to serve him?

Trade is so far here from being inconsistent with a gentleman, that in short trade in England makes gentlemen, and has peopled this nation with gentlemen; for after a generation or two the tradesmen's children, or at least their grand-children, come to be as good gentlemen, statesmen, parliament-men, privy counselors, judges, bishops and noblemen, as those of the highest birth and the most ancient families; and nothing too high for them. Thus the earl of Haversham was originally a merchant; the late Secretary Craggs was the son of a barber; the present Lord Castlemaine's father was a tradesman, the great grandfather of the present Duke of Bedford the same, and so of several others. . . .

We see the tradesmen of England, as they grow wealthy, coming every day to the herald's office, to search for the coats of arms of their ancestors, in order to paint them upon their coaches, and engrave them upon their furniture, or carve them upon the pediments of their new houses; and how often do we see them trace the registers of their families up to the prime nobility, or the most ancient gentry of the kingdom?

Source: From Daniel Defoe, *The Complete English Tradesman, Volume I,* 1726.

dred titled noblemen, known as peers, took precedence over some 50,000 families that belonged to the gentry. In Poland the nobility, known as the *szlachta,* was divided between a tiny, powerful group of magnates and some 700,000 noblemen of much more modest means who constituted more than 10 percent of the entire population.

The aristocracy was not completely closed to outsiders. Commoners could gain entrance to it, especially its lower ranks, on the basis of acquired wealth or government service. It was not unusual for lawyers, wealthy merchants, or accomplished state servants to accumulate wealth during their careers, use that wealth to purchase land, and then receive a recognition of their new status in the form of a title of nobility. Many of the men to whom Peter the Great of Russia gave titles of nobility in the early eighteenth century were commoners. In France, where the old "nobility of the sword" could be distinguished from the "nobility of the robe" that ascended through state service, more than 20 percent of mid-eighteenth-century noblemen could not trace their noble status back further than two generations.

It was also possible for prosperous farmers to enter the aristocracy by purchasing land, hiring manual laborers to perform agricultural work, and then adopting the leisured lifestyle, dress, and manners of aristocrats. These men did not bear titles, but they expected to be regarded as having the same status as other members of the lesser aristocracy. Occasionally women of nonnoble birth gained entry into aristocratic society by marriage. This usually occurred when a nobleman who was greatly in debt arranged to marry his son to the daughter of a wealthy merchant in order to secure the dowry from the father of the bride. The dowry became the price of the daughter's admission to the nobility.

In the sixteenth and seventeenth centuries the size of the aristocracy had grown faster than the general population, as a result of both economic prosperity and the expansion of the state bureaucracy. In eastern Europe monarchs had increased the number of hereditary noblemen in order to gain their services for the state. In the eighteenth century the size of the aristocracy stabilized and in many countries declined, as nobles took steps to restrict the number of newcomers from the lower orders. It was never a very large social group. The number of titled nobles was almost always less than 1 percent of the total population, and even when lesser nobles or gentry are taken into account, their total numbers usually amounted to no more than 4 percent. Only in Poland and Hungary did the percentages climb to more than 10 percent. Because of the small size of this social group, many nobles knew each other, especially those who were members of the same political assembly or who served together at court. The aristocracy was in fact the only real class° in European society before the early nineteenth century, in the sense that they formed a cohesive social group with similar economic and political interests, which they were determined to protect.

Size of the Aristocracy in European States in the Eighteenth Century

Country	Date	Number of Nobles and Lesser Aristocrats	Percent of the Population
Austria	1800	90,000	1.15%
France	1775	400,000	1.60
Great Britain & Ireland	1783	50,000	3.25
Hungary	1800	400,000	11.25
Poland	1800	700,000	11.66
Russia	1800	600,000	1.66
Spain	1797	402,000	3.80
Sweden	1757	10,000	0.50
Venice	1797	1,090	0.80

Sources: A. Corvisier, *Armies and Society in Europe, 1494–1789* (1976), pp. 113, 115; J. Meyer, *Noblesses et pouvoirs dans l'Europe d'Ancien Régime* (1973); M. Reinard and A. Armenguard, *Histoire Générale de la Population Modiale* (1961); J. Dewald, *The European Nobility* (1996), pp. 22–27.

The Wealth of the Aristocracy

The aristocracy was without question the wealthiest social group in all European countries, and during the eighteenth century many members of this group became even wealthier. The most prosperous aristocratic families lived in stupendous luxury. They built magnificent homes on their country estates and surrounded them with finely manicured gardens. In the cities, where service at court demanded more of their time, they built spacious palaces, entertained guests on a lavish scale, and purchased everything from expensive clothes to artistic treasures. They consumed the best food and wines they could find at home or abroad. This ostentatious display of wealth was intended to confirm their social importance and status.

Most of the income that supported the lifestyle of the aristocracy came directly or indirectly from land. In all European countries the aristocracy owned at least one-third of all the land, and in some countries, such as England and Denmark, they owned more than four-fifths of it. Even in the Italian states, where many of the nobility had come from families of merchants, they controlled large estates. Land provided the aristocracy with either feudal dues or rents from the peasants who lived and worked on their estates. Because noblemen did not engage in manual labor themselves, it is not surprising that they later came to be seen as unproductive parasites living off the labor of others.

During the first half of the eighteenth century the collective wealth of the European aristocracy reached new heights. In eastern Europe that increase in wealth derived mainly from the dramatic increase in the size of the population. With more serfs under their control, the landed nobility could increase the wealth they gained from their labor and dues. In western European countries, most notably Britain and France, the members of the aristocracy increasingly participated in other forms of economic activity. They operated rural industries such as mining and forestry. They entered the financial world by lending money to the government, thus serving the state in the process. They became involved in urban building projects and in the economic development of overseas colonies. Those who came from old families considered these pursuits to be beneath the status of a nobleman, but by investing at a distance nobles could give the impression that they were not actually engaged in the sordid transactions of the marketplace.

The members of the eighteenth-century aristocracy are often described as social and economic conservatives who were unable or unwilling to act in an entrepreneurial manner. The financial and commercial projects that many noblemen engaged in suggest that this reputation of the aristocracy is not fully deserved. Even on their landed estates, the aristocracy often behaved in a capitalistic manner during the seventeenth and eighteenth centuries. Many members of the aristocracy, both titled and untitled, adopted capitalist techniques of estate management to make their lands more productive. In England a nobleman, Charles Townshend, became widely known as "Turnip Townshend" when he introduced a crop rotation that included the lowly turnip. This type of agrarian entrepreneurship accounts for the accumulation of many great eighteenth-century aristocratic fortunes.

The Political Power of the Aristocracy

The mid-eighteenth century also marked the apex of political power for the aristocracy in Europe. Having recovered from the economic and political turmoil of the mid-seventeenth century, when they suffered economic losses and experienced a temporary eclipse of their power, noblemen pursued various strategies to increase or preserve their share of local and national political power. In

Marriage into the Nobility

This painting by William Hogarth, in a series titled *Marriage à la Mode,* depicts the negotiation of a marriage contract between an English earl and a wealthy London merchant. The earl, seated to the left and pointing to his family tree, is negotiating with the merchant sitting across the table. The marriage will take place between the earl's vain son, sitting to the far right, and the distracted daughter of the merchant, sitting next to him. The two individuals who are about to be married have no interest in each other. The earl has incurred large debts from building the large mansion depicted in the rear, and he intends to use the dowry to recover financially. By virtue of this transaction the daughter will enter aristocratic society.

England, where royal power was greatly restricted as a result of the Glorious Revolution, the aristocracy gained political dominance. A small group of noblemen sat in the House of Lords, while the gentry formed the large majority of members of the House of Commons. After 1689 the English king could not rule without the cooperation of these two Houses of Parliament. The monarchy tried to control the proceedings of that assembly by creating parties of royal supporters within both houses. Because those parties were controlled by the king's ministers, who were themselves members of the nobility, the system allowed the aristocracy to dominate.

A similar situation prevailed in Poland and Hungary, where only the nobility were represented in the legislative assemblies of those countries. In Sweden and most German states the nobility formed a separate group that voted by themselves within the representative assemblies of those kingdoms. The country in Europe where members of the aristocracy exercised the least power and influence was the Dutch Republic. The traditional Dutch landed nobility remained a force to be reckoned with in eighteenth-century politics, but wealthy merchants and bankers held the balance of power in the seven Dutch provinces.

In absolute monarchies, where rulers had succeeded in restricting independent aristocratic power, members of the aristocracy exercised political power by controlling the institutions through which royal power was exercised. As we have seen in Chapter 15, absolute monarchs appeased the aristocracy by giving them control over provincial government and by recruiting them to occupy offices in the central bureaucracy of the state. The large bureaucracy of the eighteenth-century French state, for example, was run mainly by noblemen of the robe, a privileged group of approximately 2,000 officials who owed their noble status to their appointment to office rather than to heredity. In Russia during the early eighteenth century, tsars granted the nobility privileges and strengthened their powers over their serfs in order to secure the assistance the tsars needed to administer the Russian state at the local level.

The aristocracy also exercised political power through the judiciary. Members of the aristocracy often served as judges of the law courts of their kingdoms. In England noblemen and gentry served as the judges of almost all the common law courts, hearing cases both at the center of government at Westminster and in the provinces. In France noblemen staffed the nine regional *parlements* that registered royal edicts and acted as a court of appeal in criminal cases. The nobility controlled the central tribunals of the German kingdoms and principalities. At the local level the nobility exercised either a personal jurisdiction over the peasants who lived on their lands or an official jurisdiction as magistrates, such as the justices of the peace in each English county.

Britain provides a vivid example of the way in which the members of the landed class could use their judicial power to keep the lower classes in line: punishing petty crimes with harsh penalties. During the eighteenth century the incidence of crimes against property increased, especially when war created shortages of basic commodities. Those who occupied the middle ranks of society were the most frequent victims of these crimes, but as men of great wealth the aristocracy believed that all crimes against property threatened them as well. The aristocracy responded to this threat by passing legislation making even minor crimes against property, such as petty theft, capital offenses punishable by death. One victim of this harsh policy was John Burton, a lowly paid wagon driver who was hanged in 1744 for stealing two woolen caps.

Not all those convicted of such petty crimes suffered the same punishment as Burton. A few public executions every year were deemed sufficient to deter crime in a country that did not have a police force. Most convicted criminals were pardoned or had their sentences reduced. These displays of judicial mercy also served the purposes of the aristocracy by making people from the lower ranks of society dependent upon them for their lives. Exercising the power of pardon also strengthened their authority and made them appear sympathetic to the poor. In this way the British aristocracy helped to maintain the traditional deference paid to them from the lower ranks of society.

The Cultural World of the Aristocracy

During the eighteenth century the aristocracies in western European countries followed a lifestyle that emphasized their learning, refinement, and appreciation of the fine arts. It had not always been that way. As late as the fifteenth century the aristocracy, which in the Middle Ages had been a warrior class, had a reputation for their indifference or even hostility to learning, and their conduct was often uncouth if not boorish. In eastern Europe a tradition of aristocratic illiteracy persisted into the eighteenth century. In western and central Europe, however, the pattern began to change in the sixteenth century, when members of the aristocracy started providing for the education of their children either at universities or in private academies. Even more important, aristocratic families began to acquire the manners and social graces that would be acceptable at court. By the eighteenth century the aristocracy, especially its upper ranks, became the backbone of what was then called "polite society."

The aristocracy also developed a sophisticated appreciation of high culture. Their homes housed large private collections of artwork that occasionally rivaled or even surpassed those of contemporary European monarchs. They were the main participants in the cultural life of European cities, especially Paris, London, Rome, Vienna, and Berlin. They formed the audiences of musical recitals, attended plays and operas in large numbers, and frequented the art galleries that were established in all the capitals of Europe. They also became the patrons of musicians, writers, and artists.

The homes of the eighteenth-century aristocracy reflected their preference for classicism°, a style in art, architecture, music, and literature that emphasizes proportion, adherence to traditional forms, and a rejection of emotion and enthusiasm. The classicism of the eighteenth century marked a step away from the more dynamic, imposing baroque style, which had flourished in the seventeenth century. Classicism celebrated the culture of ancient Greece and Rome. The revival of that culture in the eighteenth century in art and architecture is often referred to as neoclassicism°. The residences of the eighteenth-century aristocracy built in the classical style were perfectly proportioned and elegant without being overly decorated. Their Greek columns and formal gardens, lined with statues of classical figures, served as symbols of their cultural heritage. The classical architecture of the eighteenth century reflected the quiet confidence of the aristocracy that they, like their Greek and Roman forebears, occupied a dominant position in society.

Eighteenth-century music, which is likewise referred to as classical, reflected a concern for formal design, proportion, and concise melodic expression. The two greatest composers of the eighteenth century, Franz Joseph Haydn (1732–1809) and Wolfgang Amadeus Mozart (1756–1791), whose music was played before predominantly aristocratic audiences, became the most famous composers in this tradition. Classical music appealed less to the emotions than either the baroque music of the seventeenth century or the romantic music of the nineteenth century. The dominance of classicism in music as well as architecture during the eighteenth century reflected broader cultural currents in

Chiswick House
This house was built by Lord Burlington as a library and reception hall on his estate near London about 1725. Symmetrical, balanced, and restrained, the building embodies many of the features of classicism. Chiswick House was modeled on the architecture of the Italian Andrea Palladio (1518–1580), who in turn drew his inspiration from the buildings of ancient Rome.

European intellectual life, when science and philosophy placed the highest value on the rationality and order of all material and human life.

Challenges to Aristocratic Dominance

- **How did subordinate social groups, most notably the rural peasantry and those who lived in the towns, challenge the aristocracy during the late eighteenth century?**

Starting around the middle of the eighteenth century, the aristocracy endured increasingly acrimonious challenges to their power and criticisms of their values and lifestyles. They gradually lost the respect that they commanded from the lower ranks of society. By the end of the century European aristocracies had been significantly weakened. Their values had been called into question, while their political power and privileges had been eroded. A claim of nobility began to be viewed more as a sign of vanity than as a natural right to rule. The revolution that took place in France in the last decade of the eighteenth century, followed by the reform movements that developed in its wake throughout Europe in the early nineteenth century, brought the age of aristocracy to an end. Members of the aristocracy managed to regain some of what they had lost in the French Revolution, and they also showed their resourcefulness by accommodating themselves to the new order, but they never recovered the dominant position they had held in the eighteenth century.

Encounters with the Rural Peasantry

One set of challenges to the aristocracy came from the peasants and serfs who lived and worked on landed estates. This was the social group over whom the aristocracy exercised the most direct control. The control was most oppressive in central and eastern Europe, where the rural masses were serfs and therefore had no personal freedom. Landlords not only determined where serfs lived and when they married, but they also collected burdensome financial duties from them. Their plight was relieved only partially by the elimination of some of the burdens of serfdom. In Prussia and Austria these obligations were abolished by royal edict. The monarchs who instituted these reforms may have been responding to the demands of philosophes°, the intellectuals and writers of the age, who condemned the institution of serfdom for its cruelty and inefficiency. (See the section on the Enlightenment later in this chapter.) A more powerful motive, however, was the desire of monarchs to collect taxes from a peasantry that was spending the greater part of its income on financial duties owed to aristocratic landowners. Because the peasants still remained overburdened by financial obligations, emancipation did little to improve their lot.

In western Europe, where serfdom had for the most part given way to tenant ownership and leasehold tenure, the condition of the rural masses was only marginally better. After 1720, famines became less common than they had been in the late seventeenth century, making it possible for peasants to eke out an existence, but other economic pressures, including the elimination of common pasture rights and an increase in taxation, continued to weigh down on them. Over the course of the eighteenth century the number of peasants owning small plots of land declined. Many of those who leased land were forced to sell it as landowners consolidated their holdings. Consequently the number of landless laborers who worked for wages increased. By 1789 almost half the peasants in France had no land at all.

Under these circumstances the relationship between peasants and landowners continued to deteriorate. The realities of the marketplace gradually eroded the paternalistic concern that the nobility had traditionally shown for the welfare of their serfs or tenants. As the relationship between landlord and peasant became predominantly economic, the two parties became more distant. At the same time the gap between the culture of the elite and that of the common people, which as we have seen in Chapter 16 began in the seventeenth century, became more pronounced. The distance between landlord and peasant assumed real geographical form as landlords built their mansions away from the local village. By surrounding their homes with acres of parkland and gardens, they shielded themselves from the sight of the peasants working in the fields. Visual and personal contact between lord and peasant therefore became less frequent. The most direct contact a landlord made with the members of the lower classes was with the servants who worked in their homes.

As economic pressures on the peasants mounted, conflict between them and the aristocracy increased. Peasant resistance to their landlords could take a number of different forms. In some countries, most notably France, peasants could bring their grievances before village assemblies. These democratic institutions often succeeded in upholding peasants' demands, especially when royal officials in the provinces, who wished to collect their own taxes from the peasants, sided with them against the nobility.

Another option was to file a lawsuit against the lord, often with the assistance of the royal government. In Burgundy numerous peasant communities hired lawyers to take their seigneurs° or lords to court in order to prevent the imposition of new financial dues or the confiscation of communal village land. They were often aided in these efforts by the agents of the royal government, who wanted the peasants to be able to pay higher taxes imposed by the king. In these lawsuits, which became very common in the second half of the eighteenth century, peasants challenged not only the imposition of seigneurial dues but the very institution of aristocratic lordship. In 1765 one lawyer representing a peasant community in Champagne argued that the rights claimed by landowners "derive from the violence of seigneurs" and had always been "odious." The language used in these cases inspired much of the rhetoric employed in the abolition of feudal privilege at the time of the French Revolution (see Chapter 19).

Peasants occasionally took more direct action against their landlords. In eastern France the number of incidents of rural violence against the property of seigneurs who tried to collect new duties increased toward the end of the eighteenth century. In Ireland a group known as the Whiteboys maimed cattle and tore down fences when landowners denied tenants their common grazing rights. Other forms of peasant action included poaching on the lands of landowners who claimed the exclusive right to hunt or trap game on their estates. The hunting activities of the tenants of the Earl of Uxbridge discussed at the beginning of this chapter are just one example of this type of lower-class resistance to aristocratic privilege.

In western Europe these acts of resistance did not develop into widespread peasant rebellion until the outbreak of the French Revolution in 1789. During the late eighteenth century incidents of rural violence were largely confined to individual villages. The reduction in the incidence of famine in the eighteenth century provides one possible explanation for this pattern of isolated, localized resistance. Without recurrent subsistence crises, the plight of the rural masses was not sufficiently desperate to provoke large-scale rebellion. The only expressions of collective unrest over the supply of food in western Europe during the eighteenth century were urban riots. These food riots usually took place in market towns or ports where grain was being exported. The violence was not directed against landlords but merchants or officials who were suspected of hoarding grain or fixing the price of bread.

The economic and social situation in eastern Europe differed from that of France, Britain, and other western European countries. In the east the deteriorating economic condition of the peasantry led to large-scale rebellion. Bohemia, Hungary, and Croatia, all of which lay within the boundaries of the Austrian Habsburg monarchy, witnessed large peasant revolts in the 1780s. The bloodiest of these revolts occurred in the province of Transylvania in 1784, when 30,000 peasant rebels butchered hundreds of noblemen and their families after those landowners had raised the dues owed to them as much as 1,000 percent.

The largest eastern European rural rebellion took place in Russia between 1773 and 1774. Pretending to be the murdered Tsar Peter III (d. 1762), the Cossack Emelian Pugachev (1726–1775) set out to destroy the Russian government of Catherine the Great and the nobility that served it. Pugachev assembled an army of 8,000 men, which staged lightning raids against government centers in the southern Urals. The most serious phase of this uprising took place when these troops marched into the agricultural regions of the country and inspired as many as three million serfs to revolt. Pugachev promised to abolish serfdom, end taxation, and eliminate the lesser aristocracy. The rebellion took a heavy toll, as the serfs and soldiers murdered some 3,000 nobles and officials. The Russian upper class feared that the rebellion would spread and destroy the entire social order, but government troops prevented that from happening by brutally suppressing the rising. Pugachev was transported to Moscow in an iron cage, where he was hanged, quartered, and burned.

Neither Pugachev nor the serfs who joined his rebellion envisioned the creation of a new social order. They still spoke in conservative terms of regaining ancient freedoms that had been lost. But this massive revolt, like others that resembled it, reflected the depth of the tension that prevailed between landlord and peasant, between nobleman and serf, in the apparently stable world of the eighteenth century. That tension serves as one of the most striking and ominous themes of eighteenth-century social history.

Joshua Reynolds, *Mary, Duchess of Richmond* (ca. 1765)

At a time when most European noblewomen were attracting criticism for their luxury and vanity, this prominent English duchess was depicted as being engaged in the simple domestic task of needlepoint. Some members of the aristocracy were able to deflect criticism of their lifestyle by adopting the habits of the bourgeoisie.

The Social Position of the Bourgeoisie

In the cities and towns the most serious challenges to the aristocracy came not from the urban masses, who posed an occasional threat to all urban authorities, but from the bourgeoisie°. This social group was more heterogeneous than the aristocracy. It consisted of untitled people of property who lived in the cities and towns. The word *bourgeoisie* refers to those who were burghers—or those who had voting rights in the towns. Prosperous merchants and financiers formed the upper ranks of the bourgeoisie, while members of the legal and medical professions, second-tier government officials, and emerging industrialists occupied a social niche just below them. The bourgeoisie also included some skilled artisans and shopkeepers, sometimes referred to as the "petty bourgeoisie," who were far more prosperous than the large mass of urban laborers. The size of the bourgeoisie grew as the urban population of Europe expanded during the eighteenth century, even before the advent of industrialization. This social group was far more numerous in the North Atlantic countries of France, the Dutch Republic, and Britain than in the states of central and eastern Europe. In England the bourgeoisie accounted for about 15 percent of the total population in 1800, whereas in Russia they constituted no more than 3 percent.

Because it was possible for some members of the bourgeoisie to achieve upward social mobility and join the ranks of the aristocracy, the social and economic boundaries separating these wealthy townsmen from the lower ranks of the nobility could become blurred. In French towns it was often difficult to distinguish between wealthy financiers and noble bureaucrats. Although the two groups received their income from different sources, they both belonged to a wealthy, propertied elite. The middle and lower ranks of the bourgeoisie, however, gradually emerged as a social group that acquired its own social, political, and cultural identity distinct from that of the aristocracy.

Bourgeois identity was rooted in the towns, which had their own political institutions and their own social hierarchies. The bourgeoisie also possessed the means of effectively communicating with each other and thus were capable of forming common political goals. Their high rates of literacy made them the core of the new political force of public opinion that emerged in the cities and towns in the eighteenth century. The bourgeoisie made up the main audience of the thousands of newspapers, pamphlets, and books that rolled off the presses during the eighteenth century. A "public sphere" of activity, in which politically conscious townsmen participated, became a peculiar feature of bourgeois society. During the eighteenth and early nineteenth centuries the bourgeoisie became the leaders of movements seeking political change. They organized and became the main participants in the protest movements,

The Human Body in History

Bathing in the West

One of the personal habits that members of the European aristocracy and bourgeoisie began to adopt in the eighteenth century was frequent bathing. Until that time people in the West had been reluctant to immerse their bodies in water. In this respect there was a clear difference between Western and Eastern practice. Among Asians who practiced the Hindu religion, bathing had deep religious significance and was a daily ritual. The same was true for Muslims, for whom water possessed a sacred purifying role and prepared the bather for prayer or sacrifice. In the West bathing was not invested with similar religious significance. Christianity had emphasized purity of heart, not of the body. Without a religious inspiration, bathing the body rarely occurred in Western nations during the early modern period. Europeans might wash various parts of their body, especially the hands and face, but total immersion was almost unheard of. The few who did bathe usually did so no more than once a year, and tubs and basins were not widely available. Swimming in rivers and lakes was dangerous and often resulted in drowning. Even medical opinion conspired against bathing. According to one seventeenth-century French doctor, "bathing outside the practice of medicine was not only superfluous but very damaging to health."

By the beginning of the nineteenth century, many Europeans had begun to take regular baths. The sale of washbasins and commercially produced soap soared. This change occurred as a result of three distinct factors. The first was the insistence by many eighteenth-century Protestants that Christianity did indeed demand a clean body as well as a clean soul. The eighteenth-century founder of Methodism, the English preacher John Wesley, coined a new proverb when he declared that "cleanliness is indeed next to godliness."

A second reason was that cleanliness became associated with gentility and good manners. Bodily cleanliness became one of the ways in which members of society who considered themselves civilized made themselves attractive to the people with whom they associated. This explains why bathing the body all over was first adopted by the upper classes, who contrasted themselves with the dirty lower classes. It also became more common among women than men. The third reason was a change in medical opinion, which began to view bathing as a means to keep the pores of the skin open and thus promote perspiration. Bathing came to be viewed as a means of curing numerous diseases and as a key to long life.

The acceptance of bathing in the West owed something to Eastern influence. Eighteenth-century Western writers often commented on the daily bathing of Turks and Hindus, and Europeans who lived in the East had the opportunity to witness firsthand a custom that contrasted strikingly with their own. The period of most pronounced influence was the mid-eighteenth century, when many other features of Eastern culture penetrated the West. In the early nineteenth century a Hindu noted that bathing in the West was still very different from that practiced in his own country. Nevertheless, the reluctant European adoption of immersing the body in water had brought about a minor accommodation between Eastern and Western practice.

For Discussion

What does the widespread practice of bathing in Asia and the reluctance of Europeans to adopt this practice tell us about the differences between Eastern and Western cultures in the eighteenth century?

Jean-Jacques Henner, *Chaste Susanna at Her Bath* (1865)
By the nineteenth century, Europeans had adopted the practice of bathing the entire body.

petitioning drives, and ultimately the revolutionary steps taken to challenge and replace established regimes.

The Bourgeois Critique of the Aristocracy

At the core of bourgeois identity lay a set of values that contrasted with those attributed to the aristocracy, especially the noblemen and noblewomen who gathered at court. Not all members of the bourgeoisie shared these values, nor did all members of the nobility embody those attributed to them. Nonetheless, the bourgeois critique of aristocratic society, which flourished mainly among the lower or petty bourgeoisie rather than the great merchants and financiers, contributed to the formation of bourgeois identity and helped to erode respect for the traditional aristocracy.

The bourgeois critique of the aristocracy consisted of three related themes. First was the allegation that the aristocracy lived a life of luxury, hedonism, and idleness that contrasted with the thrifty, sober, hardworking petty bourgeoisie. Unlike the aristocracy, the bourgeoisie did not display their wealth. Second, court nobles were accused of being sexually promiscuous and immoral, while their wives were depicted as vain flirts. There was some foundation to this charge, especially because the predominance of arranged marriages within the nobility had induced many noble husbands and wives to seek sexual partners outside marriage, a practice that was widely tolerated within aristocratic circles. By contrast, the bourgeoisie tended to enter into marriages in which both partners remained faithful to each other. Third, the members of the aristocracy were considered participants in a decadent international culture that often ignored or degraded the more wholesome, patriotic values of the bourgeoisie.

This critique of the aristocracy had profound political implications. It laid the foundation for the demands for equal political rights and the advancement of careers on the basis of talent rather than inherited wealth. These demands came not from the wealthy financiers, merchants, and capitalists who had the opportunity to ascend into the ranks of the nobility but from men of more modest wealth: holders of minor political offices, shopkeepers, and even skilled artisans. These people from the middle ranks of society, especially those who lived in the cities and towns, were most responsible for eventually reducing the influence of the aristocracy in European political and social life.

Criticism of aristocratic values and demands for liberty and equality received support from intellectuals who are usually identified with the movement known as the Enlightenment°. Not all of these thinkers and writers came from the middle ranks of society. Many of them were in fact members of the aristocracy or the beneficiaries of aristocratic patronage. Nevertheless their goal was to bring about the reform of society, and that inevitably led to a critique of aristocratic values and practices.

The Enlightenment

■ **What were the main features of Enlightenment thought and how did it present a threat to the old order?**

The Enlightenment was the defining intellectual and cultural movement of the eighteenth century. This complex movement had roots in the seventeenth century; the Scientific Revolution and the growth of philosophical skepticism were particularly important influences (see Chapter 16). Contemporaries used the word *Enlightenment* to describe their own intellectual outlook and achievements. For Immanuel Kant (1724–1804), the renowned German philosopher and author of *Critique of Pure Reason* (1781), enlightenment was the expression of intellectual maturity, the attainment of understanding solely by using one's reason without being influenced by dogma, superstition, or another person's opinion. For Kant enlightenment was both the process of thinking for oneself and the knowledge of human society and human nature that one achieved as a result. His famous exhortation, "Have the courage to know!" could serve as a slogan for the entire Enlightenment.

The Enlightenment is often referred to as a French movement, and it is true that the most famous of the European writers and thinkers of the Enlightenment, known as philosophes, were French. It was also in France that the Enlightenment first became a campaign to change people's minds and reform institutions. But French philosophes were inspired by seventeenth-century English sources, especially the writings of Isaac Newton (1647–1727) and John Locke (1632–1704), while German, Scottish, Dutch, Swiss, and Italian writers made their own distinctive contributions to Enlightenment thought. The ideas of the Enlightenment also spread to the Americas, where they inspired movements for political reform and national independence. The men and women of the Enlightenment thought of themselves not so much as French, British, or Dutch but as members of an international Republic of Letters, not unlike the international community of scholars that had arisen within the ancient Roman Empire and again at the time of the Renaissance. This cosmopolitan literary republic knew no geographical boundaries, and it was open to ideas from all lands (see Map 18.1). Its literary achievements, however, bore a distinctly Western stamp, and the ideas its members promoted became essential components of Western civilization.

Themes of Enlightenment Thought

Because the Enlightenment spanned the entire continent and lasted for more than a century, it is difficult to establish characteristics that all its participants shared. The Enlightenment was more a frame of mind, an approach to

Map 18.1 The European Enlightenment

The map shows the birthplaces of thinkers and writers of the Enlightenment. The greatest number of them came from France and Britain, but all European countries were represented, and the men and women of the Enlightenment thought of themselves as belonging to an international "Republic of Letters" that knew no political boundaries.

obtaining knowledge, as Kant claimed, than a set of clearly defined beliefs. Enlightenment writers, however, emphasized several intellectual themes that gave the entire movement a certain degree of unity and coherence.

Reason and the Laws of Nature

The first theme emphasized by Enlightenment thinkers was the elevation of human reason to a position of paramount philosophical importance. Enlightenment thinkers placed almost unlimited confidence in the ability of human beings to understand how the world operates. In previous ages philosophers had always found a place for human reason, but they also placed limits on it, especially when it came into conflict with religious faith. Medieval scholastic philosophers had tried to reconcile faith and reason, and that effort continued through the seventeenth century, particularly in scientific circles. In the eighteenth century, however, greater emphasis was placed on reason alone, which was believed to be superior to religious faith and the final arbiter of all disputes.

Confidence in human reason was closely associated with the belief that the operation of the entire universe was governed by natural laws that human reason could discover. This belief in natural law can be traced back to the ancient Greeks and to its revival and assimilation to Christian theology by the scholastics in the Middle Ages. Natural law acquired a distinctive character at the time of the Scientific Revolution. The search for and discovery of the laws governing such phenomena as gravitation, the circulation of the blood, and dynamics gradually led to the belief that all activity, including the behavior of human beings, was governed by similar laws.

The application of natural law to human society was the most novel and distinctive feature of Enlightenment thought. According to Enlightenment thinkers, scientific laws governed the functioning of society. There were even laws governing the passions and the operation of the human psyche. In his *Treatise of Human Nature* (1739–1740), the Scottish philosopher David Hume (1711–1776) offered a science of the human mind, which could be applied to politics and other human endeavors. Economics, too, received the same treatment. The Scottish economist Adam Smith (1723–1790), who described the operation of economic life in *The Wealth of Nations* (1776), believed that the economy was subject to inviolable laws, just like those that governed the movement of the heavens. The Enlightenment therefore gave birth to modern social science. Economics, political science, sociology, anthropology, and psychology all trace their origins as intellectual disciplines to this time. They were all based on the premise that reason could discover the laws or principles of human nature.

Adam Smith, Introduction to *The Wealth of Nations* (1776)

The search for natural laws governing all human life provides one explanation for the unprecedented interest of eighteenth-century writers in non-European cultures. During the Enlightenment a vast literature subjected the peoples of the world to detailed description, classification, and analysis. The first thorough, scholarly studies of Indian, Chinese, and Arab cultures were published during the middle and late eighteenth century. Egypt, a country that had been a part of the Ottoman Empire and isolated from the West since the sixteenth century, became the subject of a sizable literature, especially after the French occupied the country in 1798. There also was an increase in travel literature describing the societies that Europeans were encountering, some of them for the first time. Descriptions of the indigenous peoples of northwestern Canada, Australia, and Tahiti became readily available in the bookshops of Paris and London.

This cross-cultural scholarship, which was facilitated by the rapid growth of overseas empires after 1660, served the purpose of providing intellectuals with information enabling them to discover laws governing the behavior of all people. Some of the non-European countries that these scholars studied, such as China, had highly developed civilizations, whereas those of Native Americans and the indigenous people of the South Sea islands were far less developed. In both cases, however, educated people in the West began to consider these non-Western societies valid subjects of intellectual inquiry.

David Hume, Scottish Philosopher
Like John Locke, Hume explored the process by which the human mind reaches an understanding of the material world. Hume was committed to the application of science to the human psyche.

Religion and Morality

The spread of scientific knowledge in the eighteenth century gave the thinkers of the Enlightenment a new understanding of God and his relationship to humankind. The Christian God of the Middle Ages and the Reformation period was an all-knowing, personal God who often intervened in the life of human beings. He could be stern and severe or gentle and merciful, but he was always involved in the affairs of humankind, which he governed through Providence. The gradual recognition that the universe was of unfathomable size and that it operated in accordance with natural laws made God appear more remote. Most philosophes believed that God was still the creator of the universe and the author of the natural laws that governed it, but they did not believe that he was still actively involved in its operation. God was the playwright of the universe, but not its director. This belief that God had created the universe, given it laws, and then allowed it to operate in a mechanistic fashion is known as deism°. In deism there was no place for the traditional Christian belief that God became human in order to redeem humankind from original sin.

Enlightenment thinkers, especially those who were deists, believed that human beings could use reason to discover the natural laws God had laid down at the time of creation. This inquiry included the discovery of the principles of morality, which no longer were to be grounded in Scripture. To observe the laws of God now meant not so much keeping his commandments but discovering what was natural and acting accordingly. In a certain sense God was being remade in a human image and was being identified with the natural instincts of human beings. In this way religion could become equated with the pursuit of human happiness.

If one believed that God established natural laws for all humanity, then doctrinal differences between religions became less important. All religions were valid to the extent that they led to an understanding of natural law. There was no one true religion, a point that the German dramatist and philosopher Gotthold Lessing (1729–1781) made in his play *Nathan the Wise* (1779) in response to the persistent questioning of a fictional Turkish sultan. This denial of the existence of one true religion led naturally to a demand for toleration of all religions, including those of non-Western peoples.

Enlightenment thinkers were highly critical of the superstitious and dogmatic character of contemporary Christianity, especially Roman Catholicism. French philosophes in particular had little use for priests, whom they castigated relentlessly in their letters and pamphlets. They minimized the importance of religious belief in the conduct of human life and substituted rational for religious values. They had little respect for the academic discipline of theology. The German-born Parisian writer Baron d'Holbach (1723–1789), one of the few philosophes who could be considered an atheist—denying the existence of God at all—dismissed theology as a "pretended science." He claimed that its principles were "only hazardous suppositions, imagined by ignorance, propagated by enthusiasm or knavery, adopted by timid credulity, preserved by custom which never reasons, and revered solely because not understood."[1]

Epitomizing the new religious outlook of the Enlightenment was the Scottish moral philosopher David Hume, who is most famous for his treatise *An Enquiry Concerning Human Understanding* (1748). In that work he challenged the argument of the great rationalist philosopher René Descartes that God implants a number of clear and distinct ideas in our minds, from which we are able to deduce other truths. Hume's position was that our understanding derives from sense perceptions, not innate ideas. Even more important, he denied that there was any certain knowledge,

William Hogarth, *Credulity, Superstition, and Fanaticism* (1762)

Hogarth was a moralist who embodied the rationalism and humanitarianism of the Enlightenment. In this engraving he exposes the effects of fanatical religion, witchcraft, and superstition. The sermon has whipped the entire congregation into a highly emotional state. The woman in the foreground is Mary Tofts, who was believed to have given birth to rabbits. The boy next to her, allegedly possessed by the Devil, vomits pins. The Protestant preacher's wig falls off, exposing the shaven head of a Roman Catholic monk. An unemotional Turk observes this scene from outside the window.

thereby calling into question the authority of revealed truth and religious doctrine.

Hume's writing on religion reflected his skepticism. Raised a Presbyterian, he nevertheless rejected the revealed truths of Christianity on the ground that they had no rational foundation. The concept of Providence was completely alien to his philosophical position. An avowed deist, he expressed contempt for organized religion, especially Catholicism in France and Anglicanism in England. Organized religion, according to Hume, "renders men tame and submissive, is acceptable to the magistrate, and seems inoffensive to the people; till at last the priest, having firmly established his authority, becomes the tyrant and disturber of human society."[2]

Progress and Reform

Theories regarding the stages of human development, coupled with the commitment of philosophes to the improvement and ultimate transformation of society, contributed to a belief in the progress of civilization. Until the eighteenth century the very notion of progress was alien to even the most highly educated Europeans. Those who held political power had dedicated themselves to maintaining the social and political order, not its transformation. Programs of reform were almost always associated with the restoration of a superior golden age rather than the realization of something new and different. If movement took place, it was cyclical rather than progressive. Even the original meaning of the word *revolution* was the path of a planet that came full circle in its orbit, not the creation of a new order. Now, however, the possibility of improvement began to dominate philosophical and political discussion. The Enlightenment was largely responsible for making this belief in progress, especially toward the attainment of social justice, a prominent feature of modern Western culture.

Some Enlightenment thinkers, using evidence gained from encounters with non-Western people, argued that all civilizations progressed gradually from relatively simple to more complex economies and societies. David Hume, Adam Smith, and their fellow Scotsman Adam Ferguson (1723–1816) identified four stages of human development. The first was characterized by hunting and gathering, the second by pastoral farming, the third by agriculture, and the last by commerce. The French philosophe the Marquis de Condorcet (1743–1794) focused more on intellectual progress. In *A Sketch for a Historical Picture of the Progress of the Human Mind* (1795), Condorcet identified nine distinct epochs in human history. He predicted that in the tenth and final epoch humankind would achieve a state of perfection in which rational moral judgments would inform efficient government policy.

Another source of the Enlightenment's belief in progress was the conviction that corrupt institutions could be reformed, thereby allowing societies to advance to a higher level and realize their full potential. The system of taxation, bureaucratic institutions, established churches, and the institution of monarchy itself all became the targets of Enlightenment reformers. The judicial institutions of government were particularly susceptible to this type of reforming zeal. Campaigns arose to eliminate the administration of judicial torture as well as capital punishment. All of this was intended to establish a more humane, civilized society.

The intellectual inspiration to this movement for legal reform was the work of the Italian jurist Cesare Beccaria (1738–1794). In his *Essay on Crimes and Punishments* (1764), Beccaria argued that punishment should be used not to exact retribution for crimes but to rehabilitate the criminal and to serve the interests of society. "In order that every punishment may not be an act of violence committed by one or by many against a private member of society," wrote Beccaria, "it should be above all things public, immediate, and necessary, the least possible in the case given, proportioned to the crime, and determined by the laws."[3] He called for the abolition of capital punishment and the imprisonment of convicted felons. The prison, which prior to the eighteenth century had been little more than a jail or holding facility, was now to become a symbol of the improvement of society.

Voltaire and the Spirit of the Enlightenment

The philosophe who captured all the main themes as well as the spirit of the Enlightenment was the writer and philosopher François Marie Arouet (1694–1778), known universally by his pen name, Voltaire. Born into a French bourgeois family, Voltaire became one of the most prominent and prolific writers of the eighteenth century. Although he wrote for a fairly broad, predominantly bourgeois audience, and although he waged war against the injustices of aristocratic society, he was comfortable in the homes of the nobility and at the courts of European monarchs, especially that of Frederick the Great of Prussia. Voltaire's main career was as an author. He wrote plays and novels as well as poems, letters, essays, and history. These writings revealed his commitment to scientific rationality, his contempt for established religion, and his unflagging pursuit of liberty and justice.

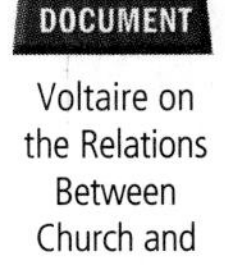

Voltaire on the Relations Between Church and State (mid-18th c.)

Like many men of the Enlightenment, Voltaire developed a deep interest in science. He acquired much of his scientific knowledge from a learned noblewoman, Madame du Châtelet (1706–1749), a scientist and mathematician who translated the works of Newton into French. Madame du Châtelet became Voltaire's mistress, and the two lived together with her tolerant husband in their country estate in eastern France. The sexual freedom they experienced was characteristic of many Enlightenment figures, who rejected the Christian condemnation of

A Case of Infanticide in the Age of the Enlightenment

A mid-eighteenth-century trial of a young French woman charged with killing her newborn child provides a window into the life of women who occupied the lower rungs of French society, in contrast to those who frequented the court and met in salons. The trial also raises the larger questions, debated in French and European judicial circles during the time of the Enlightenment, of how society should deal with the mothers of illegitimate children and whether the punishments prescribed for infanticide, or the killing of a young child, were proportionate to the crime.

In August 1742 Marie-Jeanne Bartonnet, a 21-year-old unmarried woman from a small French village in Brie, moved to Paris, where she took up residence with Claude le Queux, whom she had known in her youth, and Claude's sister. At that time Bartonnet was seven months pregnant. On October 22 Bartonnet caused a ruckus in the middle of the night when she went to the toilet and began groaning loudly and bleeding profusely. When her neighbors found her, and when she asked for towels for the blood, they suspected that she had had a miscarriage and called for a midwife. By the time the midwife arrived, it was clear that the delivery had already taken place and that the infant had fallen down the toilet to the cesspool five stories below. Suspecting that Bartonnet had killed the baby, the proprietress of the building reported her to the nearest judicial officer. The next day judicial authorities returned to the building and found the dead infant in the cesspool. An autopsy revealed that the child's skull had been dented by either a blunt instrument or a fall. After a medical examination of Bartonnet revealed the signs of having just delivered a baby, she was arrested and imprisoned for the crime of infanticide.

Bartonnet came very close to being executed, but the strict procedures of French justice saved her from paying the ultimate price for her apparent crime. In the seventeenth and eighteenth centuries French criminal justice had established clear criteria for determining the guilt or innocence of a person accused of a crime. These procedures involved a systematic interrogation of the accused (only rarely under torture), the deposition of witnesses, the evaluation of physical evidence, and the confrontation of the accused with the witnesses who testified against her. There also was a mandatory review of the case, which involved a further interrogation of the defendant, before the Parlement of Paris, the highest court in northern France.

The interrogations of Bartonnet did not give her judges much evidence on which they could convict her. When asked the name of the village where she had lived in Brie, she told her interrogators, "It's none of your business." She denied that she had even known she was pregnant, refused to name the man with whom she had had intercourse, and claimed that she had mistaken her labor pains for colic or diarrhea. She denied picking her baby off the floor of the toilet after the delivery and throwing it into the cesspool. When presented with the baby's corpse, she claimed she did not recognize it.

After this interrogation, Bartonnet was given the opportunity to challenge the testimony of the witnesses who had seen her the night of the delivery. The most damning testimony came from Madame Pâris, the wife of the proprietor, who had found Bartonnet on the toilet and thus could verify the circumstances of the clandestine delivery. Bartonnet's inability to challenge the testimony of Madame Pâris led directly to her initial conviction. After reviewing the entire dossier of evidence, the king's attorney recommended conviction for concealing her pregnancy, hiding her delivery, and destroying her child. French criminal procedure entrusted the decision of guilt or innocence to the judges themselves, and on November 27 they voted that Bartonnet should be executed by hanging.

Marie-Jeanne Bartonnet's fate, however, was not yet sealed. When her case went on appeal to the Parlement of Paris, Bartonnet repeated her statement that she had gone to the toilet but did not know whether she had given birth. Even though her execution was warranted by terms of an edict of 1557 that defined the crime of infanticide, the judges of this court voted to commute her sentence to a public whipping, banishment from the jurisdiction of the Parlement of Paris, and confiscation of her property. The basis of this decision appears to have been the absence of any proof that she had deliberately killed her baby. Indeed, its injuries could have been caused by its fall down the drain pipe into the cesspool. There was also the persistent refusal of the defendant to make a confession. She may have been lying, but it is equally possible that once she had delivered the baby, which happened very quickly, she convinced herself that it had not happened.

Bartonnet's trial for infanticide stands at the end of a long period of intense prosecution of this crime. Trials of this sort declined as cities and towns built foundling hospitals for abandoned infants and as the moral outrage for illegitimacy was redirected from the pregnant mother to the illegitimate father. The new legal values promoted at the time of the Enlightenment, moreover, made it less likely that any woman or man would be executed for this or any other crime.

Questions of Justice

1. As in many trials, the facts of this case can be used to support different claims of justice. If you had been the prosecutor in this trial, what position would you have taken to prove the crime of infanticide? If you had been defending Marie-Jeanne Bartonnet, what arguments would you have used in her defense?
2. In his *Essay on Crimes and Punishments* (1764), Beccaria recommended that punishments be determined strictly in accordance with the social damage committed by the crime. What would Beccaria have said about the original sentence of death in this case? What would he have said about the modified sentence handed down by the Parlement of Paris?

Taking It Further

Michael Wolfe, ed. *Changing Identities in Early Modern France.* 1997. Gives a full account of Marie-Jeanne Bartonnet's trial for infanticide.

A Woman Accused of Murder in the Eighteenth Century
With the exception of infanticide—the crime for which Marie-Jeanne Bartonnet was tried and convicted—few women were tried for capital crimes in the eighteenth century. One exception was Sarah Malcolm, a 22-year-old Englishwoman, shown here in a portrait by William Hogarth (1733). Malcolm was executed for slitting the throat of a wealthy lady in London.

sexual activity outside marriage and who justified their behavior on the basis of natural law and the pursuit of happiness. From Madame du Châtelet, Voltaire acquired not only an understanding of Newton's scientific laws but also a commitment to women's education and equality. Voltaire lived with her until she died in 1749 while giving birth to a child that was fathered neither by Voltaire nor her husband.

Madame du Châtelet

In her *Institutions de physique* (1740) this French noblewoman, the mistress of Voltaire, made an original and impressive attempt to give Newtonian physics a philosophical foundation.

Voltaire's belief in a Newtonian universe—one governed by the universal law of gravitation—laid the foundation for his deism and his attacks on contemporary Christianity. In his *Philosophical Dictionary* (1764), he lashed out at established religion and the clergy, Protestant as well as Catholic. In a letter to another philosophe attacking religious superstition he pleaded, "Whatever you do, crush the infamous thing." In Voltaire's eyes Christianity was not only unreasonable; it was vulgar and barbaric. He condemned the Catholic Church for the slaughter of millions of indigenous people in the Americas on the grounds that they had not been baptized, as well as the executions of hundreds of thousands of Jews and heretics in Europe. All of these people were the victims of "barbarism and fanaticism."[4]

Voltaire's indictment of the Church for these barbarities was matched by his scathing criticism of the French government for a series of injustices, including his own imprisonment for insulting the regent of France. While living in England for three years, Voltaire became an admirer of English legal institutions, which he considered more humane and just than those of his native country. Using England as a model, he appealed for the implementation of various political reforms in France. He deplored those "who reduce men to a state of slavery by force and downright violence." A tireless advocate of individual liberty, he became a regular defender of victims of injustice, including Jean Calas, a Protestant shopkeeper from Toulouse who had been tortured and executed for allegedly murdering his son because he had expressed a desire to convert to Catholicism. The boy had in fact committed suicide.

Voltaire showed a commitment to placing his knowledge in the service of humanitarian causes. In his most famous novel, *Candide* (1759), the character by that name challenges the smug confidence of Dr. Pangloss, the tutor who repeatedly claims that they lived in "the best of all possible worlds." At the end of the novel Candide responds to this refrain by saying that "we must cultivate our garden." Voltaire, instead of being content with the current condition of humankind, was demanding that we work actively to improve society.

Enlightenment Political Theory

Enlightenment thinkers are known most widely for their political theories, especially those that supported the causes of liberty and reform. The men and women of the Enlightenment did not, however, share a common political ideology, nor did they agree on the most desirable type of political society. They did share a belief that politics was a science that, like the cosmos, had its own natural laws. The title of one of David Hume's treatises, *That Politics May Be Reduced to a Science* (1741), reflects a belief that most Enlightenment political writers endorsed. They also thought of the state in secular rather than religious terms. There was little place in Enlightenment thought for the divine right of kings. Nor was there a place for the Church in the government of the state. On other issues, however, there was little consensus. Three thinkers in particular illustrate the range of Enlightenment political thought: Montesquieu, Rousseau, and Paine.

Baron de Montesquieu: The Separation of Powers

The most influential political writer of the Enlightenment was the French philosophe Charles-Louis de Secondat, Baron de Montesquieu (1689–1755). The son of a nobleman of the robe from Bordeaux, Montesquieu had a legal education and also developed an early interest in science. His political thought owed as much to his study of history and anthropology as to the study of law and science. His first book, *The Persian Letters,* published anonymously in Holland in 1721, was a brilliant satire of Western government and society through the eyes of two Persian aristocrats traveling in Europe. It laid the groundwork for a much more scholarly and substantial contribution to political theory, *Spirit of the Laws* (1748). Often compared to Aristotle because of the range of his thought, Montesquieu interwove commentaries on natural law, religion, morals, virtue, climate, and liberty. Unlike Hobbes, Locke, and the other natural-law philosophers who preceded him, Montesquieu was not concerned with the origin of government or with the establishment of a universal model of politics. Rather, he treated the laws of a country in historical perspective and within the context of that country's religion, morality, climate, geography, and culture. His political writing was scientific mainly in its empirical approach to its subject, and in the comparisons it made between politics on the one hand and Newtonian physics on the other.

Montesquieu argued that there were three forms of government: republics, monarchies, and despotisms, each of which had an activating or inspirational force. In republics that force was civic virtue, in monarchies it was honor, and in despotisms it was fear. In each form of government there was a danger that the polity could degenerate: The virtue of republics could be lost, monarchies could become corrupt, and despotisms could lead to repression. The key to maintaining moderation and preventing this degeneration of civil society was the law of each country. Ideally the law of a country should provide for the separation and balance of political powers. Only in that way could degeneration be avoided and moderation ensured.

Montesquieu used his knowledge of the British political system, which he had studied firsthand while living in England for two years, to propose that the key to good government was the separation of executive, legislative, and judicial power. He was particularly concerned about the independence of the judiciary. Montesquieu was unaware of how legislative and executive powers actually overlapped in eighteenth-century Britain, but his emphasis on the importance of a separation of powers became the most durable of his ideas. It had profound influence on the drafting of the Constitution of the United States of America in 1787.

CHRONOLOGY

Literary Works of the Enlightenment

1687	Isaac Newton, *Mathematical Principles of Natural Philosophy*
1690	John Locke, *An Essay Concerning Human Understanding*
1721	Baron de Montesquieu, *The Persian Letters*
1738	Voltaire, *Elements of the Philosophy of Newton*
1739	David Hume, *Treatise of Human Nature*
1748	Baron de Montesquieu, *Spirit of the Laws*
1748	David Hume, *An Enquiry Concerning Human Understanding*
1751	First volume of Diderot and d'Alembert's *Encyclopedia*
1755	Jean-Jacques Rousseau, *Discourse on the Origin of Inequality Among Men*
1759	Voltaire, *Candide*
1762	Jean-Jacques Rousseau, *The Social Contract* and *Emile, or on Education*
1763	Voltaire, *Treatise on Toleration*
1764	Cesare Beccaria, *Essay on Crimes and Punishments*
1764	Voltaire, *Philosophical Dictionary*
1776	Adam Smith, *The Wealth of Nations*
1781	Immanuel Kant, *Critique of Pure Reason*
1791	Thomas Paine, *The Rights of Man*
1792	Mary Wollstonecraft, *A Vindication of the Rights of Woman*
1795	Marquis de Condorcet, *Progress of the Human Mind*

Jean-Jacques Rousseau: The General Will

Also influential as a political theorist was the Swiss philosophe Jean-Jacques Rousseau (1712–1778), who as a young man moved from Geneva to Paris and became a member of a prominent intellectual circle. Rousseau does not conform to the model of the typical Enlightenment thinker. His distrust of human reason and his emotionalism separated him from Hume, Voltaire, and another

Differences Among the Philosophes
This satirical print shows Rousseau, to the left, and Voltaire engaged in heated debate. The two men were both major figures in the Enlightenment, but they differed widely in temperament and in their philosophical and political views. Rousseau was very much the rebel; unlike Voltaire, he distrusted reason and articulated highly egalitarian political principles.

great French philosophe, Denis Diderot (1713–1784). That distrust laid the foundations for the romantic reaction against the Enlightenment in the early nineteenth century (see Chapter 21). Instead of celebrating the improvement of society as it evolved into higher forms, Rousseau had a negative view of the achievements of civilization. In his novel *Emile, or on Education* (1762) he wrote, "All our wisdom consists of servile prejudices, all our customs are but enslavement, constraint, or bondage. Social man is born, lives and dies enslaved. At birth he is bound up with swaddling clothes; at his death he is nailed down in a coffin. For the whole of his existence as a human being he is chained up by our institutions."[5] Rousseau idealized the uncorrupted condition of human beings in the state of nature, supporting the theory of the "noble savage." Human beings could not ever return to that original natural state, but Rousseau held out the hope of recreating an idealized golden age when they were not yet alienated from themselves and their environment.

Rousseau's political theories were hardly conventional, but they appealed to some segments of the reading public. In his *Discourse on the Origin of Inequality Among Men* (1755) and *The Social Contract* (1762) he challenged the existing political and social order with an uncompromising attack on aristocracy and monarchy. He linked absolute monarchy, which he referred to as despotism, with the court and especially with the vain, pampered, conceited, and overdecorated aristocratic women who wielded political influence with the king and in the salons. As an alternative to this aristocratic, monarchical, and feminized society Rousseau proclaimed the sovereignty of the people. Laws were to be determined by the General Will, by which he meant the consensus of a community of citizens (but not necessarily the vote of the majority).

As a result of his writings Rousseau became associated with radical republican and democratic ideas that flourished at the time of the French Revolution. One indication of that radicalism was the fact that *The Social Contract* was banned not only in absolutist France but in the republics of the Netherlands and Switzerland as well. Rousseau was also criticized for justifying authoritarian rule. His argument that the General Will placed limits on individual civil liberty encouraged autocratic leaders, such as the radical Maximilien Robespierre at the time of the French Revolution, to claim that their dictatorial rule embodied that General Will.

Thomas Paine: The Rights of Man

Of all the Enlightenment political theorists, the English publicist and propagandist Thomas Paine (1737–1809) was arguably the most radical. Paine was influenced by Rousseau, Diderot, and Voltaire, but his radicalism was cultivated mainly by his intense involvement in the political world of revolutionary America, where he became politically active in the 1770s. In *Common Sense* (1776) Paine presented the case for American independence from Britain. This included a passionate statement of human freedom, equality, and rationality. It also involved a vicious attack on hereditary monarchy and an eloquent statement for the sovereignty of the law. At the time of the French Revolution, Paine continued to call for the establishment

DOCUMENT

Rousseau Places Limits on Civil Liberty

In his Social Contract *(1762) Rousseau discussed the effect that the formation of the civil state had on individual liberty. Rousseau is careful to distinguish between the liberty one enjoys in the state of nature and the liberty one acquires by entering civil society. As he explains in this passage, the establishment of the civil state limits one's natural liberty, but contrary to what some scholars have maintained, he does not justify totalitarian rule. Passionately committed to human liberty, Rousseau claims that the democratic and egalitarian society he envisions would serve as an alternative to the despotic systems of government that existed in late-eighteenth-century Europe.*

The passage from the state of nature to the civil state produces a very remarkable change in man, by substituting justice for instinct in his conduct and giving his actions the morality they had formerly lacked. Then only, when the voice of duty takes the place of physical impulses and right of appetite, does man who so far had considered only himself, find that he is forced to act on different principles, and to consult his reason before listening to his inclinations. Although in this state he deprives himself of some advantages which he got from nature, he gains in return others so great, his facilities are so stimulated and developed, his ideas so extended, his feelings so ennobled, and his whole soul so uplifted that, did not the abuses of this new condition often degrade him below that which he left, he would be bound to bless continually the happy moment which took him from it forever and, instead of a stupid and unimaginative animal, made him an intelligent being and a man.

Let us draw up the whole account in terms easily commensurable. What man loses by the social contract is his natural liberty and an unlimited right to everything he tries to get and succeeds in getting; what he gains is civil liberty and the proprietorship of all he possesses. If we are to avoid mistake in weighing one against the other, we must clearly distinguish natural liberty, which is bounded only by the strength of the individual, from civil liberty, which is limited by the general will; and possession, which is merely the effect of force or the right of the first occupier, from property, which can be founded only on a positive title.

Source: Jean-Jacques Rousseau, *The Social Contract* (1762).

of a republic in France and in his native country. In his most widely circulated work, *The Rights of Man* (1791), he linked the institution of monarchy with the aristocracy, which he referred to as "a seraglio of males, who neither collect the honey nor form the hive but exist only for lazy enjoyment."

The title of *The Rights of Man* identified a theme that appeared in much Enlightenment writing. Like Diderot and Rousseau, Paine spoke the language of natural rights. Until the Enlightenment, rights were considered legal privileges acquired by royal charter or by inheritance. One had a right, for example, to a particular piece of land or to elect representatives from one's county or town. Those rights could be surrendered under certain circumstances, such as when a person sold land. The new emphasis on natural law, however, led to the belief that simply by being a human being one acquired natural rights that could never be taken away. The American Declaration of Independence (1776), drafted by Thomas Jefferson, presented an eloquent statement of these God-given inalienable rights, which included "life, liberty and the pursuit of happiness." In defending that independence, Paine claimed that "a government of our own is our natural right." Since the eighteenth century those rights have been extended to include newly defined activities, such as the right to privacy, but the language in which such rights are asserted is a legacy of the Enlightenment.

Women and the Enlightenment

The claim advanced by Enlightenment thinkers that all human beings are equal in a state of nature did not lead to a widespread belief that on the basis of natural law men and women are equal. Quite to the contrary, many philosophes, including Diderot and Rousseau, argued that women are different in nature from men and that they should be confined to an exclusively domestic role as chaste wives and mothers. Rousseau also insisted on the separate education of girls.

This patriarchal argument supported the emerging theory of separate spheres°, which held that men and women should conduct their lives in different social and political environments. The identification of women with the private, domestic sphere laid the foundation for the ideology of female domesticity, which became popular in bourgeois society in the nineteenth century. But it denied them the freedom that aristocratic women in France had acquired during the eighteenth century, especially those who participated in polite society. It also continued to deny them civil rights. Like women in ancient Sparta, whose situation served as the model for a number of Enlightenment thinkers, eighteenth-century women could not vote and could not initiate lawsuits on their own authority. They were not full members of civil society.

DOCUMENT

Montesquieu Satirizes European Women

Montesquieu's first publication, The Persian Letters *(1721), is a clever satire on French society. The book consists of a series of letters written to and from two fictional Persian travelers, Usbek and Rica. Because the characters come from a radically different culture, Montesquieu was able to avoid official censure for presenting his irreverent views. The Persians refer to the king as a great magician who has the power to persuade men to kill one another though they have no quarrel, and to the pope as "an old idol worshipped out of habit." Montesquieu's satire was all the more biting because Europeans harbored deep contempt for the world of the Middle East, which they thought of as a region ruled by oriental despots and inhabited by people with lax standards of sexual morality. In this passage from one of Usbek's early letters to one of his wives in the harem, Montesquieu presents a favorable image of the oriental harem to contrast with the aristocratic women of eighteenth-century France.*

Usbek to Roxana, at the seraglio in Ispahan

How fortunate you are, Roxana, to live in the gentle land of Persia and not in these poisoned regions where neither shame nor virtue are known! You live in my seraglio as in the bower of innocence, inaccessible to the assaults of mankind; you rejoice in the good fortune that makes it impossible for you to fall. No man has sullied you with lascivious glances; even your father-in-law, during the freedom of the festivals, has never seen your lovely mouth, because you have never failed to cover it with a sacred veil . . . .

If you had been raised in this country, you would not have been so troubled. Women here have lost all restraint. They present themselves barefaced to men, as if inviting conquest; they seek attention, and they accompany men to the mosques. On walks, even to their rooms; the service of eunuchs is unknown. In place of the noble simplicity and charming modesty which is the rule among you, one finds here a barbaric impudence, to which one cannot grow accustomed. . . .

When you enhance the brilliance of your complexion with lovely coloring, when you perfume all your body with the most precious essences, when you dress in your most beautiful garments, when you seek to distinguish yourself from your companions by the charm of your dancing or the delight of your song, when you graciously compete with them in beauty, sweetness and vivacity, then I cannot imagine that you have any other object than that of pleasing me. . . .

But what am I to think of European women? Their art in making up their complexions, the ornaments they display, the care they give to their bodies, their preoccupation with pleasing are so many stains on their virtue and outrages to their husbands.

Source: From Baron de Montesquieu, *The Persian Letters,* translated by George R. Healy (Hackett, 1999), Letter 26.

Only in the 1790s did writers begin to use the language and ideas of the Enlightenment to advance the argument for the full equality of men and women. The first of these appeals came from Condorcet, who published *On the Admission of Women to the Rights of Citizenship* in 1789. In that pamphlet he proposed that all women who own property be given the right to vote. He later called for universal suffrage for all men and women on the grounds that they all shared a common human nature. A similar appeal came from the French dramatist and revolutionary activist Marie Olympe Aubrey de Gouges (1748–1793). At the very beginning of the French Revolution, de Gouges, the daughter of a butcher, proposed that the revolutionary manifesto adopted by the French National Assembly, *Declaration of the Rights of Man and Citizen* (1789), be extended to include women as well as men.

De Gouges drafted her most famous publication, *The Rights of Woman* (1791), as a proposed appendix to that constitutional document. She took the authors of the *Declaration* to task for their failure to address the problem of women's civil rights and responsibilities with the same determination and enthusiasm they had manifested in proclaiming the rights of men. Revealing her debt to Rousseau, she proposed in Article VI of her document that "the law must be the expression of the general will. All citizens, men and women, must concur, personally or through their representatives, in its creation. It must be the same for everyone: every citizen, man and woman, being equal in its eyes, must be equally eligible for all high honors, public offices, and positions according to their merits. . . . " Using more of Rousseau's language, she went on to propose a "social contract" between man and woman that recognized, among other things, common ownership of property. None of de Gouges's proposals were implemented by the French government, but she did succeed in drawing attention to the contradictions between the rhetoric and the reality of natural rights.

De Gouges's English contemporary, Mary Wollstonecraft (1759–1797), was the most famous of the Enlightenment's advocates of women's rights. Inspired by the events of the French Revolution and angered by the conservative English response to the events taking place in France,

Wollstonecraft wrote *A Vindication of the Rights of Woman* (1792). This treatise, which embodies a stinging critique of eighteenth-century polite society, has become a founding document of modern feminism. In it Wollstonecraft made an eloquent appeal for extending civil and political rights to women and even proposed that women elect their own representatives to legislatures. Her most original and innovative proposals, however, dealt with education. She claimed that in order for women to take control of their lives and to become the full equals of men within marriage and in the political realm, girls had to acquire greater knowledge and skill and learn how to support themselves. Wollstonecraft insisted that the education of women must be made equal and identical to that of men. In this way she challenged the arguments presented by Rousseau and many other male Enlightenment thinkers that cultural and social differences between men and women should be maintained because they were "natural."

The Enlightenment and Sexuality

One facet of Enlightenment thought that had a profound effect on the position of women in society was the appeal for greater sexual permissiveness. Many philosophes, including Voltaire, Diderot, and Holbach, remained openly critical of the strict standard of sexual morality enforced by Christian churches. The basic argument of the philosophes was that sexual activity should not be restricted, because it was pleasurable and a source of happiness. The arbitrary prohibitions imposed by the Church contradicted human nature. European encounters with pagan natives of the South Pacific, who were reported to have enjoyed great sexual permissiveness, were used to reinforce this argument based on human nature. Diderot appealed to the sexual code of the Tahitians in his attack on Christian sexual morality.

Many philosophes, including Voltaire, practiced what they preached and lived openly with women out of wedlock. Other members of wealthy society adopted an even more libertine lifestyle. The Venetian adventurer and author Giacomo Casanova (1725–1798), who was expelled from a seminary for his immorality, gained fame for his life of gambling, spying, and seducing thousands of women. To one young Spanish woman, who resisted his advances in order to protect her virginity, he said: "You must abandon yourself to my passion without any resistance, and you may rest assured I will respect your innocence." Casanova's name soon became identified with sexual seduction.

The violent excesses to which this type of eighteenth-century sexual permissiveness could lead can be seen in the career of Alphonse Donatien François, the Marquis de Sade (1740–1814). The author of licentious libertine narratives, including his own memoirs and an erotic novel, *Justine* (1793), de Sade described the use of violence in sexual encounters and thus gave rise to the word *sadism* to describe the pleasurable administration of pain. He spent twenty-seven years in prison for his various sexual offenses.

It makes sense that noblemen like Casanova and de Sade would have adopted the libertine values of the Enlightenment thinkers. Somewhat more remarkable was the growth of public sexual permissiveness among all social groups, including the rather prim and proper bourgeoisie and the working poor. Erotic literature, such as John Cleland's *Memoirs of a Woman of Pleasure* (1749), and pornographic prints achieved considerable popularity in an increasingly commercialized society, while prostitution became more open and widespread. Voltaire and Diderot might not have approved of this literature or these practices, but their libertine, anti-Christian, materialist outlook helped to prepare the ground for their acceptance.

The Impact of the Enlightenment

■ **What impact did the Enlightenment have on Western culture and politics?**

The ideas of the Enlightenment spread to every country in Europe as well as to the Americas. They inspired programs of reform and radical political movements. Enlightenment thought, however, did not become the property of the entire population. It appealed mainly to the educated and the relatively prosperous and failed to penetrate the lower levels of society.

The Spread of Enlightened Ideas

The ideas of the Enlightenment spread rapidly among the literate members of society, mainly by means of print. During the eighteenth century, print became the main medium of formal communication. The technology of printing allowed for the publication of materials on a scale unknown a century before. Pamphlets, newspapers, and books poured off presses, not only in the major cities but in provincial towns as well. Literacy rates increased dramatically throughout western Europe. The highly educated still constituted a minority of the population, but the better part of the aristocracy and many of those who occupied the middle ranks of society could read and write. By 1750 more than half the male population of France and England could read basic texts. The foundation of public libraries in all the major cities of western Europe made printed materials more widely available. In many bookshops, rooms were set aside for browsing in the hope that readers would eventually purchase the books they consulted.

One of the most widely circulated publications of the Enlightenment was the *Encyclopedia* compiled by the philosophe Denis Diderot and the mathematician Jean le Rond d'Alembert. This massive seventeen-volume work, which was published between 1751 and 1765, contained thousands of articles on science, religion, politics, and the economy. The entries in the *Encyclopedia* were intended not only to promote knowledge but also to advance the ideas of the Enlightenment. Included, for example, were two entries on natural law, which was described as being "perpetual and unchangeable." The entry on intolerance makes a passionate plea against religious persecution, asserting that "If we may tear out one hair of anyone whose opinions differ from ours, we could also claim the whole head, for there is no limit to injustice." Other articles praised the achievements of science and technology and gave special attention to industrial crafts and trades. Underlying the entire enterprise was the belief that knowledge was useful, that it could contribute to the improvement of human life. In these respects the *Encyclopedia* became the quintessential statement of the worldview of the Enlightenment, and its publication stands as a crowning achievement of the entire movement.

IMAGE
Diderot's *Encyclopedia*, Plate Illustrating Agricultural Techniques

Encyclopedias, pamphlets, newspapers, and novels were not the only means by which the ideas of the Enlightenment spread. A number of informal institutions promoted the exchange of ideas. Literary societies and book clubs, which proliferated in the major cities of western Europe, encouraged the public reading and discussion of the latest publications. Scientific societies sponsored lectures on the latest developments in physics, chemistry, and natural history. One of the most famous of these lectures demonstrated the power of electricity by charging a young boy, suspended from the ground, with static electricity. This "electrified boy," who was not harmed in the process, attracted objects from a stool placed below him. Lectures like this one attracted large crowds.

Equally important in the spread of the scientific and cultural ideas of the Enlightenment were museums, where scientific and cultural artifacts, many of them gathered from around the world, could be viewed by an increasingly curious and educated public. The museums often sponsored exhibits and lectures. Paris became home to a number of these museums in the 1780s, and they could be found in all the major cities of Europe by the end of the eighteenth century. A more informal set of cultural institutions were the coffeehouses that sprang up in cities across Europe. These commercial establishments were open to everyone who could pay the fare, and therefore they proved immensely successful in facilitating the spread of ideas within the bourgeoisie. Newspapers were often read aloud at coffeehouses, and they became the setting for many political debates.

Another set of institutions that promoted the ideas of the Enlightenment were the secret societies of men and women known as freemasons°. Freemasons strove to create a society based on reason and virtue, and they were committed to the principles of liberty and equality. Freemasonry first appeared in England and Scotland in the seventeenth century and then spread to France, the Dutch Republic, Germany, and as far east as Poland and Russia during the eighteenth century. Some of the most famous figures of the Enlightenment, including Voltaire, belonged to masonic lodges. In the 1770s there were more than 10,000 freemasons in Paris alone. The lodges were places where philosophes interacted with merchants, lawyers, and government leaders. The pope condemned the freemasons in 1738, and many civil authorities expressed deep suspicion of the political and religious ideas they fostered.

The most famous informal cultural institutions of the Enlightenment were the salons, the private sitting rooms or parlors of wealthy women where discussions of philosophy, science, literature, and politics took place. Salons became particularly prominent in Paris, where the salons of Madame Geoffrin and Madame du Deffand won international fame. The women who hosted these meetings invited the participants, entertained those who attended, and used their conversational skills to direct and facilitate the discussions that took place in the salons. They also used their influence to secure aristocratic patronage of the young male writers and scientists whom they cultivated. The success of a new book was often determined by its initial reception in the salon. Most of the prominent male figures of the French Enlightenment participated in these meetings, at least during the early years of their careers. (See the illustration at the beginning of this chapter.)

Madame Geoffrin
Her salon was called "one of the wonders of the social world."

The salons became the target of contemporary criticism not only because they allowed women to participate in public life but also because they were bastions of aristocratic society. While most of the salon women came from the aristocracy, many of their fathers had recently risen into the nobility or had merely purchased their noble status. The men who attended the meetings had even fewer ties to the traditional aristocracy. The salons were places where old and new noble blood intermingled, where social refinement was even more important than inherited nobility. What mattered most in the salons was the quickness of one's wit, the quality of one's conversational skills, and the appeal of one's views. Thus the salon succeeded in opening elite society to the talented. In this way the salons helped to dissolve the bonds that held together the Old Regime and contributed to the creation of a society based on merit rather than birth alone.

The Limits of the Enlightenment

The ideas of the Enlightenment spread rapidly across Europe, but their influence was limited. The market for books by philosophes such as Voltaire and Rousseau was quite small. Diderot and d'Alembert's *Encyclopedia* sold a remarkable 25,000 copies by 1789, but that was exceptional, and many sales were to libraries. Paine's *The Rights of Man* also reached a fairly broad audience, mainly because it was written in a simple direct style and its price was deliberately kept low. Most books on social and political theory, however, like scholarly works on science, did not sell very well. Rousseau's *The Social Contract* was a commercial failure.

Books on other topics had much better sales. Inspirational religious literature continued to be published in large quantities, indicating the limits of Enlightenment secularism. Novels, a relatively new genre of fiction that appealed to the bourgeoisie, were almost as successful. We can readily see why Rousseau and Voltaire both used novels to advance their radical social views. In France, books that were banned because of their pornographic content or their satirical attacks on the monarchy, the clergy, or ministers in the government also proved to be best-sellers in the huge underground French book market.

One segment of the popular press that revealed a limited influence of the Enlightenment was the literature on popular science. The reading public did not show much interest in technical scientific books, but they did purchase publications on such technological developments as hot-air balloons, which became a new fad in the 1780s. Descriptions of monsters found in distant lands and other extraordinary natural occurrences also sold thousands of copies. Some of this interest in the preternatural originated in the work of highly educated scholars, but the reports of new discoveries increasingly lent themselves to sensational treatment in the popular press.

Another subject of popular literary interest was mesmerism°. The Viennese physicist and physician Franz Anton Mesmer (1734–1815), who moved to Paris in 1778, claimed that he had discovered a fluid that permeated and surrounded all bodies and was the source of heat, light, electricity, and magnetism. Sickness was caused by the obstruction to the flow of this fluid in the human body. To restore this flow patients were massaged, hypnotized, or "mesmerized" with the intention of producing a convulsion or crisis that restored health. Mesmerism developed into a form of spiritualism in which its patients engaged in séances with spirits, and its practitioners dabbled in the occult. This pseudoscience, which was rejected by the French Academy of Science as a hoax, became the subject of numerous pamphlets and newspaper articles that fascinated the reading public.

Those who read books about mesmerism had only a tenuous connection with the learned world of the Enlightenment. Among those who were illiterate or barely literate, Enlightened ideas made even fewer inroads. The only exposure these people may have had to the ideas we associate with the Enlightenment would be through the actions and attitudes of their social superiors. From the elitist perspective of the philosophes, the intellectual world of the illiterate was characterized by the superstition and ignorance that the philosophes were determined to eliminate.

The growing gap between a learned culture shared by philosophes and members of salons on the one hand and the popular culture of the lower classes on the other can be seen in the perpetuation of beliefs regarding magic and witchcraft among the uneducated. During the late seventeenth and eighteenth centuries, educated people in Europe gradually abandoned their belief in magic and witchcraft. As we have seen in Chapter 16, belief in the operation of a mechanical universe, religious skepticism, and rationalism had gradually eroded many beliefs regarding the operation of a supernatural realm, especially the possibility of demonic intervention in the natural world. Among the lower classes, however, this skeptical outlook found very little fertile ground. Popular belief in a world charged with supernatural and magical forces continued to lead villagers to accuse their neighbors of having harmed them by means of witchcraft. After European courts stopped prosecuting witches in the late seventeenth and early eighteenth centuries, local communities often took justice into their own hands and lynched the suspects themselves. It was left to the government to prosecute those who engaged in this illegal form of local justice.

The gap between the high culture of the Enlightenment and that of the lower classes can also be seen in the condemnations of certain sports and amusements. Popular culture was known for its blood sports, especially cockfighting, and the baiting of bulls, bears, and badgers by tying the animals down and allowing dogs to attack them. These blood sports, which could attract thousands of spectators at a single event, resulted in the serious injury or death of animals. Enlightenment thinkers, especially those from the bourgeoisie, condemned this activity for its cruelty and its barbarism. Just like the torture and execution of criminals, these "barbarous" pastimes had no place in polite society. Popular sports, however, could not be easily eradicated. It was not until the nineteenth century that they began to disappear, often as the result of campaigns conducted by clergymen rather than philosophes. The persistence of blood sports reveals the strength of popular culture and the inability of the Enlightenment to transform it.

Enlightened Absolutism

When we turn to Enlightened political ideas, we confront an even more difficult task of determining the extent of their impact. The main figures of the Enlightenment were intellectuals—men of letters who did not occupy positions of great political importance and who did not devote much thought to the challenging task of putting their theories into practice. The audience for their books did not always include people with the power to implement their proposals. Rulers often treated Enlightenment thinkers with suspicion, if only because they criticized established authority. Nevertheless, Enlightenment thought did make its mark on eighteenth-century politics in two strikingly different ways.

The first was through the reforms enacted by rulers who are often referred to as enlightened despots°. These rulers exercised absolute power and used that power to implement changes that Enlightenment thinkers had proposed. The term *despot* is misleading, as these enlightened rulers were rarely despotic in the sense of exercising power cruelly and arbitrarily. The connection between Enlightenment and royal absolutism is not as unnatural as it might appear. It is true that philosophes tended to be critical of the Old Regime°, the eighteenth-century political order that was dominated by an absolute monarch and a privileged nobility and clergy. But many of them, including Voltaire, had little sympathy with democracy and social equality, and preferred to entrust absolute monarchs with the implementation of the reforms they advocated. Among the philosophes the prospect of a philosopher-king had widespread appeal.

Rulers of central and eastern European countries were particularly open to Enlightenment thought. These monarchs had read widely in the literature of the Enlightenment and introduced Western intellectuals to their courts. The most famous of the enlightened absolutists was King Frederick II of Prussia, known as Frederick the Great (r. 1740–1786). Frederick, a deist who wrote poetry and played the flute, was enamored of all things French. When the French philosophe d'Alembert visited his court, the king hosted a dinner at which he spoke only French, leaving many of the Prussian guests to sip their soup in stunned silence. Frederick corresponded extensively with Voltaire and invited him to take up residence at his French-style royal palace, "Sans Souci," at Potsdam. The relationship between king and philosopher, however, was often stormy, and when Frederick publicly burned a publication in which Voltaire had lampooned a royal favorite, Voltaire left Potsdam in 1752.

The departure of Voltaire did not weaken Frederick's determination to implement a number of policies that reflected the ideals of the Enlightenment. The most noteworthy of these was the introduction of religious toleration throughout his predominantly Lutheran kingdom. Protestants of all denominations and Catholics (but not Jews) received the protection of the law and even benefited from royal patronage. Frederick also introduced a number of legal reforms with the intention of realizing the Enlightenment ideal of making the law both rational and humane. He authorized the codification of Prussian law (which was completed after his death in 1794), abolished judicial torture, and eliminated capital punishment. In order to provide for the training of future servants of the state, he began a system of compulsory education throughout the country. Like most enlightened rulers, Frederick never abandoned his commitment to absolute rule, which he strengthened by winning the support of the nobility. He also remained committed to the militaristic and expansionist policies of his father, Frederick William I. For him there was no contradiction between his style of rule and his commitment to Enlightenment ideals.

In neighboring Austria two Habsburg rulers, Maria Theresa (r. 1740–1780) and her son Joseph II (r. 1780–1790), pursued reformist policies that gave them the reputation of being enlightened monarchs. Most of Maria Theresa's reforms were of an administrative nature. Stunned by the Prussian invasion and occupation of the Habsburg province of Silesia in 1740, Maria Theresa set out to strengthen the Habsburg monarchy by gaining complete control over taxation and by reorganizing the military and civil bureaucracy. She also took steps to make the serfs more productive, mainly by restricting the work they performed on their lords' lands and by abolishing the feudal dues they paid.

These efforts won the applause of philosophes, but the policies of Maria Theresa's that most clearly bore the stamp of the Enlightenment were her legal reforms. Inspired by Beccaria and Montesquieu, she established a commission to reform the entire corpus of Austrian law. A new code of criminal law was promulgated in 1769, and seven years later Maria Theresa issued an edict abolishing judicial torture. Joseph continued this program of legal reform by reorganizing the entire central court system and by eliminating capital punishment. He also revealed the influence of the Enlightenment by granting religious toleration, first to Protestants and eastern Orthodox

Torture
The torture of a defendant as depicted in the published version of the criminal code promulgated by Empress Maria Theresa in 1769. This form of torture, the *strappado,* used a pulley to hang the accused from the ceiling. Weights could be attached to the feet to make the pain more excruciating. The purpose of judicial torture was to extract a confession. Torture was eliminated from the law codes of most continental European countries during the Enlightenment.

Christians in 1781, and then to Jews in 1782. With respect to social issues, he completed his mother's work of abolishing serfdom altogether.

The efforts of Catherine II of Russia (r. 1762–1796) to implement the ideas of the Enlightenment followed a different course from those of Maria Theresa and Joseph. The daughter of a German prince, Catherine received an education grounded in a traditional curriculum of history, geography, and Lutheran theology. In 1745 she was married to a distant cousin, Peter, who was in line to inherit the Russian throne from his aunt, the childless Empress Elizabeth (r. 1741–1762). After arriving in St. Petersburg Catherine not only acquired a knowledge of Russian language, literature, and religion but also read widely in western European sources, including the works of Enlightenment thinkers. She later corresponded with Voltaire and d'Alembert and employed the famous salon hostess Madame Geoffrin at her court. At Catherine's invitation Diderot visited St. Petersburg for six months.

Early in her reign, Catherine embarked on a program of reform similar to those of other enlightened absolutists. In 1767 she appointed a commission to codify Russian law on the basis of western European principles. Her recommendations to the commission included the abolition of torture and inhumane punishment and the establishment of religious toleration. She was eventually forced to disband the commission, which could not agree on a new code, but she later abolished torture and capital punishment on her own authority. Like Maria Theresa, she instituted a number of administrative and educational reforms, including the introduction of primary schooling in the provinces. Catherine, who became known as Catherine the Great, also tried unsuccessfully to provide for the education of girls as well as boys.

Catherine the Great's Constitution (1767)

Catherine gained a reputation for being an enlightened European monarch, but her acceptance of traditional Russian culture and the need to maintain her rule prevented her from fully embracing the ideals of the Enlightenment. She even admitted that it was much easier to subscribe to the ideals of the Enlightenment than actually to implement them. The strength of vested interests within Russian society accounted for the failure of the law commission of 1767. After putting down the Pugachev rebellion in 1774, she began to question the desirability of social reform, and the experience of the French Revolution in the 1790s (see Chapter 19) led her to disavow the ideals of the Enlightenment.

On the issue of serfdom, which most Enlightenment thinkers wished to see abolished, she would not yield. She preserved that social system in order to secure the loyalty of the Russian nobility, and she extended it to Ukraine and parts of Poland after Russia incorporated those regions into the empire. Catherine also catered to the imperialistic ambitions of the Russians, gaining vast territories in eastern Europe, East Asia, and Alaska. Thus she expanded the Russian Empire at the very time when the ideals of the Enlightenment were leading some philosophes to call for the dissolution of large imperial structures.

The Enlightenment and Revolution

The second mark that Enlightenment thought made on eighteenth-century politics was the inspiration it gave to movements for reform and revolution in western Europe and the Americas. The emphasis placed by Enlightenment

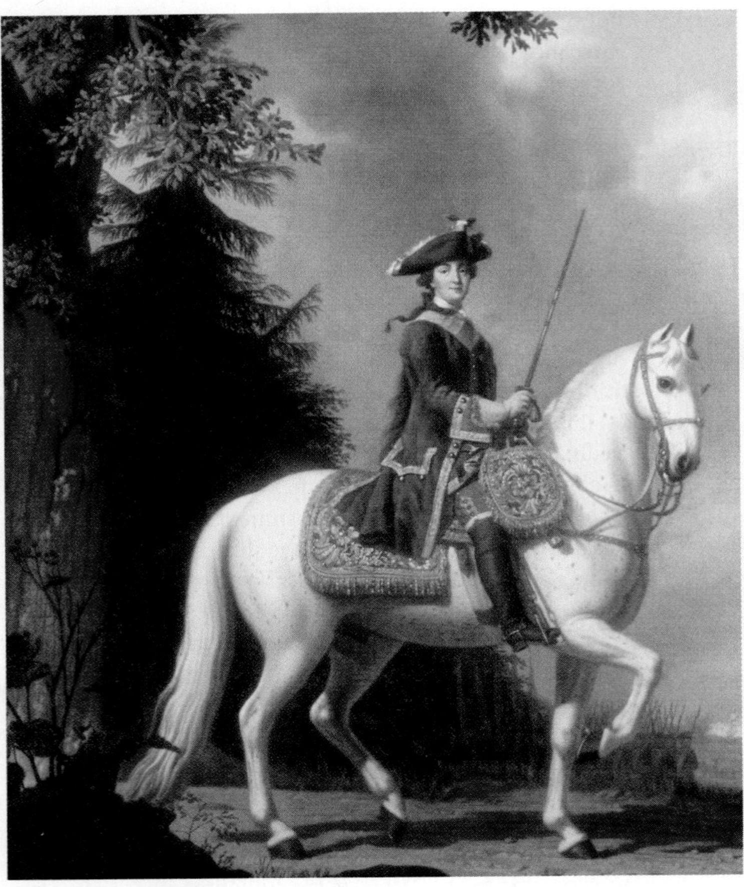

Catherine the Great
Catherine II of Russia on the day she succeeded in taking the throne from her husband, Peter III, at Peterhof in 1762. Catherine, who despised her husband, joined a conspiracy against him right after his accession to the throne. Catherine, like Peter, had a number of lovers, and her two children, including the future emperor Paul, were reputedly conceived by members of the nobility.

thinkers on individual liberty, natural rights, and political reform put pressure on both monarchs and the traditional nobility either to make concessions or to relinquish power altogether.

In Britain, for example, the movement for parliamentary reform and the expansion of the franchise°, as well as the first appeals for women's rights, were partially inspired by the Enlightenment. The radical democrat Thomas Paine, the feminist Mary Wollstonecraft, and the parliamentary reformer Joseph Priestley all based their demands for political reform on Enlightenment ideas of natural rights and civil liberty. It took considerable time, however, for these reforms to be realized. Only in 1832 did the British Parliament agree to a modest extension of the franchise, and women did not receive the vote until the early twentieth century. Nevertheless the movements to achieve these reforms were inspired by ideals born of the Enlightenment.

In France the influence of the Enlightenment on the momentous changes that took place during the French Revolution (1789–1799) has been a matter of debate among historians. The complexity of the revolution, which will be discussed in Chapter 19, and the diversity of Enlightenment thought make this a particularly difficult debate to resolve. Many of the revolutionaries of the 1790s were steeped in the ideas of the Enlightenment, but those ideas did not necessarily inspire the revolution itself. The French philosophes of the eighteenth century denounced the evils of the Old Regime and proposed many ideas about how governments should function, but they did not make serious efforts to introduce actual reforms, much less topple the government. Many philosophes, including Voltaire, had personal connections with aristocratic society, and very few shared the democratic and egalitarian ideas that came to the fore at the time of the Revolution. Some lesser journalists and literary hacks were more successful than the most renowned philosophes in fostering contempt for the Old Regime before the Revolution. Their merciless satires of the court and the clergy were more responsible than the grand treatises of the philosophes for stimulating a crisis of confidence in the French government and eroding the traditional respect for authority that made possible the violent overthrow of the Old Regime.

We can nevertheless establish some connections between the ideas and programs of the philosophes and the events that transpired in France during the 1790s. Some of the figures of the Enlightenment contributed to the new critical spirit evident after 1750 or provided some inspiration for the creation of a new political culture once the revolution began. The towering reputation of Voltaire during the French Revolution—and the anger of conservatives who exhumed and burned his bones after it had ended—suggest that his passionate criticisms of the Old Regime and his pleas for human freedom at the very least helped to set the stage for the revolutionary events of the 1790s. The same is true of the radical Rousseau, whose concept of the General Will served as the basis of a revolutionary ideology. Rousseau's democratic and republican ideas were used to justify some of the most important changes that took place during the revolution. Contemporaries glorified or attacked him, depending on their political philosophy, for having actually caused the revolution. One book published in 1791 was titled *On Jean-Jacques Rousseau Considered as One of the First Authors of the Revolution.*

Yet another application of enlightened ideas to politics took place in the Americas. The advocates of colonial independence from their mother countries, such as Thomas Jefferson in Virginia and Símon Bolívar in Venezuela and Colombia, were all deeply influenced by the Enlightenment concepts of natural law, natural rights, liberty, and popular sovereignty. The Declaration of Independence, which was written by Jefferson, betrayed its debt to the Enlightenment in its reference to the inalienable rights of all men and to the foundation of those rights in "the law of nature and Nature's God." Of course the American Revolution cannot be explained solely in terms of these Enlightenment ideas. The colonists found inspiration in many different sources, including English common law. But the American colonists did wish to create an entirely new world order, just as did many Enlightenment thinkers. They also adopted some of the most radical political ideas of the Enlightenment, which identified the people as the source of political power.

More generally, the Enlightenment fostered a critique of all efforts to establish overseas empires. The French priest Guillaume Thomas Raynal, mentioned in Chapter 17, wrote a condemnation of colonialism titled *The Philosophical and Political History of the Settlement and Commerce of Europeans in the Two Indies* (1770). Diderot and a number of lesser-known philosophes contributed to the final version of this massive work, which was published at Geneva in 1780. The book, which was the first to treat European imperialism in both hemispheres in the same context, praised the civilizing effects of commerce but condemned colonialism for the effects it had on those who emigrated. Cut off from their homeland, colonists brought with them only the prejudices of the civilizations they left behind and became hopelessly corrupt and degenerate. The English political theorist Richard Price developed a similar critique of all overseas empires, claiming that simply by their size and their diversity they could not promote the happiness of a community and the "fellow-feeling that takes place between persons in private life." According to Price, sprawling overseas empires by their very nature violated the standards of humanity.

Conclusion

The Enlightenment and Western Identity

The Enlightenment was a distinctly Western phenomenon. It arose in the countries of western Europe and then spread to central and eastern Europe (Germany, Austria, Poland, and Russia) and to the Americas. Most traditions that are identified today as "Western values" either had their origin or received their most cogent expression in the Enlightenment. In particular, the commitment to individual liberty, civil rights, toleration, and rational decision making all took shape during this period.

It would be misleading to make a simple equation between the ideas of the Enlightenment and the Western intellectual tradition. First, the ideals of the Enlightenment have never been fully accepted within Western societies. Ever since their original formulation, the ideas of the philosophes and publicists of the Enlightenment have been challenged by conservatives who argued that those ideas would lead to the destruction of religion and the social order. Those conservative criticisms, which are voiced even today, became intense at the time of the French Revolution and during the early years of the nineteenth century, and we shall discuss them in Chapters 19 and 21. Second, claims that the ideas promoted by the Enlightenment are exclusively Western can also be disputed. A celebration of reason and an insistence on religious tolerance, for example, can be found in the cultures of ancient India and China. The claim that the West is more rational than the East is itself a product of long-standing Western prejudice, an assertion that studies of other cultures undertaken by Enlightenment writers only served to strengthen.

Nevertheless, the ideas and traditions of the Enlightenment, despite the challenges they have endured, have become deeply ingrained in Western law and politics. They are less often found embedded in the political and legal traditions of non-Western lands, and when they are, such as in the twentieth-century socialist legal system of China, their presence is more often the result of Western influence than the legacy of native Eastern thought.

The acquisition of the values of the Enlightenment, even though they were never universally adopted, gave Europeans a clear sense of their own identity with respect to the rest of the world. Educated people who prided themselves on being enlightened knew that their scientific, rational worldview was not shared by Asians, Africans, indigenous Americans, or South Pacific islanders. It did not matter whether Enlightenment thinkers had a positive view of those other cultures, like Voltaire or Rousseau, or a negative one, like Montesquieu. What mattered was that they shared a similar mental outlook and a commitment to individual liberty, justice, and the improvement of civilization. For all of them religious faith was less important, both as an arbiter of morality and as a source of authority, than it was in these other cultures. The men and women of the Enlightenment all looked to the law as a reflection of natural law and as the guardian of civil liberty. Their writings helped their European and colonial public audiences think of themselves as even more distinct from non-Western people than they had in the past.

As these enlightened Western cultural values were spreading, the boundaries between East and West remained fluid and contested. The geographical region where this contest took place was what we now call eastern Europe. As we have seen in Chapter 15, the countries that occupied this buffer zone between East and West had long-standing cultural ties with Asia, especially the Middle East, but they also developed an attraction to Western culture beginning in the late seventeenth century. In Russia, this process of westernization began with Peter the Great, who integrated his country into European social, political, and diplomatic life. But it was carried further by Catherine the Great, who invited *philosophes* to her court and introduced Western reforms. This adoption of Western ideas made her appear to be a model Enlightened ruler and her country part of the Western world, but Russia's inclusion became and has remained a matter of debate. The very term "eastern Europe," which was coined during the Enlightenment, reflected the ambiguous relationship between this part of the world and the West. It provides a further illustration of the fact that the West was a cultural realm whose geographical boundaries have frequently changed.

Suggestions for Further Reading

For a comprehensive listing of suggested readings, please go to www.ablongman.com/levack2e/chapter 18

Alexander, John T. *Catherine the Great: Life and Legend.* 1989. A lively biography of the remarkable "enlightened despot."

Beckett, J. V. *The Aristocracy in England, 1660–1914.* 1986. A comprehensive study of this landholding and governing elite. Makes the important distinction between the aristocracy and the nobility.

Darnton, Robert. *The Forbidden Best-Sellers of Pre-Revolutionary France.* 1995. A study of the salacious, blasphemous, and subversive books that sold more copies than those of the philosophes in eighteenth-century France.

Dewald, Jonathan. *The European Nobility, 1500–1800.* 1996. A comprehensive study of this social class that emphasizes its adaptability.

Doyle, William. *The Old European Order, 1660–1800.* 2nd ed. 1999. The best general study of the period.

Houston, R. A. *Literacy in Early Modern Europe: Culture and Education.* 1991. The best survey of the subject for the entire period.

Lugee, Carolyn. *Le Paradis des Femmes: Women, Salons and Social Stratification in 17th-Century France.* 1976. A social study of the women of the salons.

Outram, Dorinda. *The Enlightenment.* 1995. A balanced assessment of the major historiographical debates regarding the Enlightenment.

Root, Hilton. *Peasants and King in Burgundy: Agrarian Foundations of French Absolutism.* 1979. A study of peasant communal institutions and their relationship with the crown as well as the nobility.

Williams, David, ed. *The Enlightenment.* 1999. An excellent collection of political writings with a long introduction.

Notes

1. Baron d'Holbach, *Good Sense* (1753).
2. David Hume, *Essays Moral, Political, and Literary* (1742), Essay X: "Of Superstition and Enthusiasm."
3. Cesare Beccaria, *An Essay on Crimes and Punishments* (1788), Chapter 47.
4. Voltaire, "Religion," in *The Philosophical Dictionary* (1802).
5. Jean-Jacques Rousseau, *Emile, or on Education* (1762).

The Age of the French Revolution, 1789–1815

19

CHAPTER OUTLINE

- The First French Revolution, 1789–1791
- The French Republic, 1792–1799
- Cultural Change in France During the Revolution
- The Napoleonic Era, 1799–1815
- The Legacy of the French Revolution

On July 12, 1789, the French journalist Camille Desmoulins addressed an anxious crowd of Parisian citizens gathered outside the Palais-Royal, where public debate often took place. Playing upon fears that had been mounting during the past two months, Desmoulins claimed that the royal government of Louis XVI was preparing a massacre of Parisians. "To arms, to arms," Desmoulins cried out, as he roused the citizens to their own defense. That night Parisians responded to his call by invading arsenals in the city in anticipation of the violence they thought was about to descend upon them. The next day they continued to seize weapons and declared themselves members of the National Guard, a volunteer militia of propertied citizens.

On the morning of July 14, crowds of Parisians moved into a district of the city where royal troops were stationed in an ancient fortress known as the Bastille. The Parisians feared that the troops in the Bastille would take violent action against them, and they also wanted to capture the ammunition stored inside the building, which served as both an arsenal and a prison. Negotiations with the governor of the Bastille were interrupted when some of the militia, moving into the courtyard of the fortress, demanded the surrender of the troops. Shots were fired from both sides, and the exchange led to a full-scale assault upon the Bastille by the National Guard.

After three hours of fighting and the death of eighty-three people, the governor surrendered. He was then led by his captors, bearing the arms they had seized, to face charges before the officers of the city government. The crowd, however, crying for vengeance against their oppressors, attacked the soldiers and crushed some of them underfoot. The governor was stabbed hundreds of times, hacked to pieces, and decapitated. The chief magistrate of the city suffered the same fate for his reluctance to issue arms to its citizens. The crowd then placed the heads of the two men on pikes and paraded through the city.

Jacques-Louis David, *The Oath of the Tennis Court* The oath taken by the members of the Third Estate not to disband until France had a constitution led to the creation of the National Assembly and the legislation that destroyed royal absolutism and feudalism.

The storming of the Bastille was the first of many violent episodes that occurred during the sequence of events called the French Revolution. That revolution brought about some of the most fundamental changes in European political life since the end of Roman rule. It heralded the destruction of the Old Regime, the eighteenth-century political order that had been dominated by an absolute monarch and a privileged nobility and clergy. It led to the submission of the Catholic Church to state control. A more radical phase of the revolution, beginning in 1792, resulted in the destruction of the French monarchy and the declaration of a republic. It also led to a period of state-sponsored terrorism in 1793 and 1794, during which one group of revolutionaries engaged in a brutal campaign to eliminate their real and imagined enemies.

The Storming of the Bastille, July 14, 1789

The Bastille was attacked not because it was a symbol of the Old Regime, but because it contained weapons that the Parisian citizens needed to protect themselves from royalist troops.

The excesses of the revolution led to a conservative reaction. Between 1795 and 1799 a moderate republican government, known as the Directory, modified the egalitarianism of the revolution by limiting the right to vote to men of property. Between 1799 and 1814 the reaction continued under the direction of Napoleon Bonaparte, a military officer who dominated the Consulate, a new political structure established in 1799, and then proclaimed himself emperor in 1804. Although Napoleon declared his loyalty to many of the principles of the revolution, his authoritarian rule undermined or reversed many of its achievements. In 1815 Napoleon fell from power and the monarchy was restored, marking the end of the revolutionary period. The ideas of the revolution, however, especially its commitment to democratic republicanism and its concept of the nation, continued to dominate politics in the West for the next hundred years. The French Revolution permanently changed the political culture of the West.

This chapter will address the question of how the encounters between different political and social groups in France at the end of the eighteenth century brought about some of the most important and far-reaching changes in the history of the West. In pursuing this broad objective, the individual chapter sections will address the following questions:

- **Why did the Old Regime in France collapse in 1789, and what revolutionary changes took place in French government and society during the next two years?**
- **How did a second, more radical revolution, which began with the establishment of the Republic in 1792, lead to the creation of a regime that used the power of the state to institute the Reign of Terror?**
- **In what ways did the political events of the revolution change French cultural institutions and create a new political culture?**
- **How did the authoritarian rule of Napoleon Bonaparte from 1799 to 1814 confirm or betray the achievements of the French Revolution, and what impact did his military conquests have on Europe and the world?**

- **What did the French Revolution ultimately achieve and in what ways did it change the course of European and Western history?**

The First French Revolution, 1789–1791

- **Why did the Old Regime in France collapse in 1789, and what revolutionary changes took place in French government and society during the next two years?**

One of the main characteristics of political revolutions is that they involve a fundamental change in the political *system,* not simply in the personnel of government. On the basis of this criterion the French Revolution consisted of two distinct revolutions. The first revolution, which began in 1789, resulted in a destruction of royal absolutism and the drafting of a constitution. The second and more radical revolution began in 1792 with the abolition of the monarchy and the formation of the French Republic.

Like all revolutions, the first French revolution had deep-seated causes. As we discussed in Chapter 18, a constant barrage of satirical literature directed at the royal family and the court lowered the prestige of the government and thus weakened its authority. The publication of thousands of pamphlets advocating reform, including many written by philosophes of the Enlightenment, fostered a critical attitude toward the French government and led to demands for political and economic change. Conflicts between the nobility and the crown over constitutional issues, a source of tension throughout the age of absolutism, led to charges that the government was acting despotically. Encounters between the landowning nobility and the peasantry, which increased in the last half of the eighteenth century, also contributed to the disaffection with the Old Regime and played a major role in stimulating demands for a restriction of the privileges enjoyed by the nobility. Ongoing food shortages in the cities created a militant citizenry ready to take action against authorities they considered responsible for the high price of bread.

De Stael on the Ancien Regime (1789)

The immediate cause of the revolution was a major economic crisis that bankrupted the monarchy and deprived it of its authority. This crisis led to a revolt of the nobles against the crown and brought down the entire system of royal absolutism. Only after this collapse of royal government did various groups that had had long-standing grievances against the regime take the initiative and establish a new political system. These groups never actually planned the revolution; they simply filled a void created by the absence of effective governmental power.

The Beginning of the Revolution

The financial crisis that brought about the collapse of the French government peaked in the late 1780s. The government of Louis XVI (r. 1774–1792) had inherited considerable debts from that of his grandfather, Louis XV (r. 1715–1774) as a result of protracted periods of warfare with Great Britain. The opening of a new phase of this warfare in 1778, when France intervened in the American War of Independence on the side of the United States, pushed the government further into debt and put a strain on the entire French economy. Attempts to solve the crisis by implementing financial reforms made the situation only worse. In 1787 the government had a revenue of 475 million livres and expenses of just under 600 million livres. More than half of the revenue went to pay interest on the accumulated debt. As the crisis deepened, protests from the ranks of the nobility against royal policy became more vocal.

In 1787 the king made efforts to win the support of the nobility by convening an Assembly of Notables, a handpicked group of 144 nominees, the great majority of whom were noblemen. The purpose of the meeting was to gain approval for a new system of taxation that would include a direct tax on all landowners. These proposals encountered formidable opposition from the members of the assembly, and the meeting was adjourned. Some of the nobles in the assembly had been willing to pay the taxes, but only if the king would convoke the Estates General, a national legislative body that had not met since 1614. Convening the Estates General, they argued, would provide them with guarantees against royal despotism. Louis resisted these pressures because he did not want to give up the right to make law by his own authority.

The king then tried to gain approval of new taxes from the regional parlements, the provincial law courts whose powers included the registration of royal edicts. There too the crown met resistance. The Parlement of Paris, which was the most important of all the parlements, refused to comply with the king's request. The other parlements followed suit, claiming that only the Estates General had the power to approve new taxes. Constitutional tension was heightened when the king demanded the registration of edicts for new loans without the approval of the parlements, a step that even he acknowledged was illegal. He then suspended the parlements, thereby deepening the constitutional crisis.

The deterioration of the government's financial condition finally forced the king to yield to the demands of the nobles and the increasingly hostile popular press. When tax returns dried up as the result of an agricultural crisis in the summer months of 1788, the government could no longer pay its creditors. In a desperate effort to save his regime, Louis announced that he would convene the Estates General. By this time there was little hope for Louis. His absolutist government had completely collapsed.

CHRONOLOGY

The First French Revolution, 1789–1791

1787	
February 22	Convening of the Assembly of Notables
1788	
August 8	Announcement of the meeting of the Estates General
1789	
May 5	The Estates General opens at Versailles
June 17	The Third Estate adopts the title of the National Assembly
June 20	Oath of the Tennis Court
July 11	The king dismisses his finance minister, Jacques Necker
July 14	The storming of the Bastille
Late July	The Great Fear in rural areas
August 4	Abolition of feudalism and privileges
August 26	*Declaration of the Rights of Man and Citizen*
October 5	March to Versailles; Louis XVI and National Assembly move to Paris
November 2	Church property is nationalized
1790	
July 12	Civil Constitution of the Clergy
July 14	Feast of the Federation
November 27	Decree requiring oath of loyalty from the clergy
1791	
June 20	Royal family flees to Varennes, is apprehended by the National Guard
October 1	Newly elected Legislative Assembly opens

The meeting of the Estates General was set for May 1789, and during the months leading up to its opening, public debates arose over how the delegates should vote. The Estates General consisted of representatives of the three orders or social groups, known as estates, that made up French society: the clergy, the nobility, and the Third Estate. The Third Estate technically contained all the commoners in the kingdom (about 96 percent of the population), ranging from the wealthiest merchant to the poorest peasant. The elected representatives of the Third Estate, whose numbers had doubled by a recent order of the king, were propertied nonnoble elements of lay society, including many lawyers and military officers.

Before the meeting a dispute arose among the representatives whether the three groups would vote by estate, in which case the first two estates would dominate the assembly, or by head, in which case the Third Estate would have numerical parity. Each side claimed that it was the best representative of the "nation," a term meaning the entire body of French people. The nobles maintained that the nation was represented by the nobility and clergy from all the provinces, especially the members of the provincial parlements, who had been critical of royal power during the past few decades. The members of the Third Estate advanced the claim that *they* represented the nation. The cleric Emmanuel-Joseph Sieyès (1748–1836), who joined the Third Estate during this dispute, claimed that it "has within itself all that is necessary to constitute a nation. . . . Nothing can go on without it, and everything would go on far better without the others. . . . This privileged class (nobility and clergy) is assuredly foreign to the nation by its do-nothing uselessness."[1]

The question of voting within the Estates General was not resolved when that body met at Versailles on May 5, 1789. After the king indicated that he would side with the clergy and nobility, the Third Estate took the dramatic step of declaring itself a National Assembly and asking members of the other estates to vote with them on the basis of "one man, one vote." Many members of the lower clergy and a few noblemen accepted this invitation. In a conciliatory response to this challenge, the king planned to summon all three estates to a special "royal session" to announce some concessions. In preparation for this meeting, however, he locked the Third Estate out of its meeting hall without explanation. The outraged members of the Third Estate went to a nearby indoor tennis court and took a solemn oath that they would not disband until the country had been given a constitution. One week later, after more clerics and noblemen had joined the ranks of the Third Estate, the king ordered the nobility and the clergy to join the National Assembly.

As this political crisis was reaching a climax, a major social crisis fueled by the high price of bread was causing a breakdown of public order. For many years French agriculture had had difficulty meeting the demands of an expanding population. These problems, aggravated in the 1780s by a succession of poor harvests, climaxed in a widespread harvest failure in 1788. As the price of bread soared, demand for manufactured goods shrank, thus causing widespread unemployment among artisans. An increasing number of bread riots, peasant revolts, and urban strikes contributed to a sense of panic at the very time that the government's financial crisis deepened. In Paris the situation reached a critical point in June 1789.

At this point the king, a man with little political sense, made two ill-advised decisions. The first was to send 17,000 royal troops to Paris to restore order. The arrival of the troops gave the impression that the government was planning an attack on the people of the city. The second decision was the dismissal of the king's popular finance minister, Jacques Necker, who had favored the meeting of the Estates General and demonstrated real concern for the welfare of the populace. His dismissal sent a signal that the king was contemplating a move against the National Assembly. It was in this atmosphere of public paranoia that Parisians formed the National Guard and stormed the Bastille.

The fall of the Bastille unnerved the king. When he asked one of his aides, "Is it a revolt?" the aide replied, "No, sire, it is a revolution." The revolution had just begun. It moved into high gear two weeks later when the National Assembly responded to the outbreak of social unrest in the provinces. The scarcity of grain in the countryside gave rise to false rumors that the nobles were engaged in a plot to destroy crops and starve the people into submission. Peasants armed themselves and prepared to fight off the hired agents of the nobility. Some of these peasants burned the mansions of noblemen, together with the deeds that gave the nobles title to their lands and the right to collect dues from their tenants. A widespread panic, known as the "Great Fear," gripped many parts of the country. Townspeople and peasants amassed in large numbers to defend themselves and save the harvest. In response to this panic, which reached its peak in the last two weeks of July, the National Assembly began to pass legislation that destroyed the Old Regime and created a new political order.

The Creation of a New Political Society

Between August 1789 and September 1790 the National Assembly took three revolutionary steps. The first was the elimination of noble and clerical privilege. In August the assembly abolished the feudal dues that peasants paid their lords, the private legal jurisdictions of noblemen, the collection of tithes by the clergy, and the exclusive rights of noblemen to hunt game on their lands. The privileges of provinces and local towns met the same fate, and ten months later the nobility lost their titles. Instead of a society divided into various corporate groups, each with its own privileges, France would now have only citizens, all of them equal at law. Social distinctions would be based on merit rather than birth. There were no longer any intermediary powers between the king and the individual subject.

The second step, taken on August 26, was the promulgation of the *Declaration of the Rights of Man and Citizen.* This document reveals the main influence of the Enlightenment on the revolution. It declared that all men, not just Frenchmen, had a natural right to liberty, property, equality before the law, freedom from oppression, and religious toleration. The statement that the "law is the expression of the general will" reflects the influence of Rousseau's *The Social Contract* (1762), while the statement that every citizen has the right to participate in the formation of that law either personally or through a representative embodies the basic principle of democracy. The *Declaration* differed from the English Bill of Rights of 1689 by grounding the rights it proclaimed in natural law rather than in the law of one country. The provisions of the French document therefore serve as statements of broad principle rather than as confirmations of specific rights that the government had allegedly been violating.

The third step in this revolutionary program was a complete reorganization of the Church. In order to solve the problem of the national debt, the National Assembly placed land owned by the Church (about 10 percent of all French territory) at the service of the nation. The Civil Constitution of the Clergy of July 1790 in effect made the Church a department of the state, with the government paying the clergy directly. In order to retain their positions, the clergy were required to take an oath of loyalty to the nation. At the same time the Church was reorganized into eighty-three dioceses, one for each of the departments or administrative units into which the country was also now divided. The bishops of these dioceses were to be elected by laymen. The parishes, which were the basic units of ecclesiastical administration, would become uniform in size, each administering to some 6,000 parishioners.

In 1791 a newly elected Legislative Assembly—replacing the National Assembly—confirmed and extended many of these changes. A constitution, put into effect in October, formalized the end of royal absolutism. The king became a constitutional monarch, retaining only the power to suspend legislation, direct foreign policy, and command the armed forces. The constitution did not, however, give all men the right to vote. Only "active citizens," who paid the equivalent of three days' wages in direct taxes, had the right to vote for electors, who in turn chose representatives to the legislature.

The new constitution formally abolished hereditary legal privileges, thus providing equality of all citizens before the law. Subsequent legislation granted Jews and Protestants full civil rights and toleration. A law eliminating primogeniture (inheritance of the entire estate by the eldest son) gave all heirs equal rights to inherited property.

DOCUMENT

Declaration of the Rights of Man and Citizen (1789)

The passage of the Declaration of the Rights of Man and Citizen *by the National Assembly on August 26, 1789, is one of the earliest and most enduring acts of the French Revolution. A document of great simplicity and power, it was hammered out during many weeks of debate. Its concern with the natural rights of all people and equality before the law reflected the ideas of the Enlightenment.*

1. Men are born free and remain free and equal in rights. Social distinctions may be founded only on the common good.
2. The aim of all political association is the preservation of the natural and imprescriptible rights of man. These rights are liberty, property, security and resistance to oppression.
3. The principle of all authority rests essentially in the nation. No body nor individual may exercise any authority which does not emanate expressly from the nation.
4. Liberty consists in the freedom to do whatever does not harm another; hence the exercise of the natural rights of each man has no limits except those which assure to the other members of society the enjoyment of the same rights. These limits can only be determined by law. . . .
6. Law is the expression of the general will. Every citizen has the right to participate personally or through his representative in its formation. It must be the same for all, whether it protects or punishes. All citizens, being equal in the eyes of the law, are equally eligible to all dignities and to all public positions and occupations, according to their abilities, and without distinction except that of their virtues and talents.
7. No man may be indicted, arrested, or imprisoned except in cases determined by the law and according to the forms prescribed by law. . . .
10. No one should be disturbed for his opinions, even in religion, provided that their manifestation does not trouble public order as established by law.
11. The free communication of thoughts and opinions is one of the most precious of the rights of man. Every citizen may therefore speak, write, and print freely, but shall be responsible for any abuse of this freedom in the cases set by the law. . . .
17. Property being an inviolable and sacred right, no one may be deprived of it except when public necessity, determined by law, obviously requires it, and then on the condition that the owner shall have been previously and equitably compensated.

Source: From P.-J.-B. Buchez and P.-C. Roux, *Histoire parlementaire de la Révolution française.* (Paris: Paulin, 1834).

The establishment of marriage as a civil contract and the right to end a marriage in divorce supported the idea of the husband and wife as freely contracting individuals. The largely symbolic abolition of slavery in France was consistent with the proclamation of equality of all men, but the failure to extend that emancipation to French colonies suggests that there were limits to the concept of liberty proclaimed by the assembly.

This body of legislation amounted to nothing less than a revolution. The Old Regime had been destroyed and a new one had taken its place. Although the form of government remained a monarchy, the powers of that monarchy were drastically curtailed. Unlike the English revolutions of the 1640s and 1688, this revolution did not disguise the extent of the changes that had transpired by using the language of conservatism, claiming that the revolution had recovered lost freedoms. It did not appeal to the French past at all. It promoted a new view of French society as a nation composed of equal citizens possessing natural rights, in place of the older concept of a society consisting of different corporate groups, each with its own privileges. Contemporaries recognized the significance of these changes. The Portuguese ambassador to France, who witnessed the events of 1789 firsthand, reported back to his government, "In all the world's annals there is no mention of a revolution like this."

Responses to the First French Revolution

During the early years of the revolution, events in Paris and Versailles dominated the political scene. The revolution was not confined, however, to the metropolis. In the provinces groups of ordinary townspeople and peasants, frightened that the members of the nobility might be taking counteraction against them, took the law into their own hands and brought about a new revolutionary political and social order. In many places the local rulers who had exercised political power in towns and villages were overthrown and replaced by supporters of the new regime. At the same time there was considerable opposition to the revolutionary government. In many parts of the country the clergy's refusal to take the oath of loyalty to the nation led to violent clashes with the provincial authorities. In the south nobles began to organize resistance to the new regime, while militant Catholics attacked Protestants, who had been granted toleration and who generally supported the revolution.

The revolutionary events of 1789–1791 quickly gained the attention of countries outside France. In England the nonconformist Protestant minister Richard Price urged members of the British Parliament to follow the example of their French neighbors and abolish the laws that restricted

DOCUMENT

Edmund Burke Deplores the Events of the French Revolution

The first French Revolution met with both praise and criticism abroad. The strongest attack came from Edmund Burke, an Irish-born lawyer who sat in the British Parliament. Burke, who is recognized as the father of modern conservatism, attacked the leaders of the revolution for destroying religion and the social order in the interests of an abstract philosophy, subverting the law, and introducing a new tyranny.

. . . France has bought undisguised calamities at a higher price than any nation has purchased the most unequivocal blessings. France has bought poverty by crime. France has not sacrificed her virtue to her interest; but she has abandoned her interest that she might prostitute her virtue. All other nations have begun the fabric of a new government, or the reformation of an old, by establishing originally, or by enforcing with greater exactness, some rites or other of religion. All other people have laid the foundation of civil freedom in severer manners and a system of a more austere and masculine morality. France, when she let loose the reins of regal authority, doubled the license of a ferocious dissoluteness in manners, and of an insolent religion in opinions and practices; and has extended through all ranks of life, as if she were communicating some privilege or laying open some secluded benefit, all the unhappy corruptions that usually were the disease of wealth and power. This is one of the new principles of equality in France.

France, by the perfidy of her leaders, has utterly disgraced the tone of lenient council in the cabinets of princes, and disarmed it of its most potent topics. She has sanctified the dark, suspicious maxims of tyrannous distrust, and taught kings to tremble at . . . the delusive plausibilities of moral politicians. Sovereigns will consider those who advise them to place an unlimited confidence in their people as subverterrs of their thrones—as traitors who aim at their destruction, by leading their easy good—nature, under specious pretenses, to admit combinations of bold and faithless men into a participation of their power. . . . They have seen the French rebel against a mild and lawful monarch, with more fury, outrage, and insult than ever any people has been known to rise against the most illegal usurper or the most sanguinary tyrant. . . .

They have found their punishment in their success. Laws overturned; tribunals subverted; industry without vigour; commerce expiring; the revenue unpaid, yet the people impoverished; a church pillaged, and a state not relieved; civil and military anarchy made the constitution of the kingdom; everything human and divine sacrificed to the idol of public credit, and national bankruptcy the consequence. . . .

Were all these dreadful things necessary? Were they the inevitable results of the desperate struggle of determined patriots, compelled to wade through blood and tumult to the quiet shore of a tranquil and prosperous liberty? No! Nothing like it. The fresh ruins of France, which shock our feelings wherever we can turn our eyes, are not the devastation of civil war: they are the sad, but instructive monuments of rash and ignorant counsel in a time of profound peace. . . .

Source: Edmund Burke, *Reflections on the Revolution in France* (1790).

hunting on aristocratic lands. Prussian reformers took heart that the events of the revolution would portend the destruction of absolutism in their country and in other European lands. A Prussian official who had studied with the philosopher Immanuel Kant called the revolution "the first practical triumph of philosophy . . . the hope and consolation for so many of those ancient ills under which mankind has suffered."

Not all foreign assessments of the revolution were positive. In November 1790 the British politician Edmund Burke published *Reflections on the Revolution in France,* in which he expressed horror at the way in which abstract philosophy had destroyed the traditional social order in France. Pope Pius VI condemned the *Declaration of the Rights of Man and Citizen* and then, outraged at the attack upon the Roman Catholic Church, issued a sweeping condemnation of the Civil Constitution of the Clergy. The absolute monarchs of western Europe, sensing rightly that their regimes were in danger of a contagious revolutionary ideology, not only planned an invasion of France to restore the old order but took action against dissent in their own territories. When Polish legislators wrote a new constitution in 1791, modeled on that of France, Catherine the Great of Russia, who controlled a portion of Poland at the time, claimed that it was the product of French radicalism. She shut down the presses, revived censorship, turned against the philosophes whom she had admired, and banned the works of Voltaire.

The French Republic, 1792–1799

- **How did a second, more radical revolution, which began with the establishment of the Republic in 1792, lead to the creation of a regime that used the power of the state to institute the Reign of Terror?**

Beginning in 1792 France experienced a second revolution that was much more radical than the first. During this revolution France was transformed from a constitutional monarchy into a republic. The state claimed far greater power than it possessed under the constitutional monarchy established in 1791, and it used that power to bring about a radical reform of French society.

The Establishment of the Republic, 1792

During the first two years of the revolution it appeared that the building of a new French nation would take place within the framework of a constitutional monarchy. Absolutism had suffered an irreversible defeat, but there was little sentiment among the members of the Legislative Assembly, much less among the general population, in favor of abolishing the institution of monarchy. The only committed republicans—those supporting the establishment of a republic—in the Legislative Assembly belonged to a party known as the Jacobins°, who found support in political clubs in Paris and in other parts of the country. By the late summer of 1792 this group of radicals, drawing upon the support of militant Parisian citizens known as *sans-culottes* (literally, those without breeches, the pants worn by noblemen), succeeded in bringing about the second, more radical revolution.

King Louis himself was in part responsible for this destruction of the monarchy. The success of constitutional monarchy depended on the king's willingness to play the new role assigned to him as a constitutional figurehead. In October 1789 Louis had agreed, under considerable pressure, to move his residence from Versailles to Paris, where the National Assembly had also relocated. The pressure came mainly from women, who formed the large majority of 10,000 demonstrators who marched from Paris to Versailles demanding a reduction in the price of bread. The king yielded to their demands and came to Paris. As he entered the city, accompanied by soldiers, monks, and women carrying guns and pikes, he reluctantly agreed to wear the tricolor cockade (a badge) to symbolize his acceptance of the revolution. Louis, however, could not disguise his opposition to the revolution, especially to the ecclesiastical settlement. This opposition led many people to suspect that he was encouraging the powers of Europe to invade France to restore the Old Regime.

Louis XVI had few personal resources upon which he might draw to win the confidence of his subjects. He was not as intelligent as his grandfather, Louis XV, nor did he have the skills necessary to dispel his subjects' growing distrust of him. Neither Louis nor his Austrian wife, Marie Antoinette, commanded much respect among the people. For many years the royal couple had been the object of relentless, sometimes pornographic satire. He had been lampooned for his rumored sexual inadequacies and she for a series of alleged infidelities with the king's brother and a succession of female partners. Whatever confidence Parisian citizens might have retained in the royal couple evaporated in June 1791, when the king and queen attempted to flee the country. The National Guard apprehended them at Varennes, close to the eastern French border, and forced them to return to Paris, where they were kept under guard at the palace of the Tuileries. Even that development, however, failed to destroy the monarchy,

Sans-Culottes

Male and female dress of the *sans-culottes,* the armed Parisian radicals who supported the Republic. The men did not wear the breeches (*culottes*) that were in style among the members of the French nobility.

which had been preserved in the constitution implemented in October.

The development that actually precipitated the downfall of the monarchy and led to the establishment of a republic was the decision to go to war. Until the summer of 1791 European powers had been involved in various conflicts and had resisted pleas from French émigrés to support a counterrevolutionary offensive against the new French regime. After the flight to Varennes and the capture of the royal family, however, Frederick William II of Prussia (r. 1786–1797) and Emperor Leopold II of Austria (r. 1790–1792), the brother of Marie Antoinette, signed an alliance and called upon the other monarchs of Europe "to restore to the King of France complete liberty and to consolidate the bases of monarchical government." No action would be taken, however, unless all European sovereigns agreed to cooperate.

The actual declaration of war came not from the monarchs of Europe but from the French Legislative Assembly. A small group of republicans, headed by the eloquent orator Jacques-Pierre Brissot (1754–1793), convinced the assembly that an international conspiracy against the revolution would end in an invasion of their country. Brissot and his supporters also believed that if France could be lured into a foreign war, the king and queen would be revealed as traitors and the monarchy would be destroyed. Exploiting xenophobic as well as revolutionary sentiment, and claiming that the strength of a citizen army would win a quick and decisive victory, Brissot and his allies won the support of the entire assembly. They also appealed to the international goals of the revolution, claiming that the French army would inspire revolution against "the tyrants of Europe" everywhere they went.

The Legislative Assembly declared war on Austria in April 1792. Instead of a glorious victory, however, the war resulted in a series of disastrous defeats at the hands of Austrians and their Prussian allies in the Netherlands. This military failure contributed to a mood of paranoia in France, especially in Paris. Fears arose that invading armies, in alliance with nobles, would undermine the revolution. In May members of the assembly learned that the Austrian minister, in cooperation with a group of the king's advisers, was plotting the destruction of the assembly itself. In July the assembly officially proclaimed the nation to be in danger, calling for all citizens to rally against the enemies of liberty at home and abroad. Women petitioned for the right to bear arms. When the Austrians and Prussians threatened to torch the entire city of Paris and slaughter its population if anyone laid a hand on the royal family, citizens in Paris immediately demanded that the king be deposed.

Tricolor Cockade

Louis XVI wearing the red liberty bonnet with the tricolor cockade on October 20, 1792. Refusing to be intimidated by a crowd of 20,000 people outside the royal palace, he donned the cap and proclaimed his loyalty to the constitution.

On August 10 a radical republican committee overthrew the Paris commune, the city government that had been installed in 1789, and set up a new, revolutionary commune. A force of about 20,000 men, including volunteer troops from various parts of the kingdom, invaded the Tuileries, which was defended by about 900 Swiss guards. When the members of the royal bodyguard fled, they were pursued by members of the Paris crowds, who stripped them of their red uniforms and hacked 600 of them to death with knives, pikes, and hatchets. The attack on the Tuileries forced the king to take refuge in the nearby Legislative Assembly. The assembly promptly suspended the monarchy and turned the royal family over to the commune, which imprisoned them in the Temple, a medieval fortress in the northeastern part of the city. The assembly then ordered its own dissolution and called for the election of a new legislative body that would draft a new constitution.

The fall of the monarchy did nothing to allay the siege mentality of the city, especially after further Prussian victories in early September escalated fears of a Prussian invasion. Individuals suspected of plotting against the regime were imprisoned, and when it was rumored that they would escape and support the Prussian enemy, angry crowds pulled 1,200 prisoners (most of whom were being held for nonpolitical crimes) from their cells and killed them. The feared foreign invasion that had inspired this "September Massacre" never did materialize. On September 20, 1792, a surprisingly well-disciplined and well-trained army of French citizens, inspired by dedication to France and the revolution, repulsed the armies of Austria and Prussia at Valmy. This victory saved the revolution. The German poet Johann Wolfgang von Goethe (1749–1832) claimed that the battle marked the beginning of "a new epoch in the history of the world." Delegates to a new National Convention, elected by universal male suffrage°, had already arrived in

The Attack on the Palace of the Tuileries
On the night of August 10, 1792, Parisian crowds and volunteer soldiers attacked the royal palace in Paris. The puffs of smoke in the building are coming from the Swiss guards, who were entrusted with the defense of the royal family and the palace. The royal family escaped and took refuge in the Legislative Assembly, but 600 of the Swiss guards were killed. Those that retreated were hunted down in the streets of Paris and stripped of their uniforms, and their heads were placed on the ends of pikes.

Paris to write a new constitution. On September 22 the convention declared that the monarchy was formally abolished and that France was a republic. France had now experienced a second revolution, more radical than the first, but dedicated to the same principles of liberty, equality, and fraternity.

The Jacobins and the Revolution

Before the Republic was established, different political factions had begun to vie for power, both in the Legislative Assembly and in the country at large. The first major division to emerge was between the Feuillants, who supported a constitutional monarchy, and the Jacobins, many of whom favored the creation of a democratic republic. By the time the Republic had been declared, the Jacobins had become the major political party. Soon, however, factional divisions began to develop within Jacobin ranks. The main split occurred between the followers of Brissot, known as Girondins°, and the radicals known as Montagnards°, or "the Mountain." The latter acquired their name because they occupied the benches on the side of the convention hall, where the floor sloped upward. The Girondins occupied the lower side of the hall, while the uncommitted deputies, known as "the Plain," occupied the middle. Both the Mountain and the Girondins claimed to be advancing the goals of the revolution, but they differed widely on which tactics to pursue. The Mountain took the position that as long as the state was endangered by internal and external enemies, the government needed to centralize authority in the capital. The Mountain thought of themselves as the representatives of the common people, especially the *sans-culottes* in Paris. Many of their leaders, including

Georges-Jacques Danton (1759–1794), Jean-Paul Marat (1743–1793), and Maximilien Robespierre (1758–1794), were in fact Parisians. Their mission was to make the revolution even more egalitarian and to establish a republic characterized by civic pride and patriotism, which they referred to as the Republic of Virtue.

The Girondins, known as such because many of their leaders came from the southwestern department of Gironde, took a more conservative position than the Mountain on these issues. Favoring the economic freedom and local control desired by merchants and manufacturers, they were reluctant to support further centralization of state power. They believed that the revolution had advanced far enough and should not become more radical. They were also afraid that the egalitarianism of the revolution, if unchecked, would lead to a leveling of French society and result in social anarchy.

The conflict between the Girondins and the Mountain became apparent in the debate over what to do with the deposed king. Louis had been suspected of conspiring with the enemies of the revolution, and the discovery of his correspondence with the Austrian government led to his trial for treason against the nation. The Girondins had originally expressed reluctance to bring him to trial, preferring to keep him in prison. Once the trial began, they joined the entire National Convention in voting to convict him, but they opposed his execution. This stance led the Mountain to accuse the Girondins of being secret collaborators with the monarchy. By a narrow vote the convention decided to put the king to death, and on January 21, 1793, Louis was executed at the Place de la Révolution.

The instrument of death was the guillotine, an efficient and merciful but nonetheless terrifying decapitation machine first pressed into service in April 1792. It took its name from Dr. Joseph-Ignace Guillotin, who had the original idea for such a device, although he did not invent it. The guillotine was inspired by the conviction that all criminals, not just those of noble blood, should be executed in a swift, painless manner. The new device was to be put to extensive use during the next eighteen months, and many Girondins fell victim to it.

The split between the Mountain and the Girondins became more pronounced as the republican regime encountered increasing opposition from foreign and domestic enemies. Early in 1793 Great Britain and the Dutch Republic allied with Prussia and Austria to form the First Coalition against France, and within a month Spain and the kingdoms of Sardinia and Naples joined them. The armies of these allied powers defeated French forces in the Austrian Netherlands in March of that year, and once again an invasion seemed imminent. At the same time internal rebellions against the revolutionary regime took place in various outlying provinces, especially in the district of the Vendée in western France. These uprisings were led by noblemen and clerics, but they also had popular support, especially from tenant farmers who resented the increased taxation imposed by the new revolutionary government.

In the minds of Robespierre and his colleagues, the Girondins were linked to these provincial rebels, whom they labeled as federalists° because they opposed the centralization of the French state and thus threatened the unity of the nation. In June twenty-nine Girondins were expelled from the convention for supporting local officials accused of hoarding grain. This purge made it apparent that any political opponent of the Mountain, even those with solid republican credentials, could now be identified as an enemy of the revolution.

CHRONOLOGY

The French Republic and the Terror, 1792–1794

1792	
April 20	Declaration of war against Austria
August 10	Attack on the Tuileries; monarchy is suspended
September 2–6	September Massacre of prisoners in Paris
September 20	French victory at the Battle of Valmy
September 21	National Convention meets
September 22	Abolition of the monarchy and establishment of the Republic
1793	
January 21	Execution of Louis XVI
February 1	Declaration of war against Great Britain and the Dutch Republic
March 11	Beginning of rebellion in the Vendée
June 2	Purge of Girondins from the Convention
June 24	Ratification of a republican constitution
July 27	Robespierre elected to the Committee of Public Safety
August 23	The Convention decrees the *levée en masse*
October 5	Adoption of the revolutionary calendar
October 16	Execution of Marie Antoinette
1794	
July 28	Tenth of *Thermidor;* execution of Robespierre
November 12	Jacobin clubs are closed

Justice in History

The Trial of Louis XVI

After the abolition of the monarchy and the proclamation of the French Republic in September 1792, the National Convention considered the fate of the deposed king. There was a broad consensus that Louis was guilty of treason against the nation and that he should answer for his crimes, but how he should do so was a matter of heated debate. The convention was divided between the Girondins and the Mountain. Of the two, the Girondins were more inclined to follow legal forms, whereas those of the Mountain considered themselves to be acting as a revolutionary tribunal that should adhere to standards of justice not specifically included in the law of the land. The convention thus became a forum where Louis's accusers expressed competing notions of revolutionary justice.

The most divisive and revealing issue was whether there should be a trial at all. The Mountain originally took the position that because the people had already judged the king on August 10, when the monarchy had fallen and the king taken prisoner, there was no need for a second judgment. They should proceed immediately to carrying out the death sentence. Robespierre argued that to have a trial would be counterrevolutionary, for it would allow the revolution itself to be brought before the court to be judged. A centrist majority, however, decided that the king had to be charged with specific offenses in a court of law and found guilty by due process before being sentenced.

A second issue, closely related to the first, was the technical legal question of whether the king could be subject to legal action. Even if the legislative branch of the government was considered the equal of the king in a constitutional monarchy, it did not possess authority over him. A further argument was that the king could not be tried for actions for which he had already suffered abdication. This claim was challenged on the most basic principle of the revolution—that the nation was higher than the king and his crimes were committed against that nation, which is the people. The king, moreover, was no longer king but was now a citizen and therefore subject to the law in the same way as anyone else.

The third issue was Louis's culpability for the specific charges in the indictment. These crimes included refusing to call the Estates General, sending an army to march against the citizens of Paris, and conducting secret negotiations with France's enemies. The journalist and deputy Jean-Paul Marat added that "he robbed the citizens of their gold as a subsidy for their foes" and "caused his hirelings to hoard, to create famine, to dry up the sources of abundance that the people might die from misery and hunger."

Nonetheless the king, who appeared personally to hear the indictment and then to respond to the charges on December 26, presented a plausible defense. He based it on the laws in force at the various times he was supposed to have committed his crimes. Thus he defended his sending of troops to Paris on the grounds that in June and July 1789 he could order troops wherever he wanted. In the same vein he argued that he had used force solely in response to illegal intimidation. These legalisms, however, only made the members of the convention more contemptuous of the king. His defense failed to persuade a single convention deputy. He was convicted of treason by a vote of 693–0.

This unanimous conviction of the king did not end the factional debates over the king's fate. Knowing that there was extensive support for the king in various parts of the country, the Girondins asked that the verdict be appealed to the people. Their argument was that the convention, dominated by the Mountain and supported by militants in Paris, had usurped the sovereignty of the people. Pierre-Victurnien Vergniaud, a lawyer from Bordeaux, pleaded that "To take this right from the people would be to take sovereignty from them, to transfer it . . . to the hands of the representatives chosen by the people, to transform their representatives into kings or tyrants." Vergniaud's motion to submit the verdict to the people for ratification lost by a vote of 424–283.

The last vote, the closest of all, determined the king's sentence. Originally it appeared that a majority might vote for noncapital punishment. The Marquis de Condorcet, for example, argued that although the king deserved death on the basis of the law of treason, he could not bring himself to vote for capital punishment on principle. The radical response to this argument came from Robespierre, who appealed to the "principles of nature" in stating that the death penalty could be justified "only in those cases where it is vital to the safety of private citizens or of the public." Robespierre's impassioned oratory carried the day. By a vote of 361–334 the king was sentenced to "death within 24 hours" rather than the alternatives of imprisonment followed by banishment after the war or imprisonment in chains for life. The following day Louis was led to the guillotine.

All public trials, especially those for political crimes, are theatrical events, in that the various parties play specific roles and seek to convey certain messages to their audiences. The men who voted to put Louis XVI on trial

MORT DE LOUIS CAPET 16e DU NOM, LE 21 JANVIER 1793.

Execution of Louis XVI, January 21, 1793
Although the king was convicted of treason by a unanimous vote, the vote to execute him carried by a slender majority of only twenty-seven votes.

wanted to create an educational spectacle in which the already deposed monarch would be stripped of any respect he might still have commanded among the people. Louis was to be tried like any other traitor, and he was to suffer the same fate, execution by the guillotine. The attempt to strip him of all privilege and status continued after his death. His corpse, with his head placed between his knees, was taken to a cemetery, placed in a wooden box, and buried in the common pit. The revolutionaries were determined to guarantee that even in death the king would have the same position as the humblest of his former subjects.

Questions of Justice

1. How would you describe the standard of justice that the members of the National Convention upheld in voting to execute the king? How did this standard of justice differ from the standard to which King Louis XVI appealed?
2. Evaluate the argument of Robespierre that the death penalty can be justified only in cases of public safety. Compare his argument to that of Enlightenment thinkers such as Cesare Beccaria that capital punishment was an unjust, unnecessary, and uncivilized punishment.

Taking It Further

Jordan, David P. *The King's Trial: The French Revolution vs. Louis XVI.* 1979. The most thorough account of the trial.

Walzer, Michael, ed. *Regicide and Revolution: Speeches at the Trial of Louis XVI.* 1974. A valuable collection of speeches with an extended commentary.

In order to repel the coalition of foreign powers, the convention ordered a *levée en masse,* a conscription of troops from the entire population. This step, taken in August 1793, created an unprecedented military force, a massive citizen army drawn from all segments of the population and committed to the prosecution of the war. In the past the rank and file of European armies, whether mercenaries or regular troops, had been filled with men on the margins of society: the poor, the unemployed, and even criminal outcasts. The conscription of males from all ranks of society might have promoted a sense of national unity among the troops, but it also caused resentment and resistance against this use of state power. It led to increased federalist resistance to the radical Jacobin government.

The Reign of Terror, 1793–1794

In order to deal with its domestic enemies, the republican government claimed powers that far exceeded those exercised by the monarchy in the age of absolutism. The convention passed laws that set up special courts to prosecute enemies of the regime and authorized special procedures that deprived those accused of their legal rights. These laws laid the legal foundation for the Reign of Terror°, a campaign to rid the state of its internal enemies. A Committee of Public Safety, consisting of twelve members entrusted with the executive power of the state, superintended this process. Although technically subordinate to the convention, the Committee of Public Safety became in effect a revolutionary dictatorship.

The man who emerged as the main figure on the Committee of Public Safety was Maximilien Robespierre. A brilliant student as a youth, Robespierre was affronted when the king's carriage splashed him with mud as he was waiting to read an address to the king. A man with little sense of humor, he was passionate in his quest for justice. As a lawyer who defended indigent clients, Robespierre was elected to the Third Estate in 1789 and became a favorite of the *sans-culottes,* who called him "The Incorruptible." That he may have been, but he was also susceptible to the temptation to abuse power for partisan political purposes. Like Rousseau, whose work he admired, he was also willing to sacrifice individual liberty in the name of the collective General Will. His logic was that since the General Will was indivisible, it could not accommodate dissent. Robespierre was primarily responsible for pushing the revolution to new extremes and for establishing the program of state repression that began in the autumn of 1793.

Saint-Just on Democracy, Justice and the Terror (1790s)

The most intense prosecutions of the Terror took place between October 1793 and June 1794, but they continued until August 1794. By that time the revolutionary courts had executed 17,000 people, while 500,000 had suffered imprisonment. Another 20,000 either died in prison or were killed without any form of trial. Among the victims of the Terror were substantial numbers of clergy and nobility, as we might expect, but the overwhelming majority were artisans and peasants. One Parisian stableboy was guillotined for having said "f . . . the Republic," while a baker from Alsace lost his head for predicting that "the Republic will go to hell with all its partisans."[2] Many of the victims came from the outlying regions of the country, especially the northeast, where foreign armies were threatening the Republic, and the west, where a brutal civil war between the French army and Catholics and Royalists was raging. These provincial enemies of the regime were identified by special surveillance committees and then were tried by revolutionary tribunals. The guillotine was by no means the only method of execution. In November and December 1793, about 1,800 rebels captured during the uprising in the Vendée were tied to other prisoners, placed in sinking boats, and drowned in the chilly waters of the Loire River.

The most visible and alarming of the executions took place in the capital. The execution of Marie Antoinette and other royalists might have been justified on the basis of their active subversion of the regime, but trumped-up charges against Girondins exposed a process that would destroy republicans as well. As one Girondin said in a speech to the Convention, the revolution, like the mythical Roman god Saturn, devoured its own children. Some of the most prominent figures of the Enlightenment fell victim to this paranoia. Among them was the Marquis de Condorcet, who believed passionately that all citizens, including women, had equal rights. Having campaigned against capital punishment, he committed suicide in a Parisian prison, just before he was to be executed. Another figure of the Enlightenment, the famous chemist Antoine Lavoisier (1743–1794), who had devoted himself to improving social and economic conditions in France, was executed at the same time. So too was the feminist Olympe de Gouges, who as we discussed in Chapter 18 had petitioned for the equal political rights of women. Many French revolutionaries, including Robespierre, used the political ideas of the Enlightenment to justify their actions, but the Terror struck down some of the most distinguished figures of that movement. In that sense the Terror marked the end of the Enlightenment in France.

The Committee of Public Safety then went after Danton and other so-called "Indulgents," who had decided that the Terror had gone too far. Danton's execution made everyone, especially moderate Jacobins, wonder who would be the next victim of a process that had spun completely out of control. In June 1794 the Terror reached a climax, as 1,300 people were sent to their deaths. In order to stop the process, a group of Jacobins in the convention, headed by Joseph Fouché (1759–1820) and Paul Barras (1755–1829), organized a plot against Robespierre. Calling him a tyrant, they arrested him and more than 100 of his followers and guillotined them in late July 1794. An equally swift retaliation was exacted against the Jacobins in the provinces, when members of the White Terror, so named for the white Bourbon flag they displayed, executed leaders of the local revolutionary tribunals. With these reprisals, which used the very same methods that had been perfected by Robespierre and his followers, the most violent and radical phase of the French revolution came to an end.

The Reign of Terror had ended, but its memory would never be extinguished. Its horrors served as a constant warning against the dangers inherent in revolutionary movements. The guillotine, the agent of a dysfunctional and indiscriminate state terrorism, became just as closely identified with the French Revolution as its famous slogan of "Liberty, Equality, Fraternity." The contrast between those two symbols, each of them emblematic of a different stage of the revolution, helps to explain how both conservatives and liberals in the nineteenth century would be able to appeal to the experience of the revolution to support their contradictory ideologies.

The Directory, 1795–1799

A desire to end the violence of the Terror allowed moderates in the National Convention to regain control of the state apparatus that Robespierre and his allies had used to such devastating effect. The Paris Commune was dismantled and the Committee of Public Safety stripped of most of its powers. In November 1794 the Jacobin clubs throughout the country, which had provided support for the Terror, were closed. The moderates who now controlled the government still hoped to preserve the gains of the revolution, while returning the country to more familiar forms of authority. A new constitution of 1795 bestowed executive power on a five-man Directorate, while an assembly consisting of two houses, the Council of Elders and the Council of Five Hundred, proposed and voted on all legislation. The franchise was limited to property holders, allowing only 2,000,000 men out of an adult male population of 7,000,000 to vote. A system of indirect election, in which a person voted for electors who then selected representatives, guaranteed that only the wealthiest members of the country would sit in the legislative assembly.

The establishment of the Directory formed part of a more general reaction against the culture of the republic. The austere, egalitarian dress of the *sans-culottes* gave way once again to fancy and opulent clothes, at least among the bourgeoisie. Low necklines, officially out of favor during the Reign of Terror, once again came back into fashion among wealthier members of society. The high social life of the capital experienced a revival. Some dances took place on the sites of churches that Jacobins had desecrated. Jacobin theaters were shut down and Jacobin works of art destroyed. France was still a republic, but it was no longer Robespierre's Republic of Virtue.

Some of the more entrepreneurial citizens of Paris welcomed the new regime, but opposition soon arose, mainly from Jacobins and *sans-culottes.* When the government relaxed the strict price controls that had been in effect under the Jacobins, the soaring price of bread and other commodities caused widespread social discontent among the population. This situation was aggravated by the continuation of the interminable war against the foreign powers in the First Coalition. Wherever French troops went, their constant need of food and other goods resulted in serious shortages of these commodities.

By the end of 1798 conditions had grown even worse. Inflation was running out of control. The collection of taxes was intermittent at best. The paper money known as *assignats,* first issued by the government in 1791 and backed by the value of confiscated church lands, had become almost worthless. Late in 1797 the Directory had been forced to cancel more than half the national debt, a

CHRONOLOGY

The Directory, 1795–1799

1795	
August 22	The National Convention approves a new constitution
October 5	Napoleon suppresses a royalist insurrection in Paris
October 26	End of the Convention; beginning of the Directory
1796	
February 19	The issuing of *assignats* is halted
April 12	Beginning of a series of victories by Napoleon in Italy
1798	
May 13	Napoleon's expedition departs for Egypt
May	Second Coalition (Britain, Austria, Russia, Naples, and Turkey) is formed against Napoleon
July 21	Napoleon wins the Battle of the Pyramids
August 1	Nelson destroys the French fleet at the Battle of the Nile
1799	
November 9–10	Napoleon's coup on the eighteenth of *Brumaire;* Consulate is established

***The 25th December 1799. The Three Consuls: Bonaparte, Cambecérès and Lebrun* (1856)**

This painting by Louis-Charles-Auguste Couder shows the three consuls taking the oath of office before the presidents of the Assembly on December 25, 1799. Napoleon, the First Consul, stands at the center of the three to the left.

step that further alienated wealthy citizens who had lent money to the government. Military setbacks in 1798 and 1799 brought the situation to a critical point. An expedition to Egypt, which was intended to gain for France a foothold in the Middle East, had resulted in a number of victories against the Turks, but the British destroyed the French fleet at the Battle of the Nile in 1798. The next year a series of revolts against French rule in Italy and in the Austrian Netherlands pushed the French armies back to France's earlier boundaries. The formation of a Second Coalition of European powers in 1799, which included Russia, Naples, and Turkey as well as Britain and Austria, represented a formidable challenge to French power and ensured that the war would not end soon. These military events produced a swing to the political left and raised the specter of another Jacobin coup.

In the face of this instability, Emmanuel-Joseph Sieyès, who had been elected as one of the directors two years earlier, decided to overthrow the government. Sieyès provided a link between the early years of the revolution, when he had defended the Third Estate, and the current government of the Directory. Unlike many other prominent political figures, he had managed to avoid prosecution as the revolution had become more radical. When asked what he had done during the Reign of Terror, Sieyès replied, "I survived." The goal of the planned coup was to provide the country with strong government, its greatest need in a period of political, economic, and social instability. The person Sieyès selected as his partner in this enterprise, and the man who immediately assumed leadership of the coup, was Napoleon Bonaparte (1769–1821), a 30-year-old general who in 1795 had put down a royalist rebellion in Paris with a "whiff of grapeshot."

Napoleon had already established impressive credentials as a military leader. In 1796 and 1797 he had won major victories in Italy, leading to the Treaty of Campo Formio with Austria in 1797. Those victories and his short-lived success at the Battle of the Pyramids in Egypt had made him enormously popular in Paris, where he was received as a hero when he assumed command of the armed forces in the city in 1799. His popularity, his demonstrated military leadership, and his control of a large armed force made this "man on horseback" appear to have the best chance to replace the enfeebled civilian regime of the Directory.

On November 9, 1799, Napoleon addressed the two legislative councils. He reported that another Jacobin conspiracy had been uncovered and that in order to deal with such insurrections a new constitution must be written to give the executive branch of the government more authority. Napoleon encountered resistance from some members of the Council of Five Hundred, who demanded that he be declared an outlaw. At this stage the president of the council, Napoleon's brother Lucien, intervened and called in troops to evict the members who opposed him. The following day France had a new government, known as the Consulate.

Executive power in the new government was to be vested in three consuls. It soon became clear, however, that Napoleon would be the dominant member of this triumvirate, and in the new constitution of December 1799, which the electorate ratified by means of a plebiscite, Napoleon was named First Consul. This appointment made him the most powerful man in France and for all practical purposes a military dictator. Republican forms of government were preserved in the new constitution, but they were easily manipulated to produce what the consuls desired. A Senate appointed by the consuls chose men from a list of 6,000 "notables" to form a body known as the Tribunate, which would discuss legislation proposed by the consuls. Another assembly, the Legislative Body, would vote on those measures without debate.

With the establishment of the Consulate the French Republic was a thing of the past. It had been replaced by a military dictatorship in all but name. This transformation of the republic into a military dictatorship had been predicted by both the radical democrat Robespierre and the British conservative Edmund Burke many years before. The dictatorship became more apparent in 1802, when Napoleon was named Consul for Life, and in 1804, when he crowned himself emperor of the French.

Cultural Change in France During the Revolution

- **In what ways did the political events of the revolution change French cultural institutions and create a new political culture?**

The French Revolution was primarily a political revolution. It brought about fundamental change in the system of government. It resulted in the destruction of the monarchy and the establishment of a republic. It inspired the drafting of new constitutions, led to the creation of new legislative assemblies, and endowed the state with unprecedented power. The French revolution also brought about profound changes in French culture. It transformed the cultural institutions of the Old Regime and created a new revolutionary culture.

The Transformation of Cultural Institutions

Between 1791 and 1794 most of the cultural institutions of the Old Regime were either destroyed or radically transformed, and new institutions under the control of the state took their place.

Schools

The confiscation of church property in 1790, followed by the abolition of the monastic religious orders, had a devastating effect on the traditional parish schools, colleges, and universities, most of which were run by the clergy. Without sufficient endowments, many of these schools were forced to close. During the Terror, schools suspected of having aristocratic associations and teaching counterrevolutionary doctrines came under further assault. Thousands of teachers lost their salaries and sought employment elsewhere. In September 1793 the universities were suppressed.

The government gradually realized that the entire educational process was collapsing. Recognizing the necessity of using education to encourage loyalty to the republican regime, the National Convention established a system of universal primary education. Instruction would be free, and the teachers would receive their salaries from the state. Unfortunately, the state did not have enough money to pay for the system, so the schools continued to languish.

The state was only slightly more successful in providing secondary education by converting abandoned colleges, monasteries, and libraries into "central schools," which were intended to provide a standardized form of state education. By 1799, the central schools had 10,000 students, 40,000 fewer than were in the colleges in 1789. The system was improved significantly during the Napoleonic period when the government established thirty-six secondary schools known as *lycées* while also allowing private and religious schools to continue to function.

Academies

The Parisian scientific and artistic academies established by Louis XIV (see Chapter 15) had a monopoly over the promotion and transmission of knowledge in the sciences and the visual arts. The academies were the epitome of privilege. They controlled their own membership, determined the recipients of their prizes, and had a monopoly of their particular branch of knowledge. They were also heavily aristocratic institutions; as many as three-quarters of their members were nobles or clergy.

During the revolution the academies were abolished as part of a general attack on corporate bodies. The work they did was taken over by various government committees. For example, the Commission on Weights and Measures, which had been part of the Academy of Science, became an independent commission. Its task had been to provide uniform weights and measures for the entire kingdom. In 1795 it established the meter, calculated as one ten-millionth of the distance from the North Pole to the equator, as the standard measure of distance. The metric system and the decimal system, which were introduced at the same time, have subsequently been adopted as universal standards in all European countries except Great Britain.

The Royal Academy of Arts, dissolved by a vote of the National Convention in 1793, was replaced by the Popular and Republican Society of the Arts. The inspiration for this new republican society, which was open to artists of all social ranks, was Jacques-Louis David (1748–1825), the greatest painter of his generation. Employed at the court of Louis XVI, David became a vocal main critic of the academy at the time of the revolution. He painted some of the most memorable scenes of the revolution, including the oath taken at the tennis court by the members of the National Assembly in 1789. During the Republic David depicted heroes of the revolution such as Jean-Paul Marat, and after the empire was established he was appointed First Painter to Napoleon. David presided over a revival of classicism in French painting, employing Greek and Roman motifs and exhibiting a rationalism and lack of sentiment in his work.

Libraries

Shortly after the revolution had begun, thousands of books and manuscripts from the libraries of monasteries, royal castles, residences of the nobility, and academies came into the possession of the state. Many of these were funneled into the Royal Library, which grew five times in size between 1789 and 1794 and was appropriately renamed the National Library. The government also intended to inventory and catalog all the books held in libraries throughout the country. This effort to create the General Bibliography of France was never completed, and while the books were being cataloged, the government decided to get rid of those that dealt with "theology, mysticism, feudalism, and royalism" by sending them to foreign countries. This decision did not lead to the export of books to other parts of Europe, but it initiated a frenzy of book sales, mainly to private individuals. Altogether about five million books were lost or sold during these years.

Museums and Monuments

The day after the abolition of the monarchy the National Assembly created a Commission of the Museum, whose function was "to collect paintings, statues and other precious objects from the crown possessions" as well as from the churches and houses of the émigrés. The museum was to be located in the Louvre, a royal palace that also served as an art gallery. When it opened in August 1793 the Louvre included a majority of paintings with religious themes, most of them confiscated from royal and émigré residences. The incompatibility of these religious works of art with the republican rejection of Christianity can be explained only by the assumption that this museum was intended to be entirely historical and to have no relevance to contemporary politics. The Louvre and the Museum of French Monuments represented an attempt to quarantine the religious French past from its secular present, lest it contaminate the revolution itself.

The revolutionaries did not have the same respect for the bodies of their former kings. On August 10, 1793, the first anniversary of the deposition of Louis XVI, the National Convention ordered the destruction of all the tombs of past French kings. One by one the tombs were opened and the corpses, embalmed in lead, were removed. Metals and valuables were melted down for use in the war effort. The corpses were either left to disintegrate in the atmosphere or dragged unceremoniously to the cemetery, where they were

Le XI Aout 1792, les parisiens reprennent une mesure qu'ils avoient eu tort de ne pas mettre a execution le 20 Juin 1791. Ils abbatirent les Statues de Louis XIV, Place des victoires, et place vendôme.

Destruction of the Statue of Louis XIV in the Place de Victoires, August 11, 1792

The leaders of the Republic attempted to eliminate the memory of the institution of monarchy by destroying statues as well as the tombs of France's kings.

thrown into the common pit. The corpse of Louis XIV landed on top of that of Henry IV. This disrespectful treatment of the remains of France's former kings was intended to erase the memory of monarchy.

The Creation of a New Political Culture

As the state was taking over and adapting the cultural institutions of the Old Regime, revolutionaries engaged in a much bolder and original undertaking: the production of a new, revolutionary political culture. Its sole purpose was to legitimate and glorify the new regime. It symbolized the political values of that regime: liberty, equality, and fraternity in 1789 and republicanism after 1792. This culture was almost entirely political; all forms of cultural expression were subordinated to the realization of a pressing political agenda.

One of the main characteristics of this culture was that it was popular—it was shared by the entire populace, not simply by a small upper-class or literate elite. The fundamental political doctrine of the revolution was popular sovereignty°: the claim that the people were the highest political power in the state. The revolutionaries claimed that this power could never be alienated. The move of the National Assembly from Versailles to Paris actually enabled the people to be present in the gallery during political debate, and deputies were always conscious of their presence. "Learn," claimed one of them in 1789, "that we are deliberating here in front of our masters and we are answerable to them for our opinions." The political culture that emerged—the textual and literary symbols spoken, written, and drawn to reflect this sovereignty of the people—would become the property of the entire population, especially in Paris, where the revolutionary cause found its most passionate popular support. The very words used to identify revolutionary institutions, such as the National Assembly and the National Guard, formed the texture of this new political culture.

The common people who embraced this new culture most enthusiastically were the *sans-culottes*—the radical shopkeepers, artisans, and laborers of Paris. The dress of these people influenced a change in fashion among the wealthier segments of society. A simple jacket replaced the ruffled coat worn by members of the upper classes, their powdered wigs gave way to natural hair, and they too now wore long trousers. They also donned the red liberty cap, to which a tricolor cockade was affixed. The tricolor, which combined the red and blue colors of Paris with the white symbol of the Bourbon monarchy, identified the adherents of the revolution.

Symbols of revolution could be found everywhere. The commercialization of the revolution guaranteed that the tricolor flag, portraits of revolutionary figures, and images of the Bastille would appear on household objects as constant reminders of the public's support for the revolution. By an order of the government in 1792 all men were required to wear the tricolor cockade. Liberty trees, first planted by peasants as protests against local landlords, became a symbol of the revolution. By May 1792 more than 60,000 had been planted throughout the country.

The press, no longer tightly controlled by the government and the printers' guild, became a crucial agent of revolutionary propaganda and a producer of the new culture. Pamphlets, newspapers, brochures, and posters all promoted a distinctive revolutionary language, which became one of the permanent legacies of the revolution. Political leaders used the same rhetoric in their political speeches. *Sans-culottes* sang satirical songs and ballads, many of them to the same tunes well known in the Old Regime. The most popular of the songs of the revolutionary period was the *Marseillaise,* first sung by soldiers preparing for battle against the Austrians but soon adopted by the civilian population and sung at political gatherings. The theaters, which had been privileged corporations in the Old Regime but also carefully regulated, were now free to engage in political satire that strengthened the ties of the people to the revolution.

Much of this new political culture stemmed from the conviction that the doctrine of popular sovereignty should be practiced in everyday life. *Sans-culottes* did this by joining the political clubs organized by different factions within the National Assembly, by addressing others as citizens, and by using the more familiar form of the pronoun *you* (*tu* rather than *vous*) in all conversations. They also participated in the revolution by taking public oaths. On the first anniversary of the fall of the Bastille, as many as 350,000 people, many of them members of the "federations" of National Guards throughout the country, gathered on the royal parade ground outside Paris to take an oath "to the Nation, to the Law, to the King." Direct democracy was not possible in a society of 27 million people, but these cultural practices allowed people to believe that they were participating actively in the political process.

The new revolutionary culture was emphatically secular. In its most extreme form, it was blatantly anti-Christian. In September 1793 the radical Jacobin and former priest Joseph Fouché inaugurated a program of de-Christianization°. Under his leadership, radical Jacobins closed churches and removed religious symbols such as crosses from cemeteries and public venues. In an effort to establish a purely civic religion, they forbade the public practice of religion and renamed churches "temples of reason." In their public pronouncements the architects of de-Christianization avoided reference to the Christian period of French history, which covered the entire national past.

This de-Christianization campaign became the official policy of the Paris Commune, and the National Convention issued a few edicts to enforce it. The program, however, did not win widespread support, and even some Jacobins

Oath Taking

On July 14, 1790, the first anniversary of the fall of the Bastille, as many as 350,000 people gathered on a field outside Paris to take an oath of loyalty to the new French nation. The event was referred to as the Feast of the Federation, because most of the oath takers were members of the regional federations of National Guards. The oath taking, which had many characteristics of a religious gathering, was led by the king himself, and it marked the most optimistic period of the revolution.

claimed that in rejecting Christianity it had undermined a belief in God and the afterlife. In 1794 Robespierre attempted to modify the excesses of de-Christianization by launching the Cult of the Supreme Being. He promoted a series of festivals acknowledging the existence of a deity and the immortality of the soul. This new cult paid lip service to traditional religious beliefs, but it still served secular purposes. In fact, the cult was designed to direct the spiritual yearnings of the French people into patriotic undertakings and promote republican virtue.

The new secular revolutionary culture incorporated many elements of the Christian culture that had prevailed before the revolution began. The new pageants and festivals designed to promote a civic religion were modeled on traditional Catholic processions. Revolutionaries co-opted some of the religious holy days for their own purposes. Churches were converted to temples honoring revolutionary heroes. An effigy of Jean-Paul Marat, who was murdered in 1793, appeared on the altar of a Parisian church, next to a female statue of liberty. Jacques-Louis David's portrait of the murdered Marat depicted the slain victim in the manner of the dead Christ in Michelangelo's *Pietà*. Meetings of revolutionaries often took on the atmosphere of religious revivals, as men and women wept in response to orations. Secular catechisms taught young children the virtues of republicanism in the same way that they had in-

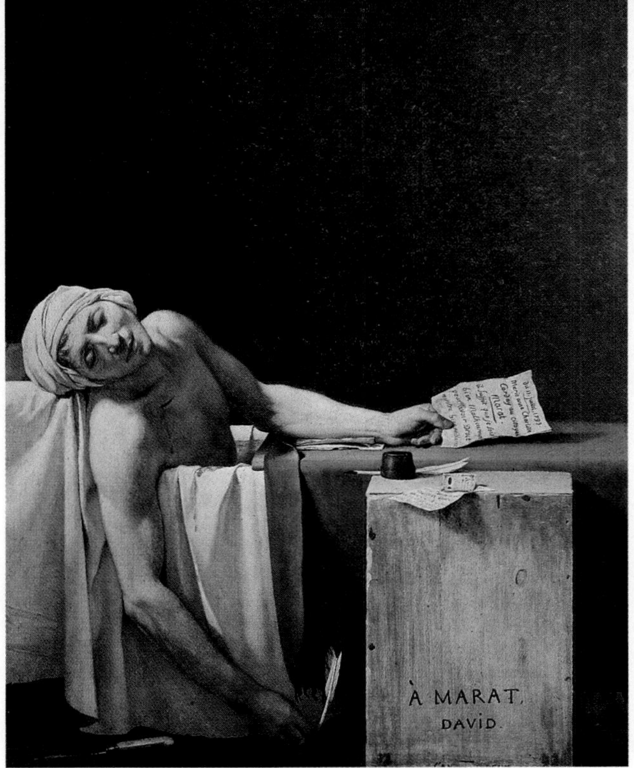

Jacques-Louis David, *The Death of Marat* (1793)
The Jacobin journalist Jean-Paul Marat was stabbed to death in his bathtub by a noblewoman, Charlotte Corday, in July 1793. The painting depicts Marat as having suffered a martyr's death. Marat holds the letter from his murderer that gave her entrance to his residence.

structed them in Christian doctrine during the Old Regime.

In order to destroy all vestiges of the Old Regime, the government also instituted a new calendar in October 1793. The dates on the calendar began with September 22, 1792, the day the Republic was established. That became the first day of the year I, while the weeks now had ten days instead of seven. The new months were given names to evoke the different seasons, such as *Brumaire* for the first month of wintry weather, *Germinal* for the season of planting, and *Thermidor* for the warmest month of the summer. Hostile British contemporaries gave their own humorous renditions of these names, translating them as Freezy, Flowery, Heaty, and so on. The new calendar was intended to make the revolution a part of people's everyday consciousness. It remained in effect until the last day of 1805.

The new revolutionary culture was disseminated widely, but it was always contested. Royalists trampled on the tricolor cockade, refused to adopt the new style of dress, and pulled up the liberty trees. This resistance from counterrevolutionary forces guaranteed that when the revolution was reversed, much of the new political culture would disappear. Napoleon did little to perpetuate it, and the restored monarchy was openly hostile to it. Like the political revolution, however, some elements of revolutionary culture, such as the tricolor and the rhetoric of the revolutionary press, could never be suppressed. Not only did these cultural innovations inspire revolutionaries for the next hundred years, but they also became part of the mainstream of Western civilization.

Cultural Uniformity

One of the most striking features of the new revolutionary culture was its concern for standardization and simplicity. The division of France into *départements,* all roughly equal in size, population, and wealth, and the further subdivision of each *département* into uniform districts and communes, serves as one manifestation of this compulsion. The establishment of a national school system, at least on paper, serves as another. When the *lycées* were founded by Napoleon, each of the schools was given the exact same curriculum, and the same 3,000 books, chosen by a central committee, were deposited in all *lycée* libraries. The adoption of the metric system and the decimal system and the plan to establish one body of French law for the entire country, eventually brought to fruition by Napoleon, reflected the same impulse. So too did the efforts begun during the Terror to make French the official language in regions of the country that spoke Breton, Occitan, Basque, or other regional dialects.

The main source of this drive toward cultural uniformity was the desire to build a new French nation composed of equal citizens. Linguistic, legal, educational, or administrative diversity only made the realization of that program more difficult. The quest for cultural and political standardization did not, however, originate during the revolution. Many of the projects of the 1790s, especially the desire to establish standard weights and measures, began during the Old Regime. They were often the product of the rationalism of the Enlightenment, which, as we have seen in Chapter 18, sought to make society conform to the operation of universal laws.

The Napoleonic Era, 1799–1815

■ **How did the authoritarian rule of Napoleon Bonaparte from 1799 to 1814 confirm or betray the achievements of the French Revolution, and what impact did his military conquests have on Europe and the world?**

The coup d'état on November 9, 1799, or the eighteenth of *Brumaire* on the revolutionary calendar, marked a turning point in the political history of France. The Consulate ushered in a period of authoritarian rule. Liberty was restricted in the interest of order; republicanism gave way to dictatorship. The French Revolution had apparently run its course. But the period between 1799 and 1815 was also a time of considerable innovation, especially in the realm of politics and diplomacy. Those innovations were primarily the work of one man, Napoleon Bonaparte, who controlled the French government for the next fifteen years.

Napoleon's Rise to Power

Napoleon Bonaparte was born on the Mediterranean island of Corsica. His father, Charles-Marie de Buonaparte, was an attorney who had supported the Corsican patriot Pascale de Paoli in winning the independence of the island from the Italian state of Genoa. His mother, Letizia, had come from an old noble family from Lombardy in Italy. In 1770 the new French government, which had gained control of the island the previous year, accepted the Buonaparte family as nobility. In 1779 the young Napoleon, whose native language was Corsican, received an appointment to a French military school. He survived both the rigors of the course of study and the taunting of his classmates, who mocked him for his accent and his poverty. Displaying a natural gift for military science, he won a position in the artillery section of the national military academy in Paris.

Until the beginning of the French Revolution, Napoleon seemed destined to pursue a successful but unspectacular career as an officer in the royal army. The events of the revolution made possible his rapid ascent to military prominence and political power. When the revolution broke out, Napoleon returned to Corsica, where he organized the National Guard and petitioned the government to grant full rights of citizenship to his people. As the revolution became more radical he became a Jacobin, and he was commissioned to attack federalist and royalist positions in the south of France. Unlike many of his fellow Jacobins, he managed to survive the Terror and then found favor with the Directory. In 1796 Napoleon was given command of the Army of Italy, at which time he abandoned the Italian spelling of his name for Bonaparte. His decisive victories against the Austrians and his popularity in Paris attracted the attention of Sieyès and others who wished to give the country strong, charismatic leadership.

Napoleon's personality was ideally suited to the acquisition and maintenance of political power. A man of unparalleled ambition, he was driven by an extraordinarily high assessment of his abilities. After one of his military victories he wrote, "I realized I was a superior being and conceived the ambition of performing great things." To the pursuit of his destiny he harnessed a determined and a stubborn will. Temporary setbacks never seemed to thwart his single-minded pursuit of glory. He brought enormous energy to his military and political pursuits. He wrote more than 80,000 letters during his life, many of them transmitting orders to his officers and ministers. Authoritarian by nature, he used intimidation as well as paternal concern to cultivate the loyalty of his subordinates. Like many authoritarian leaders, he had difficulty delegating authority, a trait that was to weaken his regime. Finally, in an age dominated by high-minded causes, he exhibited an instinctive distrust of ideology and the doctrinaire pronouncements of philosophes such as Rousseau. Napoleon's military training led him to take a pragmatic, disciplined approach to politics, in which he always sought the most effective means to the desired end.

Napoleon's acquisition of power was systematic and shrewd. Playing on the need for a strong leader, and using the army he controlled as his main political tool, he maneuvered himself into the position of first consul in 1799. In 1802 he became consul for life, and two years later he crowned himself emperor of the French and his wife Josephine empress. The title of emperor traditionally denoted the height of monarchical power. It identified a ruler who not only ruled more than one kingdom or state but also did not share power with any other political authority. That was certainly the case with Napoleon. During his rule the Legislative Body, the Senate, and the Tribunate, all of which had been instituted during the Consulate, were reduced to performing only ceremonial functions.

It is certainly ironic that Napoleon, while continuing to hunt down and execute royalists, accepted a title of royalty himself and made his position, just like the French kingship, hereditary. In 1804 a group of royalists, including the members of the Bourbon family, were convicted of and executed for trying to assassinate Napoleon. One of them declared ironically, "We have done more than we hoped. We meant to give France a king, and we have given her an emperor." That emperor, moreover, appeared to the royalists and to many others to be a tyrant who would trample on the rights of the French people. Napoleon's coronation also made a negative impression outside France. The great German composer Ludwig van Beethoven, having dedicated his *Third Symphony* (1803) to Napoleon for overthrowing tyranny in France, scratched Napoleon's name from the dedication after Napoleon assumed his new position as emperor.

Napoleon and the Revolution

What was the relationship between Napoleon's rule and the French Revolution? Did Napoleon consolidate the gains of the revolution or destroy them? Did he simply redirect the revolutionary commitment to liberty, equality, and fraternity into new and more disciplined channels of expression after 1799? Or did he reverse the political trends that had prevailed from 1789 to 1799, crushing liberty in all its forms and establishing a ruthless, authoritarian dictatorship? Napoleon always thought of himself as the heir of the

Emperor Napoleon Crowning His Wife, Josephine, Empress of the French in the Cathedral of Notre Dame, 1804

This painting by Jacques-Louis David depicts secular and religious figures gathered around Napoleon not as members of privileged orders but as representatives of the nation. Pope Pius VII remains seated as Napoleon places the crown on Josephine's head. Napoleon had already crowned himself emperor of the French.

revolution rather than its undertaker. Certainly he was able to use the radical vocabulary of the revolution to characterize his domestic programs and his military campaigns. He presented himself as the ally of the common man against entrenched aristocratic privilege. He proclaimed a love for the French people and gave his support to the doctrine of popular sovereignty. He often referred to the rulers of other European countries as tyrants and presented himself as the liberator of their subjects.

This view of Napoleon as a true revolutionary, however, ignores the fact that his commitment to liberty was almost entirely rhetorical. Behind the appeals to the slogans of the revolution lurked an authoritarian will that was far stronger than that of any eighteenth-century absolute monarch. He used the language of liberty and democracy to disguise a thoroughgoing authoritarianism, just as he used the rhetoric of republicanism to legitimize his own dictatorial regime. The practice of holding carefully orchestrated and controlled elections to ratify the changes he made in French government guaranteed that his rule would appear to have emanated from the will of the people. At the establishment of the Consulate, Napoleon paid lip service to representative forms of government, which he maintained but then proceeded to render totally ineffective. When the empire was established he told his troops that they had the freedom to vote for or against the new form of government but then told them that if they voted against it, they would be shot.

We can make a stronger case for Napoleon's egalitarianism. He spoke of equality of opportunity. He synthesized the egalitarianism of the revolution with the authoritarianism of the Old Regime. He supported the equality of all Frenchmen (but not Frenchwomen) before the law. This egalitarianism laid the foundation for the support he received from the peasants, soldiers, and workers. It might be said that he brought both equality and political stability to France in exchange for political liberty.

There are two other ways in which we might legitimately consider Napoleon the heir of the revolution. The first is that he continued the centralization and growth of state power and the rational organization of the administration

DOCUMENT

The French People Accept Napoleon as Emperor, 1804

The Countess de Rémusat was the wife of one of Napoleon's chamberlains. In this letter she explains why the French people accepted Napoleon as their emperor. Her comments reflect the fear of disorder that permeated French society at the end of the eighteenth century.

I can understand how it was that men worn out by the turmoil of the Revolution, and afraid of that liberty which had long been associated with death, looked for repose under the dominion of an able ruler on whom fortune was seemingly resolved to smile. I can conceive that they regarded his elevation as a decree of destiny and fondly believed that in the irrevocable they should find peace. I may confidently assert that those persons believed quite sincerely that Bonaparte, whether as Consul or Emperor, would exert his authority to oppose the intrigues of faction and would save us from the perils of anarchy.

None dared to utter the word Republic, so deeply had the Terror stained that name, and Directorial Government had perished in the contempt with which its chiefs were regarded. The return of the Bourbons could only be brought about by the aid of a revolution; and the slightest disturbance terrified the French people, in whom enthusiasm of every kind seemed dead. Besides, the men in whom they had trusted had one after the other deceived them; and as, this time, they were yielding to force, they were at least certain that they were not deceiving themselves.

The belief, or rather the error, that only despotism could at that epoch maintain order in France, was very widespread. It became the mainstay of Bonaparte; and it is due to him to say that he also believed it. The factions played into his hands by imprudent attempts which he turned to his own advantage; he had some grounds for his belief that he was necessary; France believed it too; and he even succeeded in persuading foreign sovereigns that he constituted a barrier against Republican influences which, but for him, might spread widely. At the moment when Bonaparte placed the imperial crown upon his head, there was not a king in Europe who did not believe that he wore his own crown more securely because of that event. Had the new emperor granted a liberal constitution, the peace of nations and of kings might, in sober seriousness, have been for ever secured.

Source: *Memoirs of Madame de Rémusat,* translated by C. Hoey and John Lillie (D. Appleton and Co., 1880).

that had begun in 1789. Each of the successive regimes between 1789 and 1815, even the Directory, had contributed to this pattern of state building, and Napoleon's contribution was monumental. The second was his continuation and extension of France's military mission to export the revolution to its European neighbors. The two achievements are related to each other, because the war effort necessitated the further growth and centralization of state power.

Napoleon and the French State

Once Napoleon had gained effective control of the French state, he set about the task of strengthening it, making it more efficient, highly organized, and powerful. In addition to turning the government into a de facto dictatorship, he settled the long struggle between Church and state, laid down an entirely new law code that imposed legal uniformity on the entire country, and made the civil bureaucracy more centralized, uniform, and efficient. All of this was done with the intention of making the state an effective instrument of social and political control.

Concordat with the Papacy

Napoleon's first contribution to the development of the French state, achieved during the Consulate, was to bring about a resolution of the bitter struggle between Church and state. A committed secularist, Napoleon was determined to bring the Church under the direct control of the state. This had been the main purpose of the Civil Constitution of the Clergy of 1790. Napoleon also realized, however, that this policy had divided the clergy between those who had taken an oath to the nation and those who had refused. Clerical independence had also become a major rallying cry of royalists against the new regime, thereby threatening the stability of the country.

Napoleon's solution to this problem was to reach an agreement with the Church that would satisfy clerics and royalists yet not deprive the state of its authority over the Church. With the Church safely under state control, Napoleon could also use religion to maintain respect for authority and to encourage loyalty and service to the state. "In religion," he wrote, "I do not see the mystery of the Incarnation but the mystery of the social order." In a new catechism published after Napoleon became emperor, children were taught: "Christians owe to the princes who govern them, and we owe in particular to Napoleon I, our Emperor, love, respect, obedience, fidelity, military service, and the tributes laid for the preservation and defense of the Empire."

The death of Pope Pius VI (r. 1775–1799), the implacable foe of the revolution, gave Napoleon the opportunity to address this problem. The new pope, Pius VII (r. 1800–1823), who was more sympathetic to liberal causes, was eager to come to terms with a French government that had become more moderate under the Consulate. The Concordat, which Napoleon and Pope Pius agreed to in 1801 and which was published the following year, gave something to both sides, although Napoleon gained more than he conceded. The pope agreed that all the clergy who refused to swear their loyalty to the nation would resign their posts, thus ending the bitter divisions of the past twelve years. The pope would appoint new bishops, but only with the prior approval of Napoleon. The state would pay all clerical salaries, and the Church would abandon any claims it still had to the ecclesiastical lands seized by the state at the beginning of the revolution.

These provisions represented formidable concessions to state power, and many French bishops found the terms of the Concordat too unfavorable to the Church. But the pope did manage to secure a statement that Roman Catholicism was the religion of the majority of citizens, and Napoleon agreed to scrap the secular calendar introduced in 1793, thereby restoring Sundays and holy days. Church attendance began to increase, having reached historic lows during the period of the Republic. The Church regained its respect as well as its legitimacy and its freedom to function in French society. More young recruits joined the clergy. Napoleon did not make many concessions to the Church, but they were significant enough to alienate a group of liberal philosophers and writers known as the Ideologues°, who objected to what they saw as the return of "monkish superstition."

With the pope at least somewhat appeased, Napoleon took unilateral steps to regulate the administration of the French Church. In a set of regulations known as the Organic Articles, which were added to the Concordat in 1802, the French church became a department of state, controlled by a minister of religion, just like the treasury or any other bureaucratic ministry. Pronouncements from the pope required prior government approval, and the clergy were obliged to read government decrees from the pulpit. Protestant congregations, which were also given freedom of worship and state protection by the terms of the Concordat, were likewise brought under state control, and their ministers were paid by the state. Jews received the protection of the state, but the government did not pay the salaries of rabbis.

The Civil Code

Napoleon's most enduring achievement in the realm of state building was the promulgation of a new legal code, the Civil Code of 1804, later known as the Napoleonic Code°. A legal code is an authoritative and comprehensive statement of the law of a particular country. The model for modern legal codes in Europe was the *Corpus Juris Civilis* of the Roman Empire, which Justinian decreed at Constantinople between 529 and 534 C.E. That code had replaced the thousands of constitutions, customs, and judicial decisions that had been in effect during the Roman Republic and Empire. In compiling the new French code Napoleon, who had just proclaimed himself emperor of the French, was imitating Justinian's legal achievement.

The Napoleonic Code also met a long-standing set of demands to reform the confusing and irregular body of French law. Ever since the Middle Ages, France had been governed by a multiplicity of laws. In the southern provinces of the country, those closest to Italy, the law had been influenced by Roman law. The *Corpus Juris Civilis* had been revived in the Middle Ages and had been incorporated into the written law of these southern French provinces and municipalities. In the north the law was based on local or provincial customs that had not originally existed in written form. France needed a common law for all its people. Efforts to produce an authoritative written code began during the revolution, but Napoleon completed the project and published the code.

The Civil Code, which consisted of more than 2,000 articles, reflected the values that were ascendant in Napoleonic French society. The ideals of the revolution were enshrined in the articles guaranteeing the rights of private property, the equality of all people before the law, and freedom of religion. The values it promoted, however, did not include the equality of the sexes. It granted men control of all family property. Women could not buy or sell property without the consent of their husbands. Only adult men could witness legal documents. All male heirs were entitled to inherit equal shares of a family estate, but daughters were excluded from the settlement.

The Civil Code, which dealt only with the rights and relationships of private individuals, was the first and most important of six law codes promulgated by Napoleon. Others dealt with civil procedure (1806), commerce (1807), and criminal law (1811). Renamed the Napoleonic Code in 1806, the Civil Code had an impact on the law of several countries outside France. It became the basis for the codification of the laws of Switzerland, northern Italy, and the Netherlands, and it served as a model for the numerous codes that were compiled in the German territories controlled by France during the Napoleonic period. The Napoleonic Code also influenced the law of French-speaking North America, including the civil law of the state of Louisiana, which bears signs of its influence even today.

Administrative Centralization

Napoleon laid the foundation of modern French civil administration, which acquired the characteristics of rational organization, uniformity, and centralization. All power emanated from Paris, where Napoleon presided over a Council of State. This body consisted of his main ministers, who handled all matters of finance, domestic affairs, and war and oversaw a vast bureaucracy of salaried,

CHRONOLOGY

The Consulate and the Early Years of the Empire, 1799–1806

1799	
December 15	Proclamation of the Constitution of the Consulate
1801	
July 15	Signing of the Concordat with the Papacy
1802	
March 27	Peace of Amiens
April 8	Organic Articles added to the Concordat
1803	
May	Renewal of the war with Britain
1804	
March 21	The Civil Code is promulgated
December 2	Napoleon is crowned emperor of the French
1805	
August	Third Coalition (Britain, Austria, and Russia) is formed against France
October 21	Defeat of the French navy in the Battle of Trafalgar
October 29	The French defeat the Austrian army at Ulm
December 2	The French defeat Russian and Austrian armies at Austerlitz
December 31	End of the revolutionary calendar
1806	
October 14	French victories at the battles of Jena and Auerstädt
November 21	Proclamation of the Continental Blockade of British goods
August 6	Formal dissolution of the Holy Roman Empire

trained officials. The central government also exercised direct control over the provinces, which lost the local privileges they had possessed under the Old Regime. In each of the departments an official known as a *prefect,* appointed by the central government, implemented orders emanating from Paris. Paid the handsome annual salary of 20,000 francs, the prefects were responsible for the maintenance of public order. The power of the prefects was far greater than that of the *intendants* of the Old Regime. The prefects enforced conscription, collected taxes, and supervised local public works, such as the construction and improvement of roads.

The men who served in the government of the French Empire belonged to one of two elaborate, hierarchical institutions: the civil bureaucracy and the army officer corps. The two were closely related, because the main purpose of the administrative bureaucracy was to prepare for and sustain the war effort. Both institutions were organized hierarchically, and those who held positions in them were trained and salaried. Appointment and promotion were based primarily on talent rather than birth.

The idea of "a career open to all talents," as Napoleon described it, ran counter to the tradition of noble privilege. This was one of the achievements of the revolution that Napoleon perpetuated during the empire. All of the twenty-six marshals who served under him in the army were of nonnoble blood. Three of them had been sergeants in the army before 1789 and another three had been privates. The new system did not amount to a pure meritocracy, in which advancement is determined solely by ability and performance, because many appointments were made or influenced by Napoleon himself on the basis of friendship or kinship. Napoleon's brother, Lucien, for example, became minister of the interior. The system did, however, allow people from the ranks of the bourgeoisie to achieve rapid upward social mobility. In order to recognize their new status, Napoleon created a new order of nonhereditary noblemen, known as *notables.* As men ascended through the ranks of the bureaucracy and army they were given the titles of duke, count, baron, and chevalier. Instead of earning status based on their ancestry, these men acquired their titles by virtue of their service to the state. Napoleon created more than 3,500 notables during his rule. In this way he encouraged service to the state while also strengthening loyalty to it.

Napoleon, the Empire, and Europe

Closely related to Napoleon's efforts to build the French state was his creation of a massive European empire. The French Empire was the product of a series of military victories against the armies of Austria, Prussia, Russia, and Spain between 1797 and 1809. By the latter date France controlled, either directly or indirectly, the Dutch Republic, the

Austrian Netherlands, Italy, Spain, and large parts of Germany and Poland. The instrument of these victories was the massive citizen army that Napoleon assembled. Building on the *levée en masse* of 1793, which he supplemented with soldiers from the countries he conquered, Napoleon had more than one million men under arms by 1812. More than three times the size of Louis XIV's army in 1700, it was the largest military force raised under the control of one man up to this time in European history.

These troops engaged in a military offensive that was more massive, wide-ranging, and sustained than Alexander the Great's invasion of Egypt, Persia, and northern India between 334 and 326 B.C.E. Napoleon's invasion began with the great victories against Austria and Prussia in 1797. Two years later, shortly after Napoleon had become first consul, he directed his army to further military successes that paved the way to French dominance of Europe. The defeat of Austria in 1800 confirmed earlier territorial gains in Italy as well as French control over the southern Netherlands, now called Belgium. With Austria defeated and Russia involved with the Ottoman Turks, France and Britain concluded peace at Amiens in 1802. This peace gave Napoleon free rein to reorganize the countries that bordered on France's eastern and southeastern boundaries. In Italy he named himself the president of the newly established Cisalpine Republic, and he transformed the cantons of Switzerland into the Helvetic Republic. These acquisitions gave substance to the title of emperor that he assumed in 1804, because now he controlled many different kingdoms. France had not had an emperor since the ninth century, when Charlemagne and his heirs had ruled as Roman emperors, and Napoleon's territories were more extensive than those under Charlemagne's jurisdiction.

These stunning military successes as well as those that were to follow have secured Napoleon's reputation as one of the most brilliant and successful military leaders in modern history. The reasons for that reputation are a matter of some controversy. Napoleon made terrible strategic blunders in many of his campaigns and tactical mistakes in many of his battles. Somehow he seemed to make up for these mistakes by his careful planning, unbounded energy, and decisive moves. He spent hours studying his opponents' position beforehand but made quick decisions once the battle had begun. "Everything," he once said, "is in the execution." The combination of infantry, artillery, and cavalry in the same units or *corps* allowed him to move these forces easily on the battlefield. He struck quickly, usually at the center of enemy lines, using superior numbers to overwhelm his opponent. Attacks on enemy lines of communication often prevented his opponents from calling up reinforcements. Once they began their retreat, he would pursue them rather than stop to celebrate. In his campaigns he benefited from the loyalty of his troops and the ideological zeal that continued to inspire them, even as his wars lost their ideological purpose of exporting the ideals of the revolution.

Napoleon was far less successful at sea than on land. With no real experience in naval warfare, he could not match the dominance of the British navy, which retained its mastery of the seas throughout the entire revolutionary period. Only in the West Indies, where Britain was never able to send sufficient naval forces, did the French navy manage to hold its own. This naval weakness also explains Napoleon's failure to build or regain an overseas empire. His expedition to Egypt in 1798, which was dominated by dreams of colonial conquest in the Middle East and South Asia, was checked by the British destruction of the French fleet at the Battle of the Nile. In the Western Hemisphere financial problems and a false hope of limiting British power induced Napoleon to sell the vast North American territory of Louisiana, which he had regained from Spain in 1800, to the United States in 1803. The following year the French Caribbean colony of St. Domingue became independent as the result of the violent revolution staged by free blacks and slaves, as discussed in Chapter 17. Informed of that loss, Napoleon shouted "Damn sugar, damn coffee, damn colonies!"

The most significant French naval defeat came in 1805, shortly after Britain, Austria, and Russia had formed the Third Coalition against France. As Napoleon was preparing for an invasion of Britain from northern French ports, the British navy, under the command of the diminutive, one-eyed Admiral Horatio Nelson, won one of the most decisive battles in the history of naval warfare. Nelson broke the line of a Franco-Spanish fleet that was preparing to strike off the Cape of Trafalgar near Gibraltar. The British destroyed or captured half the enemy ships, thus breaking the back of French sea power. The battle is commemorated at Trafalgar Square in London, which is overlooked by a towering statue of Nelson, who died of wounds inflicted during the battle. Nelson might have survived if he had not insisted on wearing glimmering medals on his uniform, thereby attracting the notice of French marksmen.

The monumental naval defeat at Trafalgar did not prevent Napoleon from continuing his wars of conquest in central Europe. In October 1805 he defeated an Austrian army at Ulm, and in December of that year he overwhelmed the combined forces of Austria and Russia at Austerlitz. These victories brought him new German and Italian territory, which he ceded to some of the larger German states; the smaller German states became satellites of France and fought with him until the collapse of his empire. A defeat of Prussian forces at Jena and Auerstädt in 1806 and the subsequent occupation of Berlin gave him the opportunity to carve the new German kingdom of Westphalia out of Prussian territory in the Rhineland and to install his brother Jerome as its ruler. In the East he created the duchy of Warsaw out of Polish lands controlled by Prussia. In 1806

The French Encounter the Egyptians, 1798–1801

Napoleon's expedition to Egypt in 1798 marked one of the few times during the revolutionary period that the French came in direct contact with non-Western peoples. The expedition resulted in the military occupation of the country for three years and set the stage for the first extensive encounters between Egyptians and Europeans since the Ottoman conquest of Egypt in the sixteenth century. At that time Egypt had become a semiautonomous province of the Ottoman Empire and had very little contact with the West. Egypt's isolation from the West meant that it had little exposure to the scientific and technological discoveries that had taken place in western Europe during the previous 300 years.

In addition to 38,000 soldiers, Napoleon brought with him 165 scholars who were organized in a Commission of Science and Arts. These men came from virtually every branch of learning: surveyors, cartographers, civil engineers, architects, botanists, physicians, chemists, and mineralogists. The commission also included artists, archaeologists, writers, and musicians. Their purpose was to give Napoleon information on the people and the resources of the country so that he could more easily subject it to French domination. A small group of these scholars set up an Institute of Egypt, whose mission was to propagate the Enlightenment and to undertake research on the history, people, and the economy of the country. This involved the scholarly study of Egyptian antiquities, including the pyramids.

This work of the institute ushered in a long period in which many artifacts of Egyptian antiquity were taken from the country and transported to European museums and palaces. Members of the institute encouraged this cultural plundering, arguing that their addition to the collections of the Louvre would embellish the glory of France. This plundering of native Egyptian antiquities represented a form of cultural imperialism that continued unabated during the nineteenth century.

Cultural imperialism of a different sort can be found in a widely disseminated description of Egypt, *Travels in Upper and Lower Egypt* (1802), by a member of the institute, Dominique Vivant-Denon. This two-volume work contained extensive descriptions of the different "races" of people in Egypt whom the expedition encountered in the thriving port town of Rosetta. Vivant-Denon described the Copts, the most ancient Egyptians, as "swarthy Nubians" with flat foreheads, high cheekbones, and short broad noses. They displayed the moral qualities of "ignorance, drunkenness, cunning, and finesse." The Arabs, who were the most numerous group, and the Turks had more appealing physical and personal characteristics, although they were often reduced to the "degraded state of animals."

Expressions of French cultural superiority permeate other contemporary accounts of Napoleon's expedition. A multivolume work, *The Description of Egypt,* claimed that Napoleon wanted to procure for Egyptians "all the advantages of a perfected civilization." It praised him for bringing modern knowledge to a country that had been "plunged into darkness." These attitudes provided a justification for the subsequent economic exploitation of Egypt, first by the French and later by the British, during the nineteenth century.

For Discussion

In what ways did Vivant-Denon's work reflect the values that were cultivated during the Enlightenment?

Jean Charles Tardieu, *The French Army Halts at Syene, Upper Egypt, on February 2, 1799*
This painting depicts a cultural encounter between French soldiers and Egyptians in the city of Syene (now Aswan) during the Egyptian campaign of 1798–1799. The soldiers are scribbling on the ruins of ancient Egypt, indicating a lack of respect for Egyptian culture.

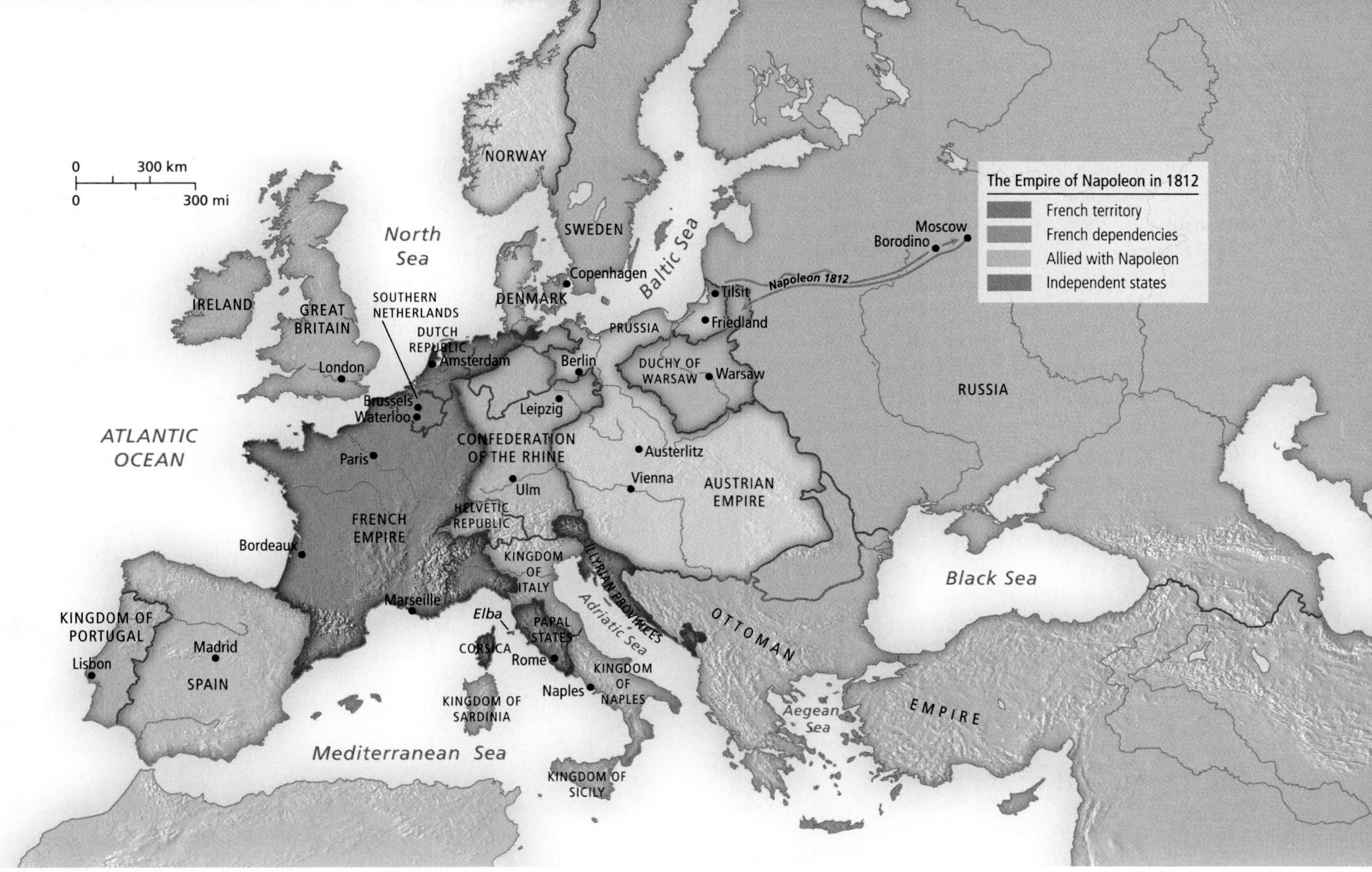

Map 19.1 The Empire of Napoleon in 1812
By establishing dependent states in Spain, Italy, Germany, and Poland, France controlled far more territory than the areas technically within the French Empire.

he formally dissolved the ancient Holy Roman Empire and replaced it with a loose association of sixteen German states known as the Confederation of the Rhine. By 1807, in the words of one historian, Napoleon had "only allies and victims" on the Continent (see Map 19.1).

Napoleon inserted the last piece in this imperial puzzle by invading and occupying the kingdom of Spain in 1808. This campaign began as an effort to crush Portugal, the ally of Britain, which he was never able to defeat. In May 1808, as French armies marched through Spain en route to Lisbon, the Portuguese capital, a popular insurrection against Spanish rule occurred in Madrid. This spontaneous revolt, which led to the abdication of King Charles IV and the succession of his son Ferdinand VII, was the first of many developments that caused the collapse of the Spanish Empire in America. In Europe it led to the absorption of Spain into the French Empire. Sensing that he could easily add one more territory to his list of conquests, Napoleon forced Ferdinand to abdicate and summoned his own brother, Joseph Bonaparte, who was then ruling the dependent kingdom of Naples, to become king of Spain.

Joseph instituted some reforms in Spain, but the abolition of the Spanish Inquisition and the closing of two-thirds of the Spanish convents triggered a visceral reaction from the Spanish clergy and the general populace. Fighting for Church and king, small bands of local guerillas subjected French forces to intermittent and effective sabotage. An invasion by British forces under the command of Arthur Wellesley, later the Duke of Wellington (1769–1852), in what has become known as the Peninsula War (1808–1813), strengthened Spanish and Portuguese resistance.

The reception of the French in Spain revealed that the export of revolution, which had begun with the French armies of 1792, was a double-edged sword. The overthrow of authoritarian regimes in other European states won the support of progressive, capitalist, and anticlerical forces in those countries, but it also triggered deep resentment against French rule. The ideology of nationalism in Germany and Italy arose more because of a reaction against French rule than because the armies of France had tried to stimulate it. In Italy during the 1790s young educated *patrioti,* imbued with enthusiasm for liberty, equality, and progress, supported the newly proclaimed republics and envisioned the establishment of a single Italian state, at least in the north of Italy. By the middle of the Napoleonic years that vision had changed. Many of the *patrioti* had become disillusioned and joined secret societies to press for further political and social change and to plot insurrections against the new republics.

In Germany many of those who supported the French cause during the early years of the Republic turned away from it during Napoleon's wars of expansion. In 1809 a German student who attempted to assassinate Napoleon shouted "Long live Germany!" at his execution. In 1813 the German writer Johann Gottlieb Fichte (1762–1814) appealed to the German nation to resist Napoleon in order to regain their liberty. For all his political astuteness, Napoleon could not comprehend that his own policies were responsible for the growth of this reactive sentiment, which formed one of the foundations of nineteenth-century nationalism. We shall discuss this topic more fully in Chapter 21.

Francisco Goya, *The Third of May 1808*
This painting of the suppression of the popular revolt in Madrid in 1808 captures the brutality of the French occupation of Spain. A French unit executes Spanish citizens, including a monk in the foreground. Goya was a figure of the Enlightenment and a Spanish patriot.

The Art of Francisco Goya

The Downfall of Napoleon

The turning point in Napoleon's personal fortunes and those of his empire came in 1810. After securing an annulment of his marriage to Josephine in late 1809, he married Marie-Louise, the daughter of the Habsburg emperor. This marriage, which the following year produced a son and heir to the throne, should have made the French Empire more secure, but it had the opposite effect. For the first time during his rule, dissent from both the right and the left became widespread. Despite the most stringent efforts at censorship, royalist and Jacobin literature poured off the presses. The number of military deserters and those evading conscription increased. Relations with the papacy reached a breaking point when Napoleon annexed the Papal States, at which point Pope Pius VII, who had negotiated the Concordat of 1801, excommunicated him.

Dissent at home had the effect of driving the megalomaniacal emperor to seek more glory and further conquests. In this frame of mind Napoleon made the ill-advised decision to invade Russia. The motives for engaging in this overly ambitious military campaign were not completely irrational. Victory over Russia promised to give France control of the Black Sea, and that in turn would ultimately lead to the control of Constantinople and the entire Middle East. More immediately, defeating Russia would be necessary to enforce the French blockade of British goods, which Russia had refused to support.

The problem with a Russian invasion was that it stretched Napoleon's lines of communication too far and his resources too thin, despite the support of the Austrians and Prussians whom he had defeated. Even before the invasion it was becoming increasingly difficult to feed, equip, and train the huge army he had assembled. The Grand Army that crossed from Poland into Russia in 1812 was not the efficient military force that Napoleon had commanded in the early years of the empire. Many of his best soldiers were fighting in the guerilla war in Spain. Casualties and desertions had forced Napoleon to call up new recruits who were not properly trained. Half the army, moreover, had been recruited from the population of conquered countries, making their loyalty to Napoleon uncertain.

The tactics of the Russians contributed to the failure of the invasion. Instead of engaging the Grand Army in combat, the Russian army kept retreating, pulling Napoleon further east toward Moscow. On September 7 the two armies clashed at Borodino, suffering a staggering 77,000 casualties in all. The Russian army then continued its retreat eastward. When Napoleon reached Moscow he found it deserted, and fires deliberately set by Muscovites had destroyed more than two-thirds of the city. Napoleon, facing the onset of a dreaded Russian winter and rapidly diminishing supplies, began the long retreat back to France. Skirmishes with the Russians along the way, which cost him 25,000 lives just crossing the Beresina River, conspired with the cold and hunger to destroy his army. During the entire Russian campaign his army lost a total of 380,000 men to death, imprisonment, or desertion. In the midst of this horror Napoleon, oblivious to the suffering of his troops, reported back to Paris, "The health of the emperor has never been better."

Not to be discouraged, Napoleon soon began preparing for further conquests. Once again his enemies formed a coalition against him, pledging to restore the independence of the countries that had become his satellites or dependents. Napoleon scored a few victories in the late summer of 1813, but in October allied forces inflicted a crushing defeat on him in the Battle of the Nations at Leipzig. Austrian troops administered another blow to the French in northern Italy, and the British finally drove them out of Spain. As a result of these defeats, Napoleon's army was pushed back into France. A massive allied force advanced into Paris and occupied the city. After extensive political maneuvering, including a vote by the Senate to depose Napoleon, the emperor abdicated on April 6, 1814. The allies promptly exiled him to the Mediterranean island of Elba. As he made the journey to the coast, crowds surrounding his coach shouted "Down with the tyrant!" while some villagers hanged him in effigy.

This course of events led to the restoration of the Bourbon monarchy. By the terms of the first Treaty of Paris of May 1814, the allies restored the brother of Louis XVI, the Count of Provence, to the French throne as Louis XVIII (r. 1814–1824). Louis was an implacable foe of the revolution, and much of what he did was intended to undermine its achievements. The white Bourbon flag replaced the revolutionary tricolor. Catholicism was once again recognized as the state religion. Exiled royalists returned to their high-ranking positions in the army. Nonetheless, Louis accepted a Constitutional Charter that incorporated many of the changes made between 1789 and 1791. Representative government, with a relatively limited franchise, replaced the absolutism of the Old Regime. Equality before the law, freedom of religion, and freedom of expression were all reaffirmed. Even more important, the powers of the state that the National Assembly and the Directory had extended and Napoleon had enhanced were maintained. The administrative division of France into departments continued, and the Napoleonic Code remained in force. France had experienced a counterrevolution in 1814, but it did not simply turn the political clock back to 1788. Some of the political achievements of the previous twenty-five years were indeed preserved.

Despite his disgrace and exile, Napoleon still commanded loyalty from his troops and from large segments of the population. While in power he had constructed a legend that drew on strong patriotic sentiment. Supporters throughout France continued to promote his cause in the same way that royalists had maintained that of the Bourbon monarchy since 1792. The Napoleonic legend held great appeal among the lower classes, who were persuaded that Napoleon, the patriot and the savior of the revolution, had made it possible for every Frenchman to achieve wealth and fame. The strength of the Napoleonic legend became apparent in March 1815, when Napoleon escaped from Elba and landed in southern France. Promising to rid the country of the exiled royalists who had returned and to save the revolutionary cause that he claimed had been abandoned, he won over peasants, workers, and soldiers. Regiment after regiment joined him as he marched toward Paris. By the time he arrived, Louis XVIII had gone into exile once again, and Napoleon found himself back in power.

CHRONOLOGY

The Downfall of Napoleon, 1807–1815

1807	
November–December	French military intervention in Spain and Portugal begins
1808	
May	Beginning of the Spanish rebellion
July 20	Joseph Bonaparte appointed king of Spain
1809	
December 15	Annulment of marriage of Napoleon and Empress Josephine
1810	
April 2	Marriage of Napoleon to Marie-Louise
1812	
September 7	Battle of Borodino
September 14	Napoleon enters Moscow
October	Retreat from Moscow begins
1813	
October 16–19	Battle of the Nations at Leipzig
1814	
April 6	Abdication of Napoleon
May 30	First Treaty of Paris
September	Congress of Vienna assembles
1815	
March	Napoleon escapes from Elba
June 18	Battle of Waterloo
November 20	Second Treaty of Paris

But not for long. The allied European powers quickly began to assemble yet another coalition. Fearing that the allies would launch a massive invasion of France, Napoleon decided to strike first. He marched an army of 200,000 men into the Austrian Netherlands, where the allies responded by amassing 700,000 troops. Near the small village of Waterloo, south of Brussels, he met the British forces of the Duke of Wellington, who had turned the tide against him during the Peninsula War. Reinforced by Prussian troops, Wellington inflicted a devastating defeat on the French army, which lost 28,000 men and went into a full-scale retreat. Napoleon, captured in the battle, abdicated once again. He was exiled to the remote South Atlantic island of St. Helena, from which escape was impossible. He died there in 1821.

DOCUMENT
Napoleon's Exile to St. Helena (1815)

Even before the battle of Waterloo, the major powers of Europe had gathered in Vienna to redraw the boundaries of the European states that had been created, dismembered, or transformed during the preceding twenty-five years (see Map 19.2). Under the leadership of the Austrian foreign minister, Prince Clemens von Metternich (1773–1859), this conference, known as the Congress of Vienna°, worked out a settlement that was intended to preserve the balance of power in Europe and at the same time uphold the principle of dynastic legitimacy. By the terms of a separate Treaty of Paris (the second in two years) the boundaries of France

Map 19.2 Europe After the Congress of Vienna, 1815
The four most important territorial changes that took place in 1815 were the scaling back of the boundaries of France to their status in 1790, the Austrian acquisition of territory in western and northeastern Italy, the establishment of the new kingdom of the Netherlands, and the formation of the new German Confederation.

were scaled back to what they had been in 1790, before it had begun its wars of expansion. To create a buffer state on the northern boundary of France, the Congress annexed the Austrian Netherlands to the Dutch Republic, which now became the kingdom of the Netherlands with William I, a prince of the House of Orange, as its king. Territory along the Rhineland in the state of Westphalia was ceded to Prussia, while Austria gained territory in Italy, both along the French border in the west and in northern Italy to the east. In place of the defunct Holy Roman Empire, the Congress established a new German Confederation, a loose coalition of thirty-nine separate territories with a weak legislative assembly, whose members were appointed and instructed by their governments. The five major powers that had drawn this new map of Europe—Britain, Austria, Prussia, Russia, and France—agreed to meet annually to prevent any one country, especially France but also Russia, from achieving military dominance of the European Continent.

The Legacy of the French Revolution

- **What did the French Revolution ultimately achieve and in what ways did it change the course of European and Western history?**

With the conclusion of the Congress of Vienna a tumultuous period of European and Western history finally came to an end. Not only had France experienced a revolution, but every country in Europe and America had felt its effects. Governments were toppled in countries as far apart as Poland and Peru. Added to this turbulence was the experience of incessant warfare. France was at war for more than twenty years during the period of the Republic and the empire, and it had brought almost all European powers into the struggle. With armies constantly in need of provisions and supplies, high taxation, galloping inflation, and food shortages inflicted economic hardship on a large portion of the European population.

The cost of all this instability and warfare in terms of human life was staggering. Within the space of one generation almost two million European soldiers were killed in action, wasted by disease, or starved or frozen to death. In France alone just under 500,000 soldiers died during the revolutionary wars of 1792–1802 and another 916,000 during the wars of the empire. Internal political disturbances took the lives of hundreds of thousands of civilians from all ranks of society, not only in France but throughout Europe. The violence was fed at all levels by unprecedented fears of internal and external subversion. Government officials, collaborators, counterrevolutionaries, and imagined enemies of the state were all executed. This spate of violence and death—much of it in the name of liberty—was inflicted almost entirely by the state or its enemies.

What was achieved at this extraordinary price? How did the France of 1815 differ from the France of 1788? What on balance had changed? For many years historians, especially those who believed that economic forces determined the course of history, claimed that as a result of the revolution the bourgeoisie, composed of merchants, manufacturers, and other commoners of substantial wealth, had replaced the nobility as the dominant social and political class in the country. The bourgeoisie, so they argued, had started the revolution in order to acquire political power that was commensurate with their economic power, and they had ultimately prevailed.

This assessment can no longer be sustained. The nobility certainly lost many of their privileges in 1789, and many of them went into exile during the revolutionary period, but the position they had in French society in 1815 did not differ greatly from what it had been under the Old Regime. In both periods there was considerable blurring of the distinctions between nobility and bourgeoisie. Nor did the revolutionary period witness the emergence of a new class of industrial entrepreneurs. The only group who definitely profited from the revolution in the long run were men of property, regardless of their membership in any social category or "class." Men of property emerged triumphant in the Directory, found favor during the Napoleonic period, and became the most important members of political society after the monarchy was restored.

It would be difficult to argue that *women* of any social rank benefited from the revolution. During the early years of the revolution, women participated actively in public life. They were involved in many demonstrations in Paris, including the storming of the Bastille and the march to Versailles to pressure the king to move to Paris. Women as well as men filled the ranks of the *sans-culottes,* and women donned their own female version of nonaristocratic dress. During the early years of the revolution, many women joined patriotic clubs, such as the Club of Knitters or the unisex Fraternal Society of Patriots of Both Sexes. In 1790 the Marquis de Condorcet published *On the Admission of Women to the Rights of Citizenship,* and the following year Olympe de Gouges published *The Rights of Women,* in which she called for the granting of women's equal rights. Both of these advocates of women's rights had been influenced by Enlightenment thought, as we have discussed in Chapter 18.

The goal advanced by Condorcet and de Gouges was not to be realized. The radical Jacobins dealt it a terrible setback when they banned all women's clubs and societies on the grounds that their participation in public life would harm the institution of the family. This action, coupled with the imprisonment and death of both de Gouges and Condorcet during the Terror, signaled an end to the extensive participation of women in political life, which had begun during the eighteenth century, especially in the salons. During the nineteenth century women were generally considered to occupy a separate sphere of activity from that of men. They were expected to exercise influence in the private sphere of the home, but not in the public sphere of politics. As we shall discuss in Chapter 20, the changes wrought by the Industrial Revolution reinforced this segregation of men and women by excluding many married women from the workforce.

It is even more difficult to identify permanent economic changes as a result of the revolution. The elimination of the remnants of feudalism may have made France marginally more capitalist than it had been before the revolution, but agricultural and mercantile capitalism had long been entrenched in French society. Nor did the Continental System, the blockade of British goods from all European ports initiated in 1806, allow French industry to catch up with that of Great Britain. Whatever economic gains were made under the protective shield of the state were offset by the adverse economic effects of twenty-two years of nearly continuous warfare. In the long run the revolutionary period delayed the process of industrialization that had entered its preliminary stages in France during the 1780s and retarded the growth of the French economy for the remainder of the nineteenth century.

The permanent legacy of the French Revolution lies in the realm of politics. First, the period from 1789 to 1815 triggered an enormous growth in the competence and power of the state. This trend had begun before the revolution, but the desire of the revolutionaries to transform every aspect of human life in the service of the revolution, coupled with the necessity of utilizing all the country's resources in the war effort, gave the state more control over the everyday life of its citizens than ever before. Fifteen years of Napoleonic rule only accentuated this trend, and after 1815 many of those powers remained with the government.

An even more significant and permanent achievement of the French Revolution was the promotion of the doctrine of popular sovereignty. The belief that the people constituted the highest political authority in the state became so entrenched during the revolution that it could never be completely suppressed, either in France or in the other countries of Europe. Napoleon recognized its power when he asked the people to approve political changes he had already made by his own authority. He also arranged for such plebiscites to secure approval of the new states he had set up in Europe. After the restoration of the monarchy the doctrine of popular sovereignty was promoted mainly by the press, which continued to employ the new revolutionary rhetoric to keep alive the high ideals and aspirations of the revolution. The doctrine also contributed to the formation of two nineteenth-century ideologies, liberalism and nationalism, which will be discussed in Chapter 21.

The third permanent political change was the active participation of the citizens in the political life of the nation. This participation had been cultivated during the early years of the revolution, and it had been accompanied by the creation of a new political culture. Much of that culture was suppressed during the Napoleonic period, but the actual habit of participating in politics was not. The franchise was gradually expanded in Europe during the nineteenth century. The press spread political ideas to a large segment of the population. People from all walks of life participated in marches, processions, and demonstrations. All of this followed from the acceptance of the French revolutionary doctrine that the people are sovereign and have a right therefore to participate in the political life of the state.

Conclusion

The French Revolution and Western Civilization

The French Revolution was a central event in the history of the West. It began as an internal French affair, reflecting the social and political tensions of the Old Regime, but it soon became a turning point in European and Western history. Proclamations of the natural rights of humanity gave the ideals of the revolution widespread appeal, and a period of protracted warfare succeeded in disseminating those ideals outside the boundaries of France.

Underlying the export of French revolutionary ideology was the belief that France had become the standard-bearer of Western civilization. French people believed they were *la grande nation,* the country that had reached the highest level of political and social organization. They did not believe they had acquired this exalted status by inheritance. Unlike the English revolutionaries of the seventeenth century, they did not claim that they were the heirs of a medieval constitution. French republicans of the 1790s attributed none of their national preeminence to the monarchy, whose memory they took drastic steps to erase. They considered the secular political culture that emerged during the French Revolution to be an entirely novel development.

The export of French revolutionary political culture during the Republic and the empire brought about widespread changes in the established order. Regimes were toppled, French puppets acquired political power, boundaries of states were completely redrawn, and traditional authorities were challenged. Liberal reforms were enacted, new constitutions were written, and new law codes were promulgated. The Europe of 1815 could not be mistaken for the Europe of 1789.

The ideas of the French Revolution, like those of the Enlightenment that had helped to inspire them, did not go unchallenged. From the very early years of the revolution they encountered determined opposition, both in France and abroad. As the revolution lost its appeal in France, the forces of conservatism and reaction gathered strength. At the end of the Napoleonic period, the Congress of Vienna took steps to restore the legitimate rulers of European states and to prevent revolution from recurring. It appeared that the revolution would be completely reversed, but that was not the case. The ideas born of the revolution would continue to inspire demands for political reform in Europe during the nineteenth century, and those demands, just like those in the 1790s, would meet with fierce resistance.

Suggestions for Further Reading

For a comprehensive listing of suggested readings, please go to www.ablongman.com/levack2e/chapter19

Andress, David. *The French Revolution and the People.* 2004. Focuses on the role played by the common people of France—the peasants, craftsmen and those living on the margins of society—in the revolution.

Blanning, T. C. W. *The French Revolutionary Wars, 1787–1802.* 1996. An authoritative political and military narrative that assesses the impact of the wars on French politics.

Chartier, Roger. *The Cultural Origins of the French Revolution.* 1991. Explores the connections between the culture of the Enlightenment and the cultural transformations of the revolutionary period.

Cobban, Alfred. *The Social Interpretation of the French Revolution.* 1964. Challenges the Marxist interpretation of the causes and effects of the revolution.

Doyle, William. *The Oxford History of the French Revolution.* 1989. An excellent synthesis.

Ellis, Geoffrey. *Napoleon.* 1997. A study of the nature and mechanics of Napoleon's power and an analysis of his imperial policy.

Furet, François. *The French Revolution, 1770–1814.* 1992. A provocative narrative that sees Napoleon as the architect of a second, authoritarian revolution that reversed the gains of the first.

Hardman, John. *Louis XVI: The Silent King.* 2000. A reassessment of the king that mixes sympathy with criticism.

Higonnet, Patrice. *Goodness Beyond Virtue: Jacobins During the French Revolution.* 1998. Explores the contradictions of Jacobin ideology and its descent into the Terror.

Hunt, Lynn. *Politics, Culture and Class in the French Revolution.* 1984. Analyzes the formation of a revolutionary political culture.

Kennedy, Emmet. *The Culture of the French Revolution.* 1989. A comprehensive study of all cultural developments before and during the revolution.

Landes, Joan B. *Women and the Public Sphere in the Age of the French Revolution.* 1988. Explores how the new political culture of the revolution changed the position of women in society.

Lefebvre, Georges. *The Great Fear of 1789: Rural Panic in Revolutionary France.* 1973. Shows the importance of the rural unrest of July 1789 that provided the backdrop of the legislation of August 1789.

Schama, Simon. *Citizens: A Chronicle of the French Revolution.* 1989. Depicts the tragic unraveling of a vision of liberty and happiness into a scenario of hunger, anger, violence, and death.

Notes

1. Emmanuel-Joseph Sieyès, *What Is the Third Estate?* (1789).
2. H. Wallon, *Histoire du tribunal révolutionnaire de Paris* (1880–1882), Vol. 4, 511.

The Industrial Revolution

20

IN 1842 A 17-YEAR-OLD GIRL, PATIENCE KERSHAW, TESTIFIED BEFORE A BRITISH parliamentary committee regarding the practice of employing children and women in the nation's mines. When the girl made her appearance, the members of the committee observed that she was "an ignorant, filthy, ragged, and deplorable-looking object, such as one of uncivilized natives of the prairies would be shocked to look upon." Patience, who had never been to school and could not read or write, told the committee that she was one of ten children, all of whom had at one time worked in the coal mines, although three of her sisters now worked in a textile mill. She went to the pit at five in the morning and came out at five at night. Her job in the mines was to hurry coal, that is, to pull carts of coal through the narrow tunnels of the mine. Each cart weighed 300 pounds, and every day she hauled eleven of them one mile. The carts were attached to her head and shoulders by a chain and belt, and the pressure of the cart had worn a bald spot on her head. Patience hurried coal for twelve hours straight, not taking any time for her midday meal, which she ate as she worked. While she was working, the men and boys who dug the coal and put it in the carts would often beat her and take sexual liberties with her. Patience told the committee, "I am the only girl in the pit; there are about 20 boys and 15 men. All the men are naked. I would rather work in a mill than a coal pit."[1]

Patience Kershaw was one of the human casualties of an extraordinary development that historians usually refer to as the Industrial Revolution. This process, which brought about a fundamental transformation of human life, involved the extensive use of machinery in the production of goods. Much of that machinery was driven by steam engines, which required coal to produce the steam. Coal mining itself became a major industry, and the men who owned and operated the mines tried to hire workers, many of them children, at the lowest possible wage. It was this desire to maximize profits that led to the employment, physical hardship, and abuse of girls like Patience Kershaw.

Exhibit of Machinery at the Crystal Palace Exhibition in London in 1851
During the Industrial Revolution the manufacture of heavy machinery itself became an industry.

CHAPTER OUTLINE

Child Labor in the Mines
A child hurrying coal through a tunnel in a mine.

The story of the Industrial Revolution cannot be told solely in terms of the exploitation of child or even adult workers. Many of its effects can be described in positive or at least morally neutral terms. The Industrial Revolution resulted in a staggering increase in the volume and range of products made available to consumers, from machine-produced clothing to household utensils. It made possible unprecedented and sustained economic growth. The Industrial Revolution facilitated the rapid transportation of passengers as well as goods across large expanses of territory, mainly on the railroads that were constructed in all industrialized countries. It brought about a new awareness of the position of workers in the economic system, and it unleashed powerful political forces intended to improve the lot of these workers.

The Industrial Revolution played a crucial role in redefining and reshaping the West. Until the late nineteenth century industrialization took place only in Western nations. During that century "the West" gradually became identified with countries that had industrial economies. When some non-Western countries introduced mechanized industry in the twentieth century, largely in imitation of Western example, the geographical boundaries of the West underwent a significant alteration.

The main question this chapter sets out to answer is why this fundamental transformation of Western civilization began in Europe in the late eighteenth and nineteenth centuries. The individual sections of the chapter will address the following questions:

- **What do historians mean when they refer to the Industrial Revolution of the late eighteenth and nineteenth centuries?**
- **What social and economic changes made industrial development possible?**
- **How did industrialization spread from Great Britain to the European continent and America?**
- **What were the economic, social, and cultural effects of the Industrial Revolution?**
- **What was the relationship between the growth of industry and Britain's dominance in trade and imperial strength during the middle years of the nineteenth century?**

The Nature of the Industrial Revolution

- **What do historians mean when they refer to the Industrial Revolution of the late eighteenth and nineteenth centuries?**

The Industrial Revolution was a series of economic and social changes that took place in Great Britain during the late eighteenth and early nineteenth centuries and on the European continent and in the United States after 1815. Some economic historians claim that the use of the term *revolution,* which suggests radical and abrupt change, is misleading in this context, because the economic and social changes to which the term refers occurred gradually over a long period of time. Even so, the term is still appropriate because it conveys the radical nature and profound significance of the changes it identifies. Like the Scientific Revolution of the seventeenth century, which also took place gradually, the Industrial Revolution reshaped Western civilization.

The Industrial Revolution consisted of four closely related developments: the introduction of new industrial technology, the utilization of mineral sources of energy, the concentration of labor in factories, and the development of new methods of transportation.

New Industrial Technology

The Industrial Revolution ushered in the machine age, and to this day machines are the most striking feature of modern industrial economies. In countries that have become industrialized, virtually every human-made commodity can be mass-produced by some kind of machine. In the late eighteenth century such machines were novelties, but their numbers increased dramatically in the early nineteenth century. For example, the power loom, a machine used for weaving cloth, was invented in Britain in 1787 but not put into widespread use until the 1820s. By 1836 there were more than 60,000 power looms in just one English county.

Machines became so common in Britain that machine making itself became a major industry, supplying its products to other manufacturers rather than to individual consumers. Machines were introduced in the textile, iron, printing, papermaking, and engineering industries and were used in every stage of manufacture. Machines extracted minerals that were used as either raw materials or sources of energy, transported those materials to the factories, saved time and labor in the actual manufacturing of commodities, and carried the finished products to market. Eventually machines were used in agriculture itself, facilitating both the plowing of fields and the harvesting of crops.

The most significant of the new machines, which changed the entire industrial process, were those used for spinning and weaving in the textile industry and the steam engine, first used in mining and the iron industry. These pieces of machinery became almost synonymous with the Industrial Revolution, and their invention in the 1760s appropriately marks its beginning.

Textile Machinery

Until the late eighteenth century, the production of textiles throughout Europe, which involved both the spinning of yarn and the weaving of cloth, was done entirely by hand, on spinning wheels and hand looms respectively. This was the practice for wool, which was the main textile produced in Europe during the early modern period, as well as for a new material, cotton, which became immensely popular in the early eighteenth century, mainly because of its greater comfort. The demand for cotton yarn was greater than the quantities spinners could supply. To meet this demand a British inventor, James Hargreaves, in 1767 constructed a new machine, the spinning jenny, which greatly increased the amount of cotton yarn that could be spun and thus made available for weaving. The original jenny, a hand machine used in the homes of spinners, consisted of only eight spindles, but it later accommodated as many as 120.

The spinning of yarn on the jenny required a stronger warp, the yarn that ran lengthwise on a loom. A power-driven machine, the water frame, introduced by the barber and wigmaker Richard Arkwright in 1769, made the production of this stronger warp possible. In 1779 Samuel Crompton, using tools he had purchased with his earnings as a fiddle player at a local theater, combined the jenny and the frame in one machine, called the mule. Crompton worked on his machine only at night, in order to keep it secret, and the strange noises that came out of his workshop made his neighbors think his house was haunted. The mule, which could spin as much as 300 times the amount of yarn produced by one spinning wheel, became the main spinning machine of the early Industrial Revolution. Both the water frame and the mule required power, and that requirement led to the centralization of the textile industry in large rural mills located near rivers so that their water wheels could drive the machinery.

The tremendous success of the mule eventually produced more yarn than the weavers could handle on their hand

Broadlie Mill in the 1790s

The earliest textile mills were built in the rural areas, near rivers that supplied water power. This mill was built on the Broadlie farm, near the village of Neilston in southwestern Scotland, about twelve miles from Glasgow. The power to run the mill came from the Levern River. By 1815 there were six cotton mills in the area, supporting a community of about 1,500 workers. Housing for the workers, including some houses for single women, was constructed near the mills.

looms. Edmund Cartwright, an Oxford-educated clergyman, supported by monies from his heiress wife, addressed that need with the invention of the power loom in 1787. In that same year he put his new invention to use in a weaving mill he built near the town of Doncaster. The power loom, like the spinning jenny, the water frame, and the mule, met a specific need within the industry. It also gave the producer a competitive advantage by saving time, reducing the cost of labor, and increasing production. Two power looms run by a 15-year-old boy, for example, could produce more than three times what a skilled hand loom weaver could turn out in the same time using only the old hand device, the flying shuttle. The net effect of all these machines was the production of more than 200 times as much cotton cloth in 1850 as in 1780. By 1800 cotton became Britain's largest industry, producing more than 20 percent of the world's cloth, and by 1850 that percentage had risen to more than 50 percent. Indeed, by midcentury, cotton accounted for 70 percent of the value of all British exports.

The Steam Engine

The steam engine was even more important than the new textile machinery because it was used in almost every stage of the productive process, including the operation of textile machinery itself. The steam engine was invented by a Scottish engineer, James Watt, in 1763. It represented an improvement over the engine invented by Thomas Newcomen in 1709, which had been intended mainly to drain water from deep mines. The problem with Newcomen's engine was that the steam, which was produced in a cylinder heated by coal, had to be cooled in order to make the piston return, and the process of heating and cooling had to be repeated for each stroke of the piston. The engine was therefore inefficient and expensive to operate. Watt created a separate chamber where the steam could be condensed without affecting the heat of the cylinder. The result was a more efficient and cost-effective machine that could provide more power than any other source. Watt's pride in his invention was matched only by his pride in his Scottish nationality. Upon receiving a patent for the new device, he boasted, "This was made by a Scot."

After designing the steam engine, Watt teamed up with a Birmingham metal manufacturer, Matthew Boulton, to produce it on a large scale. Boulton provided the capital necessary to begin this process and to hire the skilled laborers to assemble the machines. He also had ambitious plans for marketing the new invention throughout the world. "It would not be worth my while to make for three countries only," Boulton said, "but I find it well worth my while to make for the whole world."

The steam engine soon became the workhorse of the Industrial Revolution. Not only did it pump water from mines, but it helped raise minerals such as iron ore that were extracted from those mines. It provided the intense blast of heat that was necessary to resmelt pig iron into cast iron, which in turn was used to make industrial machinery, buildings, bridges, locomotives, and ships. Once the engine was equipped with a rotating device, it was used to drive the factory machinery in the textile mills, and it eventually powered the railroad locomotives that carried industrial goods to market.

The widespread adoption of steam power came fairly late in the Industrial Revolution. Only in the 1840s and 1850s, after its efficiency had been greatly improved, did it become the main source of energy in the textile industry. Until then rural water power was the preferred method of running the cotton mills. Only after the introduction of coal-driven steam power did the factories locate in the cities, especially those of northern England, such as Manchester. The 1840s and 1850s were also the decades when the railroads, using the steam locomotive invented by the English engineer George Stephenson in 1815, began to crisscross the European continent. By midcentury the steam engine had become the predominant symbol of the Industrial Revolution.

CHRONOLOGY

Technological Innovations of the Industrial Revolution

1763	James Watts's rotative steam engine
1767	James Hargreaves's spinning jenny
1769	Richard Arkwright's water frame
1779	Samuel Crompton's mule
1787	Edmund Cartwright's power loom
1815	George Stephenson's steam locomotive
1846	Elias Howe's sewing machine

Mineral Sources of Energy

Until the late eighteenth century, most economic activity, including the transportation of goods, was powered by either humans or beasts. Either people tilled the soil themselves, using a spade, or they yoked oxen to pull a plow. Either they carried materials and goods on their backs or they used horses to transport them. In either case the energy for these tasks came ultimately from organic sources, the food that was needed to feed farmers or their animals. If workers needed heat, they had to burn an organic material, wood or charcoal, to produce it. The amount of energy that could be generated in a particular region was therefore limited by its capacity to produce sufficient wood, charcoal, or food. By the middle of the eighteenth

Philippe Jacques de Loutherbourg, *Coalbrookdale by Night* (1801)
This painting depicts the intense heat produced by the coal bellows used to smelt iron in Coalbrookdale, an English town in the Severn Valley that was one of the key centers of industrial activity at the beginning of the nineteenth century.

century, for example, the forests in Britain were no longer capable of producing sufficient quantities of charcoal for use in the iron industry.

Organic sources of energy were of course renewable, in that new crops could be grown and forests replanted, but the long periods of time that these processes took, coupled with the limited volume of organic material that could be extracted from an acre of land, made it difficult to sustain economic growth. The only viable alternatives to these organic sources of energy before the eighteenth century were those that tapped the forces of nature: windmills, which were used mainly in the Netherlands for purposes of field drainage, and water wheels, which were driven by water pressure from river currents, waterfalls, or human-made channels that regulated the flow of water. The potential of those natural sources of energy was both limited and difficult to harness, and it could be tapped only in certain locations or at certain times. Moreover, those sources could not produce heat.

The decisive change in the harnessing of energy for industrial purposes was the successful use of minerals, originally coal but in the twentieth century oil and uranium as well, as the main sources of energy used in the production and transportation of goods. These minerals were not inexhaustible, as the decline of coal deposits in Europe during the twentieth century has shown, but the supplies could last for centuries, and they were much more efficient than any form of energy produced from organic materials, including charcoal and peat. Coal produced the high combustion temperatures necessary to smelt iron, and unlike charcoal it was not limited by the size of a region's forests. Coal therefore became the key to the expansion of the British iron industry in the nineteenth century. That industry's dependence on coal was reflected by the relocation of iron works from the mines that supplied the ore itself to the coal fields that supplied the energy. Coal also became the sole source of heat for the new steam engine.

As the Industrial Revolution progressed, it relied increasingly on coal as its main fuel. The change, however, occurred gradually. In 1830 a majority of factories still used water power, and steam power did not realize its most spectacular increases until after 1870. Nevertheless, largely because of the demands of the mining, textile, and metal industries, coal mining became a major industry itself with an enormous labor force. By 1850 British mines employed about 5 percent of the entire national workforce. These miners were just as instrumental as textile workers in making Britain an industrial nation.

The Growth of Factories

One of the most enduring images of the Industrial Revolution is that of the large factory, filled with workers laboring amid massive machinery driven by either water or steam power. Mechanized factory production evolved out of forms of industry that had emerged only during the early modern period (1500–1750). In the Middle Ages virtually all industry in Europe was undertaken by skilled craftsmen who belonged to urban guilds. These artisans, working either by themselves or with the assistance of apprentices or journeymen, produced everything from candlesticks and hats to oxcarts and beds. During the early modern period the urban craftsman's shop gave way to two different types of industrial workplaces, the rural cottage and the large handicraft workshop. Both of these served as halfway houses to the large factory.

Beginning in the sixteenth century, entrepreneurs began employing families in the countryside to spin and weave cloth and make nails and cutlery. By locating industry in the countryside the entrepreneurs were able to escape the regulations imposed by the guilds regarding employment and the price of finished products. They also paid lower wages, because the rural workers, who also received an income from farming, were willing to work for less than the residents of towns. Another attraction of rural industry was that all the members of the family, including children, participated in the process. In this "domestic system" a capitalist entrepreneur provided the workers with the raw materials and sometimes the tools they needed. He later paid them a fixed rate for each finished product. The entrepreneur was also responsible for having the finished cloth dyed and for marketing the commodities in regional towns.

Rural household industry was widespread not only in certain regions of Britain but also in most European countries. In the late eighteenth century it gradually gave way to the factory system. The great attraction of factory production was mechanization, which became cost-efficient only when it was introduced in a central industrial workplace. In factories, moreover, the entrepreneur could reduce the cost of labor and transportation, exercise tighter control over the quality of goods, and increase productivity by concentrating workers in one location. Temporary labor shortages sometimes made the transition from rural industry to factory production imperative.

DOCUMENT

Adam Smith Describes the Division of Labor

Adam Smith, a Scottish economist who is considered the founder of the classical school of economics, was the great theorist of modern laissez-faire *capitalism. In* An Inquiry into the Nature and Causes of the Wealth of Nations *(1776), he challenged the mercantilist assumption that there was only a fixed supply of wealth for which nations had to compete. He also argued that in an unregulated economy, the pursuit of self-interest would work in the interest of the public welfare. In this selection Smith discusses the division of labor. Smith wrote* The Wealth of Nations *during the very early stages of industrialization. The place of production that he uses in this example is not a large mechanized factory but a small urban workshop, often referred to as a manufactory.*

To take an example, therefore, from a very trifling manufacture; but one in which the division of labour has been very often taken notice of, the trade of the pin-maker; a workman not educated to this business (which the division of labour has rendered a distinct trade), nor acquainted with the use of the machinery employed in it (to the invention of which the same division of labour has probably given occasion), could scarce, perhaps, with his utmost industry, make one pin in a day, and certainly could not make twenty. But in the way in which this business is now carried on, not only the whole work is a peculiar trade, but it is divided into a number of branches, of which the greater part are likewise peculiar trades. One man draws out the wire, another straits it, a third cuts it, a fourth points it, a fifth grinds it at the top for receiving the head; to make the head requires two or three distinct operations; to put it on is a peculiar business, to whiten the pins is another; it is even a trade by itself to put them into the paper; and the important business of making a pin is in this manner, divided into about eighteen distinct operations, which in some manufactories, are all performed by distinct hands, though in others the same man will sometimes perform two or three of them. I have seen a small manufactory of this kind where ten men only were employed, and where some of them consequently performed two or three distinct operations. But though they were very poor and indifferently accommodated with the necessary machinery, they could, when they exerted themselves, make about twelve pounds of pins a day. There are in a pound upwards of four thousand pins of a middling size. Those ten persons, therefore, could make among them upwards of forty-eight thousand pins in a day. Each person, therefore making a tenth part of forty-eight thousand pins, might be considered as making four thousand eight hundred pins in a day.

Source: From Adam Smith, *An Inquiry into the Nature and Causes of the Wealth of Nations,* 5th Edition, 1789, Book I, Chapter 1.

Mule Spinning
A large mechanized spinning mill in northern England, about 1835. The workers did not require any great skill to run the machinery.

The second type of industrial workplace that emerged during the early modern period was the large handicraft workshop. Usually located in the towns and cities, rather than in the countryside, these workshops employed relatively small numbers of people with different skills who worked collectively on the manufacture of a variety of items, such as pottery and munitions. The owner of the workshop supplied the raw materials, paid the workers' wages, and gained a profit from selling the finished products.

The large handicraft workshop made possible a division of labor°—the assignment of one stage of production to each worker or group of workers. The effect of the division of labor on productivity was evident even in the manufacture of simple items such as buttons and pins. In *The Wealth of Nations* (1776), the economist Adam Smith (1723–1790) used a pin factory in London to illustrate how the division of labor could increase per capita productivity from no more than twenty pins a day to the astonishing total of 4,800.

Like the cottages engaged in rural industry, the large handicraft workshop eventually gave way to the mechanized factory. The main difference between the workshop and the factory was that the factory did not require a body of skilled workers. When production become mechanized, the worker's job was simply to tend to the machinery. The only skill factory workers needed was manual dexterity to operate the machinery. Only those workers who made industrial machinery remained craftsmen or skilled workers in the traditional sense of the word.

With the advent of mechanization, factory owners gained much tighter control over the entire production process. Indeed, they began to enforce an unprecedented discipline among their workers, who had to accommodate themselves to the boredom of repetitive work and a timetable set by the machines. Craftsmen who had been accustomed to working at their own pace now had to adjust to an entirely new and more demanding schedule. "While the engine runs," wrote one critical contemporary, "the people must work—men, women, and children yoked together with iron and steam. The animal machine—breakable in the best case, subject to a thousand sources of suffering—is chained fast to the iron machine which knows no suffering and no weariness."[2]

Despite the growth and development of the factory system, the factory did not become the most common type of industrial workplace until the early twentieth century. In Britain, Germany, France, and the United States most manufacturing continued to take place in handicraft workshops in the cities or in rural households. Indeed, many of the industries that became mechanized spawned a variety of secondary crafts and trades, such as the dyeing and finishing of cloth and the sewing of clothes, which were conducted mainly in rural households.

New Methods of Transportation

As industry became more extensive and increased its output, transport facilities, such as roads, bridges, canals, and eventually railroads, grew in number and quality. Increased industrial productivity has always depended on efficient movement of raw materials to places of production and transportation of finished products to the market. During the early phase of the Industrial Revolution in Britain, water transportation supplied most of these needs. A vast network of navigable rivers and human-made canals, eventually more than 4,000 miles in length, was used to transport goods in areas that did not have access to the coast. The canals that were built after 1760, with their systems of locks and their aqueducts spanning roads and rivers, were a product of the technology that the Scientific Revolution had made possible. For routes that could not be reached by water, the most common method of transportation was by horse-drawn carriages on newly built turnpikes or toll roads, many of them made of stone so that they were passable even in wet weather.

The most significant innovation in transport during the nineteenth century was the railroad. Introduced as the Industrial Revolution was gaining momentum, the railroad provided quick, cheap transportation of heavy materials such as coal and iron over long distances. Its introduction in Britain during the 1820s and throughout Europe and America during the following decades serves as one of the best illustrations of the transition from an economy based on organic sources of energy to one based on mineral sources of energy. Driven by coal-burning, steam-powered locomotives, the railroads freed transport from a dependence on animal power, especially the horses that were used to pull coaches along turnpikes, barges along canals, and even carts along parallel tracks in mines. Railroads rapidly became the main economic thoroughfares of the industrial economy. They linked towns and regions that earlier had not been easily accessible to each other. They also changed the travel habits of Europeans by making it possible to cover distances in one-fifth the time it took by coach.

The construction and operation of railroads became a major new industry, employing thousands of skilled and unskilled workers and providing opportunities for investment and profit. The industry created an unprecedented demand for iron and other materials used to build and equip locomotives, tracks, freight cars, passenger cars, and signals, thus giving a tremendous boost to the iron industry and the metalworking and engineering trades. By the 1840s the railroads had become the main stimulus to economic growth throughout western Europe and the United States. Transport in industrialized economies continues to experience frequent innovation. During the twentieth century, for example, new methods of transportation, including automobiles, airplanes, and high-speed rails, have sustained economic growth in all industrialized countries, and like the railroads they have become major industries themselves.

Transport facilities, unlike factories, can seldom be built entirely by their individual owners. The cost of building locomotives and laying railroad tracks is almost always too great to come from the profits accumulated in the normal conduct of one's business. The funds for these facilities must come from either private investment, governments, or international financial institutions. In Britain the capital for

The Stockton and Darlington Railway

A locomotive and two cars used on the first major railroad in Britain, which opened in 1825. The railroad carried materials and goods to and from towns producing iron in the northern counties of England.

the railroads came entirely from individual investors. In the United States, which built the world's largest railroad system in the nineteenth century, most of the capital also came from private investment, but many state and city governments helped finance early railroads. In other industrialized countries, governments played a more important role. In Belgium, which was the second European country to experience an Industrial Revolution, and in Russia, which was one of the last, the governments of those countries assumed the responsibility for building a national railroad system.

Conditions Favoring Industrial Growth

- **What social and economic changes made industrial development possible?**

The immediate causes of the Industrial Revolution were the competitive pressures that encouraged technological innovation, the transition to coal power, the growth of factories, and the building of the railroads. These developments, however, do not provide a full explanation for this unprecedented economic transformation. Certain social and economic conditions were present in Britain that allowed industrialization to progress—a large population, improved agricultural productivity, the accumulation of capital, a group of people with scientific knowledge and entrepreneurial skill, and sufficient demand for manufactured goods. In this section we will look at the historical experience of Great Britain, which was the first country to industrialize, to see how these conditions made industrial economic development possible.

Population Growth

Industrialization requires a sufficiently large pool of labor to staff the factories and workshops of the new industries. One of the main reasons why the Industrial Revolution occurred first in Britain is that its population during the eighteenth century increased more rapidly than that of any country in continental Europe. Between 1680 and 1820 the population of England more than doubled, while that of France grew at less than one-third that rate, and that of the Dutch Republic hardly grew at all. One of the reasons this growth took place was that famines, which had occurred periodically throughout the early modern period, became less frequent during the eighteenth century. The last great famine in Britain took place in 1740, only a generation before industrialization began. There was also a decrease in mortality from epidemic diseases, especially typhus, influenza, and smallpox. Bubonic plague, which had decimated the European population periodically since the fourteenth century, struck England for the last time in the Great Plague of London of 1665. It made its last European appearance at Marseilles in 1720 but did not spread beyond the southern parts of France.

Increase in European Population, 1680–1820

Population Totals (millions)	1680	1820
France	21.9	30.5
Italy	12.0	18.4
Germany	12.0	18.1
Spain	8.5	14.0
England	4.9	11.5
Netherlands	1.9	2.0
Western Europe	71.9	116.5

Percentage Growth Rates, 1680–1820	
England	133%
Spain	64
Italy	53
Germany	51
France	39
Netherlands	8
Western Europe	73

Source: E. A. Wrigley, "The Growth of Population in Eighteenth-Century England: A Conundrum Resolved," *Past and Present* 98 (1983): 122.

Even more important than this reduction in mortality was an increase in fertility. More people were marrying, and at a younger age, which increased the birth rate. The spread of rural industry seems to have encouraged this early-marriage pattern. Wage-earning textile workers tended to marry a little earlier than agricultural workers, probably because wage earners did not have to postpone marriage to inherit land or to become self-employed, as was the case with farm workers.

This increase in population facilitated industrialization in two ways. First, it increased demand for the goods that were being manufactured in large quantities in the factories. The desire for these products, especially the new cottons, played an important role in enlarging the domestic market for manufactured goods, as we shall see shortly. Second, it increased the supply of labor, freeing a substantial portion of the population for industry, especially for factory labor. At the same time, however, this increase was not so large as to have had a negative effect on industrialization, as it did in a number of underdeveloped countries in the twentieth century. If population growth is too rapid, it can lead to declining incomes, put pressure on agriculture to feed more people than is possible, and prevent the accumulation of wealth. Most important, it can discourage factory owners from introducing costly machinery, because if labor is plentiful and cheap, it might very well cost less for workers to produce the same volume of goods by hand. Industrialization therefore requires a significant but not too rapid increase in population—the exact scenario that occurred in Britain during the eighteenth century.

Agricultural Productivity

Between 1700 and 1800 British agriculture experienced a revolution, resulting in a substantial increase in productivity. A major reason for this increase was the consolidation of all the land farmed by one tenant into compact fields. During the Middle Ages and most of the early modern period, each tenant on a manorial estate leased and farmed strips of land that were scattered throughout the estate. The decisions regarding the planting and harvesting of crops in these open fields were made collectively in the manorial court. Beginning in the sixteenth century, some of the wealthier tenants on these estates agreed to exchange their strips of land with their neighbors in order to consolidate their holdings into large compact fields, whose boundaries were defined by hedges, bushes, or walls. The main benefit of this process of enclosure° was that it allowed individual farmers to exercise complete control over the use of their land. In the eighteenth and nineteenth centuries the number of these enclosures increased dramatically, as the British Parliament passed legislation that divided entire estates into a number of enclosed fields. This legislation benefited all landowners, including the members of the aristocracy who passed the legislation.

With control of their lands, farmers could make them more productive. The most profitable change was to introduce new crop rotations, often involving the alternation of grains such as rye or barley with root crops such as turnips or grasses such as clover. These new crops and grasses restored nutrients to the soil and therefore made it unnecessary to let fields lie fallow once every three years. Farmers also introduced a variety of new fertilizers and soil additives that made harvests more bountiful. Farmers who raised sheep took advantage of discoveries regarding scientific breeding that improved the quality of their flocks.

More productive farming meant that fewer agricultural workers were required to feed the population. This made it possible for more people to leave the farms to work in the factories and mines. The expanded labor pool of industrial workers, moreover, was large enough that factory owners did not have to pay workers high wages; otherwise the prospect of industrializing would have lost much of its appeal. The hiring of children and women to work in the factories and mines also kept the labor pool large and the costs of labor low.

Capital Formation and Accumulation

The term capital° refers to all the assets used in production. These include the factories and machines that are used to produce other goods (fixed capital) as well as the raw materials and finished products that are sent to market (circulating capital). Other forms of capital are the railroads and barges used for transporting raw materials to the place of production and finished products to market. Mechanized industry involves the extensive and intensive use of capital to do the work formerly assigned to human beings. An industrial economy therefore requires large amounts of capital, especially fixed capital.

Capital more generally refers to the money that is necessary to purchase these physical assets. This capital can come from a number of different sources: It can come from individuals, such as wealthy landlords, merchants, or industrialists who invest the profits they have accumulated in industrial machinery or equipment. In many cases the profits derived from industrial production are reinvested in the firm itself. Alternatively, capital can come from financial institutions in the form of loans. Very often a number of individuals make their wealth available to an industrial firm by buying shares of stock in that company's operations. This of course is the main way in which most capital is accumulated today. In countries that have only recently begun to industrialize in Latin America and Southeast Asia, capital often comes from public sources, such as governments, or from international institutions, such as the International Monetary Fund.

In Great Britain the capital that was needed to achieve industrial transformation came almost entirely from private sources. Some of it was raised by selling shares of stock to people from the middle and upper levels of society, but an even larger amount came from merchants who engaged in domestic and international trade, landowners who profited from the production of agricultural goods (including those who owned plantations in America), and the industrial entrepreneurs who owned mines, ironworks, and factories. In Britain, where all three groups were more successful than in other parts of Europe, the volume of capital made available from these sources was substantial. These people could invest directly in industrial machinery and mines or, more commonly, make their wealth available to others indirectly in the form of loans from banks where they kept their financial assets.

Banks supplied a considerable amount of the funds necessary for industrialization. In Britain the possibilities for such capital were maximized in the late eighteenth century when financial institutions offered loans at low interest rates and when the development of a national banking system made these funds readily available throughout the country, especially in the new industrial cities such as Leeds, Sheffield, and Manchester. The number of English banks went from a mere dozen in 1750 to more than 300 in 1800. Many bankers had close ties with industrialists, thereby facilitating the flow of capital from the financial to the industrial sector of the economy. Banks played an even more central role in the industrialization of Germany, which was economically not as advanced as Britain and less capable, therefore, of generating capital through the accumulation of profits.

Technological Knowledge and Entrepreneurship

The process of industrialization involves the application of technological knowledge to the manufacturing process. It also involves entrepreneurship, the ability to make business ventures profitable. The mechanization of industry demanded scientifically trained people not only to introduce new forms of machinery but also to mass-produce that machinery for other manufacturers. The development of new modes of transportation required the skill of an entire class of civil engineers who could design and construct locomotives, ships, canals, railroads, and bridges. At the same time, industrialization required a group of business experts who knew how to run the factories and market their products. These requirements help explain why countries that are industrializing today often import technological and financial personnel from other countries to assist them in the process of industrialization and take steps to train and educate people from their own countries to carry on this work.

As we have discussed in Chapter 16, the geographical center of the Scientific Revolution shifted from the Mediterranean to the North Atlantic, especially to England, in the late seventeenth century. At the same time, England took the lead in making science an integral part of the nation's culture. In no other European country was so much attention given to the dissemination of scientific knowledge in public lectures, the meetings of local scientific societies, and the publication of scientific textbooks. Much of this popular scientific education focused on Newtonian mechanics and dynamics. These were precisely the areas of science that lent themselves most readily to technological application. The only area that was developed more fully in France than in Britain was thermodynamics, the branch of physics dealing with heat and its conversion into other forms of energy, such as steam power. To some extent the technological innovations and engineering achievements that took place in Britain during the Industrial Revolution can be considered the product of this unparalleled diffusion of scientific knowledge. Those who made these innovations also required extensive mathematical skill. The education given to British schoolchildren in the eighteenth century included more instruction in mathematics than was given in any other European country.

Industrial entrepreneurs, the people who actually ran the factories and superintended the industrial process, also needed a certain level of technological and mathematical skill, but their talents lay much more in their ability to run a variety of capitalist enterprises for a profit. Britain had no shortage of this type of talent in the eighteenth century. Even before the advent of mechanization there had developed an entire class of merchant capitalists who had organized the domestic system of rural industry or run the large handicraft workshops in London and other towns.

The invention and production of the steam engine readily illustrate the way in which technological and entrepreneurial skills reinforced and complemented each other. The partnership between the Scotsman James Watt, who invented the steam engine, and the Englishman Matthew Boulton represented a dynamic British alliance of science and capitalism. Of the two men, Watt had more scientific and mathematical knowledge, having taught himself geometry and trigonometry as well as having read textbooks on mechanics. He was familiar with the work of Joseph Black, the chemist at the University of Glasgow who studied steam, and he had acquired a knowledge of scientific instruments from his father's business as an outfitter of ships. Even though he was not an academic, he thought he was as smart as the famous French chemist Antoine Lavoisier. He was also a shrewd businessman who figured out various ways to use his knowledge of engineering to turn a profit and acquire a competitive advantage over others. Boulton was the classic eighteenth-century English entrepreneur who manufactured a variety of small metal objects from toys and buttons to teakettles and watch chains. His contribution to the partnership was assembling workers with the requisite skills to mass-produce the engine. Boulton was also scientifically knowledgeable, and both he and Watt were members of the Lunar Society of Birmingham, a voluntary scientific society in which they shared similar interests. Both men thought of themselves as scientists, just as both of them acted as entrepreneurs.

Demand from Consumers and Producers

The conditions for industrialization that we have discussed so far all deal with supply°, that is, the amounts of capital, labor, food, and skill that are necessary to support the industrial process. The other side of the economic equation is demand°, that is, the desire of consumers to purchase industrial goods and of producers to acquire raw materials and machinery. Much of the extraordinary productivity of the Industrial Revolution arose from the demand for industrial products. Many of the technological innovations that occurred at the beginning of the revolution also originated as responses to the demand for more goods. For example, the demand for more cotton goods spurred the introduction of the spinning jenny, the water frame, and the mule. Likewise the demand for coal for industrial and domestic use led to the development of an efficient steam engine in order to drain mines so that those supplies of coal could be extracted.

During the early years of industrialization, only about 35 percent of all British manufactured goods were exported. This statistic indicates that as the Industrial Revolution was taking hold, the domestic market was still the main source of demand for industrial products. The demand was especially strong among the bourgeoisie. Within that group a "consumer revolution" had taken place during the eighteenth century. This revolution was based on an unprecedented desire to acquire goods of all sorts, especially clothing and housewares, such as pottery, cutlery, furniture, and curtains. The consumer revolution was fueled in large part by a desire to imitate the spending habits of the aristocracy. It was assisted by commercial manipulation of all sorts, including newspaper advertising, warehouse displays, product demonstrations, and the distribution of samples. An entirely new consumer culture arose, one in which women played a leading role. Advertisements promoting the latest female fashions, housewares, and children's toys became more common than those directed at adult male consumers. One ad in a local British paper in 1777, capitalizing on reports that mice were getting into ladies' hair at night, promoted "night caps made of silver wire so strong that no mouse or even a rat can gnaw through them." Advertisements therefore created a demand for new products as well as increasing the demand for those already on the market.

If this consumer revolution had been restricted to the middle class, it would have had only a limited effect on the Industrial Revolution. The bourgeoisie in the eighteenth century constituted at most only 20 percent of the entire population of Britain, and most of the goods they craved, with the exception of the pottery produced in Josiah Wedgwood's factories (which is still made today), were luxury items rather than the types of products that could be easily mass-produced. A strong demand for manufactured goods could develop only if workers were to buy consumer goods such as knitted stockings and caps, cotton shirts, earthenware, coffeepots, nails, candlesticks, watches, lace, and ribbon. The demand for these products came from small cottagers and laborers as well as the middle class. The demand for stockings for both men and women was particularly strong. In 1831 the author of a study of the impact of machinery on British society declared, "Two centuries ago not one person in a thousand wore stockings; one century ago not one person in five hundred wore them; now not one person in a thousand is without them."

Demand for manufactured products from the lower classes was obviously limited by the amount of money that wage earners had available for nonessential goods, and real wages did not increase very much, if at all, during the eighteenth century. Nevertheless the income of families in which the wife and children as well as the father worked for wages did increase significantly both during the heyday of rural industry and during the early years of industrialization. With these funds available, a substantial number of workers could actually afford to buy the products they desired. As the population increased, so too did this lower-class demand, which helped sustain an economy built around industrial production.

The Spread of Industrialization

- **How did industrialization spread from Great Britain to the European continent and America?**

The Industrial Revolution, like the Scientific Revolution of the sixteenth and seventeenth centuries, did not occur in all European countries at the same time. As we have seen, it began in Britain in the 1760s and for more than four decades was confined exclusively to that country (see Map 20.1). It eventually spread to other European and North American countries, where many industrial innovations were modeled on those that had taken place in Britain. Belgium, France, Germany, Switzerland, Austria, Sweden, and the United States all experienced their own Industrial Revolutions by the middle of the nineteenth century. Only in the late nineteenth century did countries outside the traditional boundaries of the West, mainly Russia and Japan, begin to industrialize. By the middle of the twentieth century, industrialization had become a truly global process, transforming the economies of a number of Asian and Latin American countries.

Great Britain and the Continent

Industrialization occurred on the European continent much later than it did in Great Britain. Only after 1815 did Belgium and France begin to industrialize on a large scale, and it was not until 1840 that Germany, Switzerland, and Austria showed significant signs of industrial growth. Other European countries, such as Italy and Spain, did not begin serious efforts in this direction until the late nineteenth century. It took continental European nations even longer to rival the economic strength of Britain. Germany, which emerged as Britain's main competitor in the late nineteenth century, did not match British industrial output until the twentieth century.

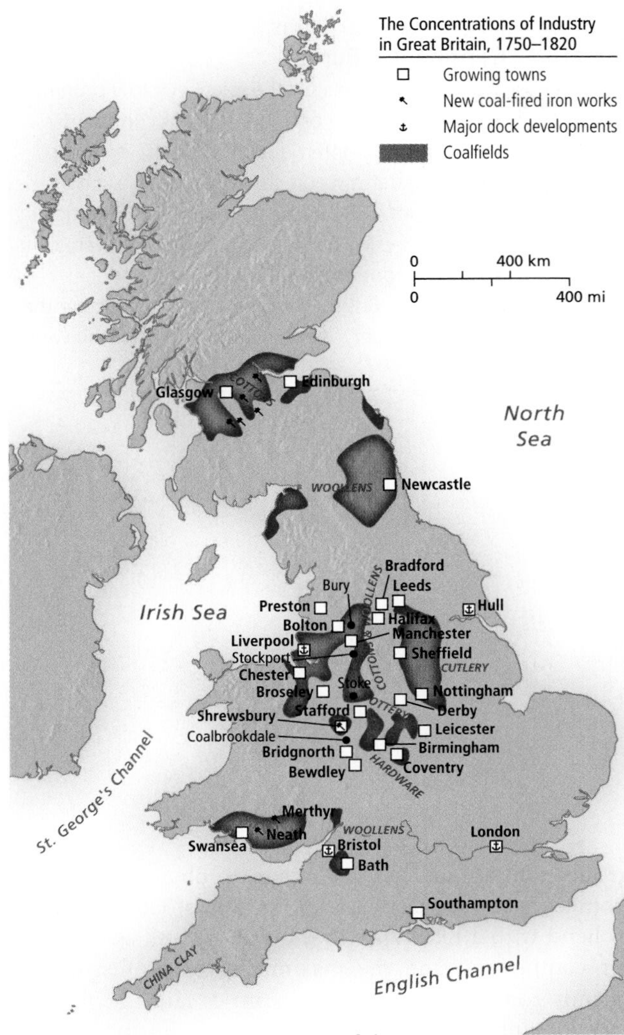

Map 20.1 The Concentrations of Industry in Great Britain, 1750–1820
The most heavily industrialized regions were in northern England, where the population of cities such as Manchester, Liverpool, and Sheffield grew rapidly.

Why did it take so long for other countries to industrialize? Virtually all of them had developed extensive rural industry in the late eighteenth century. The governments of European countries, in keeping with mercantilist philosophy, had a long tradition of encouraging the development of domestic industry. Population growth on the Continent during the late eighteenth century, while less dramatic than in Great Britain, should have been sufficient to stimulate consumer demand and increase the supply of labor. Overall economic growth in France during that time almost matched that of Great Britain. Scientific education, while not as widespread as in Britain, was hardly lacking, especially in France. Nonetheless, industrialization on the Continent, especially in heavy industry, lagged far behind that of Great Britain, and the process was for the most part painfully slow.

One explanation for the slower development of industrialization on the Continent relates to the political situations in those countries. Well into the nineteenth century, most continental European countries had numerous internal political barriers that could impede the transportation of raw materials and goods from one part of the country to another. In Germany, for example, which was not politically united until 1871, scores of small sovereign territorial units charged tariffs whenever goods crossed their territorial boundaries. Only in 1834 was a customs union, the *Zollverein,* created to eliminate some of these barriers. In France, which had achieved a formal territorial unity during the reign of Louis XIV, local rights and privileges impeded internal trade until the early nineteenth century. This political situation was aggravated by the relatively poor state of continental roads and the inaccessibility of many seaports from production sites.

The contrast between the situation on the Continent and that which prevailed in Great Britain is striking. After 1707, when Scotland was united to England and freedom of internal trade was established between the two countries, the United Kingdom of Great Britain constituted the largest free-trade zone in Europe. Thus raw materials and finished products could pass from one place within Great Britain to another, up to a distance of more than 800 miles, without payment of any internal customs or duties. The system of inland waterways was complete by 1780, and seaports were accessible from all parts of the country.

The industrial potential of many continental European countries was also weakened by the imposition of protective tariffs on goods imported from other countries. The purpose of this mercantilist policy was to develop national self-sufficiency and to maintain a favorable balance of trade, but it also had the negative effect of limiting economic growth. For example, in the Dutch Republic (the kingdom of the Netherlands after 1815) a long tradition of protecting established industries prevented that country from importing the raw materials and machines needed to develop new industries. Because protectionism invited retaliation from trading partners, it also tended to shrink the size of potential overseas markets. Britain adopted a policy of free trade during the 1840s, and it pressured other European countries to adopt the same policy.

A further obstacle to European industrialization was aristocratic hostility, or at least indifference, to industrial development. In Britain the aristocracy, which consisted of noblemen and gentry, were themselves often involved in capitalist enterprise and did not have the same suspicion of industry and trade that their counterparts in France and Spain often harbored. Many members of the British aristocracy, such as

Map 20.2 Customs Unions in Continental Europe

One of the reasons for the relatively slow progress of industrialization on the European continent was the existence of internal tariff barriers. This map shows the dates when customs unions, such as the *Zollverein* of 1834 in the German Confederation, were established or the customs barriers were eliminated. By contrast, all internal customs duties within Great Britain had been eliminated more than a century earlier when England and Scotland were united in 1707.

the entrepreneur "Turnip Townshend" (see Chapter 18), were agricultural capitalists who improved the productivity of their estates. Others were involved in mining. The Duke of Devonshire encouraged the exploitation of the copper mines on his estate, while the Duke of Bridgewater employed the engineer James Brindley to build a canal from the duke's coal mines in Worsley to Manchester in 1759. He later had Brindley extend the canal from Manchester to the mouth of the Mersey River, connecting the textile region of Manchester with the large northern industrial city of Liverpool.

One reason for the British aristocracy's support for economic growth was that many of its members, especially the gentry, rose into its ranks from other social and economic groups. These individuals tended to be sympathetic to the values of a commercial and an industrial society. The same attitude toward commerce and industry simply did not exist among the nobility in France before the revolution, much less among German *Junkers.* These groups had little connection with industrial or commercial society, whose values they held in very low regard. Consequently they rarely invested in industry.

Even among the European middle classes, the same type of competitive entrepreneurial spirit that was exhibited by men like Matthew Boulton seems to have been in large part lacking. Capitalism was by no means absent in European countries, but the conduct of business was characterized by greater caution and less willingness to obtain new capital from loans or the sale of stock to investors. This went hand in hand with a reluctance to innovate as well as a distaste for competition and the maximizing of profits. Consequently continental European countries failed to produce many counterparts to the captains of industry who had contributed much of the capital, technology, and entrepreneurial spirit to the Industrial Revolution in Britain.

A final reason for the slow industrialization of continental European countries was that they lacked the abundant raw materials that were readily accessible in Britain. The natural resources that Britain had in greatest quantities were coal and iron ore, both of which were indispensable to industrialization. At the same time British farms provided ample supplies of raw materials for the wool and leather industries. The French and the Germans had some coal deposits, but they were more difficult to mine, and they were not located near ocean ports. Continental countries also lacked the access to other raw materials that Britain could import through its vast trading network, and in particular from its overseas colonies. With a large empire on four continents and the world's largest merchant marine, Britain had abundant supplies of raw materials such as cotton as well as the capacity to import them cheaply and in large quantities. The greater difficulty European countries had in obtaining these raw materials did not prevent them from industrializing; it simply made the process slower.

Features of Continental Industrialization

During the first half of the nineteenth century, especially after 1830, Belgium, France, Switzerland, Germany, and Austria began to introduce machinery into the industrial process, use steam power in production, concentrate labor in large factories, and build railroads. This continental European version of the Industrial Revolution is usually described as an imitative process, one in which entrepreneurs or government officials simply tried to duplicate the economic success that Britain had achieved by following British example. Continental European nations did indeed rely to some extent on British industrial machinery. Some of them also relied on British skilled labor when they began to build their first factories and ironworks. In a few instances, in violation of British law, foreign agents actually smuggled blueprints, models, or machine parts out of Britain. British engineers, entrepreneurs, and managers were also occasionally hired to run British-style factories in France and Germany. But each European nation, responding to its own unique combination of political, economic, and social conditions, followed its own course of industrialization.

One distinctive feature of continental European industrialization was that once countries such as Belgium and Germany began to industrialize, their governments played a much more active role in encouraging and assisting in the process. In contrast to Britain, whose government allowed private industry to function with few economic controls, continental governments became active partners in the industrial process. They supplied capital for many economic ventures, especially the railroads and roads. In Prussia the state owned a number of manufacturing and mining enterprises. Many continental governments also imposed protective tariffs to prevent an influx of cheap British goods from underselling the products of their own fledgling industries. In a few cases continental European governments even provided financial support for investors in an effort to encourage capital formation. In some places, such as Austria, the state eliminated the regulations of urban guilds that had restricted industrial development in rural regions.

A second major feature of continental European industrialization was that banks, particularly in Germany and Belgium, played a central role in industrial development. This was necessitated by the low level of capital formation on the Continent and the reluctance of entrepreneurs to take risks by investing money themselves. Banks in Germany and Belgium played a particularly active role in stimulating industry. Drawing on the resources of both small and large investors, these corporate banks became in effect industrial banks, building railroads and factories themselves in addition to making capital available for a variety of industrial ventures.

A third distinct feature of continental European industrialization was that the railroads actually contributed to the beginning of industrial development. In Great Britain the railroads were introduced some sixty years after industrialization had begun and thus helped sustain a process of economic development that had been long afoot. By contrast the railroads on the Continent provided the basic infrastructure of its new economy and became a major stimulus to the development of all other industries. Railroads also gave continental European governments the ability to transport military troops quickly in time of war, which helps to explain why governments supported railroad construction with such enthusiasm. In Belgium, which was the first continental European nation to industrialize, the new government built a national railroad system during the 1830s and 1840s, not only to stimulate industry but also to unify the newly independent nation.

Of all the European countries that industrialized, only Belgium appears to have followed the British model closely by developing coal, iron, and textiles as the three main sectors of the new economy. Other countries tended to concentrate their activity in one specific area. France emphasized textiles, especially those such as worsted woolens that did not compete with British cottons. France's coal production and consumption never matched that of Great Britain or Belgium, and after 1850 it fell behind that of Germany as well. In 1860 France was importing 43 percent of its coal, and it was still relying on charcoal rather than coal to smelt pig iron. In Germany the main economic advances, which did not begin until 1850, occurred mainly in the area of heavy industry, that is, coal, iron, and engineering rather than

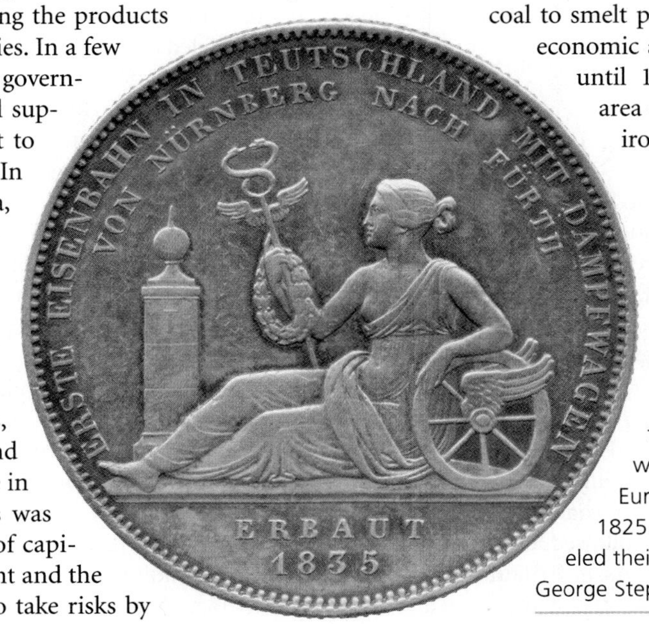

Medal Struck in 1835 to Commemorate the First German Railroad, from Nuremberg to Fürth
Industry is depicted as a female figure with her arm resting on a winged wheel. The first railroad in Europe had opened in England in 1825. German engineers had modeled their first locomotive on that of George Stephenson.

A Colossal Steam-Driven Hammer, Nicknamed "Fritz," Installed by Alfred Krupp at His Steelworks in Essen in 1861

Krupp's factory was located in the Ruhr region of Germany, the main center in that country for heavy industry.

textiles. Together with the United States, Germany began to offer the main economic competition to the British economy by the end of the nineteenth century.

Industrialization in the United States

Industrialization in the United States began during the 1820s, not long after Belgium and France had begun to experience their own industrial revolutions. It occurred first in the textile industry in New England, where factories using water power produced goods for largely rural markets. New England also began producing two domestic hardware products—clocks and guns—for the same market. Between 1850 and 1880 a second region between Pittsburgh and Cleveland became industrialized. This region specialized in heavy industry, especially steelmaking and the manufacture of large machinery, and it relied on coal for fuel.

American industrialization followed both British and continental European patterns. As in Britain and France, the development of cottage industry in the United States preceded industrialization. Most of the industrial machinery used in the United States during the nineteenth century was modeled on imports from Britain. The most significant American technological innovation before 1900 was the sewing machine, which was patented by Elias Howe in 1846 and then developed and improved upon by Isaac Singer in the 1850s. This new machine was then introduced in Europe, where it was used in the production of ready-to-wear garments.

The state played an ambivalent role in early American industrialization. The U.S. federal government, whose powers were greatly limited, especially during the early nineteenth century, followed a policy of nonintervention in the economy, similar to the policy followed by the British government. The individual states in America, however, played a much more active role, especially in facilitating the growth of railroads. One of the ironies of early industrialization is that Prussia, with its tradition of strong state government and its control of the mines, did far less to promote the building of railroads than did the individual states in America.

After 1865, when American industrialization began to spread rapidly across the entire country, American entrepreneurs made a distinctive contribution to the industrial process in the area of business organization, especially the operation of international firms. Toward the beginning of the twentieth century, American manufacturers streamlined the production process by introducing the assembly line, a division of labor in which the product passes from one operation to the next until it is fully assembled. The assembly line required the production of interchangeable parts, another American innovation, first used in the manufacture of rifles for the U.S. government.

Like Great Britain, the United States possessed vast natural resources, including coal. It also resembled Britain in the absence of governmental involvement in the process of industrialization. The main difference between the industrializations of the two countries is that during the nineteenth century labor in America was in relatively short supply. This placed workers in a more advantageous situation in dealing with their employers and prevented some of the horrors of early British industrialization from recurring on the other side of the Atlantic. Only with the influx of European immigrants in the late nineteenth century did the condition of American workers deteriorate and begin to resemble the early-nineteenth-century British pattern.

Industrial Regionalism

Although we have discussed the industrialization of entire nations, the process usually took place within smaller geographical regions. There had always been regional specialization in agriculture, with some areas emphasizing crops and others livestock. During the Industrial Revolution, however, entire economies acquired a distinctly regional character. Regional economies began to take shape during the days of the domestic system, when merchants employed families in certain geographical areas, such as Lancashire in England, to produce textiles. In these regions there was a close relationship between agricultural and industrial production, in that members of the same household participated in both processes. Related industries, such as those for finishing or dyeing cloth, also sprang up close to where the cotton or wool yarn was spun and the cloth woven.

As industrialization spread outside Britain, this regional pattern became even more pronounced. In France the centers of the textile industry were situated near the northeastern border near Belgium and in the area surrounding Lyons in the east-central part of the country. Both of these areas had attracted rural household industry before the introduction of textile machinery. In Germany the iron industry was centered in the Ruhr region, where most of the country's coal was mined. In the city of Essen on the Ruhr River the industrialist Alfred Krupp (1812–1887) established an enormous steelmaking complex that produced industrial machinery, railroad equipment, and guns for the Prussian army. Within the Habsburg Empire most industry was located in parts of Bohemia (now the Czech Republic).

The development of regional economies did not mean that markets were regional. The goods produced in one region almost always served the needs of people outside that particular area. Markets for most industrial goods were national and international, and even people in small agricultural villages created a demand for manufactured goods. The French iron industry, for example, was centered in the eastern part of the country, but it catered to the needs of the wealthier segments of its own and other European populations, as did the iron industry in the Ruhr region in Germany and the textile industry in the north of England.

The development of regional industrial economies helps to explain the striking contrast that persisted well into the twentieth century between the parts of countries that had become heavily industrialized and those that retained at least many of the appearances of a preindustrial life. In Britain and the rest of Europe industrial machinery and factories were not introduced into every village. Some areas remained exclusively agricultural, while others continued a tradition of rural industry. This pattern was particularly evident in France, where mechanized industry was concentrated in a limited number of centers in the northeastern half of the country. In 1870 more than two-thirds of the French population still lived in rural areas. As economic growth and industrial development continued, however, agricultural regions eventually began to lose their traditional character. Even if industry itself did not arrive, the larger industrial economy made its mark. Agriculture itself became mechanized, while railroads and other forms of mechanized transport integrated these areas in a national economy.

The Effects of Industrialization

- **What were the economic, social, and cultural effects of the Industrial Revolution?**

The Industrial Revolution had a profound impact on virtually every aspect of human life. It encouraged the growth of the population and the economy, affected the conditions in which people lived, changed family life, created new divisions within society, and transformed the traditional rural landscape. The changes that it brought about were most evident in Britain, but in time they have occurred in every country that has industrialized, including the United States.

Population and Economic Growth

The most significant of these changes was the sustained expansion of both the population and the economy. As we have seen, the Industrial Revolution in Britain was facilitated by a significant population increase in the eighteenth century. That growth had created a plentiful supply of relatively cheap labor, which in turn had helped to bring about a marked increase in industrial output. As industry grew, population kept pace, and each provided a stimulus to the growth of the other.

Most contemporary observers in the late eighteenth century did not believe that this expansion of both the population and the economy could be sustained indefinitely. The most pessimistic of these commentators was Thomas Malthus (1766–1834), an English cleric who wrote *An Essay on the Principle of Population* in 1798. Malthus argued that population had a natural tendency to grow faster than the food supply. Thus, unless couples exercised restraint by marrying late and producing fewer children, the population would eventually outstrip the resources necessary to sustain it, resulting in poor nutrition, famine, and disease. These "positive checks" on population growth, which sometimes were initiated or aggravated by war, would drive population back to sustainable levels. These checks would also end periods of economic expansion, which generally accompany increases in population. For example, in the fourteenth century the Black Death, which killed about one-third of the European population, also ended a significant period of economic growth. A similar but less severe contraction of the European population and economy occurred in the second half of the seventeenth century, marking the end of the economic expansion that had begun in the sixteenth century. In both these instances the increase in population put pressure on the food supply, raised the price of food, reduced employment, and lowered wages. The scarcity of food and the reduced nutritional levels that followed had made the population vulnerable to disease. If these demographic and economic patterns were to recur, we might expect that the significant expansion of the population and the economy that took place in eighteenth-century England would likewise reach its limits, just around the time that Malthus was writing.

Thomas Malthus, *Laws of Population Growth* (1798)

This predicted cyclical contraction of both the population and the economy did not take place. Europe for the first time in its history managed to escape the "Malthusian population trap." Instead of being sharply reduced after 1800, the population continued to expand at an ever-faster rate, doubling in Great Britain between 1800 and 1850 and following a similar pattern of rapid growth in all other countries that had industrialized. At the same time the economy, instead of contracting or collapsing, continued to grow and diversify.

It is not absolutely clear how Europe avoided the Malthusian trap in the nineteenth century. Part of the answer lies in the greater productivity of agriculture, which resulted from either private initiative, as in Britain, or governmental agrarian reforms, as in Austria. The importation of grain from central and eastern Europe also helped to feed the larger, more urbanized population. Improvements in medicine and public health reduced mortality during the nineteenth century, helping to maintain the size of the industrial population. But it was mainly developments in industry itself, especially the increased accumulation of capital, that kept Europe from succumbing to yet another cycle of depopulation and economic contraction. The accumulation of capital over a long period of time was so great that industry was able to employ large numbers of workers even during the 1790s and 1800s, when Europe was at war. Because they had income from wages, workers were willing to marry earlier and have larger families, and with lower food prices because of higher agricultural productivity they could afford to maintain a healthier diet and purchase more manufactured goods as well. Thus the Industrial Revolution itself, coupled with the changes in agriculture that accompanied it, proved Malthus wrong.

While the rapid growth of population in industrialized societies up until the late twentieth century is incontestable, the record of economic growth is not so clear. In order to claim that the Industrial Revolution has resulted in sustained economic growth, we have to take a broad view, looking at an overall pattern of growth and ignoring certain cyclical recessions and depressions. Nations that have industrialized, beginning with European countries in the nineteenth century, have all experienced a significant increase in both gross national product and per capita income over the long run. Although the contrast between the size of these industrial economies and those of preindustrial, agrarian countries is staggering, economic growth in industrialized countries was not always rapid or continuous. During the first six decades of industrialization in Britain, for example, economic growth was actually fairly slow, mainly because so much capital went into subsidizing the long war against France (1792–1802; 1804–1815). During this period Britain spent an average of 60 million English pounds, or 25 percent of its national income, on war. Nevertheless, there still was steady growth, and more important, the type of Malthusian economic contraction or collapse that had followed all previous periods of expansion did not occur. To that extent we can say that the Industrial Revolution has resulted in sustained economic growth in the West.

Standards of Living

Ever since the early years of the Industrial Revolution, a debate has raged over the effect of industrialization on the standard of living and the quality of life of the laboring population. The supporters of the two main schools of thought on this issue have been called the optimists and the

DOCUMENT

A French Geologist's Impressions of Birmingham, 1784

Barthélemy Faujas de Saint-Fond (1741–1819), a French scientist who rose to become professor of geology at the Muséum d'Histoire Naturelle in Paris, recorded the following impressions of the industrial city of Birmingham on a journey through England and Scotland in 1784. He was especially impressed by the variety of products made there, the number of workers in the various industries, and the dramatic increase in the city's population,

From the activity of its manufactures and its commerce, Birmingham is one of the most curious towns in England. If any one should wish to see in one comprehensive view the most numerous and varied industries, all combined in contributing to the arts of utility, of pleasure, and of luxury, it is hither that he must come. Here all the resources of industry, supported by the genius of invention and by mechanical skill of every kind are directed towards the arts and seem to be linked together to cooperate for their mutual perfection.

I know some travelers who have not given themselves the trouble to reflect on the importance and advantage of these kinds of manufactures in such a country as England have disapproved of most of these industrial establishments. I know that even an Englishman who has only taken a hasty, I would almost say an inconsiderate view of these magnificent establishments, William Gilpin, has said that it was difficult for the eye to be long pleased in the midst of so many frivolous arts, where a hundred men may be seen, whose labours are confined to the making of a tobacco box. But besides that this statement is exaggerated and ill-considered, the author has not deigned to cast his eyes over the vast works where steam-pumps are made, these astonishing machines, the perfecting of which does so much honour to the talents and knowledge of Mr. Watt; over the manufactories in constant activity making sheet-copper for sheathing ships' bottoms; over those of plate-tin and plate-iron, which make France tributary to England, nor over that varied and extensive hardware manufacture which employs to so much advantage more than thirty thousand hands and compels all Europe, and a part of the New World, to supply themselves from England, because all ironmongery is made here in greater perfection, with more economy, and in greater abundance than anywhere else. Once more I say with pleasure, and it cannot be said too often to Frenchmen, that it is the abundance of coal which has performed this miracle and has created, in the midst of a barren desert, a town with forty thousand inhabitants, who live in comfort and enjoy all the conveniences of life. . . .

The population of Birmingham has made such an advance that during the war with the United States of America, a war which weakened the resources of England, at least three hundred new homes were added annually to the town, and this rate doubled as soon as peace was concluded. A well-informed person assured me that this was true, and he showed me, during my stay in the town, a whole street which was in process of erection with such rapidity that, all the houses being built on a given plan at the same time, one could believe that the street would be entirely completed in less than two months.

Source: From Faujas de Saint-Fond, *A Journey through England and Scotland to the Hebrides in 1784* (1907), pp. 345–50.

pessimists. The optimists have always emphasized the positive effects of both the process of mechanization and the system of industrial capitalism that arose during the revolution. They have focused on the success that industrialized nations have achieved in escaping the Malthusian trap and in achieving sustained economic growth. The Industrial Revolution, so they argue, has resulted in an unprecedented rise in individual income, which has made it possible for the mass of a country's population to avoid poverty for the first time in human history. In the second half of the twentieth century many optimists claimed that the industrialization of Western nations provided a blueprint for African, Asian, and Latin American countries that wished to escape from the poverty of a predominantly agrarian economy relying on organic sources of energy.

The main yardstick that the optimists have used to measure the improvement in living standards is per capita real income, that is, income measured in terms of its actual purchasing power. Real income in Great Britain rose about 50 percent between 1770 and 1850 and more than doubled during the entire nineteenth century. This increase in income allowed workers to improve their diets as well as to purchase more clothing and other basic commodities. These improvements, however, did not affect the lives of most workers for a long period of time—in Great Britain not until 1820, about sixty years after the beginning of industrialization. The increases that occurred after that date, moreover, were only averages, concealing disparities among workers with different levels of skill. Only in the late nineteenth and twentieth centuries did industrialization raise the real income of all workers to a level that made the benefits of industrialization apparent.

Even if the pessimists concede a long-term increase in real income, it has never been substantial enough to persuade them that industrialization was on balance a positive good, at least for the working class. The pessimists have always stressed the negative effects of industrial development on the life of the lower classes. In their way of thinking, industrialization was an unmitigated disaster. The cause of this disaster in their eyes was not the process of mechanization but the system of industrial capitalism°. This form of capitalism is characterized by the ownership of factories by private individuals and by the employment of wage labor. Like earlier forms of mercantile and agricultural capitalism, it involved a systematic effort to reduce costs and maximize profits. In the pursuit of this goal, employers tried to keep wages as low as possible and to increase production through labor-saving technology, thus preventing workers from improving their lot.

Pessimists regarding the Industrial Revolution over the past two centuries have usually claimed a moral basis for their position. In this respect they follow in a tradition begun by the poet William Blake (1757–1827), who referred to the new factories as "satanic mills," and the socialist Friedrich Engels, who in *The Condition of the Working Class in England in 1844* (1845) accused the factory owners in England of mass murder and robbery. Much pessimist writing has also been used to support a program of social or political reform. The German social philosopher Karl Marx (1818–1883), with whom Engels often collaborated and whose views we shall discuss more fully in Chapter 21, used his critique of industrial capitalism to call for a communist revolution in which the working class would seize political power and acquire ownership of the means of production.

Most of the evidence that social critics have used to support the pessimist position has come from the early period of industrialization in Britain, when incomes were either stagnant or declining and when conditions in factories and industrial and mining towns were most appalling. It is difficult to measure these living standards statistically, but the weight of qualitative evidence suggests that they deteriorated during the nineteenth century. Working-class housing was makeshift and crowded, and there were few sanitary facilities. A new word, *slum*, was coined to refer to these poverty-stricken working-class neighborhoods. Poor drainage and raw sewage gave rise to a host of new hygienic problems, especially outbreaks of typhus and cholera. Between 1831 and 1866 four epidemics of cholera killed at least 140,000 people in Britain, most of whom lived in poorer districts.

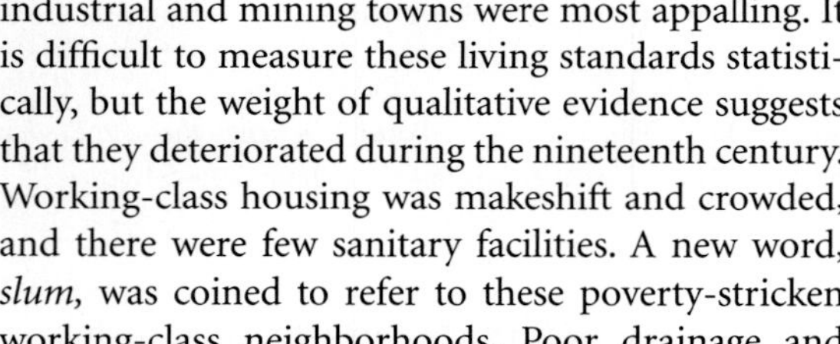

DOCUMENT

Chadwick's Report on Sanitary Conditions

The impact of industrialization and urbanization on the environment was no less harrowing. The burning of coal and the use of industrial chemicals polluted the urban atmosphere. The famous London fogs, which were actually smogs caused by industrial pollutants, presented a serious public health problem throughout the nineteenth century and did not begin to disappear until the introduction of strict regulations on the burning of coal in the 1950s.

While life in the city was bleak and unhealthy, working conditions in the factory were monotonous and demeaning. Forced to submit to a regimen governed by the operation of the machine, workers lost their independence as well as any control whatsoever over the products of their labor. They were required to work long hours, often fourteen hours a day, six days a week, with few breaks. Factory masters locked the doors during working hours, and they assessed fines for infractions such as opening a window when the temperature was unbearable, whistling while working, and having dirty hands while spinning yarn. Work in the mines was a little less monotonous, but it was physically more demanding and far more dangerous.

Women, Children, and Industry

During the early Industrial Revolution in Great Britain, large numbers of children and women were recruited into the workforce, especially the textile and mining industries. In the woolen industry in the western part of England, for example, female and child labor together accounted for 75 percent of the workforce. Children under age 13 made up 13 percent of the cotton factory workforce, and those under age 18 made up 51 percent. This pattern of employment reflects the demands of industrialists, who valued the hand skills and dexterity that children possessed as well as the greater amenability of both children and women to the discipline of factory labor. Some of the machines that were introduced into the textile industry in the late eighteenth century were specifically designed for women and children.

DOCUMENT

Industrial Society and Factory Conditions (early 1800s)

Female and child labor was both plentiful and cheap. Children received only one-sixth to one-third the wages of a grown man, while women generally took home only one-third to one-half of that adult male income. There was no lack of incentive for women and children to take one of these low-paying jobs. In a family dependent on wages, everyone needed to work, even when a large labor pool kept wages depressed.

The participation of both women and children in the workforce was not new. In an agricultural economy all members of the family contributed to the work, with parents and children, young and old, all being assigned specific roles. Rural industry also involved the labor of all members of the family. When people began working in the factories, however, they were physically separated from the home, making it impossible for workers to combine domestic and occupational labor.

As the workplace became distinct from the household, family life underwent a fundamental change, although this change did not occur immediately. During the early years of the Industrial Revolution, members of many families found employment together in the factories and mines. Factory owners also tried to perpetuate many aspects of family life in the new industrial setting, defining the entire factory community as an extended family, in which the factory owner played the paternalistic role. Gradually, however, mothers found it impossible to care for their youngest chil-

DOCUMENT

The Employment of Women

The German social philosopher Friedrich Engels (1820–1895) was one of the founders of modern socialism. He and Karl Marx collaborated in writing The Communist Manifesto *(1848), and he edited the final two volumes of Marx's* Capital *after Marx died. Having served as a manager in a factory in Manchester, Engels described these conditions throughout Britain in one of his earliest works,* The Condition of the Working Class in England in 1844 *(1845). He emphasized the exploitation and brutalization of the lower classes as they were turned into a wage-earning proletariat. In this passage Engels describes the negative effects of factory labor on women and the family.*

The employment of women at once breaks up the family; for when the wife spends twelve or thirteen hours every day in the mill, and the husband works the same length of time there or elsewhere, what becomes of the children? They grow up like weeds; they are put out to nurse for a shilling or eighteen pence a week, and how they are treated may be imagined. Hence the accidents to which little children fall victims in the factory districts multiply to a terrible extent. . . . Women often return to the mill three or four days after confinement, leaving the baby of course; in the dinner hour they must hurry home to feed the children and eat something, and what kind of suckling that can be is also evident. Lord Ashley repeats the testimony of several work women: "M.H., twenty years old, has two children, the youngest a baby, that is tended by the other, a little older. The mother goes to the mill shortly after five o'clock in the morning, and comes home at eight at night; all day the milk pours from her breasts so that her clothing drips with it". . . . The use of narcotics to keep the children still is fostered by this infamous system and has reached a great extent in the factory districts. Dr. Johns, Registrar in Chief for Manchester, is of opinion that this custom is the chief source of the many deaths from convulsions. The employment of the wife dissolves the family utterly and of necessity, and this dissolution in our present society, which is based upon the family, brings the most demoralising consequences for parents and children. A mother who has no time to trouble herself about her child, to perform the most ordinary loving services for it during its first year, who scarcely indeed sees it, can be no real mother to the child, must inevitably grow indifferent to it, treat it unlovingly like a stranger. The children who grow up under such conditions are utterly ruined for later family life, can never feel at home in the family which they themselves found, because they have always been accustomed to isolation, and they contribute therefore to the already general undermining of the family in the working-class.

Source: From Friedrich Engels, *The Condition of the Working Class in England in 1844,* translated by F. K. Wischnewtzky (London: S. Sonnenshein, 1892).

dren on the job, and most of them dropped out of the full-time workforce. The restriction of child labor by the British Factory Act of 1833 reinforced this trend and led to the establishment of a fairly common situation in which the male wage earner worked outside the home while his wife stayed home with the children. As one young girl who worked in the mines testified before a parliamentary commission investigation of child labor in 1842, "Mother takes care of the children."

As more and more mothers left the factories, the female workforce became increasingly dominated by those who were unmarried. The few female workers who were married with children either came from the very poorest segments of society or took jobs only because their husbands were ill or unemployed. Neither the pay these women received nor the jobs they performed gave them financial autonomy or social prestige. Becoming an independent wage earner meant little when women's wages were on average one-third to one-half those of men. The jobs assigned to women within industry, such as operating textile machinery, generally required the least skill. When men and women were employed in the same workplace, the women were invariably subordinated to the authority of male workers or foremen, thereby perpetuating the patriarchal patterns that prevailed in preindustrial society. The Industrial Revolution did nothing to improve the status of women, and even their exclusion from certain occupations, such as mining by an act of Parliament in 1842, only reinforced a new sexual division of labor that was even more rigid than that which had prevailed in preindustrial society.

Class and Class Consciousness

As Europe became more industrialized and urbanized, and as the system of industrial capitalism became more entrenched, writers began to use a new terminology to describe the structure of society. Instead of claiming that society consisted of a finely graded hierarchy of ranks to which individuals belonged by virtue of their occupations or their legal status, they divided society into three classes that could be distinguished by the type of property people owned and the manner in which they acquired it. At the top of this new social hierarchy was the aristocracy, consisting

Justice in History

The Sadler Committee on Child Labor

The widespread use of child labor in Britain during the early decades of the Industrial Revolution led to efforts by social reformers and members of Parliament to regulate the conditions under which children worked. Parliament passed legislation restricting the number of hours that all children could work in textile mills in 1819 and 1829, but neither of these laws was enforced effectively, and they did not apply to all industries. Complaints of inhumane treatment, moral degradation, and exploitation of child workers continued to surface. In 1831 Michael Sadler (1780–1835), a Tory member of the British Parliament, introduced a bill in Parliament to limit the number of hours that all children could work to ten hours per day. Like many social reformers, Sadler was inspired by what he considered his Christian duty to protect dependent members of the community.

Sadler chaired the committee to which his bill was referred. In order to muster support for the bill, Sadler held hearings in which child workers themselves came before the committee to report on the conditions under which they lived and worked. The success of his bill was by no means guaranteed. Many members of Parliament were deeply committed to the policy of *laissez-faire,* according to which the government should not intervene in the operation of the economy, treating it instead as a self-regulating machine. Sadler had to convince his colleagues that they should modify that policy in the case of children, on the grounds that the state was obliged to provide for the welfare of children when their parents were unable to do so. He also needed to make the members of Parliament and the broader public aware of the brutality of the conditions under which the children worked.

The hearings that took place were not a trial in the strict sense of the word, but they possessed many of the features of a judicial investigation, not unlike those conducted by grand juries in criminal cases. The committee's proceedings were intended to expose, condemn, and ultimately remedy misconduct by the factory owners. Procedurally the committee members had more latitude than did courts of law. Because these parliamentary committees were designed to extract information rather than to bring offenders to trial, they did not need to adhere to any established judicial guidelines. There was no cross-examination of witnesses, nor could factory owners present a defense. The witnesses in this investigation were chosen because Sadler knew they would reveal the evils of the factory system.

The testimony presented to the Sadler Committee produced abundant evidence of the exploitation and physical abuse of child workers. Some of the most harrowing testimony came from the examination of a 17-year-old boy, Joseph Hebergam, on July 1, 1832. Hebergam revealed that he had begun the work of worsted spinning at age 7, that he worked at the factory from five A.M. until eight P.M., and that he had only thirty minutes for lunch at noon, leaving him to eat his other meals while standing on the job. In the factory there were three overlookers, one of whom was responsible for greasing the machinery and another for whipping the workers. The latter overlooker walked continually up and down the factory with whip in hand.

When asked where his brother John was working, Joseph replied that he had died three years before at age 16. Sadler then inquired into the cause of his brother's death. The boy responded, "It was attributed to this, that he died from working such long hours and that it had been brought on by the factory. They have to stop the flies [part of the textile machinery] with their knees, because they go so swift they cannot stop them with their hands; he got a bruise on the shin by a spindle-board, and it went on to that degree that it burst; the surgeon cured that, then he was better; then he went to work again; but when he had worked about two months more his spine

Child Workers
These children are on their way to work in the Yorkshire textile mills.

Child Labor in the Textile Industry
Factory girls operate machinery in a textile mill under the tight supervision of the factory owner.

became affected, and he died." The witness went on to explain that his own severe labor had damaged his knees and ankles so much so that he found it painful to walk. His brother and sister would help carry him to the factory, but when they arrived late, even by as little as five minutes, the overlooker beat all three of them "till we were black and blue."[3] At the request of the committee, Joseph then stood up to show the condition of his limbs. He reported the death of another boy who had sustained massive injuries when he was caught in the shaft of the machinery he was running. Joseph concluded his testimony by recounting how the factory owners had threatened him and his younger brothers with losing their jobs if they testified before the committee.

The hearings of the Sadler Committee were widely publicized, but they fell short of realizing their original objective. The bill, which eventually was approved by Parliament as the Factory Regulations Act of 1833, prohibited the employment of children under age 9 in all factories. Boys and girls were allowed to work up to nine hours a day from age 9 until their thirteenth birthday, and up to twelve hours a day from age 13 until their eighteenth birthday. The long-term effect of this legislation was to establish in Western industrialized countries the principle that early childhood was a period of life set aside for education rather than work.

Questions of Justice

1. This investigation was concerned with the achievement of social justice rather than the determination of criminal culpability. What were the advantages of using legislative committees in such an undertaking?
2. Child labor was not a new phenomenon in the early eighteenth century. Why did the Industrial Revolution draw attention to this age-old practice?

Taking It Further

Horn, Pamela. *Children's Work and Welfare, 1780–1890.* 1996. An examination of the scale and nature of child employment in Britain and changing attitudes toward the practice.

of those who owned land and received their income in the form of rent. The middle class or bourgeoisie, which included the new factory owners, possessed capital and derived their income from profits, whereas the working class owned nothing but their own labor and received their income from wages.

This new model of society served a number of different purposes. Marx and Engels used it to construct a comprehensive theory of historical development. According to this theory, the middle class had struggled for centuries to seize power from the aristocracy, while the working class would eventually take power from the middle class. For Marx and Engels, conflicts over control of the means of production created a state of continuous class conflict. David Ricardo (1772–1823), an English social philosopher whose political and social allegiances were very different from those of Marx, used a similar model of society to illustrate the crucial role that the middle class played in the economy. Ricardo compared society to a coach in which the middle class was the driver guiding the vehicle, the working class was the horse that provided the labor, and the aristocracy was the nonpaying passenger.

Historians and social scientists disagree over the extent to which men and women in the nineteenth century were actually conscious of their membership in these classes. Marxist historians have claimed that the growth of wage labor, the exploitation of the working class, and conflicts between capital and labor encouraged workers to think of themselves not so much as individuals who claimed a certain social status but as members of a large class of workers who shared the same relationship to the means of production. These historians have pointed to the growth of trade unions, political campaigns for universal male suffrage, and other forms of working-class organization and communication as evidence of this awakening of class consciousness.

Other historians have claimed that people were less conscious of their class position. True, at certain times in the early nineteenth century some workers thought of themselves as members of a class whose interests conflicted with those of factory owners and financiers. It was much more common, however, for them to think of themselves primarily as practitioners of a particular craft, as members of a local community, or as part of a distinct ethnic minority, such as the Irish. When they demanded the right to vote, workers based their claim on their historic constitutional rights, not on the interests of all wage earners. When they demonstrated in favor of the ten-hour working day, they did so to improve the conditions in which they worked, not to advance the struggle of all workers against the middle class. The work experiences of laborers were too varied to sustain an awareness among most of them that they belonged to one homogeneous group.

The various capitalists, shopkeepers, and factory owners who belonged to the bourgeoisie also lacked a clear sense of their membership in a single middle class. These people were capable of achieving solidarity on certain occasions, such as when they feared that workers threatened their interests. As we discussed in Chapter 18, the bourgeoisie often criticized the lifestyle and values of the landed aristocracy in print. But like the working class, the bourgeoisie was too diverse to allow for the development of a unifying class consciousness inspired by an identity of economic interest

Capital and Labor

This cartoon, drawn by the illustrator Gustave Doré, depicts wealthy industrialists gambling with workers tied together as chips.

The Industrial City of Birmingham in 1829
Factories dominated the landscape of the city of Birmingham in this watercolor attributed to Frederick Calvert. By this time contemporaries were already complaining about the poor quality of air caused by the smelting of iron.

against those who occupied social positions either above or below them.

Working men and women showed a marked reluctance to engage in militant or violent action against their employers. Appeals for working-class solidarity to a large extent fell on deaf ears. It is true that on certain occasions workers took violent action against their employers. In 1812 groups of hand loom weavers in the highly industrialized Midland region of England engaged in a determined campaign to destroy the new power looms that they blamed for rising unemployment and low wages. Often disguised and operating at night, these "Luddites," who took their name from their mythical leader Ned Ludd, smashed the new textile machinery that factory owners had introduced. (Even today people who object to the introduction of new technology are referred to as Luddites.) The government sent an army of 12,000 men to suppress the Luddites, a task made difficult by the protection given them by their communities.

The Luddites did not, however, represent the majority of the English working class. Factory workers in particular seemed reluctant to join working-class organizations. Most of the workers who participated in these associations and who campaigned for the rights of the workers were independent artisans who had little interest in the struggle that Marx and Engels had predicted would result in the victory of the working class.

Nevertheless, the growing tensions between industrial capitalists and labor, coupled with the recognition that those who had political power were reluctant to give workers the right to vote, led to the gradual emergence of class consciousness in England. A violent encounter between workers demonstrating for the right to vote and better working conditions in Manchester in 1819, described in detail in the Encounters & Transformations feature in this chapter, contributed to a growing awareness among workers and the members of the bourgeoisie alike that British society was divided into classes that were engaged in continual conflict with each other.

The Industrial Landscape

As industry spread throughout Europe and reached into areas that previously had been untouched by mechanization, urban and rural areas underwent dramatic changes. The most striking of these changes took place in the new industrial towns and cities, some of which had been little more than country towns before the factories were built. Manchester, for example, grew from a modest population of 23,000 people in 1773 to a burgeoning metropolis of 105,000 by 1820. Large factories with their smokestacks and warehouses, ringed by long rows of houses built to accommodate the armies of new industrial workers, gave these cities an entirely new and for the most part a grim appearance.

Cities experienced the most noticeable changes in physical appearance, but the countryside also began to take on a new look, mainly as a result of the transport revolution. The tunnels, bridges, and viaducts that were constructed to accommodate the railroad lines and the canals that were built to improve inland water transportation made an indelible imprint on the traditional terrain. In many ways this alteration of the landscape served as a statement of the mastery over nature that human beings had achieved at the time of the Scientific Revolution. The Industrial Revolution finally fulfilled the technological promise of that earlier revolution, and one of its effects was the actual transformation of the physical world.

The Peterloo Massacre, 1819

The most dramatic encounter between the middle class and the working class in early nineteenth-century Britain took place in the northern industrial city of Manchester. During the first fifty years of the Industrial Revolution Manchester had grown into a major textile-producing metropolis—known to some as "Cottonopolis"—with a population of some 120,000 people. With thousands of workers finding employment in the mills, the city provided an environment in which demands for a wide suffrage and an improvement in working-class conditions attracted widespread support. In August 1819 some 60,000 people, most of them workers and their families, gathered at St. Peter's Field to demonstrate support for universal male suffrage, annual parliaments, and relief from low wages, high prices, and long working hours. The fact that many of the workers had served in the Napoleonic wars and had been preparing for the demonstration by marching in military style had raised the fears of the middle-class establishment. Shortly after the meeting began, a violent confrontation took place between the demonstrators and the volunteer cavalry (known as yeomen), who belonged to the city's bourgeoisie. Frightened by the size of the demonstration and determined to prevent concessions that would reduce their profits, the yeomen decided to disperse the meeting by force. In the confrontation that ensued, the yeomen trampled hundreds of demonstrators and slashed many others with their swords, killing eleven people and wounding more than 400. "Over the whole field," wrote one observer, "were strewed caps, bonnets, hats, shawls, and shoes, and other parts of male and female dress, trampled, torn and bloody."

The violence that erupted at St. Peter's Field may have occurred too spontaneously to claim that the middle class deliberately attacked the workers who had assembled, but there is little doubt that the demonstration and the brutal response to it contributed to the growth of class solidarity, especially among the workers. The massacre inspired a number of calls for working class revolution. The young poet Percy Shelley (1792–1822), who was in Italy at the time, upon hearing of what had occurred in Manchester, called the working class to action:

Rise like lions after slumber
In unvanquishable numbers
Shake your chains to earth like dew
Which in sleep had fallen on you.
You are many—they are few.

The British working class did not respond to Shelley's summons. The Peterloo Massacre did not lead to a working-class revolution in Britain. It did, however, lead to the transformation of Britain into a society that was increasingly divided along class lines. It led directly to the organization of British labor in unions as well as to the birth of the Chartist movement, which staged a number of demonstrations in favor of parliamentary reform and the improvement of working conditions in the 1830s and 1840s. The Peterloo Massacre also contributed to the growth of class consciousness. British workers did not always identify themselves as members of a single class, but incidents such as this violent clash encouraged them to think in such terms. Consequently Britain, the first country in the West to industrialize, gained a reputation, which it has not completely lost today, of being a society in which one's identity is based more on class than the place of one's origins.

For Discussion

The historian E. P. Thompson has referred to the Peterloo Massacre as class warfare. Is this an appropriate characterization of the events that transpired at St. Peter's Field?

The Peterloo Massacre, 1819
This drawing of the Peterloo Massacre shows the mounted yeomen with drawn swords attacking the demonstrators, who had gathered to hear the speeches by the reformers on the platform above.

Joseph M. W. Turner, *Rain, Steam and Speed: The Great Western Railway* (1844)
This was one of the first oil paintings that had the railroad locomotive as its theme.

The advent of modern industry also brought about a change in attitudes toward the landscape. The destruction of natural beauty in the interest of economic progress stimulated an appreciation of nature that had not been widespread during the medieval and early modern periods. Before the Industrial Revolution many features of the countryside, especially mountains, were viewed as obstacles to either travel or human habitation, not as sources of aesthetic appreciation. Urbanization and industrialization changed those perceptions, triggering a nostalgic reaction that became one of the sources of the romantic movement, which we shall consider in greater detail in the next chapter. Some of the idyllic landscapes of the English romantic painter John Constable (1776–1837), for example, represented an imaginative recreation of a countryside that had already been transformed by the advent of industry by the time he painted them.

Industry did not always form a blight on the landscape or offend artistic sensibilities. Some of the new industrial architecture, especially the viaducts and aqueducts that traversed valleys in the mountainous regions of the country, were masterpieces of modern engineering and architecture. Sir Walter Scott (1771–1832), the Scottish romantic novelist, claimed that the cast-iron Pont Cysyllte aqueduct in Wales, which carried the waters of the Caledonian Canal 127 feet above the River Dee, was the most beautiful work of art he had ever seen. The railroads also had the ability to inspire the artistic imagination, as they did in Joseph Turner's (1775–1851) romantic painting *Rain, Steam and Speed,* which captured the railroad's speed and beauty.

Industry, Trade, and Empire

- **What was the relationship between the growth of industry and Britain's dominance in trade and imperial strength during the middle years of the nineteenth century?**

As the middle of the nineteenth century approached, Britain towered above all other nations in the volume of its industrial output, the extent of its international trade, and the size of its empire. In industrial production it easily outpaced all its competitors, producing two-thirds of the world's coal, about half of its cotton cloth, half of its iron, and 40 percent of its hardware. Little wonder that Britain became known as "the workshop of the world." Britain controlled about one-third of the world's trade, and London had emerged as the undisputed financial center of the global economy. Britain's overseas empire, which included colonies in Canada, the Caribbean, South America, India, Southeast Asia, and Australia, eclipsed that of all other European powers and would continue to grow during the second half of the century.

These three great British strengths—industry, trade, and empire—were closely linked. Britain's colonies in both Asia and the Americas served as trading depots, while the promotion of trade led directly to the acquisition of new imperial possessions. Even when Britain did not formally acquire territory, it often established exclusive trading relationships with those countries, thereby creating an informal "empire of trade." Trade and empire in turn served the purposes of industry. Many of the raw materials used in industrial production, especially cotton, came from Britain's imperial possessions. At the same time, those possessions provided markets for Britain's mass-produced manufactured goods. Such imperial markets proved immensely valuable when France blockaded its ports during the Napoleonic wars and thereby cut into British trade with the entire European continent (see Chapter 19).

The great challenge for Britain during the nineteenth century was to find new markets for its industrial products. Domestic demand had been strong at the beginning of the Industrial Revolution, but by the 1840s British workers did not possess sufficient wealth to purchase the increasingly large volume of hardwares and textiles manufactured in the mills and factories. Britain had to look overseas to find markets in which to sell the bulk of its industrial products. One possibility was to market them in other European countries, such as France and Germany, where demand for manufactured goods was high. These countries, however, were in the midst of their own industrial revolutions, and their governments had often legislated high protective tariffs against British goods to encourage the growth of their own industries. Britain therefore chose instead to market its goods in the less economically developed parts of the world, including its own colonies. We can see this trading pattern in the relationships that Britain had with three different regions: East Asia, India, and Latin America. In all three areas, moreover, British military power and diplomatic influence were enlisted in the cause of industry, trade, and empire.

East Asia: The Opium War, 1839–1842

British conflict with China provides the best illustration of the way in which the British desire to promote trade led to the acquisition of new colonies. For three centuries the Chinese had tightly controlled their trade with European powers. By 1842, however, British merchants, supported by the British government, managed to break down these barriers and give Britain a foothold in China, allowing it to exploit the East Asian market.

The conflict arose over the importation of opium, a narcotic made from poppy seeds and produced in great quantities in India. This drug, which numbed pain but also had hallucinogenic effects and could cause profound lethargy, was in widespread use in Europe and had an even larger market in Asia. In China opium had became a national addiction by the middle of the eighteenth century, and the situation became much worse when British merchants increased the volume of illegal imports from India to China in the early nineteenth century. The Chinese government prohibited the use of opium, but because it had difficulty enforcing its own edicts, it decided to put an end to the opium trade.

Chinese efforts to stop British merchants from importing opium led to an increase in tensions between China and Britain. The situation reached a climax in 1839, when the Chinese seized 20,000 chests of opium in the holds of British ships and spilled them into the China Sea. It is unknown what effect the opium had on the fish, but the incident led to a British attack on Chinese ports. In this conflict, the first Opium War (1839–1842), the British had the advantage of superior naval technology, itself a product of the Industrial Revolution. The first iron-clad, steam-driven gunboat used in combat, the *Nemesis,* destroyed Chinese batteries along the coast, and an assault by seventy-five British ships on Chinkiang forced the Chinese to come to terms. In a treaty signed in 1842 China ceded the island of Hong Kong to the British, reimbursed British merchants for the opium it had destroyed, and opened five Chinese ports to international trade. As part of this settlement, each of these ports was to be governed by a British consul who was not subject to Chinese law. In this way Britain expanded its empire, increased its already large share of world trade, and found new markets for British manufactured goods in East Asia.

India: Annexation and Trade

The interrelationship of industry, trade, and empire became even clearer in India, which became known as the jewel in Britain's imperial crown. As we have seen in Chapter 17, Britain gained control of the Indian province of Bengal in the eighteenth century and subsequently acquired a number of other Indian states. After the Sepoy Mutiny of 1857 the British government brought all of India under its direct control.

Political control of India during the nineteenth century served the interests of British trade in two ways. First, it gave British merchants control of the trade between India and other Asian countries. Second, Britain developed a favorable balance of trade with India, exporting more goods to that country than it imported. Taxes paid to the British government by India for administering the country and interest payments on British loans to India increased the flow of capital from Calcutta to London. The influx of capital from India was in large part responsible for the favorable balance of payments that Britain enjoyed with the rest of the world until World War I. The capital that Britain received from these sources as well as from trade with China was funneled into the British economy or invested in British economic ventures throughout the world.

Control of India also served British interests by supplying British industries with raw materials while giving them access to the foreign markets they needed to make a profit. This promotion of British industry was done at the expense of the local Indian economy. The transportation of cotton grown in India to British textile mills only to be returned to India in the form of finished cloth certainly retarded, if it did not destroy, the existing Indian textile industry. Resentment of this economic exploitation of India became one of the main sources of Indian nationalism in the late nineteenth century.

Latin America: An Empire of Trade

British policy in Latin America developed differently from the way it had in China and India, but it had the same effect of opening up new markets for British goods. Great Britain was a consistent supporter of the movements for independence that erupted in South America between 1810 and 1824 (see Chapter 17). Britain supported these movements not simply because it wished to undermine Spanish and Portuguese imperialism, but because it needed to acquire new markets for its industrial products. Britain did not need to use military force to open these areas to British trade, as it did in China. Once the countries became independent, they attracted large volumes of British exports. In 1840 the British cotton industry shipped 35 percent of all its exports to Latin American countries, especially to Argentina, Brazil, Uruguay, Mexico, and Chile. Britain also exported large amounts of capital to these Latin American countries by investing vast sums of money in their economies. Britain thus established an informal "empire of trade" in Latin America. These countries were not controlled by Britain, but they had the same economic relationship with Britain as other parts of the British Empire.

British investment and trade brought the newly independent nations of Latin America into the industrial world economy. In so doing, however, Britain assigned these countries to a dependent position in that economy, not unlike the position that India occupied in Asia about the same time. One effect of this dependence was to transform the small, self-sufficient village economies that had developed alongside the large plantations in Central and South America. Instead of producing goods themselves and selling them within their own markets, these villages now became suppliers of raw materials for British industry. At the same time the Latin American population became more dependent upon British manufactured goods. This transformation not only retarded or destroyed native Latin American industry but also created huge trade deficits for Latin American countries by the middle of the nineteenth century.

Ireland: The Internal Colony

Of all the imperial possessions with which Britain engaged in trade, the position of Ireland was the most anomalous. Despite its proximity to England, Ireland had always been treated as a colony. In 1801, after the unsuccessful Irish rebellion of 1798 discussed in Chapter 17, Ireland was incorporated into the United Kingdom, the Irish parliament was abolished, and Irishmen elected representatives to sit in the British Parliament at Westminster. Even though Ireland thus became formally a part of the British state, Britain nonetheless continued to treat the country as an imperial possession, especially with respect to its economy.

Throughout the nineteenth century Ireland remained almost entirely agricultural; only in the north, in the province of Ulster, which produced ready-to-wear undergarments for women and shirts for men, did industrialization take place, and that usually took the form of cottage industry. At the same time, large agricultural estates in Ireland, many of them owned by absentee British landlords, provided Britain with large imports of grain. Unable to afford the high cost of grain, which British protectionist legislation kept artificially high, and without the opportunity to find employment in industry, Irish tenants eked out an existence on the land, relying on a diet consisting almost entirely of potatoes. When a blight destroyed the potato crop in 1845, the country experienced a devastating famine that killed more than one million Irish people and forced another million to emigrate—many of them to the United States and Canada—between 1845 and 1848. The famine occurred despite the fact that Irish lands produced enough grain to feed the entire population. As the Lord Mayor of Dublin complained in 1845, British commercial policy inflicted on the Irish "the abject misery of having their own provisions carried away to feed others, while they themselves are left contemptuously to starve."[4] Thus, even in this internal colony, the British government's policy of promoting industry at home while importing resources from its imperial possessions promoted British economic interests at the expense of the countries under its control.

Conclusion

Industrialization and the West

By 1850 the Industrial Revolution had begun to bring about some of the most dramatic changes in human life recorded in historical documents. Not since the Neolithic Age, when people began to live in settled villages, cultivate grains, and domesticate animals, did the organization of society, the patterns of work, and the landscape undergo such profound changes. In many ways the Industrial Revolution marked the watershed between the old way of life and the new. It gave human beings unprecedented technological control over nature, made employment in the home the exception rather than the rule, and submitted industrial workers to a regimentation unknown in the past. It changed family life, gave cities an entirely new appearance, and unleashed new and highly potent political forces, including the ideologies of liberalism and socialism, which shall be discussed in depth in the next chapter.

Industrialization changed the very definition of the West. In the Middle Ages the predominant cultural values of Western countries were those of Christianity, while in the eighteenth century those values were more often associated with the rational, scientific culture of the Enlightenment. Now, in the nineteenth century, the West was increasingly becoming identified with industrialization and the system of industrial capitalism it had spawned. In discussing the prospects of industrialization in the Ottoman Empire in 1856, a British diplomat wrote that "Europe is at hand, with its science, its labor, and its capital," but that the Qur'an and other elements of traditional Turkish culture "are so many obstacles to advancement in a Western sense."[5] The Industrial Revolution was creating new divisions between the West and the non-Western world.

Until the late nineteenth century, industrialization took place only in nations that have traditionally formed a part of the West. Beginning in the 1890s, however, countries that lay outside the West or on its margins began to introduce industrial technology and methods. Between 1890 and 1910 Russia and Japan underwent a period of rapid industrialization, and in the second half of the twentieth century a number of countries in Asia and Latin America, as well as Turkey, followed suit. This process of industrialization and economic development is often described as one of westernization, and it has usually led to conflicts within those countries between Western and non-Western values. The industrialization of these nations has not always been fully successful, and even when it has, doubt remains as to whether those nations should now be included within the West. Industrialization outside Europe and the United States reveals once again that the composition of the West changes from time to time and that its boundaries are often difficult to define.

Suggestions for Further Reading

For a comprehensive listing of suggested readings, please go to www.ablongman.com/levack2e/chapter20

Ashton, T. A. *The Industrial Revolution,* reprint edition with preface by P. Hudson. 1992. The classic statement of the optimist position, identifying the benefits of the revolution.

Berg, Maxine. *The Age of Manufactures, 1700–1820: Industry, Innovation and Work in Britain.* 1994. A study of the process and character of specific industries, especially those employing women.

Brinley, Thomas. *The Industrial Revolution and the Atlantic Economy: Selected Essays.* 1993. Essays challenging the view that Britain's Industrial Revolution was a gradual process.

Deane, Phyllis. *The First Industrial Revolution.* 1967. The best study of technological innovation in Britain.

Gutmann, Myron. *Toward the Modern Economy: Early Industry in Europe, 1500–1800.* 1988. A study of cottage industry, especially in France.

Hobsbawm, E. J. *Industry and Empire.* 1968. A general economic history of Britain from 1750 to 1970 that analyzes the position of Britain in the world economy.

Jacob, Margaret. *Scientific Culture and the Making of the Industrial West.* 1997. An exploration of the spread of scientific knowledge and its connection with industrialization.

Morris, R. J. *Class and Class Consciousness in the Industrial Revolution, 1780–1850.* 1979. A balanced treatment of the link between industrialization and class formation.

Pollard, Sidney. *Peaceful Conquest: The Industrialization of Europe, 1760–1970.* 1981. A linking of coal supplies to economic development.

Rule, John. *The Vital Century, England's Developing Economy, 1714–1815.* 1992. A general economic history establishing the importance of early eighteenth-century developments.

Stearns, Peter. *The Industrial Revolution in World History.* 2nd ed. 1998. The best study of industrialization in a global context.

Teich, Mikulas, and Roy Porter, eds. *The Industrial Revolution in National Context: Europe and the USA.* 1981. Essays illustrating similarities as well as national differences in the process of industrialization.

Wrigley, E. A. *Continuity, Chance and Change: The Character of the Industrial Revolution in Britain.* 1988. Includes the best discussion of the transition from an advanced organic economy to one based on minerals.

Notes

1. Lord Ashley's Commission on Mines, *Parliamentary Papers,* Vols. 15–17 (1842), Appendix 1, Note 26.
2. Sir James Kay-Shuttleworth (1832), quoted in John Rule, *The Labouring Classes in Early Industrial England* (1986).
3. "Report of the Select Committee on the Factories Bill," *Parliamentary Papers,* Vol. 20 (1833).
4. John O'Rourke, *The History of the Great Irish Famine of 1847* (1902).
5. David Gillard, ed., *British Documents on Foreign Affairs,* Vol. 1: *The Ottoman Empire in the Balkans, 1856–1875* (1984–1985), 20.

Ideological Conflict and National Unification, 1815–1871

21

On March 18, 1871, the president of the French government, Adolphe Thiers, sent a small unit of troops to Paris to seize cannons that had been used against Prussian forces during their siege of the city a few months before. The artillery was in the possession of the National Guard, the citizen militia of Paris. The members of the National Guard felt that the government had abandoned them by recently concluding an armistice with the Prussians, who were still camped outside the city. They also believed that the government was determined to gain control of the city, which had refused to comply with the orders of the national government. When the troops reached the city, they encountered a hostile crowd of Parisians, many of whom were armed. The crowd surrounded the two generals who led the detachment, placed them up against a wall, and executed them.

This action led to a full-scale siege of Paris by government troops. In the city a committed group of radicals formed a new municipal government, the Paris Commune, which was a revival of the commune established during the French Revolution in 1792. The Commune took steps to defend the city against the government troops, and during its short life it implemented several social reforms. The Communards, as the members were known, set up a central employment bureau, established nurseries for working mothers, and recognized women's labor unions. For many decades the Commune served as a model of working-class government.

The Paris Commune lasted only a few weeks. On May 21 the troops of the provisional government poured through the gates of the city, and during the "bloody week" that followed they took the city street by street, demolishing the barricades and executing the Communards. The Communards retaliated by executing a number of hostages, including the archbishop of Paris. They also burned down the Tuileries Palace, the hall of justice, and the city

Eugene Delacroix, *Liberty Leading the People* (1830) The romantic representation of Liberty carrying the French tricolor during the Paris revolution of 1830 conveys the ideological inspiration as well as the violence of that armed uprising.

CHAPTER OUTLINE

hall. During this one week at least 25,000 Communards were killed, and because many bodies were burned in the fires that consumed the city, the numbers were probably much higher.

The short life of the Paris Commune marks the climax of a tumultuous period of European history. Between 1815 and 1871 Europe witnessed numerous movements for reform, periodic uprisings, and several revolutions. The people who participated in these momentous developments were inspired in large part by ideologies°, theories of society and government that lay at the basis of political programs. The ideologies that developed during this period—liberalism, conservatism, socialism, and nationalism—were the product of historical developments that had arisen in the West, and they endowed the West with a distinctive political culture. These four ideologies also provide a framework for understanding the complex and often confusing political and social history of the West from 1815 until 1871.

The main question that this chapter will address is how the ideological encounters of this period influenced the course of Western political development. More specifically, the individual sections of the chapter will address the following questions:

- **What were the main features of the ideologies that inspired people to political action during the period from 1815 to 1871?**
- **How did the encounters among the people who espoused these ideologies shape the political history of Europe between 1815 and 1848?**
- **How did liberal and conservative leaders use the ideology of nationalism as a tool to unite the people of various territories into nation-states between 1848 and 1871?**
- **What role did ideology play in international warfare and diplomacy, especially in efforts to maintain the balance of power during this period?**

New Ideologies in the Early Nineteenth Century

- **What were the main features of the ideologies that inspired people to political action during the period from 1815 to 1871?**

In the wake of the French Revolution, four new ideologies—liberalism, conservatism, socialism, and nationalism—led thousands of Europeans to call for profound changes in the established political order. These ideologies had their roots in the works of eighteenth-century writers, but they developed into integrated systems of thought and inspired political programs in the first half of the nineteenth century. All four were influenced by the two great transformations of the West that we have discussed in the last two chapters: the French Revolution and the Industrial Revolution.

Liberalism: The Protection of Individual Freedom

Liberalism° is anchored in the beliefs that political, social, and economic freedoms are of supreme importance and that the main function of government is to protect those freedoms. The political agendas of nineteenth-century liberals varied from one country to another, but they all pursued three main objectives. The first objective was to establish and protect individual rights, such as the freedom of the press, freedom of religion, and freedom from arbitrary arrest and imprisonment. Liberals sought to guarantee these rights by having them enumerated in written constitutions. Opposed to aristocratic privilege, liberals supported the principle of equality before the law. They also tended to be anticlerical, a position that led to frequent tension between them and the Roman Catholic Church. As defenders of individual freedom they often campaigned to end slavery and serfdom.

The second objective of liberals was the extension of the franchise (the right to vote) to all property owners, especially those in the middle class. For the most part liberals were opposed to giving the vote to the lower classes, on the grounds that poor people, with little property of their own, could not be trusted to elect representatives who would protect property rights. Liberals also were opposed to giving the vote or any other form of political power to women. They justified the exclusion on the grounds that the proper arena for female activity was the home, where women occupied their natural domain. In this way liberals subscribed to the theory of separate spheres, which assigned men and women different gender roles. As we know from Chapter 18, this theory was based on the belief that women were different in nature from men and that they should be confined to an exclusively domestic role as chaste wives and mothers. Liberals believed that only male property holders should be allowed to participate in public affairs.

The third objective of liberals was to promote free trade with other nations and to resist government regulation of the domestic economy. This economic dimension of liberal ideology, which is grounded in the writings of the Scottish economist Adam Smith and other advocates of free-market capitalism, is usually referred to as laissez-faire°, a phrase that means "let (people) do (as they choose)." Advocates of *laissez-faire* held that the government should intervene in the economy only if it is necessary to maintain public order and protect property rights. As merchants and manufacturers, liberals favored a policy of *laissez-faire* because it offered them the freedom to pursue their own self-interest without governmental interference and thereby realize greater profits.

Some of the earliest expressions of liberal ideology appear in the works of John Locke and his fellow Whigs in England during the late seventeenth century (see Chapter 15). In arguing against the absolutist policies of Charles II and James II, the Whigs emphasized the inviolability of private property rights, freedom from state economic control, and the rights of those who held property to participate in government. In the eighteenth century these ideas were developed by Enlightenment thinkers who defended natural rights, and they found eloquent expression at the time of the American Revolution and the early years of the French Revolution. Liberal ideas were also embodied in the constitutions implemented in France, Germany, and Spain at the end of the Napoleonic period. When those constitutions and their principles came under attack after 1815, liberals sought to restore the freedoms they had lost without destroying public order. At that time liberalism became a distinct ideology.

Some liberals sought to realize their goals through the establishment of a republic, but the ideal form of government for most early nineteenth-century liberals was a limited monarchy—one in which the ruler did not act arbitrarily and suppress representative assemblies. As we shall see, liberal reformers in Britain during the 1830s wished to preserve the monarchy, and in France Louis-Philippe, the bourgeois citizen king installed during the Revolution of 1830, sought to implement liberal programs. In Germany, Belgium, and Greece, liberal revolts ended in the establishment of a constitutional monarchy.

DOCUMENT

John Stuart Mill Argues for the Sovereignty of the Individual in the Liberal State

John Stuart Mill (1806–1873) belonged to a group of British utilitarian social philosophers who gave liberalism its classic definition. In his most famous work, On Liberty *(1859), Mill discusses the nature and limits of the power that can be legitimately exercised over the individual. Mill recognized that this issue, the balance between freedom and authority, "has divided mankind almost from the remotest ages." His solution, which lies at the core of nineteenth-century liberalism, is that while the state can restrict one's liberty for the benefit of society, such as by compelling a person to pay taxes or to testify in court, in all undertakings that do not affect others, the individual has complete freedom over his actions and his opinions.*

The object of this essay is to assert one very simple principle, as entitled to govern absolutely the dealings of society with the individual in the way of compulsion and control, whether the means used be physical force in the form of legal penalties or the moral coercion of public opinion. That principle is that the sole end for which mankind are warranted, individually or collectively, in interfering with the liberty of action of any of their number, is self-protection. That the only purpose for which power can be rightfully exercised over any member of a civilized community, against his will, is to prevent harm to others. His own good, either physical or moral, is not a sufficient warrant. He cannot rightfully be compelled to do or forbear because it will be better for him to do so, because it will make him happier, because in the opinion of others to do so would be wise or even right. . . . The only part of the conduct of any one, for which he is amenable to society, is that which concerns others. In the part which merely concerns himself, his independence is, of right, absolute. Over himself, over his own body and mind, the individual is sovereign. . . .

But there is a sphere of action in which society, as distinguished from the individual, has, if any, only an indirect interest; comprehending all that portion of a person's life and conduct which affects only himself, or, if it also affects others, only with their free, voluntary, and undeceived consent and participation. . . . This, then, is the appropriate region of human liberty. It comprises, first, the inward domain of consciousness; demanding liberty of conscience, in the most comprehensive sense; liberty of thought and feeling; absolute freedom of opinion and sentient on all subjects, practical or speculative, scientific, moral or theological. The liberty of expressing and publishing opinions may seem to fall under a different principle, since it belongs to that part of the conduct of an individual which concerns other people; but, being almost of as much importance as the liberty of thought itself, and resting in great part on the same reasons, is practically inseparable from it. Secondly, the principle requires liberty of tastes and pursuits; of framing the plan of our life to suit our own character; of doing as we like, subject to such consequences as may follow; without impediment from our fellow creatures, so long as what we do does not harm them, even though they should think our conduct foolish, perverse, or wrong. Thirdly, from this liberty of each individual follows the liberty, within the same limits, of combination among individuals; freedom to unite for any purpose not involving harm to others: the persons combining being supposed to be of full age, and not forced or deceived.

Source: John Stuart Mill, *On Liberty* (1901).

Liberalism found its greatest strength among the urban middle class: merchants, manufacturers, and members of the professions. These people formed the group that felt most aggrieved by their exclusion from political life during the eighteenth and early nineteenth centuries and most eager to have government protect their property. Their substantial wealth provided the basis for their claim to acquire a share of political power, and as manufacturers and merchants they had the most to gain from an economy unfettered by government regulations.

Liberal economic theory found its most articulate proponents in England, where industrial capitalism achieved its earliest and most significant successes. Two of the most prominent liberals in early nineteenth-century Britain were the utilitarians Jeremy Bentham and David Ricardo. Utilitarians° advocated economic and social policies that in their view would provide the greatest good to the greatest number of people. In pursuit of that goal, Bentham (1748–1832), a legal scholar and political philosopher, proposed that a government should give its people as much freedom as possible and impose only those laws that were socially useful. The economist Ricardo (1772–1823), the son of a Dutch Jewish banker, argued that the absence of government intervention would spur economic growth and thus contribute to the benefit of all people. This *laissez-faire* argument was far more persuasive to manufacturers than to workers. In *Principles of Political Economy and Taxation* (1819), Ricardo argued that if wages were left to the law of supply and demand, they would fall to near subsistence levels. This "iron law of wages" made it clear that *laissez-faire* liberalism would not benefit the working class.

Conservatism: Preserving the Established Order

Throughout human history people have demonstrated a desire to maintain the established order and to resist change. In the early nineteenth century, however, the ideals of the Enlightenment and the radical changes ushered in by the French Revolution led to the formulation of a new ideology of conservatism°, a set of ideas intended to prevent a recurrence of the revolutionary changes of the 1790s. The main goal of conservatives after 1815 was to preserve the monarchies and aristocracies of Europe against liberal and national movements.

The new conservatism justified the existing political order as the product of gradual change. This defense was most clearly expressed in the writings of the fiery, Irish-born parliamentary orator Edmund Burke (1729–1797). Burke was no reactionary; he advocated a number of changes in British public life, including electoral reform and a reorganization of the British Empire. But Burke, who is regarded as the founder of modern conservatism, had enormous respect for the existing social order, which he considered the handiwork of God. Society according to Burke was a partnership between the living, the dead, and those who had yet to be born. Only within this historical partnership could change take place, and all changes would have to be gradual.

On the basis of this view of the social order, Burke attacked the liberal and radical ideas that had inspired the French Revolution. In *Reflections on the Revolution in France* (1790), he asserted that equality was a dangerous myth; its effect would be to allow those at the bottom to plunder those at the top and thus destroy the hierarchical order of society. Unlike the French revolutionaries, Burke had no faith in the people, whom he referred to as the "swinish multitude." In Burke's view rights did not derive from human nature, as they did for the philosophes of the Enlightenment; rights were privileges that had been passed down through the ages and could be preserved only by a hereditary monarchy. By claiming abstract rights for all men, the French had rejected their inheritance.

Conservative ideology justified the institution of monarchy on the basis of religion. The French writer Louis de Bonald (1754–1840) argued that Christian monarchies were the final creation in the development of both religious and political society. Only monarchies of this sort could preserve public order and prevent society from degenerating into the savagery witnessed during the French Revolution. De Bonald and his fellow French writer, Joseph de Maistre (1754–1821), rejected the entire concept of natural rights and reiterated the traditional doctrine of divine right, by which all political power came from God. De Maistre also reinforced the alliance between the throne and the altar by considering the monarchy and the Church as the foundations of the social order. In the nineteenth century, conservatives throughout Europe thought of religion as the basis of society. This view was especially strong in Catholic countries such as France and Austria, but Burke had put forth the same argument in Protestant England.

A fine line separates conservatism, which allows for gradual change, and reaction, which is the effort to reject any changes that have taken place and return to the old order. Early nineteenth-century conservatism provided an ideological foundation for the reactionary movements that arose throughout Europe after 1815. These movements had both national and international dimensions. In all western European countries, groups of influential and powerful individuals, usually nobles and churchmen, were determined to return to the days when they had more power. Internationally, the rulers of Europe, under the leadership of the Austrian foreign minister Clemens von Metternich, established a mechanism known as the Concert of Europe° to preserve the map of Europe as it was drawn at the Congress of Vienna (see Chapter 19). To do so meant taking concerted action against liberals and nationalists who attempted to unseat dynastic rulers.

In keeping with the identification of conservatism with religion, three of the four original powers in the Concert of Europe—Prussia, Russia, and Austria—gave their alliance a religious mission. At the Congress of Vienna Tsar Alexander I drafted a document in which the cooperation among European monarchs, whom he referred to as "the delegates of Providence," would be based "upon the sublime truths which the holy religion of Our Savior teaches." The British refused to subscribe to this document, claiming that it was "sublime mysticism and nonsense." So too did the future Louis XVIII of France (which was only a probationary member of the Concert of Europe until 1818) and even the pope. But Alexander's commitment to defend Christian values in what he called the Holy Alliance provided a religious foundation for the reactionary and repressive policies that Russia, Prussia, and Austria took steps to implement.

Socialism: The Demand for Equality

Socialism, the third new ideology of the early nineteenth century, arose in response to the development of industrial capitalism and the liberal ideas that justified it. Socialism calls for the ownership of the means of production (such as factories, machines, and railroads) by the community, with the purpose of reducing inequalities of income, wealth, opportunity, and economic power. In small communities, such as some early nineteenth-century socialist settlements, ownership could be genuinely collective. In a large country, however, the only practical way to introduce socialism would be to give the ownership of property to the state, which represents the people.

The main appeal of socialism was the prospect of remedying the deplorable social and economic effects of the Industrial Revolution. As we have seen in Chapter 20, the short-term effects of industrialization included wretched working conditions, low wages, a regimentation of the labor force, and a declining standard of living. Socialists did not object to the mechanization of industry as such. Like liberals, they wanted society to be as productive as possible. They did, however, object to the system of industrial capitalism that accompanied industrialization and the liberal economic theory that justified it.

The earliest socialists were known as Utopian socialists, a name given to them because they envisioned the creation of ideal communities in which perfect social harmony and cooperation would prevail. One of these Utopian socialists, the British industrialist and philanthropist Robert Owen (1771–1858), actually turned his mill in New Lanark, Scotland, into a model socialist community in which the principles of cooperation prevailed and where the workers were housed and their children were educated. In 1825 he established a similar community in New Harmony, Indiana. Utopian socialism was not particularly concerned with the granting of political rights to workers, nor did it encourage class consciousness or class tensions.

A second generation of socialists became more concerned with using the power of the state to improve their lot. The most influential of these socialists was the French democrat Louis Blanc (1811–1882), who proposed that the state guarantee workers' wages as well as employment in times of economic depression. He also wanted the state to support the creation of workshops in which workers would sell the product of their labor directly without an intermediary. The principle underlying Blanc's concept of the social order was, "From each according to his abilities; to each according to his needs." Blanc's brand of socialism began a long tradition in which workers tried to improve their lot by influencing government. This initiative was closely related to the radical democratic goal of universal male suffrage, which became one of the main objectives of many socialists after 1840.

The most radical form of nineteenth-century socialism was formulated by the German social philosopher Karl Marx (1818–1883). Marx was much more preoccupied than

Karl Marx

Karl Marx, the German social philosopher who developed the revolutionary socialist doctrine of communism.

DOCUMENT

Karl Marx and Friedrich Engels, *The Communist Manifesto* (1848)

These excerpts from the final pages of The Communist Manifesto *summarize the communist plan for establishing a socialist society by means of revolution. They reveal Marx's view of history as a succession of class conflicts and his prediction that the proletariat will become the ruling class. The appeal for working-class solidarity and revolution illustrates the power of socialist ideology to inspire people to action.*

The history of all past society has consisted in the development of class antagonisms, antagonisms that have assumed different forms at different epochs. But whatever form they may have taken, one fact is common to all past ages, viz., the exploitation of one part of society by the other. . . .

We have seen above that the first step in the revolution by the working class is to raise the proletariat to the position of ruling class, to win the battle of democracy. The proletariat will use its political supremacy to wrest, by degrees, all capital from the bourgeoisie, to centralize all means of production in the hands of the state, i.e., of the proletariat organized as the ruling class, and to increase the total of productive forces as rapidly as possible.

If the proletariat during its contest with the bourgeoisie is compelled by the force of circumstances, to organize itself as a class, if by means of a revolution it makes itself the ruling class, and as such sweeps away by force the old conditions of production, then it will, along with these conditions, have swept away the conditions for the existence of class antagonisms and of classes generally, and will thereby have abolished its own supremacy as a class. . . .

Communists disdain to conceal their views and aims. They openly declare that their ends can be attained only by the violent overthrow of all existing social conditions. Let the ruling classes tremble at a Communist revolution. The proletarians have nothing to lose but their chains. They have a world to win. WORKING MEN OF ALL COUNTRIES UNITE!

Source: From Karl Marx and Friedrich Engels, *The Communist Manifesto,* 1848, translated in English by Friedrich Engels in 1888.

other socialists with the collective identity and political activities of the working class. Reading about working conditions in France during the early 1840s, he became convinced that workers in industrial society were the ultimate example of human alienation and degradation. In 1844 he began a lifetime association with another German-born philosopher, Friedrich Engels (1820–1895), who as we have seen in the preceding chapter exposed the wretchedness of working-class life in Manchester. Marx and Engels began to think of workers as part of a capitalist system, in which they owned nothing but their labor, which they sold to capitalist producers for wages.

Marx and Engels worked these ideas into a broad account of historical change in which society moved inevitably and progressively from one stage to another. They referred to the process by which history advanced as the dialectic°. Marx acquired the idea of the dialectic from the German philosopher Georg Wilhelm Friedrich Hegel (1770–1831), who believed that history advanced in stages as the result of the conflict between one idea and another. Marx disagreed with Hegel on the source of historical change, arguing that material or economic factors rather than ideas determined the course of history. Hence Marx's socialist philosophy became known as dialectical materialism°.

According to Marx and Engels, the first stage of the dialectic had taken place when the bourgeoisie, who received their income from capital, seized political power from the aristocracy, who received their income from land, during the English and French revolutions. Marx and Engels predicted that the next stage of the dialectic would be a conflict between the bourgeoisie and the working class or proletariat°, which received its income from wages. This conflict, according to Marx and Engels, would result in the triumph of the working class. Led by a committed band of revolutionaries, the proletariat would take control of the state, establish a dictatorship so that they could implement their program without opposition, and usher in a classless society.

Marx and Engels issued this call to action in *The Communist Manifesto* (1848), which ended with the famous words, "Working men of all countries unite!" Marx's brand of socialism, communism°, takes its name from this book. Communism is a revolutionary ideology that advocates the overthrow of "bourgeois" or capitalist institutions and the transfer of political power to the proletariat. Communism differs from other forms of socialism in its call for revolution, its emphasis on class conflict, and its insistence on complete economic equality. Communism belongs to a tradition that originated among members of the extreme wing of the democratic movement at the height of the French Revolution. One of those radicals, François-Noël Babeuf (1760–1797), demanded economic as well as political equality, called for the common ownership of land, and

DOCUMENT Karl Marx, On the Question of Free Trade (1848)

spoke in terms of class warfare. Marx's achievement was to place Babeuf's radical ideas in a new philosophical and historical framework. That framework, dialectical materialism, was explained in great detail in Marx's monumental three-volume work, *Das Kapital,* or *Capital* (1867–1894).

Nationalism: The Unity of the People

Nationalism, the fourth new ideology of the early nineteenth century, also took shape during and after the French Revolution. A nation° in the nineteenth-century sense of the word refers to a large community of people who possess a sense of unity based on a belief that they have a common homeland and share a similar culture. The ideology of nationalism° is the belief that the people who form this nation should have their own political institutions and that the interests of the nation should be defended and promoted at all costs.

The geographical boundaries of nations do not often correspond to the geographical boundaries of states, which are administrative and legal units of political organization. For example, in the early nineteenth century Germans often referred to their nation as comprising all people who spoke German. At that time, however, there were several German states, such as Prussia, Bavaria, and Baden, and there were also many German speakers living in non-German lands, such as Bohemia. A primary goal of nationalists is to create a nation-state°, a single political entity that governs all the members of a particular nation. The doctrine that justifies this goal is national self-determination°, the claim that any group that considers itself a nation has the right to be ruled only by members of its own nation and to have all the members of the nation included in this state.

The ideology of nationalism had roots in the French Revolution. Most of the revolutionary steps taken in France during the 1790s were undertaken in the name of a united French people. Article 3 of the *Declaration of the Rights of Man and Citizen* (1789) declared that "the principle of all authority rests essentially in the nation." The French Republic was constructed as the embodiment of the French nation. It gave an administrative unity to the French people and encouraged them to think of themselves as sharing a common cultural bond. Instead of a collection of regions, France had become *la patrie,* or the people's native land.

Nationalists emphasized the antiquity of nations, arguing that there had always been a distinct German, French, English, Swiss, or Italian people living in their respective homelands. This claim involved a certain amount of fiction, because in the past the people living in those lands possessed little cultural unity. There was little uniformity, for example, in the languages spoken by people who were identified as German, French, or Italian. Until the eighteenth century most educated Germans wrote in French, not German. Only a small percentage of Italians spoke Italian, and the main language of many Italian nationalists of the nineteenth century was French. Even after nation-states were formed, a large measure of linguistic, religious, and ethnic diversity has persisted within those states and has made true cultural unity impossible. The nation is therefore something of a myth—an imagined community to which nationalists believe they belong, but which in reality has never existed.

The ideal of the nation-state has proved almost impossible to realize. The boundaries of nations and states have never fully coincided. Patterns of human settlement are too fluid to prevent some members of a particular cultural group from living as a minority in a neighboring state. Germans, for example, have always lived in Poland, Spaniards in Portugal, and Italians in Switzerland. France at the time of the French Revolution probably came closest to realizing the ideal of a nation-state, claiming jurisdiction over most French people. Nevertheless, different regional identities and languages, such as that of the people of the southern province of Languedoc who spoke their own dialect, prevented the emergence of a powerful sense of national identity in all parts of France until the late nineteenth or early twentieth century.

In Britain the creation of a nation-state has been a complicated process. National consciousness, which is a people's belief that they belong to a nation, developed earlier in England than in any other country in Europe. In the sixteenth century almost all English people spoke the same language, and they were also subject to the same common law. In 1536, however, Wales was united to the kingdom of England, thereby including two nations, the English and the Welsh, in the same state. In 1707 England and Scotland were united in a new state, the United Kingdom of Great Britain, and in 1801 Ireland was brought into the United Kingdom as well. Thus the United Kingdom now included four nations: the English, the Welsh, the Scots, and the Irish. The task of building a British, as opposed to an English or a Scottish, nation in this multinational state has taken time, and to this day Britons are more accustomed to think of themselves as primarily English or Scottish than as British.

Other peoples have faced even more daunting obstacles than the British in constructing nation-states. Many nations have been subsumed within large empires, such as Hungarians and Croatians in the Habsburg Empire and Greeks and Serbs in the Ottoman Empire. In those empires, nationalist movements have often taken the form of separatist revolts or wars of independence, in which a nationalist group attempted to break off and form a nation-state of its own. A very different situation prevailed in Germany and Italy, where people who shared some linguistic and cultural traditions lived under the control of many different sovereign states of varying size. In these cases nationalist movements have sought to unite the smaller states into a larger nation-state.

One of the great paradoxes of nationalism is that the acquisition of colonies overseas often strengthened nationalist sentiment at home. The military conquest of these lands became a source of pride for the people in the metropolis, and also gave them a sense of cultural superiority. The main source of British national pride was the rapid spread of British control over one-quarter of the world's surface during the eighteenth and nineteenth centuries. Nationalism could also promote the supremacy of one's own nation over others. The French revolutionaries who conquered a large part of the European continent in the early nineteenth century justified their expansion on the grounds that they were superior to the rest of the human race. In 1848 a fervent German nationalist declared his support for "the preponderance of the German race over most Slav races." The Italian national leader Giuseppe Mazzini (1805–1872), whom we shall discuss in detail shortly, preferred to be called a patriot rather than a nationalist on the grounds that nationalists were imperialists who sought to encroach on the rights of other peoples.

Nationalism was often linked to liberalism during the early nineteenth century, when both movements supported revolutionary programs to realize the goal of national self-determination. Liberals believed that representative government and a limited expansion of the franchise would provide a firm foundation for the establishment of the nation-state, both in nations like Spain with a long tradition of self-rule and in countries like Greece that were seeking their independence from autocratic rulers. In Germany and Italy, where there was no central state, nationalists and liberals joined together to create one. There was, however, a difference of emphasis between the two ideologies, even in the early years of the nineteenth century. Liberalism stressed individual freedom, whereas nationalism was more concerned with political unity. At times those different ideals came into conflict with each other. The liberal doctrine of free trade, for example, ran into conflict with the doctrine of economic nationalism, which encouraged the protection of national industries. The nationalist German economist Friedrich List (1780–1846) claimed that free trade benefited only the wealthy and the powerful; he advocated instead protective tariffs to benefit German businesses.

Nationalism was just as capable of supporting conservatism as liberalism in the early nineteenth century. Because the nation was often viewed as having deep roots in the distant past, some nationalists glorified the monarchical and hierarchical political arrangements that prevailed in the Middle Ages. In 1848 conservative Prussian landlords rallied around the cause of "God, King, and Fatherland." Later in the nineteenth century, nationalism became identified almost exclusively with conservatism when the lower middle classes began to prefer the achievement of national glory, either in warfare or in imperialistic pursuits, to the establishment of individual freedom.

Culture and Ideology

As the four great ideologies of the Western world were developing during the nineteenth century, they were influenced by two powerful cultural traditions: scientific rationalism and romanticism. These two traditions represented two sharply divergent sides of modern Western culture.

Scientific Rationalism

Scientific rationalism is a manner of thinking that traces its origins to the Scientific Revolution and reached its full flowering in the Enlightenment. This tradition has provided a major source of Western identity ever since the late eighteenth century. It has stressed the powers of human reason and considered science superior to all other forms of knowledge. Scientific rationalism is essentially a secular tradition, in that it does not rely on theology or Christian revelation for its legitimacy. The effort to construct a science of human nature, which was central to Enlightenment thought, belongs to this tradition, while the Industrial Revolution, which involved the application of scientific knowledge to production, was one of its products.

During the nineteenth century, scientific rationalism continued to have a powerful influence on Western thought and action. As scientific knowledge continued to grow, and as more people received a scientific education, the values of science and reason were proclaimed more boldly. Scientific knowledge and an emphasis on the importance of empirical data (that which can be tested) became essential components of much social thought. The clearest statement that science was the highest form of knowledge and would lead inevitably to human progress was the secular philosophy of positivism°.

The main elements of positivism were set forth by the French philosopher Auguste Comte (1798–1857). Like many thinkers in the Enlightenment tradition, Comte argued that human society passed through a succession of historical stages, each leading to a higher level. It had already passed through two stages, the theological and the metaphysical, and it was now in the third, the positive or scientific stage. The word *positive* in this context means that which has substance or concrete reality, as opposed to that which is abstract or speculative. Comte predicted that in the final positive stage of history the accumulation of factual or scientific knowledge would enable thinkers, whom we now call sociologists, to discover the laws of human behavior and thus make possible the improvement of society. This prediction of human progress, and Comte's celebration of the liberation of knowledge from its theological shackles, had particular appeal to liberals, especially those who harbored hostility to the Roman Catholic Church.

The values of science and the belief in its inevitable advance also influenced the social thought of Karl Marx. His ideology of communism has been referred to as scientific socialism, in that it too is based on a vision of history determined solely by positive, in this case material or economic, developments. Marxism rejects the metaphysical, idealistic world of Hegel and the theology of all Christian religion and thus fits into the same scientific tradition to which positivism and earlier Enlightenment thought belongs.

Romanticism

The cultural tradition that posed the greatest challenge to scientific rationalism was romanticism°. This tradition originated as an artistic and literary movement in the late eighteenth century, but it soon developed into a more general worldview. The artists and writers who identified themselves as romantics recognized the limits of human reason in comprehending reality. Unlike scientific rationalists, they used intuition and imagination to penetrate deeper levels of being and to comprehend the entire cosmos. Romantic art, music, and literature therefore appealed to the passions rather than the intellect.

Romantics did not think of reality as being simply material, as did the positivists. For them it was also spiritual and emotional, and their purpose as writers and artists was to communicate that nonempirical dimension of reality to their audiences. Romantics also had a different view of the relationship between human beings and nature. Instead of standing outside nature and viewing it objectively, in the manner of a scientist analyzing data derived from experiments, they considered themselves a part of nature and emphasized its beauty and power.

As an art form, romanticism was a protest against classicism and in particular the classicism that prevailed in the late eighteenth century. As we discussed in Chapter 18, classicism reflects a worldview in which the principles of orderliness and rationality prevail. Classicism is a disciplined style that demands adherence to formal rules that governed the structure as well as the content of literature, art, architecture, and music. By contrast, romanticism allows the artist much greater freedom. In literature the romantic protest against classicism led to the introduction of a new poetic style involving the use of imagery, symbols, and myth. One example of this new approach is "Rime of the Ancient Mariner" (1798) by the English romantic poet Samuel Taylor Coleridge (1772–1834), which uses the sun and moon as powerful symbols in describing a nightmarish sea voyage.

Many romantic works of literature, such as the novels of the Scottish author Sir Walter Scott (1771–1832), were set in the Middle Ages, a period often associated with superstition rather than science and enlightenment. Other romantic prose works explore the exotic, the weird, the mysterious, and even the satanic elements in human nature. Mary Shelley's introspective novel *Frankenstein* (1818), an early example of science fiction that embodies a critique of scientific rationalism, incorporates many of these themes.

Within the visual arts, romanticism also marked a rebellion against the classicism that had dominated eighteenth-century culture. Classicism emphasized formality and symmetry in art, and it celebrated the culture of an ideal Greek

F. G. Lardy, *Entrance to Chamonix Valley*
This painting reflects the romantic concern with the majesty and power of nature.

Mary Shelley's *Frankenstein*: The Body in Romantic Literature

In 1818, Mary Shelley, the 20-year-old daughter of the feminist Mary Wollstonecraft and the wife of the poet Percy Shelley, published a novel, *Frankenstein: or, The Modern Prometheus,* that became a literary sensation in contemporary England and has inspired books and films down to the present day. The depiction of the human body in the novel reflects the attitude of romantic writers toward nineteenth-century science.

The novel tells the story of an idealistic Swiss scientist, Victor Frankenstein, who discovers the secret of giving life to inanimate matter. Using his knowledge of chemistry, anatomy, and physiology, Frankenstein pieces together bones and flesh from corpses to construct the frame of a human being, which he then infuses with life. The creature turns out to be a freak of nature: a gigantic, ugly, and deformed monster with watery eyes, yellow shriveled skin, and straight black lips. Frankenstein is horrified by what he has wrought, and his rejection leads the monster to turn on his creator, eventually killing his brother, his friend, and his wife on their wedding night. Frankenstein pursues the creature to the Arctic region, but the monster brings about Frankenstein's death. Filled with self-loathing for having murdered "the lovely and the helpless," the monster declares that Frankenstein will be his last victim and sets off to throw himself on his own funeral pyre.

The body of the monster created by Frankenstein is unnatural in the manner of creation, its size, its features, and its preternatural strength. The depiction of monstrous creatures in literature was common during the early modern period, as a way of indicating supernatural intervention in the world. Shelley's depiction of this monster, which reflects the preoccupation of romantic literature with the exotic and the mysterious, differs from that older tradition in that it identifies modern science, not supernatural forces, as the source of the monster's abnormality. In trying to unite the body and the soul, Frankenstein produced a creature he called a daemon, a body inhabited by an evil spirit who commits multiple murders. Science had produced a moral and a physical aberration.

One of the important theological questions in the history of Christianity has been whether an evil spirit or demon can inhabit or possess a human body. Shelley was preoccupied by this issue, as evidenced by Victor Frankenstein's deep interest in the figure of Satan in the novel. Frankenstein's monster was a demonic figure, but unlike the Satan of the Bible, he was the product of science and its attempt to control nature. The real monster becomes science itself, whose power nineteenth-century intellectuals desired but at the same time feared.

Mary Shelley, like many romantic writers, thought of nature as a life force with which human beings should be in harmony. The novel reinforces this theme by showing how a human being's attempt to control nature leads to nature's revenge. Frankenstein's loss of physical and mental health, the thwarting of his ability to have children with his wife, and his eventual death are all penalties for his violation of nature.

For Discussion

How does *Frankenstein* reflect the themes of romanticism and in particular its critique of scientific rationalism?

Depiction of the Monster Created by Victor Frankenstein
The creation of the monster in Mary Shelley's novel embodied a critique of scientific rationalism.

and Roman past. By contrast, romantic painters depicted landscapes that evoked a mood and an emotion rather than an objective pictorial account of the surroundings. Romantic paintings were intended to evoke feeling rather than to help the viewer achieve intellectual comprehension. Some of them conveyed the power of nature while others depicted its majesty and grandeur.

Romantic music, which also appealed to the emotions, marked a similar but more gradual departure from the formal classicism that was triumphant during the eighteenth century. The inspirational music of Ludwig van Beethoven (1770–1827), the son of a German court musician from Bonn, marked the transition from classical to romantic forms. Beethoven's early work conformed to the conventions of classical music, but his later compositions, which were completed as he became progressively deaf and which defied traditional classical harmonies, were intended to evoke an emotional response. His famous "Ode to Joy," in his ninth and final symphony, remains unequaled in its ability to rouse the passions. In the view of one critic, Beethoven's music "opens the floodgates of fear, of terror, of horror, of pain, and arouses that longing for the eternal which is the essence of romanticism."

Another early romantic composer, Franz Schubert (1797–1828), who was born in Vienna, blended classical forms with romantic themes by incorporating Hungarian and gypsy folk music into his compositions. The emotionally powerful operas of the German composer Richard Wagner (1813–1883), which were set in the mythical German past, marked the height of the romantic movement in music. That style attained its greatest popularity during the second half of the nineteenth century with the lyrical symphonies and concertos of Johannes Brahms (1833–1897) in Germany and the symphonies, ballets, and operas of Peter Tchaikovsky (1840–1893) in Russia.

Romanticism, like the rational and scientific culture it rejected, had powerful political implications, leaving its mark on the ideologies of the modern world. In the early nineteenth century, romanticism appealed to many liberals because it involved a protest against the established order and emphasized the freedom of the individual. Romantic writers were themselves often outsiders, and therefore their protests took many different forms. The French romantic author Victor Hugo (1802–1885), whose epic novels *The Hunchback of Notre Dame* (1831) and *Les Misérables* (1862) depicted human suffering with great compassion, identified romanticism as "liberalism in literature." For Hugo a relationship existed between liberty in art and liberty in society. In France wealthy liberal bourgeoisie generally patronized romantic music and literature, while nobles and clerics denounced them. Romanticism could, however, support conservatism by idealizing the traditional social and political order of the Middle Ages and the central importance of religion in society. The hostility of romantics to the culture of the Enlightenment could also lead to political conservatism. Sir Walter Scott and Samuel Taylor Coleridge were both conservatives, while the German writer Johann Wolfgang von Goethe (1749–1832), whose poems reflected many of the themes of romantic literature, opposed all liberal and republican movements in Germany.

Romanticism has a closer association with nationalism than with any other ideology. In the most general sense romanticism invested the idea of "the nation" with mystical qualities, thus inspiring devotion to it. Romantics also had an obsessive interest in the cultural, literary, and historical roots of national identity. This connection between romanticism and nationalism can be seen in the work of the German philosopher and literary critic Johann Gottfried von Herder (1744–1803), who was one of the leaders of the *Sturm und Drang* (storm and stress) literary movement. This movement, which developed in the 1770s and 1780s and included works by Goethe and Friedrich von Schiller (1759–1805), encouraged subjectivity and the youthful revolt of genius against accepted classical standards. Herder promoted the study of German language, literature, and history with the explicit purpose of giving the German people a common sense of national unity. He claimed that "a people may lose its independence, but it will survive as long as its language survives." Like many romantics, Herder idealized the Middle Ages and cultivated many of the myths that surrounded that epoch in Germany's history.

In other parts of Europe, especially in Poland and the Balkans, romantic writers and artists gave nationalists the tools necessary to construct a common culture and history of their nations. The Polish romantic composer Frédéric Chopin (1810–1849), who emigrated to Paris in 1831, inspired Polish nationalists by drawing on native Polish dances in his works for the piano. At the same time the romantic poet Adam Mickiewicz (1798–1855), another Polish exile in Paris, wrote *The Books of the Polish Nation* (1832), exalting his country as the embodiment of freedom and predicting that by its long suffering it would eventually liberate the human race.

Ideological Encounters in Europe, 1815–1848

- **How did the encounters among the people who espoused these ideologies shape the political history of Europe between 1815 and 1848?**

The four new ideologies of the nineteenth century—liberalism, conservatism, socialism, and nationalism—interacted in a variety of ways, sometimes reinforcing each other and at other times leading to direct and violent political conflict. During the years between 1815 and 1831 the main ideological encounters occurred between liberalism, sometimes infused with nationalism, and conservatism. In 1815, at the time of the Congress of Vienna, it appeared that conservatism would carry the day. The determination of Metternich, the Austrian minister, to employ all the resources of the Holy Alliance to suppress any signs of revolutionary activity made the future of liberalism and nationalism appear bleak. The power of the new ideologies, however, could not be completely contained. Liberal and nationalist revolts took place in three distinct periods: the early 1820s, 1830, and 1848. During the latter two periods the demands of workers, sometimes expressed in socialist terms, added to the ideological mixture. In all these encounters conservatives had their say, and in most cases they emerged victorious.

Liberal and Nationalist Revolts, 1820–1825

Between 1820 and 1825 a sequence of revolts in Europe revealed the explosive potential of liberalism and nationalism and the determination of conservatives to crush those ideologies. These revolts also reflected the strength of movements for national self-determination. The three most significant revolts took place in Spain, Greece, and Russia.

The Liberal Revolts of 1820 in Spain and Portugal

The earliest clash between liberalism and conservatism occurred in Spain, where liberals ran into determined opposition from their king, Ferdinand VII (r. 1808–1833). Ferdinand had been restored to power in 1814 after his forced abdication in 1808. In 1812, during the rule of Joseph Bonaparte, the Spanish *cortes*—the representative assembly in that kingdom—had approved a liberal constitution. This constitution provided a foundation for a limited monarchy and the protection of Spanish civil liberties. In keeping with the ideas of the French Revolution, it also declared that the Spanish nation, not the king, possessed sovereignty. The tension began when King Ferdinand declared that he would not recognize this constitution. Even worse for the disheartened liberals was Ferdinand's decision to reestablish the Spanish Inquisition, invite exiled Jesuits to return, and refuse to summon the *cortes*. In 1820, when the Spanish Empire in the New World had already begun to collapse (see Chapter 17), liberals in Madrid, in alliance with some military officers, seized power.

This liberal revolt proved to be a test for the Concert of Europe. Metternich urged intervention, and although the British refused because they wanted to protect their trading interests with the Spanish colonies, the members of the Holy Alliance supported the invasion of Spain by a French army of 200,000 men. Ferdinand was restored once again to the throne, and once again he renounced the liberal constitution of 1812. The liberals not only lost this struggle, but they also suffered bitter reprisals from the government, which tortured and executed their leaders. The situation became only marginally better in 1833, when Ferdinand died and the liberal ministers of his young daughter, Queen Isabella II (r. 1833–1868), drew up another constitution. Her reign was marked by civil war, instability, and factional strife in which liberals made few substantial gains.

Shortly after the Spanish revolt of 1820, a similar rebellion based on liberal ideas took place in Portugal. The royal family had fled to Brazil during the Napoleonic wars, leaving Portugal to be governed by a regent. A group of army officers removed the regent and installed a liberal government, which proceeded to suppress the Portuguese Inquisition, confiscate church lands, and invite King John (r. 1816–1826) to return to his native land as a constitutional monarch. After the king returned in 1822, his enthusiasm for liberal government waned. His granddaughter, Maria II (r. 1826–1853), kept the liberal cause alive, relying on support from Portugal's traditional ally, Britain, but she struggled against the forces of conservatism and had only limited success.

The Nationalist Revolt of 1821 in Greece

A revolt in Greece in 1821, inspired more by nationalism than liberalism, achieved greater success than did the rebellions of 1820 in Spain and Portugal. It succeeded because other members of the Concert of Europe, not just Britain, lent their support to the revolt. Greece had long been a province in the sprawling Ottoman Empire, but a nationalist movement, organized by Prince Alexander Ypsilantis (1792–1828), created a distinct Greek national identity and inspired the demand for a separate Greek state. In 1821 a series of revolts against Ottoman rule took place on the mainland of Greece and on some of the surrounding islands. These rebellions received widespread support in Europe from scholars who considered Greece the cradle of Western civilization and from religiously inspired individuals who saw this as a struggle of Christianity against Islam. Hundreds of European volunteers joined the Greek rebel forces. Thus the insurrection became not only a liberal and national revolt but a broad cultural encounter between East and West. The English romantic poets George Lord Byron (1788–1824) and Percy Shelley (1792–1822) became active and passionate advocates for Greek independence, while the romantic painter Eugène Delacroix (1798–1863) depicted the horror of the Turkish massacre of the entire population at the island of Chios in 1822. The link between nationalism and romanticism could not have been made more explicit.

The Greek revolt placed the powers allied in the Concert of Europe in a quandary. On the one hand they were committed to intervene on behalf of the established order to crush any nationalist or liberal revolts, and they condemned the insurrection on those grounds when it

Eugène Delacroix, *The Massacre at Chios* (1824)
In 1821 the Greeks on the Aegean Islands rebelled against their Turkish rulers, and in April 1822 Turkish reprisals reached their peak in the massacre of the inhabitants of Chios. Romantic paintings were intended to evoke feelings, in this case horror, at the genocide perpetrated by the Turks against the Greek rebels. The painting reveals the close association of romantic art with the causes of liberalism and nationalism.

first erupted. On the other hand they were Western rulers who identified the Ottoman Turks with everything that was alien to Christian civilization. Moreover, Russia wanted to use this opportunity to dismember its ancient enemy, the Ottoman Empire. The European powers eventually took the side of the Greek rebels. In 1827 Britain, France, and Russia threatened the Turks with military intervention if they did not agree to an armistice and grant the Greeks their independence. When the Turks refused, the combined naval forces of those three countries destroyed the fleet of the Turks' main ally, Egypt, at Navarino off the Greek coast. This naval action turned the tide in favor of the Greeks, who in 1833 finally won their independence and placed a Bavarian prince, Otto I (r. 1833–1862), on the throne. Thus the Greek war of independence effectively ended the Concert of Europe. Originally intended to crush nationalist and liberal revolts, the Concert had in this case helped one succeed.

The Decembrist Revolt of 1825 in Russia

The least successful of the early liberal revolts took place in Russia, where a number of army officers, influenced by liberal ideas while serving in western Europe during the Napoleonic wars, staged a rebellion against the government of Tsar Nicholas I (r. 1825–1855) on the first day of his reign. The officers, together with other members of the nobility, had been meeting for almost a decade in political clubs, such as the Society of True and Faithful Sons of the Fatherland in St. Petersburg. In these societies they articulated their goals of establishing a constitutional monarchy and emancipating the serfs.

The rebels, known as Decembrists° for the month in which their rebellion took place, could not agree on the precise form of government they wished to institute. That disagreement, coupled with a reluctance to take action at the critical moment, led to their failure. When Tsar Alexander I died suddenly in 1825, the Decembrists hoped to persuade his brother Constantine to assume the throne and establish a representative form of government. Their hopes were dashed when Constantine refused to tamper with the succession and accepted the reign of his brother Nicholas. The reactionary Nicholas had no difficulty suppressing the revolt, executing its leaders, and leaving Russian liberals to struggle against police repression for the remainder of the nineteenth century.

Liberal and Nationalist Revolts, 1830

A second cluster of early-nineteenth-century liberal and national revolts in 1830 achieved a greater measure of success than the revolts of the early 1820s. These revolutions took place in France, the kingdom of the Netherlands, and the kingdom of Poland.

The French Revolution: The Success of Liberalism

The most striking triumph of liberalism in Europe during the early nineteenth century occurred in France, where a revolution took place fifteen years after the final defeat of Napoleon at Waterloo. This liberal success did not come easily. During the first few years of the restored monarchy conservatives had their way, as they did elsewhere in Europe. Louis XVIII had approved a Charter of Liberties in 1814, but he was hardly receptive to any further liberal reforms.

CHRONOLOGY

Liberal and Nationalist Revolts, 1820–1833

1820	Liberal revolt in Spain; liberal army officers seize power in Portugal
1821	Beginning of Greek revolt against the Ottoman Empire
1825	Decembrist revolt in Russia against Nicholas I
1829	Liberals gain majority in French Chamber of Deputies
1830	Revolution in Paris, Louis-Philippe I becomes king of France; Belgium becomes independent and adopts a liberal constitution; beginning of the Polish rebellion against Nicholas I of Russia
1833	Greece becomes independent; Otto I becomes king

Between 1815 and 1828 French politics was dominated by the ultraroyalists, who sponsored a "white terror" (so called because they displayed the white flag of the Bourbon monarchy) against liberals and Protestants. The terror was led by two men nicknamed Three Slices and Four Slices, indicating the number of pieces into which they butchered their Protestant enemies.

In 1824, when the conservative Charles X (r. 1824–1830) ascended the throne and took steps to strengthen the Church and the nobility, there appeared to be little hope for liberalism. Nevertheless liberal opposition to the monarchy gained support from merchants and manufacturers, as well as from soldiers who still kept the memory of Napoleon alive. When liberals feared that Charles would claim absolute power, and when a serious economic crisis afflicted the country in 1829, liberals at last gained a majority in the Chamber of Deputies, the French legislature.

Charles then embarked upon a perilous course. In what became known as the July Ordinances he effectively undermined the principles of the Charter of 1814. These ordinances dissolved the new Chamber of Deputies, ordered new elections under a highly restrictive franchise, and censored the press. The public reaction to this maneuver caught the king by surprise. Thousands of students and workers, liberals and republicans alike, poured onto the streets of Paris to demonstrate. Skirmishes with the king's troops only made the situation worse, and when the tricolor flag of the French Revolution appeared on top of Notre Dame Cathedral, protesters blocked the streets with barricades. Unable to restore order, the king abdicated in favor of his grandson, but the liberals offered the crown instead to the Duke of Orléans, who was crowned as Louis-Philippe I (r. 1830–1848).

Louis-Philippe accepted a revised version of the Charter of 1814 and doubled the franchise, giving the vote to middle-class merchants and industrialists. The king catered to this bourgeois constituency by encouraging economic growth and restricting noble privilege. His reign, which is often referred to as the "bourgeois monarchy," also achieved a measure of secularization when the Chamber of Deputies declared that Roman Catholicism was no longer the state religion. In keeping with mainstream liberal ideals, however, he did nothing to encourage republicanism or radical democracy, much less socialism. Efforts to depict him as the heir to the French Revolution did not persuade the bulk of the population. When the government brought the ashes of Napoleon from St. Helena to Paris, thousands of French men and women turned out to pay homage to the former emperor. Much to his disappointment, Louis-Philippe gained little political benefit from the move. France had acquired a liberal monarchy, but it stood on a precarious foundation.

The Belgian Revolution: The Success of Nationalism

The French Revolution of 1830 triggered the outbreak of a liberal and nationalist revolution in the neighboring country of Belgium. At the Congress of Vienna the Austrian Netherlands were united with the Dutch Republic in a new kingdom of the Netherlands. This union of the Low Countries did not work out, and soon after the formation of the new kingdom the Belgians began pressing for their independence as a nation. With a Dutchman, William I, as king and with the seat of government in Holland, the Dutch were the dominant partner in this union, a situation that caused considerable resentment in Belgium. Belgians spoke Flemish or French rather than Dutch, which had become the kingdom's official language. Moreover, most Belgians were Catholics, whereas the majority of Dutch people were Protestants. With their own language, religion, and culture, as well as their own history, Belgians thought of themselves as a separate nation. They also were more liberal than their Dutch neighbors, advocating free trade and the promotion of industry, while resenting the high tariffs imposed by the Dutch government.

The two main political parties in Belgium, the Liberals and the Clericals, joined forces to achieve autonomy. When the news of the Revolution in Paris reached Brussels, fighting broke out between workers and government troops. A national congress gathered to write a new constitution, and when the Dutch tried to thwart the rebellion by bombarding the Belgian city of Antwerp, Britain assembled a conference of European powers to devise a settlement. The powers agreed to recognize Belgium's independence, and they arranged for a German prince,

Scene from the French Revolution of 1830 in Paris
Demonstrations by students and workers led to the abdication of King Charles X and the establishment of a liberal government. Tricolor flags of the French Revolution hang from the windows.

Leopold of Saxe-Coburg, uncle of the future British Queen Victoria, to become king. The Dutch, however, refused to recognize the new government, and they renewed their military attacks on Belgium. Only in 1839 did all sides accept the new political arrangement.

The Polish Rebellion: The Failure of Nationalism

The French Revolution of 1830 triggered a second uprising, this one unsuccessful, in the kingdom of Poland (see Map 21.1). Poland had suffered many partitions at the hands of European powers during the eighteenth century, and in 1815 the Congress of Vienna had redefined its borders once again. After incorporating much of the eastern portion of the country into the Russian Empire, the Congress established a separate Polish kingdom, with Warsaw as its capital and the Russian tsar, Alexander I (r. 1815–1825), as its king.

With a Russian king the independence of Poland was a mere fiction, but Alexander had approved a liberal Polish constitution in 1815. He grew to regret this decision, and his rule as king of Poland gradually alienated Polish liberals within the national legislature, the *sejm.* The accession of Nicholas in 1825 only aggravated those tensions. An uncompromising conservative, Nicholas accused the Polish opposition of complicity with the Russian Decembrist rebels, and he brought them to the brink of rebellion when he made plans to send the Polish army, together with Russian troops, to suppress the French Revolution of 1830 and to prevent the Belgians from receiving their independence.

The revolt began within the school of army cadets, who attacked the residence of the Grand Duke Constantine, but it quickly gained the support of the entire army and the urban populace. The revolt appealed to both liberals and nationalists, and it drew inspiration from a group of romantic poets who celebrated the achievements of the Polish past. A provisional government was established at Warsaw, but the liberal members of the elected national assembly were unwilling to enlist the peasantry in the conflict, fearful that they would rise against Polish landlords rather than the Russians. When the powers of western Europe refused to intervene on behalf of this liberal cause, Nicholas was able to crush the rebellion, abolish the *sejm,* and deprive the

DOCUMENT
Adam Mickiewicz, Excerpts from *The Books of the Polish Nation*

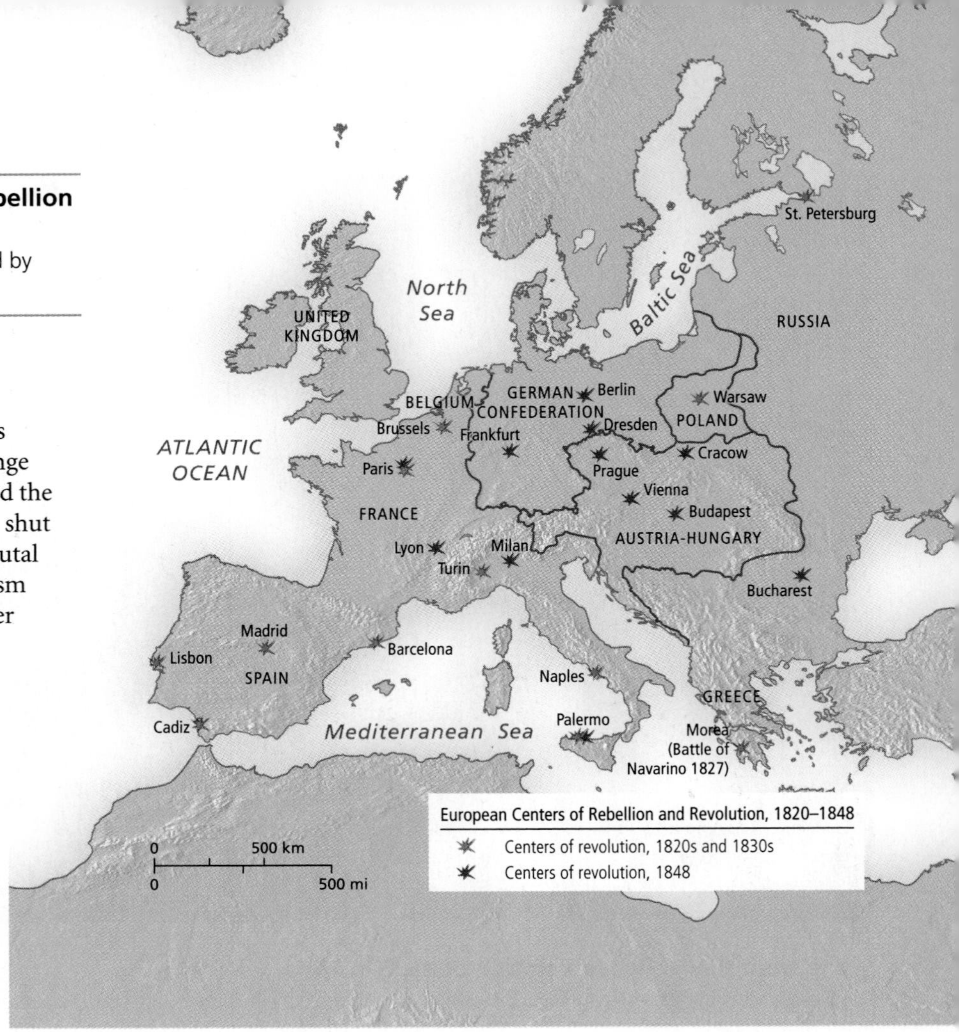

Map 21.1 European Centers of Rebellion and Revolution, 1820–1848

All these political disturbances were inspired by ideology.

kingdom of Poland of its autonomous status. Nicholas visited a terrible revenge upon the leaders of the revolt, confiscated the lands of those who had emigrated, and shut down the University of Warsaw. His brutal repression set back the cause of liberalism and nationalism in Poland for another two generations.

Liberal Reform in Britain, 1815–1848

The challenges that liberals faced in Britain were somewhat different from those they confronted in most other European countries. Having maintained the status quo during the era of the French Revolution, the forces of British conservatism, which bore the ideological stamp of Edmund Burke, remained formidable. At the same time, however, Britons already enjoyed many of the rights that liberals on the European continent demanded, such as freedom of the press and protection from arbitrary imprisonment. The power of the British monarchy was more limited than in almost any other European country. The ideology of liberalism, which originated in England and had deep roots in British political and social philosophy, defined the political creed of many Whigs, who formed the main opposition to the ruling Conservative or Tory party after 1815.

In this relatively favorable political climate, British liberals pursued three major goals, which amounted to a program for reform rather than revolution. The first was parliamentary reform and the expansion of the franchise. The British had a long tradition of representative government, which had been secured by the Glorious Revolution of 1688, but the titled nobility in the House of Lords effectively controlled elections to the House of Commons, while the members of the gentry or lesser aristocracy held most of the seats in the House of Commons. In some boroughs real representation was a sham; the electorate consisted entirely of the borough councils, who elected the nominees of the noblemen who controlled them. Very few people lived in some of these "rotten boroughs"—one was nothing but a pasture—whereas large segments of the population in the recently industrialized north had no representation at all in Parliament.

The Great Reform Bill of 1832, which was pushed through Parliament by the Whig prime minister, Lord Grey, marked a victory for British liberalism. The bill expanded the franchise to include most of the urban middle class. It eliminated the rotten boroughs and created a number of new ones in heavily populated areas. It also established a uniform standard for the right to vote in all parliamentary boroughs. In keeping with the principles of liberalism, however, the bill restricted the vote, and hence active citizenship, to property owners. It rejected the demands of radicals for universal male suffrage, and by using the phrase "male person" to identify eligible voters, the bill denied all women the vote.

IMAGE Reform Bill of 1832 Cartoon

The second liberal cause was the repeal of legislation that denied political power to Catholics and also to Protestants who did not attend the services of the Anglican Church. In the seventeenth century a body of legislation had denied both of these religious minorities the right to hold national or local political office. Catholics suffered the additional liability of being denied the right to sit in Parliament. Liberals provided the basis of support for the political "emancipation" of Catholics and Protestant nonconformists. Liberals were opposed on principle to religious discrimination, and many of them belonged to Protestant nonconformist congregations. Conservatives opposed the repeal of this legislation, but they feared a civil war in Ireland if Catholics were not allowed to sit in the British Parliament. The Tory prime minister, the Duke of Wellington, who had defeated Napoleon at Waterloo, eventually agreed to liberal demands. The Protestant nonconformists were emancipated in 1828, while the Catholics had to wait until one year later. One of the first Catholics elected to Parliament in 1830 was Daniel O'Connell (1775–1847), an Irishman who worked tirelessly to improve the lot of his countrymen within the limits of the Irish union with Britain.

The third liberal cause was free trade. The target of this campaign was a series of protective tariffs on the import or export of hundreds of commodities, including raw materials used in production. The most hated protective tariff was on grain (known in Britain as corn), which kept the price of basic food commodities high in order to protect the interests of landlords and farmers. In this respect the determination of liberals for free trade conflicted with the determination of Parliament to defend the economic interests of its largely aristocratic membership. In 1837 a group of industrialists and radical reformers formed the Anti-Corn Law League with the purpose of bringing about the repeal of the Corn Law of 1815, which greatly restricted the importation of foreign grain into Britain. This campaign against protectionism did not succeed until 1845, when the Conservative prime minister, Sir Robert Peel, brought about repeal by securing the votes of some of his own party and combining them with those of the Whigs, all of whom favored free trade. Peel took this action only after the potato famine in Ireland, which was discussed in Chapter 20, had begun to cause widespread starvation. The repeal of the corn laws allowed the importation of foreign grain into Ireland, but this change in government policy occurred too late to alleviate the suffering of the Irish people.

Unlike the liberals, socialists and radical democrats achieved little success in Britain during the first half of the nineteenth century. In 1834 the Utopian socialist Robert Owen established the Grand National Consolidated Trades Union, the purpose of which was to unite all workers in a peaceful struggle to realize his idealist goals. One of Owen's supporters hoped that the union would give "the productive classes a complete dominion over the fruits of their own industry." The refusal of many unions to join this association, coupled with opposition from the government, led to its disintegration. In its wake workers and radicals decided that economic improvement could come only through political means. In 1837 the newly formed London Workingman's Association, in collaboration with a few radical Members of Parliament, drew up a People's Charter, calling for the implementation of a program of radical democracy. Their demands included universal male suffrage, annual parliaments, voting by secret ballot, equal electoral districts, the elimination of property qualifications for Members of Parliament, and the payment of salaries to those same members. The workers who supported this cause became known as Chartists.

The Last Great Chartist Rally in Britain, April 10, 1848

Government precautions, including the appointment of special constables to handle the crowd, and rain kept the number of demonstrators in London lower than anticipated. The government ordered the leader of the movement, Feargus O'Connor, to stop the planned march to Parliament.

The strength of the Chartist movement fluctuated between 1837 and 1848, gaining the greatest popular participation when economic conditions deteriorated. Most Chartists restricted their activities to meetings to support candidates for Parliament and petitioning Parliament. A few of the more militant, such as the Irish immigrant Feargus O'Connor, called for "a holy and irresistible crusade" against the government. The British government and the upper classes became most frightened in 1848, when revolution broke out in France, Italy, and Germany, and when the Chartists decided to draft a new charter and threatened to form a revolutionary national assembly like that of France if Parliament were to reject the new document.

Within the next few years the Chartist movement died. British workers revealed, as they would throughout the remainder of the nineteenth century, that they had little inclination to take to the streets, especially after good economic times returned. The government's reduction of indirect taxes during the 1840s, coupled with the effective use of the police force and the strict enforcement of the criminal law, also helped prevent Britain from experiencing revolution in 1848. The price of this failure was that further liberal reforms, such as the extension of the franchise, did not take place in Britain for another two decades.

The Revolutions of 1848

Unlike Britain, almost every country in Europe experienced revolution in 1848. A wave of revolutionary activity spread rapidly throughout the Continent. The revolutions took place during a period of widespread economic discontent. European countries had suffered bad harvests in 1845 and 1846 and an economic recession in 1847, leading to a temporary decline in the standard of living among industrial as well as agricultural workers. Discontent took the form of mass protests and demonstrations, which increased the likelihood of violent confrontation. The revolutions of 1848 were more widespread than the revolts of the 1820s and 1830, and they involved greater popular participation. These revolutions also gave greater attention to both nationalist and socialist issues.

CHRONOLOGY

The Revolutions of 1848

1848	
February	Revolution in Paris
March	Insurrection in Berlin, peasant unrest in the countryside, formation of liberal governments in Prussia and other German states; revolutions in Milan and Venice, Ferdinand II issues a new constitution in Naples
April	Elections for a new National Assembly in France
May	Meeting of the Frankfurt Parliament; meeting of the Prussian Assembly
June	Suppression of working-class resistance in Paris; Pan-Slav Congress in Prague; suppression of the rebellion in Prague
October	Suppression of revolution in Vienna
December	Election of Louis-Napoleon as president of the Second French Republic; Frankfurt Parliament issues *Declaration of the Basic Rights of the German People;* Frederick William dissolves Prussian Assembly
1849	
March	King Frederick William rejects the German crown offered by the Frankfurt Parliament
April	Frankfurt Parliament promulgates a new constitution; Hungarian Diet proclaims Magyar independence
May–June	Fall of the liberal ministries in German states
August	Venetian Republic surrenders to Austrian forces; suppression of the Hungarian movement for independence

The French Revolutions of 1848

The first of the revolutions of 1848 took place in France, where the liberal government of Louis-Philippe faced mounting criticism. Declining economic conditions, which prevailed throughout Europe during the 1840s, provided an environment that brought the country to a crisis point. A series of demonstrations in Paris in favor of the right of workers to vote and to receive state assistance for their trades was the final precipitant. When troops from the Paris National Guard fired on the demonstrators and killed forty people, the barricades once again appeared in the streets and the rebels seized government buildings. France was experiencing its third revolution in sixty years. In an effort to save his regime, Louis-Philippe abdicated in favor of his grandson, but the revolutionaries abolished the monarchy and declared the Second French Republic.

A provisional government selected by the Chamber of Deputies was headed by nine republicans, but it included liberals and radical democrats. Most significantly it also included two socialists, Louis Blanc and a worker who preferred to be called by the single name of Albert. The French Revolution of 1848 offered the socialists the first opportunity to realize their goal of a democratic and socialist republic. Many of the 200 clubs formed in Paris at this time, some of which were exclusively female, were either republican or socialist in their orientation. The socialist agenda included not only universal male suffrage, which was granted immediately by the government, but also active support for the masses of unemployed workers. Louis Blanc secured the establishment of national workshops to give the unemployed jobs on public projects. Ordinances reduced the length of the workday to ten hours in the city and twelve hours in rural areas, and the government authorized a commission to study working conditions.

These bold socialist initiatives did not last long. By the summer the euphoria of the revolution had dissipated and the aspirations of workers had been crushed. The elections held in April 1848 to constitute a new National Assembly and write a new constitution seated an overwhelming majority of conservative monarchists and only a small minority of republicans and socialists. Resentment of the provisional government's assistance to urban workers and anger at the levying of a surtax to pay for government programs revealed the lack of broad popular support for radical political programs. Tension between the new conservative assembly and the forces of the left mounted when the government closed the workshops and Parisian workers were either drafted into the army or sent to the provinces.

These newly adopted policies led to further working-class violence in Paris in June 1848. When General Louis Cavaignac, known as "the butcher," was called in to suppress this insurgency with regular army troops, there was a devastating loss of life. No fewer than 1,500 insurgents were killed in the streets or in summary executions, while another 4,000 were sent into exile in French colonies. These confrontations appeared to Karl Marx to constitute class warfare, a prelude to the proletarian revolution he predicted for the future. Louis Blanc, who was implicated in these uprisings, fled to England, where Marx himself would soon arrive and spend the rest of his life.

The revolution ended with the election of Napoleon's nephew, Louis-Napoleon Bonaparte (1808–1873), as the president of the Second French Republic in December 1848. Until the February Revolution it seemed highly unlikely that Louis-Napoleon, an impetuous adventurer and conspirator, would ever come to power. After staging two unsuccessful coups against the government of Louis-Philippe in 1836 and 1840, he was sentenced to life imprisonment. He managed to escape to England, however, and the events of February 1848 gave him the opportunity to return to France. He became a member of the new National Assembly, and then easily defeated Cavaignac in the presidential election.

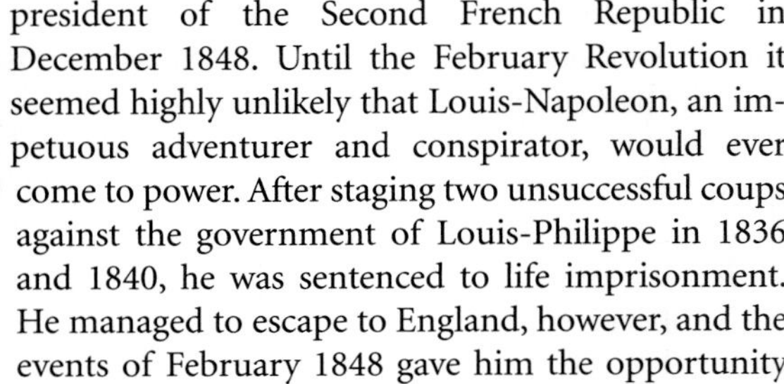

Louis-Napoleon v. General Cavaignac—British Cartoon, 1848

As president, Louis-Napoleon drew support from conservatives, liberals, and moderate republicans. He also benefited from the legend that his uncle had created and the nationalist sentiment it inspired. Because the first Napoleon had become emperor, even those who preferred an empire to a republic could vote for his nephew. The younger Napoleon followed in his uncle's footsteps, dissolving the National Assembly in December 1851 and proclaiming himself emperor of the French one year later. This step brought the Second Republic to an end and established the Second Empire. The new emperor called himself Napoleon III, in deference to the dynastic rights of the uncrowned Napoleon II, the son of Napoleon I who had died in 1823.

The Revolutions of 1848 in Germany, Austria, Hungary, and Bohemia

Until French revolutionaries built barricades in the streets of Paris in 1848, liberalism and nationalism had achieved little success in Germany. German university students, inspired by the slogan "Honor, Freedom, Fatherland," had staged a number of large rallies during the early years of the nineteenth century, but the forces of conservatism had kept them in check. The Carlsbad Decrees of 1819, intended to suppress university radicalism, inaugurated a period of severe repression throughout Germany. The only success achieved by German liberals and nationalists prior to 1848 was the establishment of the *Zollverein,* a customs union of the various German states, in 1834. Even that project, which promoted free trade within German lands, did not attract support from all liberals.

A major opportunity for the liberal cause in Germany came in 1848 in the immediate wake of the February Revolution in France. As in France, however, this opportunity was complicated by the more radical demands of democrats and socialists for universal suffrage, including equal rights for women. German radicals also demanded government assistance for artisans and workers who had suffered economic hardship as a result of industrialization. In Berlin, the capital of Prussia, these discontents led radicals to barricade the streets. The situation became more serious after troops fired into the crowd, killing some 250 people. The violence spread to the countryside, where peasants demanded that landlords renounce their privileges and grant them free use of their lands. In response to these pressures, King Frederick William IV summoned an assembly, elected by universal male suffrage, to write a new Prussian constitution. Other German states also yielded to liberal pressure, establishing liberal governments known as the "March ministries."

As these events were unfolding, the contagion of revolution spread to Austria, the other major German kingdom, which formed the nucleus of the sprawling Habsburg Empire. News of the revolution in Paris led to demonstrations by students and workers in Vienna. An assortment of

DOCUMENT

The Carlsbad Decrees, 1819

The main source of liberal and national ideas in Germany after 1815 were university students, who often belonged to secret societies or fraternities. Conservatives considered these students dangerous revolutionaries and tried to expel them from the universities. When a student assassinated a conservative writer in 1819, the princes of the German Confederation issued a set of decrees that called for the monitoring of the lectures given at the universities, the removal of liberal professors, the expulsion of students, and the censorship of the press.

2. The confederated governments mutually pledge themselves to remove from the universities or other public educational institutions all teachers who, by obvious deviation from their duty, or by exceeding the limits of their functions, or by the abuse of their legitimate influence over youthful minds, or by propagating harmful doctrines hostile to public order or subversive to existing governmental institutions, shall have unmistakably proven their unfitness for the important office entrusted to them. No teacher who shall have been removed in this manner shall be again appointed to a position in any public institution of learning in another state of the Confederation.
3. Those laws which have for a long period been directed against secret and unauthorized societies in the universities shall be strictly enforced. The governments mutually agree that such persons as shall hereafter be shown to have remained in secret or unauthorized associations, or shall have entered such associations, shall not be admitted to any public office.
4. No student who shall be expelled from a university by a decision of the university senate which was ratified or prompted by the agent of the government, or shall have left the institution in order to escape expulsion, shall be received in any other university.

So long as this decree shall remain in force no publication which appears in the form of daily issues, or as a serial not exceeding twenty sheets of printed matter, shall go to press in any state of the union without the previous knowledge and approval of the state officials.

Source: From *Readings in European History: 1789 to the Present*, 2nd Edition by John L. Heineman.

Austrian liberal aristocrats, middle-class professionals, and discontented workers demanded an end to the long rule of the conservative minister, Clemens von Metternich. In response to the demands of these groups, Emperor Ferdinand I (r. 1835–1848) summoned a constitutional assembly and installed a moderate government. A conservative Prussian observer feared that these concessions had broken "the most secure dam against the revolutionary tide."

The main difference between the revolutions of 1848 in Austria and the other German lands was that events in Vienna awakened demands of Hungarians and Czechs for national autonomy within the empire. In Hungary the nationalist leader Lajos Kossuth (1802–1894) pushed for a program of liberal reform and national autonomy. This initiative created further tensions between the Magyars and the various national minorities within the kingdom of Hungary. Similar problems arose in Bohemia, where a revolution in Prague led to demands from the Czechs for autonomy within the Habsburg Empire. In June 1848 the Czech rebels hosted a Pan-Slav Congress in Prague to advance a nationalist plan for achieving unity of all Slavic people within the empire. This idealistic proposal could not be realized, for there were many distinct Slavic nationalities, each of which had a desire to preserve its autonomy. In addition, there was a large German-speaking population within Bohemia that identified with other German territories in the Confederation.

The most idealistic and ambitious undertaking of the revolution in central Europe was the meeting of the Frankfurt Parliament in May 1848. Some 800 middle-class liberals, many of whom were lawyers, officials, and university professors, came from all the German states to draft a constitution for a united Germany. The parliament produced powerful speeches in support of both liberal and nationalist ideals, and in December 1848 it promulgated a *Declaration of the Basic Rights of the German People.* This document recognized the equality of all German people before the law; freedom of speech, assembly, and religion; and the right to private property. Like so many liberal assemblies, however, the Frankfurt Parliament failed to address the needs of the workers and peasants. The delegates rejected universal male suffrage as a "dangerous experiment" and refused to provide protection for artisans who were being squeezed out of work by industrialization. For these reasons the parliament failed to win broad popular support.

In April 1849 the Frankfurt Parliament drafted a new constitution for a united Germany, which would have a hereditary "emperor of the Germans" and two houses of parliament, one of which would be elected by universal male suffrage. Austria, however, voted against the new plan, and without Austrian support the new constitution had little hope of success. The final blow to German liberal hopes came when King Frederick William of Prussia refused the Frankfurt Parliament's offer of the crown, which he referred to as coming from the gutter and "reeking of the stench of revolution." At that point the Frankfurt Parliament disbanded and the efforts of German liberals to unite their country and give it a new constitution came to an inglorious end.

By the middle of 1849, conservative forces had triumphed in the various German territories and the Habsburg Empire. In Prussia the efforts of the newly elected assembly to restrict noble privilege triggered a reaction from the conservative nobles known as Junkers. Frederick William dismissed his liberal appointees, sent troops to Berlin, and disbanded the assembly. A similar fate befell the other German states, such as Saxony, Baden, and Hanover, all of which had installed liberal governments in the early months of the revolution. In Austria Prince Alfred Windischgrätz, who had crushed the Czech rebels in June, dispersed the rebels in Vienna in October. When Hungary proclaimed its independence from the empire in April 1849, Austrian and Russian forces marched on the country and crushed the movement.

The Revolutions of 1848 in Italy

The revolutions of 1848 also spread to Austrian possessions in the northern Italian territories of Lombardy and Venetia. In Milan, the main city in Lombardy, revolutionary developments followed the same pattern as those in Paris, Berlin, and Vienna. When the barricades went up, some of the Milanese insurgents used medieval pikes stolen from the opera house to fight off Austrian troops. Their success triggered rebellions in other towns in Lombardy, in Venice, and in the southern Kingdom of the Two Sicilies. In that kingdom the Spanish Bourbon king, Ferdinand II (r. 1830–1859), after suppressing a republican revolt in January, was forced to grant a liberal constitution. The spread of these revolts inspired the hope of bringing about the unification of all Italian people in one state.

This Italian nationalist dream had originated among some liberals and republicans during the first half of the nineteenth century. Its most articulate proponent was Giuseppe Mazzini, a revolutionary from Genoa who envisioned the establishment of a united Italian republic through direct popular action. In his youth Mazzini had been a member of the *Carbonari,* a secret conspiratorial society pledged to drive foreigners out of the Italian states, to secure constitutional liberties, and to bring about some form of Italian unity. His arrest led to one of many periods of exile in London, where he continued to pursue the cause of republicanism and democracy. In 1831 Mazzini founded Italy's first organized political party, Young Italy, which was pledged to realize national unification, democracy, and greater social equality. Mazzini combined a passionate commitment to the ideals of liberalism, republicanism, and nationalism. For him the nation was the highest ideal to which one could pledge devotion, one possessing almost

The German National Assembly Gathered in St. Paul's Church in Frankfurt, 1848
The parliament ultimately failed in its goal to give a liberal constitution to a united Germany.

Prostitution, Corporal Punishment, and Liberalism in Germany

In March 1822 Gesche Rudolph, a poor, uneducated 25-year-old woman from the northern German city of Bremen, was arrested by municipal authorities for engaging in prostitution without registering with the police. Ever since the days when troops from five different European nations had occupied her neighborhood, Rudolph had been selling her sexual services as her only form of livelihood. After her arrest she was not given a formal trial but was summarily expelled from the city and banned from ever returning. Unable to earn a living through prostitution in a village outside the city, where she resided with a brother who physically abused her, Rudolph returned to the city, where she was arrested once again for prostitution. This time she was sentenced to fifty strokes of the cane and six weeks in jail, after which she was once again expelled from the city. Returning again to Bremen, she was arrested in a drunken stupor in a whorehouse and subjected to a harsher sentence of three months' imprisonment and 150 strokes before another expulsion. This pattern of arrest, punishment, expulsion, and return occurred repeatedly during the next two decades, with the number of strokes rising to 275 and the period of imprisonment to six years. During a portion of her prison sentence she was given only bread and water for nourishment.

Rudolph's arrest in 1845 at the end of a six-year imprisonment and her subsequent expulsion and return to Bremen led to the appointment of a liberal lawyer, Georg Wilhelm Gröning, to represent her. After reviewing her case and calculating that she had been whipped a total of 893 times and imprisoned for a cumulative period of eighteen years, Gröning appealed her sentence to the senate of Bremen on the grounds that her treatment was not only futile but immoral. His appeal addressed an issue that went far beyond this particular case or even the prosecution of the crime of prostitution. Gröning's action raised the highly controversial issue of the legitimacy and value of corporal punishment, an issue that divided liberals and conservatives, who had different notions of justice.

Until the eighteenth century the penal systems of Europe had prescribed corporal punishments, administered publicly, for most crimes. These punishments ranged from whippings and placement in the stocks for minor offenses to mutilation, hanging, and decapitation for felonies. They were justified mainly on the grounds that they provided retribution for the crime and deterred the criminal and those who witnessed the punishment from committing further crimes. These two main functions of retribution and deterrence are the same functions that capital punishment allegedly serves today. Corporal punishments were also intended to humiliate the criminal both by violating the integrity of the body and by subjecting the prisoner to the mockery and sometimes the maltreatment of the crowd. The torture of suspects to obtain evidence also served some of these functions, although judicial torture took place during the trial, not as part of the sentence.

The entire system of corporal punishment, as well as that of torture, came under attack during the eighteenth century. In Prussia torture was abolished in 1754, and the General Law Code of 1794 eliminated many forms of corporal punishment. The General Law Code reflected the concern of Enlightenment thinkers that all such assaults on the body were inhumane and a denial of the moral dignity of the individual. Because corporal punishments in Prussia and elsewhere were administered mainly against people from the lower classes, they also were a violation of the liberal principle of equality before the law.

Despite these efforts at reform, the illegal administration of corporal punishment by public and private authorities continued in Prussia and the other German states. Conservatives, who had a different notion of justice from that of the liberals, defended these sentences on the grounds that all punishment, including imprisonment, was intended to deny the criminal freedom and hence his or her dignity. For them any reference to natural rights and human dignity were "axioms derived from abstract philanthropic speculation." The president of the Prussian police, Julius Baron von Minutoli, expressing the conservative position on the issue, claimed that corporal punishment was more effective than imprisonment in preventing crime, as it alone could instill terror in the criminal.

It was apparent that in the case of Gesche Rudolph, 893 strokes had not instilled terror in her or brought about any transformation of her spirit. The Senate made the young woman Gröning's ward and suspended her sentence. Gröning arranged for Rudolph to live in the countryside under the strict supervision of a competent countryman. This compromise solution at least broke the cycle of expulsion, return, and punishment that had failed to reform her. We do not know whether she gave up her life of prostitution.

Soon after Gesche Rudolph became Gröning's ward, the liberal critics of corporal punishment in

Germany celebrated a victory. King Frederick William IV of Prussia formally abolished the practice in his kingdom in May 1848. Shortly thereafter the Frankfurt Parliament included freedom from physical punishment by the state in its *Declaration of the Basic Rights of the German People*. Most German states and municipalities, including Bremen, wrote this right into law in 1849. The failure of the Frankfurt Parliament, however, and the more general failure of liberalism in Germany after 1849 led to a strong conservative campaign to reinstate corporal punishment in the 1850s. They succeeded only in maintaining corporal punishment within the family, on manorial estates, and in the prisons. Liberalism had not succeeded in completely establishing its standard of justice, but it did end exposure to public shame as a punishment for crime.

Questions of Justice

1. What elements of liberalism led those who adhered to this ideology in the nineteenth century to object to corporal punishment?
2. In addition to inflicting physical pain, corporal punishment produces social shame. What is the difference between social shame and legal guilt? In what ways does shame still play a role in punishments today?

Taking It Further

Evans, Richard. *Tales from the German Underworld: Crime and Punishment in the Nineteenth Century.* 1998. Provides a full account of the prosecution of Gesche Rudolph.

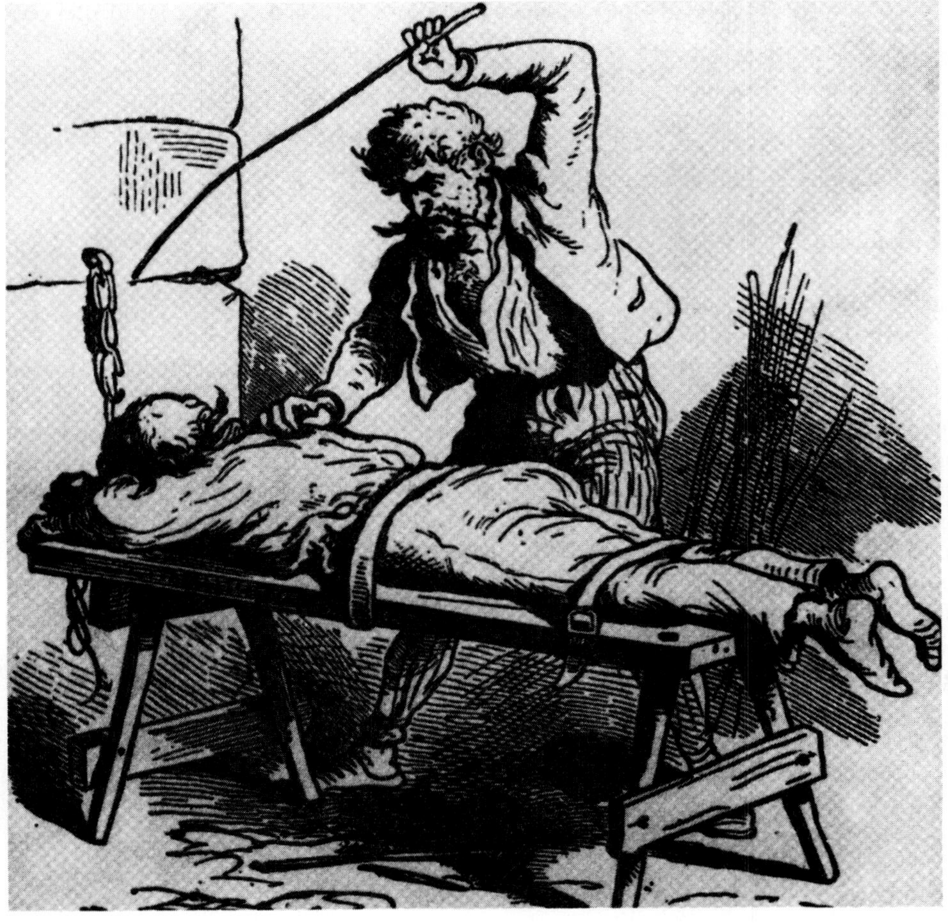

Corporal Punishment in Nineteenth-Century Germany
Whipping in prisons continued long after public corporal punishment was abolished in the middle of the nineteenth century.

mystical qualities. "We have beheld in Italy," he wrote, "the purpose, the soul, the consolidation of our thoughts, the country chosen of God and oppressed by men."

The ruler who assumed the nationalist mantle in 1848 was Charles Albert of Piedmont-Sardinia, the most economically advanced of the Italian states. This initiative began successfully, as Charles Albert's army, which included volunteers from various parts of Italy, marched into Lombardy and defeated Austrian forces. Instead of moving forward against Austria, however, Charles Albert decided to consolidate his gains, hoping to annex Lombardy to his own kingdom. This decision alienated republicans in Lombardy and in other parts of Italy as well as the rulers of the other Italian states, who feared that Charles Albert's main goal was to expand the limits of his own kingdom at their expense. By August 1848 the military tide had turned. Fresh Austrian troops defeated the Italian nationalists outside Milan. The people of that city turned against Charles Albert, forcing him to return to his own capital of Turin. The Italian revolutions of 1848 had suffered a complete defeat.

The Failure of the Revolutions of 1848

The revolutions of 1848 in France, Germany, the Habsburg Empire, and Italy resulted in victory for conservatives and defeat for liberals, nationalists, and socialists. All the liberal constitutions passed during the early phase of the revolutions were eventually repealed or withdrawn. The high hopes of national unity in Germany, Italy, and Hungary were dashed. Workers who built the barricades in the hope of achieving improvements in their working conditions gained little from their efforts.

Divisions among the different groups that began the revolutions were in large part responsible for their failure. The most serious division—in fact, one that was fatal—was the split between the liberals who formulated the original goals of the revolution and the lower-class participants who took to the streets. Liberals used the support of the masses to bring down the governments they opposed, but their ideological opposition to broad-based political movements and their fear of further disorder sapped their revolutionary fervor. Divisions also emerged between liberals and nationalists, whose goals of national self-determination required different strategies from those of the liberals who supported individual freedom.

The failure of the revolutions of 1848 did not, however, portend the death of the ideologies of liberalism, nationalism, and socialism. They all continued to manifest strength during the following two decades, and they often influenced the policies of the conservative governments that returned to power after the revolutions. In Germany, for example, the goal of nationalists was realized under conservative auspices and even mustered a measure of liberal support, while in France liberalism made some inroads into the conservative and nationalist government of the Second French Empire after 1860.

National Unification in Europe and America, 1848–1871

- **How did liberal and conservative leaders use the ideology of nationalism as a tool to unite the people of various territories into nation-states between 1848 and 1871?**

Prior to 1848 the forces of nationalism, especially when combined with those of liberalism, had little to show for their efforts. Besides the Greek rebellion of 1821, which succeeded largely because of international opposition to the Turks, the only successful nationalist revolution in Europe took place in Belgium. Both of these nationalist movements were secessionist in that they involved the separation of smaller states from larger empires. Efforts in 1848 to form nations by combining smaller states and territories, as in Italy and Germany, or by uniting all Slavic people, as proposed at the Pan-Slav Congress, had failed. Between 1848 and 1871, however, movements for national unification succeeded in Italy, Germany, and the United States, each in a different way. In the vast Habsburg Empire a different type of unity was achieved, but it did little to promote the cause of nationalism.

Italian Unification: Building a Fragile Nation-State

The great project of Italian nationalists, the unification of Italy, faced formidable obstacles. Austrian military control over the northern territories, which in the end had thwarted the nationalist movement of 1848, meant that national unification would not be achieved peacefully. The dramatic economic disparities between the prosperous north and the much poorer south posed a challenge to any plan for economic integration. A long tradition of local autonomy within the kingdoms, states, and principalities made submission to a strong central government unappealing. The unique status of the papacy, which controlled its own territory and which influenced the decisions of many other states, served as another challenge. Despite these obstacles, the dream of a resurgence of Italian power, reviving the achievements of ancient Rome, had great emotive appeal. Hatred of foreigners who controlled Italian territory, which dates back to the fifteenth century, gave further impetus to the nationalist movement.

The main question for Italian nationalism after the failure of 1848 was who could provide effective leadership of the movement. It stood to reason that Piedmont-Sardinia, the strongest and most prosperous Italian kingdom, would be central to that undertaking. Unfortunately the king, Victor Emmanuel II (r. 1849–1861), was more known for his hunting, his carousing, and his affair with a teenage mistress than his statesmanship. Victor Emmanuel did, however, appoint as his prime minister a nobleman with liberal leanings, Count Camillio di Cavour (1810–1861). Cavour displayed many of the characteristics of nineteenth-century liberalism. He favored a constitutional monarchy, the restriction of clerical privilege and influence, and the development of a capitalist and industrial economy. He was deeply committed to the unification of the Italian peninsula, but only under Piedmontese leadership, and preferably as a federation of states. In many ways he was the antithesis of the republican Mazzini, the other central figure in Italian unification. Mazzini's idealism and romanticism led him to think of national unification as a moral force that would lead to the establishment of a democratic republic, which would then undertake an extensive program of social reform. Mazzini often wore black, claiming that he was in mourning for the unrealized cause of unification.

Mazzini's strategy for national unification involved a succession of uprisings and invasions. Cavour, however, adopted a diplomatic course of action intended to gain the military assistance of France against Austria. In 1859 French and Piedmontese forces defeated the Austrians at Magenta and Solferino and drove them out of Lombardy. One year later Napoleon III signed the Treaty of Turin with Cavour, allowing Piedmont-Sardinia to annex Tuscany, Parma, Modena, and the Romagna, while ceding to France the Italian territories of Savoy and Nice. This treaty resulted in the unification of all of northern and central Italy except Venetia in the northeast and the Papal States in the center of the peninsula (see Map 21.2).

The main focus of unification efforts now turned to the Kingdom of the Two Sicilies in the south. A rebellion against the Bourbon monarch Francis II, protesting new taxes and the high price of bread, had taken place there in 1860. At that point the militant republican adventurer Giuseppe Garibaldi (1807–1882) intervened with decisive force. Garibaldi, who was born in Nice and spoke French rather than Italian as his main language, was determined no less than Cavour and Mazzini to drive all foreigners out of Italy and achieve its unification. Originally a supporter of Mazzini's republican goals, Garibaldi gave his support in the 1860s for Italian unification within the framework of a monarchy. A charismatic military leader, Garibaldi put together an army of volunteers, known as the Red Shirts for their colorful makeshift uniforms. In 1860 he landed in Sicily with an army of 1,000 men, took the main Sicilian city of Palermo, and established a dictatorship on behalf of King Victor Emmanuel. He then landed on the mainland and took Naples. Shortly thereafter the people of Naples, Sicily, and most of the Papal States voted their support for union with Piedmont-Sardinia. In March 1861 the king of Sardinia assumed the title of King Victor Emmanuel of Italy (r. 1861–1878). Complete unification was achieved when Austria ceded Venetia to Italy in 1866 and when French troops, which had been protecting a portion of the Papal States, withdrew from Rome in 1870.

Garibaldi Surrendering Power—British Cartoon, 1860

The unification of Italy owed more to the statecraft of Cavour than the passion of Mazzini and Garibaldi. Their achievement did not fully realize the lofty nationalist goals of creating a culturally unified people or a powerful central state. Economic differences between northern and southern Italy became even greater after unification than before. The overwhelming majority of the people continued to speak their local dialects or even French rather than Italian. Traditions of local political autonomy and resentment

Giuseppe Garibaldi
The uniform he is wearing was derived from his days as a guerilla fighting in the civil war in Uruguay (1842–1846). Garibaldi also spent two years in asylum in the United States.

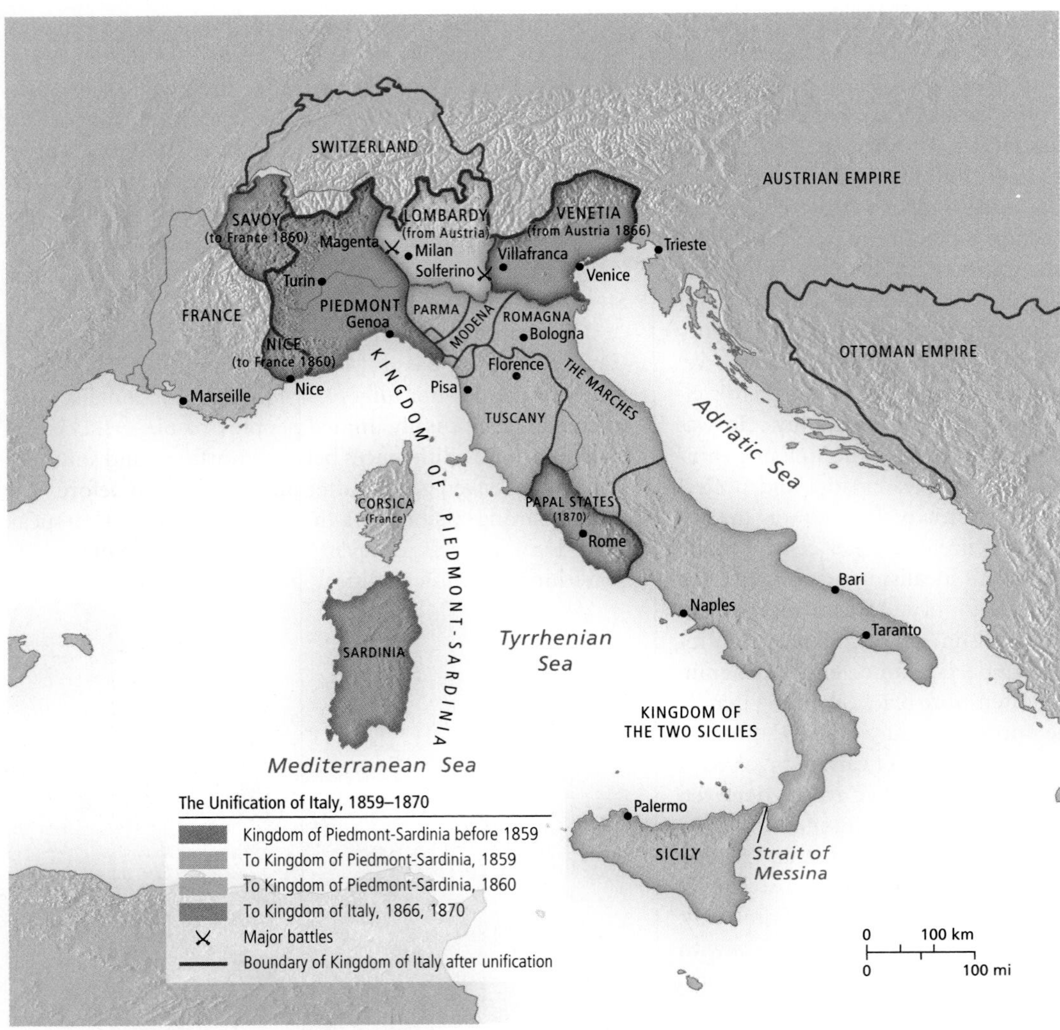

Map 21.2 The Unification of Italy, 1859–1870
The main steps to unification took place in 1860, when Piedmont-Sardinia acquired Tuscany, Parma, Modena, and the Romagna and when Garibaldi seized control of the Kingdom of the Two Sicilies in the name of King Victor Emmanuel of Piedmont-Sardinia.

against the concentration of wealth in the north retarded the development of loyalty to the new Italian state and inspired a series of bloody rebellions in the former Kingdom of the Two Sicilies during the 1870s and 1880s.

This instability was aggravated by the widespread practice of banditry in the southern mainland. Bandits were peasants who, in the hope of maintaining a world that appeared to be vanishing, swept through towns, opened jails, stole from the wealthy, and sacked their houses. Closely related to banditry was the growth in Sicily of the Mafia°, organizations of armed men who took control of local politics and the economy. The Mafia originated during the struggle for unification in the 1860s and strengthened their position in Sicily once the country had been unified. Their power, the prevalence of banditry, and the enduring strength of Italian loyalty to the local community all made it difficult for the new Italian state to flourish. The movement for national unification had driven the French and the Austrians out of the peninsula, but it had failed to create a model nation-state.

German Unification: Conservative Nation-Building

Like Italy, Germany experienced a successful movement for national unification after the disappointments of 1848. The German movement, like the Italian, benefited from the actions of crafty statesmen and from the decisions made by other states. Unlike Italy, however, Germany achieved unification under the direction of highly conservative rather than liberal forces. One reason for this was that the severity of the reaction to the Revolution of 1848 had forced the emigration of many German liberals and nationalists to Great Britain and the Netherlands and as far west as the hill country of central Texas. Nevertheless a number of liberals, such as those who belonged to a Pan-German association known as the National Union, still kept alive the hopes of the Frankfurt Parliament for a German constitutional republic.

The main dilemma regarding German unification was whether Prussia or Austria would form the nucleus of any new political structure. In the end, Prussia, with its almost entirely German-speaking population, its wealth, and its strong army, assumed leadership of the movement. The key figure in this process was Count Otto von Bismarck (1815–1898), a lawyer and bureaucrat from an old Junker family whom King William I of Prussia appointed as his prime minister in 1862. By birth, training, and instinct Bismarck was an inflexible conservative, determined to preserve and strengthen the Prussian nobility and monarchy and to make the Prussian state strong and powerful. In the words of the liberal British ambassador to Berlin, Robert Morier, "not one mustard seed of faith in liberal principles exists in Count Bismarck's nature." Bismarck did not hesitate, however, to make alliances with any political party, including the liberals, to achieve his goals. This subordination of political means to their ends, and Bismarck's willingness to use whatever tactics were necessary, regardless of any moral considerations, made him a proponent of *Realpolitik*, the adoption of political tactics solely on the basis of their realistic chances of success.

The Proclamation of the German Empire in the Hall of Mirrors at Versailles, January 21, 1871

King William I of Prussia, standing on the dais, is being crowned emperor of Germany. At the center of the picture, dressed in a white uniform jacket, is Otto von Bismarck, the person most responsible for the unification of all German territory in one empire.

Bismarck pursued the goal of national unification through the exercise of raw military and political power. "The great questions of the day," he said in 1862, "will not be settled by speeches and majority decisions—that was the error of 1848 and 1849—but by iron and blood." Bismarck did not share the romantic devotion of other German nationalists to the Fatherland or their desire to have a state that embodied the spirit of the German people. His determination to achieve German national unification became synonymous with his goal of strengthening the Prussian state. This commitment to the supremacy of Prussia within a united Germany explains his steadfast exclusion of the other great German power, Austria, from his plans for national unification.

Bismarck's achievement of German unification was based mainly on Prussian success in two wars (see Map 21.3). The first, the Austro-Prussian War of 1866, resulted in the formation of a new union of twenty-two states, the North German Confederation. This new structure replaced the old German Confederation, the loose association of thirty-nine states, including Austria, that had been established in 1815 by the Congress of Vienna. The North German Confederation had a centralized political structure with its own legislature, the *Reichstag;* the king of Prussia became its president and Bismarck its chancellor. The foundation of the North German Confederation was, however, only one step toward the unification of all Germany. Bismarck laid the foundation for the realization of this larger goal by strengthening the *Zollverein,* which included the southern German states. By encouraging free trade among all the German states he also won support for unification from German liberals.

The second war, which completed the unification of Germany, was the Franco-Prussian War of 1870–1871. This

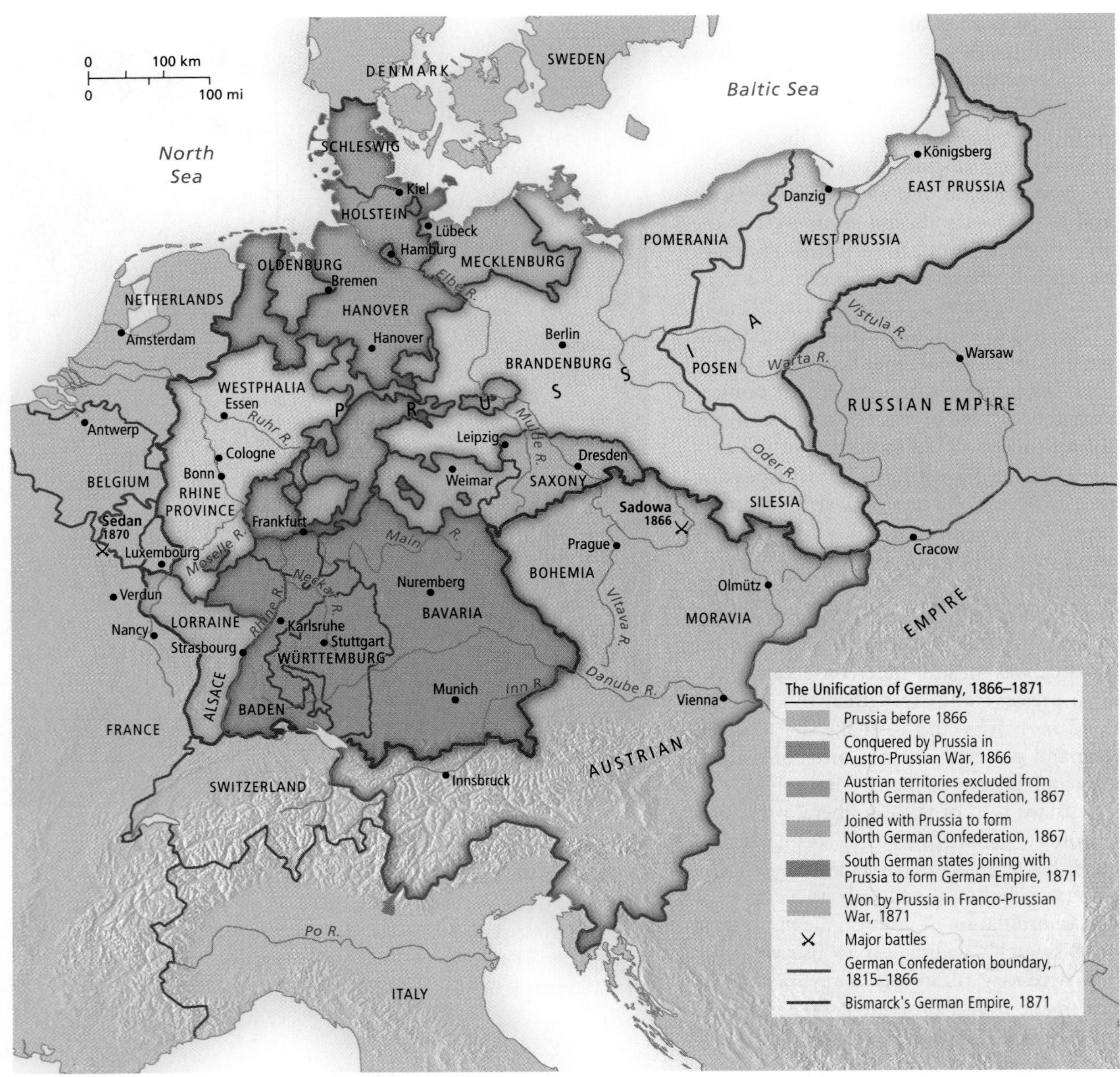

Map 21.3 The Unification of Germany, 1866–1871

Prussia assumed leadership in uniting all German territories except Austria. Prussia was responsible for the formation of the North German Confederation in 1866 and the German Empire in 1871.

conflict began when Napoleon III, the French emperor, challenged Prussian efforts to place a member of the Prussian royal family on the vacant Spanish throne. Bismarck welcomed this opportunity to take on the French, who controlled German-speaking territories on their eastern frontier and who had cultivated alliances with the southern German states. Bismarck played his diplomatic cards brilliantly, guaranteeing that the Russians, Austrians, and British would not support France. He then used the army that he had modernized to invade France and seize the towns of Metz and Sedan. The capture of Napoleon III during this military offensive precipitated the end of France's Second Empire and the establishment of the Third French Republic in September 1870.

As a result of the war Prussia annexed the predominantly German-speaking territories of Alsace and Lorraine. Much more important, it led to the proclamation of the German Empire with William I of Prussia as emperor. Officially the structure of the new empire, a term used to indicate that it embraced many separate states, was that of a federation, just like that of the North German Confederation that preceded it. In fact the government of the empire, like that of

Prussia, was highly centralized as well as autocratic, and the liberal middle classes did not participate in it, as they did in the governments of Britain, France, and Italy. The German imperial government won the support of the middle class by adopting policies supporting free trade, but the ideologies that underpinned the new German Empire were those of conservatism and nationalism, which encouraged devotion to "God, King, and Fatherland."

Unification in the United States: Creating a Nation of Nations

At the same time that Italy and Germany were achieving national unification, the United States of America engaged in a bitter process that preserved and strengthened the federal union it had instituted in 1787. The thirteen colonies that proclaimed their independence from Great Britain in 1776 shared common constitutional grievances against the mother country or metropolis, but each colony had its own identity. The U.S. Constitution, drawn up in 1787, sought to preserve this balance between the states and the federal government by dividing sovereignty between them, leaving to the states control over all matters it had not specifically given to the federal government. This arrangement generated friction and debate between the Federalists, who wished to strengthen the central government, and the Anti-Federalists, who feared that a strong central government would lead to corrupt, arbitrary rule. The Federalists won some early victories, including the establishment of a national bank, but they were unable to create a truly united people. The great victory of the Anti-Federalists was the Bill of Rights, the first ten amendments to the U.S. constitution, which was ratified by the states in 1791. By enumerating the rights of the citizens in a formal constitution, including freedom of speech and freedom of assembly, the Bill of Rights embodied one of the main elements of liberal ideology.

Throughout the early years of the republic Americans continued to think of themselves as citizens of particular states more than as members of a single national community. In the early nineteenth century, President Thomas Jefferson (1801–1809) imagined a new American nation, a people "with one heart and one mind," but nationalist sentiment, such as had developed in European countries on the basis of a common language and culture, had difficulty materializing in the United States. The American republic was originally the product of English-speaking colonists who shared the same language and culture as the British against whom they had rebelled. After the revolution, efforts were made to build a new nation on the basis of a distinctly American culture. *The American Dictionary of the English Language,* compiled by Noah Webster (1758–1843) in 1812, made one contribution to this endeavor by listing hundreds of American words that had never been included in English dictionaries. Patriotic sentiment, especially after the defeat of British forces at the Battle of New Orleans in 1815, also helped give Americans a sense of common purpose and destiny.

These efforts at building an American nation became more challenging as the young republic began to incor porate Western territories into the federal union. Lands acquired by purchase or conquest were formed into territories and then gradually admitted into the union as states. This process of unification, which proceeded in a piecemeal fashion, took much longer than the unifications of Italy and Germany in the 1860s. It was marked by sustained military action against the Native American population and a war against Mexico between 1846 and 1848. Florida was annexed in 1819, while Texas, an independent republic for nine years, was admitted in 1845 and California in 1850. This process of gradual unification did not end until 1912, when New Mexico and Arizona, the last territories in the contiguous forty-eight states, were admitted to the union.

As the United States expanded westward into the Spanish-speaking Southwest, and as immigrants from various European nations swelled the population of the eastern as well as the western states, the country became more rather than less culturally diverse. Assimilation to a dominant Protestant English-speaking culture, even one that was gradually becoming distinct from that of Great Britain, could not provide the same commitment to the homeland that inspired Italians and Germans to support national unification. Americans might be patriotic, in that they proclaimed their allegiance to the federal republic, but they had more difficulty thinking that they shared a common culture with the people from different parts of the country. Building a nation-state in America was a task fraught with obstacles.

The great test of American national unity came during the 1860s, when eleven southern states, committed to the preservation of the economic system of slavery, and determined that it should be extended into new territories acquired by the federal government, seceded from the union and formed a confederation of their own. The issue of slavery had helped to polarize North and South, creating deep cultural and ideological divisions that made the goal of national unity appear even more distant. America had its own ideological and cultural encounters that paralleled those that prevailed in European countries.

The constitutional issue underlying the civil war was the preservation of the union. In a famous speech President Abraham Lincoln (1861–1865) declared that "a house divided against itself cannot stand . . . this government cannot endure permanently half slave and half free." When the war ended and slavery was abolished, that union was not only preserved but strengthened. Amendments to the U.S. Constitution provided for equal protection of all citizens under the law. The South, which had its own regional economy, was integrated into the increasingly commercial and industrial North. The whole process of national unification, both economic and social, was greatly facilitated by the building of railways. In the United States, even more than in Europe, railroads linked otherwise isolated communities and facilitated the spread of products and ideas across vast distances. Gradually the people of the United States began to think of themselves as a united people, drawn from many different nations of the world. The United States became "a nation of nations."

Nationalism in Eastern Europe: Preserving Multinational Empires

The national unifications that took place in Germany, Italy, and the United States formed part of a *western* European pattern in which the main units of political organization would be nation-states. Ethnic minorities would of course always live within the boundaries of these states, but the state itself would encourage the growth of a national identity among all its citizens. We can observe this process at work in France, Britain, and Spain, all of which had undergone a process of national unification before the nineteenth century. Minority populations within these large western European states have occasionally threatened to establish a separate political identity as nations, but with the one notable exception of Ireland, the southern portion of which became independent of Britain in the twentieth century, the large states of western Europe have maintained their unity and promoted nationalist sentiment to sustain it.

In *eastern* Europe a very different pattern prevailed, especially in the Habsburg and Russian Empires. Instead of becoming unified nation-states, these two empires remained large, multinational political formations, embracing many different nationalities. This pattern was most obvious in the large, sprawling Habsburg Empire, which encompassed no fewer than twenty different ethnic groups, each of which thought of itself as a nation (see Map 21.4). The largest of these nationalities were the Germans in Austria and Bohemia and the Magyars in Hungary, but the Czechs, Slovaks, Poles, Slovenes, Croats, Rumanians, Bulgarians, and Italians (before 1866) all formed sizable minority populations. Map 21.4 only begins to reveal the full complexity of this diversity. The various nationalities within the empire had little in common except loyalty to the Habsburg emperor, who defended the Catholic faith and the privileges of the nobility. National unification of the empire would have presented a much more formidable task than the ones that confronted Cavour and Bismarck.

During the era of national unification the ideology of nationalism threatened to tear apart this precariously unified empire. It awakened demands of Hungarians, Czechs, and others for national autonomy and also spawned a movement for the national unity of all Slavs. The emperor,

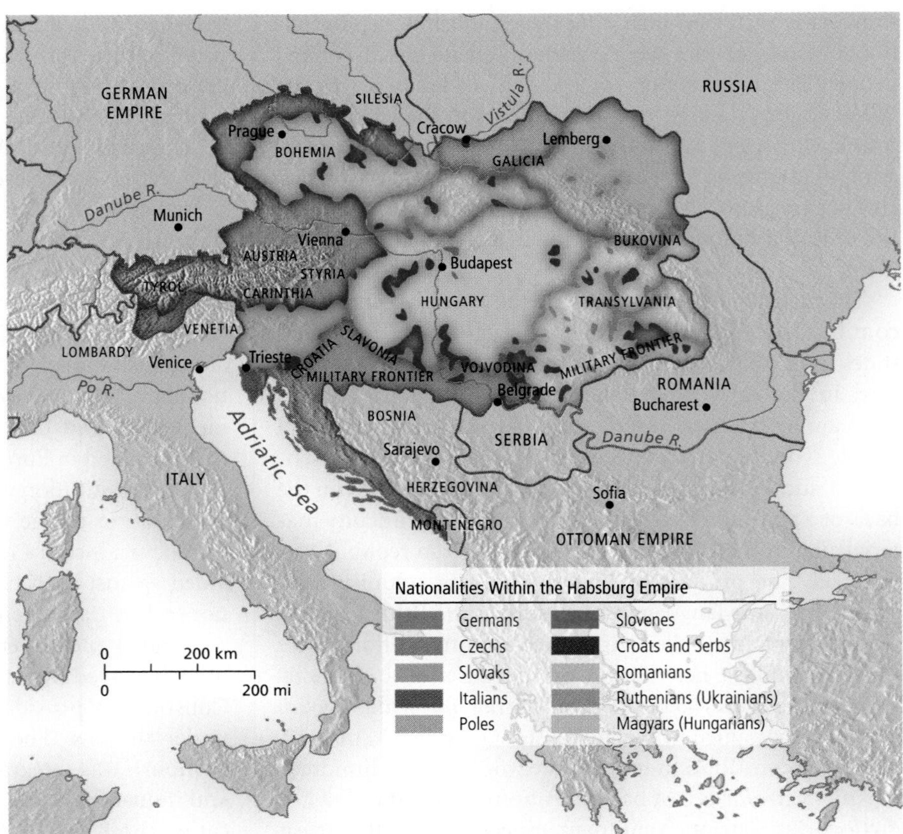

Map 21.4 Nationalities Within the Habsburg Empire The large number of different nationalities within the Habsburg Empire made it impossible to accommodate the demands of all nationalities for their own state.

Francis Joseph (r. 1848–1916), recognized the danger of nationalist ideology. He also feared that liberalism, which was often linked to nationalism, would at the same time undermine his authority, which he had reasserted with a vengeance after the failure of the revolutions of 1848. He therefore repressed these nationalist aspirations at every turn. This policy had disastrous consequences for the future history of Europe, as Slavic nationalism and separatism have remained a source of political instability of southeastern Europe until the present day.

The one concession that Francis Joseph did make during this volatile period was to establish the Dual Monarchy of Austria-Hungary in 1867. This significant increase of Hungarian power within the empire came in the wake of the disastrous defeats of Austrian forces by the French and Piedmontese in 1859 and the Prussians in 1866. Austrian liberals took this opportunity to call for the introduction of constitutional government, while the second-largest ethnic group within the empire, the Magyars, demanded more autonomy for Hungary. The *Ausgleich* (Settlement) of 1867, which was proposed by the wealthy Hungarian nobleman and lawyer Ferenc Deák (1803–1876), created a dual monarchy in which Francis Joseph would be both king of Hungary and emperor of Austria. Each monarchy would have its own parliament and bureaucracy, although matters of foreign policy and finance would be handled in Vienna. This arrangement represented a concession to Magyar nationalism but gave very little to all the other nationalities within both kingdoms. The *Ausgleich* officially recognized the equality of all nationalities within the empire and allowed schooling to be conducted in the local language, but it permitted only Germans in Austria and Magyars in Hungary to acquire their own political identity. Instead of a unified nation-state the emperor now presided over two multinational monarchies.

Ideology, Empire, and the Balance of Power

■ **What role did ideology play in international warfare and diplomacy, especially in efforts to maintain the balance of power during this period?**

The new ideologies of the early nineteenth century, and the movements for national unification to which they gave rise, had a disruptive impact on the conduct of international affairs. The original framework for international action after 1815 was the Concert of Europe, which was intended to prevent the recurrence of revolution and preserve the balance of power. It achieved much greater success in pursuing the second goal than it did the first. The five European powers in the Concert—Britain, Austria, Russia, Prussia, and France—could never contain the liberal and national forces that the French Revolution had unleashed, but as a group the five powers prevented any one of them from establishing a dominant position in Europe.

Challenges to the balance of power during this period came mainly from governments engaged in a process of imperial expansion. The first of these challenges arose in the Western Hemisphere during the 1820s, the second occurred in the 1850s in the Balkans, and the third took place after the Franco-Prussian War of 1870–1871.

Britain, the United States, and the Monroe Doctrine of 1823

In North America a clash of empires threatened to engulf European powers in a new round of imperial expansion and warfare during the early 1820s. As Spanish power in the Western Hemisphere began to collapse, the young republic of the United States feared that Austria or France might intervene in the new Latin American nations. The United States was also alarmed about Russian expansion down the western coast of North America, as we have discussed in Chapter 17. In order to prevent imperial expansion by any of these European powers, the United Sates found an ally in Britain, which even after the loss of the thirteen North American colonies still ruled a large empire of its own in Canada, the Caribbean, and South America. Britain did not wish to compromise the dominant influence it exercised in this area.

British and U.S. resistance to continental European imperialism in the Western Hemisphere had a foundation in liberal ideology. The United States, with its constitutional protection of individual liberty and its success in achieving national self-determination in the American Revolution, had become the very embodiment of European liberalism. No wonder it supported the independence of Latin American nations on ideological as well as diplomatic grounds. In Britain, as we have already seen, the liberal tradition was stronger than in other parts of Europe. Britain's liberal heritage also helps to explain its refusal to join the Holy Alliance of 1815. The British government viewed the Concert of Europe as a mechanism for preserving the balance of power, not for supporting autocratic regimes.

In 1823, President James Monroe (1817–1825) declared that the United States would consider any future attempts by European powers to colonize the Americas as hostile acts. The enforcement of this policy, which became known as the Monroe Doctrine, depended mainly on the support of the British navy, because the United States was not yet capable of taking on the powers of Europe by itself. During the next ten years Britain provided that naval support.

The main effect of the Monroe Doctrine, and Britain's enforcement of it, was to preserve the balance of power in the Western Hemisphere. The doctrine also created the concept of two hemispheres, one old and one new, each refraining from interference in each other's affairs. The broader ideological significance of the Monroe Doctrine was that it provided support for liberalism and nationalism both in Europe and in the Americas. Monroe's speech made explicit reference to the opposition of the United States to the repressive political systems of the allied powers, support for the liberal revolutions that had taken place in Spain and Portugal in 1820, and approval of the revolutions against Spanish rule in Latin America.

Russia, the Ottoman Empire, and the Crimean War, 1853–1856

The second major challenge to the balance of power occurred as a result of Russian imperial ambitions in the Balkans, resulting in the first major war among European powers since the defeat of Napoleon at Waterloo in 1815. The Crimean War (1853–1856), which claimed almost a million casualties on all sides, was the direct result of Russian imperial expansion. It began when Russia occupied the principalities of Moldavia and Wallachia (present-day Romania) in the Ottoman Empire in order to gain access to the Straits of Constantinople and thus to the Aegean and Mediterranean seas. The weakness of the Ottoman Empire had invited Russian expansion into this area, which Russians justified by claiming they were protecting the Orthodox Christianity of people in the Balkans from their Turkish Muslim oppressors. They also claimed that they were promoting the national unity of all Slavic people under Russian auspices. This Russian version of Pan-Slavism differed from that developed by Czech Slavs at the Pan-Slav Congress of 1848. In effect it was an extreme form of Russian imperialism that rivaled the nationalism of individual Slavic nationalities.

Britain resisted the Russian occupation of Moldavia and Wallachia, ostensibly to protect its trade with the Turks but more urgently to prevent Russia from becoming too powerful. In this respect it was adhering to the principles of the Concert of Europe by trying to preserve the balance of power in Europe. The underlying British fear was that Russia might invade India, Britain's most important colony. When the Turks declared war on the Russians, therefore, the British followed suit and were joined by the French. Both powers sent large armies to begin a siege of the port of Sebastopol on the Black Sea.

CHRONOLOGY

French Politics, 1848–1871

1848	
February 25	Establishment of the Second Republic
December	Election of Louis-Napoleon as president of the Second Republic
1851	
December 2	Louis Napoleon dissolves the National Assembly
1852	
November	Establishment of the Second Empire under Napoleon III
1870	
July 19	Beginning of the Franco-Prussian War
September 2	Surrender of Napoleon III to Prussia at Sedan
September 4	End of the Second Empire and proclamation of the Third Republic
1871	
February	National Assembly meets at Bordeaux
March	Rising of the Paris Commune
May 10	End of the Franco-Prussian War
May 21–27	"Bloody Week"; suppression of the Paris Commune

The poorly trained British forces, commanded by officers who had purchased their commissions and who had no sound knowledge of military tactics, suffered staggering losses, more of them from disease than from battle. The most senseless episode of the war occurred when a British cavalry unit, the Light Brigade, rode into a deep valley, only to be cut down by Russian artillery perched on the surrounding hills. The slaughter was memorialized in a poem by the British poet Alfred Lord Tennyson (1850–1892), "The Charge of the Light Brigade."

Nevertheless, the British, French, and Turks prevailed, handing Russia its most humiliating defeat of the nineteenth century. The defeat led to a curtailment of Russian expansion for the next twenty years and preserved the balance of power in Europe. Within Russia the defeat contributed to a crisis that led to a series of liberal reforms during the rule of Tsar Alexander II (1855–1881). Alexander, an indecisive man who had inherited the throne in the middle of the Crimean War, was hardly a liberal (he once referred to the French system of government as "vile"), but he did yield to mounting liberal pressure to emancipate the serfs in 1861, a step that occurred two years before the emancipation of slaves in the United States.

The German Empire and the Paris Commune, 1870–1871

A third, and in the long run the most serious, challenge to the balance of power in Europe came from Prussia. As we have seen, Prussian victories over

Execution of Paris Communards, May 1871
Troops of the provisional French government killed at least 25,000 Parisians during the uprising.

Austria in 1866 and France in 1871 allowed Bismarck to complete the unification of Germany. The newly created German Empire, which now possessed the strongest army in Europe, replaced Austria as the predominant power in central Europe. The growth of German military power, coupled with its expansionist territorial ambitions, soon made it a formidable rival to other European countries and threatened to upset the delicate balance of power. In the twentieth century Germany's territorial ambitions led ultimately to two world wars.

German military success in the Franco-Prussian War of 1870–1871 played a crucial role in French politics, exposing the complex ideological contradictions of the Second French Empire and laying the groundwork for the Third French Republic. After Napoleon III had established the Second Empire in 1852, he tried to mask his usurpation of power by preserving the tradition of universal male suffrage and by submitting his rule to popular ratification, just as his uncle had done. During the 1860s his government became known as "the Liberal Empire," a strange mixture of conservatism, liberalism, and nationalism. Although "the little Napoleon" ruled as an emperor, he gradually allowed a semblance of real parliamentary government to return, relaxed the censorship of the press, and encouraged industrial development. To this mixture he added a strong dose of nationalist sentiment by evoking the memory of Napoleon I.

These efforts failed to save Napoleon III's regime. His moderate liberal policies angered conservatives on the one hand and failed to satisfy the demands of republicans and socialists on the other. These complex ideological encounters came to a head in 1870 during the Franco-Prussian War, which Napoleon himself was in large part responsible for starting. Napoleon took the field at the Battle of Sedan and was captured. The Prussians allowed him to go into exile in England, where he lived until his death in 1873. On September 4, 1870, a large crowd invaded the Legislative Assembly in Paris and forced the deputies who still remained to join them in declaring the end of the Second Empire and the beginning of the Third Republic. Shortly thereafter Prussian troops surrounded Paris and began a long siege of the city, forcing hungry city dwellers to eat cats and dogs roaming the streets and an elephant seized from the Paris zoo.

In January 1871 Adolphe Thiers (1797–1877), a veteran statesman who had served as prime minister during the liberal government of the 1830s, negotiated an armistice with Bismarck. Thiers hoped to establish a conservative republican regime or possibly a restoration of the monarchy at the conclusion of the war. This prospect gained strength when elections to the new National Assembly, which Bismarck permitted so that the French legislature could conclude a formal peace treaty, returned a majority of monarchists.

The National Assembly then elected Thiers as president of the provisional government.

The National Assembly, which sat at Bordeaux, and the provisional government, which took up residence at Versailles, were determined to assert their authority over the entire French nation. In particular, they wanted to curb the independence of the city of Paris, which was determined to carry on the struggle against Prussia and to keep alive the French radical tradition that had flourished in the city in 1792 and again in 1848. The radicalism of the Paris Commune drew its strength from the large working-class population in the industrialized districts on the northern, eastern, and southern edges of the city. The socialist and republican ideals of the Commune's leaders, coupled with their determination to preserve the independence of the city, culminated in the bloodshed described at the beginning of this chapter. The crushing of the Commune marked a bitter defeat for the forces of French socialism and radicalism. The Third French Republic that was established in September 1870 endured, but its ideological foundation was conservative nationalism, not liberalism or socialism.

Conclusion

The Ideological Transformation of the West

The ideological encounters that took place between 1815 and 1871 resulted in significant changes in the political culture of the West. As the early nineteenth-century ideologies of liberalism, conservatism, socialism, and nationalism played out in political movements and revolutions, the people who subscribed to these ideologies often redefined their political objectives. Many British and French socialists, for example, recognizing the necessity of assistance from liberals, abandoned their call for creating a classless society and sought instead to increase wages and improve working conditions of the lower classes. The demands of socialists for greater economic equality pressured liberals to accept the need for more state intervention in the economy. The realities of conservative politics led liberal nationalists in Germany and Italy to accept newly formed nation-states that were more authoritarian than they had originally hoped to establish. Recognizing the strength of the ideologies to which they were opposed, conservative rulers such as Emperor Napoleon III and Tsar Alexander II agreed to adopt liberal reforms. Liberals, conservatives, socialists, and nationalists would continue to modify and adjust their political and ideological positions during the period of mass politics, which began in 1870 and which will be the subject of the next chapter.

The Western ideologies that underwent this process of adaptation and modification had a broad influence on world history. In the twentieth century, three of the four ideologies discussed in this chapter have inspired political change in parts of the world that lie outside the geographical and cultural boundaries of the West. Liberalism has provided the language for movements seeking to establish fundamental civil liberties in India, Japan, and several African countries. In its radical communist form, socialism inspired revolutions in Russia, a country that for many centuries had straddled the boundary between East and West, and in China. Nationalism has revealed its explosive potential in countries as diverse as Nepal, Thailand, and Zaire. Ever since the nineteenth century, Western ideologies have demonstrated a capacity both to shape and to adapt to a variety of political and social circumstances.

Suggestions for Further Reading

For a comprehensive listing of suggested readings, please go to www.ablongman.com/levack2e/chapter21

Anderson, Benedict. *Imagined Communities: Reflections on the Origin and Spread of Nationalism.* 1991. A discussion of the ways in which people conceptualize the nation.

Clark, Martin. *The Italian Risorgimento.* 1999. A comprehensive study of the social, economic, and religious context of Italian unification as well as its political and diplomatic dimensions.

Gellner, Ernest. *Nations and Nationalism.* 1983. An interpretive study that emphasizes the social roots of nationalism.

Hamerow, Theodore S. *Restoration, Revolution, Reaction: Economics and Politics in Germany, 1815–1871.* 1966. An investigation of the social basis of ideological encounters in Germany.

Honour, Hugh. *Romanticism.* 1979. A comprehensive study of romantic painting.

Hunczak, Tara, ed. *Russian Imperialism from Ivan the Great to the Revolution.* 1974. A collection of essays that illuminate Russian nationalism as well as imperialism over a long period of time.

Lichtheim, George. *A Short History of Socialism.* 1970. A good general treatment of the subject.

Nipperdey, Thomas. *Germany from Napoleon to Bismarck, 1800–1866.* 1996. An exploration of the creation of German nationalism as well as the failure of liberalism.

Onuf, Peter S. *Jefferson's Empire: The Language of American Nationhood.* 2000. A study of Jefferson's expansionary nationalism.

Pflanze, Otto. *Bismarck and the Development of Germany: The Period of Unification, 1815–1871.* 1963. The classic study of both Bismarck and the unification movement.

Pinckney, David. *The French Revolution of 1830.* 1972. The best treatment of this revolution.

Seton-Watson, Hugh. *Nations and States.* 1977. A clearly written study of the nation-state.

Sperber, Jonathan. *The European Revolutions, 1848–1851.* 1994. The best study of the revolutions of 1848.

Tombs, Robert. *The War Against Paris, 1871.* 1981. A narrative history of the Paris Commune.

The Coming of Mass Politics: Industrialization, Emancipation, and Instability, 1870–1914

22

CHAPTER OUTLINE

- Economic Transformation
- Defining the Political Nation
- Broadening the Political Nation
- Outside the Political Nation? The Experience of Women

IN THE SPRING OF 1881, A HARROWING SCENE TOOK PLACE IN ST. PETERSBURG, capital of the vast Russian Empire. A 28-year-old woman, Sofiia Perovskaia, was scheduled to be executed for her part in the assassination of Tsar Alexander II. Born into the ranks of wealth and privilege, Perovskaia had rejected her traditional role in order to join the revolutionary socialist movement. She became a leader of the People's Will, a small revolutionary group that sought to undermine the tsarist regime through a program of sabotage and assassination. These revolutionaries dared to set their sights on assassinating the tsar himself, and on March 1, 1881, they achieved this goal. Led by Perovskaia, six People's Will members (all under age 30) stationed themselves at prearranged points along the streets of St. Petersburg. At Perovskaia's signal, they released their bombs and assassinated one of the most powerful men in Europe.

Despite the death of the tsar and the audacity of the crime, however, the tsarist regime did not crumble. The six assassins were quickly arrested and sentenced to death by hanging. (One of the six was pregnant and therefore allowed to live.) On the day of Perovskaia's execution, she mounted the scaffold calmly, but when the noose was placed around her neck, she grabbed hold of the platform below with her feet. It took the strength of two men to pry her feet loose so that she could hang.

The image of Sofiia Perovskaia clinging to the platform with her bare feet while her two executioners strained to push her to her death captures the ferocity of political struggle not only in Russia but throughout Europe at the end of the nineteenth century. As Chapter 21 explained, the ideological

Mass Society at Play Pierre Auguste Renoir, *Le Moulin de la Galette* (1876). The growing cities offered both middle- and working-class men and women new opportunities for leisure and relaxation.

competition among liberals, conservatives, socialists, and nationalists shaped the political culture of the West in the nineteenth century. Economic developments after 1870 both intensified and widened this competition. Individuals and groups that had traditionally been excluded from power demanded a voice in political affairs. Even in authoritarian Russia, the political nation could not long remain the preserve of the titled and wealthy. Neither economic modernization nor the coming of mass politics ensured the victory of democracy, however. Like Sofiia Perovskaia's executioners, the governing classes often struggled hard to pry newcomers off the platform of political power—and they often won.

How did the new mass politics reshape definitions of the West by the beginning of the twentieth century? Four questions will structure our exploration of mass politics and its impact:

- **How did the economic transformation of Europe after 1870 help shape the encounters between established political elites and newcomers to the political process?**
- **How did the ruling classes of the Western powers respond to the new threats and opportunities provided by mass political participation?**
- **What forms did mass politics assume during this time of industrial expansion and the spread of modern nationalist ideology?**
- **In what ways did the emergence of feminism in this period demonstrate the potential as well as the limits of political change?**

Economic Transformation

- **How did the economic transformation of Europe after 1870 help shape the encounters between established political elites and newcomers to the political process?**

Europe's political development between 1870 and 1914 is inextricably linked to its economic transformation. Four important economic developments helped shape European actions and attitudes during these years: the onset of economic depression in 1873, the expansion of the Industrial Revolution into new geographic regions and economic sectors, the emergence of new patterns in the production and consumption of industrial goods, and accelerated urbanization and immigration. Together, these developments not only altered the daily life of the ordinary European, they also exacerbated social tensions and accelerated political change. The resulting series of often violent encounters within societies helped transform the political structures and ideologies of the West.

Economic Depression

In 1873, Europe's economy tilted sharply downward—prices, interest rates, and profits all fell, and remained low in many regions until the mid-1890s. Contemporaries referred to this as the Great Depression in Trade and Agriculture°. In hindsight, "Great Depression" may seem an inaccurate label for a period that saw a continuing rise in world production and growing levels of foreign investment in new industrial economies, but to many Europeans living in these decades, this Great Depression seemed depressing indeed. Agriculture was hardest hit of all economic sectors. By the 1890s, the price of wheat had fallen to only one-third of what it had been in the 1860s. Farm owners and laborers across Europe found it difficult to remain on the land and make a living. Business, too, faced hard times after 1873. Profit margins were squeezed as the prices of finished products fell, often by as much as 50 percent, while labor and production costs tended to remain much more static.

What caused this depression? Ironically, it was rooted in the very success of the Industrial Revolution. The development of the steamship and the expansion of railway lines across Europe and the United States sharply reduced the cost of transporting both agricultural and industrial goods. Cheaper transportation costs opened the breadbaskets of the American Midwest and Ukraine to European consumption. With wheat and other agricultural goods now flooding the market, farmers were forced to accept increasingly lower prices for their products. More generally, as regions and nations industrialized, they of course produced more goods. Yet many industrial workers, agricultural laborers, and landowning peasants still stood on the very edge of subsistence, with little money to spend on industrial products. In other words, by the 1870s, a mass consumer society had not yet emerged. Thus in many regions of Europe production exceeded consumption, and the result was a long-term agricultural and industrial depression.

Industrial Expansion

The onset and impact of economic depression is, then, closely linked to the second important economic development of this period—the continued expansion of the Industrial Revolution. As Chapter 20 detailed, the period between 1760 and 1860 saw gradual, spotty, but still dramatic changes in economic production, first in Britain, then in portions of western Europe. But throughout much of the nineteenth century many of the inhabitants of central, eastern, and southern Europe continued to live and work in ways not far removed from those of their great-grandparents. They used simple horse- or oxen-drawn plows, they harvested with scythes fueled by their own arms and backs, they celebrated births and mourned deaths with

Pre-Industrial Continuities
This photograph of French peasant women taking time off for a meal highlights the patchy nature of industrialization even in western Europe. Not until the 1880s and 1890s did many rural regions come within the embrace of the modern industrial economy.

rituals embedded in centuries-old peasant cultures. And they had little contact with unsettling ideas as high rates of illiteracy continued—almost 90 percent in some rural regions of the Austrian Empire, for example.

This cultural and economic isolation was breaking down by the time World War I erupted in 1914. Railways, which increasingly linked Europe's diverse regions into a single economic network, played a crucial role. Between 1870 and 1914 the world's rail network grew by 500 percent. In the 1880s, agriculture still employed the majority of Europe's population in all countries except Britain, Belgium, France, the Netherlands, and Switzerland, but even peasants still farming in traditional ways were caught up in the momentum of the industrial economy.

Imperial Russia serves as a good example of the breakdown of social and cultural isolation. By 1914 Russia had developed a significant industrial zone, one that tied it more closely than ever before to Western economic structures. In the 1890s, Russia underwent dramatic industrialization under the leadership of Sergei Witte (1849–1915), Alexander III's finance minister. Before serving the tsar in this capacity, Witte had a successful career in the railway industry. He used this experience to carry out a program of planned economic development. The state-owned railway network doubled in size. This impressive engineering achievement, which included the 5,000-mile trans-Siberian railway (begun in 1891), accelerated the movement of both goods and laborers across the vast expanse of Russian territory. Witte also placed Russia on the gold standard, making the Russian ruble easily convertible into other currencies and so fostering international trade. High taxes and protective tariffs generated some of the capital to fuel industrial expansion, but foreign investment was also crucial. French, British, German, and Belgian capital poured into Russia, up from 98 million rubles in 1880 to 911 million by 1900. By the turn of the century, as a result of such policies, Russian steel production was ranked fourth worldwide—behind only Britain, Germany, and the United States—and Russia supplied 50 percent of the oil used by the industrialized world. Coal mines and steel mills dotted Ukraine, and huge state-run factories dominated Moscow and St. Petersburg.

The Second Industrial Revolution

The expansion of the Industrial Revolution coincided with a shift in the processes of industrialization itself. The decades after 1870 witnessed a new phase in the techniques and technologies of both production and consumption, a phase that some historians regard as so important that they call it the "Second Industrial Revolution°." Mechanical processes were altered with the development of more specialized lathes and the mechanization of tasks such as grinding that had previously been completed by hand. By the late 1870s, a series of technological innovations ensured that for the first time steel could be produced cheaply and in huge quantities. The availability of steel, more durable and more flexible than iron, expanded production in industries such as railroads, shipbuilding, and construction.

The Eiffel Tower Reaches to the Sky

Engineer Gustave Eiffel designed the Eiffel Tower for the Paris Universal Exposition of 1889. French politicians intended the exposition to highlight the "progress resulting from one hundred years of freedom," yet many of its displays featured artifacts from cultures France had conquered.

The construction industry itself was transformed. New technological advances in the production of not only steel but also iron, cement, and plate glass, combined with the inventions of the mechanical crane and stone cutter, allowed architects and builders to reach to the skies. Cityscapes changed dramatically as these spectacular new constructions thrust upward. In 1885, the engineering firm of Gustave Eiffel (1832–1923) proposed the construction of an iron and steel tower to celebrate the Paris World's Fair of 1889. Modeled on the structural supports of railway viaducts, the Eiffel Tower was ridiculed by critics as a "truly tragic street lamp" and a "half-built factory pipe," but it soon came to symbolize both Paris and the new age of modernity.

This same era saw the development of electric power. In 1866 the English scientist Michael Faraday (1791–1867) designed the first electromagnetic generator. Four years later the first commercially viable generator was produced. Once electricity could be cheaply generated and delivered to homes and shops, it then needed to be converted into usable forms. In 1879, the American Thomas Edison (1847–1931) invented the lightbulb and illuminated the practical possibilities of electric power. These developments created a huge new energy-producing industry. They also accelerated the production and distribution of other industrial goods as factories and shops, as well as the train and tram lines that serviced them, were linked to the city power grid.

One important characteristic that distinguished this new phase of industrialization was the role of the state in encouraging economic modernization. Governments implemented policies of economic regulation and intervention, such as the construction of state-owned and -operated railway networks and the provision of financial assistance to private business ventures. The challenge posed by the Great Depression hastened the retreat from the free-trade principles of economic liberalism. Faced with declining profits and increased competition, businessmen demanded that their governments act to protect domestic industries from foreign competition. In this period, only Britain, Denmark, and the Netherlands retained the liberal commitment to free trade and refused to construct tariff walls designed to overprice the goods of outside competitors.

The emergence of much larger and more complicated organizational structures also characterized this new industrial phase. As a result of the economic pressures of the Great Depression, businesses grew much bigger. Faced with the necessity of trimming production costs in a time of declining profits, business owners developed new organizational forms, including both *vertical integration*—buying up the companies that supplied their raw materials and those that bought their finished products—and *horizontal integration,* linking up with companies in the same industry to fix prices, control competition, and ensure a steady profit. The Standard Oil Company exemplifies both trends. Formed in 1870 by the American industrialist John D. Rockefeller (1839–1937), Standard Oil monopolized 75 percent of the petroleum business in the United States by the 1890s, and in addition controlled iron mines, timberland, and various manufacturing and transportation businesses.

Within these new, huge, often multinational companies, organization grew more complex and impersonal. The small family firm run by the owner who knew the name of every employee grew increasingly rare as an ever-expanding layer of managers and clerical staff separated worker from owner. Moreover, identifying "the owner" grew increasingly difficult. The need for capital to fuel these huge enterprises drove businesses to incorporation—the sale of "shares" in the business to numerous stockholders, each of whom now shared ownership in the company.

The development of more complicated organizational patterns at the production end of the economic process interacted with changes in the way goods were marketed.

DOCUMENT

The Ladies' Paradise

The French novelist Émile Zola recognized in the new department store a revolutionary force of modernization. His novel The Ladies' Paradise, *first published in 1883, explored the social and economic changes associated with this retail revolution. As this excerpt makes clear, Zola, through his fictional character Mouret, the fiercely competitive department store owner, saw women as playing a central role in the revolution.*

It was the cathedral of modern business, strong and yet light, built for vast crowds of customers. In the central gallery on the ground floor, after the bargains near the door, came the tie, glove, and silk departments; the Monsigny Gallery was occupied by the household linen and the printed cotton goods, the Michodiere Gallery by the haberdashery, hosiery, cloth, and woolen departments. Then, on the first floor, there were the ready-made clothes, lingerie, shawls, lace, and other new departments, while the bedding, carpets, and furnishing materials, all the bulky goods and those which were difficult to handle, had been relegated to the second floor. By this time there were thirty-nine departments and eighteen hundred employees, of whom two hundred were women. A whole world was springing up amidst the life echoing beneath the high metal naves.

Mouret's [the department store owner's] sole passion was the conquest of Woman. He wanted her to be the queen in his shop; he had built this temple for her in order to hold her at his mercy. His tactics were to intoxicate her with amorous attentions, to trade on her desires, and to exploit her excitement. He racked his brains night and day for new ideas. Already, to spare delicate ladies the trouble of climbing the stairs, he had installed two lifts lined with velvet. In addition, he had just opened a buffet, where fruit cordials and biscuits were served free of charge, and a reading-room, a colossal gallery decorated with excessive luxury, in which he even ventured to hold picture exhibitions. But his most inspired idea, which he deployed with women devoid of coquetry, was that of conquering the mother through the child; he exploited every kind of force, speculated on every kind of feeling, created departments for little boys and girls, stopped the mothers as they were walking past by offering pictures and balloons to their babies. Presenting a balloon as a free gift to each customer who bought something was a stroke of genius; they were red balloons, made of fine indiarubber and with the name of the shop written on them in big letters; when held on the end of a string they traveled through the air, parading a living advertisement through the streets!

Source: Émile Zola, *The Ladies' Paradise* (1883; NY: Oxford University Press, 1995), pp. 232–3. Translation by Brian Nelson.

During these decades, a revolution in retailing occurred, one that culminated in a new type of business aimed at middle-class customers—the department store. In a traditional shop, the retailer (who was often also the producer) offered a single product—gloves, for example—in limited quantity at a fairly high price. Often, this price was not set. The customer haggled with the tradesperson until they agreed on a price. "Browsing" was unheard of; an individual who entered a shop was expected to make a purchase. The department stores changed these practices. These new commercial establishments—Bon Marche in Paris, Macy's in New York, Marshall Field's in Chicago, Whiteley's in London—offered a vast array of products in huge quantities. They made their profits not from high prices, but from a quick turnover of a very large volume of low-priced goods. To stimulate sales, they sought to make shopping a pleasant experience. Thus, they provided huge, well-lighted expanses filled with appealing goods sold by courteous, well-trained clerks. In-store reading rooms and restaurants pampered the weary shopper. Another innovation, mail-order catalogs, offered the store's delights to potential customers stranded in distant rural regions and traditionally reliant for their goods on the itinerant peddler and the seasonal fair. Advertising became a crucial industry in its own right, as business sought to persuade potential customers of new needs and desires.

On the Move: Emigration and Urbanization

These three economic developments—the onset of the Great Depression, the expansion of industrialization, and the Second Industrial Revolution—accelerated already existing patterns of urbanization and immigration, and so helped widen the borders of local, regional, and national communities across Europe. The Great Depression hit agricultural regions particularly hard, at just the same time that continuing population growth exerted greater pressure on land and jobs. In addition, industrial expansion undercut rural manufacturing and handicraft production, crucial sources of income for rural populations. As a result, men and women from traditional villages sought new economic opportunities in the industrializing cities of Europe, or further abroad, in the United States, Canada, South America, and Australia.

European cities grew dramatically after 1870. In 1800, only 23 European cities had more than 100,000 inhabitants.

The Bicycle Revolution

The bicycle revolutionized daily life for ordinary Europeans. The introduction of equal-sized wheels in 1886 and of pneumatic tires in 1890 allowed for a far more comfortable ride than had been the case with the bone-breaking cycles built earlier. Mass industrial production made the bicycle affordable; for the first time, ordinary individuals, far too poor to afford a horse or motorcar, could dare to purchase their own private means of transportation that would get them where they wanted to go in one-quarter of the time that walking required. No longer confined to their village for work opportunities or social contacts, bicycle owners discovered that their daily world had widened fourfold. As this engraving shows, the bicycle also contributed to the expansion of the woman's sphere.

By 1900, 135 cities of such a size had sprung up. The European population as a whole continued to expand in this period, but the cities increased at a much faster pace. For example, in 1800 the city of Odessa in Ukraine held 6,000 inhabitants. By 1914, Odessa contained 480,000 people. In the same period, Hungary's Budapest expanded from 50,000 to 900,000 inhabitants.

The migration flow was not all one-way. Farm laborers moved to the cities when times were tough and then moved home again after they had earned some money. Most urban immigrants came to the cities from the surrounding countryside, and often stayed for less than a year. Duisberg, a steel- and tool-making center located in Germany's Ruhr Valley, grew in population from 8,900 to 106,700 between 1848 and 1904. Almost one-third of its newcomers in the 1890s came from villages less than fifteen miles away. No fewer than two-thirds of these immigrants eventually returned to their rural villages.

By 1910, however, one-sixth of Duisberg's immigrants came from other countries, particularly Italy and the Netherlands. The combined impact of agricultural crisis and urban industrial expansion broke down national boundaries to create an international industrial workforce by 1914. Inhabitants of industrially underdeveloped regions were drawn to more economically advanced areas. Italians headed to France and Switzerland, while the Irish poured across the Irish Sea into Liverpool and Glasgow.

Some immigrants headed not for the nearest city, but for an entirely different continent. Between 1860 and 1914, more than 52 million Europeans crossed the ocean in quest of a better life. Seventy-two percent of these transoceanic immigrants traveled to North America, 21 percent to South America, and the rest to Australia and New Zealand.[1] Irish and English immigration to the United States remained high throughout this period, but after the 1880s eastern Europeans accounted for an ever-larger share of those bound for America. One hundred thousand Poles moved to the United States over the course of the 1880s; in the first decades of the twentieth century, between 130,000 and 175,000 Poles were immigrating to the United States each year.

By the 1890s, a truly global labor market had developed. Both technological developments (primarily the shift from sailing to steam ships) and competition among shipping firms considerably reduced the cost of transoceanic travel. As a result, men from villages in southern Italy and Spain could cross the Atlantic in time for the fall harvest of wheat in Argentina, travel to Brazil to pick coffee beans, and then head back home in May. Clearly, in such societies, the borders between local villages and the rest of the world had become permeable.

Growing Social Unrest

M. I. Pokzovskaya on Working Conditions of Women in the Factories (early 20th c.)

Rapid economic change, combined with accelerated urbanization and immigration, heightened social tensions and destabilized political structures. The freefall in prices that characterized the Great Depression eroded capitalist profit margins, shattered business confidence, and increased middle-class resistance to workers' demands. Class hostilities rose as workers responded angrily to businessmen's efforts to protect their profit margins by reducing the number of their employees and increasing labor productivity.

In rural regions such as Spain and Ireland, the devastating collapse in agricultural prices fostered serious social and economic crises. Increasingly desperate, agricultural laborers and peasants turned to violence to enforce their calls for a fairer distribution of land. The spread of industrialization into southern and eastern Europe also led to social unrest as handicraft producers and independent artisans fought to maintain their traditional livelihoods in the face of the industrial onslaught.

In regions such as Britain and parts of Germany, traditional producers had lost that battle against industrialization in the preceding generation, but the onset of the Second Industrial Revolution brought new social strains. The expansion of office and sales jobs widened the ranks of the lower middle class (or *petty bourgeoisie*). This increasingly important social group exhibited extreme class consciousness and an often fierce hostility toward the working class. With an income no higher than that of a skilled worker, the clerk had to fight hard to maintain middle-class status. The erosion of objective differences such as income levels accentuated the importance of subjective differences—wearing the correct clothing, speaking with the proper accent, living on the right street, keeping the children in school.

The flow of immigrants into Europe's cities also sent social and ethnic tensions soaring. Cities were often unable to cope with the sudden and dramatic increases in population, despite the spread of public health provisions such as water and sewer systems. Housing shortages and poor living conditions exacerbated social tensions as newcomers battled with established residents for jobs and apartments. The mixture of different nationalities and ethnic groups often proved particularly explosive.

Defining the Political Nation

- **How did the ruling classes of the Western powers respond to the new threats and opportunities provided by mass political participation?**

The economic and social changes examined in the last section helped create mass politics—a new political culture characterized by the participation of men (but not yet women) outside the upper and middle classes. Mass politics was in many ways an industrial product. In general terms, industrial expansion broke down local and regional cultures, loyalties, and mindsets; it thus cleared the way for the development of national political identities and interests. More specifically, the new transportation and communication technologies introduced by industrialization made mass political participation possible. The railroads, telegraph, and telephone, for example, shattered the barriers of distance between province and capital, while new printing technologies made newspapers cheap and available to ordinary people. With access to information, they could now form opinions and participate in national and international debate as never before. At the same time, the dramatic growth of cities associated with industrialization created the environments in which mass political movements could grow.

Faced with the challenge of adapting to this new political culture, political leaders sought ways to quell social discontent and ensure the loyalty of their populations. They did so in the context of the turbulent international climate created not only by the spread of industrialization but also by the national unification of both Italy and Germany and the continuing decline of the Ottoman Empire (see Chapter 21). As the European balance of power shifted, governments scrambled to create policies that would strengthen their states both at home and abroad.

Nation Making

After 1870, all but the most authoritarian of European political leaders recognized the importance of "nation-making," of creating a sense of national identity powerful enough to overcome the conflicting regional, social, and political loyalties that divided their citizens and subjects. But while European political elites sought to make ordinary men feel a part of political life, they endeavored, through such nation-making policies, to retain their dominant social and political position. As socialism mounted an increasingly powerful challenge to both liberal and conservative regimes, those in power had to figure out how to stay there.

Franchise Expansion

One way to stay in power was by sharing power. The British political system proved the most flexible in this regard. In the first half of the nineteenth century, Britain's landed elite had accommodated middle-class demands for greater influence without relinquishing its own political dominance. Aristocrats and landed gentlemen played leading roles in both major political parties—the Liberals and the Conservatives (also called "Tories")—but both parties also pursued policies that encouraged industrial growth and benefited the middle classes. In the last third of the century, this system expanded to include working-class men. In 1867, many urban working men won the right to vote, and in 1884 this right was extended to rural male laborers. Although Britain did not achieve universal male suffrage until after World War I, these gradual measures of franchise expansion convinced many British working-class men that they could be a part of the political nation and that the political system did respond to demands for reform.

Across Europe in the last third of the nineteenth century and the opening decades of the twentieth century, we see similar patterns as both aristocratic and middle-class politicians enacted measures extending the vote to lower-class men. These political leaders regarded franchise reform as a preventive measure, a way to avoid socialist revolution by incorporating potential revolutionaries within the system. Even strongly conservative politicians came to realize that mass suffrage did not always mean radical political change, as the political structure of Germany attested. The new German state remained politically authoritarian, despite its democratic appearance. All adult males had the right to elect representatives to the German Reichstag (the lower house of parliament) but the Reichstag was fairly powerless. Real power lay in the hands of William I (r. 1861–1888), the first emperor (or *kaiser*) of the unified Germany, and his chancellor, the conservative aristocrat Otto von Bismarck.

Regardless of conservative or liberal intentions, however, the widened franchise was a key development in the creation of mass politics. New voters had to be wooed and wowed; they had to be persuaded to vote the way their leaders, or aspiring leaders, wished. Again, Germany provides a potent example. Even Bismarck could not entirely ignore the democratically elected Reichstag, because it possessed the power of the purse: It approved the budget and appropriated the funds necessary to run the government.

Social Reform

To attract workers' votes, but more important, to ensure working-class loyalty to the nation and its political leaders, political parties turned to social welfare legislation. In the

Map 22.1 Europe at the End of the Nineteenth Century

A comparison of this map with Map 19.2 ("Europe After the Congress of Vienna in 1815," page 638) shows the impact of modern nationalism on European political geography. The most striking change is the formation of the new states of Italy and Germany (the German Empire). In addition, nationalist movements succeeded in carving away large chunks of the Ottoman Empire's European territories. By the 1880s, Bosnia and Herzegovina were under Austrian administration, and Greece, Serbia, Montenegro, Rumania, and Bulgaria had all achieved independence.

1880s, for example, Bismarck introduced to Germany some of the most thoroughgoing social welfare measures yet seen in Europe. He initiated sickness benefits in 1883, coverage for industrial accidents in 1884, and old-age pensions and disability insurance in 1889. Bismarck, a fiercely conservative aristocrat, might seem an unlikely social welfare crusader, but his policies suited his overall goal of ensuring German stability, prosperity, and international power. Alarmed by the growing popularity of the German Social Democratic Party (SPD), Bismarck had outlawed it in 1878 and authorized the federal police to disband all socialist meetings and organizations. This attack on the SPD appealed to antisocialist groups such as conservative landowners, Roman Catholics, and liberal businessmen, but risked alienating the growing urban working class. To attract the support of this vital social segment and weaken the appeal of the SPD's call for violent revolution at the same time, Bismarck turned to social welfare legislation.

Bismarck was not the only or even the first conservative political leader to advocate social welfare as a means of winning the loyalty of the expanding industrial working classes. In Britain, the Conservative Party leader Benjamin Disraeli (1804–1881) argued that the traditional aristocratic policy of *noblesse oblige,* of the privileged caring for those below them, made the Conservatives the natural party of social reform. In the 1870s, his government strengthened trade union rights, established the beginnings of a public housing program, expanded the state's program of inspecting factories, and assumed some responsibility for the population's safety by beginning to monitor the sale of food and drugs.

The most substantial foundations of Britain's welfare state were, however, constructed in the early twentieth century by a Liberal government. Between 1906 and 1912, the Liberals enacted a series of welfare measures, including state-funded lunches for schoolchildren, pensions for the elderly, and sickness and unemployment benefits for some workers. This legislation, like Bismarck's two decades earlier, was a direct response to the political threat posed by working-class socialism. In 1906, British trade unionists and socialists allied together to form the Labour Party. Seeking to maintain their hold on working-class voters, the Liberals turned to social welfare measures.

A similar process occurred in Italy. Alarmed by the growing appeal of Italy's revolutionary socialist parties, the liberal leader Giovanni Giolitti (1842–1928) embarked on a conscious policy of improving workers' lives and so convincing their political leaders that real change did not require revolution. Giolitti legalized trade unions, nationalized the railroads, established public health and life insurance programs, cracked down on child labor, and established a six-day workweek.

Schooling the Nation

Social welfare was part of a broader nation-making agenda that sought to unite the masses with the elite in a strong national community. In this nation-making effort, schools also played an essential role. State elementary schools served as important tools in the effort to build internally united and externally competitive nation-states. During the last third of the nineteenth century, most of the nations of western and central Europe established free public elementary education systems. In Austria-Hungary, for example, free and compulsory education was decreed in 1869.

Of course, passing legislation is one thing, ensuring compliance another. Because children's wages contributed to the family income, many poor families deeply resented the laws that made school attendance mandatory. In poorer districts of Austria-Hungary such as Bukovina, only 36 percent of children attended school, despite the law. In Italy communities were required to provide free education to needy children as early as 1859, but as late as 1912 only 31 percent of the children in the southern region of Calabria were in school.

Despite these difficulties, the schools constituted an essential link in the chain of national identity. Schools broke the cultural barriers imposed by illiteracy. Individuals who could read had access to newspapers, magazines, and books that drew them far beyond the borders of their local village or neighborhood. Both political leaders and intellectuals recognized the power of education in creating a national community. In the 1880s, for example, French student teachers were instructed that "their first duty is to make [their pupils] love and understand the fatherland."[2]

Schools thus helped forge a national identity in very specific ways. First, they ensured the triumph of the national language. Required to abandon their regional dialect (and sometimes brutally punished if they did not), children learned to read and write in the national language. Second, history and geography lessons taught children particular versions of the past that buttressed their sense of belonging to a superior people and often served a specific political agenda. For example, French classrooms after 1870 displayed wall maps of France—maps that clearly included the provinces of Alsace and Lorraine, even though these regions belonged to Germany, which had seized them as the spoils of victory after the Franco-Prussian War. Finally, the schools, with their essentially captive populations, participated fully in newly designed nationalistic rituals, including singing aggressive patriotic songs such as "*Deutschland Über Alles*" ("Germany Over All") or "Rule Britannia," and observing special days to commemorate military victories or national heroes.

Inventing Traditions

Nationalistic ritual was not confined to the schoolroom and playground. Making nations often meant *inventing* traditions to captivate the imagination and capture the loyalty of the mass electorate. German policymakers, for example, developed "Sedan Day." This national holiday, which celebrated the battle that helped create the new German state, featured parades, flag raisings, and special services to foster a sense of German nationalism among its citizens. At the

German Emperor William II and His Entourage

William preferred to wear military regalia when he appeared in public. In this way, William himself symbolized the link between the German state and Germany's military might.

same time, the person of the emperor, or *kaiser,* became the center of nationalistic ceremony and loyalty, particularly after the accession of William II (r. 1888–1918), the first emperor to identify himself as truly German rather than Prussian. William used personal appearances, militaristic pageantry, and civic ritual to link together monarchy and subjects in a sturdy chain of nationalism.

The monarchy was even more central to British nationalism. Whereas Queen Victoria's coronation in 1837 had been a small, disorganized affair, by the final decades of the century the anniversaries of her accession to the throne (the Silver Jubilee of 1887 and the Diamond Jubilee of 1897) were dramatically different. Elaborately staged, beautifully costumed, and carefully orchestrated, these events were designed to make ordinary individuals feel part of a wider, powerful, meaningful national community. The new technologies of mass printing and mass production helped support this new mass politics of nationality. At the Jubilees, participants could purchase colorfully illustrated commemorative pamphlets, ceramic plates etched with the queen's silhouette, teapots in the shape of Victoria's head, or even an automated musical bustle that played "God Save the Queen" whenever the wearer sat down.

Crisis, Revolution, and Civil War: The Examples of France, Russia, and Ireland

In the climate of heightened international competition that followed Germany's unification and the spread of industrialization, political leaders recognized domestic unity as a vital ingredient of national strength as well as a strong bulwark against revolution. The very different examples of France, Russia, and Ireland demonstrate both the crucial importance and the complexity of creating a sense of national identity and fostering national unity in the years before World War I.

France: A Crisis of Legitimacy

A century of almost continuous political revolution ensured that in the final decades of the nineteenth century no consensus existed on who or what France actually was. After Napoleon III's capture by Prussian troops in 1871, his empire collapsed and the French returned to a republican form of government, based on universal manhood suffrage (see Chapter 21). Born in the humiliation of military defeat, the Third Republic faced a crisis of legitimacy. Key sectors of the population argued that the Republic had been foisted on the French by their Prussian conquerors, and that it was therefore not a legitimate state and not worthy of their loyalty or support.

This crisis of legitimacy was worsened by the failure of French politicians to generate much enthusiasm. A dozen different parties jostled for control of the legislature. Because no single party controlled a majority, the only way to form a government was through forging coalitions, and thus compromise, political wheeling and dealing, financial corruption, and constant reshuffling of office holders became the common tools of parliamentary politics.

The lackluster nature of French politics accentuated the appeal of those who wished to destroy the French Republic—monarchists who wanted a king back on the throne, Bonapartists longing for the glory days of Napoleonic empire, Roman Catholics disturbed by republican efforts to curb the political power of the Church, aristocrats opposed to democracy. To perceive the

The Mass Marketing of National Identity
Advertising and mass production allowed ordinary Britons to participate in the glamour of royalty by purchasing inexpensive trinkets, such as this 1902 coronation souvenir.

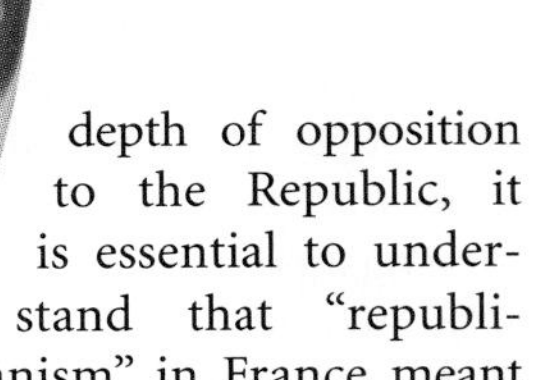

depth of opposition to the Republic, it is essential to understand that "republicanism" in France meant more than "no king, no emperor." Rooted in the radical Jacobin Republic of 1792, republicanism rested on a vision of an ideal France consisting of male equals—small shopkeepers and independent artisans, governed by reason rather than religion. Such a vision directly conflicted with the interests and ideals of monarchists, Bonapartists, and Roman Catholics, as well as of the growing number of working-class socialists. The encounter of these rival ideologies generated chaos in French politics throughout this era.

This fundamental lack of consensus about the nature or shape of France was strikingly revealed by the eruption of the Dreyfus Affair°. In 1894, on the basis of hearsay evidence and forged documentation, a French military court convicted Captain Alfred Dreyfus (1859–1935) of espionage. Prominent French intellectuals took up Dreyfus's case, and it became a full-fledged "affair," as supporters and opponents of Dreyfus battled in the streets and in the legislature. Support for Dreyfus, who was Jewish, became linked to support for the secular and egalitarian ideals of the Republic; the anti-Dreyfusards, in contrast, saw Dreyfus's Jewishness as a threat to France's Catholic identity and argued that to question the army hierarchy was to undermine France's military might. The Dreyfus Affair so dominated French politics that in 1899, when René Waldeck-Rousseau, a prominent politician, formed a governing coalition comprising members of a number of political parties, its unifying principle was support for Dreyfus.

Dreyfus was finally declared not guilty in 1906, but the consequences of the affair were far-reaching. The Dreyfus Affair revealed the strength of antirepublicanism in France, and so drove the Republic's supporters to seize the offensive. The government pushed through measures placing the army under civilian control, prohibiting members of Catholic religious orders from teaching in public *or private* schools, and removing the Catholic Church from its privileged position in French political life. With these measures politicians aimed to separate citizenship from religious affiliation and social rank and to redefine France in republican terms.

In 1914 on the eve of World War I, the success of this effort at redefinition remained unclear. National political life was dominated by the Radical Party, which represented the interests of small shopkeepers and independent artisans, not industrial workers, and drew its support from rural and small-town constituencies, not the growing cities. The Radicals' grip on power thwarted any significant efforts to address the grievances of the urban working class. Radicals opposed the high taxes necessary to establish social welfare programs and dragged their feet on social legislation such as the ten-hour workday (not passed until 1904) and old-age provisions (not established until 1910). As a result, workers increasingly turned to violent ideologies and actions, such as anarchism and sabotage. Although by 1914 the Third Republic was far stronger than it had been in the early 1870s, it clearly had not yet gained the approval of all segments of French society.

Russia: Revolution and Reaction

The success of French republican efforts to redefine the French nation may have remained unclear in 1914, but no one could have doubted the failure of the Russian imperial regime to construct any sense of national identity among the Russian masses at all. Convinced that God had appointed them to rule, Russia's tsars clung to absolutism. To catch up with the West, the tsarist regime adopted Western industrialization but it had no intention of accepting Western ideas of representative government. It could not, however, completely block the flow of these ideas into the Russian Empire. By the 1880s, many members of Russia's small but growing middle class espoused liberal political goals such as a written constitution and limited representational government. Other Russians went further and embraced socialism. Both liberalism and socialism constituted revolutionary ideological challenges to tsarist absolutism, and both liberals and socialists met with fierce repression.

As we saw at the opening of this chapter, some of these political dissenters turned to terrorism. In 1881, the revolutionary People's Will succeeded in assassinating Tsar Alexander II, but not in toppling the tsarist regime. With the use of repressive legislation and an ever-expanding

The Dreyfus Affair: Defining National Identity in France

On September 27, 1894, the five officers who made up the counterespionage section of France's War Ministry examined a disturbing document—an unsigned, undated, torn piece of paper that had clearly served as a cover letter for a packet of documents containing information on French military equipment and training. The officers found no envelope, but they concluded that the letter was intended for Lieutenant Colonel Maximilian von Schwartzkoppen, the German military attaché in Paris. Thus, this torn piece of paper constituted evidence of treason. Someone in the French officer corps was selling military secrets to the Germans.

After a brief investigation and a cursory comparison of handwriting samples, the French investigators concluded that the traitor was Captain Alfred Dreyfus, a candidate officer on the General Staff. An unlikely traitor, Dreyfus had compiled a strong record during his military career and, by all accounts, was a staunch French patriot. Moreover, because of his marriage to a wealthy woman, he had no need to sell his country for money. He was, however, an aloof and arrogant man, disliked by most of his fellow officers and without a strong backer among his superiors. He was also a Jew.

Despite the lack of solid evidence, Dreyfus was convicted of treason. After a ceremony of military degradation, he was exiled in 1895 to a specially constructed prison hut on Devil's Island, a former leper colony twelve miles off the coast of French Guyana. Many French men and women believed he had gotten off too lightly. Both public and press clamored for his execution.

With Dreyfus safely imprisoned on his island, his case seemed closed. But in July 1895, Major Marie-Georges Picquart was named chief of the Intelligence Bureau. An ambitious man determined to make a name for himself, Picquart soon discovered that the sale of military secrets to the Germans had continued even after Dreyfus's imprisonment. Ignoring his superiors' instructions to leave the Dreyfus case alone, Picquart set out to trap the man he first believed to be Dreyfus's accomplice. The evidence he uncovered, however, led him to conclude that Dreyfus was in fact innocent.

Picquart's investigations raised serious doubts about Dreyfus's conviction. These doubts were transformed into sensational charges on January 13, 1898, when one of France's most famous authors, Émile Zola, alleged in a Paris daily newspaper that the French military was engaged in a colossal cover-up. In an article headlined *"J'accuse!"* ("I accuse!"), Zola charged that the General Staff had knowingly convicted an innocent man. Zola's accusations aroused enormous public attention, and over the next six weeks, riots broke out in French cities.

Retried before a second military court in 1899, Dreyfus was again found guilty—although this time "with extenuating circumstances," a ridiculous verdict (there are no extenuating circumstances for the crime of treason) concocted to salvage the military's position despite Dreyfus's obvious innocence. In the subsequent riots that broke out in Paris, 100 people were wounded and 200 jailed. Ten days later, the French president pardoned Dreyfus in an effort to heal the divisions opened by the trial. Finally, in 1906, a French high court set aside the court-martial verdict and exonerated Dreyfus. Not until 1995, however, did the French military acknowledge the captain's innocence.

The Dreyfus Affair drew international attention, polarized French politics, and tore apart Parisian society. It sparked not only violent protests but also numerous duels and a series of related trials for assault, defamation, and libel. To uphold Dreyfus's conviction, high-ranking military officials falsified evidence, even to the point of forging entire documents. The question "Are you for or against Dreyfus?" divided families and destroyed friendships. During the height of the controversy, for example, the painter Edgar Degas spoke contemptuously of paintings by Camille Pisarro. When reminded that he had once admired these very same works, Degas said, "Yes, but that was before the Dreyfus Affair." Degas was a passionate anti-Dreyfusard; Pisarro believed Dreyfus was innocent.[3]

What about the Dreyfus Affair so aroused personal passion as to alter one painter's perception of another's work? What made this trial not simply a case, but an *affair,* a matter of public debate and personal upheaval, a cause of violent rioting and political turmoil?

To comprehend the Dreyfus Affair, we must understand that it was less about Captain Alfred Dreyfus than about the very existence of the French Third Republic, founded in 1871 in the wake of military defeat in the Franco-Prussian War and the collapse of Napoleon III's empire. The intellectuals and politicians who rallied in support of Dreyfus were defenders of the Republic, men and women who sought to limit the army's involvement in France's political life, who linked both monarchy and empire to national disaster rather than national glory, and who believed in a secular definition of the nation that would treat Roman Catholics no differently from Protestants, Jews, or atheists.

The Dreyfus Affair
Captain Alfred Dreyfus before his judges, 1899.

Dreyfus's opponents, in contrast, regarded the establishment of the Third Republic as a betrayal of the true France—a hierarchical, Roman Catholic, imperial state, steeped in military traditions. Defending the military conviction of Dreyfus became a way to express support not only for the army, but also for the authoritarian traditions that the Republic had jettisoned. The Dreyfus Affair was thus an encounter between competing versions of French national identity.

The question "What is France?," however, could not be answered without considering a second question: "Who belongs in France?"—or more specifically, "What about Jews?" France's small Jewish community (less than 1 percent of the total population) had enjoyed the rights of full citizenship since 1791—much longer than in most of Europe. Yet the Dreyfus Affair clearly demonstrated that even in France, the position of Jews in the national community was far from assured. Although anti-Semitism probably played little role in the initial charges against Dreyfus, it quickly became a dominating feature of the affair. More than seventy anti-Semitic riots ravaged France during this period. Anti-Semitic politicians and publications placed themselves in the vanguard of the anti-Dreyfus forces. For many anti-Dreyfusards, Dreyfus's Jewishness explained everything. The highly acclaimed novelist and political theorist Maurice Barres insisted, "I have no need to be told why Dreyfus committed treason. . . . That Dreyfus is capable of treason I conclude from his race."[4]

Anti-Semites such as Barres regarded Jewishness as a kind of genetic disease that made Jews unfit for French citizenship. To the anti-Semitic nationalist, the Jew was a person without a country, unconnected by racial or religious ties to the French nation—the very opposite of a patriot. As a symbol of rootlessness, "the Jew" came to represent for many anti-Dreyfusards the forces of unsettling economic and political change that appeared to be weakening the French nation. Anti-Semites pointed to the successes of assimilated Jews such as Dreyfus—not only in the army but also in the universities, the professions, and business life—as evidence of what they perceived as the threat of Jewish "domination" of French culture.

Declared innocent in 1906, Dreyfus resumed his military career and served his country with distinction in the First World War. Like Dreyfus, the Third Republic survived the Dreyfus Affair. It was probably even strengthened by it. Outrage over the army's cover-up led republican politicians to limit the powers of the military and so lessened the chances of an anti-republican military coup. Anti-Semitism, however, remained a pervasive force in French politics and cultural life well into the twentieth century.

Questions of Justice

1. What does the Dreyfus Affair reveal about definitions of national identity in late-nineteenth-century Europe?
2. Once Dreyfus was convicted, many French men and women believed that for the sake of the national interest, his conviction had to be upheld—whether he was actually guilty or not. In what situations, if any, should "national interest" override an individual's right to a fair trial?

Taking It Further

Cahm, Eric. *The Dreyfus Affair in French Society and Politics.* 1994. A wide-ranging history.

Kleeblatt, Norman, ed. *The Dreyfus Affair: Art, Truth, and Justice.* 1987. This richly illustrated collection of essays explores the cultural as well as political and legal impact of the case.

Lindemann, Albert S. *The Jew Accused: Three Anti-Semitic Affairs (Dreyfus, Beilis, Frank), 1894–1915.* 1991. An illuminating comparative study.

Snyder, Louis L. *The Dreyfus Case: A Documentary History.* 1973. An accessible collection of primary documents.

CHRONOLOGY

Instability Within the Russian Empire

1881	Assassination of Tsar Alexander II; accession of Alexander III
1882	May Laws reimpose restrictions on Russian Jews
1890s	Industrialization accelerates under Witte
1894	Accession of Nicholas II
1904	Outbreak of Russo-Japanese War
1905	Revolution
1906–1910	Nicholas II stifles political revolution

secret police force, both Alexander III (r. 1881–1894) and Nicholas II (r. 1894–1917) drove aspiring revolutionaries underground or into exile. They could not, however, quell the social unrest produced by economic change. By the turn of the century, rapid, state-sponsored industrialization had built an industrial structure in Russia, but it stood on a very faulty foundation. Russia remained a largely agricultural nation, with peasants still accounting for more than 75 percent of the population. Heavy taxation and rapid population growth, which increased competition for land, heightened social and economic anxiety among the peasant masses.

Within the industrial cities, social unrest also simmered. Factory workers labored more than twelve hours a day in wretched working conditions for very little pay. Any protest against these conditions was regarded as protest against the tsar and was quickly repressed. The workers themselves remained peasants in their loyalties and mindset. Separated from their families, who remained behind in the village, they lived in crowded state dormitories and traveled regularly back to their villages to plant and harvest. They had little sense of belonging to the Russian nation or of participating in the political structures that governed their lives.

In 1905, popular discontent flared into revolution. That year Japan trounced Russia in a war sparked by competition for territory in Asia. The military debacle of the Russo-Japanese War revealed the incompetence of the tsarist regime and provided an opening for reformers to demand political change. On a day that became known as "Bloody Sunday" (January 22, 1905), a group of 100,000 workers and their families attempted to present to the tsar a petition calling for higher wages, better working conditions, and the right to participate in political decision making. Government troops opened fire on the unarmed crowd; at least 70 people were killed and more than 240 were wounded.

The massacre horrified and radicalized much of Russian society. Across the Russian Empire, cities came to a standstill as workers went on strike and demanded both economic and political rights. In June, portions of the navy mutinied. By the fall, the empire was in chaos, with transportation, communications, energy, and water supplies all facing disruption. Taking advantage of this upheaval, states on the fringes of the empire, such as the Baltic regions, rose up in revolt against imperial rule, and middle-class liberals demanded limited representative government. In October, Tsar Nicholas II gave in and acceded to demands for the election of a legislative assembly. The Revolution of 1905 appeared to be a success.

The Revolution of 1905 in the Movies
On Bloody Sunday, January 22, 1905, Russian troops opened fire on more than 100,000 citizens who had gathered in St. Petersburg to present a petition to the tsar. Rather than subduing the revolt, the massacre sparked a revolution. This photograph, supposedly of the moment when the tsar's troops began to shoot the demonstrators, is one of the most familiar images of the twentieth century—yet it is *not* in fact a documentary record. Instead, it is a still taken from *The Ninth of January,* a Soviet film made in 1925.

By 1910, however, the tsar had regained much of his autocratic power. Revolutionary fervor dissipated as rival groups jostled for political influence. The tsar, with his army still loyal, refused to carry out many of the promised reforms. Tsarist autocracy remained intact, but so too did the causes of the discontent that had led to the revolution. Russia lacked an authentic national community, as Nicholas would discover during the First World War, when a new revolution would destroy the Russian imperial state.

The Irish Identity Conflict

In France, competing notions of "Frenchness" erupted into the Dreyfus Affair. In Russia, the lack of a widespread sense of Russian national identity increased the vulnerability of the tsarist state to revolutionary challenges. In Ireland, two very different forms of national identity took root during this era and led to the brink of civil war.

Theoretically, Ireland was not an imperial or conquered territory, but rather (since 1801) part of the United Kingdom, comprising England, Wales, Scotland, and Ireland. In reality, as we saw in Chapter 20, a chasm yawned between the first three overwhelmingly Protestant and industrialized nations, and the Roman Catholic, economically backward, peasant culture of Ireland. While the English, Scottish, and Welsh economies flourished under the impact of industrialization, the Irish economy stagnated. Peasant desperation fueled revolutionary Irish nationalism, as the economic grievances of Irish Catholics fused with their sense of political and religious repression, and convinced many of the need for independence from Britain. In the 1860s, the Irish Republican Brotherhood, or Fenian movement, endeavored to overthrow British rule by force. The Fenian "Rising" of 1867 failed dismally, but it planted a seed that took deep root in Irish soil—the belief that the British constituted an occupying force that must be violently resisted.

Faced with growing Irish Catholic nationalism, the British resorted to military rule, accompanied by attempts to alleviate peasant grievances through land reform. Such reform measures were always too little, too late. In 1898 Irish nationalists organized themselves as Sinn Fein (pronounced "shin fane"—Gaelic for "Ourselves Alone"), a political movement devoted to complete independence for Ireland by any means necessary. Sinn Fein grew rapidly, and by 1914 could call to arms a paramilitary force of 180,000 fighters. The success of Sinn Fein demonstrated that Irish Catholics had developed their own sense of nationhood, which refused to be subordinate to or absorbed by Britain.

But the refusal of Irish *Catholics* to accept British national identity was matched by the refusal of Irish *Protestants* to consider themselves as anything but British. The descendants of English and Scottish settlers in Ireland, these Protestants constituted a minority of the Irish population as a whole, but made up the majority in the northernmost province of Ulster. Frightened by the idea of belonging to a Catholic state, the Ulster Protestants opposed the British Liberal government's plans to grant Ireland "Home Rule," or limited autonomy, by 1914. The Ulstermen, or "Unionists," made it clear that they would fight to the death to preserve the union of Ireland with Britain. By 1914, they too were smuggling in arms and setting up clandestine paramilitary organizations. Only the outbreak of war in Europe postponed the coming civil war in Ireland.

Broadening the Political Nation

- **What forms did mass politics assume during this time of industrial expansion and the spread of modern nationalist ideology?**

Through nation making, liberal and conservative political leaders sought both to strengthen their states and to ensure the loyalty of new political participants—industrial workers, peasants, the petty bourgeoisie. But in this era, mass support for socialist and racist-nationalist political parties challenged the political authority of traditional elites.

The Politics of the Working Class

The rise of working-class socialist political parties and the emergence of new, more radical forms of trade unionism reflected an escalation of class hostilities. Workers often rejected the political vision offered by their bosses and landlords, and instead fought hard to broaden the political nation on their own terms.

The Workers' City

In the decades after 1870, the combined impact of agricultural crisis and industrial expansion created large working-class communities in the rapidly growing industrial cities. These working-class communities tended to be increasingly isolated from the middle and upper class. Technological developments such as electrified tram lines, together with the expansion of the railway system, enabled Europe's middle classes to retreat from overcrowded, dirty, disease-ridden city centers to new and burgeoning suburbs. Workers knew members of the middle class only within the limited context of the "boss-employee" relationship—a relationship that was growing more hostile as economic depression drove middle-class employers to try to limit wages and raise productivity.

Within the sprawling industrial cities, industrial workers created a vibrant community life. They developed what sociologists call "urban villages," closely knit neighborhoods in which each family had a clear and publicly acknowledged

Urban Villages

Packed into slums, European workers developed a separate working-class culture. This painting by the Belgian painter Léon Frédérick (1856–1940) gives a sense of the crowded, tumultuous, community-oriented world of the urban worker. Painted in 1895, *The Stages of a Worker's Life* also illustrates the gender divisions in working-class culture: The left panel of the triptych shows the man's work world, while the right panel features the nurturing role of women as they care for their children in front of the market stalls where they buy their families' food. In the center panel workers of all ages commingle, with the funeral coach in the background reminding them of their inevitable end.

place. Sharply defined gender roles played an important part in ordering this world. The home became the woman's domain (although many working-class women continued to work outside the home as well). In many regions, the wife controlled the family income and made most of the decisions about family life. Men built up their own cultural and leisure institutions, free from middle-class (and from female) participation and control—the corner pub, the music hall, the football club, the choral society, the brass band. These institutions provided an escape from the physical and emotional confines of work and home; they also secured the bonds of male working-class identity, one that rested on a sharp distinction between "Us"—the ordinary men, the workers, the neighbors—and "Them," the bosses, the owners, the landlords, the people with privilege and power.

Working-Class Socialism and the Revolutionary Problem

This heightened class identity and hostility were embodied in the emergence of working-class socialist political parties. In the decades after 1870, socialism established itself as a powerful force in European parliamentary politics, the means by which workers sought to claim a place in the political nation. By 1914, socialist parties had been formed in twenty European countries.

Why socialism? As we saw in Chapter 21, by 1870 Karl Marx had published a series of books outlining his economic and political theory of revolutionary socialism. Not many workers had the time, education, or energy necessary for the study of Marx's complex ideas. But Marx's basic points, presented to workers by socialist party activists and organizers, resonated with many workers. Quite simply, most workers had already identified their boss as the enemy, and Marx assured them that they were right. His insistence that class conflict was inherent within the industrial system accorded with their own experience of social segregation and economic exploitation. In addition, the onset of economic depression in the 1870s appeared to confirm Marx's prediction that capitalism would produce ever more serious economic crises, until finally it collapsed under its own weight.

The most dramatic socialist success story was in Germany. Even after it was outlawed in 1878, the German Social Democratic Party (SPD) continued to attract supporters. In 1890, the SPD emerged from the underground as the largest political party in Germany. By 1914, it held 40 percent of the seats in the German Reichstag and served as the model for socialist parties founded in the Netherlands, Belgium, Austria, and Switzerland. Even more important, German socialists constructed a set of institutions that provided

Socialism: The Gotha Program

German workers with an alternative community. If they chose, they could send their children to socialist day care centers and bury their parents in socialist cemeteries. They could spend their leisure time in socialist bicycling clubs and gymnastic groups and choral societies and chess teams. They could read socialist newspapers, sing socialist songs, save their money in socialist savings banks, and shop at socialist co-operatives.

By the 1890s, the rapid growth of socialist parties such as the SPD persuaded many socialists that working-class revolution was just around the corner. In 1885 SPD leader August Bebel (1840–1913) told Marx's colleague Friedrich Engels, "Every night I go to sleep with the thought that the last hour of bourgeois society strikes soon."[5] Six years later in a speech before the SPD congress, Bebel told the gathered crowd, "I am convinced that the fulfillment of our aims is so close, that there are few in this hall who will not live to see the day."[6]

By the time Bebel made this promise, however, unexpected economic and political developments were creating serious problems for Marxist theory and practice. In 1890, the new German emperor, William II, fired Bismarck. Bismarck's antisocialist legislation was not renewed and the now-legal SPD faced a time of new opportunity, but also new challenges. To improve workers' wages and working conditions, the SPD worked in close connection with the rapidly growing German trade union movement—from 300,000 members in 1890 to 2.5 million in 1913. Such activity raised the fundamental question, what was the role of a socialist party within a nonsocialist state? To continue to attract voters, the SPD needed to push through legislation that would appeal to workers; yet the passage of such legislation, by improving workers' lives within a nonsocialist system, made the possibility of socialist revolution ever more remote. Why should workers resort to violent revolution when participation in parliamentary politics was clearly paying off?

The SPD's dilemma was shared by socialist parties across western Europe. According to Marx, capitalism would generate its own destruction—the growing misery of workers would fuel a social and political revolution. But in western European industrial nations in the last decades of the nineteenth century, working-class living standards were generally rising rather than deteriorating. In addition, the expansion of the franchise seemed to indicate that workers could gain political power without violent revolution. As socialist political parties grew in strength, then, they faced crucial and often divisive questions: Should they work for gradual reforms that would make life better for the worker—and risk making capitalism more acceptable? Could socialists participate in coalition governments with nonsocialists—and so lend legitimacy to parliamentary systems they condemned as oppressive and unequal?

The quest for answers to these questions led some socialists to socialist revisionism°, a set of political ideas most closely associated with the German socialist theorist Eduard Bernstein (1850–1932). Bernstein rejected the Marxist faith in inevitable violent revolution and argued instead for the gradual and peaceful evolution of socialism through parliamentary politics. Questioning Marx's insistence on the centrality of class struggle in modern politics, Bernstein called for German socialists to abandon their commitment to revolution, to form alliances with liberals, and to carry out immediate social and economic reforms.

In 1899, the German socialist party congress condemned Bernstein's revisionism and reaffirmed its faith in the inevitability of capitalism's collapse and working-class revolution. Bernstein had lost the battle—but he won the war. For regardless of what the congress affirmed as socialist theory, in practice the SPD acted like any other parliamentary party. It focused on improving the lot of its constituency through immediate and incremental legislative change. In the words of one socialist intellectual, the SPD was "a party which, while revolutionary, does not make a revolution."[7]

DOCUMENT

The Socialist Culture

Songs played a vital role in the socialist culture developed in Germany at the end of the nineteenth century. Workers organized singing societies, which competed in local, regional, and national competitions. Rejecting the nationalist and religious songs of the middle-class choral society repertoire, workers often expressed their political ideals in their music. These overly didactic lyrics reveal not only the rage against economic injustice that fueled the socialist movement, but also its fundamental faith in human rationality and in parliamentary politics as an avenue of change.

"You Men, All of You" by Ernst Klaar

Already on all sides and throughout the world
The proletariat rises up together—
The fate of the poor is to be changed,
And to be changed through the state.
O, if we stand together firmly,
Who will be able to refuse us our right?
Upward, upward, you new generation,
Defiant let your banner wave!
Put in the eight-hour day!
Reduce the misery of toil!
To our victorious march
The drum now beats.
Eight hours are enough!

Source: From "You Men, All of You" by Ernst Klaar, translated by Vernon L. Lidtke in *The Alternative Culture,* 1985. Reprinted by permission.

Its effect, although not its aim, was thus to make the existing political system more responsive to the needs of working-class constituents. Despite the almost hysterical fears of many middle- and upper-class Europeans, the successes of socialist political parties probably worked less to foment revolution than to strengthen parliamentary political systems.

Radical Trade Unions and the Anarchist Threat

To many at the end of the nineteenth century, however, revolution appeared a genuine possibility. The Great Depression, which shattered middle-class confidence and shrank capitalists' profit margins, led businesses to look for ways to cut costs. As management sought to reduce the number of laborers, to increase the rate of production, and to decrease wages, workers began to organize themselves in new and threatening ways.

The expansion and radicalization of trade unions highlighted growing working-class militancy. For example, in Britain between 1882 and 1913, union membership increased from 750,000 to 4,000,000. While size alone set apart the new unions from their midcentury predecessors, two additional differences marked them as much more subversive. First, the new unions were much more willing to resort to large-scale strikes and to violence. Second, the unions sought to better the lives of a wide range of workers, not just an elite of the highly skilled. In contrast to the unions of the 1850s and 1860s, which had tended to be small, craft-based groupings of skilled workers, the new unions aimed to organize all the male workers in an entire industry—for example, all male textile workers, rather than just the skilled weavers. (Unionists, fighting for higher pay, often resisted the unionization of female workers both because women earned much less than did men and because a central union aim was the "family wage"—a pay rate high enough for a man to support a family without his wife's second income.)

Political leaders reacted ferociously to the unionist challenge. In the coastal port of Hull in Britain, striking dockworkers in 1893 confronted Royal Navy gunboats. A little more than a decade later, the British government responded to a transport workers' strike in Liverpool by quartering 14,000 soldiers in the city and stationing two warships off the coast. Increasingly, "class war" seemed an appropriate label for interactions between workers and their middle-class employers. Even the simple act of getting a shave could prove dangerous for a member of the bourgeoisie: Unionized workers in barbershops were encouraged to "inflict nonfatal cuts on the clients of their capitalist masters."[8]

In the first decade of the twentieth century, the European labor movement became further radicalized by its encounter with the new ideology of syndicalism°. Syndicalists worked to overturn the existing social and political order by marshaling the economic might of the laboring classes. They focused on the general strike as a means of change. In the syndicalist vision, if every worker in a nation went on strike, the resulting disruption of the capitalist economy would lead to working-class revolution. Thus they placed their revolutionary faith in economic rather than political action—in unions rather than parties, in the strike rather than the vote, and in compulsion rather than compromise. According to the French syndicalist theorist Georges Sorel (1847–1922), workers had to embrace violence to destroy the capitalist state. Sorel did not actually believe that a general strike was possible, but he believed that the idea of the general strike was crucial. In Sorel's view, the general strike served as an essential myth, an inspirational idea that would give workers the motivation and self-confidence they needed to overthrow the state.

The Unions' Challenge

In 1911 the British government deployed troops in the city of Liverpool to put down working-class labor unrest. In one confrontation, two people were killed.

In their rejection of parliamentary politics and in their willingness to utilize violent means to achieve their revolutionary ends, syndicalists were heavily influenced by anarchism°. In contrast to socialists who formed political parties to claim for workers a place in the political nation, anarchists shunned parliamentary politics. Opting for direct and violent action such as street fighting and assassination, anarchists aimed to destroy rather than control the state. The Russian anarchist Mikhail Bakunin (1814–1876) insisted that the great obstacle to achieving a just and egalitarian society was the state itself, not capitalism or the industrial middle class.

The combined impact of both syndicalism and anarchism created a climate of social unrest and political turmoil in much of Europe before 1914. In France, where a strong non-Marxist revolutionary tradition already existed, both syndicalism and anarchism possessed significant appeal. Impatient with parliamentary politics, anarchists resorted in the 1890s to a terrorist campaign in Paris, which began with a series of bombings and culminated in the fatal stabbing of President Sadi Carnot in 1894. Other prominent victims of assassination included Empress Elisabeth of Austria-Hungary in 1898, King Humbert of Italy in 1900, and U.S. president William McKinley in 1901.

The Politics of Race and Nation

The rise of socialist political parties and the spread of revolutionary ideologies such as anarchism and syndicalism fostered middle- and upper-class fears of a worker revolution. But the emergence of mass politics was not limited to left-wing ideologies. In the age of the masses, the right-wing ideas offered by nationalist, racist, and anti-Semitic parties also answered the demands of many ordinary people for a political voice. These parties possessed a special appeal in areas that industrialized late and so still contained a large peasant class profoundly threatened by the economic changes wrought by the continuing Industrial Revolution. Socialist politics also possessed little appeal for members of the petty bourgeoisie, who regarded the vision of working-class rule as a frightening nightmare. Instead, they turned to the new mass politics of nationalism.

Unlike the men who had dominated politics in the past, most newly enfranchised voters possessed only a basic education; they had little time for reading or sustained intellectual work; they worked long hours and therefore needed to be entertained. They needed a new style of politics—one based more on visual imagery and symbolism than on the written word, one that relied on emotional appeals rather than on intellectual debate. Nationalist politics fit the bill perfectly. Unlike socialists, who placed great faith in education and in rational persuasion, nationalist politicians did not recruit supporters with reasoned arguments. Instead, by waving flags, parading in historical costumes or military uniforms, and singing folk songs, they tapped into powerful personal and community memories to persuade voters of their common identity, one based not on shared political ideas or economic interests but rather on ethnic, religious, or linguistic ties. This was as much a politics of exclusion as of inclusion—it defined the nation by identifying who was "not in" as well as who belonged.

Nationalism in the Ottoman Empire and Austria-Hungary: The Politics of Division

Nationalist mass politics proved very powerful in eastern Europe, particularly in the multiethnic, industrially underdeveloped Ottoman and Austrian-Hungarian Empires. These regions lacked a large, politically conscious urban working class. What they possessed was an abundant diversity of ethnic, linguistic and religious groups. Modern nationalist ideology taught these groups to identity themselves as nations, and to demand political statehood.

By the 1870s, nationalism had already diminished the Ottoman Empire's European territories. As we saw in Chapter 21, in 1833 Greece won its independence from the Ottomans. In the same period, the Ottomans granted autonomy, although not complete independence, to Serbia and the provinces that became Romania. Determined to hold on to what remained of his European empire, the Ottoman sultan in 1875 and 1876 suppressed nationalist uprisings in Bosnia-Herzegovina and Bulgaria with great ferocity. This repression backfired, however; it gave Russia the excuse it needed to declare war on the Ottoman Empire on behalf of its Slavic "little brothers" in the Balkans. In the aftermath of the Russo-Turkish War (1877–1878), Montenegro, Serbia, and Romania became independent states and Austria-Hungary received oversight of Bosnia-Herzegovina (see Map 22.2). Bulgaria received limited autonomy, which the Bulgars widened into full independence in 1908. The Ottomans had lost the bulk of their territory west of Istanbul.

Ottoman weakness appeared to make Austria-Hungary stronger. The Habsburg Empire not only gained territory—granted the administration of Bosnia-Herzegovina in 1878, Austria-Hungary annexed it outright in 1908—but it also benefited from the weakening of its once-formidable rival. The appearance of strength, however, was deceptive. Straining under the social and economic pressures of late industrialization, Austria-Hungary contained numerous ethnic and linguistic groups competing for power and privileges (see Map 21.4, page 704).

This competition intensified as the franchise was gradually widened in the 1880s and 1890s. (The Austrian half of the empire achieved universal manhood suffrage in 1907.) Various parties emerged that appealed to voters on the basis of ethnic identity and linguistic practice rather than economic interest. Language became a key battleground in this political competition. In a multilingual empire, which language would be taught in the schools? Which language would be required in official communications? Which language would guarantee career advancement? Not surprisingly, politicians tended to agitate for

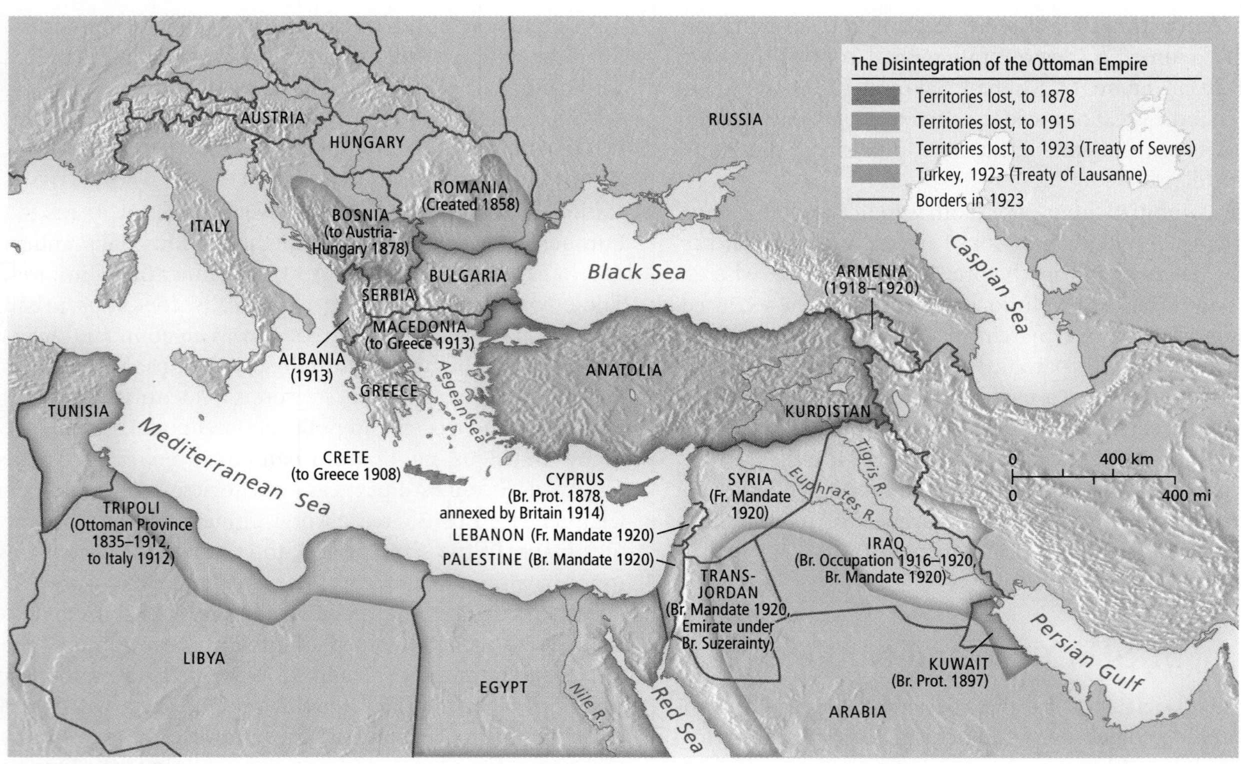

Map 22.2 The Disintegration of the Ottoman Empire

As Map 22.2 shows, the disintegration of the Ottoman Empire was a slow process that began at the end of the seventeenth century. By 1870, the Ottoman regime had already lost territory and political control over much of its once-mighty empire to both nationalist independence movements and to rival European powers. From the 1870s on, mass nationalism accelerated Ottoman disintegration. The Ottoman Empire would finally disappear as a consequence of the peace settlement of World War I.

the primacy of their own native language, and to jostle for the political power needed to ensure that primacy.

In Hungary, the ruling Magyar-speaking Hungarian landlords redrew constituency boundaries to give maximum influence to Magyar speakers and to undercut the power of other ethnic and linguistic groups. This policy of "Magyarization" in governmental offices and in the schools bred widespread resentment among non-Hungarians and fostered their own nationalist ambitions and their own political parties.

At the same time in the Austrian half of the empire, Czechs succeeded in gaining greater political power and official support for the Czech language. In response, German nationalist parties within Austria grew more aggressive in asserting German primacy. They called for closer ties with Germany and even a complete break of the link with Hungary. By 1900 the struggle over language laws in the Czech portion of the Austrian Empire had become so intense that no party could establish a majority in the Reichsrat (the legislative assembly), and Emperor Francis Joseph (r. 1848–1916) resorted to ruling by decree.

In this context of nationalist divisions, anti-Semitic politics proved extremely powerful, particularly in the capital city of Vienna. In the last two decades of the nineteenth century, Vienna's Jewish population swelled, as Austrian Jews from the surrounding countryside came in search of jobs and Russian Jews fled the tsar's anti-Semitic regime.

The growing Jewish presence provided the opportunity for Karl Lueger (1844–1910), a lawyer, self-made man, and power-hungry politician. Lueger's Christian Social party demonstrates how hate-based politics could overcome social and economic divisions among members of a single ethnic or religious community. Lueger used both anti-Semitism and promises of social reform to unite artisans and workers with conservative aristocrats in a German nationalist party. His proposals to exclude Jews from political and economic life proved so popular that he was elected mayor of Vienna in 1897, despite the opposition of

Emperor Francis Joseph. Lueger was still the mayor in 1908, when 18-year-old Adolf Hitler, hoping to attend art school, moved to Vienna. Hitler's application to study art was denied, but he remained in Vienna for several years, soaking in the anti-Semitic political culture.

Anti-Semitism in Mass Politics

Anti-Semitism played a central role not only in Vienna but across Europe in the new nationalist mass politics. Across Europe, explicitly anti-Semitic parties emerged, while established conservative parties adopted anti-Semitic rhetoric to attract voters. In Germany, the widespread belief that Jews had conspired to cause the Great Depression fueled anti-Semitic politics; by the 1890s anti-Semitic parties had won seats in the Reichstag. In France, nationalists linked Jewish prosperity to French national decline and grew increasingly anti-Semitic in their ideology and rhetoric, until finally the Dreyfus Affair made explicit the connections between hatred of Jews and extremist French nationalism. Many of Dreyfus's opponents saw "Jewishness" and "Frenchness" as incompatible and regarded Dreyfus himself as part of a vast Jewish conspiracy to undermine France's religious, military, and national strength.

To explain the heightened anti-Semitism of this period, we need to understand three developments: the increased emphasis on racial identity, the upsurge in the numbers of Jewish immigrants into Western cities, and Jewish success in the new industrial economy. First, the triumph of nationalism meant a new concern with group boundaries and a greater focus on racial identity. Nationalism raised the question, "Who does *not* belong?" For many Europeans and Americans, race provided the answer. The new nationalism meant new perceptions of common "racial roots." Ideas about "the English race" or of the shared racial heritage of the French had no scientific basis, but these perceptions of racial links nonetheless proved extremely powerful. In this new nationalistic climate, then, "Jewishness" was increasingly defined not only as a matter of religious belief but also as a racial identity. As a racial marker, Jewishness was not a matter of choice but of blood—something that could not be changed. A Jew who no longer ascribed to the Jewish faith or even a Jew who converted to Christianity remained a Jew. This shift to a more racial definition of Jewishness is one of the factors behind the upsurge in anti-Semitic actions and attitudes at the end of the nineteenth century. If national identity grew from supposedly racial roots, then in the eyes of many Europeans, Jews were a foreign plant. They were non-English, or non-French, or non-German—essentially outsiders whose very presence threatened national unity.

This perception of Jews as outsiders was also exacerbated by the growth in immigrant Jewish urban populations in the 1880s and 1890s. The Russian tsar Alexander III believed that a Jewish conspiracy was responsible for his father's assassination in 1881. He responded by reimposing restrictions on Jewish economic and social life with the May Laws of 1882. Pogroms—mass attacks on Jewish homes and businesses, sometimes organized by local government officials—also escalated. Fleeing this persecution, Jews from the Russian Empire settled in Paris, London, Vienna, and other European cities.

The encounter between these immigrant Jewish communities and their hosts was often hostile. Extremely poor, the immigrants spoke Yiddish rather than the language of their new home, dressed in distinctive clothing,

The Results of Anti-Semitism

In this 1905 painting by Samuel Hirszenberg, Hasidic Jews in Russian-governed Poland bury the victim of a pogrom. Hirszenberg called his painting *The Black Banner* in reference to both "The Black Hundreds," armed thugs who belonged to the anti-Semitic "Union of the Russian People," and *The Russian Banner,* the Union's newspaper that was partially funded by the tsar.

and sometimes practiced an ardently emotional style of Judaism that resisted assimilation. As the numbers of Jews escalated in Europe's cities, these new, impoverished, clearly identifiable immigrants received the blame for unemployment, the spread of disease, soaring crime rates, and any other difficulty for which desperate people sought easy explanations.

Many anti-Semites, however, associated Jews not with poverty but with wealth and power. A few Jewish families, such as the internationally connected Rothschild banking dynasty, did possess spectacular fortunes and corresponding political clout, but far more important in explaining the outburst of anti-Semitism in this era is what one historian has labeled the "rise of the Jews,"[9] or Jewish prominence in modern European societies. At the start of the nineteenth century, Jews were barred from political participation in most of Europe and often confined to certain economic roles and even certain territories or city districts. Jews in Russia, for example, could not live outside the area defined as the "Pale of Settlement." In the second half of the century, Jews throughout much of Europe gained civil and political rights. No longer barred from certain sectors of the economy, no longer required to live in certain territories, many Jews moved into new regions and into new economic and political roles. As newcomers, they often took up positions in the newest sectors of the industrial economy. They became department store owners or newspaper editors rather than farmers. At the same time, many Jews assimilated into European societies: They dropped distinctive dress styles and abandoned or modernized their practice of Judaism. They secularized the traditional Jewish emphasis on studying the Torah into an emphasis on education.

As a result of these developments, Jewish communities quickly assumed a significant presence in European economic and political life. In Budapest in 1900, for example, Jews formed 25 percent of the population, yet they accounted for 45 percent of the city's lawyers, more than 40 percent of its journalists, and more than 60 percent of its doctors. In Germany, almost all the large department stores were owned by Jewish businessmen, and in the cities of Frankfurt, Berlin, and Hamburg all the large daily newspapers were in the hands of Jewish proprietors.

The "rise of the Jews" meant that many Europeans linked Jewishness to economic modernity. For independent shopowners and traditional artisans with a great deal to lose from economic modernization, Jews became targets. Fearing the power of corporate capitalism as well as the revolutionary threat of socialism, they perceived both as somehow Jewish. Like Tsar Nicholas II, who blamed the Russian Revolution of 1905 on Jewish conspirators, ordinary men and women reacted to their own personal reversals of fortune by seeking a scapegoat. Jews became the embodiment of threatening change to many newly enfranchised European voters.

Zionism: Jewish Mass Politics

The heightened anti-Semitism of the last quarter of the nineteenth century convinced some Jews that the Jewish communities of Europe would be safe only when they gained a political state of their own. The ideology of Jewish nationalism was called Zionism°, as Jewish nationalists called for a return to Zion, the biblical land of Palestine. Most Jews in western nations such as France and Britain viewed Zionism with skepticism, but it had a potent appeal in eastern Europe, home to more than 70 percent of the world's Jewish community—and to the most vicious forms of anti-Semitism.

Zionism became a mass movement under the guidance of Theodor Herzl (1860–1904). An Austrian Jew born in Budapest, Herzl was living in Vienna when Karl Lueger was elected mayor. Confronted with the appeal of anti-Semitism to the mass electorate, Herzl began to doubt whether Jews could ever be fully accepted as Austrian citizens. His experience as a journalist reporting on the Dreyfus Affair from Paris confirmed these doubts. The vicious display of anti-Jewish hatred in a prosperous, industrialized, western European state convinced Herzl that Jews would always be outsiders within the existing European nations. In 1896, he published *The Jewish State,* a call for Jews to build a nation-state in Palestine. Herzl gained the financial support of wealthy Jewish businessmen such as Baron Edmund James de Rothschild, but he recognized that for Zionism to succeed, it must capture the imagination and loyalties of ordinary Jews. Through newspapers, popular publications, large rallies, and his own enthusiasm, Herzl made Zionism into an international mass movement.

As a mass movement, Zionism faced strong opposition. Many Jewish leaders argued that Zionism played into the hands of anti-Semites by insisting that Jews did not belong in Europe. In addition, by marking out Palestine as the Jewish "homeland," Zionists ran into a huge political obstacle: Arab nationalism. By the 1890s, Arab leaders had begun to dream of an Arab state, one that would be independent of the Ottoman Empire and that would include Palestine, home to 700,000 Arabs. Nevertheless, by 1914 some 90,000 Jews had settled in Palestine, where they hoped to build a Jewish state.

Outside the Political Nation? The Experience of Women

- **In what ways did the emergence of feminism in this period demonstrate the potential as well as the limits of political change?**

Extending the suffrage to men outside the middle and upper classes also called attention to gender differences, as middle-class women demanded that they, too,

DOCUMENT

John Stuart Mill on Enfranchisement of Women (1869)

be made part of the political nation. The campaign for women's suffrage, however, was only part of a multifaceted international middle-class feminist movement° that, by the 1870s, demanded a reconsideration of women's roles. To the feminist movement, the vote was not an end in itself, but a means to an end, a way of achieving a radical alteration in cultural values and expectations. At the core of nineteenth-century feminism stood a rejection of the liberal ideology of separate spheres—the insistence that both God and biology destined middle-class men for the public sphere of paid economic employment and political participation, and women for the private sphere of the home. In seeking a place in the political nation, feminists sought not just to enter the public, masculine sphere, but in fact to obliterate many of the distinctions between the public and private spheres altogether and so to reconfigure political and social life.

During this period the feminist movement remained largely middle class in its membership and its concerns. Working-class and peasant women were occupied by the struggle for survival; obtaining the vote seemed fairly irrelevant to a woman listening to her children cry from hunger. Politically active working-class women tended to agree with Karl Marx that class, not gender, constituted the real dividing line in society. For help in bettering their lives, they turned to labor unions and to working-class political parties rather than middle-class feminist organizations. The British working-class feminist Selina Cooper (1868–1946), for example, fought hard for women's rights, but within the context of the British Labour movement. Cooper, who was sent to work in a textile mill at age 10, viewed the widening of women's opportunities and the achievement of working-class political power as two sides of the same coin. Similarly, in Germany, the SDP activist Clara Zetkin (1857–1933) argued that the fight against class oppression was inextricably linked to the fight against women's oppression.

Changes in the Position of Middle-Class Women

The middle-class women's movement operated within changing economic and social conditions that were pushing middle-class women into more public positions in European society. Married women moved into a new public role as consumers during this period. It was the woman who was the principal target of the new advertising industry, the woman whom the new department stores sought to entice with their lavish window displays and courteous shop clerks, the woman who rode the new tram lines and subways to take advantage of sale days.

The largest change for married middle-class women was much more basic, however. In the last third of the nineteenth century, middle-class men and women began to limit the size of their families. In Britain in the 1890s, the average middle-class family had 2.8 children, a sharp reduction in family size from the middle of the century, when the typical middle-class family had 6 children. This enormous change, characteristic of all the advanced industrial nations, reflected both economic and social developments. As the Great Depression cut into business profits and made economic ventures ever more precarious, middle-class families looked for ways to cut expenses and yet maintain a middle-class lifestyle. At the same time, the growing tendency to keep both boys and girls in school longer meant added financial obligations for the middle-class family. Limiting births, through the use of already well-known methods such as abstinence, withdrawal, and abortion, provided the answer. In working-class families, in which children left school by age 11 or 12 and so began to contribute to the family income much earlier, family size continued to remain large, but in the middle class, married women no longer spent much of their adult life pregnant or nursing, and were thus free for other activities and interests, including feminist activism.

The expectations of unmarried middle-class women were also transformed during this period. In 1850, the unmarried middle-class woman who had to support herself had little choice but to become a governess or a paid companion to an elderly widow. By 1900 her options had widened. As we shall see, the women's movement played a crucial role in this expansion of opportunity, but so also did two more general economic and political developments: the expansion of the state and the Second Industrial Revolution.

The expansion of state responsibilities in this period significantly widened opportunities for women. By the final decade of the nineteenth century, local governments took over many tasks traditionally assigned to church volunteers and especially women charity workers, such as training the poor in proper hygiene and nutrition. Middle-class women quickly claimed both paying and elected positions in the new local bureaucracies, on the argument that women possessed an expertise in managing households and raising children that could be directly translated into managing poorhouses and running schools. Women served on school and welfare boards, staffed government inspectorates, voted in local elections, and were elected to local office. For example, in Britain between 1870 and 1914, approximately 3,000 women were elected to county and municipal governing bodies. In Germany, 18,000 women worked as local welfare officials by 1910. But the largest employers of middle-class women before 1914 were the new state-funded elementary schools. The implementation of compulsory mass education created a voracious demand for teachers and thus a new career path for unmarried women from the middle class as well as from the upper ranks of the working class.

The emergence of new technologies and the retail revolution also created new jobs for women, positions that did

Men in Black

Within a span of about fifty years, upper- and middle-class European and American men transformed the way they presented their bodies to the world. Before the late eighteenth century, social rank outweighed gender in determining clothing styles. Thus an aristocratic man dressed more like an aristocratic woman than like a male laborer. Aristocrats, both men and women, decorated themselves with expensive jewels, shaped their bodies with corsets and pads, powdered their faces and hair, sported huge hats decorated with ribbons, carried lacy fans, wore high heels, and dressed in brightly colored and elaborately ruffled silks and taffetas. By the middle of the nineteenth century, however, the man had lost his plumage, and decoration had become a distinctly female attribute. The aristocratic man of the 1850s looked like his middle-class counterpart. He dressed in darkly colored, loose-fitting trousers and jackets; wore sensible shoes; and put on a top hat when he went outside. Cosmetics, perfume, ruffles and lace, elaborate jewelry, hats, and fans all retreated to the woman's sphere.

Whether he was engaged actively in business or lived a life of leisure, the new man in black now presented a sharp contrast to his female companions. His clothing associated him with the world of practicality and production; her costume, however, was designed to reinforce the prevailing notions about women's incapacity for public or economic roles. Middle- and upper-class women's clothing not only remained brightly colored, decorative, and luxurious, it also became increasingly constrictive. The full crinolines and hoop skirts of the 1850s and 1860s, for example, made the simple task of sitting down a tricky endeavor, while tight corseting placed strenuous physical activity beyond reach of fashionable women.

Changes in clothing reflect new ideas about the relationships between a man's and a woman's identities and their physical bodies. After 1850 men's clothing styles de-emphasized their bodies. Whereas eighteenth-century aristocrats wore attention-grabbing colors, silk stockings that outlined their legs, short jackets that emphasized their waist, and tight-fitting breeches that highlighted the sexual aspects of the male body, the long loose jackets and trousers of the later nineteenth-century man masked rather than highlighted their wearer's physical characteristics. In contrast, women's fashions increasingly accentuated female sexuality. By shrinking the waist, tightly laced corsets made the bust and hips appear fuller. In the 1880s, the addition of the bustle emphasized the woman's bottom. Such clothing styles fortified the view that a woman's body in many ways determined her destiny, that women were designed to be wives and mothers.

Economic developments led to important changes in women's fashions in the 1890s. As middle-class women began to enter the workforce in large numbers, fashions adapted to fit their new roles. Dresses became more streamlined: Skirts moved slightly above the ankles and shrank in width, and bustles disappeared. But it took the demands of the First World War, when women assumed previously all-male positions in industry, agriculture, and transportation, to effect radical alterations in the way women presented their bodies and themselves to the world.

For Discussion

Changes in women's employment patterns clearly had an impact on women's dress styles. What other economic developments during this period may help explain changes in fashion?

Loose-fitting jackets and trousers hide, rather than highlight, physical characteristics, and are more practical for a day of business.

Dark colors have replaced the bright colors of earlier times; lace, ribbons, and jewelry have disappeared.

Men in Black
Painting by James Tissot, *Cercle de la Rue Royale,* detail (1868). Although most are barons, marquises, or counts, the men whose portraits Tissot captured in this high-society painting dress like bankers or stockbrokers.

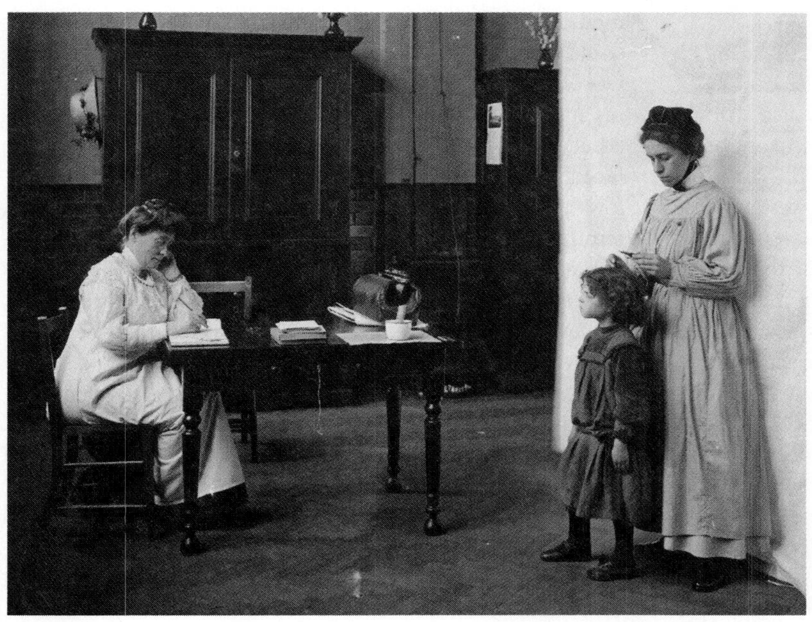

Women at Work
The expansion of local and central government interference in daily life created many opportunities for women's paid employment. Here government health inspectors check a schoolgirl for head lice.

not involve manual labor and so did not mean a descent into the working class. Middle-class women moved into the work world as typists, telephone and telegraph operators, sales clerks, and bank tellers. During the 1860s in England, the number of women working as commercial clerks and accountants increased tenfold.

Middle-class women thus found new ways to make a living; they did not, however, find the same opportunities as their male counterparts. A woman earned an average of between one-third and two-thirds less than a man working in the same job. The entry of large numbers of women into any job was certain to result in a recasting of that position as unskilled and low-paying. Unlike men, women lost their jobs when they married and found most supervisory positions closed to them.

By the 1880s, an international women's movement had emerged to challenge the legal, political, and economic disabilities facing European and American women. Consisting of a vast web of interconnected organizations, publications, and correspondence networks, the middle-class women's movement sought to challenge the ideology of separate spheres and to establish a new basis for both private and public relations. Its multifaceted campaigns focused on four fronts: the legal impediments facing married women, employment opportunities and higher education for girls and women, the double standard of sexual conduct enshrined in European laws, and national women's suffrage.

Women and the Law

European legal systems strongly reinforced the liberal ideology of separate spheres for men and women. Law codes often classified women with children, criminals, and the insane. Article 231 of the Napoleonic Code, the legal system of France and the basis of the legal codes of much of western and central Europe, declared that the wife was the dependent of the husband; hence, "the husband owes protection to his wife; the wife owes obedience to her husband." The Russian legal code agreed: "The woman must obey her husband, reside with him in love, respect, and unlimited obedience, and offer him every pleasantness and affection as the ruler of the household." In Russia a woman could not travel without her father's or husband's permission. The husband was also the legal guardian of all children; he alone had the authority to pick their schools, determine their punishments, and approve their marriage partners. Similarly, in Prussia the law declared that only the husband could decide when his baby should stop breastfeeding. English common law, based on tradition and precedent rather than on a single, systematized code, proclaimed much the same idea. As Sir William Blackstone explained in his famous *Commentaries on the Laws of England* (1765–1769), "the husband and wife are one person in law," and that person was the husband. A married woman simply disappeared in the eyes of the British common law. Most property brought into a marriage, or given to her or earned by her while married, became the property of her husband.

From the middle of the nineteenth century on, women's groups fought to improve the legal rights of married women. By the end of the 1880s, English married women had won rights to own their own property, control their own income, and keep their children. Two decades later, French women could claim similar rights. In contrast, the German women's movement suffered a sharp defeat with the promulgation of the Civil Code in 1900. The Civil Code, which formulated a single uniform legal system for Germany, proclaimed that "the husband takes the decisions in all matters affecting married life." It granted all parental authority to the husband—over his stepchildren as well as his own children. By German law, "if the parents disagree, the father's opinion takes precedence." While it allowed married women to keep money they earned while married, it declared that all property owned by the wife before marriage or given to her after marriage became the husband's.

Finding a Place: Employment and Education

In addition to their legal campaigns, feminists also worked to widen women's educational and employment opportunities as part of their effort to enter the public sphere. At the core of this aspect of the women's movement was a simple demographic reality—women outnumbered men in almost every region in Europe. In England by 1900, the higher rates of male emigration and infant mortality meant that there were 1,064 females for every 1,000 males. Clearly, not all women could marry. Thus, providing respectable jobs for middle-class single women was a high priority for early European and American feminists.

The problem of women's jobs quickly proved to be inseparable from the issue of women's education. Even girls from privileged families rarely received rigorous educations before 1850. The minority of girls who did go to school spent their time learning ladylike occupations such as fancy embroidery, flower arranging, and piano playing. Proper posture was more important than any literary or scientific attainments. Widening the world of women's education, then, became a crucial feminist aim and proved to be an area in which they achieved considerable, but still limited, success.

Feminists' educational campaigns in the second half of the nineteenth century had two main emphases: first, improving the quality as well as expanding the number of girls' secondary schools, and second, opening universities to women. The fight to upgrade the quality of girls' secondary education was often difficult. Many parents opposed an academic curriculum for girls, a position reinforced by medical professionals who argued that girls' brains simply could not withstand the strain of an intellectual education. Dorothea Beale (1831–1906), a pioneer in girls' education in England, established one of the first academically oriented high schools for girls in London in the 1850s, but she faced an uphill battle in persuading reluctant parents to allow her to teach their daughters mathematics. In France, feminists achieved their goal of a state-funded and state-run system of secondary schools for girls in the 1880s. They lost the battle for a university-preparatory curriculum, however, which made it difficult for girls to pass the exams necessary to enter the French university system.

Not surprisingly, the number of women in French universities remained very small throughout this period. Opportunities for university education for women varied enormously. In the United States, women accounted for one-third of all students in higher education as early as 1880, while in Germany, women were not admitted to full-time university study until 1901. In Russia, the development of women's higher education was particularly sporadic. Full-time university study became available to women in Moscow in 1872, and by 1880, women in Russia had some of the best opportunities for higher education in all of Europe. But the involvement of Sofiia Perovskaia—an educated woman—in the assassination of Tsar Alexander II in 1881 convinced the authorities that revolutionary politics and advanced female education went hand in hand. Most educational avenues for Russian women were blocked for more than two decades after the assassination.

Despite such limitations and reverses, the range of jobs open to women did broaden during this period. In 1900, French women won the right to practice law, and in 1903

On the Way to School
By the 1880s, the sight of middle-class girls in secondary and university education was not yet commonplace, but no longer rare.

in the French city of Toulouse, a woman lawyer presented a case in a European court for the first time. In 1906, the physicist and Nobel Prize winner Marie Curie became the first woman to hold a university faculty position in France. By the opening decades of the twentieth century, women doctors, although still unusual, were not unheard of. In Russia, women accounted for 10 percent of all physicians by 1914.

No More Angels

The campaigns for women's legal rights and an expansion of employment and educational opportunities helped women move out of the private and into the public sphere. But the third goal of feminist activity—to eradicate the double standard of sexual conduct—posed a more radical challenge to nineteenth-century middle-class culture and its ideology of separate spheres. By arguing that the same moral standards should apply to both men and women, feminists questioned whether two separate spheres should exist at all.

The ideology of separate spheres glorified women's moral purity and held that the more aggressive, more animal-like natures of men naturally resulted in such male pastimes as heavy drinking and sexual adventurism. The laws as well as the wider culture reflected these assumptions. For example, in France, a woman with an illegitimate child could not institute a paternity suit against the father: Premarital sex was a crime for the woman, but not for the man. Similarly, the English divorce legislation of 1857 declared that a woman's adultery was all that was necessary for a husband to sue for divorce, but a man's adultery was not a sufficient reason to end a marriage. For a wife to divorce her husband, she had to prove that he had committed additional crimes such as bigamy, incest, or bestiality.

To feminists, applying different moral standards to men and women degraded men and blocked women's efforts to better their own lives and society as a whole. As the French feminist leader Maria Desraismes explained, "To say that woman is an angel is to impose on her, in a sentimental and admiring fashion, all duties, and to reserve for oneself all rights. . . . I decline the honor of being an angel."[10]

In their effort to erase the moral distinctions between men and women, feminists fought on a variety of fronts. One key area of struggle was the regulation of prostitution. By the 1870s, many European countries, as well as the United States, had established procedures that made it safer for men to hire prostitutes, while still treating the women involved as criminals. In England, the Contagious Diseases Act, passed in 1870 to address the problem of venereal disease, declared that any woman suspected of being a prostitute could be stopped by the police and required to undergo a genital exam. Men, however, were subject to no such indignities. Feminists such as Josephine Butler (1857–1942) contended that such legislation made it easier for men to indulge their sexual appetites, while punishing the impoverished women who were forced to sell their bodies to feed themselves and their children. For almost twenty years Butler led a concerted campaign both to repeal the legislation that regulated prostitution and to focus public attention on the lack of employment opportunities for women.

Abuse of alcohol was another key battleground for the women's movement. Arguing that the socially accepted practice of heavy male drinking had devastating consequences for women, in the form of both family poverty and domestic violence, feminist activists backed the temperance or prohibitionist cause. The movement triumphed in the United States in 1919 when decades of agitation from groups such as the Women's Christian Temperance Union led to the passage of the Eighteenth Amendment prohibiting the manufacture and sale of alcoholic beverages. "Prohibition," however, did little to transform gender relations; instead, it simply created new ways for organized crime syndicates to make money. The American prohibition experiment ended in 1933 with the repeal of the Eighteenth Amendment.

In general, feminist moral reform campaigns achieved only limited success. The regulation of prostitution did end in England in 1886 and in the United States, France, and the Scandinavian countries by 1914, but remained in effect in Germany. By 1884 in France, a husband's adultery, like a wife's, could end a marriage, but in England, the grounds for divorce remained differentiated by gender until 1923. In all European countries and in the United States, the sexual double standard remained embedded in both middle- and working-class culture far into the twentieth century.

The Fight for Women's Suffrage

The slow pace and uneven progress on both the legal and moral fronts convinced many feminists that they would achieve their goals only if they possessed the political clout of the *national* suffrage. In 1867 the National Society for Women's Suffrage was founded in Britain; over the next three decades suffrage societies emerged on the Continent. The French suffragist Hubertine Auclert (1848–1914) described the vote as "the keystone that will give [women] all other rights." As the editor of *La Citoyenne* ("The Citizeness"), Auclert agitated for full citizenship rights for adult women. In an imaginative move, she refused to pay taxes, on the grounds of "no taxation without representation." Auclert was also the first woman to describe herself as a "feminist," a word that entered the English language from the French around 1890.

Auclert and other American and European suffragists had little success. Only in Finland (1906) and Norway (1913) did women gain the national franchise in this period. (By 1913, women also possessed the vote in twelve American

DOCUMENT

In Favor of the Vote for Women

Many supporters of women's suffrage believed that education, reason, and persuasion would achieve the vote. If suffragists made their case in logical, reasonable terms, they would be able to convince a majority of male voters of the rightness of their cause. This excerpt from a French suffragist pamphlet, published in 1913, is very typical both in its effort to persuade its reader through a careful marshaling of factual evidence and in its belief that the women's vote would transform political life. French women did not win the vote for another thirty years.

We are going to try to prove that the vote for women is a just, possible and desirable reform. . . .

A woman has responsibility in the family; she ought to be consulted about the laws establishing her rights and duties with respect to her husband, her children, her parents.

Women work—and in ever greater numbers; a statistic of 1896 established that . . . the number of women workers was 35 per cent of the total number of workers, both male and female.

If she is in business, she, like any businessman, has interests to protect. . . .

If a woman is a worker or a domestic, she ought to participate as a man does in voting on unionization laws, laws covering workers' retirement, social security, the limitation and regulation of work hours, weekly days off, labor contracts, etc.

. . .

Finally, her special characteristics of order, economy, patience and resourcefulness will be as useful to society as the characteristics of man and will favor the establishment of laws too often overlooked until now.

The woman's vote will assure the establishment of important social laws.

All women will want:

To fight against alcoholism, from which they suffer much more than men;

To establish laws of health and welfare;

To obtain the regulation of female and child labor;

To defend young women against prostitution;

Finally, to prevent wars and to submit conflicts among nations to courts of arbitration.

Source: From a report presented to Besancon Municipal Council by the Franc-Comtois Group of the Union Française pour le Suffrage des Femmes. Besancon, March 1913, pp. 6–9.

states.) The social upheaval of World War I brought women the vote in Russia (1917), Britain (1918), Germany (1919), Austria (1919), the Netherlands (1919), and the United States (1920). Women in Italy had to wait until 1945; French women did not gain the vote until 1946, Greek women not until 1949. Women in Switzerland did not vote until 1971.

Feminists faced a number of significant obstacles in their battle for the national franchise. In Catholic countries such as France and Italy, the women's suffrage movement failed to become a political force not only because the Church remained fiercely opposed to the women's vote, but also because in Catholicism—in its veneration of the Virgin Mary and other female saints, in its exaltation of family life, in the opportunity for religious vocation as a nun—women found a great many avenues for emotional expression and intellectual satisfaction. Feminism had a much harder time taking root in these countries.

In central and eastern Europe the obstacles were even greater. In much of this region, economic development was far behind that of the western areas of Europe, and thus middle-class culture—the social base of feminism—was also underdeveloped. In the Russian Empire, the middle class was small and any political organization independent of the tsar was seen as a form of treason. No women's suffrage movement existed there until the Revolution of 1905 dramatically changed the political equation. After the revolution won the vote for men but failed to extend it to women, an organized and vocal women's suffrage campaign emerged.

In contrast to Russia, in England the middle class was both large and politically powerful, and the political structure had shown itself capable of adaptation and evolution. Yet even in England, the site of the first and the strongest European female suffrage movement, women failed to win the vote in the nineteenth century. As a result, a small group of activists resorted to more radical tactics. Led by the imposing mother-and-daughters team of Emmeline (1858–1928), Christabel (1880–1958), and Sylvia Pankhurst (1882–1960), the suffragettes° formed a breakaway women's suffrage group in 1903. Convinced that the mainstream suffragists' tactics such as signing petitions, publishing reasoned arguments, and lobbying politicians would never win the vote, the suffragettes threw respectability to the winds. They adopted as their motto the slogan "Deeds, Not Words," and declared that women would never earn the vote through rational persuasion. Instead, they had to grab it by force. The suffragettes broke up political meetings with the cry "Votes for Women!," chained themselves to the steps of the Houses of Parliament, shattered shop windows, burned churches, destroyed mailboxes, and even, in a direct attack on a cherished citadel of male middle-class culture, vandalized golf courses.

In opting for violence, the suffragettes staged a full frontal assault on a central fortification of middle-class culture—the ideal of the passive, homebound woman. The fortress they were attacking proved well-defended, however. Their opponents reacted with fury. Police broke up suffragette rallies with sexually focused brutality: They dragged suffragettes by their hair, stomped on their crotches, punched their breasts, and tore off their blouses. Once in jail, hunger-striking suffragettes endured the horror of forced feedings. Several jailers pinned the woman to her bed while the doctor thrust a plastic tube down her throat, often lacerating her larynx in the process, and pumped in food until she gagged.

Conclusion

The West in an Age of Mass Politics

The clash between the suffragettes and their jailers was only one of a multitude of encounters, many of them violent, among those seeking access to political power and those seeking to limit that access, in the era from 1870 to the start of World War I in 1914. At the same time, changing patterns of industrialization and accelerated urbanization gave rise to other sorts of encounters—between the manager seeking to cut production costs and the employee aiming to protect his wages, for example, or among the newly arrived immigrants in the city, struggling to survive in an unfamiliar culture, and the long-established residents who spoke a different language.

Out of such encounters emerged key questions about the definition of "the West." Where, for example, did the West end? Did it include Russia? "Yes," replied the small revolutionary groups who embraced Karl Marx's socialist theories and argued that Russia would follow Western patterns of economic and political development. Other Russian revolutionaries, however, rejected Western models and sought a revolutionary path unique to Russia. The expansion of the franchise and the processes of making nations raised even more fundamental questions. Was the West defined by democracy? Should it be? Was it synonymous with white, western European men or could people with olive-colored or black skin—or women of any color—participate fully in Western culture and politics? Was "the West" defined by its rationality? In the eighteenth century, Enlightenment thinkers had praised the power of human rationality and looked to reason as the path to social improvement. The rise of a new style of politics, based on emotional appeal and often irrational racist hatred, challenged this faith in reason. But at the same time, developments in industrial organization and technologies, which helped expand European national incomes, seemed to point to the benefits of rational processes.

As we will see in the next chapter, the expansion of Western control over vast areas of Asia and Africa in this period led an increasing number of Europeans and Americans to highlight economic prosperity and technological superiority as the defining characteristics of the West. Confidence, however, was accompanied by anxiety as these years also witnessed a far-reaching cultural and intellectual crisis. Closely connected to the development of mass politics and changes in social and gender relations, this crisis slowly eroded many of the pillars of middle- and upper-class society and raised searching questions about Western assumptions and values.

Suggestions for Further Reading

For a comprehensive listing of suggested readings, please go to www.ablongman.com/levack2e/chapter22

Evans, Richard. *The Feminists: Women's Emancipation Movements in Europe, America, and Australasia, 1840–1920.* 1977. A helpful comparative overview.

Kern, Stephen. *The Culture of Time and Space, 1880–1918.* 1983. An innovative work that explores the cultural impact of technological change.

Lidtke, Vernon. *The Alternative Culture: Socialist Labor in Imperial Germany.* 1985. Looks beyond the world of parliamentary politics to assess the meaning and impact of working-class socialism.

Lindemann, Albert. *Esau's Tears: Modern Anti-Semitism and the Rise of the Jews.* 1997. A comprehensive and detailed survey that challenges many assumptions about the roots and nature of modern anti-Semitism.

Mayer, Arno. *The Persistence of the Old Regime: Europe to the Great War.* 1981. Argues that landed elites maintained a considerable amount of economic and political power throughout the nineteenth century.

Milward, A. S., and S. B. Saul. *The Development of the Economies of Continental Europe, 1850–1914.* 1977. A helpful survey.

Moch, Leslie. *Moving Europeans: Migration in Western Europe Since 1650.* 1992. Filled with maps and packed with information, Moch's work explodes many easy assumptions about the movement of Europeans in the nineteenth century.

Nord, Philip. *The Republican Moment: Struggles for Democracy in Nineteenth-Century France.* 1996. Illuminates the struggle to define and redefine France.

Pilbeam, Pamela. *The Middle Classes in Europe, 1789–1914: France, Germany, Italy, and Russia.* 1990. A comparative approach that helps clarify the patterns of social change.

Richards, Thomas. *The Commodity Culture of Victorian England: Advertising and Spectacle, 1851–1914.* 1990. Fascinating study of the manufacturing of desire.

Stearns, Peter N. *Lives of Labor: Work in a Maturing Industrial Society.* 1975. Explores changing economic and social patterns.

Steenson, Gary P. *After Marx, Before Lenin: Marxism and Socialist Working-Class Parties in Europe, 1884–1914.* 1991. Examines both ideology and political practice within Europe's socialist parties.

Weber, Eugen. *Peasants into Frenchmen: The Modernization of Rural France, 1870–1914.* 1976. A very important work that helped shape the way historians think about "nation making."

Notes

1. Leslie Moch, *Moving Europeans: Migration in Western Europe Since 1650* (1992), 147.
2. Quoted in Eugen Weber, *Peasants into Frenchmen: The Modernization of Rural France, 1870–1914* (1976), 332–333.
3. Norman Kleeblatt, *The Dreyfus Affair: Art, Truth, and Justice* (1987), 96.
4. Quoted in Eric Cahm, *The Dreyfus Affair in French Society and Politics* (1994), 167.
5. Quoted in Robert Gildea, *Barricades and Borders: Europe, 1800–1914* (1987), 317.
6. Quoted in Leslie Derfler, *Socialism Since Marx: A Century of the European Left* (1973), 58.
7. Karl Kautsky, quoted in Eric Hobsbawm, *The Age of Empire, 1875–1914* (1987), 133.
8. Eugen Weber, *France, Fin-de-Siècle* (1986), 126.
9. Albert Lindemann, *Esau's Tears: Modern Anti-Semitism and the Rise of the Jews* (1997).
10. Maria Desraismes, "La Femme et Le Droit," *Eve dans l'humanite* (1891), 16–17.

The West and the World: Cultural Crisis and the New Imperialism, 1870–1914

23

CHAPTER OUTLINE

- Scientific Transformations
- Cultural Crisis: The Fin-de-Siècle and the Birth of Modernism
- The New Imperialism

In the autumn of 1898, British troops moved into the Sudan in northeast Africa to claim the region for the British Empire. On September 2, the British Camel Corps faced an army of 40,000 fighters. The Sudanese soldiers, Islamic believers known as dervishes who possessed a reputation for military fierceness, were fighting on their home ground against an invading force. Nevertheless, after only five hours of fighting, 11,000 dervishes lay dead. Their opponents lost just forty men. While the dervishes, armed with swords and spears, surged forward in a full-scale frontal assault, the British troops sat safely behind fortified defenses, and, using repeating rifles and Maxim guns (a type of early machine gun), simply mowed down their attackers. According to one participant on the British side, the future prime minister Winston Churchill, the biggest danger to the British soldiers during the battle of Omdurman was boredom: "The mere physical act [of loading, firing, and reloading] became tedious." The dervishes had little chance of boredom. Churchill recalled, "And all the time out on the plain on the other side bullets were shearing through flesh, smashing and splintering bone; blood spouted from terrible wounds; valiant men were struggling through a hell of whistling metal, exploding shells, and spurting dust—suffering, despairing, dying."[1]

The slaughter of 11,000 Sudanese in just over five hours formed but one episode in what many historians call the age of new imperialism, a period that witnessed both the culmination of, and a new phase in, Europe's conquest of the globe. This often-violent encounter between Europe and the regions that Europeans emphatically defined as non-Western was closely connected to the political and economic upheavals examined in Chapter 22. An understanding of the new imperialism, however, demands a close look not

Paul Gauguin, *Matamoe* ("Peacocks in the Country"), 1892 The Fauvist painter Paul Gauguin fled Europe for Tahiti in an effort to restore to his art the strong colors and emotions that he believed characterized non-Western cultures. The sights, sensibilities, and symbolism of Tahitian society profoundly affected his painting—and helped shape modernist art.

only at political rivalries and economic structures, but also at scientific, intellectual, and cultural developments in the last third of the nineteenth century. At the same time that European and American adventurers risked life and limb to chart Africa's rivers, exploit its resources, and subjugate its peoples, Western artists and scientists embarked on explorations into worlds of thought and perception far deeper than the surface reality accessible to the senses, and in so doing challenged the social order and even the meaning of reality itself. The final decades of the nineteenth century and the opening years of the twentieth thus comprised an era of internal fragmentation and external expansion.

This chapter examines the scientific, artistic, and physical explorations that characterized the period between 1870 and 1914 to answer a key question: In what ways did these explorations redefine the West and its relationship with the rest of the world? Three more specific questions guide this examination:

- **How did scientific developments during this period lead to not only greater intellectual and cultural optimism but also deepened anxiety?**
- **What factors led many Europeans in this period to believe they were living in a time of cultural crisis?**
- **What were the causes and consequences of the new imperialist ideology for both the West and non-Western societies?**

Scientific Transformations

- **How did scientific developments during this period lead to not only greater intellectual and cultural optimism but also deepened anxiety?**

During the final third of the nineteenth century, Europeans encountered in new ways both the human body and the wider physical universe. Forced by urbanization to cram more bodies into limited space, men and women grew increasingly aware of the human body, and of the way it interacted with other bodies, both human and microscopic. At the same time, the work of geologists and biologists highlighted the way the body itself had evolved to meet the challenges of survival, while the experiments of chemists and physicists revealed the inadequacies of accepted models for understanding the physical world.

These developments affirmed a central assumption of the dominant middle-class worldview—that human reason and endeavor can guarantee social, intellectual, and moral progress. Scientific advances in the final third of the nineteenth century helped improve the health and hygiene of the Western world. Yet these changes in scientific understandings of both the body and the cosmos also threatened to destabilize Western society and therefore deepened the cultural anxiety of Europeans and Americans in this period.

Medicine and Microbes

In the second half of the nineteenth century, and particularly after 1870, a series of developments transformed the practice of Western medicine. Before this time, Western physicians assumed that illness was caused by bad blood and so relied on practices such as leeching (attaching leeches to the skin) and bloodletting (slicing open a vein). These procedures drained large amounts of blood, further weakening already ill patients. Admission into a hospital was sometimes a death sentence. Ignorant of the existence of bacteria and viruses, doctors commonly attended one patient after another without bothering to wash their hands or surgical instruments. The only anesthetic available was alcohol; pain was regarded as inevitable, something to be endured rather than eased.

Urbanization posed a fundamental challenge to such traditional medical practice and helped transform Western medicine. Expanding urban populations served as fertile seedbeds for contagious diseases. Cholera outbreaks, such as the epidemics that ravaged British cities in 1831 and 1848, forced doctors and public officials to pay attention to the relationship between overcrowding, polluted water, and epidemic disease. Hamburg was one of the first cities to undertake the construction of a modern water and sewer system in 1842; in 1848 the London cholera epidemic persuaded public officials to build a vast sewer system (most of which is still in use today).

It was not until the 1860s, however, that germ theory was developed. By exploring the transmission of disease among plants and animals in the French agricultural industry, the chemist Louis Pasteur (1822–1895) discovered the source of contagion to be microscopic living organisms—bacteria. Astonishingly productive, Pasteur developed vaccines against anthrax, hog fever, sheep pox, various poultry and cattle diseases, and rabies. (His process of purifying milk and fermented products is still known as pasteurization.) Following Pasteur, Robert Koch (1843–1910), professor of public health in Berlin, isolated the tuberculosis bacillus in 1882 and the bacteria that cause cholera in 1883.

The work of Pasteur, Koch, and other scientists in tracing the transmission of disease was crucial in improving Western medical practice. Between 1872 and 1900, the number of European deaths from infectious diseases dropped by 60 percent. Once physicians and surgeons accepted that microscopic organisms caused disease, they began to develop techniques to control their spread. The development of antiseptic surgery in the later 1860s improved the patient's odds of surviving the operating table.

The increasing use of anesthetics in the second half of the nineteenth century also improved those odds. In 1847 a

Scottish physician performed the first delivery of a baby using chloroform to dull the mother's pain. Although condemned by many Christian theologians (who regarded pain as both ennobling and a necessary part of sinful human existence), the use of anesthetics spread fairly quickly. Britain's Queen Victoria, who gave birth to nine children, probably articulated the feelings of many patients when she greeted the use of anesthetics in the delivery room with unfettered delight: "Oh blessed chloroform!"

Medical advances such as anesthetic techniques and an understanding of how diseases are spread gave Europeans genuine confidence that the conquest of nature through science would create a healthier environment. But the widespread awareness of germs also heightened anxiety. Isolation of the bacilli that caused an illness did not immediately translate into its cure, and viral infections remained often lethal. Measles, for example, continued to kill at least 7,000 people per year in Britain throughout the nineteenth century. After the 1870s, Europeans were aware that they lived in a world populated by potentially deadly but invisible organisms, carried on the bodies of their servants, their employees, their neighbors, and their family members. Those who could afford to isolate themselves from the danger often did so. As a result, this era witnessed striking growth in the number of seaside resorts as middle- and upper-class Europeans fled from urban centers of contagion.

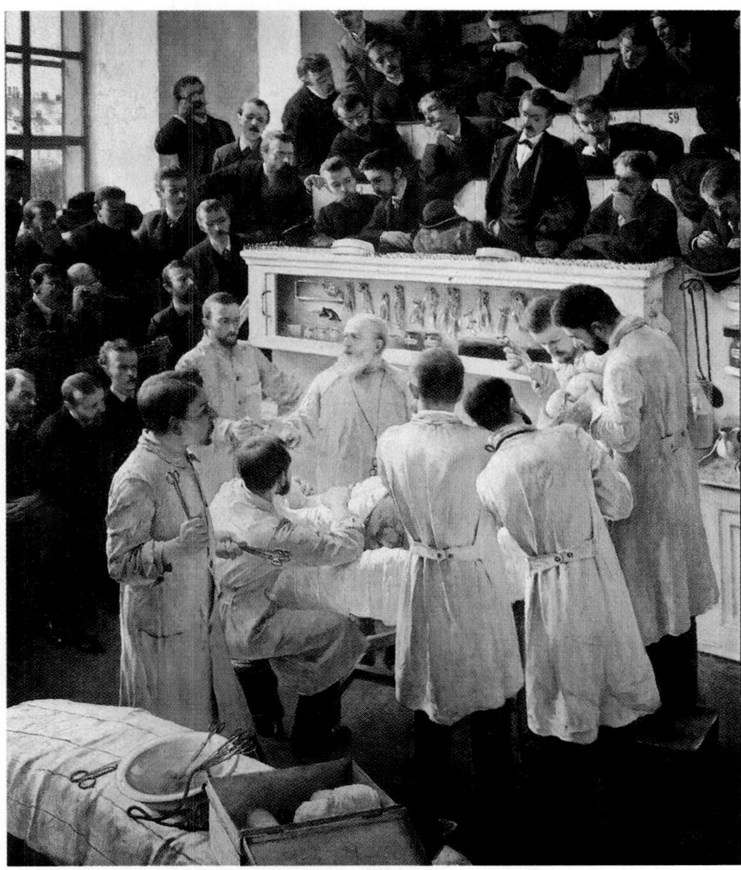

Adelbert Seligmann, *German Surgeon Theodor Billroth at Work in Vienna* (1890)
Modern surgery in the making: The patient has been anesthetized, but the modern operating room does not yet exist, nor are the doctors wearing gloves or masks. Billroth, the director of the Second Surgical Clinic in Vienna, pioneered surgical techniques for gastrointestinal illnesses and cancer.

The Triumph of Evolutionary Science

Developments in geology and biology also led to both confidence and anxiety. Evolutionary science provided a scientific framework in which educated Europeans could understand and justify their own superior social and economic positions. It also, however, challenged basic religious assumptions and depicted the natural world in new and unsettling ways.

Traditionally, Europeans had relied on the opening chapters of the Bible to understand the origins of both nature and humanity. By the 1830s, however, the work of geologists challenged the biblical account. Although a literal reading of the Bible dated the Earth at only 6,000 years old, geologists such as Charles Lyell (1797–1875) argued on the basis of the fossil record and existing geological formations that the Earth had formed over millions of years. Lyell's most famous work was the *Principles of Geology,* first published in 1830 and a nineteenth-century best-seller that went through eleven editions. In three volumes of very readable prose, packed with illustrative examples, Lyell gently but rigorously refuted the orthodox Christian position that geological change and the extinction of species could be explained by the biblical account of the flood or other such supernatural interventions. Instead, he and others argued that the material world must be seen as the product of natural forces still at work, still observable today.

But how could one explain the tremendous variety of plant and animal species in the world on the basis of natural processes? In 1859, the British scientist Charles Darwin (1809–1882) answered this question in a way that proved quite satisfying to large numbers of educated Europeans—and quite horrifying to others. Darwin had spent two decades thinking about the data he collected during a five-year expedition to the South Pacific in the 1830s. Serving as an unpaid naturalist on the H.M.S. *Beagle* between 1831

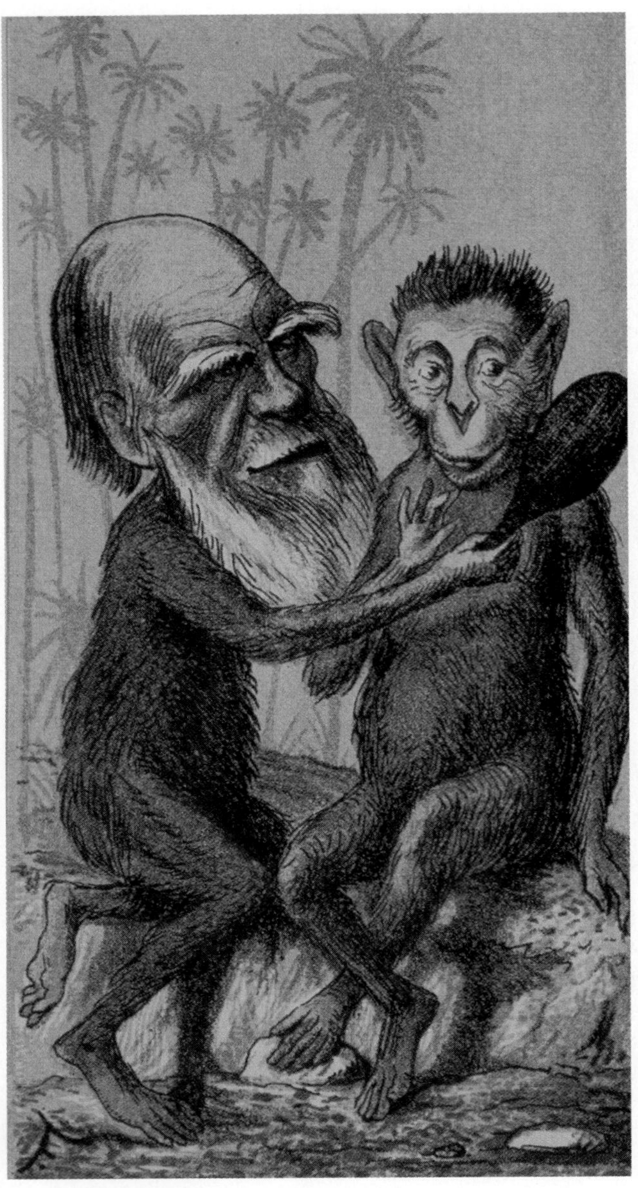

Darwin's Disturbing Mirror

Simplified and often ridiculous versions of Darwin's ideas almost immediately entered popular culture. Here a monkey version of Darwin holds up a mirror to his fellow creature, who seems surprised by his reflection.

and 1836, Darwin observed that certain species of animal and plant life, isolated on islands, had developed differently from related species on the coast. After returning to Britain, Darwin read the population theory of Thomas Malthus (1766–1834). Malthus argued that population growth would outstrip food supply, and that in all species, more offspring are produced than can actually survive. Putting together Malthus's theory with his own observations, Darwin concluded that life is a struggle for survival, and that even quite small biological variations might help an individual member of a species win out in this struggle. From this understanding came the Darwinian theory° of the evolution of species.

Darwin's evolutionary hypothesis rested on two basic ideas: *variation* and *natural selection.* Variation refers to the small but crucial biological advantages that assist in the struggle for survival: A bird with a slightly longer beak, for example, might gain easier access to scarce food supplies. Over generations, the individuals more adapted for survival displace those without the positive variation. Variation, then, provides the means of natural selection, the process by which new species evolve.

Darwin provided a persuasive explanation for evolutionary change, but the fact that the laws of genetic heredity were not yet understood resulted in two key weaknesses in his formulation—first, its extreme gradualness, in that the process of variation required many, many generations; and second, the lack of a precise explanation of how variations first emerge and how they are inherited. Answers to both problems lay embedded in the research of an Austrian monk, Gregor Mendel (1822–1884). Experimenting in his vegetable garden with what we now call selective breeding, Mendel developed the laws of genetic heredity. Mendel's work was ignored almost completely until the end of the century, when the Dutch botanist Hugo DeVries (1848–1935) used his data to hypothesize that evolution occurred through radical mutations in the reproductive cells of an organism. These mutations are passed on to offspring at the moment of reproduction and, if they offer an advantage in the struggle for existence, enable the offspring to survive and to produce more mutant offspring. Thus evolution can proceed by leaps, rather than gradually over a very long period of time.

Long before these genetic underpinnings of evolution were understood, however, Darwin's theories proved extraordinarily influential. Published in 1859, *The Origin of Species* aroused immediate interest and controversy. This controversy intensified when, in 1871, Darwin published *The Descent of Man,* in which he firmly placed humanity itself within the evolutionary process. Many Christians reacted with horror to a theory that they believed challenged the biblical narrative of Creation and denied a special place for humankind within the physical universe. But the most troubling aspect of Darwin's theory was its view of nature. According to orthodox Christian theology, nature, like the Bible, reveals God to the believer. In the Darwinian universe, however, nature was not a harmonious, well-ordered system that revealed the hand of God. Instead, it was the arena of brutal and bloody competition for survival—"nature red in tooth and claw," as the British poet Alfred Lord Tennyson put it. In such a universe, ideas of purpose and

DOCUMENT
On Darwin (1860s)

DOCUMENT

The Descent of Man

First published in 1871, The Descent of Man *continued and completed Charles Darwin's theory of the evolution of species first introduced in his* Origin of Species *(1859). Darwin's work in many ways affirmed central prejudices and assumptions of his middle-class readers, as the following excerpts demonstrate.*

We have now seen that man is variable in body and mind; and that the variations are induced, either directly or indirectly, by the same general causes, and obey the same general laws, as with the lower animals. Man has spread widely over the face of the earth, and must have been exposed, during his incessant migration, to the most diversified conditions. . . . The early progenitors of man must also have tended, like all other animals, to have increased beyond their means of subsistence; they must, therefore, occasionally have been exposed to a struggle for existence, and consequently, to the rigid law of natural selection. Beneficial variations of all kinds will thus, either occasionally or habitually, have been preserved and injurious ones eliminated. . . .

Man in the rudest state in which he now exists is the most dominant animal that has ever appeared on this earth. He has spread more widely than any other highly organised form, and all others have yielded before him. He manifestly owes this immense superiority to his intellectual faculties, to his social habits, which lead him to aid and defend his fellows, and to his corporeal structure. . . .

The belief that there exists in man some close relation between the size of the brain and the development of the intellectual faculties is supported by the comparison of the skulls of savage and civilized races, of ancient and modern people, and by the analogy of the whole vertebrate series . . . the mean internal capacity of the skull in Europeans is 92.3 cubic inches; in Americans 87.5; in Asiatics 87.1; and in Australians only 81.9 inches. . . . Nevertheless, it must be admitted that some skulls of very high antiquity, such as the famous one of the Neanderthal, are well developed and capacious.

Source: From *The Descent of Man,* 2nd edition, by Charles Darwin, 1874.

meaning seemed to disappear. Faced with this disturbing vision, many Christians opposed Darwinian science.

Many other Christians, however, welcomed Darwin's evolutionary theory. They argued that evolution did not banish divine purpose from the universe but instead showed God's hand at work in the gradual development of more perfect species. Enthusiastically applying the idea of evolution to the ethical universe, they contended that the history of humanity showed that the morally fittest proved victorious in the ethical sphere, just as the strongest triumphed in the natural world.

By 1870, three-quarters of British scientists surveyed accepted evolutionary theory. More important, many middle-class Europeans and Americans welcomed Darwin's ideas as providing a coherent explanation of change that accorded with their worldview. They saw Darwin's work as a scientific confirmation of their faith in the virtues of competition and in the inevitability of progress. As Darwin himself wrote in *The Origin of Species,* because "natural selection works solely by and for the good of each being, all corporeal [bodily] and mental development will tend to progress toward perfection."

Social Darwinism and Racial Hierarchies

Darwin's explanation of evolution contributed to a new understanding of biological relationships and of the connections between humanity and the natural world. In the last quarter of the nineteenth century, however, a growing number of writers and social theorists insisted that evolutionary theory could and should be applied more broadly. One of the most influential of this group was the British writer Herbert Spencer (1820–1902). Trained as a civil engineer, Spencer became convinced that evolution held the key to engineering a better human society. A self-confident, eminently practical thinker, Spencer coined the phrase "the survival of the fittest" to describe what he viewed as the most basic explanation of development in both nature and human society. He believed that human societies evolve like plant and animal species. Only the fittest, those able to adapt to changing conditions, survive. A great champion of *laissez-faire* economics (see Chapter 21), Spencer contended that government interference in economic and social affairs interfered with the natural evolutionary process and so hindered rather than assured progress.

Spencer's essentially biological vision of society proved influential in shaping the theories of Social Darwinism°. Arguing that racial hierarchy was the product of natural evolution, the Social Darwinists applied Spencer's ideas about the importance of individual competition and the survival of the fittest to entire races. In their view, the nonwhite races in Africa and Asia had lost the game. Their so-called backward way of life showed they had failed to compete successfully with white Europeans and thus displayed their biological inferiority. The very popular British novelist Rider Haggard, in his best-selling thriller *She* (1887), summed up the Social Darwinist worldview: "Those who are weak must perish; the earth is to the strong . . . We run to place and power over the dead bodies of those who fail and fall; ay, we win the food we eat from out the mouths of starving babes. It is the scheme of things."

In their effort to construct a scientifically based racial hierarchy, Social Darwinists made use not only of Darwin's idea of natural selection but also of the theory of "recapitulation," first proposed by the German zoologist Ernst Haeckel (1834–1919). According to Haeckel, as an individual matures, he or she moves through the same stages as did the human race during the course of its evolution. For example, the gill slits of a human embryo "recapitulate" the fish stage through which the human race had evolved. The idea of recapitulation enabled scientists to fill in the gaps left by the fossil record. By observing the development of children into adults, they argued, we can witness the evolutionary maturation of the human race.

Social Darwinists used the theory of recapitulation to argue that only white European males had reached the pinnacle of evolutionary development. They contended that nonwhite men, as well as all women, embodied the more primitive stages of evolution through which the white European male had already passed. In other words, the nonwhite races and white women were suffering from arrested development. Their bodies and brains bore witness to their low-ranking position on the evolutionary ladder. Such ideas permeated much of Western culture in the late nineteenth century. Sigmund Freud, for example, argued that "the female genitalia are more primitive than those of the male," while Gustave LeBon compared the average female brain to that of a gorilla. G. A. Henty, a best-selling British novelist, insisted that the "intelligence of the average negro is about equal to that of a European [male] child of ten years old."[2]

Firmly convinced that the inferiority of women and nonwhites was a biological fact, nineteenth-century scientists and large sections of the European public welcomed evolutionary theory as scientific proof of deeply embedded cultural assumptions, such as the benefits of competition, the rightness of white rule and male dominance, and the superiority of Western civilization. Yet evolutionary science also worked to undermine European confidence because with the idea of evolution came the possibility of regression: Was the traffic on the evolutionary ladder all one-way, or could species descend to a lower evolutionary level? Could humanity regress to its animal origins?

The concept of the "inheritance of acquired characteristics," associated with the work of the French scientist Jean-Baptiste Lamarck (1744–1829), played a crucial role in fostering these fears of regression. More than fifty years before Darwin published his *Origin of Species,* Lamarck theorized that acquired characteristics—traits that an individual develops in response to experience or the environment, such as the stooped back of a miner, the poor vision of a lace maker, or the deep tan of an agricultural laborer—could be passed on to the individual's offspring. Because the process of genetic reproduction was not understood until the twentieth century, Lamarck's theories remained very influential throughout the nineteenth century and possessed deeply disturbing implications. Middle-class Europeans began to speculate that the conditions of urban industrial life were producing undesirable characteristics among urban workers. In their view, characteristics such as physical weakness, sexual promiscuity, and violent criminality were being passed from one generation to the next and were threatening to reverse the evolutionary ascent of Western civilization.

The Revolution in Physics

Darwin's work revolutionized the field of biology. Between 1880 and 1910 a revolution in physics occurred as well. Although the most dramatic consequences of this revolution—atomic weapons and nuclear energy—would not be realized for another half century, this transformation in scientific understanding contributed to both the exhilaration and the uncertainty that characterized the intellectual and cultural history of Europe in the decades before World War I.

At the core of the revolution in physics lay the question, "What is matter?" For most of the nineteenth century, the answer was simple: Matter was what close observation and measurement, as well as common sense, showed it to be. Material bodies, made up of the building blocks called atoms, rested and moved against a fixed backdrop of space and time. Matter was three-dimensional, defined by height, width, and depth. Accessible to reason, observation, and common sense, the material world could be understood and controlled. The triumph of the theories of Isaac Newton had ensured that for 200 years, educated Westerners regarded the natural world as a precise and predictable machine (see Chapter 16).

As the new century opened, this picture of the universe began to crumble. A series of discoveries and experiments challenged this commonsense view of the universe and offered in its place a much more mysterious and unsettling vista. The discovery of the X-ray in 1895 had already disrupted prevailing assumptions about the solidity and predictability of matter. They were shaken even further in 1898 when the Polish-French chemist Marie Curie (1867–1934) discovered a new element, radium, which did not behave the way matter was supposed to behave. Because it continually emitted subatomic particles, radium did not possess a constant atomic weight. Two years later, the German scientist Max Planck (1858–1947) theorized that a heated body radiates energy not in the continuous, steady, predictable stream most scientists envisaged, but rather in irregular clumps, which he called *quanta.* Although at first dismissed by most scientists as contrary to common sense, Planck's quantum theory accorded with the emerging picture of a changeable universe.

These scientific discoveries provide the context for the work of Albert Einstein (1879–1955), certainly the most famous and readily recognizable scientist of the twentieth century. Bored by his job as a patent clerk, Einstein passed the time speculating on the nature of the cosmos. In 1905, he rang the death knell for the Newtonian universe by publishing an article that introduced to the world the theory of relativity. Einstein rejected the nineteenth-century assumption of the absolute nature of time and space. Instead, he argued, time and space shift relative to the position of the observer. Similarly, matter itself shifts. Mass depends on motion, and thus time, space, and matter intermingle in a universe of relative flux. The result of Einstein's vision was a revolution in perspective. The universe is not three- but four-dimensional: To height, width, and depth, Einstein added *time.*

This new understanding was much harder to grasp than that offered by Newtonian science. With the revolution in physics, much of science became incomprehensible to ordinary men and women, even educated ones. The new science also challenged the basic assumptions that governed nineteenth-century thought by offering a vision of the universe in which what you see is *not* what you get, in which objective reality might well be the product of subjective perception.

Social Thought: The Revolt Against Positivism

Just as the revolution in physics presented a new and more disturbing picture of the physical universe, so social thinkers in the last third of the nineteenth century began to formulate troubling theories about the nature of human society. As Chapter 21 explained, the mainstream of nineteenth-century thought was positivist: It placed great faith in human reason and therefore in the validity of applying methods drawn from the natural sciences to the study of human affairs. Positivism viewed the world as eminently knowable and progress as ultimately guaranteed, given the capacity of rational human beings to understand and therefore control both physical and human nature. This faith in human reason, however, came under attack in the last decades of the century. In this era, social thinkers (writers and scientists whose work would lay the foundations for new academic disciplines such as sociology, psychology, and anthropology) began to emphasize the role of nonrational forces in determining human conduct.

Social thinkers confronted the power of the nonrational first in the new mass politics of this era. The rise of racist and nationalist political parties demonstrated that individuals were often swayed more by emotion than by rational argument. In an effort to understand and therefore to manipulate political demonstrations, the French theorist Gustave LeBon (1841–1931) developed the discipline of crowd or collective psychology. He showed how appeals to emotion, particularly in the form of symbols and myths, can influence crowd behavior. In LeBon's view, democracy relinquished political control to the easily swayed masses and so would lead only to disaster.

Unlike LeBon, the German social theorist Max Weber (1864–1920) believed in democracy, but he, too, recognized the role of the nonrational in influencing the mass electorate. Weber was both fascinated and frightened by the development of modern industrial society. His studies focused on the "bureaucratization" of modern life—the tendency of both political and economic institutions to become increasingly standardized and to grow ever larger and more impersonal. Weber judged the triumph of bureaucracy as the victory of reason and science over individual prejudice and interest-group politics, and so as a generally progressive force. But at the same time he recognized that because growing bureaucracies could crush both ideals and individuals, they posed a real threat to personal and political freedom. Troubled by the vision of individuals trapped within "the iron cage of modern life," Weber in 1898 suffered a nervous breakdown. After four years Weber was able to free himself from the grip of debilitating depression, but he remained profoundly pessimistic about the future, which he described as "a polar night of icy darkness and hardness."[3]

According to his wife, when Weber fell into depression, "an evil something out of the subterranean unconscious . . . grasped him by its claws."[4] This view of the individual as a captive of the unconscious was central to the revolt against positivism and reached its fullest development in the highly influential work of the Viennese scientist and physician Sigmund Freud (1856–1939). Freud argued that the conscious mind plays only a very limited role in shaping the actions of each individual. His effort to treat patients suffering from nervous disorders led him to hypnosis and dream analysis, and to the conviction that behind the conscious exterior existed a deeper, far more significant reality—the unconscious. In *The Interpretation of Dreams* (1900), Freud argued that beneath the rational surface of each human being surge all kinds of hidden desires, including such irrational drives as the longing for death and destruction.

Freud thought of himself as a scientist. He believed that he could understand human behavior (and treat mental illness) by diving below the rational surface and exploring the submerged terrain of unconscious desire. Yet the emergence of Freudian psychology convinced many educated Western individuals not that the irrational could be uncovered and controlled, but rather that the irrational was *in* control.

Cultural Crisis: The Fin-de-Siècle and the Birth of Modernism

- **What factors led many Europeans in this period to believe they were living in a time of cultural crisis?**

The growing recognition of the power of irrational forces in shaping human society contributed to a growing cultural crisis. The sense of crisis, and more specifically the fear that Western civilization was declining, that degeneration and decay characterized the contemporary experience, was summed up in a single French phrase: fin-de-siècle°. Literally translated as "end of the century," fin-de-siècle served as a shorthand term for the mood of cultural uneasiness, and even despair, that characterized much of European society in the final decades of the nineteenth century and the opening years of the twentieth. Uncertainty colored many aspects of European thought and culture. Fast-moving economic and social change, coupled with the new scientific ideas, convinced many Europeans that old solutions were no longer sufficient. The quest for new answers fostered the birth of what would become known as *modernism,* a broad label for a series of unsettling developments in thought, literature, and art. Many Europeans celebrated modernism as a release from the restraints imposed by middle-class cultural codes. Others, however, responded fearfully. Both exhilaration and anxiety, then, characterize this time of cultural crisis.

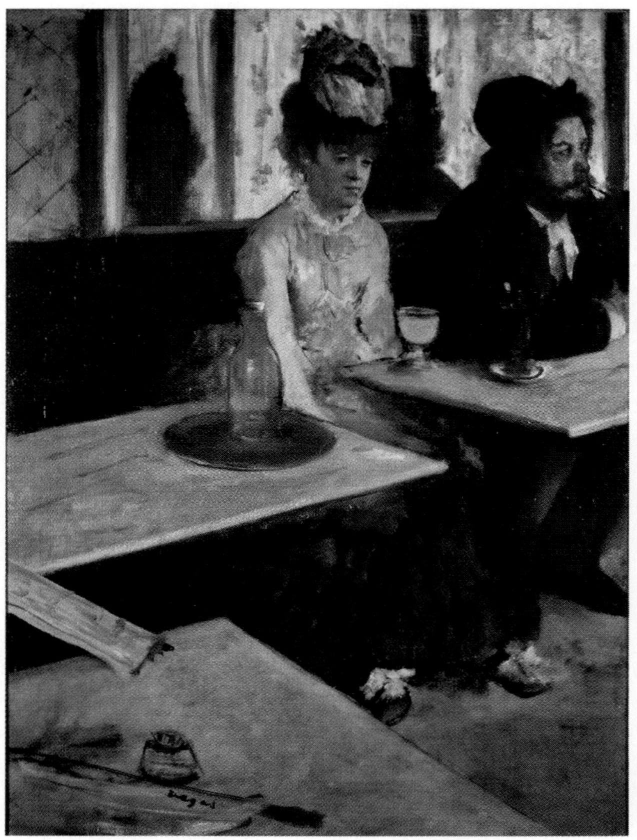

Edgar Degas, *Absinthe* (1876–1877)
Parisian café-goers often indulged in absinthe, a strong alcoholic drink flavored with anise. Degas's portrait of one such absinthe drinker is a picture of deterioration: This woman's lined face and weary posture, as well as her sense of isolation, provide an evocative image of the fin-de-siècle.

The Fin-de-Siècle

A series of social problems common to increasingly urbanized nations reinforced Europeans' fear of degeneration. As cities spread, so too did the perception of a rising crime rate. This perception of a more criminal society went hand-in-hand with the reality of increasing drug and alcohol use. Diners in high society finished their sumptuous meals with a dessert course consisting of strawberries soaked in ether; respectable bourgeois men offered each other cocaine as a quick "pick-me-up" at the end of the working day; middle-class mothers fed restless babies opium-laced syrups; workers bought enough opium-derived laudanum on Saturday afternoon to render them unconscious until work on Monday morning. Using Lamarck's theory of the inheritance of acquired characteristics, scientists contended that addictions could be passed on from generation to generation, thus contributing to national decline and a culture of decadence.

Popular novels of the fin-de-siècle also contributed to the fear of degeneration by depicting Western culture as diseased or barbaric. In a twenty-volume work, the French novelist Émile Zola (1840–1902) traced the decline of a once-proud family to symbolize the decay of all of France. As alcoholism and sexual promiscuity pollute succeeding generations, the family disintegrates. In *Nana* (1880), Zola used the title character, a prostitute, to embody his country. Watching as French soldiers march off to defeat in the Franco-Prussian War, Nana is dying of smallpox, her face "a charnel-house, a heap of pus and blood, a shovelful of putrid flesh."[5] Novels such as *Dr. Jekyll and Mr. Hyde* (1886) and *Dracula* (1897) showed that beneath the cultured exterior of a civilized man lurked a primitive, bloodthirsty beast and so revealed a deep sense of anxiety.

The most influential advocate of the idea that Western culture had degenerated was the German philosopher and poet Friedrich Nietzsche (1844–1900). In Nietzsche's view, most people were little more than sheep, penned in by outdated customs and conventions. Bourgeois morality, rooted in Christianity, helped sap Western culture of its vitality. "Christianity has taken the side of everything weak," Nietzsche claimed. He traced the weakness of Western culture beyond Christianity, however, and back to ancient Greece, to Socrates' exaltation of rationality. In Nietzsche's view, an overemphasis on rational thought had deprived Western culture of the power of more primal urges, such as the irrational, emotional, and instinctive aspects of human nature.

Even more fundamentally, Nietzsche argued that the belief that human reason has direct access to scientific fact is an illusion. Trained as a classical philologist, Nietzsche's study of language convinced him that everything we know must be filtered through a symbolic system—through language or some other means of artistic or mathematic representation. We can know only the representation, not the thing itself. Not even science can uncover "reality." Even the style of Nietzsche's publications worked to expose the limits of reason. Rather than write carefully constructed essays that proceeded in a logical, linear fashion from fact to fact, Nietzsche adopted an elusive, poetic style characterized by disconnected fragments, more accessible to intuitive understanding than to rational analysis.

Nietzsche's writings attracted little attention until the 1890s, when his ideas first exploded in Germany and Austria, and then spread throughout Europe. Nietzsche's call to "become what you are" attracted young enthusiasts, who embraced his conviction that the confining assumptions and aspirations of bourgeois society held back the individual from personal liberation. "God is dead," Nietzsche proclaimed, "and we have killed him." If God is dead, then "there is nobody who commands, nobody who obeys, nobody who trespasses."

Tightening Gender Boundaries

The fear of degeneration evident throughout European culture and society in the last decades of the nineteenth century also expressed itself in a multifaceted effort to draw more tightly the boundaries around accepted definitions of "maleness" and "femaleness." Both the feminist and the homosexual joined the alcoholic, the drug addict, the prostitute, and the criminal in the list of dangerous and degenerate beings.

As discussed in Chapter 22, the years after 1850 and particularly after 1880 witnessed the birth of modern feminism. The emergence of legal, educational, and political reform campaigns challenged nineteenth-century middle-class domestic ideology. Antifeminists viewed these campaigns with alarm. They insisted that a woman's physiology demanded that she remain in the home. In the view of antifeminists, a woman who chose political activism or paid employment not only risked her own physical and mental breakdown, she also tended to produce physically and morally degenerate children.

Like feminists, homosexuals were also singled out as threats to the social order. Before 1869, *homosexual* was not a word: Coined by a Hungarian scientist seeking a new label for a new concept, it entered the English language in 1890. Traditionally, Europeans and Americans had viewed same-sex sexual practice as a form of immoral behavior, indulged in by morally lax—but otherwise normal—men. (Few considered the possibility of female homosexual behavior.) In the last third of the nineteenth century, however, the emphasis shifted from *actions* to *identity*, from condemning a specific type of sexual behavior to denouncing a certain group of people now considered abnormal and dangerous. Scientists argued that "the homosexual" was diseased—and that he could communicate this disease to others.

These ideas gained in force as homosexual subcultures increased in number in European and American cities. The anonymity and mobility of urban life offered homosexuals the possibility of creating a space for themselves in which a new, more confident and assertive homosexual identity could be expressed. But these subcultures soon encountered fierce repression as the moral and medical condemnation of male homosexuality became enshrined in legislation. The Penal Code of the new Germany stipulated severe punishment for homosexuality, while the British government in 1885 made illegal all homosexual acts, even those between consenting adults in the privacy of their own home.

The new concern about homosexuality was nurtured by a wider anxiety about the man's role in society, an anxiety provoked not only by the challenge of feminism, but also by the economic changes associated with the rise of corporate capitalism (see Chapter 22). Required by liberal ideology to be aggressive, independent, self-reliant initiators, middle-class males increasingly found themselves bound to desks, demoted from being those who delivered orders to those who received them. No longer masters of their own fates, they were now bit players in the drama of corporate capitalism. Thus the fear of both feminism and homosexuality arose in part from the compelling need to shore up masculine identity.

The new science of sexuality also heightened this concern about the definition of the "normal" man and woman. During the final decades of the nineteenth century, scientists invaded the most intimate areas of human behavior and made important breakthroughs in the understanding of human reproduction and sexual physiology. In 1875, for example, a German physiologist discovered the basic process of fertilization—the union of male and female sex cells. Four years later, scientists for the first time witnessed, with the aid of the microscope, a sperm cell penetrating an egg. In the following decade, scientific research uncovered the link between hormonal secretions and sexual potency, affirmed the existence of erogenous zones, and began to explore the role of chromosomes in reproduction.

The Trial of Oscar Wilde

In March 1895 the Marquis of Queensberry left a message with the porter of a gentleman's club in London. The message, written on Queensberry's calling card, read "To Oscar Wilde, posing as a *somdomite.*" What Queensberry meant to write was *sodomite,* a common term for a man who engaged in sexual relations with other men. By handing the card to the porter, Queensberry openly accused Wilde, a celebrated novelist and playwright, of homosexual—and therefore criminal—activity. Ten years earlier the British Parliament had declared illegal all homosexual activity, even consensual relations between adults in a private home. Queensberry's accusation, then, was extremely serious. Oscar Wilde responded by suing Queensberry for libel—and set in motion a legal process that led to Wilde's imprisonment, and indirectly, to his early death.

Wilde made a reckless mistake when he chose to sue for libel, for in fact Queensberry had not libeled him. Wilde was a homosexual, and he and Queensberry's son, Lord Alfred Douglas, were lovers. Why, then, did Wilde dare to challenge Queensberry? Perhaps the fact that he was married, with two children, seemed to provide a certain shield against the charge of homosexuality. Or perhaps Wilde's successes as a novelist and playwright gave him a misguided sense of invulnerability. With two of his plays currently appearing on the London stage to favorable reviews, Wilde stood at the pinnacle of his career in the spring of 1895.

Wilde had built that career on a deliberate flouting of middle-class codes of morality. He saw himself as an artist, and insisted that art should be freed from social convention and moral restraint. His "High Society" comedies about privileged elites living scandalous lives and exchanging witty epigrams were far from the morally uplifting drama expected by middle-class audiences.

He also used his public persona to attack the conventional, the respectable, and the orthodox. Widely recognized for his outrageous clothing and conversation, Wilde had consciously adopted the mannerisms of what nineteenth-century Britons called a "dandy"—a well-dressed, irreverent, artistic, leisured, and most of all, effeminate man. Before the Oscar Wilde trial, such effeminacy did not serve as a sign of, or a code for, homosexual inclinations, but it did signal to many observers a lavish—and loose—lifestyle. Oscar Wilde, then, was a man many British men and women loved to hate.

Even so, when his trial opened Wilde appeared to be in a strong position, the prosecutor rather than the defendant. Because Wilde had Queensberry's card with the "sodomite" charge written right on it, Queensberry faced certain conviction unless he could show that Wilde had engaged in homosexual activity. Wilde knew, of course, that Queensberry would not risk bringing the legal spotlight to bear on his own son's homosexuality.

At first, Queensberry's attorney, Edward Carson, focused on Wilde's published works, trying to use Wilde's own words against him. It proved an ineffective strategy. On the witness stand, Wilde reveled in the attention and ran circles around Carson.

On the second day of the libel trial, however, Wilde's witticisms proved insufficient as Carson began to question him about

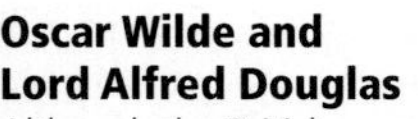

Oscar Wilde and Lord Alfred Douglas
Although the British government pursued its case against Wilde, it made no effort to put together a case against Douglas.

his frequent visits to a male brothel and his associations with a number of young, working-class men who worked as male prostitutes. Suddenly the issue was no longer the literary merit or moral worth of Wilde's published writings, but rather his sexual exploitation of working-class boys. At this point, Wilde withdrew his libel charge against Queensberry, and the court declared the marquis not guilty.

If Queensberry was not guilty of libel in calling Wilde a sodomite, then by clear implication, Wilde was guilty of homosexual activity and therefore a criminal. Within days he was charged with "gross indecency" with another male. The jury in that case failed to reach a verdict, but the state was determined to obtain a conviction and brought the charges again. Wilde was refused bail, and on May 20 he was back in court.

On May 25, 1895—just three months after Queensberry had left his misspelled message with the club porter—Wilde's promising literary career ended. He was found guilty of seven counts of gross indecency with other men. The presiding judge, Sir Alfred Wills, characterized the trial as "the worst case I have ever tried," and declared, "I shall under the circumstances be expected to pass the severest sentence the law allows. In my judgment it is totally inadequate for such a case." He sentenced Wilde to two years at hard labor. The physical punishment took its toll. Wilde died in 1900 at age 46.

In sentencing Wilde, Wills described him as "the centre of a circle of extensive corruption of the most hideous kind." How do we account for the intensity of Wills's language, as well as the severity of Wilde's sentence? Homosexual activity had long been condemned on religious grounds, but this condemnation grew much more fierce in the closing decades of the nineteenth century. In a time of rapid and threatening change, the marking of gender boundaries became a way to create and enforce social order. Wilde crossed those boundaries, and so had to be punished.

Moreover, by the end of the nineteenth century, the state had assumed new responsibilities. Desperate to enhance national strength in a period of heightened international competition, governments intervened in areas previously considered to be the domain of the private citizen. By the turn of the century, western European governments were compelling working-class parents to send their children to school, regulating the hours adults could work, supervising the sale of food and drugs, providing limited forms of old-age pensions and medical insurance—and policing sexual boundaries.

The policing of sexual boundaries became easier after the Wilde trial because it provided a homosexual personality profile, a "Wanted" poster to hang on the walls of Western culture. For many observers of his very well-publicized trial, Wilde became the embodiment of "the homosexual," a particular and peculiar type of person, and a menace to cultural stability. The Wilde trial linked "dandyism" to the new image of the homosexual. Outward stylistic choices such as effeminacy, artistic sensibilities, and flamboyant clothing and conversation became, for many observers, the telltale signs of substantial inner corruption. Thus the Wilde case marked an important turning point in the construction, as well as the condemnation, of a homosexual identity.

Questions of Justice

1. How does this trial illustrate the role of medical, legal, and cultural assumptions in shaping sexual identity in the late nineteenth century?
2. Did the trial of Oscar Wilde achieve justice? If so, of what kind and for whom?

Taking It Further

An Ideal Husband. 1999. A film adaptation of Oscar Wilde's very funny play, which exemplifies his lighthearted but devastating critique of conventional manners and morals.

Ellman, Richard. *Oscar Wilde.* 1988. An important biography of Wilde.

Hyde, H. Montgomery. *The Trials of Oscar Wilde.* 1962. Includes extensive quotations from the trial transcripts as well as photographs of some of the documentary evidence.

McLaren, Angus. *The Trials of Masculinity: Policing Sexual Boundaries, 1870–1930.* 1997. Places the Wilde trial within a wider cultural context.

This greater understanding of sexual *physiology* went hand in hand with the effort to apply the scientific method to sexual *practice.* With data drawn from biology, anthropology, and human physiology, scientists in Europe and the United States sought to define "normal" sexual behavior. In seven weighty volumes, the British scientist Havelock Ellis (1859–1939) explored the range of child and adult sexuality. Ellis used his data to argue for sex education, legalization of contraception and nudism, and tolerance of homosexuality. Other sex researchers, however, turned to science to buttress middle-class moral codes. The German scientist Richard von Krafft-Ebing labeled homosexuality a pathology in 1886, while many publications condemned masturbation and frequent sexual intercourse. Other works offered support for antifeminism by arguing that female physiology incapacitated women for public life.

Heightened concern about gender boundaries also pervaded the visual art of late-nineteenth-century Europe. Women often appeared as elemental forces, creatures of nature rather than civilization, who threatened to trap, emasculate, engulf, suffocate, or destroy the unwary man. In *Medicine,* by the Austrian painter Gustav Klimt (1862–1918), the liquid portraits of women flow between and into images of sex and death in a disturbing and powerful painting. Such images recur even more graphically in the work of Klimt's student, Egon Schiele (1890–1918). In his very short life Schiele created more than 3,000 works on paper and 300 paintings, many of these depictions of the dangerous female. In works such as *Black-Haired Girl with Raised Skirt* (1911), harsh colors and brazen postures present an unsettling vision of female sexuality. A series of Schiele's paintings with titles such as *Dead Mother* place children in the arms of dead or expressionless women—a direct challenge to the middle-class glorification of motherhood.

Gustav Klimt, *Medicine* (1901)

Klimt was commissioned by the University of Vienna to create a work that would celebrate medicine's great achievements. Not surprisingly, the painting he produced provoked great controversy. The woman in the forefront is Hygeia, the Greek goddess of health, but behind her swim images of female sexuality and death. Klimt's paintings often featured women as alluring but engulfing elemental forces.

The Birth of Modernism

Schiele's disturbing paintings exemplify the new modernist movement. Although the term modernism° was not commonly used until the 1920s, the main developments it embraced were well underway by 1914. It is a difficult term to define, in part because it refers to a variety of artistic, literary, and intellectual styles. Despite this variety, however, modernist art and literature expressed a set of common attitudes and assumptions that centered on a rejection of established authority. In the final decades of the nineteenth century, many artists tossed aside accepted standards and rules and embarked on a series of bold experiments. Oscar Wilde (1854–1900), the British playwright whose dramas mocked Victorian conventions and outraged middle-class sensibilities, wrote, "It is enough that our fathers believed. They have exhausted the faith-faculty of the species. Their legacy to us is the skepticism of which they were afraid."[6] At the core of modernism was a questioning of all accepted standards and truths, particularly those that shaped the middle-class liberal worldview.

In that liberal worldview, the arts served a useful purpose and were a vital part of civilized society. Going to art galleries, for example, was a popular activity, rather like going to the movies today. Respectable workers and middle-class men and women crowded into exhibitions where they viewed paintings that told an entertaining story and had a clear moral message. Modernism shattered this community between artist and audience. It rejected the idea of art as an instrument of moral or emotional uplift. Modernists argued that art is autonomous—it stands alone, of value in and of itself rather than for any impact it may have on society. Modernist painters, for example, did not seek to tell a story or to preach a sermon, but rather to experiment with line, color, and composition.

In addition to rejecting the idea that art must be useful, modernists also challenged middle-class liberalism by insisting that history is irrelevant. Nineteenth-century culture was "historicist." Fascinated with the process of change over time—with the evolution not only of species but also of ideas and societies—the middle-class mindset viewed history as the orderly forward march of progress. In contrast, modernists argued that fast-moving industrial and technological change had shattered the lines connecting history and modernity. Painters such as the Futurists in Italy and the Vorticists in Britain (two of the many artistic movements that clustered under the modernist umbrella) reveled in the new machine age, a world cut off from anything that had gone before. In their paintings they depicted human beings as machines in motion, moving too fast to be tied down to history.

New musical styles emerging in both popular and high culture in these decades also demonstrated the modernist sense of discontinuity. Ragtime, for example, combined syncopation with unexpected rhythms and sudden stops, while jazz, which developed around the turn of the century in black urban neighborhoods in the United States, created a musical universe of constant change. At the same time, symphonic musicians such as Russian composer Igor Stravinsky (1882–1971) and his Austrian counterpart Arnold Schoenberg (1874–1951) shocked their audiences by tossing aside the convention that a piece should state a central theme, which is then repeated in a sequence of variations. In Stravinsky's ballet *The Rite of Spring* (1913), the meter changes no fewer than twenty-eight times in the final thirty-four bars of the central dance. Similarly, Schoenberg eliminated repetition from his works and used rapid tempo changes.

Modernism also rejected the dominant nineteenth-century faith in the power of human reason and observation, and instead emphasized the role of individual emotion and experience in shaping human understanding. In Paris, for example, a group of artists centered on the Spaniard Pablo Picasso (1881–1973) dared to juxtapose different perspectives and points of view on a single canvas. They called themselves Cubists°. Just as Albert Einstein revolutionized physics by arguing that time and space shift as the position of the observer changes, so Cubism transformed Western visual culture by revealing the incompleteness and even incoherence of individual perception. In one cultural historian's apt description, "Cubists cracked the mirror of art."[7] Their fragmented, jagged, energetic works no longer reflected the world "out there," but instead revealed the artist's fluid and contradictory vision (see page 762).

Léon Bakst, *Nijinsky in The Afternoon of a Faun* (1912)

The Russian dancer Vaslav Nijinksy (1890–1950) brought modernism to the ballet, with startling, awkward poses and sudden, jerky moves. In this painting, however, the Russian artist Bakst uses the flowing lines of the Art Nouveau style to evoke Nijinsky in movement.

This emphasis on art as a form of personal expression is also seen in the Expressionist° movement, centered not in France as was Cubism, but in central and eastern Europe. Expressionists such as Egon Schiele argued that art should express the artist's interior vision, not the exterior world. In nude self-portraits, Schiele depicted himself as ugly and emaciated, a graphic expression of his tormented internal universe. His fellow Expressionist, the Russian painter Wassily Kandinsky (1866–1944), went even further in shattering artistic boundaries and splashing his emotions all over the canvas. Kandinsky sought to remove all form from his painting, to create a universe of pure color that would express a fundamental spiritual

DOCUMENT

Cubist Painters

Born in 1880, the Frenchman Guillaume Apollinaire became part of the modernist circle of artists and poets that dominated Parisian cultural life at the turn of the century. His Cubist Painters, *written in 1911 and published two years later, is both a study and an example of modernism. In its fragmentary style it resembles a Cubist painting; it rejects a point-by-point reasoned narrative for the use of juxtaposition, contrast, and poetic analogies.*

The rainbow is bent, the seasons quiver, the crowds push on to death, science undoes and remakes what already exists, whole worlds disappear forever from our understanding, our mobile images repeat themselves, or revive their vagueness, and the colors, the odors, and the sounds to which we are sensitive astonish us, then disappear from nature—all to no purpose.

The monster, beauty, is not eternal . . .

You cannot carry around on your back the corpse of your father. You leave him with the other dead. You remember him, miss him, speak of him with admiration. And if you become a father yourself, you cannot expect one of your children to be willing to split in two for the sake of your corpse.

. . .

Many new painters limit themselves to pictures which have no real subjects. . . . These painters, while they still look at nature, no longer imitate it, and carefully avoid any representation of natural scenes which they may have observed, and then reconstructed from preliminary studies.

Real resemblance no longer has any importance, since everything is sacrificed by the artist to truth, to the necessities of a higher nature, whose existence he assumes, but does not lay bare. The subject has little or no importance any more.

Generally speaking, modern art repudiates most of the techniques of pleasing devised by the great artists of the past.

. . .

Cubism differs from the old schools of painting in that it aims, not at an art of imitation, but an an art of conception, which tends to rise to the height of creation . . . .

I love the art of today because above all else I love the light, for man loves light more than anything; it was he who invented fire.

Source: Guillaume Apollinaire. *The Cubist Painters: Aesthetic Meditations,* trans. Lionel Abel (1913; New York: Wittenborn and Company, 1944), pp. 9, 10–11, 14, 15.

Wassily Kandinsky, *Composition VII* (1913)
Kandinsky's experiments in color and form led him to pure abstraction.

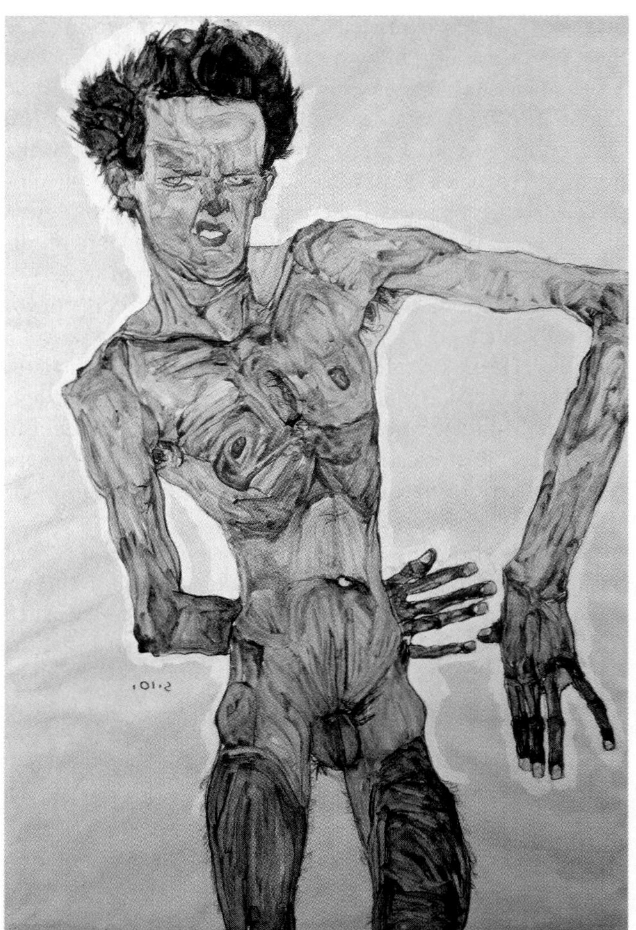

Egon Schiele, *Nude Self-Portrait with Open Mouth* (1910)
Schiele's paintings exemplify the Expressionist movement with their bold use of color and their no-holds-barred exploration of human emotion and sexuality.

reality. In the process, he produced the first purely abstract paintings in Western art.

Because they so radically challenged middle-class and liberal standards and assumptions, modernist works were greeted with incomprehension and outrage. At the first performance of Schoenberg's *Five Orchestral Pieces* (1909) in London in 1912, one listener reported that "the audience laughed audibly all through . . . and hissed vigorously at the end." The next year in Vienna, the performance of a different Schoenberg piece had to be abandoned after the audience rioted. Modernist painting was routinely condemned as sick, pornographic, anarchic, and simply insane. One London reviewer dismissed the painter Paul Cézanne (1869–1954) as "an artist with diseased retinas." Most middle-class men and women remained firmly within a cultural milieu in which paintings revealed pretty scenes, novels told a moral tale, and music offered harmonious charm. At the same time that Picasso was shattering perspective, one of the most popular pieces of art in the English-speaking world was *The Light of the World* by William Holman Hunt (1827–1910). This moralistic piece with its easy-to-understand and uplifting story, completely at odds with every modernist principle, triumphantly toured the British Empire from 1905 to 1907. In cities throughout Australia, South Africa, Canada, and Britain, enthusiastic crowds jostled for tickets and hailed the painting as both a religious and an artistic masterpiece.

William Holman Hunt, *The Light of the World* (1903)
This devotional painting is rich in Christian symbolism. Jesus, the light of the world, stands knocking at the closed door of a lost soul. The overgrown weeds and fallen fruit symbolize sin; the lantern stands for Christ's illuminating power, while the stars and crescents on it represent Christ's appeal to Jews and Muslims.

Popular Religion and Secularization

As the response to Holman Hunt's depiction of Jesus shows, religious belief remained a powerful force in the decades after 1870. In Britain, regular Sunday worship continued to be a central aspect of middle-class culture, and the still-strong Sunday School movement as well as religious instruction in state schools ensured that working-class children were taught the fundamentals of the Christian faith. On the Continent, many Europeans connected revolutionary anarchy with unbelief after revolutionaries executed the Archbishop of Paris in 1871 (see Chapter 21). The excesses of the Paris Commune thus contributed to a religious revival. Much of this popular Catholic religiosity focused on the cult of the Virgin Mary: By the 1870s, the shrine at Lourdes, site of Mary's miraculous appearance in 1858, was attracting hundreds of thousands of Catholic pilgrims.

Three additional factors contributed to the religiosity of late-nineteenth-century Europe. First, the high rate of immigration, which meant that large groups of people often found themselves searching for something familiar in foreign cities, fostered attachments to the religious cultures of the homeland. In English cities, for example, Irish immigrants looked to the local Roman Catholic Church for spiritual solace, material support, and social contacts. Second, in many regions nationalism also shored up religious belief and practice. Hence, for Polish nationalists dreaming of independence from Russian rule, Roman Catholicism was a key part of a separate national identity. Finally, as we shall see in the next section, imperialism became interwoven with Western Christianity. Missionary publications and societies not only lobbied intensely for continued Western expansion abroad, but also served to inspire and unite Western Christians at home. Foreign mission work gave Western Christians a sense of both purpose and power as imperial expansion appeared to provide clear evidence of the ongoing triumph of Christianity.

Yet this triumphalism met growing anxiety as Christians faced a series of challenges, most obviously those posed by science. As we saw in our discussion of Darwin, developments in geology and biology undermined the orthodox Christian view of a harmonious, divinely directed, natural world. Medical advances also worked to narrow the appeal of traditional religion. Tragedies once accepted as "acts of God," such as epidemic disease, now appeared to be curable and controllable. Increasingly, scientists seemed able to answer questions once thought the province of the theologians.

At the same time, the emergence of the social sciences posed a direct challenge to Christian belief by simply dismissing the question of religious truth and asking instead, what is the function of religious belief in a society? Emile Durkheim (1858–1917), one of the founders of French sociology, dared to lump Christianity with "even the most barbarous and the most fantastic rites and the strangest myths." Durkheim insisted that no religion is more true than any other; each fills a social need.[8]

The Christian response to these challenges varied. Some Christians embraced the scientific method as a gift from God, and argued that the Christian faith must adapt to the ongoing expansion of human knowledge. To many theologians as well as ordinary believers, the study of the Bible as a historical and literary document—as a collection of divinely inspired texts produced by all-too-human writers—promised to free Christians *from* antiquated beliefs impossible to sustain in the new scientific age, and *for* a more worldly, reform-oriented religious life. Other Christians, however, resisted any accommodation to the scientific age. Protestant fundamentalists insisted on retaining a belief in the literal, historical, and scientific accuracy of the Christian scriptures, a stance that led them to oppose science as the enemy of religion.

Similarly, the Roman Catholic papacy adopted a defiant pose in the face of the scientific challenge. In 1864, Pope Pius IX (r. 1846–1878) issued a *Syllabus of Errors,* which condemned not only materialism but also the idea that the pope should "harmonize himself with progress, with liberalism, and with modern civilization." Five years later, a church council—the first called since the sixteenth-century Catholic Reformation—proclaimed the doctrine of papal infallibility. According to this doctrine, any decrees issued by the pope with regard to faith and morals were free from error and good for all time and all places. The proclamation of the doctrine of papal infallibility was a sharp rebuff to those Catholic theologians who argued that Christianity must adapt to the modern world.

The Roman Catholic Church also faced a crucial political challenge from both liberal and socialist movements. In Roman Catholic countries, the Church's alliance with conservatism pushed anticlericalism° to a dominant position on the liberal agenda. In France, for example, Roman Catholics were in the forefront of the conservative forces seeking to overturn the Republic established in 1871 and to return to monarchical or authoritarian rule. As a result, Frenchmen who wanted the Republic to survive fought to reduce the Church's influence over French politics and culture. At the same time, the spread of socialism provided European workers with an alternative belief system and source of communal life. The result was to widen the secular sphere and limit the influence of traditional Christianity.

The most significant challenge faced by Christianity after 1870, however, emerged not from scientific laboratories, parliamentary assemblies, or socialist rallies but rather from the department stores and playing fields. In the growing industrial cities, both working- and middle-class individuals enjoyed new, secular sources of entertainment, inspiration, and desire. Energies once focused on Christian devotion were now increasingly displaced onto the activities of consumption and recreation. Whereas shared religious worship had once cemented community life, the increasingly elaborate rituals of spectator sports now forged new bonds of loyalty and identity. At the same time, the delectable array of colorful products displayed in shop windows promised fulfillment and satisfaction in the here and now, an earthly paradise rather than a heavenly reward.

The New Imperialism

- **What were the causes and consequences of the new imperialist ideology for both the West and non-Western societies?**

Many of those items on display behind the new plate-glass shop windows were the products of imperial conquest. After 1870, Europe entered not only a new age of mass consumption but also a new era of imperialist expansion. Imperialism intertwined with many of the economic, scientific, and cultural developments already examined in this chapter. Telegraphs ensured rapid communication from far-flung empires while mass printing technologies guaranteed that illustrated tales of imperial achievement made their way into homes and schools; Social Darwinism supplied a supposedly scientific justification for the conquest of peoples deemed biologically inferior; swift and decisive victories over other lands and societies helped quell anxiety about European degeneration. For many Europeans—particularly the British, who presided over the largest empire in the world—imperialist domination served as reassuring, even incontrovertible, evidence of the superiority of Western civilization.

Understanding the New Imperialism

Imperialism was not, of course, new to Europe. In the fifteenth century, Europeans had embarked on the first phase of imperialism, with the extension of European control across coastal ports of Africa and India, and into the New World of the Americas. In the second phase, which began in the late seventeenth century, European colonial empires in both Asia and the Western Hemisphere expanded as governments sought to augment their profits from international trade. Trade motivated much of the imperial activity after 1870 as well, with the need to protect existing imperial possessions often impelling further imperialist conquests. The desire to protect India—the "Jewel in the Crown" of the British Empire—explains much of British imperial acquisition throughout the nineteenth century. Britain's annexation of Burma and Kashmir, its establishment of spheres of influence in the Middle East, and its interests along the coast of Africa were all vitally linked to its concerns in India.

Neither defense of existing empires nor commercial considerations, however, fully explain the headlong rush into empire in the later nineteenth century. After 1870 and particularly after 1880, Europe's expansion into non-European territories became so much more aggressive that historians label this third phase the age of new imperialism°. A few figures illustrate the contrast: Between 1800 and 1880, European colonial empires grew by 6,500,000 square miles, but between 1880 and 1910, these empires increased by an astonishing 8,655,000. In just thirty years, European control of the globe's land surface swelled from 65 to 85 percent. In addition, new players joined the expansionist game. Recently formed nation-states such as Germany and Italy jostled for colonial territory in Africa, the United States began to extend its control over the Western Hemisphere, and Japan initiated its imperialist march into China and Korea. What factors lay behind this new imperialism?

Technology, Economics, and Politics

Part of the answer lies in the economic developments examined in Chapter 22. The new technologies characteristic of the Second Industrial Revolution meant that industrial Europe increasingly depended on raw materials available only in non-Western regions such as Asia, Africa, and South America. Rubber, for example, was essential not only for tires on the new automobiles, but also for insulating the electrical and telegraph wires now encircling the globe. Palm oil from Africa provided the lubricant needed for industrial machinery. Africa's once-plentiful elephant herds were slaughtered to provide the ivory for many of the new consumer goods now displayed prominently in department store windows and middle-class parlors—piano keys, billiard balls, knife handles. Increasingly dependent on these primary resources, European states were quick to respond to perceived threats to their economic interests. The Germans even coined a word to describe this fear of losing access to essential raw materials: *Torschlusspanik,* or "fear of the closing door."

Competition for markets also accelerated imperial acquisition. With the onset of economic depression in 1873 (discussed in Chapter 22), industrialists were faced with declining demand for their products in Europe. Imperial expansion seemed to provide a solution, with annexed territories seen as captive markets. As an editorial in the largest French mass-circulation newspaper explained in 1891, "every gunshot opens another outlet for French industry."[9]

By the mid-1890s, however, the depression had ended in most regions, and Europe embarked on the longest investment boom it had yet experienced. Western European capital spread across the globe, underwriting railway lines, digging mines, and erecting public utilities in the United States, Latin America, Russia, Asia, and Africa. This global investment boom also contributed to new imperialism. With each railroad or coal mine or dam, European interests in non-European regions expanded, and so did the pressure on European governments to assume formal political control should those interests be threatened, whether by the arrival of other European competitors or by local political instability.

Britain provides an important example of the link between empire and economics. By the end of the nineteenth century, the British Empire covered one-quarter of the globe and contained one-quarter of the world's population. This empire reflected Britain's position at the center of the world's economy, as the chief agent of global economic exchange. Despite the emergence of Germany and the United States as industrial powerhouses, Britain remained the world's largest trading nation. Even more important, British stockbrokers, currency traders, and banks managed the global exchange system that emerged in the last third of the nineteenth century. In this era British loans abroad were larger than the combined investments of Britain's five largest competitors—France, Germany, the Netherlands, the United States, and Belgium.

Imperialism was motivated by more than economic concerns. Political pressures also contributed to imperialist acquisition. First, in the age of mass politics, political leaders needed to find issues that would both appeal to new voters and strengthen the status quo. Imperialism was one such issue. It assured ordinary men that they were part of a superior, conquering people. Tales of dangerous explorations and decisive military victories engaged the emotions and prodded the ordinary individual to identify more closely with the national group.

A second political factor motivating new imperialism was nationalist competition. Newly formed nations such as Italy and Germany sought empires outside Europe as a way to gain both power and prestige within Europe. The nineteenth-century German historian Heinrich von Treitschke explained, "All great nations in the fullness of their strength have desired to set their mark on barbarian lands and those who fail to participate in this great rivalry will play a pitiable role in time to come." Similar concerns about status and strategic advantages motivated nations such as Britain and France both to defend and expand their existing empires.

Imperialism from the European Perspective
France here brings the peoples of Morocco the wealth of Western education, technology, and military discipline.

The Imperial Idea

New imperialism was not simply a policy embraced by elites for economic, political, and strategic advantage. One of its most distinctive features was the way it functioned as a belief system, as an idea that permeated middle-class and mass culture in the decades after 1870. Images of empire proliferated, appearing in boys' adventure stories, glossy ads for soap and chocolates, picture postcards, cookie tins, and cheap commemorative china plates and mugs. In the music halls and theaters, imperialist songs and dramas received popular applause. At exhibitions and world's fairs, both goods and peoples from conquered regions were put on display to educate the crowds of viewers in the "imperial idea."

At the center of this idea stood the assumption of the *rightness* of white European dominance over the world. Europeans would not have sought to remake the world in the European image had they not been convinced of the superiority of that image. What led white Europeans to believe they had both the right and the responsibility to take charge of other cultures and continents?

One key factor was the perceived link between Western Christianity and "civilization." Christian missionaries served as a vanguard of Western culture throughout the nineteenth century. The celebrated Scottish explorer David Livingstone (1813–1873), who mapped out much of central and southern Africa, was a Protestant missionary (although not a very successful one—his only convert eventually renounced the Christian faith). Moreover, missionary society publications introduced their readers to exotic territories, while the societies themselves served as powerful political interest groups that often lobbied for Western territorial expansion to promote the spread of Christian missionary activity.

Europeans also pointed to their advanced technologies as evidence of their material and moral superiority, and as a justification for their imperial rule. Before the nineteenth century, the technological gap between European and non-European societies had not loomed large; in some cases, such as China, non-European societies had held the technological advantage. Industrialization, however, gave Europe the technological edge. Thus Mary Kingsley (1862–1900), a British adventurer who was actually unusually admiring of African culture and customs, wrote, "when I come back from a spell in Africa, the thing that makes me proud of being one of the English is . . . a great railway engine . . . [I]t is the manifestation of the superiority of my race."[10]

Mary Kingsley and the Bubi of Fernando Po (1890s)

Although many European Christians regarded the West's technological advantages as a sign that God intended Europe to Christianize (that is, westernize) the globe, a growing number of prominent thinkers, writers, and policymakers viewed the force that conferred this civilizing duty upon Europeans as natural rather than supernatural—biology rather than God. Social Darwinism lent a seemingly scientific authority to the imperial idea by supposedly proving the mental and moral superiority of white Europeans over all peoples of color. Thus the British Lord Milner (1854–1925) explained in a speech in South Africa in 1903: "The white man must rule, because he is elevated by many, many steps above the black man; steps which it will take the latter centuries to climb, and which it is quite possible that the vast bulk of the black population may never be able to climb at all."

Often white Europeans presented the idea of a biologically ordained imperial destiny in somber terms. They saw imperial rule as a heavy responsibility that must be shouldered by the civilized. Men and women in the West had a moral duty to bring the benefits of their civilization to the rest of the world. This idea of the burden of imperialism was dramatically expressed by Rudyard Kipling (1865–1936), the preeminent British poet of new imperialism. In 1899, Kipling urged American policymakers to complete their conquest of the Philippines with these words:

Imperialism and the White Man's Burden (1899)

Take up the White Man's burden—
Send forth the best ye breed—
Go bind your sons to exile,
To serve your captives' need;
To wait in heavy harness
On fluttered folk and wild—
Your new-caught sullen peoples,
Half devil and half child.

Not all Europeans embraced the idea of the "White Man's burden," and many rejected the imperialist assumption of Western superiority. Some modernist artists, for example, looked to non-Western cultures for artistic inspiration and argued that these societies had much to teach the West. The Fauves ("wild beasts"), a Paris-based circle of artists that included Henri Matisse (1869–1954) and Paul Gauguin (1848–1903), condemned most Western art as overrefined and artificial, and sought in their own brilliantly colored works to rediscover the vitality that they found in non-Western cultures (see page 742).

Critics of empire often focused on its domestic political and economic implications. The British economist J. A. Hobson (1858–1940) charged that overseas empires benefited only wealthy capitalists while distracting public attention from the need for domestic political and economic reform. Hobson argued that unregulated capitalism led almost inevitably to imperialist expansion. While impoverishing the masses, the capitalist system generates huge surpluses in capital for a very small elite, who must then find somewhere to invest these surpluses. Hobson's ideas proved very influential among European socialists, who condemned imperialism along with capitalism.

Many liberals also condemned imperialism. The British prime minister William Gladstone (1809–1898) clung fast to the liberal belief that free trade between independent nations fostered international peace. Gladstone and other liberals were uneasy about the expense of empire and acutely aware of the contradictions between liberal ideals and imperialist practice. It was difficult, for example, to reconcile the liberal commitment to individual freedom with the widespread use of forced labor in colonial Africa.

Yet between 1880 and 1885—while Gladstone was prime minister—the British Empire expanded at the rate of 87,000 square miles per year, with Gladstone himself ordering the bombardment of Alexandria and the military occupation of Egypt. When Gladstone did hold firm to his anti-imperialist ideals and ordered British troops to withdraw from the Sudan in 1885, he outraged the British public. Critics of empire were in the minority, not only in Britain but throughout Europe. The imperial idea permeated European and much of American culture in the final decades of the nineteenth century.

The Scramble for Africa

New imperialism reached its zenith in Africa. In 1875 European powers controlled only 11 percent of the African continent. By 1905, 90 percent of Africa was under European control. In just thirty years, between 1875 and 1905, Europeans established thirty new colonies and protectorates encompassing ten million square miles of territory and controlling 110 million Africans (see Map 23.1). The conquest of the African continent was so rapid and

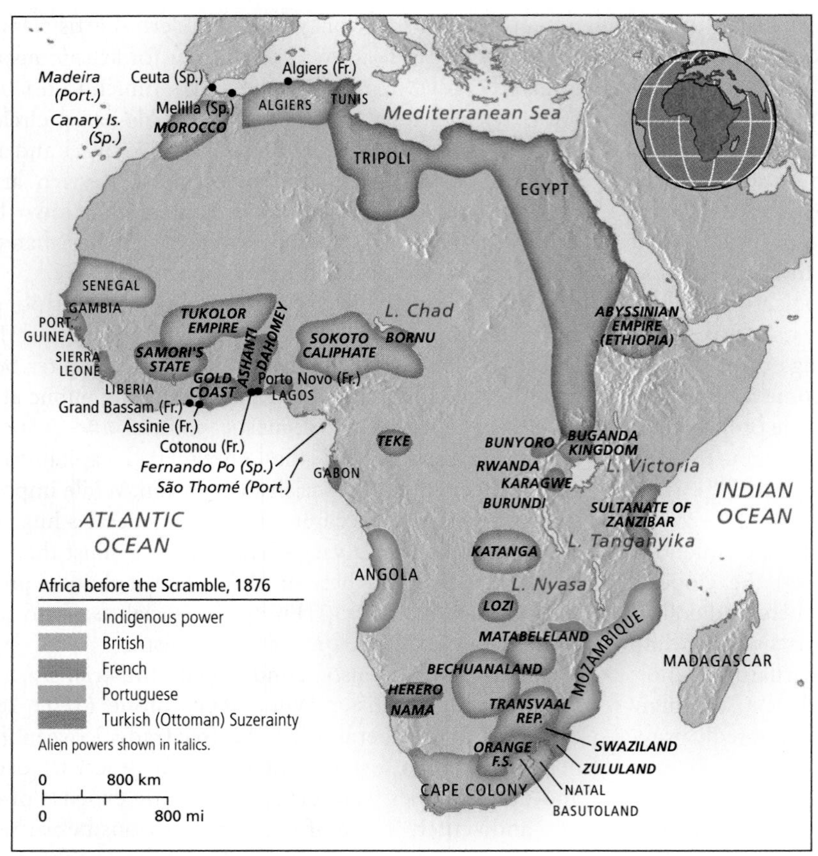

Map 23.1 (a) Africa Before the Scramble, 1876 and (b) Africa After the Scramble, 1914

A comparison of these two maps reveals the dramatic impact of the new imperialism on African societies. Indigenous empires such as the Sokoto Caliphate in West Africa came under Western rule, as did tribal societies such as the Herero. Even indigenous states ruled by whites of European descent came under European rule, as the examples of the Transvaal and the Orange Free State in South Africa illustrate. Only Ethiopia preserved its independence.

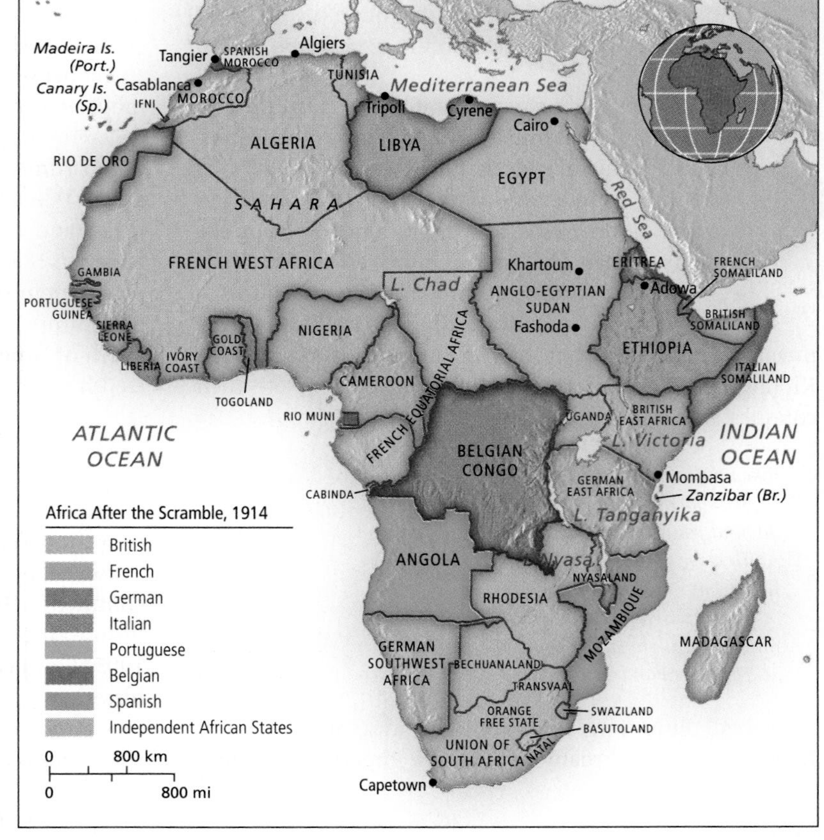

A Lesson in the Imperial Idea
As this alphabet reader makes clear, education in imperial ideology began early.

dramatic that as early as 1884 mystified Europeans began to talk about the Scramble for Africa°.

Overcoming the Obstacles

When the nineteenth century began, Europeans knew little more about the continent of Africa than the ancient Greeks had known. A vast and profitable trading network between European merchants and Africa's coastal regions had developed, centering on the exchange of European goods for African gold and slaves. European efforts to establish settlements in the interior, however, faced three key obstacles—the climate, disease, and African resistance.

Africa was known as "the white man's grave," deservedly so. Seventy-seven percent of the white soldiers sent to West Africa in the early nineteenth century died there, and another 21 percent became invalids. Temperatures of more than 100 degrees Fahrenheit in some regions and constant rainfall in others made travel extremely difficult. The mosquito and the tsetse fly made it deadly. Mosquito bites brought malaria, while the tsetse fly carried trypanosomiasis, or sleeping sickness, an infectious illness that began with a fever and ended in a deadly paralysis. Sleeping sickness also posed a grave danger to livestock and so aggravated the problem of transportation within the African interior. In regions with endemic trypanosomiasis, such as equatorial, southern, and eastern Africa, the use of horses and oxen was impossible. Despite the dangers posed by the climate and disease, Europeans did endeavor to establish inland settlements in Africa but then faced the obstacle of African resistance. In the seventeenth century, for example, the Portuguese set up forts and trading centers in modern Zimbabwe but were driven out by local African populations.

Beginning around 1830, a series of developments altered the relationship between Europe and Africa and prepared the groundwork for European conquest. First, the efforts of European explorers changed the Western vision of Africa. Between 1830 and 1870, adventurers mapped out the chief geographical features of Africa's interior and so illuminated the "Dark Continent" for Europeans. They discovered that central Africa was not the vast, empty desert that Europeans had assumed, but rather a territory with abundant agricultural and mineral resources—and lots of people, all of them potential consumers of European goods.

The shift in the European vision of Africa—from empty desert to potential treasure house—coincided with important changes within Africa itself. In the first half of the nineteenth century, various forces destabilized African political structures and so weakened the African ability to withstand conquest in later decades. Although the precise nature of the destabilizing forces varied by region, one common denominator prevailed—the unsettling impact of early encounters with the West. In the 1830s, for example, Britain and other European powers, pressured by humanitarian and missionary lobby groups, embarked on an effort to stamp out the West African slave trade. They succeeded but only in West Africa. The slave trade shifted to the central and eastern regions of the continent and wreaked havoc with political arrangements there. African slaving nations relied on frequent military raids to obtain their human merchandise. These raids—carried out by Africans against Africans—disrupted agricultural production, shattered trade networks, and undermined the authority of existing political rulers. With political systems in disarray, many African regions were vulnerable to European encroachment.

Encounters & Transformations

Picasso Goes to the Museum

After months of work and more than 800 preparatory sketches, Picasso judged the painting finished at last. But when he showed *Les Demoiselles d'Avignon* to his friend and rival Matisse, the Frenchman thought the work a joke. Another friend and fellow painter, Georges Braques, found it appalling. Picasso did not exhibit the painting for several years; it remained largely unknown until 1939 when it went on display at the Museum of Modern Art in New York City. Today, *Demoiselles* is one of the most well-known modernist works of art in the western world, "the amazing act on which all the art of our century is built."[11] It helped transform the history of Western art and even, perhaps, the history of perception itself.

With its in-your-face sexuality, *Demoiselles* retains its ability to shock. Five naked whores (*demoiselles* means "prostitutes") advertise for trade, twisting their bodies into erotic, even pornographic poses. The painting's eroticism alone, however, does not explain its impact.

The painting as we now know it resulted from a very specific encounter that occurred when Picasso went to a museum in Paris. Some time in 1906 or 1907, when he was already deeply involved in this painting, Picasso viewed African tribal masks on exhibit at the Ethnographic Museum in the Trocadero. This museum visit profoundly excited and upset the Spanish painter. His girlfriend Fernande Olivier reported, "Picasso is going crazy over Negro works and statues."[12] In Picasso's view, these "Negro works and statues" possessed the vitality and authenticity missing from Western art. Picasso and many modernists believed that Western civilization, with its urbanization and industrialism, its organizations and academies, its codes and regulations, had stifled artistic expression. They saw most modern art as weak and lifeless—the tired-out product of a worn-out society. In contrast, they argued, African art resembled the pictures drawn by children: energetic, playful, creative, colored outside the lines.

This notion of African culture as childlike, of course, reflected the imperialist idea of "backward peoples." Picasso and other modernists rejected the imperialist notion of Western superiority and often sharply criticized Western empires, yet clearly they could not escape imperialist stereotypes. Within the limits of these stereotypes, however, modernists turned the cultural relationship of the West and Africa upside down. Picasso went to African art to learn, not to conquer.

Picasso's encounter with the African masks transformed both this specific painting and modern art itself. After his Trocadero visit, Picasso reconfigured the faces of the two women on the right so that their masklike appearances now clash awkwardly with those of the three other prostitutes. This step destroyed any unity of narrative or composition in the painting: The five figures are no longer part of a single story or share a single point of view. At the same time that Picasso fragmented the painting, he fragmented each of the bodies, flattening them and reducing them to jutting geometric forms. Thus *Demoiselles* pushed Picasso toward Cubism, one of the most influential artistic styles of the twentieth century (see page 755). As the art historian John Golding has written, "In the *Demoiselles* Picasso began to shatter the human figure. . . . He spent the rest of his artistic life dissecting, reassembling, and reinventing it."[13] After Picasso, Western artists spent the rest of the twentieth century dissecting, reassembling, and reinventing the way we see and depict our world.

For Discussion

Clearly Picasso's encounter with the African sculptures on display at the Trocadero transformed this specific painting. But why is this single work of art so important?

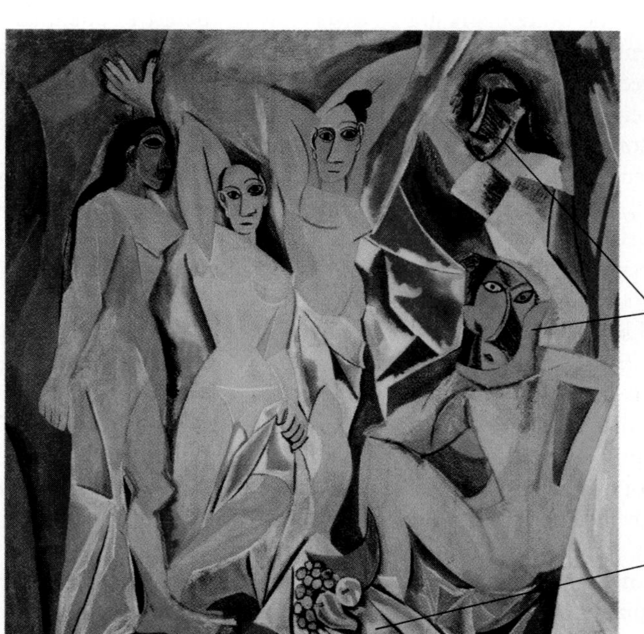

Pablo Picasso, *Les Demoiselles d'Avignon* (1907)

The mask-like features of the prostitutes reflect the influence of African tribal art on Picasso.

The edge of the table engages the viewer as a participant in the painting: the viewer's perspective is that of a customer sitting at a table in a brothel.

Finally, three specific developments shifted the balance of power in the West's favor—the steamship, the "quinine prophylaxis," and the repeating, breech-loading rifle. The steam revolution was inaugurated in 1807 when the *Clermont*, a ship powered by a steam engine invented by the American Robert Fulton, chugged its way along the Hudson River between Albany and New York City. By the 1820s, steamships were widely in use on European lakes and rivers. Steam proved crucial in enabling Western imperialists to overcome the obstacles to traveling through Africa by allowing them to use the continent's extensive but shallow river system.

But until the 1850s and the development of the "quinine prophylaxis," such journeys almost guaranteed death sentences because of the risk of malaria. Steam enabled Westerners to penetrate the African interior; quinine helped them survive once they got there. Produced commercially from 1827 on, quinine was prescribed by doctors for malaria. Death and disability rates from the disease remained high, however, until a series of chance discoveries revealed the importance of taking quinine prophylactically—of saturating the system with quinine before any risk of infection. By the 1860s, Westerners were routinely ingesting quinine in preparation for postings in Africa—and their death rates dropped dramatically.

African death rates, however, soared because of the third crucial technology of imperialism—the repeating, breech-loading rifles carried by Europeans from the 1870s on. Before the invention of these rifles, Europeans used muskets or muzzle-loading rifles that had to be loaded one ball or cartridge at a time while standing up, and were prone to foul easily, particularly in damp weather. Such weapons did not provide Europeans with much of a military advantage, even over spears. With the repeating rifle, however, "any European infantryman could now fire lying down, undetected, in any weather, fifteen rounds of ammunition in as many seconds at targets up to half a mile away." As we saw at the beginning of this chapter, in regions such as the Sudan, where armor-clad cavalrymen fought with spears, swords, and arrows like medieval knights, the repeating breech-loader and its descendant the machine gun made the European conquest "more like hunting than war."[14]

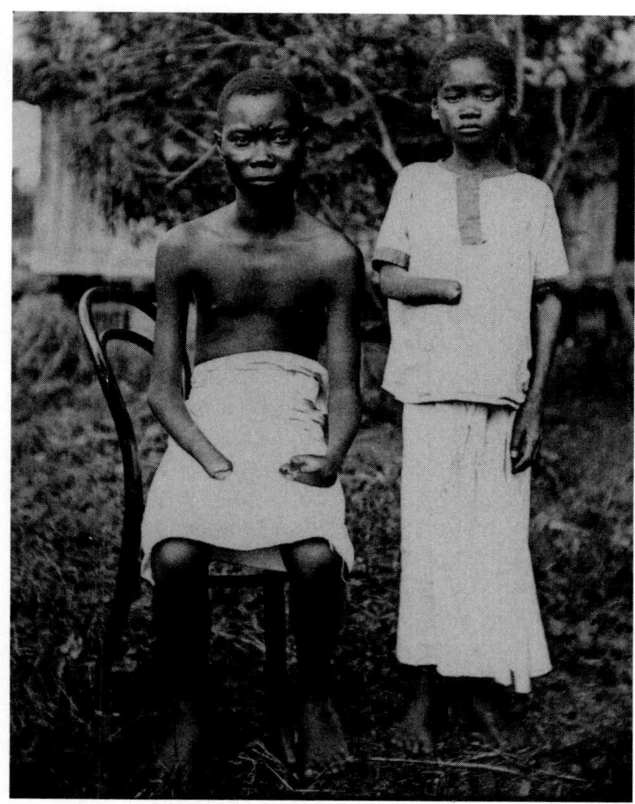

Congo Atrocities
Harsh punishments were used by Leopold's forces to subdue the Congolese people and increase his personal profits.

Slicing the Cake: The Conquest of Africa

In the decades after 1870, convinced that the conquest of African territories would guarantee commercial prosperity and strengthen national power, European states moved quickly to beat out their rivals and grab a piece of the continent. As King Leopold II of Belgium (1865–1909) explained in a letter to his ambassador in London in 1876, "I do not want to miss a good chance of getting us a slice of this magnificent African cake."[15]

Leopold's slice proved to be enormous. Presenting himself as a humanitarian whose chief concern was the abolition of the slave trade, he called on the other European leaders to back his claim to the Congo, a huge region of central Africa comprising territory more than twice as large as central Europe. After a decade of controversy and quarreling, representatives of the European powers met in Berlin in 1884 and agreed to Leopold's demands. At the same time, they used the Berlin Conference to regulate the Scramble for Africa. According to the terms established in Berlin, any state claiming a territory in Africa had to establish "effective occupation" and to plan for the economic development of that region.

But as the history of the Congo Free State demonstrated, colonialism in Africa was far from a humanitarian endeavor. Leopold's personal mercenary army turned the Congo into a hellhole of slavery and death. By claiming all so-called vacant land, Leopold deprived villagers of the grazing, foraging, and hunting grounds they needed to survive. He levied impossibly high rubber quotas for each village, forcing villagers to harvest wild rubber for up to twenty-five days each month while their families starved. Brutal punishments ensured compliance: Soldiers chopped off the hands of villagers who failed to meet their rubber quota. In other cases, babies were chained in sweltering huts until

Belgian King Crushing the Congo Free State—Cartoon

their mothers delivered their quota. At the same time, the Belgians forced black Africans to serve as human mules. This practice spread sleeping sickness from the western coast into the interior. Between 1895 and 1908, an epidemic of sleeping sickness decimated the already weakened population. As an estimated three million people died from the combined effects of forced labor, brutal punishments, starvation, and disease, the enormous profits from the Congo enabled Leopold II to indulge his hobby of building elaborate tourist resorts on the Riviera.

King Leopold's personal brand of imperialism proved so scandalous that in 1908 the Belgian government replaced Leopold's personal rule with state control over the Congo. Yet the king's exploitation of the Congo differed only in degree, not in kind, from the nature of European conquest elsewhere in Africa. Forced labor was common throughout European-controlled areas, as were brutal punishments for any Africans who dared resist. Faced with tribal revolt in Southwest Africa, the German colonial army commander in 1904 ordered that the entire Herero tribe be exterminated. Twenty thousand Africans, including children, were forcibly driven from their villages into the desert to die of thirst.

African Resistance

As the Herero rebellion demonstrates, Africans frequently resisted the imposition of these often-brutal imperial regimes, but to no avail. The only successful episode of African resistance to European conquest occurred in northern Africa, in the kingdom of Ethiopia (also called Abyssinia). After four centuries of isolation, Ethiopia modernized in the 1850s. By the time of the European Scramble for Africa, Ethiopia had developed not only a modern standing army but also an advanced infrastructure and communications system. These factors enabled the Ethiopian nation, in 1896, to defeat the Italian army at the battle of Adowa.

Adowa, however, was the exception. Most African resistance was doomed by the technological gap that yawned between the indigenous peoples and their European conquerors. A booming arms trade developed between European rifle manufacturers and African states desperate to obtain guns. Frequently, however, the arms shipped to Africa were inferior models—muskets or single-firing muzzle-loaders rather than the up-to-date and deadly efficient repeating rifles and early machine guns possessed by the European invaders.

African military leaders who did obtain advanced weaponry often did not make the strategic leap necessary to adapt their military tactics to new technologies. (As we will see in Chapter 24, European military leaders made similar mistakes in World War I.) In the 1890s, for example, the West African state of Dahomey imported repeating rifles to enable it to resist French annexation. A prosperous, highly centralized state, Dahomey possessed a 4,000-soldier standing army with a deservedly fierce reputation. Dahomey's military command, however, failed to change the attack drill devised for a musket-based regiment. The troops advanced forward at a run, fired from the hip, and withdrew—a strategy that worked well with muskets because they did not have to be aimed, but that proved disastrous with more advanced weapons. In 1892, French forces, outnumbered six to one, annihilated the Dahomian army. By 1900, Dahomey had become part of the French empire.

Yet even African resistance leaders who did adapt military strategy as well as adopt modern military weapons could not stand for long against the industrial might of Western powers. The most famous African resistance leader, Samori Ture (1830–1900), built a vast West African empire of 115,000 square miles and held off the forces of French imperialism for fifteen years, but he, too, was conquered in the end. Utilizing information obtained by spies sent to infiltrate the French military, Samori trained his massive infantry in modern military maneuvers and armed his elite cavalry troops with 6,000 repeating rifles, used with deadly effect against the French in a series of battles in the 1880s. Even more important, Samori was one of the first military commanders to conceive of the tactics of modern guerilla warfare—hit-and-run attacks, night battles, the crucial advantage of knowing the land. These measures enabled him to elude French capture for more than seven years after the French in 1891 sent a massive force to destroy the Samorian state. Yet 6,000 repeating rifles and guerilla tactics could not hold off the vast weight of French imperialism. Ambushed in 1898, Samori died in exile two years later, with his empire in European control.

The Scramble for Africa provides the most dramatic illustration of new imperialism but certainly not the only one. The same era witnessed the extension of European empires throughout Asia. Moreover, it was in Asia that non-European powers—the United States and Japan—entered the imperial game, and that Russia made its bid for empire.

Asian Encounters

Unlike most of Africa, many of the diverse states of Asia had already been woven into the web of the Western economy well before 1870. Pacific states such as Java and Malaysia formed a part of the eighteenth-century mercantilist empires established by Dutch, British, Portuguese, and French trading companies. (See Chapter 17.) Throughout the nineteenth century, European governments formalized their control over many of these island states, primarily to protect trade routes or to ensure access to profitable commodities such as rubber, tin, tobacco, and sugar. The Dutch, for example, gradually expanded their East Indies empire, moving from control of the island of Java in 1815 to domination over almost the entire archipelago several decades later. Similarly, Britain steadily expanded its control over India throughout the nineteenth century (see Map 23.2).

A number of factors accelerated the pace of imperialist acquisition in Asia beginning in the 1870s. In the age of steam, the Pacific islands took on strategic significance because European powers and the United States needed coaling stations for their commercial and naval fleets. At the same time, new industrial processes often heightened the economic value of many of these regions. The development of a process for producing dried coconut, for example, made Samoa so valuable that Germany, Britain, and the United States competed for control over the tiny islands.

As in Africa, however, the most important factor in imperialist expansion after 1870 was a phenomenon we can call the *scramble effect:* Imperialist gains by one power led to anxiety and a quicker pace of expansion by its rivals. The steady erosion of Chinese political stability—itself a result of encounters with the West—intensified this Asian scramble. Competition for access to Chinese markets was an important factor in determining the course of Western imperialism throughout much of Asia. The quest for a protected trade route to China, for example, impelled the French to extend their control over neighboring Indochina. By 1893, the Union of French

Map 23.2 Imperialism in Asia, 1914

The impact of the new imperialism on Asia was not as dramatic as in Africa, but the spread of Western rule is significant nonetheless. This map shows a key development: the entry of non-European powers—Japan and the United States—into the imperialist game. What it does not show is the extent of Western and Japanese influence in China. Profoundly destabilized by foreign intervention, China in 1914 was in the midst of revolution.

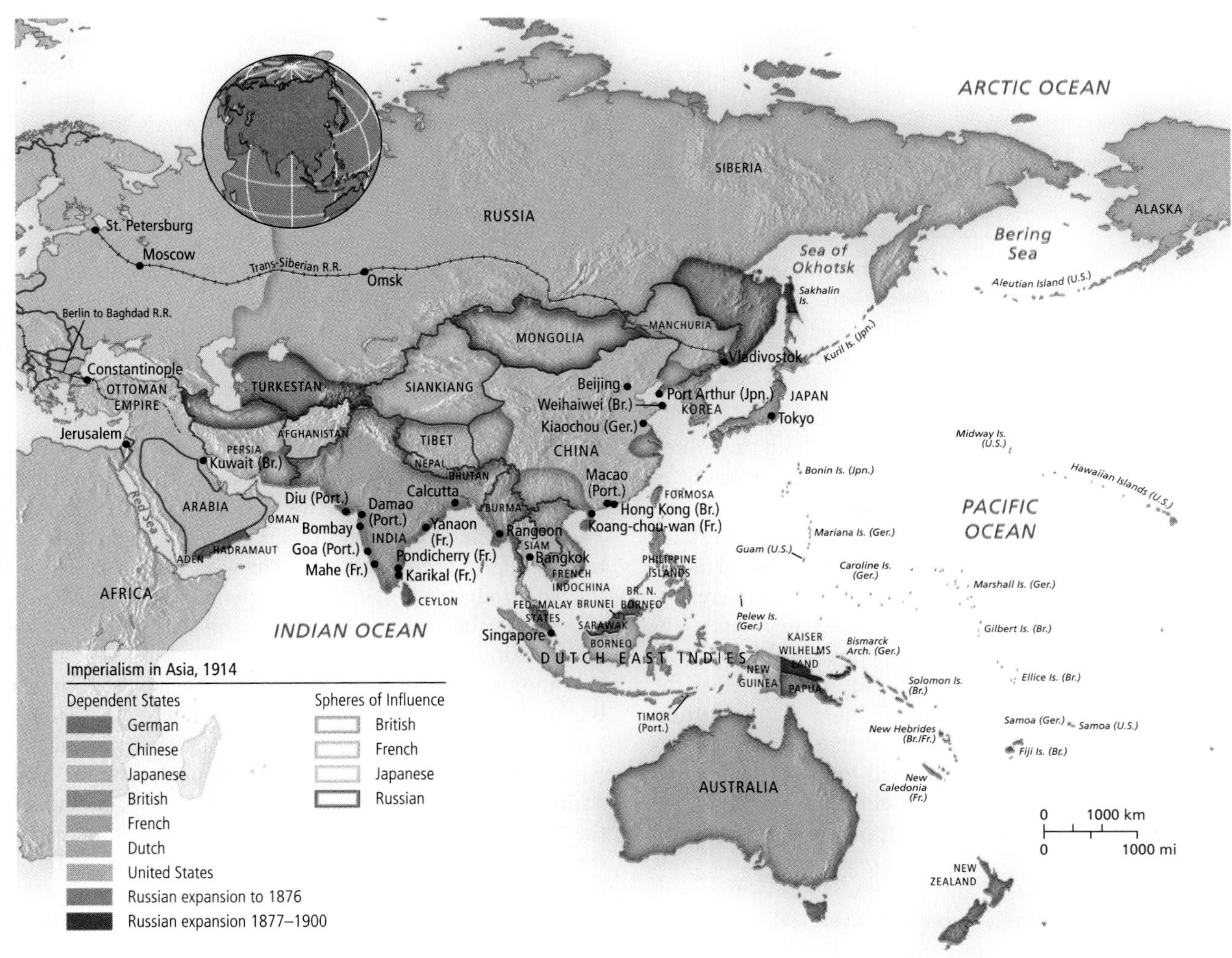

CHRONOLOGY

Asia Encounters the West

1840–1842	The Opium War: Western powers begin to chip away at Chinese territorial sovereignty in China
1853	Commodore Matthew Perry forces Japan to open its markets to the United States
1868	The Meiji Restoration in Japan; Japan begins rapid modernization
1885	Russia establishes control over Central Asia
1893	Union of French Indochina includes Laos, Cambodia, Tonkin, and Annam
1894–1895	The Sino-Japanese War: China defeated
1898	Spanish-American War; United States annexes Puerto Rico, Philippines, Hawaii, and Guam; establishes protectorate over Cuba
1899	"Open door" policy in China proclaimed by United States
1900–1903	Boxer Rebellion in China
1901	Commonwealth of Australia formed
1904–1905	Russo-Japanese War: Russia defeated
1911	Revolution in China: overthrow of Manchu Dynasty

Indochina included the formerly independent states of Laos, Cambodia, Annam, and Tonkin—the latter two better known by their contemporary name of Vietnam.

Expanding the West: The United States and Australia

In the latter half of the nineteenth century, both the United States and Australia established themselves as extensions of the West. In both of these regions, the nineteenth century was a period of internal consolidation, territorial expansion, and the subjugation of the indigenous populations. Both regions also witnessed a determined effort to create a national identity that explicitly excluded Asian peoples.

For the United States, the acquisition of an empire in Asia followed consolidation of control over much of the North American continent. After emerging victorious from a war with Mexico in 1846, the United States gained the territory of California (which included today's New Mexico and part of Arizona) and so extended its reach to the Pacific. The completion of the transcontinental Union Pacific railroad in 1869 both symbolized this coast-to-coast dominion and accelerated the pace of westward settlement.

The conquest of the continent, however, depended on the defeat of its indigenous peoples. The decades from 1860 through 1890 were punctuated by a series of Indian wars throughout the American West. As in Africa, even those Indians who acquired repeating rifles, such as Crazy Horse's troops who wiped out General George Armstrong Custer (1839–1876) at Little Big Horn in 1876, could not hold out for long against the industrial might of the United States.

With its borders now touching the Pacific Ocean, the United States quickly emerged as an imperialist power in Asia. In 1853, Commodore Matthew Perry used the potent threat of his squadron of four warships to force the opening of Japan to American commerce, and during the 1860s and 1870s the United States participated with the European powers in chipping away at China's national sovereignty to ensure favorable terms of trade there. By the end of the century, the United States had annexed Hawaii and part of Samoa, and as a result of the Spanish-American War had acquired Guam, the Philippines, Cuba, and Puerto Rico.

American acquisition of empire in Asia heightened anti-Asian sentiment within the United States, as many Americans of European descent sought to construct a version of national identity that excluded not only Asians but all peoples of color. The Chinese Exclusion Act, passed in 1882 and renewed in 1902, prohibited Chinese immigration. In 1913, the Alien Land Law, which outlawed land ownership by noncitizens, sought to restrict the property rights of Japanese immigrants. During this same period, legislators in the American South deprived blacks of their right to vote through literacy tests, poll taxes, and violent intimidation, while Jim Crow° or segregation laws defined blacks as second-class citizens, in but not really of the West.

Australia's conquest and consolidation as a Western zone paralleled many of the American developments. Discovered and claimed for the British Crown by Captain James Cook in 1770, Australia was first used by Britain as a dumping ground for convicts. But with the expansion of the wool industry in the decades after 1830, the six British colonies established in Australia became a center of British immigration. In 1901, these colonies joined together in the Commonwealth of Australia, part of the British Empire but a self-governing political entity—and a self-defined "Western" nation, despite its geographical location in the Eastern Hemisphere. Many Australians, including the new nation's first prime minister, Edmund Barton, identified the "West" as "white." Barton, who campaigned on a platform calling for a "White Australia," regarded his country as an outpost of Western civilization.

As in the United States, the process of extending Western civilization demanded the defeat of the indigenous population. At the very start of Britain's occupation of Australia in 1787, King George III had forbidden anyone to "wantonly destroy [the Aboriginal peoples] or give them any unnecessary interruption in the exercise of their several occupations."[16] But the landing of whites intent on building cities, planting farms, and fencing in land for pastures clearly interrupted the nomadic way of life for the estimated 500,000 inhabitants of Australia, living in scattered tribal groupings. In 1795, the first major clash between Aborigines and British settlers occurred. Over the next hundred years, these clashes were frequent—and disastrous for the Aboriginal populations.

The British divided over how to treat the Aborigines. To many British settlers, and as the decades passed, to many in the growing group of Australia-born whites, the Aborigines constituted a clear and violent threat that had to be eradicated. Massacres of Aborigines resulted. Christian and humanitarian groups, as well as the British government in London, opposed this sort of violence and insisted that the Aborigines should be westernized and Christianized. From the 1820s on, mission stations housed and educated Aboriginal children. Forcibly removed from their homes, these children were schooled in British ways and then at age 15 placed in employment as apprentices and domestic servants. Despite these missions, few Aborigines assimilated to the Western way of life. Thus the final decades of the nineteenth century saw a shift in official policy from assimilation to "protection." Aborigines and mixed-race individuals were declared legal wards of the state and required to live on reserves. Aborigines did not receive Australian citizenship until 1967.

White Australians perceived not only the Aborigines but also Asian immigrants as threats to their Western identity. By the 1850s, tens of thousands of Chinese had emigrated to Australia. Arriving as indentured servants, they worked under brutal conditions. Many, for example, labored in the gold mines, where they received one-twelfth of the wages paid to a European. As the numbers of Chinese immigrants grew, so, too, did anti-Chinese sentiment. Most British immigrants and white native Australians, often fiercely divided in their vision of what sort of nation Australia should be, agreed that it should be colored white. One newspaper editor noted, "The Chinese question never fails. At every meeting, somebody in the hall has a word to say in regard to it, and visions of millions of the barbarians swooping upon the colony in a solid body rise in the mental horizons of every man present."[17] In 1888, the Australian government turned back ships containing Chinese immigrants; restrictive immigration legislation soon followed.

The Continued Expansion of the Russian Empire

As in the United States and Britain, in nineteenth-century Russia, imperial expansion took the form of territorial consolidation across a continent. During this era, Russia continued the colonization of Siberia that had begun in the sixteenth century, when Russian serfs had first fled to Siberia in search of land and freedom. The end of serfdom actually accelerated the Siberian exodus, because peasants now needed to escape the debts imposed on them by the emancipation legislation of 1861 (see Chapter 21). The completion of the trans-Siberian railway in the 1890s made this journey even more appealing. Between 1800 and 1914, seven million Russians settled in or were deported to Siberia.

Just as American expansion westward and the British conquest of Australia dramatically depleted Indian and Aboriginal numbers, so Russian migration into Siberia displaced much of that region's original population. Until 1826 Russians could trade Siberians as slaves; many died because of brutal treatment. Two additional factors were even more devastating to the indigenous Siberians. First, the immigrants brought with them new epidemic diseases. And second, the booming fur trade depleted the animal herds that served as the aborigines' main food source. Disease and famine decimated the Siberian population.

Russia also expanded southward into central Asia, primarily as a preemptive response to the growth of British power in India. Fearing that the British might push northward, the Russians pushed south. By 1885, the Black Sea region, the Caucasus, and Turkestan had all fallen to Russian imperial control, and Muslims now constituted a significant minority of the tsar's subjects. Over the next three decades the oil fields of the Caucasus would become a crucial part of the Russian industrial economy.

By 1914, the Russian Empire stretched from Warsaw in central Europe to Vladivostok on the Sea of Japan—8,660,000 square miles, or one-seventh of the global land surface. Ethnic Russians composed only 45 percent of the population of this vast empire.

As the tsarist regime expanded its Asian empire, it increasingly encroached upon Chinese territory, a move that contributed to the destabilization of China and to growing hostilities between Russia and Japan. By 1860, Russia had gained from China a sizable chunk of land along the Pacific coast and began pressing into Manchuria. Manchuria, however, was a region also coveted by Japanese imperialists. The growing antagonism between Russia and Japan led to the outbreak of the Russo-Japanese War in 1904 and, as we noted in Chapter 22, to a dramatic Japanese victory. Military defeat by a people regarded as racially inferior shocked Russians and led to demands for radical political change. With Tsar Nicholas II's regime clearly weakened and his troops tied up in Manchuria, this domestic discontent exploded in the Russian Revolution of 1905. The return of his soldiers from the Manchurian front enabled Nicholas to withstand this challenge to his authoritarian rule. His regime, however, was fundamentally weakened: Imperialism could be a risky business.

Japanese Industrial and Imperial Expansion

Japan's victory over Russia in 1905 vividly illustrated its remarkable rise to global power and its emergence as an imperialist player. Until 1853, Japan had remained sealed off from the West, a result of a decision made by the Japanese emperor in the 1630s to close Japanese ports to all foreigners except a small contingent of Dutch and Chinese traders confined to the city of Nagasaki. The Japanese government rebuffed all Western overtures until 1853, when Commodore Perry used warships to force Japan to open two of its ports to American ships. Over the next fifteen tumultuous years, Western powers pushed to expand their economic influence in Japan and Japanese elites fought over the question of how to respond to the West. Anti-Western terrorism became endemic, civil war broke out, and a political revolution ensued.

In 1868, Japan emerged from this turbulent time with a new government. For more than 200 years effective political control had rested in the hands not of the Japanese emperor, but rather of the "Shogun," the military governor of Japan. When the Shogun adopted pro-Western policies, Japan's warrior nobility tossed him from power and restored the young Emperor Mutsuhito (1867–1912) to effective rule—the Meiji Restoration.

The Meiji Constitution, 1889

Even more dramatically, these anti-Western elites determined that the only way to resist Western domination was to adopt Western industrial and military technologies and techniques. The next four decades witnessed a thoroughgoing revolution from the top as a modern centralized state, modeled on France, replaced Japan's feudalist political system. Young Japanese men traveled to Europe and the United States to learn Western ways. Western technologies and techniques helped modernize the Japanese economy.

Modernization was not an end in itself, however. The purpose of opening Japan to the West was to build up its

DOCUMENT

"A Dream of the Future"

In 1878, Tachibana Mitsuomi published his "Dream of the Future" in Hochi Shimbun, *the newspaper that he edited. Tachibana's dream is a nightmare. It reveals the anxiety prevalent in Japan during its time of rapid modernization and increasing contact with Western economies and ideas. In this excerpt, Tachibana projects the consequences of an imaginary decision to lift regulations on the importation of Western capital. In actual fact, no such decision was made. The Japanese government borrowed technology, techniques, and institutions from the West, but restrained the inflow of Western capital, thus retaining control over the Japanese economy.*

Tachibana's story opens with his bewilderment at suddenly finding himself on a busy street in Tokyo in 1967:

The houses in the surrounding streets were splendidly built and some of them three, and others five stories high; flags from every merchant's house were waving in the air; all kinds of precious articles were displayed in the shops and carriages and horses were incessantly passing to and fro. Indeed, a most flourishing trade was actually before my eyes. Greatly puzzled at this, I went into a shop and found that the master of the shop was a White man with blue eyes and red hair, wearing handsome clean clothes and sitting in an easy position by a desk; and that those wearing scanty and torn apparel and in the employment of the master of the house, were none but the yellow-coloured and high-cheek-boned brethren of ours. . . . I was informed that . . . all the large houses in the main streets [were] occupied by the Whites. . . .

. . . I then passed into the [side] streets and on looking at the state of the houses, I saw none but immense numbers of my countrymen flocking together like sheep or pigs, in a few poorly-built houses . . . their scanty dress leaving portions of their body uncovered . . . their wives were weeping from the cold, and the children crying from hunger, the husbands being employed by the Western people, and were earning scarcely sufficient wages to fill the mouths of their families. . . .

I, seeing this, could hardly keep from weeping and was sorely puzzled why my countrymen should have fallen to such misery . . . I saw a respectable looking gray-haired old man standing on the bridge . . . I approached him and after bowing to him, I asked, "Is this country Japan? Is this the capital, Tokei [Tokyo]? How is it that the Western people alone are enjoying such great wealth, whilst the Japanese are in such a miserable state? . . . "

The old man explains to Tochibana that the Japanese "were outdone by the superior strength of capital and intellect" from the West. As a result of lifting regulations on Western investment and ownership within Japan, "those who have control over the wealth of Japan . . . are none but the Western people." Tochibana concludes, "At this, I was very sad and deeply affected, and I was on the point of bursting into tears, when I suddenly awoke and found that it was all a dream."

Source: From Tachibana Mitsuomi, "A Dream of the Future," *Hochi Shimbun,* October 17, 1878. For the full version and a commentary, refer to Ian Inkster, *Japanese Industrialisation: Historical and Cultural Perspectives* (Routledge: London and New York, 2001), pp. 1–6.

Japanese Sailors Waiting for Battle Against Russia, 1904
The Japanese began the war with a surprise attack on Russian ships in Port Arthur. Many in Britain and the United States admired the Japanese for the audacity of their offensive—rather ironically, given the moral outrage that greeted a similar surprise attack carried out by the Japanese against American forces at Pearl Harbor in 1941.

national wealth, and with this wealth, to remake Japan as a global military power. Thus funds poured into building a modern navy, modeled on Britain's, and a powerful conscript-based army, modeled on Germany's. Beginning in the 1890s, Japan used its now formidable military force to push its way into the imperialist game. War with China in 1894 and Russia in 1904 led to the Japanese seizure of Taiwan and Korea, and to expanded Japanese economic influence in Manchuria. One Japanese writer, Tokutomi Soho (1863–1957) proclaimed that Japan's imperial conquests showed that "civilization is not a monopoly of the white man."[18] Certainly imperialist violence was not a white man's monopoly: The Japanese brutally punished Koreans and Taiwanese who dared to protest against their new rulers.

Scrambling in China

While Japan used its encounter with the West to modernize and militarize its society, China proved far less successful in withstanding Western hegemony. Throughout the nineteenth century, Chinese national sovereignty slowly eroded, as European powers, soon joined by Russia, the United States, and Japan, jostled for access to China's markets and resources.

We saw in Chapter 20 that Britain's victory over China in the First Opium War in 1842 marked the beginnings of Western encroachment on Chinese territory. During the 1890s, Western influence expanded rapidly. Following China's defeat in the Sino-Japanese War of 1894–1895, Western powers scrambled to claim spheres of influence throughout China. The European powers and the United States did agree in 1899 to back the American "open door" policy, which opposed the formal partitioning of China (as had just occurred in Africa), but this policy increased rather than blocked Western interference in Chinese economic and political affairs.

Chinese opposition to intensified Western encroachment provoked even greater outside interference—and the collapse of the Manchu dynasty that had governed China since the seventeenth century. In 1900, a secret society devoted to purging China of Western influence began attacking foreigners. The Boxer Rebellion (a rough translation of "Harmonious Fists," a name that refers to the society's commitment to the discipline of martial arts) received the covert support of the Chinese government. With more than 200 missionaries and several thousand Chinese Christians killed, and European diplomatic headquarters under attack in Beijing, the West responded in fury. A combined military force, drawing 16,000 soldiers from Russia, Germany, Austria-Hungary, France, Britain, Japan and the United States, crushed the rebellion and sacked Beijing. Required to pay a large indemnity to the West and to grant further trade and territorial concessions to its invaders, the Chinese central government was fatally weakened. In 1911, revolution engulfed China and propelled it into four decades of political and social tumult.

Concentration Camps
This illustration, which appeared in the French magazine *Le Petit Journal* in 1901, attempts to depict the anxiety and suffering of both the Boer families and their black servants who were imprisoned in English camps during the Boer War, yet it cannot convey the lack of sanitation that led to rampant disease.

A Glimpse of Things to Come: The Boer War

Writing at the time of the Opium War (1840–1842), a British journalist in China urged the Chinese to accept what he regarded as the crucial lesson of history: "Ever since the dispersion of man, the richest stream of human blessings has, in the will of Providence, followed a western course." To many Europeans, Australians, and Americans, the rapid expansion of Western imperial control over much of the world after 1870 confirmed this lesson. At the very end of the nineteenth century, however, the British found themselves embroiled in a bloody imperial conflict that challenged this complacent view. The Boer War of 1899–1902 shook British self-confidence and in many ways foreshadowed both the total warfare and the crumbling of empires that would mark the experience of the West in the twentieth century.

The Boer War was the culmination of a century of hostility among British imperialists, Dutch settlers (called Boers, the Dutch word for "farmer"), and indigenous Africans in the southern triangle of Africa. Germany's move into Southwest Africa in 1884 worsened this conflict: The British in the Cape Colony feared that the Boers would work with Germany to limit British expansion in the region. But even more important was the discovery in 1886 of diamonds and gold in the Transvaal, an independent Boer republic. British investors in the profitable diamond and gold mines resented Boer taxation and labor policies, and

CHRONOLOGY

The Struggle for Control in South Africa

1806	Britain takes control of the Cape Colony from the Dutch
1837	Boers establish independent republics of Transvaal and Orange Free State
1884	German annexation of Southwest Africa
1886	Gold discovered in the Transvaal
1899	Anglo-Boer War begins
1910	Self-government granted to South Africa

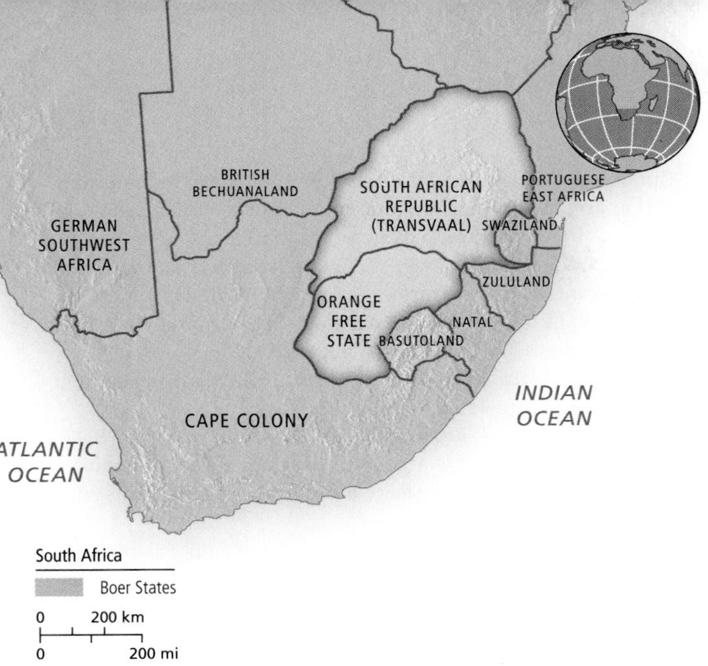

Map 23.3 South Africa
After the defeat of the Boer states—the Transvaal and the Orange Free State—in the Boer War, the Union of South Africa comprised the Cape Colony and the two Boer republics.

pressed the British government to use military force to place the Boer republics under British rule.

In 1899, these imperialists got the war they had demanded, but it turned out to be rather different from what they expected. Skilled riflemen who were fighting for their very homes, the Boers proved to be fierce enemies who successfully adopted guerilla tactics against their numerically superior foe. By the spring of 1901, the war had reached a stalemate. The British military command in South Africa then decided to smoke out the Boer fighters through a scorched-earth policy: British troops burned more than 30,000 farms to the ground and confined the Boer women and children, and their black African servants, in poorly provisioned concentration camps. Diseases such as diphtheria and typhus soon took their toll. Almost 20,000 Boer women and children, and at least 14,000 blacks, died in these camps.The British finally defeated the Boers in April 1902, but this victory was limited. The Boer states were brought under British control but the Boers (or Afrikaners, as they were increasingly called) outnumbered other whites in the newly created Union of South Africa (see Map 23.3). After South Africa received self-government in 1910, the Afrikaners dominated the political system and created a nation founded on segregation and racist oppression.

More immediately, Britain emerged from the war with both its military and its humanitarian reputation severely tarnished. The war aroused strong opposition inside Britain and made clear that popular support for imperialism could be rapidly eroded if the costs of imperial conquest proved too high. The conflict between the war's opponents and supporters inside Britain was one that would be repeated within imperialist countries many times over the course of the next several decades as nationalist challenges against imperial rule multiplied and as the imperial idea grew less and less persuasive. More ominously, the sight of noncombatants confined—and dying—in concentration camps would soon become all too familiar. The Boer War thus served as a fitting opening to the twentieth century.

The Boer War and Queen Victoria—Dutch Caricature

Conclusion

Reshaping the West: Expansion and Fragmentation

Africans and Asians who saw their political and social structures topple under the imperialist onslaught would probably have agreed with the Austrian poet Hugo von Hoffmansthal (1874–1929) when he wrote in 1905 that "what other generations believed to be firm is in fact sliding." Hoffmansthal, however, was commenting not on Africa or Asia or any other region of imperialist conquest, but rather on the Western cultural and intellectual landscape, which, like colonial political boundaries, underwent enormous and disturbing change in the period between 1870 and the outbreak of World War I in 1914. In this era, matter itself began to slide, as the Newtonian conception of the world gave way to a new, much more unsettling picture of the physical universe. At the same time, changes in medical practice, the revolt against positivism, and the triumph of Darwin's evolutionary theory helped undermine established assumptions and contributed to the sense that the foundations of Western culture were shifting; so, too, did the birth of modernism as well as broader cultural changes such as the move of middle-class women into the public sphere and the redefinition of sexual boundaries.

In the decades after 1870, then, a series of encounters reshaped the West. Its geographic boundaries expanded as non-European regions such as the United States emerged as significant economic and imperial powers. With Australians claiming Western identity, "the West" even spilled over into the Eastern Hemisphere. Yet fragmentation as well as expansion characterized the Western experience after 1870. At the same time that some social thinkers were proclaiming white cultural superiority, European artists such as Gauguin and Picasso were embracing the visual forms of non-European, nonwhite societies in an effort to push open the boundaries of Western culture. While scientific and technological achievements convinced many Europeans and Americans that the West was destined to conquer the globe, others regarded these scientific and technological changes with profound uneasiness.

The next chapter will show that the sense that old certainties were slipping led some Europeans to welcome the outbreak of war in 1914 as a way to restore heroic values and clear purpose to Western society. The trenches of World War I, however, provided little solidity. Many nineteenth-century political, economic, and cultural structures slid into ruin under the impact of total war.

Suggestions for Further Reading

For a comprehensive listing of suggested readings, please go to www.ablongman.com/levack2e/chapter23

Adas, Michael. *Machines as the Measure of Men: Science, Technology, and Ideologies of Western Dominance.* 1989. A superb study of the way in which the ideology of empire was inextricably connected with cultural and intellectual developments within the West.

Betts, Raymond F. *The False Dawn: European Imperialism in the Nineteenth Century.* 1975. A general survey that looks at the ideas that underlay imperialism as well as the events that shaped it.

Bowler, Peter. *Evolution: The History of an Idea.* 1989. Looks at the development of evolutionary theory both before and after Darwin.

Butler, Christopher. *Early Modernism: Literature, Music, and Painting in Europe, 1900–1916.* 1994. Wide-ranging and nicely illustrated.

Dijkstra, Bram. *Idols of Perversity: Fantasies of Feminine Evil in Fin-de-Siècle Culture.* 1986. This richly illustrated work shows how anxiety over the changing role of women permeated artistic production at the end of the nineteenth century.

Dodge, Ernest. *Islands and Empires: The Western Impact on the Pacific and East Asia.* 1976. A useful study of Asian imperialism.

Ellis, John. *The Social History of the Machine Gun.* 1975. Lively, nicely illustrated, and informative.

Gould, Stephen Jay. *The Mismeasure of Man.* 1996. A compelling look at the manipulation of scientific data and statistics to provide "proof" for racist and elitist assumptions.

Headrick, Daniel R. *The Tools of Empire: Technology and European Imperialism in the Nineteenth Century.* 1981. Highlights the important role played by technology in determining both the timing and success of Western imperialism.

Hochschild, Adam. *King Leopold's Ghost.* 1998. Blistering account of Leopold's imperialist rule in the Congo.

Pick, Daniel.*Faces of Degeneration: A European Disorder, c. 1848–1918.* 1993. Argues that concern over degeneration formed a central theme in European culture in the second half of the nineteenth century.

Showalter, Elaine. *Sexual Anarchy: Gender and Culture at the Fin de Siècle.* 1990. An illuminating look at the turbulence that characterized gender relations in the fin de siècle.

Sperber, Jonathan. *Popular Catholicism in Nineteenth-Century Germany.* 1984. A look at the religious dimensions of popular culture.

Thornton, A. P. *The Imperial Idea and Its Enemies: A Study in British Power.* 1959; reprinted 1985. An older but still-important look at imperialist ideology and opposition.

Vandervort, Bruce. *Wars of Imperial Conquest in Africa, 1830–1914.* 1998. An up-to-date study by a military historian.

Wesseling, H. L. *Divide and Rule: The Partition of Africa, 1880–1914.* 1996. A solid survey of complex developments.

Notes

1. Winston Churchill, *The River War: An Account of the Re-Conquest of the Sudan* (1933); quoted in Daniel Headrick, *The Tools of Empire: Technology and European Imperialism in the Nineteenth Century* (1981), 118.
2. Quoted in Anne McClintock, *Imperial Leather: Race, Gender, and Sexuality in the Colonial Contest* (1995), 50.
3. Quoted in H. Stuart Hughes, *Consciousness and Society: The Reorientation of European Social Thought, 1890–1930* (1958), 332.
4. Quoted in Hughes, *Consciousness and Society,* 296.
5. Quoted in Shearer West, *Fin de Siècle* (1993), 24.
6. Quoted in Christopher Butler, *Early Modernism: Literature, Music, and Painting in Europe, 1900–1916* (1994), 2.
7. Stephen Kern, *The Culture of Time and Space, 1880–1918* (1983), 195.
8. From *Elementary Forms.* Quoted in Hughes, *Consciousness and Society,* 284–285.
9. Quoted in William Schneider, *An Empire for the Masses: The French Popular Image of Africa, 1870–1900* (1982), 72.
10. Mary Kingsley, in *West African Studies* (1901), 329–330.
11. Yve-Alain Bois, "Painting as Trauma," in Christopher Green, *Picasso's* Les Demoiselles d'Avignon (2001), 49.

12. Brassaï, *Conversations with Picasso,* trans. Jane Marie Todd (1999), 32.

13. John Golding, "*Les Demoiselles D'Avignon* and the Exhibition of 1988," in Green, *Picasso's* Les Demoiselles, 29.

14. Headrick, *The Tools of Empire,* 101. Headrick is the historian who identified the crucial role of the steamship, the quinine prophylaxis, and the breech-loading, repeating rifle in the conquest of Africa.

15. Quoted in Thomas Pakenham, *The Scramble for Africa, 1876–1912* (1991), 22.

16. Quoted in F. K. Crowley (ed.), *A New History of Australia* (1974), 6.

17. Ibid., 207.

18. Quoted in W. G. Beasley, *Japanese Imperialism, 1894–1945* (1987), 31–33.

The First World War

24

CHAPTER OUTLINE

- The Origins of the First World War
- The Experience of Total War
- The Home Fronts
- War and Revolution

On the morning of July 1, 1916, in the fields of northern France near the Somme River, tens of thousands of young British soldiers crawled out of ditches and began to walk across a muddy expanse filled with shards of metal and decomposing human bodies. Encumbered with backpacks weighing more than sixty pounds, the men trudged forward. For the past week their heavy artillery had pummeled the Germans who lay on the other side of the mud. Thus they expected little opposition. In less than sixty seconds, expectations and reality horribly diverged. The German troops, who had waited out the bombardment in the safety of "dugouts"—fortified bunkers scooped from the earth beneath the trenches—raced to their gunnery positions and raked the evenly spaced lines of British soldiers with machine-gun fire. The slowly walking men made easy targets. Those who were lucky enough to make it to the enemy lines found their way blocked by barbed-wire fences—still intact, despite the bombardment. Standing in front of the wire, they were quickly mown down. More than 20,000 British soldiers died that day, thousands within the first minutes of the attack. Another 40,000 were wounded. Yet the attack went on. Between July 1 and November 18, 1916, when the Battle of the Somme finally ended, almost 420,000 British soldiers were killed or wounded. Their French allies lost 200,000 men to death or injury. German casualties are estimated at 450,000.

Such carnage became commonplace during the First World War. At the Battle of Verdun, which began before the Somme conflict and continued after, the French and Germans suffered total casualties of at least 750,000, while in the disastrous Gallipoli offensive of 1915, ANZAC (Australia and New Zealand) troops experienced a casualty rate of 65 percent. Between 1914 and 1918, European commanders sent more than eight million men to their deaths in a series of often futile attacks. The total number of casualties—killed, wounded, and missing—reached more than 37 million.

Death on the Western Front This movie still comes from *The Battle of the Somme*, a documentary filmed during the battle and the first "war movie" shown in Britain.

These casualty figures were in part the products of the Industrial Revolution. Between 1914 and 1918 the nations of the West used their factories to churn out ever more efficient tools of killing. The need for machine guns, artillery shells, poison gas canisters, and other implements of modern warfare meant that World War I was the first total war°, a war that demanded that combatant nations mobilize their industrial economies as well as their armies, and thus a war that erased the distinction between civilian and soldier. In total war, victory depended on the woman in the munitions factory as well as the man on the front lines.

The First World War helped redefine the West. By shattering the authoritarian empires of eastern and central Europe and integrating the United States more fully in European affairs, the war ensured that commitment to democratic values became central to one dominant twentieth-century definition of "the West." But the war also strengthened antidemocratic forces: It catapulted into power a communist regime in Russia, intensified eastern Europe's ethnic and nationalist conflicts, and undermined many of the economic structures on which Western stability and prosperity rested. The years after the war, then, would see an acceleration of the fragmentation of Western cultural and social life already underway in the prewar period.

How did the encounter with total war transform Western cultures? Four questions inform this chapter's examination of the origins and experience of the First World War:

- **What factors led Europe into war in 1914?**
- **When, where, and how did the Allies defeat the Central Powers?**
- **How did total war structure the home fronts?**
- **What were the consequences of this war for the European and the global political and international order?**

The Origins of the First World War

- **What factors led Europe into war in 1914?**

On June 28, 1914, the heir to the throne of the Austrian-Hungarian Empire, Archduke Franz Ferdinand (1863–1914), was assassinated by ethnic Serbian terrorists. Austrian officials accused the Serbian government of involvement with the assassination. One month after the archduke's death, Austria declared war on Serbia. One week later, Europe was at war. Germany entered the war on Austria's side. These two Central Powers°, as they were known, squared off against not only small Serbia but also the colossal weight of Russia, France, and Britain, called the Allies°. By the time the war ended in late 1918, the conflict had embraced not only most of Europe, but also nations from around the globe.

Why did the murder of one man on the streets of a Balkan city lead to the deaths of millions in theaters of war ranging from muddy ditches in northern France to beaches along the Mediterranean, from the mountains of Italy to the deserts of northern Africa and the depths of the Atlantic? To understand the war's origins, we need to exam-

Arrest of Gavrilo Princip
Princip was only 18 years old when he assassinated Archduke Franz Ferdinand and set into motion the sequence of events that led to the First World War. Because of his young age, he did not receive the death penalty but instead was sentenced to twenty years in prison. He did not serve out his term; he died at age 22 of tuberculosis.

ine four interlocking factors: first, eastern European nationalism; second, the creation of rival alliance systems; third, the requirements of an industrialized military; and finally, the "will to war," the conviction among both policymakers and ordinary people that war would provide a resolution to social and cultural crisis.

Nationalism in Eastern Europe: Austria-Hungary and the Problem of Serbia

The roots of the First World War extend deep into the soil of nationalist conflict in eastern Europe. Western European national identities coalesced in accordance with existing political boundaries; in eastern Europe, however, the "nation" was defined by ethnic, religious, or linguistic identities rather than political citizenship. More than 27 million subjects of the Habsburg monarchy, for example, did not identify themselves with the Austrian-Hungarian Empire's dominant German or Magyar (Hungarian) peoples.[1] For the Czechs or Slovenians or Serbs, translating national into political identity—creating a "nation-state"—demanded the breakup of empires and a radical redrawing of political boundaries. Unlike in much of western Europe, then, in the East nationalism served as an explosive rather than a unifying force.

The divisive impact of nationalism explains why officials within the vast Austrian-Hungarian Empire regarded the small state of Serbia as a major threat. As a multiethnic, multilinguistic empire, Austria-Hungary's very survival depended on damping down the fires of nationalism wherever they flamed up. Yet much of Serbian politics centered on fanning the nationalist flame. In 1903, a group of Serbian army officers had shot Serbia's despised king and queen, chopped their bodies into little bits, and threw the pieces out the window. The new king, a member of a rival Serbian royal dynasty, recognized that his position on the throne was precarious, to say the least. To remain in power he catered to the demands of radical nationalists, who sought the unification of all Serbs into a Greater Serbian state. Given the fact that more than seven million Serbs lived not in Serbia but in Austria-Hungary, it is not surprising that the Austrian monarchy regarded the call for Serbian unification as a direct threat to its existence.

The hostile relations between Serbia and Austria-Hungary led directly to the outbreak of World War I. In 1908 Austria annexed Bosnia, a region with a large Serbian population. The Serbian government, which viewed Bosnia as an integral part of what it hoped would become Greater Serbia, responded to the Austrian annexation by encouraging Bosnian Serb separatist and terrorist groups. After one such group, the Black Hand, succeeded in assassinating Archduke Franz Ferdinand in the summer of 1914, Austrian officials decided to crush Serbia once and for all. On July 23 a representative of the Austrian-Hungarian Empire presented the Serbs with an ultimatum, a set of demands that would have given Austria-Hungary the right to an unprecedented degree of involvement in Serbian internal affairs. Austrian diplomats informed the Serbian government that anything short of unconditional acceptance of the impossible ultimatum within just forty-eight hours would be taken as a declaration of war. Serbian officials agreed to comply with every demand except one. On July 28 Austria-Hungary declared war on Serbia.

Borijove Jevtic: The Murder of Archduke Franz Ferdinand

International Competition and Rival Alliance Systems

But why did war between Austria-Hungary and Serbia mean war across Europe? To understand what transformed this Austro-Serbian conflict into a continental war, we need to look beyond the unsettling impact of nationalism in eastern Europe to the heightened international competition that divided Europe into rival alliance systems. Concerned with protecting and enhancing the economic and military might of their states in an increasingly unsettled international climate, diplomats wove a web of alliances across Europe. As we will see, these alliances helped escalate a regional conflict into a European and then a global war.

One crucial factor in the growing intensity of international competition in the prewar years was Germany's unification as a state in 1871. By creating a military and economic powerhouse in the middle of Europe, the unification of the German states upset the balance of power on the Continent. Until 1890, however, the diplomatic maneuvers of Otto von Bismarck (1815–1898), the chancellor of the new nation, ensured a certain degree of stability. Bismarck recognized that Germany's position in the center of Europe made it vulnerable to encirclement by hostile powers. To avoid such an encirclement, Bismarck patched up relations with Austria in the aftermath of the Austrian-Prussian War, an effort that resulted in the signing of the Dual Alliance between Germany and the Austrian Empire in 1879. In 1882, the Dual Alliance became the Triple Alliance° when Italy joined the two Central Powers in a defensive treaty. At the same time, Bismarck was careful to maintain an alliance with Russia. By the terms of the Reinsurance Treaty of 1887, Russia and Germany agreed to remain neutral if either was attacked. Bismarck thus ensured that if Germany were to go to war against its old enemy, France, it would not face battle on two fronts.

But in 1888, a new emperor, Kaiser William II (r. 1888–1918), ascended the German throne. William, an ambitious and impatient young man, dismissed Bismarck in 1890 and launched Germany down a more dangerous path. The new kaiser made a fatal break with Bismarck's policies in two areas. First, William let the Reinsurance Treaty with Russia lapse, thus allowing fiercely anti-German France to form a partnership with Russia, formalized as the Franco-Russian Alliance of 1894. Germany now faced exactly the sort of encirclement by hostile powers, and the resulting threat of a two-front war, that Bismarck had sought to avoid.

Second, William favored a new "world policy" (*Weltpolitik*) for Germany that pushed Britain toward allying with Russia and France. Whereas Bismarck had insisted that Germany's interests were confined to Europe, William and many prominent Germans wanted to see Germany claim its "place in the sun" as a global imperial and naval power. In 1898 Germany passed a naval law mandating the construction of nineteen battleships; a second law passed in 1900 doubled the number of ships. At the same time Germany adopted a more aggressive stance in Africa.

Such policies were guaranteed to aggravate and alienate Britain. As an island nation with a vast overseas empire, Britain based its military defense system on its naval su-

Map 24.1 Europe, August 1914

In August 1914 each of the Central Powers faced the challenge of war on two fronts, but the entry of the Ottoman Empire into the war on the side of the Central Powers in November 1914 blocked Allied supply lines to Russia through the Mediterranean.

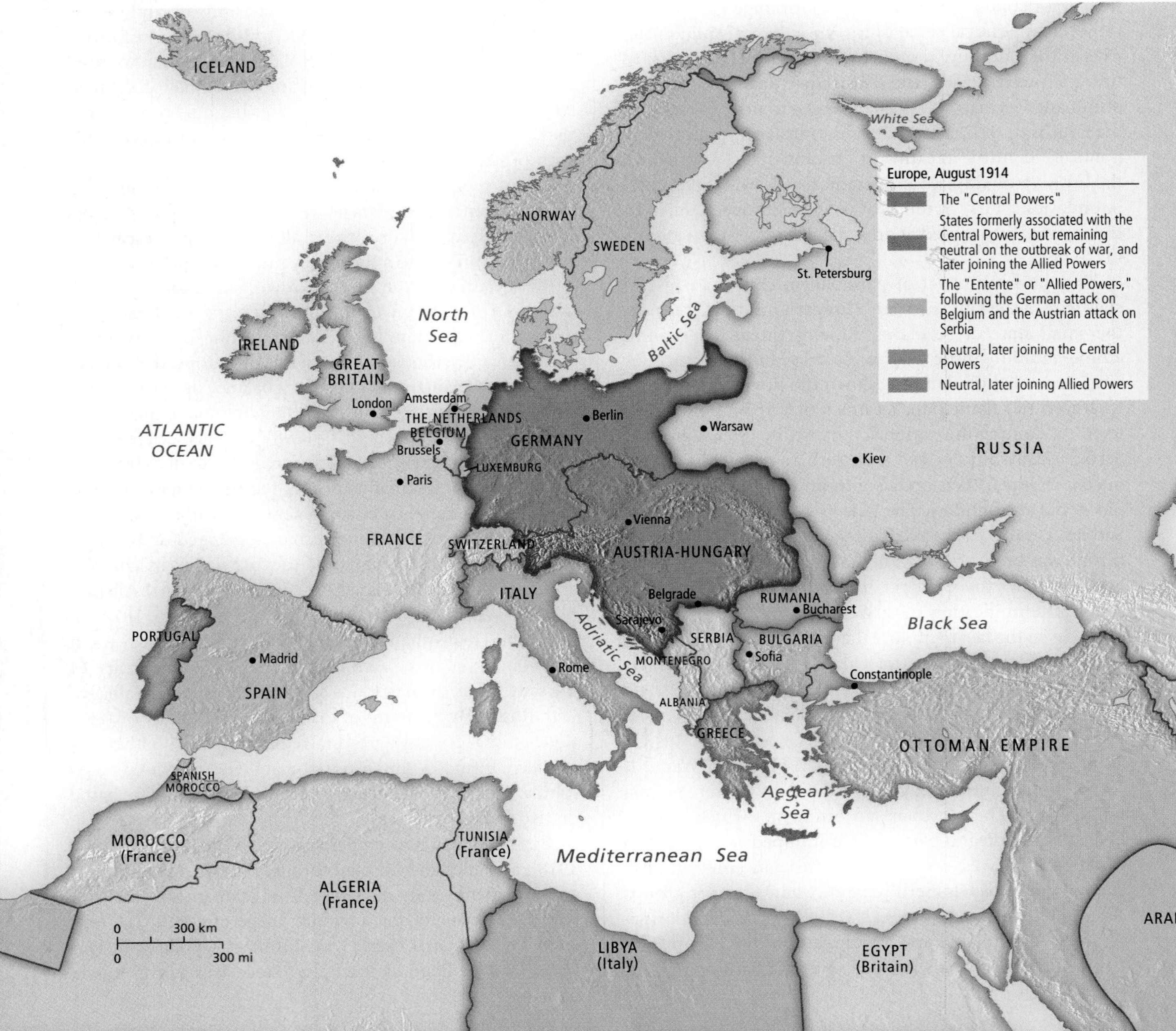

premacy. From the British point of view, a strong German navy was nothing less than a direct challenge to British national security, just as an expanding German empire was bound to conflict with British imperial interests.

Hostility toward German ambitions overcame Britain's long tradition of "splendid isolation" from continental entanglements. In the first decade of the twentieth century, a series of military, imperial, and economic arrangements formed ever-tighter links between Britain and both Russia and France. These arrangements cleared the way for the formation of the Triple Entente° among France, Russia, and Britain. An informal association rather than a formal alliance, the Triple Entente did not *require* Britain to join in a war against Germany. There is no doubt, however, that British officials increasingly viewed Germany as the major threat to British interests.

By the first decade of the twentieth century, then, Europe had split into two opposing camps: the Triple Alliance versus the Triple Entente. To German policymakers, it appeared that Germany stood surrounded by hostile powers. With Italy regarded as unreliable, Germany's alliance with Austria-Hungary took on greater and greater importance. Strengthening this crucial ally became paramount.

These considerations guided German policymaking in July 1914. When Austrian officials debated their response to the assassination of Franz Ferdinand, Kaiser William and his chancellor Theobold von Bethmann-Hollweg (1856–1921) urged a quick and decisive blow against Serbia. According to the Austrian ambassador, the kaiser told him "he would regret if we did not make use of the present moment, which is all in our favour."[2] In what some historians have described as an act akin to issuing a "blank check," the kaiser assured the ambassador that Germany would stand by Austria, even at the risk of a war with Russia.

Why would an Austrian move against Serbia heighten the risk of a wider war with Russia? The basic answer is that such a move threatened Russian interests. Eager to expand its influence in the Balkan region (and so gain access to the Mediterranean Sea), the Russian Empire had for decades positioned itself as the champion of Slavic nationalism in the Balkans and as the protector of small independent Slavic states such as Serbia. Thus both German and Austrian policymakers recognized that if Austria attacked Serbia, Russia might well mobilize against Austria and its ally, Germany (see Map 24.1).

German officials gambled, however, that Russia was not strong enough to wage war on Serbia's behalf. After all, in 1905, Russia had exposed its military shortcomings to the world with its loss in the Russo-Japanese War of 1905 (discussed in Chapter 23). And if they were wrong and Russia did mobilize for war? Then, as Bethmann-Hollweg explained, Germany's chances of winning were "better now than in one or two years' time."[3] German officials were well aware that the tsarist government, in response to its humiliating defeat in 1905, had implemented a military reform and rearmament program. Given a few more years, the Russian Empire would constitute a formidable foe.

Mobilization Plans and the Industrialized Military

Germany's alliance with Austria emboldened Austrian policymakers to embark on an aggressive attack on Serbia. In addition, the links between Serbia and Russia made it very likely that this attack against Serbia would pull in the Russian Empire, which of course did not stand alone but was allied with France. Alliances alone do not explain the transformation of the Austro-Serbian conflict into a European war, however. Consider the case of Italy. Although a member of the Triple Alliance, Italy did not join Germany and Austria in August 1914. In fact, when Italy did enter the war in 1915, it did so on the opposing side. Even more significantly, no alliance *required* either Russia or Britain to enter the fray. We need to look at a third factor in the origins of World War I—the widening gap between the expectations of traditional diplomacy and the requirements of an increasingly industrialized military. This growing gap ensured that when preparations for war were underway in the summer of 1914, control of the situation slipped out of the hands of the diplomats and their political superiors and into the grasp of the generals. The generals had planned for a European war. Once set in motion, their plans began to dictate events.

In the decades before 1914 military planning was dominated by a new reality, the railroad. The criss-crossing of the European continent with train tracks gave military planners a new and powerful weapon: the ability to move large numbers of men quickly to precise locations. The speed with which nations could now throw armies into battle almost obliterated the distinction between mobilization and actual war. *Mobilization* refers to the transformation of a standing army into a fighting force—calling up reserves, requisitioning supplies, enlisting volunteers or draftees, moving troops to battle stations. Traditionally, mobilization meant preparation for a possible fight, a process that took months and could be halted if the diplomats succeeded in avoiding war. But the railroads accelerated the mobilization process and thereby changed the very nature of military plans. Aware that the enemy could also mobilize quickly, military planners stressed the importance of preventive attacks, of striking before being struck. Once a nation mobilized, the momentum toward war became almost irresistible.

These factors help explain the origins and impact of the Schlieffen Plan°, the military blueprint that structured German actions—and Allied reactions—in the summer of 1914. The Franco-Russian Alliance, signed in 1894, meant that German military planners had to prepare for the possibility of a two-front war. They devised the Schlieffen Plan for just that eventuality. The plan called for a quick knockout blow against France, which would then allow the German army to concentrate on defeating the much larger force of Russia. The key assumption here was that Russia's mobilization would take time: The vastness of its territory and its underdeveloped industrial infrastructure would slow its military mobilization and so guarantee that Russian troops would not pose an immediate threat to German borders. According to the Schlieffen Plan, the smaller Austrian army would hold off the slowly mobilizing Russians while the German army moved with lightning speed against France (see Map 24.2).

The need for speed dictated the next step in the plan—an attack against France via Belgium. German planners knew that the French expected any German attack to come from the northeast, through Alsace and Lorraine (the provinces taken from France by the victorious Germans after the Franco-Prussian War in 1870). The Schlieffen Plan called for the bulk of the German army to avoid France's heavily fortified northeastern border and instead swing to the west. Moving rapidly in a wide arc, the German army would flood into France through Belgium, encircle Paris, and scoop up the French forces before their generals knew

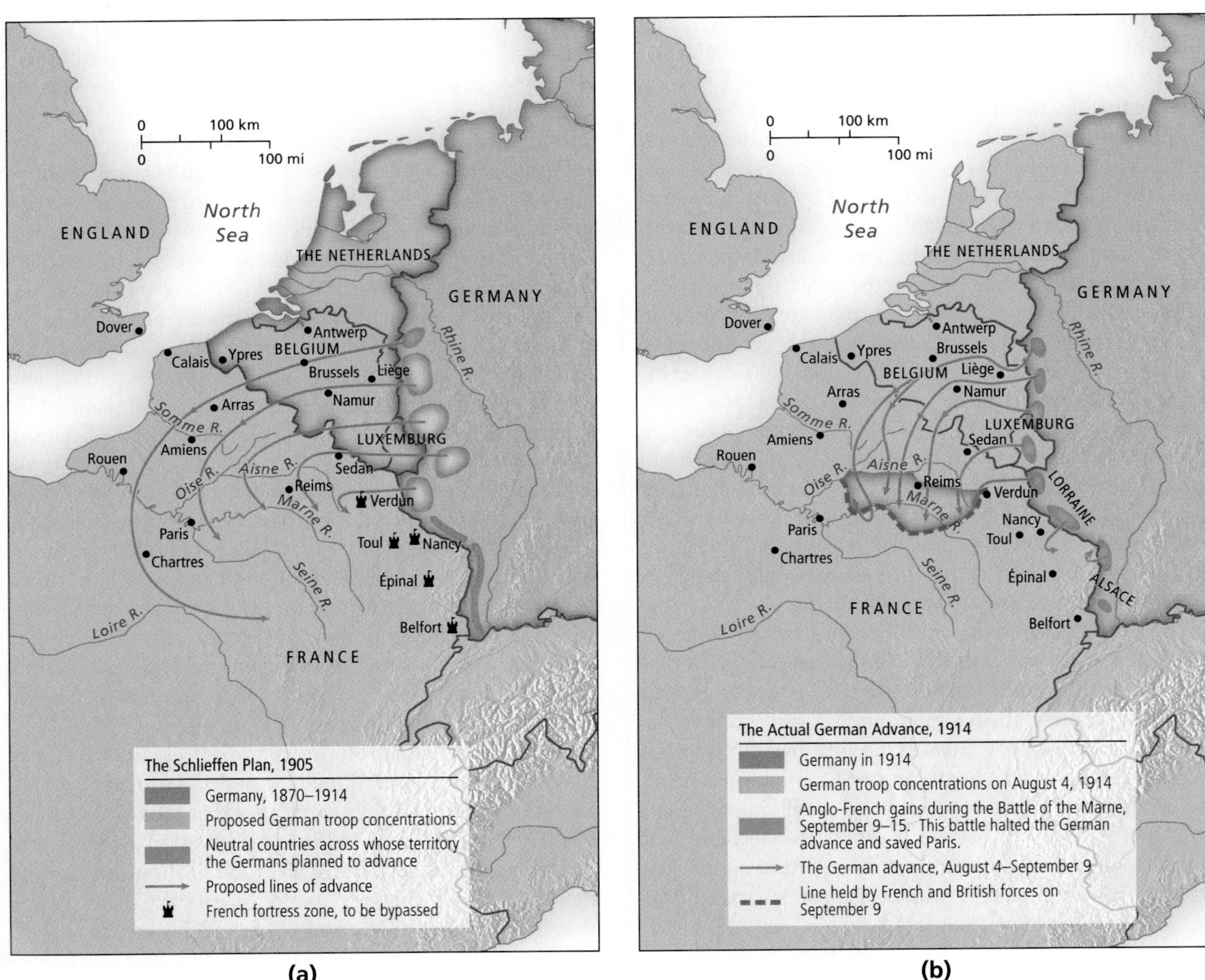

Map 24.2 The Schlieffen Plan, 1905 (a) and The Actual German Advance, 1914 (b)

Count Alfred von Schlieffen's original plan of 1905 called for the sleeves of the German soldiers on the right flank to brush the English Channel—in a daring move, the German army would sweep in a huge arching movement west. In the fall of 1914 Helmut von Moltke modified Schlieffen's plan: The crucial right flank was only three times as strong as the left, rather than eight times as strong as Schlieffen stipulated, and Moltke moved his troops north and east of Paris instead of south and west. Military historians today still argue over whether Schlieffen's original plan could have succeeded.

what had hit them. With France out of the fight, the German troops would then board trains and speed back to the Eastern Front to join their Austrian allies in defeating the Russians.

The need for speed—the key factor in the Schlieffen Plan—placed enormous pressure on German politicians to treat a Russian declaration of mobilization as a declaration of war itself. And that is what happened. Only two days elapsed between Russia's order of mobilization and the German declaration of war. As soon as Russia began to mobilize, German military leaders pressured their political counterparts to break off diplomatic negotiations so that the troop-laden trains could set off.

Moreover, the plan for a speedy thrust into France meant that Germany went ahead with its invasion of Belgium—a decision that brought Britain into the war. Belgium was a neutral nation, with its neutrality protected by Britain under a long-standing treaty. German policymakers gambled that Britain would stay out of the conflict, but their gamble failed. Germany's unprovoked and brutal invasion of Belgium provided the British government with the public-pleasing moral justification it needed to enter the war with mass support. Thus, just six weeks after a Bosnian terrorist shot an Austrian archduke in Sarajevo, British and German soldiers were killing each other in the mud of northern France.

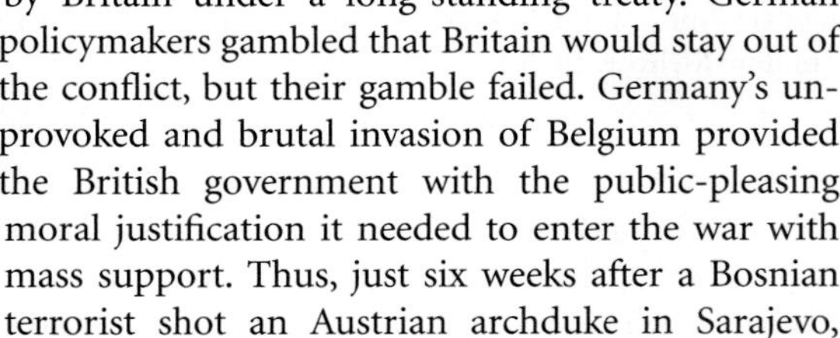

Bravo, Belgium-British Cartoon, WWI

CHRONOLOGY

The Outbreak of the First World War, 1914

June 28	Assassination of Archduke Franz Ferdinand
July 28	Austrian-Hungarian declaration of war against Serbia
July 30	Russian mobilization
July 31	French, Austrian, and German mobilization
August 1	German declaration of war on Russia
August 3	German declaration of war on France
August 4	German invasion of Belgium; British declaration of war against Germany

The Will to War

The events that pushed those soldiers into that mud were dictated not by diplomatic maneuvers but by the needs of an industrialized military. Unable to rein in the new forces of industrial warfare, diplomats also faced new pressures from public opinion. This public pressure, or the "will to war," constitutes the fourth factor that helps explain the outbreak of World War I in 1914.

Still drawn largely from the aristocracy, diplomats moved from elaborate hall to exclusive dinner, secure in their belief that with their secret agreements and coded dispatches they could manipulate international affairs. Mired in traditional protocol, they also remained enmeshed in traditional assumptions. Prominent among these assumptions was the notion of balancing power among the principal European states. But they sought to maintain a balance of power in a world increasingly unbalanced by the forces of nationalism, mass politics, and industrial change. To these men, the traditions of secret diplomacy made perfect sense. They believed that only a small elite possessed the education, temperament, and background to understand and control international affairs. Increasingly, however, foreign affairs interested and excited the mass public, whose assumptions about the course of international events clashed strongly with those of the career diplomats.

A number of developments accounted for this mass interest in foreign affairs. First, new technologies such as the telegraph, telephone, and camera collapsed distances and made international news much more immediate and accessible. Second, the rise of the popular press—cheap newspapers marketed to a semiliterate public—changed the coverage of foreign affairs. The competition to attract readers increased the pressure on editors and reporters to simplify and color their coverage, to make the often dull, dense, gray complexities of foreign relations into a compelling drama of Good Guys versus Bad Guys. Finally, the emergence of mass nationalism played an important role in shaping public opinion. Well-schooled in national identity, the European masses by 1914 viewed international relations as a vast nationalistic competition. They wanted evidence that "we" were ahead of "them."

Public opinion, therefore, constituted a new ingredient in international affairs in the years before the outbreak of World War I. Public opinion also constituted a real although impossible-to-measure factor in the war's outbreak. In the last weeks of July, pro-war crowds gathered in large cities. In Berlin, for example, a crowd of 30,000 young men and women paraded through the streets on the evening of July 25, singing patriotic songs and massing around statues of German heroes. Not all Europeans greeted the prospect of war with enthusiasm. Middle-class men and women, particularly students, predominated in the cheering crowds. In the countryside, farmers and villagers were more fearful, while in working-class neighborhoods anti-war demonstrations received solid support in July. The declaration of war, however, silenced these demonstrations. Opposition to the war was very much a minority movement after August 1914, even among working-class socialists. The German Social Democratic Party (SPD), for example, sponsored anti-war parades in July, but when war was declared in August, voted overwhelmingly to approve war appropriations. Socialist parties throughout Europe did likewise; national loyalties proved far stronger than class solidarity. In Britain, a total of 2.5 million men

DOCUMENT

War As a Unifying Force

Many Europeans welcomed the outbreak of war because it offered a chance to step aside from peacetime quarrels and factions. This excerpt from The Diary of a French Army Chaplain, *first published in 1915, illustrates the way political party competition was forgotten as French society mobilized for war. The author, Felix Klein, contrasts the prewar political infighting of the French legislature with the spirit of unity expressed in the declaration of war on August 4, 1914.*

Where, but a few weeks ago, could be found a more grievous spectacle than the first sittings of the new Chamber? And where, even in turning over the annals of many Parliaments, could be found a more admirable scene than that it offered on the 4th August. . . . And in this hot-bed of dissensions, quarrels, selfish desires, boundless ambitions, what trace remained of groups, of rivalries, of hates? Unanimous the respect with which the Presidential message was received; unanimous the adhesion to the Chief of the Government and his noble declaration: "It is the liberties of Europe that are being attacked of which France and her allies and friends are proud to be the defenders. . . . " And without debate, with no dissentient voice, all the laws of national defense, with the heavy sacrifices they imply, are at once voted. . . .

The fact is that we know ourselves no longer; barriers are falling on every side which, both in public and private life, divided us into hostile clans. . . . The relations between citizens are transformed. In the squares, in the streets, in the trains, outside the stations, on the thresholds of houses, each accosts the other, talks, gives news, exchanges impressions; each feels the same anxiety, the same hopes, the same wish to be useful, the same acceptance of the hardest sacrifices.

Source: From *Diary of a French Army Chaplain* by Felix Klein. London: Melrose, 1915.

volunteered to fight in the war, with 300,000 enlisting in the first month.

What made the idea of war so appealing to so many men and women in 1914? For some Europeans, war constituted a purging force, a powerful cleanser that would scour the impurities and corruptions from European society. As Chapter 23 explained, the years before 1914 witnessed a widespread cultural crisis in Europe, marked by fears of racial degeneration and gender confusion. War seemed to provide an opportunity for men to reassert their virility and their superiority. It also offered them the chance to be part of something bigger than themselves—to move beyond the boundaries of their often-restricted lives and join in what was presented as a great national crusade. As Carl Zuckmayer, a German playwright and novelist and a volunteer in the conflict, explained later, men like him welcomed the war as bringing "liberation . . . from . . . the saturation, the stuffy air, the petrifaction of our world."[4]

For political leaders, war provided the opportunity to mask social conflicts, to displace domestic hostilities onto the battlefield. We saw in Chapter 22 that the decades before 1914 were characterized by the rise of aggressive and often violent trade union movements and the increasing strength of socialist political parties, as well as anarchist-inspired

The Will to War

In western Europe, much of the public welcomed the news that war had begun. Here the crowds cheer as a French regiment embarks for the front. Enthusiasm for the war was less marked in working-class and peasant communities than in middle-class areas.

assassinations, ethnic terrorism, and feminist protests. To many European elites, their society seemed on the verge of disintegration. But, as the future British prime minister Winston Churchill explained, war united societies with "a higher principle of hatred."

The war for which university students cheered and for which the politicians and generals had planned was not anything like the war that actually happened, however. Most anticipated a short war. Theorists argued that in the new industrial age, the cost of waging war was so high that no nation would be able to sustain a conflict for very long. Everything depended on throwing as many men and as much materiel as possible into the battlefield at the very beginning. The men who marched off in August 1914 expected that they would be home by Christmas. Instead, if they survived, which few of them did, they would spend not only that Christmas, but the next three, in the midst of unspeakable and unprecedented horror.

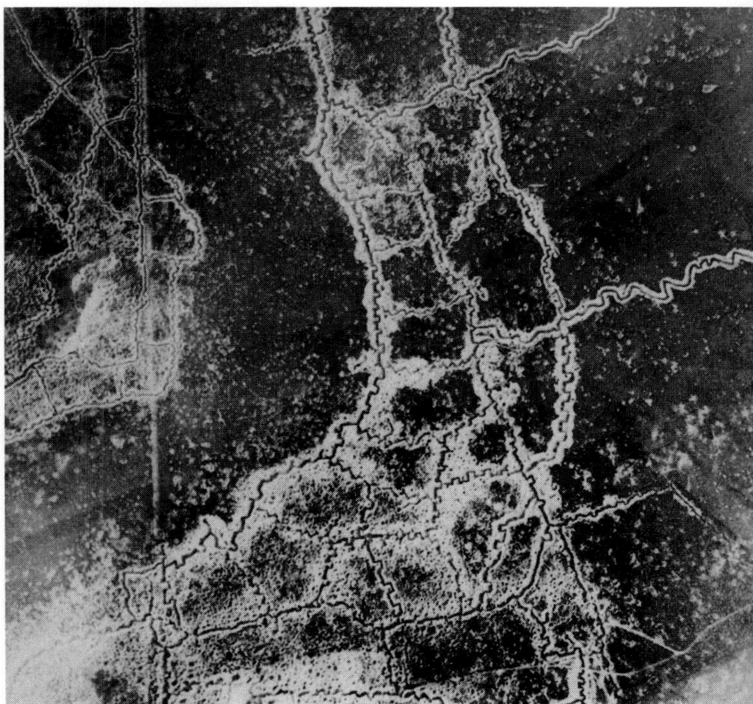

The Trench System

In this British reconnaissance photo, we can see the three lines of German trenches on the right, no-man's-land in the center, and the British trenches partly visible on the left. A trench system consisted of three parallel lines: the front or fire trenches, the support trenches, and the reserve trenches, all connected by intersecting communications trenches. If the enemy succeeded in gaining the front trenches, the defending forces could withdraw to the support or even the reserve trenches and still hold the line.

The Experience of Total War

- **When, where, and how did the Allies defeat the Central Powers?**

Expecting a German attack through Alsace and Lorraine, French military commanders in August 1914 poured their troops into these provinces. Counting on élan, the French military spirit, to see them to victory, the French troops swung into battle sporting bright red pants and flashy blue tunics. At their head rode the cream of the French military education system, the graduates of the elite Saint-Cyr military academy, who charged forward wearing their parade dress of white gloves and plumed hats. All that color and dash made easy targets for the German machine guns. As one military historian has written, "Never have machine-gunners had such a heyday. The French stubble-fields became transformed into gay carpets of red and blue."[5] Those "gay carpets," colored with the blood and broken bodies of young French men, signaled that this would be a war that shattered expectations, a war of revolutionary possibilities and devastating slaughter.

The Western Front: Stalemate in the Trenches

Implementing a modified version of the Schlieffen Plan (see Map 24.2), the German troops swept into Belgium in August 1914. By the first week of September the German troops had swung into France and seemed poised to take Paris. The Germans had overstretched their supply lines, however, and French and British forces turned back the German offensive at the Marne River. In an episode that provided a glimpse of how important the internal combustion engine—and the oil that fueled it—was to become to modern warfare, an ingenious French commander was able to exploit a gap in the German lines by moving troops rapidly from the city of Paris to the front in the only vehicles available: taxicabs. (The army paid the drivers full fare for the trip.)

The taxicabs had saved Paris, but the French and British forces were unable to push the German army out of France. By the middle of October, the German, British, and French forces were huddling in trenches that eventually extended more than 300 miles from the Belgian coast to the borders of Switzerland. There they stayed for the next four years.

The Troglodyte War

Literary scholar Paul Fussell has used the phrase "the troglodyte war" to sum up what the soldiers experienced on the Western Front.[6] Like prehistoric cavemen, the men on both sides of the conflict found themselves confined to underground dwellings. As British poet and World War I veteran Siegfried Sassoon explained, "when all is said and done, this war was a matter of holes and ditches."[7]

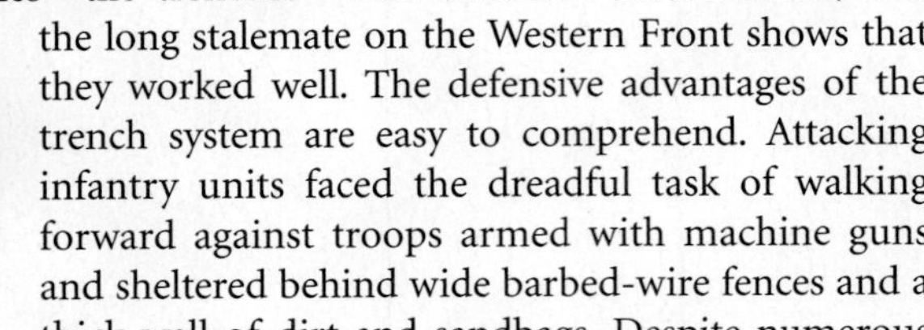

A Typical British Trench System

From the strategic point of view, these holes and ditches—the trenches—were defensive fortifications, and the long stalemate on the Western Front shows that they worked well. The defensive advantages of the trench system are easy to comprehend. Attacking infantry units faced the dreadful task of walking forward against troops armed with machine guns and sheltered behind wide barbed-wire fences and a thick wall of dirt and sandbags. Despite numerous attempts between the fall of 1914 and the spring of 1918, neither side was able to break through the enemy line.

A discussion of trench strategy, however, conveys nothing of the appalling misery summed up by the term "trench warfare." Imagine standing in a ditch that is about seven or eight feet deep and about three or four feet wide. The walls of the ditches are packed mud, propped up with sandbags. Wooden boards cover the floor, but the mud squelches between them. The top side of the ditch facing the enemy is reinforced with piled sandbags and barbed-wire barricades, thus deepening your sense of being underground. Moreover, the trenches do not run in tidy straight lines. Instead, the trenches zigzag at sharp angles, restricting the range of fire for enemy snipers and limiting the impact of explosives, but also ensuring that everywhere you look you see a wall of mud. Because you are in northern France, it is probably raining. Thus you are standing not on but *in* mud—if you are lucky. In some parts of the line, soldiers stand in muddy water up to a foot deep. On the other side of your sandbag defenses stretches no-man's-land°, the territory dividing the British and French trench systems from the German. Pocked with deep craters from heavy shelling, often a sea of mud churned up by the artillery, no-man's-land is littered with stinking corpses in various states of decomposition—all that is left of the soldiers who died during previous attacks. Your constant companions are lice (the term *lousy* was coined on the Western Front) and rats. For the rats, the war is an endless feast as they grow enormously fat, nibbling their way through the piles of dead.

From 1915 on, the horror of the Western Front escalated with the introduction of a new killing tool—poison gas, first deployed against enemy troops by the Germans in the spring of 1915. The Allies condemned the use of poison gas as inhumane, but within a matter of months the British and French, too, were firing poison gas canisters across the lines. The consequences were appalling: blinded eyes, blistered skin, seared lungs, death by asphyxiation. Gas proved to be an unreliable weapon, however. With a sudden wind shift, artillery units found they had asphyxiated their own troops. By 1916, with the gas mask a standard part of every soldier's uniform, military companies resembled hordes of insects. And, like insects, they were easily squashed. In the summer of 1915 an average of 300 British men became casualties on the Western Front every day, not because they were wounded in an attack but because they were picked off by snipers, felled by an exploding shell, or wasted by disease brought on by living in the mud amid putrefying corpses.[8]

Life and Death in the Trenches
The dead, the dying, and the surviving jostle one another in a French trench.

The Offensives

The offensives, the attacks launched by both sides on the Western Front, sent the numbers of dead and wounded soaring. None of the elderly commanders—the Germans Helmut von Moltke and Erich von Falkenhayn, the French Joseph Joffre and Ferdinand Foch, and the British Douglas Haig and John French—knew what to make of trench warfare. Schooled to believe that war is about attacking, they sought vainly to move this conflict out of the ditches by throwing vast masses of both artillery and men against the enemy lines. But time and time again these mass attacks were foiled by the machine gun.

DOCUMENT

Expectations vs. Reality

Written by two young upper-middle-class British writers, the following poems illustrate the shift from the initial enthusiasm for the war to later disillusionment and despair. In the first poem, written just as the war began, Rupert Brooke welcomes the war as an ennobling and purifying force that will bring genuine peace. In contrast, Wilfred Owen's later piece flatly describes a soldier asphyxiated by poison gas. Brooke died of blood-poisoning on his way to Gallipoli in 1915; Owen was killed in battle in 1918, just days before the war ended.

1914. *Peace* by Rupert Brooke

Now, God be thanked Who has matched us with His hour,
And caught our youth, and wakened us from sleeping,
With hand made sure, clear eye, and sharpened power,
To turn, as swimmers into cleanness leaping,
Glad from a world grown old and cold and weary
Leave the sick hearts that honor could not move,
And half-men, and their dirty songs and dreary,
And all the little emptiness of love.

Dulce et Decorum Est by Wilfred Owen

Bent double, like old beggars under sacks,
Knock-kneed, coughing like hags,
we cursed through sludge,
Till on the haunting flares we turned our backs
And towards our distant rest began to trudge.
Men marched asleep. Many had lost their boots
But limped on, blood-shod. All went lame; all blind;
Drunk with fatigue; deaf even to the hoots
Of tired, outstripped Five-Nines that dropped behind.
Gas! Gas! Quick, boys!—An ecstasy of fumbling,
Fitting the clumsy helmets just in time;
But someone still was yelling out and stumbling
And flound'ring like a man in fire or lime . . .
Dim, through the misty panes and thick green light,
As under a green sea, I saw him drowning.
In all my dreams, before my helpless sight,
He plunges at me, guttering, choking, drowning.
If in some smothering dreams you too could pace
Behind the wagon that we flung him in,
And watch the white eyes writhing in his face,
His hanging face, like a devil's sick of sin;
If you could hear, at every jolt, the blood
Come gargling from the froth-corrupted lungs,
Obscene as cancer, bitter as the cud
Of vile, incurable sores on innocent tongues,—
My friend, you would not tell with such high zest
To children ardent for some desperate glory,
The old Lie: "Dulce et decorum est
Pro patria mori."*

*"*It is good and right to die for one's country.*"

Sources: From "Peace" from *"1914" Five Sonnets* by Rupert Brooke. London: Sidgwick & Jackson, 1915; "Dulce et Decorum Est" from *Poems* by Wilfred Owen, with an Introduction by Siegfried Sassoon. London: Chatto and Windus, 1920.

A New Kind of War
From 1915 on, nerve gas became a part of the soldier's experience. Here tradition meets modernity as horses as well as soldiers are equipped with gas masks.

The Battle of the Somme, described in the opening of this chapter, provides a classic illustration of a failed offensive. The Somme, however, was only one of a number of fruitless attacks launched by both sides on the Western Front. By the end of 1917, the death tolls on the Western Front were astonishing, yet neither side had gained much ground. Soldiers, who enlisted not for a specific term or tour of duty but "for the duration"—until the war ended—became convinced that only the dead escaped from the trenches.

A Modernist War

To the artists and intellectuals who took up arms and found themselves in the trenches, the war often seemed like a modernist painting that had escaped its frame. The characteristics of modernist art—fragmentation, an emphasis on the isolation and the incommunicability of each individual's perception, surprising juxtaposition—also described the soldier's experience on the Western Front. Confined on all sides by mud walls, he glimpses only a bit of sky. When sent "over the top" in an attack, he knows only his own little part; he is unable to see the battlefield, or comprehend the battle plan, in its entirety. In letters home he finds he cannot communicate to his parents or to his lover the reality in which he is living and expects to die. Yet the front is often close enough to home to receive food packages sent just a few days earlier, so that he might find himself sitting in the mud, a few yards from the skeletal remains of other soldiers, eating a piece of his mother's best lemon tart.

Like modernist artists, soldiers quickly learned to question accepted truths, to mistrust the past, and to doubt the power of human reason. Recruited with promises of glory, they watched rats eat the bodies of their friends. While the generals clung to their history books, which taught that offensives won wars, soldiers died in great numbers. Not surprisingly, the modernist rejection of history resonated in the trenches. The past seemed to offer little of value in this new kind of war. Similarly, the war revealed the absurdity of the nineteenth-century faith in rationality. As the weeks, months, and years wore on, and the death tolls climbed higher and higher, many soldiers were struck by the senselessness, the sheer irrationality, of the conflict. The war often seemed to be governed not by reasoning men but rather by unthinking machines.

The mechanical nature of this war became a dominant theme in soldiers' accounts, just as machines dominated prewar modernist art. Seeking the chance to be heroes, men volunteered to fight and found themselves reduced to interchangeable parts in a colossal war machine. Like mechanical gears, army companies moved in circles: from the firing trenches to the reserve trenches to the support trenches to behind the lines and back to the firing trenches. Thus in works such as *Returning to the Trenches,* British artist Christopher Nevinson (1889–1946) used modernist techniques to represent the reality of mechanized war. In Nevinson's work, the men cease to be individuals. Welded into a single machine, they are propelled into the trenches by a force beyond their control, components of a purely mechanized landscape. French war veteran and writer Georges Duhamel (1884–1966) even likened the front-line ambulances to factory repair shops. The function of the ambulances was to repair the broken-down parts (the soldiers) of the war machine and get them back into production.

We saw in Chapter 23 that in the decades before 1914 members of the press and the general public often condemned modernist styles and idioms as outrageous,

***Returning to the Trenches* by Christopher Nevinson (1914–1915)**

Nevinson's work demonstrates the close parallels between wartime reality and modernist representation.

***We Are Making a New World* by Paul Nash (1918)** Nash's title drips in irony. His paintings are often considered among the finest produced during the war.

degenerate, and removed from reality. By 1918, however, as Nevinson's painting shows, these forms seemed to offer an accurate, even realistic means of conveying the horror of the war experience. Thus the British cultural historian Samuel Hynes has argued, "modernism had not changed, but reality had."[9]

Yet the realities of this war did change modernism. Horrified by the mass slaughter, many modernist artists abandoned the modernist principle of "art for art's sake," the idea that art has no moral purpose or social responsibility, that it conveys no message. Instead, they used modernist techniques to communicate their outrage. Paul Nash (1889–1940), a British landscape painter and army volunteer, explained in 1918, "I am no longer an artist, interested and curious, I am a messenger who will bring back word from the men who are fighting to those who want the war to go on forever. . . . may it burn their lousy souls."[10] Nash's depiction of the Western Front, *We Are Making a New World* (1918), transformed the landscape genre from an evocation of pastoral tranquility into a cry of pain.

The War in Eastern Europe

The Western Front was only one in a number of theaters of war. Floundering in the snows of the Italian Alps, the Italian and Austrian armies fought each other along a stationary front for two brutal years after Italy, enticed by the promise of territorial gain, joined the war on the Allies' side. Characterized by futile offensives and essential immobility, the war in Italy mirrored the conflict on the Western Front. In eastern Europe, however, a different plot unfolded. For three years, massive armies surged back and forth, as the plains and mountains of eastern Europe echoed with the tumult of spectacular advances, headlong retreats, and finally political revolution.

The Eastern Front: A War of Movement

Much of the movement in eastern Europe consisted of Russians running—running forward in surprising advances, running back in terrifying retreats. When the war began in August 1914, Russia shocked its enemies by fielding a much stronger army much more quickly than German and Austrian military planners had expected. In a two-pronged onslaught, Russian troops headed against the Germans in East Prussia and against the Austrians in Galicia, the northeastern region of the Austrian Empire. Surprised by the speed of the Russian advance, German troops in East Prussia at first fell back, but skillful maneuvering by the German commanders Paul von Hindenburg (1847–1934) and Erich von Ludendorff (1865–1937) turned the Russian tide at the Battle of Tannenberg at the end of August. Within two weeks the Germans had shoved the Russian troops back across the border. In the subsequent months, the Germans advanced steadily into Russian imperial territory. At the same time, a combined German and Austrian assault forced the Russian army to retreat from Austrian Galicia—and more than 300 miles into its own territory. Russian casualties in the offensive stood at 2.5 million.

Over the next two years the pattern of Russian advances and retreats continued. Russian soldiers pushed into Austria-Hungary in June 1916, but could not sustain the attack. The summer of 1917 saw another initially successful Russian advance, but it too soon disintegrated into a retreat (see Map 24.3).

These retreats revealed that Russia's economic and political structures could not withstand the pressures of total war. Russian supply lines were so overextended that the poorly fed and inadequately clothed Russian troops found themselves without ammunition and unable to press ahead. Demoralized by defeat and by the daily grind of life without adequate rations or uniforms or weapons, Russian soldiers began to desert in ever-larger numbers. On the home front Russian workers and peasants grew ever more impatient with wartime deprivations and demands. This disaffection led to revolution. As we will explore in detail later in this chapter, revolution forced the tsar to abdicate in March 1917. In November, the Bolsheviks, a small group of socialist revolutionaries, seized control and moved quickly to pull Russia out of the war.

The Bolshevik military withdrawal finally freed Germany from the burden of waging a two-front war. Signed in March 1918, the Treaty of Brest-Litovsk° ceded to Germany all of Russia's western territories, containing a full one-third of the population of the prewar Russian Empire. Germany now controlled the imperial Russian territories in Poland, the Baltic states, and part of Byelorussia. But because it had to commit large numbers of troops to controlling this new territory, Germany reaped less advantage from this victory than might have been expected.

Map 24.3 The Eastern and Middle Eastern Fronts, 1915–1918
Unlike the Western Front, the Eastern Front was far from stationary. By 1918, the Central Powers occupied Serbia, Romania, and much of European Russia. The entry of the Ottoman Empire on the side of the Central Powers in November 1914 extended the conflict into the Middle East. In 1915 Ottoman forces not only repelled an initial British advance toward Baghdad but also threatened Egypt. By the end of 1917, however, Arab nationalists helped the British defeat the Central Powers in the Middle East.

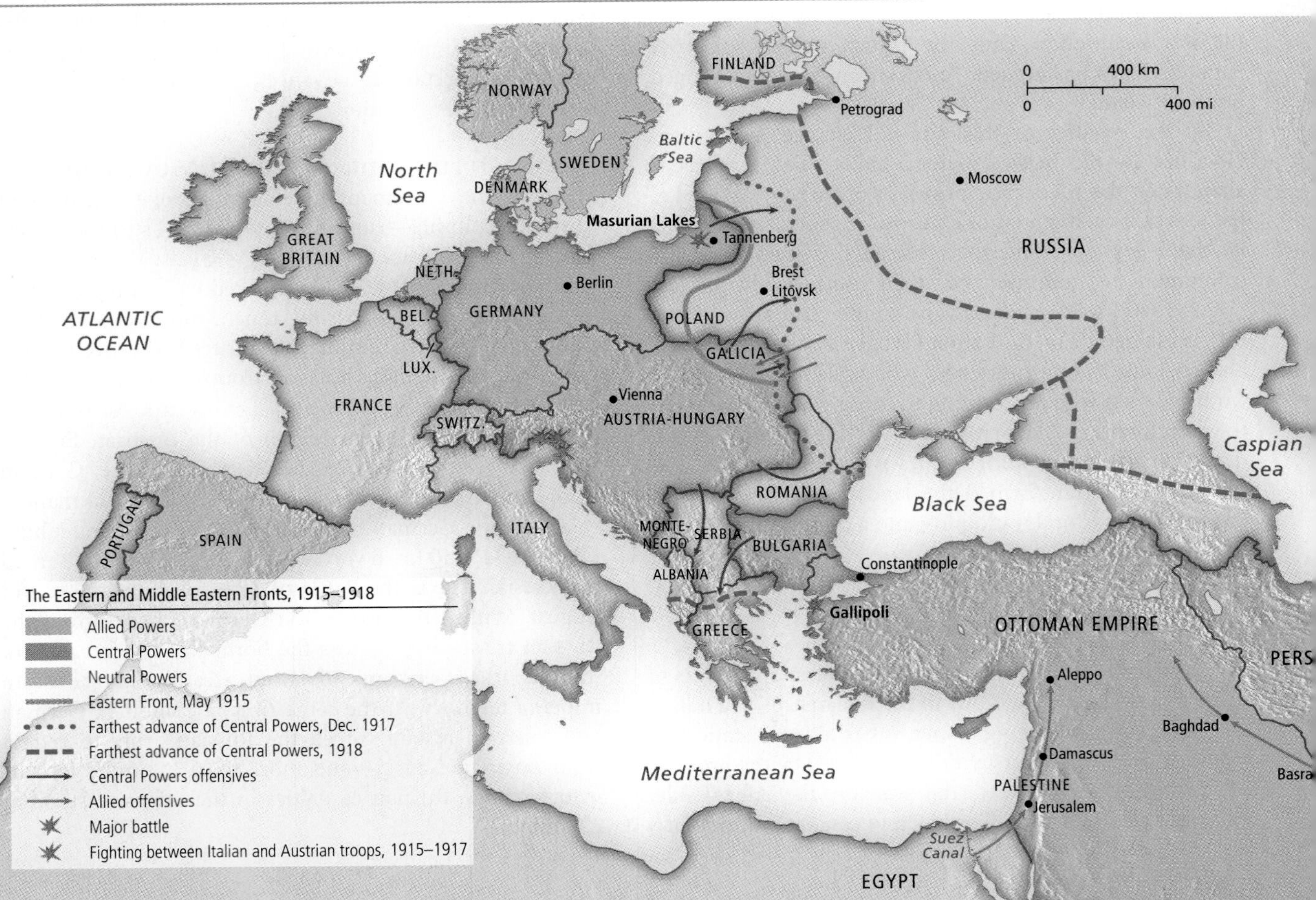

The Forgotten Front: The Balkans

The new Balkan states were no strangers to war by 1914. After shrugging off Ottoman control, Greece, Bulgaria, Romania, and Serbia fought each other in the First and Second Balkan Wars of 1912 and 1913. In southeastern Europe, World War I was thus in many ways the "Third Balkan War," yet another installment in an ongoing competition for territory and power. Bulgaria joined the Central Powers in 1915, hoping to gain back the territory it had lost in the Second Balkan War. To protect its hold on this territory, Romania entered the war on the Allies' side in August 1916 and quickly found itself crushed between invading Bulgarian, German, and Austrian-Hungarian troops.

The Serbian experience was even more bleak. In the first year of the war Austrian and Serbian troops jostled back and forth for control of the country, but in October 1915 Bulgarian, German, and Austrian forces advanced into Serbia from three different directions. By November, the Serbian army had been pushed to the Albanian border. Two hundred thousand Serbian soldiers fled over the snow-swept mountains of Albania to the Adriatic Sea, in a disastrous "Winter March." Austrian troops occupied Serbia and placed the country under military rule. Like most military occupations, this one was brutal. By the war's end, approximately 25 percent of Serbian citizens lay dead.

The Winter March

Of the 200,000 Serbian soldiers who attempted the "Winter March" in 1915, at least 40,000 died and another 60,000 were wounded.

The World at War

The imperialist expansion of the later nineteenth century ensured that as soon as the war began, it jumped outside European borders. The British and French Empires supplied the Allies with invaluable military and manpower resources. Australia, New Zealand, Canada, India, South Africa, and Ireland supplied no less than 40 percent of Britain's military manpower during the war. More than 650,000 men from Indochina, Algeria, and French West Africa assisted the French war effort. (One of these men was

A World at War: Sikh Cavalry Officers

Sikh cavalry officers from India patrol the Western Front. India provided 1.3 million men to assist the British war effort. Indian troops fought—and more than 49,000 Indian soldiers died—in battles in the Middle East, in East Africa, and on the Western Front. Similarly, black Senagalese soldiers fought for France on various fronts; 30,000 Senagalese died during the war.

Ho Chi Minh, who would later lead the Vietnamese struggle against France and then the United States.)

Fighting fronts multiplied around the globe as the major combatants struggled for imperial as well as European supremacy (see Map 24.4). Portugal joined the Allies largely because it hoped to expand its colonial possessions in Africa. Japan, too, entered the war for colonial gain. When the war began in August 1914, Japan seized the opportunity to snatch German colonial possessions in China. In return, Japan contributed to the Allied war effort by using its navy to protect Allied troop and supply ships in both the Pacific and the Mediterranean. By the end of 1914, most of Germany's colonies in the Far East had been occupied by Japanese and ANZAC troops.

The Middle East also became a key theater. When the Ottoman Empire joined the war on the side of Germany and Austria-Hungary in 1914, it posed a serious threat to Britain's economic and military interests in the Mediterranean and Middle East. Britain was desperate to protect Allied access both to the Suez Canal—a vital link to the soldiers and supplies of India, Australia, and New Zealand—and to Persian oil fields, an important source of fuel for the British navy. In a move that would have far-reaching consequences for twentieth-century geopolitics, the British joined forces with Arab nationalists. Led by a British soldier named T. E. Lawrence (1888–1935)—better known as "Lawrence of Arabia"—and inspired by promises of postwar national independence, Arab nationalists used guerilla

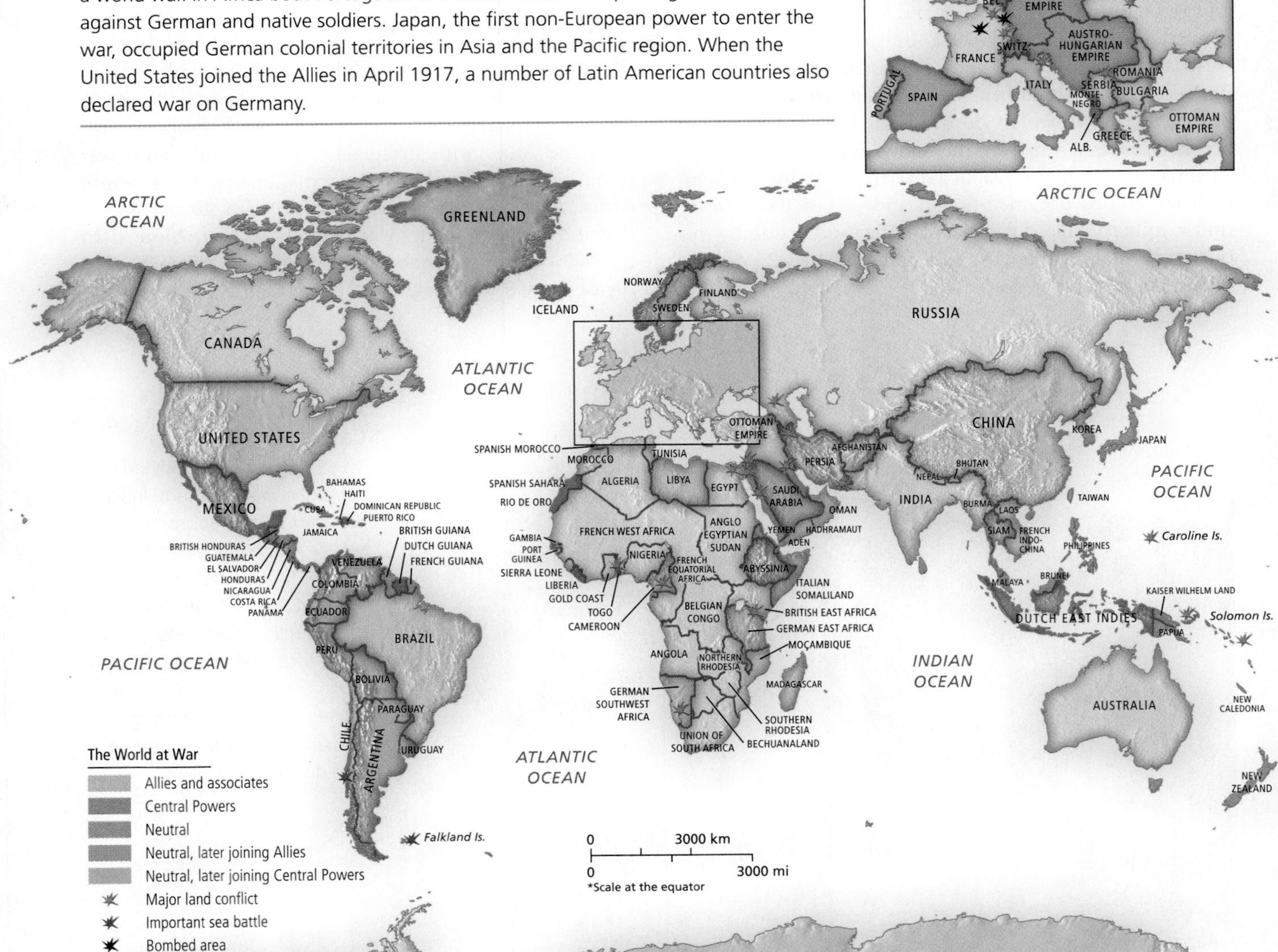

Map 24.4 The World at War

Imperialist relationships and global economics ensured that a European conflict became a world war. In Africa both Portuguese and South African troops fought a bush war against German and native soldiers. Japan, the first non-European power to enter the war, occupied German colonial territories in Asia and the Pacific region. When the United States joined the Allies in April 1917, a number of Latin American countries also declared war on Germany.

warfare to destroy what remained of Ottoman rule in the Middle East. By 1917 the Ottomans had lost control of almost the entire coastal region of the Arabian peninsula bordering the Red Sea, and Lawrence and his Arab allies had captured Jerusalem.

CHRONOLOGY

The End of the War, 1917–1918

1917	Stalemate continues on the Western Front
March	Collapse of the Russian imperial government
April	U.S. declaration of war on Germany
November	Bolshevik Revolution in Russia
December	Bolsheviks sign armistice with Germany; capture of Jerusalem by British troops
1918	
March	Treaty of Brest-Litovsk
March–July	German offensive on Western Front, rapid gains
July–November	Allied counteroffensive begins
September	Bulgaria and Allies sign armistice
November 3	Austria-Hungary sues for peace with Allies
November 9	Kaiser William abdicates
November 11	Fighting ends on Western Front at 11:00 A.M.

The War at Sea and the Entry of the United States

Despite the losses of its ally in the Middle East, at the beginning of 1918 Germany looked to be in a winning position. Engulfed in revolution, Russia had dropped out of the war and relieved Germany of the burden of fighting on two fronts. With Serbia and Romania both occupied by their forces, the Central Powers could claim to have won the war in eastern Europe. Yet Germany was far weaker than any map of its eastern conquests in 1917 could indicate. Germany was being strangled from the sea.

While infantrymen rotted in trenches and froze in mountain passes, the German and British navies fought a critical war at sea. German submarines sought to cut Britain's imperial lifeline and starve out its civilian population by sinking ships before they could reach British ports. Almost 14,000 British sailors and civilians died in these submarine attacks. In turn, British destroyers stretched a blockade across all ocean and sea passageways to Germany and its allies.

The Allied blockade proved effective in preventing food and other essential raw materials from reaching Germany, Austria-Hungary, and their associates. Food shortages sparked riots in more than thirty German cities in 1916. When the potato crop that year failed and eliminated one of the only sources of nutrition left, children's rations were limited to *one-tenth* of their actual needs.

Desperate to win the war quickly, German policymakers in 1917 took a huge gamble when they decided to up the tempo of their submarine war against Britain. Suspecting that supposedly neutral American passenger ships were delivering essential war materiel to Britain, they ordered their submarines to sink without warning any ship heading for British shores. The Germans were well aware that this policy of unrestricted submarine warfare would very likely pull the United States into the war. In May 1915, a German submarine had torpedoed the British passenger liner *Lusitania* and killed almost 1,200 people, including 128 Americans. The furious response from the United States had forced Germany to restrict its submarine attacks. By 1917, however, Germany stood on the brink of economic collapse, and German policymakers decided they had no choice but to resume unrestricted attacks on ships heading for British ports. They gambled they could defeat Britain in a last-ditch effort before the addition of the United States to the Allies could make much of a difference. Over the next eight months German submarines sank 500 British merchant ships.

The United States declared war on Germany in April 1917. Outrage over American deaths at sea served as the most immediate cause of American entry into the war. Four other factors, however, also played a role. First, Franco-British news stories about German atrocities during the invasion of Belgium had persuaded many Americans that right rested on the Allied side. Second, the Russian Revolution of March 1917 removed an important obstacle to American cooperation with the Allies—the tsarist regime. Americans had balked at the idea of allying with the repressive government of Tsar Nicholas II, but the March Revolution, which overthrew Nicholas, reminded many in the United States of the American Revolution and offered American policymakers a more ideologically acceptable wartime partner. Third, by the time President Woodrow Wilson asked the U.S. Congress for a declaration of war, the American economy was thoroughly intertwined with that of the Allies. Trade between the United States and the Allied nations had grown from $825 million in 1914 to more than $3 billion in 1916, and American bankers had loaned more than $2 billion to the Allied governments. Finally, the German government committed a serious blunder in the spring of 1917 when it offered to back Mexico in recovering New Mexico, Arizona, and Texas in exchange for Mexican support should war break out between Germany and the United States. The interception of a telegram sent by the German foreign minister Arthur Zimmermann exposed this offer and inflamed anti-German sentiment in the

United States. The German resumption of unrestricted submarine warfare, then, simply put flame to kindling that was already in place.

The U.S. declaration of war (followed by those of Brazil, Costa Rica, Cuba, Guatemala, Haiti, Honduras, Nicaragua, and Panama) provided an immediate psychological boost for the Allies, but several months passed before American troops arrived on the battlefield in significant numbers. By July 1918, however, the United States was sending 300,000 fresh soldiers to Europe each month. The Allies now had access to an almost unlimited supply of materiel and men. Eventually nearly two million American soldiers were sent to Europe and almost 49,000 American soldiers died in battle.

Back in Motion: The Western Front in 1918

Faced with the prospect of having to fight fresh American forces, German policymakers decided to gamble one more time. On March 2, 1918—before the bulk of the U.S. army had been deployed—the German army launched a massive ground assault against British and French lines. The gamble almost succeeded. In just thirty minutes the German troops broke through the British front line; in seven days, German soldiers advanced forty miles; by April the German army stood just fifty miles from Paris.

What explains this sudden shift on the Western Front from a conflict characterized by stalemate and deadlock to a war of rapid and decisive movement? The answer is that after three and a half years of relentless, pointless slaughter, the German High Command in 1918 finally developed strategies that matched offensive techniques with industrialized killing technology. As we have seen, in the first years of the war commanders remained committed to offensive techniques suited to an age of preindustrial warfare—the mass charge, the cavalry attack. What they failed to realize was that industrial technologies such as the machine gun had transformed the power of defensive war. Certainly Western commanders were well-acquainted with the power of the machine gun. In the imperial conflicts discussed in Chapter 23, the machine gun enabled small European forces to mow down enormous indigenous armies. But on the Western Front, both sides possessed the machine gun. In other words, both sides were good on defense but poor on offense.

In 1918, however, the Germans came up with a new offensive strategy. They did not simply throw masses of men against machine guns. Instead of a frontal assault dictated by commanders sitting well behind the lines, Germany's offensive of 1918 consisted of a series of small group attacks aiming to cut behind British and French positions rather than straight on against them. In addition, the Germans in 1918 scrapped the massive preliminary artillery barrage that signaled when and where an attack was about to begin. In place of the barrage they employed sudden gas and artillery bursts throughout the offensive. The rapid German advance in the spring of 1918 showed that technique had caught up with technology.

In July, however, the Allies stopped the German advance; in August they broke through the German lines and began to push the German army backward. Throughout the summer the push continued. By September the Western Front, which had stood so stationary for so long, was being rolled eastward at a rapid clip.

The final German gamble failed for three reasons: First, the German advance was so rapid that it overstrained German manpower and supply lines; second, the Allies learned from their enemies and adopted the same new offensive strategies; and third, the Allies figured out how to make effective use of a new offensive technology—the tank. Developed in Britain, the tank obliterated the defensive advantages of machine-gun-fortified trenches. A twentieth-century offense met a twentieth-century defense, and the war turned mobile.

1916 Debut of the British Tank

Reinforced with fresh American troops and the promise of more to come, the Allied forces surged forward against the hungry and demoralized Germans. When the Bulgarian, Ottoman, and Austrian armies collapsed in September and October, Germany stood alone. On November 11, 1918, German leaders signed an armistice and the war ended.

The Home Fronts

- **How did total war structure the home fronts?**

The term *home front* was coined during World War I to highlight the fact that this conflict was fought not only by soldiers on the front lines, but also by civilians at home. Created by industrialization, total war demanded the wholehearted mobilization of a combatant nation's productive capacity. Total war recast and in some cases revolutionized not only the economic but also the political, social, and gender relations of the nations involved.

Industrial War

World War I was the first industrial war. Poison gas, the machine gun, barbed wire, canned foods, mass-produced uniforms and boots, and of course shovels all poured out of Europe's factories and helped shape this war. Even more important, industrialization made it possible for governments to deploy the vast masses of men mobilized in this conflict. Consider this comparison: The Battle of Waterloo, which ended the Napoleonic Wars in 1815, involved 170,000 men; the Battle of Sedan, which ended the Franco-Prussian War in 1870, involved 300,000 soldiers. The first Battle of the Marne, however, fought between the Germans and the

French in September 1914, involved one million combatants. By the war's end, more than 70 million men had been mobilized; in France and Germany, approximately 80 percent of the men of draft age were called up. Only industrialized production could keep these huge armies supplied with weapons, ammunition, and other necessities.

It thus became clear that this war would be won in the factories as much as on the front lines. Those nations that collapsed did so at least in part because they lost the war at home. In Austria-Hungary, factories could not produce enough uniforms to clothe the empire's soldiers. Similarly, Russia's underdeveloped industrial sector and infrastructure meant that its soldiers failed to receive needed supplies. In the end, the Allies (minus Russia) won the war in large part because of their greater economic power.

The Expansion of the State

At first, no government realized the crucial role that industrial labor would play in this war. Both military and political leaders believed that the war would end quickly, and that success depended on throwing as many men as possible into the front lines. In France, even munitions factories were shut down and their workers sent to the front. Governments practiced "business as usual"—letting the free market decide wages, prices, and supply—with disastrous results. Soaring rates of inflation, the rapid expansion of the black market, growing public resentment over war profiteering (the practice of private businessmen making huge profits off the war), and, most crucially, shortages of essential military supplies, including shells, proved that a total war economy needed total regulation.

Beginning in 1915, both the Allied and Central Powers' governments gradually assumed the power to requisition supplies, dictate wages, limit profits, and forbid workers to change jobs. In Germany, the increasing regulation of the economy was called "war socialism," a misleading term because it was big business rather than ordinary workers who benefited. The German army worked in partnership with large industrial firms to ensure the supply of war materiel to the front lines, while the Auxiliary Service Law of 1916 drafted all men age 17 to 60 for war work. Measures such as these greatly expanded the size and power of the central governments in the combatant states. For example, in 1914 the British office in charge of military purchases employed twenty clerks. By 1918, it had become the Department of Munitions, an enormous bureaucratic empire with 65,000 employees overseeing more than three million men and women working in government-owned and -operated munitions plants.

This expansion of governmental power was one of the most striking aspects of the war experience on the home front. Even in Britain, bastion of liberalism, the demands of total war seriously restricted individual freedom. Flying in the face of tradition, in 1916 Britain's government imposed the draft—a clear example of the requirements of the state overriding the desires of the individual. By the war's end, governments had moved further, not only dictating all aspects of economic life but also controlling many areas of social and intellectual choice. The British government restricted the hours that pubs could be open, as a way of encouraging workers to show up for work sober. It also tampered with time itself, introducing Daylight Saving Time as a means of maximizing war production.

The Politics of Total War

The war's reliance on industrial production greatly empowered industrial producers—the workers. In 1915 both France and Britain abandoned political party competition and formed coalition governments, which included socialist and working-class representatives. At the same time, political leaders welcomed labor unionists as partners in shaping the wartime economy. In return, French and British union leaders agreed to a ban on labor strikes and the "deskilling" of certain jobs—a measure that allowed unskilled laborers, particularly women, to take the place of skilled workers at much lower rates of pay.

Despite these "no strike" agreements, both Britain and France witnessed a sharp rise in the number of labor strikes in 1916 and in 1917. Faced with the potential of disintegration on the home front, political leaders in Britain and France reacted similarly. Both countries witnessed the emergence of war governments committed to total victory. In Britain, David Lloyd George (1863–1945) became prime minister at the end of 1916. A Welsh artisan's son who had fought hard to reach the top of Britain's class-bound, English-dominated political system, Lloyd George was not a man to settle for a compromise peace. One year later, Georges Clemenceau (1841–1929) became prime minister of France. Nicknamed the "Tiger," Clemenceau demanded victory. When asked to detail his government's program, he replied simply, "*Je fais la guerre!*" ("I make war!").

Making war, however, was not possible without public support, as officials in both France and Britain realized. They cultivated this support in two ways. First, they sought to depict the war as a struggle between democracy and authoritarianism—a crusade not simply for national power or economic gain but for a better world. Second, they recognized that if civilian morale were to be sustained, the basic needs of ordinary citizens had to be met. Both governments intervened regularly in the economy to ensure that workers received higher wages, better working conditions, and a fair distribution of food stocks. In state-owned munitions factories, workers for the first time received benefits such as communal kitchens and day care. Food rationing (although not implemented until quite late in the war) actually improved the diets of many poor families.

The situation in Germany differed significantly. The parliamentary political voice of the German working class, the Social Democratic Party (SPD), was not invited to participate in a coalition government. Instead, until the very last weeks of the war German political leadership remained in the hands of the conservative aristocracy. Increasingly, the aristocratic generals Hindenburg and Ludendorff—the heroes of the Battle of Tannenberg—called the political shots. The army and big industrial firms seized control of German economic life. Given the power to set prices and profit margins, industrialists—not surprisingly—made a killing. Their incomes soared, while ordinary workers were ground down by escalating inflation and chronic food shortages. By 1917, industrial unrest had slowed German war production, and civilian discontent had reached dangerous levels. Unlike the British and the French, the German government proved unable to control the unrest. The success of the Allied blockade meant Germans were starving. In contrast, living standards among employed workers in France and in Britain rose during the war.

The World Turned Upside Down

By the war's end, changes in the relations among classes and between men and women caused many Europeans to feel as if their world had turned upside down. European workers grew more radical as they realized the possibilities of their own collective power, as well as the potential of the state as an instrument of social change. The fact that by 1917 many of these workers were women also had revolutionary implications. In the work world and in society at large, gender roles, like class relations, underwent a marked shift.

The War's Impact on Social Relations

In the trenches and on the battlefields, World War I had a leveling effect. For many young middle- and upper-class soldiers, the war provided their first sustained contact with both manual labor and manual laborers. In letters home, they testified to a newfound respect for both, as the horrors of the war experience broke down rigid class barriers.

On the home front, however, social relations grew more rather than less hostile. During the war years, inflation eroded the savings of the middle class and left bourgeois men and women desperately seeking ways to maintain their social and economic status. In Germany and throughout eastern Europe, drastic food shortages and falling real wages produced a revolutionary situation. By contrast, in both Britain and France, a rising standard of living demonstrated to workers the benefits of an active and interventionist state. Yet class hostilities rose in western Europe, too. Workers, having finally tasted the economic pie, fought for a bigger piece, while the middle class fought to defend its shrinking share. Working-class activists demanded that the state continue to regulate the economy in peacetime as it did in waging total war, to improve the standard of living of ordinary workers.

The War's Impact on Gender Relations

By 1916, labor shortages in key military industries, combined with the need to free up as many men as possible for fighting, meant that governments on both sides actively recruited women for the paid workforce. Women were suddenly everywhere in very visible roles: as bus drivers, eleva-

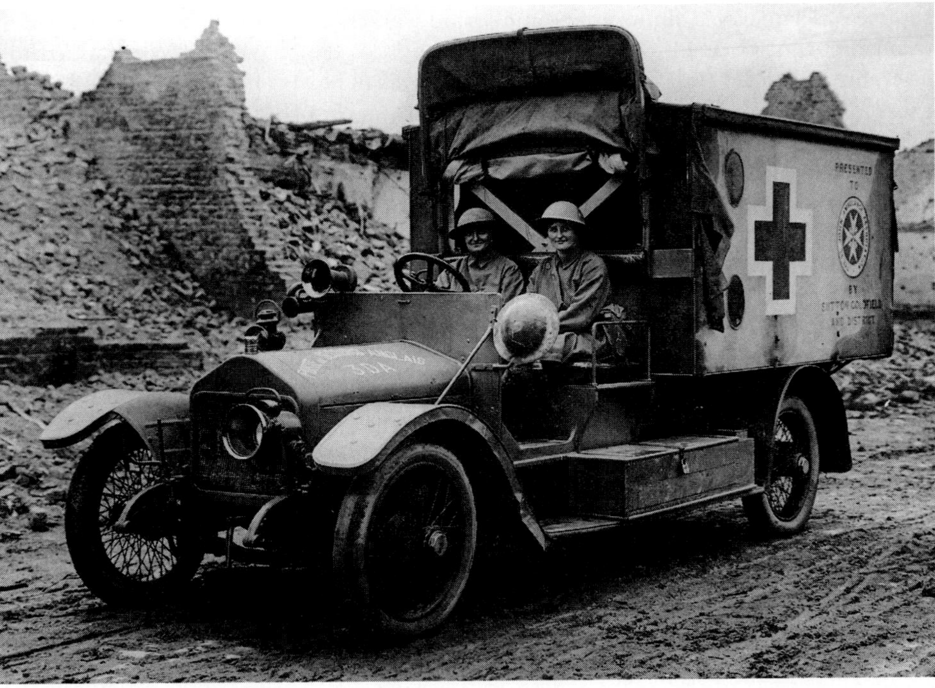

Women in the War
Women often served at the front in extremely dangerous conditions. The two women in this photograph set up a dressing station to treat the wounded just five yards behind the trenches.

tor operators, train conductors, and sales clerks. In eastern Europe, the agricultural labor force came to consist almost entirely of women. In western Europe, women joined labor unions in unprecedented numbers. They took on extremely dangerous positions in munitions factories; they worked just behind the front lines as ambulance drivers and nurses; in 1917 and 1918, they often led the way in walking off the job to demand better conditions.

The impact of the war on women's roles should not be exaggerated, however. Throughout the war, more women continued to work in domestic service—as cooks, maids, nannies—than in any other sector of the economy. The great majority of the women who did move into skilled industrial employment were not new to the world of paid employment. Before 1914 they had worked in different, lower-paying jobs. And they certainly were not treated as men's equals. In government-run factories in Britain, women received as little as 50 percent of men's wages for the same job.

Nevertheless, for many women, the war constituted a profoundly liberating experience. With their husbands away, many wives made decisions on their own for the first time. The average wages of female munitions workers in Britain were three times their prewar earnings. But just as crucially, the war validated women's claims to citizenship. Total war made the female civilian into a combatant. For example, the *Win the War Cookery Book* (1917) urged British housewives to view the preparation of meals in a time of food shortages as part of the war effort: "The British fighting line shifts and extends now *you* are in it. The struggle is not only on land and sea; it is in *your* larder, *your* kitchen and *your* dining room. Every meal you serve is now literally a battle."[11] With "women's work" as central to national survival as men's work, women came to see themselves as an integral part of the national community.

Middle-class women, especially, testified to the freedom the war brought. Before 1914, the position of middle-class women in Europe had undergone important changes, as Chapter 22 detailed. From 1870 on, the numbers of women in higher education and paid employment expanded, women increasingly served in local government, and a European-wide women's suffrage campaign emerged. Despite the rise of these strong challenges to the ideology of separate spheres, however, the predominant idea remained that women were biologically suited for the private confines of home and family and men for the public arena of work and politics. Many middle-class girls continued to live lives marked by immobility and passivity—sheltered within the family home, subject to paternal authority, waiting for a marriage proposal. The war, however, threw women into the public space. The middle-class girl who before 1914 was forbidden to travel without a chaperone might be driving an ambulance, splashing through the mud and blood, or washing the bodies of naked working-class soldiers.

At the same time that the war smashed many of the boundaries to which women had been confined, it sharply narrowed the world of the middle-class male soldier. While women were in charge and on the move—driving buses, flying transport planes, ferrying the wounded—men were stuck in the mud, confined to narrow ditches, waiting for orders. Expecting to be heroes, men of action, they found themselves instead living the sort of immobile, passive lives that had characterized the prewar middle-class women's experience. Ironically, then, at the same time the war gave women new power, it introduced many men, particularly middle-class men, to new levels of powerlessness. In total war, even gender roles turned upside down.

Yet when the war ended, some of these radical changes proved to be very temporary indeed. The much-heralded wartime movement of women into skilled factory jobs and public positions such as bus drivers and train conductors was rapidly reversed. For example, by the terms of the British Restoration of Pre-War Practices Act (1919), women who had taken up skilled factory jobs received two weeks' pay and a train ticket home.

Other changes appeared more permanent. France in 1919 possessed ten times as many female law students and three times as many female medical students as it had in 1914. British women over age 30 received the vote on a limited basis while in the United States, Germany, and most of the new states in eastern Europe, the achievement of female suffrage was more complete. (Women in France, Italy, Switzerland, and Greece remained unenfranchised.) Cultural changes also seemed to signal a gender revolution. Women began to smoke in public; trousers became acceptable female attire; hemlines rose dramatically; the corset and bustle disappeared for good.

Identifying the Enemy: From Propaganda to Genocide

We have seen that total war demanded an unprecedented expansion of state control over economic affairs. To ensure that their citizens remained committed to the war effort, governments also regulated the production and distribution of ideas. First, they eliminated ideas they viewed as dangerous. Pacifists and war objectors faced prison sentences and even execution. French prime minister Clemenceau adopted a particularly harsh stance toward all dissenting opinion. Journalists and rival politicians—even the former prime minister—who dared suggest that France negotiate with Germany rather than fight on for total victory were thrown in prison.

At the same time, governments worked to create ideas that would encourage a total war mentality. Propaganda now emerged as a crucial political tool. The careful censorship of newspapers and doctoring of photographs ensured that the public received a positive image of the war. In

Shell Shock: From Woman's Malady to Soldier's Affliction

Broken in mind as well as body, the casualties of World War I forced medical practitioners to think anew about the connections among emotional anguish, physical disabilities, and gender roles. Doctors discovered to their horror and surprise that in the trenches of total war, men's bodies began to act like women's. Pouring into hospital units came thousands of men with the symptoms of a malady that before the war was considered a woman's disease—hysteria.

The word *hysteria* comes from the Greek word *hystera,* for "womb" or "uterus," and for much of Western history doctors believed that women were doomed to suffer from hysteria because of their physical makeup—because they were afflicted with wombs. Physicians long considered the uterus to be an inherently weak and unstable organ, prone even to detach itself from its proper place and wander about the body causing havoc. By the end of the nineteenth century, however, the diagnosis had changed. Doctors continued to regard hysteria as primarily a woman's disease but they were more inclined to view it as a neurosis, a mental and emotional disorder. The symptoms varied enormously but included bouts of shrieking, emotional problems such as depression or breakdown, and physical ailments without any clear physical cause—ranging from abnormal fatigue or insomnia to the inability to walk.

With war came thousands of soldiers with the symptoms of hysteria—men who could not stop shaking, men with healthy limbs who could not move, men certain that rats were nibbling at their bodies. At first, doctors dismissed such symptoms as signs of cowardice: These were men faking illness to avoid doing their duty. But by 1916, with such men accounting for 40 percent of the casualties in British combat zones alone, doctors realized they were dealing with an epidemic of male hysteria.

The war illustrated that hysteria was linked not to the uterus or the weak female nervous system but rather to an environment of immobility and passivity. Neither the length of time a soldier had served nor the intensity or horror of his combat experience were significant in producing breakdowns. Instead, the most important factor was his level of immobility. Men on the Western Front suddenly found themselves in positions of passivity and confinement. Deprived of the ability to make decisions, to determine their future, to act, many men broke down.

Yet the reincarnation of what had been considered a woman's malady as a soldier's affliction did not lead doctors to reexamine their understanding of the woman's body or the woman's role. Instead, they reconfigured the disease. Hysteria became "shell shock." The treatment differed as well. Convinced that female hysteria was a result of the overstimulation of the nervous system, doctors prescribed total rest cures for their female patients. Women found themselves confined to rooms with bare walls and shuttered windows, forbidden to read or to receive visitors. In contrast, doctors ordered male soldiers with shell shock to engage in intense physical and mental activity. Thus, despite the upheaval in gender roles caused by total war, doctors continued to view women's bodies as inherently passive and men's as naturally active. The findings of medical science remained linked to cultural conventions.

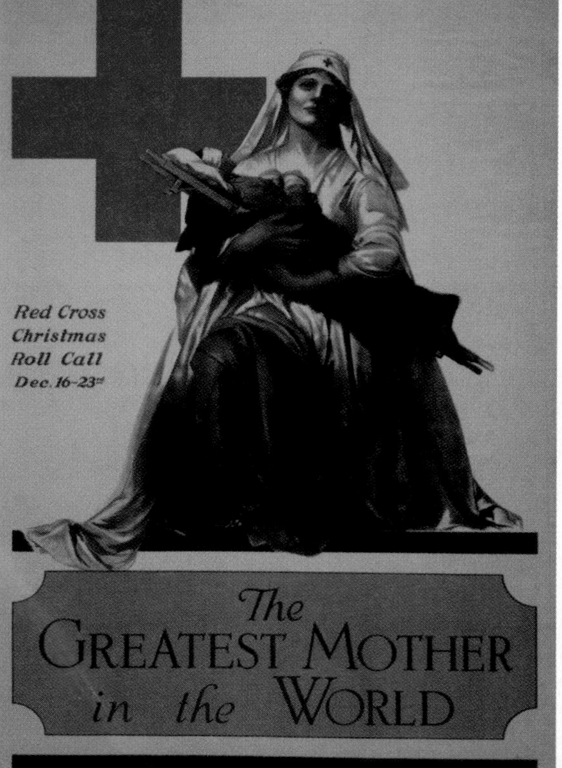

Red Cross
Christmas
Roll Call
Dec. 16-23rd
The
GREATEST MOTHER
in the WORLD

Role Reversal
In this British Red Cross poster, the soldier is infantilized in the arms of the nurse. Many men found their forced confinement and passivity profoundly unsettling.

For Discussion

Why does the contrast between the medical treatment of hysteria and that of shell shock indicate that the war had a limited impact on gender roles? What evidence in this chapter points to the opposite conclusion?

Never Forget!
This French poster uses the image of a raped woman and her murdered child to arouse anti-German passions. The image recalls the German invasion of neutral Belgium, which soon came to be called "the rape of Belgium." All combatant states produced similar propaganda pieces.

Germany, giant wooden statues of the war hero Hindenburg were paraded to rally war enthusiasm, while in all the combatant nations, poster campaigns used the techniques developed in the new mass advertising industry to arouse patriotic fervor.

Fostering a total war mentality meant not only cultivating love for the Father- or Motherland, but also stirring up hatred for those labeled as the Enemy. In words that were soon set to music and became a popular wartime song, the poet (and army private) Ernst Lissauer (1882–1937) urged Germans to "hate [England] with a lasting hate . . . Hate of seventy millions, choking down."[12] In Britain, anti-German sentiment was so strong that the royal family changed its name from Hanover to Windsor in an effort to erase its German lineage.

In the ethnic cauldron of eastern Europe, this hatred was often directed at minority groups who were perceived as the enemy within: In Austria-Hungary, for example, more than 500 Bosnian Serbs and hundreds of Ukrainians were shot without trial because they were seen as Russian sympathizers.

The most horrific result of the tendency to look for the enemy at home occurred not in Austria-Hungary but in the Ottoman Empire, where suspicion of the Armenian minority resulted in mass murder. Massacres of Armenians under Ottoman rule had punctuated the decades before 1914. The war accentuated the Turkish-Armenian conflict. Recognizing that Armenian loyalty to imperial rule was shaky, to say the least, the Ottoman government decided to eliminate the Armenian population from Turkey. This brutal "solution" to what was described as the "Armenian question" began in April 1915. After arresting Armenian elites (and thus removing potential resistance leaders from Armenian communities) Turkish troops rounded up and killed Armenian men. In some cases, special

A Turkish Officer Describes the Armenian Massacres

The Harvest of War
The Turkish massacre of more than one million Armenians illustrates the destructive consequences of combining nationalist hatred with total war. This criminal horror is often seen as foreshadowing the Jewish Holocaust during World War II.

forces marched the men outside their town or village and then shot them; in other instances, they were pushed into caves and asphyxiated by fires blocking the entrances. The Ottoman government then ordered the women, children, and the elderly deported to Syria. Driven from their homes on short notice, they marched through mountain and desert terrain without food or water. Rapes and executions were commonplace. Between 1915 and 1918, more than one million Armenian men, women, and children died in this attempt at genocide, the murder of an entire people.

War and Revolution

- **What were the consequences of this war for the European and the global political and international order?**

The machinery of total war tore at the social and political fabric of European societies. As seams began to fray and gaping holes appeared, many welcomed what they saw as the opportunity to tear apart the old cloth and create something entirely new. Some of these revolutionaries were Marxists aiming to build a socialist world order. Others were nationalists, determined to assert the rights of their ethnic or linguistic group, or to overthrow their colonial rulers. Not all revolutionaries belonged to underground or terrorist groups. One individual who dared to demand a new world order was the president of the United States, Woodrow Wilson. The peace settlement, however, fell far short of creating a new world. In Europe, many of the conflicts that had caused the war remained unresolved, with disastrous consequences for the next generation. Outside Europe, redesigned imperialist regimes encountered anti-Western forces that emerged from the war stronger than ever before.

The Russian Revolutions

Tsarist Russia began the war already sharply divided, its 125 million inhabitants splintered into more than one hundred different national groups—from Inuits in the north to Kazakhs in the southeast to Germans in the west. Ethnic hostilities sapped Russia's defenses from the very start. In Poland, for example, many of the four million Jews under Russian imperial rule welcomed the German army as liberators from tsarist violence and repression. In the regions of Latvia and Lithuania, anti-Russian sentiment flared high, and nationalists saw the war as opening the door to national independence.

The war brought political chaos to Russia. Nicholas II (r. 1894–1917), a man of limited intelligence and a remarkable capacity for self-delusion, insisted on going to the front and commanding his army. He left political affairs in the hands of his wife Alexandra (1872–1918) and her spiritual mentor Grigorii Rasputin (1869–1916). Rasputin is one of the more intriguing characters in twentieth-century history. An illiterate, unwashed faith healer from a peasant background, he possessed a well-documented and still-unexplained ability to stop the bleeding of Alexei, the young hemophiliac heir to the throne. To many high-ranking Russians, however, Rasputin was not a miracle worker but a traitor. Because Rasputin opposed the war against Germany, they perceived him as a voice of treason whispering in the German-born tsarina's ear. In 1916 Russian noblemen murdered Rasputin, in hopes of restoring authority and stability to the tsarist government.

The March Revolution

Rasputin's removal was not enough to stop the forces of revolution stirred up by total war. The political disarray he observed at the highest levels of government dumbfounded the French ambassador, who wrote in January 1917, "I am obliged to report that, at the present moment, the Russian Empire is run by lunatics."[13] The lack of effective political leadership, combined with Russian losses on the battlefield, brought to a boil the simmering disaffection with the tsarist government. Almost two million Russian soldiers had died and many more had been wounded or taken prisoner. Economic and communications networks had broken down, bread prices were rising, and people were hungry. Even members of the tsarist government began to ask not *if* revolution would occur, but *when.*

The answer came on March 8, 1917. A group of women workers in Petrograd staged a demonstration to protest inadequate food supplies. Over the course of the next few days, similar demonstrations flickered across the city; on March 11, they coalesced into a major revolutionary fire when the troops who were ordered to put down the protest joined it instead. Governmental orders lost all authority, and on March 15 Tsar Nicholas was forced to abdicate. The Russian Revolution had begun.

Who now controlled Russia? Two competing centers of power soon emerged: the Provisional Government and the Petrograd Soviet. On March 12, the Duma, or Russian parliament, created a Provisional Government from among its members. Like the Duma, the new Provisional Government was dominated by members of the gentry and middle classes: professionals, businessmen, intellectuals, bureaucrats. These men tended to be liberals who believed that Russia was now moving along the path toward a parliamentary democracy. They quickly enacted important reforms such as universal suffrage, the eight-hour workday, and civic equality for all citizens.

But at the same time that the Provisional Government was struggling to bring order to the chaos of revolutionary Russia, across the empire industrial workers and soldiers formed soviets°, or councils, to articulate their grievances and hopes. As Russian revolutionary socialists in exile

DOCUMENT

Revolution in the Front Lines

At age 25, Maria Botchkareva, a poor Russian woman who had been forced to work as a prostitute, volunteered for service as a soldier. Women served as nurses, ambulance drivers, and transport plane pilots on both sides of the war, but only in Russia did women serve in combat, and even there the presence of a woman on the front lines was quite exceptional. Botchkareva earned a well-deserved reputation as a fierce fighter, and was honored for her bravery. In 1917, she was serving at the front with her company when she heard startling news from the capital.

The first swallow to warn us of the approaching storm was a soldier from our Company who had returned from a leave of absence at Petrograd: "Oh my! If you but knew, boys, what is going on in the rear! Revolution! Everywhere they talk of overthrowing the Tsar. The capital is aflame with revolution." . . . Finally, the joyous news arrived. The Commander gathered the entire Regiment to read to us the glorious words. . . . The miracle had happened! Tsarism, which enslaved us and thrived on the blood and marrow of the toiler, had fallen. Freedom, Equality and Brotherhood! How sweet were these words to our ears! We were transported. There were tears of joy, embraces, dancing. It all seemed a dream, a wonderful dream. Who ever believed that the hated regime would be destroyed so easily and in our own time?

The Commander read to us the manifesto, which concluded with a fervent appeal to us to hold the line with greater vigilance than ever, now that we were free citizens, to defend our newly won liberty from the attacks of the Kaiser and his slaves. . . . Then came Order No. 1, signed by the Petrograd Soviet of Workmen and Soldiers. Soldiers and officers were now equal, it declared. All the citizens of Free Russia were equal henceforth. . . .

We were dazzled by this shower of brilliant phrases. The men went about as if intoxicated. For four days the festival continued unabated. . . . There were meetings, meetings, and meetings. . . . All duty was abandoned. . . . The front became a veritable insane asylum.

One day, in the first week of the revolution, I ordered a soldier to take up duty at the listening-post. He refused.

Source: From Maria Botchkareva, *Yashka: My Life as Peasant, Officer and Exile* (New York: Frederick A. Stokes Company, 1919), 139–145.

across Europe returned to their homeland in the weeks after the March Revolution began, they assumed leading roles in the Petrograd Soviet, which soon became a powerful political rival to the less radical Provisional Government.

The revolution, however, did not originate with nor was it controlled by either the liberals in the Provisional Government or the socialists in the Petrograd Soviet. Nicholas II was overthrown by a popular revolution, and at the core of this popular revolution stood a simply stated demand: "Peace, Land, Bread." Soldiers—and most Russians—wanted an immediate end to a war that had long ceased to make any sense to them. Peasants, as always, wanted land, their guarantee of survival in a chaotic world. And city dwellers wanted bread—food in sufficient quantities and at affordable prices.

The Provisional Government could not satisfy these demands. It did promise the gradual redistribution of royal and monastic lands, but peasants, inspired by the revolution and unconstrained by the liberal regard for law and the rights of private property, wanted land immediately. More important, by the summer of 1917 no Russian government could have provided bread without providing peace. Russia no longer had the resources both to continue its war effort and to reconstruct its economy. The population of the cities began to dwindle as food disappeared from the shops, factories ceased operation because of shortages of raw materials, and currency had little value. Peace appeared impossible, however. Not only did Russia have commitments to its allies, but German armies stood deep within Russian territory. A separate peace with Germany would mean huge territorial losses. And so the war continued.

But so, too, did the revolution. Peasants effected their own land reform by simply seizing the land they wanted. Soldiers declared their own peace by deserting in huge numbers. (Of every 1,000-man troop sent to the front, fewer than 250 men actually made it into combat. The rest deserted.) The Provisional Government grew increasingly unpopular. Not even the appointment of the popular socialist and Petrograd Soviet member Alexander Kerensky (1881–1970) as prime minister could stabilize the government's position.

The November Revolution

This tumultuous situation created the opportunity for the Bolsheviks°, one of the socialist factions in the Petrograd Soviet, to emerge as a powerful revolutionary force. In April 1917, the Bolshevik leader, Vladimir Lenin (1870–1924), returned from almost twenty years in exile. While still in his teens, Lenin had committed himself to revolution after his older brother was executed for trying to assassinate Tsar Alexander III. Iron-willed and ruthlessly pragmatic, Lenin argued that a committed group of professional revolutionaries could force a working-class revolution on Russia immediately.

The Revolution's Hero
In this heroic portrait by Gemalde von A. M. Gerassimow, Lenin pushes the revolution and the Russian people forward.

By the fall of 1917, Bolshevik membership had grown from 10,000 to 250,000, and the party had achieved a majority in the Petrograd Soviet. Lenin now demanded the immediate overthrow of the Provisional Government. "Insurrection is an art," he declared, something to be made, not something that happens spontaneously. By promising "Peace, Land, Bread," Lenin would take control. On November 9, Bolshevik fighters captured the Winter Palace in Petrograd, where the Provisional Government had been sitting.

The *second* Russian Revolution was underway. The Bolsheviks declared a policy of land and peace—land partition with no payment of compensation to estate owners and an immediate peace with Germany, regardless of the cost. (And as we have seen, the cost was high: According to the terms of the Treaty of Brest-Litovsk, signed with Germany in 1918, Russia lost its western territories.) Not everyone in Russia was won over by promises of peace and land, however. Confronted with a diverse array of opponents, the Bolsheviks turned to the methods of terror. After an assassination attempt against Lenin in August 1918, the Bolshevik secret police received the power to execute without trial. More than 500 individuals were shot in a single day in Petrograd.

During the next two years, the Bolsheviks waged a brutal war against domestic and international opponents of their Communist Revolution. This civil war proved Lenin's promises of "Peace, Land, Bread" to be hollow. Peasant farms were transformed into battlefields as five years of civil war killed off more combatants than had World War I. In the resulting famine, death tolls reached as high as five million. Yet, as the next chapter shows, the Bolsheviks emerged victorious. The Russian Empire was remade as the Soviet Union, a communist state.

The Spreading Revolution

The victory of the Bolsheviks in Russia inspired socialists across Europe and around the world. In January 1919, communists in Buenos Aires, Argentina, led by Russian immigrants, controlled the city for three days until they were crushed by the Argentine army. British dockworkers struck in support of the Bolshevik Revolution, and in French cities general strikes caused chaos. In Austria, revolutionaries attempted to take control of government buildings in Vienna but were quickly defeated by the Austrian army. In Hungary, Bela Kun, a journalist who had come to admire the Bolsheviks while a prisoner of war in Russia, established a short-lived soviet regime in the spring of 1919.

Revolution also swept through defeated Germany. Disillusion with the kaiser's regime had set in long before Germany had lost the war. Defeat simply accentuated the desire for radical political change. But the first revolutionary step in Germany was a response not to popular desire but to American demands. In October 1918, Germany's military commanders recommended that the German government enter into peace negotiations. U.S. president Woodrow Wilson, however, saw the war as a democratic crusade and so refused to allow the Allies to negotiate with representatives of the kaiser's authoritarian regime. To placate Wilson, the kaiser was forced to overhaul Germany's political system. For the first time, representatives of left-wing and centrist parties—including the SPD, the largest socialist party in Europe—were invited to join the government.

This "revolution from above" coincided with and was challenged by a "revolution from below." Inspired by the success of the Bolshevik Revolution, many German workers rejected the SPD's vision of socialism as too moderate. The members of the SPD believed in working for gradual social reform through parliamentary action and debate. A much more radical alternative was offered by a breakaway socialist faction called the Spartacists (after Spartacus, the gladiator who led a slave revolt against Rome in the first century B.C.E.). Directed by Karl Liebknecht (1871–1919) and Rosa Luxemburg (1870–1919), the Spartacists wanted Germany to follow Russia down the path to communist revolution.

The Spartacist Revolution in Germany
The effort to establish a soviet government in Berlin took the form of street fighting. This photograph shows one street skirmish that occurred in the city's newspaper district.

In Berlin, thousands rallied behind Liebknecht and Luxemburg. By November 8, communists had declared the establishment of a Soviet republic in the province of Bavaria; the Red Flag—symbol of communism—was flying over eleven German cities; and revolutionaries had seized control of all the main railroad junctions.

On November 9, the head of the SPD, Friedrich Ebert (1871–1925), became chancellor of Germany and the kaiser abdicated. One of Ebert's colleagues in the SPD triumphantly proclaimed from the window of the Reichstag building in Berlin that Germany was now a parliamentary democracy. Almost at that very moment, Karl Liebknecht stood at another window (in the occupied royal palace) and announced that Germany was now a revolutionary communist state. With two opposing versions of revolution on offer, civil war raged until the spring of 1919, when the SPD defeated the communists for control of the new Germany.

The Failure of Wilson's Revolution

At the beginning of 1919, the representatives of the victorious Allied nations gathered in Paris to draw up the treaties that would wrap up the war. Yet their aims were far higher than simply ending the war; they wished to construct a new Europe and to reconfigure the conduct of international affairs. At the center of this high endeavor was the American college-professor-turned-president Woodrow Wilson. Like the Bolsheviks, Wilson offered a vision of a radical new future. He based *his* version of revolutionary change on the ideal of national self-determination—a world in which "every people should be left free to determine its own polity, its own way of development, unhindered, unthreatened, unafraid, the little along with the great and powerful." The map of Europe would be redrawn, the old empires replaced with independent, ethnically homogenous, democratic nation-states.

These new nation-states would interact differently from the empires of the past. In what he called his Fourteen Points, Wilson demanded a revolution in international affairs. He argued that "Points" such as freedom of the seas, freedom of trade, and open diplomacy (an end to secret treaties) would break down barriers and guarantee peace and prosperity for all peoples. The cornerstone of this new world order would be an international organization, the League of Nations°, which would oversee the implementation of these new measures and would have the power to resolve disputes between nations. Wilson and other planners

CHRONOLOGY

Revolution in Russia, 1917–1921

1917	
March 8	St. Petersburg/Petrograd women's protest; revolution begins
March 12	Establishment of Provisional Government
March 15	Abdication of Tsar Nicholas II
November 9	Bolshevik overthrow of the Provisional Government
1918–1921	Civil war

Revolutionary Justice: The Nontrial of Nicholas and Alexandra

On July 16, 1918, Bolshevik revolutionaries shot and killed Nicholas II, tsar of Russia; his wife, the tsarina Alexandra; his heir, 14-year-old Alexei; their four daughters—Olga (age 23), Tatiana (age 21), Maria (age 19), and Anastasia (age 17); their three servants; and their physician. When news of the deaths reached other countries, the killings were condemned as murders. The Bolsheviks, however, termed them executions, acts of revolutionary justice.

When Nicholas II abdicated on March 15, 1917, after twenty-three years on the throne, he expected to embark on a life of exile in Britain. Instead, the Provisional Government placed the tsar and his family under house arrest and appointed a Commission of Inquiry to investigate the persistent rumors that the tsar's German-born wife had conspired with Germany to destroy Russia. The commission found no evidence to convict the tsar or his wife of treason, but by the autumn of 1917, its findings were irrelevant. The war with Germany was effectively over, whereas the war against all that the tsar had stood for had just begun.

The civil war that followed the Bolshevik Revolution proved fatal for the royal family. Faced with counterrevolutionary challenges on all sides, the Bolsheviks feared that if Nicholas escaped, he would serve as a symbolic center for these antirevolutionary forces. They decided to move him to a region firmly under Bolshevik control. In April 1918, a special train transported the tsar and his family to Ekaterinburg (about 900 miles east of Moscow), where they were placed in the hands of the Bolshevik-dominated Ural Regional Soviet. Meanwhile, the revolutionary Bolshevik government prepared to try Nicholas publicly for his crimes against the Russian people. The charge was no longer secret contacts with Germany—the Bolsheviks themselves had negotiated with Germany and ended Russia's participation in the war—but rather the tsar's both real and symbolic leadership of a politically repressive regime. Leon Trotsky, the head of the Petrograd Soviet, planned to present the case against Nicholas.

But the case was never made. By July, an anti-Bolshevik army was approaching Ekaterinburg from the east. If these troops freed the imperial family, they would score a crucial victory. Told that Ekaterinburg might fall to the enemy within days, the Ural Soviet decided to execute the tsar and his family immediately, most likely with Lenin's approval.

Pavel Medvedev, one of the tsar's guards, later offered a detailed account of the events of the evening of July 16. His interviewer recorded what Medvedev had told him:

> *[He said,] The Tsar, the Tsaritsa [Tsarina], the Tsar's four daughters, the doctor, the cook and the lackey came out of their rooms. The Tsar was carrying the heir [Alexei] in his arms. . . . In my presence there were no tears, no sobs and no questions. . . .*

Medvedev then testified that he was ordered out of the room. When he returned a few minutes later:

> *. . . he saw all the members of the Tsar's family lying on the floor with numerous wounds to their bodies. The blood was gushing. The heir was still alive—and moaning. [The commander] walked over to him and shot him two or three times at point blank range. The heir fell still.*[14]

What Medvedev's understated account did not relate were the more gruesome details of the execution. In an effort to preserve part of the family fortune, the tsar's daughters were wearing corsets into which had been sewn diamonds. When they were shot, the bullets, in the words of one eyewitness, "ricocheted, jumping around the room like hail."[15] Even after several pistols were emptied, one of the girls remained alive. The guards resorted to bayonets.

The killing of not only the tsar but also his wife and children was a startling act, as the Bolsheviks themselves recognized. The Ural Regional Soviet announced the tsar's execution, but said nothing about his family, while the official statement from Moscow reported that "the wife and son of Nicholas Romanov were sent to a safe place."[16]

These omissions and lies reveal the Bolsheviks' own uneasiness with the killings. Why, then, was the entire family shot? The Bolsheviks' determination to win the civil war regardless of the cost provides part of the answer. According to Trotsky, Lenin "believed we shouldn't leave the Whites [the anti-Bolshevik forces] a live banner to rally around."[17] Any of the tsar's children could have served as such a banner. The rapid approach of the White army meant the royal family had to be disposed of quickly. But Trotsky also viewed the killings as an essential and absolute break with the past. In his words, "the execution of the Tsar's family was needed not only to frighten, horrify, and to dishearten the enemy, but also in order to shake up our own ranks, to show them that there was no turning back, that ahead lay either complete victory or complete ruin."[18] For the Bolsheviks, there was no middle ground.

The killing of Tsar Nicholas and his family thus forms part of the pattern of escalating violence that characterized the First World War's

Tsar Nicholas II and Family
Tsar Nicholas II, the Tsarina Alexandra, and their family.

revolutionary aftermath. But in the blood of these killings we can also see reflected two ideas that had a powerful impact on postwar political life—first, the subordination of law to the revolutionary state; second, the concept of collective guilt.

The Bolsheviks offered a different idea of justice. As a Bolshevik publication explained in a discussion of the tsar's killing:

> *Many formal aspects of bourgeois justice may have been violated. . . . However, worker-peasant power was manifested in the process, making no exception for the All-Russian murderer, shooting as if he were an ordinary brigand. . . . Nicholas the Bloody is no more.*[19]

In the Bolshevik model, the law was not separate from but rather subordinate to the state. Legal rights and requirements—the "formal aspects of bourgeois justice"—could be suspended in the service of "worker peasant power," as embodied in the revolutionary state.

This concept of the law subordinate to the state helps us understand the tsar's execution without trial; the concept of collective guilt provides a context for the killing of his children. The Bolshevik model of socialism assumed that *class* constituted objective reality. Simply by belonging to a certain social class, an individual could be—and was—designated an enemy of the revolution. The Bolshevik constitution equated citizenship with social class. Workers and peasants received the vote, but seven categories of people, such as those who lived off investment interest, were disenfranchised. For the next two decades, aristocratic and middle-class origins served as an indelible ink, marking a person permanently as an enemy of the revolutionary state—regardless of that person's own actions or inclinations. Thus, from the Bolshevik perspective, the tsar's children bore the taint of their royal origins. When their continuing existence threatened the revolution, they were shot. Over the next four decades, the concept of collective guilt would result in the deaths of millions in the new Soviet Union.

When World War I ended and representatives of the Allied victors met in Paris in 1919 to build the new postwar world, they sought to establish nationalist-based democracies, in which the rule of law would guarantee the rights of individuals. These two interlinked concepts of law and human rights became for many the defining features of "the West," of democracy, and of civilization itself. The Bolsheviks challenged this definition. They offered instead a definition of democracy based on class and an understanding of the law resting on the demands of continuing revolution.

Questions of Justice

1. In what ways was the murder of the Russian royal family the by-product of total war rather than the result of any revolutionary ideals?
2. In what ways, if any, were the Bolsheviks correct in arguing that "justice" is never blind, that legal systems always reflect the interests of a society's dominant groups? Is there such a thing as impartial justice?

Taking It Further

Kozlov, Vladimir, and Vladimir Khrustalëv. *The Last Diary of Tsaritsa Alexandra.* 1997. A translation of the tsarina's diary from 1918.

Rosenberg, William, ed. *Bolshevik Visions: First Phase of the Cultural Revolution in Soviet Russia.* 1990. The section on "Proletarian Legality" explores the Bolsheviks' effort to develop a legal system that embodied their revolutionary ideals.

Steinberg, Mark, and Vladimir Khrustalëv. *The Fall of the Romanovs.* 1999. A detailed account of the last two years of the tsar and his family, based on recently opened archives.

Wilson and the Peace
Setting sail for the Paris Peace Conference on December 4, 1918, Wilson believed he was also embarking on a journey in which he would lead Europe into political democracy and international peace.

of the postwar era envisioned the league as a truly revolutionary organization, one that would guarantee that World War I was "the war to end all wars." To replace the system of secret diplomacy and Great Power alliances that had led to the horrors of total war, the league offered an international forum in which all states, big and small, European and non-European, would have a voice and in which negotiations would be conducted openly and democratically. War would become outmoded.

These soaring social and political expectations went largely unrealized. In Paris in 1919 and 1920, the Allies and their defeated enemies signed a series of treaties.* In drawing up these agreements, the treaty writers sought to create a new international order based on three features: a democratic Germany, national self-determination in eastern Europe, and a viable system of international arbitration headed by the League of Nations. They failed in all three.

**These treaties were named after the French palaces in which they were signed—the Treaty of Versailles, with Germany; the Treaty of St. Germain, with Austria; the Treaty of Neuilly, with Bulgaria; the Treaty of Trianon, with Hungary; and the Treaty of Sèvres, with Turkey.*

The Treaty of Versailles and German Democracy

At the center of the new Europe envisioned by Woodrow Wilson was to be a new democratic Germany. French leader Georges Clemenceau did not share this vision. He had lived through two German invasions of his homeland and wished to ensure that Germany could never again threaten France. Clemenceau proposed the creation of a Rhineland state out of Germany's industrialized western region, both as a neutral buffer zone between France and Germany and as a way to reduce Germany's economic power. The British leader, David Lloyd George, who had just won an election on the campaign slogan "Hang the Kaiser" and who had promised his people that he would squeeze Germany "until the pips squeak," publicly supported Clemenceau's hardline approach to the peace settlement with Germany. In private, however, he expressed fear that such an approach would backfire by feeding the flames of German resentment and undermining the structures of German democracy.

Lloyd George's fears proved well-grounded. The German people bitterly resented the Versailles Treaty°, which they perceived as unjustly punitive. By the terms of the treaty, Germany lost all of its overseas colonies, 13 percent of its European territory, 10 percent of its population, and its ability to wage war. The German army was limited to a defensive force of 100,000 men and allowed no aircraft or tanks. Clemenceau failed in his effort to create a separate Rhineland state, but the Rhineland was demilitarized, emptied of German soldiers and fortifications. In addition, the coalfields of the Saar region were ceded to France for fifteen years (see Map 24.5).

Even more significantly, the Versailles Treaty declared that German aggression had caused the war, and therefore that Germany must recompense the Allies for its cost. In 1921, the Allies presented Germany with a bill for reparations° of 132 billion marks ($31.5 billion). As we will see in the next chapter, this reparations clause helped set up an economic cycle that was to prove devastating for both global prosperity and German democratic politics.

The Failure of National Self-Determination

The map of Europe drawn by the peace treaties appeared to signal the establishment of a new international order. The old authoritarian empires of eastern and central Europe disappeared, replaced with independent nation-states. In keeping with the principle of national self-determination, Poland once again became an independent nation, with pieces carved out of the German, Austrian, and Russian Empires. One entirely new state was formed out of the rubble of the Austrian-Hungarian Empire—Czechoslovakia. Romania, Greece, and Italy all expanded as a result of serv-

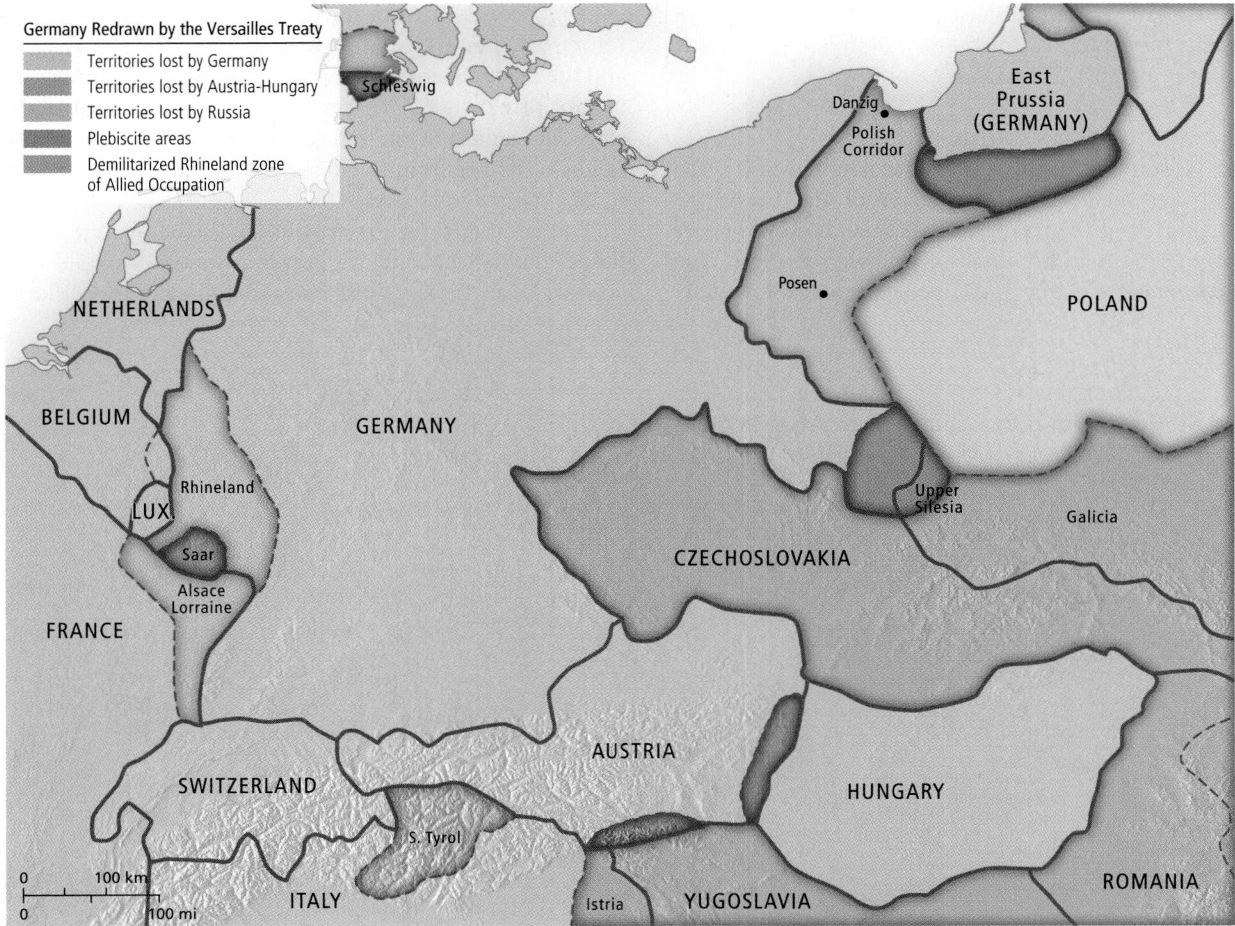

Map 24.5 Germany Redrawn by the Versailles Treaty
By the terms of the Versailles Treaty, Germany lost 13 percent of its prewar territory and 10 percent of its prewar population. France regained Alsace and Lorraine; reconstructed Poland was given a corridor to the sea; and the industrialized Rhineland became a demilitarized zone.

ing on the winners' side, while Serbia became the heart of the new Yugoslavia. The defeated nations shrank, some dramatically. Austria, for example, became a mere rump of what had been the mighty Habsburg Empire, while Hungary was reduced to one-third of its prewar size. All that remained of the Ottoman Empire was Turkey.

These changes were heralded as the victory of "national self-determination." But as Woodrow Wilson's own secretary of state, Robert Lansing, complained, "This phrase is simply loaded with dynamite. It will raise hopes which can never be realized." Wilson had called for "every people" to be left free to determine its political destiny—but who constituted "a people"? Did the Macedonians? Should there be an independent Macedonia? Macedonians said yes, but the Paris peace negotiators answered no. Macedonia was enveloped by Yugoslavia and Greece, and in consequence, throughout the 1920s and 1930s Macedonians waged a terrorist campaign in the Balkans. Wilson's peaceful new world seemed far, far away when in 1923, a Macedonian nationalist group kidnapped the Bulgarian prime minister, chopped off his head, and sliced off his limbs.

The Macedonians were not the only dissatisfied ethnic group in eastern Europe. Even after the peace settlements redrew the map, no fewer than 30 million eastern Europeans remained members of minority groups. Less than 70 percent of Hungarians, for example, lived in Hungary—more than three million were scattered in other states. Over nine million Germans resided outside the borders of Germany. In the newly created Czechoslovakia, one-third of the population was neither Czech nor Slovak. The new state of Yugoslavia contained an uneasy mixture of several ethnic groups, most resentful of the dominant Serbs.

Rather than satisfying nationalist ambitions, then, the peace settlements served to inflame them, thus creating a volatile situation for the post–World War I world.

The Limits of the League

True to Wilson's vision of a new international order, the treaty makers included the Covenant of the League of Nations in each of the treaties. The league, however, never realized Wilson's high hopes of making war obsolete. One crucial weakness was that it did not represent every state. When the league met for the first time in 1920, three significant world powers had no representative present: Germany and the Soviet Union were excluded, and, in a stunning defeat for President Wilson, the U.S. Senate rejected membership. The failure of these three states to participate in the league at its beginning stripped the organization of much of its potential influence.

Two additional factors explain the league's failure. First, the league had no military power. Although it could levy economic sanctions against states that flouted its decisions,

Map 24.6 Europe and the Middle East After World War I
A comparison of this map with Map 24.1 on page 780 illustrates the vital role played by the war in shaping eastern Europe and the Middle East.

it could do nothing more. And perhaps most important, the will to make the league work was lacking. With Wilson removed from the picture, European leaders were free to pursue their own rather more traditional visions of what the league should be. French politicians, for example, believed that the league's primary reason for existence was to enforce the provisions of the Versailles Treaty—in other words, to punish Germany rather than to restructure international relations.

The Making of the Modern Middle East

The high hopes that accompanied the end of the war extended beyond the borders of Europe and invigorated nationalist movements throughout Europe's empires. In the Middle East, the war's end meant an entirely new map, but not the end of European dominance. Under terms set by the new League of Nations, the Allies carved Ottoman territory in the Middle East into separate and nominally independent states. These states, however, were judged "not yet able to stand by themselves under the strenuous conditions of the modern world" and so were placed under French or British control (or "Mandate"). Syria and Lebanon fell to the French, while Britain claimed Iraq (Mesopotamia), Palestine, and Transjordan (later called simply Jordan). Britain also continued to exercise its influence over Egypt, Iran (Persia), and what would become Saudi Arabia.

This remaking of the Middle East failed to effect a lasting settlement in the region. First, the new map clashed with promises made to indigenous groups during the war, and so created a long-lasting legacy of mistrust and resentment against the West. Second, the new states imposed on the region were artificial, the creation of the Allied victors rather than a product of historical evolution or of the wishes of the inhabitants themselves. And finally, Western mandatory supervision (which in actual practice differed little from old-fashioned imperial rule) brought with it Western practices and concepts that destabilized regional social and economic structures.

The early history of Iraq exemplifies these three developments. First, the drawing of Iraq, together with Syria, Lebanon, Palestine, and Jordan, betrayed promises made by the British to their Arab allies during the war. In 1915, the British High Commissioner in Egypt, Sir Henry McMahon, wrote to Sharif Husayn (Hussein) ibn Ali, head of the Hashemite dynasty that acted as traditional guardian of Islamic holy sites, and agreed to grant him control over Arab areas liberated from Ottoman rule in exchange for his military support against the Central Powers. This "McMahon-Husayn Correspondence" did not establish precisely the actual boundaries under discussion, but the Hashemites and their supporters believed that they had been promised an independent Arab kingdom centered on Damascus—the same area that the Allies carved up into the five mandatory states. The British argued they had kept their promise when they placed Husayn's son Faisal on the throne of Iraq and his other son Abdullah on the throne of Jordan, but many Arabs felt betrayed.

The artificiality of Iraq, as well as the other new states, also created a revolutionary situation. In creating Iraq, the Allies glued together three Ottoman provinces—Basra, Baghdad, and Mosul—that had never been treated as a single political or economic unit by the Ottomans, nor regarded as in any way united by the inhabitants themselves. The population of this new state consisted of a volatile mixture of both ethnicities (including Arab, Kurd, and Assyrian) and religions (including not only the majority Shia Muslim community but also Sunni Muslims, Christians, Jews, and Zorastrians). None of these diverse groups identified themselves as "Iraqi." Many of the inhabitants of the new state also lacked a sense of allegiance to their new ruler; they regarded Faisal (along with his brother Abdullah in Jordan) as an imperialist puppet, jumping as British "advisers" pulled the strings.

Finally, the British inadvertently destabilized Iraq's social structures when they set out to make the new state into a friendly regime that would protect British access to both air bases and oil resources. The introduction of British legal and economic concepts destroyed indigenous traditions. For example, by applying the concept of private land ownership to Iraqi customary relations, the British transformed the traditional tie between tribal sheikh and tribesmen into an economic arrangement between landowner and tenants—an arrangement that tended to enrich the landowner while impoverishing the tenants.

Iraq erupted into full-scale rebellion in 1920, a revolt the British quelled with mustard gas bombs. Similar rebellions—and similar use of brutal force, often airborne, to crush such rebellions—occurred throughout much of the Middle East immediately after World War I.

The settlement of the region labeled Palestine destabilized the region even further. As we noted, the Hashemites and their supporters believed that the British had promised that Palestine would be included in an independent Arab kingdom after the war ended. Yet at the same time, British officials pledged support for a Jewish state in Palestine. In making this pledge, British policymakers were influenced by the anti-Semitic myth of a powerful Jewish elite wielding influence over world affairs: More specifically, they believed that Jewish influence could determine whether the U.S. would enter and Russia would remain in the war. Desperate to ensure both, the British government in 1917 issued the Balfour Declaration°. This declaration announced that Britain favored the Zionist goal of a Jewish national homeland in Palestine (the biblical land of Israel).

Palestine in 1920 passed into British hands in the form of a United Nations mandate formally committed to the Balfour Declaration. Ninety percent of the inhabitants of

Palestine in 1920 were Arabs (both Christians and Muslims) who viewed the Zionist dream of a Jewish Palestine as a form of European imperialism that threatened to dispossess them of their land. But as Arthur Balfour (the Conservative politician who gave the Balfour Declaration its name) explained, "in Palestine we do not propose even to go through the form of consulting the wishes of the present inhabitants of the country."[20] Arab protests and riots in Palestine erupted and by 1922, the British government decided to slow the pace of Jewish immigration into the region to alleviate Arab fears. This decision was only a stopgap solution, however; over the next two decades the British faced continuous pressure from both Arab and Jewish nationalist forces. Like the remaking of eastern Europe, the remaking of the Middle East ushered in decades of political turmoil and violence.

Conclusion

The War and the West

Sparked by nationalist fervor, international competition, and a widespread will to believe that in war lay the solution to political divisions and cultural fears, World War I quickly slipped out of the control of both the diplomats and the generals. Industrialization changed the face of combat. Total war smashed the boundaries of the battlefield, eroded the distinction between soldier and civilian, and demanded an overhaul of each combatant nation's political, economic, and social structures.

The idea of "the West" also changed as a result of the impact of this war. The entry of American forces in the final year of the war signaled that in the twentieth century, the United States would have to be factored into any definition of "Western culture" or "Western civilization." At the same time, the spread of the war to the Middle East and Africa and the significant role played by soldiers from imperial territories such as Tunisia, India, and Australia demonstrated the global framework that complicated and constrained Western affairs. The war's revolutionary aftermath also had profound consequences for formulations of "Western identity." With the triumph of the Bolshevik Revolution, two versions of modernity now presented themselves—one associated with the United States and capitalism, and the other represented by the new Soviet Union and its communist ideology. Soviet communism's intellectual roots lay in Marxism, a quintessentially Western ideology, one shaped by Western ideals of evolutionary progress and the triumph of human reason. But after the Russian Revolution, communism was increasingly viewed in the West as something foreign, essentially Eastern, the Other against which the West identified itself.

The carnage of World War I also challenged the faith of many Europeans that through industrial development the West was progressing morally as well as materially. In the final decades of the nineteenth century, European and American soldiers had used repeating rifles and machine guns to conquer huge sections of the globe in the name of Western civilization. In 1914, European and American soldiers turned their machine guns on each other. The world the war had created was one of unprecedented destruction. Millions lay dead, with millions more maimed for life. Vast sections of northern France and eastern Europe had been turned into giant cemeteries filled with rotting men and rusting metal. Across central and eastern Europe, starvation continued to claim thousands of victims, while a worldwide influenza epidemic, spread in part by the marching armies, ratcheted up the death tolls even higher. In the new world shaped by relentless conflicts such as the Battle of the Somme, the pessimism and sense of despair that had already invaded much of the arts in the decade before the war became more characteristic of the wider culture. For many Europeans, the optimism and confidence of nineteenth-century liberalism died in the trenches.

Yet, paradoxically, the war also fostered high hopes. Wilson declared that this had been the war to end all wars. The fires of revolution burned high and many in the West believed that on top of the ashes of empire they would now build a better world. The task of reconstruction, however, proved immense; as we shall see in Chapter 25, in many areas, retrenchment replaced revolution. Seeking stability in an increasingly unsettled world, many Europeans and Americans did their best to return to prewar patterns. The failure of the peace settlement ensured that the "war to end all wars" set the stage for the next, far more destructive total war.

Suggestions for Further Reading

For a comprehensive listing of suggested readings, please go to www.ablongman.com/levack2e/chapter24

Cork, Richard. *A Bitter Truth: Avant-Garde Art and the Great War.* 1994. A beautifully illustrated work that looks at the cultural impact of the war.

Eksteins, Modris. *Rites of Spring: The Great War and the Birth of the Modern Age.* 1989. Explores the links among modernism, the war experience, and modernity.

Ferguson, Niall. *The Pity of War.* 1999. A bold reconsideration of many accepted interpretations of the origins and experience of the war.

Fitzpatrick, Sheila. *The Russian Revolution, 1917–1932.* 1994. As the title indicates, Fitzpatrick sees the revolutions of 1917 as the opening battle in a more than ten-year struggle to shape the new Russia.

Gilbert, Martin. *The First World War: A Complete History.* 1994. A comprehensive account, packed with illuminating detail.

Gilbert, Martin. *The Routledge Atlas of the First World War.* 1994. Much more than a set of maps, Gilbert's atlas provides a very clear and useful survey of both the causes and results of the war.

Higonnet, Margaret. *Lines of Fire: Women's Visions of World War I.* 1998. An important study of women's experiences.

Joll, James. *The Origins of the First World War.* 1984. One of the best and most carefully balanced studies of this complicated question.

Read, Christopher. *From Tsar to Soviets: The Russian People and Their Revolution, 1917–1921.* 1996. An up-to-date study of the popular revolution and its fate.

Winter, J. M. *The Experience of World War I.* 1989. Despite the title, this richly illustrated work not only covers the war itself but also explores the factors that led to its outbreak and outlines its chief consequences.

Winter, J. M., and R. M. Wall, eds. *The Upheaval of War: Family, Work and Welfare in Europe, 1914–1918.* 1988. A series of essays examining the home front experiences.

Notes

1. Figures from Alan Sharp, "The Genie That Would Not Go Back into the Bottle: National Self-Determination and the Legacy of the First World War and the Peace Settlement," in Seamus Dunn and T. G. Fraser, eds., *Europe and Ethnicity,* (1996), 10.
2. Quotation from Karl Kautsky et al., eds., *The Outbreak of the World War: German Documents* (1924), 76.
3. Quoted in Niall Ferguson, *The Pity of War* (1999), 152.
4. Quoted in Eric Leeds, *No Man's Land: Combat and Identity in World War I* (1979), 17.
5. Allister Horne, *The Price of Glory: Verdun, 1916* (1967), 27.
6. Paul Fussell, *The Great War and Modern Memory* (1975), ch. 2.
7. Siegfried Sassoon, *Memoirs of an Infantry Officer* (1937), 228.
8. Figure from Tony Ashworth, *Trench Warfare, 1914–1918* (1980), 15–16.
9. Samuel Hynes, *A War Imagined: The First World War and English Culture* (1991), 195.
10. Quoted in Richard Cork, *A Bitter Truth* (1994), 198.
11. Quoted in Sheila Rowbotham, *A Century of Women* (1997), 72.
12. Ernst Lessauer, "Hymn of Hate" (1914), in *Jugend* (1914). Translated by Barbara Henderson, *New York Times,* October 15, 1914.
13. Quoted in W. Bruce Lincoln, *Red Victory: A History of the Russian Civil War* (1989), 32.
14. Quoted in Edvard Radzinsky, *The Last Tsar,* trans. Marian Schwartz (1993), 336.
15. From the written account of Yakov Yurovsky, quoted in Radzinsky, *The Last Tsar,* 355.
16. Quoted in William Henry Chamberlin, *The Russian Revolution, 1917–1921,* Vol. 2: *From the Civil War to the Consolidation of Power* (1987), 91.
17. Quoted in Lincoln, *Red Victory,* 151.
18. Ibid., 155.
19. Quoted in Radzinsky, *The Last Tsar,* 326.
20. Quoted in Walid Khalidi (ed.), *From Haven to Conquest: Readings in Zionism and the Palestine Problem Until 1948* (1987), 208.

ПРОЛЕТАРИИ ВСЕХ СТРАН
СОЕДИНЯЙТЕСЬ!

Reconstruction, Reaction, and Continuing Revolution: The 1920s and 1930s

25

CHAPTER OUTLINE

- Cultural Despair and Desire
- Out of the Trenches: Reconstructing National and Gender Politics in the 1920s
- The Rise of the Radical Right
- The Polarization of Politics in the 1930s
- The West and the World: Imperialism in the Interwar Era

On September 14, 1927, an open car accelerated down a street in Nice in southern France. In its passenger seat sat a woman, who let her long silk shawl whip in the wind. This woman in free-flowing clothing, speeding down the streets in a convertible, provides a fitting image for Western culture in the decade after World War I. Entranced by the automobile, Americans and Europeans embraced its promise of mobility and freedom. They perceived themselves as moving ahead, breaking through traditional barriers and heading off into new directions. Even more fitting was the identity of that female passenger: Isadora Duncan, by 1927 one of the most famous artists in Europe. In the years before World War I, the American-born Duncan had rejected classical ballet as an artificial form that restricted and deformed the female body. She cast aside ballet's confining toe shoes and tutus, and opted for bare feet and simple tunics. For Duncan, dance was not a force imposed on the body from outside; instead, dance flowed from the body itself. In her break with the highly regulated system of classical ballet, her quest for more natural forms, and her desire to liberate women, both physically and artistically, Duncan serves as an apt symbol for modernity. Moreover, as an American, Duncan appeared to personify the new culture that for many Europeans represented the world of the future. Even her clothing—loose tunics, free-flowing scarves, fluid shawls—symbolized a love of freedom and movement.

Yet freedom is sometimes dangerous and movement can be violent. On that autumn day in 1927 Duncan's long scarf became entangled in the wheel of her car and strangled the dancer. Gruesome as it is, the image of Duncan's sudden death serves as an appropriate introduction to the history of the West in the 1920s and 1930s, the turbulent interlude between two tragic

"The World Will Soon Be Yours" This Soviet propaganda poster promises workers around the world a global communist revolution. In *The Communist Manifesto,* Karl Marx had addressed the working classes in these famous words: "Workers of the world, unite! You have nothing to lose but your chains!" Adapting this call, the poster's banner declares, "You have nothing to lose but your chains, but the world will soon be yours."

world wars. The American president Woodrow Wilson had hailed World War I as the "final war for human liberty." Many Europeans agreed; they thought that the war would propel their society down a new road, yet in much of Europe the drive toward freedom ended quickly. The interwar period saw the strangulation of democracy in eastern and southern Europe and the rise of political and cultural ideologies that viewed human liberty as an illusion and mass murder as a tool of the state.

These developments had profound implications for the idea of the West. In the Wilsonian vision, "the West" stood as a culture that promoted individual freedom through democratic politics and capitalist economics. But the success of antidemocratic and anticapitalist ideologies in capturing the hopes and allegiances of large numbers of Europeans illustrated that Wilson's definition of the West was only one among many.

Why was the link between "Western" and "democratic" so fragile? To answer this question, we will look closely at diverse responses to the revolutionary aftermath of World War I. Five more specific questions will guide our examination:

- **What was the impact of the war on European cultural life?**
- **In what ways did reconstruction rather than revolution characterize the postwar period?**
- **What circumstances explain the emergence of the Radical Right?**
- **What factors led to the polarization of European politics in the 1930s?**
- **How did the interaction between the West and the world outside change after World War I?**

Cultural Despair and Desire

- **What was the impact of the war on European cultural life?**

To many Europeans in the 1920s and 1930s, World War I seemed to have torn a huge and irreparable gash in the fabric of culture and society. It appeared as the sudden and horrifying end to an age of science and progress, an era of technological improvement and social optimism. Yet this perception of a radical cultural break masked fundamental continuities. As we observed in Chapter 23, beginning in the 1870s, anxiety intermingled with optimism in European culture, and widespread fear of degeneration and decay marked Western society. Well before World War I, modernist painters, musicians, and poets pushed beyond the limits of nineteenth-century art and articulated disturbing visions of a world in purposeless flux. The real change in the years after the war was that modernism's fragmented canvases and dissonant choruses no longer seemed alien; they echoed the sensibilities of societies shattered by total war. But the war had also injected art with an often passionate political intensity. Excitement as well as anxiety thus marked the art and the age. The interwar era was a time of contradictions, one in which many Europeans despaired at the future of their society but many others dreamed of building a new and better world.

The Waste Land

Within just a few years of the war's end, war memorials were erected in cities, towns, and villages throughout France and Britain. Significantly, these memorials rarely celebrated the Allies' victory; instead, they focused on dead soldiers. Slaughter, not success, was the dominant theme. At Verdun, for example, the memorial was an ossuary, a gigantic receptacle for the skulls and bones of 130,000 men. In some ways, European culture after the war took on the form of an ossuary, as intellectuals and artists looked at the death tolls from the war and concluded that the end product of human reason and scientific endeavor was mass destruction.

In the English-speaking world, the American expatriate poet T. S. Eliot (1888–1965) supplied the most evocative portrait of postwar disillusion. In 1922, Eliot published a lengthy poem called "The Waste Land," which became a metaphor used by many Europeans to express their own sense of the waste wrought by the war. Arising out of Eliot's own personal anguish, "The Waste Land" contains no straightforward narrative. Instead, like a Cubist collage painting, it comprises fragments of conversation, literary allusions, disjointed quotations, mythological references, all clashing and combining in a modernist cry of despair.

The heightened anxiety and loss of certainty that characterized much of Western literature after the war is also clear in the realms of theology and philosophy. In the nineteenth century, theologians emphasized the harmony of religion and science. Their argument that God is present in the world, guiding its rational and progressive evolution, was difficult to sustain in a society that had experienced the absurd slaughter of World War I. In his postwar writings, the Swiss theologian Karl Barth (1886–1968) emphasized human sinfulness and argued that an immense gulf separated humanity from God. Neither scientific analysis nor historical inquiry could bridge the gap. Reaching God demanded a radical leap of faith.

Barth's German colleague Rudolf Bultmann (1884–1976) made the leap of faith even more radical. Bultmann argued that the Jesus Christ depicted in the New Testament—the foundation of Christianity—was largely fictional. In Bultmann's view, the Gospels were something like Eliot's "Waste Land" poem, a collection of fragments originating from myth and folk tale, layered on one another and capable of multiple interpretations. Rational inquiry and scientific methods cannot deliver a certain image of the historical Jesus, who remains essentially unknowable, obscured by the myths built up over centuries. Yet Bultmann, a Lutheran pastor, did not discard his Christian beliefs. Instead, he argued that within and through the Christian mythology rests ultimate spiritual—although not scientific or historical—truth.

Bultmann's form of Christianity is often called Christian existentialism° because Bultmann put a Christian twist on the existentialist philosophy taught by his friend, the philosopher Martin Heidegger (1889–1976). At the core of existentialism was a profound despair. The human condition is one of anxiety and alienation, even *Nausea,* as Heidegger's student Jean-Paul Sartre (1905–1980) entitled one of his most famous works. For Barth and Bultmann, the way out from this anxiety was through submission to God. As an atheist, Heidegger found this route blocked. Instead, he taught that the individual must struggle to rise above mere existence to a consciousness of the genuine and authentic. Sartre's version of existentialism was more pessimistic. At a time when, as we will see, dictatorships were rising across Europe, Sartre insisted that the fundamental fact of human existence is that "man is condemned to be free" in a universe devoid of meaning or reason. Yet Sartre, too, offered a way out from this prison of freedom: Individuals must recognize that they are free to make choices, and then must do so. During World War II, Sartre's own heroic acts in the French Resistance against the Nazis exemplified his insistence on the necessity of making moral choices in an absurd world.

A sense of absurdity and waste dominates much of the visual art of the period. War veteran Otto Dix (1891–1969) filled his canvases with crippled ex-soldiers. The vivid colors and distorted figures of the Expressionist style enabled Dix to articulate his outrage at the world he saw about him. In *Flanders,* painted in 1934, Dix depicted a nightmare of trench soldiers, rotting like blasted trees. Here there is no heroism, only horror.

DOCUMENT

The Waste Land

T. S. Eliot's "The Waste Land" comprises 434 lines; the excerpt given here is thus just one small piece of a much larger and complex poetic work that provides an evocative portrait of a despairing age. One of its central images, drawn from the English legends of King Arthur, is of an impotent and sickly king, reigning over a dried-up land.

April is the cruellest month, breeding
Lilacs out of the dead land, mixing
Memory and desire, stirring
Dull roots with spring rain.
Winter kept us warm, covering
Earth in forgetful snow, feeding
A little life with dried tubers.
. . .
But at my back in a cold blast I hear
The rattle of the bones, and chuckle spread from ear to ear.
A rat crept softly through the vegetation
Dragging its slimy belly on the bank
While I was fishing in the dull canal
On a winter evening round behind the gashouse
Musing upon the king my brother's wreck
And on the king my father's death before him.
White bodies naked on the low damp ground
And bones cast in a little low dry garret,
Rattled by the rat's foot only, year to year.

Source: From "The Waste Land" by T. S. Eliot. First published in 1922. Reprinted by permission of Faber and Faber Ltd.

Building Something Better

Stuck in the mud, the soldiers in Dix's *Flanders* provide a haunting image of European culture in the interwar years. A very different image takes shape when we examine the work of Dix's contemporaries in the *Bauhaus.* Established in Berlin in 1919 as a school for architects, craftsmen, and designers, the Bauhaus epitomized not the despair but rather the near-utopianism of much of European society after the war. The Bauhaus sought to eliminate the barriers between "art" (what we put on our walls or see in museums) and "craft" (what we actually use in daily life: furniture, textiles, dishes, and the like), and so to enhance daily living by making it more effective, efficient, and beautiful. Its founder, Walter Gropius (1883–1969), hoped his students would become nothing less than "the architects of a new civilization."[1]

Gropius's belief that the arts could serve a social purpose was commonly shared in the interwar years. As the British poet W. H. Auden (1907–1973) explained, although good poetry is "not concerned with telling people what to do," it should "[lead] us to the point where it is possible for us to make a rational and moral choice."[2] Many artists abandoned the prewar modernist ideal of "art for art's sake" and produced work steeped in political passion and a desire for a better world.

Machinery and Movement

Much of the near-utopianism of European culture focused on the transforming power of technology. The "machine aesthetic" triumphed most completely in the Soviet Union, where the Bolsheviks encouraged artistic experiment and

Otto Dix, *Flanders* (1934–1935)
In this painting, the Flanders landscape is literally shaped by the bodies of soldiers. Like these soldiers—and much of postwar European culture—Dix could not escape the war. His paintings reveal a man permanently wounded.

innovation as part of their revolution. The engineer became the image of a communist hero, and industrial motifs permeated Soviet culture in the 1920s. In the revolutionary theater of Vsevelod Meyerhold, mechanical gestures replaced naturalistic expressions and sets consisted of scaffolding. Similarly, a factory whistle opens the chorus of Dmitri Shostakovich's *Second Symphony* (1927), written to praise industrial labor.

Postwar architecture in the West also provides a vivid illustration of this mechanical faith. A house, explained the Swiss architect Le Corbusier (1887–1965), was "a machine for living in." Le Corbusier and his fellow modernist architects stripped their buildings of all ornament and frequently exposed the essential machinery—the supporting beams, the heating ducts, the elevator shafts. Concrete, steel, and glass became the building materials of choice as modernist skyscrapers—glittering rectangles—transformed urban skylines and testified to the triumph of the human-made.

Closely related to the worship of the machine in the interwar period was a celebration of movement and speed. The automobile evolved from a rich man's toy to a middle-class necessity, made possible by the assembly-line techniques developed in Henry Ford's Detroit factories. The assembly line, which reduced the entire industrial workforce of a factory to a single efficient machine, was imported from the United States into Europe in the later 1920s. The airline industry also took off in this era. In 1919 the first air passenger service between London and Paris began; the next decade saw Europe's major cities linked by air networks. The car and the plane became potent symbols of a new age of possibility and opportunity. In 1927, when the American Charles Lindbergh (1902–1974) became the first person to fly across the Atlantic alone, he was hailed not only as a national but as an international hero, an icon of human resourcefulness and technological mastery.

The idea that Western society was moving rapidly and that anything was possible in a world of change shaped much of the culture of the interwar era. Take the popular dance craze of the 1920s—the Charleston. Arms outstretched and legs firing like pistons, the entire body becomes a fast-moving machine. Another American import, Hollywood's "moving pictures," even more clearly represented and stimulated the ideal of a society in motion. The Italians and the French had dominated the movie industry before 1914, but during the war film production in Europe halted. American filmmakers quickly filled the void. After the war, moviegoing became a truly popular pastime—and most of the movies on the screen were made in America. Hollywood presented European audiences with an appealing, if unrealistic, picture of the United States as a land of fabulous wealth, technological modernity, and unlimited mobility.

Scientific Possibilities

While the United States dominated the fantasy land of popular films in the interwar years, Germany and Britain still clung to their leadership positions in the ongoing scientific revolution. At its most basic level, this revolution overthrew

Building Something Better
Built between 1929 and 1930, the Villa Savoye exemplified Le Corbusier's goal to build "a machine for living (in)." The villa's ribbon windows echo industrial architecture but provide openness and light. True to modernist principles, the house has no historical or traditional ornamentation and uses ramps, spiral staircases, and built-in furniture to create a sense of fluidity.

the mechanistic explanation of the universe that had held sway since the first scientific revolution in the seventeenth century. From the 1890s on, scientists began to replace Isaac Newton's now-discredited universe with a new, more complicated model based on Albert Einstein's theory of relativity. As Chapter 23 explained, Einstein's model replaced Newton's static universe with a world in which space, time, matter, and energy are all interchangeable.

In the 1920s and 1930s, this effort to construct an entirely new understanding of the cosmos electrified the discipline of physics and attracted some of the most brilliant young thinkers of the twentieth century. Students from all over the world traveled to Germany and Britain in pursuit of the best teachers and in hopes of joining research teams in both university and state-funded laboratories.

Much of the excitement in physics stemmed from Einstein's concept of matter as "frozen energy." In theory, if the energy could be "thawed out," then this energy could be released. But could this theory become reality? In 1936, the distinguished British scientist Ernest Rutherford (1871–1937), head of one of the most important research laboratories in the Western world, answered that question with a resounding "no." He dismissed the idea of unlocking the atom to release energy as "moonshine." Yet four years earlier, a scientist working in Rutherford's own laboratory had in fact found the key to unlocking the atom. In 1932, James Chadwick (1891–1974) discovered that atoms contain not only positively charged protons and negatively charged electrons, but also neutrons. Because neutrons possess no electrical charge, they are not repelled by either an atom's protons or its electrons. In theory, then, a bombardment of heavy neutrons could split open an atom's nucleus—a process called nuclear fission. The split nucleus would itself emit neutrons, which would then burst open other atoms, which in turn would emit further neutrons . . . and on and on in a nuclear chain reaction. The result: a colossal burst of energy, energy so abundant that it could perhaps satisfy industrial society's insatiable appetite for energy resources—or produce an atom bomb.

Such possibilities remained purely theoretical—pure "moonshine," in Rutherford's words—until 1938, when two scientists working in Berlin proved Rutherford wrong. Otto Hahn (1879–1968) and Fritz Strassmann (1902–1980) bombarded uranium with a stream of neutrons and broke open the uranium atom. Matter had been unlocked. Within a year, more than 100 articles on the implications of this discovery were published in scientific journals around the world. As one historian has noted, "Physicists viewed the discovery of nuclear fission like the finding of a lost treasure map."[3]

Out of the Trenches: Reconstructing National and Gender Politics in the 1920s

■ **In what ways did reconstruction rather than revolution characterize the postwar period?**

As we saw at the end of Chapter 24, in the years immediately following World War I Europe stood on the brink of revolutionary change. The war toppled empires and redrew the map of eastern and central Europe. Gender roles turned upside down, imperial patterns shattered, and social expectations were raised. The American president Woodrow Wilson promised a radically new world of peace and democracy. In Russia, the Bolshevik revolution offered an even more radical vision of communist freedom. Despite these expectations and fears, however, retrenchment rather than revolution characterized much of the immediate postwar period. In many areas, World War I was the turning point that failed to turn, as Europeans sought to reconstruct the structures toppled by total war.

The Reconstruction of Russia: From Tsar to Commissar

Even in the newly formed Soviet Union, the nation that epitomized revolution, important aspects of prewar society reemerged in the postwar period. By 1922 and against all odds, the Bolsheviks had won the civil war and established their authority over most of the regions of the old tsarist empire. The Bolsheviks also reestablished many features of the tsarist regime: authoritarian rule built on violent coer-

Map 25.1 Europe in the 1920s and 1930s

The map shows the consequences of not only World War I but also such successor conflicts as 1. the Irish-English struggles, which resulted in the partition of Ireland: Northern Ireland remained a part of Britain while the rest of the island became the independent nation-state of Eire (see p. 840); 2. the war between Bolshevik Russia and its enemies, which widened the western frontiers of the Soviet state (see p. 819); and 3. the Turkish uprising, which kept Turkey intact and independent (see pp. 842–843).

cion, a highly centralized state, a large bureaucratic elite living in conditions of privilege that cut it off from ordinary people, and a peasant economy.

How do we explain the continuity of authoritarian rule in Russia? The first crucial factor was the impact of civil and international war. Across Russia in 1919 the Bolsheviks faced fierce opposition from rival bands of socialists, middle-class liberals, and aristocratic supporters of the tsar. These opponents of the Bolshevik revolution—called the "Whites" to distinguish them from the "Red" Bolsheviks—were supported by foreign troops. Fearing the spread of communist revolution, fourteen different countries (including the United States, Britain, France, and Japan) sent more than 100,000 soldiers to fight in Russia. In addition to these forces, the new Bolshevik state confronted numerous attempts by non-Russian nationalists to throw off the yoke of Russian rule. This was warfare at its most savage. When Ukrainian peasants resisted Russian control, the Bolsheviks resorted to methods of mass reprisal. Entire villages were burned, the men executed, the women and children sent to slower deaths in prison camps. The Bolsheviks did not have a monopoly on murder, however. White forces in the Ukraine massacred more than 100,000 Jews.

As the scale of savagery escalated, so too did Russia's economic disintegration. In the cities, residents faced anarchic conditions. Transportation systems shut down, the water supply ceased to run, and furniture became the only source of fuel. When the furniture ran out, entire families froze to death inside apartment blocks. The urban areas emptied as their inhabitants fled to the countryside. By 1921, Moscow had lost half its residents and Petrograd (formerly St. Petersburg) had lost two-thirds. Yet conditions in the countryside were also brutal. To feed the cities, the Bolsheviks adopted the policy of "War Communism": requisitioning (stealing) food and seed stores from the peasants. The peasants resisted, both actively, in violent revolt, and passively, by reducing the amount they planted. Food shortages and other war-related hardships increased the population's vulnerability to epidemic disease. Between 1918 and 1921, the number of deaths from the combined impact of the civil war, starvation, and typhus surpassed the number of those who died in World War I.

The need to impose order on this chaotic situation led the Bolsheviks to adopt increasingly authoritarian measures. Like the Jacobins in 1792 during the French Revolutionary Wars, the Bolsheviks turned to terror to defeat their enemies, both domestic and foreign. In the first six years of Bolshevik rule, the Cheka (Lenin's secret police force) executed at least 200,000 people. In contrast, in the fifty years before the Bolsheviks came to power, 14,000 Russians had died at the hands of the tsarist secret police.

But the antidemocratic nature of the Bolshevik regime was not solely a response to the pressures of war. Ideology also helps explain the continuity of authoritarian rule in post-tsarist Russia. Faced with the task of building a communist state in an isolated, economically backward, peasant society, the Bolshevik leader Vladimir Lenin modified Marxist theory. In a peasant society, Lenin argued, the agent of revolutionary change could not be the working class alone: There simply were not enough industrial workers in Russia. Instead, the Bolshevik or Communist Party, an elite of highly disciplined, politically aware and committed individuals, would be the "vanguard" of revolution. Because the masses could not be trusted to make their own decisions, government officials, strictly controlled by the party, would make these decisions for them. The number of

The High Costs of Civil War
Civil War raged in Russia between 1918 and 1922 as the Bolsheviks fought not only tsarist supporters but also other revolutionary groups and ethnic nationalists. The chaos in the countryside, exacerbated by the Bolshevik policy of seizing peasant produce, resulted in famine.

bureaucrats multiplied and by 1925 had become a privileged elite, with access to the best jobs, food, clothing, and apartments. The rule of the tsar had been replaced not with democracy but with the rule of the commissar, the Communist Party functionary.

In the economic sphere, as in the political system, important continuities shaped the Russian experience. Famine and widespread peasant unrest forced Lenin to revise his program. In 1921 Lenin announced a New Economic Policy (NEP)°. Under NEP, peasants were allowed to sell their produce for profit. Although the state continued to control heavy industry, transport, and banking, NEP encouraged the proliferation of small private businesses and farms—just as the tsar's economic policymakers had done before the war.

The Reconstruction of National Politics in Eastern and Central Europe

U.S. president Woodrow Wilson's vision of a new international order based on democratic politics offered the war-torn states of Europe a sharp alternative to Bolshevik one-party rule. But in the new states of eastern Europe, democracy proved to be fragile, and in most cases short-lived. Much of old Europe survived the war intact.

The Defeat of Democracy in Eastern Europe

After the peace negotiations concluded in 1922, postwar eastern Europe certainly looked markedly different from its prewar counterpart (see Map 25.1). The Russian, Austrian-Hungarian, and Ottoman Empires had all disappeared, replaced by a jigsaw puzzle of small independent nations. But lines on the map did not change key political and economic realities. Three important threads tied these new states to their prewar past: ethnic disputes, economic underdevelopment, and antidemocratic politics.

As we saw at the end of Chapter 24, the Allies paid lip service to the ideal of national self-determination but found it impossible to create ethnically homogenous nation-states in eastern Europe. As a result, nationalist-ethnic divisions continued to haunt postwar political structures. In the new Yugoslavia, for example, Croats and Slovenes had expected a federalist system that would grant them local autonomy. Instead, they found themselves in a centralized state under Serbian control. As a result, Croat representatives refused even to sit in the new parliament, and ethnic struggles dominated Yugoslav politics.

Economic difficulties also threatened eastern European stability. In many regions, eastern Europe remained a world of peasants and aristocratic landlords. In Romania, Poland, and Hungary, at least 60 percent of the population worked the land; in Bulgaria and Yugoslavia the figure was 80 percent—versus 20 percent in industrialized Britain. With little industrial growth in these regions and few cities to absorb labor, unemployment rates and land hunger were both high.

Thus ethnic divisions and economic underdevelopment helped destabilize eastern Europe's new democratic political systems. The result was the collapse of democracy across eastern Europe. As the chronology (left) shows, with the exception of Czechoslovakia, every eastern European nation returned to authoritarian politics during the 1920s or early 1930s. In Poland, for example, democracy crumbled in 1926 when the World War I hero Marshal Josef Pilsudski (1867–1935) seized power in a military coup, after parliamentary representatives proved unable to overcome class and ethnic divisions. Pilsudski told the squabbling legislators, "The time has come to treat you like children, because you behave like children."[4] In Yugoslavia, the death of democracy was even more dramatic. Years of escalating ethnic violence peaked in 1928 when a popular Croatian political leader was shot to death on the floor of the legislature. The ensuing ethnic unrest gave King Alexander (a Serb) the excuse he needed to abolish the constitution and replace parliamentary democracy with a royal dictatorship. A brutal repression of Alexander's opponents followed. In Bulgaria, Albania, Hungary, and Romania, too, continuing ethnic conflicts and economic underdevelopment ensured the destruction of democracy.

CHRONOLOGY

The Return of Authoritarian Rule to Eastern Europe

1923	Boris III establishes a royalist dictatorship in Bulgaria
1926	Marshal Josef Pilsudski establishes a military dictatorship in Poland
1928	A new constitution gives King Zog in Albania almost unlimited powers
1929	Alexander I establishes a royal dictatorship in Yugoslavia
1932	Fascist leader Gyula Gombos appointed prime minister in Hungary
1938	King Carol establishes a royal dictatorship in Romania

The Weakness of the Weimar Republic

In Germany, as in the new states of eastern Europe, the appearance of radical change masked crucial continuities between the pre- and postwar eras. The kaiser's empire gave way to the Weimar Republic°, led by a democratically elected parliamentary government. This democratic political structure, however, sat uneasily atop fundamentally antidemocratic social and political foundations.

The survival of authoritarian attitudes and institutions resulted in part from the civil war that raged throughout Germany in the fall of 1918 and the first months of 1919. In this struggle, communists, inspired by the Bolshevik revolution, fought their one-time colleagues in the more moderate socialist party (the SPD) for control of the new Germany. Anxious to impose order on a potentially anarchic situation, the SPD leaders who now controlled the German government chose not to replace the existing state bureaucracy—the elite corps of aristocratic civil servants that had served the kaiser—but to work with it. To put down the communist threat, they also abandoned their longstanding loathing of the German military and deployed both regular army units and the "Free Corps" (volunteer paramilitary units, often comprising demobilized soldiers addicted to violence). By the spring of 1919, this strange alliance of moderate socialists, traditional aristocrats, soldiers, and thugs had triumphed. In January 1919, Free Corps officers murdered the communist leaders Karl Liebknecht and Rosa Luxemburg in Berlin. Three months later, an equally savage repression crushed the communist soviet in Munich, with the Free Corps killing more than 600 people.

The SPD had won. Yet it lost. By allying with the aristocratic civil service, the army, and the Free Corps, the SPD crushed more than the communist revolution; it also crushed its own chances of achieving significant social change. The officers in the army and the bureaucrats in the civil service were representatives of the old Germany, vehemently opposed to not only communism but also parliamentary democracy. Continuing in positions of authority and influence, they constituted a formidable antidemocratic force at the very heart of the new Germany. The approximately 400,000 men who made up the Free Corps also regarded democratic ideals and the new German republic with contempt—"an attempt of the slime to govern."[5] The attitude of the Free Corps men is summed up in their slogan: "Everything would still have been all right if we had shot more people."[6]

The antidemocratic nature of the Free Corps became clear in 1920, after the Allies imposed restrictions on the size of Germany's military force and most Free Corps units were officially dissolved. Disaffected corpsmen joined the right-wing politician Wolfgang Kapp (1858–1922) and the World War I hero Erich von Ludendorff in an effort to overthrow the Weimar regime. This "Kapp Putsch" quickly fizzled out, defeated by both divisions in the ranks of the rebels and a general strike, but the threat posed by the Free Corps did not disappear. Disguising themselves as athletic societies, haulage companies, and even circuses, many corps units continued their violent anti-Weimar activities. In 1923, some of these corpsmen tried once again to overthrow the Weimar government by force, with another "putsch," this time originating in a beer hall in Munich and led by a former army corporal named Adolf Hitler. Like the Kapp Putsch, Hitler's "Beer Hall Putsch°" did not succeed. The laughably light sentences imposed on its participants, however, made clear the strength of antirepublican sentiments not only among disgruntled Free Corps men but also far up the ranks of the Weimar judicial system.

Antidemocratic forces in the Weimar Republic fed on the widespread resentment among Germans aroused by the severity of the Versailles Treaty. Many Germans could not separate the birth of the republic from the national humiliation imposed by Versailles. They blamed the moderate socialist government that signed the treaty for this humiliation. Army officers encouraged the idea that Germany could have kept on fighting had it not been "stabbed in the back" by the socialists. This "stab-in-the-back" legend helped undermine support not only for the SPD's moderate socialism but even for democracy itself.

The shaky foundations of democracy in Weimar Germany were eroded further by the dramatic events of 1923. In that year, the German mark collapsed completely and paper money ceased to have any value. This hyperinflation was the unintended by-product of the Weimar government's effort to force the Allies to reconsider reparations. In 1922, the Weimar government halted payments and demanded a new economic settlement. The French retaliated by sending troops into Germany's Ruhr Valley to seize coal as a form of reparations payment. German laborers in the Ruhr Valley resisted the invasion by going on strike. Already relying on a policy of inflationary spending to meet its budget deficit, the German government began printing money with abandon to pay the striking Ruhr workers. The inflation rate surged upward. By January 1923, the mark, which in 1914 could be traded for the American dollar at a rate of 4:1, had plummeted to an exchange rate of 22,400:1. By October, the exchange rate from mark to dollar was at 440,000,000:1. Families who had scrimped for years found they had only enough savings to buy a loaf of bread.

France Demands War Reparations from Germany—*L. A. Times* Cartoon

As a result of this disaster, the French army pulled out of the Ruhr Valley and in 1924 Allied and German representatives drew up the Dawes Plan, which renegotiated reparations. By the end of 1924, the German economy had stabilized; the later 1920s were years of relative prosperity. Yet for many Germans, the memory of hyperinflation tainted the Weimar Republic. Many Germans concluded that democracy meant disorder and degradation. They looked with longing back to the prewar period, an era of supposed social stability and national power.

The Trial of Adolf Hitler

On February 24, 1924, Adolf Hitler appeared in court in Munich to confront a charge of high treason following his pathetic attempt three months earlier to overthrow the Weimar government by armed rebellion. The trial marked a crucial point in Hitler's career. It gave him a national platform and, even more important, convinced him of the futility of an armed offensive against the state. From 1925 on, Hitler would work through the parliamentary system in order to destroy it. But the trial of Adolf Hitler is also significant in what it reveals about the power of antidemocratic forces in the new Germany. The trial made clear that many in positions of authority and responsibility in the Weimar Republic shared Hitler's contempt for the democratic state. By treating Hitler not as a traitorous thug but rather as an honorable patriot, his prosecutors helped weaken the already fragile structures of German democracy.

Hitler's attempt to overthrow the Weimar Republic by force occurred at the height of hyperinflation and the ensuing political chaos. By November 8, 1923, when Hitler took up arms, the German mark was worth only one-trillionth of its prewar value. As its currency eroded, the Weimar Republic saw its political legitimacy seeping away as well. Separatist movements in several states threatened the sovereignty of the central government in Berlin. Separatist politics attracted the support of many men from aristocratic backgrounds, members of the traditional conservative elite who viewed Weimar democracy as a foreign and unwelcome import.

Hitler had little interest in the separatist movement, but he believed he could channel its antidemocratic sentiments into a national revolution. He attracted a number of supporters, including one of the most important men in Germany, the World War I hero General Erich von Ludendorff. Seeking to avoid the blame for Germany's defeat in 1918, Ludendorff insisted that his army could have won the war had it not been stabbed in the back by the Social Democratic politicians who now ran the government. Like many German conservatives—and like Hitler—he viewed the Weimar Republic as illegitimate.

On November 8 Hitler made his move. His men surrounded a Munich beer hall where 2,000 supporters of Bavarian separatism had gathered. Hitler declared that both the Bavarian and the national governments had been overthrown and that he was now the head of a new German state, with Ludendorff as his commander-in-chief. Around noon the next day, Hitler, Ludendorff, and several thousand of their followers marched toward the regional government buildings located on one of Munich's main squares. Armed police blocked their passage. In the ensuing firefight, seventeen men were killed. Despite the bullets whizzing through the air, Ludendorff marched through the police cordon and stood in the square awaiting arrest. Hitler ran away. Police found him two days later, cowering in a supporter's country house about thirty-five miles outside Munich.

The Beer Hall Putsch had clearly, utterly, completely failed. In jail awaiting trial, Hitler contemplated suicide. Yet later he described his defeat as "perhaps the greatest stroke of luck in my life." The defeat meant a trial; the trial meant a national audience—and an opportunity for Hitler to present his case against the Weimar Republic. He admitted that he had conspired to overthrow the democratically elected Republican government, but he insisted he was not therefore guilty of treason. The real treason had occurred in November 1918, when the Social Democratic government had surrendered to the Allies: "I confess to the deed, but I do not confess to the crime of high treason. There can be no question of treason in an action which aims to undo the betrayal of this country in 1918. . . . I consider myself not a traitor but a German." He argued that he was not aiming for personal power: "In what small terms small minds think! . . . What I had in mind from the very first day was a thousand times more important than becoming a [Cabinet] minister. I wanted to become the destroyer of Marxism." Thus Hitler depicted himself as a patriot, a nationalist motivated by love of Germany and hatred of communists and socialists. "The eternal court of history," according to Hitler, would judge him and his fellow defendants "as Germans who wanted the best for their people and their Fatherland, who were willing to fight and to die."[7]

Despite Hitler's own admission of conspiring against the government, the presiding judge could persuade the three lay judges (who took the place of a jury) to render a guilty verdict only by arguing that Hitler would most likely be pardoned soon. The reluctance of the judges to convict Hitler highlights the extraordinary sympathy shown to him and his political ideas throughout the trial and during his imprisonment. The chief prosecutor offered a rather surprising description of an accused traitor: "Hitler is a highly gifted man, who has risen from humble beginnings to achieve a respected position in public life, the result of much hard work and dedication. . . . As a soldier he did his duty to the utmost. He cannot

Hitler in Landsberg Prison, 1924
This photo of Hitler during his short imprisonment was made into a postcard, to be purchased by his supporters.

be accused of having used the position he created for himself in any self-serving way." In delivering the verdict, the judge emphasized Hitler's "pure patriotic motives and honorable intentions." Rather than being deported as a foreign national convicted of a serious crime (Hitler was still an Austrian citizen), Hitler was given a slight sentence of five years, which made him eligible for parole in just six months. In prison he was treated like a visiting dignitary—exempted from work and exercise requirements, provided with prisoners to clean his rooms, even given a special table decorated with a swastika banner in the dining hall. When he was released in September, his parole report described him favorably as "a man of order."[8]

Hitler's gentle treatment reveals the precarious state of democratic institutions in Germany after World War I. Many high-ranking Germans in positions of power and influence (such as judges and prosecutors) viewed parliamentary democracy with loathing. The trial also reveals the willingness of conservative aristocrats to ally with Radical Right groups such as the Nazis. Still not very strong, the Nazis in 1923 were easily reined in. A decade later, however, the conservatives who thought they could ride Hitler to power suddenly found that they were no longer in control.

Questions of Justice

1. Imagine you are a German war veteran reading about this case in the newspaper in 1924. Why might you be attracted to the party of Adolf Hitler?
2. Hitler appealed to the "eternal court of history." What do you think he meant? How would Hitler have defined "justice"?

Taking It Further

Gordon, Harold, Jr. *Hitler and the Beer Hall Putsch.* 1972. This lengthy study (more than 600 pages) provides a detailed account of the putsch and its aftermath.

The Hitler Trial Before the People's Court in Munich, trans. H. Francis Freniece, Lucie Karcic, and Philip Fandek (3 vols.). 1976. An English translation of the court transcripts.

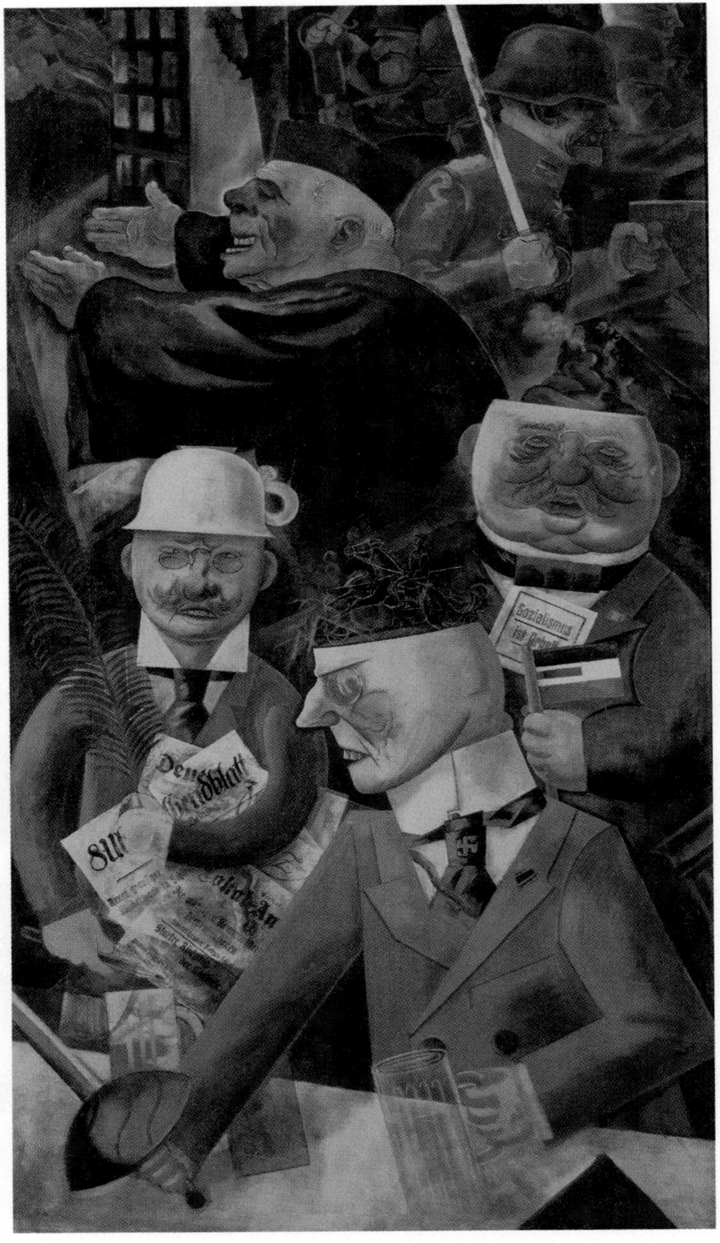

George Grosz, "The Pillars of Society" (1926)
The Expressionist artist George Grosz was, like Otto Dix (see page 816), a World War I veteran and a sharp critic of Weimar Germany. In Grosz's scathing critique, the Weimar state had failed to carry out essential social reforms and thus the old order still survived. In this painting, a drunken military chaplain continues to preach while soldiers slaughter behind his back. In the foreground sits a lawyer, supposedly a modern professional, but out of his head bursts a cavalry officer bent on destruction. To the lawyer's right, a press baron, his limited intelligence indicated by the chamber pot on his head, clutches the newspapers that guarantee his fortune and that delude the masses. To the lawyer's left totters an SPD politician. Both his pudgy, drink-reddened cheeks and the pamphlet he presses to his chest (headlined "Socialism is Work") indicate Grosz's contempt for the gradual reformism of the SPD.

The Reconstruction of Gender

Many of the patterns that shaped interwar national politics also characterized the politics of gender in these years. World War I wrought a profound upheaval in gender roles in European society. The demands of total war had meant that women moved into economic areas previously designated as "men only." The war, therefore, seemed an important turning point in the history of women in the West. But here again the turning point failed to turn. Important changes in women's expectations did occur, but nineteenth-century gender roles were quickly reconstructed after the war.

The New Woman

At first sight, the postwar period seems an era of profound change in the roles of women. In the films, magazines, novels, and popular music of the 1920s, the "New Woman" took center stage. Living, working, and traveling on her own, sexually active, she stepped out of the confines of home and family. Women's dress reinforced this idea of a new woman. Whereas nineteenth-century women's clothing had accentuated the womanly body while restricting the woman's movement, the clothing of the 1920s ignored a woman's curves and became much less confining. Complementing this revolution in clothing came a revolution in hairstyle. Women chopped off the long locks regarded for generations as a sign of femaleness and sported fashionable new bobs.

This perception of the New Woman rested on important changes in women's political and economic expectations. By 1920 women in the United States and many European countries had received the right to vote in national elections and to hold national office. In all the industrialized countries, the expansion of both the health care and service sectors meant new jobs for women as nurses, social workers, secretaries, telephone exchange operators, and clerks. Women's higher-education opportunities also widened in this period.

The biggest change affecting the lives of ordinary women was the spreading practice of limiting family size. We saw in Chapter 22 that by the 1870s middle-class women in Western nations were practicing forms of birth control. In the 1920s and 1930s, an increasing number of working-class women began to do so as well. In Britain, for example, between 1911 and 1931 the average number of

The "New Woman"
Almost every aspect of the "New Woman" captured in this 1928 French photograph offended traditionalists: short skirts and bobbed hair, smoking in public, the association with a car and therefore with mobility and illicit sex—all crossing the border into masculine terrain.

DOCUMENT

The Threat of the New Woman

The perceived movement of women into less traditional roles was profoundly upsetting to many Europeans after the war. Much of this distress focused on a clearly visible target: the dramatically different dress and hairstyles sported by fashionable women, as is evident in this description of the New Woman by a French law student in 1925:

Can one define *la jeune fille moderne* [the young modern woman]? No, no more than the waist on the dresses she wears. Young girls of today are difficult to locate precisely. If you want to be true to French tradition, it would be barbaric, in my opinion, to call our pretty young *parisiennes* young girls.

These beings—without breasts, without hips, without "underwear," who smoke, work, argue, and fight exactly like boys, and who, during the night at the Bois de Boulogne, with their heads swimming under several cocktails, seek out savory and acrobatic pleasures on the plush seats of 5 horsepower Citroens—these aren't young girls!

There aren't any more young girls! No more women either!

Source: Quoted in Mary Louise Roberts, *Civilization Without Sexes: Reconstructing Gender in Postwar France, 1917–1927* (1994), p. 20.

children per family fell from 3.4 to 2.2, with most of this decrease resulting from changes in working-class family size. Fewer pregnancies and fewer mouths to feed meant a significant improvement in women's health and living standards.

The Reconstruction of Traditional Roles

Despite these important changes, however, women's roles actually altered little in the two decades after World War I. These years witnessed a strong reaction against the wartime gender upheaval and a concerted effort to reconstruct nineteenth-century masculine and feminine ideals.

Both the war's lengthy casualty lists and the drop in the average family size provoked widespread fear about declining populations—and thus declining national strength. Governments, religious leaders, and commercial entrepreneurs joined together to convince women that their destiny lay in motherhood. Sale and purchase of birth control devices became illegal during the 1920s in France, Belgium, Italy, and Spain. France outlawed abortions in 1920. In Britain after 1929, a woman who had an abortion could be sentenced to life imprisonment.

To encourage population growth, governments also turned to more positive incentives ranging from the symbolic to the economic. Mother's Day, an American invention, crossed into Europe during the 1920s. In France from 1920 on, women who gave birth to at least five children received a bronze medal; those who bore seven or more children earned the silver; and mothers who produced ten offspring brought home the gold. German women had an easier time: They needed only seven children to get the gold. Of more lasting importance was the expansion of welfare services—family allowances, subsidized or state-provided housing, school lunches, health insurance, prenatal and well-baby clinics—with the express aim of strengthening the family, encouraging women to stay at home, and raising the birth rate. Eugenics played an important role in this legislation. National leaders wanted to increase not only the quantity but the quality of the population. On the positive side, this meant improving the health of babies and mothers. More ominously, much of the rhetoric focused on separating the "fit" from the "unfit," with both class and race among the factors that determined who was "fit" to produce children for the nation.

Despite the calls for women to remain at home, many women had to work in paid employment. In the work world, just as in the family, traditional roles were strengthened after World War I. Most working women returned to jobs in domestic service or to factory positions labeled unskilled and therefore low-paying. Women tended to be barred from management positions, assigned to the most repetitive tasks, and paid by piecework, with the result that the wage gap between male and female laborers remained wide. In both Germany and Britain, unemployment benefits were frequently denied to married women workers, even though they had regularly paid into the insurance system while they were working. The numbers of women employed in the clerical and service sectors did rise in this era, but the movement of women into these positions meant such jobs were reclassified as "women's work," a guarantee of low pay and little power.

Women and the Bolshevik Revolution

In sharp contrast to these efforts to buttress the traditional family structures, in Russia the Bolsheviks promised to revolutionize gender roles. Lenin believed that the family was a middle-class institution doomed to "wither away." In the ideal communist society, marriage would be a mutually beneficial—and in many cases temporary—arrangement between two equally educated and equally waged partners, and both housework and child care would move from the private domestic household into the public sphere of paid employment. To create such a society, the Bolsheviks turned to legislation. One month after seizing power, they legalized divorce and civil marriages. In October 1918, a new family legal code declared women and men equal under the law, made divorce readily available, and abolished the distinction between legitimate and illegitimate children. To free women from housework—described by Lenin as "barbarously unproductive, petty, nervewracking, and stultifying drudgery"[9]—the Bolsheviks established communal child care centers, laundries, and dining rooms. In 1920, just as other nations were outlawing abortion, the practice became legal in Bolshevik Russia.

By 1922, however, the newly created Soviet Union seemed about to self-destruct, and as we have already seen, Lenin retreated from rigorous communist economic ideology to institute the New Economic Policy. NEP also meant significant reversals in the gender revolution. By 1923, the dining halls had been closed and more than half of the day care centers had shut down. The decade of the 1920s was a time of high unemployment for Soviet women. Those who did find jobs received wages that averaged only 65 percent that of men's. An increasing number turned to prostitution. In addition, the traditional patriarchal peasant household—with women in a clearly subordinate role—remained firmly intact. Even in revolutionary Russia, therefore, certain continuities linked the pre- and postwar experience of women.

The Rise of the Radical Right

■ **What circumstances explain the emergence of the Radical Right?**

As the revolution in gender roles was reversed, as Lenin's communist revolution shifted into a lower gear, and as Wilson's democratic revolution ran out of gas, a very different sort of revolution was occurring in Italy, a region long on the periphery of European power. The fascist revolution introduced Europe to a new sort of politics, the politics of the Radical Right. Like conservatism, the new Radical Right ideologies—fascism° and its younger cousin, Nazism—dismissed equality as a socialist myth and emphasized the importance of authority. But neither fascism nor Nazism was conservative. These radical political systems sought to use the new technologies of the mass media to mobilize their societies for a program of violent nationalism.

The Fascist Alternative

Conceived in the coupling of wartime exhilaration and postwar despair, fascism offered an alternative to the existing political ideologies. Fascism was more than a set of political ideas, however. As presented by its creator, Benito Mussolini (1883–1945), fascism was an ongoing performance, a spectacular sound-and-lights show with a cast of millions.

Mussolini's Rise to Power

Fascism originated in Italy. In 1915 after a fierce internal debate that widened the already huge gaps in Italian society, Italy entered the war on the side of the Allies. Many pro-war Italians viewed the war as a cleansing force, a powerful disinfectant that would leave Italian society stronger and more powerful. Mussolini, a socialist journalist, shared these views. Because the Socialist Party opposed Italy's entry into the war, Mussolini broke with the socialists, joined the army in 1915, and fought until he was wounded in 1917. When the war ended, he sought to create a new form of politics that would translate the military camaraderie and the exhilaration of violent action that he had experienced during the war. The result was fascism.

In March 1919, Mussolini and a little more than 100 men and some women gathered in Milan and declared themselves the fascist movement. Like Mussolini, many of these "fascists of the first hour" were war veterans; a number had served in the *arditi,* elite commando units that fought behind enemy lines. The arditi uniform, a severe black shirt, became the fascist badge of identity. The arditi slogan, "*me ne frego*" ("I don't give a damn") became the blackshirts' creed, a fitting summary of their willingness to throw aside conventional standards and politics.

The March on Rome, October 28, 1922
The fascist march on Rome was a carefully orchestrated show of power, not an armed rebellion. Mussolini had already been offered the premiership of Italy, as is clear from his clothing: He has changed his black shirt for a proper suit.

Just three and a half years after the first fascist meeting in Milan, Mussolini became prime minister of Italy. His astonishing rise to power occurred against a backdrop of social turmoil. In 1919 and 1920, more than one million workers were on strike, factory occupations became commonplace, and a wave of land seizures spread across the countryside. Increasingly frightened that revolution would engulf Italy just as it had destroyed tsarist Russia, large landowners and industrialists, as well as the professional and commercial middle classes, looked to Mussolini's fascists for help. Fascist squads disrupted Socialist Party meetings, vandalized the offices of socialist newspapers, broke up strikes, beat up trade unionists, and protected aristocratic estates from attack. By 1922, the fascists were a formidable political force and Mussolini was engaged in negotiations aimed at bringing the fascists into a coalition government. In October 1922, King Victor Emmanuel III (r. 1900–1946) asked Mussolini to become not only a member of the government but its prime minister. Mussolini agreed. In a carefully orchestrated display of muscle, fascists from all over Italy converged in the "March on Rome," a piece of street theater designed to demonstrate Mussolini's mass support, as well as the disciplined might of his followers.

The Fascist Revolution in Italy

Over the next four years Mussolini used both legal and illegal methods, including murder, to eliminate his political rivals and remake Italy as a one-party state. By 1926, he had succeeded. Party politics, an independent press, and the trade union movement ceased to exist. Victor Emmanuel

CHRONOLOGY

Mussolini's Rise to Power

1915–1917	Serves in the Italian army
1919	Participates in the creation of the fascist movement
1921	Fascist Party wins thirty-five seats in parliament
1922	Becomes prime minister
1925–1926	Abolishes party politics and establishes himself as dictator
1929	Signs Lateran Accords with the Roman Catholic Church

remained on the throne, the official head of state, but power lay in Mussolini's hands. The restored death penalty and a strong police apparatus stood ready to enforce Mussolini's will and to remake Italy into a fascist society.

But what was fascism? Mussolini conceived of fascism as the politics of modernity. He condemned the existing political ideologies as outdated. Socialism exalted the working class; liberalism viewed the individual as the core of society; conservatism clung to social hierarchy. Fascism, however, identified the *nation* as the dominant social reality. With a strong leader at the wheel, with violent action as its fuel, the fascist nation would crash through social and economic barriers and transport its people into a new and more powerful age.

Yet Mussolini's supposedly radical revolution reinforced traditional elite interests. Early fascist promises of land redistribution were quickly forgotten, and the end of democracy meant that the control of local government rested not with elected officials but rather with Mussolini's appointees—usually drawn from the ranks of the traditional agrarian elite. Fascist economic theory, such as it was, promised to replace capitalist competition and the profit motive with corporatism: Committees (or "corporations") made up of representatives of workers, employers, and the state were to direct the economy for the good of the nation. In actuality, workers' rights disappeared while industrialists' profits remained untouched.

Mussolini's revolution, then, was not about leveling society. Mussolini had no intention of giving *actual* political power to ordinary people; he did, however, recognize the importance of giving them the *illusion* of power. The fascist revolution offered individuals a sense of power by making them feel a part of the nation. A series of "after-work" occupational and recreational groups served as a channel for fascist propaganda and connected ordinary people more closely to the fascist state, while at the same time occupying their leisure hours. By 1939, four million Italians were participating in fascist sporting clubs, holiday camps, and cultural outings.

The "Cult of the Duce" also provided an important means of fostering a sense of participation in the life of the nation. Mussolini insisted, "I am Fascism." Carefully choreographed public appearances gave ordinary Italians the chance to see, hear, and adore their Duce ("Leader"), and through contact with his person, to feel a part of the new Italy. To stimulate public adoration of himself, Mussolini paid careful attention to his public image. He ordered that the press ignore his birthdays and the births of his grandchildren: The Duce could not be seen to age. Instead, in photograph after photograph, Mussolini appeared as a man of action. Depicted in planes, in trains, and in racing cars, he was always on the move, always pressing forward.

At the same time, Mussolini combined up-to-date advertising and the latest mass media technologies with age-old rituals inspired largely by the Catholic Church. Huge public rallies set in massive arenas, carefully staged with lighting and music, inspired his followers. A popular fascist slogan summed up the leadership cult: "Believe, Obey, Fight." Italians were not to think or question; they were to *believe*. What were they to believe? Another slogan provides the answer: "Mussolini is always right."

The Great Depression and the Spread of Fascism After 1929

The simple certainty offered by a slogan such as Mussolini's proved highly appealing throughout much of Europe after 1929. During the 1930s, fascist movements emerged in almost every European state. The key factor in the spread of fascism was the Great Depression°. On October 24, 1929, the American stock market collapsed. Over the next two years, the American economic crisis evolved into a global depression. Banks closed, businesses collapsed, and unemployment rates rose to devastating levels. Even by the end of the 1930s, the production rates of many nations remained low. Desperate people looked for desperate answers. Fascism provided some of these.

Why did the Depression spread so quickly and last so long? The explanation lies with the changing role of the United States in Europe. World War I accelerated the shift of the world's economic center away from Europe and toward America. New York's stock market emerged to rival London's, and U.S. businesses increasingly displaced European competitors as the chief suppliers of industrial goods to regions such as Latin America. While European nations sold off their domestic and foreign assets and borrowed heavily to pay for the war, the United States moved from the position of debtor to creditor nation. By the end of 1918 Allied nations owed the United States more than $9 billion—and American officials made it clear that they expected this money to be repaid in full, with interest.

The problem of wartime indebtedness quickly became entangled with the issue of German reparations. Britain, France, and Italy could pay off their debts to the United States only if Germany paid reparations to them. Hyperinflation and the near-collapse of the German economy in 1923, however, forced the revision of the reparations schedule established by the Versailles Treaty. In 1924 and again in 1928 American and European financial representatives met to reconfigure (and in 1928 to reduce) the payments. American credit became the fuel that kept the European economy burning. From 1925 on, American investors loaned money to Germany, which used the money to pay reparations to the Allies, which in turn used the money to pay back the United States. The system worked for a short time. Fueled by loans, the German economy kicked into gear. Currencies stabilized, production rose, and American money flowed not only into Germany but into all of Europe. If these loans dried up, however, Europe faced disaster.

In 1929 that disaster struck. With the collapse of the U.S. stock market, savings portfolios lost between 60 and 75 percent of their value almost overnight. Scrambling to scrape up any assets, American creditors liquidated their European investments, and European economies tumbled. Germany, the country whose economy was most directly linked to the United States, saw its industrial output fall by 46 percent, while its number of jobless grew to more than six million.

The political and social disarray that accompanied the Great Depression enhanced the appeal of fascist promises of stability, order, and national strength. In the 1930s, fascist movements emerged across Europe. Few succeeded in seizing the reins of government, but existing authoritarian regimes adopted many fascist trappings in order to stay in power. For example, Romania's King Carol II (r. 1930–1940) faced a strong challenge to his rule from the Iron Guard, the first mass fascist movement in the Balkans. To compete with the guard, Carol embraced its language of national renewal, as well as typically fascist features such as uniformed paramilitaries, a youth group, and mass rallies. In 1938 he abolished all political parties, placed the judicial system under military control, and declared himself a royal dictator. He then dissolved the Iron Guard and garroted its leader.

CHRONOLOGY

Hitler's Rise to Power

1914–1918	Serves in the German army
1919–1923	Establishes himself as a right-wing activist in Munich
1923	Fails to overthrow the government with the Beer Hall Putsch
1929	Collapse of the U.S. stock market; onset of Great Depression
1930	Nazis win 107 seats in German parliament
1932	Nazis win 230 seats; become largest party in German parliament
1933	
January	Becomes chancellor
February	Uses Reichstag fire as pretext to gain emergency powers
March	Uses the Enabling Act to destroy democracy in Germany

The Nazi Revolution

In Germany, the Nazi Party offered a different version of Radical Right ideology. Just as the emergence of fascism was inextricably linked to the career of one man, Benito Mussolini, so Nazism° cannot be separated from Adolf Hitler (1889–1945). To understand the Nazi revolution in Germany, we need first to explore Hitler's rise to power and then to examine the impact of Nazi rule on ordinary people.

Hitler's Rise to Power

Hitler, an ardent German nationalist, was not a citizen of Germany for most of his life. Born in Austria, Hitler came of age in Vienna, where he made a meager living as a painter while absorbing the anti-Semitic German nationalism that permeated the capital city of the Habsburg Empire. When World War I broke out, Hitler grabbed at the chance to fight the war in a German rather than an Austrian uniform. He regarded army life as "the greatest of all experiences." Hitler served as a German soldier for almost the entire length of the war until he was temporarily blinded by poison gas in 1918. After the war he settled in Munich, home to large bands of unemployed war veterans and a breeding ground for nationalist and racist groups.

The Nazi Party began as one of these small fringe groups, with Hitler quickly emerging as its leader. *Nazi* is shorthand for *National Socialist German Workers' Party,* but this title, like all of Nazi ideology, was a lie. Nazism fiercely opposed socialism, communism, trade unionism, and any political analysis that emphasized class conflict or workers' rights. For the Nazis, race, not class, constituted the key social reality. To Hitler, all history was the history of racial struggle, and in that racial struggle, the Jews were always the principal enemy. Hitler regarded Jewishness as a biological rather than a religious identity, as a sort of toxic infection that could be passed on to future generations and that posed a threat to the racially pure "Aryans"—white northern Europeans.*

Like Mussolini, Hitler exalted the nation. He believed Germany was destined to become a powerful empire controlling central and eastern Europe. This new age would dawn, however, only after a mighty battle between the racially superior Germans and their numerically superior enemy: the forces of "Judeo-Bolshevism." In Hitler's distorted vision, Jewishness and communism formed two parts of the same evil whole. He saw the Bolshevik victory in Russia and the call for communist world revolution as part of a much larger struggle for Jewish world domination.

In its early days Nazism appealed to men like Hitler, individuals without much power or, apparently, much chance of getting it—demobilized and now unemployed soldiers, small shopkeepers wiped out by postwar inflation, lower-middle-class office clerks anxious to preserve their shaky social status, and workers who had lost their jobs. Nazism

*Aryan *is actually a linguistic term referring to the Indo-Aryan or Indo-European language groups. Anti-Semites such as Hitler misapplied the term to racial groups to lend a supposedly scientific authority to their racism.*

offered a simple explanation of history, a promise of future glory, and a clear and identifiable scapegoat for both personal and national woes. By the time of the Beer Hall Putsch in November 1923, party membership stood at about 55,000.

As we saw earlier in the discussion of postwar Germany, the Beer Hall Putsch failed in its aim to overthrow the Weimar Republic, but it did bring Hitler a national audience. Both his speeches during the ensuing trial for treason and *Mein Kampf* ("My Struggle"), the book he wrote while in prison, publicized his racialized view of German political history. After Hitler emerged from prison, he concentrated on transforming the Nazis into a persuasive political force. To infiltrate German society at all levels, Nazis formed university and professional groups, labor unions, and agrarian organizations, while the Nazi paramilitary organization, the SA (*Sturmabteilung*), terrorized opponents. The party held meetings and rallies incessantly, not just during election periods, and so ensured that Germany was saturated with its message. Even so, in the elections of 1928, Nazi candidates won only 2.6 percent of the vote.

It was the Great Depression that gave the Nazis their chance at power. After 1929, unemployment rates skyrocketed and the Weimar political system began to collapse. No German political leader could put together a viable governing coalition. Parliamentary power dwindled; in all of 1932 the federal parliament met for only thirteen days. As the mechanisms of parliamentary democracy faltered, the German chancellor Heinrich Bruning increasingly relied on a stopgap measure in the German constitution—the presidential emergency decree. The constitution declared that in emergency situations, decrees signed by the German president could become law without parliamentary consent. But this practice meant that power shifted from the parliament to the president, the World War I hero General Paul von Hindenburg. Already in his eighties, Hindenburg was a weak man easily manipulated by a small circle of aristocratic advisors and cronies.

In this unstable climate, political polarization accelerated as Germans looked for extreme solutions to extreme problems. By July 1932, the Nazis had become the largest party in the parliament, winning the support of 37 percent of the German voters. Support for their communist rivals also continued to grow.

Terrified of the threat posed by communism and convinced that Hitler could be easily controlled, a small group of conservative politicians persuaded Hindenburg to offer Hitler the position of chancellor in January 1933. One of the group, Baron Franz von Papen, reassured a friend that Hitler posed "no danger at all. We have hired him for our act. In two months' time we'll have pushed Hitler so far into the corner, he'll be squeaking."[10] But von Papen was wrong.

Within six months Hitler had destroyed what remained of democracy in Germany and established a Nazi dictatorship. Almost as soon as he took office he persuaded Hindenburg to pass an emergency decree mandating the seizure of all Communist Party presses and buildings. Then in February a fire destroyed the German parliament building. Declaring (wrongly) that the fire was part of a communist plot against the state, Hitler demanded the power to imprison without warrant or trial. Mass arrests of more than 25,000 of his political opponents followed—not only communists but also social democrats and anyone who dared oppose him openly. At the end of March, German politicians, cowed by Nazi threats of imprisonment, passed the Enabling Act. This key act gave Hitler the power to suspend the constitution and pass legislation without a parliamentary majority. By the summer of 1933, parliamentary political life had ceased to exist in Germany and a dictatorship had destroyed democracy.

Often presented as a model of authoritarian efficiency, the Nazi dictatorship was actually a confusing mass of overlapping bureaucracies, in which ambitious officials competed with each other for power and influence. This planned chaos ensured that none of Hitler's deputies acquired too much authority. It also enhanced the mystery of the state. The individual citizen attempting to make a complaint or resolve a problem would soon feel as if he were engaged in a battle with a multilimbed monster.

This multilimbed monster, however, had only one head: Adolf Hitler. The entire system was designed to make clear that there was only one man in charge, one leader—the *Führer*. Like Mussolini, Hitler realized the importance of personalizing his rule. During election campaigns before 1933 and in the early years of power after, Hitler was constantly on the move, using cars and planes to hit city after city, to deliver speech after speech, to touch person after person. In 1932 and 1933, he conducted election campaigns from the sky, often visiting four or five cities in a single night. He always arrived late, so that his plane could fly above the packed stadium, the focus of every upturned face. Leaders of the Hitler Youth were required to take this oath: "Adolf Hitler is Germany and Germany is Adolf Hitler. He who pledges himself to Hitler pledges himself to Germany."[11]

National Recovery

Jews, communists, socialists, and other groups defined as enemies of the state faced the constant threat of persecution and imprisonment under the Nazi regime during the 1930s. But for many Germans not in these groups, life got better. Nazi rule brought full employment, restoration of national pride, and a cultural revolution that linked the power of nostalgia to the dynamism of modernity.

Economic depression gave the Nazis the chance at power; economic prosperity (or the appearance of it) enabled them to hold on to this power. Because Hitler perceived himself as a revolutionary, bound by no existing rules, he was able to intensify and accelerate unorthodox economic programs put in place by the preceding government. The rules of economic orthodoxy dictated that in times of depression, a government should cut spending and maintain a balanced budget. Struggling to cope with the broken economy, Hitler's predecessors had set aside the rules and instead began devising a program of deficit spending on things such as a national network of highways (the *Autobahnen*). Hitler took up these plans and ran with them. He made the autobahn a reality, invested heavily in other public works, and after 1936 poured marks into rearmament. These programs created thousands of jobs. By 1938, unemployment in Germany had been defeated, dropping from 44 percent in 1932 to 14.1 percent in 1934 to less than 1 percent in 1938. In contrast, double-digit unemployment rates persisted in much of western Europe.

"Heil (Hail) Hitler!"
An enthusiastic crowd salutes Hitler at a Nazi party rally. The women in the traditional costumes illustrate a key aspect of the Nazis' appeal: their promise to restore women to their traditional domestic roles. The men in military uniform indicate a second source of Nazi popularity: the restoration of military strength and national pride.

Germans and non-Germans alike hailed Nazi Germany as an economic success. In many ways, they were wrong. Under Nazi rule, real wages fell and the concentration on rearmament led to shortages in food supplies and in consumer goods. In 1938, meat consumption remained below the level of 1929. Yet many Germans *believed* themselves to be much better off. The expansion of social welfare assistance (for those considered "Aryan") helps explain this perception, as does the establishment of the "Strength through Joy" program (directly inspired by Mussolini's "after-work" organizations), which provided workers with cheap vacations, theater and concert tickets, and weekend outings. But most important, under the Nazis, Germans were working. The abundance of jobs—despite the low wages, despite the disappearance of workers' rights, despite the food shortages—made Hitler an economic savior to many Germans.

Many also viewed him as a national savior, a leader who restored Germany's pride and power. Payment of war reparations, demanded by the humiliating Versailles Treaty, halted in 1930 because of the global economic crisis. Hitler never resumed payment. He also ignored the treaty's military restrictions and rebuilt Germany's armed forces. By 1938, parades featuring row after row of smartly uniformed troops, impressive displays of tanks, and flybys of military aircraft all signaled the revitalization of German military might. For many ordinary Germans, traumatized and shamed by the sequence of national disasters—military defeat, loss of territory, hyperinflation, political and fiscal crises, unemployment—the sight of troops goose-stepping under the German flag meant a personal as well as a national renaissance. As one Nazi song proclaimed, "And now the me is part of the great We."[12]

German Painting Idolizing Hitler

To create the "great We," Hitler utilized modern techniques and technology. The Nazis published a glossy illustrated magazine, produced their own films, and littered cities with propaganda posters. Impressed by Mussolini's use of the radio to popularize fascism, Hitler subsidized the production of radios in Germany so that by the end of the 1930s most Germans had access to a radio—and to Hitler's radio talks. He also recognized the power of the cinema, and hired the brilliant filmmaker Leni Riefenstahl (1902–2003) to film Nazi rallies. These still-astonishing films show an overwhelming mass spectacle in which an entire nation appears to be marching in step behind Hitler.

But Hitler also perceived the power of nostalgia for many Germans, and so used modern techniques and technologies to establish the Nazis as bulwarks of tradition. In speeches, posters, and films, the Nazis painted a picture of a mythic Germany, an idyllic community peopled by sturdy blond peasants, small shopkeepers, and independent craftsmen. The Nazis promised that under their leadership, individual Germans would regain meaning and purpose as part of a single national community. Nazi ideology condemned international corporations, large department stores, and supermarket chains as elements of a vast Jewish-controlled conspiracy to deprive ordinary people of their livelihoods.

Campaigns of Repression and Terror

Part of the appeal of the "great We" that Hitler was creating relied on the demonization and violent repression of the "not Us," those defined as outside or opposed to the nation. Hitler used the existing German police force as well as his own paramilitary troops—the brownshirted SA and the blackshirted SS (*Schutzstaffeln*)—to terrorize those he defined as enemies of the nation. The Nazis first targeted political opponents. By 1934 half of the 300,000 German Communist Party members were in prison or dead; most of the rest had fled the country. The Nazis also persecuted specific religious groups on the basis of their actual or presumed opposition to the Nazi state. Roman Catholics could no longer work in the civil service and faced constant harassment, and about half of Germany's 20,000 Jehovah's Witnesses were sent to concentration camps.

The groups that the Nazis deemed biologically inferior suffered most severely. Beginning in 1933, the Nazi regime forced the sterilization of the Roma (Gypsies), the mentally and physically handicapped, and mixed-race children (in most cases, the offspring of German women and black African soldiers serving in the French occupation force in the Rhineland). By 1939, 370,000 men and women had been sterilized.

The Jewish community—less than 1 percent of the German population—bore the brunt of Nazi racial attacks. To Nazi anti-Semites, Hitler's accession to the German chancellorship was like the opening of hunting season. They beat up Jews in the streets, vandalized Jewish shops and homes, threatened German Christians who associated with Jews, and violently enforced boycotts of Jewish businesses. Anti-Jewish legislation piled up in an effort to convince Germans of the separateness, the "non-Germanness," of Jewish cultural and racial identity. In 1933, "non-Aryans" (Jews) were dismissed from the civil service and the legal profession, and the number of Jewish students in high schools and universities was restricted. Every organization in Germany—youth clubs, sports teams, labor unions, charitable societies—underwent "Nazification," which meant the dismissal of all Jewish members and the appointment of Nazis to leadership roles. In 1935, the "Nuremberg Laws" labeled as Jewish anyone with three or more Jewish grandparents. Marriage or sexual relations between German Jews and non-Jews now became a serious crime.

Women and the Radical Right

Much of the appeal of both fascism and Nazism lay in the promise to restore order to societies on the verge of disintegration. Restoration of order meant, among other things, the return of women to their proper place. According to Nazi propaganda, "the soil provides the food, the woman supplies the population, and the men make the action."[13] Hitler proclaimed, "the Nazi Revolution will be an entirely male event." Mussolini agreed: "Woman must obey. . . . In our State, she must not count."[14]

In Nazi Germany, the restoration of order translated into a series of financial and cultural incentives to encourage women to stay at home and produce babies. These measures ranged from marriage loans (available only if the wife quit her job) and income tax deductions for families to the establishment of discussion, welfare, and leisure groups for housewives. Not surprisingly, the Nazis also used disincentives. One of the first actions of the new Nazi government was to dismiss women from the civil service and to rule that female physicians could work only in their husbands' practices. By 1937, both women physicians and women Ph.D.s had lost the right to be addressed as "Doctor" or "Professor." Women could no longer work as school principals. Coeducational schools were abolished. Birth control became illegal and penalties for abortion increased while prosecutions doubled.

In fascist Italy, Mussolini's government focused its legislation on both men and women. Unmarried men over age 30 had to pay double income tax (priests were exempt), homosexual relations between men were outlawed, and fatherhood became a prerequisite for men in high-ranking public office. A wide-ranging social welfare program that included family allowances, maternity leaves, and marriage loans sought to strengthen the traditional family. Quotas limited the number of women employed in both the civil service and in private business, while women found themselves excluded entirely from jobs defined as "virile," a varied list that included boat captains, diplomats, high school principals, and history teachers.

The Polarization of Politics in the 1930s

- **What factors led to the polarization of European politics in the 1930s?**

The apparent successes of fascist Italy and Nazi Germany appealed to many Europeans and Americans disenchanted with democracy in the era of the Great Depression. During this period, the Soviet Union also seemed a success story. While the capitalist nations struggled with high unemployment rates and falling industrial output, the Soviet Union appeared to be performing economic miracles. Politics in the West thus became polarized between communism on the radical left and fascism and Nazism on the radical right. In both the United States and Europe, however, politicians and policymakers sought to maintain the middle ground, to retain democratic values in a time of extremist ideologies.

The Soviet Union Under Stalin: Revolution Reconstructed, Terror Extended

Many Europeans looked with envy at the Soviet Union in the 1930s. Unemployment had disappeared; huge industrial cities transformed the landscape; the development of new industries such as chemicals and automobiles, together with a full-scale exploitation of the Soviet Union's massive natural resources, sent production indices soaring. But this economic transformation rested on dead bodies, millions of dead bodies. During the 1930s, mass murder became an integral part of the Soviet regime under Joseph Stalin (1879–1953).

Stalin's Rise to Power

By 1928, Stalin was the uncontested head of the party. At the time of Lenin's death in 1924, however, few observers would have predicted Stalin's success. Although a stalwart Bolshevik, he stood in the shadow of more charismatic, intellectually able colleagues. How, then, did Stalin seize control of the Communist Party and the Soviet state?

One key factor in Stalin's rise to power was the changing nature of the Communist Party. The party that made the revolution in 1917 comprised only 24,000 members. Following a massive recruitment campaign to honor Lenin's memory, party membership in 1929 stood at more than one and a half million—and only 8,000 of these had been members in 1917. In other words, the vast majority of communists in 1929 had not fought in the revolution. For them, communism was not a revolutionary ideology challenging the tsarist political order; it was itself the political order. Party membership was not a revolutionary act; it was a guarantee of privileged status and career opportunities. Moreover, unlike the original Bolshevik revolutionaries, most of the new members were not well educated or well versed in communist ideology. In fact, 25 percent of the party membership was functionally illiterate.

As party secretary from 1922 on, Stalin led the recruitment drive that enlisted many of these new party members. Other party leaders dismissed Stalin as the "card-index Bolshevik"—the paper-pusher, the gray guy with the boring job. But Stalin, an astute politician, recognized that his card index held enormous power. Not only did he determine the fate of party membership applications, he also decided who got promoted to what and where. Thus, throughout the 1920s Stalin slowly built up a broad base of support within the party. Vast numbers of ordinary communists owed their party membership, and in many cases their livelihoods, to Stalin.

CHRONOLOGY

Stalin's Rise to Power

1917	
March	Popular Russian Revolution
November	Bolshevik revolution
1918–1921	Russian civil war
1921	New Economic Policy (NEP) begins
1922	Stalin appointed general secretary of the Central Committee of the Communist Party
1924	Death of Lenin
1925–1928	Leadership disputes; Stalin emerges as the head of the Communist Party
1929	NEP ended; collectivization begins
1934	The Congress of Victors
1934–1938	The Great Purge

While Stalin expanded his support at the grassroots, a fierce ideological struggle at the highest levels of the Communist Party distracted his rivals for the party leadership. By the time of Lenin's death, the New Economic Policy (NEP) had restored economic stability to the Soviet Union. The nation, however, remained far behind its capitalist competitors in both agricultural and industrial productivity. All communists agreed on the need to launch the Soviet economy into industrialization. The problem was, how could this backward nation obtain the capital it needed for industrial development? One faction of the party, led by Leon Trotsky (1879–1940), argued that the answer was to squeeze the necessary capital out of the peasantry through high taxation and even, if necessary, the confiscation of crops. Trotsky wanted to abandon NEP and its encouragement of small private farming initiatives. The opposing faction, led by Nikolai Bukharin (1888–1938), pointed to the lessons taught by western European industrialization. In the West, industrial capital came from agricultural profits. Bukharin insisted on the need for gradualism: Agricultural development must precede industrialization. "Enrich the peasant," Bukharin argued.

Stalin at first backed Bukharin and those who wished to continue on the NEP course, because he perceived the charismatic Trotsky as the more immediate threat to his ambitions. Once Trotsky had been expelled from the party, however, Stalin reversed course and turned on Bukharin. In 1928, Stalin emerged as the sole leader of the party and as a fierce advocate of the abandonment of NEP, the total socialization of the Soviet economy, and a fast march forward into full-scale industrialization.

The "Revolution from Above": Collectivization and Industrialization, 1928–1934

As party leader, Stalin placed the Soviet Union firmly back on a revolutionary course, with the aim of catapulting the Soviet Union into the ranks of the industrialized nations.

Stalin Demands Rapid Industrialization of the USSR (1931)

The first step in what was called "the revolution from above" was collectivization°, the replacement of private and village farms with large cooperative agricultural enterprises run by communist managers according to directives received from the central government. Collectivization had both economic and political aims. Regarded as more modern and efficient, collective farms were expected to produce an agricultural surplus and thereby raise the capital needed for industrialization. But in addition, collectivization would realize communist ideals by eradicating the profit motive, abolishing private property, and transforming the peasants into modern state employees.

The peasants resisted this transformation, however. They burned their crops and slaughtered their livestock. Famine followed. The numbers of deaths resulting from collectivization and the famine of 1931–1932 remain the subject of intense controversy; the available quantitative evidence points to death figures between five million and seven million. Ukraine and Kazakhstan were hardest hit. Almost 40 percent of the Kazakh population died from starvation or typhus; the number of dead in Ukraine alone may have reached four million.[15] Perhaps as many as ten million peasants were deported in these years; many of these died either on the way to or in forced labor camps.

While class war raged in the countryside, city dwellers embarked on the second stage of the "revolution from above"—industrialization. In 1931 Stalin articulated the task facing the Soviet Union: "We are fifty or a hundred years behind the advanced countries. We must catch up this distance in ten years. Either we do it or we go under."[16] Doing it demanded, first, unprecedented levels of labor output. Despite the massive investment in heavy industry, the Soviet Union throughout the 1930s remained undermechanized. What it lacked in technology, however, it possessed in population. Thus Soviet industry was highly labor intensive. To ensure that workers produced at the levels needed, the Soviet state under Stalin imposed fierce labor discipline. Only productive workers received ration cards. Internal passports restricted workers' freedom of movement. If fired, a worker was automatically evicted from his or her apartment and deprived of a ration card.

Catching up with the West also demanded reducing already low levels of personal consumption. Eighty percent of all investment went into heavy industry, while domestic construction and light industry—clothing, for example, and furniture—were ignored. Scarcity became the norm, long lines and constant shortages part of every urban resident's existence. Economists estimate that Soviet citizens endured a 40 percent fall in their already low standard of living between 1929 and 1932.

While millions starved in the countryside, young communists acclaimed these years of hardship and horror as an era of heroism. They volunteered to organize collective farms, to work in conditions of extreme brutality at construction sites, to labor long hours in factories and mines. Babies born in this decade received names like "Little Five Years" (for girls) and "Plan" (for boys), reflecting their parents' enthusiasm for the series of Five-Year-Plans issued by the central government as outlines for the new world order. Much of this enthusiasm was stirred up by propaganda campaigns aimed at persuading laborers to work ever harder and sacrifice ever more. Ordinary workers who achieved record-breaking feats of production earned medals, special ceremonies, and material gifts. Immense publicity focused on the gargantuan engineering achievements of the era—the cities built atop swampland, the hydroelectric projects with their enormous dams and power plants, the Moscow subway system. Such publicity made party members feel part of a huge and powerful endeavor. A popular song announced, "We were born to make fairy tales come true."[17]

Just as important as the propaganda campaigns was the reality of unprecedented opportunity. The Soviet Union in the 1930s has been called "the quicksand society," one in which traditional structures and relations (and people too) were swallowed up at a breathtaking pace. As these traditional structures disappeared, new ones emerged, bringing tremendous geographic and social mobility to Soviet society. For example, Nikita Khrushchev (1894–1971), who would succeed Stalin as the head of the party and state in the 1950s, was the son of a poor peasant.

No propaganda campaign and no amount of effort from enthusiastic young communists, however, could provide the Soviet Union with the labor it needed to catch up with the West in ten years. Forced labor was crucial. Throughout the 1930s, as many as five million men, women, and children—peasants, political opponents of Stalin, religious dissenters, ethnic minorities—labored in prison camps.[18] By some estimates, forced labor accounted for no less than 25 percent of all construction work in the Soviet Union in the 1930s. Many of the huge engineering triumphs of the decade rested on the backs of prisoners and deportees.

By the end of the 1930s, Stalin's "revolution from above" had achieved its aim. The pouring of resources into heavy industry and the wringing of every ounce of labor out of an exhausted, cold, and hungry populace succeeded in building the foundations of an industrial society. This society would stand the test of total war in the 1940s.

But Stalin's revolution failed to convert Soviet agriculture into a modern, prosperous sector of the economy. Rural regions remained backward. Peasant villages, for example, were not electrified until the later 1950s. Most peasants regarded the collective farm as belonging not to them or to the community but to the state, just another in a long line of harsh landlords. Under Stalin, peasants were second-class citizens, ineligible for internal passports, with little access to the benefits of Soviet industrialization. Like their ancestors under serfdom, peasants at the end of the 1930s found themselves tied to a particular village, saddled with forced labor obligations, and compelled to spend the bulk of their time farming for someone else's profit. Most peasants viewed the communist state as the enemy, to be ignored when possible, tricked if necessary, and endured no matter what.

Stalin's Consolidation of Power: The Great Purge and Soviet Society, 1934–1939

By the mid-1930s, the worst seemed to be over. Most villages were collectivized and the mass violence had ended. The 17th Party Congress in 1934 was known as the "Congress of Victors," as the party celebrated its industrial successes and the achievement of collectivization. But for many of the men and women at this congress, the worst was yet to come. Within five years, half of the 2,000 delegates had been arrested; of the 149 elected members of the congress's Central Committee, 98 were shot dead. These Congress delegates, and hundreds of thousands of other Soviet citizens, were victims of the "Great Purge°." In the purge, Stalin's effort to eliminate any possible rival to his power converged with widespread paranoia and economic crisis to produce a nationwide witch-hunt and mass executions.

The early victims of the purge tended to be top-ranking Communist Party officials, many of whom had opposed Stalin on various issues during the 1920s. By charging these powerful men with conspiring against the communist state, Stalin reduced the chances that any competitor might oust him. In a series of three spectacular show trials attended by journalists from all over the world, leading Bolsheviks—some of the Soviet Union's most respected men, such as Nikolai Bukharin—pleaded guilty to charges of conspiracy and sabotage, and were immediately executed. Numerous smaller trials replicated the process throughout the Soviet Union. Non-Russians suffered heavily. By the end of the 1930s, for example, 260 of the 300 party secretaries in Georgia had been killed. The purge also swept the armed forces. Those executed included three of the five Soviet marshals, thirteen of fifteen army commanders, and fifty-seven of eighty corps commanders.

The purge quickly spread beyond the top ranks of the party and military. With the show trials indicating that even the highest-level Bolsheviks were not to be trusted, people began to suspect that traitors lurked within every factory and local party gathering. At the same time the shortcomings of an overly centralized and poorly run economy were multiplying: Subject to an endless stream of ever-changing and often irrational program and policy directives, managers falsified key economic statistics, while poorly trained workers misused machines and cut all available corners.

"Pictures Can't Lie . . . "

Stalin was not Lenin's closest associate, nor did Lenin select him as his successor. To claim and consolidate his position as sole leader of the Communist Party and of the Soviet Union, Stalin had to falsify history and present himself as Lenin's chosen heir. Murder and mass executions could remove competitors from the present, but to erase them from the past, Stalin turned to the airbrush and the scissors rather than the gun. Pictures showing other Bolsheviks standing next to Lenin were cropped, leaving him with Stalin, or if such a pairing could not be achieved, standing alone. Compare these two photos, taken by the same photographer, within five seconds of each other. In the first, Lev Kamenev and Leon Trotsky—leading Bolsheviks and rivals with Stalin for the party leadership after Lenin's death—stand on the steps to Lenin's left. But in the second, Kamenev and Trotsky have been cut out and some steps have been drawn in. Stalin sought to airbrush Trotsky and Kamenev out of Soviet history, just as he eliminated them from Soviet politics. Trotsky was forced into exile in 1929 and murdered in 1940; Kamenev was executed in 1936.

People were anxious and hungry, and eager to find someone to blame for breakdowns and failures. The purge made it easy to point the finger, to charge this manager with deliberately failing to order tractors or that engineer with implementing the wrong system of crop rotation to sabotage production. Thus the Great Purge quickly spun out of control to embrace low-level party members, managers in state agencies, factory directors, and engineers. Many were killed without trial, others executed after a legal show, and still others deported to slave labor camps to be worked to death on Stalin's vast construction projects. Death estimates vary widely; at least 750,000 people died, with the numbers of those arrested, imprisoned, or deported running into the millions.[19]

The Great Purge consolidated Stalin's hold on the Soviet Union. It not only eliminated all potential competitors, it also tied huge numbers of people more tightly to Stalin and his version of revolution. The shocking thing about the Great Purge was its popularity. The purge hit primarily urban managers. For the most part, ordinary workers and peasants were safe from its onslaught. These ordinary citizens, who had been ordered about, reprimanded, fined, insulted, and assaulted by these self-same managers, tended to believe that the purge's victims got what they deserved. Moreover, the purge can also be seen as a huge job creation program. Individuals who moved into the positions left vacant by the purge's victims had an enormous material as well as psychological stake in viewing the purge as an act of justice.

Stalin and the Nation

The popularity of the purge was also closely linked with the emergence of a Stalin-centered personality cult. By the time the purge began, the cult was an omnipresent part of Soviet urban life. Huge posters and statues ensured that Stalin's figure remained constantly in front of Soviet citizens. Textbooks rewrote the history of the Bolshevik revolution to highlight Stalin's contribution and linked every scientific, technological, or economic advance in the Soviet Union to the person and power of Stalin. The scores of letters personally addressed to Stalin that poured into central government offices testify to the success of this cult. To many Soviet citizens, Stalin personified the nation.

Increasingly the *nation*—not the worker, not socialism, not the revolution—assumed the central role in Soviet propaganda. Lenin had condemned Russian nationalism as a middle-class ideology to be eradicated along with capitalism. The working class, not the nation, mattered. But Stalin reversed this aspect of Lenin's revolution. In the 1930s, "Russia" and "the motherland/fatherland" both reappeared in political discourse. The tsarist past, which Lenin had condemned or ignored, was resurrected to emphasize Russian greatness. The imperial anthem resounded once again, while films and books praised strong Russian leaders such as Peter the Great. While this resurgence of Russian nationalism was popular in Russia itself, it spelled real difficulties for the 50 percent of the Soviet population who lived outside Russia and who found it necessary to repress their own sense of national identity—or face deportation.

Exalting the motherland went hand in hand with exalting the mother. Just as Stalin resurrected Russian nationalism in the 1930s, so he sought to resurrect the Russian family. He promoted the family as a vital prop of the national order, an institution to be strengthened rather than encouraged to wither away (as Lenin had insisted). In 1936, Stalin's regime outlawed abortion and made divorce more difficult.

"People's Dreams Have Come True!"
In this typical example of "Socialist Realism," an older Soviet citizen points proudly to the achievements of Stalinist industrialization while the young boy, in the uniform of the Pioneers, the Stalinist youth organization, listens eagerly.

DOCUMENT

The Cult of the Leader

The personality cult *characterized not only the Radical Right ideologies of Italian fascism and German Nazism, but also the ideological system that stood at the opposite end of the political spectrum: Stalinist communism. Searching for a way to mobilize the masses without granting to them actual political power, Mussolini, Hitler, and Stalin erected around themselves leadership cults. Their own images came to embody the nation. As the following set of excerpts shows, the cults of Mussolini, Hitler, and Stalin took on religious dimensions, with all three men adored as secular saviors.*

I. Description of Mussolini's Visit to Trieste in 1938

Finally we have seen and heard Him! . . . These first reactions, expressed with indescribable joy, eyes moved to tears and an ineffable, agonizing joy. . . . It is not easy to describe the expression on most faces, on those of the little people as on those of the educated, of the mass as a whole. Expressions of wonderful contentment and pride among those who saw Him pass close by—especially among the dockworkers He visited yesterday—and those whose eyes He met, those who caught His eye. "Never such eyes! The way he looks at you is irresistible! He smiled at me . . . I was close, I could almost touch him. . . . When I saw him my legs trembled" . . . and a thousand other similar statements show and confirm the enormous fascination exercised by his person.

II. Description of an Early Nazi Rally by Louise Solmitz, Schoolteacher

The April sun shone hot like summer and turned everything into a picture of gay expectation. There was immaculate order and discipline . . . the hours passed. . . . Expectations rose. There stood Hitler in a simple black coat and looked over the crowd. Waiting. A forest of swastika pennants swished up, the jubilation of this moment was given vent in a roaring salute. . . . How many look up to him with a touching faith! As their helper, their savior, their deliverer from unbearable distress—to him who rescues the Prussian prince, the scholar, the clergyman, the farmer, the worker, the unemployed, who leads them from the parties back into the nation.

III. Speech by a Woman Delegate at a Workers' Conference in the Soviet Union

Thank you comrade Stalin, our leader, our father, for a happy, merry kolkhoz life!

He, our Stalin, put the steering-wheel of the tractor in our hand. . . . He, the great Stalin, carefully listens to all of us in this meeting, loves us with a great Stalinist love (*tumultuous applause*), day and night thinks of our prosperity, of our culture, of our work. . . .

Long live our friend, our teacher, the beloved leader of the world proletariat, comrade Stalin! (*Tumultuous applause, rising to an ovation. Shouts of "Hurrah!"*)

Sources: "I. Description of Mussolini's Visit to Trieste in 1938," reprinted by permission of the publisher from *The Sacralization of Politics in Fascist Italy* by Emilio Gentile, translated by Keith Botsford, p. 147, Cambridge, Mass.: Harvard University Press. Copyright © 1996 by the President and Fellows of Harvard College. "II. Description of an Early Nazi Rally by Louise Solmitz, Schoolteacher," copyright © 1988 by Claudia Koonz. From *Mothers in the Fatherland: Women, the Family, and Nazi Politics* by Claudia Koonz. Reprinted by permission of St. Martin's Press, LLC. "III. Speech by a Woman Delegate at a Worker's Conference in the Soviet Union," from *Stalin's Peasants: Resistance and Survival in the Russian Village After Collectivization* by Sheila Fitzpatrick. Copyright © 1996 by Oxford University Press, Inc. Published by Oxford University Press, Inc.

Like Western leaders, Stalin also sought to increase the national birth rate by granting pregnant women maternity stipends and increasing the number of prenatal health clinics. There was no effort to pull women out of the workforce, however. Of the more than four million new workers entering the labor force between 1932 and 1937, 82 percent were women. The Soviet Union continued to provide women with access to higher education and professional jobs—women worked as doctors, engineers, scientists, and high-ranking public officials. (And women were deported and executed in huge numbers—one could argue that Stalin was an equal-opportunity killer.)

In the arts, too, Stalinism meant a retreat from the radicalism of Lenin's revolution. Whereas Soviet artists under Lenin had been in the vanguard of modernism, under Stalin art came firmly under state control. Artists knew that their literal survival depended on their conforming to the principles of "Socialist Realism": *Partinost* (loyalty to the state), *Ideinost* (correct ideology and content), and *Narodnost* (easy accessibility to ordinary viewers). The abstract experiments of the early Soviet period gave way to pretty pictures of happily collectivized peasants and portraits of Stalin in heroic poses.

The Response of the Democracies

The apparent economic successes of fascism and Nazism on the right, and Stalinism on the left, polarized European politics. For many Europeans in the 1930s, it seemed that the middle ground was collapsing beneath their feet, that democracy had failed and that they had no choice but to scramble to one extreme or the other. Yet in both western Europe and in the United States, important steps were taken to ensure not only that democracy survived but that it eventually delivered a decent standard of living to the great mass of ordinary people.

A Third Way? The Social Democratic Alternative

The effort to meet the challenge of the depression without embracing either Nazism or Stalinism accelerated the development of the political model that would dominate western Europe after World War II: social democracy°. In a social democracy, a democratically elected parliamentary government accepts the responsibility of ensuring a decent standard of living for its citizens. To achieve this goal, the government assumes two important functions—first, regulating an economy containing both private enterprise and nationalized or state-controlled corporations; second, overseeing a welfare state, which guarantees the citizen access to unemployment and sickness benefits, pensions, family allowances, and health services. Although social democracy did not triumph in western Europe until after the massive bloodletting of another total war, the interwar years witnessed important steps toward this third path, an alternative to the extremes of both the Radical Right (fascism and Nazism) and the Radical Left (Stalinism).

One of the most striking experiments in changing the relationship between democratic governments and the economy occurred in the United States. Franklin Delano Roosevelt (1882–1945) became president in 1932 at the height of the Great Depression, when unemployment stood at 24 percent (15 million workers were without jobs) and Washington, D.C., witnessed federal troops called out to quell rioting among unemployed veterans. Promising a "New Deal" of "Relief, Recovery, Reform," Roosevelt tackled the depression with an activist governmental policy that included agricultural subsidies, public works programs, and the Social Security Act of 1935, which set the foundations of the U.S. welfare program.

Yet even with this sharp upswing in government activity, unemployment remained high—ten million workers were without jobs in 1939—and the gross national product (GNP) did not recover to 1929 levels until 1941. In the view of some economists, Roosevelt failed to solve the problem of unemployment because he remained committed to the ideal of a balanced budget. In contrast, the British economist John Maynard Keynes (1883–1946) insisted that in times of depression, the state should not reduce spending and endeavor to live within its budget, but instead should adopt a program of deficit spending to stimulate economic growth. Only when prosperity returned, Keynes advised, should governments increase taxes and cut expenditures to recover the deficits.

The experience of Sweden appeared to confirm Keynes's theory. The Swedish Social Democratic Party took office in 1932 with the intention of using the powers of central government to revive the depressed economy. The government allowed its budget deficit to climb while it financed a massive public works campaign, as well as an increase in welfare benefits ranging from unemployment insurance to maternity allowances to subsidized housing. By 1937 unemployment was shrinking rapidly as the manufacturing sector boomed.

Throughout most of western Europe, however, governments proved far more reluctant to advocate radically new policies, despite an expansion of the state's role in economic affairs. For example, Britain's limited economic recovery in the later 1930s was based largely on private initiatives such as an expansion in housing construction and the emergence of new industries aimed at domestic consumption (radios and other small electronics, household goods, automobiles). In the areas hardest hit by depression—the heavy export industries such as coal, shipbuilding, textiles, and steel, located primarily in northern Britain—the lack of government intervention meant continuing high unemployment rates and widespread poverty and deprivation throughout the 1930s.

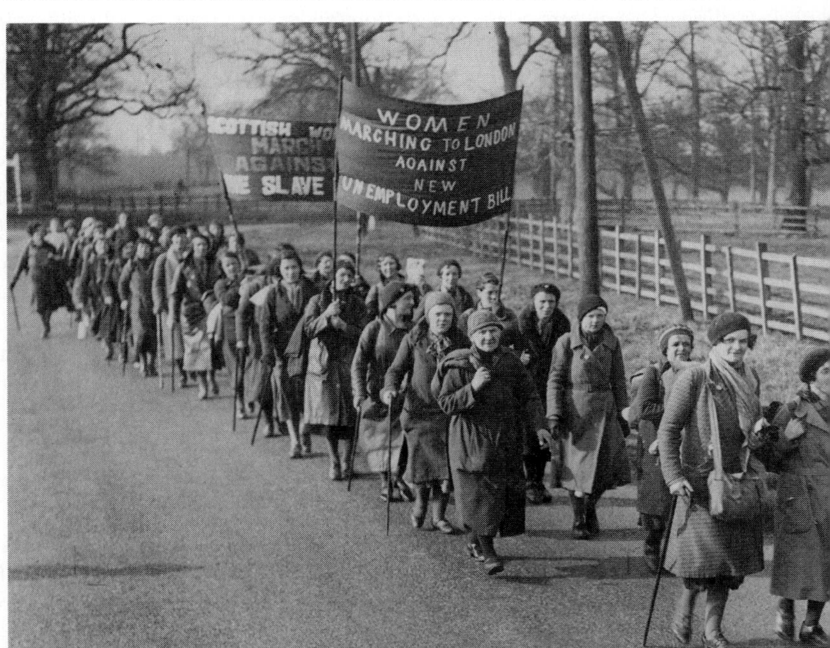

Taking a Stand

British women demonstrate against legislation that tightened requirements for receiving unemployment benefits and caused widespread suffering.

The Popular Front in France

The limited success of democratic governments in addressing the problems of the Great Depression meant that many experienced the 1930s as a hard, hungry decade when democracy failed to deliver a decent standard of living. The example of France illustrates both the political polarization occurring in Europe in the 1930s and the sharp limits on governments seeking both to maintain democratic politics and to improve the living conditions of their citizens. France lacked such basic welfare benefits as old-age pensions and unemployment insurance. As the economy plummeted, therefore, social unrest rose, and so, too, did the appeal of the fascist movement. In 1934, fascist riots left 17 dead and more than 2,000 injured.

The increasing strength of fascism, combined with the deepening national emergency, led to the formation of the Popular Front, a coalition comprising the centrist Radical Party, the moderate leftist Socialist Party, and the far-left Stalinist Communist Party. In 1936, the Popular Front won the national elections. The Socialist leader Leon Blum (1872–1950) took office as prime minister in the midst of a general strike involving two million workers. He settled the strike to the workers' benefit by granting them a 15 percent pay raise and the right to collective bargaining. Over the next year, Blum nationalized the key war industries and gave workers further pay increases, paid holidays, and a forty-hour workweek.

Many conservative French voters saw Blum's policies of social reform as the first step on the road to Stalinism. Thus they cried, "Better Hitler than Blum!"—in other words, better the Radical Right than the Stalinist Left. The global business community pulled capital out of France, resulting in a major financial crisis and the devaluation of the French franc. Dependent on foreign loans, Blum's government faced sharp pressure to pull back from its program of social and economic reforms. When it tried to do so, its working-class constituency rose in revolt. In May 1937 the suppression of a left-wing demonstration left 7 dead and 200 injured. Blum resigned the next month. The Popular Front in France quickly disintegrated.

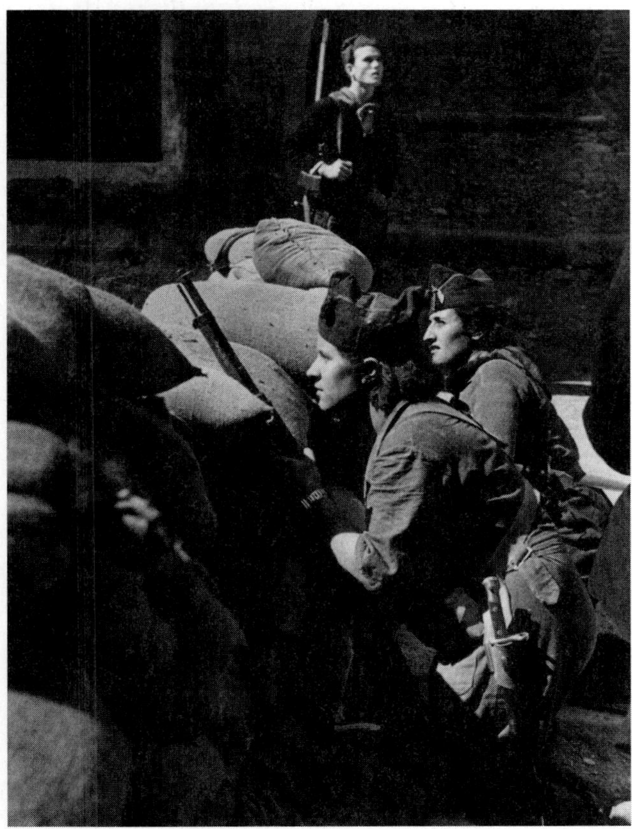

The Spanish Civil War
The Spanish Civil War mobilized women as well as men. These soldiers, fighting in the uniform of the anarchist militia, are defending the barricades of Barcelona against rebel attack.

The Spanish Civil War

Spain became the arena in which the struggle of Europe's polarized political forces turned into outright war. In 1931, a democratically elected republican government replaced the Spanish monarchy and in 1936, a Popular Front government, comprising both socialists and communists, took office. In July, army officers led a right-wing rebellion against this government.

The struggle between the left-wing Republican government and the right-wing rebels quickly became an international issue. Both fascist Italy and Nazi Germany supported the rebellion, enabling General Francisco Franco (1892–1975) and his crack Moroccan troops to cross into Spain from their station in North Africa and launch an all-out offensive against the republic. The Republican government appealed to the democracies for aid, but the only government that came to its assistance was that of the Soviet Union. Soviet tanks and aircraft enabled the besieged city of Madrid to hold out against Franco's forces but at the same time the Soviet intervention split the Republican movement, with anarchists and socialists resisting Stalinist control. Unnerved by the Soviet involvement, the governments of France, Britain, and the United States remained neutral. Appalled by this official inaction, many citizens of these countries served in the International Brigade, which fought for the cause of democracy in Spain.

The Spanish Civil War raged until March 1939, when the last remnants of the Republican forces finally surrendered to Franco. Four hundred thousand men and women died in the war; in the following four years, another 200,000 were executed. Franco established an authoritarian government that crushed Spanish democracy. Spain became a potent symbol for all of Europe. To both fascists and their democratic opponents, Franco's victory illustrated how easily democracy could be destroyed.

The West and the World: Imperialism in the Interwar Era

- **How did the interaction between the West and the world outside change after World War I?**

In the interwar struggle between authoritarian and democratic forms of politics, we can see contrasting definitions of "the West" competing for dominance. In this same period, the clash between advocates and enemies of Western imperialism revealed multiple notions of "Western culture" as well. The Allies claimed to have fought during World War I for national self-determination, but they had no intention of allowing their overseas empires the right to determine their own national selves. Britain and France emerged from the war with not only their imperialist ideologies intact but their empires greatly expanded. They divided up Germany's overseas colonies in Africa and Asia, and as we saw in Chapter 24, became the dominant powers in the Middle East.

During the 1920s and 1930s, popular imperialism reached its zenith in Europe. Filmmakers and novelists found that imperial settings formed the perfect backdrop for stirring tales of individual heroism and limitless adventure. Governments also played a role in strengthening the culture of empire. In both Britain and France, imperial history became a required part of school curricula. British children learned to identify the pink-colored sections of the world map as "ours," while a series of colonial exhibitions impressed on the British public the importance of the empire to Britain's economic prosperity. In Belgium, the government promoted the Congo as a "model colony." The economic ties between European states and their imperial territories grew tighter. For example, by 1940 more than 45 percent of French overseas investment went to regions within its empire (see Map 25.2).

The Irish Revolution

This period, however, also witnessed the emergence of important challenges to the imperial idea. The most successful of these occurred in Ireland. Many Irish men, both Catholic and Protestant, fought for Britain during World War I, but a small group of revolutionary nationalists saw the war as an opportunity for revolt. They mounted an armed rebellion on Easter Monday in 1916. Although quickly and brutally suppressed, the "Easter Rising" became for Irish nationalists a key moment in the fight for an independent Ireland. The executed leaders of the rising became martyrs for the sacred cause of nationhood, while the ease with which the British crushed the revolt convinced Irish nationalist leaders of the necessity of employing guerilla tactics rather than open military assault to defeat their much more powerful foe.

In 1921, ground down by more than two years of guerilla warfare waged with consummate skill by the Irish Republican Army (IRA), the British government offered Ireland independence. The offer, however, came with strings attached. The new state would remain within the British Empire and Ireland itself would be partitioned. Its six northern counties, dominated by Protestants who opposed Irish independence, were to remain part of Britain. A delegation led by the charismatic IRA chief Michael Collins (the "Big Fella") accepted this offer. It took two years of civil war—a war that cost Collins his life—to persuade many Irish nationalists to do the same. Ireland continued as an uneasy member of the British Empire until the end of the 1930s, when it cut all constitutional ties to Britain. Northern Ireland remains a part of Britain to this day.

Changing Power Equations: Ideology and Economics

Ireland's revolt against British imperial rule, while unusual in its success, revealed the growing power of anti-imperialist forces across the world. The triumph of communism in Russia helped strengthen these forces. In his publications, Lenin argued that imperialism was the logical consequence of capitalism and its quest for markets, and thus that anticapitalism and anti-imperialism went hand in hand. Under Lenin, the Soviet Union declared itself the defender of oppressed nationalities everywhere, and provided ideological and material assistance to nationalist independence movements in Indonesia, Indochina, Burma, and most significantly, China, where Soviet advisers helped form the Communist Party in 1921.

Communism alone, however, does not account for the spread of anti-imperialist nationalist movements in the interwar years. Changing economic relationships were crucial. During World War I, the demands of industrial warfare forced Europe's imperial powers to utilize fully their colonial resources, a strategy that brought with it unintended but far-reaching social change. Throughout Europe's empires, wartime economic demands escalated labor migration rates, expanded urban populations, and enveloped once-isolated villages in the global economic web. These changes were not often welcomed by the peoples involved. In Africa, for example, the Allies tailored their colonial economies to meet wartime demands for commodities such as rubber. This policy benefited multinational companies such as Unilever, which pocketed increasing profits, but had a negative impact on local populations: Native merchants

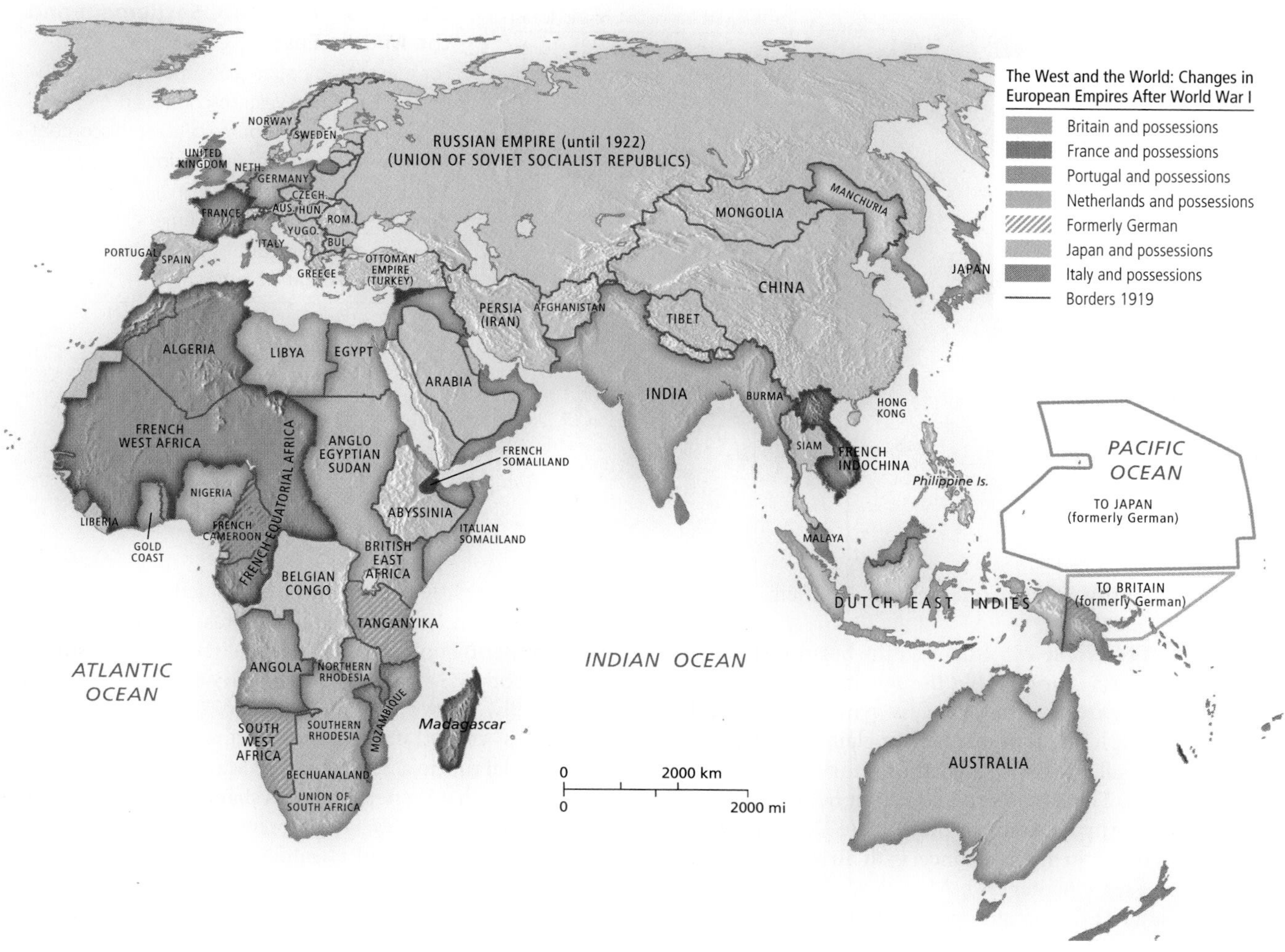

Map 25.2 The West and the World: Changes in European Empires After World War I
Britain, France, and Japan were the principal beneficiaries of Germany's loss of empire after World War I.

saw their independence and their incomes disappearing; African peasants lost their land and became waged laborers; the concentration on cash crops reduced food production at a time when the population was growing steadily.

In the 1930s, economic conditions grew worse in the wake of the Great Depression. The sharp fall in the prices of primary products spelled disaster for regions of the world that had shifted their agricultural economies to the production of cash crops for export. At the same time, the benefits of imperial governance diminished. Looking for ways to reduce expenditures, European governments cut funds to colonial schools, public services, and health care. Direct taxation rates rose while unemployment rates soared. So, too, did the numbers attracted to nationalist movements.

Postwar Nationalism, Westernization, and the Islamic Challenge

These economic and social developments not only helped subvert the legitimacy of imperialist rule but also fostered the growth of anti-Western movements, often in religious form. In Africa, for example, a revival of animist religion expressed both an explicit rejection of the Christian teachings brought by European and American missionaries and an implicit refusal of Western cultural and political styles. Throughout many African regions, however, Islam possessed the most potent appeal. In the growing cities, immigrants cut off from their village and its religious practices found that Islam provided an alternative

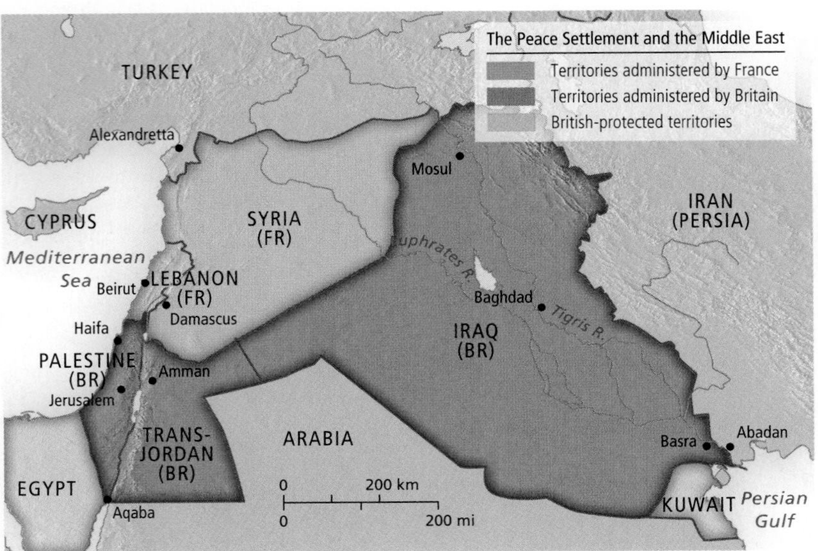

Map 25.3 The Peace Settlement and the Middle East
For many Arab nationalists, the division of the Middle East into Western-controlled "Mandates" was a source of deep discontent. After widespread anti-British riots in Iraq in 1920, the British ceded nominal independence to King Faisal's government. The British, however, retained control over financial, military and diplomatic matters.

cultural identity to that one offered by their European rulers.

The end of World War I marked the beginning of a new era in Islamic history. Feeble though it was by 1914, the Ottoman Empire had nevertheless symbolized a unified Islam: As caliph, the Ottoman sultan claimed religious authority over all Muslims, even those not under Ottoman political rule. The sultan's role as caliph helps explain why the vast majority of Arabs in the Middle East did not join the Hashemites in their alliance with Britain against the Ottomans (see Chapter 24). Most Arabs did not see the Turkish sultan as a foreign oppressor; instead, as Muslims, they regarded him as their rightful leader. For similar reasons, Muslims in British India experienced a profound conflict of loyalties during the war.

The collapse of the Ottoman Empire and the abolition of the Ottoman caliphate in the wake of World War I created a new religious and political environment for Muslims. Many followed Western secular models and turned to ethnic nationalism. Others, however, found both spiritual solace and political identity in Islamic revival movements that sought to unify Muslims under an Islamic ruler and Islamic law once again.

The Emergence of Pan-Arabism

In the Middle East, pan-Arabism° emerged in the interwar era as a powerful form of nationalism. Just as pan-Slavism promoted the ideal of a single Slavic state, so pan-Arabism insisted that all Arabs—including the minority who were not Muslim—should unite in an Arab state. Three postwar developments nourished pan-Arabism. First, as already noted, the collapse of the Ottoman regime shattered traditional loyalties. But second, the new map of the Middle East drawn by the postwar peace settlement placed Arabs in states they regarded as artificial, unrelated to dynastic or tribal identities. (See Chapter 24.) Thus nationalist movements centering on these new states—Iraqi nationalism, for example, or Syrian, or Lebanese—possessed little appeal. And finally, as we saw in Chapter 24, the system of "Mandates" created in the wake of the war actually continued imperial rule in a new form (see Map 25.3). As it quickly became clear that Western interests shaped policy in the new Middle Eastern states, resentment grew toward both Western imperialism and toward the state system imposed by the West. These sentiments nourished the pan-Arabist movement.

State Nationalism on the Western Model

Not all Arab nationalists, however, embraced pan-Arabism. In states such as Egypt, with a national identity not imposed by Western imperialists or the peace settlement, nationalism tended to coalesce around the state itself. Hence in Egypt, the nationalist political party, Wafd, called not for Arabic unity but for Egyptian national freedom. Wafd, whose full name translates as "Egyptian delegation," originated as precisely that, a delegation of Egyptian representatives to the Paris peace conferences after World War I. When the Allies refused to let the delegation participate in the peace process, Wafd organized into a political movement fighting against not only the British but also the British-backed Egyptian monarchy for full Egyptian independence. Although Wafd opposed the monarchical government as too subservient to Western economic and political interests, it sought social and economic reforms that would Westernize and modernize Egypt.

For nationalists such as those in Wafd, the successful nationalist revolution in Turkey provided an important source of inspiration. After World War I, the Allies forced the defeated Ottoman government to sign a humiliating treaty: The Treaty of Sèvres not only dispossessed the Ottoman government of its Middle Eastern empire, it also gave territories in the Anatolian heartland (modern Turkey) to Greece, Italy, an autonomous Kurdistan, and an independent Armenia. In addition, Sèvres stripped the Ottoman government of national sovereignty by ceding to the Allies the right of intervention in economic, military, and foreign affairs. Turkish nationalists, led by Mustafa Kemal Pasha, rejected the Treaty of Sèvres and rose up against the government that dared sign such a document. Kemal's nationalist rebellion overthrew the sultan, defeated a Greek invasion, and forced the Allies to draw up a new settlement. In 1923, the Treaty of Lausanne restored to Turkey much of its territory and its full national sovereignty.

But while Kemal had no intentions of letting Western powers govern in Turkey, he was not anti-Western. He viewed the West as modern; to modernize Turkey, he believed he had to reconfigure its culture as Western. Thus Kemal declared Turkey a secular republic, outlawed polygamy, granted women civil and legal rights, and required all Turks to take surnames—he became known as Kemal "Ataturk" ("Father of the Turks"). A mass literacy program aimed not only to teach Turks how to read and write, but how to do so using the Latin alphabet. Schoolmasters who dared use Arabic lettering were arrested. Ataturk even condemned the traditional form of Turkish headwear, the fez, as "an emblem of ignorance, negligence, fanaticism, hatred of progress and civilization."[20] To represent Turkey's new Western orientation, Turkish men were ordered to wear bowler hats and Western suits. But while he favored the English bowler hat, Ataturk was less enthusiastic about English political freedom. Despite setting up a parliament elected by universal suffrage, he made full use of emergency executive powers to govern with an iron grip over a one-party state. He also continued the Ottoman policies of repression toward Turkey's Armenian minority.

Ataturk (Mustafa Kemal)

Kemal Ataturk's secularist, Westernized model of nationalism proved powerful. During the 1920s and 1930s nationalists in the Middle East, Africa, and Asia tended to embrace Western models, even as they rejected Western (or Western-imposed) rulers. They formed parliamentary political parties, advocated Western political ideologies such as liberalism and communism, regarded the state as essentially secular, and saw political independence as a crucial step toward industrial modernization and economic prosperity.

The Islamic Challenge

Beneath the surface of political life, however, different styles of movements, with very different aims, were coalescing. Throughout the new states of the Middle East, for example, the soaring sales of popular biographies of the Prophet Muhammad and other caliphs, as well as the proliferation of Islamic leagues and clubs, hinted that many inhabitants of these new states found the secularism of the nationalists as alien as the faces of their Western-imposed rulers or the boundaries on the new European-drawn map.

These sentiments would not harden into explicitly political movements until the 1940s, but both the Wahhabi religious revival in central Arabia during the 1920s and 1930s and the foundation of the Muslim Brotherhood in Egypt in 1928 proved crucial in shaping the relationship of Islam and the West in the later twentieth century.

Founded by Muhammad Abd al-Wahhab (1703–1787) in the eighteenth century, Wahhabism demanded the purification of Islam by ridding it of centuries of heretical accretions such as saint worship and other forms of mysticism, and by returning to a strict interpretation of the *Sharia,* or Islamic law. Over the next century, this militant form of religious revival inspired a number of popular revolts—on the Arabian peninsula (against the Ottomans), in India (against the British), in Algeria (against the French), and in Daghistan (against the Russians). Although all of these revolts were defeated, Wahhabism's call to return to fundamental truths and practices continued to appeal to Muslims, particularly in times of unsettling political change. It is not surprising, then, that Wahhabism revived in the tumultuous period after World War I. The Wahhabi revival in Arabia had a powerful patron: Abd al-Aziz Ibn Saud (ca. 1888–1953), the head of the Saudi dynasty whose conquests on the Arabian peninsula became the basis for the kingdom of Saudi Arabia.

Like Wahhabism, the Islamic Brotherhood (or *Ikhwan*) rejected modernizing interpretations of Islam and sought to reassert the universal jurisdiction of Islamic law. For the Brotherhood, Islam governed not just religious belief but all areas of life. The Brotherhood rejected Western practices and political institutions less because they were foreign than because they were associated with infidels. Working through youth groups, educational institutes, and business enterprises, the Brotherhood spread from its Egyptian base throughout the Middle East during the 1930s.

Moral Revolution in India

During this same era, a very different sort of anti-Western protest movement took shape in India. In 1916 a British-educated lawyer returned from South Africa, where he had spent twenty years fighting to improve the lot of indentured Indian laborers and developing a revolutionary approach to the fight for national independence. Mohandas Gandhi (1869–1948) called on his followers to fight British rule in India not with armed weapons but with moral force—with nonviolent protest and civil disobedience. As the war ended, Gandhi led a mass protest movement in India against British rule. In this *Satyagraha* ("hold fast to

From Mohandas to Mahatma: Gandhi's Transformation

Encounters & Transformations

In April 1893, a young, well-dressed Indian lawyer purchased a first-class train ticket from Durban to Pretoria (South Africa). The first part of the journey proceeded uneventfully, but then another traveler, a white man, entered the first-class compartment. He turned around and returned with two guards, who demanded that the Indian man sit in third class, with the other "colored" passengers. The young lawyer refused, and so was thrown off the train at the next stop.

Mohandas Gandhi's experience on the train to Pretoria was not unusual. The Indian immigrant community in South Africa had long endured legal discrimination, economic exploitation, and frequent violence; the black African community suffered far worse. But the 24-year-old Gandhi knew little about such things. Growing up as the spoiled youngest son in an upper-caste family in India, he had known privilege rather than prejudice. Even the three years he spent in London studying law did not expose him to racial discrimination. Gandhi, in fact, felt that when he left Britain he was leaving "home." He returned to India in 1891 convinced of the superiority of British law and culture. He banned Indian-style clothing from his household, insisted that his illiterate young wife learn English, and decreed that oat porridge and cocoa be served at breakfast. He saw himself as a successful British lawyer.

But others did not see him that way. When Gandhi asked a British official for a favor for his brother, he was humiliated, actually pushed out the door by a servant. "This shock changed the course of my life," Gandhi later noted.[21] Offered a job in South Africa, he went—and on that train to Pretoria encountered further humiliation. By the time Gandhi finally reached Pretoria, he had decided to fight. He became the leader of the Indian civil rights movement in South Africa.

Gandhi lived in South Africa for 21 years. During these decades, the westernized, Britain-loving lawyer became a Hindu holy man; Mohandas became Mahatma, the "great-souled one." This transformation occurred in part because of Gandhi's sense of betrayal as he encountered the racial discrimination embedded in British imperialism. From his London experience, Gandhi had concluded that Britain epitomized the Western ideals of impartial justice and individual rights. But the British colonial regime he encountered in South Africa violated those ideals. Disillusioned, Gandhi turned back to his Hindu roots.

Western culture also, however, played a positive role in Gandhi's transformation. During his time in South Africa, Gandhi read widely in Christian and Western texts, including Jesus' Sermon on the Mount in the New Testament, and books by nineteenth-century European social and cultural critics that exposed the spiritual and material failures of industrial society. Gandhi's intellectual encounter with these texts helped him formulate the idea of *Satyagraha* ("Truth-Force"). In its most specific sense, Satyagraha is a political tool. Through nonviolent mass civil disobedience, the powerless persuade the powerful to effect political change. But Satyagraha is also a spiritual act, the victory of goodness over violence and evil.

Gandhi's specific encounters with the injustice of imperial rule, first in the home of a British official in India and then on his South African train ride, forced him to embark on a different sort of spiritual and political journey, an exploration of both Western and Hindu thought. This journey transformed Gandhi from Mohandas into Mahatma and led him to Satyagraha—and the transformation of Indian nationalism into a mass movement. By 1948, this movement had made it impossible for the British to govern India.

For Discussion

Both negative and positive encounters with Western ideas and Western people contributed to Gandhi's transformation "from Mohandas to Mahatma." In what ways have Gandhi's ideas transformed Western culture and politics?

The Mathatma
Gandhi drew on both Hindu and Western traditions in formulating his ideal of moral protest.

the truth") campaign, Indians refused to cooperate with the imperial system in any way, including wearing British-made cloth.

Before Gandhi's arrival, the cause of Indian independence belonged to the educated, westernized elite. Gandhi transformed the Indian National Congress into a mass movement by appealing to traditional Indian customs and religious identities. He did not oppose modernization, but he argued that modernization did not necessarily mean westernization, that India could follow its own path. Thus Gandhi rejected Western dress and presented himself in the role of the religious ascetic, a familiar and deeply honored figure in Indian culture. In his insistence that the nationalist struggle be one of "moral force" rather than a physical fight, Gandhi drew on the Hindu tradition of nonviolence. He was careful, however, not to equate "Indian" with "Hindu." He worked hard to incorporate the minority Muslim community into the nationalist movement, and he broke with the traditional Hindu caste system by campaigning for the rights of those deemed "untouchable." Ordinary Indians surged into the movement, calling Gandhi "Mahatma," or "great-souled," a term of great respect.

Unable to decide whether to arrest Gandhi as a dangerous revolutionary or to negotiate with him as a representative of the Indian people, the British did both. In 1931, Gandhi and the viceroy of India (literally the "vice-king," the highest British official in India) met on equal terms for a series of eight meetings. A few months later Gandhi was in prison, along with 66,000 of his nationalist colleagues. Successive British governments did pass a series of measures granting Indians increasing degrees of self-government, but Gandhi and the Indian National Congress demanded full and immediate national independence. The resulting impasse led to escalating unrest and terrorist activity, despite Gandhi's personal commitment to nonviolence. India remained the jewel in Britain's imperial crown, but the glue holding it in place was deteriorating rapidly by the end of the 1930s.

The Power of the Primitive

When asked what he thought of "Western civilization," Gandhi replied, "I think it would be a very good idea." Just as nationalists outside of the West such as Gandhi began to challenge the equation of the West with civilization, so too did Westerners themselves. For nineteenth-century European culture, "civilization" was what gave the West the right to rule the rest of the world. In the latter decades of the nineteenth century, ideologues had described inhabitants of Asia, Africa, and South America as barbarians who needed the guidance and discipline of the more advanced European white races. But by 1918, in the wake of the war, at least some Europeans were asking, "Who is the barbarian now?"

Developments in psychology further undermined the idea of Western superiority by eroding the boundaries between so-called primitive and modern cultures. In his postwar writings, Sigmund Freud (1856–1939) emphasized that human nature was fundamentally aggressive, even bestial. Freud's three-part theory of personality, developed in the 1920s, argued that within each individual the *id,* the unconscious force of primitive instinct, battles against the controls of the *ego,* or conscious rationality, and the *superego,* the moral values imposed by society. Although Freud taught that the continuity of civilization depended on the repression of the id, many Freudian popularizers insisted that the individual should allow his or her primitive self to run free.

The work of Freud's onetime disciple Carl Jung (1875–1961) also stressed the links between the primitive and the modern. Jung contended that careful study of an individual's dreams will show that they share common images and forms—"archetypes"—with ancient mythologies and world religions. These archetypes point to the existence of the "collective unconscious," shared by all human beings, regardless of when or where they lived. Thus, in Jung's analysis the boundary between "civilized" and "primitive," "West" and "not West," disappeared.

In the work of other thinkers and artists, that boundary remained intact, but Western notions of cultural superiority were turned upside down. The belief that white Western culture was anemic, washed out, and washed up led to a new openness to alternative intellectual and artistic traditions. This era saw a lasting transformation of popular music as the energetic rhythms of African-American jazz worked their way into white musical traditions. Many writers argued that the West needed to look to outside its borders for vibrancy and vitality. The German novelist Herman Hesse (1877–1962) condemned modern industrial society as spiritually barren and celebrated Eastern mysticism as a source of power and wisdom.

Similarly, the *Négritude* movement stressed the history and intrinsic value of black African culture. Founded in Paris in 1935 by French colonial students from Africa and the West Indies, Négritude condemned European culture as weak and corrupted and called for blacks to recreate a separate cultural and political identity. The movement's leading figures, such as Leopold Senghor (1906–2001), who later became the first president of independent Senegal, vehemently opposed the continuation of European empires and demanded African self-rule. Drawing together Africans, Afro-Caribbeans, and black Americans, Négritude assumed the existence of a common black culture that transcended national and colonial boundaries. The movement stole the white racists' stereotype of the "happy dancing savage" and refigured it as positive: Black culture fostered the emotion, creativity, and human connections that white Western industrial society destroyed.

The Power of the Primitive

When the American dancer Josephine Baker first hit the stage in Paris in 1925, her audience embraced her as the image of African savagery, even though Baker was a city kid from Philadelphia. A Parisian sensation from the moment she arrived, Baker's frenetic and passionate style of dancing, as well as her willingness to appear on stage wearing nothing but a belt of bananas, seemed to epitomize for many Europeans the essential freedom they believed their urbanized culture had lost, and that both the United States and Africa retained. As Baker's belt of bananas, designed by her white French employer, makes clear, much of this idealization of the primitive was deeply embedded in racist stereotypes. But it is also clear that both Baker's blackness and her Americanness represented a positive image of liberation to many Parisians.

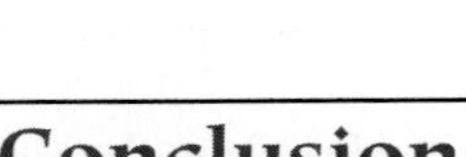

Conclusion

The Kingdom of Corpses

In 1921, the Goncourt Prize, the most prestigious award in French literature, was awarded not to a native French writer but to a colonial: René Maran, born in the French colony of Martinique. Even more striking than Maran's receiving the prize was the content of the novel for which he was honored. In *Batouala,* Maran mounted a fierce onslaught against Western culture: "Civilization, civilization, pride of the Europeans and charnel house of innocents. . . . You build your kingdom on corpses."[22]

For many in the West, Maran's description of Europe as a kingdom of corpses seemed apt in the aftermath of total war. The 1920s and 1930s witnessed a dramatic reevaluation of Western cultural and political assumptions. Both Soviet communism on the left and Nazism and fascism on the right rejected such key Western ideals as individual rights and the rule of law. Such extremist ideologies seemed persuasive in the climate of despair produced not only by the war, but by the postwar failure of democracy in eastern Europe and the collapse of the global economy after 1929. As a result, the kingdom of corpses grew: in Nazi Germany, in Spain, and most dramatically in the Soviet Union. The kingdom of corpses was, however, a particularly expansionist domain. As the 1930s ended, the West and the world stood on the brink of another total war, one in which the numbers of dead would spiral to nearly incomprehensible levels.

Suggestions for Further Reading

For a comprehensive listing of suggested readings, please go to www.ablongman.com/levack2e/chapter25

Bookbinder, Paul. *Weimar Germany: The Republic of the Reasonable.* 1996. An innovative interpretation.

Brendon, Piers. *The Dark Valley: A Panorama of the 1930s.* 2000. Fast-paced but carefully researched and comprehensive overview of the histories of the United States, Germany, Italy, France, Britain, Japan, Russia, and Spain.

Carrère D'Encausse, Hélène. *Stalin: Order Through Terror,* Vol. 2: *A History of the Soviet Union, 1917–1953.* 1981. A brief but convincing account of the way Stalin seized and held power in the Soviet Union.

Fischer, Conan. *The Rise of the Nazis.* 1995. Summarizes recent research and includes a section of primary documents.

Fitzpatrick, Sheila. *Everyday Stalinism. Ordinary Life in Extraordinary Times: Soviet Russia in the 1930s.* 1999. Explores the daily life of the ordinary urban worker in Stalinist Russia.

Fitzpatrick, Sheila. *Stalin's Peasants: Resistance and Survival in the Russian Village After Collectivization.* 1995. A superb history from the bottom up.

Getty, J. Arch, and Oleg V. Naumov. *The Road to Terror: Stalin and the Self-Destruction of the Bolsheviks, 1932–1939.* 1999. Interweaves recently discovered documents with an up-to-date interpretation of the Great Purge.

Gilbert, Bentley Brinkerhoff. *Britain 1914–1945: The Aftermath of Power.* 1996. Short, readable overview, designed for beginning students.

Jackson, Julian. *The Popular Front in France: Defending Democracy, 1934–1938.* 1988. A political and cultural history.

Kershaw, Ian. *Hitler.* 1991. A highly acclaimed recent biography.

Kitchen, Martin. *Nazi Germany: A Critical Introduction.* 2004. Short, clearly written, up-to-date. An excellent introduction and overview.

Lewis, Bernard. *The Shaping of the Modern Middle East.* 1994. Concise but comprehensive analysis.

Mack Smith, Denis. *Mussolini: A Biography.* 1983. An engaging read.

Pedersen, Susan. *Family, Dependence, and the Origins of the Welfare State: Britain and France, 1914–1945.* 1993. Shows how welfare policy was inextricably linked to demographic and eugenic concerns.

Rothschild, Joseph. *East Central Europe Between the Wars.* 1974. An older source, but still one of the best accounts of this tumultuous region in this tumultuous time.

Thomas, Hugh. *The Spanish Civil War.* 1977. An authoritative account.

Whittam, John. *Fascist Italy.* 1995. A short synthesis of recent research. Includes a section of primary documents and an excellent bibliographic essay.

Wolpert, Stanley. *Gandhi's Passion: The Life and Legacy of Mahatma Gandhi.* 2001. An intellectual and spiritual biography by one of the foremost historians of modern India.

Notes

1. Quoted in Peter Gay, *Weimar Culture* (1970), 99.
2. Quoted in T. W. Heyck, *The Peoples of the British Isles from 1870 to the Present* (1992), 200.
3. Martin J. Sherwin, *A World Destroyed: Hiroshima and the Origins of the Arms Race* (1987), 17.
4. Quoted in Martin Gilbert, *A History of the Twentieth Century, Vol. I* (1997), 700.
5. Quoted in Michael Burleigh, *The Third Reich: A New History* (2000), 36.
6. Quoted in Burleigh, *The Third Reich,* 52.
7. Quoted in Joachim Fest, *Hitler* (1973), 190–193.
8. Ibid., 192, 218.
9. Quoted in Wendy Goldman, *Women, the State, and Revolution: Soviet Family Policy and Social Life, 1917–1936* (1993), 5.
10. Quoted in Claudia Koonz, *Mothers in the Fatherland* (1987), 130.
11. Quoted in Fest, *Hitler,* 445.
12. Quoted in Koonz, *Mothers in the Fatherland,* 194.
13. Ibid., 178.
14. Ibid., 56; Victoria DeGrazia, *How Fascism Ruled Women: Italy, 1922–1945* (1992), 234.
15. See J. Arch Getty and Roberta Manning, *Stalinist Terror: New Perspectives* (1993), 11, 265, 268, 280, 290.
16. Quoted in Mark Mazower, *Dark Continent: Europe's Twentieth Century* (1998), 123.
17. Quoted in Sheila Fitzpatrick, *Everyday Stalinism* (1999), 68.
18. See Stephen G. Wheatcroft, "More Light on the Scale of Repression and Excess Mortality in the Soviet Union in the 1930s," in Getty and Manning, *Stalinist Terror,* 275–290.
19. "Appendix 1: Numbers of Victims of the Terror," in J. Arch Getty and Oleg V. Naumov, *The Road to Terror: Stalin and the Self-Destruction of the Bolsheviks, 1932–1939* (1999), 587–594.
20. Quoted in Felix Gilbert, *The End of the European Era* (1991), 162.
21. Mohandas K. Gandhi, *An Autobiography: The Story of My Experiments with Truth* (1957), 120.
22. Quoted in Tyler Stovall, *Paris Noir: African Americans in the City of Light* (1996), 32.

World War II

26

IN THE WEEKS IMMEDIATELY PRECEDING THE END OF THE SECOND WORLD WAR in Europe, many Allied soldiers faced their most difficult assignment yet. Hardened combat veterans, accustomed to scenes of slaughter and destruction, broke down and wept as they encountered a landscape of horror beyond their wildest nightmares: the world of the Nazi concentration and death camps. As one American war correspondent put it, "we had penetrated at last to the center of the black heart, to the very crawling inside of the vicious heart."[1] The American soldiers who opened the gates of the camp in Mauthausen, Austria, never forgot their first sight of the prisoners there: "By the thousands they came streaming . . . Hollow, pallid ghosts from graves and tombs, terrifying, rot-colored figures of misery marked by disease, deeply ingrained filth, inner decay. . . . squat skeletons in rags and crazy grins."[2]

Similarly, the British troops who liberated Bergen-Belsen in Germany were marked indelibly by what they encountered within the camp's walls. Bergen-Belsen had become the dumping ground for tens of thousands of prisoners evacuated from camps in eastern Europe, as the Nazi SS desperately retreated in front of the advancing Soviet army. Already sick and starving, these prisoners were jammed, 1,200 at a time, into barracks built to accommodate a few hundred. By March 1945, both drinking water and food had disappeared, human excrement dripped from bunk beds until it coated the floors of the barracks, and dead bodies piled up everywhere. In these conditions, the only living beings to flourish were the microorganisms that cause typhus. Floundering in this sea of human want, British soldiers, doctors, and nurses did what they could; even so, 28,000 of Bergen-Belsen's 60,000 inmates died in the weeks following liberation.

In Mauthausen and Bergen-Belsen, in the piles of putrefying bodies and among the crowds of skeletal survivors, American and British soldiers encountered the results of Adolf Hitler's effort to redefine the West. In Hitler's vision, Western civilization comprised ranks of white, northern Europeans, led by Germans, marching in step to a cadence dictated by the antidemocratic

CHAPTER OUTLINE

- The Coming of War
- Europe at War, 1939–1941
- The World at War, 1941–1945
- The War Against the Jews
- The Home Front: The Other Wars

Wilhelm Becker, *Bombing Raid in Berlin* (1943) The intentional and intensive bombing of civilian centers was one of the defining characteristics of the Second World War.

state. To realize this vision, he turned to total war and to mass murder. This quest to reconfigure the West as a race-based German empire also led Hitler to join hands with an ally outside the West: Japan. The German-Japanese alliance between transformed a European war into a global conflict. Thus, understanding World War II demands that we look not only at the results of Nazi racial ideology but also at global power relations and patterns of economic dependency. Like Hitler, Japan's governing elites longed for empire—in their case, an Asian empire to ensure both Japanese access to the resources and Japanese domination over the peoples of the Pacific region. With such access and such domination, they hoped to insulate Japan's economic and political structures from Western influence or control. The Pacific war thus constituted the most brutal in a long series of encounters between Japanese elites and the West. As we examine both the European and the Pacific theaters of war, we will need, then, to ask how competing definitions of "the West" helped shape this conflict. We will also confront the question of results: How did the cataclysm known as World War II re-define the West?

To organize its exploration of the many facets of World War II, this chapter focuses on five questions:

- **What were the expectations concerning war in the 1920s and 1930s, and how did these hopes and fears lead to armed conflict in both Europe and Asia?**
- **How did Nazi Germany conquer the continent of Europe by 1941?**
- **Why did the Allies win in 1945?**
- **How and why did the war against the Jews take place, and what were its consequences?**
- **What did total war mean on the home front?**

The Coming of War

- **What were the expectations concerning war in the 1920s and 1930s, and how did these hopes and fears lead to armed conflict in both Europe and Asia?**

The 1914–1918 war had been proclaimed the "war to end all wars." Instead, a little more than twenty years later, total war once again engulfed Europe and then the world. Adolf Hitler's ambitions for a German empire in eastern Europe account for the immediate outbreak of war in September 1939. But other, longer-term factors also contributed and help explain the origins of World War II. During the 1930s, the uneasy peace was broken by a series of military conflicts. These confrontations underlined the fragility of the post–World War I international settlement and foreshadowed the horrors to come in World War II.

An Uneasy Peace

The origins of the Second World War are closely tied to the settlement of the First. Rather than ending war for all time, the treaties negotiated after 1918 created an uneasy peace, one that could not be sustained. As we have already seen, much of Hitler's appeal to his German followers lay in his openly displayed contempt for the economic and military terms of the Versailles Treaty. But the peace settlement of World War I led to World War II in other, less direct ways as well. First, the redrawing of the map of eastern and central Europe fostered political instability in these regions. The mapmakers failed to fulfill the nationalist ambitions of many groups—the Macedonians, the Croats, the Ukrainians, and a host of others—and created as many territorial resentments as they resolved. For example, Germans could not forget that parts of Silesia now belonged to Poland, and Hungarians mourned the loss of traditionally Hungarian lands to Czechoslovakia, Romania, and Yugoslavia. Demands for boundary revisions, as well as ethnic hostilities and economic weaknesses, debilitated the new central and eastern European states carved out of the prewar Austrian-Hungarian, Russian, and German Empires.

Second, the League of Nations, created to replace the competitive alliance systems that many blamed for starting World War I, could not realize the high hopes of its planners. Poorly organized, lacking military power, boycotted by the United States and at various times excluding the key nations of Germany and the Soviet Union, the league proved too weak to serve as the basis of a new international order. Instead, alliances, such as that between the French and Polish governments or the "Little Entente" of Czechoslovakia, Yugoslavia, and Romania, formed the framework of a more traditional and very precarious international system.

Finally, the peace settlements created resentments among the war's winners as well as its losers. Italian nationalists argued that their nation's contribution to the Allies' victory should have been more fully compensated and looked longingly at territories granted to Yugoslavia, Austria, and Albania. Japanese nationalists, too, felt betrayed by the peace. Japan had cooperated fully with Britain and the United States during the First World War and expected this cooperation to be rewarded in the postwar era. Instead, many Japanese contended that the peace settlement disregarded Japan's economic needs and international ambitions. The results of the postwar Washington Conference particularly enraged Japanese nationalists. The conference, convened in Washington, D.C., in 1921, assembled representatives of the war's nine victorious powers—Britain, France, Italy, the United States, Belgium, the Netherlands, Portugal, China, and Japan—who pledged themselves to uphold China's territorial integrity and political independence as a means of restoring stability to the region. European and especially American capital poured into China during the

1920s while Western advisers assisted in the reform of the Chinese tax and currency systems. Japanese nationalists, however, viewed a united, Western-oriented China not as a guarantor of regional stability but rather as a threat to Japanese political power and economic development.

The 1930s: Prelude to World War II

The onset of the Great Depression in 1929 heightened international instability. Throughout Europe economic nationalism intensified as nations responded to economic collapse by throwing up tariff walls in an effort to protect their own industries. In addition, leaders sought escape from economic difficulties through territorial expansion. In Japan, the collapse of export markets for Japanese raw silk and cotton cloth made it difficult for the Japanese to pay for their vital imports of oil and other industrial resources. Anti-Western Japanese nationalists contended that Western capitalism was terminally ill and that the time had come for Japan to embark on a course of aggressive imperialist expansion to ensure its access to vital resources. In 1931, Japanese forces seized Manchuria.

Similarly, Mussolini proclaimed empire as the answer to Italy's economic woes, as well as a way to recreate the glories of ancient Rome. Seeking

CHRONOLOGY

On the Road to World War II

1919	Versailles Treaty
1921–1922	Washington Conference
1929	Onset of the Great Depression
1931	Japan invades Manchuria
1933	Hitler becomes chancellor of Germany
1935	Hitler announces a German air force and military conscription; Italy invades Ethiopia
1936	German troops occupy the Rhineland; civil war breaks out in Spain; Hitler and Mussolini form the Rome-Berlin Axis
1937	Japan advances against China; Rape of Nanking
1938	
March	Germany annexes Austria (the *Anschluss*)
September	Munich Conference: Germany occupies the Sudetenland
1939	
March 15	Germany invades Czechoslovakia
August 23	German-Soviet Non-Aggression Pact
September 1	Germany invades Poland
September 3	Great Britain and France declare war on Germany

The Prelude to World War II
The Japanese resumption of their war in China in 1937 added to the horrors of the 1930s. Here a photographer captured the agony of a baby separated from its parents in the railway station in Shanghai.

to expand Italy's North African empire and to avenge Italy's humiliating defeat at the Battle of Adowa in 1896, when Ethiopian troops had beaten back an Italian invasion, Mussolini ordered his army into Ethiopia in 1935. The Italian forces inflicted on the Ethiopian people many of the horrors soon to come to the European continent, including the saturation bombing of civilians, the use of poison gas, and the establishment of concentration camps. At the end of June 1936, Ethiopia's now-exiled Emperor Haile Selassie (1892–1975) addressed the Assembly of the League of Nations and warned, "It is us today. It will be you tomorrow."[3]

One year after Italian troops invaded Ethiopia, civil war broke out in Spain. As Chapter 25 explained, the war between the elected republican government and General Franco's rebels quickly became an international conflict. Hitler and Mussolini sent troops and equipment to assist Franco, and Stalin responded by sending aid to communists fighting on the republican side. Reluctant to ally with Stalin, the governments of France, Britain, and the United States remained neutral, and seemed, therefore, to signal that aggressors could act with impunity.

While the Spanish Civil War raged, the Japanese resumed their advance in China. The Japanese conquest was brutal. In what became known as the Rape of Nanking (Nanjing), soldiers used babies for bayonet practice, gang-raped as many as 20,000 young girls and women, and left the bodies of the dead to rot in the street. The League of Nations had condemned Japan's seizure of Manchuria in 1931 but could do little else.

Map 26.1 The Expansion of Germany in the 1930s

Beginning with the remilitarization of the Rhineland in 1936, Hitler embarked on a program of German territorial expansion. This map also indicates the expansion of the Soviet Union into Poland as a result of the secret terms of the German-Soviet Non-Aggression Pact.

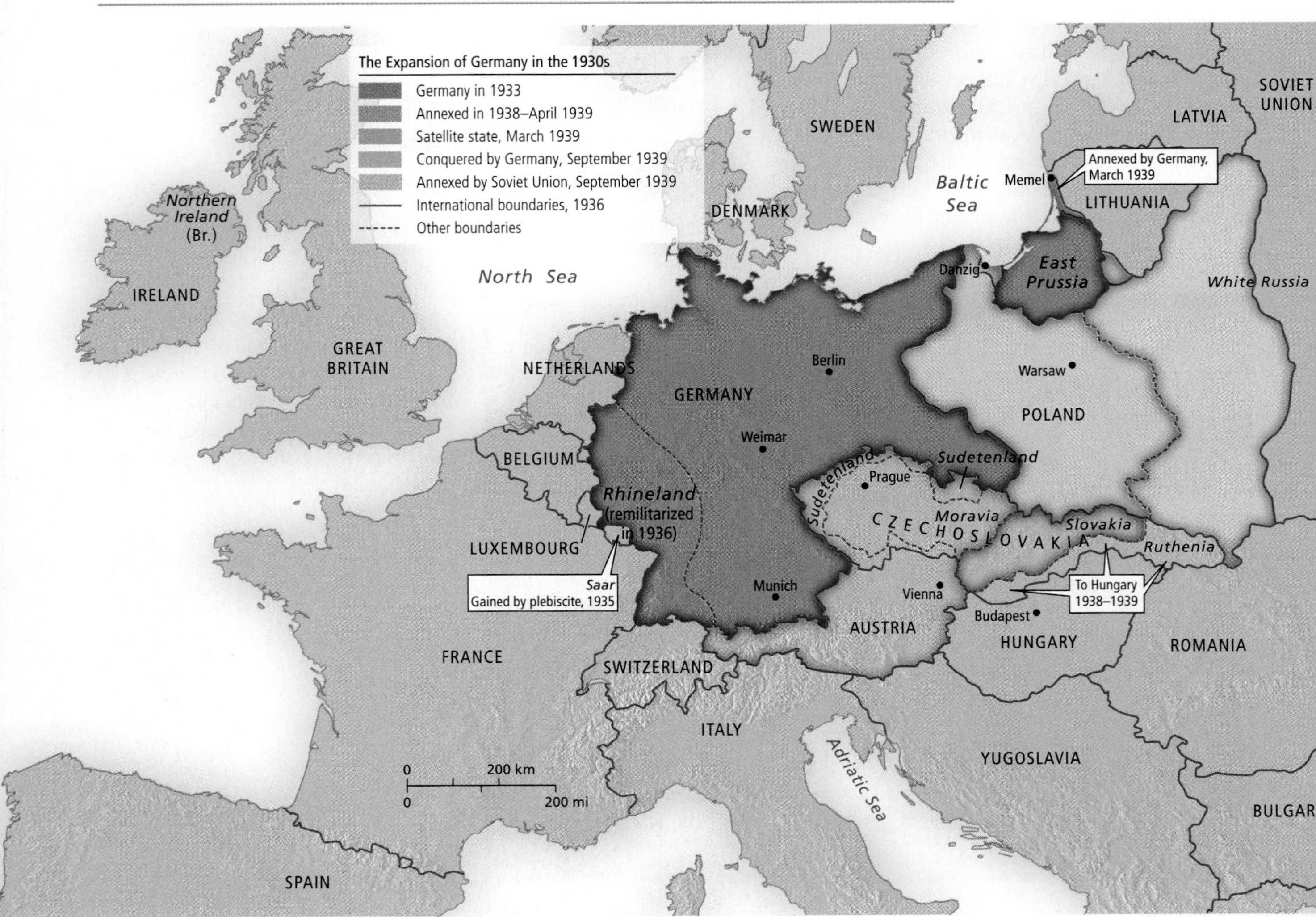

Against this backdrop of military aggression and the democracies' inaction, Hitler made his first moves to establish a German empire in Europe (see Map 26.1). In 1933, he withdrew Germany from the League of Nations and two years later announced the creation of a German air force and the return of mass conscription—in deliberate violation of the terms of the Versailles Treaty. In 1936, Hitler allied with Mussolini in the Rome-Berlin Axis° and again violated his treaty obligations when he sent German troops into the Rhineland, the industrially rich region on Germany's western border. Yet France and Britain did not respond. Two years later, in March 1938, Germany broke the Versailles Treaty once more by annexing Austria after an intense Austrian Nazi propaganda campaign punctuated by violence.

After the successful *Anschluss* ("joining") of Germany and Austria, Hitler demanded that the Sudetenland, the western portion of Czechoslovakia inhabited by a German-speaking majority, be joined to Germany as well. He seemed finally to have gone too far. France and the Soviet Union had pledged to protect the territorial integrity of Czechoslovakia. In September 1938, Europe stood on the brink of war. The urgency of the situation impelled Britain's prime minister Neville Chamberlain (1869–1940) to board an airplane for the first time in his life and fly to Munich to negotiate with Hitler. After intense negotiations that excluded the Czech government, Chamberlain and French prime minister Edouard Daladier agreed to grant Hitler the right to occupy the Sudetenland immediately. Assured by Hitler that this "Munich Agreement" satisfied all his territorial demands, Chamberlain flew home to a rapturous welcome. Crowds cheered and church bells rang when he claimed to have achieved "peace in our time."

"Peace in our time" lasted for six months. In March 1939, German troops occupied the rest of Czechoslovakia and Hitler's promises proved to be worthless. On August 23, Hitler took out an insurance policy against fighting a two-front war by persuading Stalin to sign the German-Soviet Non-Aggression Pact°. The pact publicly pledged the two powers not to attack each other; it also secretly divided Poland between them and promised Stalin substantial territorial gains—much of eastern Poland and the Baltic regions of Latvia, Estonia, and parts of Lithuania. On September 1, 1939, German troops invaded Poland. The British and French declared war against Germany on September 3. Two weeks after German troops crossed Poland's borders in the west, the Soviets pushed in from the east and imposed a regime of murderous brutality. The Second World War had begun.

Evaluating Appeasement

Could Hitler have been stopped before he catapulted Europe into World War II? The debate over this question has centered on British policy during the 1930s. France advocated an aggressive policy toward Germany in the 1920s, even to the point of sending troops into the Rhineland in 1923 to seize reparations. But during the 1930s, debilitating economic and political crises left France too weak to respond strongly to Hitler. With the United States remaining aloof from European affairs and the now-communist Soviet Union regarded as a pariah state, Britain assumed the initiative in responding to Hitler's rise to power and his increasingly aggressive actions.

After World War II broke out, one term came to be equated with passivity and cowardice in the face of aggression. That term was appeasement°—the policy of conciliation and negotiation that British policymakers,

"Peace in Our Time"
In September 1938, British prime minister Neville Chamberlain announced his diplomatic triumph: With the German annexation of the Sudetenland, Hitler declared himself satisfied and Chamberlain announced "peace in our time."

particularly Neville Chamberlain, pursued in their dealings with Hitler in the 1930s. Chamberlain, however, was not a coward and was far from passive. Convinced he had a mission to save Europe from war, he actively sought to accommodate Hitler. Chamberlain thought like the businessmen who voted for him. He believed that through negotiation a suitable agreement—the "best price"—can always be found. His fundamental failure was not passivity or cowardice but rather his insistence that Hitler was a man like himself. Chamberlain could not believe that Hitler would find a war worth the price Germany would need to pay.

For Chamberlain, and many other Europeans, the alternative to appeasement was a total war that would surely destroy Western civilization. They remembered the last war with horror and agreed that the next war would be even worse, for it would be an air war. The years after 1918 saw the aviation industry come into its own in Europe and the United States, and both military experts and ordinary people recognized the disastrous potential of airborne bombs. Stanley Baldwin (1867–1947), Chamberlain's predecessor as prime minister, told the British public that there was no defense against a bomber force: "The bomber will always get through." The horrendous civilian casualties inflicted by the Italian air force in Ethiopia and by the bombing of Spanish cities in the Spanish Civil War convinced many Europeans that Baldwin was right, and that war was completely unacceptable. Just two years after the British Peace Pledge Union was founded in 1934, it had 100,000 supporters pledged not to fight in a war.

Motivated by the desire to avoid another horrible war, appeasement also rested on two additional pillars—first, the assumption that many of Germany's grievances were legitimate; second, the belief that only a strong Germany could neutralize the threat posed by Soviet communism. During the 1920s, many historians, political scientists, and policymakers studied the diplomatic records concerning the outbreak of World War I and concluded that the treaty makers at Versailles were wrong in blaming Germany for starting the war. During the 1920s, then, British leaders sought to renegotiate reparations, to press the French into softening their anti-German policies, and to draw Germany back into the network of international diplomatic relations. Hitler's rise to power gave added impetus to a policy already in place. British leaders argued that they could rob Hitler of much of his appeal by rectifying legitimate German grievances.

British policymakers' fear of communism reinforced their desire to stabilize Germany. Many politicians applauded Hitler's moves against German communists and welcomed the military resurgence of Germany as a strong bulwark against the threat posed by Soviet Russia. The startling announcement of the German-Soviet Non-Aggression Pact in the summer of 1939 revealed the hollowness of this bulwark, just as the German invasion of Czechoslovakia in March had exposed Hitler's promises of peace as worthless.

Europe at War, 1939–1941

■ **How did Nazi Germany conquer the continent of Europe by 1941?**

German soldiers crossed the Polish border on September 1, 1939; just two years later, Hitler appeared to have achieved his goal of establishing a Nazi empire in Europe. By the autumn of 1941, almost all of continental Europe was either allied to or occupied by Nazi Germany.

A New Kind of Warfare

During these two years, the German army moved from triumph to triumph as a result of its mastery of the new technology of offensive warfare. Executing a strategy of attack that fully utilized the products of modern industry, the German military demonstrated the power of a mobile, mechanized offensive force. Germany's only defeat during these years came in the Battle of Britain, when Germany confronted a mobile, mechanized defense. Like Germany's victories, this defeat highlighted the central role of industrial production in modern warfare.

The Conquest of Poland

In its attack on Poland, the German army made use of a new kind of warfare. As Chapter 24 explained, in World War I a full frontal infantry assault proved no match for a deeply entrenched defensive force armed with machine guns. In the 1920s and 1930s, military strategists theorized that the way to avoid the stalemate of trench warfare was to use both the airplane and the tank to construct an "armored fist" strong and swift enough to break through even the most well-fortified enemy defenses. The bomber plane provided a mobile bombardment, one that shattered enemy defenses, broke vital communication links, and clogged key transport routes. Simultaneously, motorized infantry and tank formations punched through enemy lines.

Germany's swift conquest of Poland provided the world with a stunning demonstration of this new offensive strategy. Most of the German army, like all of the Polish, moved on foot or by horseback, as soldiers had done for centuries. Fast-moving motorized divisions, however, bludgeoned through the Polish defenses, penetrated deep into enemy territory, and secured key positions. While these units wreaked havoc on the ground, the Luftwaffe—the German air force—rained ruin from the air. Thirteen hundred planes shrieked across the Polish skies and in just one day destroyed the far smaller, less modern Polish air force, most of whose planes never left the ground. Warsaw surrendered after just ten days.

Blitzkrieg in Western Europe

Western newspaper reporters christened this new style of warfare blitzkrieg°—lightning war. Western Europeans experienced blitzkrieg firsthand in the spring of 1940. The German army invaded Denmark and Norway in early April, routed the French and British troops sent to aid the Norwegians, and moved into western Europe in May. The Netherlands fell in just four days; Belgium, supported by French and British units as in World War I, held out for two weeks.

On May 27, 1940, the British army and several divisions of the French force found themselves trapped in a small pocket on the northern French coast called Dunkirk. Their destruction seemed certain. But over the next week, the only Allied success in the campaign unfolded. The British Royal Air Force (RAF) succeeded in holding off the Luftwaffe and enabling the British navy and a flotilla of fishing and recreational boats manned by British civilians to evacuate these troops. By June 4, 110,000 French and almost 240,000 British soldiers had been brought safely back to Britain. But, as the newly appointed British prime minister Winston Churchill (1874–1965) reminded his cheering people, "wars are not won by evacuation."

Over the next two weeks the Germans steadily advanced through northern France, and on June 14, German soldiers marched into Paris. The French Assembly voted to disband and to hand over power to the World War I war hero Marshal Philippe Pétain (1856–1951), who established an authoritarian government. On June 22 this new Vichy regime° (named after the city Pétain chose for his capital) signed an armistice with Germany that pledged French collaboration with the Nazi regime. Theoretically, Pétain's authority extended over all of France, but in actuality the Vichy regime was confined to the south, with Germany occupying France's western and northern regions, including Paris, as well as the Atlantic seaboard. One million French

CHRONOLOGY

Europe at War

1939	
September	German-Soviet conquest of Poland
1940	
April 9	German blitzkrieg against Denmark and Norway begins
May 10	Germans attack western Europe
June 22	Fall of France
July 10	Battle of Britain begins
September 7	London Blitz begins
September 17	Hitler cancels plans for invasion of Britain
1941	
March	U.S. Congress passes Lend-Lease Act
April	German invasion of the Soviet Union postponed; German offensives in Yugoslavia, Greece, and North Africa
June 22	German invasion of the Soviet Union begins
September	German siege of Leningrad begins
December	German advance halted outside Moscow

Blitzkrieg
In blitzkrieg, the tank and bomber plane worked together to punch openings in the enemy's defenses. Motorized infantry divisions then poured through the holes.

soldiers became prisoners of war. Germany, with its allies and satellites, held most of the continent.

The Battle of Britain

After the fall of France, Hitler hoped that Britain would accept Germany's domination of the continent and agree to a negotiated peace. But his hopes went unrealized. Military disaster in Norway had thoroughly discredited Prime Minister Chamberlain and his halfhearted approach to war making. A member of Chamberlain's own party, Leo Amery, spoke for the nation when he shouted at Chamberlain, "In the name of God, go!" Chamberlain went. Party politics were suspended for the duration of the war, and the British government passed to an all-party coalition headed by Winston Churchill, a vocal critic of Britain's appeasement policy since 1933. Never a humble man, Churchill wrote that when he accepted the position of prime minister, "I felt as if I were walking with Destiny, and that all my past life had been but a preparation for this hour and this trial . . . I was sure I should not fail." In his first speech as prime minister, Churchill promised, "Victory—victory at all costs."

Faced with the British refusal to negotiate, Hitler ordered his General Staff to prepare for a land invasion of Britain. But placing German troops in the English Channel while Britain's Royal Air Force still flew the skies would be a certain military disaster. Thus, a precondition of invasion was the destruction of the RAF. On July 10, German bomber raids on English southern coastal cities opened the Battle of Britain, a battle waged in the air—and in the factories. Fortunately for Britain, from 1935 on the government's defense policy had accorded priority to the RAF. In the summer of 1940, British factories each month produced twice the number of fighter aircraft coming out of German plants in the same period. Preparing for air attack, the British had constructed a shield comprising fighter planes, anti-aircraft gun installations, and a chain of radar stations. These preparations, its higher production rates of aircraft, and the fact that RAF pilots were fighting in the skies above their homes gave the British the advantage. On September 17, 1940, Hitler announced that the invasion of Britain was postponed indefinitely.

The Invasion of the Soviet Union

War against Britain had never been one of Hitler's central goals, however. His dreams of the "Third Reich," a renewed Germanic European empire that was to last a thousand years, centered on conquest of the Soviet Union. Hitler believed that the rich agricultural and industrial resources of the vast Russian empire rightly belonged to the superior German race. He also believed that Soviet communism was an evil force and a potential threat to German stability and prosperity. Moreover, one of Hitler's aims in invading the Soviet Union was to realize his dream of a new racial order

DOCUMENT

In the Tanks

If World War I was the war of the trenches, then World War II was the war of the tanks. In the Battle of Kursk on the eastern front, for example, the Russians and Germans sent a thousand tanks into combat on a single day (July 12, 1943). In the first two years of the war, just the sight of these armored monsters crashing through barriers could demoralize an entire infantry regiment. By 1942, however, both sides had developed effective antitank defensive systems. For the men in the tanks, the experience of combat was harrowing.

Alan Gilmour, 48th Royal Tank Regiment (Britain), Tunisia, 1943

In the low padded compartment . . . we crouch, the two of us shapeless figures engulfed in a miasma of smoke and dust through which the facia lights barely penetrate. Behind us in the turret the crew are choking with the fumes of cordite which the fans are powerless to dissipate. Cut off from visible contact with the outside world, the wireless operator, wedged in his seat, cannot possibly know in which direction the vehicle is moving. To all five of us, the intercom, our lifeline, relays a bedlam of orders, distortions, and cries from another world.

Nat Frankel, American Private, France, 1944

It takes twenty minutes for a medium tank to incinerate; and the flames burn slowly, so figure it takes ten minutes for a hearty man within to perish. You wouldn't even be able to struggle for chances are both exits would be sheeted with flame and smoke. You would sit, read *Good Housekeeping,* and die like a dog. Steel coffins indeed!

Anonymous British Tank Company Commander, Italian Front, 1944

We were ordered to make the attack in the face of an anti-tank screen firing down the line of advance. We knew that we should not get far. . . . armour-piercing shot seemed to come from all directions. . . . the tanks were knocked out one by one. Most of them burst into flames immediately. A few were disabled, the turrets jammed or the tank made immobile. As the survivors jumped out, some of them made a dash across the open. . . . but they were almost all mown down by German machine gun fire.

Sources: From Bryan Perrett, *Through Mud and Blood: Infantry.* Published by Robert Hale, 1975. Reprinted by permission of Watson, Little, Ltd., licensing agents; from Nat Frankel and Larry Smith, *Patton's Best: An Informal History of the 4th Armored Division.* Hawthorne Books, New York, 1978; and from Douglas Orgill, *The Gothic Line,* Heinemann, 1967. Reprinted by permission of John Johnson Limited.

in Europe. This dream demanded a war against the Jews, the majority of whom lived in Poland and the Soviet Union.

A Crucial Postponement

In July 1940, at the very start of the Battle of Britain, Hitler ordered his military advisers to begin planning a Soviet invasion. By December the plan was set: German troops were to invade the Soviet Union in April 1941. But they did not. Hitler postponed the invasion for two crucial months because the ambitions of an incompetent ally—Mussolini—threatened to undermine the economic base of the Nazi war machine.

Italy was ill-equipped to fight a broad-based war. Its military budget was only one-tenth the size of Germany's, its tanks and aircraft were outdated, it had no aircraft carriers or anti-aircraft defenses, and most crucially, it lacked an adequate industrial base. Yet in 1940 Mussolini's hopes of rebuilding the Roman Empire drove him to launch just such a war. In July 1940, Italian troops invaded British imperial territories in North Africa, and in October Mussolini's soldiers marched into Greece. By the spring of 1941, the Italian advance was in trouble. The British army in North Africa pushed the Italians back into Libya while the Greeks mounted a fierce resistance against the invaders.

Hitler feared the consolidation of British power in Africa and was even more terrified that Mussolini's adventurism would pull the British into eastern Europe. If Britain were able to build air bases in Greece, the Balkans

Map 26.2 The Nazi Empire in 1942

By 1942, Nazi Germany occupied or was allied to not only most European countries but also much of North Africa and the Middle East. Spain, Portugal, Ireland, Iceland, Sweden, and Switzerland remained neutral. Great Britain and the Soviet Union east of Moscow remained unconquered.

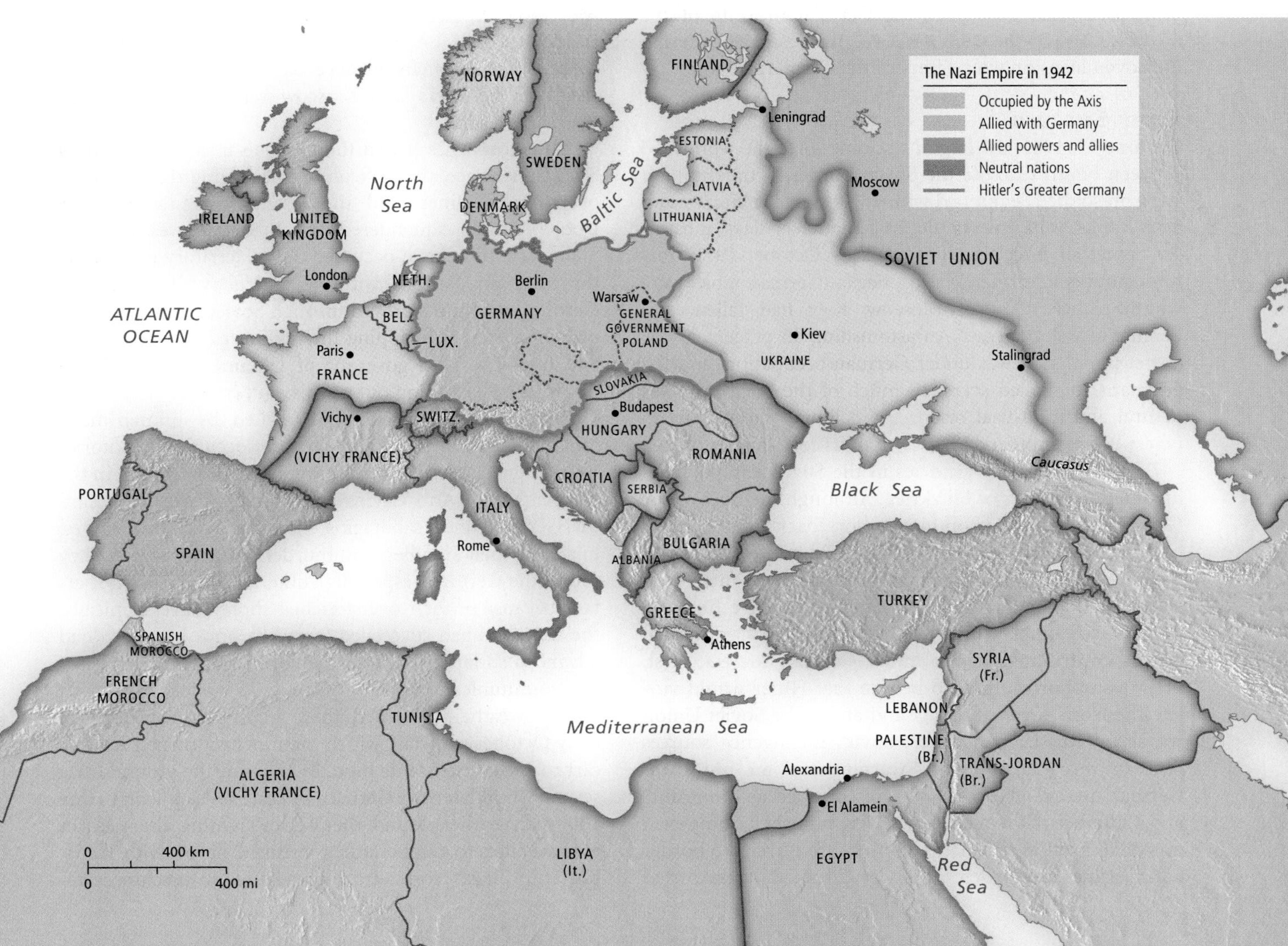

would lie open to British bombing runs. The British could then cripple the German war effort. Germany received 50 percent of its cereal and livestock from the Balkan region, 45 percent of its aluminum ore from Greece, and 90 percent of its tin from Yugoslavia. Most crucially, the oil fields of Romania constituted Germany's chief source of this vital war-making resource. Without oil, there would be no *blitz* in *blitzkrieg*.

These economic considerations led Hitler to delay the invasion of the Soviet Union while the German army mopped up Mussolini's mess in the Balkans and North Africa. In April 1941, German armored units punched through Yugoslavian defenses and encircled the hapless Yugoslav army. Greece came next. The British sent troops as well as state-of-the-art tanks and airplanes to aid the Greeks, but by the end of April Greece was in German hands. Meanwhile, in North Africa German field marshal Erwin Rommel's (1891–1944) Afrika Korps recaptured all the territory taken by the British the previous year.

In the summer of 1941, then, Germany stood triumphant, with dramatic victories in North Africa and the Balkans (see Map 26.2). But these victories came at a high price. They had postponed the German invasion of the Soviet Union. By the winter of 1941, the delay in beginning the Soviet invasion would imperil the German army.

Early Success

On June 22, 1941, the largest invading force the world had yet seen began to cross the Soviet borders. Three million German soldiers, equipped with 2,770 modern aircraft and 3,350 tanks, went into battle. In a matter of days, most of the Soviet air force was destroyed. By October 1941, only four months after the invasion began, German tanks were within eighty miles of Moscow, Kiev had fallen, and Leningrad was besieged. An astonishing 45 percent of the Soviet population was under German occupation, and the Germans controlled access to much of the Soviet Union's natural and industrial resources, including more than 45 percent of its grain and 65 percent of its coal, iron, and steel.

The early German victories in the Soviet campaign illustrated the power of blitzkrieg. Although the bulk of the German army traveled on foot or horseback (the Germans went into the Soviet Union with 700,000 horses), its spearhead force consisted of tank and motorized infantry divisions. This force shattered the Soviet defensive line and then moved quickly to seize key targets. Two additional factors contributed to the initial German success. First, Stalin's stubborn refusal to believe that Hitler would violate the Non-Aggression Pact and attack the Soviet Union weakened Russian resistance. Soviet intelligence sources sent in more than eighty warnings of an imminent German attack; all, however, were classified as "doubtful" and a number of the messengers were punished, some even executed. Even as German troops poured over the border and German bombs fell on Soviet cities, Stalin distrusted the news of a German invasion and ignored his generals' pleas for a counterassault.

A second factor that contributed to the early German victories was the popularity of the invasion among many of the peoples being invaded. The initial German advance occurred in territories where Stalin's rule had brought enormous suffering. In areas that had come under Soviet rule in the previous two years—eastern Poland and the Baltic states—anti-Soviet sentiment was especially high. Ceded to the Soviets by the German-Soviet Non-Aggression Pact, these regions were still bleeding from the imposition of Stalinist terror after 1939. Over two million ethnic Poles had been thrown into cattle cars and sent to Siberian labor camps. Thousands had been shot, including 10,000 Polish army officers who were marched to the Katyn forest and gunned down in front of mass graves. To many in these regions, then, the Germans at first seemed like liberators.

The Fatal Winter

On October 10, Hitler's spokesman announced to the foreign press corps that the destruction of the Soviet Union was assured. German newspapers proclaimed, "CAMPAIGN IN THE EAST DECIDED!"[4] But within just a few months, the German advance had stalled. Leningrad resisted its besiegers and Moscow remained beyond the Germans' reach.

Three obstacles halted the German invasion: stiffening Soviet resistance, the difficulty of supplying the Germans' overstretched lines, and the Russian weather. German troops rapidly squandered the huge reserves of anti-Stalinist sentiment in occupied Soviet territory by treating the local populations with fierce cruelty. Both SS and German army units moved through Soviet territories like a plague of locusts, stripping the regions of livestock, grain, and fuel. The Nazi governor of Ukraine insisted, "I will pump every last thing out of this country."[5] By 1941, both Ukraine and Galicia were devastated by human-made famine. German atrocities in the occupied territories strengthened the will to resist among the Soviets still in the Germans' path. Anti-German partisan units worked behind the German lines, sabotaging their transportation routes, hijacking their supplies, and murdering their patrols. They found the Germans especially vulnerable to this sort of attack because of their overstretched supply lines. Ironically, the Germans had succeeded too well: Since June they had advanced so far so fast that they overstrained their supply and communication lines.

The weather worsened these logistical problems. An early October snowfall, which then melted, turned Russia's dirt roads to impassable mud. By the time the ground froze several weeks later, the German forces, like Napoleon's army 130 years earlier, found themselves fighting the Russian winter. Subzero temperatures wreaked havoc with transportation lines. Horses froze to death, and machinery refused to start. Men fared just as badly. Dressed in lightweight spring uniforms and forced to camp out in the cold, German soldiers fell victim to frostbite. By the end of the winter, the casualty list numbered more than 30 percent of the German East Army.

At the close of the winter of 1941–1942, the German army still occupied huge sections of the Soviet Union and controlled the vast majority of its agricultural and industrial resources. More than three million Soviet soldiers had been killed and another three million captured. But the failure to deal the Soviets a quick death blow in 1941 gave Stalin and his military high command a crucial advantage—*time.* In the zones soon to be occupied by the German army, Soviet laborers dismantled entire factories and shipped them eastward to areas out of German bombing range. Between August and October 1941, 80 percent of the Soviet war industry was in pieces, scattered among railway cars, heading to safety in Siberia. With time, these factories could be rebuilt and the colossal productive power of the Soviet Union geared for the war effort. And that is what happened. By 1943, Russia was outproducing Germany: 24,000 tanks versus 17,000; 130,000 artillery pieces versus 27,000; 35,000 combat aircraft versus 25,000. In a total war, in which victory occurs on the assembly line as well as on the front line, these were ominous statistics for Hitler and his dreams of a German empire.

The World at War, 1941–1945

■ **Why did the Allies win in 1945?**

In December 1941, as the German advance slowed in the Soviet Union, Japanese expansionism in the Pacific fused with the war in Europe and drew the United States into the conflict. Neither Japan nor Germany could compete with the United States on the factory floor. Over the next four years, as millions of soldiers, sailors, and civilians lost their lives in a gargantuan and complicated conflict, industrial production continued to supply a crucial advantage to the Allies.

The Globalization of the War

Even before 1941, Europe's imperialist legacy ensured that World War II was not confined to Europe. As we have seen, Mussolini's desire to expand his North African empire pushed the fighting almost immediately outside European borders. In addition, Britain would never have been able to stand alone against the German-occupied continent without access to the manpower and materials of its colonies and Commonwealth. German efforts to block British access to these resources spread the war into the Atlantic, where British merchant marines battled desperately against German submarines to keep open the sea lanes into Britain.

Britain also drew heavily on the resources of the United States. Throughout 1941 the United States maintained a precarious balance between neutrality and support for the British war effort, as American naval escorts accompanied supply ships loaded with goods for Britain across the Atlantic. In March, the U.S. Congress passed the Lend-Lease Act°, which guaranteed to supply Britain all needed military supplies, with payment postponed until after the war ended. The passage of Lend-Lease was one of the most important decisions in all of World War II. It gave first Britain and then the Soviets access to the incredible might of American industry.

At the same time that the United States was drawing closer to Britain, its relations with Japan were growing increasingly hostile. In 1941 the Japanese occupied Indochina, and the United States responded by placing an embargo on trade in oil with Japan. Threatened with the loss of a key resource, Japanese policymakers viewed this boycott as tantamount to an act of war. Japan's imperial ambitions demanded that it move decisively before its oil ran out. The South Pacific, a treasure house of mineral and other resources, beckoned.

Between December 7 and 10, 1941, Japanese forces attacked American, British, and Dutch territories in the Pacific—Hong Kong, Wake and Guam Islands, the Philippines, Malaya, Molucca in the Dutch East Indies, and most dramatically, the U.S. Pacific fleet base at Pearl Harbor. After an attack that lasted only a few hours, the American Pacific fleet in Hawaii lay gutted. Guam fell immediately; Wake held out until December 23; Hong Kong surrendered on Christmas Day; by February, Malaya had been defeated. On February 15, 1942, the garrison of 130,000 British, Indian, Australian, and local troops surrendered Singapore to a Japanese force less than half its size. By May, this astounding success had been cemented with the conquest of Indonesia, Burma, and the Philippines. In just a few months, the Japanese had established themselves as imperial overlords of the South Pacific, with its wealth of raw materials (see Map 26.3).

The audacity of the Japanese attack impressed Hitler. Although he had long feared American industrial power, he declared war on the United States on December 11, 1941. In Europe Germany now faced the alliance of Britain, the Soviet Union, and the United States. Even against such an alliance, Germany appeared to occupy a strong position. By January a spectacular offensive in North Africa had brought Rommel's forces within two hundred miles of the strategically vital Suez Canal. And in June the German army resumed its advance in the Soviet Union. Within a few months German troops stood at the borders of Russia's oil fields in the southern Caucasus. With Germany on the offensive in the east and Japan controlling the Pacific, the Allies looked poised to lose the war.

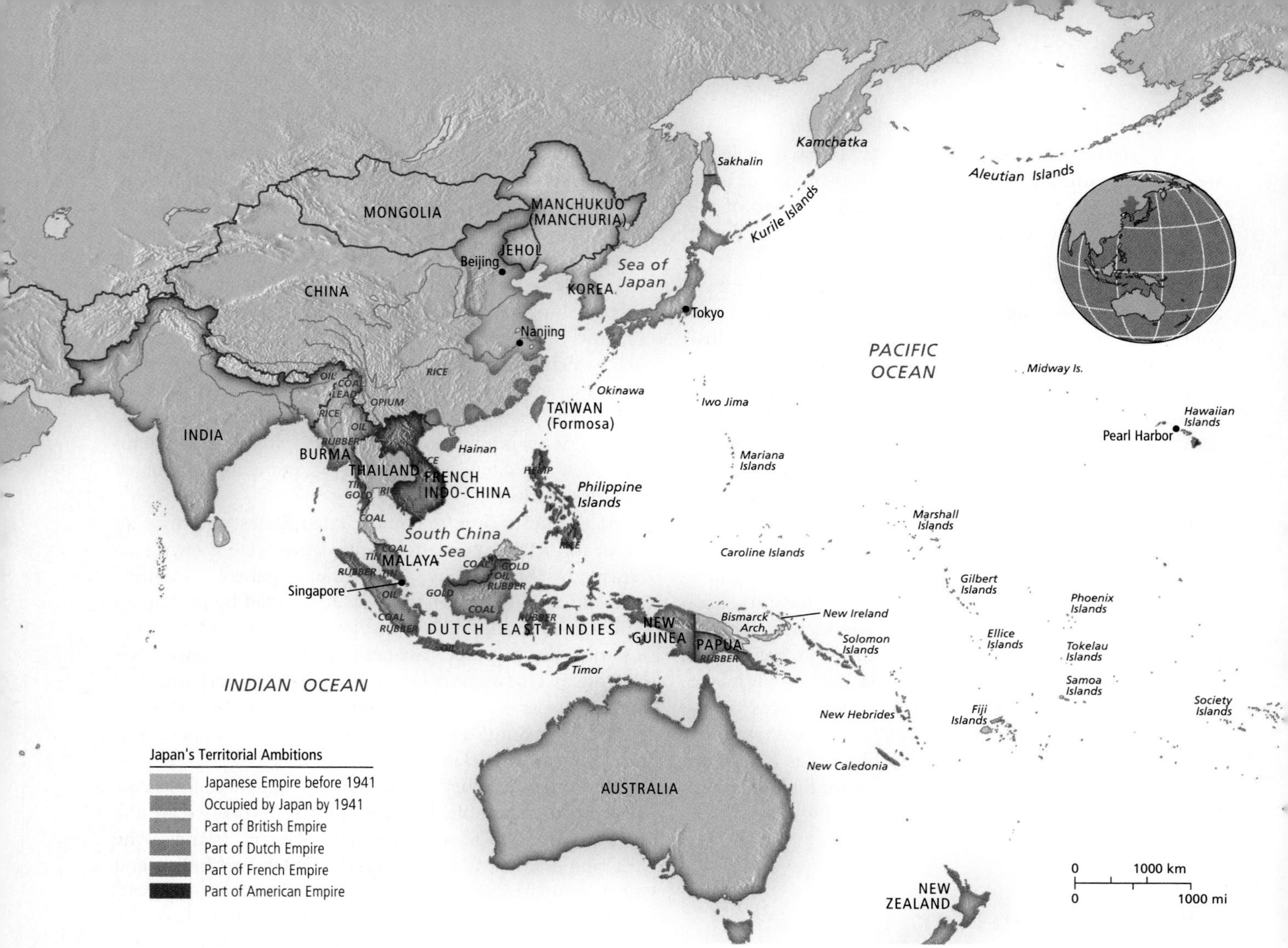

Japan's Territorial Ambitions

- Japanese Empire before 1941
- Occupied by Japan by 1941
- Part of British Empire
- Part of Dutch Empire
- Part of French Empire
- Part of American Empire

Map 26.3 Japan's Territorial Ambitions
Lacking its own supply of natural resources, Japan embarked on imperial conquest.

From Allied Defeat to Allied Victory

Twelve months later the situation had changed, and the Allies were on the road to eventual victory. This road, however, proved long and arduous. The period from 1943 through 1945 was marked by horrendous human suffering, unprecedented attacks on civilians, and cataclysmic military battles. Yet in the end American and Soviet industrial supremacy, allied with a superior military strategy, pushed the balance in the Allies' favor.

FDR on Winning the War

The Turning Point: Midway, El Alamein, and Stalingrad

The second half of 1942 proved the turning point as three very different battles helped transform the course of the war. In the Pacific, victory at the Battle of Midway gave the U.S. forces a decisive advantage. In North Africa, British forces experienced their first battlefield victory at El Alamein. And in Europe, the Battle of Stalingrad dealt Germany a blow from which it never recovered.

The Battle of Midway resulted from the Japanese effort to ensure its air supremacy by drawing the U.S. Pacific fleet's aircraft carriers into battle. To do so, the Japanese attacked Midway Island, a U.S. outpost, on June 4, 1942. By midmorning the Japanese had shot down two-thirds of the American planes. But then an American dive-bomber group, which had gotten lost, suddenly found itself above the main Japanese carriers. Caught in the act of refueling and rearming the strike force, their decks cluttered with gas lines and bombs, the carriers made remarkably combustible targets. In five minutes, three of Japan's four carriers were destroyed; the fourth was sunk later in the day. Japan's First

The Surrender of Singapore
In one of the most humiliating moments in British military history, General Arthur Percival surrenders the Union Jack, and Singapore, to the Japanese in February 1942. More than 130,000 troops were taken prisoner by a Japanese force containing half that number. The Japanese had captured the island's water reservoirs and so had placed Percival in a helpless situation.

Air Fleet was decimated. The destruction of the Japanese fleet dealt Japan a blow from which it could not recover. The United States possessed the industrial resources to rebuild its lost ships and airplanes. Japan did not. In five explosive minutes at Midway the course of the Pacific war changed.

In contrast, the battle of El Alamein marked the culmination of over two years of fighting in North Africa. In September 1940, Mussolini had ordered his troops to advance from Libya (an Italian colony) into Egypt, as part of his effort to establish an Italian empire in the Mediterranean. That winter British and Australian troops not only pushed the Italians back but drove far into Libya itself. The stakes were too high for Hitler to let his Italian ally lose: Control over North Africa and the Middle East meant control over both the strategically and economically vital Suez Canal and the southern shipping lanes of the Mediterranean, as well as access to key oil fields. The Germans entered the conflict and by June 1941, the German Afrika Korps, led by Field Marshal Erwin Rommel, had muscled the British back into Egypt. For more than a year the two armies pushed each other back and forth across the desert. But finally British field marshal Bernard Montgomery, an abrasive, arrogant man whose meticulous battle strategy included the leaking of false plans, caught the Germans by surprise at El Alamein in October 1942. One month later combined British and American forces landed in Morocco and Algeria, and over the next six months pushed Germany out of North Africa. The following year North Africa served as the Allies' jumping-off point for their invasion of southern Italy in July 1943. El Alamein thus marked a crucial turning point in the war. Churchill

CHRONOLOGY

1942: The Turning Point

1941	
December 7	Japan bombs Pearl Harbor
December 11	Germany declares war on United States
1942	
January 21	Rommel's Second Offensive begins in North Africa
February 15	Surrender of British forces to Japan at Singapore
April 22	British retreat from Burma
May 6	Japan completes conquest of the Philippines
June 4	Battle of Midway
August 7	First U.S. Marine landing on Guadalcanal
August 23	German Sixth Army reaches Stalingrad
October 23	Battle of El Alamein begins
November 8	Anglo-American landing in North Africa begins
November 23	German Sixth Army cut off at Stalingrad

said of it, "It is not the beginning of the end, but it may be the end of the beginning."[6]

Churchill's apt description fits the third turning point of 1942, the battle of Stalingrad, as well. In July the German army was sweeping southward toward the oil-rich Caucasus. Hitler ordered the southern offensive split into two, with one arm reaching up to conquer Stalingrad on the Volga River. The conquest of Stalingrad would give the Germans control over the main waterway for the transport of oil and food from the Caucasus to the rest of the Soviet Union: The Soviet lifeline would be cut. But by dividing his offensive, Hitler widened his front from 500 to 2,500 miles. By the time the German Sixth Army reached Stalingrad on August 23, German resources were fatally overstretched.

Recognizing Germany's vulnerability, Stalin's generals assured him they could attack the exposed German lines and then encircle the German Sixth Army—but only if Stalingrad's defenders could hold on for almost two months while they assembled the necessary men and machinery. An epic urban battle ensued, with the Russian and German soldiers fighting street by street, house by house, room by room. By November, the Russians had surrounded the Germans. When the German commander, General Friedrich von Paulus (d. 1953), requested permission to surrender, Hitler replied, "The army will hold its position to the last soldier and the last cartridge."[7] Paulus finally disobeyed orders and surrendered on January 30, 1943, but by then his army had almost ceased to exist. The Germans were never able to make up the losses in manpower, material, or morale they suffered at Stalingrad.

Stalingrad: Turning Point on the Eastern Front
The battle for Stalingrad proved to be not only the turning point in the European war, but also a conflict that tested human endurance to the utmost. German and Russian soldiers fought street by street, house by house, room by room in the bitter Russian winter.

The Allies on the Offensive

The Allies were now on the offensive. In 1942 British bomber command ordered the intensive bombing of German civilian centers. Soon joined by the American air force, the RAF bombers brought the war home to the German people.

The Allies followed their victory in North Africa with an invasion of Italy. This campaign was a response, first, to Stalin's pleas that his Allies open a "Second Front" in Europe and so relieve the pressure on Russian troops and, second, to Churchill's desire to protect British economic and imperial interests in the Mediterranean. The Italian offensive began on July 10, 1943, when Anglo-American forces landed in Sicily, prepared to push up into what Churchill called the "soft underbelly" of German-controlled Europe. Within just fifteen days, Mussolini had been overthrown in a high-level coup and his successor opened peace negotiations with the Allies. But then German muscle hardened the "soft underbelly": The German army occupied Italy. British and American soldiers faced a long, brutal, slow-moving push up the peninsula. Ridged with mountains and laced with rivers, Italy formed a natural defensive fortress. In an eight-month period, the Allied forces advanced only seventy miles.

The European war was decided, then, not in the mountains of Italy but on the eastern front. Beginning in the summer of 1943, the Russians steadily pushed back the Germans. By the spring of 1944 the Red Army had reached the borders of Poland. In August Soviet troops turned south into Romania and Hungary. By February 1945 they were within 100 miles of Berlin (see Map 26.4).

Two interconnected factors proved vital in the Soviet victory over the Germans in the east. The first was the evolution of Soviet military strategy. By 1943, the Red Army had learned important lessons from being on the receiving end of blitzkrieg. It had not only increased its tank units, but it had concentrated these into armies in which motorized infantry regiments accompanied massive numbers of tanks, antitank battalions, and mobile anti-aircraft artillery. In addition, a vast expansion in the number of radios and field telephones overcame the organizational chaos that had greeted the German invasion in 1941.

These changes in technique and technology were closely connected to achievements in industrial production, the second key factor in the Soviet victory. Mobile armored forces depended on factories churning out steel, rubber, oil, and all the various machine parts needed by a modern army. Access to the industrial wealth of the United States provided the Soviet Union with assistance in this task. By 1943, Lend-Lease deliveries of aircraft and tanks were pouring into Soviet ports. Lend-Lease supplied the Soviet Union with the basics needed to keep its army moving: rails and locomotives, jeeps, trucks and gasoline, and 15 million pairs of boots. Yet the Soviets did not rely only on imports. The Soviet industrial effort was enormous. In 1943, Russia manufactured four times as many tanks as it imported, and Soviet production of tanks and antitank guns was double that of Germany.

The Fall of Germany

As the Red Army closed in on Germany from the east, the British and Americans pushed in from the west. On June 6, 1944, the Allies carried out the largest amphibious operation the world had ever seen. Five seaborne divisions (two American, two British, and one Canadian) and three airborne divisions (two American and one British) crossed the English Channel and landed on a sixty-mile stretch of coastline in northern France. The "D-Day" landings illustrated the Allied advantage in manpower and material. Against the Allies' eight divisions, the Germans had four; against the Allies' 5,000 fighter planes, the Germans could send up 169.

Yet the strength of the German resistance—particularly on Omaha Beach, where the U.S. landing encountered more than 4,000 casualties—signaled that the road to Berlin would not be easy. The Allies faced the formidable task of uprooting the Germans from territory where they had planted themselves five years earlier. For ten long months, the British, American, Canadian, and imperial troops fought a series of hard-won battles. By March 1945, as the Russian army approached Berlin from the east, the British and American armies reached Germany's Rhine border and by mid-April stood within fifty miles of Berlin.

The Allies agreed, however, to leave the conquest of Berlin to the Soviet Army. In this climactic battle of the European war, 320,000 Germans, many of them young

Map 26.4 Allied Victory in Europe, 1942–1945
Beginning in late 1942, Allied forces moved onto the offensive.

The GI

On January 26, 1942, the first soldiers from the United States arrived in Britain to prepare for the invasion of Nazi-controlled Europe. By the spring of 1944, Britain was host to a million and a half American soldiers, sailors, and airmen, awaiting the opening of the Second Front in Europe. The coming of the "Yanks" to war-weary, bomb-blasted Britain was an event of more than military significance. For the majority of individuals on both sides, it was their first prolonged encounter with another culture, another way of life. Cultural clashes were commonplace. Forgetting that most essential items were strictly rationed, the GIs (slang that comes from the military label "government issue") at times infuriated their hosts with insensitive complaints about cold rooms, inadequate food, and the shabby style of British dress. The British found the Americans naive, supremely self-confident, alarmingly friendly, and most of all, BIG.

The bigness of the GI is a constant theme in British descriptions and recollections. One British man, urging greater toleration for the GIs, explained to his countrymen, "An American is like a large dog trying to be friendly with everyone in the room, whilst wrecking everything with its tail wagging." A Lancashire nurse recalled her first sight of GIs: "They all seemed to be handsome six-footers with friendly grins and toothpaste advert teeth." But we know that not every GI stationed in Britain was tall and husky; the average height of American servicemen in this era was 5'10". How do we explain this focus on the bigness of the GI body?

A number of factors helped shape British perceptions. First, the bigness of America in general was a constant obsession of both the GIs and their British hosts. *Meet the U.S. Army,* a publication distributed in British schools, told the children, "In the USA, you can get in a car—a high-powered car at that—and drive for a week or more in a comparatively straight line without running into the sea." Second, the Americans *looked better.* The GI's uniform was of a higher-quality fabric and a closer fit than that of the average British soldier's: American privates often found that their flashy uniforms led not only British civilians but even British soldiers to mistake them for officers. Third, compared to the British, the Americans were big eaters and big spenders. An American private earned five times as much as his British counterpart—and spent it with abandon. British pubgoers were sometimes dismayed to find that American soldiers had already consumed the pub's entire stock of beer. Undisciplined by rationing, American appetites seemed huge to the British. One soldier enjoyed his dinner in a British home: "Only afterwards did I discover that I had eaten the family's special rations for a *month.*" GIs also had access to items such as chocolate and canned fruit that had long been unobtainable in Britain. And finally, different cultural norms magnified the impact of the GI's presence. Americans spoke more loudly. They used exaggerated expressions that struck the more understated British as boastful. They tended to lounge, to slouch, to lean against walls, to throw their bodies around in ways that startled many British, schooled in more restrained patterns of public behavior. All of these factors combined to ensure that the GI made an indelible impression on British culture.

Embraced with enthusiasm by many British citizens (particularly women), derided by others (particularly men) as "overfed, overpaid, oversexed, and over here," the GI's body became a symbol, a shorthand reference to American power, influence, and plenty. As World War II ended and the Cold War began, and as the United States took on a new role as the undisputed leader of the "West," the American soldier became a familiar figure throughout western Europe, the visible reminder of the reconfiguration of military and economic dominance.[8]

For Discussion

What other bodies became symbols or shorthand references during World War II? What did these bodies symbolize?

Wartime Encounters
British women entertain GIs headed for the front in France.

boys, fought three million Soviet troops. Even so, it took eleven days before the city's commander surrendered on May 2. Two days earlier, Hitler had taken a cyanide capsule and then shot himself with his service pistol. On May 7, 1945, General Alfred Jodl (1890–1946) signed the unconditional surrender of German forces.

CHRONOLOGY

The Long March Toward Allied Victory

1943	
February	German surrender at Stalingrad; Red Army goes on the offensive; Allied round-the-clock bombing of Germany begins; Japanese surrender at Guadalcanal
May	German surrender in North Africa
July 10	Allied invasion of Italy begins
1944	
January	Lifting of the siege of Leningrad
June 4	Allies liberate Rome
June 6	D-Day landings; Allied offensive in France begins
August 24–26	Allied liberation of Paris
September	Allies liberate the Netherlands, Belgium, and Luxembourg
October	U.S. invasion of Philippines

The Air War, the Atom Bomb, and the Fall of Japan

When Germany surrendered, the war in the Pacific was still raging. After the Midway battle of 1942, the United States steadily, but slowly, agonizingly, pushed the Japanese back island by island. Japanese industry could not make up for the weapons and ammunition expended in these brutal battles. In contrast, American factories were just gearing up. Whereas in 1940 American assembly lines produced only a little more than 2,000 aircraft, by 1944 they had manufactured over 96,000 bombers and fighters. American productivity per worker hour was five times that of Japan.

While U.S. troops moved closer to the Japanese mainland, British and Indian troops rebuffed a Japanese attempt to invade India and pushed the Japanese out of Burma. Australian forces, with American assistance, held the line at New Guinea and forestalled a Japanese invasion of Australia. By February 1945, then, when U.S. Marines landed on the small island of Iwo Jima, just 380 miles from Japan's home islands, the Japanese war effort was in tatters and an Allied victory was ensured.

Obtaining this final victory, however, proved far from easy. In the month of fighting for the island of Iwo Jima, one-third of the American landing force died or suffered injury. The April conquest of Okinawa was even more hard-won. Outnumbered two to one, the Japanese endured

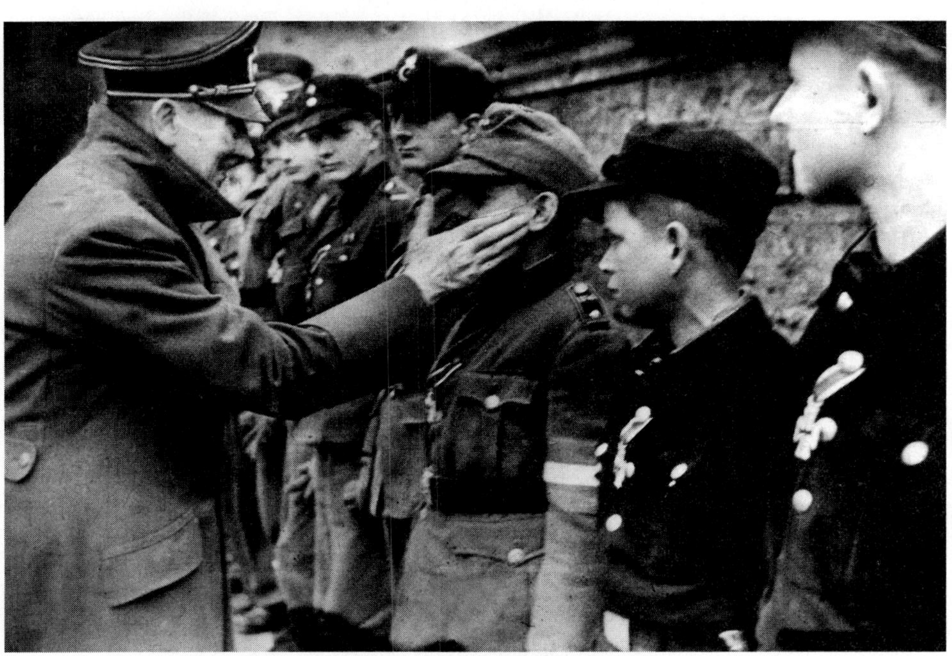

The Battle for Berlin
On April 20, 1945, Hitler celebrated his fifty-sixth birthday and made a rare visit out of his Berlin bunker to visit with the troops defending his city. As this photograph shows, these "soldiers" were just children. Ten days later, Hitler committed suicide.

unbelievable losses—110,000 of the 120,000 soldiers on the island died. Yet they still inflicted serious damage on the attacking force, killing or wounding 50,000 Americans before the fight was over. (Nobody bothered to count how many Okinawans died in a battle they had done nothing to provoke; estimates range as high as 160,000.)

The Air War

Despite the high price exacted to win them, the battles of Iwo Jima and Okinawa were significant victories: The United States now had the bases it needed to bomb Japanese cities. This air war utilized tactics and technologies developed over the previous five years in Europe. For many European civilians, World War II was the war of the bomber. In Britain, until late 1941, civilian deaths outnumbered military, and most civilians died in bombing raids. During autumn 1940, Londoners endured the "Blitz"—seventy-six consecutive nights of mass bombing. By May 1941, almost every main industrial city in Britain had been bombed, and 43,000 noncombatants lay dead. British bombers, joined in 1943 by the American air force, retaliated in kind, and as the war wore on, developed new techniques of airborne destruction. In May 1942, British planes destroyed Cologne with the world's first 1,000-bomber raid, and one year later, introduced the world to the horror of the firestorm with the bombing of Hamburg. In this human-made catastrophe, fires caused by incendiary bombs combine with winds to suck the oxygen out of the air and raise temperatures to combustible levels. As one survivor recalled, "The smallest children lay like fried eels on the pavement."[9] In a single night, 45,000 of Hamburg's residents were killed. In total, more than 500,000 German civilians died in bombing attacks. Twenty percent of the dead were children.

In 1945 the conquests of Iwo Jima and Okinawa enabled the U.S. air command to adopt the British tactics perfected in the skies over Germany as a key strategy to defeat Japan. On one March evening, American bombs and the ensuing firestorm killed 85,000 residents of Tokyo. Over the next five months, American bombers hit sixty-six Japanese cities, burned 180 square miles, and killed approximately 330,000 Japanese. At the same time, a U.S. naval blockade cut Japan off from its supply lines.

The Manhattan Project

While American bombers pulverized Japanese cities during the spring and summer of 1945, a multinational group of scientists fought a very different sort of battle in a secret military installation in New Mexico. The Manhattan Project°, the code name for the joint British-American-Canadian effort to construct an atom bomb, was an extraordinary endeavor, the biggest and most expensive weapons research and development project up to that point in history. Comprising thirty-seven installations in nineteen

DOCUMENT

Living Under the Bombs

During the 1930s, European statesmen and politicians condemned the aerial bombing of civilian populations as an act of barbarity and criminality. Once World War II began, the targeting of civilians in order to break home front morale and impede industrial production became commonplace. Analysts disagree about the military effectiveness of urban bombing, but no one can dispute the human horror.

In this first excerpt, an elderly air warden from Hull, one of Britain's northern port cities, is speaking. One night, when he returned from his post, he found that his street:

Was as flat as this 'ere wharfside—there was just my 'ouse like—well, part of my 'ouse. My missus were just making me a cup of tea for when I come 'ome. She were in the passage between the kitchen and the wash'ouse, where it blowed 'er. She were burnt right up to 'er waist. 'Er legs were just two cinders. And 'er face—The only thing I could recognize 'er by was one of 'er boots—I'd 'ave lost fifteen 'omes if I could 'ave kept my missus. We used to read together. I can't read mesen [myself]. She used to read to me like. We'd 'ave our armchairs on either side o' the fire, and she read me bits out o' the paper. We 'ad a paper every evening. Every evening.

In the following excerpt, a German woman, 19 years old on July 28, 1943, recalls the bombing of Hamburg and the firestorm it induced:

We came to a door which was burning just like a ring in a circus through which a lion has to jump. . . . I struggled to run against the wind in the middle of the street but could only reach a house on the corner. . . . We got to the Loschplatz [park] all right but I couldn't go across the Eiffestrasse [street] because the asphalt had melted. There were people on the roadway, some already dead, some still lying alive but stuck in the asphalt. They must have rushed on to the roadway without thinking. Their feet had got stuck and then they put out their hands to try to get out again. They were on their hands and knees screaming.

Sources: Excerpt from a Mass-Observation typescript report, filed at Mass-Observations offices, no. 844, August 23, 1941. Copyright © by the Trustees of the Mass-Observation Archive. Reprinted by permission; and from Martin Middlebrook, *The Battle of Hamburg*, Allen Lane, 1980. Reprinted by permission of the author.

American states and in Canada, it employed 120,000 individuals. Yet this gargantuan effort was top-secret, unknown even to American vice president Harry Truman, who first learned of the project only after President Roosevelt died.

The Manhattan Project originated as part of the war against Germany, not Japan. When the European war began, a number of scientists—many of them eastern and central European émigrés who had fled the Nazis, many of them Jewish—feared that Germany, with its stellar tradition of scientific research and state-of-the-art laboratories, possessed the potential for developing an atom bomb. They pressured the British and American governments to build the Bomb before Hitler did so. Britain took the initial lead by creating a committee to oversee atomic research in spring 1940. By the following summer, British research had persuaded the Americans that an atom bomb could be constructed. In October 1941—two months before Japan bombed Pearl Harbor—Roosevelt and Churchill agreed to create an atomic partnership.

For three years the Manhattan Project scientists labored to unlock the atom's power. They finally succeeded on July 16, 1945, when the world's first atomic explosion—the Trinity test—detonated over the desert of New Mexico. The date of the Trinity test is crucial because by the time of the test, Nazi Germany had already fallen to the Allies, and Japan was staggering under the combined effects of the American naval blockade and nightly bombing raids (see Map 26.5). Given this situation, the decision to use atom bombs against Japan generated controversy from the very start. Many of the scientists on the Manhattan Project opposed the decision, as did important American military officials such as General Dwight Eisenhower (1890–1969), supreme commander of the Allied forces in Europe; General Douglas MacArthur (1880–1964), supreme commander of the Allied forces in the Pacific; and Admiral William Leahy (1875–1959), chairman of the U.S. Joint Chiefs of Staff.

Advocates of dropping the atom bomb on Japan argued that the fierce Japanese resistance encountered by Americans at Iwo Jima and Okinawa and by the British in Burma signaled that an invasion of Japan's home islands would result in horrifying casualties. Leahy noted to Truman that if casualty rates were as high as those on Okinawa, then the numbers of Americans killed in the first phase of the invasion could reach 50,000.

An invasion of Japan was, however, not a foregone conclusion in the spring and summer of 1945. Leahy and others argued that the naval blockade would end the war *without* an invasion, and in 1946, the U.S. Strategic Bombing Survey concluded that "in all probability prior to 1 November 1945, Japan would have surrendered . . . even if no invasion had been planned or contemplated." Survey officials, of course, had the benefit of hindsight, an advantage denied to Truman and his advisers in the summer of 1945. But more important, from Truman's perspective, continuing to blockade and to drop conventional bombs on Japan meant continuing to put American soldiers in harm's way, a cost he was unwilling to pay. The atom bomb's appeal was not in its potential to kill tens of thousands in a single night; conventional bombs were already doing that, and doing it rather effectively. But the idea of massive casualties, caused by a single atomic bomb, dropped by a single plane, promised to have an enormous psychological impact on the Japanese, and so to end the war more quickly and to bring Allied servicemen home.

The Mushroom Cloud
The detonation of the atomic bomb over Hiroshima on August 6, 1945, produced what would become one of the most familiar images of the post–World War II age.

A Light Brighter Than a Thousand Suns

As a result, at 8:15 A.M. on August 6, 1945, an American plane named the *Enola Gay* (after the pilot's mother) dropped an atom bomb above the city of Hiroshima. A

Map 26.5 Japan in 1945
By the summer of 1945, American bombing raids had decimated many Japanese cities, including Tokyo. Hiroshima escaped unscathed until August 6, 1945. Nagasaki received the second atom bomb on August 9 only because clouds obscured the primary target of Kokura.

light "brighter than a thousand suns" flashed in the sky. Temperatures at the site of the atomic explosion reached 5,400 degrees Fahrenheit. All those exposed within two miles of the center suffered primary thermal burns—their blood literally boiled and their skin peeled off in strips. Scientists calculated that the atom bomb produced casualties 6,500 times more efficiently than an ordinary bomb. Of Hiroshima's wartime population of 400,000, 140,000 died by the end of 1945, with another 60,000 dying in the next five years.

An Eyewitness to Hiroshima (1945)

The Japanese reacted to the atomic bombing of Hiroshima with incomprehension and confusion. They literally did not know what had hit them. Within the high levels of the Japanese government, gradual realization of the atomic bomb's power strengthened the position of those officials who recognized that Japan must now give up. A hardline faction of the military, however, wished to fight on.

Then, on August 8, the Soviet Union declared war on Japan. The next day American forces dropped an atom bomb on the city of Nagasaki and killed 70,000 outright, with another 70,000 dying over the next five years. On August 10, Emperor Hirohito (1901–1989) told his military leaders to surrender. Viewed in the West as an implacable warlord, Hirohito was actually a man with fairly limited political power who had been pressing for peace since June. Negotiations between the Allies and the Japanese continued until August 15, when the war officially ended.

In Hiroshima and Nagasaki, however, another war was raging, this time against an unseen and at first unrecognized enemy—radiation. The lingering horror of radiation sickness, accounts of which were at first dismissed by many Americans as Japanese propaganda, signaled that the atom bomb was not just a bigger weapon, not simply more bang for the buck. In the months after the war's end, Europeans and Americans came to recognize that the revolutionary new force of atomic power had introduced the world to new possibilities—and new horrors.

CHRONOLOGY

The End of World War II

1945	
March 16	American victory on Iwo Jima
April	Berlin encircled by Red Army
April 11	American troops reach Elbe River in Germany
April 30	Hitler commits suicide
May 7	Official German surrender
June 22	American victory at Okinawa
August 6	U.S. drops atomic bomb on Hiroshima
August 8	Soviet Union enters war against Japan
August 9	United States drops atomic bomb on Nagasaki
September 2	Official Japanese surrender

The War Against the Jews

■ **How and why did the war against the Jews take place, and what were its consequences?**

In the months following the war's end, the world also confronted a very different sort of horror, as people began to piece together the story of Hitler's war against the Jews. For European Jews, World War II brought unprecedented terror and, for millions, death. Chapter 25 explained that hatred of the Jewish people stood at the heart of Hitler's world view and Nazi ideology. Yet anti-Semitism alone cannot explain the mass murder that we now call the

Holocaust°, nor was the Holocaust the product of a detailed plan carefully plotted by Hitler long before he came to power. The decision to murder Europe's Jews evolved over time, in the context of total war.

The Holocaust Underway in Lithuania, July 1941
Nazi soldiers adopt a supervisory role while citizens in the Lithuanian city of Kovno murder their Jewish neighbors.

From Emigration to Extermination: The Evolution of Genocide

During the 1930s, Nazi policies focused on forcing German Jews to emigrate. By 1938, these policies had driven out about 25 percent of Germany's Jewish population. At the same time, however, the unification of Germany and Austria, followed by the seizure first of the Sudetenland and then all of Czechoslovakia, meant 300,000 more Jews in the expanded Germany. These numbers skyrocketed with the outbreak of the war. The invasion of Poland brought almost two million more Jews under German control. Pushing Jews to emigrate no longer seemed a workable solution to what the Nazis defined as the "Jewish Problem." But even more important, the fact of war itself made a radicalization of policy and a turn toward murderous violence much more acceptable.

The German occupation of Poland marked the first step toward the Nazi construction of a new racial order in Europe. Hitler intended the Slavic populations, defined in his racist hierarchy as biologically inferior, to serve as a vast labor pool for their German superiors. To reduce the Polish people to slaves, the Nazis embarked on a wholesale destruction of Polish society and culture. They seized businesses and bank accounts, replaced Polish place names with German, closed universities and high schools, and murdered Polish intellectuals and professionals. By the time the war ended in 1945, more than 20 percent of Poland's population had died.

Within the context of their larger plan of racial reordering, Nazi officials talked about "eliminating" Jews from Poland. At this point, however, "elimination" did not yet mean total extermination but instead referred to vaguely articulated plans for mass deportations. German policy toward the Jews in Poland initially focused on "ghettoization." The Nazis forcibly expelled Jews from their homes and confined them in ghettos sealed off from their non-Jewish neighbors. Packed into overcrowded apartments, with inadequate food rations and appalling sanitary conditions, the ghetto populations lived in a nightmare of disease, starvation, and death.

In the almost two-year period between the invasion of Poland and the invasion of the Soviet Union, an estimated 30,000 Jews died, killed outright by German soldiers or dying a more lingering death from starvation and disease as a result of deportation and ghettoization. Yet the suffering had only begun. In the summer or fall of 1941, the Nazis decided on what they termed the Final Solution° to the "Jewish problem": genocide.

The German invasion of the Soviet Union helped shape the "Final Solution." Marching with the forces of the regular army were special mobile units of the SS called Einsatzgruppen° ("strike forces"). With the army providing logistical support, these small motorized units (about 3,000 men in all) took on the task of liquidating those designated as enemies of the Nazi Reich—which meant killing communists and Jews.

Most of these murders followed the same general pattern: SS soldiers rounded up all of the Jewish men, women, and children in a town or village and marched them in batches to a field or woods. They ordered the first batch to dig a large ditch. They then stripped their victims of their clothing, lined them up on the edge of the ditch, and shot them at point-blank range. Subsequent batches were lined up and shot as well, so that by the end of a day's worth of killing, dead and dying bodies filled the ditch. A thin layer of soil was then thrown on top, transforming the ditch into a mass grave. Estimates of the final death count of the Einsatzgruppen actions range from 1.5 to 2 million.

In their war against the Jews, the Einsatzgruppen found ready allies among large sectors of the occupied population. Recall that the earliest stages of the German invasion of the

Einsatzgruppen Action
A soldier shoots the last remaining Jew in a Ukrainian village.

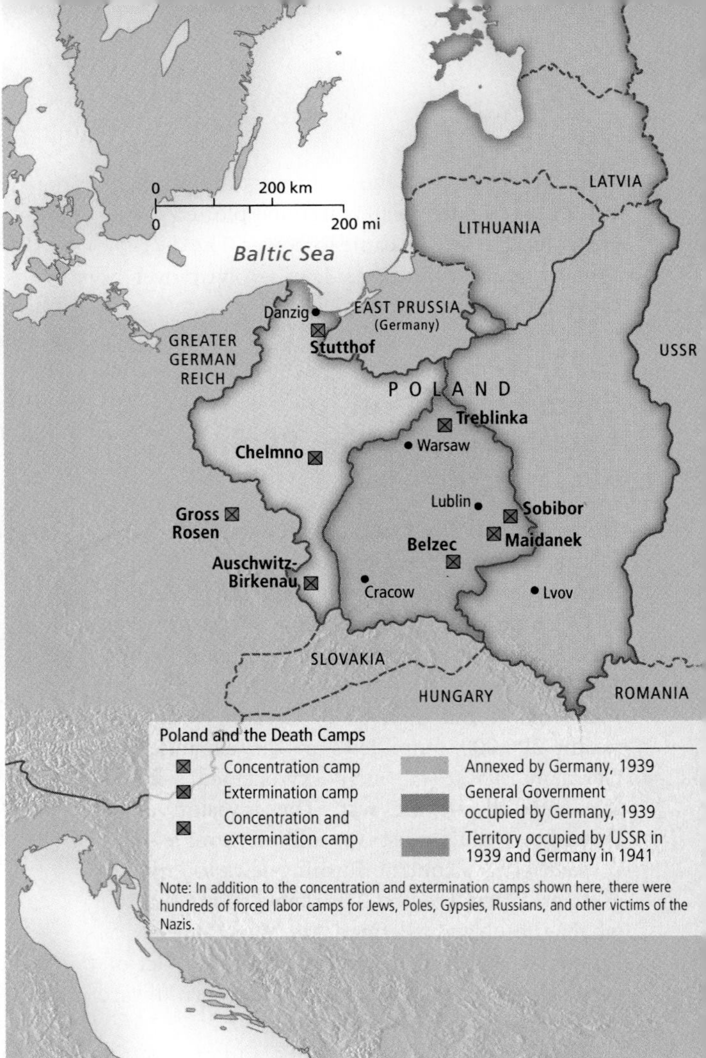

Map 26.6 Poland and the Death Camps
The Nazis set up a vast network of concentration and labor camps across Europe, but built death camps only in Poland.

Soviet Union took place in the territories that had been seized by the Soviets in 1939 as a result of the German-Soviet Non-Aggression Pact. Hence the local populations often welcomed the German troops as liberators and aided the SS in hunting down and killing Jews. In Lvov in eastern Galicia, for example, anti-Soviet Ukrainian fighters turned on the large Jewish community and in two days of violence killed at least 7,000 Jews—*before* the Einsatzgruppen had even arrived.

The Death Camps: Murder by Assembly Line

On January 20, 1942, senior German officials met in a villa in Wannsee, outside Berlin, to finalize plans for killing every Jew in Europe. SS lieutenant colonel Adolf Eichmann (1906–1962) listed the number of Jews in every country; even the Jewish populations in neutral countries such as Sweden and Ireland showed up on the target list. The Wannsee Conference marked the beginning of a more systematic approach to murdering European Jews, one that built on the experience gained by the Einsatzgruppen in the Soviet war.

To accomplish mass murder, the Einsatzgruppen had become killing machines. By trial and error, they discovered the most efficient ways of identifying and rounding up Jews, shooting them quickly, and burying the bodies. But the Einsatzgruppen actions also revealed the limits of conventional methods of killing. Shooting took time, used up valuable ammunition, and required large numbers of men. Moreover, even the best-trained and carefully indoctrinated soldiers eventually cracked under the strain of shooting unarmed women and children at close range. A systematic approach was needed, one that would utilize advanced killing technology and provide a comfortable distance between the killers and the killed. This perceived need resulted in a key Nazi innovation: the death camp.

The death camp was a specialized form of a concentration camp. From 1933 on, Hitler's government had sentenced communists, Jehovah's Witnesses, the Roma, and anyone else defined as an enemy of the regime to forced labor in concentration camps. After the war began, the concentration camp system expanded dramatically. Scattered throughout Nazi-controlled Europe, concentration camps became an essential part of the Nazi war economy. Some firms, such as the huge chemical conglomerate I. G. Farben, established factories inside or right next to camps, which provided vital supplies of forced labor. All across Europe during the war, concentration camp inmates died in huge numbers from the brutal physical labor, torture, and diseases brought on by malnutrition and inadequate housing and sanitary facilities. But it was only in Poland that the Nazis constructed death camps, specialized concentration camps with only one purpose—murder, primarily the murder of Jews (see Map 26.6).

Emaciated Woman at Bergen-Belsen

The death camps marked the final stage in a vast assembly line of murder. In early 1942 the trains conveying Jewish victims to the death camps began to rumble across Europe. Jewish ghettos across Nazi-occupied Europe emptied as their inhabitants moved in batches to their deaths. Individuals selected for extermination followed orders to gather at the railway station for deportation to "work camps" farther east. They were then packed into cattle cars, more than 100 people per car, all standing up for the entire journey. Deprived of food and water, with hardly any air, and no sanitary facilities, often for several days, many Jews died en route. The survivors stumbled off the trains into a nightmare world. At some camps, SS guards culled stronger Jews from each transport to be worked to death as slave laborers. Most, however, walked straight from the transport trains into a reception room, where they were told to undress, and then herded into a "shower room"—actually a gas chamber. Carbon monoxide gas or a pesticide called Zyklon-B killed the victims. After the poison had done its work, Jewish slaves emptied the chamber and burned the bodies in vast crematoria, modeled after industrial bake ovens.

The Holocaust: Memoirs from the Commandant of Auschwitz (1940s)

The Nazis thus constructed a vast machine of death. In this machine, slave laborers constituted key components, each with identification numbers tattooed onto their

DOCUMENT

The "Jager Report"

Karl Jager was a German businessman who joined the SS in 1932. In 1941 he was appointed Commander of Einsatzkommando 3 of Einsatzgruppe A, which was given the task of ridding Lithuania of Jews. The following is an excerpt from his nine-page report on his squad's activities in the summer and fall of 1941. The first six pages contain a day-by-day tally of the number of "executions" (murders) carried out. The final total: 137,346 Jews killed. Jager became a farm laborer after the war, but in 1959 he was arrested; he hanged himself before he could be tried for war crimes.

Kauen [Kaunas], 1 December 1941. Secret Reich Business!

. . .

Today I can confirm that our objective, to solve the Jewish problem for Lithuania, has been achieved by EK 3. In Lithuania there are no more Jews. . . . It was only possible to achieve our objective . . . by forming a raiding squad consisting of specially selected men led by SS-Obersturmfuhrer Hamann, who grasped my aims completely and understood the importance of ensuring cooperation with the Lithuanian partisans and the relevant civilian authorities.

The execution of such actions is first and foremost a matter of organization. The decision to clear each district of Jews systematically required a thorough preparation of each individual action and a reconnaissance of the prevailing conditions in the district concerned. The Jews had to be assembled at one or several places. Depending on the number of Jews a place for the graves had to be found and then the graves dug. . . .

In Rokiskis 3,208 people had to be transported 4½ km before they could be liquidated. In order to get this work done within 24 hours, over sixty of the eighty available Lithuanian partisans had to be detailed for cordon duty. The rest, who had to be relieved constantly, carried out the work together with my men. . . . It was only through the efficient use of time that it was possible to carry out up to five actions of week, while still coping with any work that arose in Kauen, so that no backlog was allowed to build up.

The actions in Kauen itself, where there was an adequate number of reasonably well-trained partisans available, were like parade-ground shootings in comparison with the often enormous difficulties which had to be faced elsewhere.

All the officers and men in my Kommando took an active part in the major actions in Kauen. . . . I consider the Jewish action more or less terminated as far as Einsatzkommando 3 is concerned.

Source: *"The Good Old Days": The Holocaust as Seen by Its Perpetrators and Bystanders.* Eds. Ernst Klee et al. (1991), pp. 46–58.

forearms, a type of human "bar coding." Along a murderous assembly line the human raw material moved from arrival through selection to the undressing rooms to the gas chamber to the crematoria. Approximately three million Jews died in these factories of death. The death camp victims joined the millions who starved or died of disease in the ghettoes, suffocated in the cattle cars, were shot in mass graves, or worked to death in the labor camps. Children were especially vulnerable. Of the Jewish children living in 1939 in the regions already or soon to be under German control, only 11 percent survived.

In total, the Holocaust claimed the lives of approximately six million Jews. The numbers of Roma victims remains unclear. Somewhere between 200,000 and 600,000 died in what the Roma call the *Porajmos*—the Devouring. Jews and Gypsies were the only groups singled out for total extermination based on their supposed biological identity. But Hitler's drive to create his new Germany claimed three to five million other victims as well. Five to fifteen thousand homosexuals perished. So, too, did at least three million Polish Christians.

The Allies' Response

Allied leaders had access to surprisingly accurate information about the Holocaust from very early on. British code breakers translated German military radio transmissions throughout the summer of 1941 so that as the German army—and the Einsatzgruppen—moved into the Soviet Union, British officials confronted intercepted messages such as this one from August 27: "Regiment South shot 914 Jews; the special action staff with police battalion 320 shot 4,200 Jews." By June 1942, Allied leaders knew that death camps existed.

Such information quickly became accessible to ordinary people. British and American newspaper readers and radio listeners received numerous reports about Jewish massacres; after 1942, these reports told about the death camps. But this information had to compete with other war news and many of these articles were written in a skeptical tone, as both reporters and editors had a difficult time believing that such atrocities could be taking place. Pressure from Jewish and non-Jewish public-interest groups did succeed in pushing the British and American governments to issue an inter-Allied declaration in December 1942 that in no uncertain terms announced and condemned Hitler's effort to exterminate European Jewry. This declaration was broadcast all over the world.

Despite this official acknowledgment of the mass murder of Jews, the Allies did not act directly to stop the killings. Should the Allies then be considered bystanders in the crime of the Holocaust? Some historians contend that anti-Semitism in both British and American society structured the Allies' military priorities and prevented leaders from exploring strategies such as sending in commando units, bombing the rail lines into the death camps, or even bombing the camps themselves. Other historians argue these alternatives were not militarily feasible, and that the Allies did the only thing they could do on the Jews' behalf—win the war as quickly as possible.

In the months after the war ended, Allied leaders struggled to bring Nazi leaders to trial to account for their crimes. What one participant called "the greatest trial in history" opened on November 14, 1945. For eleven months, a tribunal of four judges—American, British, French, and Soviet—sat in a courtroom in the German city of Nuremberg to judge nineteen prominent German military, political, and industrial leaders. The Nuremberg trials°, broadcast by the crowds of journalists packed into the courtroom, offered the world its first encounter with the Holocaust. The trials highlighted the Nazi onslaught against European Jewry as one of the most horrendous of the Nazis' many "crimes against humanity," a category first introduced into international law at Nuremberg.

IMAGE
Liberating the Concentration Camps

The Home Front: The Other Wars

■ **What did total war mean on the home front?**

As the Holocaust made vividly clear, for many Europeans during World War II the home front was not a place of safety or normalcy but a place where other wars were fought. The spreading resistance against the Nazi regime, as well as bombing raids and forced labor obligations, obliterated the distinction between combatant and noncombatant, blurred gender roles, and provoked calls for radical social change.

The Limits of Resistance

Throughout the war individuals and groups in occupied Europe performed heroically, hiding Jews and others on the run, sabotaging equipment, disrupting transportation systems, and relaying secret information to the Allies. In the Soviet Union and in mountainous regions of Yugoslavia, Italy, and southern France, where the terrain offered shelter for guerillas, anti-Nazi fighters formed partisan groups that attacked German army units. In one of the best-known cases of resistance, the Jews in the Warsaw ghetto rose up in the spring of 1943. Armed with only one or two submachine guns and a scattering of pistols, rifles, hand grenades, and gasoline bombs, Jewish fighters held off the far superior German military force for more than a month. In the

Mass Grave at Bergen-Belsen
British soldiers liberated the camp of Bergen-Belsen on April 15, 1945. For many prisoners, however, death provided their only "liberation." The Allies forced German civilians living in the regions around camps such as these to view the mass graves, in an effort to compel them to face up to their passive participation in the Holocaust. Few Germans accepted responsibility.

end, however, the ghetto was leveled, and all its survivors deported to Nazi death camps.

Both men and women participated in the Resistance, the struggle against Nazi rule. In Yugoslavia, 100,000 women fought as soldiers in the partisan ranks: 25,000 were killed and 40,000 injured. Most women in the Resistance were not in combat units. Instead, they played gender stereotypes to great advantage: They hid bombs in baby carriages, tucked vital messages under their shopping, disarmed Germans with feminine charm. One Italian partisan used to catch rides on German trucks to deliver her illegal communications: "What was there to fear? You only had to give them a few smiles."[10] With men at risk of being rounded up for forced labor in Germany, women often shouldered the burden of distributing clandestine publications, delivering supplies and arms, and finding safe houses.

But only a minority of Europeans, men or women, fought in the Resistance. As the Dutch historian Louis de Jong has noted of European actions and attitudes under Nazi occupation, "Unwilling adjustment was the rule, intentional resistance the exception."[11] Why did so few Europeans join the Resistance? Important factors include the Germans' military might, their success at infiltrating Resistance organizations, and their willingness to use brutal force to crush any threat. The German network of concentration camps throughout occupied Europe possessed enormous deterrent value. Concerned for their own and their families' safety, most Europeans hoped simply to keep their heads down and survive the war.

The German practice of exacting collective retribution for Resistance actions particularly undercut mass support for anti-German efforts. In 1942, for example, British intelligence forces parachuted Czech agents into German-held Czechoslovakia. The agents assassinated the chief SS official in the region, Reinhard Heydrich (1904–1942), but they were immediately betrayed by one of their own. In retaliation, the Germans massacred the entire population of the village of Lidice. Similarly, an assassination attempt against Hitler in 1944 led to mass arrests and the executions of an estimated 5,000 Germans.

In Germany itself and in countries allied to rather than conquered by the Germans, potential resisters had to convince themselves that patriotism demanded working against their own government. In France until 1943, resistance meant opposing the lawfully instituted but collaborationist Vichy government of Marshal Pétain. As a World War I hero, Pétain had an almost godlike reputation in France and was popular even with those who did not share his authoritarian conservatism. As a result, in the early years of the war many French men and women viewed the members of the Resistance as traitors against France, rather than as heroes fighting against the Nazis. By 1943, however, an alternative focus of national loyalty had emerged: the Free French headed by General Charles De Gaulle (1890–1970), a career military man who had gone into exile rather than accept the armistice with Nazi Germany. After the Anglo-American landing in North Africa in November 1942, De Gaulle claimed Algeria as a power base and declared himself

Justice in History

The Trial of Adolf Eichmann

On May 23, 1960, David Ben-Gurion (1886–1973), the prime minister of Israel, made a spectacular announcement: Israeli secret service agents had kidnapped Adolf Eichmann, a wanted Nazi war criminal, and smuggled him into Israel to await trial. Eichmann, the head of the Gestapo's Jewish Affairs unit, had implemented Nazi policies on Jewish emigration and deportation. His office sorted through the complicated bureaucratic procedures to ensure that the trains laden with Jews kept to their schedules and delivered their human cargo to the gas chambers on time. It was to Eichmann that Jewish leaders came to plead for emigration visas and for work permits. It was with Eichmann that Jewish leaders negotiated about the timing, size, and composition of deportations. For many Jews, then, Eichmann represented German power and came to personify Nazi evil. He had disappeared in the chaotic final days of World War II and eventually made his way to Argentina, where, as "Ricardo Klement," he lived a quiet, respectable life with his wife and children—until 1960.

From the moment of Ben-Gurion's sensational announcement, the Eichmann case occupied the attention of the world. Six hundred foreign correspondents attended the trial, which was one of the first to be filmed by television cameras. More than 1,500 documents were submitted and 120 witnesses testified in the 114 sessions held between April 11 and August 14, 1961. Three judges, each of whom had been born in Germany and had emigrated to Palestine in 1933, heard the evidence. On December 15, they sentenced Eichmann to death. He died by hanging on May 31, 1962, the first execution in Israel, which had abolished capital punishment for all crimes except genocide.

The Eichmann trial told the story of Jewish suffering during World War II to the widest possible audience. Both Ben-Gurion and the chief prosecutor, Gideon Hausner, stated publicly that the trial aimed to construct "a living record of a gigantic human and national disaster," and so educate both young Israelis and the entire world in the causes and consequences of the Holocaust.[12] As Hausner explained in his emotional opening statement, he saw himself as the spokesman for "six million accusers . . . [whose] ashes were piled up in the hills of Auschwitz and in the fields of Treblinka, or washed away by the rivers of Poland."[13] Hausner (who, like many Israelis, had lost most of his relatives in the Nazi death camps) called more than 100 witnesses, many of them death camp survivors. Their testimony, published or broadcast throughout the world, painted an unforgettable and detailed picture of the horror of genocide.

By the time the prosecution rested its case, no one could doubt that Eichmann was a guilty man, one who had played an essential role in the murder of millions. Yet the Eichmann trial attracted an enormous amount of criticism and continues to arouse great controversy. Critics charged that to achieve moral justice for Holocaust victims and survivors, the Israeli court committed a legal injustice against Eichmann. The trial was not only made possible by a violation of international law (Eichmann's kidnapping), it also was filled with irregularities, including the introduction of testimony that did not pertain to the specific crimes charged. Critics also disputed Israel's legal right to try Eichmann: The crimes had not occurred in Israeli territory, nor were Eichmann's victims Israeli citizens. (Israel did not exist until 1948.)

In reply to these critics, Hausner and other supporters of the prosecution insisted that justice demanded that Eichmann be brought to trial, and that the Israeli government had pursued the only course of action open to it. In the Eichmann trial, then, we confront a case in which what was legal on the one hand and what was just on the other appeared very much at odds. There is no doubt that Eichmann was guilty of horrendous crimes; there is also no doubt that the Israeli government stepped beyond the boundaries of international law in kidnapping Eichmann.

The Eichmann trial also raised important questions about the nature of the Holocaust. Was it a crime perpetrated by a few very evil men, or did the evil penetrate deep into German, and European, society? The prosecution's case sought to depict Eichmann as a monster, a brilliant and demonic mastermind responsible for the deaths of millions of Jews. As Hausner contended, "it was [Eichmann's] word that put gas chambers into action; he lifted the telephone, and railway trains left for the extermination centers; his signature it was that sealed the doom of tens of thousands."[14] Such a depiction provided a comforting explanation for the Holocaust—it was perpetrated not by ordinary human beings but by monstrous devils.

Yet many trial observers and subsequent historians argued that such a depiction was simply wrong. This argument appeared in forceful terms in the most well-known critique of the prosecution—Hannah Arendt's *Eichmann in Jerusalem: A Report on the Banality of Evil,* published in 1963. Arendt (1906–1975), a Jewish philosopher who had fled Nazi Europe in 1941, argued that the evidence provided in the trial

Eichmann sits on the left in a cage of bulletproof glass.

The three judges hear the case from the high table on the right.

Eichmann on Trial

showed Eichmann to be a fairly commonplace man, motivated by ambition as much as by ideology, a rather plodding bureaucrat obsessed with trivial details—in other words, an ordinary man, capable of extraordinary evil.

Must ordinary men be held responsible for following evil orders? This is the final question raised by the Eichmann trial. Defense attorney Robert Servatius insisted that the Holocaust was an "act of state," a crime carried out by a political regime, for which no civil servant could bear the blame. Eichmann only followed orders. Servatius concluded his arguments by asking Eichmann how he viewed "this question of guilt." Eichmann replied,

> *Where there is no responsibility, there can be no guilt. . . . The questions of responsibility and conscience are for the leadership of the state. . . . I condemn and regret the act of extermination of the Jews which the leadership of the German state ordered. But I myself could not jump over my own shadow. I was a tool in the hands of superior powers and authorities.*[15]

Eichmann's judges disagreed. In declaring Eichmann guilty of genocide, they argued,

> *We reject absolutely the accused's version that he was nothing more than a "small cog" in the extermination machine. . . . He was not a puppet in the hands of others. His place was among those who pulled the strings.*[16]

Questions of Justice

1. Even if Eichmann's assertion that he was simply "a tool in the hands of superior powers and authorities" could be proven correct, to what degree was he culpable for his actions?
2. In the Eichmann case, the letter of the law and justice appeared to be at odds. In what situations—if any—must the law be broken to ensure that justice prevails? Who has the authority to make such a judgment?

Taking It Further

Laqueur, Walter. "Hannah Arendt in Jerusalem: The Controversy Revisited," in Lyman H. Legters, ed., *Western Society After the Holocaust.* 1983. Examines the impact of Arendt's critique of the trial.

The Trial of Adolf Eichmann: Record of Proceedings in the District Court of Jerusalem. Vols. 1–9. 1993–1995. The basic primary source.

the head of a Free French provisional government. French patriots could declare themselves loyal to this alternative government and fight in the Resistance against both Nazi rule and Vichy collaboration.

In many areas—for example, much of Italy after the German army occupied the country in 1943—a genuine spirit of unity characterized the Resistance struggle, with socialists, communists, and Catholics working together not only to defeat the Nazis but also to create the foundations of a better society. In other areas, divisions within the Resistance limited its impact. Conservative army officers fighting to preserve the prewar status quo clashed with guerilla groups that espoused radical political goals. Fighting among Resistance factions shaded into civil war. In Ukraine, nationalists fought against communist partisans as well as the Germans. In Greece, the communist-dominated National Liberation Front battled not only the Nazis but also a rival Resistance group, the royalist National Greek Democratic Union.

Civil War in Yugoslavia

The fiercest struggle occurred in Yugoslavia, where political and ethnic divisions split both the country and the Resistance. Wartime Yugoslavia experienced a bloodletting unmatched anywhere in Europe except in the German-occupied regions of Poland and the Soviet Union. Parts of the country such as Slovenia and Macedonia were occupied by German or German-allied armies and endured brutal repression. The scale of violence peaked in the fascist state of Croatia, created after the German invasion of 1941. This Nazi-sponsored regime immediately embarked on a savage program of ethnic homogenization, with a ferocious campaign of terror against Jews, Bosnian Muslims, and Serbs.

In Yugoslavia, therefore, the Resistance was not simply or even primarily aimed at the Germans. Guerilla bands of Serbian soldiers called *Chetniks* supported the now-exiled Yugoslav monarchy and regarded the Croatian regime as their main enemy, although, like the Croatian fascists, the Chetniks also slaughtered both Muslims and Jews. In the midst of this bloody free-for-all, a second Resistance group emerged, one based not on ethnicity but on political ideology. Led by communist Josip Broz (1892–1980), alias "Tito," these partisans saw the war as a chance for social revolution and promised equality for all in a reunited Yugoslavia. Tito's partisans focused on fighting Germans (diverting ten German divisions from the eastern front), but they also fought their fellow Yugoslavs, with the royalist Chetniks fiercely opposing Tito's aim of a communist state.

Tito's partisans won the civil war. In 1944 they fought alongside the Soviet army and liberated Yugoslavia from German control. With 90 percent of the vote in the first postwar election, Tito assumed control of the new communist state of Yugoslavia, a position he held for the next thirty-five years. Beneath the uniform surface created by communist ideology, however, the jagged edges of ethnic division remained sharp.

Under Occupation

In occupied Europe, Nazi racial ideology shaped the experience of both soldiers and civilians. The Nazis drew a sharp line between the peoples of western Europe—the Dutch, Norwegian, Danes, and Flemish, all considered of racially superior "Germanic stock"—and the Slavs of eastern Europe. The ferocity of Nazi brutality increased exponentially in the eastern occupied regions.

The German treatment of prisoners of war (POWs) illustrates the contrast between the western and eastern European experience during World War II. By the end of 1941, 2.5 million Soviet soldiers had been captured. By February 1942, two million of these had died, both from starvation and from epidemic diseases nurtured by the poor conditions in the camps. In contrast, of the more than one million French soldiers captured by the Germans in 1940, nineteen out of twenty returned home at the end of the war. When dealing with western European POWs, the Germans abided by international rules; in eastern Europe, World War II was a game without rules and without limits.

The German occupation of western Europe was less heavy-handed than in the east, particularly during the first half of the war. The Nazis believed that "Germanic" peoples such as the Dutch could be taught to become good Nazis and therefore spared them the extreme violence and mindless brutality that characterized the German occupation in the east. Moreover, in western Europe the Germans sought to work with rather than to annihilate political and economic elites. For example, in both Belgium and the Netherlands civil servants continued to do their prewar jobs. Nonetheless, the German occupation in the west, even in the first two years of the war, was far from lenient. The Nazis forced occupied countries to pay exorbitant sums to cover the costs of their own occupation. In addition, they were required to sell both manufactured products and raw materials to Germany at artificially low prices. Anyone who spoke out against the Nazis faced imprisonment or death. The occupation grew even more harsh after 1943 as German military losses piled up, stocks of food and essential supplies dwindled, and German demands for civilian labor increased.

For millions of European men and women, the war meant forced labor in Germany. With the need to free up German men for the front lines, the Nazis faced crucial labor shortages in almost every sector of the economy. Placing the economy on an all-out war footing would have meant imposing unpopular measures such as the conscrip-

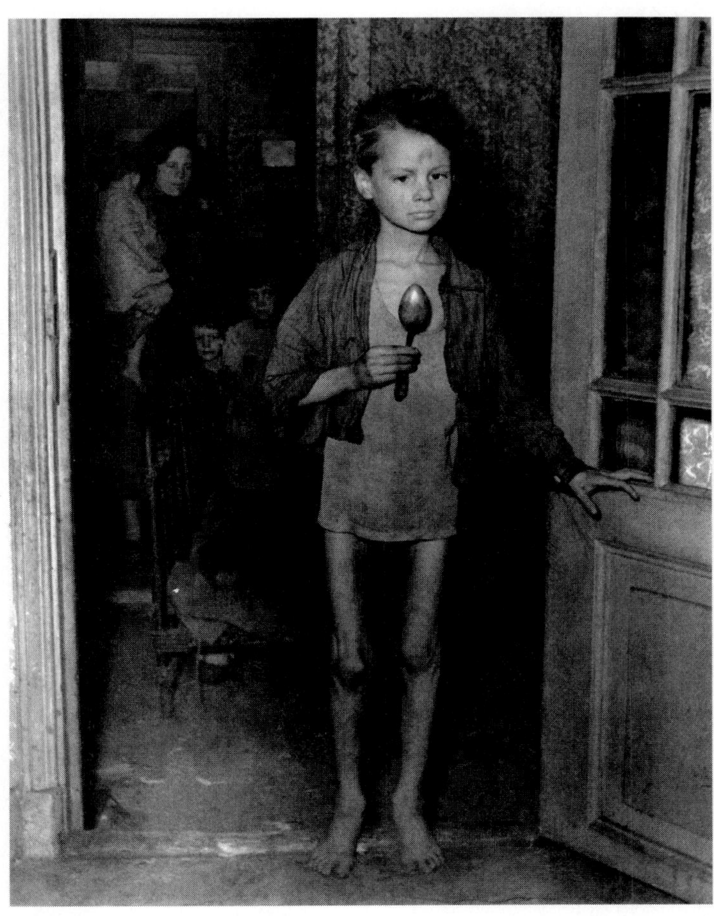

The *Hongerwinter*

By the fall of 1944, the southern provinces of the Netherlands were liberated, but the north remained under German occupation. After Dutch railway employees refused to transport any more German troops, the Germans retaliated by blocking all food shipments to the north. Twenty thousand Dutch civilians died in the resulting "Hunger Winter."

tion of women for industrial labor, lengthening working hours, and prohibiting holidays. The Nazis chose instead to recruit labor from conquered territories. Within days of the invasion of Poland, Polish POWs were working in German fields. By August 1944, German farmers and factory owners employed over 5.7 million foreign civilian laborers (one-third of whom were women) and almost two million POWs. These foreign workers accounted for more than half the labor in German agriculture and in German munitions plants and one-third of the labor force in key war industries such as mining, chemicals, and metals.

Hostile, hungry, and often untrained for the jobs in which they were placed, foreign workers proved to be less productive than German laborers. Nevertheless, foreign labor played a crucial role in wartime Germany, not only in fueling the German war machine but also in maintaining German civilian morale. Foreign labor cushioned German civilians from the impact of total war and reassured them that they belonged to a superior race. Many German factory owners were relieved to find they now had a labor force with few political rights. The director of one aircraft manufacturing firm explained, "The great advantage of employing foreigners . . . is that we only have to give orders. There is no refusal, no need to negotiate."[17] The labor of foreigners also benefited the German working class. Nazi regulations stipulated that German workers were to regard themselves as the masters of the foreign laborers working alongside them. Thus ordinary Germans held positions of privilege and power. Some families even found themselves able to afford new luxuries. Beginning in 1942, the Nazi regime brought Russian women into Germany to serve as maids in German households. As a result, according to a report in January 1943, "even those households with many children, whose financial situation previously did not permit them to hire domestic help, can now afford to maintain a worker."[18]

The Women's War

As we have seen, women joined the ranks of the Resistance and were forced to labor in German industries. Women also tended to bear the brunt of home front deprivation, as they were the ones who had to get a meal on the table and clothe their children in the face of severe rationing. Basic household goods such as frying pans, toothbrushes, bicycle tires,

Some Women's War

British women did not have to endure the hell of Nazi occupation or forced labor. They did, however, participate fully in the war effort. Only the Soviet Union mobilized its women more completely.

baby bottles, and batteries almost disappeared; food was in short supply; clothing had to be recycled. It was Europe's women who became experts at "make do and mend," as British government pamphlets advised.

British women were fully mobilized. They did not serve in combat, but they were drafted for service in civilian defense, war-related industry, or the armed forces. Women accounted for 25 percent of the civilians who worked in Britain's Air Raid Protection services as wardens, rescuers, and telephone operators. All citizens—male or female—working less than 55 hours per week had to perform compulsory fire-watching duties from 1941 on. The numbers of women employed in male-dominated industries such as metals and chemicals rose dramatically.

Only the Soviet Union mobilized women more fully than Britain. Soviet women constituted 80 percent of the agricultural and 50 percent of the industrial labor force. All Soviet adult men and women under age 45 who were not engaged in essential war work were required to work eleven hours a day constructing defenses. Unlike in Britain, Russian women also served in combat. By 1944, 246,000 women were in front-line units. For all Soviet citizens, male and female, life on the home front meant endless labor, inadequate food supplies, and constant surveillance under martial law. Stalin demanded an all-out war against not only the German invaders but also anyone at home who undermined the war effort in any way. The Soviet government established a compulsory sixty-hour workweek and issued ration cards only to those who worked.

Until 1943, the German home front contrasted sharply with that of Britain and the Soviet Union. The Nazi policy toward female employment rested on Hitler's conviction that Germany had lost World War I in part because of the collapse of morale on the home front. As a result, Hitler placed a high priority on maintaining civilian morale. Generous allowances for soldiers meant that their wives, unlike in Britain, did not have to work to feed their families. In the first years of the war, the Nazi government rationed clothing and food supplies but did not dramatically cut consumption levels. Moreover, Hitler hesitated to conscript middle-class German women for industrial labor. For Hitler, ideology came before economics. He believed that the future of the "German race" depended on middle-class women being protected from the strains of paid labor so that they could bear healthy Aryan babies.

In Germany the use of foreign labor took the place of the full-scale mobilization of women. Top-ranking Nazis explicitly linked the use of foreign workers to gender considerations. At the end of 1941, for example, Hermann Göring (1893–1946) announced that Soviet workers would be brought into Germany to guarantee "that in future, the German women should not be so much in evidence in the work process."[19] The number of women in the German workforce actually fell by 500,000 between 1939 and 1941. German women who did work were prohibited from working long hours or at night, and from performing heavy physical labor. Instead, eastern European workers (many of them women) were given the tough jobs and the poor hours. At the Krupp metalworks factory, for example, German women worked for six hours at light jobs during the day; Russian women did the heavy labor during the twelve-hour night shift.

Military necessity eventually undercut Nazi gender ideology. The fall of Stalingrad marked a turning point in Nazi policy toward German women at work. With losses on the eastern front averaging 150,000 men per month, the German army desperately needed more men. At the same time, the German war economy demanded more workers. In response, Hitler's deputy Joseph Goebbels (1897–1945) declared that Germany must fight a total war, which meant total mobilization of the home front. The final, desperate year of the war saw a concentrated use of female labor in Nazi Germany.

Of all the combatant states, the United States stands out as unique with regard to the home front. The United States never fully mobilized its economy, and more than 70 percent of its adult women remained outside the paid workforce. Rationing was comparatively minimal and consumption levels in the United States high. In fact, for many families, the war years brought prosperity after years of economic depression. But most important, American cities were never bombed, and thus the United States was able to maintain a clear distinction between soldier and civilian, man and woman—a distinction that was blurred in other combatant nations.

What Are We Fighting For?

To mobilize their populations for total war, governments had to convince their citizens of the importance of the war effort. Maintaining morale and motivating both civilians and soldiers to endure deprivation and danger demanded that leaders supply a persuasive answer to the question: What are we fighting for?

Myth Making and Morale Building

All nations—democratic or authoritarian—rely on myths, on stories of national origins and identity, to unify disparate individuals, classes, and groups. In times of total war, such myths become crucial. During World War II, the process of myth making was institutionalized by government agencies responsible for propaganda. In Britain, the newly formed Ministry of Information (democracies tend to shy away from using the word *propaganda*) took on the task of propping up civilian morale. Staffed by upper-class men, the MOI's efforts often betrayed its class composition: Many of its posters and leaflets adopted a hectoring tone, subjecting ordinary citizens to a barrage of do's and don'ts. Far more effective were the speeches of Prime Minister Winston Churchill, whose romantic vision of Britain as a still-great power destined to triumph was exactly the myth that the beleaguered British needed. In Germany, strict censorship had already subordinated the arts and entertainment industries to the demands of the state. The war heightened this control as censorship tightened even further, paper shortages limited the production of books and periodicals, and the threat of being drafted for the eastern front kept artists in line.

In all the combatant nations, governments enlisted artists, entertainers, and the technologies of the mass media for myth making and morale building. The British artist Henry Moore's (1898–1986) drawings of ordinary people in air raid shelters (completed under an official commission) evoke the survival of civilized values in the midst of unspeakable degradation. Perhaps the most famous musical work from the war is Dmitri Shostakovich's (1906–1975) *Seventh Symphony*—now universally known as the *Leningrad Symphony* and a symbol of human resilience. Shostakovich composed the early drafts of this work in Leningrad while German shells were falling, and it was actually performed in Leningrad in August 1942, while the city was still under siege.

During the war, film came into its own as an artistic form capable of creating important myths of national unity. Laurence Olivier's version of Shakespeare's *Henry V* (1944) comforted British moviegoers with its classic story of a stirring English military victory against huge odds. In Italy, a group of filmmakers known as the Neo-Realists created a set of films that dramatized the Resistance spirit of national unity. Shot on location, with amateur actors and realistic sets, films such as Roberto Rossellini's *Open City* (1945) depicted lower-class life with honesty and respect and called for the creation of a better society from the rubble of the old.

Planning for Reconstruction

Rossellini's call for the creation of a new society was echoed throughout Europe during the war. Across Europe a consensus emerged on the need for *social democracy,* a society in which the state intervenes in economic life to ensure both public welfare and social justice. As early as December 1942, a government committee set out a radical plan for a new Britain. In rather unusual language for an official document, the committee's report identified "five giants on the road to reconstruction": Want, Disease, Ignorance, Squalor, and Idleness. To slay these giants, the committee recommended that the state assume responsibility for ensuring full employment and a minimum standard of living for all through the provision of family allowances, social welfare programs, and a national health service. The Beveridge Report (named after the committee's chairman) became a bestseller in Britain and the basis for a number of postwar European social welfare plans. Churchill, however, reacted lukewarmly to its proposals—a major reason for his defeat in the election of June 1945. The Labour Party, which enthusiastically endorsed the Beveridge Report and campaigned with slogans such as "Fair Shares for All," won by a landslide. Similarly, Charles De Gaulle found that in order for his Free French Committee to be recognized as the provisional government of France, he had to display a commitment to democracy and radical social reform. Thus he espoused women's suffrage, and his government promised not only free medical services and expanded family allowances, but also the nationalization of key industries and economic planning.

Four factors explain this radical reorientation of European politics. First, and most important, as the war dragged on and the death tolls mounted, European men

Wartime Gains
British children began enjoying free school milk during the war, as part of the state's efforts both to ensure equitable distribution of resources and to shore up the health of the population. Popular sentiment demanded that such communal efforts be continued in peacetime as well.

and women demanded that their suffering be worthwhile. They wanted to know that they were fighting not to rebuild the depressed and divided societies of the 1930s, but to construct a new Europe. Second, the war (and the ongoing revelations of Nazi atrocities) completely discredited the politics of the far right. This sort of politics, whether fascist, Nazi, or conservative-authoritarian, disappeared from legitimate political discussion. But in Europe (although not in the United States) the liberal ideal of the free and self-interested individual competing in an unregulated economy also lay in ruins, the victim of the prewar Great Depression. The new Europe, then, had to be built along different lines. The third factor that explains the radical reorientation of European politics was the combatant nations' success in mobilizing their economies for total war. If governments could regulate economies to fight wars, why could they not regulate economies for peacetime prosperity? Finally, the important role of socialists and communists in the Resistance enhanced the respectability of radical political ideas. Out of the Resistance came a determination to break the mold of prewar politics and create a new Europe. In France, for example, the Resistance Charter of 1944 demanded the construction of a "more just social order" through the nationalization of key industries, the establishment of a comprehensive social security system, and the recognition of the rights of workers to participate in management.

More generally, the Resistance raised key questions about the role of the individual in modern society. In the 1930s, many Europeans had been persuaded by Hitler, Mussolini, and other far-right theorists that the individual was not important, that only the state mattered. But what the Resistance revealed is the power of human choice and the need for individual action in a world run amok. Despite—even because of—the horrors of the war, Europeans such as the French writer Albert Camus (1913–1960) emerged convinced of the power of human action: "A pessimist with respect to the human condition, I am an optimist with respect to man." Thus democracy reclaimed the activist state from fascism and Nazism on the one hand, and Stalinism on the other. Europeans saw that the power of the state could be used to improve the well-being of its citizens without at the same time trampling on the rights of the individual.

Conclusion

The New West: After Auschwitz and the Atom Bomb

The wartime encounter with the Nazi vision of the West as a race-based authoritarian order was crucial; from it emerged a sharpened commitment within the West to the processes and values of democracy. But to present the Second World War as a conflict between democracy and Nazism is to oversimplify. To defeat Nazi Germany, the democracies of Britain and the United States allied with Stalin's Soviet Union, a dictatorial regime that matched Hitler's Germany in its contempt for democratic values and human rights and that surpassed it in state-sanctioned mass murder.

The Soviet Union emerged from the war as the dominant power in eastern Europe; as we will see in the next chapter, the presence of the Red Army obliterated any chance to establish democratic governments in this region. The tensions inherent in the Anglo-American alliance with the Soviets led directly to the Cold War, the ideological and political conflict that dominated the post-World War II world and that once again forced a redefinition of the West. From 1949 until 1989, it was easy to draw the West on any map: One simply shaded in the United States and the countries allied to it—and against the Soviet Union. At the same time, however, a new division emerged. World War II marked the beginning of the end of European imperial control over the non-European world. The postwar era would thus see growing tensions between "North" and "South"—between the industrially developed nations and the underdeveloped regions seeking to shrug off their colonial past.

Much of the impetus for imperial control over non-European regions had come from the conviction of Western supremacy. During World War II, however, Japanese victories had exposed the illusion of Western military invincibility. And after the war, the gradual realization of the full horror of the Holocaust demolished any lingering claim to Western cultural superiority. What sort of superior position could be claimed by a culture in which educated, supposedly civilized men sent children into gas chambers disguised as showers? The atomic bombings of Hiroshima and Nagasaki added more questions to the ongoing debate about the meaning of the West. With the best of intentions, some of the greatest minds in the Western world had produced weapons designed to kill and maim tens of thousands of civilians within seconds. Had Western technology outdistanced Western ethics? And what about the implications of such technologies in a democratic society? For example, would the need to control such weapons lead to measures that eroded individual freedoms? Thus the assembly-line techniques of mass murder developed by the Nazis and, in very different ways, the sheer efficiency of the atom bomb in obliterating urban populations forced both individuals and their political leaders to confront the destructive potential of Western industrialism. For centuries, the use of the methods of scientific inquiry to uncover truth and achieve both material and moral progress had supported Westerners' self-identification and their sense of cultural superiority. But World War II demonstrated that the best of science could produce the worst of weapons, that technology and technique could combine in the death factory. The task of accepting this knowledge, and facing up to its implications, helped shape Western culture after 1945.

Suggestions for Further Reading

For a comprehensive listing of suggested readings, please go to www.ablongman.com/levack2e/chapter26

Alperovitz, Gar. *Atomic Diplomacy: Hiroshima and Potsdam. The Use of the Atomic Bomb and the American Confrontation with Soviet Power.* 1994. The first edition of this book, published in 1965, sparked an ongoing scholarly debate about the role of Cold War concerns in shaping U.S. decision making at the end of World War II.

Browning, Christopher. *Ordinary Men: Reserve Police Battalion 101 and the Final Solution in Poland.* 1992. A powerful account of the participation of a group of "ordinary men" in mass murder.

Calder, Angus. *The People's War: Britain, 1939–1945.* 1969. Lengthy—but worth the effort for students wishing to explore the war's impact on British society. (Those who want a shorter account can turn to Robert Mackay, *The Test of War: Inside Britain 1939–45* [1999].)

Frayn, Michael. *Copenhagen.* 1998. A remarkable play in which Frayn dramatizes a meeting (that actually did occur) between the German atomic physicist Werner Heisenberg and his Danish anti-Nazi colleague Niels Bohr. Contains both extremely clear explanations of the workings of atomic physics and a provocative exploration of the moral issues involved in the making of the atom bomb.

Friedlander, Saul. *Nazi Germany and the Jews, 1933–1939.* 1998. An important study of the evolution of Nazi anti-Semitic policy before the war.

Hilberg, Raul. *Perpetrators, Victims, Bystanders: The Jewish Catastrophe, 1933–1945.* 1992. As his title indicates, Hilberg looks at the three principal sets of participants in the Holocaust.

Iriye, Akira. *The Origins of the Second World War in Asia and the Pacific.* 1987. Part of Longman's "Origins of Modern Wars" series aimed at university students, this short and readable study highlights the major issues and events.

Keegan, John. *The Second World War.* 1989. Provides clear explanations of military technologies and techniques; packed with useful maps and vivid illustrations.

Kitchen, Martin. *Nazi Germany at War.* 1995. A short and nicely organized survey of the German home front.

Marrus, Michael R. *The Holocaust in History.* 1987. A clearly written, concise account of historians' efforts to understand the Holocaust. Highly recommended.

Moore, Bob, ed. *Resistance in Western Europe.* 2000. A collection of essays that explores recent research on this controversial topic.

Overy, Richard. *Russia's War: A History of the Soviet War Effort, 1941–1945.* 1997. A compelling account, written to accompany the television documentary *Russia's War.*

Paxton, Robert. *Vichy France: Old Guard and New Order, 1940–1944.* 1972. A now-classic study of the aims and evolution of France's collaborationist government.

Rhodes, Richard. *The Making of the Atomic Bomb.* 1986. A lengthy but very readable account; very good at explaining the complicated science involved.

Rhodes, Richard. *Masters of Death: The SS-Einsatzgruppen and the Invention of the Holocaust.* 2002. Compelling account of the Einsatzgruppen actions during the German invasion of the Soviet Union.

Rock, William R. *British Appeasement in the 1930s.* 1977. A balanced and concise appraisal.

Weinberg, Gerhard. *A World at Arms: A Global History of World War II.* 1994. Places the war within a global rather than simply a European context.

Notes

1. Quoted in Robert H. Abzug, *Inside the Vicious Heart: Americans and the Liberation of Nazi Concentration Camps* (1985), 19.
2. Quoted in Gordon Horwitz, *In the Shadow of Death: Living Outside the Gates of Mauthausen* (1991), 167.
3. Quoted in Piers Brendon, *The Dark Valley: A Panorama of the 1930s* (2000), 282.
4. Quoted in Richard Overy, *Russia's War* (1998), 95.
5. Quoted in Mark Mazower, *Dark Continent: Europe's Twentieth Century* (1999), 157.
6. Quoted in Peter Clarke, *Hope and Glory: Britain, 1900–1990* (1996), 204.
7. Quoted in Joachim Fest, *Hitler* (1973), 665.
8. Quotations from Juliet Gardiner, *"Over Here"—The GIs in Wartime Britain* (1992), 62, 53, 132.
9. Quoted in Richard Rhodes, *The Making of the Atomic Bomb* (1988), 474.
10. Quoted in Jane Slaughter, *Women in the Italian Resistance 1943–1945* (1997), 63.
11. Quoted in Bob Moore, ed., *Resistance in Western Europe* (2000), 210.
12. Gideon Hausner, *Justice in Jerusalem* (1966), 291.
13. Ibid., 323–324.
14. From Hausner's opening statement; quoted in Moshe Pearlman, *The Capture and Trial of Adolf Eichmann* (1963), 149.
15. Ibid., 463–465.
16. Ibid., 603; Hausner, *Justice in Jerusalem*, 422.
17. Quoted in Ulrich Herbert, *Hitler's Foreign Workers* (1997), 306.
18. Ibid., 149, 189.
19. Ibid., 149.

НЕТ!

Redefining the West After World War II

27

CHAPTER OUTLINE

- A Dubious Peace, 1945–1949
- The West and the World: Decolonization and the Cold War
- The Soviet Union and Eastern Europe in the 1950s and 1960s
- The West: Consensus, Consumption, and Culture

On one apparently ordinary day in August 1961, western European television viewers witnessed an extraordinary sight. While the news cameras rolled, policemen from East Berlin—the section of Berlin controlled by East Germany's communist government—played tug-of-war with firemen from West Berlin, the half of the city that belonged to the democratic state of West Germany. Between them was not a length of rope, but rather a middle-aged German woman. This horrifying contest had been set in motion by the construction of the Berlin Wall. Appalled by the growing numbers of East German citizens who were fleeing communist rule through the gateway of West Berlin, the East German and Soviet authorities decided to shut the gate. In the early morning hours of August 13, East German workers erected a barbed-wire fence along Berlin's east-west dividing line. In some cases, this line ran right through apartment buildings. For the next few weeks, these apartments provided literal "windows to the west." West Berlin firemen waited with blankets ready to catch anyone willing to jump out of a window—and out of communist eastern Europe. The woman caught on camera was one of a number of Berliners who sought to jump out a window in search of freedom.

These windows closed quickly. The communist authorities bricked them up; later they leveled entire apartment buildings to create a moat in front of what was now the armed fortress of East Berlin. The barbed-wire fence became a concrete wall buttressed by gun towers, lit by searchlights, and patrolled by armed guards with "shoot to kill" orders.

The unidentified woman literally caught between West and East serves as an appropriate symbol for Europe during the 1950s and 1960s. In these decades, the Cold War between the United States and the Soviet Union influenced European politics, culture, and society. European governments and their populations found their freedom of maneuver checked by Cold War constraints. The woman's desperation to reach the West reminds us that American influence in western Europe should not be equated with Soviet

No! The fear of nuclear war colored the post–World War II decades, as this 1958 poster from the Soviet Union attests.

Tug-of-War at the Berlin Wall
Caught by the television cameras, this woman sought to escape through her window into West Berlin. She succeeded.

control of eastern Europe: Cultural and economic dominance are not the same as political tyranny. Nevertheless, many Europeans in the West as well as the East felt that they no longer controlled their own societies.

The Cold War was in part an encounter of two clashing ideologies, as much a battle of ideas and values as weapons and warriors. Both sides laid claim to universal cultures—to have achieved a way of life that would benefit *all* human societies. This ideological encounter forced a redefinition of "the West." Previous chapters have described the way in which this cultural construct shifted over time. By the late nineteenth century, Christianity, although still important, played a less central role in defining "the West" than did a mix of other factors, including the possession of industrial technology, the illusion of white superiority based on pseudoscientific racist theorizing, and faith in both capitalist economics and liberal political values. The Cold War added an anti-Soviet stance and a fear of communist ideology to the mix. These additions at times eroded the Western commitment to democracy, particularly within the developing world.

Significantly, the Cold War turned "hot" not in Europe but in places such as Korea, Cuba, and Vietnam. The developing world served as the site of crucial Cold War conflicts in this era. The postwar years witnessed the widening of the economic gap between "North" and "South"—between the industrialized nations, largely located in the Northern Hemisphere, and the economically underdeveloped regions (many but certainly not all of which were situated south of the equator), now shrugging off colonial rule and seeking both political independence and economic prosperity. Thus, as Europeans encountered each other across the Cold War divide, they also encountered non-Europeans across a huge economic gulf. Two very different contests—North versus South and West versus East—quickly became entangled with each other as the Cold War moved beyond Europe's borders to the developing regions.

To explore the impact of these encounters on the postwar West, this chapter addresses four questions:

- **Why and how did the world step from World War II to the Cold War?**
- **What was the impact of decolonization and the Cold War on the global balance of power?**
- **What patterns characterized the history of the Soviet Union and eastern Europe after the death of Stalin?**
- **What patterns characterized the history of western Europe in the 1950s and 1960s?**

A Dubious Peace, 1945–1949

- **Why and how did the world step from World War II to the Cold War?**

World War II ended in the spring of 1945, but the killing did not. Postwar purges and deportations ensured that the death totals continued to mount, while in many regions, world war gave way to civil war. Most significantly, as the "hot" war waned, the Cold War between the Soviet Union and the countries it controlled, and the United States and its Western allies, began.

Devastation, Death, and Continuing War

If there was peace in Europe and Asia in 1945, it was the "peace of a graveyard," with an estimated 55 million people dead. In the immediate postwar period, the death statistics continued to rise as the victors turned with vengeful fury against the vanquished. In Czechoslovakia, purges killed 30,000 collaborators between 1945 and 1948. In Yugoslavia, Tito ordered the massacre of anticommunists. No one knows how many died; some estimates range as high as 60,000.

Those left alive faced the overwhelming task of reconstruction. Throughout Europe, the bombers had rendered most highways, rail tracks, and waterways unusable. With laborers, seed, fertilizer, and basic equipment all in short supply, agricultural production in 1945 stood below 50 percent of prewar levels. Less visible, but just as devastating, was the destruction of the financial system. Few European currencies were worth much. In occupied Germany, cigarettes replaced marks as the unit of exchange.

One of the most serious problems facing Europe was that of the refugees or displaced persons (DPs). The war, and Hitler's attempt at racial reordering, had uprooted millions from their homes. The DP problem grew even larger as a result of the peace settlement. The Soviet Union kept the Polish territories it had claimed in 1939 and Poland received a large chunk of what had been prewar Germany. The new Polish government then expelled the German inhabitants from this region. In Czechoslovakia, Romania, Yugoslavia, and Hungary, too, ethnic Germans were forced out. More than 11 million Germans suffered from these

Map 27.1 Europe in the Cold War
As this map shows, during the Cold War the "West" was defined culturally and politically, rather than in geographic terms. Greece and Turkey stand far to the east in Europe, yet their membership in NATO placed both within the "West."

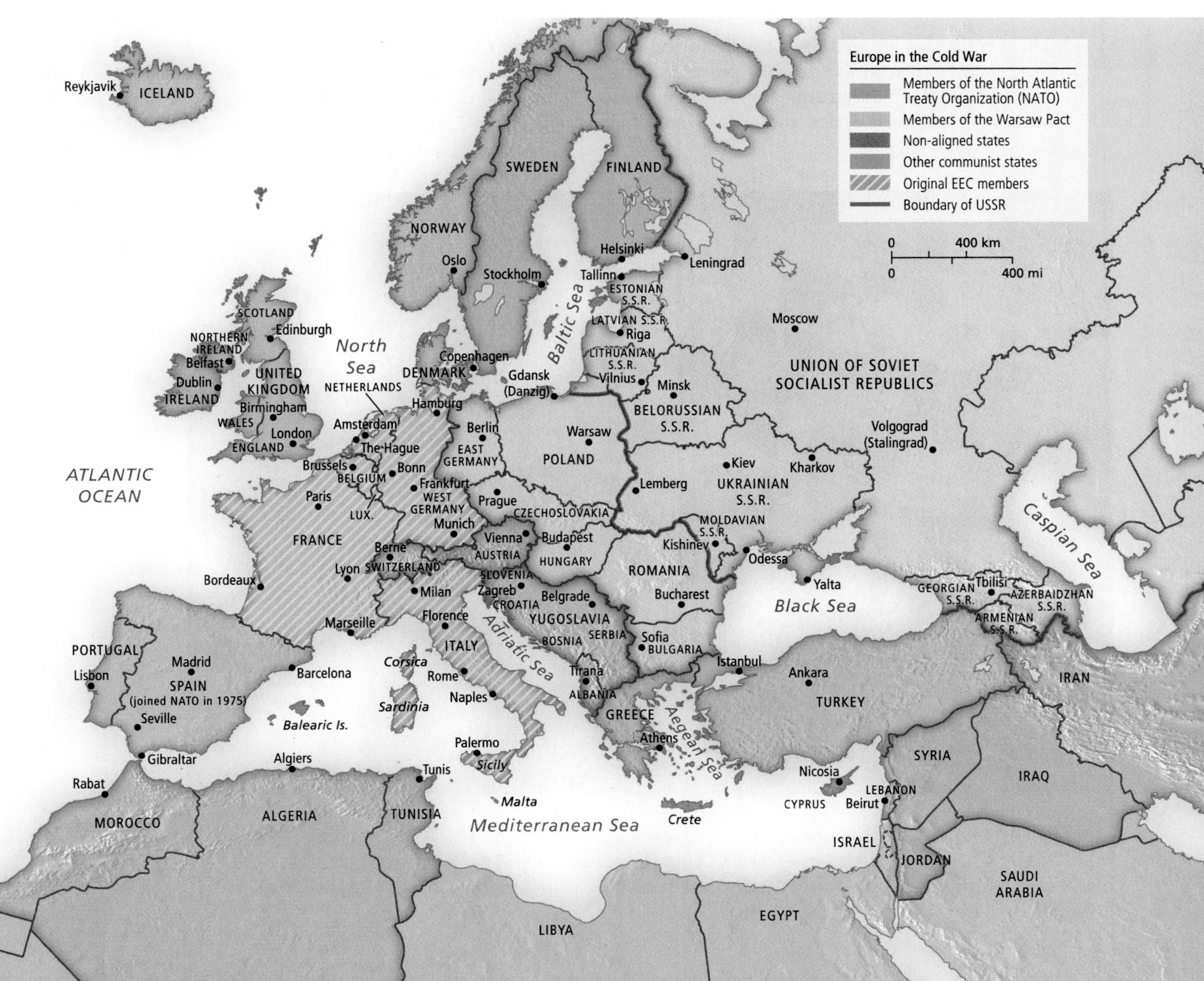

deportations. As many as two million died en route to Germany. In addition, between 1945 and 1948, eastern European governments forcibly transferred seven million non-German refugees, in a brutal solution to the ethnic divisions that had destabilized prewar political structures.

Forced deportation can be understood as a continuation of war—a war carried out by governments against groups marked as dangerous because of their ethnic makeup. Other forms of war also continued after 1945. Ukrainian nationalists kept up a guerilla war against the Soviets until the early 1950s. In Greece civil war between communist and anticommunist forces raged until 1949, while in Trieste (along the Italian-Yugoslav border) civil war continued until 1954. In the forests and marshes of Poland, anticommunist guerilla groups fought against the new communist regime until 1956.

From Hot to Cold War

The Cold War Military Stand-off

The conflict that aroused the most alarm and posed the greatest threat to the dubious peace after 1945 was the Cold War°, the struggle for global supremacy between the United States and the Soviet Union. Within just a few years of the defeat of Germany and Japan, the allies became enemies, and what Winston Churchill called an "Iron Curtain" dropped between eastern and western Europe. The divisions of the Cold War were rooted in World War II, nurtured by the fears and hopes it aroused.

Fraying Seams, 1943–1945

Each of the Allied leaders had different aims and interests. To ensure his own and the Soviet Union's security, Stalin demanded communist-controlled governments along the Soviet borders. In contrast, U.S. president Franklin D. Roosevelt believed that global international security and economic prosperity depended on the establishment of European democracies, committed to capitalist economic principles and practices. British prime minister Winston Churchill possessed a third set of aims. Concerned about the postwar balance of power in Europe and the maintenance of the British Empire, Churchill recognized that once Germany was defeated, a power vacuum would exist in central and eastern Europe. He feared that the Soviets might prove too eager to fill that vacuum. A permanent Soviet presence in the Balkans particularly threatened British military and economic interests throughout the Mediterranean. The "Big Three°," then, came to the negotiating table with

The Big Three I (Yalta, February 1945)

From 1941 until April 1945, the Big Three meant Churchill, Roosevelt, and Stalin. At the very end of the war, however, the composition of the Big Three suddenly changed, as Harry Truman replaced Roosevelt and Clement Attlee replaced Churchill.

clashing interests and aims; even before the war ended, the fabric of the alliance was under strain.

Reluctant to place too much pressure on the alliance's fraying seams, Roosevelt opted for postponing the hard decisions. He was not seeking simply to sidestep controversy. Rather, he hoped that the controversial questions would be settled after the war by a new international body, the United Nations (UN). In Roosevelt's vision, such a body could succeed where the now-discredited League of Nations had failed: It could guarantee that conciliation and negotiation would replace armed conflict in settling disputes between countries. Roosevelt recognized that if the Soviet Union refused to participate in the United Nations, the UN, like the league, would be a failure. Therefore he sought to avoid confrontations that might give Stalin a reason to block Soviet membership in the UN.

Roosevelt also hoped that new international economic structures would provide a framework for settling the disputes that divided the Allies. In 1944 leading American and European economists gathered in New Hampshire to construct a system for postwar economic revival. Well aware of the economic chaos that had followed World War I, and desperate to avoid a repeat of the Great Depression of the 1930s, they drew up the Bretton Woods Agreement°, which became the basic framework for the Western postwar economic order. To keep the global economy running smoothly, Bretton Woods established the American dollar as the world's reserve currency and fixed the currency exchange rates of its forty-four participating nations. It also established two new international economic institutions—the International Monetary Fund (IMF), to maintain the stability of member currencies, and the World Bank, to encourage global economic development.

Through the establishment of such international organizations as the IMF and the UN, Roosevelt sought "the end of the system of unilateral action, the exclusive alliances, the spheres of influence, the balances of power, and all the expedients that have been tried for centuries and have always failed." Yet neither Stalin nor Churchill shared Roosevelt's vision. Standing on opposite ends of the political spectrum, the Russian communist and the English aristocrat both continued to believe in precisely those "spheres of influence, the balances of power" that Roosevelt proclaimed outmoded. In the worldview of both Stalin and Churchill, armed force, not a new international organization, would determine the shape of the postwar world. As Stalin pointed out to Tito, the Yugoslav communist leader, "Everyone imposes his own system as far as his armies can reach. It cannot be otherwise."

By 1945, Stalin's army had a long reach. When the Big Three met in Yalta in February 1945, the communist partisans controlled Yugoslavia, and the Soviet Army had occupied Romania, Bulgaria, Hungary, and much of Czechoslovakia. This situation was in part the result of earlier Big Three negotiations. Throughout 1942 and 1943, Stalin had pressed his Allies to open a Second Front in Europe and so relieve the pressure on Soviet forces. Churchill, concerned about the prospect of Soviet armies moving into eastern Europe, wanted to push into German-dominated Europe through the Balkans—and thus ensure that British and American forces were on the ground in eastern Europe when the war ended. But at the first Big Three summit in Tehran in 1943, Stalin and Roosevelt overruled Churchill and agreed that the Anglo-American invasion would be a single, concentrated attack across the English Channel into France (the D-Day invasion of June 1944). This decision left eastern Europe open to the Red Army.

The presence of the Red Army in eastern Europe weakened the negotiating positions of Churchill and Roosevelt at Yalta. Roosevelt's desire to obtain Stalin's commitment to enter the war against Japan also reduced his bargaining power. A series of problematic compromises resulted. Stalin signed a declaration promising free elections in eastern Europe; at the same time, Roosevelt and Churchill agreed that such freely elected governments should be pro-Soviet. Germany's future remained undecided although the Big Three agreed to share the postwar occupation by dividing Germany, as well as the symbolically and strategically vital city of Berlin, into occupation zones controlled by the United States, the Soviet Union, France, and Britain.

The final Big Three summit in the German city of Potsdam in July 1945 did not bridge the gap between the Soviet Union and its allies. At this summit, Stalin faced two unfamiliar negotiating partners. The new U.S. president Harry Truman (1884–1972) replaced Roosevelt, who had died in April, and midway through the summit, the new British prime minister, Labour Party leader Clement Attlee, arrived to take Churchill's place. The change of personnel made little difference, however. Stalin was determined to maintain control over the territories occupied by his armies, while the British and Americans increasingly saw Stalin's demands as a threat to both democratic ideals and the European balance of power. Moreover, during the summit Truman received a telegraph informing him of the successful Trinity test of the atomic bomb in New Mexico (see Chapter 26). This news meant that the war against Japan would soon be over—and that the Americans and British no longer needed or wanted Stalin to join the war in the Pacific. With Western incentives for placating Stalin now removed, the tone of the negotiations became more hostile.

Yet the wartime alliance had not yet completely torn apart. Throughout the rest of 1945 and 1946 Truman hoped to resolve the allies' differences and resisted the idea of a permanent American military presence in Europe. Stalin, too, was unwilling to push too far. He not only feared American military might, but also wished to retain access to Western economic assistance and expertise. In addition, to get his economy moving again, Stalin needed to scale back military expenditures. Thus he proceeded with rapid demilitarization: Soviet army strength went from 12 million men in 1945 to 3 million by 1948. He also adopted a policy of passivity for communist parties operating in regions that he viewed as part of the Western sphere of influence. He refused to assist Greek communists seeking to overthrow the British-backed monarchical regime, and he ordered communist parties in western Europe to participate with non-communists in coalition governments.

During this period, however, the British pushed Truman to adopt a hard line toward Stalin and his demands. British foreign policy was in the hands of the foreign secretary, Ernest Bevin (1881–1951). A labor leader with a history of fighting against communist efforts to control British unions, Bevin was a fierce anti-Stalinist. He was also an ardent British nationalist who regarded the maintenance of the British Empire, particularly in the Mediterranean and the Middle East, as crucial to preserving Britain's Great Power status in the postwar world. Bevin thus urged the United States to stand tough when the Soviets demanded a stake in what had been Italy's North African empire and he urged a strong response when Stalin delayed pulling Russian troops out of Iran. (Soviet and British troops had occupied Iran during the war to keep its oil supplies out of German hands.)

Torn in Two, 1946–1949

Within just a few years of the war's end, clashing aims and interests had shredded the wartime alliance. Three key developments—the breakdown of cooperation over Germany, the Truman Doctrine°, and the Marshall Plan°—tore apart the former allies.

Allied cooperation in the occupation of defeated Germany quickly broke down over economic issues. At Potsdam, Truman and Attlee had agreed to Stalin's demand for German reparations. By 1946, however, British and American authorities became convinced that Germany faced mass starvation. To feed the Germans in the British zone, Attlee's government imposed bread rationing on the British public—a drastic step never taken during the war itself. The British and Americans decided that the immediate priority must be German economic recovery. To stabilize Germany's economy, they combined their zones into a single economic unit and, much to Stalin's fury, stopped reparations deliveries to Soviet territory.

The announcement of the Truman Doctrine the following year intensified the hostilities between Stalin and the West. In February 1947 Attlee's government informed Truman's administration that it could not afford to continue its fight against communist rebels in Greece. The United States immediately assumed Britain's role in Greece, but more importantly, Truman used this development to issue the Truman Doctrine, which committed the U.S. to the policy of containment°, resisting communist expansion wherever in the world it occurred.

President Harry Truman: The Truman Doctrine (1947)

DOCUMENT

Curtains and Camps

The Cold War gave rise to a new set of metaphors, as politicians, diplomats, and journalists struggled to find ways to explain the new world order. Two of the most compelling metaphors arose very early: the "Iron Curtain," coined by Winston Churchill in 1946, and "the two camps," used in a speech by Stalin's spokesman Andrei Zhdanov in 1947.

In 1946, Churchill was still the leader of Britain's Conservative Party but was no longer prime minister. On a visit to the United States, he gave a pivotal speech that warned of a divided Europe.

From Stettin in the Baltic to Trieste in the Adriatic, an iron curtain has descended across the Continent. Behind that line lie all the capitals of the ancient states of Central and Eastern Europe. Warsaw, Berlin, Prague, Vienna, Budapest, Belgrade, Bucharest and Sofia, all these famous cities and the populations around them lie in what I must call the Soviet sphere, and all are subject in one form or another, not only to Soviet influence but to a very high and, in many cases, increasing measure of control from Moscow. . . .

At the founding meeting of the Cominform in September 1947, Zhdanov delivered a speech that clearly articulated the postwar division of the world into two hostile blocs.

In the post-war period sharp changes have taken place in the international situation. . . . Two opposite political lines took shape: at one pole, the policy of the USSR and the democratic countries, aimed at undermining imperialism and strengthening democracy; at the other pole the policy of the USA and Britain, aimed at strengthening imperialism and strangling democracy. . . .

Thus two camps have come into being. . . .

The Truman-Marshall Plan is only one component part . . . of a general plan of worldwide expansionist policy that is being carried out by the USA in all parts of the world. . . . Yesterday's aggressors, the capitalist magnates of Germany and Japan, are being groomed by America for a new role, that of serving as an instrument of the USA's imperialist policy in Europe and Asia. . . . Under these conditions it is essential for the anti-imperialist and democratic camp to close ranks, work out a common programme of actions and develop its own tactics against the main forces of the imperialist camp. . . .

Sources: From a speech by Winston Churchill, delivered to Westminster College, Fulton, Missouri, March 5, 1946; and from G. Procacci (ed.), *The Cominform: Minutes of the Three Conferences 1947, 1948, 1949*, Milan, 1994.

A War of Words

The poster on the left demonstrates the official Soviet view of NATO: an American device to dominate Europe. The poster on the right warns Italian voters that if they vote for the Italian Communist Party, the Soviet Union will be their boss.

The Marshall Plan further divided Europe into two hostile camps. In 1947, U.S. secretary of state General George Marshall (1880–1959) toured Europe and grew alarmed at the devastation and despair that he witnessed across the Continent. Fearing that hungry Europeans might turn to communism, Marshall proposed that the United States underwrite Europe's economic recovery. Initially, Marshall's proposal received little attention in the United States, but in Britain, Foreign Secretary Ernest Bevin heard a report of it on the radio. Believing that British interests demanded a firm American commitment to Europe, Bevin perceived the Marshall Plan as the first step toward establishing this ongoing U.S. presence. He called the plan "a lifeline to sinking men." Bevin's French counterpart, Foreign Minister Georges Bidault (1899–1983), shared his enthusiasm, and together they helped make the Marshall Plan a reality. With representatives from twelve other European states, Bevin and Bidault drew up a list of European resources and requirements and devised a four-year plan for European economic reconstruction. In 1948, the first food shipments from the United States reached European ports. Eventually $17 billion in aid poured into Europe, while a new international body, the Organization for European Economic Cooperation (OEEC), worked to coordinate aid, eliminate trade barriers, and stabilize currencies.

The Marshall Plan helped integrate the economies of western Europe and accelerated Europe's leap into postwar prosperity. Stalin's response to the plan, however, cemented the division of East and West. The United States offered aid to any country that chose to accept it, including the Soviet Union and the states of eastern Europe, but required participating governments to join the OEEC. Stalin viewed the OEEC as an instrument of American economic domination and so refused to allow eastern European governments to accept Marshall aid. When the Czechs tried to do so, he engineered a communist coup that destroyed what remained of democracy in Czechoslovakia.

CHRONOLOGY

The Outbreak of the Cold War

1943	
November	Tehran Conference
1944	
August	Soviet Army advances into Balkans
October	Soviets link up with Tito's partisans in Yugoslavia
1945	
January	Soviet Army advances into Poland
February	Yalta Conference
July	Potsdam Conference
August	United States drops atomic bombs on Hiroshima and Nagasaki
1946	
March	Churchill gives his "Iron Curtain" speech in Missouri
1947	
February	Truman Doctrine announced
June	Marshall Plan announced
1948	Stalinist terror in eastern Europe underway
1949	
April	Formation of North Atlantic Treaty Organization (NATO)
May	Official formation of West Germany (Federal Republic of Germany)
August	Soviet atomic bomb test

In 1949, the basic Cold War pattern that would hold for forty years took shape. The British and American zones of occupied Germany, joined with the French zone, became the Western-allied state of West Germany. The Soviet zone became communist East Germany. In April 1949 nine western European nations[1] allied with the United States and Canada in the North Atlantic Treaty Organization (NATO)°, a military alliance specifically aimed at repelling a Soviet invasion of western Europe. Months later, on August 29, 1949, the Soviet Union tested its own atomic bomb. Over the next few years, Stalin forced his eastern European satellites into an anti-Western military alliance (finalized as the Warsaw Pact° in 1955) and both the United States and the Soviet Union developed hydrogen bombs. Europe stood divided into two hostile military blocs, each dominated by a superpower in possession of a nuclear arsenal.

The West and the World: Decolonization and the Cold War

■ **What was the impact of decolonization and the Cold War on the global balance of power?**

While the conflict between East and West dominated much of the postwar period, it soon blended with a very different struggle, that between the peoples of the developing nations and European imperialism. By the end of the 1960s, the age of the vast European overseas empires had finally ended. As decolonization became entangled with Cold War rivalries, superpower influence replaced European imperial control in many areas of the world. The Soviet Union and the United States used economic and military aid, as well as covert action, to cajole and coerce newly independent nations into choosing sides in the global Cold War conflict. The superpowers served as magnetic poles, drawing competing nationalist forces toward themselves and so entangling Cold War concerns with nationalist independence struggles throughout the world.

The End to the Age of European Empires

In the economic hard times following World War II, European governments regarded their empires as more crucial than ever. Faced with the reality of superpower domination in Europe, nations such as Britain and France looked to their imperial possessions to give them international power and prestige. The war, however, had aroused nationalists' demands for independence from European rule to a fever pitch. They pointed to the inherent contradiction between the Allies' claim to be fighting for democracy and the fact that many Allied states denied democratic rights to their imperial subjects. In the Pacific region, many colonial nationalists had sided with the Japanese against the British, Dutch, and French, whom they regarded not as defenders of democracy but as imperial overlords. The Japanese internment of the Dutch population in Indonesia in 1942 allowed nationalists to assume positions in the country's government. In Burma, the student-based nationalist movement, led by Aung San (1915–1947), supported the Japanese invasion. Similarly, the Indian nationalist Subhas Chandra Bose

(1897–1945) formed a National Army that fought alongside the Japanese and against the British. Of the 45,000 Indian troops captured by the Japanese in the conquests of Malaya and Singapore, 40,000 chose to join Bose's army.

When the war ended, these nationalists resisted European efforts to reimpose imperial rule, and a series of bloody colonial conflicts resulted. In Indonesia, for example, war raged from 1945 to 1949, as the Dutch fought bitterly to keep hold of a region they viewed as vital to their economic survival. They lost the fight, however, and in 1949 the nationalist Ahmed Sukarno led his country into independence.

Like the Dutch, the British found their empire in revolt in the postwar period. Throughout the war Churchill had placed a high priority on preserving the British Empire, but the economic and military demands of total war significantly weakened Britain's ability to control its far-flung possessions. Clement Attlee, who succeeded Churchill as prime minister in July 1945, sought to retain Britain's hold on its essential imperial interests by jettisoning those that Britain no longer needed—or could no longer afford.

CHRONOLOGY

The End to European Empire

1946	French colonial war in Indochina begins
1947	India, Pakistan, and Burma achieve independence
1948	State of Israel established; apartheid regime in South Africa comes into power
1949	Indonesia achieves independence from Dutch rule
1954	Defeat of French forces in Indochina; partition Vietnam; beginning of Franco-Algerian War
1955	Bandung Conference: the "Third World" is born
1957	Kwame Nkrumah becomes first prime minister of Ghana
1960	Congo, Nigeria, and most French colonies in Africa become independent
1962	Algeria achieves independence from French rule
1963	Jomo Kenyatta becomes first prime minister of Kenya
1965	U.S. bombing of North Vietnam begins
1967	Suharto ousts Sukarno as leader of Indonesia

Map 27.2 After Empire: Independent Asia

Dates of national formation often give no indication of the continuing political upheaval and violence that afflicted the countries of Asia in the postwar period. The formation of the nations of Vietnam, Laos, and Cambodia in 1953–1954, for example, did not mean an end to warfare in Indochina.

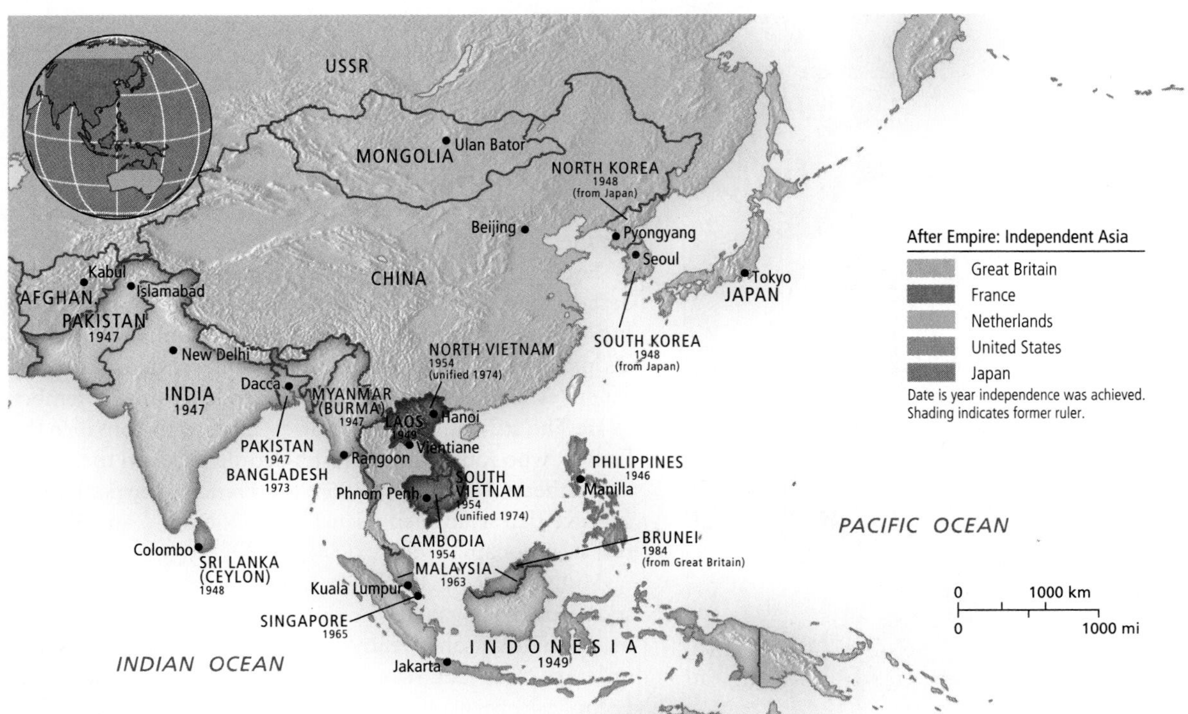

The British first jettisoned the Indian subcontinent. During World War II, the refusal of Indian nationalists to cooperate with the war effort made clear that Britain could no longer rule India. After the war, therefore, Attlee's government opened negotiations with nationalist leaders. Muslim nationalists led by Muhammad Ali Jinnah (1876–1948) refused to accept citizenship in an independent state dominated by Hindus, and won from the British the creation of a separate Muslim state—Pakistan. India and Pakistan, as well as Burma, received independence in August 1947 (see Map 27.2). The partition of the Indian subcontinent sparked widespread devastation, just as the redrawing of boundary lines in eastern Europe had resulted in brutal deportations and mass death. More than ten million people fled their homes and became refugees—Muslims fearing Hindu rule, Hindus fearing Muslim rule, Sikhs fearing both. Mahatma Gandhi traveled from village to village in some of the most afflicted areas and begged for an end to the killing, but the death tolls reached 250,000—and included Gandhi himself, who was shot by an assassin just six months after India achieved independence.

The Tandon Family at Partition (1947)

In Palestine, too, British retreat led to bloodshed. After the war in Europe ended, European Jewish refugees, persuaded by Hitler that a Jew could be safe only in a Jewish state, poured into British-controlled Palestine. Many soon found themselves waging guerilla warfare against the British, who sought to maintain regional political stability by limiting Jewish immigration. Faced with mounting violence as well as growing international pressure to grant Jewish demands for statehood, the British turned the problem over to the new United Nations. At the end of 1947, the UN adopted a plan calling for the partition of Palestine into a Jewish and Arab state. Arab leaders rejected the plan, however, and the British pulled out their troops in May 1948 without transferring authority to either party. Jewish leaders immediately proclaimed the new state of Israel, and the region erupted into all-out war. After nine months of fighting, an uneasy peace descended, based on a partition of Palestine among Israel, Jordan, and Egypt (see Map 27.3). Approximately 750,000 Palestinian Arabs became stateless refugees.

Map 27.3 Israel and Its Neighbors, 1949

The map inset outlines the United Nations' plan to partition Palestine into Jewish and Arab states, with Jerusalem as an international zone. This plan was not implemented.

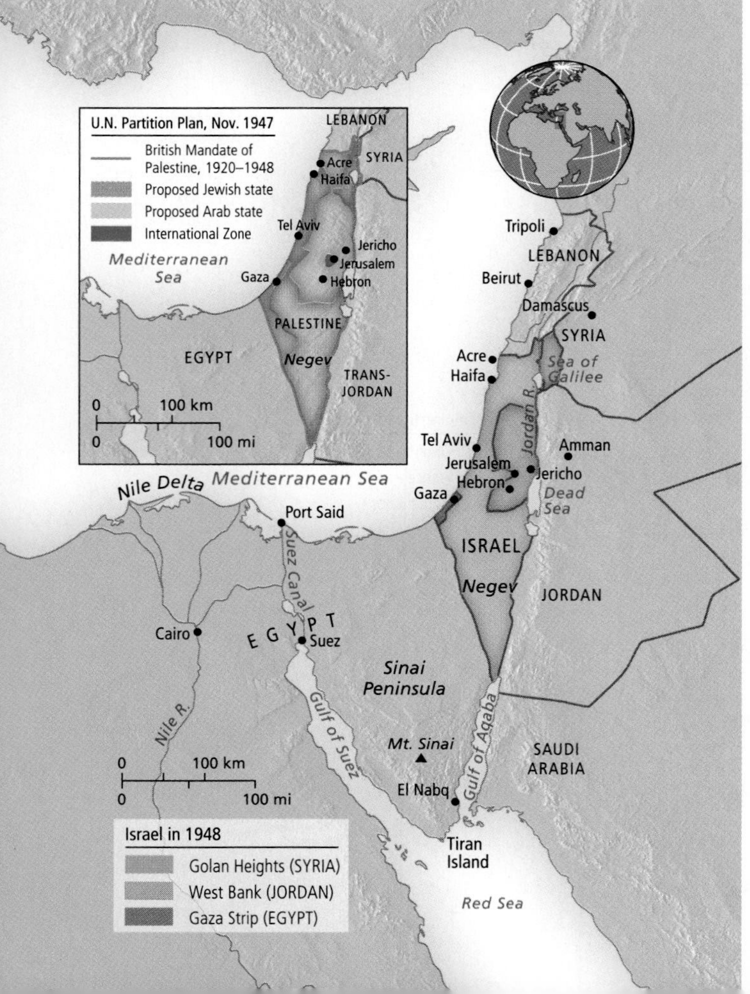

By withdrawing from hot spots such as India and Palestine, the British hoped to preserve and stabilize what remained of the British Empire. During the 1950s, successive British governments sought to diminish the force of nationalism throughout their colonial territories by diverting it down channels of constitutional reform and systems of power sharing—and then fiercely stomping down on nationalists who broke out of these channels. Many African leaders, such as Kwame Nkrumah (1957–1966) in Ghana and Jomo Kenyatta (1963–1978) in Kenya, moved from British prison cells to prime ministerial or presidential offices. Neither compromise nor coercion could stem the tide of nationalism, and by the end of the 1960s, the British Empire had been reduced to an assortment of island territories.

France, too, saw its empire disintegrate in the postwar decades despite efforts to resist nationalist movements. In Indochina, the nationalist leader Ho Chi Minh (1890–1969) adopted the U.S. Declaration of Independence for his model when he proclaimed independence in September 1945. The stirring rhetoric, however, failed to convince the French, who fought for almost a decade to retain their hold in southeast Asia. But in 1954, the French army suffered a decisive defeat at Dien Bien Phu in Vietnam, and French rule in Indochina ended.

Humiliated by this defeat, French army officers responded ferociously to the outbreak of a nationalist revolt in Algeria that same year. Many prominent politicians and ordinary men and women shared the army's view that France had been pushed too far and must now stand fast.

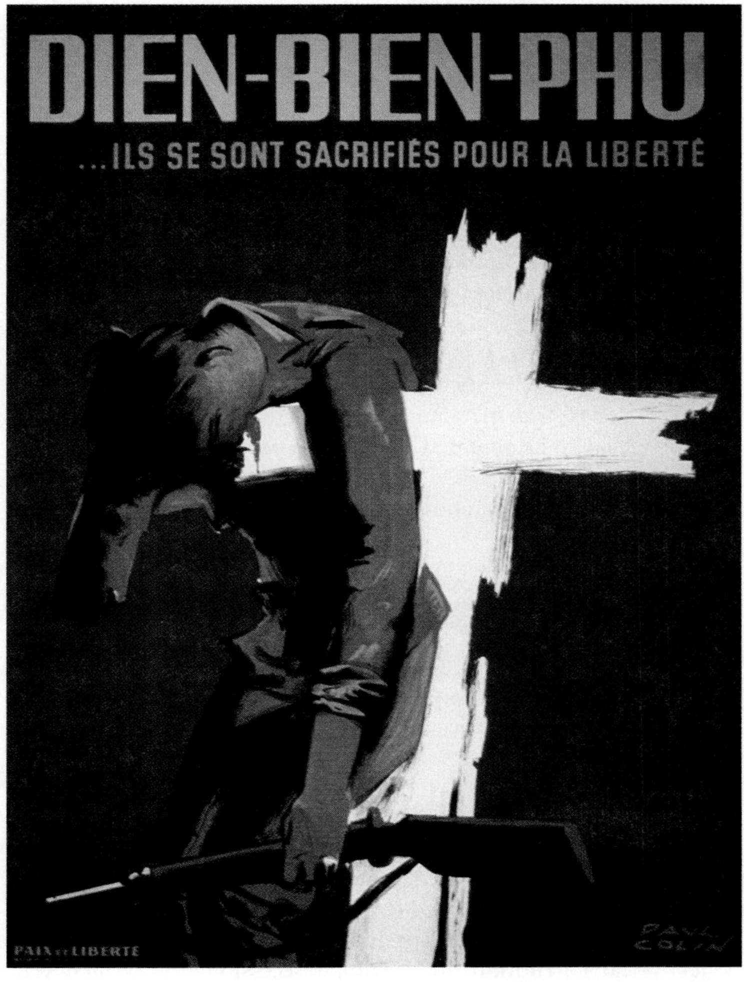

Imperial Sacrifice
This poster reminds French men and women of the sacrifice made by their army at the Battle of Dien Bien Phu in Vietnam: "They sacrificed themselves for your liberty." The memory of the army's defeat at Dien Bien Phu helped strengthen French determination to hold on to Algeria.

The result was the Franco-Algerian War, a brutal fight that raged from 1954 until the early 1960s. By the time Algeria claimed independence in 1962 (see Map 27.4), approximately 200,000 Algerian nationalist fighters had been killed or imprisoned. Fifteen thousand French soldiers and auxiliary forces were dead, as were almost 23,000 civilians in both France and Algeria.

The Franco-Algerian War seriously divided French society, called into question the meaning of French democracy, and transformed France's political structure. Supporters of the French army in Algeria saw it as a force fighting on behalf of Western civilization against barbarism (both Muslim and communist). Critics, pointing to the evidence that the French army used torture against its enemies, argued that the war threatened to corrupt French society. By 1958 France teetered on the brink of civil war, with French army officers preparing for an assault on Paris. The World War II hero Charles De Gaulle forced through a new constitution, which sharply tilted the balance of power in French domestic politics toward the president (conveniently De Gaulle himself).

The Imperialist Legacy

As the Algerian crisis showed, decolonization was not something that just happened "out there" in the world beyond the West; rather it had an often profound impact on Western politics. In the United States, for example, the burgeoning African-American civil rights movement directly linked its struggle to the colonial independence movements happening at the same time. As the civil rights leader Martin Luther King Jr. (1929–1968) asserted, "the determination of Negro Americans to win freedom from all forms of oppression springs from the same deep longing that motivates oppressed peoples all over the world."[2] Organizations such as the National Association for the Advancement of Colored People (NAACP), founded in 1910, had long fought against racial discrimination in the United States, but in the 1950s, in part inspired by nationalists' battles around the globe, the civil-rights struggle became a mass movement with an innovative program of "freedom rides," lunch counter sit-ins, boycotts, and voter registration campaigns.

The legacy of imperialist rule lingered long, particularly in areas with large white European settlements such as Rhodesia and South Africa. Despite UN sanctions and a violent black nationalist movement, white settlers in Rhodesia (present-day Zimbabwe) retained a lock on political and economic power until 1980. In South Africa, the white supremacist Afrikaner Nationalist Party assumed control in 1948 and implemented the policies of apartheid°, the rigid segregation of communities based on race. To break down any chance of resistance, the apartheid regime deliberately accentuated tribal divisions among black South Africans and denied them basic human rights. The "No Trial Act" of 1963, for example, gave the government the right to detain anyone, without charge or trial, for as long as it chose.

Creating Apartheid in South Africa

Imperialism also left a long-lasting economic legacy. European states lost their monopoly on the raw materials and markets of their one-time colonies, yet in the post-colonial era, African states grew more economically dependent than ever on the West, a development that anti-Western

DOCUMENT

Rejecting the West

Born in Martinique, Frantz Fanon became a champion of Algerian independence. He died of leukemia in 1961, shortly before an independent Algeria came into being. His writings, published posthumously, articulated clearly the discontent of the colonized. Riveting dissections of the relations of power in Western capitalism, they also helped inspire the protests of 1968.

"The last shall be first and the first last."* Decolonization is the putting into practice of this sentence. . . . The naked truth of decolonization evokes for us the searing bullets and bloodstained knives which emanate from it. For if the last shall be first, this will only come to pass after a murderous and decisive struggle between the two protagonists.

. . . As soon as the native begins to pull on his moorings, and to cause anxiety to the settler, he is handed over to well-meaning souls who in cultural congresses point out to him the specificity and wealth of Western values. But . . . it so happens that when the native hears a speech about Western culture he pulls out his knife—or at least he makes sure it is within reach. The violence with which the supremacy of white values is affirmed and the aggressiveness which has permeated the victory of these values over the ways of life and thought of the native mean that, in revenge, the native laughs in mockery when Western values are mentioned in front of him.

. . . For centuries the capitalists have behaved in the under-developed world like nothing more than war criminals. Deportations, massacres, forced labour and slavery have been the main methods used by capitalism to increase its wealth, its gold or diamond reserves, and to establish its power. . . . So when we hear the head of a European state declare with his hand on his heart that he must come to the help of the poor under-developed peoples, we do not tremble with gratitude. Quite the contrary; we say to ourselves: "It's a just reparation which will be paid to us."

* *Fanon is quoting Jesus' words in Matthew 19:30. But as the rest of the excerpt makes clear, Fanon's interpretation of this verse contrasts with the usual Christian emphasis on submission.*

Source: From Frantz Fanon, *The Wretched of the Earth,* translated by Constance Farrington. Copyright © 1963 by Présence Africaine. Used by permission.

African nationalists labeled "neo-colonialism." Desperate for cash, newly independent African governments increased production of cash crops for export—cotton, coffee, nuts, sugar—and also expanded their mining industries, producing uranium, lithium, copper, tin, gold, diamonds, and zinc for Western markets. Such exports were extremely vulnerable to fluctuations in demand and prices. At the same time, African nations became ever more dependent on importing manufactured goods from the industrialized West, with aid from Western nations often contingent on trading deals requiring such imports.

For many of the newly independent nations of Africa and Asia, political stability proved as elusive as economic prosperity. To be solid, democratic political structures must rest on a foundation of popular participation, yet almost a century of imperialist rule made such participation very problematic. For example, when the Congo became independent in 1960, it possessed only sixteen university graduates out of a population of 13 million—the result of the Belgian policy of restricting Congolese children to a basic education. In Africa as a whole, 80 percent of the African people could not read or write. Not surprisingly, then, by 1966 military regimes had replaced elected governments in the former colonial territories of Nigeria, Congo Brazzaville, Burkina Faso, Algeria, the Benin Republic, and the Central African Republic. In many newly independent states, competition between rival groups for power led to civil war. Nigeria, which gained independence from Britain in 1960, was overcome by political corruption and regional secession. In its civil war, which began in 1966, at least one million people died, either in battle or from starvation. The Congo stepped directly from Belgian rule in 1960 into a protracted civil war.

The Globalization of the Cold War

The process of decolonization often became entangled with Cold War rivalries, and in many regions, superpower influence replaced imperial control. In the Congo, for example, both overt and covert superpower involvement prolonged the civil war and destabilized the post-independence political structure. Despite fears of World War III and a Europe devastated by nuclear weapons, the Cold War actually turned hot only in places like the Congo—in the developing nations, at the intersection of superpower rivalries and nationalist conflicts.

The Korean War, 1950–1953

The first such intersection occurred in Korea. Once part of the Japanese Empire, Korea, like Germany, was divided after World War II. A Soviet-linked communist regime as-

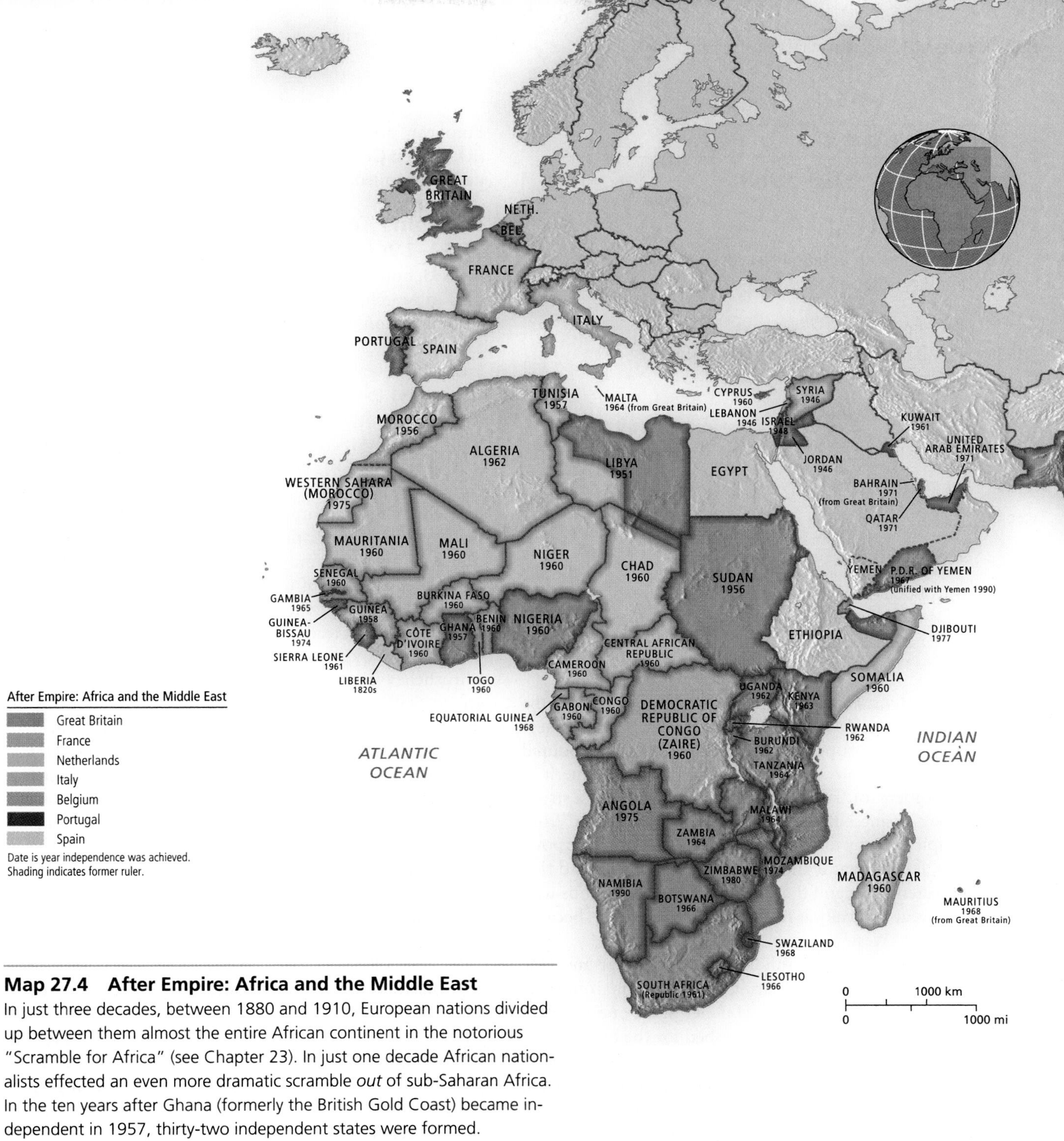

Map 27.4 After Empire: Africa and the Middle East
In just three decades, between 1880 and 1910, European nations divided up between them almost the entire African continent in the notorious "Scramble for Africa" (see Chapter 23). In just one decade African nationalists effected an even more dramatic scramble *out* of sub-Saharan Africa. In the ten years after Ghana (formerly the British Gold Coast) became independent in 1957, thirty-two independent states were formed.

sumed power in North Korea, and an anticommunist state propped up by the United States controlled the south. In 1950, North Korean troops invaded South Korea in an attempt to unite the country under communist rule. This civil war, a struggle between rival groups of Korean nationalists, was quickly swallowed up by the Cold War. A UN-sponsored, largely American army fought alongside South Korean troops, while the Soviet Union supplied arms and Communist China provided soldiers to support North Korea.

The Korean War accelerated the globalization of the Cold War. As a result of the Korean conflict, the French government was able to persuade Truman's administration to support its struggle against Ho Chi Minh and the communist nationalists in Indochina, thus drawing the United States onto the path that would lead to its war in Vietnam.

CHRONOLOGY

The Cold War, 1950–1968

1950	Outbreak of the Korean War
1953	First American and Soviet hydrogen bomb tests; death of Joseph Stalin; end of the Korean War
1955	First Geneva summit
1956	Hungarian uprising and its repression by Soviet troops
1957	Launch of *Sputnik*
1959	Khrushchev's visit to the United States
1961	Berlin Wall built
1962	Cuban missile crisis
1963	Nuclear Test Ban treaty signed
1964	Khrushchev ousted; beginning of the Brezhnev era
1965	U.S. bombing of North Vietnam begins

The conflict in Korea also welded Japan firmly into the Western alliance. As the U.S. army turned to the Japanese for vital military supplies, more than $3.5 billion poured into and rejuvenated the Japanese economy. (American military orders for trucks guaranteed the success of a struggling new Japanese firm called Toyota.) Transformed from an occupied enemy to a staunch ally and an economic powerhouse, Japan became the dam holding back "the red tide that threatens to engulf the world."[3] Thus, in a curious way, Japan—geographically as far "East" as one can get—became a part of the "West."

The Korean War also solidified the Cold War and U.S. interests within Europe. Fearing that the war's outbreak signaled a more aggressive Soviet policy in Europe as well as Asia, western European leaders pushed for the transformation of NATO from a loose defensive alliance to a coordinated fighting force. This transformation, however, came at a price. As the U.S. military budget exploded from $13.5 billion to $50 billion per year, Truman's administration demanded that its European allies strengthen their own military forces and permit the rearmament of West Germany. With the trauma of German conquest and occupation so recently behind them, many Europeans were horrified by the prospect. Britain's prime minister Clement Attlee warned, "The policy of using Satan to defeat Sin is very dangerous." Even within West Germany the proposal aroused strong opposition, although Konrad Adenauer (1876–1967), the new state's first chancellor, argued that only a rearmed West Germany could prevent the forcible reunification of Germany on Soviet terms. After four years of controversy and a failed effort to create a western European army (the European Defense Community, or EDC), West Germany rearmed, as the United States had initially demanded, under the NATO umbrella.

Changing Temperatures in the Cold War, 1953–1960

In 1953, both sides in the Cold War changed leaders. Stalin died in March, just a few months after a new Republican administration headed by President Dwight Eisenhower (1890–1969) took office in the United States. This change of leadership heralded a new phase in the Cold War. When Eisenhower took office, he condemned Truman's policy of *containing* communism as defeatist, a "negative, futile and immoral policy . . . which abandons countless human beings to a despotism and Godless terrorism."[4] Instead, he committed the United States to *roll back* communism and insisted that communist aggression would be met with massive nuclear retaliation. This newly aggressive American stance was matched on the other side of the Cold War divide. After a period of uncertainty following Stalin's death in 1953, Nikita Khrushchev (1955–1964) emerged in 1955 as the new Soviet leader. Loud and boisterous, given to off-the-cuff remarks and spontaneous displays of emotion, Khrushchev contrasted sharply with the disciplined, reserved Stalin. (It is hard to imagine Stalin taking off his shoe and beating it on a table, as Khrushchev did in front of the television cameras at an assembly of the United Nations.) Khrushchev played a dangerous game of nuclear bluff, in which he persistently and often quite successfully convinced allies and foes alike that the Soviet Union possessed a far stronger nuclear force than it actually did.

Both Khrushchev and Eisenhower recognized, however, that nuclear weapons made total war unwinnable and both sought ways to break out of the positions into which they were frozen by Cold War hostilities. Thus the period from 1953 until 1964 was characterized by thawing superpower relations followed by the icy blasts of renewed hostilities. In 1955, for example, representatives of Britain, France, the United States, and the Soviet Union met in Geneva for the first summit of the Cold War. This initial thaw ended one year later when Khrushchev sent tanks into Hungary to crush a nationalist rebellion—a clear demonstration that he would permit no challenge to Soviet authority in eastern Europe.

The Soviets' successful launch of the first human-made satellite, *Sputnik,* in 1957 was even more chilling. Khrushchev claimed—falsely—that the Soviets possessed an advanced intercontinental ballistic missile (ICBM) force and that Soviet factories were producing rockets "like sausages from a machine."[5] To western Europeans, *Sputnik* had especially ominous implications. The development of ICBMs meant that American cities were now vulnerable to a Soviet nuclear strike. Europeans began to ask themselves whether the United States would actually risk Chicago to save Paris: If the Soviets invaded western Europe with conventional forces, would the Americans respond with nuclear weapons and so open their own cities to nuclear retaliation?

Yet in the late 1950s, the Cold War ice seemed to be breaking once again. In 1958 the Soviet Union announced a voluntary suspension on nuclear testing. The United States and Britain followed suit and nuclear test ban talks opened in Geneva. The next year Khrushchev spent twelve days touring the United States—much to his regret, security concerns kept him from visiting Disneyland. The communist leader impressed Americans as a down-to-earth, ordinary sort of guy, a man rather than a monster. Khrushchev ended his U.S. visit with the promise of another four-power summit in 1960.

On the Brink: The Berlin Wall and the Cuban Missile Crisis

These warming relations, however, turned frosty in 1960 after the Soviet Union announced it had shot down an American spy plane and captured its pilot. This announcement aborted the planned summit and initiated one of the most dangerous periods in the post–World War II era, during which the construction of Berlin Wall° provided a concrete symbol of the Cold War divide. As we saw at the beginning of this chapter, the continuing outflow of East Germans to the West through Berlin led the East German communist leader Walter Ulbricht (1893–1973) and Khrushchev to take dramatic action in 1961. Two weeks after the wall went up, the Soviet Union ended a three-year moratorium on nuclear testing. The new American president John F. Kennedy (1961–1963) increased military spending and called for an expanded civil defense program to prepare for nuclear war. Across Europe men and women feared that their countries would become a nuclear wasteland.

Such a war was narrowly avoided in the fall of 1962 as once again the Cold War intersected with a nationalist struggle. In 1959, a nationalist revolutionary movement led by Fidel Castro (b. 1926) toppled Cuba's pro-U.S. dictator. Castro quickly aligned Cuba with the Soviet Union. In 1962, Kennedy learned that the Soviets were building nuclear missile bases in Cuba. What Kennedy did not know was that the Soviet forces in Cuba were armed with nuclear weapons—and with the discretionary power to use these weapons if U.S. forces attacked. Some of Kennedy's advisers urged just such an attack, but instead the president used secret diplomatic channels to broker a compromise. Khrushchev removed the missiles and in exchange, Kennedy withdrew NATO's nuclear missiles from Turkey and guaranteed that the United States would not invade Cuba.

In the aftermath of the crisis, both the United States and the Soviet Union backed off from brinkmanship. In 1963, the superpowers agreed to stop aboveground nuclear testing with the Nuclear Test Ban treaty and set up between them the "hotline," a direct communications link (at first not a telephone but a system of telegraph lines and teleprinters) to encourage immediate personal consultation in the event of a future crisis.

Cold War Arenas: Vietnam and the Middle East

Yet relations between the superpowers remained tense throughout the 1960s, and the globalization of the Cold War accelerated. In both Southeast Asia and the Middle East, as the superpowers replaced European empires as regional powerbrokers, nationalist conflicts and regional power struggles escalated.

The transformation of the Vietnam War from a nationalist struggle against European imperial rule into a Cold War conflict illustrates this process clearly. After the defeat of French imperial forces at Dien Bien Phu in 1954, rival Vietnamese nationalists fought to control the Indochinese peninsula. Ho Chi Minh and his communist regime in North Vietnam relied on the Soviet Union and China for support, while American military and economic aid propped up an anticommunist government in South Vietnam. Under the Kennedy presidency (1961–1963), the number of military advisers in Vietnam expanded rapidly, as did American involvement in South Vietnamese politics.

When Kennedy's successor, Lyndon Johnson (1908–1973), took office, he issued a clear order, "Win the war!" In 1964, the American Congress granted Johnson the authority to take "all necessary measures" to do so. By 1968, more than 500,000 American soldiers were fighting in Vietnam. Fifty-eight thousand GIs died during the war—as did well over one million Vietnamese.

Like Vietnam, the Middle East also became a Cold War arena as the superpowers replaced the French and British in the region. During the 1950s, Gamel Abdel Nasser, a vehemently anti-Western Arab nationalist who took control of Egypt after the overthrow of the monarchy in 1952, proved adept at playing the superpowers against each other. When the United States withdrew its promised funding for the Aswan High Dam power plant, a massive project intended to harness the energy of the Nile River to fuel Egypt's economic development, Nasser simply turned to the Soviet Union for military and economic assistance.

The Six-Day War of June 1967 escalated the tendency of Middle Eastern states to pick sides in the Cold War. After a decade of heightened Arab nationalist rhetoric calling for the destruction of Israel, the Israeli government moved in a preemptive strike. Facing a surprise attack on three fronts, Arab forces quickly crumbled. In just six days of fighting, Israel gained possession of the Sinai peninsula from Egypt, the West Bank from Jordan, the Golan Heights from Syria—and one million stateless Palestinian refugees. (See Map 27.5.) In the wake of the war, U.S. foreign policy shifted to decisive support for Israel. In turn, Egypt, Syria, Iraq, Sudan, and Libya aligned with the Soviet Union.

The Third World

Many newly independent nations sought to resist being pulled into the orbit of either superpower. In 1955, Ahmed Sukarno (1949–1966), the nationalist leader who had led Indonesia out from under Dutch rule six years before, hosted the Bandung Conference of "nonaligned" nations. Bandung signaled the desire of many national leaders to find a place for their nations between or apart from the United States or the Soviet Union. French journalists at the conference gave these nations a collective label—neither the first (Western, capitalist) nor the second (Eastern, communist) but rather the Third World°. Few of these nonaligned nations had much power on their own, but the General Assembly of the United Nations provided them with an important forum for making their voice heard. As the pace of decolonization accelerated, the number of independent nations voting in the UN grew.

Map 27.5 The Results of the Six-Day War

A comparison of this map with Map 27.3 ("Israel and Its Neighbors, 1949," p. 894) reveals the startling results of the war of 1967. Israel's conquest of the Sinai peninsula, the Golan Heights, and the Gaza Strip vastly increased its territorial holdings—and the resentment of Palestinians. Israel withdrew from western Sinai in 1975 and from the whole of the peninsula in 1981. The West Bank and the Gaza Strip were placed under Palestinian self-rule in 1994.

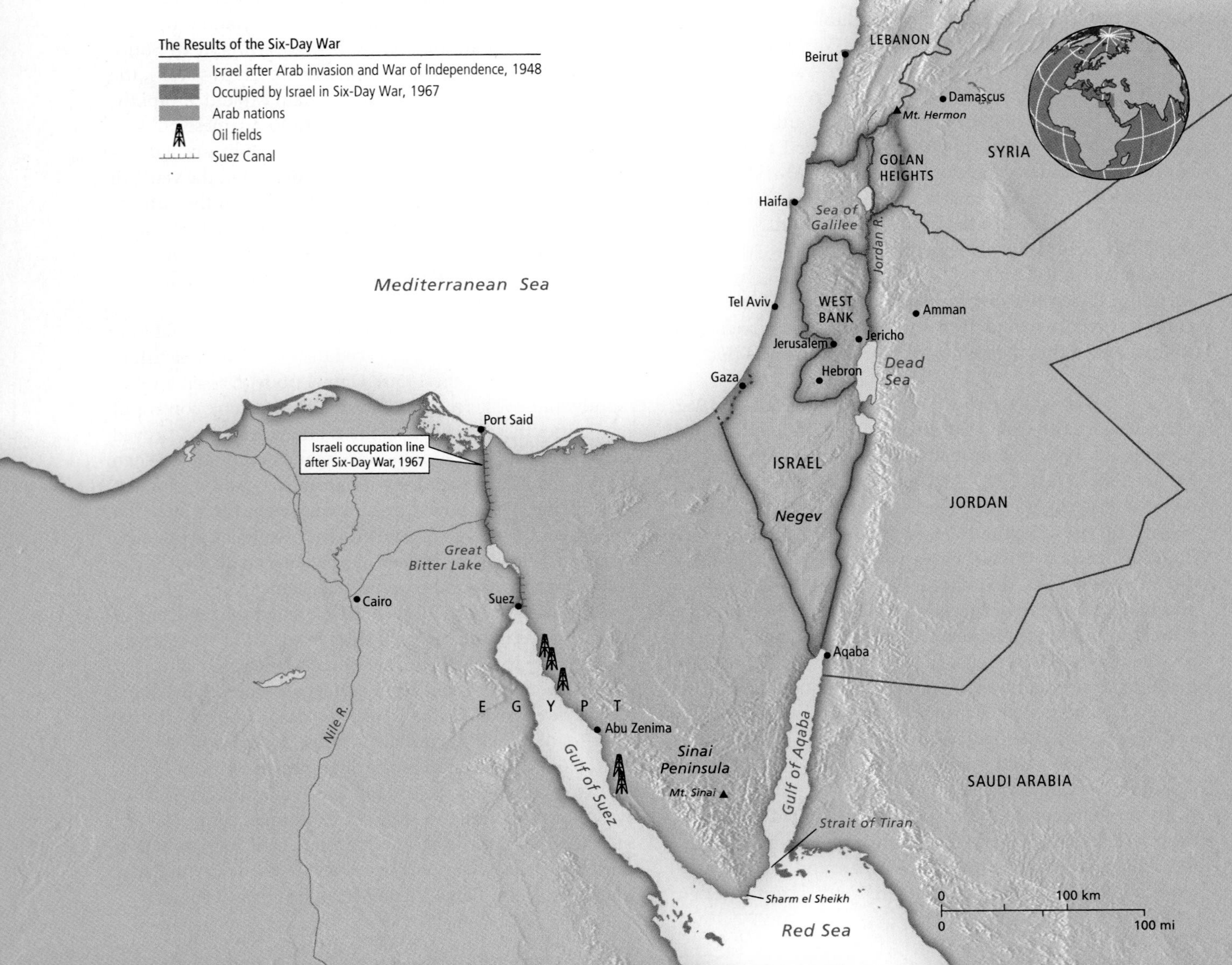

Genuine independence, however, proved difficult to retain as even Sukarno, the nonaligned movement's founder, discovered. Sukarno's quest for material and military assistance led him into the Soviet sphere of influence by the mid-1960s. In 1967, General Mohamed Suharto (b. 1921) overthrew Sukarno in a bloody coup. With his country's rivers clogged with the headless corpses of 100,000 victims, Suharto aligned Indonesia with the West.

The Soviet Union and Eastern Europe in the 1950s and 1960s

■ **What patterns characterized the history of the Soviet Union and eastern Europe after the death of Stalin?**

Divided by the Cold War, the peoples of western and eastern Europe in the 1950s and 1960s followed separate paths. For the citizens of eastern Europe and the Soviet Union, the end of World War II brought renewed terror. Stalin's death in 1953 inaugurated a period of political reform and the seeming promise of prosperity, but by the end of the 1960s, economic stagnation and political discontent characterized life in the Soviet bloc.

CHRONOLOGY

The Soviet Bloc in the Postwar Era

1948	Yugoslav leader Tito breaks with Stalin; terror underway in Eastern Europe
1953	Death of Stalin; relaxation of terror in eastern Europe and Soviet Union
1955	Khrushchev emerges as new Soviet leader
1956	Khrushchev's "Secret Speech," de-Stalinization accelerates; unrest in Poland results in new regime under Gomułka; Hungarian Revolution crushed by Soviet forces
1964	Khrushchev ousted; Brezhnev era begins
1968	Prague Spring crushed

From Stalinist Terror to De-Stalinization

As the Red Army slowly pushed the Germans out of Soviet territory and then back through eastern Europe in the final years of World War II, many of the inhabitants of these regions found that liberation from German occupation did not mean freedom, and that the end of the war did not mean peace. Stalin accused entire ethnic groups, such as the Chechens, of collaborating with the Germans. Soviet soldiers loaded hundreds of thousands of men, women, and children onto freezing freight cars without adequate supplies of food, water, or warm clothing, and shipped them eastward. An estimated 25 percent of these people died on the journey or in the first few years of barren existence in their new homes. These deportations continued into the early 1950s.

Terror also marked the daily lives of eastern Europeans in the late 1940s and early 1950s, as Stalin imposed his control over the Soviet satellite states. Developments in Yugoslavia played a crucial role in shaping the terror in eastern Europe. In 1948, Yugoslavia's communist leader, Tito, broke with Stalin and refused to let the Soviets dictate Yugoslavia's foreign and domestic policies. Alarmed by his loss of control over Yugoslavia, Stalin strove frantically to tighten his grip on the rest of eastern Europe by eliminating any potential Tito imitators from these societies. The Cold War provided Stalin with additional incentives to battle against any possible threat to his personal power. Stalin insisted that a Western conspiracy to divide and conquer the Soviet bloc could be defeated only by a thoroughgoing purge of communist ranks.

The citizens of eastern Europe thus experienced a replay of the Soviet terror of the 1930s. Labor and prison camps soon dotted eastern European maps. Between 1948 and 1953, many more communists were killed by their own party members than had died at the hands of the Nazis during World War II. Arrested, charged with sabotage or espionage, and savagely tortured, prominent communists were convicted in public show trials at which they recited the confessions that had been prepared for them. As in the Soviet Union a decade earlier, the terror quickly spread beyond the communist ranks. Factory supervisors were assigned quotas; they knew if they did not come up with a required number of names of "criminals," they would be imprisoned. In Budapest, frightened citizens watched the police vans that slid through the street every Monday, Wednesday, and Friday night at two A.M., picking up the next allotment of victims. The security forces targeted anyone remotely connected to "the West," including veterans of the Spanish Civil War and members of international organizations such as the Boy Scouts. Jews, considered "cosmopolitan" and therefore potentially pro-Western, were particularly suspect. Only Stalin's death in 1953 caused the wave of persecution to recede.

Soviet leaders jostled for power after Stalin's death but by 1955 Nikita Khrushchev had triumphed over his rivals and claimed control. A true communist success story, Khrushchev was born to illiterate peasants, began work as a coal miner at age 14, and rose to the top of the Soviet system.

Show Time: The Trial of Rudolf Slánský

On the night of July 31, 1951, Rudolf Slánský—general secretary of the Communist Party of Czechoslovakia (CPC) and the second most powerful man in Prague—left his 50th birthday party and headed home, a frightened man. Outwardly, nothing was wrong. The CPC had celebrated the day in style. The communist president, Klement Gottwald, presented to Slánský the medal of the Order of Socialism, the highest honor awarded in Czechoslovakia. Telegrams of congratulations poured in from all over the country. But the huge stack of congratulatory telegrams contained no greeting from Stalin. Slánský knew he was in trouble.

At another place and in another time, Slánský's fear could be dismissed as mere paranoia. But in the upper ranks of the Communist Party in Czechoslovakia in 1951, signs of Stalin's approval or disapproval were literally a matter of life or death. The Stalinist purge of eastern Europe was well underway, with thousands arrested, tortured, imprisoned, or killed.

Slánský knew he was vulnerable on three counts. First, he held a rank high enough to ensure a spectacular show trial. As the Soviet Great Purge of the 1930s had demonstrated, trials and executions of leading communists worked both to terrorize Stalin's potential rivals and, by rousing ordinary citizens to perpetual vigilance, to cement mass loyalty to the regime. But for a trial to be a genuine show, the defendant had to be worth showing. Slánský, as the CPC general secretary, was the perfect defendant.

Slánský was a target for Stalin's purge, second, because he was a Czech, and Stalin viewed his Czech colleagues with particular suspicion. Czechoslovakia was the only state in eastern Europe with a history of successful democracy and without Soviet troops in occupation after 1945. Moreover, the CPC had participated with noncommunists in a coalition government longer than any other eastern European communist party.

Such differences linked the CPC to the ideology of "national communism," which taught that the Soviet path to communism was not the only one, that each nation must find its own route. "National communism" became a heresy in Stalin's eyes after his break with the Yugoslav communist leader Tito in 1948. Tito had dared to lead Yugoslavia down a different path and had dared to defy Stalin's leadership. Determined to prevent any additional defections from his eastern European empire, Stalin embarked on a quest for real or potential "titoists." To save his own skin, CPC leader Klement Gottwald needed to demonstrate his willingness to uproot titoism from his party and his government. Slánský became that demonstration.

Finally, Slánský was vulnerable because he was a Jew. When the purges in eastern Europe began in 1948, anti-Semitism played no prominent role, but by 1950 the intersection of Middle Eastern power plays, Cold War hostilities, Stalin's paranoia, and the still-powerful tradition of Jew-hating in eastern European culture made Jewish communists particularly suspect. Aiming to establish a Soviet presence in the Middle East after the war, Stalin had tried to persuade the new state of Israel to align with the Soviet Union by offering the new Israeli government diplomatic recognition and arms deals. But Stalin's efforts failed. By 1950, Israel had become an ally of the United States. Stalin responded with fury. All Jews came under suspicion of "Zionist" (that is, pro-Israel and therefore pro-Western) tendencies.

Stalin's failure to send Slánský a birthday telegram signaled that Slánský was now on the list of suspects. Over the following months Soviet advisers and homegrown Czech torturers pressured prisoners already caught in the net of the purge to confess that they were part of a Slánský-led conspiracy to overthrow the communist government and to turn Czechoslovakia against the Soviet Union. These torture-induced confessions were then used to prepare a flimsy case against Slánský and thirteen other men (eleven of them Jews).

Shortly before midnight on November 24, 1951, security agents arrested Slánský at his home. A lifelong atheist, Slánský could say nothing except "Jesus Maria." He knew what was coming. Instrumental in initiating the Stalinist purge in Czechoslovakia, Slánský had approved the arrests and torture of many of his colleagues. Ironically, he had drafted the telegram asking Stalin to send Soviet advisers to assist in the Czech purge—the very same advisers who decided to target Slánský.

For the next year, Slánský endured mental and physical torture, directed by these advisers. Common torture tactics included beatings and kickings; prolonged periods without sleep, food, or water; all-night interrogation sessions; and being forced to stand in one place or march in circles for days on end. One interrogator recalled, "Instead of getting evidence, we were told that they were villains and that we had to break them."[6] Breaking Slánský took six months; the remaining months were spent defining and refining the details of his imaginary crimes against the communist regime, and rehearsing for the all-important show trial.

Slánský's trial, which began on November 20, 1952, was in every sense a show. Before the trial began, party officials had already determined the verdict and the sentences. Prosecutors, defense attorneys, judges, and the accused spoke the lines of a script written by security agents. Thus, one year after his arrest, Slánský stood up in court and pleaded guilty to the crimes of high treason, espionage, and sabotage. A founding member of the CPC, he said he had conspired to overthrow the communist government. A resistance fighter during World War II, he confessed to working with the Nazis against the communists. A zealous Stalinist, he announced that he was a titoist-Zionist who had plotted to hand Czechoslovakia to the Americans.

Why did Slánský make such a ludicrous confession? Fear of further torture is clearly one motive, but other factors also came into play. Communists such as Slánský believed that the interests of the party always came first, ahead of individual rights, ahead of abstractions such as "truth." Slánský may have believed that his confession, false though it was, served the party. As one experienced interrogator noted about a different defendant, "He'll confess; he's got a good attitude toward the party."[7] In addition, Slánský may have been promised, as were other show trial defendants, that his life would be spared and his family protected if he confessed.

In his closing statement Slánský said, "I deserve no other end to my criminal life than that proposed by the state prosecutor."[8] The prosecutor demanded the death penalty. Slánský was executed on December 3, 1952. Ten of his co-accused also hanged. Their families were stripped of their party memberships and privileges, deported with only the barest essentials to designated districts, and assigned to manual labor.

Questions of Justice

1. In what ways did Cold War concerns shape Slánský's trial?
2. What sort of justice was served in the trial of Rudolf Slánský?

Rudolf Slánský on Trial
Slánský, already a broken man, bows his head as he hears his death sentence on November 27, 1952.

Taking It Further

Lukes, Igor. "The Rudolf Slánský Affair: New Evidence." *Slavic Review* 58, 1 (Spring 1999): 160–187. Illuminating study of the role of Cold War intrigue in determining Slánský's fate.

Kaplan, Karel. *Report on the Murder of the General Secretary.* 1990. Kaplan emigrated from Czechoslovakia to West Germany in the late 1970s, with a stack of hidden documents, and wrote this report.

Recognized as a man with talent by the Communist Party, he trained as an engineer and helped build the Moscow subway system. Khrushchev owed everything to the Communist Party, and he never forgot it. Confident in the moral and material superiority of communism, Khrushchev believed that the Soviet Union would win the Cold War on the economic battlefield. But this ultimate victory would take place only if Soviet living standards substantially improved, and only if the Stalinist systems of terror and rigid centralized control were dismantled.

Nikita Khrushchev Challenges the West to Disarm

Khrushchev's determination to set communism on a new course became clear in February 1956 when, in a lengthy speech before the Twentieth Congress of the Communist Party, he shocked his listeners by detailing and condemning Stalin's crimes. This "Secret Speech" marked the beginning of de-Stalinization, a time of greater openness in the Communist bloc as governments dismantled many of the controls on speech and publication, and for the first time in years dissent and debate reappeared in public life.

The most dramatic sign of de-Stalinization was the release of at least four and a half million prisoners from slave labor camps. As one Soviet citizen recalled, their return was disturbing: "in railway trains and stations, there appeared survivors of the camps, with leaden grey hair, sunken eyes, and a faded look; they choked and dragged their feet like old men."[9] These survivors often returned to find their spouses remarried, their children embarrassed by their presence, their world destroyed. Some, such as Alexander Solzhenitsyn, wrote horrifying accounts of their experiences. Solzhenitsyn's books narrated the daily degradation of prison life and provided a detailed map of the network of slave labor camps that he christened "The Gulag Archipelago."

De-Stalinization certainly did not mean an end to all cultural controls in the Soviet Union, as artists discovered in the early 1960s. At first, Khrushchev's ascendancy seemed to promise that Soviet artists could finally break out of the prison of Socialist Realism to which Stalinist doctrine had confined them (see Chapter 25). In 1956, works by Picasso that had lain unseen in state museums for decades were finally put on exhibit. Inspired by what was to them truly revolutionary work, Soviet artists turned to producing their own nonfigurative, abstract art. But the display of some of this work in Moscow in 1962 made clear the limits of de-Stalinization. Khrushchev thundered, "What's hung here is simply anti-Soviet. It's immoral."[10] Within days, the artists who had dared to experiment found themselves censured, expelled, and unemployed.

De-Stalinization also did not mean an end to all political and religious repression. In 1959 the Gulag still held at least a million prisoners. As part of his effort to revitalize communist culture, Khrushchev embarked on a massive offensive against religious practice, which included the razing of churches, the arrest of clergy, the closure of seminaries and monasteries, and even in some cases the forcible removal of children from Christian homes. At the same time, anti-Semitism continued to mark communist policy and practice, with Soviet Jews targeted for harassment and repression.

Most ominously for the future of the Soviet Union itself, de-Stalinization failed to remedy long-term economic weaknesses. In 1962, per capita consumption of consumer goods stood at only 40 to 60 percent that of France, West Germany, and Britain. In agriculture, the economic sector where the Soviet Union lagged the furthest behind the West, Khrushchev embarked on an ambitious reform program, which included rapid mechanization, a massive chemical fertilizer program, and the plowing of virgin lands. He refused to retreat from collectivization, however. As a result, the fundamental productivity problem remained unsolved—and in fact worsened in the long term as immense ecological damage was inflicted on the Soviet countryside. Soil erosion increased exponentially, nitrogen runoff from fertilized fields contaminated water supplies, and over-irrigation led to salinization and a decline in soil fertility. The full force of these problems would not be felt until the 1980s, but as early as 1963 the Soviet Union had to import Western grain, a humiliating admission of failure for Khrushchev's regime.

Re-Stalinization and Stagnation: The Brezhnev Era

Khrushchev's reforms unsettled many high-ranking communists; as a result, he was forced out of office in 1964. After a short period of collective leadership, Leonid Brezhnev (1906–1982) emerged as the new Soviet leader, a position he held until his death in 1982. A polite man with no interest in literature, art, or original ideas, Brezhnev was far more reassuring to Soviet bureaucrats than the flamboyant Khrushchev, whose boisterous embrace of new ideas and ambitious schemes had proven so destabilizing. Fifty-eight years old and already physically ailing when he assumed the party leadership, the increasingly decrepit Brezhnev matched his era.

Under Brezhnev the Soviet economy stagnated. Growth rates in both industrial production and labor productivity slowed during the second half of the 1960s. In the 1970s, growth virtually ceased. This economic stagnation was, however, masked by improving living standards. Brezhnev continued Khrushchev's policies of free higher education and rising wages, while accelerating the expansion of consumer goods. State subsidies ensured that the cost of utilities, public transport, and rents remained far lower than in the West (although apartments were in short supply), and an extensive welfare system eased pressures on ordinary people.

By the middle of the 1960s, the Soviet Union appeared to have achieved a sort of stability. It was, however, a stability built on repression as well as stagnation. Judging de-Stalinization to be a risky business, Brezhnev and his colleagues embarked on a rehabilitation of Stalin's reputation. As statues of the dictator began to reappear, the limited cultural and intellectual freedoms introduced under Khrushchev vanished. Never subtle, state officials took to bulldozing outdoor art shows as rigid censorship and repression once again characterized Soviet society. Those who expressed dissident views soon found themselves denied employment and educational opportunities, imprisoned, sent to the Gulag, or confined indefinitely in a psychiatric ward.

De-Stalinization
On October 31, 1956, Hungarian demonstrators pulled down a huge statue of Joseph Stalin and then dragged it two miles through the city center. Stalin's head still sits at an intersection in Budapest.

Yet dissent did not disappear. Soviet society may have resembled a stagnant pond by the 1970s, but beneath the surface churned dangerous currents that, in the late 1980s, would engulf the entire communist system. Reviving a practice employed by reformers under the tsarist regime, dissidents evaded the censors by *samizdat* or "self-publishing." Novels, plays, poetry, political treatises, and historical studies were circulated privately, copied by hand or duplicated on treasured (and often confiscated) typewriters and photocopiers and distributed more widely. Nonconformist artists, banned from official exhibitions, used private apartments to show their work.

Nationalism among the non-Russian populations served as the source of much discontent within the Soviet Union during this era. As the Soviet economy grew, Russian managers and technicians were sent to places such as oil-rich Kazakhstan. Russian immigration to the Baltic states was particularly dramatic: In 1970, native Latvians made up only 59 percent of the Latvian population. Resentment of these Russian immigrants, perceived as the privileged representatives of a colonialist power, escalated. By the mid-1960s, clandestine nationalist political organizations had emerged in almost every non-Russian republic of the Soviet Union.

Diversity and Dissent in Eastern Europe

Despite the uniformity imposed by Soviet-style communist systems during these decades, the nations of eastern Europe developed in different ways. De-Stalinization contributed to this diversification. In his "Secret Speech" of 1956, Khrushchev declared, "it is ridiculous to think that revolutions are made to order"[11] and so indicated that communist nations could follow paths diverging from the road traveled by the Soviet Union.

1956 and After

But just how far from the Soviet road could those paths go? The contrasting fates of Poland and Hungary in 1956 provide the answer. In Poland, popular protests against rigid Stalinist controls proved strong enough in 1956 to bring back into power Władisław Gomułka (1905–1982). An influential Polish communist who had been purged in the Stalinist terror of 1951, Gomułka succeeded in establishing a uniquely Polish brand of communism, one that abandoned collective farming and efforts to control Polish Catholicism and yet remained loyal to the Warsaw Pact.

During these same years, Hungary also pursued a de-Stalinizing "New Course" under the leadership of a reformist communist. Unlike Gomułka, however, Imre Nagy (1896–1958) proved unable to resist demands for a break with the Soviet Union. On October 31, Hungary withdrew from the Warsaw Pact—or tried to. Four days later, Khrushchev sent in the tanks. As many as 20,000 Hungarians may have died as the Red Army crushed all resistance.[12] Nagy was executed in 1958.

The repression of the Hungarian revolt defined the limits of de-Stalinization in eastern Europe: The Soviet

Union's satellite states could not follow paths that led out of the Warsaw Pact. Within the confines of this structure and of the one-party state, however, the governments of eastern Europe continued to pursue different courses. East Germany became the most industrially advanced and urbanized country in eastern Europe, while Poland's countryside was dotted with family farms. Perhaps most surprisingly, post-1956 Hungary became the most liberal country in the Eastern bloc under Nagy's successor, János Kádár (1912–1989), a reformist communist who, like Gomułka, had survived torture and imprisonment during the Stalinist terror of the early 1950s. Kádár encouraged debate within the Communist Party, loosened censorship on film studios and publishers, and permitted private business ventures. In sharp contrast, Romanians endured the reign of the "mini-Stalins." Gheorghe Gheorghiu-Dej (1901–1965) and Nicolai Ceaușescu (1918–1989) imposed not only one-party but one-man control over the country through Stalinist methods of terror.

Within the diverse experiences of eastern Europeans, certain commonalities characterized the post-1956 era. Except in Romania and even more oppressive Albania, living standards improved. Educational opportunities expanded, the supply of consumer goods increased, and political repression became less overt. Even so, overcentralization, bureaucratic mismanagement, and political corruption ensured that living standards remained below those of the West. Moreover, the very consumer goods that were supposed to persuade eastern European citizens of the superiority of the communist system instead demonstrated its deficiencies. With a radio, a Hungarian teenager could tune into Radio Free Europe and hear of a livelier, more abundant society in the West. In East Germany, television watchers could view West German networks and catch a glimpse of Western prosperity.

The Prague Spring

Discontent and dissent simmered throughout the eastern bloc during the 1960s and then, in 1968, boiled over in Czechoslovakia. During the 1960s, a reform movement emerged in the ranks of the Czechoslovakian Communist Party. It included both Slovaks, who believed that the regime's highly centralized policies favored Czechs, and the new elite of highly educated technocrats who resented the power of poorly educated party superiors. At the beginning of 1968, this resentment fueled an intraparty revolution which brought to power the reformist Communist (and Slovak) Alexander Dubček (1921–1992). Dubček embarked on a program of radical reform, aimed at achieving "socialism with a human face." This more humane socialism included freedom of speech, press, assembly, and travel; the removal of Communist Party controls from social and cultural life; and decentralization of the economy.

Dubček's effort to reform the system from the top quickly merged with a wider popular protest movement that had arisen among intellectuals, artists, students, and workers. The result was the "Prague Spring"°—the blossoming of political and social freedoms throughout Czechoslovakia, but especially in the capital city of Prague.

Well aware of the fate of Hungary in 1956, Dubček reassured Brezhnev and the other Soviet leaders that these reforms would not lead Czechoslovakia out of the Warsaw Pact. But by the summer of 1968, many of the ideas of the Prague activists were filtering through to other eastern European countries and to the Soviet Union itself. In Ukraine, nationalist protesters looked to Prague for inspiration, while in Poland, student riots, which broke out in all the major cities, featured placards reading "Poland is awaiting its own Dubček." Frightened communist leaders throughout the eastern bloc demanded that Brezhnev act to stifle the Prague Spring.

On the night of August 20–21, 80,000 troops—drawn from not only the Soviet Union but also Poland, Hungary, and East Germany—crossed the Czech border. They were immediately confused: Czechs had removed road signs and painted over street numbers in order to confound the invaders. Thirty Czechs died on the first day of the invasion, and hundreds more were injured. The resistance spread. Workers went on strike, 20,000 Czechs marched in Prague to protest the invasion, and children ran in front of the tanks, shaking their fists. But over the next several weeks, the Prague Spring was crushed. The scientists, artists, and intellectuals who had supported the movement found themselves either in prison or unemployed. As one Communist Party journal explained, the new regime "will not permit all flowers to blossom. We will cultivate, water, and protect only one flower, the red rose of Marxism."

But that rose needed an army to hold it up. In the fall of 1968, Brezhnev acknowledged that Soviet domination in eastern Europe rested on force alone when he articulated what came to be known as the "Brezhnev Doctrine." Formally a commitment to support global socialism, the Brezhnev Doctrine was essentially a promise to use the Red Army to stomp on any eastern European effort to achieve fundamental change.

Even more important, after 1968 eastern Europeans recognized the futility of attempting to reform a system that had now been revealed as beyond reform. Many, perhaps most, eastern Europeans retreated to private worlds of friendship and family life (or to the easy escape provided by alcohol). Others, however, refused to give up or to give in to a system they now viewed as utterly corrupt. They sought, in the words of the Czech playwright and dissident Václav Havel (b. 1936), to "live in truth" in the midst of a society based on lies. As the Polish author Konstanty Gebert explained, living in truth raised "a small, portable barricade between me and silence, submission, humiliation, shame. Impregnable for tanks, uncircumventable. As long as I man it, there is, around me, a small area of freedom."

The West: Consensus, Consumption, and Culture

What patterns characterized the history of western Europe in the 1950s and 1960s?

As in eastern Europe, in western Europe both the experience of total war and Cold War concerns helped shape postwar societies. The desire to make the suffering of the war years worthwhile, as well as fear of communism, furthered the integration of Europe's economies and helped define the political centrism characteristic of western Europe in the 1950s and 1960s. The dominant fact of the postwar years was, however, material prosperity as western European economies embarked on two decades of dramatic economic growth and consumer spending.

The Triumph of Democracy

In sharp contrast to the interwar years, the parties in power in western Europe in the 1950s and 1960s, and the voters who put them there, agreed on the viability and virtues of parliamentary democracy. The new constitutions of France, West Germany, and Italy guaranteed the protection of individual rights, and French and Italian women achieved suffrage. The democratic ideal of the universal franchise had finally been realized in most of western Europe.

Citizenship, though, meant more than the right to vote after 1945. As the social democratic vision triumphed in western Europe after World War II, the meaning of citizenship broadened to include the right to a decent standard of living. Through the nationalization of key industries, the establishment of public agencies to oversee and encourage investment and trade, and the manipulation of interest rates and currency supplies, governments assumed the task of ensuring full employment and material well-being for their citizens. A slogan of the German Social Democratic Party—"as much competition as possible, as much planning as necessary"—sums up an approach common to much of western Europe at this time.

This commitment, however, embraced a variety of national styles. The British stressed the nationalization of heavy industry, while the French emphasized the role of centralized planning. Led by the pragmatic visionary Jean Monnet (1888–1979), France's postwar Planning Commission set economic targets and directed investment. In contrast, in West Germany, where centralized direction of the economy was linked to Nazism, politicians chose a more free-market path to industrial success.

Yet even in West Germany, citizens had access to an extensive welfare system. With the construction of comprehensive welfare states, postwar governments undertook to guarantee their citizens adequate incomes and medical care. By the end of the 1950s, the average western European working-class family received 63 percent of its income from wages. The substantial remaining income came from welfare benefits such as family allowances, national health services, sickness and disability insurance, and old-age pensions. In addition, state-run vaccination and inoculation programs, stricter sanitation regulation, and the development of policies to control communicable diseases all meant an improvement in the health of Europe's populations.

As we saw in Chapter 26, this triumph of social democracy was rooted in the suffering of World War II, when Europeans grew determined to create a better world out of the rubble of total war. This determination remained, but much of the radicalism of the wartime spirit quickly receded as the Cold War constricted the parameters of political debate. The mainstream political parties—Christian Democrats or Conservatives on the right, Social Democrats or Socialists on the left—agreed in refusing to allow Communist Party members to participate in governing coalitions. In France and Italy, communist parties consistently drew 20 to 30 percent of the vote but were effectively marginalized by their exclusion from office after 1948.

With the communists isolated, and with the ideologies of the extremist Right such as fascism and Nazism discredited by the horrors of the war, western European politics took on a new and marked stability during the 1950s and early 1960s. Christian Democratic° parties—which have no American or British counterpart—flourished on the Continent during the postwar era. Drawing on a Roman Catholic base for their support and espousing a largely conservative social ideology combined with a progressive commitment to the welfare state, Christian Democratic parties dominated much of European politics in the 1950s and 1960s. Christian Democrats played significant roles in the political life of France and Belgium, governed West Germany between 1949 and 1969, and provided every prime minister except two in Italy between 1945 and 1993.

Three factors account for Christian Democracy's success. First, as anticommunists and advocates of the free market, Christian Democrats benefited from Cold War anxieties and more directly from American aid and support. Second, because they were based on religion (Roman Catholicism) rather than class, Christian Democratic parties were able to appeal to both middle-class and working-class voters, and particularly to women, who tended to be more religious and to vote more conservatively than men. But finally and most important, the triumph of Christian Democracy rested on its dramatic transformation from a right-wing to a centrist political movement. In the interwar period, Christian Democracy, rooted in a religious and political tradition based on hierarchy and authoritarianism, had veered close to fascism. But during World War II, many Catholics served in the resistance movement, where they absorbed progressive political ideas. This war-inspired desire to use the power of the state to improve the lives of ordinary people blended with more traditional Catholic paternalism. After the war the Christian Democrats not only jettisoned their authoritarianism and embraced democracy, they also supported the construction of comprehensive welfare states.

Prosperity in the West

These political developments unfolded against an economic backdrop of increasing prosperity. In the first half of the 1950s, Europeans moved rapidly from the austerity of the immediate postwar years to an age of unprecedented affluence.

Economic Integration

One important factor in this new prosperity was the greater coordination of western European economies. World War II provided the impetus for this economic integration. Fighting in conditions of unprecedented horror, Europeans looked for ways to guarantee a lasting peace. In 1943, Jean Monnet (1888–1979), who would oversee French economic planning in the postwar era, declared, "there will be no peace in Europe, if the states are reconstituted on the basis of national sovereignty." In July 1944, Resistance leaders from France, Italy, the Netherlands, and a number of other countries met in Geneva to embrace Monnet's vision and declare their support for a federal, democratic Europe.

No such radical restructuring of Europe occurred, but the push toward greater European union moved forward in the years after 1945, impelled by Cold War concerns. Opposition to Stalin helped western Europeans see themselves as part of a single region with common interests. At the same time, American postwar planners—anxious to restore economic prosperity to Europe in order to lessen the appeal of communism—urged their European colleagues to dismantle trade barriers and coordinate national economic plans, and required recipients of Marshall aid to develop transnational economic institutions. Looking back on this early stage of European integration, the Belgian prime minister (and ardent proponent of European union) Paul-Henri Spaak (1899–1972) wrote in the later 1960s, "Europeans, let us be modest. It is the fear of Stalin and the daring views of Marshall which led us into the right path."[13]

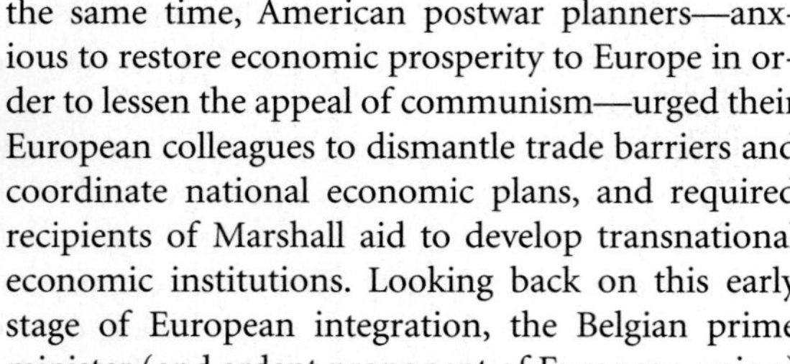

A Common Market and European Integration (1960)

Spaak was a socialist, but many Christian Democrats also promoted European economic union, including Konrad Adenauer, the first chancellor of West Germany; Alcide de Gaspari, the postwar prime minister of Italy; and the French foreign minister Robert Schuman (1886–1963). Schuman's upbringing opened him to an internationalist perspective: Reared in Alsace under both German and French rule, Schuman had served as a German army officer before he entered French politics.

Desperate to break down the nationalist and economic rivalries that had led to World War II, Schuman in 1950 proposed the merger of the German and French coal and steel industries. The resulting European Coal and Steel Community (ECSC), established in 1952, comprised not only Germany and France, but also Italy, Belgium, the Netherlands, and Luxembourg. It proved to be an economic success, stimulating economic growth throughout the member economies.

Heartened by the success of the ECSC, the six member nations in 1957 formed the European Economic Community° (EEC) or Common Market°. The EEC sought not only to establish an enormous free trade zone across member boundaries, but also to coordinate policies on wages, prices, immigration, and social security. Between 1958 and 1970, trade among its six member states increased fivefold. The rapid movement of goods, services, and even workers ensured that the economies of member states flourished. In contrast, Britain, which had chosen to remain outside the EEC in order to preserve its preferential trading relationships with its former and current colonies, struggled to compete, with growth rates below those of its continental competitors.

The Age of Affluence

If a European living in 1930 had been transported by a time machine to the Europe of 1965, he or she would probably have been most astonished, however, not by European economic integration but by the cornucopia of consumer goods spilling over the lives of ordinary Europeans. After years of wartime rationing, Europeans went on a spending spree and did not stop. A swift and unprecedented climb in real wages—by 80 percent in England, for example, between 1950 and 1970—helps explain why. So too does the construction of the welfare state. With full employment and comprehensive welfare services offering unprecedented financial security, Europeans shrugged off habits of thrift.

This spending spree transformed both the interiors of European homes and their exterior environment. The postwar period witnessed a boom in housing construction. The annual volume of construction rose by 80 percent between 1950 and 1957. With new houses came new household goods. Items such as refrigerators and washing machines, once unaffordable luxuries, now became increasingly common in ordinary homes. In France, for example, the stock of home appliances rose by 400 percent between 1949 and 1957.

At the same time, the automobile revolutionized much of both the rural and urban landscape. Highways, few and far between in 1950, cut across the countryside, and parking meters, unknown in Europe before 1959, dotted city streets. In 1964, the archbishop of Florence presided over a

DOCUMENT

The Age of Affluence

Full employment and rising real wages meant that the European working class joined the mass consumer society in the postwar era. In Alan Sillitoe's novel Saturday Night and Sunday Morning, *20-year-old Arthur Seaton seethes with unarticulated anger over continuing class divisions and his own powerlessness, yet he is well aware of the stark material contrast between the 1930s and the 1950s. Seaton credits the war, not the welfare state, with the material improvements he observes around him. He confronts his father on Monday morning before heading to work:*

"You'll go blind one day, dad," he said, for nothing, taking the words out of the air for sport, ready to play with the consequences of whatever he might cause.

Seaton turned to him uncomprehendingly, his older head still fuddled. It took ten cups of tea and as many Woodbines [cigarettes] to set his temper right after the weekend. "What do you mean?" he demanded, intractable at any time before ten in the morning.

"Sittin' in front of the TV. You stick to it like glue from six to eleven every night. It can't be good for yer. You'll go blind one day. You're bound to. I read it in the *Post* last week that a lad from the Medders went blind . . . "

"Ye're barmy," Seaton said. "Go an tell yer stories somewhere else . . . "

The subject was dropped. His father cut several slices of bread and made sandwiches with cold meat left from Sunday dinner. Arthur teased him a lot, but in a way he was glad to see the TV standing in a corner of the living-room, a glossy panelled box looking, he thought, like something plundered from a spaceship. The old man was happy at last, anyway, and he deserved to be happy, after all the years before the war on the dole [on unemployment benefit], five kids and the miserying that went with no money and no way of getting any. And now he had a sit-down job at the factory, all the Woodbines he could smoke, money for a pint [of beer] if he wanted one, though he didn't as a rule drink, a holiday somewhere, a jaunt on the firm's trip to Blackpool [a seaside resort], and a television-set to look into at home. The difference between before the war and after the war didn't bear thinking about. War was a marvellous thing in many ways, when you thought about how happy it had made so many people in England.

. . . Once out of doors they were aware of the factory rumbling a hundred yards away. . . . The thousands that worked there took home good wages. . . . With the wages you got you could save up for a motor-bike or even an old car, or you could go on a ten-day binge and get rid of all you'd saved. Because it was no use saving your money year after year. A mug's game, since the value of it got less and less and in any case you never knew when the Yanks were going to do something daft like dropping the H-bomb on Moscow.

Source: From *Saturday Night and Sunday Morning* by Alan Sillitoe,

thanksgiving service in a gas station to celebrate the completion of a highway linking Milan and Naples. Out-of-town shopping centers, geared to the convenience of car owners, proliferated while city centers decayed.

Spending begot more spending. Credit buying (what the British called "buying on the never-never") became commonplace and made possible even more consumption. Television commercials (first seen in the mid-1950s), the Yellow Pages (first distributed in Europe in the early 1960s), and color advertising supplements in the Sunday newspapers (an innovation, again, of the early 1960s) all encouraged a culture of consumption.

Western Culture and Thought in the Age of Consumption

Cultural developments in Western society highlight the shift from an era structured by the memories of World War II to a period shaped by prosperity. Existentialism and modernism retained their dominant cultural position in the later 1940s and 1950s. By the beginning of the 1960s, however, artists began to retreat from engagement with the horrors of World War II and the overwhelming challenges of the Cold War. Instead, they produced works that reflected, commented on, and reveled in the cascade of consumer abundance that was transforming Western culture.

Finding Meaning in the Age of Auschwitz and the Atom Bomb

Forged in the despair of the 1930s (see Chapter 25), existentialism remained a powerful cultural force in the early postwar era. Jean-Paul Sartre's conviction that existence has no intrinsic meaning, and yet that the individual retains the freedom to act and therefore make meaning, resounded loudly in a world that had experienced both the Holocaust and the Resistance. The existentialist emphasis on individual action as the source of meaning could lead to a life of political activism—Sartre, for example, worked with the French Resistance and became a prominent participant in left-wing political causes in the 1950s and 1960s. On the other hand, existentialism also justified political disengagement. In the Irish-French playwright Samuel Beckett's (1906–1989) existentialist masterpiece *Waiting for Godot* (1952), two tramps sit in an empty universe, waiting for someone who never comes. In this absurd void, politics has no relevance or resonance.

Existentialist themes echo throughout the visual arts in the 1950s. The sculptures of the Swiss artist Alberto Giacometti (1901–1966) are the embodiments of existentialist anguish—fragile, insubstantial, they appear ready to crack under the strain of being. While Giacometti's sculptures embody existentialist terror, the works of the preeminent British painter of the 1950s, Francis Bacon (1909–1992), evoke outright nausea. Bacon's disturbing canvases are case studies in the power of the subconscious. He painted the people he saw around him, but his perceptions were of a society disfigured by slaughter. Slabs of meat, dripping in blood, figure prominently. Bacon explained, "When you go into a butcher's shop . . . you can think of the whole horror of life, of one thing living off another."[14] By the end of the decade, solitary figures, secluded in claustrophobic settings and embodying Sartre's description of human existence as essentially isolated, recurred frequently in Bacon's work.

In this period, the terrors of the nuclear age also helped shape cultural consciousness. Because figurative painting seemed utterly incapable of capturing the power and terror of the atomic age, the Bomb reinforced the hold of abstract art over the avant-garde. But abstract art itself changed. Formal geometric abstractions had characterized much of prewar art; after the war, a new modernist movement, Abstract Expressionism, displayed more spontaneous styles. The Abstract Expressionist Jackson Pollock

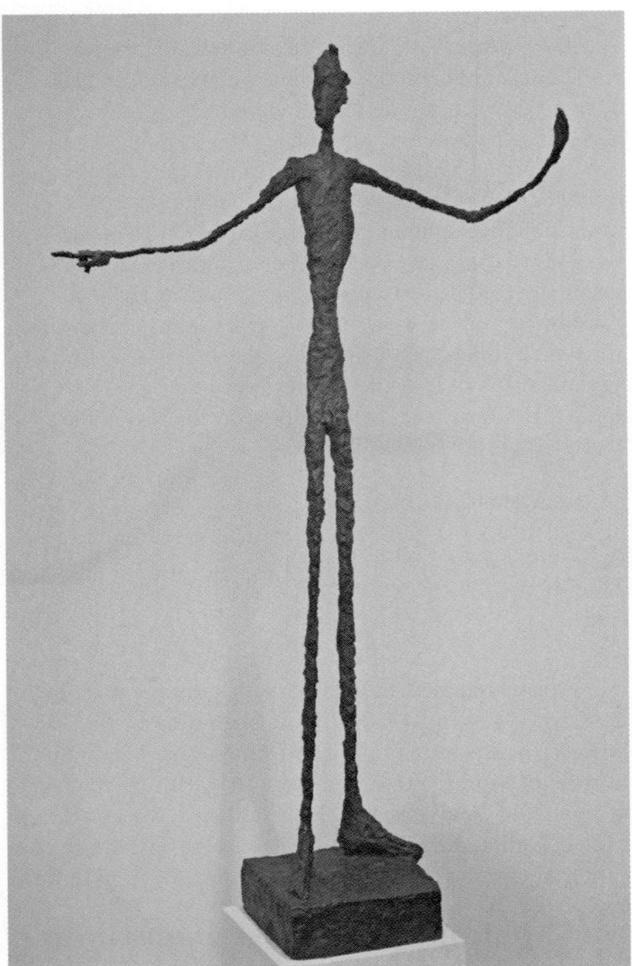

Alberto Giacometti, *Man Pointing* (1947)
Giacometti's sculptures embodied existentialist anguish. His account of this piece's creation seems to be lifted from a Samuel Beckett play or one of Jean-Paul Sartre's novels: "Wanting to create from memory [the figures] I had seen, to my terror the sculptures became smaller and smaller, they had a likeness only when they were small, yet their dimensions revolted me, and tirelessly I began again, only to end several months later at the same point."

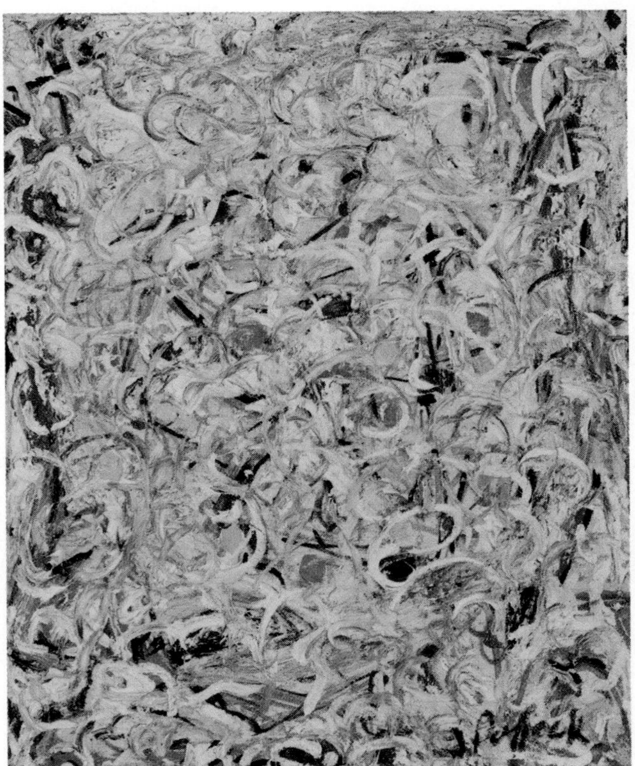

Jackson Pollock, *Shimmering Substance* (1946)
Many of Pollock's postwar works—huge paintings that pulse with power—show an obsession with heat and light, surely no coincidence in the dawn of the nuclear age.

(1912–1956), for example, invented an entirely new way of painting. Placing the canvas on the ground, he moved around and in it, dripping or pouring paint. In Pollock's works, the canvas has no clear center, no focal point. Instead, it disintegrates, like matter itself. As Pollock explained, "New needs need new techniques . . . The modern painter cannot express his age, the airplane, the atom bomb . . . in the old forms."[15]

Most people confronted their nuclear fears not in art galleries, but rather in movie theaters and popular fiction. In the movies, various nuclear-spawned horrors, including giant spiders, ants, and turtles, wreaked weekly havoc on the Western world. Fittingly enough, many of these films were produced in Japan. Throughout the 1950s, nuclear war and the postnuclear struggle for survival also filled the pages of popular fiction. Probably the most important "nuclear" novel, however, confined mention of atomic bombs to a single sentence. In *Lord of the Flies* (1954), British author William Golding (1911–1993) told the simple but brutal story of a group of schoolboys stranded on an island after they flee atomic attack. Their moral deterioration poses basic questions about the meaning of civilization, a question brought to the forefront of Western society by its use of advanced science and technology to obliterate civilian populations during World War II.

Culture and Ideas in the World of Plenty

By the early 1960s, however, artists began to turn away from such big questions and to focus instead on the material stuff of everyday existence. In works such as the British artist Richard Hamilton's *Just What Is It That Makes Today's Homes So Different, So Appealing?* (1956), artists satirized and yet celebrated postwar materialism and revealed their fascination with the plethora of material objects pouring off assembly lines. Hamilton was a leading force in the Independent Group, a loose association of British artists, designers, and architects that sought in their work to embody the "aesthetics of plenty"—the idea that consumer affluence had smashed the barriers between fine art and popular culture. The Independent Group, along with other movements such as "New Realism" in France and "Capitalist Realism" in West Germany, helped shape what became known as pop art°.

Pop artists dismissed the anguish of Bacon and Giacometti as the concerns of an older generation still mired in World War II. Pop art looked outward rather than inward, and focused on the material rather than the spiritual. Pop artists spoke in the vocabulary of mass material culture, and even relied on mass production and mass marketing.

By doing so, they challenged accepted ideas about the role of both art and the artist in Western society. When Gerhard Richter (b. 1932) placed himself in the furniture display of a West German department store and called the resulting "piece" *Living with Pop* (1963) he turned the artist, as well as art, into a commodity, something to be bought and sold just like anything else. In the age of consumption, pop advocates declared, the individual artist's intentions were unimportant, and concepts such as artistic genius were irrelevant.

Similar themes also characterized developments in social thought. Existentialism had elevated the individual as the only source of meaning in an absurd universe. In the late 1950s, however, a new social theory, structuralism°, pushed the individual off center stage. Structuralism, which French anthropologist Claude Levi-Strauss (b. 1908) first introduced to a wide audience, transformed a number of

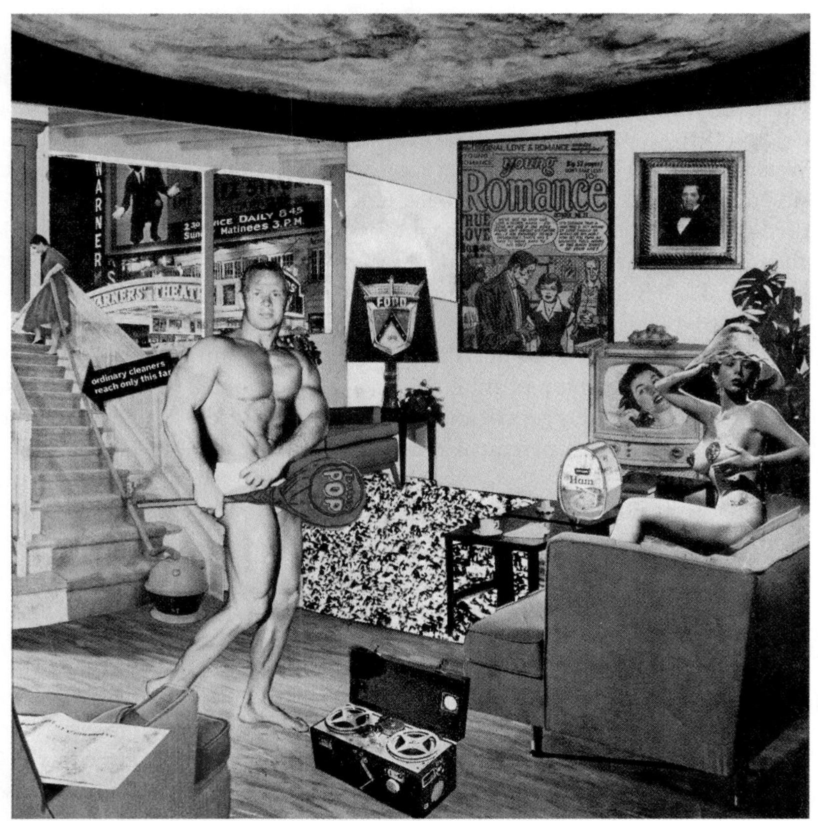

Richard Hamilton, *Just What Is It That Makes Today's Homes So Different, So Appealing?* (1956)
British artist Richard Hamilton was one of the leading figures in the pop art of the 1950s.

academic disciplines, including literary criticism, political theory, sociology, and even history. Levi-Strauss argued that the myths told in all cultures, whether that of Brazilian Indian tribes still using Stone Age tools or medieval French peasants or contemporary Londoners, shared certain "deep structures," repeated patterns such as pairings and oppositions that help give order to the cultural world. The actual stories are unimportant. To use a newspaper metaphor offered by the intellectual historian Roland Stromberg, the structuralist is interested not in the content of the articles but in the layout of the page—the arrangement of articles, the juxtaposition of images, the shape of headlines. By analyzing the "layout" of cultures, the structuralist can uncover the basic structures of human thought. In structuralism, then, as in pop art, the individual matters little. Human beings exist within a ready-built structure that shapes and dictates the way they perceive the world.

Science and Religion in an Age of Mass Consumption

At the same time that structuralists depicted the individual as stuck within a cultural and linguistic web, his or her choices firmly constrained by the sticky fibers of that web, radical breakthroughs in the biological sciences posited that perhaps the web lay inside the individual, its fibers comprising chemicals and chromosomes that determined individual capabilities. In 1953, the British biologist Francis Crick (1916–2004) and his American colleague James Watson (b. 1928) discovered the structure of DNA, the basic building block of genetic material. Crick and Watson's model of the "double helix," the intertwined spirals of chemical units that, in a sense, issue the instructions for an individual's development, caught the attention of the world. As biologists and geneticists furthered their investigations into human genetic inheritance, they raised exciting yet potentially disturbing possibilities, such as the cloning of living organisms and genetic manipulation, and added a new dimension to the perennial debate about individual freedom.

Other scientific developments assured human beings more freedom from their physical environment than ever before. Motivated by the Cold War, the space race launched humanity beyond the confines of Earth, culminating in 1969 with the American astronaut Neil Armstrong's moon walk. Medical breakthroughs in this era seemed to promise that infectious diseases could be eradicated. Large-scale production of penicillin transformed ordinary medical care, as did rapid development of vaccines against many childhood killers such as measles. In 1953, the American Jonas Salk announced the first successful clinical trial of a polio vaccine. In this era, blood transfusions become more commonplace, along with the development of organ transplants, following the first successful kidney transplant in Chicago in 1950. Like washing machines and television sets, a long and healthy life suddenly appeared accessible to many people in the West.

While scientists were claiming more control over the physical environment, the organized churches continued to offer spiritual authority and sustenance. Church attendance, which had declined in most Western countries in the interwar period, rose during the 1950s. In the United States between 1942 and 1960, church membership per capita grew faster than at any time since the 1890s. No European nation shared this dramatic religious upsurge; nevertheless, except in Scandinavia, western Europe experienced a gentle religious revival. In Britain during the 1950s, church membership, Sunday school enrollment, and the numbers of baptisms and religious marriages all increased. In West Germany, the rate of churchgoing rose among Protestants from 1952 until 1967. Throughout Catholic Europe, the vibrancy of Christian Democratic politics reflected the vital position of the Catholic Church in society.

In the 1960s, however, the situation changed dramatically. Europeans abandoned the church sanctuary in favor of the department store, the sports stadium, and the sofa in front of the television set. Declining rates of church attendance, a growing number of civil rather than religious marriage ceremonies, and an increased reluctance to obey Church teaching on issues such as premarital sexual relations all pointed to the secularization of European society. By the 1970s, churchgoing rates in both Protestant and Catholic countries were in freefall. In what had once been called "Christendom," the fastest-growing religious community was Islam.

The churches did not remain stagnant during this time of change. A number of Protestant theologians argued that Christianity could maintain its relevance in this more secular society only by adapting the biblical message to a modern context. The British theologian (and Anglican bishop) John Robinson achieved great notoriety in 1963 when he proclaimed the "death of God." Most of those who jeered at or cheered for Robinson's statement missed his point: The language in which Christians articulate their faith must be updated to make sense in the modern world.

The biggest change occurred in Roman Catholicism. In 1963 the Second Vatican Council—widely known as Vatican II°—convened in Rome, the first catholic council to

CHRONOLOGY

Medical Breakthroughs

1950	First kidney transplant
1952	First sex-change operation
1952	Polio vaccine first produced
1953	Discovery of DNA
1957	CAT scan developed
1967	First heart transplant

meet since 1870. In calling the council, Pope John XXIII (r. 1958–1963) sought to modernize and rejuvenate the Church, a process that, he recognized, would demand "a change in mentalities, ways of thinking and prejudices, all of which have a long history."[16] John did not live to see this change in mentalities take place, but his successor Paul VI (r. 1963–1978) presided over a quiet revolution.

The Church emerged from Vatican II less hierarchical and more open, with local and regional councils sharing more power with the papacy. For ordinary Catholics, the most striking changes occurred in the worship service, where a number of reforms narrowed the gap between priest and people. The priest moved from in front of to behind the altar, so that he could face the congregation; he spoke in the vernacular rather than in Latin; and all worshipers, not only the priest, received the wine at communion.

Vatican II was less revolutionary in its approach to sexual issues and gender roles. The council said nothing about homosexuality, reaffirmed the traditional doctrine of clerical celibacy, and insisted that only men could be ordained as priests. The council left open the question of birth control but three years later, the pope declared contraceptive use to be contrary to Church teaching. The issues of clerical celibacy, women's ordination, and contraceptive use would bedevil the Church for the rest of the century.

McDonald's on the Champs-Elysées in Paris
In the postwar era, the United States functioned as a symbol of modernity. The McDonald's hamburger franchise represented the United States to many Europeans because it typified modernity's standardization and mass consumerism. Assembly-line production lowered costs and made dining out affordable to the masses.

Social Encounters in the Age of Affluence

With the unprecedented prosperity of the postwar years came a series of encounters between different cultural and social groups. As trade and production increased in Europe, so, too, did the volume and variety of goods imported from elsewhere. The demand for laborers rose as well, bringing with it a rising tide of immigration and of women's employment. Affluence also permitted more young people than ever before to attend colleges and universities. The encounters that resulted from these developments both shaped and were shaped by western Europeans' efforts to make sense of the new material world.

Americanization, Coca-Colonization, and the Gaullist Protest

For many Europeans, this new world seemed overwhelmingly American, as U.S.-based corporations scattered branch offices throughout western Europe, and U.S.-produced goods filled the shelves of European shops. The U.S. presence in science and technology was also formidable. The United States invested more in scientific research and development, produced more graduates in the sciences and engineering than all other Western countries combined, and came out on top in terms of numbers of papers published and patents registered.

American domination of popular culture was even more striking. Immediately after World War II, the U.S. government forced European states to dismantle quotas on American film imports by threatening to withhold much-needed loans. By 1951, American productions accounted for more than 60 percent of film showings in western Europe. American television, too, quickly established a central position in European mass culture. In the mid-1950s, few European households had a television, while the average American family was watching more than five hours of programming every day. In the second half of the decade, then, as the number of television owners in Europe began to expand rapidly (more than doubling between 1955 and 1956), American television networks were well-situated to take advantage of this new market. By 1960, CBS, ABC, and NBC were selling their programs to the world. The popular *Lone Ranger* series, for example, appeared in twenty-four countries. Language itself seemed subject to American takeover. Words such as *babysitter* and *comics* entered directly into German, while French children coveted *les jeans* and *le chewing-gum*.

Europeans differed in their response to the new American presence. Many enthusiastically embraced American culture, equating it with greater openness and freedom. Others, however, feared that American products such as Coca-Cola would not only conquer European markets but degrade European tastes. Europeans spoke with alarm about the "brain drain" as scientists and academics headed across the Atlantic to the richer universities of the United States. They argued that even as Europe was losing its colonial possessions, it was itself undergoing colonization, or at least "coca-colonization."[17]

One of the most powerful voices protesting "coca-colonization" belonged to Charles De Gaulle, France's president throughout the 1960s. De Gaulle is usually classified as politically conservative, but the politics of "Gaullism"° are not easy to place on any simple left-right political spectrum. De Gaulle combined a fierce anticommunism and an ardent defense of traditional social values with a firm commitment to a strong state and centralized direction of the economy. Perhaps most centrally, Gaullism championed France and Frenchness. In De Gaulle's imagination, France was "like the princess in the fairy stories or the Madonna in the frescoes, as dedicated to an exalted and exceptional destiny . . . France cannot be France without greatness."[18]

De Gaulle did not sympathize in any way with the Soviet Union, but he believed that the more immediate threat to the French way of life came from American culture. Taken in 1960 to view a new highway in California, De Gaulle gazed somberly at the sight of cars weaving in and out on a traffic cloverleaf and commented, "I have the impression that all this will end very badly."[19] To reduce American influence in Europe, and thus to restore France to its rightful position of grandeur and glory, De Gaulle pursued independent foreign and military policies. He extended diplomatic recognition to China, made a state visit to Moscow, and withdrew French forces from NATO command (although France remained formally a part of the NATO alliance). In 1960 France exploded its own atomic bomb.

Like De Gaulle, Europeans across the political spectrum feared their countries' becoming secondhand versions of the United States, yet the cultural history of this era was one of reciprocal encounters rather than one-way Americanization. Europeans consumed American products with great gusto, but in the process they adapted these products to suit their own needs. In the late 1950s, for example, four young working-class men from the northern British seaport of Liverpool latched on to the new American rock and roll, mixed in their own regional musical styles, and transformed popular music not only in Europe but also in the United States. The impact of the Beatles testified to the power of European culture to remake American cultural products. Even McDonald's, when it arrived in European cities in the 1960s, made subtle changes to the composition of its fast food to appeal to the differing tastes of the new markets.

Immigration and Ethnic Diversity

A second set of encounters that transformed European societies during this era resulted from the presence of rising numbers of immigrants, who brought with them new and in many cases non-Western cultural traditions. Immigration was the by-product of both decolonization and economic prosperity. As European imperial control collapsed, white settlers retreated to their country of origin, and colonial "losers"—indigenous groups that had allied with the now-defeated colonial powers—fled because they feared discrimination, retribution, or perhaps simply a loss of status. In France, for example, Algerian independence led to the influx not only of Algeria's white French population but also of 80,000 Algerian Harkis whose loyalty to the

Immigrants Arriving in Britain, 1956

Many immigrants from regions within the British Empire had been taught that Britain was the "mother country" or "home." They were shocked to discover that once in Britain, they were regarded as foreign and as inferior.

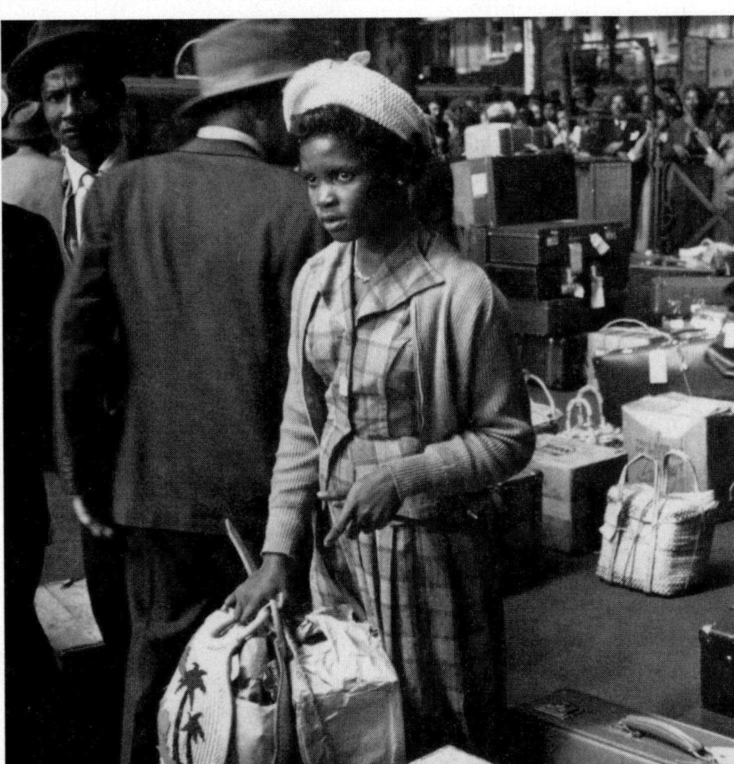

colonial administration jeopardized their place in the new Algeria.

At the same time, as northern and western European states experienced both soaring economic growth figures and a slowing rate of population increase, governments undertook to recruit foreign labor. Beginning in 1955, the West German government negotiated a series of immigration contracts with Italy, Greece, Turkey, Yugoslavia, and the North African states. In Britain, both public and private agencies turned for workers to the West Indies, India, and Pakistan. France recruited workers from Spain and Italy, as well as its colonial territories such as Algeria, Morocco, Tunisia, Senegal, Mali, and Guadeloupe. By the beginning of the 1970s, the nations of northern and western Europe were home to approximately nine million immigrants, half of these from the less prosperous Mediterranean states of Portugal, Spain, Italy, and Greece. The other half came from Turkey, Yugoslavia, and countries in Asia, Africa, and the Caribbean.

These workers did the dirtiest, most dangerous, least desirable jobs. They worked the night shifts, emptied the bedpans, dug the ditches, and cleaned the toilets. They lived in substandard housing, often confined to isolated dormitories or inner-city slums, and accepted low, often illegally low, pay rates. The reason they did so is starkly presented in the table below. Despite racial discrimination and economic exploitation, western Europe offered greater economic opportunities than were available in the immigrants' homelands.

The majority of the early immigrants were single men. They tended to see themselves, and were seen by their host countries, as "guestworkers," temporary laborers who would earn money and then return home to their native lands. By the mid-1960s, however, families were beginning to join these men, and a second generation of "immigrants" was being born. This generation changed the face of Europe. By the 1980s European societies had become multiethnic.

The Appeal of Immigration—Annual Per Capita Gross National Product in the Mid-1960s

Pakistan	$125
Turkey	$353
Jamaica	$520
Spain	$822
Italy	$1,272
Britain	$1,977
France	$2,324

Source: Leslie Page Moch, *Moving Europeans: Migration in Western Europe Since 1650* (1992), 177.

The emergence of urban ethnic subcultures immeasurably enlivened European cultures and economies (and diets); it also complicated domestic politics and raised challenging questions about the relationship between national and ethnic identity. Racism became more overt as the white settler groups who returned "home" in the wake of decolonization often brought with them hardened racist attitudes, and the presence of nonwhite minority groups, clustered in certain cities, sparked resentment in societies unused to cultural diversity.

The Second Sex?

In 1949, the French writer Simone de Beauvoir (1908–1986) published *The Second Sex.* In this influential critique of gender divisions in Western industrial society, de Beauvoir argued that women remained the "second sex"—that despite changes in their political and legal status, women were still defined by their relationship to men rather than by their own actions or achievements. Over the next two decades, the new prosperity pushed women into higher education and the labor force and so, in the long run, worked to undermine the traditional gender roles that de Beauvoir described. In the short run, however, affluence accentuated women's domestic identity.

A number of changes both reflected and reinforced postwar domesticity. The most important were demographic. Marriage rates rose and the marriage age dropped in the postwar years. In the United States between 1940 and 1957, the fertility rate rose by 50 percent. Europe experienced a baby "boomlet" rather than a baby boom. European birth rates rose in the late 1940s but dropped again in the 1950s (whereas U.S. fertility rates remained high into the 1960s). Nevertheless, although family sizes were small, a higher percentage of western European women than ever before had children.

By exalting women's maternal identity, both religion and popular culture provided a potent ideology for these demographic changes. The Roman Catholic Church of the 1950s placed renewed emphasis on Mary, the paragon of motherhood. Pope Pius XII (r. 1939–1958) particularly encouraged the growth of devotion to Mary. He proclaimed in 1950 that Mary had ascended bodily into heaven (the Doctrine of the Assumption) and designated 1954 as the Year of Mary. This Marian devotion encouraged women to regard motherhood as a holy calling, the very core of female identity. Popular culture reinforced this religious message, with its glossy images of what families should look like and how they should interact. In television programs and in the articles and advertisements of women's magazines, the woman stayed at home, presiding over an expanding array of household machines that, in theory, reduced her housework burden and freed her to focus on the satisfactions of motherhood.

At the same time, a number of cultural, economic, and technological changes transformed the Western home into a much more private place. Because of the boom in house

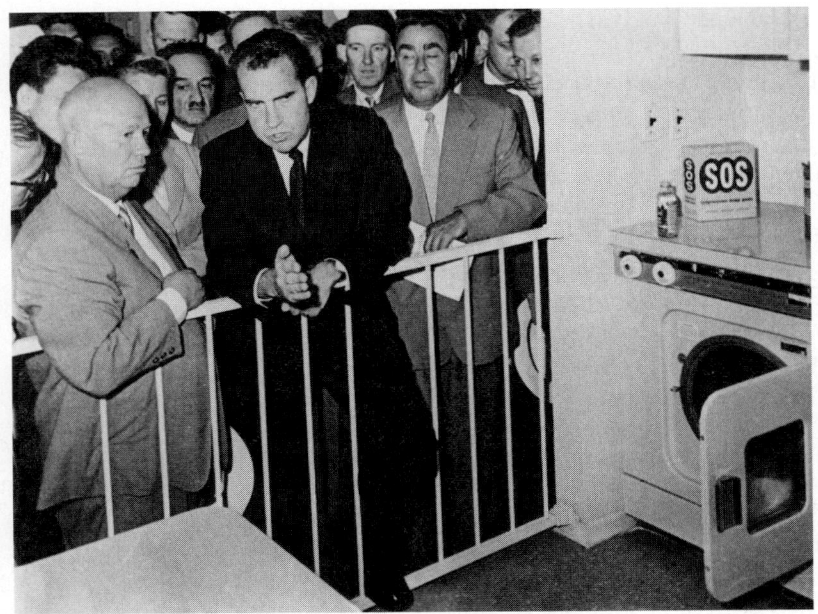

The Kitchen Debate
The kitchen—stocked with an abundance of attractively packaged foods and a glittering array of time-saving appliances—symbolized not only material plenty but also moral stability. In the Western domestic ideal, the kitchen represented the center of family life and the woman's proper domain. When Vice President Richard Nixon traveled to Moscow in 1959 to open an American exhibition, he pointed to the display model of a suburban kitchen as evidence of Western superiority. Khrushchev refused to be impressed. Nixon and Khrushchev's argument became known as the "Kitchen Debate."

building, by the mid-1950s couples forced by wartime deprivation to live with their parents could now move into their own apartment or house. Accelerated suburbanization, made possible by the expansion of private car ownership and the spread of highway networks, meant that relatives now lived farther apart. "Family" increasingly meant the nuclear family.

Prosperity accentuated the family's isolation. Economic growth translated into a rapid drop in the number of domestic servants as workers turned to better-paying jobs and household appliances took their place. Because the new houses and apartment buildings possessed modern conveniences such as indoor plumbing, communal baths, toilets, and washhouses gradually disappeared. Television moved the social center away from cinemas, cafés, and pubs to the family living room.

Cold War concerns also accentuated the Western woman's domestic role in two very different ways. First, anticommunist propaganda hailed domesticity as a sign of Western superiority, by contrasting the favorable lot of Western women to their Soviet counterparts, who led lives of almost endless labor. The vast majority of Soviet women combined their domestic duties with full-time outside employment, often in jobs involving heavy manual labor, and they spent a substantial portion of each day lining up to purchase scarce goods. Second, the nuclear age made the nuclear family seem all the more important. Feeling increasingly helpless in a superpower-dominated world on the brink of nuclear annihilation, Europeans tended to withdraw for shelter to family life.

For some women, this shelter was more like a prison. In *The Captive Wife*, published in 1966, the British sociologist Hannah Gavron (b. 1944) asked, "Have all the great changes in the position of women in the last one hundred and fifty years come to nothing?" In *The Feminine Mystique* (1963), the American journalist Betty Friedan (b. 1921) identified what she called "the problem that had no name," a crisis of identity and purpose among middle-class, educated women confined in the role of housewife and mother.

Whether a nightmare or a dream, the domestic ideal remained removed from the reality of many women's lives in the postwar era. In the poorer social classes, women by necessity continued to work outside the home, as they always had. At the same time, the new culture of consumption demanded that many women, clinging precariously to the middle rungs of the social ladder, take on paid employment to pay for the ever-expanding list of household necessities.

A new pattern of employment emerged that reconciled the new domesticity with the needs of expanding economies. Increasingly, single women, including those in the middle class, worked until they married. Many continued to do so until the first child arrived and resumed paid employment after the last child had left home or at least started school. This work was regarded, however, as secondary to their main job—the making of a home and the rearing of children. Part-time employment, with lower wages and few or no benefits, expanded accordingly. Everywhere pay rates remained unequal.

Inequalities in legal status continued as well. Until 1964 and the passage of the Matrimonial Act, for example, a married French woman could not open her own bank account, run a shop, or apply for a passport without her husband's permission. Traditional gender roles remained firmly intact, despite the material and political changes of the postwar era.

DOCUMENT

Rock and Revolution

In 1967, the Beatles, already global superstars, released Sgt. Pepper's Lonely Hearts Club Band. *Called the "most influential rock album ever produced,"* Sgt. Pepper's *revolutionized rock music. The complexity of its compositions impressed serious music critics, who for the first time acknowledged that rock music was worth listening to. The album's lyrics, too, received unprecedented praise, with one reviewer comparing the last song on the album ("A Day in the Life") to T. S. Eliot's modernist masterpiece, "The Waste Land" (see Chapter 24). Although not overtly political,* Sgt. Pepper's *illustrates many of the themes of the protests that marked the era in which it was produced. Infused with a sense of playfulness and celebration, the album called its listeners to burst out of the confines of order, authority, and rationality, and embrace instead the values of human community and emotional liberation.*

She's Leaving Home

Wednesday morning at five o'clock as the day begins
Silently closing her bedroom door
Leaving the note that she hoped would say more
She goes downstairs to the kitchen clutching her
handkerchief
Quietly turning the backdoor key
Stepping outside she is free.
She (We gave her most of our lives)
is leaving (Sacrificed most of our lives)
home (We gave her everything money could buy)
She's leaving home after living alone
For so many years. Bye, bye
Father snores as his wife gets into her dressing gown
Picks up the letter that's lying there
Standing alone at the top of the stairs
She breaks down and cries to her husband
Daddy our baby's gone.
Why would she treat us so thoughtlessly
How could she do this to me.
She (We never thought of ourselves)
is leaving (Never a thought for ourselves)
home (We struggled hard all our lives to get by)
She's leaving home after living alone
For so many years. Bye, bye
Friday morning at nine o'clock she is far away
Waiting to keep the appointment she made
Meeting a man from the motor trade.
She (What did we do that was wrong)
is having (We didn't know it was wrong) fun
Fun is the one thing that money can't buy
Something inside that was always denied
For so many years. Bye, bye
She's leaving home bye bye

Source: "She's Leaving Home" by John Lennon and Paul McCartney.

The Protest Era

The unprecedented prosperity of the West in this era permitted a dramatic expansion of higher-education systems. By the later 1960s, the expanding university campuses became the center of powerful protests as political demonstrations exploded in almost every Western country and in the developing nations well. In France, a student demonstration blossomed into a full-scale social revolt. Within a few days, eight million French men and women were on strike. "Paris '68" came to symbolize the political and social discontent of many in the West, particularly the youth, during these years.

Much of this discontent focused on the New Left° argument that ordinary people, even in democratic societies, possessed little power. Appalled by the excesses of Stalinism and concerned about the growth of large corporations and of the state itself in the West, New Left thinkers such as the German philosopher Herbert

The Protests of 1968
French students battle police in Paris during the tumultuous spring of 1968.

The Human Body in History

The Pill: Controlling the Female Body

In the postwar period, all sorts of pills appeared on the shelves of American and European pharmacies. Offered in a myriad of colors and sizes, they promised all sorts of remedies for all sorts of ailments. But only one earned the designation "*the* Pill"—the oral contraceptive, first marketed in the United States in 1960. In 1993, the *Economist* (a respected British weekly news magazine) listed the Pill as one of the seven wonders of the modern world. A revolutionary contraceptive, the Pill helped alter the place of the female body in Western culture.

The Pill's entry into the mass market coincided with two other developments. First, sexual practices and attitudes changed significantly among some sectors of the population—particularly middle-class men and women with university educations. Second, the birth rate slowed throughout the United States and western Europe. Thus it is often assumed that the Pill caused both a sexual and demographic revolution.

This assumption is incorrect. Although by 1965 the Pill was the most popular form of birth control in the United States (used by 80 percent of white, non-Catholic, college graduates between ages 20 and 24), in Europe it became a part of women's lives much more slowly. Introduced to Britain in 1961, the Pill was not mass-marketed there until the late 1960s. In France and Czechoslovakia, withdrawal remained the most popular form of birth control until well into the 1970s, when the Pill began to be distributed widely. In Italy, contraceptives of all types, including the Pill, were illegal until 1971. In Ireland, they remain illegal for unmarried men and women. In the Soviet Union, the Pill was never widely accessible. Most Soviet women relied on withdrawal, rhythm, and abortion—on the average, four to six abortions during the childbearing years. Moreover, throughout Europe and the United States, the Pill always remained more popular with the wealthier sectors of society. Because women who wanted to use it were required to visit their doctor every six months, many poor women viewed the Pill as prohibitively expensive (and many single women simply could not obtain a prescription).

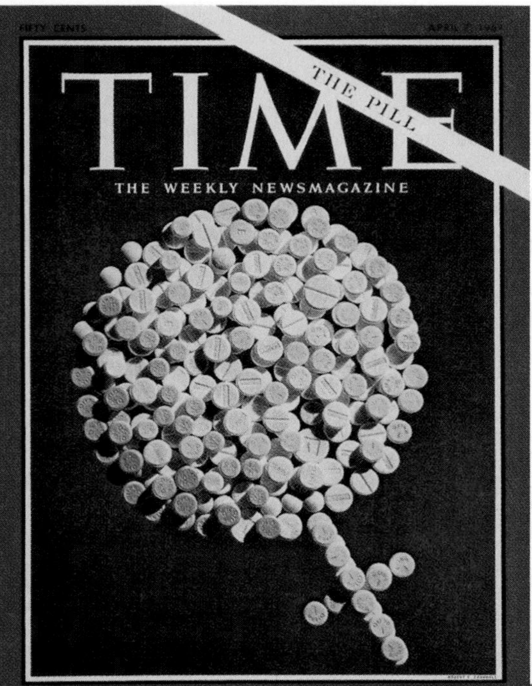

One Little Pill
In 1967, *Time* magazine's cover story on the Pill was titled "Freedom from Fear."

The Pill, then, did not cause the sexual revolution. It did, however, have a radical impact. The Pill offered a new, yet ambivalent way of viewing the female body. Other methods of birth control dealt with the consequences of sexual intercourse (the barrier methods, withdrawal, and abortion) or sought to limit its practice (rhythm). The Pill, however, was not an external object to be inserted or applied or fitted. By manipulating the female reproductive cycle, it actually altered the body itself, permitting women to experience what had been defined as an exclusively male prerogative—the detachment of sexual intercourse from pregnancy. At the same time, the Pill allowed women to distance themselves from their bodies. One of the problems with other forms of female contraceptives was that they required women to touch their genitals, a requirement that many European and American women found distasteful.

The Pill also raised important questions about controlling the female body. During the course of the twentieth century, childbirth had altered radically in the Western world. No longer occurring at home and presided over by women, childbirth now occurred in the hospital, where doctors—usually male—were in charge. It had become "medicalized": The birthing woman had become a patient, a medical problem, in need of drugs and other scientific devices. The Pill fit with this process. Although many women hailed it as a liberator that allowed them to control their own bodies, the Pill was initially marketed to doctors very differently. In its advertising, the Searle pharmaceutical company assured doctors that the Pill would allow them to supervise and regulate their patients' birth control practices. The Pill, then, offered the promise of controlling the female body; the question was, who was in charge?

For Discussion

Why has the Pill become a powerful symbol of changes in women's roles in the contemporary era?

Marcuse (1898–1979) warned that expanding corporate and state power threatened the individuality and independence of the ordinary citizen. They argued that debate might seem open, but that experts and elites, not ordinary people, made the actual choices. Hence the protesters demanded "participatory" rather than parliamentary democracy, the revitalization of citizenship through active participation in decision making.

Discarding orthodox political solutions went hand in hand with overturning traditional social rules. In their demand for "liberation," the students focused as much on cultural as on economic and political issues. Commentators began to talk about a sexual revolution as practices became commonplace that in the 1950s were labeled immoral or bohemian—couples living together before marriage or individuals engaging in sexual relationships with a variety of partners.

The protests of the later 1960s were also linked to the wider context of decolonization and the Cold War. Protesters identified their struggle for a more open politics with colonial independence movements. Rejecting both Soviet-style communism and free-market capitalism, they turned for inspiration to the newly emerging nations of Latin America and Asia. Seeking to break free from the confines of the Cold War, they fiercely criticized American involvement in Vietnam, in which they believed the United States served not as "the leader of the free world" but rather as an imperialist oppressor.

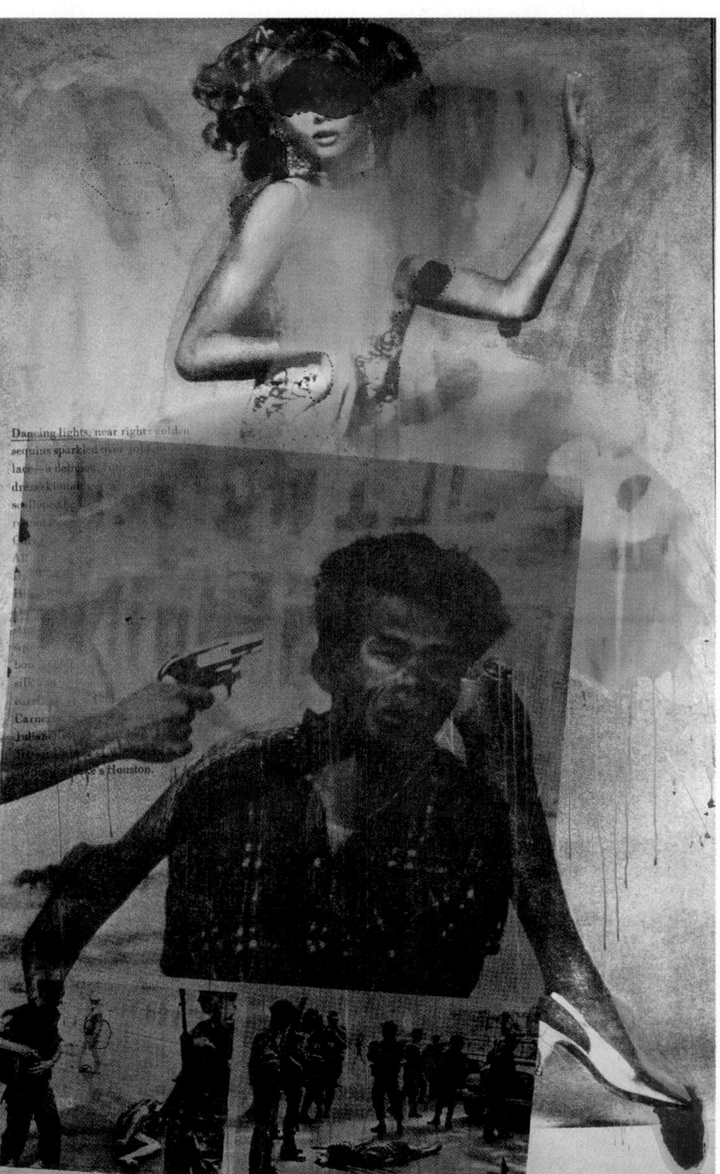

Wolf Vostell, *Miss America, 1968*

By juxtaposing Miss America, a symbol of American luxury and even decadence, with one of the most notorious photographs to come out of the Vietnam War, the German artist Wolf Vostell articulated a powerful protest. Associated Press photographer Eddie Adams won the Pulitzer Prize for the photograph of General Nguyen Ngoc Loan, the chief of the U.S.-backed South Vietnamese National Police, caught in the act of executing a Vietcong suspect (a supporter of the communist North Vietnam) on the streets of Saigon in 1968. Broadcast to 20 million viewers on the American television network channel NBC, this photograph was reproduced in countless newspapers, magazines, and books published across the world. For many, it became a symbol of a war gone wrong.

Conclusion

New Definitions, New Divisions

The Cold War was in part an ideological encounter, with both sides laying claim to the title "democratic." When Soviet tanks rolled through the streets of Budapest in 1956, they flattened not only the Hungarian Revolution but also any illusions about the democratic nature of Soviet-style communism. Yet the hope that the communist system could be reformed, that Marx's original concern for social justice and political equality could be reclaimed, remained—until twelve years later when the tanks rolled again in an eastern European city. The crushing of the Prague Spring destroyed any hope of a democratic eastern Europe within the confines of the Cold War.

In contrast, democracy took firm root in western Europe during the postwar era, even in nations with antidemocratic cultural traditions such as West Germany and Italy. Yet in 1968, protesters in Paris and in cities throughout the world challenged the easy linkage of "the West" with democracy. They pointed out that the increasing scale and complexity of industrial society deprived ordinary people of opportunities for genuine participation in political decision making. And they pointed to the way that Cold War divisions superseded democratic commitments. Despite its abandonment of democratic practices to reinforce racial apartheid, for example, South Africa considered itself, and was considered by other powers, as part of "the West." Within the Cold War context, "the West" sometimes seemed to mean simply "anti-Soviet."

By the early 1970s, the sharp bipolarities of West versus East had begun to break down. Over the next three decades, economic crisis, combined with revolutionary changes in eastern European and Soviet affairs, would reshape the contemporary world. By the early 1990s, the Cold War was over and nationalist conflicts, often fueled by vicious ethnic and religious hatreds, once again played front and center, after twenty years of being upstaged by superpower hostilities.

Suggestions for Further Reading

For a comprehensive listing of suggested readings, please go to www.ablongman.com/levack2e/chapter27

Ansprenger, Franz. *The Dissolution of Colonial Empires.* 1989. A clear and comprehensive account (that unfortunately includes no maps).

Castles, Stephen, et al. *Here for Good: Western Europe's New Ethnic Minorities.* 1984. A useful exploration of the impact of postwar immigration, despite the rather rigid Marxist analysis.

Crampton, R. J. *Eastern Europe in the Twentieth Century—And After.* 1997. Detailed chapters on the 1950s and 1960s, including a substantial discussion of the Prague Spring.

Cronin, James. *The World the Cold War Made: Order, Chaos, and the Return of History.* 1996. An intelligent and thought-provoking overview of the impact of the Cold War.

Fineberg, Jonathan. *Art Since 1940: Strategies of Being.* 1995. A big, bold, lavishly illustrated volume that makes the unfashionable argument that individuals matter.

Fink, Carole, et al. *1968: The World Transformed.* 1998. A collection of essays that explores both the international and the domestic political context for the turmoil of 1968.

Gaddis, John Lewis. *The Cold War: A New History.* 2005. A comprehensive overview by a prominent Cold war historian.

Gross, Jan T., ed. *The Politics of Retribution in Europe: World War II and Its Aftermath.* 2000. This series of essays makes clear that war did not end in Europe in May 1945.

Isaacs, Jeremy, and Taylor Downing. *Cold War: An Illustrated History.* 1998. The companion book to the CNN television series. Filled with memorable photographs.

Judge, Edward, and John Langdon. *A Hard and Bitter Peace: A Global History of the Cold War.* 1999. An extremely useful survey for students. Excellent maps.

Keep, John. *Last of the Empires: A History of the Soviet Union, 1945–1991.* 1995. Looks beyond the Kremlin to explore social, cultural, and economic developments.

Mazrui, Ali, and Michael Tidy. *Nationalism and New States in Africa.* 1984. Offers a thematic rather than chronological account of African state building.

Poiger, Uta. *Jazz, Rock, and Rebels: Cold War Politics and American Culture in a Divided Germany.* 2000. Explores the interplay among youth culture, Americanization, and political protest.

de Senarclens, P. *From Yalta to the Iron Curtain: The Great Powers and the Origins of the Cold War.* 1995. A look at the diplomatic, political and military concerns that created the Cold War.

Stromberg, Roland. *After Everything: Western Intellectual History Since 1945.* 1975. A swiftly moving tour through the major intellectual developments.

Urwin, Derek. *A Political History of Western Europe Since 1945.* 1997. Readable, reasonably up-to-date, and comprehensive.

Wyman, Mark. *DPs: Europe's Displaced Persons, 1945–1951.* 1989. An important study of an often-neglected topic.

Zubok, Vladislav, and Constantine Pleshakov. *Inside the Kremlin's Cold War: From Stalin to Khrushchev.* 1996. A close examination of the Cold War on the Soviet side.

Notes

1. The original signatories of the NATO treaty were Iceland, Norway, Great Britain, Belgium, the Netherlands, Luxembourg, France, Italy, and Portugal. Greece and Turkey joined the alliance in 1951, West Germany in 1954, and Spain in 1982. Sweden, Finland, Switzerland, Austria, Yugoslavia, and Albania remained nonaligned with either the United States or the Soviet Union.

2. Quoted in Donald W. White, *The American Century* (1996), 328.

3. Quotation from *Time* magazine, 1950; quoted in Martin Walker, *The Cold War and the Making of the Modern World* (1993), 66–67.
4. Quoted in Walker, *The Cold War,* 83.
5. Quoted in White, *The American Century*, 286.
6. Quoted in Karel Kaplan, *Report on the Murder of the General Secretary* (1990), 159.
7. Ibid., 242.
8. Ibid., 231.
9. Quoted in John L. H. Keep, *Last of the Empires: A History of the Soviet Union, 1945–1991* (1995), 79.
10. Quoted in Michael Scammell, *From Gulag to Glasnost: Nonconformist Art in the Soviet Union,* eds. Alla Rosenfeld and Norton T. Dodge (1995), 61.
11. Quoted in Walker, *The Cold War,* 105.
12. Official Hungarian statistics reported 3,000 dead. John Lewis Gaddis places the number at 20,000 in *We Now Know: Rethinking Cold War Evidence* (1997).
13. Quoted in Robert Paxton, *Europe in the Twentieth Century* (1997), 578.
14. Quoted in Jonathan Fineberg, *Art Since 1940: Strategies of Being* (1995), 144.
15. Ibid., 89.
16. Quoted in Adrian Hastings, *Modern Catholicism: Vatican II and After* (1991), 29.
17. Reinhold Wagnleitner, *Coca-Colonization and the Cold War: The Cultural Mission of the United States in Austria After the Second World War* (1994).
18. Quoted in Felix Gilbert, *The End of the European Era, 1890 to the Present* (1991), 429.
19. Quoted in Richard Kuisel, *Seducing the French: The Dilemma of Americanization* (1993), 147.

The West in the Contemporary Era: New Encounters and Transformations

28

CHAPTER OUTLINE

- Economic Stagnation and Political Change: The 1970s and 1980s
- Revolution in the East
- In the Wake of Revolution
- Rethinking the West

On the evening of November 9, 1989, East German border guards stationed at the wall that divided East and West Berlin gazed out nervously at an unprecedented sight. Thousands of their fellow citizens had gathered in front of the gates and were demanding to be let through into the western half of the city. This demand was extraordinary; in the twenty-eight years that the Berlin Wall had stood, more than 200 people had been shot trying to cross it. But the autumn of 1989 was no ordinary time. A radically reformist regime had emerged in the Soviet Union and publicly proclaimed that its eastern European allies could no longer rely on the Soviet army to assist them in putting down domestic dissent. Poland and Hungary were in the process of replacing communist governments with pluralist parliamentary systems. And in East Germany, 200,000 disaffected citizens had taken advantage of relaxed border controls in Hungary and Czechoslovakia to flee to the West in just a few weeks, while more than one million had joined illegal protest demonstrations.

On November 9, in response to overwhelming public pressure, the East German government announced that it would drastically relax the requirements for obtaining an exit visa to visit or emigrate to the West. In a press conference to announce the upcoming changes, the East Berlin Communist Party boss Gunter Schabowski gave a carelessly worded reply to a reporter's question about the new travel policy—and sparked a revolution. Schabowski indicated, wrongly, that as of the next morning, anyone who wanted to head to the West could obtain an automatic exit visa at the border. The news spread quickly, and huge crowds gathered at the checkpoints that dotted the Berlin Wall. The nervous border guards had no idea what to do. Neither did their superiors, who refused to issue the guards any clear instructions. As the crowds pressed forward, the guards gave in and

And the Wall Came Tumbling Down Berliners celebrate the fall of the Berlin Wall in November 1989.

opened the gates. While television cameras broadcast the scene to an astonished world, tens of thousands of East Germans walked, ran, and danced across the border that had for so long literally and symbolically divided West from East. Elated with their new freedom and energized with a sense of power and possibility, they then turned on the wall itself. Jumping on top of it, they transformed it from an instrument of coercion and division into a platform for partying. Caught, the East German government saw no way to close the gates. Within a few days, and again without any official approval, ordinary Germans, equipped with hammers and chisels, began to dismantle the wall that the politicians had erected almost three decades earlier.

As extraordinary as the fall of the wall was, the events that followed over the next two years proved even more dramatic—the collapse of communist regimes throughout eastern Europe, the end of the Cold War, the disintegration of the Soviet Union, and the onset of civil war in Yugoslavia and in many formerly Soviet regions. Over the next two decades, both governments and ordinary people—not only throughout Europe but across the globe—struggled to build new structures to suit the vastly changed geopolitical landscape.

How did the meaning of "the West" change with the collapse of communism and the sundering of the Iron Curtain that had once divided Europe? This chapter will look at four key questions as it seeks to understand the causes and consequences of these dramatic developments and their implications for Western identity:

- **How did economic and political developments in the 1970s and 1980s undermine the international structures of the postwar era?**
- **What factors explain not only the outbreak but also the success of the revolutions of 1989–1991?**
- **What were the consequences of these revolutions for the societies of eastern Europe?**
- **What were the implications of these developments for the meaning of "the West" itself?**

Economic Stagnation and Political Change: The 1970s and 1980s

- **How did economic and political developments in the 1970s and 1980s undermine international structures of the postwar era?**

As the 1960s drew to a close, the risk of nuclear war seemed to recede with the onset of detente°, the effort to stabilize superpower relations through negotiations and arms control. But stability remained elusive. Economic crisis heightened political and social polarization, while the renewal of the Cold War at the end of the 1970s destabilized both international and domestic relations.

The 1970s: A More Uncertain Era

In the early 1970s, the United States and Europe—both East and West—entered a new era. Detente signaled a relaxing of the Cold War tensions that had structured so much of international relations since the end of World War II. But at the same time, economic developments warned that the easy affluence of the postwar era had ended.

The Era of Detente

Changes in the Cold War climate were first felt in West Germany. In 1969 the West Berlin mayor and Social Democratic Party (SPD) leader Willy Brandt (1913–1992) became chancellor. For the first time in its history, West Germany had a government that was not led by a Christian Democrat. Brandt proceeded to implement a new *Ostpolitik* or "Eastern policy"—the opening of diplomatic and economic relations between West Germany and the Soviet Union and its satellite states. In the triumphant climax of Ostpolitik, East and West Germany recognized the legitimacy of each other's existence in 1972 and in the next year, both Germanys entered the United Nations.

During this era, the leaders of the superpowers also acted to break down the bipolarities of the Cold War. By the end of the 1960s, both the Soviet Union and the United States faced stagnating economies, and both were spending $50 million per day on nuclear weapons. These economic pressures led Soviet and American leaders to embrace detente. In November 1969 Soviet and American negotiators began the Strategic Arms Limitation Talks (SALT). Signed in 1972, the agreement froze the existing weapons balance. With both superpowers possessing sufficient nuclear weaponry to destroy the globe several times over, SALT may seem to have been inconsequential, but it helped arrest the armaments spiral and, more important, revealed a shift in Cold War power relations.

Important changes within the communist world also contributed to detente. Throughout the 1930s and 1940s, the Chinese communist leader Mao Zedong was an obedient disciple of Stalin. In the 1950s, however, relations cooled when Mao challenged Khrushchev's aim of "peaceful coexistence" with the West. Khrushchev, in turn, opposed Mao's "Great Leap Forward." This effort to transform a peasant society into an industrial powerhouse in one single year led to the deaths of an estimated 30 million Chinese, victims of starvation and Mao's fantasies. Horrified, Khrushchev suspended economic aid to China in 1960. By the time the first Chinese atomic bomb exploded in 1964, the split between China and the Soviet Union was open and irrevocable. U.S. president Richard

Detente
U.S. president Richard Nixon and Soviet leader Leonid Brezhnev joke before signing the SALT I treaty in 1972.

Nixon (1913–1994) and his national security adviser Henry Kissinger (b. 1923) decided to take advantage of this Sino-Soviet split. In 1971, Nixon announced the lifting of travel and trade restrictions with China and then sent shock waves through the world by visiting China himself. Nixon's reconciliation with communist China was a turning point: In the 1950s and 1960s, "East versus West" had formed a basic building block of international relations. In the 1970s, the shape of international politics looked much less clear.

Economic Crisis in the West

The economic outlook also blurred in this era as the 1970s brought an unprecedented combination of high inflation and high unemployment rates. Commentators labeled this new reality stagflation°—the escalating prices of a boom economy combined with the joblessness of an economy going bust. Between 1974 and 1976 the average annual growth rate within western European nations dropped to zero.

War and oil played important roles in creating this economic crisis. In October 1973, Egyptian and Syrian armies attacked Israel. When Soviet forces began airlifting supplies to the invading troops, Israel appealed to the U.S. for military aid. In retaliation for American assistance to Israel, the oil-producing states, or OPEC (Organization of Petroleum Exporting Countries), imposed an embargo on sales to the U.S. and more than quintupled the price of a barrel of oil. In 1979 political revolution in Iran doubled the price again. These price increases vastly accelerated the inflationary spiral.

Inflation and Economic Performance in the West

	France	Great Britain	Italy	United States	West Germany
Inflation over Previous Year (percent)					
1970	5.2%	6.4%	5.0%	5.9%	3.4%
1975	11.8	24.2	17.0	9.1	6.0
1979	9.1	13.4	14.8	11.3	4.1
Gross Domestic Product (Percentage Growth/Decline over Previous Year)					
1970	+5.7%	+2.3%	+5.3%	–0.3%	+5.1%
1975	+0.2	–20.6	–23.6	–0.1	–1.6
1979	+3.3	+2.4	+2.7	+2.4	+4.2

Source: Martin Walker, *Cold War: A History* (1993), 234.

Yet rising oil prices were not the sole cause of the economic crisis of the 1970s and 1980s. Two other factors also contributed. First, in 1973 U.S. president Richard Nixon took drastic action to defend the weakening dollar. He decided to let the dollar "float," to let market forces rather than fixed currency exchange rates determine the dollar's value against other currencies. This decision gutted the Bretton Woods Agreement, which had governed international economic affairs since World War II (see Chapter 27), and introduced a more volatile economic era. Whereas the Bretton Woods system had worked to direct the flow of capital to countries in need of investment, the new unregulated system allowed capital to surge into markets in which investors could reap immediate gains. National economies lay vulnerable to speculative attacks. No fewer than sixty-nine countries experienced serious banking crises, and the annual economic growth rates of the developed nations fell by one-third in the decades that followed the collapse of Bretton Woods.

A second factor in the economic crisis of the 1970s was international competition. Both western Europe and the United States struggled to compete with the emerging Asian and South/Latin American economies. Western societies possessed a politicized workforce that demanded relatively high wages and extensive social services. Increasingly, manufacturing concerns moved south and east, to take advantage of the lack of labor regulation and protection in the developing world.

Consequences of the Crisis

The economic crisis had stark social consequences. As the economic pie grew smaller, competition for slices grew fierce. The 1970s saw a resurgence of industrial unrest in western Europe. In Britain, conflict with the unions brought down three successive governments in a decade. In both Italy and West Germany, workers became increasingly militant and succeeded in winning large wage increases. These industrial settlements only worsened the problem of inflation. Workers demanded large pay increases to meet the rising cost of living, but employers, faced with having to pay higher wages, raised the prices of their goods and services. And so the cost of living continued to climb.

The new economic climate of austerity also led to heightened racial conflict throughout much of western Europe. We saw in Chapter 27 that postwar governments struggling to cope with labor shortages had encouraged immigration, both from the poorer countries of southern and eastern Europe and from colonial or former colonial regions such as Algeria, India, and Jamaica. By 1971, nine million immigrants were living in northern and western Europe.

With the onset of economic crisis, these immigrant communities soon found themselves under attack. European governments reacted to rising unemployment rates by halting labor immigration. By 1975 West Germany, France, the Netherlands, Britain, Belgium, Sweden, and Switzerland had all banned further immigration. Because it explicitly (although incorrectly) linked the presence of immigrants to unemployment, anti-immigration legislation helped solidify racist attitudes among many sectors of the European population. Violence against immigrants began to escalate.

Ironically, anti-immigration legislation actually increased the size of immigrant communities. West Germany saw its number of foreign residents rise by 13 percent between 1974 and 1982; in the same period, France witnessed a 33 percent increase. Foreign workers scrambled to get into western Europe before the doors shut, and once they were in, were reluctant to leave because of the well-grounded fear that they would not be able to return. Family members came too—only Switzerland banned the entry of dependents.

In the 1980s, then, what sociologists call "migration streams" solidified into ethnic minority communities—not "guestworkers," but rather a permanent part of western European societies. By 1991, 25 percent of the inhabitants of France were either immigrants or the children or grandchildren of immigrants. For both economic and social reasons, minority groups clustered in certain areas in certain cities. In West Germany in the early 1980s, ethnic minorities constituted 6 percent of the population as a whole, but 24 percent of the population of Frankfurt—and in the city's central district, 80 percent.

The resulting encounters among peoples of different religious and ethnic traditions reshaped European culture. In Britain, for example, Afro-Caribbean styles of dress and music had a profound influence on white working-class youth culture. These encounters also posed a potent challenge to ideas of national identity. By the 1980s, British journalists were writing about "third-generation immigrants," as if someone born in Britain to British citizenship were somehow less British than other British citizens. Such terminology indicated a deep reluctance to classify individuals with brown or black skin as British, an inability to conceive of national identity as anything but white. In France, the highly centralized education system became the site of hostile encounters, as Islamic parents fought for the rights of their daughters to attend school in traditional Muslim headdress, a practice resisted by some French authorities who feared that "Frenchness" would be diluted if immigrants failed to accept the traditions of the host society.

In both France and Britain, immigrants could become or already were legal citizens. In West Germany, Switzerland, and the Scandinavian countries, however, foreign workers remained foreign, with no chance of obtaining citizenship. Thus by the 1980s, a dangerous situation had emerged in these countries, with the children of foreign workers growing up in a society in which they had no political rights.

DOCUMENT

"Young, British, and White"

During the 1980s, racist violence increased in Britain, as throughout much of Europe. Overtly racist political parties such as the National Front capitalized on anti-immigrant sentiment to recruit new members for their movements. In this document, the American journalist Bill Buford describes a birthday party held in a pub for one young member of the National Front. The excerpt begins with a dangerous moment: football (soccer) rivalries are threatening to divide the partygoers.

On the far side, some of the new members had started in on their football chants, just as Neil had feared. These appeared to be West Ham supporters. They were then answered, from the other side of the room, by Chelsea supporters.* A contrapuntal chorus of West Ham and Chelsea songs followed, one that sent Neil scurrying through his record collection. It was time to change the music. . . . It was time to play the White Power music.

None of the songs was played on any of the established radio stations or sold in any of the conventional shops. It was a mail-order or cash-in-hand music trade, and from the titles you could see why: "Young, British, and White"; "England Belongs to Me"; "Shove the Dove"; "England" and "British Justice." These were the lyrics of "The Voice of Britain":

Our old people cannot walk the streets alone.
They fought for this nation and this is what they get back.
They risked their lives for Britain, and now Britain belongs to aliens.
It's about time Britain went and took it back.

This is the voice of Britain.
You'd better believe it.
This is the voice of Britain
C'mon and fly the flag now.
. . .

The music was delivered with the same numbing, crushing percussion that had characterized everything else that had been played that evening. . . . There was one refrain I could follow, and that was because it was played repeatedly, and because, each time, everyone joined in. It seemed to be the theme song.

Two pints of lager† and a packet of crisps.‡
Wogs§ out! White power!
Wogs out! White power!
Wogs out! White power!

It was interesting to contemplate that the high-point of the evening was organized around this simple declaration of needs: a lad needed his lager; a lad needed his packet of crisps; a lad needed his wog.

* *West Ham and Chelsea = rival English soccer teams.*
† *"Lager" = beer.*
‡ *"Packet of crisps" = bag of potato chips.*
§ *"Wog" = racially derogatory term for Southeast Asians.*

Source: From *Among the Thugs: The Experience, and the Seduction, of Crowd Violence* by Bill Buford.

These "foreigners" experienced widespread discrimination in education, housing, and employment. In West Germany in the late 1970s, more than 40 percent of "foreign" workers lived in housing without a bath or shower. (Only 6 percent of German citizens did so.) Forced to live in such substandard accommodation by poverty, immigrants were often then stereotyped as dirty and uncivilized.

Explicitly racist political parties capitalized on the new anti-immigration sentiment. In France, for example, Jean-Marie Le Pen (b. 1928), a veteran of the Algerian war, created the *Front National* in 1974 as an anti-immigration party. In Le Pen's view, "Everything comes from immigration. Everything goes back to immigration." Unemployment, rising crime rates, an increase in illegitimate births, crowded schools, AIDS—Le Pen blamed it all on nonwhite immigrants. Appealing particularly to young, male working-class voters, Le Pen's party remained a threatening political presence for the next three decades.

The 1980s: The End of Political Consensus in the West

The economic crisis of the 1970s called into question the social democratic assumptions that had governed political life since World War II. Western Europeans had emerged from the horror of total war in 1945 determined to build better societies. Rejecting the extremes of communism on the left and fascism on the right, they took the centrist social democratic path. Two features characterized social democracies—first, mixed economies that combined nationalization of key industries with private enterprise, and second, an interventionist state that took responsibility for maintaining full employment and providing extensive welfare services. The stagflation of the 1970s, however, seemed to indicate that these social democratic solutions no longer worked. Discontented voters looked for radically new answers. In Spain, Portugal, and Greece, they turned to socialist parties. Throughout most of western Europe and in the United States, however, New Conservatism° dominated political society.

The New Conservatives

Three leaders epitomized the New Conservatism: the Republican Ronald Reagan in the United States (1911–2004), the Christian Democrat Helmut Kohl in West Germany (b. 1930), and the Conservative Margaret Thatcher in Britain (b. 1925). On the most fundamental level, the New Conservatives rejected the postwar emphasis on social improvement in favor of policies intended to create more opportunities for individual achievement. Thatcher even insisted, "There is no such thing as society." In the New Conservative worldview, there was instead the individual, freely competing in a world governed by market forces rather than governmental regulations or state planning. As Kohl demanded during his 1983 campaign, "Less state, more market; fewer collective burdens, more personal performance; fewer encrusted structures, more mobility, self-initiative, and competition." Privatization of nationalized or state-owned industries constituted a key part of the New Conservative agenda—removing the state from the economy and allowing private enterprises to compete. In Britain under Thatcher, the coal industry, transport, and utilities were all shifted to private ownership.

New Conservatives also mounted an attack on the welfare state, insisting that rising social expenditures, funded by rising taxes, lay at the heart of the economic crisis that had afflicted the West since the early 1970s. They pointed to the fact that the years between 1960 and 1981 had seen a dramatic rise in social spending (for programs such as health, disability, and unemployment insurance; pensions; and family allowances). Minimizing the successes of these social programs in reducing poverty, New Conservatives instead linked rising social expenditures to surging inflation and declining economic growth rates.

Yet New Conservative fiscal policies did not actually break sharply from their social democratic predecessors. Reagan, for example, used deficit spending to finance skyrocketing military budgets (up by 40 percent during his administration). The real break lay in the New Conservatives' willingness to tolerate high unemployment rates. By imposing high interest rates on their economies, Thatcher and Reagan brought inflation under control. High interest rates, however, overvalued the British pound and the American dollar. As a result, manufacturers found it hard to sell their products abroad and many went under. In Britain, 13 percent of the workforce was unemployed by 1984. In West Germany, too, Kohl's policies of holding down taxes and government expenditures were accompanied by unemployment rates of more than 9 percent in the mid-1980s.

By the end of the 1980s, as a result of falling global oil prices and the Reagan military spending spree that primed the pump of the global economy, Western economies returned to growth. But the average late-1980s growth rates of 2 to 3 percent per year were lower than those of 5 to 6 percent that had characterized Western economies in the 1950s and 1960s. At the same time, unemployment rates tended to hover between 5 and 7 percent—levels that would have been regarded as unacceptably high in the earlier period. A new political culture, based on lowered expectations, had come into being.

Spending on Social Services as a Percentage of the Gross Domestic Product

	France	West Germany	Sweden	United Kingdom
1960	13.2	15.5	11.0	10.8
1965	15.6	16.5	13.8	11.8
1970	15.1	17.1	18.6	13.1
1975	23.9	23.7	25.0	17.1
1980	26.3	24.0	31.9	18.1
1985	28.7	23.8	30.7	20.3

Source: Susan Pedersen, *Family, Dependence, and the Origins of the Welfare State: Britain and France, 1914–1945,* 1993, p. 416. Reprinted with the permission of Cambridge University Press.

Even Europe's leftist parties had to adapt to this new political culture. Socialist and social democratic governments in Sweden, Italy, Greece, Spain, and France followed New Conservatives along the path of reduced health and social security expenditures, as well as wage cuts. The most dramatic example of this adaptation of the left occurred in France. In 1981, French voters elected Socialist Party leader François Mitterrand (1916–1996) to the presidency. In his first year in office, Mitterrand implemented a series of radical social democratic measures, including a rise in the minimum wage, a reduction in the workweek, expanded social welfare, and higher taxes for the wealthy. But in 1982, Mitterrand was forced by a series of economic catastrophes—falling exports, rising trade and budget deficits, soaring inflation rates—to cut social spending and to let unemployment rates rise.

New Challenges and New Identities: New Feminism

The triumph of New Conservatism demonstrated that economic crisis had shattered the post–World War II social democratic consensus. The protests of the 1960s also helped break apart this consensus, and in the 1970s, two offshoots of these protests—new feminism and environmentalism—offered new cultural and political alternatives. New feminism° emerged directly out of the student protest movement of the 1960s. Female activists grew frustrated at being

The Greenham Common Protests
In the spring of 1983, protesters formed a fourteen-mile human chain across Greenham Common in England to protest against NATO's deployment of cruise missiles. The protest was part of a much wider movement in western Europe and the United States, which articulated widespread public discontent with the renewal of the Cold War. It also played a pivotal role in British feminism, as female activists established a women-only camp at the Greenham Common military base.

denied a voice in the movement—"we cook while the men talk of revolution."[1] At the same time, they were increasingly eager to connect analyses of political subordination to experiences of sexual repression. Their efforts to liberate women from political and cultural limits and expectations gave birth to what was, by the 1980s, an international feminist movement.

Economic and demographic changes buttressed the new feminism. The numbers of women working outside the home rose in these decades—up by 50 percent in Italy between 1970 and 1985, for example. By the late 1970s, women in France accounted for more than 34 percent of the labor force; in Britain, 31 percent; in West Germany, 37 percent. During the same decade, the age at which men and women first married began to climb and birth rates continued to fall.

Western politics gradually responded to the changes in women's roles. By the mid-1980s, women averaged about one-third of the members of parliament in Sweden, and women members accounted for approximately half of Norway's cabinets. In the British general elections of 1992, twice as many women stood as parliamentary candidates compared to 1979.

The movement, however, refused to confine its focus to the world of party politics, arguing instead that "the personal is political." Much of the new feminist critique focused on the female body—its image, its oppression, its control. Feminists challenged feminine stereotypes through attacks on beauty pageants and critiques of the fashion industry and sought the reform of legal codes to outlaw spousal rape and to legalize abortion. Legalization of abortion occurred first in northern Europe: in Britain in 1967, in Denmark in 1970. Catholic Europe followed: In Italy abortions became legally available in 1978, in France in 1979.

In the economic and educational spheres, feminists demanded equal pay for equal work and greater access to educational and professional opportunities. They pressed for more generous parental leave policies, family allowances, and child care provisions. In addition, with women accounting for approximately half of the university students in many Western countries, feminists began to alter the content of the curriculum. Challenging the male biases that had regarded women's contributions as irrelevant and women's lives as insignificant, for example, feminist historians brought to light the "hidden history" of women.

New Challenges and New Identities: Environmentalism

Chico Mendes on the Rain Forest

Environmentalists added their voice to the political cacophony of the 1970s and 1980s. They challenged the fundamental structures of industrial economies (whether capitalist or communist), particularly their inherent emphasis on "more, bigger, faster, now." The movement embraced the ideas of unorthodox economists such as Britain's E. F. Schumacher (1911–1977), who insisted that quantitative measures of economic growth (such as the GNP) failed to factor in environmental destruction and social dislocation, and that in many contexts, "small is beautiful." At the heart of radical environmentalism was the concept of natural limits, of "Spaceship Earth"—the vision of the planet as a "single spaceship, without unlimited reservoirs of anything."[2]

New media-savvy organizations such as Greenpeace publicized the environmentalist cause with colorful protests, such as sailing in small rubber dinghies to challenge whaling fleets. The most popular of radical environmentalist targets was nuclear power. From the mid-1970s on, protests against the construction of nuclear power plants in western Europe drew tens of thousands of supporters. The movement's slogan, "Nuclear Power? No Thanks," was translated into more than forty languages.

The environmental movement helped create a new sort of political party. Green politics° drew its ideas not only from environmentalism but also from feminism. The Greens contended that the degradation of the natural environment stemmed from the same root as discrimination against women—an obsession with physical power and an unwillingness to tear down hierarchical structures. By the late 1980s Green Parties had sprouted in fifteen western European countries. The Greens were the most successful in West Germany, where they sat in the legislature from 1983 and formed an important voting bloc.

From Detente to Renewed Cold War

At the same time that economic crisis, feminist protest, and the new environmental awareness undermined political consensus, rising superpower tensions put an end to the era of detente and caused greater rifts within western European societies. In the first half of the 1970s, detente had appeared to be flourishing. In 1975 representatives of 32 European states, Canada, the United States, and the Soviet Union signed the Helsinki Accords. They declared their acceptance of all existing European borders, agreed to a policy of joint notification of all major military exercises (thus reducing the chances of accidental nuclear war), and promised to safeguard the human rights of their citizens.

Yet the Helsinki Accords marked not only the culmination but also the beginning of the end of the detente era. First, eastern European and Soviet dissidents used the Helsinki human rights clauses to publicize the human rights abuses committed by their governments and to demand fundamental reforms. Second, U.S. president Jimmy Carter, who took office in 1976, chose to place human rights at the center of his foreign policy. Carter's approach infuriated Soviet leaders, who resented what they regarded as his meddling in their internal affairs. As detente crumbled, the arms race accelerated, with both the Warsaw Pact and NATO increasing their defense budgets and deploying intermediate-range nuclear missiles. Detente finally died in December 1979, when Soviet troops invaded Afghanistan. Calling the invasion "the most serious threat to peace since the Second World War," Carter warned that if the Soviets moved toward the Middle East, he would not hesitate to use nuclear weapons.

With the election of New Conservatives such as Thatcher in 1979 and Reagan in 1980, the renewal of the Cold War took on a greater intensity. Reagan labeled the Soviet Union the "Evil Empire"—a reference to the popular *Star Wars* film series that was first released in the 1970s—and revived the anticommunist attitudes and rhetoric of the 1950s. Thatcher strongly supported Reagan's decision to accelerate the arms buildup begun by Carter. Her hard-line anticommunism won her the nickname "Iron Lady" from Soviet policymakers.

The renewal of the Cold War, like the end of economic prosperity, opened up large rifts within western European societies. NATO's decision to deploy its new generation of nuclear missiles drew hundreds of thousands of protesters into the streets of London, Bonn, Amsterdam, and other cities. Many of these protesters demanded not only the cancellation of the cruise missiles but also a withdrawal from NATO's nuclear umbrella.

War in Afghanistan

The Soviet invasion of Afghanistan in 1979 helped end the era of detente. It also catapulted the Soviet army into a winless war, one that many commentators labeled "the Soviet Vietnam."

Revolution in the East

- **What factors explain not only the outbreak but also the success of the revolutions of 1989–1991?**

Between 1989 and 1991, revolution engulfed eastern Europe and the Soviet Union. The appointment of Mikhail Gorbachev (1985–1991) as Soviet Communist Party secretary in 1985 proved pivotal. Gorbachev's efforts to reform the Soviet system led to a series of breathtaking changes: Soviet control over eastern Europe ended, the Cold War came to an abrupt halt, the Soviet Union itself ceased to exist. Ironically, Gorbachev set in motion the first two of these developments precisely to avoid the third.

The Crisis of Legitimacy in the East

While Western countries in the 1970s struggled with stagflation and disappearing economic growth rates, the Soviet Union posted record-breaking production figures. By 1984, for example, the Soviet Union was producing 80 percent more steel and six times as much iron ore than the United States. But Soviet prosperity was an illusion. Published growth and productivity statistics had little to do with actual economic performance. The Soviet economy continued to be hampered by overcentralization. The state planning commission, GOSPLAN, had the impossible task of coordinating the production of over four million different products in at least 50,000 factories. "Success" in Soviet industry meant fulfilling arbitrary quotas, regardless of the quality of goods produced, the actual demand for the product, or the cost of producing it.

The Soviet command economy also proved far too rigid to keep pace with global economic change. While triumphantly proclaiming its fulfillment of the heavy industrial expansion planned by Khrushchev in the early 1960s, Soviet leaders in the 1970s failed to recognize that increasingly, microchips counted for far more than iron ore—that fiber optics, not steel, would buttress the new modernity. When the first Soviet home computer reached the market in the 1980s, it cost ten times as much as the comparable Western model.

By the 1980s, the only growth sectors in the Soviet economy were oil and vodka—and then the bottom dropped out of the oil market. After peaking at $35 per barrel in 1981, oil prices began a steady decade-long fall. For the Soviet economy, the results were catastrophic.

The Soviet leadership proved incapable of responding to the economic crisis. Throughout the 1970s, Soviet leader Leonid Brezhnev's increasing physical frailty mirrored that of the country at large. Like many of his colleagues, Brezhnev had been a child at the time of the Russian Revolution; he knew only Soviet rule and had risen into major office very young because of the employment opportunities created by Stalin's Great Purge. In 1982, the average age of members of the Politburo was 68. These men had a vested interest in maintaining the status quo, not in carrying out fundamental reform.

The Soviet Union's satellite states in eastern Europe also lurched from apparent prosperity into economic crisis during this period. During the 1970s, the Soviets provided oil to their eastern European allies at prices far below the market value and so shielded these economies from some of the tensions afflicting their western European rivals. At the same time, eastern European governments borrowed heavily from Western banks. Western loans did not, however, solve fundamental problems such as overcentralization and the divorce of prices from production costs.

In the 1980s, the debt-laden economic structures of eastern Europe began to collapse. Governments found that they had to borrow simply to service their existing debt. And, as oil prices fell, the Soviet Union responded by charging market value for oil sales to their satellites, thus depriving these economies of a crucial support. Ordinary people soon felt the impact of this economic crisis, as governments restricted the flow of consumer goods and imposed higher prices.

The Moment of Solidarity, the Moment of Punk

Events in Poland at the end of the decade illustrated how economic discontent and political dissent could create a revolutionary situation. Faced with negative economic growth rates, the Polish government announced price increases for meat and other essentials in July 1980. Poles hit the streets in angry protest. This protest gave birth to Solidarity°. Led by a charismatic and politically savvy electrician named Lech Wałęsa (b. 1943), Solidarity was both a trade union and a political movement. It demanded not only the right to unionize and strike, but also the liberation of political prisoners, an end to censorship, and a rollback of the state's power. Within just a few months, ten million Poles had joined Solidarity's ranks.

Fearing Soviet military intervention, the Polish communist government cracked down. In December 1981 Prime Minister Wojciech Jaruzelski declared martial law and arrested more than 10,000 Solidarity members (including Wałęsa). Like the Hungarian Revolution in 1956 and the Prague Spring of 1968, Solidarity seemed to be one more futile and defeated protest in eastern Europe.

But Solidarity refused to be defeated. Both in prison and out, its members resolved to act as if they were free. They met in small groups, published newspapers and ran a radio station, and organized election boycotts. Solidarity remained a political presence and a moral force in Polish society throughout the 1980s, and in 1989 it emerged to lead Poland into democracy.

Before 1989 no other eastern European country experienced a protest movement as dramatic as Solidarity, yet

Encounters & Transformations

Rock and the Velvet Revolution

In September 1968, less than one month after the armies of the Soviet Union and its satellite states had crushed the Prague Spring, a Czech bass player named Milan Hlavsa formed a rock band. The military invasion and the subsequent political crackdown throughout Czechoslovakia appalled Hlavsa, but it never occurred to him that he could do anything to change the harsh reality of life in the communist bloc. He certainly did not see forming a rock band as a political act; he and the other members of the band liked Western rock music (particularly the "psychedelic" music of Frank Zappa, the Velvet Underground, and the Doors), and they wanted to play in a rock band. Yet the encounter between the communist state and the anarchic energy of psychedelic rock helped undermine communist rule and so contributed to the transformation of eastern Europe.

Hlavsa and his friends called their band "The Plastic People of the Universe" (PPU), after a Frank Zappa song, and PPU quickly became the most popular psychedelic group in Prague. But almost as quickly the band ran into trouble. As part of the post-1968 crackdown, the communist government insisted that rock bands conform to a set of official guidelines governing how, what, and where they performed. PPU refused and, in January 1970, lost its professional license. In the communist system, the state not only controlled broadcasting and recording, but even owned the distribution of musical instruments and electrical equipment. Without a license, PPU lost access to rehearsal and recording space, and their instruments as well. But the band played on by repairing cast-off instruments and constructing homemade amplifiers from old transistor radios. Banned in 1972 from performing in Prague, PPU moved to the countryside and when it was banned in 1974 from playing anywhere, it dove underground. Fans alerted other fans when the band would be playing at some remote farm or within some woods, while recordings made in houses and garages circulated illegally. During this period PPU became more than just a rock band; it became the center of what artistic director and manager Ivan Jirous labeled the "Second Culture." An alternative to the official communist "First Culture," the "Second Culture" comprised musicians, fans, artists, writers, and anyone else who sought to carve out a space of individuality and integrity in a society based on conformity and lies.

On March 17, 1976, the Secret Police arrested twenty-seven musicians, including every member of PPU. Six months later rock music went on trial. In response to international protests, the Czech government released most of the twenty-seven rockers. But Jirous and the band's saxophonist, Vratislav Brabenec, as well as two musicians from other groups, were found guilty of "organized disturbance of the peace" and sentenced to between eight and eighteen months in prison.

In the courtroom the day of the sentencing sat Václav Havel, an ardent Frank Zappa fan as well as a playwright who used his art to mount veiled attacks on the communist system. The imprisonment of Jirous and Brabenec infuriated Havel. For the next several years, he opened his farmhouse to PPU for illegal concerts and recording sessions. More important, Havel walked out of the courtroom convinced that the time had come to challenge communism openly. On January 1, 1977, Havel and other artists and intellectuals announced the formation of "Charter 77" to publicize human rights abuses under communism. Over the next decade many Charter members, including Havel, spent time in prison. Yet, calling the state to account for its crimes, Charter 77 helped weaken the communist regime. When revolution came in 1989, that regime toppled with astounding ease. PPU had split up two years before and so did not sing in the new era, but fittingly, one of the first individuals that President Václav Havel invited to the new free Czechoslovakia was an aging psychedelic rocker named Frank Zappa.

For Discussion

Imagine that the post-1968 Communist government in Czechoslovakia simply ignored the PPU. Would events have unfolded any differently? Why or why not?

Rocking the Bloc
In 1977, the Plastic People of the Universe play an illegal concert in Václav Havel's farmhouse.

The Moment of Solidarity

Lech Wałęsa addresses workers in the Gdansk shipyard in 1980. Note the pictures of the pope and the Virgin Mary—Roman Catholicism served as a vital source of national unity and identity, one opposed to communism.

throughout the region economic hardship fed widespread political alienation and a deepening longing for radical change. One sign of the widening gap between the communist authorities and the people they governed was the emergence of punk music as a cultural force among eastern European youth.

Punk had first appeared in Britain in the mid-1970s, the product of economic decline and social division. Dressed in clothes that deliberately mocked the consumerism and respectability of mainstream middle-class society—ripped trousers held together with safety pins, dog collars, spiked and outrageously colored hair—punks promoted a do-it-yourself style of rock music that also spat on middle-class standards. Punk rockers rarely had any musical training or expertise; even talent was not actually necessary. All that was needed was rage, which was readily available.

The nihilistic message of bands such as Britain's Sex Pistols—"no future for you, no future for me"—resonated in eastern Europe. With names like Doom, Crisis, Shortage, Paralysis, Sewage, and Dead Organism, Eastern punk bands, like their Western models, often expressed utter despair: "No goal, no future, no hope, no joy!" But this nihilism butted against explicit political protest. At punk concerts in Poland, bands and their audiences stood in silent homage to Solidarity. In Hungary, the members of one punk group received prison sentences for a performance in which they mocked their government as a "rotten, stinking communist gang" while tearing up a live chicken.[3]

Nature and the Nation

The dissatisfaction expressed by punk bands permeated eastern European society, and increasingly took political form. Just as the emergence of radical environmentalism demonstrated a strong current of dissatisfaction with the political order in the West, so similar movements in the East pushed for radical change.

For decades, the conquest of nature had been a key part of Soviet ideology: "We cannot wait for favors from nature; our task is to take from her."[4] Beginning in the 1930s, Soviet engineers sought to fill what they regarded as nature's "empty spaces" with exotic plant and animal life, thus wreaking havoc with the ecological balance of much of the Soviet environment. In the early 1960s, Khrushchev's "Virgin Lands" scheme introduced intensive chemical fertilization and irrigation across huge swathes of Soviet territory, resulting in the fall of lake water levels, the destruction of wetlands, and the salinization of extensive stretches of land.

The situation worsened in the 1970s. The rapid expansion of heavy industry focused on churning out products, not on human safety or environmental sustainability. Communist governments throughout the Soviet bloc ignored the most basic environmental precautions, dumping both untreated sewage and nuclear waste directly into lakes and rivers. By 1977, Soviet scientists concluded that Lake Baikal—the most voluminous and deepest freshwater lake in the world, home to more than 800 plant and 1,500 animal species—had experienced irreversible environmental degradation.

As a result of this wholesale destruction, environmentalist protest groups emerged in the Soviet Union and throughout eastern Europe. Because Soviet officials regarded the environment as insignificant, they tended to view environmentalist protest as unimportant, as a "safe" outlet for popular frustration. Thus environmentalism became one of the few areas in communist society that permitted ordinary people free expression and in which public opinion was allowed a voice. Environmental activism worked like a termite infestation, nibbling away from within at the structures of Soviet communism.

Environmentalism also proved crucial in underlining nationalist identity and fueling nationalist protest. The various national and ethnic groups within the vast Soviet empire watched their forests disappear, their lakes dry up, and their ancient cities bulldozed, as a result of decisions made in faraway Moscow by men they regarded as foreigners—as *Russians* rather than as *comrades.* By the 1980s, schools in Latvia issued gas masks as a routine safety precaution because of the dangers of chemical spills. Many Latvians concluded that they would be better off independent of Soviet control.

Gorbachev and Radical Reform

In 1982, the decrepit Leonid Brezhnev died—and so, in rapid succession, did his two successors, Yuri Andropov (1982–1984) and Konstantin Chernenko (1984–1985). The time had come for a generational change. When Mikhail Gorbachev succeeded Chernenko, he was 54 years old. Compared to his elderly colleagues on the Politburo, he looked like a teenager.

Gorbachev's biography encompassed the drama of Soviet history. He was born, in 1931, into the turmoil of collectivization. One-third of the inhabitants of his native village in Stavropol were executed or imprisoned or died from famine or disease in the upheavals of the early 1930s. Both of his grandfathers were arrested on trumped-up charges. Yet Gorbachev's family continued to believe in the Communist dream. During World War II his father served in the Red Army (and was twice wounded), and in 1948 Gorbachev and his father together won the Order of Red Banner of Labor for harvesting almost six times the average crop. Because of this award and his academic abilities, Gorbachev won entry to Moscow University. After earning degrees in economics and law, he rose through the ranks of the provincial Communist Party. In 1978, at age 47, he became the youngest member of the Communist Party Central Committee, the key leadership body in the Soviet Union.

Glasnost and Perestroika

Gorbachev came to power in 1985, convinced that the Soviet system was ailing, and that the only way to restore it to health was through radical surgery. What he did not anticipate was that such surgery would in fact kill the patient. His surgical tools were glasnost and perestroika, two Russian terms without direct English equivalents.

Glasnost°, sometimes translated as "openness," "publicity," or "transparency," meant abandoning the deception and censorship that had always characterized the Soviet system, for a policy based on open admission of failures and problems. To Gorbachev, "Broad, timely, and frank information is testimony of faith in people . . . and for their capacity to work things out themselves."[5]

Not surprisingly, Soviet citizens remained wary of Gorbachev's talk of glasnost—until April 1986 and the Chernobyl nuclear power plant disaster. Operator error at the Ukrainian power plant led to the most serious nuclear accident in history. In the days following the accident, thirty-five plant workers died; over the next five years the cleanup effort would claim at least 7,000 lives. The accident placed more than four million inhabitants of Ukraine and Belarus at risk from excess radiation and spread a radioactive cloud that extended all the way to Scotland. When news of the accident first reached Moscow, party officials acted as they had always done: They denied that anything had happened. But monitors in Western countries quickly

Glasnost
Mikhail Gorbachev meets with workers in Moscow in 1985.

picked up on the excess radiation spewing into the atmosphere. Gorbachev initiated an about-face and insisted that accurate information about the disaster be released to the public. Chernobyl became the first Soviet media event. In 1986, 93 percent of the Soviet population had access to a television set and what they saw on their screens convinced them that glasnost was real. A powerful change had occurred in Soviet political culture.

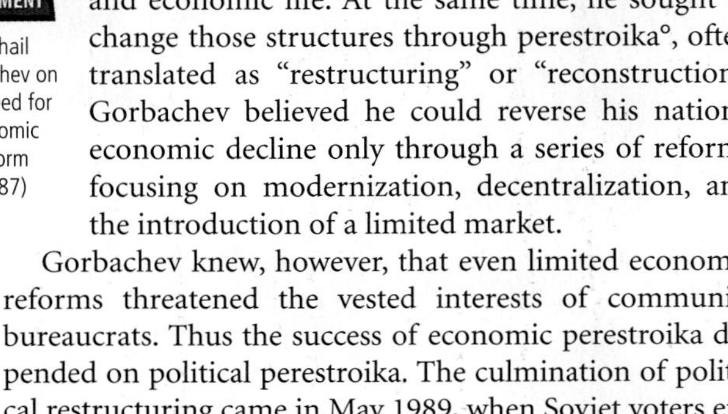

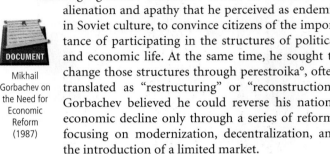

Mikhail Gorbachev on the Need for Economic Reform (1987)

Through glasnost Gorbachev aimed to overcome the alienation and apathy that he perceived as endemic in Soviet culture, to convince citizens of the importance of participating in the structures of political and economic life. At the same time, he sought to change those structures through perestroika°, often translated as "restructuring" or "reconstruction." Gorbachev believed he could reverse his nation's economic decline only through a series of reforms focusing on modernization, decentralization, and the introduction of a limited market.

Gorbachev knew, however, that even limited economic reforms threatened the vested interests of communist bureaucrats. Thus the success of economic perestroika depended on political perestroika. The culmination of political restructuring came in May 1989, when Soviet voters entered the voting booths to elect the Congress of People's Deputies, and for the first time in Soviet history they had a choice of candidates. True, all of these candidates were members of the Communist Party, but just one year later, Gorbachev ended the Communist Party's monopoly on parliamentary power, and the Soviet Union entered the brave new world of multiparty politics.

Ending the Cold War

Restructuring Soviet economics and politics led almost inevitably to restructuring international relations—and to ending the Cold War. By the 1980s, at least 18 percent of the Soviet GNP was absorbed by the arms race; Gorbachev concluded that the Soviet Union simply could not afford the Cold War. As soon as Gorbachev took office, he signaled to the West his desire to resume arms control negotiations. The results of these negotiations were startling. In December 1987, Gorbachev and U.S. president Ronald Reagan signed the INF (Intermediate Nuclear Forces) Treaty, agreeing to the total elimination of land-based intermediate-range nuclear missiles. In 1991, the Soviets and Americans signed the Strategic Arms Reduction Treaty (START I), pledging themselves to a mutual reduction of intercontinental ballistic missiles (ICBMs). The nuclear arms race had ended.

At the same time, Gorbachev signaled an end to Soviet global intervention by reducing Soviet military commitments abroad. In 1989, he brought the Red Army home from both Afghanistan and Mongolia and removed Soviet-sponsored Cuban forces from Angola.

The Revolutions of 1989 in Eastern Europe

Even more remarkably, by the end of 1990, the Red Army had pulled out of every state in eastern Europe except East Germany and Poland (and would soon withdraw from these countries as well). The Soviet Union could not afford to wage the Cold War, nor could it afford to maintain the eastern European empire that was both a cause and a consequence of that conflict.

In his first informal meetings with eastern European communist leaders in 1985, Gorbachev told them they should no longer expect Soviet tanks to enforce their will on rebellious populations. By the time Gorbachev addressed the UN General Assembly at the end of 1988 and declared that the nations of eastern Europe were free to choose their own paths, dramatic changes were already underway.

Hungary and Poland were the first to jettison communist rule. Even before Gorbachev took power, economic crisis had driven both of these states to embrace fundamental reforms. In the early 1980s Hungary moved toward a Western-oriented, market-driven economy by joining the World Bank and the International Monetary Fund (IMF) and establishing a stock market. Political reforms accompanied these economic changes. In 1983, Hungarian voters

CHRONOLOGY

Revolution in Eastern Europe

1989	
January	Noncommunist parties and unions legalized in Hungary
February	Roundtable talks between Polish government and Solidarity
June	Free elections in Poland
September	Solidarity forms government in Poland
November	Fall of Berlin Wall; reformist communists overthrow Zhivkov in Bulgaria
December	Collapse of communist government in Czechoslovakia and East Germany; execution of Ceauşescu in Romania
1990	
March	Free elections in East Germany and Hungary
October	Reunification of Germany
December	Wałęsa elected president of Poland

for the first time had a choice of candidates (all still Communist Party members); eighteen months later, independent candidates were allowed to run—and many were elected. In Poland, Jaruzelski's government also experimented with restoring some measures of a market economy and with political liberalization. Once martial law ended in 1983, censorship loosened considerably. Newspapers published criticisms of governmental policy that would never have been permitted before 1980.

With Gorbachev in power, the pace of reform in both Poland and Hungary accelerated rapidly. In January 1989, Hungary took the leap into political pluralism by legalizing noncommunist political parties and trade unions. In February, Solidarity and Polish communist officials began "roundtable talks" aimed at restructuring Poland's political system. In June, Poland held the first free elections in the Soviet bloc. Solidarity swept the contest and formed the first noncommunist government in eastern Europe since 1948.

A bewildered world waited to see if Gorbachev would send in the tanks. Only one day before the Polish elections, the Chinese communist government, oblivious to the television cameras that broadcast the horrible scenes around the globe, had used brutal force to crush a student pro-democracy uprising centered in Beijing's Tiananmen Square. Hundreds died. Horrified by the carnage, Gorbachev insisted that "the very possibility of the use or threat of force [in Poland] . . . is totally unacceptable."[6]

With the prop of the Red Army removed, the communist states of eastern Europe toppled easily. In November 1989, the Berlin Wall fell. The collapse of the wall echoed to the sound of communist governments crashing throughout eastern Europe. In December, after a year of ever-widening protest demonstrations, the communist government in Czechoslovakia resigned. Alexander Dubček, the hero of the Prague Spring of 1968, returned in triumph to assume the leadership of parliament, and the playwright and leading dissident Václav Havel (b. 1936) became the Czech president. In March 1990, the Christian Democrats took over the government from the communists in East Germany; seven months later the states of East and West Germany ceased to exist, and a single Germany was reborn. At the end of the year, reform-minded Communist Party members in Bulgaria overthrew the government of Todor Zhivkov, who had been in power for thirty-five years.

Escaping the Berlin Wall

All of these revolutions occurred with very little bloodshed. The pace of change in Czechoslovakia was so smooth, in fact, that the events earned the nickname "the Velvet Revolution." But in Romania, the revolutionary cloth came soaked in blood. In December 1989, Romania's dictator Nikolai Ceauşescu ordered the army to fire on a peaceful protest; hundreds died. In a matter of days, however, the soldiers turned against Ceauşescu. Fighting spread across the nation as the dictator's security forces battled with both the demonstrators and the army. Ceauşescu and his wife went into hiding, but on Christmas Day they were caught and executed by a firing squad. The televised pictures of their dead bodies were broadcast around the world. A new government was formed under Ion Iliescu (b. 1930), a reformist communist who had attended Moscow University with Gorbachev.

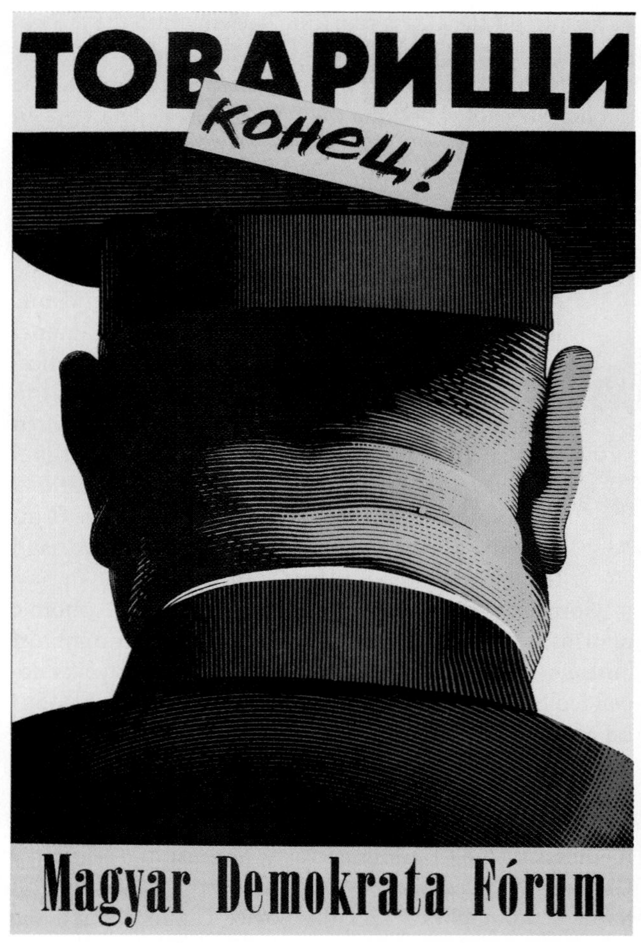

"Comrades, It's Over!"
This Hungarian political poster sums up the revolutions of 1989.

The Disintegration of the Soviet Union

By 1990, Gorbachev was one of the best-known leaders in the Western world. Both Western political leaders and ordinary people praised Gorbachev for ending the Cold War and loosening the Soviet hold on eastern Europe. But for Gorbachev, these changes in the international structure were means to an end—freeing the Soviet economy for prosperity and thereby saving the communist system. But prosperity eluded his grasp, and the system he sought to save disintegrated.

Between 1985 and 1991, Gorbachev's administration started and stopped twelve different national economic plans, in ever-more-desperate attempts to prop up the Soviet economy. These reforms seemed only to worsen the economic crisis. By 1990, food and other essential goods were scarce, prices had risen by 20 percent since the year before, and both productivity figures and incomes were falling. Dramatic increases in the number of prostitutes (accompanied by a tripling of the rate of venereal disease in Moscow), abandoned babies, and the homeless population all signaled a society in the midst of economic breakdown.

By the early 1990s Gorbachev faced fierce opposition not only from hard-line communists who opposed his reforms, but also from more liberal reformers who viewed the communist system as utterly broken, and who wanted to accelerate the shift to a capitalist economy. These reformers found a spokesman in Boris Yeltsin (b. 1931), a charismatic, boisterous politician who became the president of Russia (as distinct from the Soviet Union) in 1991. As Gorbachev increasingly began to tack toward the right, Yeltsin emerged as the leader who would keep the revolution on course. When communist hard-liners attempted to overthrow Gorbachev in August 1991, it was Yeltsin who led the popular resistance movement that defeated the coup attempt.

Gorbachev was finally ousted not by a political coup but by the power of nationalism. Glasnost had allowed separatist nationalist movements within the Soviet Union to surface from the underground, but Gorbachev, despite his commitment to freedom of choice for eastern Europe, firmly opposed the breakup of the Soviet Union. In 1990, he deployed troops to quell nationalist rioting in both Azerbaijan and Georgia and to counter independence movements in the Baltic states of Latvia, Estonia, and Lithuania. Short of an all-out civil war, however, there was little Gorbachev could do to hold the union together. By December 1991, the Soviet Union had broken apart (see Map 28.1). On December 25, Gorbachev resigned his office as president of a state that no longer existed.

IMAGE
Statue of Lenin Toppled During the Soviet Collapse

Map 28.1 The Former Soviet Union

In December 1991, the Soviet empire disintegrated. In its place stood fifteen independent and very diverse republics, ranging from tiny and impoverished Moldova to relatively affluent and Europeanized Latvia to Russia itself, still the dominant power in the region but economically stagnant.

The Disintegration of the Soviet Union
Gorbachev attempted to halt the disintegration of the Soviet Union by sending in crack Soviet troops to wrest back control of public buildings in Vilnius, Lithuania. Fourteen protesters died, and Lithuania asserted its independence.

In the Wake of Revolution

- **What were the consequences of these revolutions for the societies of eastern Europe?**

With the Cold War over and the long struggle between communism and capitalism clearly won by the latter, one best-selling author talked of the "end of history," by which he meant the end of the ideological struggles that had so defined the last two centuries of historical development.[7] But such talk was premature. "History" returned with a vengeance in the 1990s. As nationalism replaced the capitalist-communist struggle, many of the divisive issues that had led to world war in 1914 and 1939 moved back to center stage. The former Soviet Union and all the former Soviet satellite states in eastern Europe experienced high inflation rates, high unemployment, and economic instability in the wake of the revolution. Many faced nationalist hostilities from minority groups; some confronted the ultimate challenge of civil war.

Crisis Throughout the Former Soviet Union

For many ordinary Russians, the ending of the Soviet regime meant freedom of the worst kind—freedom to be hungry, freedom to be homeless, freedom to be afraid. In January 1992, Yeltsin applied "shock therapy" to the ailing Russian economy. He lifted price controls, abolished subsidies, and privatized state industries. By mid-1994, the state sector of the Russian economy had shrunk to under 40 percent. But the economy did not prosper. Prices climbed dramatically and the closure of unproductive businesses sent unemployment rates upward, while at the same time cuts in government spending severed welfare lifelines. By 1995, 80 percent of Russians were no longer earning a living wage. Food consumption fell to the same level as the early 1950s, with meat almost disappearing from the diets of many.

The economic situation worsened in 1998, when Russia effectively went bankrupt. The value of the ruble collapsed and the state defaulted on its loans. Even Russians with jobs found it difficult to make ends meet. Workers at the Moscow McDonald's, for example, had regarded themselves as privileged: They were paid regularly and well. But overnight in 1998, the value of their paycheck dropped by 70 percent. Workers in state jobs simply were not paid at all.

For many Russians, capitalism meant lawlessness. Managers of state industries were often able to manipulate privatization for their own private enrichment, so they grew fabulously wealthy, while ordinary employees experienced sharp pay cuts or the loss of their jobs. By the mid-1990s, a new force had appeared in Russian life—the "Russian Mafia," crime syndicates with international links that used extortion and intimidation to seize control of large sectors of the economy.

In the non-Russian republics, often the situation was even worse. The end of the Soviet Union meant the end of Soviet subsidies for these impoverished regions. Tajikistan, for example, had depended on Soviet financial aid to prop up the extensive irrigation system that allowed its farmers to grow cotton for export. The collapse of the Soviet Union meant the collapse of the Tajikistan economy. By the end of the 1990s, almost half of Tajikistan's 6.2 million inhabitants were struggling to survive in the face of severe food shortages. In Moldova, the economy shrank by 60 percent between 1991 and 2001, while life expectancy rates fell by five years. One Moldovan elementary school principal admitted she was "hungry for Soviet days," which she recalled as a time when salaries were steady and health care universally available.[8] In the post-Soviet era, Moldovans resorted to marketing their body organs to Western entrepreneurs for $3,000 each.

The economic and social collapse that followed the end of the Soviet Union fostered a climate of desperation in which extremist nationalism flourished. Independence did not mean stability in the republics of Georgia, Armenia, and Azerbaijan, all of which experienced civil war in the 1990s. In Russia itself, Yeltsin faced strong opposition from nationalist groups who viewed the breakup of the Soviet Union as a humiliation for Mother Russia.

The sharpest nationalist challenge to Yeltsin came from Chechnya, one of twenty-one autonomous republics within the larger Russian Federation. When the Soviet Union broke up, Chechnya became part of independent Russia. But the Chechens demanded their own state, and in 1991 declared Chechnya independent. The Chechen-Russian dispute simmered until 1994 when Yeltsin committed 30,000 troops to forcing Chechnya back within Russia's embrace. In the ensuing twenty-month conflict, 80,000 died and 240,000 were wounded—80 percent of these Chechen civilians. Yeltsin negotiated a truce in the summer of 1996, but four years later his successor, Vladimir Putin (b. 1952), renewed the war.

While Putin continued Yeltsin's battle against Chechen independence, his assumption of the presidency signaled a change in Russia's direction—but just where Russia was heading was not very clear. On the one hand, the well-manicured, tightly controlled, even austere Putin promised a more competent, stable style of government than Russia had experienced under the hard-drinking, jovial, often erratic Yeltsin. Yet Putin soon displayed authoritarian instincts. He moved quickly to centralize power under his own control and ran roughshod over such key democratic touchstones as freedom of the press and the right to a fair trial. Western governments struggled with the question of how to encourage Russia's economic stabilization without sacrificing its still fledgling democracy.

Eastern Europe: Stumbling Toward Democracy

Like the former Soviet Union, the states of Eastern Europe found the path from communist rule to democracy far from easy. The dissolution of the Soviet bloc meant that economic networks established over the last four decades suddenly disintegrated. In addition, Western advisers and the International Monetary Fund, which controlled access to much-needed loans, insisted that the new governments follow programs of "austerity" aimed at cutting government spending and curbing inflation. The result was economic hardship far beyond what any Western electorate would have endured. In Poland, for example, the new Solidarity-led government instituted the "Big Bang" on New Year's Day 1990. Controls disappeared and prices jumped between 30 and 600 percent overnight. The inflation rate for 1990 in Poland was a remarkable 550 percent. Even in 1995, when the economy had stabilized, inflation remained at 20 percent, while joblessness stood at 15 percent.

But by the second half of the 1990s, it was clear that Poland was succeeding in moving from communism to capitalism. With some measures of market reform already in place before 1988, both Poland and Hungary were the best prepared for the transition from a command to a capitalist economy. The Czech Republic and the Baltic nations also moved fairly rapidly through the most difficult stages of this transition. In countries such as Romania, Bulgaria, and Albania, economic instability continued, with the majority of their populations experiencing severe poverty.

Political stability was also hard-won during this decade. The revolutionary coalitions that had led the charge against communist rule in 1989–1990 quickly fragmented as their members moved from the heady idealism of challenging authoritarianism to the nitty-gritty of parliamentary politics. In addition, voters who were fed up with economic hardship turned to the people who represented a more stable past. Between 1993 and 1995, ex-communists returned to power in Lithuania, Hungary, Bulgaria, and Poland. In Romania, they had never left. Yet the revolutions of 1989 were not reversed. Ex-communists continued with the economic liberalization programs of their opponents, although in many cases opting for a more gradual transition. No former communist regime returned to authoritarian rule or a centralized state-run economy.

A far greater threat to eastern European democracy was posed by the revival of pre–World War II political ideas and styles. For example, the claim of Josef Antall, Hungary's prime minister in the early 1990s, to be the leader of "all Hungarians" (two million of whom lived in Romania and another 600,000 in Slovakia) recalled the vehement Hungarian nationalism of the 1920s and 1930s. Much of eastern Europe witnessed a resurgence of ethnic hostilities in the 1990s. In Czechoslovakia, Hável's government could not bridge the regional-ethnic divide that opened up between the Czech half of the country and Slovakia. In 1993, Czechoslovakia ceased to exist, replaced by the separate nations of the Czech Republic and Slovakia. The breakup of Czechoslovakia occurred peacefully, but ethnic divisions turned violent in much of eastern Europe. In Romania escalating discrimination against the Hungarian and Roma minority populations stirred up memories of interwar racist violence. Throughout eastern Europe, anti-Semitic rhetoric returned to political discourse. In 1990, Lech Wałęsa's election campaign was tainted by anti-Jewish references; graffiti appeared on the walls of Warsaw buildings: "Jews to the ovens."

The "German Problem"?

The problems that engulfed Germany after its eastern and western halves reunited in October 1990 illustrated the difficulties faced by eastern Europeans as they struggled to adjust to a post–Cold War, post-Soviet world. Almost half the population of East Germany crossed the border into West Germany in the first week after the fall of the Berlin Wall. They returned home dazzled by the consumer delights they saw in store windows and eager for a chance to grab a piece of the capitalist pie. West German chancellor Helmut Kohl recognized the power of these desires, and skillfully forced the pace of reunification. When the two Germanys united at the end of 1990, Kohl became the first chancellor of the new German state.

Kohl trusted that West Germany's economy was strong enough to pull its bankrupt new partner into prosperity, but he proved overly optimistic. The residents of the former East Germany soon found their factories closing and their livelihoods gone. These economic troubles quickly leached over into the western regions of Germany. By 1997, unemployment in Germany stood at 12.8 percent—the highest since World War II. In the eastern regions, over 20 percent of the population was out of work.

For the women of the former East Germany, life in the new Germany meant an especially intense culture clash. The concept of the male breadwinner/head of household was enshrined in the West German legal code until the end of the 1970s and prominent in West German culture for a long time after. Many women from the former East Germany found this concept alien. In East Germany, women had expected to work full time and to have access to state-provided day care, abortion, and contraceptives. In the new united Germany, which adhered to West German legal and cultural traditions, more conventional gender roles and conceptions of sexual morality dominated. For at least some East German women, then, the end of communist rule was not unambiguously liberating.

At the same time, economic despair throughout much of the former East Germany resulted in racial violence. Looking for scapegoats, eastern German youths targeted the foreign workers in their cities. Violent attacks against Turkish workers escalated in the 1990s, as did support for neo-Nazi organizations.

In 1998, these economic and social problems led German voters to reject Kohl and the Christian Democrats. The Social Democrats, out of office since 1982, took charge under the leadership of Gerhard Schroeder (b. 1944). Schroeder, however, was unable to reverse the economic slide. By 2001, the German economy was standing still, with a GDP growth rate of little more than zero. The gap between the former West and East Germanys remained wide, with easterners enduring the worst of the German economic crisis. In a hugely controversial effort to resolve the crisis, Schroeder in 2004 forced through legislation that scaled back German welfare benefits. Many Germans, however, saw this move as a repudiation of the social democratic promise of guaranteeing a decent standard of living to all Germans. In September 2005, Shroeder's Social Democrats lost their majority in the German parliament. The Christian Democrats, however, also failed to gain a majority. The inconclusive results of the election revealed a worrying lack of consensus among voters about Germany's direction in the twenty-first century.

The Breakup of Yugoslavia

In Yugoslavia the "return of history" proved most marked and, given the nature of that history, most horrific. When the communist guerilla leader Tito seized control of the Yugoslav state after World War II, he sought to free Yugoslavia from the divisive and bloody battles of its recent past. But in the 1980s and 1990s, the revival of nationalist hostilities within Yugoslavia led to civil war and

DOCUMENT

"How's the Family?"

The conflict in Yugoslavia was a civil war, which meant that frequently the fighters knew their enemy personally. Victims of ethnic cleansing testified that it was their neighbors, colleagues, or schoolmates who had thrust them out of their homes, killed their fathers and brothers, and raped their mothers and sisters. The men at the top also knew each other. In this excerpt, a transcript of a telephone conversation made in Croatia in 1991, the Serb military commander Ratko Mladic is speaking to his Croat counterpart:

"Is that you, Mladic?"

"Yes it is, you old devil, what do you want?"

"Three of my boys went missing near . . . and I want to find out what happened to them."

"I think they're all dead."

"I've got one of their parents on to me about it, so I can tell them for certain that they're gone?"

"Yep, certain. You have my word. By the way, how's the family?"

"Oh not so bad, thanks. How about yours?"

"They're doing just fine, we're managing pretty well."

"Glad to hear it. By the way, now I've got you on the line, we've got about twenty bodies of yours near the front and they've been stripped bare. We slung them into a mass grave and they're now stinking to high heaven. Any chance of you coming to pick them up because they really are becoming unbearable. . . ?"

Source: From Misha Glenny, *The Fall of Yugoslavia* (1994), p. 28.

state-sanctioned mass murder, to scenes of carnage and to mass atrocities not seen in Europe since the 1940s.

Although Yugoslavia had appeared on European maps since the end of World War I, one could argue it did not really exist until after World War II. During the 1920s and 1930s, the subjects of the Serbian monarchy did not regard themselves as "Yugoslavs"; they were Serbs or Croats, Muslims or Montenegrins, Albanians or Slovenians. And during World War II, as we saw in Chapter 26, Serbs and Croats fought each other with a savage intensity—a bitter reminder of the lack of a single national Yugoslav identity.

To construct a united nation out of Yugoslavia's diverse and often hostile cultures, Tito utilized two tools—federalism and communism. A federal political structure consisting of six equal republics prevented Serbia, or any other of the republics, from dominating Yugoslavia. Communism served as a unifying ideology, a cluster of ideas that transcended the divisions of race, religion, and language. Ethnic identities and rivalries were declared unacceptable, part of the bourgeois past that had supposedly been left behind.

Yugoslavs often said, however, that their nation consisted of "six nationalities, five languages, four religions, . . . and one Tito." According to this folk wisdom, Tito—not communism, not federalism—was the glue that held together this diverse state. In 1980, Tito died. Ominously, the year after his death saw the outbreak of riots between ethnic Albanians and Serbs in the province of Kosovo. Even more ominously, Tito's death coincided with the onset of serious economic crisis. The drastic rise in oil prices in 1979 undercut the Yugoslav economy, as did its rising debt load. Between 1979 and 1985 real wages fell in Yugoslavia by almost 25 percent. By 1987, inflation was raging at 200 percent per year; two years later it had burst through into hyperinflation—200 percent *per month.*

Under pressure from this economic crisis, the federal structure built by Tito began to collapse, as the wealthier Yugoslav republics such as Croatia sought to loosen the ties that bound them to the poorer republics such as Serbia. Then, in 1989, the revolutions that swept through the Soviet satellite states shattered the hold of communism on Yugoslavia as well. Ethnic nationalism, long simmering under the surface of Yugoslavian political life, poured into the resulting ideological void. New leaders emerged with new agendas.

In Serbia, the former communist functionary Slobodan Milošević (b. 1941) transformed himself into a popular spokesman for aggressive Serbian nationalism. Milošević used rallies and the mass media, which he controlled, to convince Serbs that their culture was under attack and to paint himself as the defender of that culture. To enhance Serbia's power—and his own—Milošević fiercely opposed any talk of destroying the Yugoslav federation. Moreover, Milošević possessed a powerful weapon to enforce his will: the Yugoslav army, the fourth-largest fighting force in Europe, dominated by Serbs.

Thus, when Croatia declared independence in June 1991, the result was civil war. Milošević mobilized the Yugoslav army against the Croatian separatists. In 1992 the war spread to Bosnia-Herzegovina after its government, too, declared independence. The war quickly degenerated into an ethnic bloodbath, with memories of World War II shaping the conflict. Serbs viewed Croats as the direct heirs of the murderous Nazi-backed Croatian fascists, responsible for the mass slaughter of Serbs (and Jews) in World War II. In turn, Croats called all Serbs "Chetniks," linking them to the anti-Croat Serbian guerilla bands of the war years. (See Chapter 26.) The presence of paramilitary forces also heightened the brutality of the war. With no military discipline and often possessing criminal records, the

CHRONOLOGY

The Shattering of Yugoslavia

1989	Slobodan Milošević becomes president of Yugoslavian Republic of Serbia
1991	
July	Civil war in Croatia begins
1992	
April	Civil war in Bosnia begins
1994	
April	NATO air strikes against Bosnian Serb positions begin
1995	
December	Dayton Accords
1998	Large-scale fighting in Kosovo between Albanians and Serbs
1999	
March	NATO air strikes against Serbia
June	Cease-fire in Kosovo
2000	
October	Milošević defeated in Serbian elections
2001	
June	Milošević extradited to the Hague to be tried for genocide

Map 28.2 The Former Yugoslavia

The breakup of Yugoslavia began in June 1991 with the Slovenian and Croatian declarations of independence. Bosnia and Macedonia soon followed.

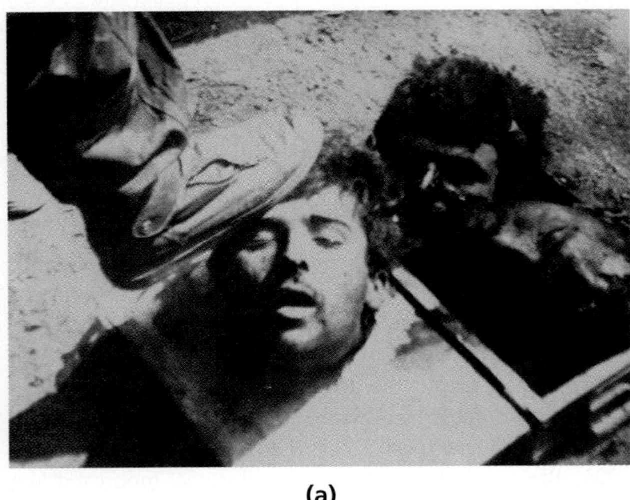

(a)

(b)

Bosnian War Atrocities

(a) Serbian heads, found after Serb fighters raided a Muslim base in northern Bosnia in 1993. (b) A mass grave of Muslim civilians in Pilica, northwest of Srebrenica, in the spring of 1996. Twelve thousand of the men and boys of Srebrenica tried to flee to safety—about half made it; many of those that didn't were forced by Serb fighters to dig their own graves and then shot in front of them. The citizens of Srebenica who did not flee were told by Bosnian Serbian general Ratko Mladic, "No one will harm you." Mladic then ordered his soldiers to shoot all Muslim men between ages 17 and 60. Reviewing the evidence against Mladic, the UN tribunal noted, "These are truly scenes from hell, written on the darkest pages of human history."

volunteers in these units plunged into a fury of plunder, murder, and rape.

This war introduced the world to the horrors of ethnic cleansing° and rape camps. By 1994, all sides within the Bosnian war were practicing ethnic cleansing, although it is clear that Serbs initiated the practice and used it most extensively. To create all-Serb zones within Croatia and Bosnia, Serb paramilitary units embarked on a campaign of terror designed to force Muslims and Croats to abandon their homes and villages. They burned mosques, closed schools, and vandalized houses. Most villagers fled; the paramilitaries tortured and often killed those who stayed. Women were sometimes rounded up and placed in special camps where they were subjected to regular, systematic rape. An estimated 20,000 women, most of them Muslim, endured this vicious effort to subjugate and humiliate a people.

With Serbia assisting the Bosnian Serbs and Croatia assisting the Bosnian Croats, the Muslim community within Bosnia suffered the most intensely, and begged western governments to abandon their positions of neutrality and to stop the atrocities. Finally, in 1994, NATO planes began bombing Serb positions, the first time in its history that NATO had gone into combat. One year later, the Dayton Accords, signed in Dayton, Ohio, brought an uneasy peace to Bosnia (see Map 28.2).

Peace eluded Serbia during this period, however. The sort of vicious nationalism embodied by Milošević demanded a constant supply of enemies and a continuous cycle of violence. In 1998, large-scale fighting between Serbs and Albanians erupted in the province of Kosovo. Ethnic cleansing, mass rape, and a huge exodus of refugees began once again. After a NATO bombing campaign in Serbia, NATO and Russian troops moved into Kosovo, and in 2001, a police helicopter transported Milošević to the Netherlands to be tried for genocide before the International War Crimes Tribunal.

Rethinking the West

- **What were the implications of these developments for the meaning of "the West" itself?**

At the start of the 1990s, a sense of triumphalism characterized much of Western culture—at its simplest, expressed as "we won the Cold War." But who was "we"? For forty years, the Cold War had provided a clear enemy and thus a clear identity: The West was anticommunist, anti-Soviet, anti–Warsaw Pact. Communism's loss of credibility, the disintegration of the Soviet Union, and the dismantling of the Warsaw Pact all demanded that the West revise itself. But so, too, did other important social, political, and cultural changes that occurred in the wake of the tumultuous events of the later 1960s and the economic downturn of the 1970s.

The European Union

With the ending of the Cold War, the nations of western Europe, united under the umbrella of the European Union° (EU), moved to take on a much more important role in global affairs. We saw in Chapter 27 that the EU began in the 1950s as the Common Market or EEC (European Economic Community), an economic free-trade organization of six western European nations. By the end of the millennium, this organization had become a powerful entity possessing not only economic but also political clout, a potential counterweight to the United States.

During the 1970s and 1980s, the EEC widened both its membership and its areas of cooperation. Britain, Denmark, and Ireland joined in 1973, Greece in 1981, Spain and Portugal in 1986. (Austria, Finland, and Sweden joined in the 1990s.) In 1979, a European Parliament chosen directly by European voters met for the first time. Throughout these decades, the European Court of Justice gradually began to assert the primacy of the European Community over national law, thus pushing western Europe down the road toward political integration. The EEC—the European Economic Community—became the EC, or the European Community, a political and cultural as well as economic organization.

The pace of change accelerated in the 1980s and 1990s as the Single European Act of 1985 and the Maastricht Agreements of 1991 replaced the European *Community* (EC) with the European *Union* (EU), defined by France's President Mitterrand as "one currency, one culture, one social area, one environment." The establishment of the EU meant visible changes for ordinary Europeans. They saw their national passports replaced by a common EU document, and border controls eliminated. The creation of a single EU currency—the euro, which replaced national currencies in 2002—tore down one of the most significant economic barriers between European countries. At the same time, the powers of the European Parliament expanded and member states moved toward establishing common social policies (such as labor rights).

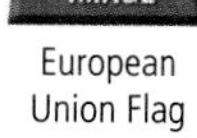

European Union Flag

While these developments occurred, Europeans also faced the unexpected challenge posed by the ending of the Cold War. Should the European Union (often called simply "Europe") now include East as well as West? Attracted by the undoubted prosperity of the EU, the nations of the former Soviet bloc answered that question with a resounding "yes." The leaders of western Europe, however, looked with trepidation at the prospect of joining their countries to eastern Europe's shattered economies and divided societies and drew up a list of rigorous qualifications for applicant nations. To be recognized as belonging to "Europe," nations applying for EU membership had to meet a set of complex financial requirements that demonstrated both the essential stability of their economies and their commitment to market capitalism. Thus "Europe" was defined, first of all, as capitalist. But a set of political requirements made clear that "Europe" also meant a commitment to democratic politics. Applicants' voting processes, treatment of minority groups, policing methods, and judicial systems were all scrutinized, as the EU used its considerable economic clout to nurture fledgling democratic structures in eastern Europe. In 2004, Estonia, Latvia, Lithuania, Poland, the Czech Republic, Slovakia, Slovenia, and Hungary, as well as Cyprus and Malta, all joined the EU (see Map 28.3).

Many Europeans greeted both the launch of the euro in 2002 and the dramatic expansion of the EU in 2004 as signs that the dream of a united Europe was being realized. Other Europeans, however, perceived this dream as a nightmare. "Euro-skeptics" questioned the economic value of unification. They pointed out that throughout the 1990s, the U.S. economy continued to outperform that of the EU, and European unemployment rates were often high. Britain, Denmark, and Sweden all refused to join the conversion to the euro, fearing that their economies would be dragged down by their slower-performing EU partners. Small traders and independent producers opposed the seemingly endless stream of orders and regulations issued by EU bureaucrats and the way in which economic integration privileged large, international firms over small, local shops. Many Europeans feared the growing political power of the EU and saw it as a threat to national sovereignty. Still others predicted that the expansion of the EU would mean the loss of jobs as western European firms moved eastward to take advantage of the lower wage rates and lax standard of work-

Map 28.3 Contemporary Europe
The revolutions of 1989 and their aftermath mark a clear turning point in European history, as a comparison of this map and that of "Europe in the Cold War" (p. 887) will show. Significant changes include the breakup of the Soviet Union and Yugoslavia, the replacement of Czechoslovakia by the Czech Republic and Slovakia, and the unification of Germany.

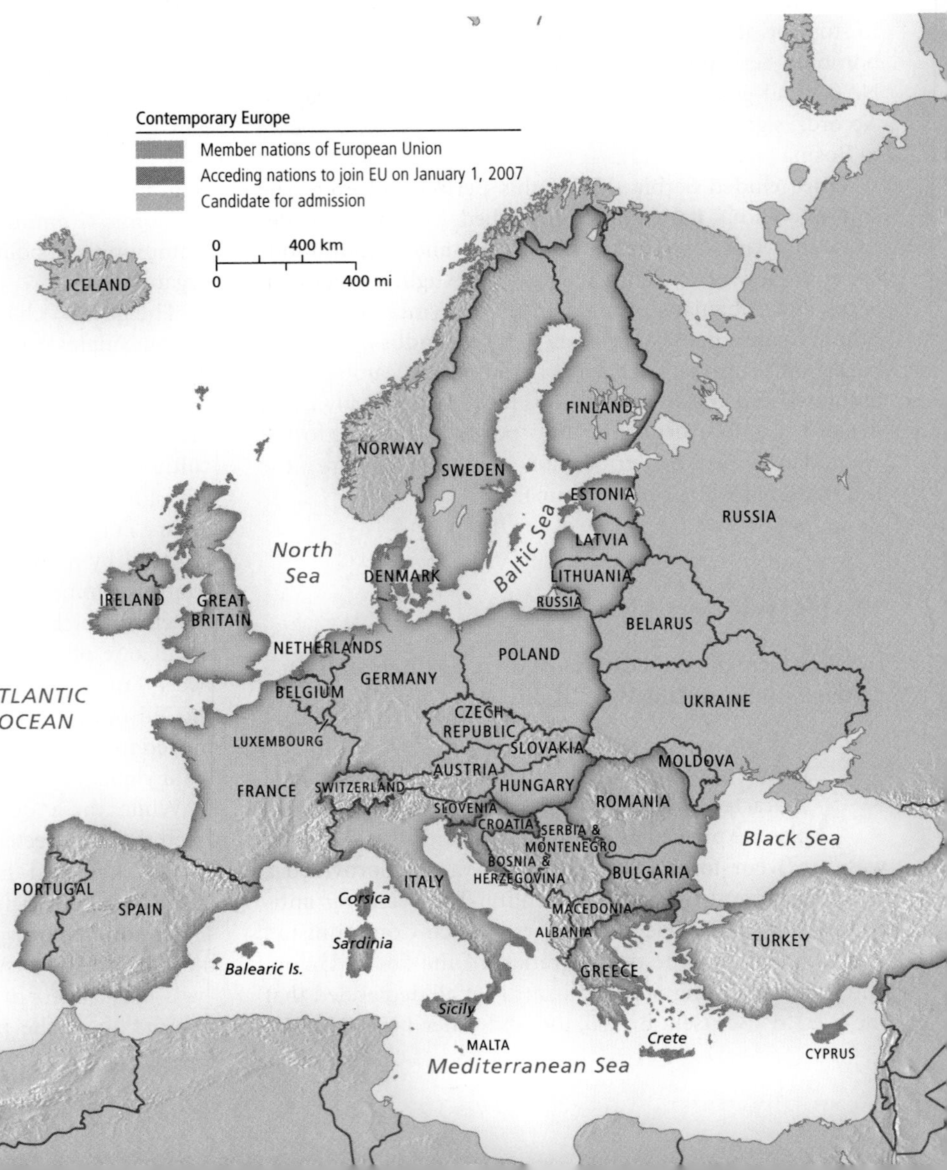

ers' protections in eastern Europe. All of these fears came into the open in the spring of 2005 when voters in both France and the Netherlands rejected a proposed EU constitution. These "no" votes from traditionally pro-EU states forced the shelving of the constitution and raised serious doubts about both the process and the pace of Europe's political and economic unification.

Islam, Terrorism, and European Identity

Significantly, the expansion of the EU in 2004 did not include Turkey. A member of NATO since 1952, Turkey first applied for associate membership in the EU (then the EEC) in 1959 but did not succeed in becoming an associate until 1991. In 2004 EU officials announced that talks on Turkey's entry as a full member would begin in 2005, but denied to the Turkish government any guarantees. A number of issues had frustrated Turkey's efforts to join the EU, including its refusal to recognize the independence of Cyprus, the clash between Turkey's repressive penal system and EU human rights legislation, and its poverty. If Turkey joined the EU, it would immediately become the most populous and the poorest member of the union. Opponents to Turkey's bid for membership feared that the European economy could not absorb the expected massive influx of impoverished Turkish migrant workers. They also, however, opposed full membership in "Europe" for Turkey because most Turks are Muslim, and for many Europeans, "European" and "Islamic" described clashing cultures.

Muslim Communities in Europe

The struggle over Turkish membership in the EU was just one of many controversies in contemporary Europe resulting from an ongoing battle to reconcile European identity with a growing Islamic cultural and political presence. By 2004, the number of European Muslims stood at 20 million—5 percent of the EU's population. Because the European Muslim birth rate is three times the non-Muslim birth rate, the percentage of Muslims within Europe is likely to continue to expand.

There is, of course, no single "Muslim Europe." In eastern European countries such as Bulgaria, Albania, and Bosnia, Muslims were part of the indigenous nation, the descendants of those who converted to Islam centuries earlier during the era of Ottoman rule. In western Europe, by contrast, most Muslims were immigrants or the children or grandchildren of immigrants, drawn to the West by greater economic and educational opportunities.

Even in western Europe, the Muslim experience varied. The majority of Britain's two million Muslims had roots in India or Pakistan, and thus received citizenship because of their Commonwealth inheritance; in contrast, until the passage of new citizenship laws in 2004, few of the three million Muslims living in Germany—most of them Turks or of Turkish descent—could claim the rights of citizenship. Many Muslims were highly educated and prosperous, but overall, the Muslim standard of living throughout Europe lagged behind that of non-Muslims: Muslims were far more likely to be unemployed; to work in low-paying, dead-end jobs; to live in substandard housing; and to possess fewer educational qualifications than their non-Muslim neighbors. Many of these "neighbors," however, lived far away, as Muslims, responding both to poverty and discrimination as well as their own desire to retain their distinct communities, tended to cluster in certain areas and cities, part of a subculture largely separate from and, in some cases, increasingly hostile to the majority culture. As minarets began to rival church steeples in the skylines of European cities, an increasing number of non-Muslim Europeans argued that Western culture itself was under threat. The decision of Iran's Ayatollah Khomeini to issue a death sentence against the British writer Salman Rushdie in 1989 forced many of these tensions and hostilities into the open but provided no easy answers to questions about Islamic, European, and Western identity.

Terrorism, the West, and the Middle East

Terrorism both deepened hostilities between Muslims and non-Muslims in the West and made the resolution of these hostilities even more urgent. This textbook has traced the way in which "the West" changed meaning, often in response to places and peoples defined as "not West." With the ending of the Cold War, the West lost its main enemy, but a replacement stood readily at hand. In 1996, the American president Bill Clinton (b. 1946) identified terrorism as "the enemy of our generation." In the post–Cold War world, terrorism in many ways replaced communism as the new foe against which the West defined itself. Many Europeans and Americans, however, not only viewed terrorism as "not West," they also linked "terrorism" with "Islam."

Terrorism directly opposes what many now regard as the bedrock of Western culture—a commitment to democracy and the rule of the law. Because terrorists seek to achieve political ends through violence and intimidation, terrorism short-circuits the democratic process: Decision-making shifts from the ballot box to the bomb. Yet the equation of the West with law and democracy conveniently ignores the history of the West and of terrorism itself. Together with fascism and Nazism, terrorism is one of the less savory products of Western political culture. Terrorism grew out of late nineteenth-century anarchism, which advocated violence as a means of political change (see Chapter 22). Like the assassins who killed Tsar Alexander II in 1881, contemporary terrorists belonged to groups lacking access to political power. Unable to achieve their goals through political persuasion (lobbying, campaigning, winning votes), they endeavored to destabilize the societies they opposed through acts of terror. In the twentieth century, thwarted

Justice in History

The Sentencing of Salman Rushdie

In February 1989, the Ayatollah Khomeini, political leader of Iran and spiritual head of the Shi'a Muslim community, issued a death sentence against the novelist Salman Rushdie and offered an award of $2.5 million to any faithful Muslim who killed him. Rushdie, a British citizen who had never been tried in any Iranian or Islamic court, immediately went into hiding, where he remained for several years. His death sentence ignited the "Satanic Verses Affair," a tumultuous international crisis caused by a resounding clash of cultural assumptions and expectations.

The crisis centered on a book. In the early autumn of 1988 Viking Penguin published Rushdie's *The Satanic Verses,* a difficult novel about the complexities and contradictions of the modern immigrant experience. Born in India and raised in an Islamic home, Rushdie wrote *The Satanic Verses* to describe "migration, metamorphosis, divided selves, love, death, London, and Bombay."[9] The novel received immediate critical acclaim, with reviewers praising it as an astonishing work of postmodernist fiction.

Other readers judged it differently. Many Muslims around the world regarded the book as a direct attack on the foundations of their religious faith. One scene in the novel particularly horrified devout Muslims. In this episode, the central character has a psychotic breakdown and falls into a dream: Muhammad appears as a corrupt businessman, and prostitutes in a brothel take on the names of the Prophet's wives.

The novel aroused intense controversy from the moment of its publication. The government of India banned it almost immediately; within a matter of weeks, several other states followed suit. Anti-Rushdie demonstrations in both India and Pakistan turned violent, resulting in fifteen deaths. Bookstores selling the novel received bombing and death threats. In western Europe, hostilities between Muslims and non-Muslims intensified. Then, on February 14, 1989, an announcer on Radio Tehran read aloud the text of a *fatwa,* or decree, issued by the Ayatollah Khomeini:

> *I would like to inform all the intrepid Muslims of the world that the author of the book entitled* The Satanic Verses, *which has been compiled, printed and published in opposition to Islam, the Prophet and the Koran, as well as those publishers who were aware of its contents, have been sentenced to death. I call on all zealous Muslims to execute them quickly, wherever they find them. . . . Whoever is killed on this path will be regarded as a martyr, God willing.*

Western governments reacted quickly against Khomeini's call for Rushdie's death. The twelve nations of the European Community, the United States, Sweden, Norway, Canada, Australia, and Brazil all condemned Khomeini's judgment, recalled their ambassadors from Tehran, and cancelled high-level diplomatic contacts with Iran. British prime minister Margaret Thatcher provided police protection for Rushdie and dismissed British Muslim demands to ban the book: "It is an essential part of our democratic system that people who act within the law should be able to express their opinions freely."[10]

Large numbers of Muslims, including many who spoke out against Rushdie's book, also condemned Khomeini's fatwa. Some Muslim scholars contended that the Ayatollah's fatwa was a scholarly opinion, not a legally binding judgment; others argued that Rushdie could not be condemned without a trial, or that because Rushdie lived in a society without an Islamic government, he was not bound by Islamic law.

But many ordinary Muslims ignored these high-level theological and legal disputes and greeted the Ayatollah's fatwa with delight. The news of the Ayatollah's fatwa brought crowds of cheering Muslims into the city streets. In Manchester and Bradford, young British Muslim men insisted they would kill Rushdie if given the chance. In Paris, demonstrators marched to cries of "We are all Khomeinists!"

Why did Khomeini's fatwa arouse such popular enthusiasm within Western Muslim communities? A partial answer to this question is that many Muslims were frustrated with what they regarded as the unequal application of the laws of censorship. Faced with what they saw as a hate-filled, pornographic caricature of Islam, they demanded that Western governments use the laws censoring pornography and banning hate crimes to block the publication of Rushdie's book. In Britain, Muslims were particularly outraged that the existing law against blasphemy protected only Christianity, the official state religion.

But the controversy was not simply a dispute about censorship. For some Muslims, Rushdie's *Satanic Verses* epitomized Western secular society, with its scant regard for tradition or religious values. As Dr. Kalim Siddiqui of the pro-Iranian Muslim Institute in Britain proclaimed, "western civilization is fundamentally an immoral civilization. Its 'values' are free of moral constraints."[11] From this perspective, Khomeini's fatwa condemned not just one book or one author, but an entire culture that seemed inherently opposed to Islam. Khomeini had already proven himself a forceful leader in the Iranian hostage crisis of 1979–1980, when he successfully thumbed his nose at American power. Now once again he seemed willing to take on the West to defend Islam.

The anti-Western stance of some radical Muslims was mirrored by the anti-Islam position soon occupied by some Rushdie supporters. In one of the most ironic twists in the entire Satanic Verses Affair, Rushdie's books, which condemned the endemic racism in British society and exposed the falsehood of Western claims to cultural superiority, were championed by individuals who articulated precisely the sort of Western cultural chauvinism against which Rushdie had written so passionately. For example, Robert Maxwell, a multimillionaire communications tycoon, offered $10 million to any individual "who will, not kill, but civilise the barbarian Ayatollah" by forcing him to recite publicly the Ten Commandments.[12] Many western Europeans agreed with the conclusion drawn in this letter to a British daily newspaper: "The lesson of the Rushdie affair is that it was unwise to let Muslim communities establish themselves in our midst."[13] The lines were drawn, with Islam standing for irrationalism, barbarity, intolerance, and ignorance, while the "West" was linked to democracy, reason, freedom, and civilization. At precisely the moment when the crumbling of communism and the ending of the Cold War deprived the West of one of its defining attributes, the Satanic Verses Affair offered up a new Other against which the West could define itself.

Questions of Justice

1. On what grounds are publications censored in secular, Western societies? Given the existence of this censorship, should Rushdie's book have been banned?
2. In what ways does the Satanic Verses Affair illuminate the tensions within many European societies from the 1970s on, as communities struggled to adapt to the challenges of ethnic and religious diversity?

Taking It Further

Bowen, David G., ed. *The Satanic Verses: Bradford Responds.* 1996. This collection of essays and documents helps explains why many British Muslims viewed the British government's failure to censor Rushdie's book as an act of injustice.

A Clash of Cultures?
In London, a policeman chases a demonstrator during a protest against the publication of *The Satanic Verses.*

nationalism provided especially fertile soil for the growth of terrorism. In Northern Ireland, assassinations and bombings became commonplace after the Irish Republican Army (IRA) turned to terror to pressure the British government to relinquish its control over the province. In Spain, the Basque separatist group Eta has for three decades waged a campaign of terror to achieve its aim of an independent Basque state. Terrorism is thus one of the negative aspects of "Western civilization." Yet by the 1990s, terrorism was often perceived as the antithesis of the West, as an outside threat, usually bearing an Arabic face and carrying a copy of the Qur'an.

Terrorist activity sparked by the Palestinian-Israeli conflict helped create this perception. Frustrated by the failure of the United Nations to implement its 1947 resolution promising a Palestinian state, Palestinian nationalists (most but not all of whom were Muslim) in 1964 formed the Palestine Liberation Organization (PLO). Like the IRA in Northern Ireland or Eta in Spain, the PLO saw violence as the only means to its nationalist ends. The PLO's commitment to terrorism deepened after the Six-Day War of 1967, which (as we saw in Chapter 27) led to Israel occupying East Jerusalem, the West Bank, and the Golan Heights. During subsequent decades the PLO took its campaign of terror around the world, bombing airports, targeting tourists, and persuading many in the West that "Arab," "Muslim," and "terrorist" were interchangeable terms.

At the same time, U.S. support for Israel convinced many Muslims that "the West" (often equated simply with the United States) was an enemy. Between 1949 and 1998, Israel received more American aid than any other country. As Israel went on the offensive against not only Palestinian terrorism but also popular Palestinian uprisings in the 1980s and 1990s (the first and second "intifadahs"), Palestinians and their supporters argued that the United States was bankrolling a repressive regime, and that Israel was a Western colonialist outpost (see Map 28.4).

Islamism and the West

Western perceptions of a link between Islam and terrorism were further strengthened by the development of Islamism°. Also called Islamic fundamentalism or *jihadism* (after the Islamic idea of "jihad," or holy war), Islamism is explicitly anti-Western—and is rejected by most Muslims as a corruption or negation of Islamic values. Islamism views Western culture as a threat to Islamic identity; regards the United States as the standard-bearer of the West and thus as a particular enemy of Muslim interests; and accepts violence, including the murder of civilians, as an acceptable means to its ends.

A confluence of developments helped swell the Islamist tide. Modernity itself created in its wake a fundamentalist surge, not only within Islam but within other religious traditions such as Christianity and Hinduism. In times of often confusing change and growing secularization, men and women sought clear answers and the guarantee of order through rigid religious systems. This guarantee of order particularly appealed to the children of Muslim immigrants in western Europe. Many in this generation, young men in particular, felt betrayed by the cultures in which they lived. Their ongoing struggle against poverty, discrimination, and disempowerment turned many European Muslims toward Islamism.

Ayatollah Khomeini's Vision of Islamic Government

A series of international developments also nourished Islamism. First, the West's willingness during the Cold War to prop up unpopular and corrupt governments turned the Western promise of democracy into a sham for many Muslims. In Iran, for example, the United States supported the autocratic regime of the Shah. In 1979 a popular revolution vaulted into power the Ayatollah Khomeini (1901–1989), who rapidly reversed the westernizing and modernizing policies of the Shah and decried the United States as the "Great Satan."

The Gulf War of 1991 sharpened these hostilities. In this conflict American and British forces led a twenty-eight-country coalition in a military intervention to drive invading Iraqi forces out of tiny but oil-rich Kuwait. The war itself could not be construed as "the West versus Islam" or "the West versus the East": One Arab and Islamic country had invaded another. But in the aftermath of the war, U.S. forces remained in American-controlled bases in Saudi Arabia, home of some of the most holy sites in Islam. For Islamists, the presence of the United States in this region both sullied Islamic purity and insulted Arabic political independence.

Finally, the wars in both Bosnia and Chechnya fed Islamist hatred of the West. The initial passivity of both western Europe and the United States while Muslim men and boys were slaughtered and Muslim women and girls raped during the Bosnian war of 1992–1995 convinced many European Muslims that Western governments had an anti-Muslim agenda. This perception grew stronger when western states refused to back the Chechens (who are Muslim) in what many view as the Chechen war of independence against Russian oppression, ongoing from 1994.

Significantly, many Islamists viewed Russia as part of the West against which they were fighting. The predominantly Muslim states of the Caucasus had a long history of fighting against Russian rule, and Soviet communism had been no more tolerant of Islam than it had been of Judaism or Christianity. Most important, however, was yet another recent war: the Soviet-Afghan War of 1979–1989. To Islamists, the Afghan guerillas fighting both the pro-Soviet Afghan regime and the Soviet army came to represent the wider struggle to free Islam from Western control and purify it from Western corruption. More practically, many Islamists received military training in this conflict.

Ironically, many of these Islamist rebels in Afghanistan were supported by the United States. Soviet troops withdrew from Afghanistan in defeat in 1989. The pro-Soviet Afghan government collapsed, and after a period of turmoil, the Taliban, a revolutionary Islamist group, seized control.

Events in Afghanistan seemed a long way away from Europe and the United States—until September 11, 2001, when Islamists declared open war on the West in one of the most deadly episodes of terrorism yet seen. Three jets hijacked by Islamist terrorists (most of them Saudi) smashed into the World Trade Center in New York City and the Pentagon (the U.S. military headquarters in Washington, D.C.), while a fourth crashed in Pennsylvania. Almost 3,000 people died. U.S. and European intelligence officers quickly linked the suicide pilots to Al Qaeda, an Islamist terrorist organization run by Osama bin Laden, a wealthy Saudi exile. Evidence of ideological and financial links between bin Laden and the Taliban led the United States to begin air attacks against Afghanistan in October 2001. The Taliban regime fell within weeks, but bin Laden remained at large and the "war against terror" continued.

In March 2003, this widely ranging war took a new turn when U.S. and British forces attacked Iraq. No direct connection linked Osama bin Laden to Iraq's government,

Map 28.4 The Middle East in the Contemporary Era
Although placed under Palestinian self-rule in 1994, the West Bank and Gaza Strip remain contested areas, sites of frequent confrontations between Palestinians and Israelis.

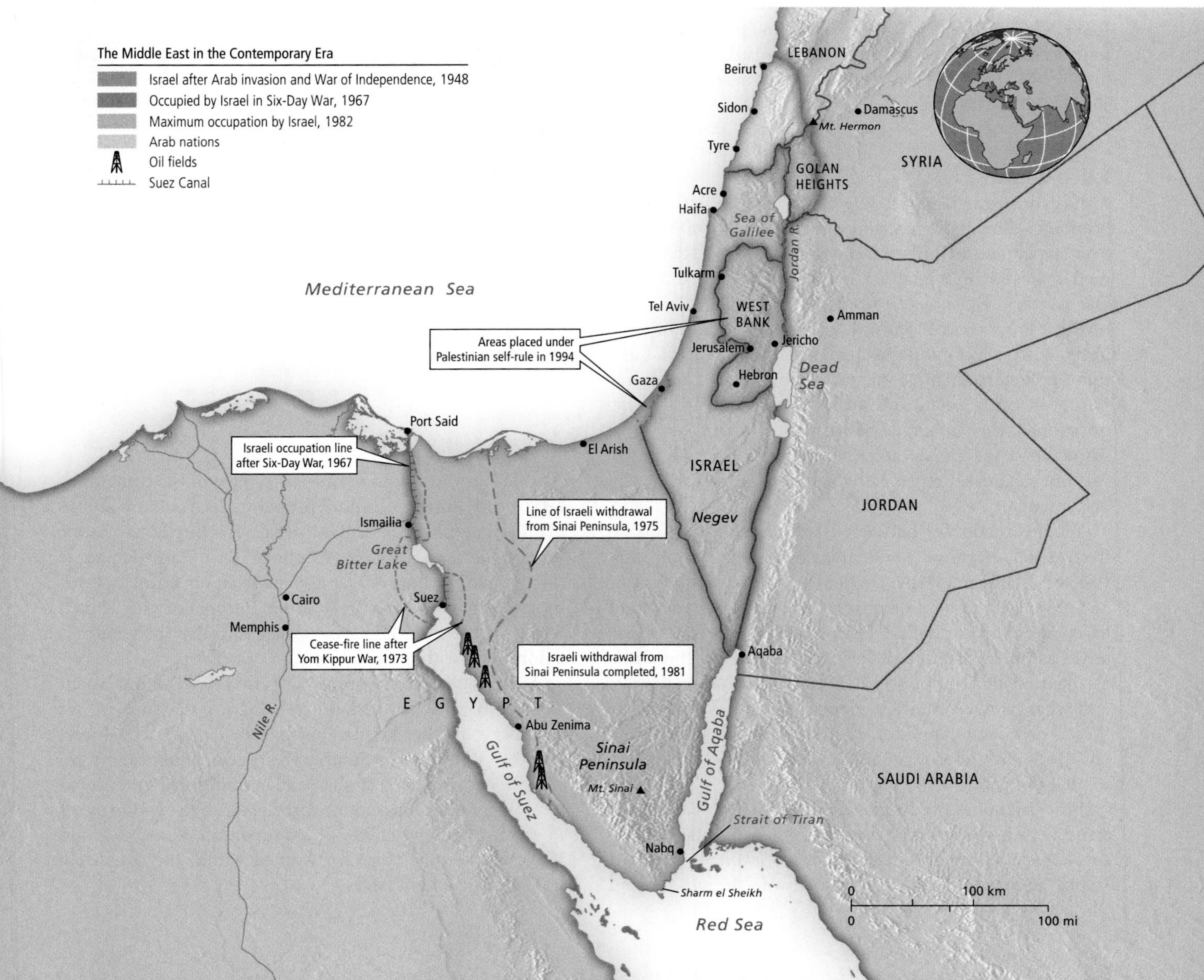

which was firmly controlled by Saddam Hussein, a secular dictator with a long history of torturing and killing Islamists like bin Laden who threatened his personal power. But in the world after "9/11," Saddam Hussein's refusal to allow UN inspections of his weapons factories convinced both the American and British governments that Iraq possessed the ability to launch a terrorist strike, in the form of biological or chemical weapons, against Western targets. The result was the first preemptive war ever waged by U.S. forces and, after a three-week conflict involving both air strikes and land battles, the toppling of Saddam Hussein's dictatorial regime. Many Iraqis cheered the dictator's overthrow, but other Iraqis—and many Arabs in the surrounding states—condemned the Anglo-American intervention as yet another episode in a long history of Western imperial intrusions on Arab territory.

The war in Iraq proved controversial, especially after Al Qaeda demonstrated its continuing ability to carry out lethal terrorist attacks. On the third anniversary of "9/11"—September 11, 2004—almost 200 people died after four bombs exploded on commuter trains during the rush hour in Madrid. Al Qaeda linked the bombing to Spain's support of the Iraq war.

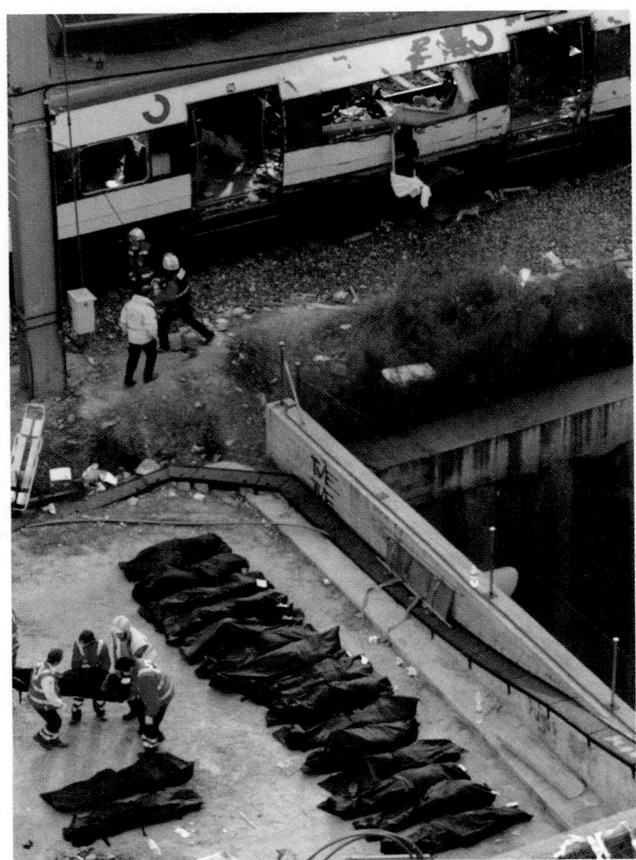

The Terrorist Age: Madrid, March 11, 2004
On March 11, 2004, a series of bombs ripped through four commuter trains in the Spanish capital city. Al Qaeda claimed responsibility for the attack, which killed 191 people and injured more than 1,500.

Euro-Islam

Almost one year later, on July 7, 2005, a similar spate of bombings during the morning rush hour in London killed over 50 people and injured more than 700. Significantly, the men involved in this attack were not only linked to Al Qaeda, they were also British. The London bombings revealed the power of Islamism within the West itself. Thus, in the wake of 9/11 and the attacks that followed, the question of Western identity was more troublesome than ever. European and American Muslims found their loyalties questioned, their religious beliefs regarded as grounds for suspicion. The long, complex history of Islam in the West was often ignored, replaced by a simplistic "Them" versus "Us" mentality.

Yet the encounter between Islam and Europe was far from wholly negative. The majority of European Muslims rejected Islamism. Many, particularly those of the second and third generations of immigrant families, endeavored to create a new identity: Euro-Islam°. Regarding themselves as fully Muslim and fully European, these individuals insisted that no contradiction existed between Islam and what many Westerners view as the core values of the West—democratic politics, respect for individual differences, and civil liberties guaranteed by law to all, regardless of race and gender.

Euro-Islam has produced significant theological innovations within the Islamic community. Traditional Islamic theology cuts the world into two: *dar al-Islam,* or "house of Islam," and *dar al-harb,* or "house of war." In *dar-al-Islam,* Islamic law prevails. In *dar-al-harb* (most of the contemporary world), Muslims cannot properly practice Islam and so live in a state of constant spiritual war. But Euro-Islamic proponents such as the Swiss scholar Tariq Ramadan argue there is a third "house": *dar ash-shahada,* or "house of testimony," regions—such as western Europe or the United States—where Muslims can profess and live their faith in community with non-Muslims.

European Muslim women have also played an important role in shaping Euro-Islam. Muslim women such as the members of the French group *Ni Putes Ni Soumises* (Neither Whores Nor Submissives) have been at the forefront of campaigns to eradicate such traditional practices as female circumcision and the forced marriage of young girls to men from their parents' or grandparents' homelands and to claim an equal place for women within the context of both Europe and of Islam.

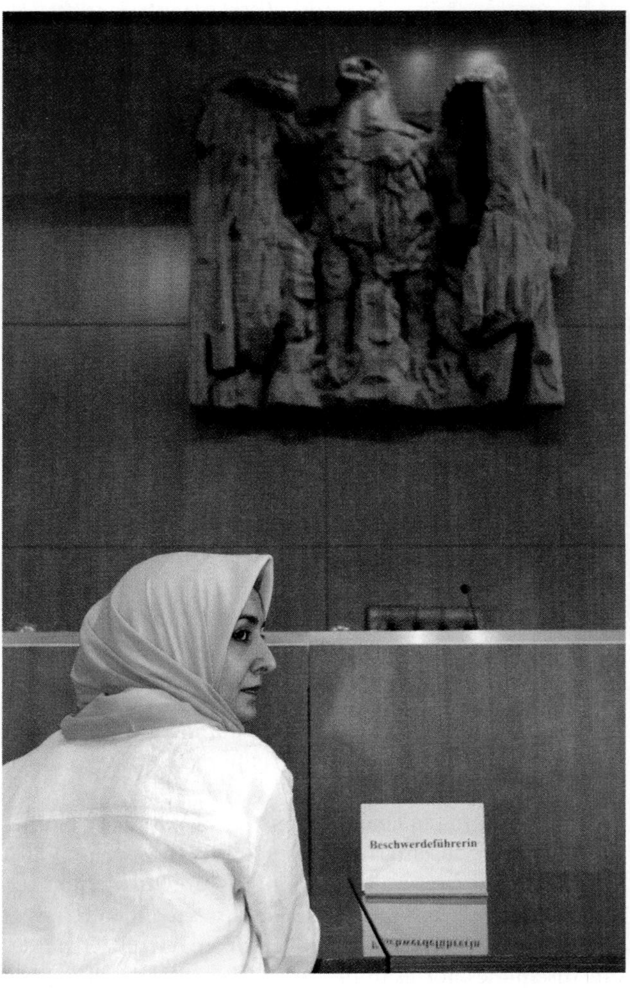

An Identity Struggle
In the wake of 9/11, European Muslims fought to assert their Western identity. Symbols became particularly important; this teacher won her battle in German courts to wear her Islamic head scarf in the classroom of a state school. In France, however, Islamic girls in head scarves were not permitted in schoolrooms.

Into the Postmodern Era

The end of the Cold War, the formation of the European Union, and the growth of significant Muslim communities within western Europe all demanded a reevaluation and redefinition of West. So, too, did a number of intellectual, artistic, and technological developments that together helped created the postmodern era. A grab-bag term covering a huge array of styles and stances, postmodernism° at its core constitutes the rejection of Western cultural supremacy and, more particularly, a challenge to the idea that Western science and rationality had constructed a single, universally applicable form of "modernity."

The Making of the Postmodern

Postmodernism resulted from the joining of three specific intellectual and cultural streams: postmodernist architecture, postmodernist art, and the literary theories of poststructuralism.

Postmodernism first clearly took form in architecture, perhaps because the failures of modernist architecture were so obvious by the early 1970s. Motivated by an intense faith in both human rationality and modern technology, modernist architects had sought to build new forms of housing that they believed would enable people to live better, more beautiful lives. But the concrete high-rises they constructed failed to connect with the needs and emotions of their inhabitants, and many became derelict, crime-ridden, graffiti-scarred tenements.

Faced with this sense of failure, a new generation—the postmodernists—insisted that architects needed to start communicating with ordinary people. The American architect Charles Jencks (b. 1939) argued that because people tend to rely on the familiar to make sense of their world, modernism was wrong to reject traditional forms. For example, most Europeans and Americans connect domestic housing with gabled roofs (ask a child to draw a picture of a house and see if he or she draws a flat roof). Was it surprising, Jencks asked, that the concrete rectangles used by modernists for housing proved profoundly alienating to many people? Postmodernist *anti-elitism* thus led to *eclecticism,* to re-creating and combining forms and styles from past eras (such as gabled roofs), and to efforts to revive local and regional styles. Why should the streets of Tokyo look like the center of London or downtown Chicago? Instead, postmodernists embraced an architecture rooted in the specifics of time and place. In addition to being anti-elitist and eclectic, then, postmodernist architecture was also *anti-universalist:* It condemned modernism for its assumption that the same modern (and Western) ideals and forms fit all individuals and all societies.

The same sorts of criticism of modernism surfaced in the art world, as the wider political context of the late 1960s and early 1970s transformed the visual arts in three ways. First, in the wake of the protests of 1968, artists—many coming out of left-wing activist environments—rejected ideologies based on hierarchy and authority. This rejection led to an attack on the modernist idea of the "avant-garde," a small elite of artistic geniuses fighting to advance the frontiers of aesthetic excellence. Even more than their modernist predecessors, postmodernist artists celebrated the possibilities of the mass media and condemned distinctions between "high" and popular culture. Second, the experience of political protest led many artists to reject the modernist ideal of "art for art's sake," insisting instead that art had to say something to the world around it. To communicate with a wider public, they plundered both the past and popular culture for familiar forms and material. As the art critic

Postmodernism at Play
Designed by the American architect Frank Gehry and his Czech collaborator Vlado Mulunić, the "Dancing Building" fills a bomb site left vacant in central Prague since World War II. Also called "Fred and Ginger" (after the famous Hollywood dancing duo Fred Astaire and Ginger Rogers), this postmodernist piece both delighted and enraged the people of Prague.

Edit DeAk explained, postmodernist art relied on "the shock of recognition instead of the shock of the new."[14] Finally, feminism proved crucial in shaping the new art. Women began to challenge the dominance of men in the art world not only by highlighting the systematic exclusion of women from gallery and museum exhibitions, but also by questioning the aesthetic hierarchy that relegated to the lower status of "craft" traditionally female art forms such as weaving.

By the end of the 1970s, postmodernist practices in art and architecture both were reinforced by and in turn strengthened a growing body of literary and cultural theory often called *poststructuralism.* The theory of poststructuralism centered on the work of an assorted group of French thinkers whose ideas were taken up in American universities and then filtered back into European intellectual circles. These thinkers included Jacques Derrida (1930–2004) and Roland Barthes (1915–1980) in literary studies, Michel Foucault (1926–1984) in history, and Jacques Lacan (1901–1981) in psychoanalytic theory.

Like postmodernist theories in architecture and art, poststructuralism began as an exploration into the problems of communication. Jacques Derrida argued that the world we see and experience is a world structured by language—we cannot even understand or express our very selves apart from language. But because there is no inherent match between a word (what Derrida called a "signifier") and the thing or idea to which that word refers (the "signified"), communication is never straightforward. An endless variety of meanings and interpretations results, and thus, Derrida argued, we must abandon the idea of a fixed or single truth, of ultimate or universal meaning. In a related argument, Roland Barthes declared the "Death of the Author," by which he meant that the purpose of literary study is not to ask, "What does the author mean?" but instead to explore the way in which the reader creates his or her own meanings.

This effort to challenge any center of authority (sometimes called "decentering") linked the poststructuralist concern with communication to its analysis of power. Michel Foucault and Jacques Lacan dissected hierarchies of authority (not only in the political sphere but also in academic disciplines, for example, or in the medical world), and the way these authorities created and manipulated seemingly objective bodies of knowledge to retain their hold on power.

Postmodernism in its most general form emerged by the later 1980s out of the blending of these poststructuralist theories of communication and power with the critique of modernism already flourishing in architecture and the arts. Thinkers, writers, and artists argued that Western elites had shaped global culture and had ignored or distorted the cultures of non-Western and minority groups. This view of culture as bound up in a global contest for power disturbed many more traditional thinkers (with "modernist" now increasingly perceived as traditional) who continued to insist that criteria of aesthetic excellence ("Beauty") and objective standards of knowledge ("Truth") did exist. These critics warned that cultural "decentering" would destroy the social cohesion and political stability of the West.

Postmodern Cultures and Postindustrial Technologies

In many ways popular culture confirmed postmodern theories. In Britain, for example, the "Big Beat" songs that dominated the club scene in the late 1990s were produced not by vocalists or instrumentalists but by disc jockeys who lifted snatches from old records, played them at different speeds, and combined them with contrasting styles. Like postmodernist paintings, Big Beat contained chunks of the past, recycled in startling new ways. More generally, a series of technological developments meant that popular culture was clearly "decentered," that at the very least a multitude of popular cultures coexisted and that the individual consumer of culture, like Barthes's reader, was free to make meaning as he or she chose. The videocassette recorder (VCR), first marketed in 1975, not only transported film viewing from the public to the private sphere, it also provided the film viewer with the possibility to tailor the film to his or her own preferences—to adjust the volume or choose another soundtrack entirely, to omit or fast-forward through certain scenes, to replay others endlessly. Similarly, the proliferation of cable and satellite television stations during the 1980s and 1990s fragmented the viewing audience and made it impossible to speak of popular culture in the singular.

Postmodernist concerns with communication and codes, with the way in which interpretations can be endlessly modified, and with the abolition of a single center of authority certainly seemed appropriate for an era that many called "the Information Age" and others called the postindustrial society°. The industrial phase of economic development had been characterized by an emphasis on production. But in the postindustrial phase, the *making* of things becomes less important than the *marketing* of them. A postindustrial society, in fact, is characterized less by *things* in general than by *images, ideas, and information.*

If the factory symbolized industrial society, then the epitome of the postindustrial era is the home computer, with its capacity to disperse information, market products, and endlessly duplicate yet constantly alter visual and verbal images. By the end of the 1990s, relatively inexpensively priced home computers gave their users access to libraries, art galleries, and retail outlets from across the world, and provided, for entrepreneurs, the opportunity to make (and lose) enormous fortunes by exploiting this new image-oriented means of marketing products and information—all without any central regulating authority. Governments scrambled desperately to impose control on the proliferating technologies of the postindustrial age, but in true postmodern fashion the centers of authority broke down. Existing laws that regulated pornography, for example, proved difficult to apply to the Internet, the vast global communications web.

Similarly, developments in medical technologies raised important questions about authority and ownership. In 1978, Louise Brown was born in Britain, the world's first "test-tube baby." Over the next twenty years, assisted fertility treatment resulted in the births of more than a million babies. As the technology grew more sophisticated, so too did the ethical and political questions. Societies struggled to determine the legality of practices such as commercial surrogate motherhood, in which a woman rents her womb to a couple, and postmenopausal motherhood, in which a woman past childbearing age is implanted with a fertilized egg.

Genetic research provoked even more debate about which authorities or what principles should guide scientific research. In 1997, British scientists introduced the world to Dolly the sheep, the first mammal cloned from an adult. Many scientists declared that the cloning of human beings, long part of science fiction and horror stories, was inevitable, even if declared immoral by religious leaders and illegal by political authorities. The announcement in February 2001 that the human genome had been decoded—that scientists had mapped the sequencing of the human genome, or set of instructions in every cell in the human body—immediately raised such questions as, Who owns this information? Who has the authority to decide how it is to be used?

CHRONOLOGY

Medical Challenges and Achievements

1977	First diagnosed case of AIDS
1978	First test-tube baby
1980	Worldwide eradication of smallpox
1982	First use of genetic engineering (insulin manufactured from bacteria)
1983	First artificially created chromosome
1984	HIV identified
1985	First use of laser surgery to clear blocked arteries
1997	Successful cloning of sheep
2001	Human genome decoded

Postmodern Patterns in Religious Life

Postmodern patterns—the fragmentation of cultures, the collapse of centers of authority, the supremacy of image—also characterized Western religious faith and practice after the 1970s. Christianity no longer served as a common cultural bond. In a time of increasing immigration and cultural diversity, Islam was the fastest-growing religious community in western Europe. In Britain, Muslims outnumbered Methodists by two to one. By the end of the twentieth century, established Protestant churches in western Europe faced a serious crisis, with regular churchgoers now a small minority of the population—less than 5 percent in most countries. The decline of the mainline churches in the United States was also dramatic, although a greater percentage of Americans—25 to 30 percent—attended church regularly. Religious faith became a private matter, the mark of subcultures (often defined by an "Us versus Them" mentality), rather than a bond tying together individuals and groups into a cohesive national culture.

At the same time, however, the long-reigning Pope John Paul II (r. 1978–2005) experienced unprecedented popularity. The most well-traveled and populist-oriented of twentieth-century popes, John Paul II became a media star, met with the same sort of cheering crowds and tee-shirt vendors that accompanied famous rock bands. Much of his popularity rested on his intimate connection with Poland's Solidarity, and therefore with an image of liberation. Born Karol Wojtyla, John Paul was the first non-Italian pope since 1523 and the first-ever Polish pope. Twelve million people—one-third of the Polish population—greeted him in Warsaw in 1979 when he made the first visit by any pope to a communist country. Many Solidarity members testified to the importance of this visit in empowering them to challenge the political order fourteen months later. But the pope's support for Solidarity did not mean he supported other forms of rebellion against authority. Opposing the promise of continuing change inherent in Vatican II (see Chapter 27), John Paul II adopted a thoroughly authoritarian approach to church government and took an uncompromising stand against birth control, married clergy, and the ordination of women. Confronted with the postmodernist message that authority had fragmented and that no universal truth existed, many Christians found the pope's uncompromising stand a source of great comfort.

Yet the papacy of John Paul II confirmed as well as contradicted postmodernist ideas; much of the pope's popularity was based on image rather than authority. Despite censoring liberal Catholic theologians, the pope was unable to bring into line an increasingly rebellious flock throughout Europe and the United States. In the United States, millions turned out to cheer the pope waving from an open car (the "popemobile"), yet the percentage of American Catholics using birth control—in direct violation of papal teachings—mirrored that of the population at large. By the 1980s, Catholic Italy boasted the second-lowest birth rate in the world (after China), with the one-child family becoming the norm. It was hard to avoid the conclusion that in much of Western Roman Catholicism, as in much of postmodern society, image ruled while authority dissipated.

The Global Challenge

At the same time that postmodern artists and theorists were questioning the validity of Western cultural forms, economic and environmental developments called into doubt other key assumptions of Western societies. Both the globalization of market capitalism and a worldwide environmental crisis crashed down national borders, limited the scope of action open to individual governments, and raised significant questions about the ecological sustainability of Western habits of consumption.

The Global Economy

In the 1990s, a number of technological and economic developments helped make national borders even more permeable and accelerated the globalization of economic production. Personal computers, fax machines, and wireless telephones all ensured that "the office" could be anywhere. Fiber-optic cables that transmitted signals 4,000 times faster than their copper predecessors made instant communication across national boundaries a reality.

Technological innovations demanded organizational change. In the postindustrial economy, firms had to be more flexible, able to respond immediately to rapidly changing markets and technologies. They did not want too much capital investment in one way of doing things, in one kind of machinery, in one labor force, in one stock of supplies. Rather than economies of scale, they looked for other economies, such as subcontracting, outsourcing, and downsizing. The worker became more vulnerable. Concepts such as "a job for life" or "loyalty to the firm" had little relevance as companies merged and fragmented, shedding large number of workers in the endless pursuit of efficiency and the competitive edge. In this global economy, multinational corporations, with quick access to cheap Third World labor and raw materials, possessed significant economic power. In 2000, corporations such as ExxonMobil and DaimlerChrysler had annual revenues that exceeded the GDP of Norway or Singapore.

Increasingly, however, it was the far more nebulous "markets" that dictated the course of economic and political affairs across the world. In the 1990s, the volatility that had characterized the global economy since the collapse of the Bretton Woods Agreement in 1973 (see Chapter 27) became even more intense as currency speculators moved their money in and out of currency markets with astonishing rapidity, and with often devastating consequences for the countries involved. In 1997, for example, Thailand was forced to devalue its currency, and the economic catastrophe of collapsing currencies and stock markets quickly spread to Indonesia, Malaysia, the Philippines, and South Korea. By 1998, the Japanese economy had slid into serious recession.

As the Asian economic crisis of the later 1990s revealed, "the markets," rather than elected leaders, played an increasingly important role in determining a country's path. So, too, did the dictates of the World Bank and the IMF, the institutions that directed the flow of aid and loans throughout much of the world. The IMF, for example, insisted that governments receiving loans follow the orthodoxy of "austerity"—cutting government spending on social and welfare programs and restricting the flow of money supply to reduce inflation. Thus economists in offices far away, not

DOCUMENT

The West and the Rest

In 1998, economic historian David Landes published The Wealth and Poverty of Nations: Why Some Are So Rich and Some So Poor. *Landes, a professor at Harvard University, had been writing on the history of industrial and technological change since the 1950s. Now he turned his attention to the present and endeavored to answer one of the most pressing problems of the contemporary era. His introduction laid out the key issues.*

The old division of the world into two power blocs, East and West, has subsided. Now the big challenge and threat is the gap in wealth and health that separates the rich and poor. These are often styled North and South, because the division is geographic; but a more accurate signifier would be the West and the Rest, because the division is also historic. Here is the greatest single problem and danger facing the world of the Third Millennium. The only other worry that comes close is environmental deterioration, and the two are intimately connected, indeed are one. They are one because wealth entails not only consumption but also waste, not only production but also destruction. It is this waste and destruction, which has increased enormously with output and income, that threatens the space we live and move in.

How big is the gap between rich and poor and what is happening to it? Very roughly and briefly: the difference in income per head between the richest industrial nation, say Switzerland, and the poorest nonindustrial country, Mozambique, is about 400 to 1. Two hundred and fifty years ago, this gap between richest and poorest was perhaps 5 to 1, and the difference between Europe and, say, East or South Asia (China or India) was around 1.5 or 2 to 1.

. . . Our task (the rich countries), in our own interest as well as theirs, is to help the poor become healthier and wealthier. If we do not, they will seek to take what they cannot make; and if they cannot earn by exporting commodities, they will export people. In short, wealth is an irresistible magnet; and poverty is a potentially raging contaminant: it cannot be segregated, and our peace and prosperity depend in the long run on the well-being of others.

. . . the best way to understand a problem is to ask: How and why did we get where we are? How did the rich countries get so rich? Why are the poor countries so poor? Why did Europe ("the West") take the lead in changing the world?

A historical approach does not ensure an answer. Others have thought about these matters and come up with diverse explanations. Most of these fall into two schools. Some see Western wealth and dominion as the triumph of good over bad. The Europeans, they say, were smarter, better organized, harder working; the others were ignorant, arrogant, lazy, backward, superstitious. Others invert the categories. The Europeans, they say, were aggressive, ruthless, greedy, unscrupulous, hypocritical; their victims were happy, innocent, weak—waiting victims and hence thoroughly victimized. . . . both of these manichean visions have elements of truth, as well as of ideological fantasy. Things are always more complicated than we would have them.

elected leaders, called the shots. Moreover, both the World Bank and the IMF embodied the characteristic Western confidence of the postwar era. Local traditions and leaders were ignored, replaced instead by outside economists and agronomists who believed that an infusion of Western economic and technological expertise would set the rest of the world on the path to economic growth.

By the 1990s, the widening gap between "North" and "South," the rich and poor nations of the world, called into question these easy assumptions. Meetings of the World Bank, the IMF, and the "G8" (Japan, the United States, Britain, Canada, France, Germany, Italy, and Russia) were disrupted by "antiglobalization" campaigners who highlighted the social costs of global capitalism, particularly the devastation wrought by what was called the "debt crisis." More than fifty of the world's poorest countries (thirty-six in Africa) were paying off their debts to Western banks and governments by withdrawing money from sanitation, health, and education programs. Relief organizations estimated that as many as seven million children died each year during the 1990s because of the debt crisis.

The Environmental Crisis

The urgency of the environmental crisis also revealed the limitations of Western expertise. By 1985, 257 multilateral treaties mandated some form of environmental protection—restrictions on trade in endangered species, wetlands preservation, forest conservation, regulation of industrial emissions. Almost half of these had been signed since 1970. Yet the degradation of the planet proceeded apace. At the end of the millennium, half of the world's rivers were polluted or running dry, and the number of people displaced by water crises stood at 25 million (versus 21 million war-related refugees). In the 1980s, almost half of the world's tropical forests were cleared, posing a serious threat to the planet's biodiversity.

The destruction of the rain forests contributed to what is perhaps the largest threat facing not only Western but global civilization at the beginning of the third millennium—global warming. Global warming is linked to industrial development. The burning of fossil fuels such as oil and coal (which releases carbon dioxide into the atmosphere) and deforestation (which reduces the "natural sinks" that absorb the gas) together produce the "greenhouse effect"—the trapping of solar radiation in the Earth's atmosphere, with rising temperatures as a result. Faced with predictions of widespread climate change (and resulting economic devastation on a colossal scale), representatives from 160 countries met in Kyoto in 1997 and agreed to cut "greenhouse gas emissions" by 10 percent. In 2001, however, U.S. president George W. Bush rejected the Kyoto Agreements. Without the cooperation of the world's largest producer of greenhouse gases, the Kyoto Agreements' impact would be minimal.

North versus South
An Ethiopian farmer wages a losing war against drought and famine.

Europeans, both political leaders and ordinary citizens, reacted with fury to the American withdrawal from the Kyoto Agreements. They condemned the unilateral American action as that of a superpower out of control, no longer constrained by the Cold War to march in step with its allies. This perception of the United States as a bullying "hyperpower" was strengthened in 2003 by the Anglo-American invasion of Iraq. Across Europe, anti-war rallies drew huge crowds as Europeans protested against what they perceived to be an unwarranted use of American military force. As new divisions and alliances emerged both within and outside Europe, the meaning of "the West" remained a subject of intense debate.

Conclusion

Where Is the West Now?

In England, the most popular fast food is not fish and chips, long the quintessential English national supper, nor is it the Big Mac, as opponents of economic globalization might predict. Instead it is curry, the gift of the minority South Asian immigrant community. In the new millennium, "the West" may no longer serve as an important conceptual border marker. By many of the criteria explored in this textbook—economic, technological, political, and cultural—Tokyo would be defined as a Western city. So, too, would Melbourne—or Budapest or Warsaw. Nevertheless, the economic and social trauma that afflicted Russia and the poorer nations of the former Soviet bloc such as Romania and Bulgaria in the 1990s and after demonstrates that the "West" retains its distinct identity, for clearly the gap between it and the "East" remains wide. The admittedly hesitant, still incomplete spread of the Western ideal of democracy has thrown a fragile bridge across that gap. But perhaps the real divide for the twenty-first century stretches between "North" and "South"—the huge and growing difference between the global Haves and the Have-Nots. Whether any bridge can stretch across that span remains to be seen.

Suggestions for Further Reading

For a comprehensive listing of suggested readings, please go to www.ablongman.com/levack2e/chapter28

Ardagh, John. *Germany and the Germans: The United Germany in the Mid-1990s.* 1996. A snapshot of a society in the midst of social and economic change.

Hughes, H. Stuart. *Sophisticated Rebels: The Political Culture of European Dissent, 1968–1987.* 1988. A perceptive and imaginative exploration of "dissenters," ranging from Solidarity and Soviet dissidents to German Greens, Welsh nationalists, and an assortment of novelists and philosophers.

Kavanagh, Dennis. *Thatcherism and British Politics: The End of Consensus?* 1987. Kavanagh answers the question posed in his title with a convincing "yes."

Lewis, Jane, ed. *Women and Social Policies in Europe: Work, Family and the State.* 1993. A series of essays exploring the position of women in western Europe. Packed with statistics and useful tables.

McNeill, John. *Something New Under the Sun: An Environmental History of the Twentieth Century.* 2000. Argues that twentieth-century human economic activity has transformed the ecology of the globe—an ongoing experiment with a potentially devastating outcome.

Ost, David. *Solidarity and the Politics of Anti-Politics: Opposition and Reform in Poland Since 1968.* 1990. Although the bulk of this account was written before the Revolution of 1989, it provides a compelling study of Solidarity's emergence, impact, and ideology.

Rogel, Carole. *The Breakup of Yugoslavia and the War in Bosnia.* 1998. Designed for undergraduates, this work includes a short but detailed historical narrative, biographies of the main personalities, and a set of primary documents.

Rosenberg, Tina. *The Haunted Land: Facing Europe's Ghosts After Communism.* 1995. Winner of the Pulitzer Prize, this disturbing account focuses on the fundamental moral issues facing postcommunist political cultures.

Sandler, Irving. *Art of the Postmodern Era: From the Late 1960s to the Early 1980s.* 1996. Much more broad-ranging than the title suggests, this well-written, blessedly jargon-free work sets both contemporary art and the theories of the postmodern within the wider historical context.

Stokes, Gale. *The Walls Came Tumbling Down: The Collapse of Communism in Eastern Europe.* 1993. A superb account, firmly embedded in history.

Young, John W. *Cold War Europe, 1945–1991: A Political History.* 1996. A solid survey.

See also the works by Crampton, Cronin, Gaddis, Isaacs and Downing, Judge and Langdon, Keep, and Urwin listed at the end of Chapter 27.

Notes

1. Quoted in Robert Paxton, *Europe in the Twentieth Century* (1997), 613.
2. Kenneth Boulding, "The Economics of the Coming Spaceship Earth," first published in 1966, reprinted in *Toward a Steady-State Economy,* ed. Herman Daly (1973).
3. Quotations from Timothy W. Ryback, *Rock Around the Bloc: A History of Rock Music in Eastern Europe and the Soviet Union* (1990), 184–185, 176.
4. Quoted in D. J. Peterson, *Troubled Lands: The Legacy of Soviet Environmental Destruction* (1993), 12.
5. Quoted in Archie Brown, *The Gorbachev Factor* (1996), 125.
6. Quoted in R. J. Crampton, *Eastern Europe in the Twentieth Century—And After* (1997), 408.
7. Francis Fukuyama, *The End of History and the Last Man* (1992).
8. Quoted in *The Observer* (London), (April 8, 2001), 20.
9. Salman Rushdie, "Please, Read *Satanic Verses* Before Condemning It," *Illustrated Weekly of India* (October 1988). Reprinted in M. M. Ahsan and A. R. Kidwai, *Sacrilege Versus Civility: Muslim Perspectives on The Satanic Verses Affair* (1991), 63.
10. Quoted in Malise Ruthven, *A Satanic Affair: Salman Rushdie and the Wrath of Islam* (1991). 562.
11. Quoted in Ruthven, *A Satanic Affair,* 100.
12. *Bookseller,* London (February 24, 1989). Quoted in Lisa Appignanesi and Sara Maitland, *The Rushdie File* (1990), 103–104.
13. *The Sunday Telegraph* (June 24, 1990). Quoted in Ahsan and Kidwai, *Sacrilege Versus Civility,* 80.
14. Quoted in Irving Sandler, *Art of the Postmodern Era* (1996), 4.

Glossary

absolutism (p. 478) A form of government in the seventeenth and eighteenth centuries in which the ruler possessed complete and unrivalled power.

acropolis (p. 70) The defensible hilltop around which a polis grew. In classical Athens, the Acropolis was the site of the Parthenon (Temple of Athena).

Aeneid (p. 157) Written by Virgil (70–19 B.C.E.), this magnificent epic poem celebrates the emperor Augustus by linking him to his mythical ancestor, Aeneas, the Trojan refugee who founded the Roman people. Considered by many to be the greatest work of Latin literature, the poem has had enormous influence in the West.

agrarian capitalism (p. 404) A form of economic organization characteristic of European colonialism in which Europeans organized the production of certain kinds of commercial crops (such as sugar, tobacco, and indigo) on land expropriated from native peoples and with slave labor.

agricultural revolution (p. 273) Refers to technological innovations that began to appear during the eleventh century, making possible a dramatic growth in population. The agricultural revolution came about through harnessing new sources of power with water and wind mills, improving the pulling power of animals with better collars, using heavy plows to better exploit the soils of northern Europe, and employing a three-field crop rotation system that increased the amount and quality of food available.

agricultural societies (p. 14) Settled communities in which people depend on farming and raising livestock as their sources of food.

alchemy (p. 518) A form of learned magic that was intended to turn base metals into precious ones.

aldeias (p. 396) Settlements for natives who had converted to Christianity in Brazil. In these settlements the Jesuit fathers protected the natives from enslavement.

Allies (p. 778) During World War I, the states allied against the Central Powers of Germany and Austria-Hungary. During World War II, the states allied against the regimes of Nazi Germany, fascist Italy and imperial Japan.

Anabaptism (p. 425) Meaning "to rebaptize"; refers to those Protestant radicals of the sixteenth century who rejected infant baptism and adopted adult baptism. Anabaptists treated the Bible as a blueprint for reforming not just the church but all of society, a tendency that led them to reject the authority of the state, to live in self-governing "holy communities," and in some cases to practice a primitive form of communism.

anarchism (p. 728) Ideology that views the state as unnecessary and repressive, and rejects participation in parliamentary politics in favor of direct, usually violent, action.

anticlericalism (p. 758) Opposition to the political influence of the Roman Catholic Church.

Antonine Decree (p. 149) In 212 C.E. the emperor Aurelius Antoninus, called Caracalla, issued a decree that granted citizenship to all the free inhabitants of the Roman Empire. The decree enabled Roman law to embrace the entire population of the empire.

apartheid (p. 895) System of racial segregation and discrimination put into place in South Africa in 1948.

Apologists (p. 164) Christian writers in the second and third centuries C.E. who explained their religion to learned non-Christians. In the process they helped Christianity absorb much of Hellenistic culture.

appeasement (p. 853) British diplomatic and financial efforts to stabilize Germany in the 1920s and 1930s and so avoid a second world war.

Arians (p. 183) Christians who believe that God the Father is superior to Jesus Christ his Son. Most of the Germanic settlers in western Europe in the fifth century were Arians.

aristocracy (p. 576) A term that originally applied to those who were considered the most fit to rule and later identified the wealthiest members of society, especially those who owned land.

Asceticism (p. 183) The Christian practice of severely suppressing physical needs and daily desires in an effort to achieve a spiritual union with God. Asceticism is the practice that underlies the monastic movement.

Auschwitz (p. 869) Technically Auschwitz-Birkenau; death camp in Poland that has become the symbol of the Holocaust.

auto-da-fé (p. 451) Meaning literally a "theater of faith," an *auto* was practiced by the Catholic Church in early modern Spain and Portugal as an extended public ritual of penance designed to cause physical pain among the sinful and promote fear of God's judgment among those who witnessed it.

Babylonian Captivity of the Church (p. 329) Between 1305 and 1378 seven consecutive popes voluntarily chose to reside in Avignon, France, in order to escape anarchy in the streets of Rome. During this period the popes became subservient to the kings of France.

Babylonian Exile (p. 64) The period of Jewish history between the destruction of Solomon's temple in Jerusalem by Babylonian armies in 587 B.C.E., and 538 B.C.E., when Cyrus of Persia permitted Jews to return to Palestine and rebuild the temple.

balance of power (p. 487) An arrangement in which various countries form alliances to prevent any one state from dominating the others.

Balfour Declaration (p. 809) Declaration of 1917 that affirmed British support of a Jewish state in Palestine.

baroque (p. 483) A dynamic style in art, architecture, and music intended to elicit an emotional response. It was closely associated with royal absolutism in the seventeenth century.

Battle of Kadesh (p. 42) The battle between Egyptian and Hittite armies in Syria in 1274 B.C.E. that set the territorial limits of both empires in Canaan and the Middle East for a century during the International Bronze Age.

Beer Hall Putsch (p. 821) Failed Nazi effort to overthrow the German government by force in 1923.

Berlin Wall (p. 899) Constructed by the East German government, the wall physically cut the city of Berlin in two and prevented East German citizens from access to West Germany; stood from 1961 to 1989.

Big Three (p. 888) Term applied to the British, Soviet, and U.S. leaders during World War II: until 1945, Churchill, Stalin, and Roosevelt; by the summer of 1945, Attlee, Stalin, and Truman.

blitzkrieg (p. 855) "Lightning war;" offensive military tactic making use of airplanes, tanks, and motorized infantry to punch through enemy defenses and secure key territory. First demonstrated by the German army in World War II.

boers (p. 548) Dutch farmers in the colony established by the Dutch Republic in South Africa.

Bolsheviks (p. 801) Minority group of Russian socialists, headed by Lenin, who espoused an immediate transition to a socialist state. It became the Communist Party in the Soviet Union.

bourgeoisie (p. 583) A social group, technically consisting of those who were burghers in the towns, that included prosperous merchants and financiers, members of the professions, and some skilled craftsmen known as "petty bourgeoisie."

Bretton Woods Agreement (p. 889) Agreement signed in 1944 that established the post-World War II economic framework in which the U.S. dollar served as the world's reserve currency.

brinkmanship (p. 899) Style of Cold War confrontation in which each superpower endeavored to convince the other that it was willing to wage nuclear war.

bronze (p. 33) An alloy of tin and copper that produces a hard metal suitable for weapons, tools, ornaments, and household objects. Bronze production began about 3200 B.C.E.

bubonic plague (p. 310) An epidemic disease spread from rats to humans via flea bites. The infection enters the bloodstream, causing inflamed swellings called buboes (hence, "bubonic" plague) in the glands of the groin or armpit, internal bleeding, and discoloration. Although disputed by some, most experts consider bubonic plague the cause of the Black Death, which killed at least one-third of the population of Europe between 1348 and the early 1350s. Bubonic plague reappeared recurrently in the West between 1348 and 1721.

caliph (p. 226) After Muhammad's death in 632, the ruler of the Islamic state was called the caliph. The sectarian division within Islam between the Shi'ites and Sunni derived from a disagreement over how to determine the hereditary succession from Muhammad to the caliphate, which combined governmental and some religious responsibilities.

caliphate (p. 223) The Islamic imperial government that evolved under the leadership of Abu Bakr (r. 632–634), the successor of the prophet Muhammad.

calling (p. 423) The Calvinist doctrine that God calls the Elect to perform his will on earth. God's calling gave Calvinists a powerful sense of personal direction.

canon law (p. 282) The collected laws of the Roman Catholic Church. Canon law applied to cases involving the clergy, disputes about church property, and donations to the Church. It also applied to the laity for annulling marriages, legitimating bastards, prosecuting bigamy, protecting widows and orphans, and resolving inheritance disputes.

capital (p. 652) All the physical assets used in production, including fixed capital, such as machinery, and circulating capital, such as raw materials; more generally the cost of these physical assets.

caravels (p. 381) Hybrid three-masted ships developed about 1450 in the Iberian peninsula by combining the rigging of square with triangular lateen sails. These ships could be sailed in a variety of winds, carry large cargoes, be managed by a small crew, and be defended by guns mounted in the castle superstructure.

Carnival (p. 455) The most popular annual festival in much of Europe before modern times. Also known as Mardi Gras, the festival took place for several days or even weeks before the beginning of Lent and included all kinds of fun and games.

Carolingian Renaissance (p. 250) The "rebirth" of interest in ancient Greek and Latin literature and language during the reign of the Frankish emperor Charlemagne (r. 768–814). Charlemagne promoted the intensive study of Latin to promote governmental efficiency and to propagate the Christian faith.

Catholic Reformation (p. 430) A series of efforts during the sixteenth century to purify the Church that evolved out of late medieval spirituality and that included the creation of new religious orders, especially the Society of Jesus.

Central Powers (p. 778) Germany and Austria-Hungary in World War I.

Chalcedonians (p. 181) Christians who follow the doctrinal decisions and definitions of the Council of Chalcedon in 451 C.E. stating that Christ's human and divine natures were equal, but entirely distinct and united in one person "without confusion, division, separation, or change." Chalcedonian Christianity came to be associated with the Byzantine Empire and is called Greek Orthodoxy. In western Europe it is known as Roman Catholicism.

chinoiserie (p. 564) A French word for an eighteenth-century decorative art that combined Chinese and European motifs.

Christian Democracy, Christian Democratic parties (p. 907) Conservative and confessionally based (Roman Catholic) political parties that dominated much of western European politics after World War II.

Christian humanists (p. 413) During the fifteenth and sixteenth centuries these experts in Greek, Latin, and Hebrew subjected the Bible to philological study in an attempt to understand the precise meaning of the founding text of Christianity.

circuit court (p. 296) Established by King Henry II (r. 1154–1189) to make royal justice available to virtually anyone in England. Circuit court judges visited every shire in England four times a year.

civic humanism (p. 356) A branch of humanism introduced by the Florentine chancellor Leonardo Bruni who defended the republican institutions and values of the city. Civic humanism promoted the ethic of responsible citizenship.

civilization (p. 12) The term used by archaeologists to describe a society differentiated by levels of wealth and power, and in which religious, economic, and political control are based in cities.

civitas (p. 143) The Roman term for a city. A city included the town itself, all the surrounding territory that it controlled, and all the people who lived in the town and the countryside.

clans or kin groups (p. 243) The basic social and political unit of Germanic society consisting of blood relatives obliged to defend one another and take vengeance for crimes against the group and its members.

class (p. 578) A large and often cohesive social group that was conscious of its shared economic and political interests.

classicism (p. 580) A style in art, architecture, music, and literature that emphasizes proportion, adherence to traditional forms, and a rejection of emotion and enthusiasm.

Cluny (p. 280) A monastery founded in Burgundy in 910 that became the center of a far-reaching movement to reform the Church that was sustained in more than 1,500 Cluniac monasteries, modeled after the original in Cluny.

Cold War (p. 888) Struggle for global supremacy between the United States and the Soviet Union, waged from the end of World War II until 1990.

collectivization (p. 834) The replacement of private and village farms with large cooperative agricultural enterprises run by state-employed managers. Collectivization was a key part of Joseph Stalin's plans for modernizing the Soviet economy and destroying peasant opposition to communist rule.

colons (p. 568) White planters in the French Caribbean colony of Saint Domingue (Haiti).

Columbian exchange (p. 400) The trade of peoples, plants, animals, microbes, and ideas between the Old and New Worlds that began with Columbus.

Columbian question (p. 402) The debate among historians and epidemiologists about whether syphilis or its ancestor disease originated in the Americas and was brought to the Old World after Columbus's voyages.

Common Market (p. 908) Originally comprising West Germany, France, Italy, Belgium, Luxembourg, and the Netherlands, the Common Market was formed in 1957 to integrate its members' economic structures and so foster both economic prosperity and international peace. Also called the European Economic Community (EEC). Evolved into the European Union (EU).

communes (p. 277) Sworn defensive associations of merchants and workers that appeared in north-central Italy after 1070 and that became the effective government of more than a hundred cities. The communes evolved into city-states by seizing control of the surrounding countryside.

communism (p. 680) The revolutionary form of socialism developed by Karl Marx and Friedrich Engels that promoted the overthrow of bourgeois or capitalist institutions and the establishment of a dictatorship of the proletariat.

Concert of Europe (p. 678) The joint efforts made by Austria, Prussia, Russia, Britain, and France during the years following the Congress of Vienna to suppress liberal and nationalist movements throughout Europe.

Conciliar Movement (p. 330) A fifteenth-century movement that advocated ending the Great Schism and reforming church government by calling a general meeting or council of the bishops, who would exercise authority over the rival popes.

Confessions (p. 450) The formal sixteenth-century statements of religious doctrine: the Confession of Augsburg for Lutherans, the Helvetic Confessions for Calvinists, the Thirty-Nine Articles for Anglicans, and the decrees of the Council of Trent for Catholics.

Congress of Vienna (p. 638) A conference of the major powers of Europe in 1814–1815 to establish a new balance of power at the end of the Napoleonic Wars.

conquistadores (p. 388) Spanish adventurers in the Americas who explored and conquered the lands of indigenous peoples, sometimes without legal authority but usually with a legal privilege granted by the king of Spain who required that one-fifth of all things of value be turned over to the crown. The conquistadores extended Spanish sovereignty over new lands.

conservatism (p. 678) A nineteenth-century ideology intended to prevent a recurrence of the revolutionary changes of the 1790s and the implementation of liberal policies.

containment (p. 890) Cold War policy of blocking communist expansion; inaugurated by the Truman Doctrine in 1947.

Corpus of Civil Law (p. 197) The body of Roman law compiled by the emperor Justinian in Constantinople in 534. The Corpus became a pillar of Latin-speaking European civilization.

cosmology (p. 514) A theory concerning the structure and nature of the universe such as those proposed by Aristotle in the fourth century B.C.E. and Copernicus in the sixteenth century.

counties (p. 250) Territorial units devised by the Carolingian dynasty during the eighth and ninth centuries for the administration of the empire. Each county was administered by a count who was rewarded with lands and sent to areas where he had no family ties to serve as a combined provincial governor, judge, military commander, and representative of the king.

courtly love (p. 302) An ethic first found in the poems of the late twelfth- and thirteenth-century troubadours that portrayed the ennobling possibilities of the love between a man and a woman. Courtly love formed the basis for the modern idea of romantic love.

creoles (p. 548) People of Spanish descent who had been born in Spanish America.

Crusades (p. 263) Between 1095 and 1291, Latin Christians heeding the call of the pope launched eight major expeditions and many smaller ones against Muslim armies in an attempt to gain control of and hold Jerusalem.

Cubism (p. 755) Modernist artistic movement of the early twentieth century that emphasized the fragmentation of human perception through visual experiments with geometric forms.

cultural relativism (p. 404) A mode of thought first explored during the sixteenth century to explain why the peoples of the New World did not appear in the Bible. Cultural relativism recognized that many (but not necessarily all) standards of judgment are specific to particular cultures rather than the fixed truths established by natural or divine law.

culture (p. 12) The knowledge and adaptive behavior created by communities that helps them to mediate between themselves and the natural world through time.

cuneiform (p. 17) A kind of writing in which wedge-shaped symbols are pressed into clay tablets to indicate words and ideas. Cuneiform writing originated in ancient Sumer.

Curia (p. 283) The administrative bureaucracy of the Roman Catholic Church.

Cynics (p. 105) Cynics followed the teachings of Antisthenes (ca. 445–360 B.C.E.) by rejecting pleasures, possessions, and social conventions in order to find peace of mind.

Darwinian theory of evolution (p. 746) Scientific theory associated with nineteenth-century scientist Charles Darwin that highlights the role of variation and natural selection in the evolution of species.

Decembrists (p. 687) Russian liberals who staged a revolt against Tsar Nicholas I on the first day of his reign in December 1825.

de-Christianization (p. 625) A program inaugurated in France in 1793 by the radical Jacobin and former priest Joseph Fouché that closed churches, eliminated religious symbols, and attempted to establish a purely civic religion.

deduction (p. 521) The logical process by which ideas and laws are derived from basic truths or principles.

deists (p. 529) Seventeenth- and eighteenth-century thinkers who believed that God created the universe and established immutable laws of nature but did not subsequently intervene in the operation of nature or in human affairs.

Delian League (p. 76) The alliance among many Greek cities organized by Athens in 478 B.C.E. in order to fight Persian forces in the eastern Aegean Sea. The Athenians gradually turned the Delian League into the Athenian Empire.

demand (p. 653) The desire of consumers to acquire goods and the need of producers to acquire raw materials and machinery.

democracy (p. 58) A form of government in which citizens devise their own governing institutions and choose their leaders; began in Athens, Greece, in the fifth century B.C.E.

demonic magic (p. 531) The invocation of evil spirits with the goal of utilizing their supernatural powers to change the course of nature or to alter human behavior.

de-Stalinization (p. 904) Khrushchev's effort to decentralize political and economic control in the Soviet Union after 1956.

detente (p. 924) During the 1970s, a period of lessened Cold War hostilities and greater reliance on negotiation and compromise.

dialectic (p. 680) The theory that history advanced in stages as the result of the conflict between different ideas or social groups.

dialectical materialism (p. 680) The socialist philosophy of Karl Marx according to which history advanced as the result of material or economic forces and would lead to the creation of a classless society.

Diaspora (p. 160) Literally "dispersion of population;" usually used to refer to the dispersion of the Jewish population after the Roman destruction of the Temple in Jerusalem in 70 C.E.

division of labor (p. 649) The assignment of one stage of production to a single worker or group of workers to increase efficiency and productive output.

domestication (p. 13) Manipulating the breeding of animals over many generations in order to make them more useful to humans as sources of food, wool, and other byproducts. Domestication of animals began about 10,000 years ago.

Dreyfus Affair (p. 721) The trials of Captain Alfred Dreyfus on treason charges dominated French political life in the decade after 1894 and revealed fundamental divisions in French society.

dualistic (p. 522) A term used to describe a philosophy, such as that of René Descartes, in which a rigid distinction is made between body and mind or between the material and the immaterial world.

Dutch Revolt (p. 466) The rebellion against Spanish rule of the seven northern provinces of the Netherlands between 1579 and 1648, which resulted in the independence of the Republic of the United Provinces.

Edict of Nantes (p. 463) Promulgated by King Henry IV in 1598, the edict allowed the Huguenots to build a quasi-independent state within the kingdom of France, giving them the right to have their own troops, church organization, and political autonomy within their walled towns, but banning them from the royal court and the city of Paris. King Louis XIV revoked the edict in 1685.

Einsatzgruppen (p. 869) Loosely translated as strike force or task force; SS units given the task of murdering Jews and Communist Party members in the areas of the Soviet Union occupied by Germany during World War II.

empires (p. 542) Large political formations consisting of different kingdoms or territories outside the boundaries of the states that control them.

enclosure (p. 652) The consolidation of scattered agricultural holdings into large, compact fields which were then closed off by hedges, bushes, or walls, giving farmers complete control over the uses of their land.

encomienda (p. 391) The basic form of economic and social organization in early Spanish America, based on a royal grant awarded to a Spaniard for military or other services that gave the grantee and his successors the right to gather tribute from the Indians in a defined area.

enlightened despots (p. 600) The term assigned to absolute monarchs who initiated a series of legal and political reforms in an effort to realize the goals of the Enlightenment.

Enlightenment (p. 585) An international intellectual movement of the eighteenth century that emphasized the use of reason and the application of the laws of nature to human society.

Epicureans (p. 104) Followers of the teachings of the philosopher Epicurus (341–271 B.C.E.). Epicureans tried to gain peace of mind by choosing pleasures rationally.

ethnic cleansing (p. 943) A term introduced during the wars in Yugoslavia in the 1990s; the systematic use of murder, rape, and violence by one ethnic group against members of other ethnic groups in order to establish control over a territory.

Etruscans (p. 111) A people native to Italy, the Etruscans established a league of militaristic cities in central Italy that grew rich from war and trade. Etruscans had a great influence on the formation of the Roman state.

Eucharist (p. 289) Also known as Holy Communion or the Lord's Supper, the Eucharistic rite of the Mass celebrates Jesus' last meal with his apostles when the priest-celebrant consecrates wafers of bread and a chalice of wine as the body and blood of Christ. In the Middle Ages the wafers of bread were distributed for the congregation to eat, but drinking from the chalice was a special privilege of the priesthood. Protestants in the sixteenth century and Catholics in the late twentieth century began to allow the laity to drink from the chalice.

Euro-Islam (p. 950) The identity and belief system being forged by European Muslims who argue that Islam does not contradict or reject European values.

European Economic Community (EEC) (p. 908) Originally comprising West Germany, France, Italy, Belgium, Luxembourg, and the Netherlands, the EEC was formed in 1957 to integrate its members' economic structures and so foster both economic prosperity and international peace. Also called the Common Market.

European Union (EU) (p. 943) A successor organization to the EEC; the effort to integrate European political, economic, cultural, and military structures and policies.

excommunication (p. 282) A decree by the pope or a bishop prohibiting a sinner from participating in the sacraments of the Church and forbidding any social contact whatsoever with the surrounding community.

existentialism (p. 815) Twentieth-century philosophy that emerged in the interwar era and influenced many thinkers and artists after World War II. Existentialism emphasizes individual freedom in a world devoid of meaning or coherence.

Expressionism (p. 755) Modernist artistic movement of the early twentieth century that used bold colors and experimental forms to express emotional realities.

factories (p. 544) Trading posts established by European powers in foreign lands.

fanatic (p. 460) Originally referring to someone possessed by a demon, a fanatic came during the sixteenth century to mean a person who expressed immoderate enthusiasm in religious matters or who pursued a supposedly divine mission, often to violent ends.

fascism (p. 826) Twentieth-century political ideology that rejected the existing alternatives of conservatism, communism, socialism, and liberalism. Fascists stressed the authoritarian power of the state, the efficacy of violent action, the need to build a national community, and the use of new technologies of influence and control.

federalists (p. 617) The name assigned by radical Jacobins to provincial rebels who opposed the centralization of the state during the French Revolution.

feminism, feminist movement (p. 733) International movement that emerged in the second half of the nineteenth century and demanded broader political, legal, and economic rights for women.

Fertile Crescent (p. 14) Also known as the Levantine Corridor, this twenty-five mile wide arc of land stretching from the Jordan River to the Euphrates River was the place where food production and settled communities first appeared in Southwest Asia (the Middle East).

feudalism (p. 255) A term historians use to describe a social system common during the Middle Ages in which lords granted fiefs (tracts of land or some other form of income) to dependents, known as vassals, who owed their lords personal services in exchange. Feudalism refers to a society governed through personal ties of dependency rather than public political institutions.

fief (p. 255) During the Middle Ages a fief was a grant of land or some other form of income that a lord gave to a vassal in exchange for loyalty and certain services (usually military assistance).

Final Solution (p. 869) Nazi term for the effort to murder every Jew in Europe during World War II.

fin-de-siecle (p. 750) French term for the "turn of the century"; used to refer to the cultural crisis of the late nineteenth century.

First Triumvirate (p. 125) The informal political alliance made by Julius Caesar, Pompey, and Crassus in 60 B.C.E. to share power in the Roman Republic. It led directly to the collapse of the Republic.

Forms (p. 85) In the philosophical teachings of Plato, these are eternal, unchanging absolutes such as Truth, Justice, and Beauty that represent true reality, as opposed to the approximations of reality that humans encounter in everyday life.

Forum (p. 111) The political and religious center of the city of Rome throughout antiquity. All cities in the empire had a forum in imitation of the capital city.

franchise (p. 602) The right to vote; also called suffrage.

freemasons (p. 598) Members of secret societies of men and women that flourished during the Enlightenment, dedicated to the creation of a society based on reason and virtue and committed to the principles of liberty and equality.

French Wars of Religion (p. 461) A series of political assassinations, massacres, and military engagements between French Catholics and Calvinists from 1560 to 1598.

Gaullism (p. 914) The political ideology associated with twentieth-century French political leader Charles DeGaulle. Gaullism combined the advocacy of a strong, centralized state with social conservatism.

German-Soviet Non-Aggression Pact (p. 853) Signed by Stalin and Hitler in 1939, the agreement publicly pledged Germany and the Soviet Union not to attack each other, and secretly divided up Poland and the Baltic states between the two powers.

Girondins (p. 616) The more conservative members of the Jacobin party who favored greater economic freedom and opposed further centralization of state power during the French Revolution.

glasnost (p. 943) Loosely translated as openness or honesty; Gorbachev's effort after 1985 to break with the secrecy that had characterized Soviet political life.

Gothic (p. 303) A style in architecture in western Europe from the late twelfth and thirteenth centuries, characterized by ribbed vaults and pointed arches, which drew the eyes of worshipers upward toward God. Flying buttresses, which redistributed the weight of the roof, made possible thin walls pierced by large expanses of stained glass.

grand jury (p. 296) In medieval England after the judicial reforms of King Henry II (r. 1154–1189), grand juries were called when the circuit court judge arrived in a shire. The sheriff assembled a group of men familiar with local affairs who constituted the grand jury and who reported to the judge the major crimes that had been committed since the judge's last visit.

Great Depression in Trade and Agriculture (p. 712) Downturn in prices and profits, particularly in the agricultural sector, in Europe from 1873 through the 1880s.

Great Depression (p. 828) Calamitous drop in prices, reduction in trade, and rise in unemployment that devastated the global economy in 1929.

Great Persecution (p. 174) An attack on Christians in the Roman empire begun by the emperor Galerius in 303 C.E. on the grounds that their worship was endangering the empire. Several thousand Christians were executed.

Great Purge (p. 835) Period of mass arrests and executions particularly aimed at Communist Party members. Lasting from 1934 to 1939, the Great Purge enabled Stalin to consolidate his one-man rule over the Soviet Union.

Great Schism (p. 329) The division of the Catholic Church (1378–1417) between rival Italian and French claimants to the papal throne.

Green movement, Green politics (p. 930) A new style of politics and set of political ideas resulting from the confluence of environmentalism, feminism, and anti-nuclear protests of the 1970s.

guilds (p. 319) Professional associations devoted to protecting the special interests of a particular trade or craft and to monopolizing production and trade in the goods the guild produced.

haciendas (p. 391) Large landed estates that began to be established in the seventeenth century replaced encomiendas throughout much of Spanish America.

Hallstatt (p. 109) The first Celtic civilization in central Europe is called Halstatt. From about 750 to about 450 B.C.E., Hallstatt Celts spread throughout Europe.

helots (p. 73) The brutally oppressed subject peoples of the Spartans. Tied to the land they farmed for Spartan masters, they were treated little better than beasts of burden.

heresies (p. 181) Forms of Christian belief that are not considered Orthodox.

hetairai (p. 80) Elite courtesans in ancient Greece who provided intellectual as well as sexual companionship.

Holocaust (p. 869) Adolf Hitler's effort to murder all the Jews in Europe during World War II.

Homo sapiens sapiens (p. 13) Scientific term meaning "most intelligent people" applied to physically and intellectually modern human beings that first appeared between 200,000 and 100,000 years ago in Africa.

hoplites (p. 72) Greek soldiers in the Archaic Age who could afford their own weapons. Hoplite tactics made soldiers fighting as a group dependent on one another. This contributed to the internal cohesion of the polis and eventually to the rise of democracy.

Huguenots (p. 461) The term for French Calvinists, who constituted some 10 percent of the population by 1560.

humanists (p. 365) During the Renaissance humanists were writers and orators who studied Latin and sometimes Greek texts on grammar, rhetoric, poetry, history, and ethics.

Hundred Years' War (p. 321) Refers to a series of engagements (1337–1453) between England and France over England's attempts to assert its claims to territories in France.

hyperinflation (p. 821) Catastrophic price increases and currency devaluation, such as that which occurred in Germany in 1923.

Iconoclasm (p. 216) The destruction of religious images in the Byzantine empire in the eighth century.

icons (p. 215) The Christian images of God and saints found in Byzantine art.

ideologies (p. 676) Theories of society and government that form the basis of political programs.

Ideologues (p. 631) A group of liberal writers and philosophers in France who objected to Napoleon's religious policy on the grounds that it would inaugurate a return of religious superstition.

induction (p. 521) The mental process by which theories are established only after the systematic accumulation of large amounts of data.

indulgences (p. 329) Certificates that allowed penitents to atone for their sins and reduce their time in purgatory. Usually these were issued for going on a pilgrimage or performing a pious act, but during the Babylonian Captivity of the Church (1305–1378) popes began to sell them, a practice Martin Luther protested in 1517 in an act that brought on the Protestant Reformation.

industrial capitalism (p. 662) A form of capitalism characterized by the ownership of factories by private individuals and the employment of wage labor.

intendants (p. 481) French royal officials who became the main agents of French provincial administration in the seventeenth century.

interdict (p. 283) A papal decree prohibiting the celebration of the sacraments in an entire city or kingdom.

Investiture Controversy (p. 282) A dispute that began in 1076 between the popes and the German emperors over the right to invest bishops with their offices. The most famous episode was the conflict between Pope Gregory VII and Emperor Henry IV. The controversy was resolved by the Concordat of Worms in 1122.

Islamism (p. 948) Islamic radicalism or *jihadism*. The ideology that insists that Islam demands a rejection of Western values and that violence in this struggle against the West is justified.

Jacobins (p. 614) A French political party supporting a democratic republic that found support in political clubs throughout the country and dominated the National Convention from 1792 until 1794.

Jim Crow (p. 768) Series of laws mandating racial segregation throughout the American South.

Junkers (p. 493) The traditional nobility of Prussia.

justification by faith alone (p. 415) Refers to Martin Luther's insight that humanity is incapable of performing enough religious good works to earn eternal salvation. Salvation is an unmerited gift from God called grace. Those who receive grace are called the Elect.

knight (p. 255) During the Middle Ages a knight was a soldier who fought on horseback. A knight was a vassal or dependent of a lord, who usually financed the knight's expenses of armor and weapons and of raising and feeding horses with a grant of land known as a fief.

Koine (p. 101) The standard version of the Greek language spoken throughout the Hellenistic world.

La Tène (p. 109) A phase of Celtic civilization that lasted from about 450 to 200 B.C.E. La Tène culture became strong especially in the regions of the Rhine and Danube Rivers.

laissez-faire (p. 676) The principle that governments should not regulate or otherwise intervene in the economy unless it is necessary to protect property rights and public order.

lapis lazuli (p. 45) A precious, deep-blue gemstone found in the Middle East that was traded widely for jewelry during the International Bronze Age.

latifundia (p. 155) These huge agricultural estates owned by wealthy Romans, including the emperor, often used large slave-gangs as labor.

Latin Christendom (pp. 181, 238) The parts of medieval Europe, including all of western Europe, united by Christianity and the use of Latin in worship and intellectual life. Latin served as an international language among the ruling elites in western Europe, even though they spoke different languages in their daily lives.

lay investiture (p. 281) The practice of nobles, kings, or emperors installing churchmen and giving them the symbols of office.

League of Nations (p. 803) Association of states set up after World War I to resolve international conflicts through open and peaceful negotiation.

Lend-Lease Act (p. 859) Passed in March 1941, the act gave Britain access to American industrial products during World War II, with payment postponed for the duration of the war.

Levantine Corridor (p. 14) Also known as the Fertile Crescent, this twenty-five mile wide arc of land stretching from the Jordan River to the Euphrates River was the place where food production and settled communities first appeared in Southwest Asia (the Middle East).

liberalism (p. 676) An ideology based on the conviction that individual freedom is of supreme importance and the main responsibility of government is to protect that freedom.

linear perspective (p. 361) In the arts the use of geometrical principles to depict a three-dimensional space on a flat, two-dimensional surface.

liturgy (p. 238) The forms of Christian worship, including the prayers, chants, and rituals to be said, sung, or performed throughout the year.

lord (p. 255) During the Middle Ages a lord was someone who offered protection to dependents, known as vassals, who took an oath of loyalty to him. Most lords demanded military services from their vassals and sometimes granted them tracts of land known as fiefs.

Macedonian Renaissance (p. 217) During the Macedonian dynasty's rule of Byzantium (867–1056), aristocratic families, the Church, and monasteries devoted their immense riches to embellishing Constantinople with new buildings, mosaics, and icons. The emperors sponsored historical, philosophical, and religious writing.

Mafia (p. 700) Organizations of armed men who took control of local politics and the economy in late nineteenth-century Sicily.

magic (p. 457) Learned opinion described two kinds of magic: natural magic, which involved the manipulation of occult forces believed to exist in nature, and demonic magic, which called upon evil spirits to gain access to power. Widely accepted as a reality until the middle of the seventeenth century.

Magisterial Reformation (p. 421) Refers to Protestant churches that received official government sanction.

Magna Carta (p. 296) In 1215 some English barons forced King John to sign the "great charter," in which the king pledged to respect the traditional feudal privileges of the nobility, towns, and clergy. Subsequent kings swore to uphold it, thereby accepting the fundamental principle that even the king was obliged to respect the law.

Manhattan Project (p. 866) Code name given to the secret Anglo-American project that resulted in the construction of the atom bomb during World War II.

marches (p. 250) Territorial units of the Carolingian empire for the administration of frontier regions. Each march was ruled by a margrave who had special powers necessary to defend vulnerable borders.

Marshall Plan (p. 890) The use of U.S. economic aid to restore stability to Europe after World War II and so undercut the appeal of communist ideology.

mechanical philosophy (p. 522) The seventeenth-century philosophy of nature, championed by René Descartes, holding that nature operated in a mechanical way, just like a machine made by a human being.

mendicant friars (p. 288) Members of a religious order, such as the Dominicans or Franciscans, who wandered from city to city and throughout the countryside begging for alms rather than residing in a monastery. Mendicant friars tended to help ordinary laypeople by preaching and administering to the sick and poor.

mercantilism (p. 484) The theory that the wealth of a state depended on its ability to import fewer commodities than it exported and thus acquire the largest possible share of the world's monetary supply. The theory encouraged state intervention in the economy and the regulation of trade.

mesmerism (p. 599) A pseudoscience developed by Franz Anton Mesmer in the eighteenth century that treated sickness by massaging or hypnotizing the patient to produce a crisis that restored health.

metropolis (p. 542) The parent country of a colony or imperial possession.

Mishnah (p. 186) The final organization and transcription of Jewish oral law, completed by the end of the third century C.E.

Modern Devotion (p. 331) A fifteenth-century religious movement that stressed individual piety, ethical behavior, and intense religious education. The Modern Devotion was promoted by the Brothers of the Common Life, a religious order whose influence was broadly felt through its extensive network of schools.

modernism (p. 754) Term applied to artistic and literary movements from the late nineteenth century through the 1950s. Modernists sought to create new aesthetic forms and values.

monastic movement (p. 183) In Late Antiquity, Christian ascetics organized communities where men and women could pursue a life of spirituality through work, prayer, and asceticism. Called the monastic movement, this spiritual quest spread quickly throughout Christian lands.

Monophysites (p. 181) Christians who do not accept the Council of Chalcedon (see Chalcedonians). Monophysites believe that Jesus Christ has only one nature, equally divine and human.

monotheism (p. 39) The belief in only one god, first attributed to the ancient Hebrews. Monotheism is the foundation of Judaism, Christianity, Islam, and Zoroastrianism.

Montagnards (p. 616) Members of the radical faction within the Jacobin party who advocated the centralization of state power during the French Revolution and instituted the Reign of Terror.

mosque (p. 222) A place of Muslim worship.

nabobs (p. 564) Members of the British East India Company who made fortunes in India and returned to Britain, flaunting their wealth.

Napoleonic Code (p. 631) The name given to the Civil Code of 1804, promulgated by Napoleon, which gave France a uniform and authoritative code of law.

nation (p. 681) A large community of people who possess a sense of unity based on a belief that they have a common homeland and share a similar culture.

nationalism (p. 681) The belief that the people who form a nation should have their own political institutions and that the interests of the nation should be defended and promoted at all costs.

national self-determination (p. 681) The doctrine advanced by nationalists that any group that considers itself a nation has the right to be ruled only by the members of their own nation and to have all members of the nation included in that state.

nation-state (p. 681) A political structure sought by nationalists in which the boundaries of the state and the nation are identical, so that all the members of a nation are governed by the same political authorities.

NATO (North Atlantic Treaty Organization) (p. 892) Defensive anti-Soviet alliance of the United States, Canada, and the nations of western Europe established in 1949.

natural magic (p. 525) The use of magical words and drawings to manipulate the occult forces that exist in nature without calling on supernatural beings for assistance.

nawabs (p. 561) Native provincial governors in eighteenth-century India.

Nazism (p. 829) Twentieth-century political ideology associated with Adolf Hitler that adopted many fascist ideas but with a central focus on racism and particularly anti-Semitism.

neoclassicism (p. 580) The revival of the classical art and architecture of ancient Greece and Rome in the eighteenth century.

Neoplatonism (pp. 189, 522) A philosophy based on the teachings of Plato and his successors that flourished in Late Antiquity, especially in the teachings of Plotinus. Neoplatonism influenced Christianity in Late Antiquity. During the Renaissance Neoplatonism was linked to the belief that the natural world was charged with occult forces that could be used in the practice of magic.

NEP (New Economic Policy) (p. 820) Lenin's economic turnaround in 1921 that allowed and even encouraged small private businesses and farms in the Soviet Union.

New Conservatism (p. 928) Political ideology that emerged at the end of the 1970s combining the free market approach of nineteenth-century liberalism with social conservatism.

new feminism (p. 928) Re-emergence of the feminist movement in the 1970s.

new imperialism (p. 759) The third phase of modern European imperialism, that occurred in the late nineteenth and early twentieth centuries and extended Western control over almost all of Africa and much of Asia.

New Left (p. 917) Leftwing political and cultural movement that emerged in the late 1950s and early 1960s; sought to develop a form of socialism that rejected the over-centralization, authoritarianism, and inhumanity of Stalinism.

nobility (p. 570) Members of the aristocracy who received official recognition of their hereditary status, including their titles of honor and legal privileges.

no-man's-land (p. 786) The area between the combatants' trenches on the Western Front during World War I.

North Atlantic Treaty Organization (NATO) (p. 892) Defensive anti-Soviet alliance of the United States, Canada, and the nations of western Europe established in 1949.

Nuremberg trials (p. 872) Post-World War II trials of members of the Nazi Party and German military; conducted by an international tribunal.

Old Regime (p. 600) The political order of eighteenth-century France, dominated by an absolute monarch and a privileged nobility and clergy.

oligarchy (p. 78) A government consisting of only a few people rather than the entire community.

opera (p. 366) A musical form invented in the final decades of the sixteenth century by a group of humanist-musicians who thought the power of ancient Greek music could be recovered by writing continuous music to accompany a full drama. The drama was performed as a kind of speech-song with the range of pitch and rhythms closely following those of natural speech.

orthodox (p. 181) In Christianity, the term indicates doctrinally correct belief. Definitions of Orthodoxy changed numerous times.

ostracism (p. 77) Developed in democratic Athens, this practice enabled citizens in the assembly to vote to expel any Athenian citizen from the city for ten years for any reason.

Ottonian Renaissance (p. 260) Under the patronage of the Saxon Emperor Otto I (936–973) and his brother Bruno, learned monks, Greek philosophers from Byzantium, and Italian scholars gathered at the imperial court, stimulating a cultural revival in literature and the arts. The writers and artists enhanced the reputation of Otto.

paganism (p. 178) The Christian term for polytheist worship (worshiping more than one god). In the course of Late Antiquity, the Christian church suppressed paganism, the traditional religions of the Roman empire.

palimpsests (p. 246) Because parchment sheets used for copying were expensive, monks often scrubbed off an old text and copied another in its place. These reused sheets of parchment often contain layers of valuable texts that can be retrieved by scientists.

pan-Arabism (p. 842) Nationalist ideology that called for the political unification of all Arabs, regardless of religious affiliation.

panhellenic (p. 72) This word means covering all Greek communities. It applies, for example, to the Olympic Games, in which competitors came from all over the Greek world.

papacy (p. 177) The bishop of the city of Rome is called the Pope, or Father. The papacy refers to the administrative and political institutions controlled by the Pope. The papacy began to gain strength in the sixth century in the absence of Roman imperial government in Italy.

paradigm (p. 525) A conceptual model or intellectual framework within which scientists conduct their research and experimentation.

parlements (p. 481) The highest provincial courts in France, the most important of which was the Parlement of Paris.

pastoralist societies (p. 14) Nomadic communities that move from place to place to find pastures for their herds of domesticated animals.

patricians (p. 113) In ancient Rome, patricians were aristocratic clans with the highest status and the most political influence.

patrons and clients (p. 119) In ancient Roman society, a powerful man (the patron) would exercise influence on behalf of a social subordinate (the client) in anticipation of future support or assistance.

Pax Romana (p. 132) Latin for "Roman Peace", this term refers to the Roman Empire established by Augustus that lasted until the early third century C.E.

perestroika (p. 935) Loosely translated as "restructuring;" Gorbachev's effort to decentralize, reform, and thereby strengthen Soviet economic and political structures.

personal rule (p. 500) The period from 1629 to 1640 in England when King Charles I ruled without Parliament.

phalanx (p. 72) The military formation favored by hoplite soldiers. Standing shoulder to shoulder in ranks often eight men deep, hoplites moved in unison and depended on one another for protection.

philology (p. 355) A method reintroduced by the humanists during the Italian Renaissance devoted to the comparative study of language, especially to understanding the meaning of a word in a particular historical context.

philosophes (p. 581) The writers and thinkers of the Enlightenment, especially in France.

pilgrimage (p. 186) Religious journeys made to holy sites in order to encounter relics.

Pillars of Islam (p. 222) The five basic principles of Islam as taught by Muhammad.

plainchant (p. 304) A medieval form of singing based on a straightforward melody sung with simple harmony by a choir to accompany the recitation of the text of the liturgy.

plantation colony (p. 382) First appearing in the Cape Verde Islands and later in the tropical parts of the Americas, these colonies were established by Europeans who used African slave labor to cultivate cash crops such as sugar, indigo, cotton, coffee, and tobacco.

plebeians (p. 113) The poorest Roman citizens.

polis (p. 70) Or city-state, developed by Greeks in the Archaic Age. A polis was a self-governing community consisting of a defensible hilltop, the town itself, and all the surrounding fields farmed by the citizens of the polis. Poleis (plural) shared similar institutions: an assembly place for men to gather and discuss community affairs, a council of elders, and an open agora, which served as a market and a place for informal discussions.

polyphony (p. 304) A form for singing the Christian liturgy developed around 1170 in which two or more independent melodies were sung at the same time.

polytheistic (p. 21) Refers to polytheism, the belief in many gods.

pop art (p. 911) Effort by artists in the 1950s and 1960s both to utilize and to critique the material plenty of post-World War II popular culture.

popular sovereignty (p. 625) The claim that political power came from the people and that the people constituted the highest political power in the state.

portolanos (p. 381) Books of sailing directions that included charts and descriptions of ports. Portolanos appeared in the Mediterranean in the Late Middle Ages.

positivism (p. 682) The philosophy developed by August Comte in the nineteenth century according to which human society passed through a series of stages, leading to the final positive stage in which the accumulation of scientific data would enable thinkers to discover the laws of human behavior and bring about the improvement of society.

postindustrialism, postindustrial society (p. 953) A service- rather than manufacturing-based economy characterized by an emphasis on marketing and information and by a proliferation of communications technologies.

postmodernism (p. 951) Umbrella term covering a variety of artistic styles and intellectual theories and practices; in general, a rejection of a single, universal, Western style of modernity.

Prague Spring (p. 906) Short-lived popular effort in 1968 to reform Czechoslovakia's political structures; associated with the phrase "socialism with a human face."

predestination (p. 423) The doctrine promoted by John Calvin that since God, the all-knowing and all-powerful being, knew everything in advance and caused everything to happen, then the salvation of any individual was predetermined.

prerogative (p. 499) The set of powers exercised by the English monarch alone, rather than in conjunction with Parliament.

Price Revolution (p. 448) After a long period of falling or stable prices that stretched back to the fourteenth century, Europe experienced sustained price increases between about 1540 and 1640, causing widespread social and economic turmoil.

priesthood of all believers (p. 417) Martin Luther's doctrine that all those of pure faith were themselves priests, a doctrine that undermined the authority of the Catholic clergy over the laity.

proletariat (p. 680) The word used by Karl Marx and Friedrich Engels to identify the class of workers who received their income from wages.

protectionism (p. 550) The policy of shielding domestic industries from foreign competition through a policy of levying tariffs on imported goods.

Radical Reformation (p. 421) Refers to Protestant movements that failed to gain official government recognition and were at best tolerated, at worst persecuted, during the sixteenth century.

Raiders of the Land and Sea (p. 49) The name given by Egyptians to the diverse groups of peoples whose combined naval and land forces destroyed many cities and kingdoms in the eastern Mediterranean and Anatolia, thereby bringing the International Bronze Age to an end.

Reign of Terror (p. 620) A purging of alleged enemies of the French state between 1793 and 1794, superintended by the Committee of Public Safety, that resulted in the execution of 17,000 people.

relics (p. 186) In Christian belief, relics are sacred objects that have miraculous powers. They are associated with saints, biblical figures, or some object associated with them. They served as contacts between Earth and Heaven and were verified by miracles.

Religious Peace of Augsburg (p. 420) In 1555 this peace between Lutherans and Catholics within the Holy Roman Empire established the principle of *cuius regio, eius religio*, which means "he who rules determines the religion of the land." Protestant princes in the Empire were permitted to retain all church lands seized before 1552 and to enforce Protestant worship, but Catholic princes were also allowed to enforce Catholic worship in their territories.

Renaissance (p. 344) A term meaning "rebirth" used by historians to describe a movement that sought to imitate and understand the culture of antiquity. The Renaissance generally refers to a movement that began in Italy and then spread throughout Europe from about 1350 to 1550.

reparations (p. 806) Payments imposed upon Germany after World War I by the Versailles Treaty to cover the costs of the war.

republicanism (p. 345) A political theory first developed by the ancient Greeks, especially the philosopher Plato, but elaborated by the ancient Romans and rediscovered during the Italian Renaissance. The fundamental principle of republicanism as developed during the Italian Renaissance was that government officials should be elected by the people or a portion of the people.

requerimiento (p. 388) A document read by conquistadores to the natives of the Americas before making war on them. The document briefly explained the principles of Christianity and commanded the natives to accept them immediately along with the authority of the pope and the sovereignty of the king of Spain. If the natives refused, they were warned they would be forced to accept Christian conversion and subjected to Spain anyway.

revisionism, socialist revisionism (p. 727) The belief that an equal society can be built through participation in parliamentary politics rather than through violent revolution.

rhetoric (p. 356) The art of persuasive or emotive speaking and writing, which was especially valued by the Renaissance humanists.

Roman Republic (p. 110) The name given to the Roman state from about 500 B.C.E., when the last king of Rome was expelled, to 31 B.C.E., when Augustus established the Roman Empire. The Roman Republic was a militaristic oligarchy.

Romanesque (p. 302) A style in architecture that spread throughout western Europe during the eleventh and the first half of the twelfth centuries and characterized by arched stone roofs supported by rounded arches, massive stone pillars, and thick walls.

romanization (p. 149) The process by which conquered peoples absorbed aspects of Roman culture, especially the Latin language, city-life, and religion.

romanticism (p. 683) An artistic and literary movement of the late eighteenth and nineteenth centuries that involved a protest against classicism, appealed to the passions rather than the intellect, and emphasized the beauty and power of nature.

Rome-Berlin Axis (p. 853) Alliance between Mussolini's Italy and Hitler's Germany formed in 1936.

Schlieffen Plan (p. 781) German military plan devised in 1905 that called for a sweeping attack on France through Belgium and the Netherlands.

scholasticism (p. 299) A term referring to a broad philosophical and theological movement that dominated medieval thought and university training. Scholasticism used logic learned from Aristotle to interpret the meaning of the Bible and the writings of the Church Fathers, who created Christian theology in its first centuries.

Scramble for Africa (p. 763) The frenzied imposition of European control over most of Africa that occurred between 1870 and 1914.

scriptorium (p. 246) The room in a monastery where monks copied books and manuscripts.

Second Industrial Revolution (p. 713) A new phase in the industrialization of the processes of production and consumption, underway in Europe in the 1870s.

Second Triumvirate (p. 126) In 43 B.C.E. Octavian (later called Augustus), Mark Antony, and Lepidus made an informal alliance to share power in Rome while they jockeyed for control. Octavian emerged as the sole ruler of Rome in 31 B.C.E.

seigneur (p. 582) The lord of a French estate who received payments from the peasants who lived on his land.

separate spheres (p. 595) The theory that men and women should conduct their lives in different social and political environments, confining women to the domestic sphere and excluding them from the public sphere of political involvement.

sepoys (p. 562) Indian troops serving in the armed forces of the British East India Company.

Septuagint (p. 103) The Greek translation of the Hebrew Bible (Old Testament).

serfs (p. 275) During the Middle Ages serfs were agricultural laborers who worked and lived on a plot of land granted them by a lord to whom they owed a certain portion of their crops. They could not leave the land, but they had certain legal rights that were denied to slaves.

settler colony (p. 382) A colony authorized when a private person obtained a license from a king to seize an island or parcel of land and occupied it with settlers from Europe who exported their own culture to the new lands. Settler colonies first appeared among the islands of the eastern Atlantic and portions of the Americas.

simony (p. 281) The practice of buying and selling church offices.

Social Darwinism (p. 747) The later-nineteenth-century application of the theory of evolution to entire human societies.

social democracy (p. 838) Political system in which a democratically elected parliamentary government endeavors to ensure a decent standard of living for its citizens through both economic regulation and the maintenance of a welfare state.

Solidarity (p. 931) Trade union and political party in Poland that led an unsuccessful effort to reform the Polish communist state in 1981; survived to lead Poland's first non-communist government since World War II in 1989.

Sophists (p. 85) Professional educators who traveled throughout the ancient Greek world, teaching many subjects. Their goal was to teach people the best ways to lead better lives.

soviets (p. 800) Workers' and soldiers' councils formed in Russia during the Revolution of 1917.

Spanish Armada (p. 465) A fleet of 132 ships, which sailed from Portugal to rendezvous with the Spanish army stationed in the Netherlands and launch an invasion of England in 1588. The English defeated the Armada as it passed through the English Channel.

Spanish Reconquest (p. 233) Refers to the numerous military campaigns by the Christian kingdoms of northern Spain to capture the Muslim-controlled cities and kingdoms of southern Spain. This long, intermittent struggle began with the capture of Toledo in 1085 and lasted until Granada fell to Christian armies in 1492.

spiritualists (p. 428) A tendency within Protestantism, especially Lutheranism, to emphasize the power of personal spiritual illumination, called the "inner Word," a living form of the Scriptures written directly on the believer's soul by the hand of God.

stagflation (p. 925) Term coined in the 1970s to describe an economy troubled by both high inflation and high unemployment rates.

states (p. 542) Consolidated territorial areas that have their own political institutions and recognize no higher political authority.

Stoicism (p. 104) The philosophy developed by Zeno of Citium (ca. 335–ca. 263 B.C.E.) that urged acceptance of fate while participating fully in everyday life.

structuralism (p. 911) Influential post-World War II social theory that explored the common structures of language and thought.

Struggle of the Orders (p. 113) The political strife between patrician and plebeian Romans beginning in the fifth century B.C.E. The plebeians gradually won political rights and influence as a result of the struggle.

suffragettes (p. 738) Feminist movement that emerged in Britain in the early twentieth century. Unlike the suffragists, who sought to achieve the vote for women through rational persuasion, the suffragettes adopted the tactics of violent protest.

supply (p. 653) The amounts of capital, labor, and food that are needed to produce goods for the market as well as the quantities of those goods themselves.

Syncretism (p. 158) The practice of equating two gods and fusing their cults was common throughout the Roman Empire and helped to unify the diverse peoples and religions under Roman rule.

syndicalism (p. 728) Ideology of the late nineteenth and early twentieth century that sought to achieve a working-class revolution through economic action, particularly through mass labor strikes.

Talmuds (p. 186) Commentaries on Jewish law. Rabbis completed the Babylonian Talmud and the Jerusalem Talmud by the end of the fifth century C.E.

Tetrarchy (p. 172) The government by four rulers established by the Roman emperor Diocletian in 293 C.E. that lasted until 312. During the Tetrarchy many administrative and military reforms altered the fabric of Roman society.

Third World (p. 900) Term coined in 1955 to describe nations that did not align with either the Soviet Union or the United States; commonly used to describe the industrially underdeveloped nations.

Thomism (p. 301) A branch of medieval philosophy associated with the work of the Dominican thinker, Thomas Aquinas (1225–1274), who wrote encyclopedic summaries of human knowledge that confirmed Christian faith.

Time of Troubles (p. 474) The period from 1604 to 1613 when Russia fell into chaos, which ended when the national assembly elected Tsar Michael Romanov, whose descendants ruled Russia until they were deposed in 1917.

total war (p. 778) A war that demands extensive state regulation of economic production, distribution, and consumption; and that blurs (or erases entirely) the distinction between civilian and soldier.

trading posts (p. 388) Built by European traders along the coasts of Africa and Asia as a base for trade with the interior. Trading posts or factories were islands of European law and sovereignty, but European authority seldom extended very far beyond the fortified post.

transubstantiation (p. 289) A doctrine promulgated at the Fourth Lateran Council in 1215 that explained by distinguishing between the outward appearances and the inner substance how the Eucharistic bread and wine changed into the body and blood of Christ.

Treaty of Brest-Litovsk (p. 790) Treaty between Germany and Bolshevik-controlled Russia, signed in March, 1918, that ceded to Germany all of Russia's western territories.

trial by jury (p. 296) When disputes about the possession of land arose after the late twelfth century in England, sheriffs assembled a group of twelve local men who testified under oath about the claims of the plaintiffs, and the circuit court judge made his decision on the basis of their testimony. The system was later extended to criminal cases.

Triple Alliance (p. 779) Defensive alliance of Germany, Austria-Hungary, and Italy, signed in 1882.

Triple Entente (p. 781) Informal defensive agreement linking France, Great Britain, and Russia before World War I.

triremes (p. 75) Greek warships with three banks of oars. Triremes manned by the poorest people of Athenian society became the backbone of the Athenian empire.

troubadours (p. 302) Poets from the late twelfth and thirteenth centuries who wrote love poems, meant to be sung to music, which reflected a new sensibility, called courtly love, about the ennobling possibilities of the love between a man and a woman.

Truman Doctrine (p. 890) Named after U.S. president Harry Truman, the doctrine that in 1947 inaugurated the Cold War policy of resisting the expansion of communist control.

Twelfth-Century Renaissance (p. 300) An intellectual revival of interest in ancient Greek philosophy and science and in Roman law in western Europe during the twelfth and early thirteenth centuries. The term also refers to a flowering of vernacular literature and the Romanesque and Gothic styles in architecture.

tyrants (p. 72) Political leaders from the upper classes who championed the cause of hoplites in Greek city-states during the Archaic Age. The word "tyrant" gained its negative connotation when democracies developed in Greece that gave more political voice to male citizens than permitted by tyrants.

Unitarians (p. 429) A religious reform movement that began in the sixteenth century and rejected the Christian doctrine of the Trinity. Unitarians (also called Arians, Socinians, and Anti-Trinitarians) taught a rationalist interpretation of the Scriptures and argued that Jesus was a divinely inspired man, not God-become-man as did other Christians.

universal law of gravitation (p. 518) A law of nature established by Isaac Newton in 1687 holding that any two bodies attract each other with a force that is directly proportional to the product of their masses and indirectly proportional to the square of the distance between them. The law was presented in mathematical terms.

universal male suffrage (p. 615) The granting of the right to vote to all adult males.

Utilitarians (p. 678) Nineteenth-century British liberals who promoted social and economic policies that in their view would provide the greatest good for the greatest number of people.

vassals (p. 255) During the Middle Ages men voluntarily submitted themselves to a lord by taking an oath of loyalty. Vassals owed the lord certain services—usually military assistance—and sometimes received in exchange a grant of land known as a fief.

Vatican II (p. 912) Popular term for the Second Vatican Council that convened in 1963 and introduced a series of changes within the Roman Catholic Church.

Versailles Treaty (p. 806) Treaty between Germany and the victorious Allies after World War I.

Vichy, Vichy regime, Vichy government (p. 855) Authoritarian state established in France after defeat by the German army in 1940.

Warsaw Pact (p. 892) Military alliance of the Soviet Union and its eastern European satellite states in the Cold War era.

Weimar Republic (p. 821) The democratic German state constructed after defeat in World War I and destroyed by the Nazis in 1933.

wergild (p. 243) In Germanic societies the term referred to what an individual was worth in case he or she suffered an injury. It was the amount of compensation in gold that the wrongdoer's family had to pay to the victim's family.

witch-hunt (p. 457) Refers to the dramatic increase in the judicial prosecution of alleged witches in either church or secular courts from the middle of the sixteenth to the middle of the seventeenth centuries.

Zionism (p. 732) Nationalist movement that emerged in the late nineteenth century and sought to establish a Jewish political state in Palestine (the Biblical Zion).

Zoroastrianism (p. 59) The monotheistic religion of Persia founded by Zoroaster that became the official religion of the Persian Empire.

Credits

Unless otherwise acknowledged, all photographs are the property of Pearson Education, Inc.
Page abbreviations are as follows: **(T)** Top, **(B)** Bottom, **(L)** Left, **(R)** Right, **(C)** Center.

What Is the West?
2 Canali Photobank **4** European Space Agency/Photo Researchers, Inc. **5** Courtesy of Adler Planetarium & Astronomy Museum, Chicago, Illinois (W-264). **8** American Museum of Natural History Library (AMNH#314372)

Chapter 1
10 Giraudon/Art Resource, NY **12** Augustin Ochsenreiter/ South Tyrol Museum of Archaeology **17** Courtesy of the Trustees of the British Museum **19** Robert Harding Picture Library **21** Scala/Art Resource, NY **23** Erich Lessing/Art Resource, NY **29** Roger Ressmeyer/Corbis

Chapter 2
33 The Art Archive/National Archaeological Museum Athens/Dagli Orti **36** Dagli Orti/The Art Archive **38** The Art Archive/ Egyptian Museum Cairo/Dagli Orti (A) **39** Osiride Head of Hatshepsut, originally from a statue. Provenance: Thebes, Deir el Bahri. Limestone, painted. H. 64 cm. H. with crown 124.5 cm. The Metropolitan Museum of Art, Rogers Fund, 1931, (31.3.157) Photograph © 1983 The Metropolitan Museum of Art **41** British Museum, London/Bridgeman Art Library **44** Nimatallah/Art Resource, NY **48** Hirmer Fotoarchiv **53** Erich Lessing/Art Resource, NY

Chapter 3
56 Erich Lessing/Art Resource, NY **61** SEF/Art Resource, NY **66** Israel Museum **71 (BR)** The American Numismatic Society **71 (BL)** The American Numismatic Society **71 (TR)** The American Numismatic Society **71 (TL)** The American Numismatic Society **75** Erich Lessing/Art Resource, NY **79 (T)** Foto Marburg/Art Resource, NY **79 (BR)** Pedicini/Index s.a.s. **79 (BL)** Louvre, Paris, France/Bridgeman Art Library **80** Staatliche Antikensammlungen und Glyptothek, Munich **81** Robert Harding Picture Library **84** Column krater (missing bowl) (detail), Greek, Archaic Period (Late Corinthian), about 550 B.C., Place of manufacture: Greece, Corinthia, Corinth, Ceramic, Black Figure, Height 33 cm (13 in); diameter: 41cm ($16\frac{1}{8}$ in.), Museum of Fine Arts, Boston, Helen and Alice Colburn Fund (63.420) Photograph © 2003 Museum of Fine Arts, Boston **85** British Museum, London, Great Britain/HIP/Art Resource, NY **87** Scala/Art Resource, NY **88** Scala/Art Resource, NY

Chapter 4
92 Scala/Art Resource, NY **96** Bildarchiv Prüßischer Kulturbesitz/ Art Resource, NY **100** Réunion des Musées Nationaux/Art Resource, NY **101** Bildarchiv Prüßischer Kulturbesitz/Art Resource, NY **102** Réunion des Musées Nationaux/Art Resource, NY **105** Erich Lessing/Art Resource, NY **110 (T)** Erich Lessing/ Art Resource, NY **110 (B)** Bildarchiv Prüßischer Kulturbesitz/Art Resource, NY **112** Robert Harding Picture Library **119** Vanni/ Art Resource, NY **121** Alinari/Art Resource, NY

Chapter 5
130 Erich Lessing/Art Resource, NY **134** Erich Lessing/Art Resource, NY **137** SEF/Art Resource, NY **139** Leo C. Curran **141** Erich Lessing/Art Resource, NY **144** Yann Arthus-Bertrand/ Corbis **148** Vasari/Index s.a.s. **150** Robert Harding Picture Library **152** akg-images **156** Scala/Art Resource, NY **159** Scala/Art Resource, NY **160** Scala/Art Resource, NY **161** Jewish Museum, London **162** Courtesy of the Trustees of the British Museum

Chapter 6
168 Österreichische Nationalbibliothek, Vienna **170** Scala/Art Resource, NY **171** SEF/Art Resource, NY **172** Erich Lessing/Art Resource, NY **177** Scala/Art Resource, NY **179** Victoria & Albert Museum, London/Art Resource, NY **182** Réunion des Musées Nationaux/Art Resource, NY **186** The Jewish Museum, New York, NY/Art Resource, NY **191** Alinari/Art Resource, NY **197** Réunion des Musées Nationaux/Art Resource, NY **199** Scala/ Art Resource, NY **202 (T)** Courtesy of the Trustees of the British Museum **202 (B)** Courtesy of the Trustees of the British Museum

Chapter 7
204 Erich Lessing/Art Resource, NY **209 (T)** Balatoni Museum, Keszthely, Hungary **209 (B)** Balatoni Museum, Keszthely, Hungary **213** David and Goliath, Byzantine, Made in Constantinople, 629–630; Early Byzantine, Silver, D. $1\frac{1}{2}$ in. (3.8 cm); Diam. $19\frac{1}{2}$ in (49.4 cm); The Metropolitan Museum of Art, Gift of J. Pierpont Morgan, 1917 (17.190.396) Photograph © 2000 The Metropolitan Museum of Art **215** British Museum/The Art Archive **216** State Historical Museum, Moscow **217** Courtesy of His Eminence Archbishop Damianos and the Holy Council of the Fathers, Saint Catherine's Monastery. Photograph © Idryma Orous Sina, Mt. Sinai Foundation **218** Pushkin Museum, Moscow, Russia/Bridgeman Art Library **220** Werner Forman/ Art Resource, NY **223** Associate Press/AP **225** Freer Gallery of Art, Smithsonian Institution, Washington, D.C.: Purchase, F1930.60a **228** Robert Harding Picture Library **230 (TR)** The Nasser D. Khalili Collection of Islamic Art **230 (TL)** The Nasser D. Khalili Collection of Islamic Art **230 (BR)** Bibliothèque Nationale de France (2001 A 83708) **230 (BL)** Bibliothèque Nationale de France (2001 A 83707) **233** Vanni/Art Resource, NY

Chapter 8
236 Art Resource, NY **251** Vanni/Art Resource, NY **252** Eric Lessing/Art Resource, NY **254** Werner Forman/Art Resource, NY **255** Werner Forman/Art Resource, NY **257** Scala/Art Resource, NY **259** akg-images **261** Werner Forman/Art Resource, NY **264** HIP/Scala/Art Resource, NY **265** Dagli Orti/The Art Archive **266** Bildarchiv Preussischer Kulturbesitz/ Art Resource, NY **274** Réunion des Musées Nationaux/Art Resource, NY

Chapter 9

270 Courtesy Achim Bednorz **272** Scala/Art Resource, NY **273** Scala/Art Resource, NY **275** Cambridge University Collection of Aerial Photography (ATV76) **278** Scala/Art Resource, NY **282** Giraudon/Art Resource, NY **285** Scala/Art Resource, NY **286** Scala/Art Resource, NY **293** Erich Lessing/Art Resource, NY **300** Bildarchiv Preussischer Kulturbesitz/Art Resource, NY **303** Scala/Art Resource, NY **304 (R)** Marc Garanger/Corbis **304 (L)** Anthony Scibilia/Art Resource, NY

Chapter 10

306 Scala/Art Resource, NY **311** Image Select/Art Resource, NY **312** Scala/Art Resource, NY **314** Art Resource, NY **321** HIP/Art Resource, NY **322** Honourable Society of Inner Temple London/ Eileen Tweedy/The Art Archive **323** Bibliothèque Nationale de France, Paris (MS. Fr. 2644 fol. 135) **325** By permission of the British Library (Addt. mss.42130 fol 147v) **327** Giraudon/Art Resource, NY **329** Vanni/Art Resource, NY **330** Snark/Art Resource, NY **332 (T)** Tomb Effigy of Jean d'Alluy, mid-13th century, Limestone, 83½ × 34¼ in. (212.1 × 87 cm) The Metropolitan Museum of Art, The Cloisters Collection, 1925. (25.120.201) Photography © 1979 The Metropolitan Museum of Art **332 (B)** Réunion des Musées Nationaux/Art Resource, NY **333** Scala/Art Resource, NY **334** Réunion des Musées Nationaux/ Art Resource, NY **335** Erich Lessing/Art Resource, NY

Chapter 11

341 Erich Lessing/Art Resource, NY **346** Scala/Art Resource, NY **349** Scala/Art Resource, NY **350** Erich Lessing/Art Resource, NY **353** Kunsthistorisches Museum, Vienna/Art Resource, NY **354** Alinari/Art Resource, NY **360 (R & L)** Orsi Battaglini/ Index s.a.s. **361** Art Resource, NY **362** Scala/Art Resource, NY **362** Scala/Art Resource, NY **363 (T)** Nimatallah/Art Resource, NY **363 (B)** Scala/Art Resource, NY **364** Brancacci Chapel, Santa Maria del Carmine, Florence, Italy/Bridgeman Art Library **364** Art Resource, NY **365 (T)** Erich Lessing/Art Resource, NY **365 (B)** Erich Lessing/Art Resource, NY

Chapter 12

376 Courtesy of the Trustees of the British Museum **381** Giraudon/Art Resource, NY **382** Science Academy Lisbon/ Dagli Orti/The Art Archive **385** Scala/Art Resource, NY **387** Snark/Art Resource, NY **389** Snark/Art Resource, NY **390** Giraudon/Art Resource, NY **391** Nick Saunders/Barbara Heller Photo Library, London/Art Resource, NY **392** Snark/Art Resource, NY **395** Georgius Hoefnagle plate from Georg Braun (1542–1622), 5 vols. Civitatis orbis terrarum (Colonia Agrippinae, 1572–1618), Maps Division, Sterling Memorial Library, Yale University **400** Werner Forman/Art Resource, NY **402** Snark/ Art Resource, NY **404** Snark/Art Resource, NY

Chapter 13

408 Scala/Art Resource, NY **411** Scala/Art Resource, NY **412** Erich Lessing/Art Resource, NY **413** Foto Marburg/Art Resource, NY **416** Snark/Art Resource, NY **419 R & L** Scala/ Art Resource, NY **426** Thyssen Bornemisza Collection, Madrid **427** By courtesy of the National Portrait Gallery, London (NPG668) **428** Erich Lessing/Art Resource, NY **432** Scala/Art Resource, NY **436 (T)** The Granger Collection, New York **436 (B)** Max Polster Archive **437** Scala/Art Resource, NY **438** Alinari/Art Resource, NY

Chapter 14

442 Erich Lessing/Art Resource, NY **446** Scala/Art Resource, NY **453** akg-images **454** Erich Lessing/Art Resource, NY **455** Erich Lessing/Art Resource, NY **456** Erich Lessing/Art Resource, NY **459** Erich Lessing/Art Resource, NY **459** Time Life Pictures/ Getty Images **463** Musée de Beaux Arts Lausanne/Dagli Orti/ The Art Archive **465** Snark/Art Resource, NY **469** By kind permission of His Grace the Duke of Bedford and the Trustees of the Bedford Estates **471** Erich Lessing/Art Resource, NY **474** Art Resource, NY

Chapter 15

476 Réunion des Musées Nationaux/Art Resource, NY **482** Philippe de Champaigne, 1602–1674. Triple Portrait of Cardinal Richelieu, oil on canvas, 58.4 × 72.4 cm. © The National Gallery, London (NG798) **483** Réunion des Musées Nationaux/ Art Resource, NY **490** Museo del Prado/Art Resource, NY **491** Scala/Art Resource, NY **492** Bildarchiv Prüßischer Kulturbesitz/Art Resource, NY **498** Stapleton Collection, UK/ Bridgeman Art Library **500** Museum of London, UK/Bridgeman Art Library **503** This item is reproduced by permission of the Huntington Library, San Marina, California **507** Museum Boijmans van Beuningen, Rotterdam **508** Rijksmuseum Foundation, Amsterdam

Chapter 16

512 Archivo Iconografico, S.A./Corbis **515 (R)** From *The Cosmographical Glass*, 1559 **515 (L)** © 1982 Instructional Resources Corporation **516 (T)** By permission of the British Library (Neg No. 2204) **516 (B)** The Library of Congress (LC USZ62-95165) **518** Giraudon/Art Resource, NY **519** Ashmolean Museum, Oxford University (BI313) **520** Wellcome Library, London **522** Erich Lessing/Art Resource, NY **529** Herzog August Bibliothek, Wolfenbuttel, Germany/ Bridgeman Art Library **533** Erich Lessing/Art Resource, NY **536** Réunion des Musées Nationaux/Art Resource, NY **538** Corbis

Chapter 17

540 Victoria & Albert Museum, London/Art Resource, NY **546** Private Collection Pairs/Dagli Orti/The Art Archive **547** British Museum/Art Resource, NY **556** Museum of London **559** Joseph Mallord William Turner, English, 1775–1851. *Slave Ship (Slavers Throwing Overboard the Dead and Dying, Typhoon Coming On)*, 1840. Oil on canvas. 90.8 × 122.6 cm (35¾ × 48¼ in.). Museum of Fine Arts, Boston. Henry Lillie Pierce Fund. 99.22. Photograph © 2006 Museum of Fine Arts Boston **560** Benson Latin American Collection, University of Texas-Austin **562** Museo de Arte, Sao Paulo, Brazil/Giraudon/ Bridgeman Art Library **565** Private Collection/The Stapleton Collection/Bridgeman Art Library **566** The Library of Congress **567** Réunion des Musées Nationaux/Art Resource, NY **571** Museo Bolivar Caracas/Dagli Orti/The Art Archive

Chapter 18

574 Erich Lessing/Art Resource, NY **579** National Gallery, London **581** akg-images **583** By courtesy of the Trustees of the Goodwood Collection **584** Erich Lessing/Art Resource, NY **587** Scottish National Portrait Gallery (PG1057) **588** *Engravings by Hogarth*, plate 95 **592** akg-images/Archives CDA/St-Genés **594** Bibliothèque Nationale de France, Paris (50C 5452)

598 Corbis **601** From *Constituto Criminalis Theresiana*, 1769 **602** Art Resource, NY

Chapter 19

606 Giraudon/Art Resource, NY **608** Erich Lessing/Art Resource, NY **614 (R)** akg-images **614 (L)** akg-images **615** Bibliothèque Nationale de France, Paris (80C 103369) **616** Bibliothèque Nationale de France, Paris (45B M89) **619** Giraudon/Art Resource, NY **622** Erich Lessing/Art Resource, NY **624** Annenberg Rare Book & Manuscript Library, University of Pennsylvania (Revolutions de Paris No. 161: Aug 4–11, 1792) **626** Photothèque des Musées de las Ville de Paris/Cliché: Andreani **627** Giraudon/Art Resource, NY **629** Réunion des Musées Nationaux/Art Resource, NY **634** Réunion des Musées Nationaux/Art Resource, NY **636** Erich Lessing/Art Resource, NY

Chapter 20

642 Guildhall Library, Corporation of London/Bridgeman Art Library **644** From *The White Slaves of England*, 1853 **645** Royal Commission on the Ancient and Historical Monuments of Scotland; SC679552 **647** Science Museum, London/Science and Society Picture Library **649** From *History of the Cotton Manufacture in Great Britain*, 1836 **650** Lewis Carroll's Album. The Gernsheim Collection, Harry Ransom Research Center, University of Texas-Austin **657** Deutsche Bahn Museum, Nürnberg **658** akg-images **664** Rickitt Collection of Slides/The Slide Center **666** *Punch*, 1847 **667** Attributed to Frederick Calvert, *South-West Prospect of Birmingham*, 1829 Birmingham Museums & Art Gallery. **668** Manchester Art Gallery, UK/ Bridgeman Art Library **669** National Gallery, London

Chapter 21

674 Réunion des Musées Nationaux/Art Resource, NY **679** The Granger Collection, New York **683** Genève, Bibliothèque publique et universitaire **684** Bridgeman Art Library **687** Réunion des Musées Nationaux/Art Resource, NY **689** Giraudon/Art Resource, NY **691** The Royal Archives © 2003 Her Majesty Queen Elizabeth II. **695** Gemälde von Anton von Werner, 1885. Friedrichsruh, Bismarck-Museum, Bildarchiv Prüßischer Kulturbesitz, Berlin **700** Getty Images **701** akg-images **707** akg-images

Chapter 22

710 Musée d'Orsay, Paris, France, Giraudon/Bridgeman Art Library **713** Roger-Viollet/Getty Images **714** Private Collection/Archives Charmet/Bridgeman Art Library **716** Private Collection, Roger Perrin/Bridgeman Art Library **720** Courtesy Special Auction Services, England **720** Getty Images **723** Bettmann/Corbis **723** Réunion des Musées Nationaux/Art Resource, NY **724** Eastphoto/Sovfoto **728** By permission of The People's History Museum **731** The Jewish Museum, New York, NY, U.S.A./Art Resource, NY **735** By Permission of The People's History Museum **736** Yale Center for British Art/ Bridgeman Art Library

Chapter 23

742 Erich Lessing/Art Resource, NY **745** Erich Lessing/Art Resource, NY **746** National History Museum, London/ Bridgeman Art Library **750** Scala/Art Resource, NY **752** The Granger Collection, New York **754** Schloss Immendorf, Austria/Bridgeman Art Library **755** Bibliothéque de L'Arsenal, Paris, France, Giraudon/Bridgeman Art Library **756** Eastphoto/ Sovfoto © 2006 Artists Rights Society (ARS), New York/ADAGP, Paris **757 (R)** Manchester City Art Galleries, UK/Bridgeman Art Library **757 (L)** Graphische Sammlung Albertina, Vienna, Austria/Bridgeman Art Library **760** The Granger Collection, New York **762** Digital Image © The Museum of Modern Art/ Licensed by SCALA/Art Resource, NY/© 2006 Estate of Pablo Picasso/Artists Rights Society (ARS), New York **763** Bodleian Library, University of Oxford, shelfmark: 2523 c.24 **765** Anti-Slavery International **771** Robert Hunt Picture Library **772** Private Collection, Archives Charmet/Bridgeman Art Library

Chapter 24

776 Trustees of the Imperial War Museum, Imperial War Museum, Photograph Archive, Q70169 **778** Getty Images **784** Roger-Viollet/Topham/The Image Works **785** Trustees of the Imperial War Museum/Imperial War Museum, Photograph Archive, Q 45786 **786** Getty Images **787** akg-images **788** National Gallery of Canada, Ottawa (No. 4800) **789** Imperial War Museum, London **791** Trustees of the Imperial War Museum, Imperial War Museum, Photograph Archive, Q2061 **796** Trustees of the Imperial War Museum/ Imperial War Museum, Photograph Archive **798** The Library of Congress, cph 3g10241 **799 (T)** Mary Evans Picture Library **799 (B)** Getty Images **802** Scala/Art Resource, NY **803** akg-images **805** Corbis **806** Associated Press/U.S. Navy

Chapter 25

812 Museum of the Revolution, Moscow/Bridgeman Art Library **816** Bildarchiv Prüßischer Kulturbesitz/Art Resource, NY © 2006 Artist Rights Society (ARS), New York/VG Bild-Kunst, Bonn **817 (T)** Jeffery Howe **817 (B)** Jeffery Howe **819** Bildarchiv Prüßischer Kulturbesitz **821** Photographie J. H. Lartigue/ © Ministère de la Culture-France/A.A.J.H.L. **823** akg-images **824** Bildarchiv Prüßischer Kulturbesitz/Art Resource, NY. Art © Estate of Georg Grosz/Licensed by VAGA, New York, NY **827** akg-images **831** Bildarchiv Prüßischer Kulturbesitz **835 (T)** David King/Sovfoto **835 (B)** Sovfoto **836** RUSU 2225, Poster Collection, Hoover Institution Archives **838** Underwood & Underwood/Corbis **839** Robert Capa/Magnum Photo, Inc. **844** Bettmann/Corbis **846** akg-images

Chapter 26

848 Courtesy of the National Museum of the U.S. Army **851** Corbis **853** Getty Images **855** akg-images **861** TRH Pictures **862** Getty Images **864** Getty Images **865** Popperfoto/ Retrofile **867** Getty Images **869** USHMM, courtesy of the Yad Vashem Photo Archives **870** akg-images **873** Getty Images **875** Bettmann/Corbis **877** ©Marius Meijboom/npa **878** The National Archives, London **880** Topham/The Image Works

Chapter 27

884 The Granger Collection, New York **886** Camera Press, London/Retna, Ltd. **888** Courtesy Franklin D. Roosevelt Library **891 (R)** su concessione del Ministero per i Beni e le Attivitá Culturali, Soprintendenza P.S.A.E. per le province di Venezia, Padova, Belluno e Traviso, Inv. 13487 "vota o sará il tuo padrone" **891 (L)** Private Collection, Archives Charmet/ Bridgeman Art Library **895** Paul Colin/Corbis © 2006 Artist Rights Society, (ARS), New York/ADAGP, Paris **903** CTK Photo **905** Getty Images **910 (R)** Digital Image © The Museum of

Modern Art/Licensed by SCALA/Art Resource, NY/© 2006 The Pollock-Krasner Foundation/Artists Rights Society (ARS), New York **910 (L)** Digital Image © The Museum of Modern Art/ Licensed by SCALA/Art Resource, NY/© 2006 Artists Rights Society (ARS), New York/ADAGP, Paris **911** Kunsthalle, Tubingen/Bridgeman Art Library/© 2006 Artists Rights Society (ARS) New York/DACS, London **913** Todd A. Gipstein/Corbis **914** Getty Images **916** William Safire/Bettmann/Corbis **917** Bettmann/Corbis **918** Time Life Pictures/Getty Images **919** Photo source: Rheinisches Bildarchiv Köln. © 2006 Artist Rights Agency (ARS), New York/VG Kunst-Bild, Bonn

Chapter 28

922 Associated Press/AP **925** SIPA Press **929** Associated Press/AP **930** Associated Press/Alexander Sekretariev Estate **932** CTK/Sovfoto **933** Jean Gaumy/Magnum Photo, Inc. **934** Tass/Sovfoto **936** Poster Collection, Hoover Institution Archives **938** Stephen Ferry/Gamma Press USA, Inc. **942 (R)** Scott Peterson/Getty Images **942 (L)** Gyori Antoine/ Corbis **947** Getty Images **950** Associated Press/AP **951** Michael Latz/AFP/Getty Images **952** Frank Chmura/Index Stock Imagery **956** Neil Cooper/Panos Pictures

Index

Atlas

How to Read a Map and Why it Matters

Maps are one of the many tools that historians use to help them understand what is happening in space and time. There is a wide array of information that maps can convey. Some provide information about political boundaries past and present; others, topographic and physical maps, show geographical features such as rivers, mountains, deserts, and other land or water formations; while still others represent historical data, such as population growth or specialized thematic topics. Maps communicate this information, allowing the viewer to analyze, interpret, and make conclusions about the subject matter. Since maps are depictions of what places look like, they help to put history in a physical context, providing a type of visual imagery to go along with the historic narrative. They can also show change over time by demonstrating growth or decline through map symbols.

It is important to recognize that maps, like other sources, come with their own point of view and that the way in which they are drawn, or the "projection" used, affects what the viewer sees. The Mercator projection, for example, originally a valuable map for sailors since it showed true direction, actually distorts what it is showing by making areas further from the equator larger than they actually are. It could be argued that this displays a Eurocentric bias since it makes it appear that Europe and the United States are larger than they are in reality. Polar projections, in which the map centers on either the north or south pole, are used for maps of the northern and southern hemispheres and are useful when discussing subjects focused on these areas, such as air traffic patterns or Cold War arsenals (missiles were aimed over the North Pole, as it represented the shortest distance between Moscow and Washington, DC). Cartograms are special maps where the size of a country is drawn relative to one its characteristics, such as the size of its population, showing an altered view of the physical world in order to make a specific point.

In history, being able to read and interpret maps matters for three main reasons: (1) knowing where places are; (2) being able to visualize the movement of peoples, ideas, and commodities; and (3) understanding the difference location can make in human endeavors.

MAPS SHOW WHERE PLACES ARE

Maps are key to understanding the absolute and relative location of places. They provide the precise location where cities and empires have been located, where battles have taken place, and where religions, ideas, and inventions have originated. Knowing the location of places is the first step in answering some of the more interesting questions of "Why there?" "Why then?" Maps also show where a place is in relation to other places or geographic features. Whether societies evolved near rivers and coasts or are land-locked is an important consideration in historical thinking. The geo-political importance of control over nearby straits, access to trading networks, or being part of a disease exchange all factor into the importance of knowing relative location.

MAPS SHOW MOVEMENT

Maps also show movement: the voluntary and forced migration of peoples, the spread of ideas, including religion, and the trade of commodities. Maps can help provide information as to directional flows as well as volume, changes over time, and patterns of movement. One cannot discuss the Atlantic slave trade without fully comprehending that most of the enslaved people were transported from West Africa to Brazil and the Caribbean, not to the American South. A map that shows the direction and volume of the slave trade provides a visual reminder of this important fact. In a similar vein, seeing on a map how vulnerable Russia and the Soviet Union were to western and eastern invasion by first the Mongols, then Napoleon, and then Hitler, helps one better understand the rationale behind Soviet expansion into Eastern Europe.

MAPS SHOW THE IMPORTANCE OF LOCATION ON HUMAN ENDEAVORS

Maps can also help us appreciate that *where* something happens can affect *what* happens in economic, physical, and human terms. Looking at a physical map of Europe, one can appreciate how port cities along the Mediterranean as well as along rivers such as the Danube, the Rhine, and the Thames were able to become great trading centers, bringing in goods from throughout the region, as well as other regions, depending on the time and place. Maps can also show climate, population data, religious composition, and natural resources, which can help us understand such questions as why cities and societies grow and diminish and how they interact in peace and at war.

HOW TO READ A MAP

To analyze maps, it helps to recognize their central parts: the title, orientation, date, author, legend (or key), and scale (TODALS). When looking at a map, first read the *title.* It will indicate the main topic of the map: political units, physical features, or a theme. Reading the title first will help you focus your attention. The *orientation,* or the direction in which the map is "pointed," will be shown on a compass rose, a design that shows direction. Most maps today have north "at the top." However, this was not always the case: Medieval maps ("T" maps) had Jerusalem in the center and the east at the top. The *date* a map is made is also important, as our understanding changes over time, and older maps may no longer be accurate. If the *author* of a map is included, this can help you establish its credibility and whether it might represent any bias. The *legend,* or key, of a map shows what the colors, symbols, or markings on the map represent and is essential to understanding the map's story. Maps will also often include a *scale,* which tells you the relationship between distance on the map and actual distance on the earth (for example, one inch on the map represents 10 miles). Understanding the scale on a map helps viewers understand how large (and near or far apart) places actually are. In addition to these central parts, many maps include a caption. Reading the caption before examining the map can help you direct your attention and gain further insight into what the map is intended to portray and its significance in a larger context. All of these elements are tools at your disposal to help you get the most out of a map.

All maps can be "read," as one would read a document or an image, for further insights into history. The 1994 Geography for Life National Standards affirm, "Students must appreciate that viewing the past from both spatial and chronological points of view can lead to a greater awareness and depth of understanding of physical and human events, and is an essential ingredient in the interpretation of the world today." Without maps, history would be missing an important conceptual and analytical tool.

Name ______________________ Date ______________________

Course Name and Number ______________________ Instructor ______________________

MAP 1.1
Egypt, Kush, and Nubia, ca. 3100 B.C.E.

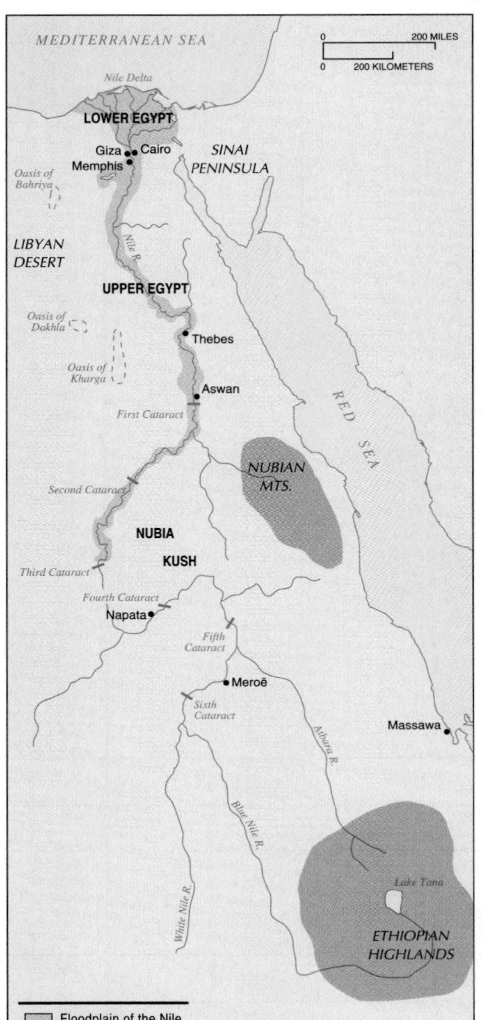

MAP ANALYSIS

1. What physical features surround the Nile River?

____

2. What cities are included in Lower Egypt?

____

3. What cities are included in Upper Egypt?

____

4. What kingdoms lay to the south of Egypt?

____

5. How far south do the floodplains of the Nile River extend?

____

MAP 1.2
The Empire of Assyria, ca. 1800 B.C.E.

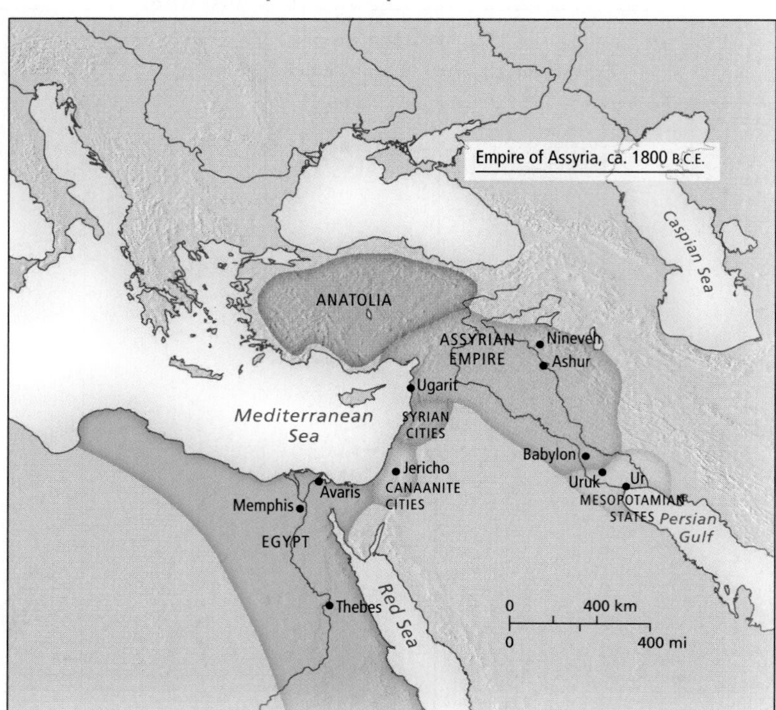

MAP ANALYSIS

1. Name the 6 major kingdoms identified on this map.

2. Name the kingdoms that have major cities located along waterways.

3. According to the depiction of the Fertile Crescent shown in the map on page 13 of this textbook, which kingdoms shown on this map are included in the Fertile Crescent?

4. According to the depiction of Sargon's Kingdom on the map on page 18 in this textbook, which cities listed on this map were part of Sargon's Kingdom in 2220 BCE?

5. By 1800 BCE, which cities had come under Assyrian control?

Name ______________________ Date ______________________

Course Name and Number ______________________ Instructor ______________________

MAP 2.1
Routes of the Raiders of the Land and Sea, ca. 1200–1150 B.C.E.

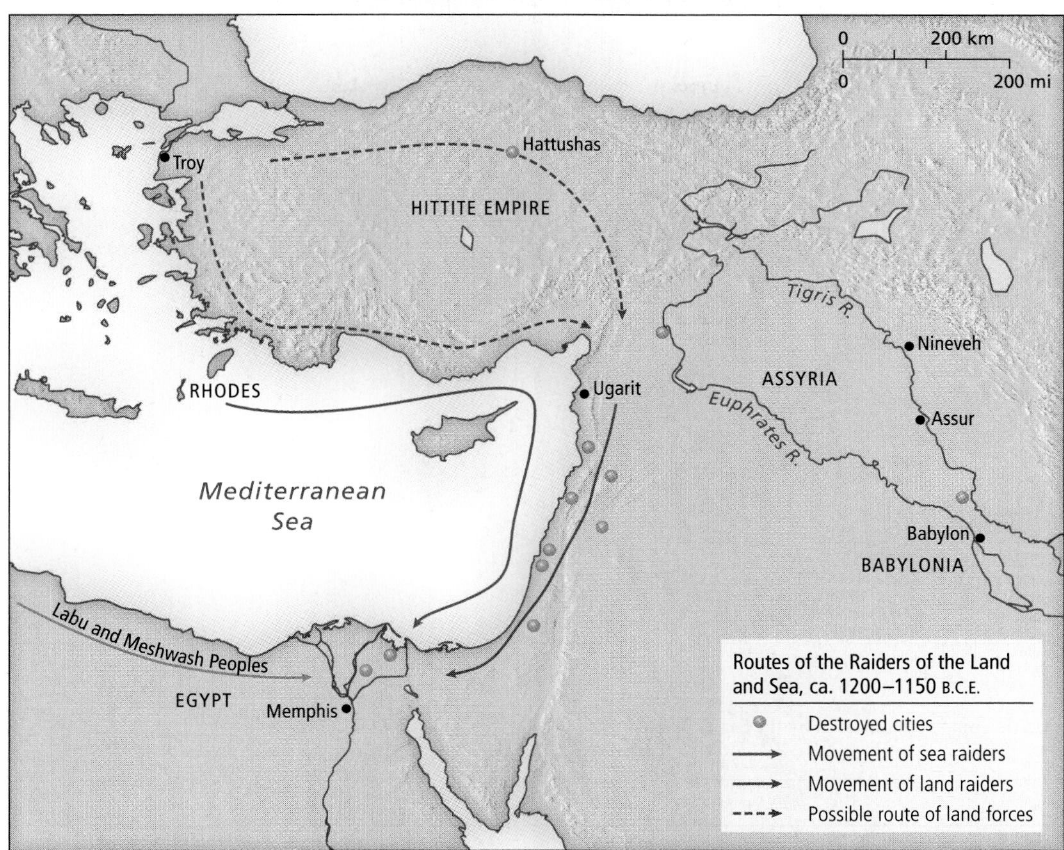

MAP ANALYSIS

1. What city in the Hittite Empire was destroyed, and how was it possibly destroyed?

____

2. How many cities were destroyed along the Tigris and Euphrates Rivers, and what cities were not destroyed?

____

3. Look at this map and the one found on page 37 in the textbook. How many cities included in the northern area of the Egyptian New Kingdom were destroyed during this period?

____

4. How were these Egyptian cities possibly destroyed?

____

MAP 2.2
The Eastern Mediterranean

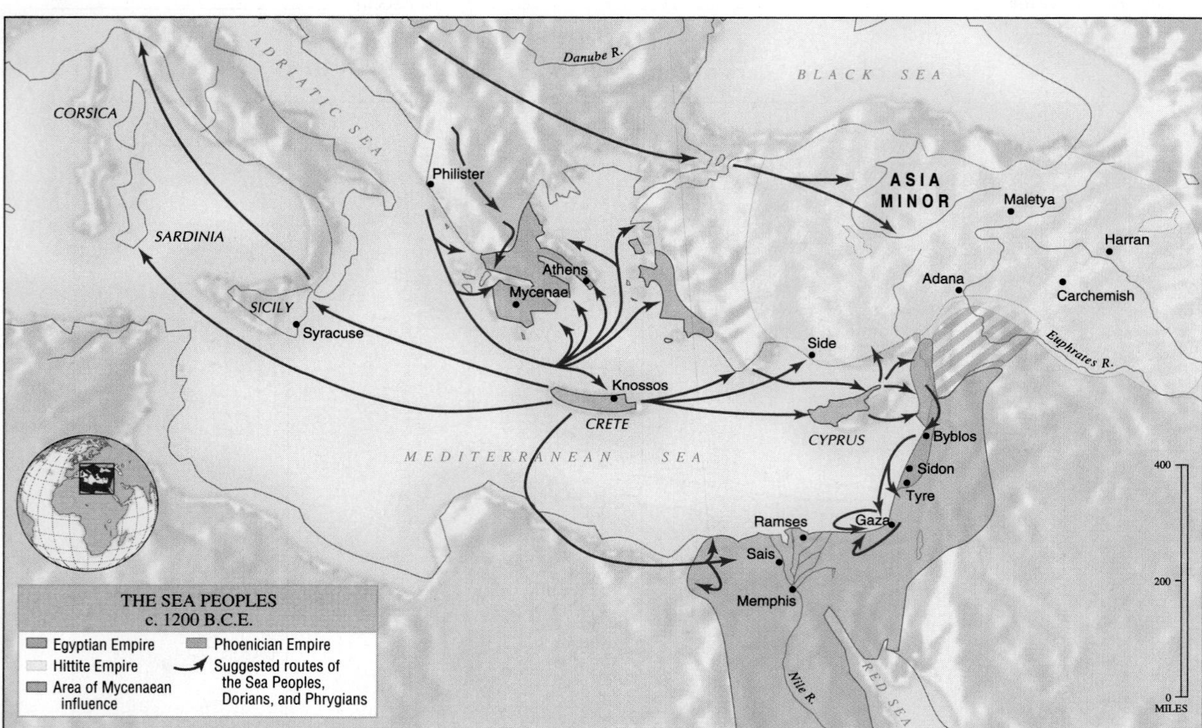

MAP ANALYSIS

1. What empires on this map were invaded by the Sea Peoples?

2. By examining the routes of the Sea Peoples on this map, where might they have migrated from?

3. Compare this map to the one found on page 26 in the textbook. How has the northern part of the Egyptian empire changed since the Middle Kingdom?

4. According to this map, what empires now border the Egyptian kingdom?

5. Compare this map to the one found on page 20 in the textbook. What former kingdoms/regions now make up the Hittite Empire?

Name ______________________ Date ______________________

Course Name and Number ______________________ Instructor ______________________

MAP 3.1
The Greek World, ca. 750–350 B.C.E.

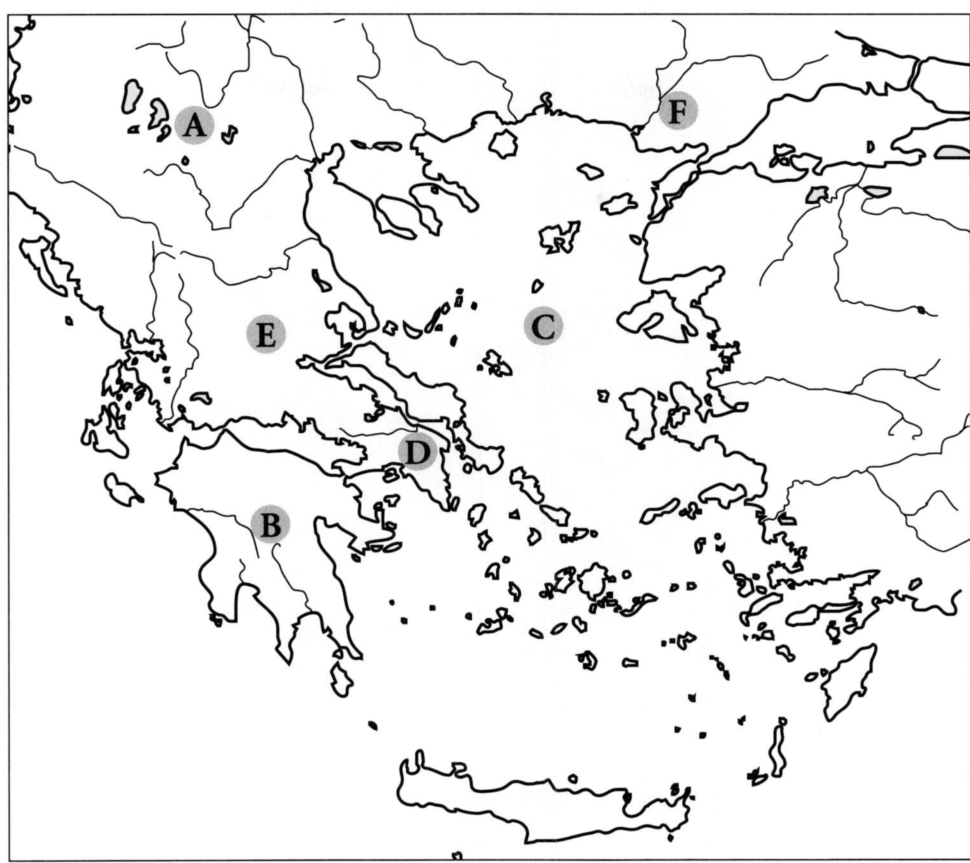

MAP ANALYSIS

1. Which letter on this map identifies Macedonia?

____

2. Which letter on this map identifies the Agean Sea ?

____

3. Which letter on this map identifies Thessaly?

____

4. Which letter on this map identifies Attica?

____

5. Which letter on this map identifies Messinia?

____

MAP 3.2
Greece and Greek Colonies of the World, ca. 431 B.C.E.

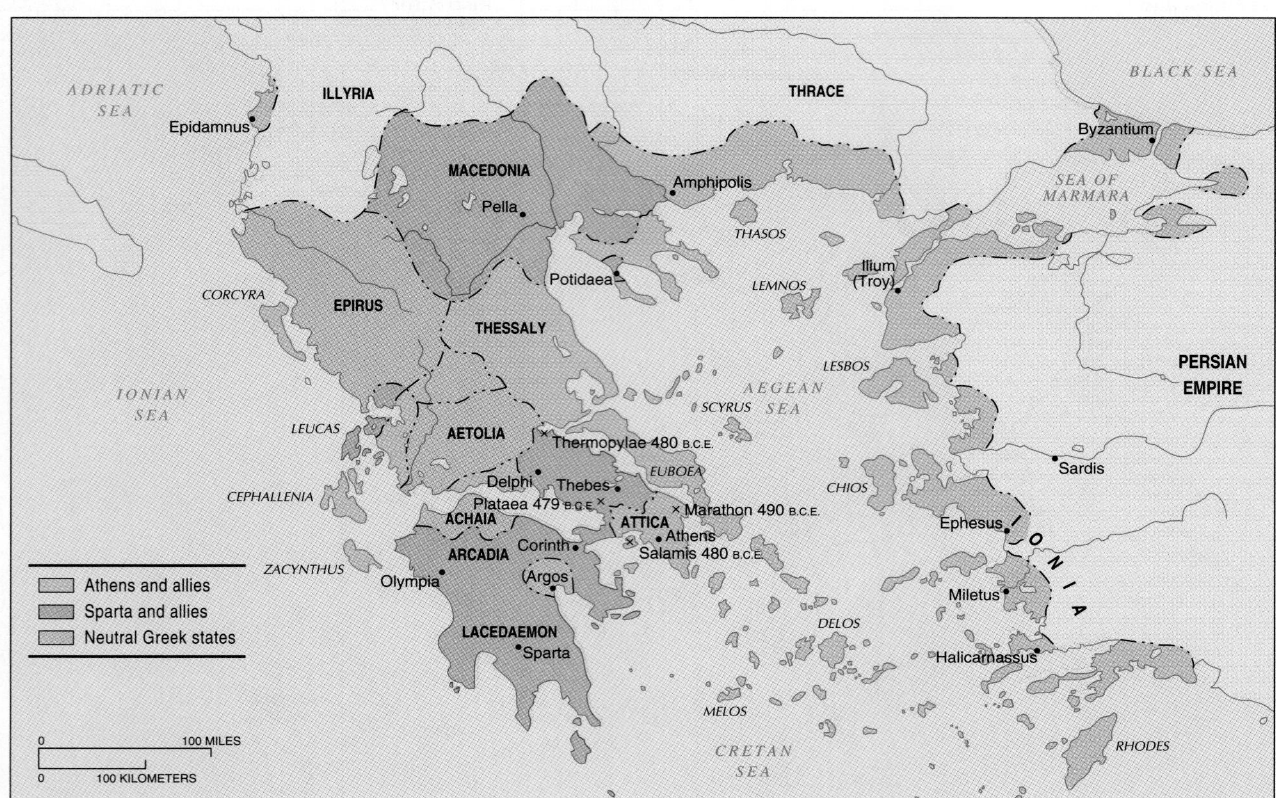

MAP ANALYSIS

1. According to Chapter 3 in the textbook, what major event took place in the Greek world around 431 BCE?

____

____

____

2. According to this map, what major city-states or regions were allied with Athens?

____

____

____

3. According to this map, what major city-states or regions were allied with Sparta?

____

____

____

4. According to this map, what major city-states or regions remained neutral?

____

____

____

5. According to this map, what major kingdoms or regions remained outside the conflict?

____

____

____

Name ______________________ Date ______________________

Course Name and Number ______________________ Instructor ______________________

MAP 4.1
Alexander's Empire

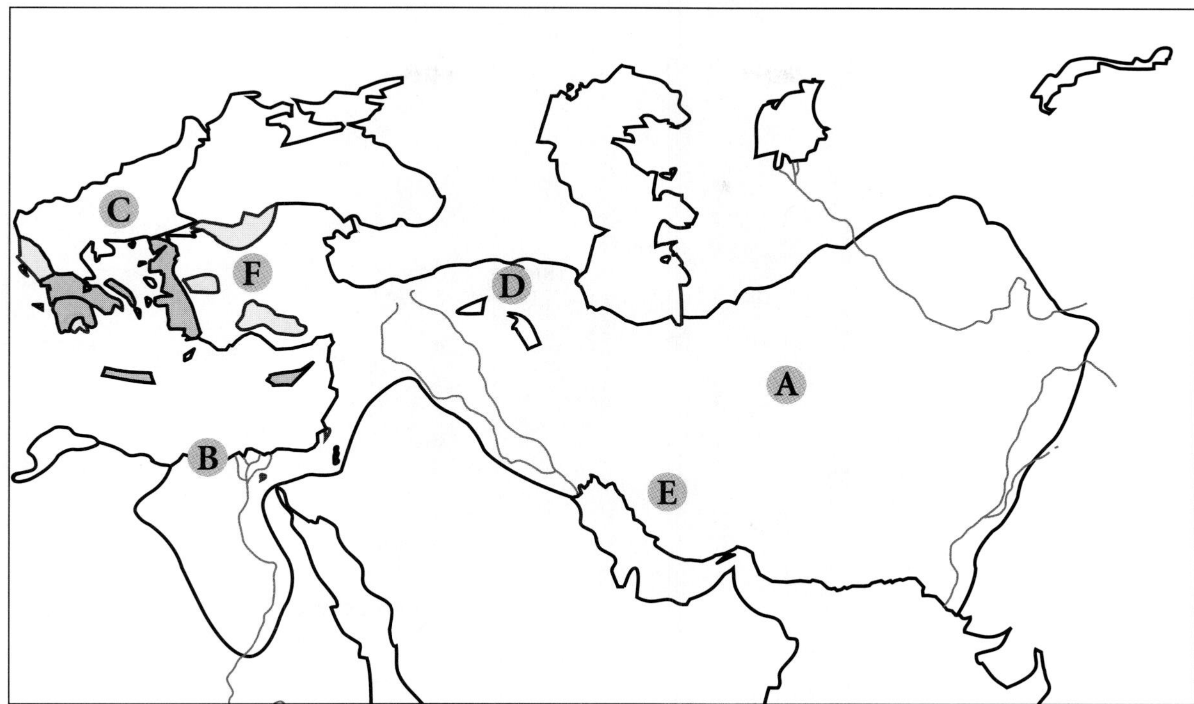

MAP ANALYSIS

1. Which letter on this map identifies Persia?

2. Which letter on this map identifies Armenia?

3. Which letter on this map identifies Macedonia?

4. Which letter on this map identifies Asia Minor?

5. Which letter on this map identifies Egypt?

6. Which letter on this map identifies Parthia?

MAP 4.2
The Expansion of the Roman Republic, 133 B.C.E.

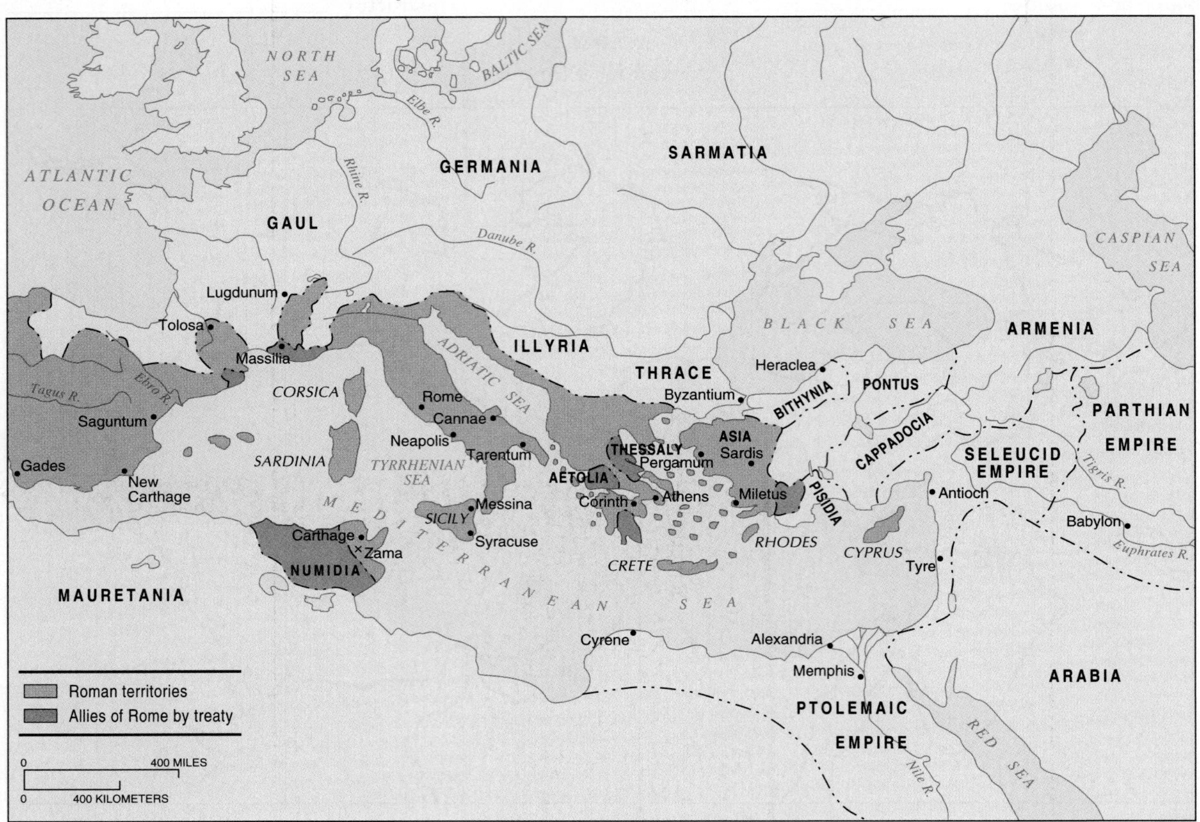

MAP ANALYSIS

1. According to the map found on page 116 in the textbook, what lands made up the Roman Republic in 218 BCE?

2. According to this map, what new territories were added to the Roman Republic by 133 BCE?

3. Using this map, name four cities or regions that became allies of the Roman Republic by 133 BCE.

4. Name the major regions not included in the Roman Republic in 133 BCE.

Name ______________________ Date ______________

Course Name and Number ______________________ Instructor ______________

MAP 5.1
The Roman Empire at its Greatest Extent

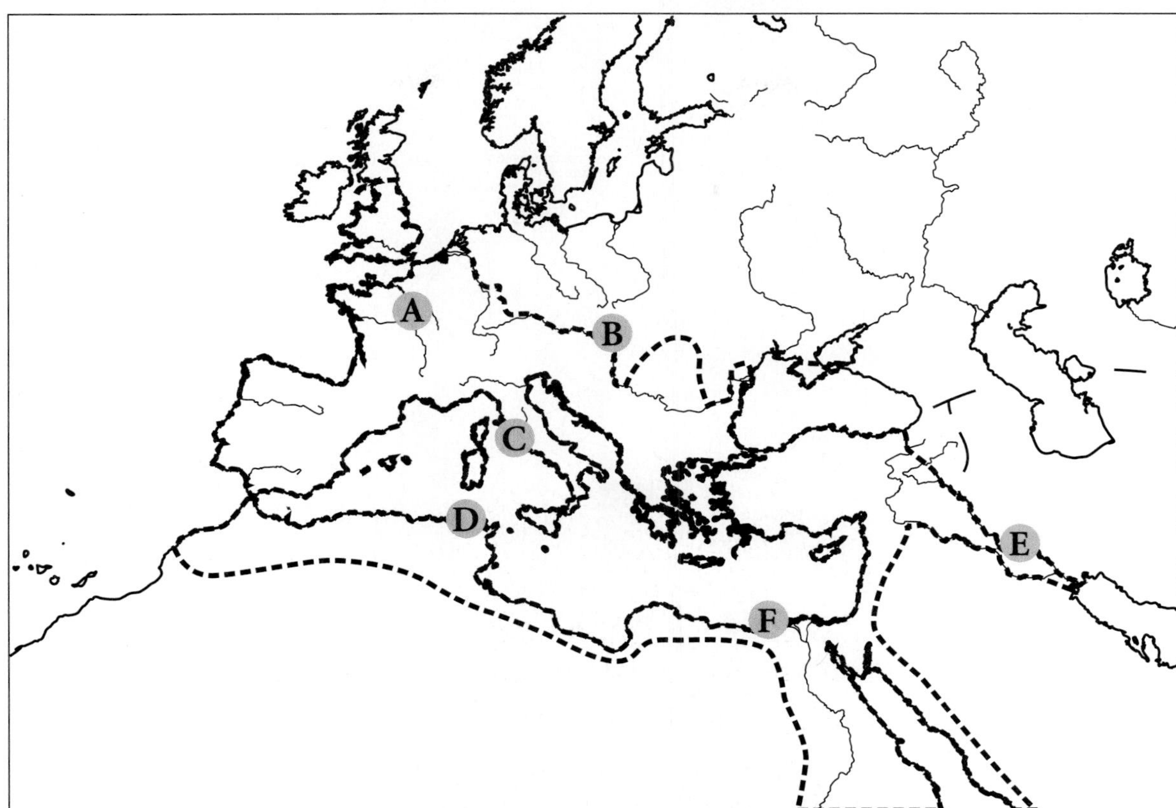

MAP ANALYSIS

1. Which letter on this map identifies the city of Rome?

2. Which letter on this map identifies the city of Carthage?

3. Which letter on this map identifies the city of Alexandria?

4. Which letter on this map identifies Gaul?

5. Which letter on this map identifies the Tigris River?

6. Which letter on this map identifies the Danube River?

MAP 5.2
The Career of Julius Caesar

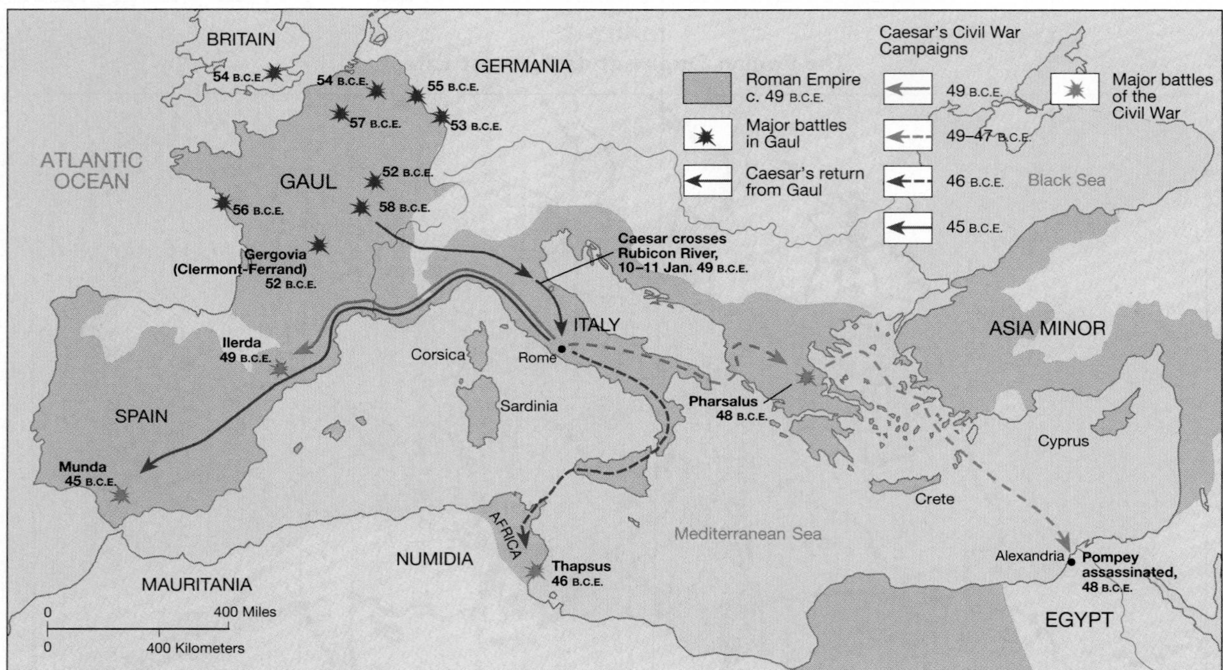

MAP ANALYSIS

1. How long was Julius Caesar fighting battles in Gaul before the Civil War?

2. What river did Julius Caesar cross on his return from Gaul, and in what year did he cross it?

3. According to this map, how many battles were fought during the Civil War?

4. When was Pompey assassinated, and during which campaign did this occur?

5. According to this map, what parts of the Roman Empire saw no battles during the Civil War?

6. Name the regions included in the Roman Empire on this map.

7. Name the regions not included in the Roman Empire on this map.

Name ______________________ Date ______________________

Course Name and Number ______________________ Instructor ______________________

MAP 6.1
The Byzantine Empire Under Justinian

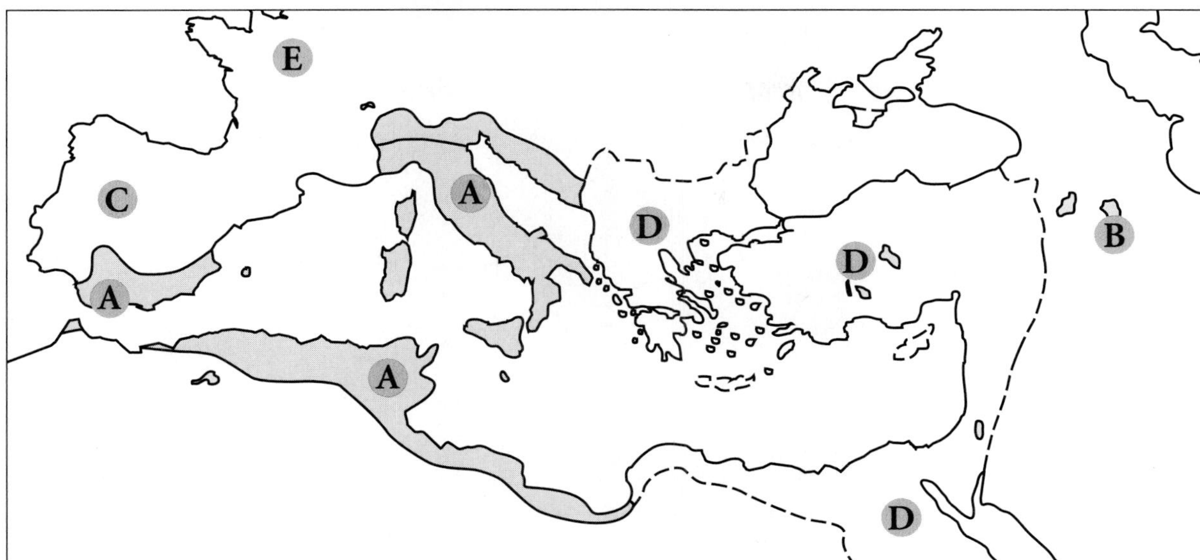

MAP ANALYSIS

1. Which letter on this map identifies the Kingdom of the Franks?

____

2. Which letter on this map identifies the Kingdom of the Visigothes?

____

3. Which letter on this map identifies the Dominions of the Sassanids?

____

4. Which letter on this map identifies lands controlled by the Vandals and Ostragoths?

____

5. Which letter on this map identifies the Eastern Roman Empire at the time of Justinian's death?

____

MAP 6.2
The Spread of Christianity

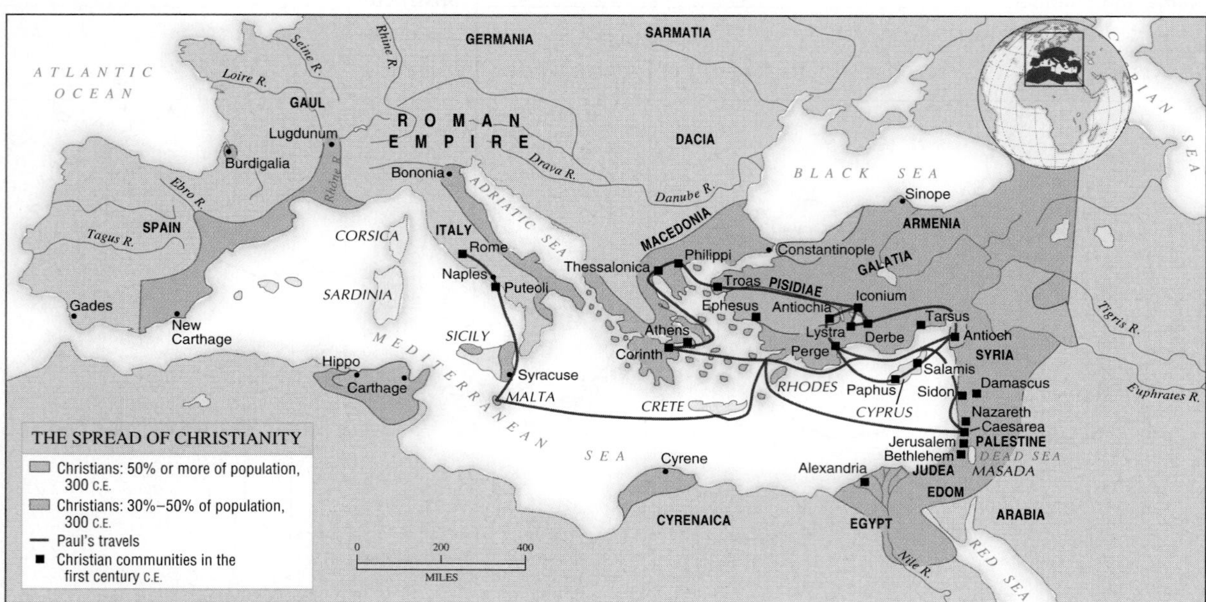

MAP ANALYSIS

1. Name the major Christian communities of the first century CE.

2. Of the cities that Paul visited, which did not have a Christian population of at least 30 percent by 300 CE?

3. Of the cities that Paul visited, which had a Christian population of 50 percent or higher by 300 CE?

4. Of the major Christian communities that existed in the first century, which did Paul not visit?

5. What minor cities had a Christian population of at least 30% by the first century?

Name ______________________ Date ______________________

Course Name and Number ______________________ Instructor ______________________

MAP 7.1
The Mediterranean, Middle East, and North Africa, ca. 500 C.E.

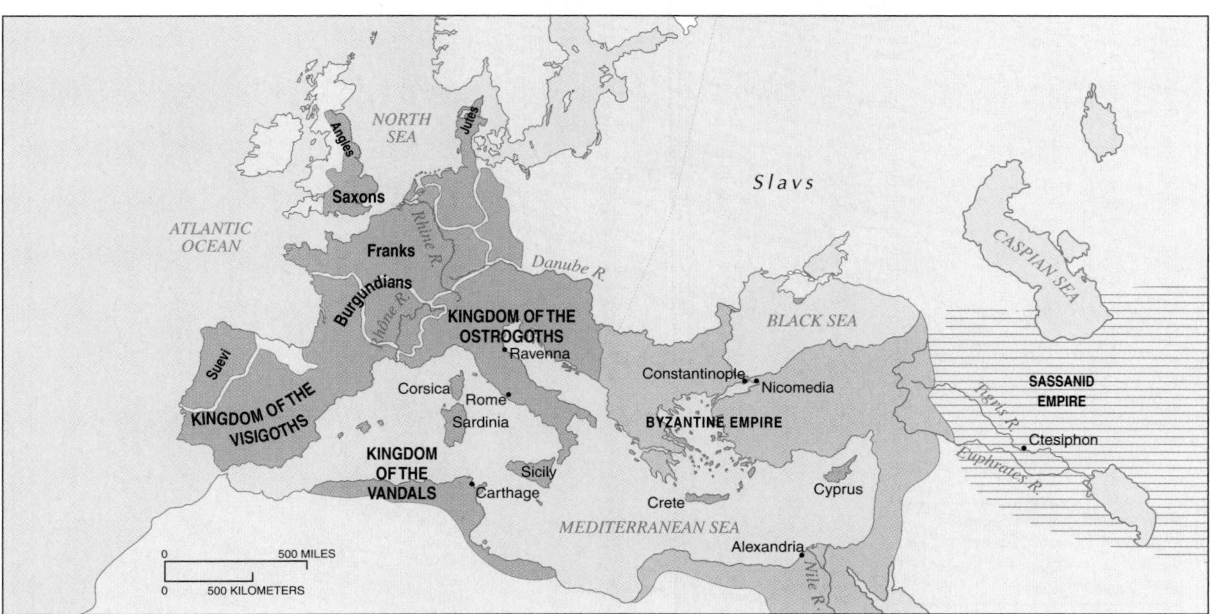

MAP ANALYSIS

1. Compare this map to the one found in the textbook on page 208 in the textbook. What military threat arose to the east of the Byzantine Empire by 600 CE?

____

____

____

2. According to this map, what kingdoms were located west of the Byzantine Empire in 500 CE?

____

____

____

3. According to the map on page 208 in the textbook, what kingdoms were located west of the Byzantine Empire in 600 CE?

____

____

____

4. Did the Byzantine Empire experience a gain or loss of territory between 500 and 600 CE?

____

____

____

MAP 7.2
The Expansion of Islam in the Seventh and Eighth Centuries

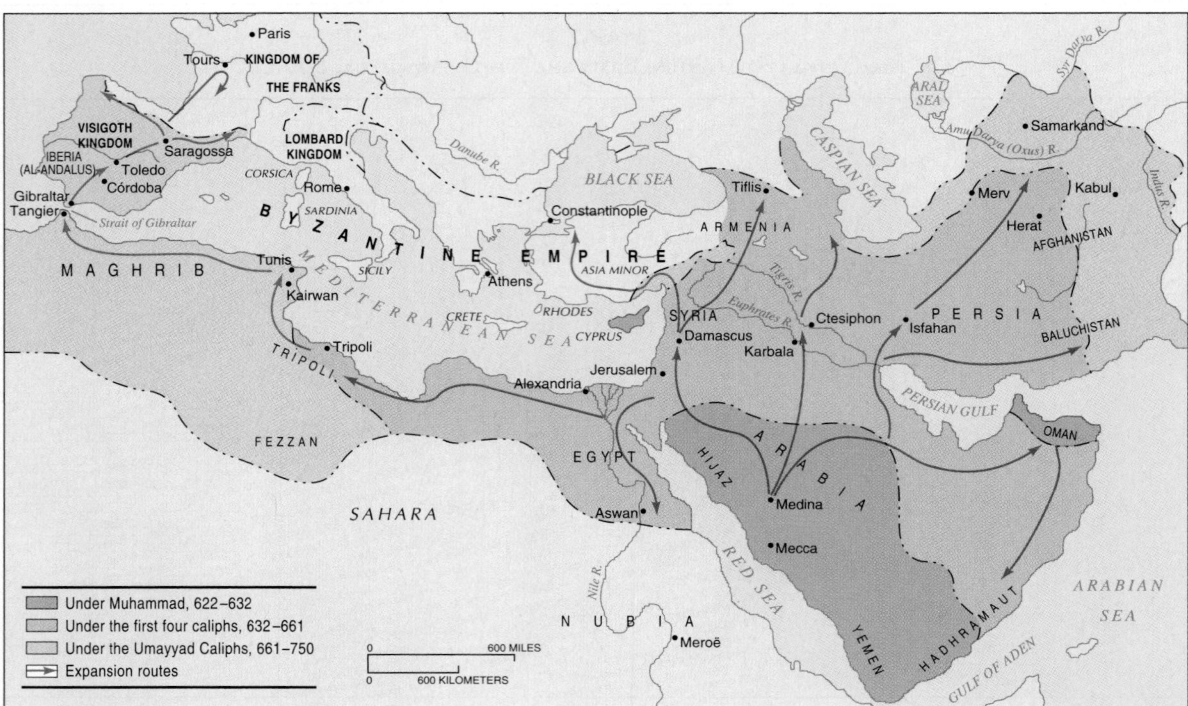

MAP ANALYSIS

1. What lands were governed by Muhammad between 622 and 632 CE?

2. What lands were gained by the first four caliphs?

3. From what city did the caliphs set out when expanding their empire after 632 CE?

4. What lands were gained under the Umayyad Caliphs?

5. What kingdoms/empires did the caliphs attempt to expand into, but did not conquer?

6. According to this map and the one found in the textbook on page 221, what two modern states evolve out of Persia?

Name ______________________________ Date ______________________________

Course Name and Number ______________________________ Instructor ______________________________

MAP 8.1
Charlemagne's Empire

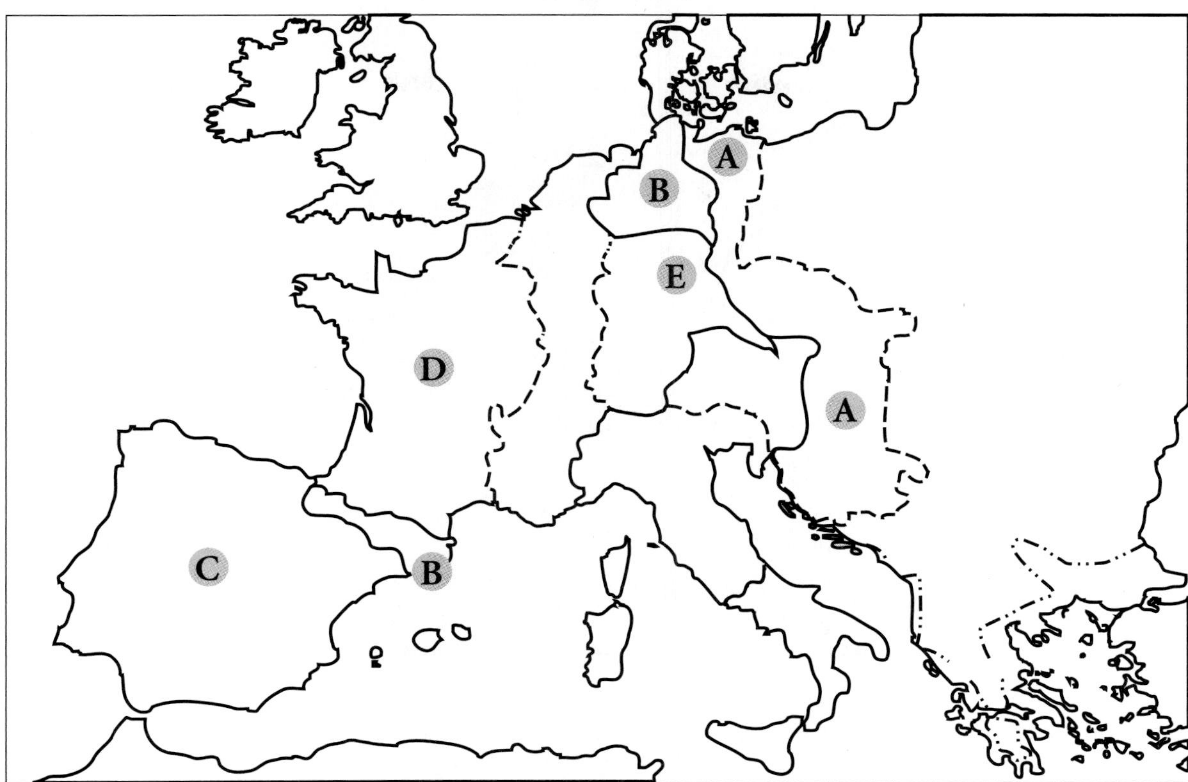

MAP ANALYSIS

1. Which letter on this map identifies land controlled by the Umayyad Empire?

____

2. Which letter(s) on this map identify lands included in Charlemagne's Empire?

____

3. Which letter on this map identifies Western Francia after the death of Charlemagne?

____

4. Which letter on this map identifies the Tributaries of the Slavic States?

____

MAP 8.2
The Crusades

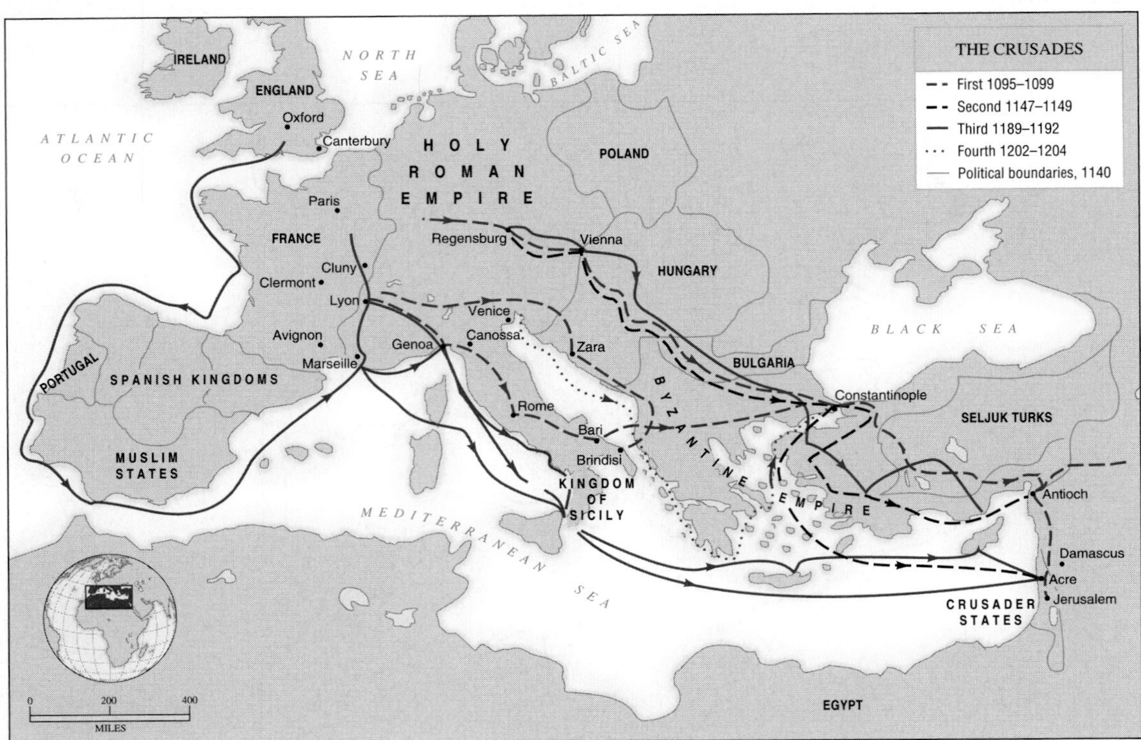

MAP ANALYSIS

1. According to this map and the one found on page 263 in the textbook, what empire launched the first crusade?

2. According to this map and the one found on page 263 in the textbook, what states launched the third crusade?

3. From what port city was the fourth crusade launched?

4. According to this map and the one found on page 263 in the textbook, what were the destinations of the first, second, and third crusades?

5. What was the destination of the fourth crusade?

Name ______________________________ Date ______________________________

Course Name and Number ______________________________ Instructor ______________________________

MAP 9.1
The Universal Monarchy of Pope Innocent III

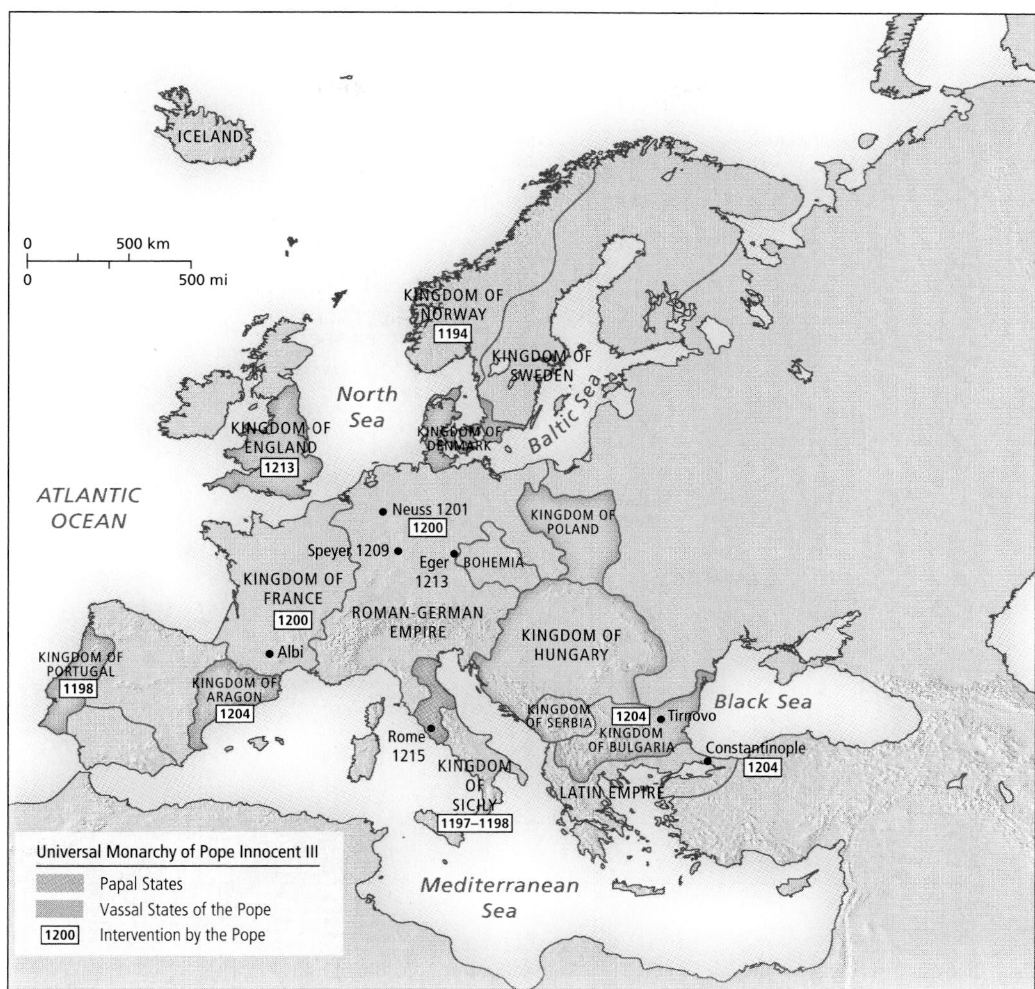

MAP ANALYSIS

1. List the kingdoms that were vassal states to the Papacy in the twelfth and thirteenth centuries.

____

____

2. List the vassal kingdoms that received no intervention from the Pope.

____

____

3. List the states that received intervention from the Pope without being a vassal state.

____

____

4. What year did Papal intervention begin and in what year did the last intervention take place?

____

____

MAP 9.2
Western Europe Toward the End of the Middle Ages, ca. 1360 C.E.

MAP ANALYSIS

1. What state on the Italian Peninsula was not included in the Holy Roman Empire according to this map?

____

____

____

2. What states shared the eastern border of the Holy Roman Empire in 1360 CE?

____

____

____

3. What state(s) shared the western border of the Holy Roman Empire in 1360 CE?

____

____

____

4. List the territories included the Holy Roman Empire as shown on this map.

____

____

____

Name ______________________ Date ______________________

Course Name and Number ______________________ Instructor ______________________

MAP 10.1
The Mongol Empire, ca. 1300

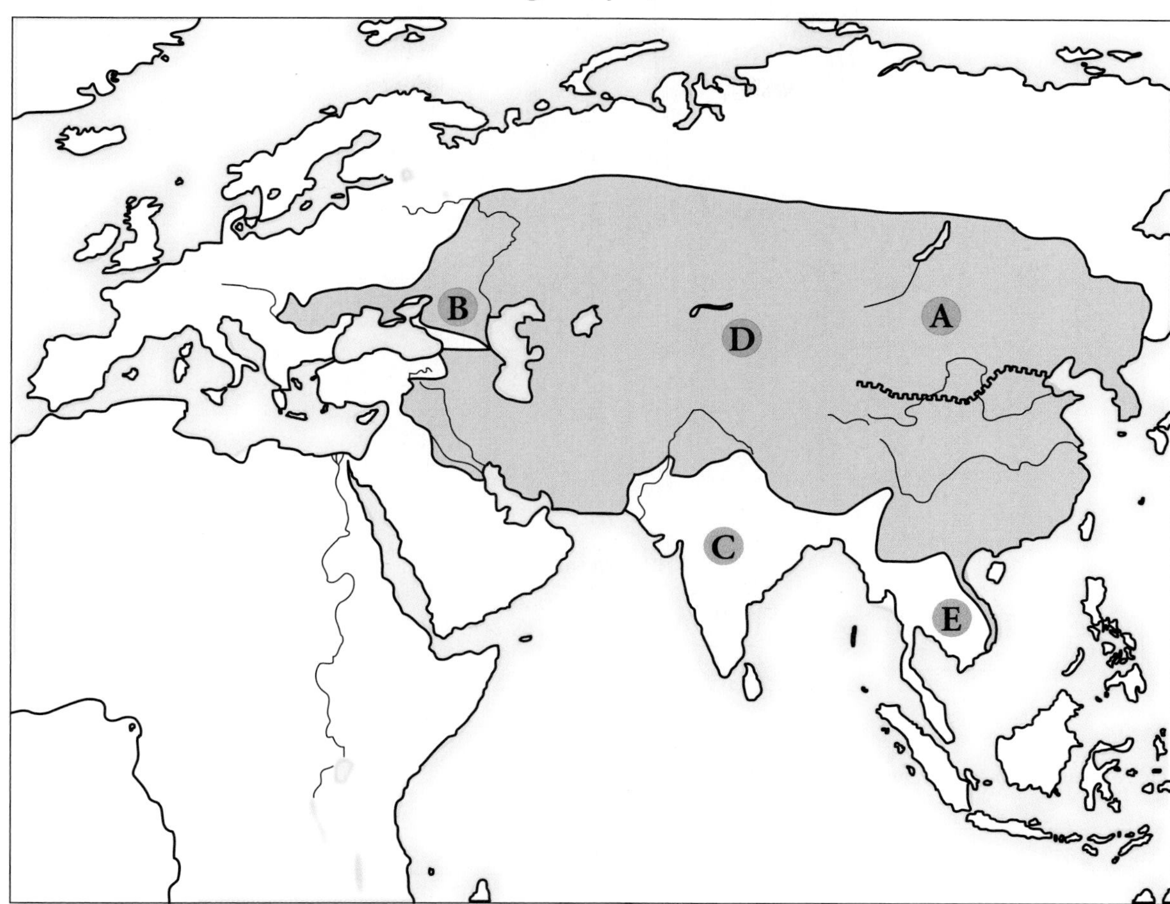

MAP ANALYSIS

1. Which letter on this map identifies the Principalities of Russia?

____

2. Which letter on this map identifies the Sultanate of Delhi?

____

3. Which letter(s) on this map identify the Mongol Empire?

____

4. What is identified on this map by the curved line beneath letter A?

____

MAP 10.2
The Expansion of the Ottoman Empire

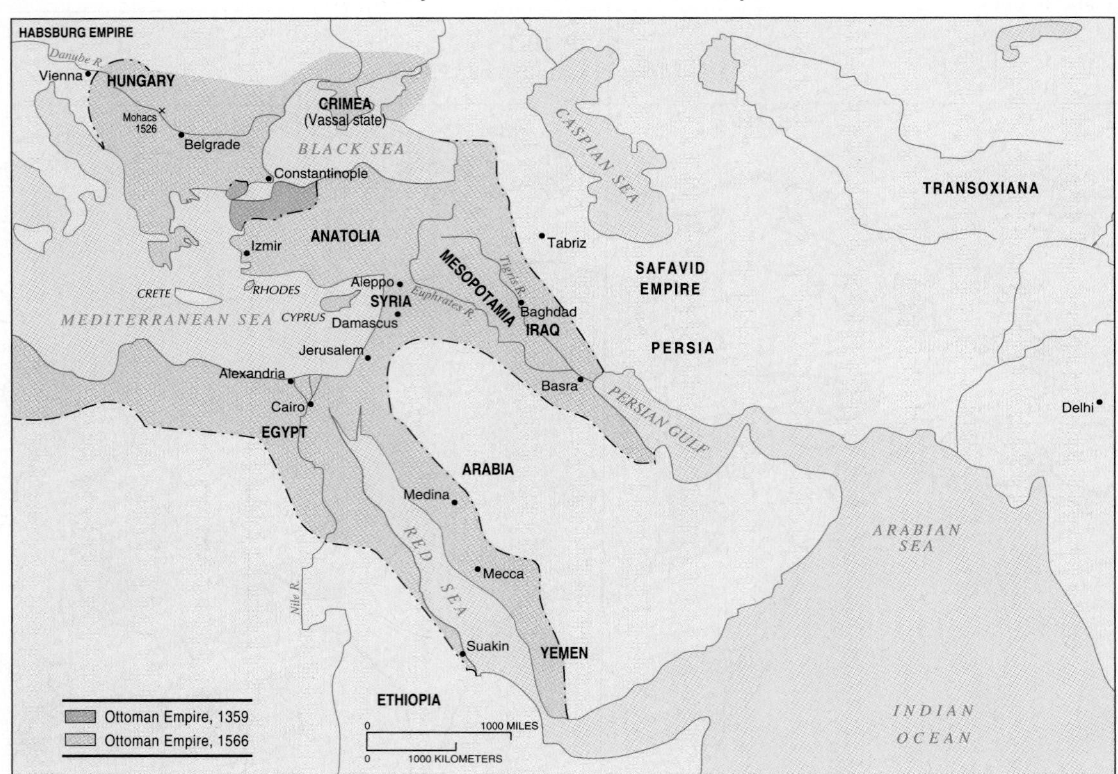

MAP ANALYSIS

1. Where, approximately, was the Ottoman Empire located in 1359?

2. By 1566, what lands were included in the Ottoman Empire?

3. What surrounding lands/empires were not included in the Ottoman Empire by 1566 CE?

4. According to the map on page 316 in the textbook, what lands were vassal states of the Ottoman Empire?

5. According to this map and the one found on page 316 in the textbook, what bodies of water did the Ottoman Empire have access to?

Name ____________________ Date ____________________

Course Name and Number ____________________ Instructor ____________________

MAP 11.1
Northern Italy in the Mid-Fifteenth Century

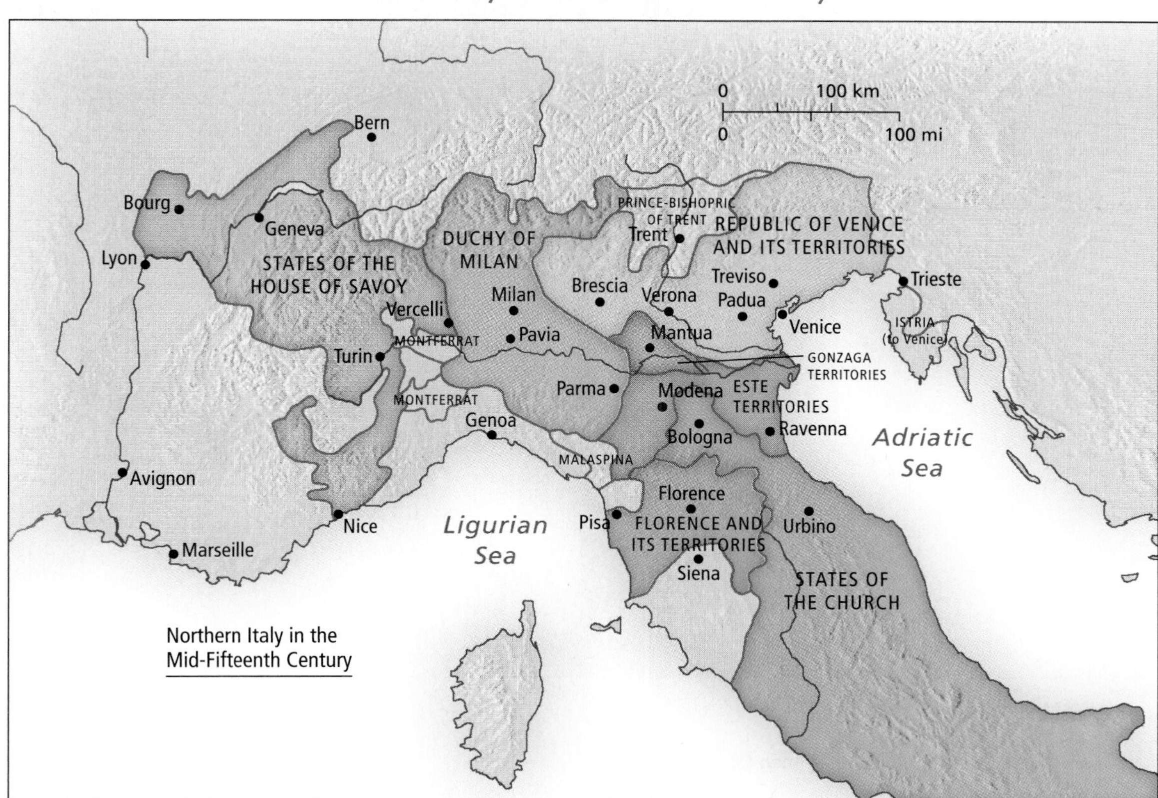

MAP ANALYSIS

1. What city-states were included among Florence and its territories, in the Dutchy of Milan, and within the Republic of Venice?

2. According to the map on page 347 in the textbook, how many colonies did Venice have in the eastern Mediterranean?

3. What city-states are included in the States of the House of Savoy and the Este Territories?

4. What state bordered the territories of Florence and the Este Territories?

MAP 11.2
Western Europe During the Renaissance and Reformation, ca. Fourteenth–Fifteenth Centuries

MAP ANALYSIS

1. What religions are included within the Holy Roman Empire?

2. What state was Anglican?

3. What states were Calvinist?

4. What states, outside of the Holy Roman Empire, were Catholic?

5. What states were Eastern Orthodox?

6. What states contained a mixture of prominent religions, and what religions did they contain?

Name ______________________ **Date** ______________________

Course Name and Number ______________________ **Instructor** ______________________

MAP 12.1
European Empires, ca. 1660

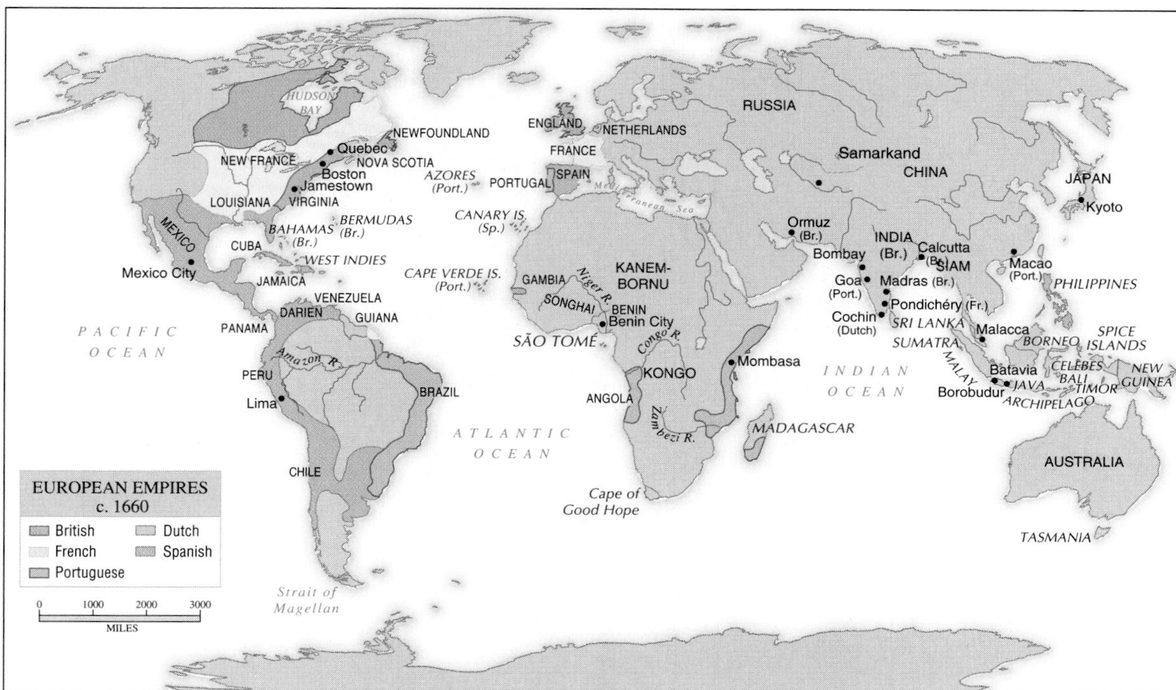

MAP ANALYSIS

1. What countries founded colonies in North America and South America?

____

____

2. What countries founded colonies in Africa?

____

____

3. According to this map and the one found on page 383 in the textbook, what countries set up colonial holdings in Southeast Asia?

____

____

4. According to the map found on page 383 in the textbook, who was the first explorer to sail to South America? According to this map, what European Empires, by 1660, controlled the cities visited by him?

____

____

5. According to the map found on page 383 in the textbook, who was the first explorer to sail to Africa? According to this map, what European Empires, by 1660, controlled the cities visited by him?

____

____

MAP 12.2
Trade Routes to Asia

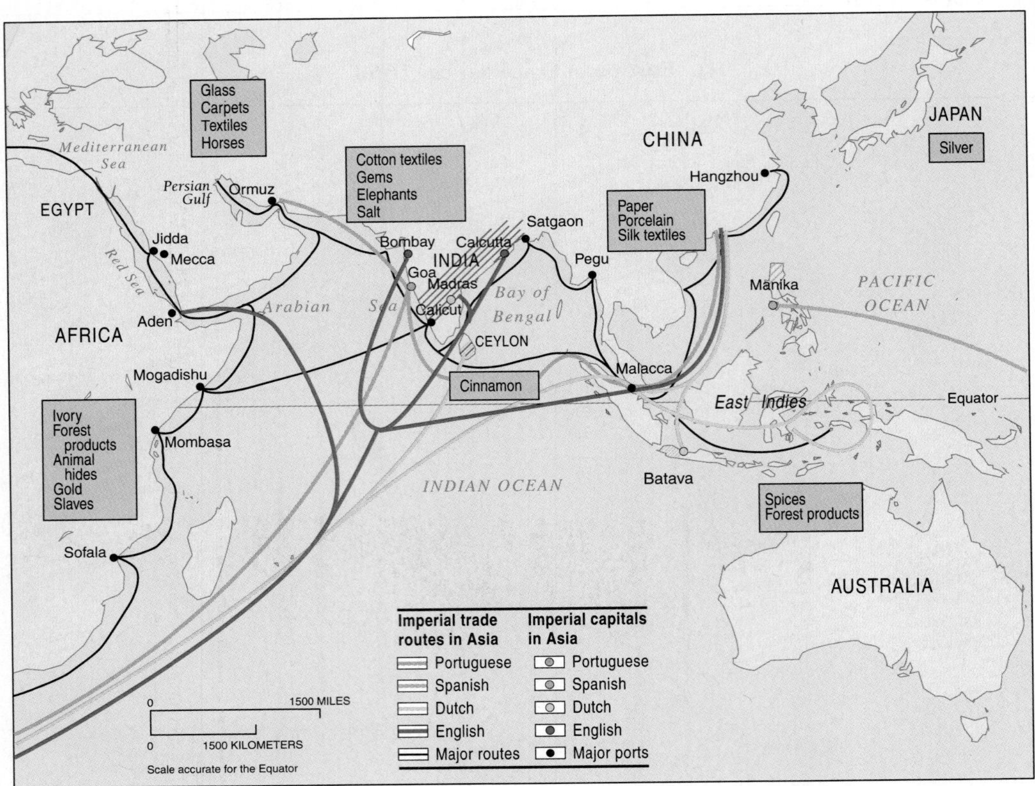

MAP ANALYSIS

1. Where did Portugal establish its trading capital in Asia, and what trading ports did they visit?

2. Where did the Dutch establish its trading capital in Asia, and what trading ports did they visit?

3. Where did England establish its trading capital in Asia, and what trading ports did they visit?

4. What major trading ports were commonly used by European nations?

Name ________________________ Date ________________________

Course Name and Number ________________________ Instructor ________________________

MAP 13.1
The Ottoman Empire, 1556

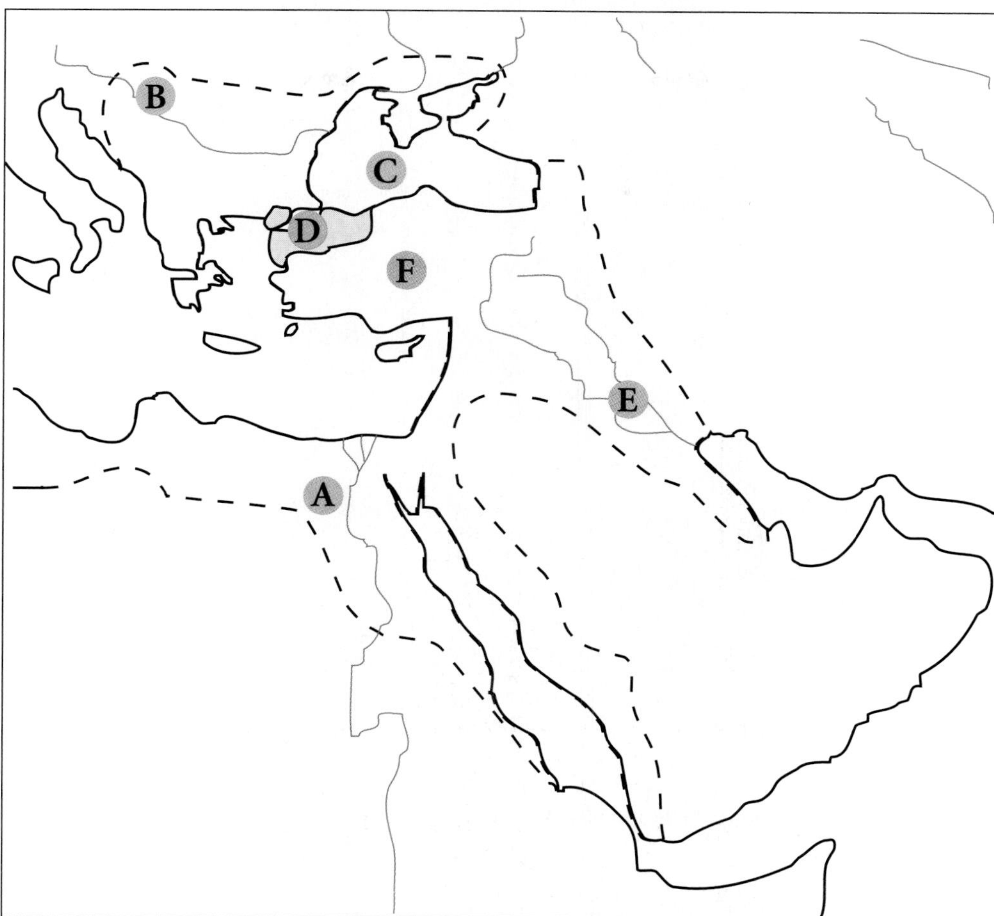

MAP ANALYSIS

1. Which letter on this map identifies Anatolia?

2. Which letter on this map identifies the Black Sea?

3. Which letter on this map identifies Hungary?

4. Which letters on this map are included within the borders of the Ottoman Empire in 1566?

MAP 13.2
Europe After the Reformation

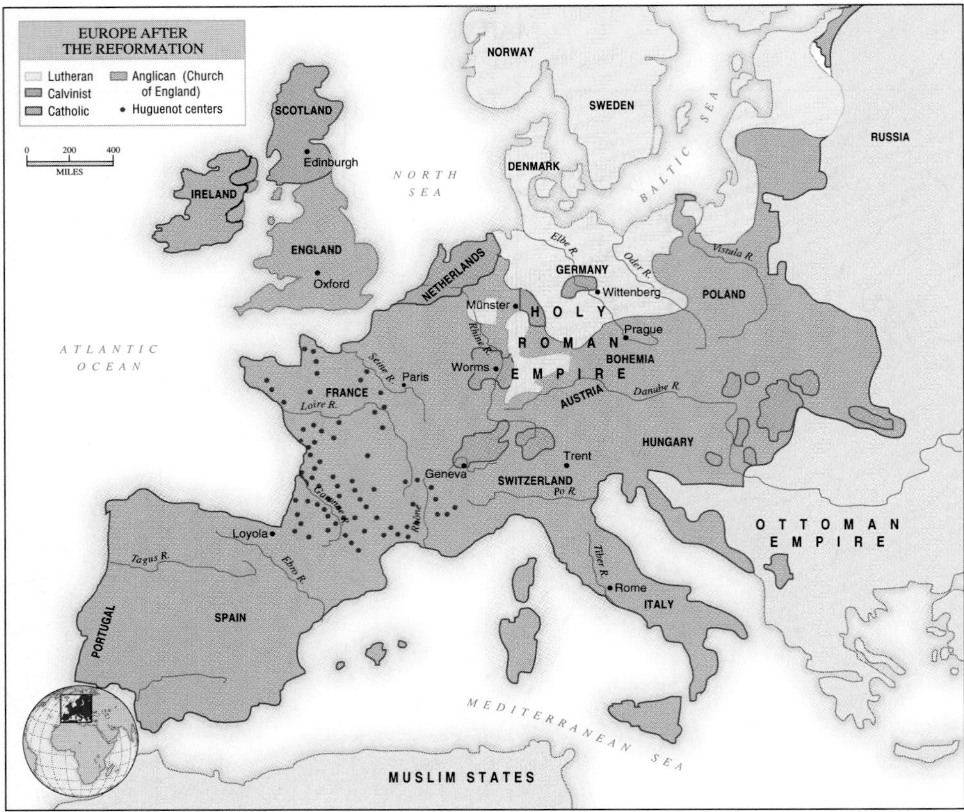

MAP ANALYSIS

1. Compare this map to the one found on page 422 in the textbook. What countries had entirely abandoned Catholicism by the end of the Reformation?

____

____

2. Compare this map to the one found on page 422 in the textbook. What countries remained predominantly Catholic at the end of the Reformation?

____

____

3. Compare this map to the one found on page 422 in the textbook. What was the religious makeup of the British Isles at the end of the Reformation?

____

____

4. Using this map, identify the religious centers that arose in France by the end of the Reformation.

____

____

5. Compare this map to the one found on page 422 in the textbook. What was the religious makeup of the Holy Roman Empire by the end of the Reformation?

____

____

Name ______________________ Date ______________________

Course Name and Number ______________________ Instructor ______________________

MAP 14.1
Russian Under Peter the Great

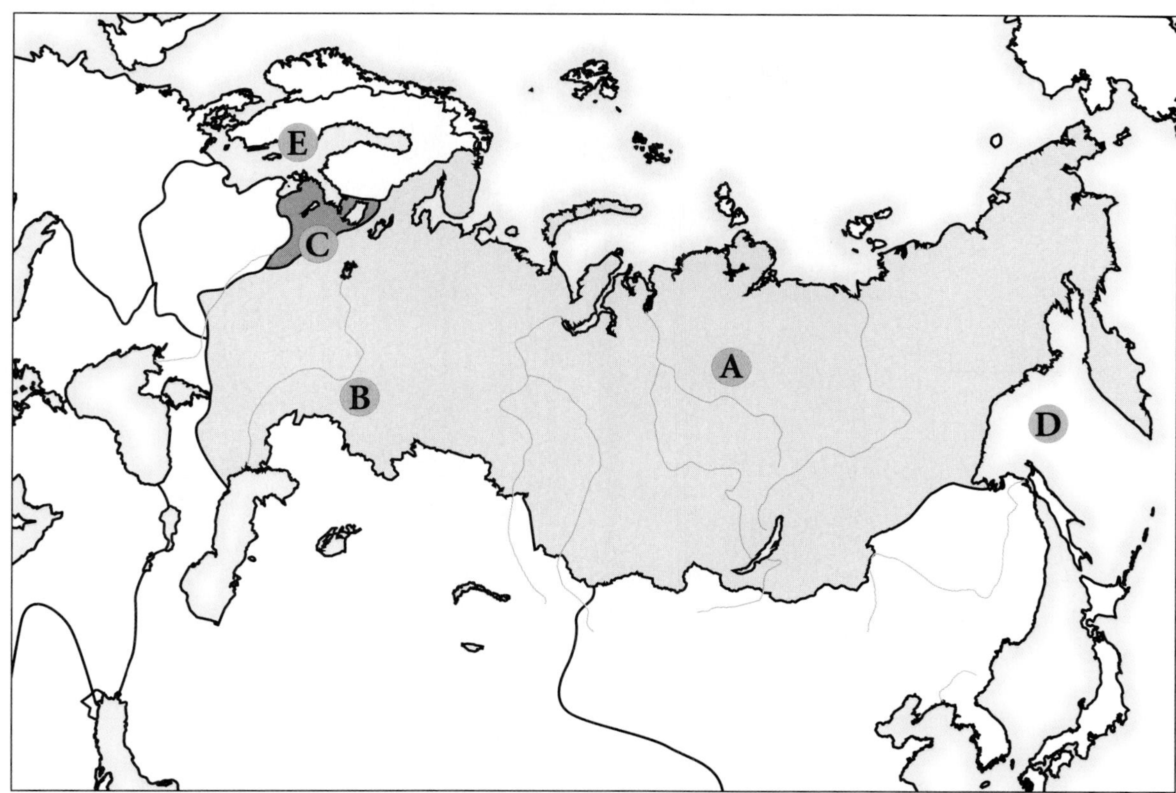

MAP ANALYSIS

1. Which letter on this map identifies the Baltic Sea?

2. Which letter on this map identifies the Volga River?

3. Which letter on this map identifies the Sea of Okhotsk?

4. Which letter on the map identifies St. Petersburg?

5. Which letter(s) on this map identify the Russian empire in 1696?

MAP 14.2
European Population Density, ca. 1600

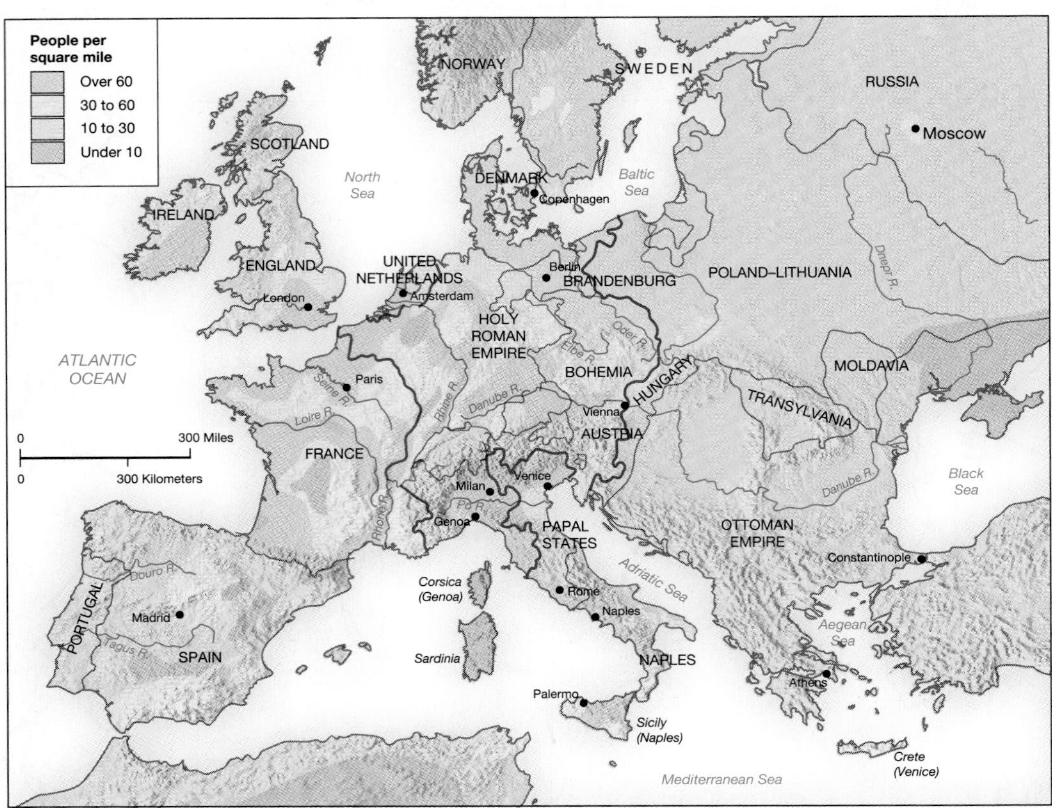

MAP ANALYSIS

1. What countries had a population density of 60 people per square mile or less?

2. What countries had areas where the population density exceeded 60 people per square mile?

3. What major cities are located in areas where the population density exceeded 60 people per square mile?

4. What major cities are located in areas where the population density did not reach 60 people per square mile, and at what density are they located?

Name ______ Date ______

Course Name and Number ______ Instructor ______

MAP 15.1
Europe After the Peace of Westphalia

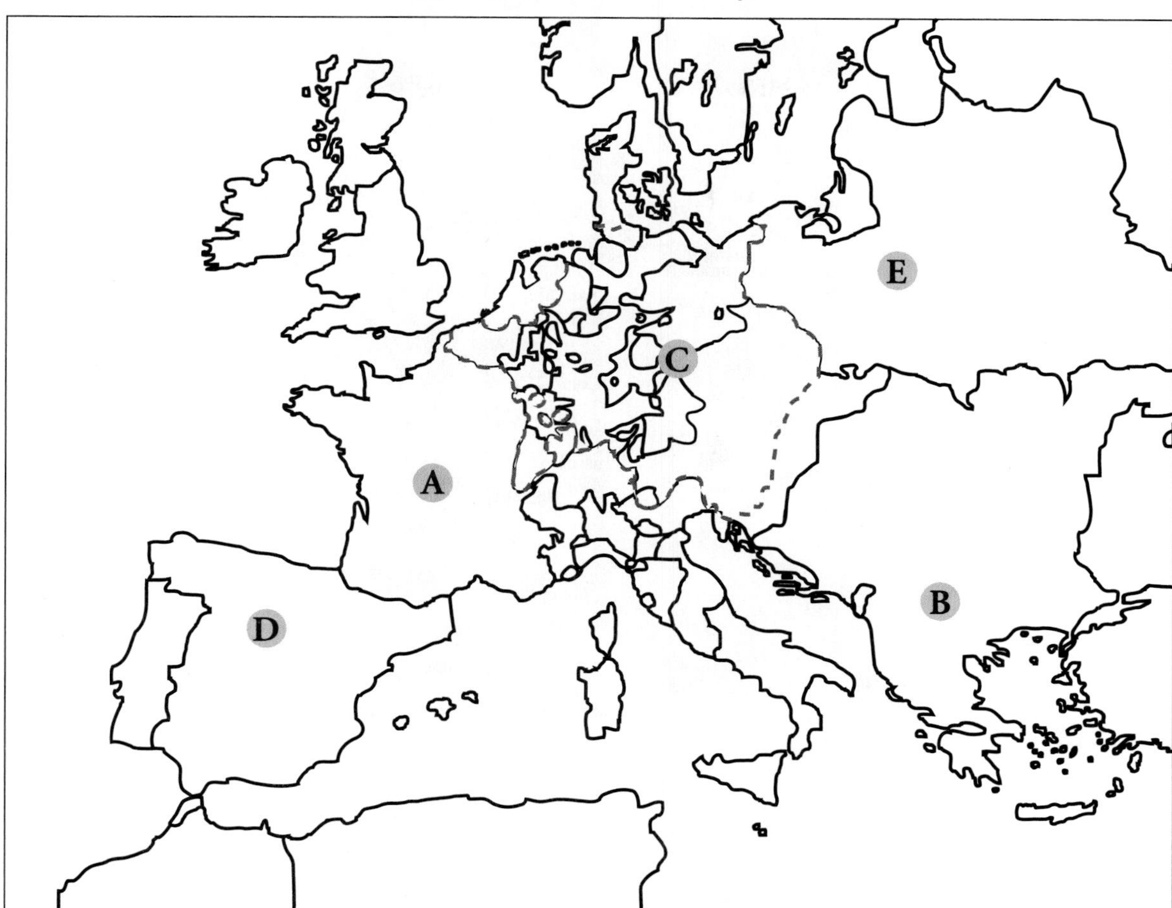

MAP ANALYSIS

1. Which letter on this map identifies France?

2. Which letter on this map identifies Poland?

3. Which letter on this map identifies Spain?

4. Which letter on this map identifies the Holy Roman Empire?

5. Which letter on this map identifies the Ottoman Empire?

MAP 15.2
Europe Under Absolute Monarchy, 1715

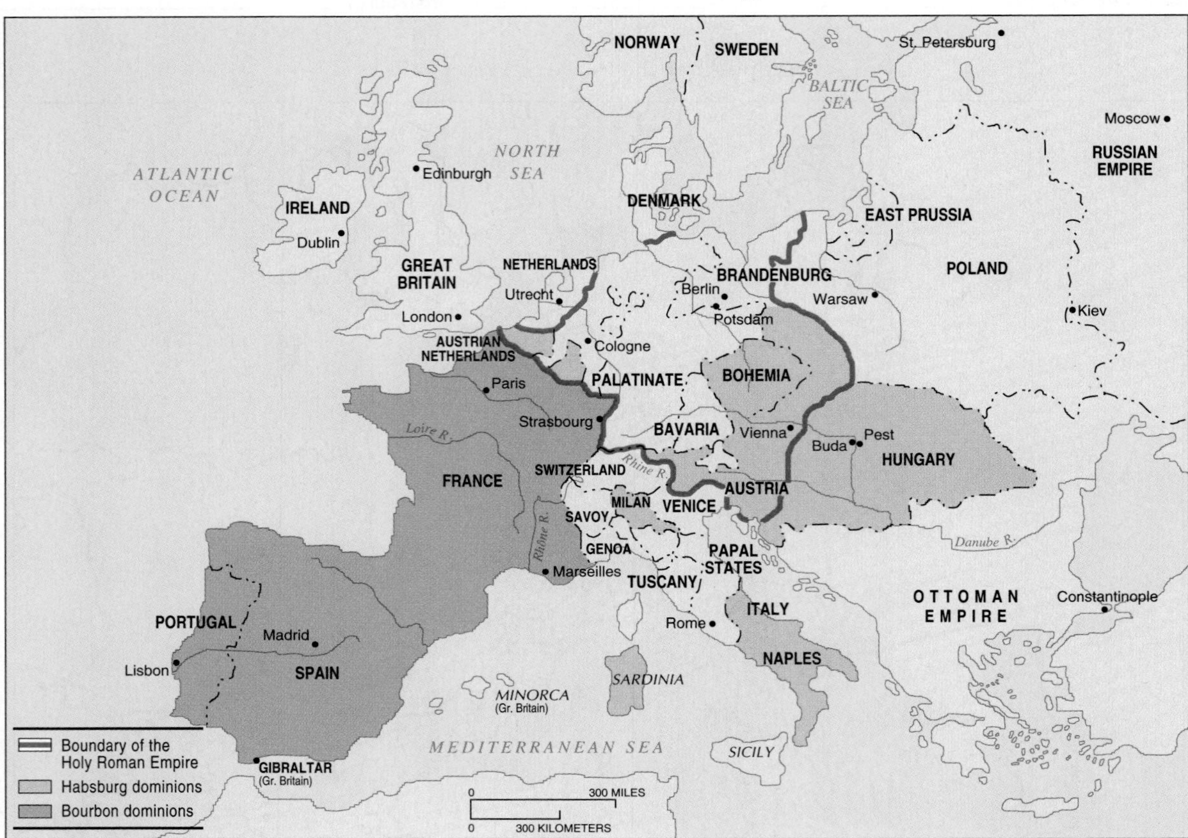

MAP ANALYSIS

1. What states were under Bourbon control in 1715?

____

____

____

2. According to the map on page 486 in the textbook, what territory was France attempting to acquire between 1679 and 1714 and was France successful in acquiring those territories?

____

____

____

3. According to the map on page 493 in the textbook, what territories given to Spain by the Treaty of Westphalia were under Habsburg control in 1715?

____

____

____

4. According to this map, what other states were under Habsburg control in 1715?

____

____

____

Name ______________________ Date ______________________

Course Name and Number ______________________ Instructor ______________________

MAP 16.1
World Boundaries, ca. 1453

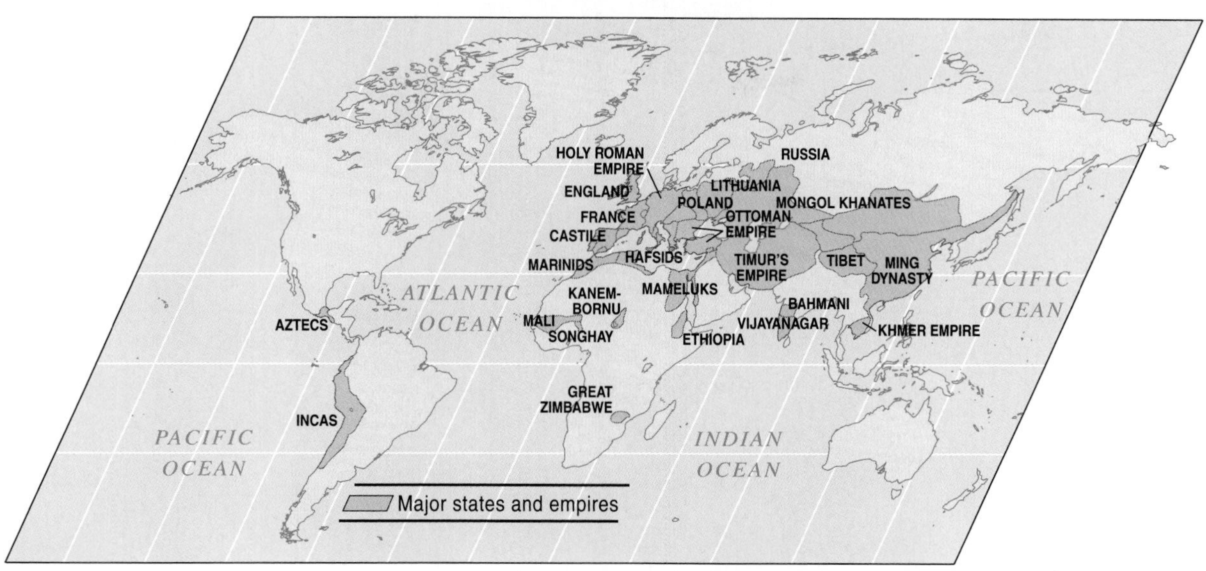

MAP ANALYSIS

1. What major European states were established by 1453?

____

2. What major states were established in the Middle East, South Asia, and East Asia by 1453?

____

3. What major states were established in Africa by 1453?

____

4. What major states were established in the Americas by 1453?

____

5. What continents had no major states or empires in 1453?

____

MAP 16.2
The Growth of Brandenburg-Prussia, 1618–1786

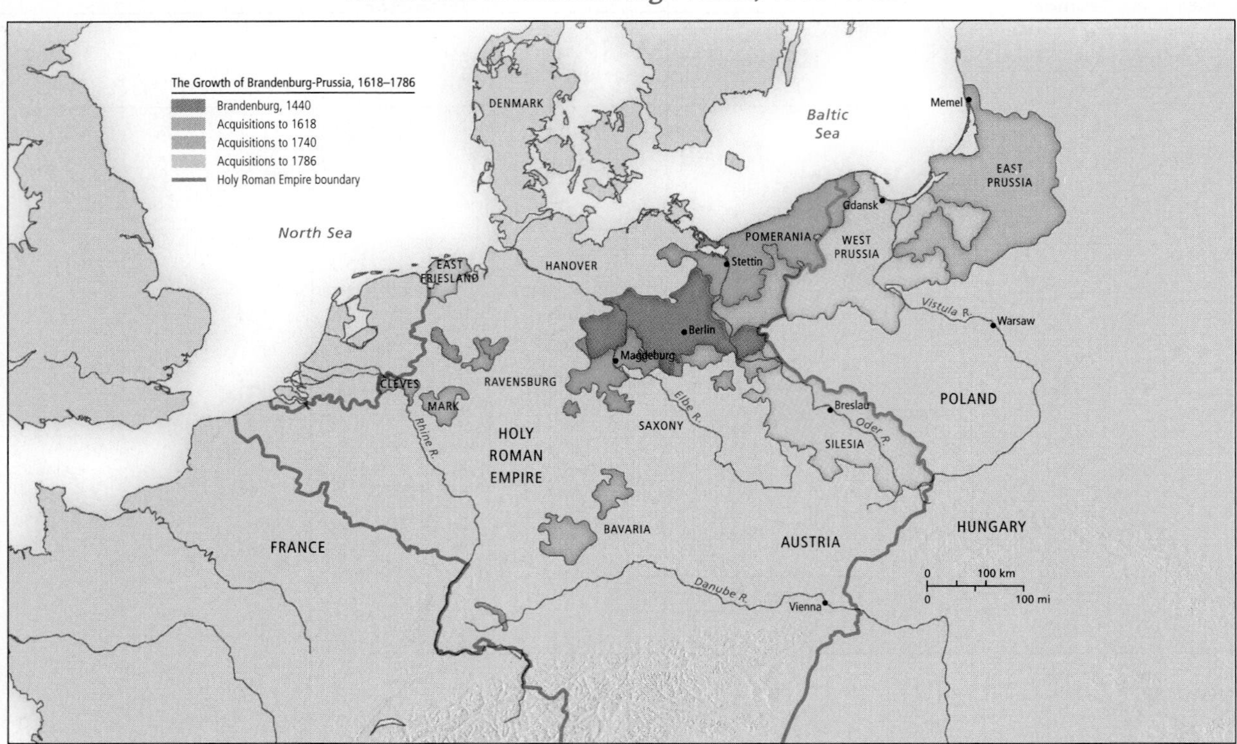

MAP ANALYSIS

1. What territories and cities were part of Brandenburg-Prussia by 1618?

2. What territory was acquired by 1740?

3. What territories were acquired by 1786?

4. What parts of Brandenburg-Prussia were included in the Holy Roman Empire?

Name _______________ Date _______________

Course Name and Number _______________ Instructor _______________

MAP 17.1
British India

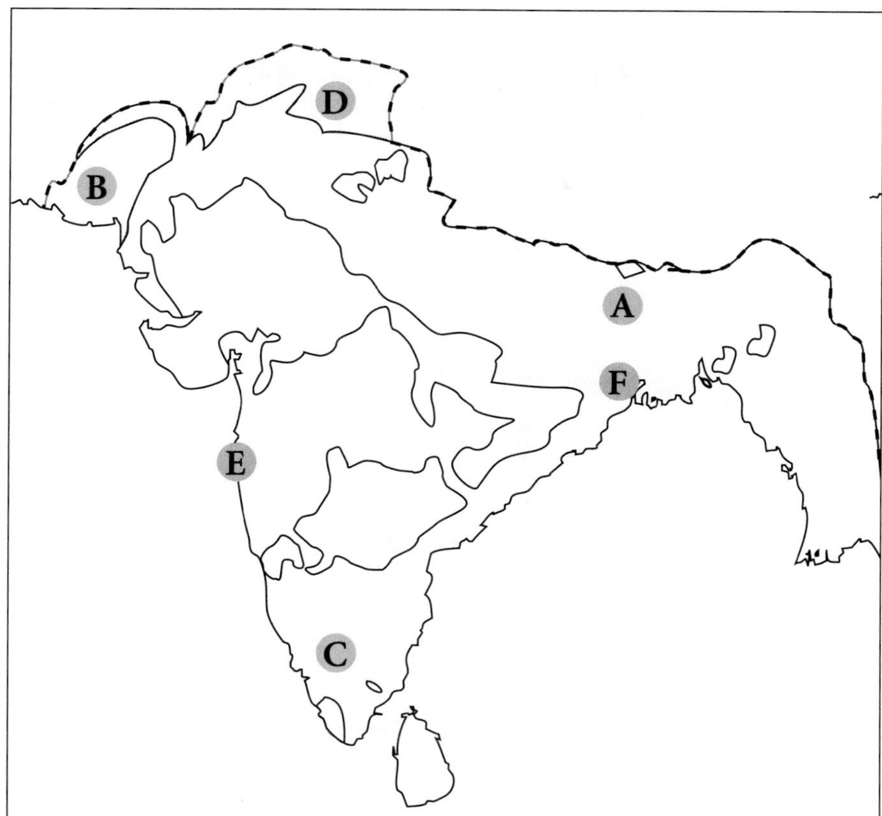

MAP ANALYSIS

1. Which letter on this map identifies Bombay?

---

2. Which letter on this map identifies Calcutta?

---

3. Which letter on this map identifies Mysore?

---

4. Which letter on this map identifies Bengal?

---

5. Which letter on this map identifies Baluchistan?

---

6. Which letter on this map identifies Kashmir?

MAP 17.2
The Beginnings of Colonial Rule in Africa

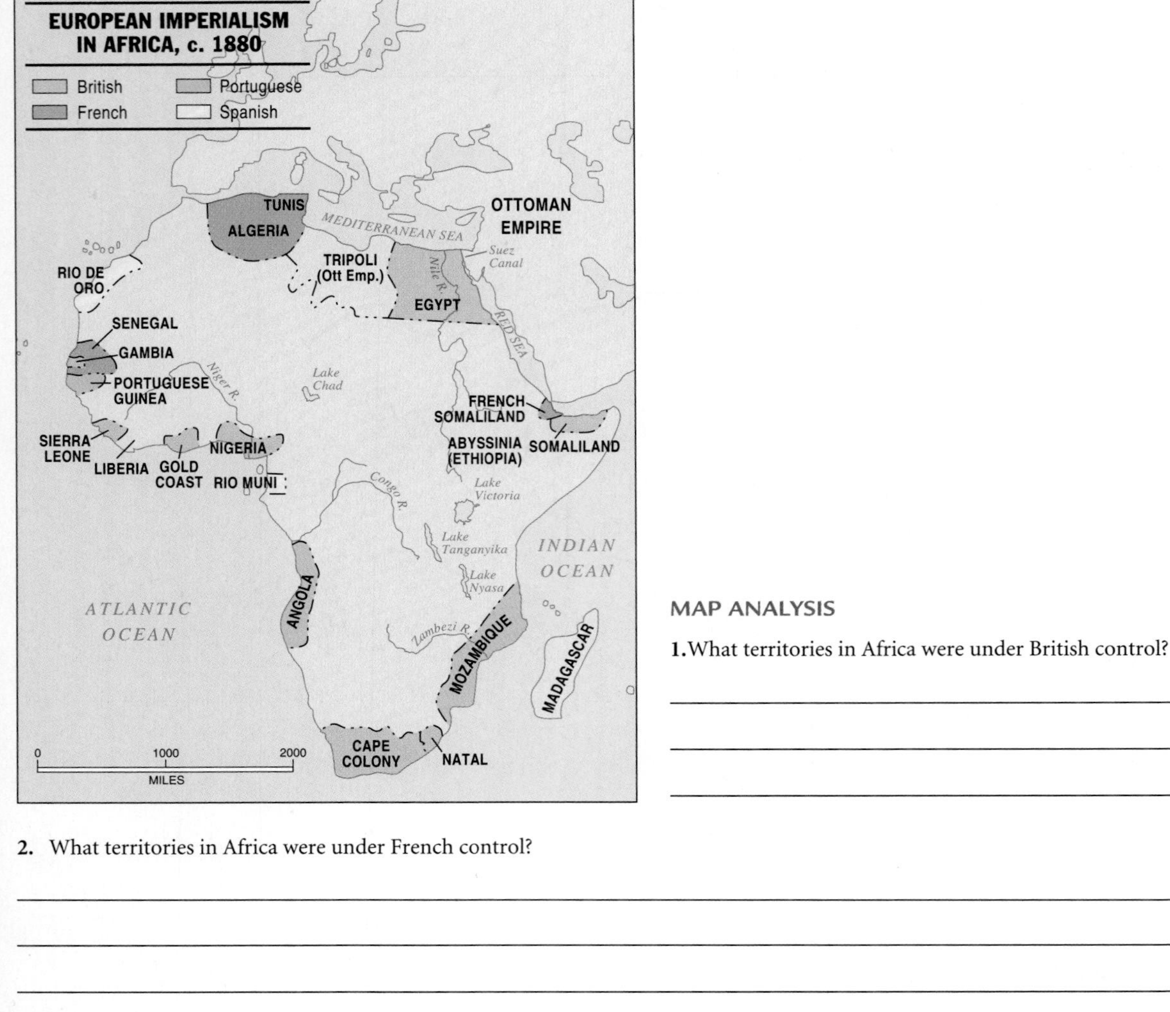

MAP ANALYSIS

1. What territories in Africa were under British control?

2. What territories in Africa were under French control?

3. What territories in Africa were under Portuguese control?

4. What territories in Africa were under Spanish control?

5. What territory in Africa was under the control of the Ottoman Empire?

6. What territories were unclaimed by foreign powers?

Name ______________________________ Date ______________________________

Course Name and Number ______________________________ Instructor ______________________________

MAP 18.1
European Empires in 1763

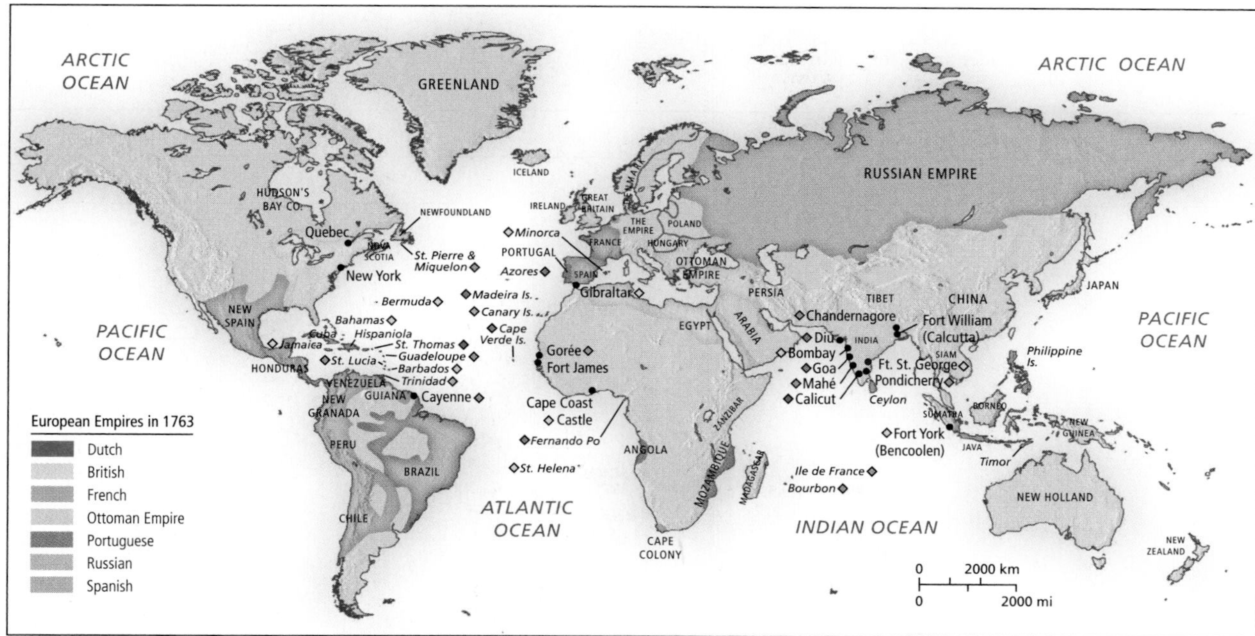

MAP ANALYSIS

1. What parts of the globe were under Dutch control by 1763?

____

____

____

2. What parts of the globe were under British control by 1763?

____

____

____

3. What parts of the globe were under French control by 1763?

____

____

____

4. What parts of the globe were under the control of the Ottoman Empire by 1763?

____

____

____

5. What parts of the globe were under Portuguese control by 1763?

____

____

____

(continued)

6. What parts of the globe were under Russian control by 1763?

7. What parts of the globe were under Spain control by 1763?

MAP 18.2
World Boundaries, ca. 1700

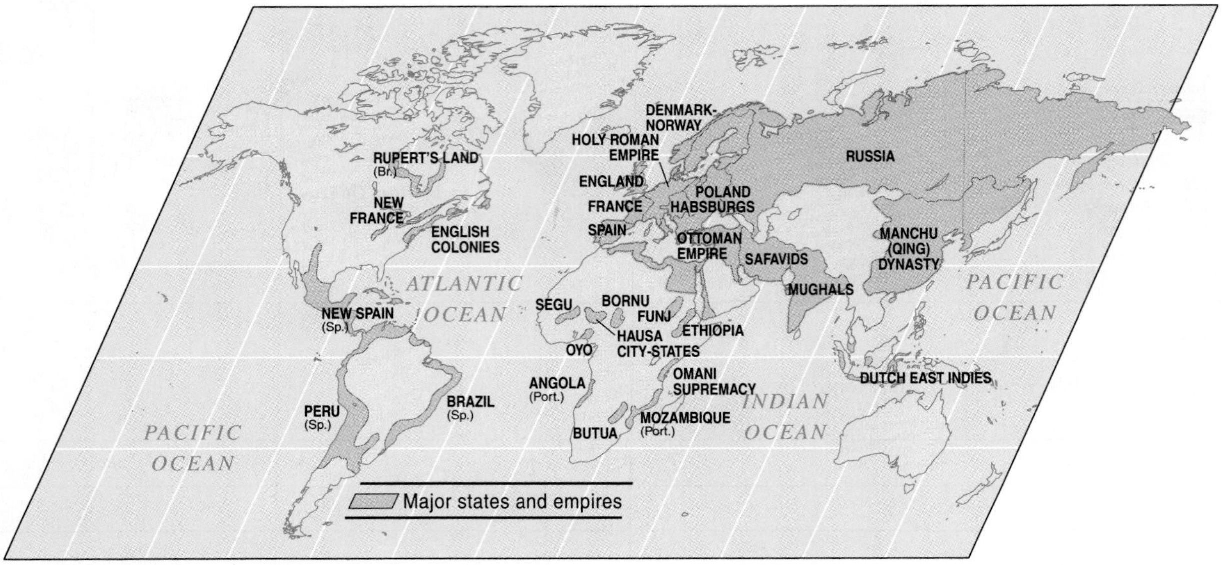

RUPERT'S LAND (Br.)
NEW FRANCE
ENGLISH COLONIES
NEW SPAIN (Sp.)
PERU (Sp.)
BRAZIL (Sp.)
ATLANTIC OCEAN
PACIFIC OCEAN
DENMARK-NORWAY
HOLY ROMAN EMPIRE
ENGLAND
FRANCE
SPAIN
POLAND
HABSBURGS
OTTOMAN EMPIRE
SAFAVIDS
RUSSIA
MANCHU (QING) DYNASTY
MUGHALS
SEGU
BORNU
FUNJ
HAUSA CITY-STATES
ETHIOPIA
OYO
ANGOLA (Port.)
OMANI SUPREMACY
MOZAMBIQUE (Port.)
BUTUA
INDIAN OCEAN
DUTCH EAST INDIES
PACIFIC OCEAN
Major states and empires

MAP ANALYSIS

1. What major European states were established by 1700?

2. What major states were established in the Middle East, South Asia, and East Asia by 1700?

3. What major states were established in Africa by 1700?

4. What major states were established in the Americas by 1700?

Name ______________________________ Date ______________________________

Course Name and Number ______________________________ Instructor ______________________________

MAP 19.1
Napoleonic Europe

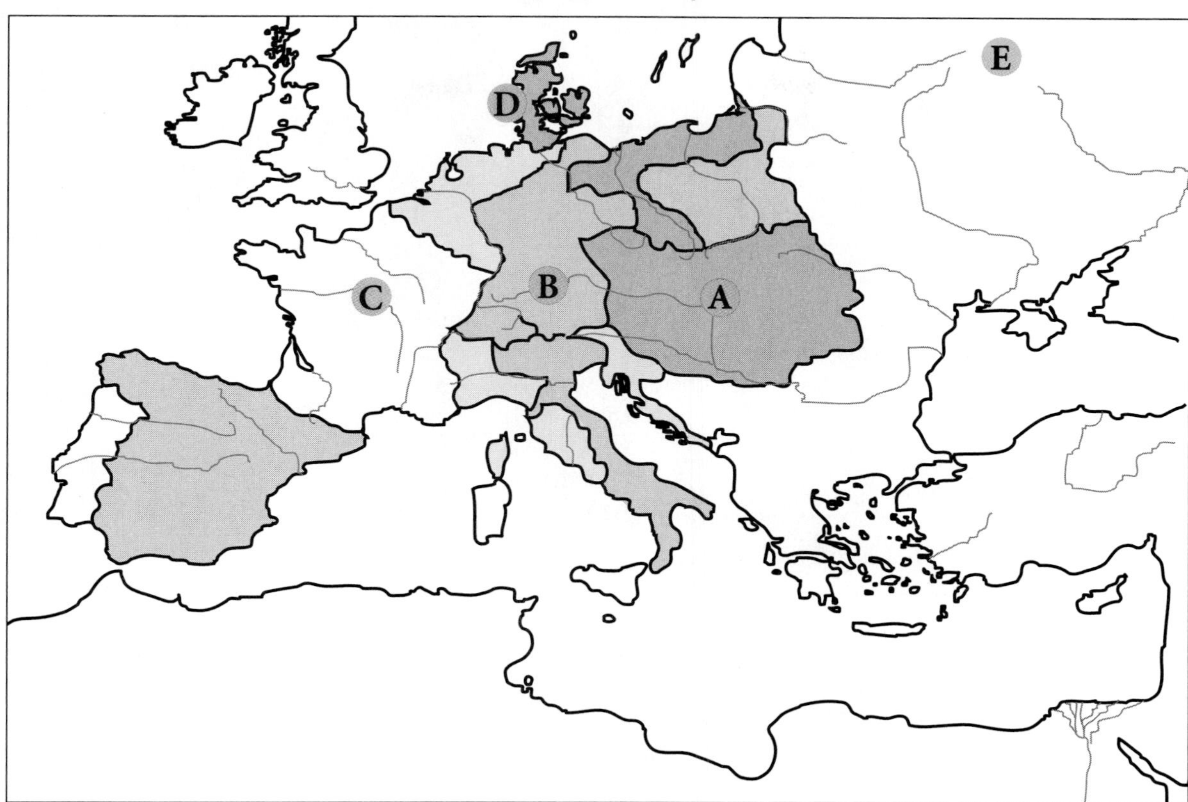

MAP ANALYSIS

1. Which letter on this map identifies the origin of Napoleon's empire?

____

2. Which letter(s) on this map identify allies of Napoleonic France?

____

3. Which letter(s) on this map identify dependent states of Napoleon's empire?

____

4. Which letter on this map identifies the site of Napoleon's final defeat?

____

MAP 19.2
Europe After the Congress of Vienna, 1815

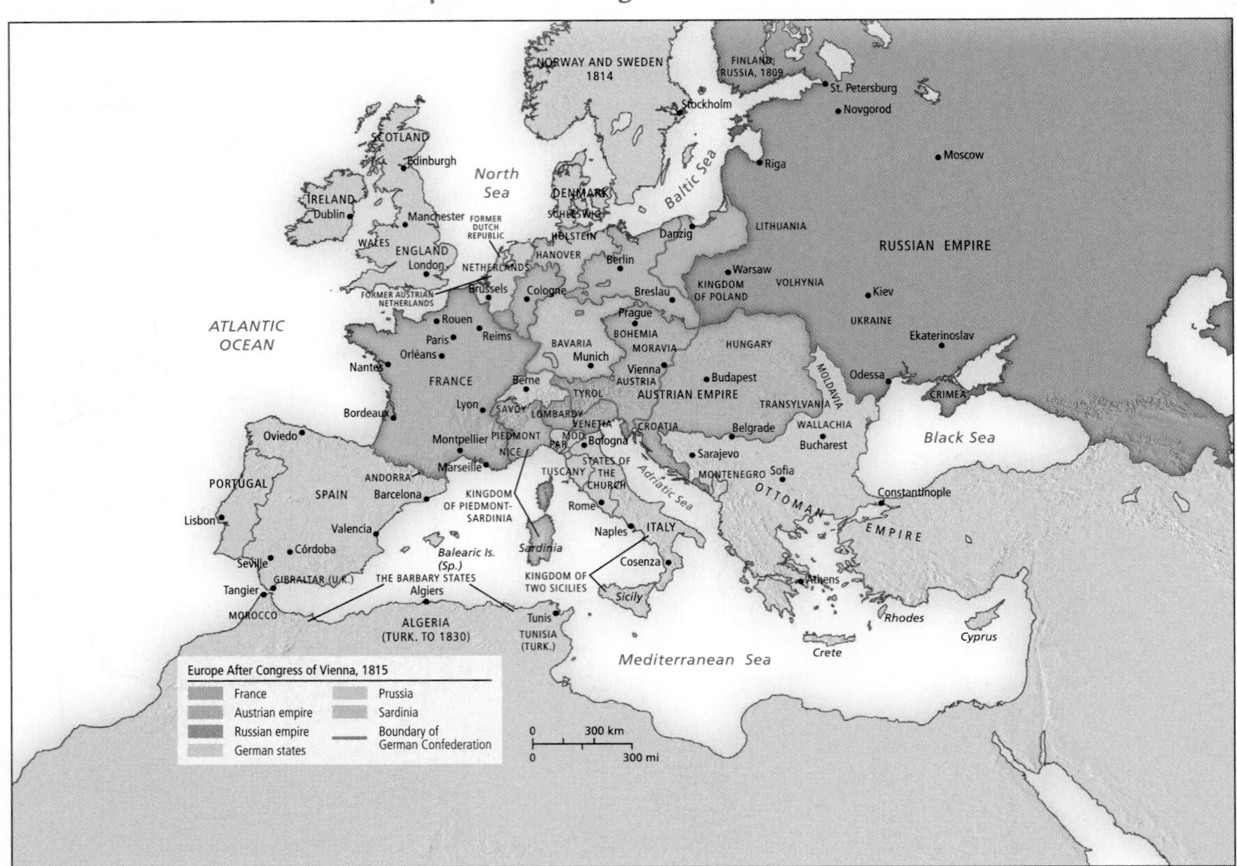

MAP ANALYSIS

1. What states were included in the German Confederation after the Congress of Vienna in 1815?

____

____

____

2. What remaining states constituted the Austrian Empire?

____

____

3. What other lands, formerly under Napoleon's control, were made independent by the Congress of Vienna?

____

____

____

4. Compare this map to the one found on page 635 in the textbook. What happened to the Duchy of Warsaw after the Congress of Vienna?

____

____

____

Name ______________________ Date ______________________

Course Name and Number ______________________ Instructor ______________________

MAP 20.1
The Industrialization of Europe, 1850

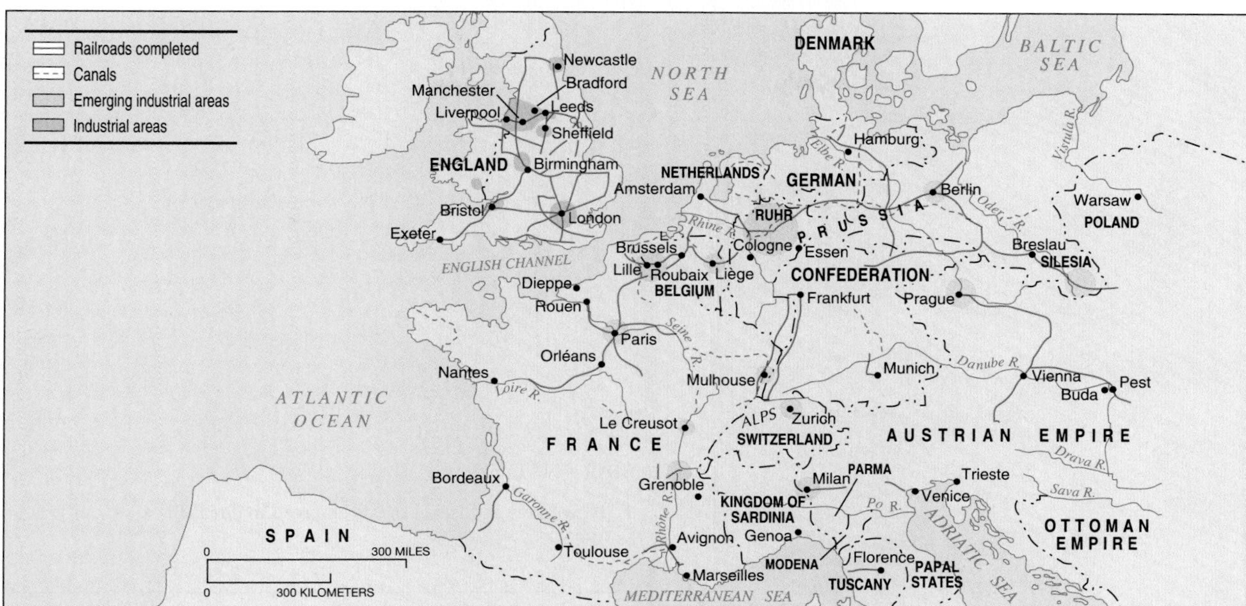

MAP ANALYSIS

1. What country had established industrial areas by 1850?

____

2. What industrial cities were located in this country?

____

3. What other cities/regions were emerging in 1850 as industrial areas?

____

4. What states had completed a system of railroads by 1850?

____

5. What is the importance of railroads and canals to industry?

____

6. What might stop a state from building or completing railroad and canal systems?

____

MAP 20.2
The Concentration of Industry in Great Britain, 1750–1820

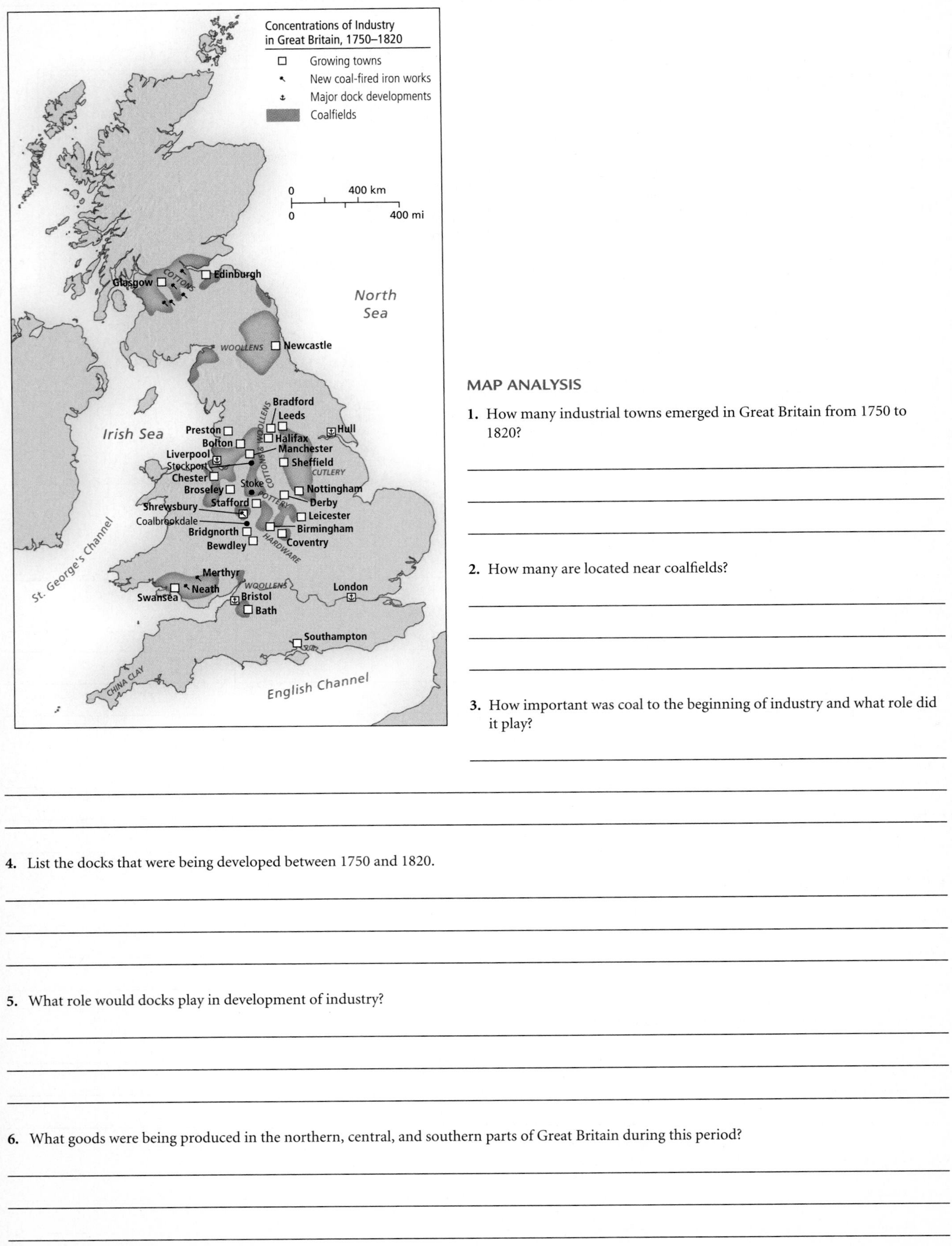

MAP ANALYSIS

1. How many industrial towns emerged in Great Britain from 1750 to 1820?

2. How many are located near coalfields?

3. How important was coal to the beginning of industry and what role did it play?

4. List the docks that were being developed between 1750 and 1820.

5. What role would docks play in development of industry?

6. What goods were being produced in the northern, central, and southern parts of Great Britain during this period?

Name ______________________ Date ______________________

Course Name and Number ______________________ Instructor ______________________

MAP 21.1
The Unification of Italy

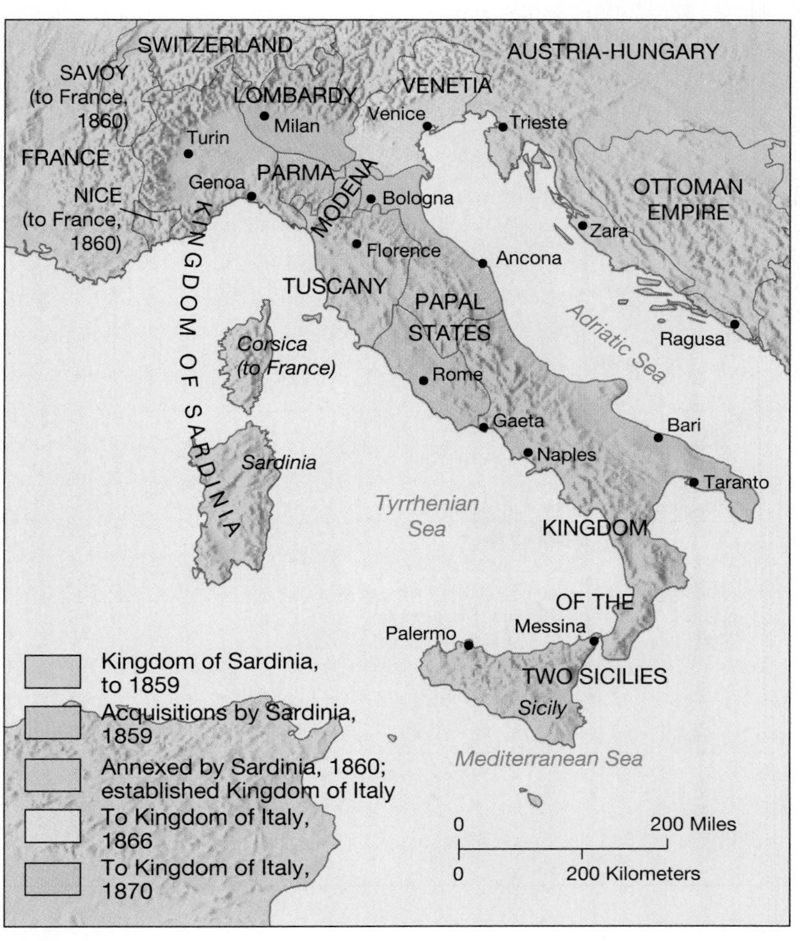

MAP ANALYSIS

1. According to this map, what state is responsible for initiating the unification of Italy?

2. What territory was acquired by Sardinia in 1859?

3. What happened in the following year?

4. What was the first territory annexed by the Kingdom of Italy and in what year did this take place?

5. What was the last territory added to the Kingdom of Italy?

MAP 21.2
Nationalities Within the Habsburg Empire

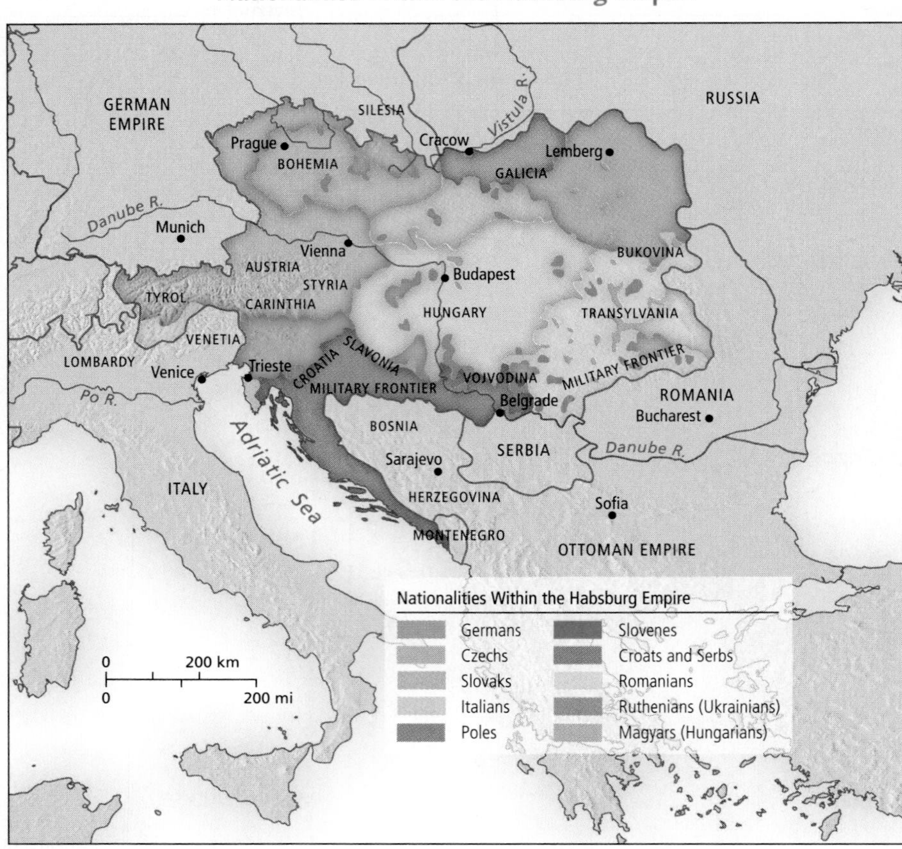

MAP ANALYSIS

1. How many separate nationalities existed within the Habsburg Empire?

____

____

____

2. What nationalities were located along military frontiers?

____

____

____

3. What major cities are included in the Habsburg Empire?

____

____

____

4. What internal setbacks might arise in trying to unify such a diverse empire?

____

____

____

Name ______________________ Date ______________________

Course Name and Number ______________________ Instructor ______________________

MAP 22.1
The Decline of the Ottoman Empire

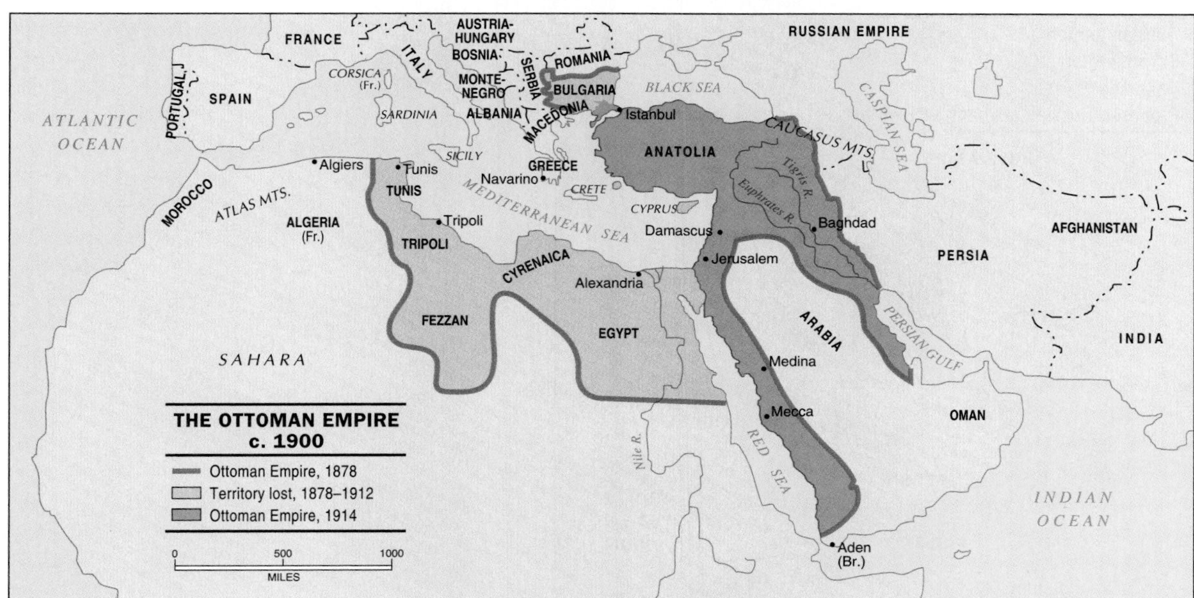

MAP ANALYSIS

1. What territories did the Ottoman Empire consist of in 1878?

____

____

____

2. According to the map on page 730 in the textbook, what territories were lost prior to 1878?

____

____

____

3. List the territories lost by the Ottoman Empire prior to 1915.

____

____

____

4. According to this map, what major cities did the Ottoman Empire still control in 1914?

____

____

____

5. According to the map on page 730 in the textbook, what territories were lost by 1923?

____

____

____

MAP 22.2
The Persian Gulf Region, ca. 1900

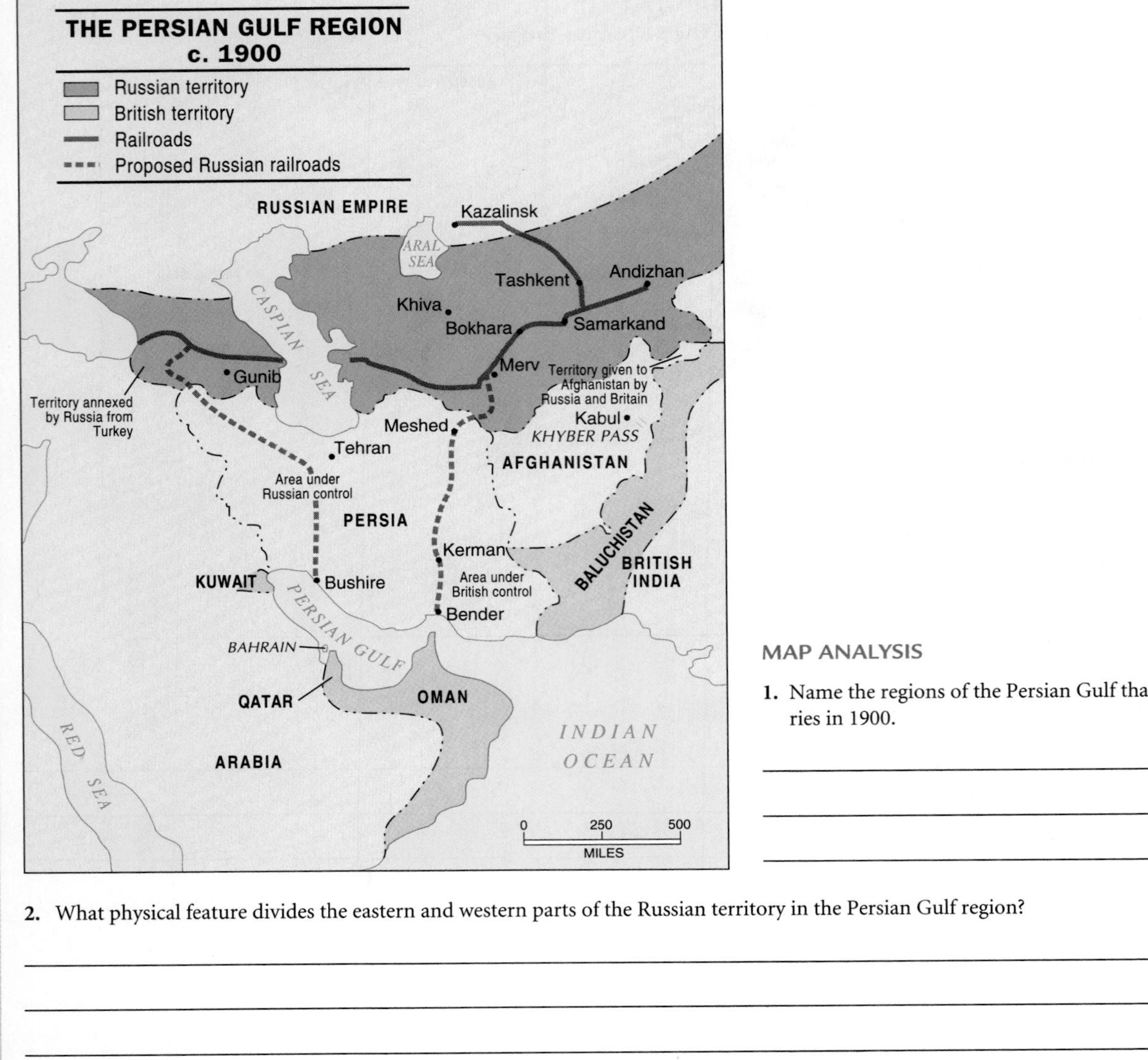

MAP ANALYSIS

1. Name the regions of the Persian Gulf that were British territories in 1900.

2. What physical feature divides the eastern and western parts of the Russian territory in the Persian Gulf region?

3. What regions of the Persian Gulf were independent of Russian or British control?

4. What region of the Persian Gulf had parts under both Russian and British control?

5. Why might Russia propose the construction of railroads through Persia?

Name ______ Date ______

Course Name and Number ______ Instructor ______

MAP 23.1
Imperialism in Southeast Asia, ca. 1914

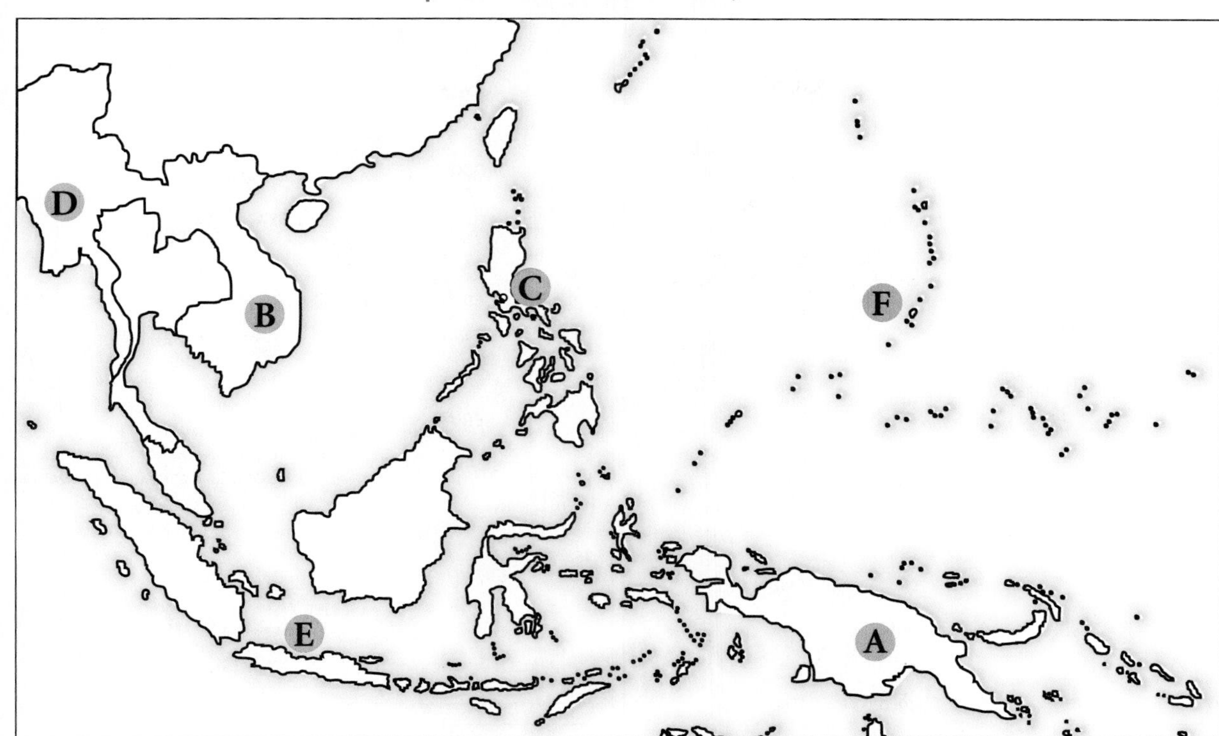

MAP ANALYSIS

1. Which letter on this map identifies the Philippines?

______

2. Which letter on this map identifies Burma?

______

3. Which letter on this map identifies Guam?

______

4. Which letter on this map identifies Papua?

______

5. Which letter on this map identifies Java?

______

6. Which letter on this map identifies Indochina?

______

MAP 23.2
The Partition of Africa Between 1870 and 1914

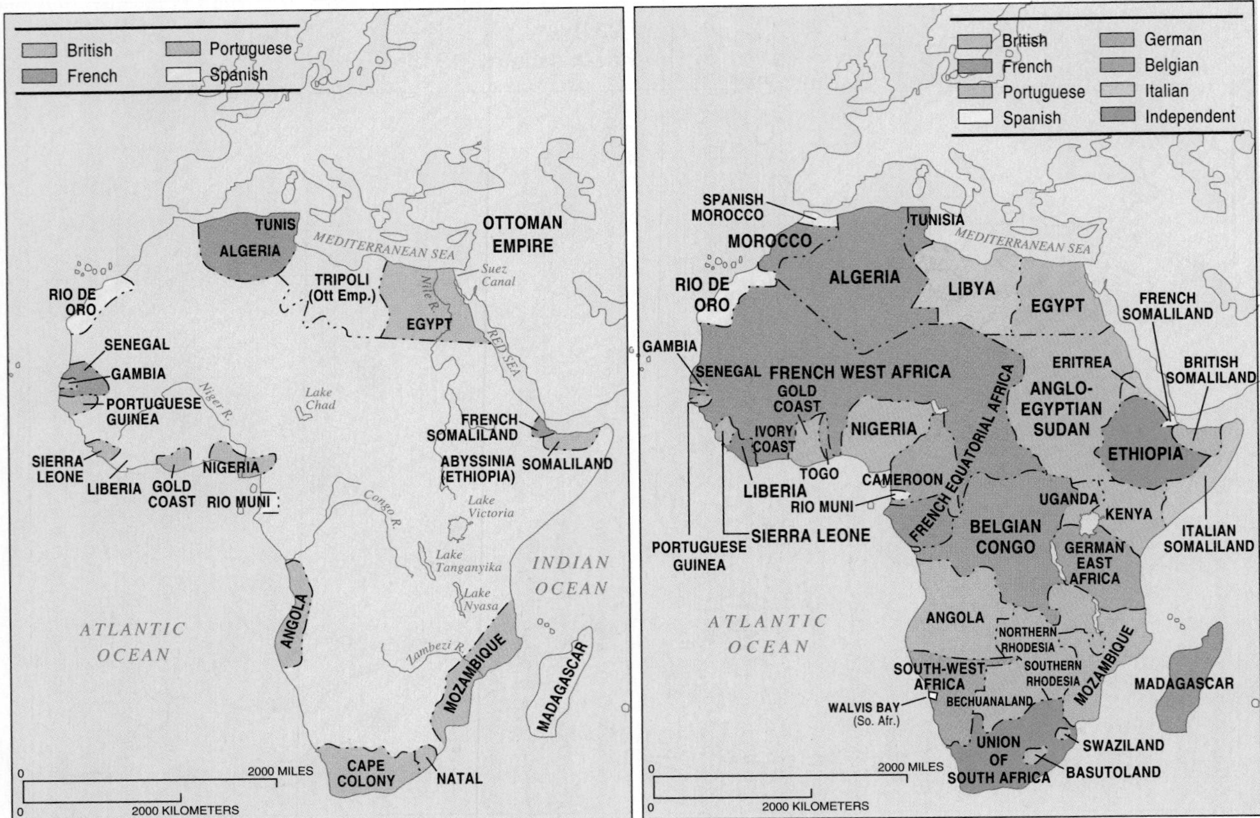

MAP ANALYSIS

1. How many African states did the British control in 1914 as opposed to 1870?

___

2. How many African states did the French control in 1914 as opposed to 1870?

___

3. How many African states did the Portuguese control in 1914 as opposed to 1870?

___

4. How many African states did the Spanish control in 1914 as opposed to 1870?

___

5. How many states come under German, Belgian, and Italian control by 1914?

___

6. What African states gained their independence by 1914?

___

___

___

Name ______________________ Date ______________________

Course Name and Number ______________________ Instructor ______________________

MAP 24.1
Europe After the Great War

MAP ANALYSIS

1. Which letter on this map identifies Austria?

2. Which letter on this map identifies Czechoslovakia?

3. Which letter on this map identifies Germany?

4. Which letter on this map identifies Syria?

5. Which letter on this map identifies Yugoslavia?

MAP 24.2
The Eastern Front, 1915–1918

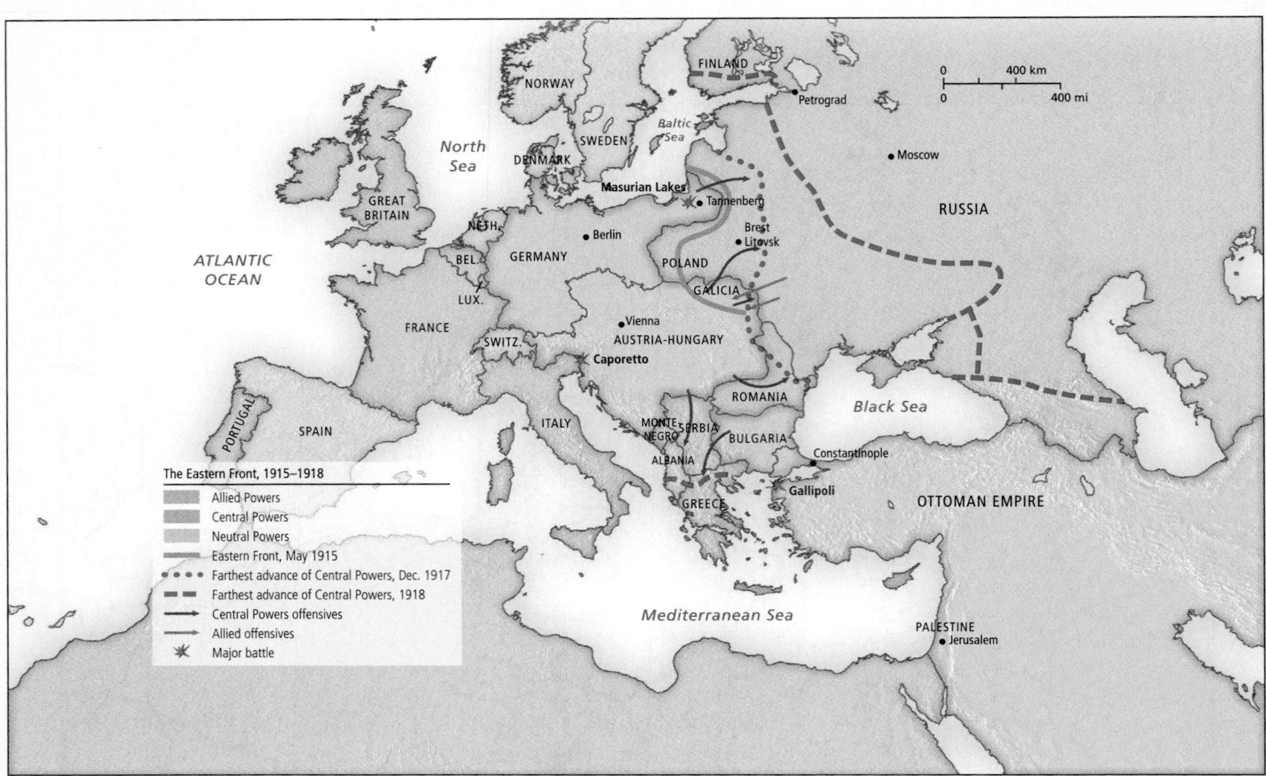

MAP ANALYSIS

1. What nations made up the Allied Powers in World War I?

2. What nations made up the Central Powers in World War I?

3. What nations remained neutral throughout the conflict?

4. What advances were made by the Central Powers in 1917 and 1918, and what might this reveal about their plan towards the end of the war?

5. How might the defeat of the Central Powers affect nations located outside of Western Europe, such as the Ottoman Empire?

Name ______________________ Date ______________________

Course Name and Number ______________________ Instructor ______________________

MAP 25.1
The Middle East in the 1920s

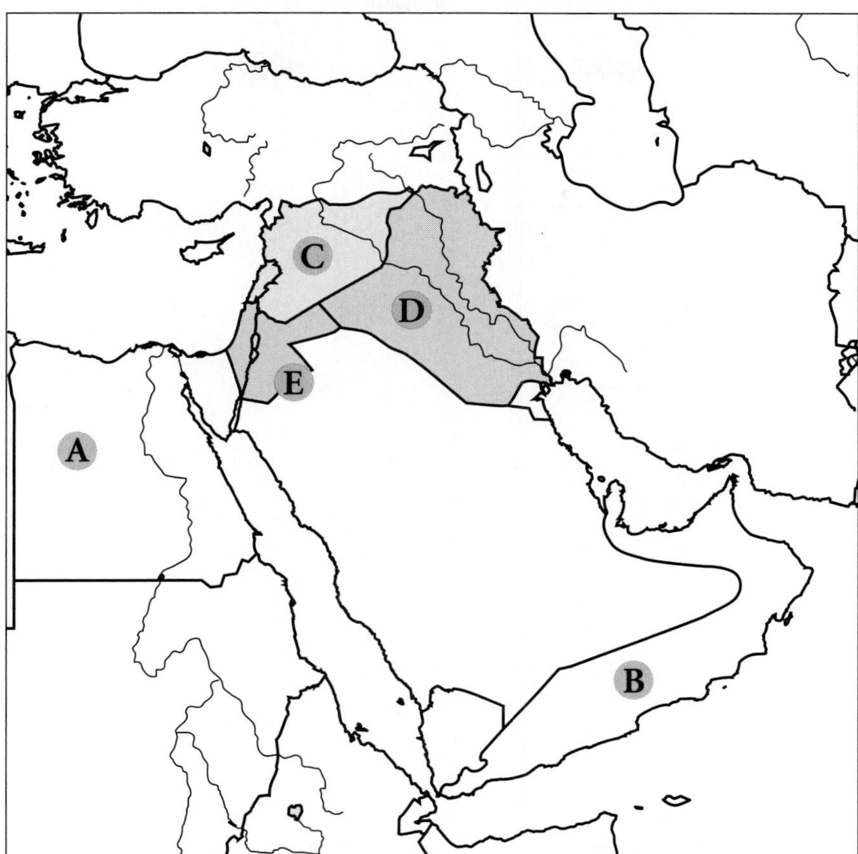

MAP ANALYSIS

1. Which letter on this map identifies Iraq?

____

2. Which letter on this map identifies Palestine and the Transjordan?

____

3. Which letter on this map identifies Syria and Lebanon?

____

4. Which letter on this map identifies Egypt?

____

MAP 25.2
Eastern Europe and the Soviet Union, 1919–1939

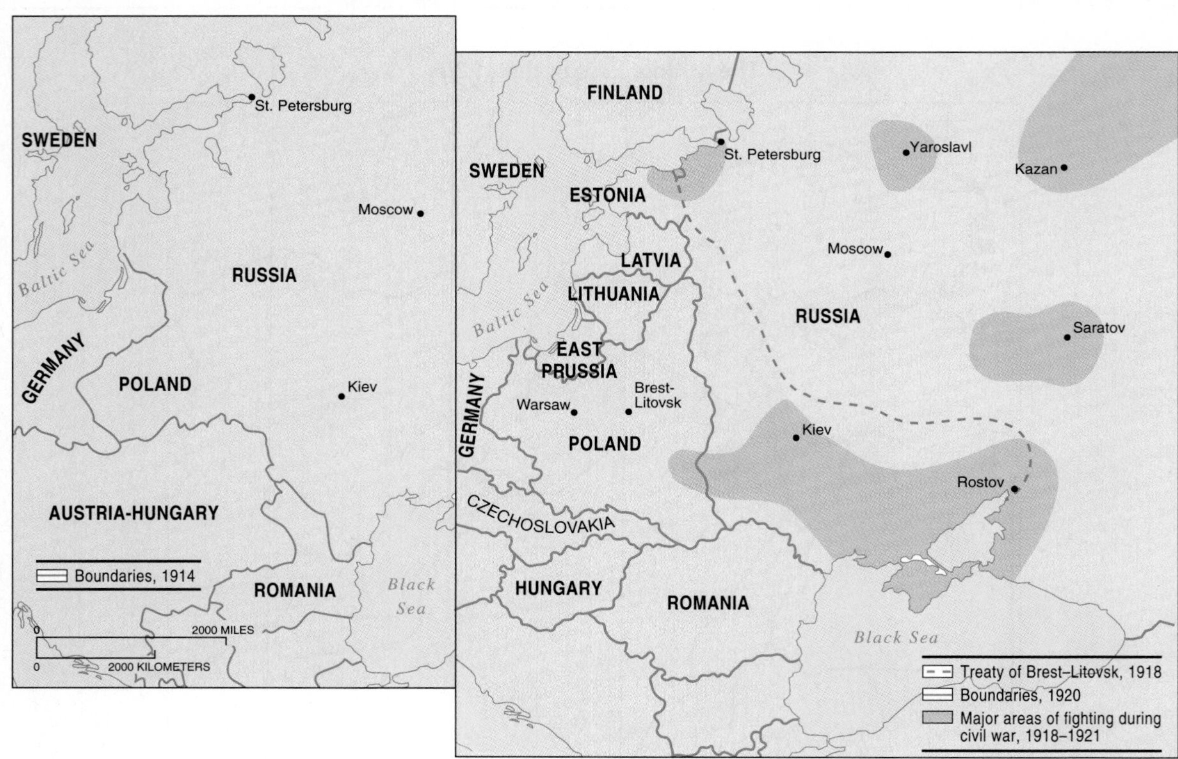

MAP ANALYSIS

1. How did the borders of Poland and Romania change between 1914 and 1919?

2. What happened to Austria-Hungary after World War I?

3. What cities were within the borders drawn for Russia by the Treaty of Brest-Litovsk?

4. What cities did Russia reclaim by 1920?

5. What new countries existed in Eastern Europe after 1920?

Name ______________________ Date ______________________

Course Name and Number ______________________ Instructor ______________________

MAP 26.1
Europe in World War II

MAP ANALYSIS

1. Which letter on this map identifies the Battle of Britain?

2. Which letter on this map identifies Vichy France?

3. Which letter on this map identifies the Battle of Stalingrad?

4. Which letter on this map identifies the Battle of Leningrad?

5. Which letter on this map identifies the Battle of the Bulge?

6. Which letter on this map identifies Normandy?

MAP 26.2
China in the Era of Revolution and Civil War

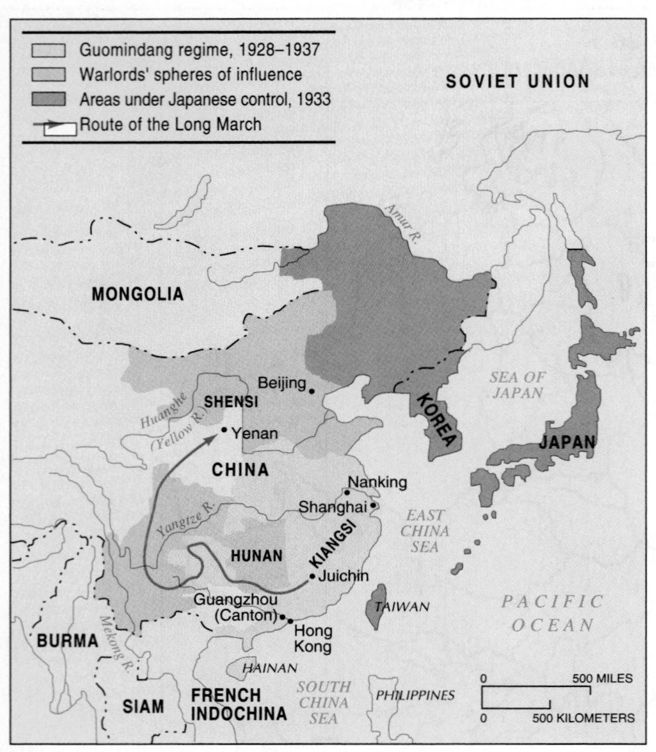

MAP ANALYSIS

1. What major cities were included in Guomandang China between 1928 and 1937?

2. Where were the warlords situated in China who posed threats to the Guomandang regime?

3. Where in China were communist power bases located in 1934?

4. Where did the Long March begin in China, what areas did it go through, and where did it end?

5. Where did Chinese nationalists, like Chiang Kai-Shek, retreat to in 1949?

Name ______________________ Date ______________________

Course Name and Number ______________________ Instructor ______________________

MAP 27.1
The Cold War Military Standoff

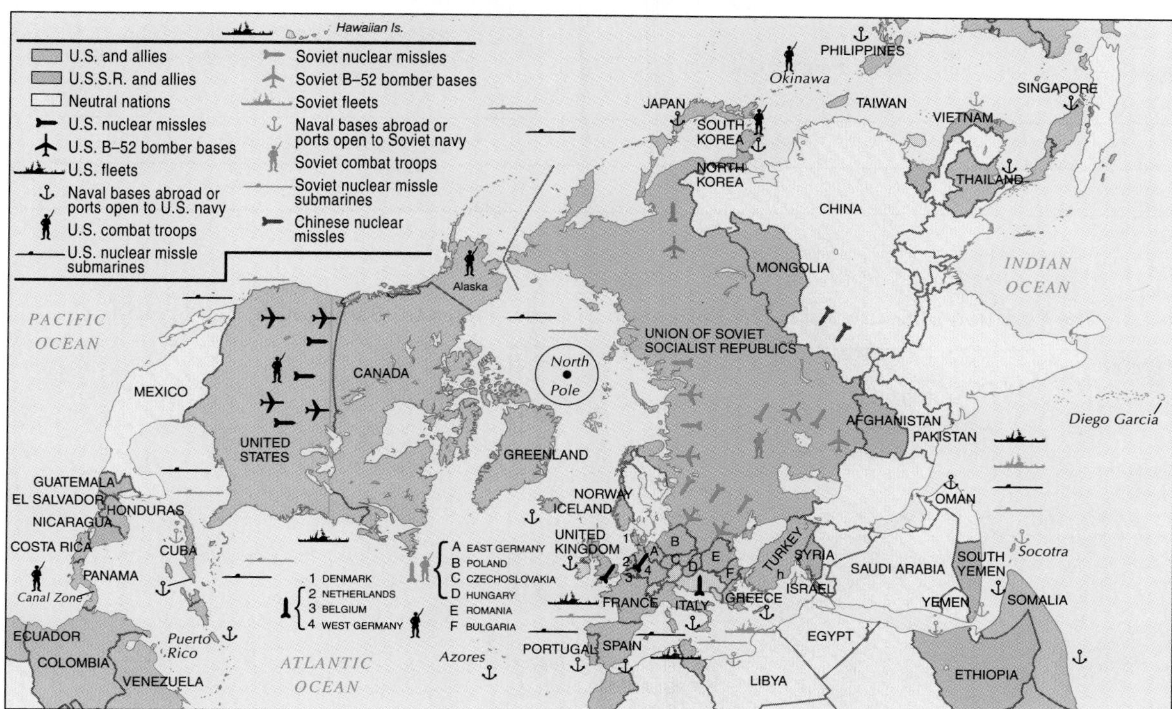

MAP ANALYSIS

1. List the allies of the United States during the Cold War.

____

____

____

2. List the allies of the U.S.S.R. during the Cold War.

____

____

____

3. What nations remained neutral during the Cold War?

____

____

____

4. What international ports were open to the U.S. navy during the Cold War?

____

____

____

5. What international ports were open to the Soviet navy during the Cold War?

____

____

______________________ (continued)

6. Where were U.S. combat troop posted during the Cold War?

7. Where were Soviet combat troops posted during the Cold War?

MAP 27.2
The Partition of South Asia: The Formation of India, Pakistan, Bangladesh, and Sri Lanka

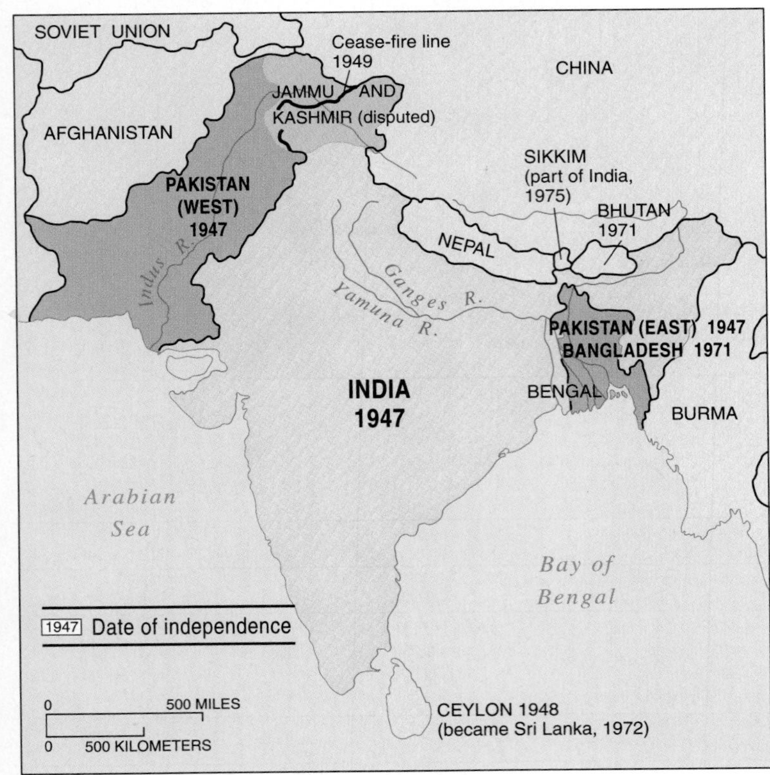

MAP ANALYSIS

1. What were the first South Asian states granted independence, and when did they become independent?

2. What was eastern Pakistan called in 1971?

3. In what year did Sri Lanka gain its independence, and by what name was it formerly known?

4. What territories were located on the eastern border of Western Pakistan?

5. What other countries bordered Pakistan and India?